A. M. D. G.

THE STUDENT'S GRADUS

AN AID TO LATIN VERSIFICATION

BY

LEO T. BUTLER, S. J.

WOODSTOCK COLLEGE
WOODSTOCK, MD.

1914

Baltimore City
Printing and Binding
Company
352-363 Equitable Building

CONTENTS

INTRODUCTION.

Experienced teachers of English know that the compassing of a style in prose is somehow connected with patient drill work in English verse, even though the pupil may never look to projecting his thoughts upon the poetic clouds of creative fancy. Few men, if any, who have successfully taught the mastery of the written and the spoken word in Latin, have doubted the value thereunto of a careful drilling in Latin verse. The familiarity with Latin idiom, rhythm, antithesis and epigram gotten by the successful grasp of the elegiac distich, for instance, is a distinct step in the security of Latin expression. So long, then, as we retain Latin as the best type for a thorough study of language and as an instrument for the development of the powers of thought-reception and thought-expression, we may count on the retention of Latin verse work in the class-room, in spite of sporadic discontent therewith. If so, the value of the present work is obvious.

For many years those of us who have put the Latin Gradus among the school-boys' tools have been constrained to fall back upon Noel's French edition of the Gradus. Thereby we complicated the problem for the student, unless he was familiar with French, and we embarrassed the college authorities concerned with book-supplies, for the reason that it was difficult and sometimes impossible to secure imported copies of Noel. More than once some of us have looked longingly for the prospect of having an edition out in English. While teaching Latin at Georgetown University some years ago, Mr. Butler emphasized to the Prefect of Studies the pressing need of such an edition and was told in reply that if he desired a Latin Gradus for the use of English students he would have to prepare it himself. He has done so. The present edition in English of the old French Noel, revised and abridged, is the result. The Prefect of Studies in the case herewith bids it welcome and Godspeed. May it do for the students of today as much good as its French forbear did for an earlier generation!

CHARLES B. MACKSEY, S.J.

Gregorian University, Rome,
Oct. 22, 1912.

PREFACE.

The compiler of the Student's Gradus makes no claim to originality either in the purpose or in the contents of this work. As was the case with any Gradus, it must be founded along the lines of those which have blazed the way to Parnassus for the student of the past. When James Vanière, S.J., uniting together all the merits of the different works, issued to aid the student of Latin poetry, brought forth his famous *Magnum Dictionarium Poeticum,* he left no room for improvement from the standpoint of originality, and when Noel, taking up the work of the scholarly Jesuit, augmented it by many more examples, phrases and quotations, no future editor could hope to extend the field covered by both. So the writer has availed himself of these two works, merely retrenching what was superfluous and making certain changes, which, from experience, seemed necessary and useful to the student of the present day.

As this volume is for the young student of the High School and College course, it has been thought advisable to omit all words not needed in his work, such as rare geographical terms, names of obscure personages, and uncommon words, found but seldom, in the classical authors. Epithets for the most part have been left out, since the young student's propensity to fill out his line at any cost has made them an occasion of abuse, while anyone, who can use them with profit, will easily select them from the authors read. Participles have been omitted, except as synonyms of adjectives, since they will be found with the verb from which they are derived. Those, however, which have been so commonly used that their connection with the verb is lost sight of, are embodied in the text.

It has seemed fit to separate from the main part of the Gradus the proper names in common use, the list of trees, plants, flowers and shrubs, as well as a complete list of the birds known to the ancients, and place them in three distinct appendices. This has been done that the body of the work should be as compact as possible, while the student, wishing to make use of these sections, may run through them with greater ease and less expenditure of time.

Such then is the work which the writer offers to the young student of Latin Verse, desiring as he does, to assist him in the great work of formation based on the time-honored study of the classics. He has been led to undertake this task, seeing the difficulty of procuring for the boys the old *Gradus Ad Parnassum,* so long out of print, and the trouble they are accustomed to have with the edition in French. If it may be of assistance in helping them to acquire a greater knowledge and love of the classics, he will feel amply repaid for the labor spent upon it.

PRAENOTANDA.

A Short Treatise On Latin Versification.

I. Quantity.

The quantity of a syllable in Latin depends upon the quantity of its vowel sound, which in turn is governed by fixed rules according to its nature and position. If the vowel is long by nature, the syllable is long. If, however, the vowel is short by nature, yet followed by two consonants, the syllable is long by position, unless the two consonants be a mute followed by a liquid in the same syllable. In the latter case, the quantity may be considered either long or short. For the sake of the student, but three symbols are used to indicate the quantity of the syllable: the long (‒), the short (⏑), and the common (⏓). The last indicates that a syllable is either long or short, by nature or position. A little practice will enable the student to discover which is meant by the common mark, since a syllable will be common by position only when the vowel is followed by two consonants, not a mute and a liquid.

II. The Foot.

The standard of all metrical measures in Latin is the foot. The following are the more ordinary ones used by the classical poets.

‒ ‒ ....The Spondee ....mōnstrūm.
⏑ ‒ ....The Iambus....................dīēs.
‒ ⏑ ....The Trochee ....ārmă.
⏑ ⏑ ....The Pyrrhic ....pĕdĕ.
‒ ⏑ ⏑ ....The Dactyl ....cārmĭnă.
⏑ ⏑ ‒ ....The Anapaest..................pĭĕtās.
⏑ ⏑ ⏑ ....The Tribrach..................ănĭmă.
‒ ⏑ ⏑ ‒ ....The Choriambus ....ēxănĭmās.

In regard to these measures it is to be noted that the last syllable of a verse may be indifferently long or short, whatsoever the metre.

III. Elision.

One of the difficulties with which the student has to contend in writing Latin verse is the elision of a vowel, diphthong, or a final syllable ending in a vowel and M before a word commencing with a vowel or H. With the ancients this combination was harsh-sounding and unpleasant, so the final syllable of the previous word was elided and not considered in the scansion. As too many elisions, however, are apt to make a line rough and harsh, it is well to be sparing of them at first.

Certain interjections are not elided: e.g. *o, ah, heu, proh, io,* etc.

IV. The Caesural Pause.

At certain points in a line of poetry, the ancients placed what was known as the caesural pause, namely a pause or slight suspension of the voice for harmony, happy effect, to give prominence to certain important words or ideas, or even to relieve the too stately effect which is apt to result in a long line such as the hexameter.

One or two things must be noted. A syllable that is elided never ends a caesura. The caesural syllable is always the end of a word. It generally comes about the middle of the verse. In the hexameter it is generally found before the last syllable of the third foot, though for grace and variety it is often found in the second and fourth feet. In the pentameter, as well as most of the other measures, the caesura has a fixed place.

V. Species and Length of Verse.

A) Hexameter Verse.

This is composed of six feet, of which the first four are indifferently dactyls or spondees, the fifth a dactyl, and the sixth a spondee. Sometimes a spondee is found in the fifth foot, but in that case a dactyl will be found in the fourth. As this latter variety is the exception rather than the rule, a spondee should not be placed in the fifth foot.

DIAGRAM.

1	2	3	4	5	6
– ⏑ ⏑	– ⏑ ⏑	– ⏑ ⏑	– ⏑ ⏑	– ⏑ ⏑	– ⏓
– –	– –	– –	– –		

A quick, light or joyful thought predominates in dactyls, while a stately, mournful theme contains more spondees. Care should be taken to have the measure fit the thought expressed. In general, however, the best effect is produced by a skilful combination of both dactyls and spondees. But the first foot should be a dactyl in preference to a spondee.

The Hexameter is the measure used in heroic and didactic poems on account of its stateliness.

B) Pentameter Verse.

This is composed of four feet, with two extra syllables called the caesural syllables, one of which is placed after the second foot, the other at the end of the line. The first two feet are indifferently dactyls or spondees, the last two necessarily dactyls. The last word in a line should never be a word of three syllables, or even a monosyllable unless the words "est," if preceded by a vowel which is elided. The best word to end the line is one of two syllables, though a word of four or even five syllables may occasionally end the verse for the sake of variety.

DIAGRAM.

1	2		3	4	
– ⏑ ⏑	– ⏑ ⏑	–	– ⏑ ⏑	– ⏑ ⏑	⏓
– –	– –				

The Pentameter verse is used with the Hexameter to form a couplet, called the Elegiac distich. It is the usual measure employed in elegies.

C) Iambic Verse.

There are two kinds of Iambic verse, the dimeter consisting of four feet, and the trimeter of six feet.

In the dimeter, the fourth foot must be an iambus, but the other feet vary according to the diagram below.

THE DIMETER.

1	2	3	4
⏑ –		⏑ –	
⏑ ⏑ –	⏑ –	– ⏑ ⏑	⏑ –
– ⏑ ⏑	⏑ ⏑ ⏑	– –	
– –		⏑ ⏑ ⏑	

The trimeter may be entirely iambic or it may be varied. In the latter case the sixth foot is always an iambus. In the mixed Iambic trimeter, the second, fourth and sixth feet must either be iambi or tribrachs, while the first, third and fifth may either be dactyls, spondees, or anapaests. The third foot, however, sometimes admits the tribrach, while the fifth is generally a spondee or an anapaest.

The Trimeter.

1	2	3	4	5	6
⏑ –		⏑ ⏑ ⏑		⏑ –	
– –	⏑ –	– ⏑ ⏑	⏑ –	⏑ ⏑ –	⏑ –
⏑ ⏑ –	⏑ ⏑ ⏑	– –	⏑ ⏑ ⏑	– –	
– ⏑ ⏑		⏑ –			

D) Sapphic and Adonic.

This measure consists of three Sapphic verses and one Adonic.

The Sapphic verse has five feet. The first is a trochee, the second a spondee, the third a dactyl and the last two trochees. The caesura comes usually after the fifth and sometimes after the sixth syllable.

The Adonic verse is composed of a dactyl followed by a spondee.

DIAGRAM.

1	2	3	4	5
– ⏑	– –	– ⏑ ⏑	– ⏑	– ⏑

– ⏑ ⏑	– –

E) Asclepiad Metres.

The general name of Asclepiad is given to five variations of metre based on the use of the choriambus. They are best explained by the diagrams below.

1. First Asclepiad.

1	2	3	4
– –	– ⏑ ⏑ –	– ⏑ ⏑ –	⏑ ⏓

2. Second Asclepiad.

1	2	3	4
– –	– ⏑ ⏑ –	⏑ –	
– –	– ⏑ ⏑ –	– ⏑ ⏑ –	⏑ ⏓

3. Third Asclepiad.

1	2	3	4
– –	– ⏑ ⏑ –	– ⏑ ⏑ –	⏑ ⏓
– –	– ⏑ ⏑ –	– ⏑ ⏑ –	⏑ ⏓
– –	– ⏑ ⏑ –	– ⏑ ⏑ –	⏑ ⏓
– –	– ⏑ ⏑ –	⏑ ⏓	

4. Fourth Asclepiad.

1	2	3	4
– –	– ⏑ ⏑ –	– ⏑ ⏑ –	⏑ ⏓
– –	– ⏑ ⏑ –	– ⏑ ⏑ –	⏑ ⏓
– –	– ⏑ ⏑ –	⏓	
– –	– ⏑ ⏑ –	⏑ ⏓	

5. Fifth Asclepiad.

1	2	3	5	5
– –	– ⏑ ⏑ –	– ⏑ ⏑ –	– ⏑ ⏑ –	⏑ ⏓

F) Alcaic Verse.

This difficult measure is composed of four lines, the first two of which are Dactylic Alcaics, the third an Archilochian Iambic, and the fourth a Dactylic Trochaic line.

The first two lines have four feet and a caesural syllable. The first foot is a spondee, rarely an iambus, the second an iambus, followed by the caesural syllable, while the last two feet are dactyls. In the third line the first foot is a spondee, rarely an iambus, the second an iambus, the third a spondee, and the last foot an iambus with a hypermetric syllable following. The fourth verse is composed of two dactyls followed by two trochees.

DIAGRAM.

	1	2		3	4
1.	⏓ =	⏑ –	–	– ⏑ ⏑	– ⏑ ⏑
2.	⏓ =	⏑ –	–	– ⏑ ⏑	– ⏑ ⏑
3.	⏓ =	⏑ –	– –	⏑ –	–
4.	– ⏑ ⏑	– ⏑ ⏑	– ⏑	– ⏑	

Another and more modern method of scanning the Alcaic metre is by considering the first syllable of the first three lines an anacrusis; in that case, the first two verses consist of an anacrusis, a trochee, spondee and two dactyls. The third and fourth lines are expansions of the first and second halves of these lines respectively; the third adding two trochees to the first half of the first line, and the fourth adding them to the second half. The following diagram will explain the method clearly.

DIAGRAM.

		1	2	3	4
1.	⏓	– ⏑	– –	– ⏑ ⏑	– ⏑ ⏓
2.	⏓	– ⏑	– –	– ⏑ ⏑	– ⏑ ⏓
3.	⏓	– ⏑	– –	– ⏑	– ⏓
4.		– ⏑ ⏑	– ⏑ ⏑	– ⏑	– ⏓

VI. General Rules of Prosody.

1. The last syllable of a verse may be long or short, no matter what species of foot be required.

2. Every vowel is long by position when it is followed by two consonants, the single consonant J, and the double consonants X and Z. The single exception to this rule is a vowel, short by nature, followed by a mute and a liquid *in the same syllable.* In this case a vowel may be long or short ad libitum.

3. A vowel followed by another vowel is short except in the case of certain words borrowed from the Greek, the genitive and dative singular of the fourth declensions, and the I in *Fio* and its compounds, except when the I is followed by ER.

4. Final O is common, except in monosyllables, the dative and ablative singular of nouns, and most adverbs.

5. Derived words follow the quantities of the words from which they are derived.

VII. Poetic Licenses.

The following licenses have been found in the works of the great Latin poets, which, however, should be used with moderation, if at all:

1. A syllable, short by nature and position, may be considered long if followed by the caesura.

e. g. Nēc quǣ prǣtĕrĭīt, hōră rĕdīrĕ pŏtēst. . . . O.

2. A vowel followed by the caesura is not elided sometimes before another vowel. Some poets have even used this license where the caesura did not follow.

e. g. Ārcădĭcō jŭvĕnī īn lǣvā pārtĕ māmīllǣ. . . . J.

3. Very rarely a vowel at the end of a line is elided by one beginning the following line.

e. g. Rōbŏră nāvĭgĭīs āptānt rēmōsquĕ rŭdēntēs*que*
Ēxĭgŭī nŭmĕrō.....V.

4. Sometimes a word is divided so that a part ends one line, and the other part begins the following line.

e. g. Pōtĕt ăcētum; ăgĕ, si ēt strāmēntīs īncŭbĕt *unde-*
Octoginta ānnōs nātŭs......H.

5. Sometimes the poet adds the suffix ER to the infinitives of passive and deponent verbs.

e. g. Ĕt īncĭpĭēbāt prīncēps īngrĕd*ĭĕr;* ĕūm
Āddūcīt prĕtĭō. Phaed.

6. Frequently two vowels generally pronounced as two separate syllables are made to form one syllable, more often a long one.

e. g. Īnvĭdĭā pōstquām pēllācĭs Ŭlŷsseī. V.

7. It is a common practice for the poet to separate the parts of a compound word by an intervening word.

e. g. *Quo* mē *cunque* răpīt tēmpēstās H.

VIII. Quantities of Final Syllables.

1. Nouns.

First Declension.

	Singular.	*Plural.*
Nom.	ă, ās, ē, ēs	ǣ.
Gen.	ǣ, ēs	ārūm.
Dat.	ǣ, ē	īs.
Acc.	ām, ān, ēn	ās.
Voc.	ă, ē, ā	ǣ.
Abl.	ā, ē	īs.

Note. In the singular, the first list is the regular declension ending. The others are the endings of Greek nouns of which there are a few used in Latin.

Second Declension.

	Singular.	*Plural.*
Nom.	ŭs, ĕr, ĭr, ūm	ī, ă.
Gen.	ī, ĕrī, rī	ōrūm.
Dat.	ō	īs.
Acc.	ūm	ōs, ă.
Voc.	ĕ, ĕr, ĭr, ūm	ī, ă.
Abl.	ō	īs.

Third Declension.

	Singular.	*Plural.*
Nom.	ŏr, ĭ̄s, ēs, ŏ̄, ūs; Neut., ă, ĕ, ŭ̄s	īs, ēs; N., ă, ĭă.
Gen.	ĭ̄s, ŏ̄s	ūm, ĭūm.
Dat.	ī	ĭbŭ̄s.
Acc.	ēm, īm, ă, ĭ̄n; N. ă, ĕ, ŭ̄s	ēs, īs; N., ă, ĭă.
Voc.	Same as Nominative.	
Abl.	ĕ, ī	ĭbŭ̄s.

Fourth Declension.

	Singular.	*Plural.*
Nom.	ŭ̄s; Neut. ū	ūs; N., ŭă.
Gen.	ūs, ū	ŭūm.
Dat.	ŭī, ū	ĭbŭ̄s, ŭbŭ̄s.
Acc.	ūm, ū	ūs, ŭă.
Voc.	Same as Nominative.	
Abl.	ū	ĭbŭ̄s, ŭbŭ̄s.

Fifth Declension.

	Singular.	*Plural.*
Nom.	ĭēs	ēs.
Gen.	ĭēī, ēī	ērūm.
Dat.	ĭēī ēī	ēbŭ̄s.
Acc.	ĭēm, ēm	ēs.
Voc.	Same as Nominative.	
Abl.	ĭē, ē	ēbŭ̄s.

2. Pronouns.

Singular.

N. & V.	Ĕgŏ̄	Tū	( )	Hīc, hǣc, hōc	Īllĕ, īllă, īllŭ̄d
G.	mĕī	tŭī	sŭī	hūjŭ̄s	īllĭ̄ŭ̄s.
D.	mĭhĭ̄	tĭbĭ̄	sĭbĭ̄	huīc	īllī.
Acc.	mē	tē	sē	hūnc, hānc, hōc.	īllūm, īllām, īllŭ̄d.
Abl.	mē	tē	sē	hōc, hāc, hōc	īllō, īllā, īllō.

Plural.

N. & V.	Nōs	Vōs	( )	Hī, hǣ, hǣc	Īllī, īllǣ, īllă.
G.	nōstrūm, ī	vēstrūm, ī	sŭī	hōrūm, hārūm	īllōrūm, īllārūm.
D.	nōbīs	vōbīs	sĭbĭ̄	hīs	īllīs.
Acc.	nōs	vōs	sē	hōs, hās, hǣc	īllōs, īllās, īllă.
Abl.	nōbīs	vōbīs	sē	hīs	īllīs.

Singular.

N. & V.	Īs, ĕă, ĭd	Īpsĕ, īpsă, īpsūm	Quī, quǣ, quŏd.
G.	ējŭs	īpsĭŭs	cūjŭs.
D.	ĕī	īpsī	cuī.
Acc.	ĕūm, ĕām, ĭd	īpsūm, īpsām, īpsūm	quēm, quām, quŏd.
Abl.	ĕō, ĕā, ĕō	īpsō, īpsā, īpsō	quō, quā, quō.

Plural.

N. & V.	Ĕī (ĭī), ĕæ, ĕă	īpsī, īpsǣ, īpsă	quī, quǣ, quǣ.
G.	ĕōrūm, ĕārūm	īpsōrūm, īpsārūm	quōrūm, quārūm.
D.	ĕīs, ĭīs	īpsīs	quĭbŭs.
Acc.	ĕōs, ĕās, ĕă	īpsōs, ipsas, ipsa	quōs, quās, quǣ.
Abl.	ĕīs, ĭīs	īpsīs	quĭbŭs.

Note. The words *Uter, Alter, Neuter,* and *Alius* are declined like *Ipse.* The interrogative pronoun *Quis, quae, quid,* is declined like *Qui.*

NUMERAL ADJECTIVES.

N. & V.	Ūnŭs, ă, ūm	Dŭŏ, dŭæ, dŭŏ	Trēs, trĭă.
G.	ūnĭŭs	dŭōrūm, dŭārūm	trĭūm.
D.	ūnī	dŭōbŭs, dŭābŭs	trĭbŭs.
Acc.	ūnūm, ūnām	dŭōs, dŭās, dŭŏ	trēs, trĭă.
Abl.	ūnō, ūnā	dŭōbŭs, dŭābŭs	trĭbŭs.

Note. *Ambo* is declined like *Duo.*

3. The Personal Endings of Verbs.

ACTIVE.

Indicative. *Subjunctive.*

Present.

	I.	II.	III.	IV.	I.	II.	III.	IV.
S.	ŏ.	ĕŏ.	ŏ.	ĭŏ.	ēm.	ĕām.	ām.	ĭām.
	ās.	ēs.	ĭs.	īs.	ēs.	ĕās.	ās.	ĭās.
	ăt.	ĕt.	ĭt.	ĭt.	ĕt.	ĕăt.	ăt.	ĭăt.
Pl.	āmŭs.	ēmŭs.	ĭmŭs.	īmŭs.	ēmŭs.	ĕāmŭs.	āmŭs.	ĭāmŭs.
	ātĭs.	ētĭs.	ĭtĭs.	ītĭs.	ētĭs.	ĕātĭs.	ātĭs.	ĭātĭs.
	ānt.	ēnt.	ūnt.	ĭūnt.	ēnt.	ĕānt.	ānt.	ĭānt.

Imperfect.

S.	ābām.	ēbām.	ēbām.	ĭēbām.	ārēm.	ērēm.	ĕrēm.	īrēm.
	ābās.	ēbās.	ēbās.	ĭēbās.	ārēs.	ērēs.	ĕrēs.	īrēs.
	ābăt.	ēbăt.	ēbăt.	ĭēbăt.	ārĕt.	ērĕt.	ĕrĕt.	īrĕt.
Pl.	ābāmŭs.	ēbāmŭs.	ēbāmŭs.	ĭēbāmŭs.	ārēmŭs.	ērēmŭs.	ĕrēmŭs.	īrēmŭs.
	ābātĭs.	ēbātĭs.	ēbātĭs.	ĭēbātĭs.	ārētĭs.	ērētĭs.	ĕrētĭs.	īrētĭs.
	ābānt.	ēbānt.	ēbānt.	ĭēbānt.	ārēnt.	ērēnt.	ĕrēnt.	īrēnt.

Future.

S.	ābŏ̆.	ēbŏ̆.	ām.	ĭām.	Wanting.
	ābĭ̆s.	ēbĭ̆s.	ēs.	ĭēs.	
	ābĭ̆t.	ēbĭ̆t.	ĕ̄t.	ĭĕ̄t.	
Pl.	ābĭmŭ̆s.	ēbĭmŭ̆s.	ēmŭ̆s.	ĭēmŭ̆s.	
	ābĭtĭ̆s.	ēbĭtĭ̆s.	ētĭ̆s.	ĭētĭ̆s.	
	ābūnt.	ēbūnt.	ēnt.	ĭēnt.	

	Perfect.	*Pluperf.*	*Fut. Perf.*	*Perfect.*	*Pluperf.*	*Fut. Perf.*
	(For all conjugations.)			*(For all conjugations.)*		
S.	ī.	ĕrām.	ĕrŏ̆.	ĕrīm.	īssēm.	Wanting.
	īstī.	ĕrās.	ĕrĭ̆s.	ĕrĭ̆s.	īssēs.	
	ĭ̆t.	ĕră̄t.	ĕrĭ̆t.	ĕrĭ̆t.	īssĕ̄t.	
Pl.	ĭmŭ̆s.	ĕrāmŭ̆s.	ĕrĭmŭ̆s.	ĕrĭmŭ̆s.	īssēmŭ̆s.	
	īstĭ̆s.	ĕrātĭ̆s.	ĕrĭtĭ̆s.	ĕrĭtĭ̆s.	īssētĭ̆s.	
	ērūnt (ērĕ).	ĕrānt.	ĕrīnt.	ĕrīnt.	īssēnt.	

Imperatives.

		I.	II.	III.	IV.
S.	2.	ā, ātŏ̆.	ē, ētŏ̆.	ĕ, ĭtŏ̆.	ī, ītŏ̆.
	3.	ātŏ̆.	ētŏ̆.	ĭtŏ̆.	ītŏ̆.
Pl.	2.	ātĕ, ātōtĕ.	ētĕ, ētōtĕ.	ĭtĕ, ĭtōtĕ.	ītĕ, ītōtĕ.
	3.	āntŏ̆.	ēntŏ̆.	ūntŏ̆.	ĭūntŏ̆.

Infinitives.

	I.	II.	III.	IV.
Pres.	ārĕ.	ērĕ.	ĕrĕ.	īrĕ.
Perf.	īssĕ.	īssĕ.	īssĕ.	īssĕ.
Fut.	ūrŭ̆s, ă, ūm ēssĕ.	ūrŭ̆s, ă, ūm ēssĕ.	ūrŭ̆s, ă, ūm ēssĕ.	ūrŭ̆s, ă, ūm ēssĕ.

Participles.

	I.	II.	III.	IV.
Pres.	āns, āntĭ̆s.	ēns, ēntĭ̆s.	ēns, ēntĭ̆s.	ĭēns, ĭēntĭ̆s.
Fut.	ūrŭ̆s, ă, ūm.	ūrŭ̆s, ă, ūm.	ūrŭ̆s, ă, ūm.	ūrŭ̆s, ă, ūm.

PASSIVE.

Indicative. *Subjunctive.*

Present.

	I.	II.	III.	IV.	I.	II.	III.	IV.
S.	ŏ̆r.	ĕŏ̆r.	ŏ̆r.	ĭŏ̆r.	ĕ̄r.	ĕă̄r.	ă̄r.	ĭă̄r.
	ārĭ̆s.	ērĭ̆s.	ĕrĭ̆s.	īrĭ̆s.	ērĭ̆s.	ĕārĭ̆s.	ārĭ̆s.	ĭārĭ̆s.
	ātŭ̆r.	ētŭ̆r.	ĭtŭ̆r.	ītŭ̆r.	ētŭ̆r.	ĕātŭ̆r.	ātŭ̆r.	ĭātŭ̆r.
Pl.	āmŭ̆r.	ēmŭ̆r.	ĭmŭ̆r.	īmŭ̆r.	ēmŭ̆r.	ĕāmŭ̆r.	āmŭ̆r.	ĭāntŭ̆r.
	āmĭnī.	ēmĭnī.	ĭmĭnī.	īmĭnī.	ēmĭnī.	ĕāmĭnī.	āmĭnī.	ĭāmŭ̆r.
	āntŭ̆r.	ēntŭ̆r.	ūntŭ̆r.	ĭūntŭ̆r.	ēntŭ̆r.	ĕāntŭ̆r.	āntŭ̆r.	ĭāmĭnī

Imperfect.

	I.	II.	III.	IV.	I.	II.	III.	IV.
S.	ābăr.	ēbăr.	ēbăr.	ĭēbăr.	ārĕr.	ērĕr.	ĕrĕr.	īrĕr.
	ābārĭs.	ēbārĭs.	ēbārĭs.	ĭēbārĭs.	ārērĭs.	ērērĭs.	ĕrērĭs.	īrērĭs.
	ābātŭr.	ēbātŭr.	ēbātŭr.	ĭēbātŭr.	ārētŭr.	ērētŭr.	ĕrētŭr.	īrētŭr.
Pl.	ābāmŭr.	ēbāmŭr.	ēbāmŭr.	ĭēbāmŭr.	ārēmŭr.	ērēmŭr.	ĕrēmŭr.	īrēmŭr.
	ābāmĭnī.	ēbāmĭnī.	ēbāmĭnī.	ĭēbāmĭnī.	ārēmĭnī.	ērēmĭnī.	ĕrēmĭnī.	īrēmĭnī.
	ābāntŭr.	ēbāntŭr.	ēbāntŭr.	ĭēbāntŭr.	ārēntŭr.	ērēntŭr.	ĕrēntŭr.	īrēntŭr.

Future.

S.	ābŏr.	ēbŏr.	ăr.	ĭăr.	Wanting.
	ābĕrĭs.	ēbĕrĭs.	ērĭs.	ĭērĭs.	
	ābĭtŭr.	ēbĭtŭr.	ētŭr.	ĭētŭr.	
Pl.	ābĭmŭr.	ēbĭmŭr.	ēmŭr.	ĭēmŭr.	
	ābĭmĭnī.	ēbĭmĭnī.	ēmĭnī.	ĭēmĭnī.	
	ābūntŭr.	ēbūntŭr.	ēntūr.	ĭēntŭr.	

Perfect. *Pluperf.* *Fut. Perf.*	*Perfect.* *Pluperf.*	*Fut. Perf.*
(*For all conjugations.*)	(*For all conjugations.*)	
Past Part. with sūm, ĕrām, & ĕrŏ, etc.	Past. Part. with sīm & ēssēm, etc.	Wanting.

Imperative.

	I.	II.	III.	IV.
S. 2.	ārĕ, ātŏr.	ērĕ, ētŏr.	ĕrĕ, ĭtŏr.	īrĕ, ītŏr.
3.	ātŏr.	ētŏr.	ĭtŏr.	ītŏr.
Pl. 2.	āmĭnī.	ēmĭnī.	ĭmĭnī.	īmĭnī.
3.	āntŏr.	ēntŏr.	ūntŏr.	ĭūntŏr.

Infinitive.

	I.	II.	III.	IV.
Pres.	ārī.	ērī.	ī.	īrī.
Perf.	ātūm ēssĕ.	ĭtūm ēssĕ.	tūm ēssĕ.	ītūm ēssĕ.
Fut.	ātūm īrī.	ĭtūm īrī.	tūm īrī.	ītūm īrī.

Participles.

	I.	II.	III.	IV.
Perf.	ātŭs, ă, ūm.	ĭtŭs, ă, ūm.	tŭs, ă, ūm.	ītŭs, ă, ūm.
Fut.	ūrŭs, ă, ūm.	ūrŭs, ă, ūm.	ūrŭs, ă, ūm.	ūrŭs, ă, ūm.

Supines.

I.	II.	III.	IV.
ātūm, ū.	ĭtūm, ū.	tūm, ū.	ītūm, ū.

4. Irregular Verbs.

Sum.

Indicative.

Pres. Sūm, ē̆s, ēst, sŭmū̆s, ēstī̆s, sūnt.
Imperf. Ĕrām, ĕrās, ĕrā̆t, ĕrāmū̆s, ĕrātī̆s, ĕrānt.
Future. Ĕrō̆, ĕrī̆s, ĕrī̆t, ĕrĭmū̆s, ĕrĭtī̆s, ĕrūnt.
Perf. Fŭī, fŭīstī, fŭī̆t, fŭĭmū̆s, fŭīstī̆s, fŭērūnt (ērĕ).
Pluperf. Fŭĕrām, fŭĕrās, fŭĕrā̆t, fŭĕrāmū̆s, fŭĕrātī̆s, fŭĕrānt.
Fut. Perf. Fŭĕrō̆, fŭĕrī̆s, fŭĕrī̆t, fŭĕrĭmū̆s, fŭĕrĭtī̆s, fŭĕrīnt.

Subjunctive.

Pres. Sīm, sīs, sī̆t, sīmū̆s, sītī̆s, sīnt.
Imperf. Ēssēm, ēssēs, ēssē̆t, ēssēmū̆s, ēssētī̆s, ēssēnt.
Perf. Fŭĕrīm, fŭĕrī̆s, fŭĕrī̆t, fŭĕrī̆mū̆s, fŭĕrī̆tī̆s, fŭĕrīnt.
Pluperf. Fŭīssĕm, fŭīssēs, fŭīssē̆t, fŭīssēmū̆s, fŭīssētī̆s, fŭīssēnt.
Infinitives. Ēssĕ, Fŭīssĕ, Fŏrĕ.
Participles. Fŭtūrū̆s, ă, ūm.

Possum.

Indicative.

Pres. Pōssūm, pŏtē̆s, pŏtēst, pōssŭmū̆s, pŏtēstī̆s, pōssūnt.
Imperf. Pŏtĕrām, pŏtĕrās, pŏtĕrā̆t, pŏtĕrāmū̆s, pŏtĕrātī̆s, pŏtĕrānt.
Fut. Pŏtĕrō̆, pŏtĕrī̆s, pŏtĕrī̆t, pŏtĕrĭmū̆s, pŏtĕrĭtī̆s, pŏtĕrūnt.
Perf. Pŏtŭī, pŏtŭīstī, pŏtŭī̆t, pŏtŭĭmū̆s, pŏtŭīstī̆s, pŏtŭērūnt (ērĕ).
Pluperf. Pŏtŭĕrām, pŏtŭĕrās, pŏtŭĕrā̆t, pŏtŭĕrāmū̆s, pŏtŭĕrātī̆s, pŏtŭĕrānt.
Fut. Perf. Pŏtŭĕrō̆, pŏtŭĕrī̆s, pŏtŭĕrī̆t, pŏtŭĕrĭmū̆s, pŏtŭĕrĭtī̆s; pŏtŭ-ĕrīnt.

Subjunctive.

Pres. Pōssīm, pōssīs, pōssī̆t, pōssīmū̆s, pōssītī̆s, pōssīnt.
Imperf. Pōssēm, pōssēs, pōssē̆t, pōssēmū̆s, pōssētī̆s, pōssēnt.
Perf. Pŏtŭĕrīm, pŏtŭĕrī̆s, pŏtŭĕrī̆t, pŏtŭĕrī̆mū̆s, pŏtŭĕrī̆tī̆s, pŏtŭ-ĕrīnt.
Pluperf. Pŏtŭīssēm, pŏtŭīssēs, pŏtŭīssē̆t, pŏtŭīssēmū̆s, pŏtŭīssētī̆s. pŏtŭīssēnt.
Infinitives. Pōssĕ, Pŏtŭīssĕ.

Eo.

Indicative.

Pres. Ĕō̆, īs, ī̆t, īmū̆s, ītī̆s, ĕūnt.
Imperf. Ībām, ībās, ībā̆t, ībāmū̆s, ībātī̆s, ībānt.
Fut. Ībō̆, ībī̆s, ībī̆t, ībĭmū̆s, ībĭtī̆s, ībūnt.
Perf. Īvī (Ĭī), īvīstī, īvī̆t (ĭī̆t), īvĭmū̆s, īvīstī̆s, īvērūnt (ĭērūnt).
Pluperf. Īvĕrām (Ĭĕrām), īvĕrās, īvĕrā̆t, īvĕrāmū̆s, īvĕrātī̆s, īvĕrānt.
Fut. Perf. Īvĕrō̆ (Ĭĕrō̆), īvĕrī̆s, īvĕrī̆t, īvĕrī̆mū̆s, īvĕrĭtī̆s, īvĕrīnt.

Subjunctive.

Pres.	Ĕām, ĕās, ĕăt, ĕāmŭs, ĕātĭs, ĕānt.
Imperf.	Īrēm, īrēs, īrĕt, īrēmŭs, īrētĭs, īrēnt.
Perf.	Īvĕrīm (Ĭĕrīm), īvĕrĭs, īvĕrĭt, īvĕrĭmŭs, īvĕrĭtĭs, īvĕrīnt.
Pluperf.	Īvīssēm (Ĭīssēm), īvīssēs, īvīssĕt, īvīssēmŭs, īvīssētĭs, īvīssēnt.

Infinitives. Īrĕ, Īvīssĕ (Ĭīssĕ).
Participles. Ĭēns (ĕūntĭs), Ĭtūrūs (ă, ūm).

Imperative. Ī, ītĕ, ītōtĕ, ĕūntŏ. *Gerundive.* Ĕūndī, ĕūndō, ĕūndūm.

Fero.

Indicative Active.

Pres.	Fĕrŏ, fērs, fērt, fĕrĭmŭs, fērtĭs, fĕrūnt.
Imperf.	Fĕrēbām, fĕrēbās, etc.
Fut.	Fĕrām, fĕrēs, etc.
Perf.	Tŭlī, tŭlīstī, etc.
Pluperf.	Tŭlĕrām, tŭlĕrās, etc.
Fut. Perf.	Tŭlĕrŏ, tŭlĕrĭs, etc.

Subjunctive Active.

Pres.	Fĕrām, fĕrās, etc.
Imperf.	Fērrēm, fērrēs, etc.
Perf.	Tŭlĕrīm, tŭlĕrĭs, etc.
Pluperf.	Tŭlīssēm, tŭlīssēs, etc.

Indicative Passive.

Pres.	Fĕrŏr, fērrĭs, fērtŭr, fĕrĭmŭr, fĕrĭmĭnī, fĕrūntŭr.
Imperf.	Fĕrēbăr, fĕrēbārĭs, etc.
Fut.	Fĕrăr, fĕrērĭs, etc.
Perf.	Lātŭs sūm, ĕs, etc.
Pluperf.	Lātŭs ĕrām, ĕrās, etc.
Fut. Perf.	Lātŭs ĕrŏ, ĕrĭs, etc.

Subjunctive Passive.

Pres.	Fĕrăr, fĕrārĭs, fĕrātŭr, fĕrāmŭr, fĕrāmĭnī, fĕrāntŭr.
Imperf.	Fērrĕr, fērrērĭs, etc.
Perf.	Lātŭs sīm, sīs, etc.
Pluperf.	Lātŭs ēssēm, ēssēs, etc.

Infinitive.

Active.	*Passive.*
Fērrĕ.	Fērrī.
Tŭlīssĕ.	Lātŭs, ă, ūm ēssĕ.

Participle.

Active.	*Passive.*
Fĕrēns, ēntĭs.	Lātŭs, ă, ūm.
Lātūrŭs, ă, ūm.	Fĕrēndŭs, ă, ūm.

Imperative.

		Active.	*Passive.*
S.	2.	Fĕr, fērtŏ.	Fērrĕ, fērtŏr.
	3.	Fērtŏ.	Fērtŏr.
Pl.	2.	Fērtĕ, fērtōtĕ.	Fĕrĭmĭnī.
	3.	Fĕrūntŏ.	Fĕrūntŏr.

Supines. Lātūm, lātū.
Gerund. Fĕrēndī, ō, ūm, ō

Fio.

Indicative.

Pres.	Fīŏ, fīs, fĭt, fīmŭs, fītĭs, fīūnt.
Imperf.	Fīēbām, fīēbās, etc.
Fut.	Fīām, fīēs, etc.
Perf.	Fāctŭs sūm, ĕs, etc.
Pluperf.	Fāctŭs ĕrām, ĕrās, etc.
Fut. Perf.	Fāctŭs ĕrŏ, ĕrĭs, etc.

Subjunctive.

Pres.	Fīām, fīās, etc.
Imperf.	Fĭĕrēm, fĭĕrēs, etc.
Perf.	Fāctŭs sīm, sīs, etc.
Pluperf.	Fāctŭs ēssēm, ēssēs, etc.
Infinitive.	Fĭĕrī, Fāctŭs ēssĕ, Fāctūm īrī.
Participles.	Fāctŭs, Făc[illegible]ndŭs.
Imperative.	S. 2. Fī, fī[illegible]. Pl. 2. Fītĕ, fītōtĕ.
	3. Fītŏ. 3. Fīūntŏ.
Supine.	Fāctū.

Note. Those compounds of *Facio* which are formed by the union with an adverb are conjugated like *Fio* in the passive. All others form the passive regularly.

Edo.

Indicative.

Pres.	Ĕdo, ĕdĭs & ēs, ĕdĭt & ēst, ĕdĭmŭs & ēstĭs, ĕdūnt.
Imperf.	Ĕdēbām, ĕdēbās, etc.
Fut.	Ĕdām, ĕdēs, etc.
Perf.	Ēdī, ēdīstī, etc.
Pluperf.	Ēdĕrām, ēdĕrās, etc.
Fut. Perf.	Ēdĕrīm, ēdĕrĭs, etc.

Subjunctive.

Pres.	Ĕdām, ĕdās, etc.
Imperf.	Ĕdĕrēm & Ēssēm, etc.
Perf.	Ēdĕrīm, ēdĕrĭs, etc.
Pluperf.	Ēdīssēm, ēdīssēs, etc.
Infinitive.	Ĕdĕrĕ & Ēssĕ, Ēdīssĕ.
Participles.	Ĕdēns (ēntĭs), Ēsūrŭs (ă, ūm), Ēsŭs, Ĕdēndŭs.
Imperative.	S. 2. Ĕdĕ & Ēs.
	Pl. 2. Ĕdĭtĕ & Ēstĕ.
Gerund.	Ĕdēndī, ĕdēndō, ĕdēndūm, ĕdēndō.

Volo.

Indicative.

Pres.	Vŏlŏ, vīs, vūlt, vŏlŭmŭ̄s, vūltī̆s, vŏlūnt.
Imperf.	Vŏlēbām, vŏlēbās, etc.
Fut.	Vŏlām, vŏlēs, etc.
Perf.	Vŏlŭī, vŏlŭīstī, etc.
Pluperf.	Vŏlŭĕrām, vŏlŭĕrās, etc.
Fut. Perf.	Vŏlŭĕrŏ, vŏlŭĕrī̆s, etc.

Subjunctive.

Pres.	Vĕlīm, vĕlīs, vĕlī̆t, vĕlīmŭ̄s, vĕlītī̆s, vĕlīnt.
Imperf.	Vēllēm, vēllēs, vēllĕ̄t, vēllēmŭ̄s, vēllētī̆s, vēllēnt.
Perf.	Vŏlŭĕrīm, vŏlŭĕrī̆s, etc.
Pluperf.	Vŏlŭīssēm, vŏlŭīssēs.

Infinitives. Vēllĕ, Vŏlŭīssĕ.

Participles. Vŏlēns (ēntī̆s).

Nolo.

Indicative.

Pres.	Nōlŏ, nōn vīs, nōn vūlt, nōlŭmŭ̄s, nōn vūltī̆s, nōlūnt.
Imperf.	Nōlēbām, nōlēbās, etc.
Fut.	Nōlām, nōlēs, etc.
Perf.	Nōlŭī, nōlŭīstī, etc.
Pluperf.	Nōlŭĕrām, nōlŭĕrās, etc.
Fut. Perf.	Nōlŭĕrŏ, nōlŭĕrī̆s, etc.

Subjunctive.

Pres.	Nōlīm, nōlīs, nōlī̆t, nōlīmŭ̄s, nōlītī̆s, nōlīnt.
Imperf.	Nōllēm, nōllēs, nōllĕ̄t, nōllēmŭ̄s, nōllētī̆s, nōllēnt.
Perf.	Nōlŭĕrīm, nōlŭĕrī̆s, etc.
Pluperf.	Nōlŭīssēm, nōlŭīssēs, etc.

Infinitives. Nōllĕ, Nōlŭīssĕ.

Participle. Nōlēns (ēntī̆s).

Imperative. Nōlī, Nōlītŏ, Nōlītĕ, Nōlītōtĕ.

Malo.

Indicative.

Pres.	Mālŏ, māvīs, māvūlt, mālŭmŭ̄s, māvūltī̆s, mālūnt.
Imperf.	Mālēbām, mālēbās, etc.
Fut.	Mālām, mālēs, etc.
Perf.	Māluī, mālŭīstī, etc.
Pluperf.	Mālŭĕrām, mālŭĕrās, etc.
Fut. Perf.	Mālŭĕrŏ̄, mālŭĕrī̆s, etc.

Subjunctive.

Pres.	Mālīm, mālĭs, mālĭt, mālīmŭs, mālītĭs, mālīnt.
Imperf.	Māllēm, māllēs, māllĕt, māllēmŭs, māllētĭs, māllēnt.
Perf.	Mālŭĕrīm, mālŭĕrĭs, etc.
Pluperf.	Mālŭīssēm, mālŭīssēs.

Infinitives. Māllĕ, Mālŭīssĕ.

Participle. Mālēns (ēntĭs).

5. Defective Verbs.

Certain verbs are only found in the following tenses, numbers and persons :—

1. *Aio.*

Indic. Pres.	Āiŏ, ăĭs, ăĭt, - , - , āiūnt.
Imperf.	Āiēbām, āiēbās, āiēbăt, - , āiēbātĭs, āiēbānt.
Subj. Pres.	- , āiās, āiăt, - , - , āiānt.
Imperative.	Ăī.
Participle.	Āiēns.

2. *Inquam.*

Indic. Pres.	Īnquām (īnquĭŏ), īnquĭs, īnquĭt, īnquĭmŭs, īnquĭtĭs, īnquĭūnt.
Imperf.	- , - , īnquĭēbăt, - , - , - .
Fut.	- , īnquĭēs, īnquĭēt, - , - , - .
Perf.	- , īnquīstī, īnquĭt, - , - , - .
Subj. Pres.	- , - , īnquĭăt, - , - , - .
Imperative.	Īnquĕ, īnquĭtŏ.

3. *Fari.*

Indic. Pres.	- , - , fātŭr, - , - , fāntŭr.
Fut.	Fābŏr, - , fābĭtŭr, - , - , - .
Imperative.	Fārĕ.
Participles.	Fāns, Fātŭs, Fāndŭs.
Infinitive.	Fārī.
Gerund.	Fāndī, fāndō.
Supine.	Fātū.

Note. In like manner the compounds *Affari, Effari,* and *Profari* are defective.

4. *Quaeso.*

Indic. Pres. Quæsŏ, - ,quæsĭt, quæsŭmŭs, - , - .
Infinitive. Quæsĕrĕ.

5. *Avere.*

Imperative. **Ăvē**, ăvētŏ, ăvētĕ.
Infinitive. Ăvērĕ.

6. *Salveo.*

Indic. Pres. Sālvĕŏ.
Fut. Sālvēbĭs
Imperative. Sālvē, sālvētŏ, sālvētĕ.
Infinitive. Sālvērĕ.

7 *Ovat.*

Indic. Pres. Ŏvăt.
Subj. Pres. Ŏvĕt.
Imperf. Ŏvārĕt.
Participles. Ŏvāns, Ŏvātŭs.
Gerund. Ŏvāndī.

8. *Fuo (obsolete).*

Subj. Imperf. Fŏrēm, fŏrēs, fŏrĕt, - , - , fŏrēnt.
Infinitive. Fŏrĕ.

LIST OF AUTHORS CITED.

(With the Abbreviations Used.)

Cat. Catullus (Gaius Valerius). b. Verona, 86 B. C. A lyric and elegiac poet.

Enn. Ennius (Quintus). b. Calabria, 239 B. C. He was the first Latin poet and wrote the *Annales* (extant only in fragments), also tragedies and comedies.

H. Horace (Quintus Horatius Flaccus). b. Venusia, 63 B. C.; d. 8 B. C. A famous lyric, satiric and didactic poet and friend of Augustus and Maecenas.

J. Juvenal (Decius Junius). b. Aquinas, 60 B. C. A famous satiric poet of the reign of Nero and Domitian.

L. & Lr. Lucretius (Titus Lucretius Carus). Disciple of Epicurus. He wrote the *De Natura Rerum*.

Mart. Martial (Marcus Valerius Martialis). b. Biblis in Spain. He came to Rome in the reign of Galba. He was a famous epigrammatic poet.

O. Ovid (Publius Ovidius Naso). b. Sulmo (Sermonetta), 43 B. C.; d. Pontus, 18 A. D. He was banished from Rome for some unknown cause by Augustus. His best-known works are his *Metamorphoses, Fasti, Ars Amatoria* and *Tristia*. His poems are noted for their elegance, smoothness and feeling.

Pers. Persius (Aulus Persius Flaccus). b. Volterra, 34 B. C. A satiric poet.

Phaed. Phaedrus. b. in Thrace about the time of Augustus. He is noted for his fables, which are mostly translated from Aesop's.

Plaut. Plautus (Titus Accius). b. about 254 B. C.; d. 184 B. C. He is noted for his comedies, of which he wrote about fifty. Though rather coarse in his language, his plays were greatly in vogue as late as the reign of Diocletian.

Prop. & Pr. Propertius (Sextus Aurelius), b. Umbria, about 50 B. C.; d. about 15 B. C. An elegiac poet of great power.

Sen. Seneca (Lucius Annaeus). b. Cordova, 4 B. C.; d. Rome, 65 A. D. Philosopher, rhetorician and poet. Nine of his tragedies are still extant.

Ter. Terence (Publius Terentius). b. Carthage about 195 B. C.; d. 159 B. C. He is celebrated for his comedies, of which six are extant. He is considered inferior to Plautus in wit, but more elegant in style. His writings are coarse and vulgar.

Tib. Tibullus (Aulus Albius). b. 55 B. C.; d. about 19 B. C. Contemporary of Ovid. Superior to the latter in style and taste, his language is much coarser.

V. Vergil (Publius Vergilius Maro). b. near Mantua, 76 B. C.; d. Rome, 15 B. C. Rome's greatest poet. He is famous for his epic, the *Aeneid,* his *Eclogues* and *Georgics.* By all he is considered one of the four greatest poets in the world.

LIST OF ABBREVIATIONS USED.

abl.	ablative.	infin.	infinitive.
acc.	accusative.	interj.	interjection.
adj.	adjective.	interr.	interrogative.
adv.	adverb.	inus.	not used.
arch.	archaic.	m.	masculine.
conj.	conjunction.	n.	neuter.
d.	dative.	nom.	nominative.
eccl.	Ecclesiastic.	pass.	passive.
Epith.	Epithet.	Phr.	Phrase.
f.	feminine.	pl.	plural.
Fig.	Figuratively.	prep.	preposition.
freq.	frequentative.	pron.	pronoun.
fut.	future.	sing.	singular.
gen.	genitive.	subst.	substantive.
impers.	impersonal.	Syn.	Synonym.
imper.	imperative.	sync.	syncopated.
indecl.	indeclinable.	voc.	vocative.

THE STUDENT'S GRADUS.

(N. B. *In the Phrases, found with each word, many are citations from different authors. These have the quantities as they are scanned. The others have the different variations possible.*)

Ā, ăb, ăbs. prep. *From, away from.* Syn.—Ē, ēx, ăb ūsquĕ prŏcŭl ăb. *By, through the agency of.* Syn.—Pĕr.

Ăbāctŏr, ōrĭs, m. *Cattle-thief.* Syn.—Fūr, prædŏ, pĕcŏrĭs rāptŏr.

Ăbāctŭs, ă, ūm. *Taken away, led away.* Syn.—Ābdūctŭs, āblātŭs, rāptŭs. *Repulsed.* Syn.—Āctŭs, ēxāctŭs, pūlsŭs, ēxpūlsŭs, ējēctŭs, ēxsŭl.

Ăbălĭēnŏ, ās, āvī, ātūm, ārĕ. *To remove, to separate, to alienate.* Syn.—Ălĭēnŏ, dīsjūngŏ, āvērtŏ, dīstrăhŏ, dīvēllŏ, sēpărŏ. *To sell.* Syn.—Vēndŏ.

Ābbās, ātĭs. m. *Abbot.* Syn.—Āntīstĕs, præsŭl, pătĕr, rēctŏr. Phr.—Cœnŏbĭī præsŭl. Mĭtră lĭtŭōquĕ dĕcōrŭs.

Ăbdĭcŏ, ās, āvī, ātūm, ārĕ. *To abdicate, to resign.* Syn.—Ēxŭŏ, dēpōnŏ, rĕpōnŏ. Phr.—Īmpĕrĭūm dēpōnŏ, pōnŏ. Măgīstrātūm ăbdĭcŏ. *To disavow, to reject.* Syn.—Ēxŭŏ, ābjĭcĭŏ, rĕnŭŏ, rējĭcĭŏ. *To deprive of one's rights.* Syn.—Ēxhærēdŏ.

Ābdīcŏ, ĭs, īxī, īctūm, ĕrĕ. *To refuse, to reject, to disapprove.* Syn.—Ēxŭŏ, rējĭcĭŏ, ābnŭŏ, rĕnŭŏ.

Ābdĭtē. adv. *Secretly.* Syn.—Clām, ōccūltē, sēcrētŏ.

Ăbdĭtūm, ī. n. *Recess.* Syn.—Lătĕbræ. Phr.—Ōbscūrŭs rĕcēssŭs, sēcrētŭs lŏcŭs. Fig.—*Secret.* Syn.—Sēcrētūm, ārcānūm. Phr.—Pŏtĕrĭt dŏlŏr ābdĭtă cōrdĭs Rūmpĕrĕ.

Ābdĭtŭs, ă, ūm. *Hidden, secreted.* Ābdĭtă frōndĕ lĕvī, dēnsā spĕcŭlābŏr ăb ūlmō. O. Syn.—Cōndĭtŭs, ābscōndĭtŭs, rĕcōndĭtŭs, ōccūltātŭs, ōccūltŭs, tēctŭs, cōntēctŭs, ōbtēctŭs, ōbdūctŭs, lătēns, lătĭtāns, ŏpērtŭs, rĕmōtŭs, ŏpācŭs, lătĕbrōsŭs, rĕdūctŭs, īnvīsŭs, claūsŭs, cæcŭs, ōbscūrŭs, ārcānŭs. Phr.—Lătĕbrīs cōndĭtŭs, īnclūsŭs. Ōccūltŭs ūmbrīs. Cūrvīs tĕnĕbrīs dēfēnsŭs. Āntrō cōntēctŭs ŏpācō. Vēprĕ lătēns. Nūbĕ căvā ămīctŭs. Sōlĭs ĭnāccēssūs rădĭīs. Fig. Phr.—Ābdĭtōs gĕrĭt sēnsūs. Ābdĭtăque īntūs spīrāmēnta ănĭmæ. Ōccūltum īnspīrēs īgnēm. Ābdĭtă fātă. Sēcrētă părēntĭs. Ānchīsæ dŏmŭs.

Ābdŏ, ĭs, dĭdī, dĭtūm, ĕrĕ. *To conceal, to bury.* Ēvŏlāt ēt nātūm frōndōsīs mōntĭbŭs ābdĭt. V. Syn.—Cōndŏ, ābscōndŏ, rĕcōndŏ, ābstrūdŏ, ōccūltŏ, ōbdūcŏ, vēlŏ, ŏpācŏ, cēlŏ, ŏpĕrĭŏ, īnvōlvŏ, tĕgŏ, ōbtĕgŏ, cōntĕgŏ. Phr.—Īnvōlvĕrĕ hōrrēntĭbŭs ūmbrīs. Cæcīs lătĕbrīs cōndĕrĕ. Dēnsā sēpĕ tĕgĕrĕ. Claūsūmquĕ căvā tē cōndĕrĕ tĕrrā. Ŏpēs tērrā prĕmĕrĕ. Fūrtūm dēpōnĕrĕ. Prĕmĭt āltūm cōrdĕ dŏlōrēm. Fāma ōbscūră rĕcōndĭt. Ŭbĭ cœlūm cōndĭdĭt ūmbrā. Ōbscūrō grădĭēntēs āĕrĕ sæpsĭt. *To remove.* Syn.—Āmŏvĕŏ, ārcĕŏ. Sē—. *To hide.* Syn.—Lătĕŏr, lătĭtŏr, dēlĭtēscŏ, ābdŏr, ābscōndŏr, tĕgŏr, vēlŏr, cēlŏr, ōccūltŏr. Phr.—Lătĕbrīs sē dărĕ. Cēlārĕ sē tĕnĕbrīs. Nōctĭs sē cōndĭdĭt ūmbrīs. Ŏcŭlōs fŭgĕrĕ. Vānīs sēse ōccŭlĭt ūmbrīs. Ēt nōctĕ tĕgūntŭr ŏpācā.

Ābdōmĕn, ĭnĭs. n. *Abdomen, belly.* Syn.—Vēntĕr, ālvŭs, ădēps, pīnguēdŏ. Phr.—Ālvī vāstă vŏrāgŏ. Īngēntī grăvĭs ābdōmĭnĕ vēntĕr.

Ābdūcŏ, ĭs, dūxī, dūctūm, ĕrĕ. *To lead away, to turn aside.* Syn.—Āmŏvĕŏ, rĕmŏvĕŏ, ābstrăhŏ, aūfĕrŏ, sūbdūcŏ, sūbmŏvĕŏ, răpĭŏ, tōllŏ, ăbĭgŏ. Phr.—Grĕmĭīs mātrūm ābdūcĕrĕ nātōs. Pĕcŭdēs ābdūcĕrĕ fūrtō. Fig.—*To turn away from.* Syn.—Āvērtŏ, āvŏcŏ, ābstērrĕŏ.

Ăbĕŏ, īs, īvī & ĭī, ĭtūm, īrĕ. *To go away, to depart.* Syn.—Ĕŏ, cēdŏ, ābcēdŏ, rĕcēdŏ, ēxcēdŏ, mīgrŏ. Phr.—Sŏlūm mūtārĕ. Pĕnātēs, ūrbēm, pătrĭām rĕlīnquĕrĕ. Tēctō, ūrbĕ, pătrĭā cēdĕrĕ. Clām sē sūbdūcĕrĕ. Pĕdēm ēffērrĕ. Sē prōrĭpĕrĕ. Quō dīvērsŭs ăbīs? Quō nūnc tē prōrĭpĭs? Cĭtō pĕdĕ dēsĕrĭt ūrbēm. Grēssūs rĕmŏvētĕ, prŏfānī. Prŏcŭl, ō prŏcŭl ēstĕ, prŏfānī. Dēcēdĕrĕ cāmpīs. Īn sīlvām pēnnīs ăblātă rĕcēssĭt. Ārdĕt ăbīrĕ fŭgā. *To go forth.* Syn.—Ēxcēdŏ, ēxĕŏ, ābsīstŏ, ēgrĕdĭŏr. *To vanish.* Syn.—Fŭgĭŏ, vānēscŏ, ēvānēscŏ.

Ăbērrŏ, ās, āvī, ātūm, ārĕ. *To wander, to lose one's way.* Syn.—Dĕērrŏ, ŏbērrŏ, dēflēctŏ, vāgŏr. Phr.—Dēvĭūs ērrŏ.

Ăbhīnc. adv. *Henceforth, henceforward.* Syn.—Ā—, ăb—; hīnc.

Ăbhōrrĕŏ, ēs, ŭī, ērĕ. *To hold in horror, to have an aversion for.* Syn.—Hōrrĕŏ, ăbhōrrēscŏ, hōrrēscŏ, pĕrhōrrēscŏ, ăbōmĭnŏr, ēxsĕcrŏr, dētēstŏr, ōdī, āvērsŏr, ēffŭgĭŏ, rĕfŭgĭŏ. Phr.—Quī crīmĕn ăbhōrrĕt. Ōmnīnō ăbhōrrērĕ ănĭmūm. *To disagree.* Syn.—Dīscrĕpŏ, dīffĕrŏ, ābsūm.

Ăbĭēs, ăbĭĕtĭs & ābiĕtĭs. f. *Spruce, fir, hemlock.* (*See Appendix under list of Trees, etc.*)

Ăbĭgŏ, ĭs, ēgī, āctūm, ĕrĕ. *To drive away.* Ō vīr cōllŏquĭō nōn ăbĭgēndĕ mĕō. O. Syn.—Pēllŏ, ēxpēllŏ, prōpēllŏ, fŭgŏ, ārcĕŏ. Phr.—Quæ dum ăbĭgō mēntĕ. Quō vōs păvŏr, īnquĭt, ăbēgĭt

Ĭmpĭŭs? Ăbĭgātquĕ mōtō nōxĭās ăvēs pānnō. Quæ cūrās
ăbĭgăt.

Ăbĭtŭs, ūs. m. *Departure.* Syn.—Dīscēssŭs, ēxcēssŭs, dīgrēssŭs,
ābscēssŭs.

Ābjĭcĭŏ, ĭs, jēcī, jēctūm, ĕrĕ. *To throw, to cast away.* Ābjĭcĭtō
pŏtĭŭs quām quō pērfērrĕ jŭbērĭs. H. Syn.—Prōjĭcĭŏ, rējĭcĭŏ,
ēxŭŏ, pōnŏ, dēpōnŏ. Phr.—Ād tērrām mīttŏ. Ābjēctŭs ĭn
hērbīs. Fig.—*To reject, to refuse.* Syn.—Rēspŭŏ, dēspĭcĭŏ.

Ābjūngŏ, ĭs, xī, ctūm, ĕrĕ *To unyoke, to separate.* Mœrēntem
ābjūngēns frātērnā mōrtĕ jŭvēncūm. V. Syn.—Ābjūgŏ, dĭs-
jūngŏ, sēpărŏ.

Ābjūrŏ, ās, āvī, ātūm, ārĕ. *To abjure, to deny with an oath.* Syn.—
Nĕgŏ, ābnĕgŏ, ējūrŏ.

Āblēgŏ, ās, āvī, ātūm, ārĕ. *To chase away, to send away.* Syn.—
Āmāndŏ, pēllŏ, ēxpēllŏ, ēxtrūdŏ, ārcĕŏ, rĕlēgŏ. Phr.—Fīnĭbŭs
āblēgārĕ sŭīs. Sēdĭbŭs āblēgāt prŏprĭīs.

Āblĭgūrĭŏ, ĭs, īvī & ĭī, ītūm, īrĕ. *To waste riotously in eating or
drinking.* Syn.—Dēcŏquŏ, ābsūmŏ, prŏfūndŏ, hēllŭŏr. Phr.—
Āblĭgūrĭērāt bŏnă pătērnă.

Āblūdŏ, ĭs, sī, sūm, ĕrĕ. *To be unlike.* Hæc ā tē nōn mūltum
āblūdĭt ĭmāgŏ. H. Syn.—Dīscrēpŏ, dīffērŏ, ābsūm. *See Dis-
crepo.*

Āblŭŏ, ĭs, ŭī, ūtūm, ĕrĕ. *To wash, to clean, to purify.* Dōnēc mē
flūmĭnĕ vīvō Āblŭĕrŏ. V. Syn.—Lăvŏ, ēlŭŏ, ābstērgŏ, pērgŏ,
mūndŏ. Phr.—Āquīs rĭgŏ. Āquā spārgŏ. Ūndīs sōrdēs, lābēs
ēlŭŏ, mūndŏ. Tūrpēs ōrĕ fŭgārĕ nŏtās. Vŭlnĕră lȳmphā
Āblŭĭt. Īrrŏrātquĕ mănūs lȳmphīs. Dāt mănĭbūs fămŭlī
lȳmphās. Spārgūntūr flūmĭnĕ lārgō. *To bathe.* Syn.—Īmmērgŏ, lăvŏr. Phr.—Cōrpūs, cōrpŏră ăquīs, ūndīs, flŭvĭō, mērgŏ,
ĭmmērgŏ. Cōrpŭs mē ĭn ăquām, ĭn ūndās īmmīttŏ, prōjĭcĭŏ.
Mē dō flŭvĭō. Ĭn āmnēm dēscēndŏ. Ĭn ūndās dēsĭlĭŏ. *To
purify, to expiate. See Expio. To efface, to make disappear.*
Syn.—Pēllŏ, fŭgŏ, dīspēllŏ, āmŏvĕŏ.

Ābnătŏ, ās, āvī, ātūm, ārĕ. *To swim away from.* Syn.—Ēnătŏ,
ēnāvĭgŏ, ēmērgŏ. Phr.—Tŭmĭdīs ābnătăt ūndīs. Tăbŭlīs frāctīs ēnătăt ēxspēs.

Ābnĕgŏ, ās, āvī, ātūm, ārĕ. *To deny, to refuse.* Ābnĕgăt ēxcīsā
vītām prōdūcĕrĕ Trōjā. V. Syn.—Nĕgŏ, pērnĕgŏ, ābnŭŏ, rĕnŭŏ.
Phr.—Jūppĭtĕr ābnĕgăt ĭmbrēm. Nēc cŏmĭtēm ābnĕgăt. Prēn-
sĭquĕ nĕgābūnt Vērbĕră lēntă pătī.

Ābnŭŏ, ĭs, ŭī, ūtūm, ĕrĕ. *To nod refusal.* Quĭs tālĭă dēmēns ābnŭăt? V. Syn.—Rĕnŭŏ, rĕcūsŏ, nĕgŏ, ābnĕgŏ, dēnĕgŏ, pērnĕgŏ, nōlŏ, rēspŭŏ. Phr.—Nēc māxĭmŭs ōmĕn Ābnŭĭt Aēnēās.

Ăbŏlĕŏ, ēs, ēvī, ĭtūm, ērĕ. *To abolish, to efface.* Nēc pŏtĕrĭt fērrūm nĕc ĕdāx ăbŏlērĕ vĕtūstās. O. Syn.—Āntīquŏ, rēscīndŏ, tōllŏ, dēlĕŏ, ēxstīnguŏ, ōblĭtĕrŏ, dēstrŭŏ. Phr.—Īrrĭtūm făcĭŏ. Īnfēctūm rēddŏ, præbĕŏ. Sī quĭd dēlēvĕrĭt æstās. Sī prōlēs dēfēcĕrĭt ōmnēs. Fērrōquĕ tŭōs ăbŏlērĕ nĕpōtēs. Ăbŏlērĕ nĕfāndī Cūnctă vĭrī mŏnŭmēntă jŭbĕt. *See Everto, Abrogo.*

Ăbŏlēscŏ, ĭs, ĕrĕ. *To be abolished, to cease.* Syn.—Ăbŏlĕŏr, āntīquŏr, rēscīndŏr, ēxŏlēscŏ, dēlĕŏr, īntĕrĕŏ, īntērcĭdŏ, vānēscŏ, ăbĕŏ.

Ăbōmĭnāndŭs, ă, ūm. *Abominable, detestable.* Syn.—Dētēstāndŭs, dētēstābĭlĭs, ēxsĕcrāndŭs, ēxsĕcrābĭlĭs, hōrrēndŭs.

Ăbōmĭnŏr, ārĭs, ātŭs sūm, ārī. *To hold in horror, to detest.* Sī mĕă sōrs rĕdĭmēndă tŭā, quŏd ăbōmĭnŏr, ēssĕt. O. Syn.—Ēxsĕcrŏr, dētēstŏr, fŭgĭŏ, hōrrĕŏ, ăbhōrrĕŏ, āvērsŏr. Phr.—Quōd dĕŭs ōmĕn āvērtăt. Ābsĭt ōmĕn.

Ābrādŏ, ĭs, rāsī, rāsūm, ĕrĕ. *To erase, to rub away.* Syn.—Rādŏ, cōrrādŏ, dērādŏ, aūfĕrŏ, tōllŏ.

Ābrĭpĭŏ, ĭs, ŭī, rēptūm, ĕrĕ. *To snatch away, to bear away.* Syn.—Răpĭŏ, ērĭpĭŏ, ābstrăhŏ, tōllŏ, aūfĕrrŏ, āvēllŏ, dīvēllŏ.

Ābrōdŏ, ĭs, sī, sūm, ĕrĕ. *To gnaw away.* Sæpĕ quŏd ābrōdūnt mĭsĕrĭs ōs ūlcĕrĕ tōtūm. O. Syn.—Rōdŏ, cōrrōdŏ, ēxĕdŏ.

Ābrŏgŏ, ās, āvī, ātūm, ārĕ. *To abolish, to abrogate.* Ēt nĭmĭūm scrīptīs ābrŏgăt īllĕ mĕīs. O. Syn.—Rēscīndŏ, ăbŏlĕŏ, āntīquŏ, dēlĕŏ, ēxpūngŏ, tōllŏ, ădĭmŏ, aūfĕrŏ, ēvērtŏ, dētrăhŏ. Phr.—Lēgēs āntīquās rĕfrīngŏ, dēlĕŏ, rēscīndŏ. Ābrŏgăt īllĕ fĭdēm.

Ābrūmpŏ, ĭs, rūpī, rūptūm, ĕrĕ. *To break, to separate.* Mănĭbūs tĕnĕrōs ābrūmpĕrĕ rāmōs. O. Syn.—Rūmpŏ, dīsrūmpŏ, frāngŏ, scīndŏ, ābscīndŏ, āvēllŏ. *To interrupt.* Syn.—Rūmpŏ, īntērrūmpŏ, īntērcĭpĭŏ.

Ābrūptūm, ī. n. *Precipice, steep declivity.* Sōrbĕt ĭn ābrūptūm rūrsūsquĕ sŭb aūrās Ērĭgĭt. V. Syn.—Prærūptūm, præcēps. Phr.—Cœlīque ābrūptă tĕnēbăt. Fērtŭr ĭn ābrūptūm mōns.

Ābrūptŭs, ă, ūm. *Broken, inaccessible.* Syn.—Rūptŭs, prærūptŭs, dīffĭcĭlĭs. Phr.—Ābrūptī nūbĭbŭs īgnēs. Ābrūptă lŏcă. Ābrūptă rīpă. *Interrupted.* Syn.—Īntērrūptŭs, īntērcēptŭs.

Ābscēdŏ, ĭs, cēssī, cēssūm, ĕrĕ. *To go away, to depart.* Pārce ŏcŭlīs, hōspēs, lūcōque ābscēdĕ vērēndō. Prop. Syn.—Cēdŏ, dīscēdŏ, ēxcēdŏ, rĕcēdŏ, ăbĕŏ, ēxĕŏ, ābsīstŏ, fŭgĭŏ, mĭgrŏ, ēvādŏ. Phr.—Nī prŏcŭl ābscēdăt. Sōmnŭs ŭt ābscēssĭt. Rēgnīs ēxcēssĭt ăvītīs. Dēcēdĕrĕ cāmpīs. Tēctīsque ābscēdĕrĕ nōstrīs. Scĕlĕrāta ēxcēdĕrĕ tērrā.

Ābscēssŭs, ūs, m. *Departure, leave.* Syn.—Dīscēssŭs, ēxcēssŭs, ēxĭtŭs, ăbĭtŭs.

Ābscīdŏ, ĭs, īdī, īsūm, ĕrĕ. *To cut off, to separate.* Syn.—Ābscīndŏ, rēscīndŏ, cædŏ, sĕcŏ, rĕsĕcŏ, dīvĭdŏ, āmpŭtŏ, ābrūmpŏ.

Ābscīndŏ, ĭs, ĭdī, īssūm, ĕrĕ. *To separate, to tear away.* Tūm pĭŭs Aēnēās hŭmĕrīs ābscīndĕrĕ vēstēm. V. Syn.—Dīvĭdŏ, sēpărŏ, dīsjūngŏ, dīvēllŏ, dīstrăhŏ. *To interrupt.* Syn.—Ābrūmpŏ, rūmpŏ, īntērrūmpŏ, īntērcĭpĭŏ.

Ābscōndŏ, ĭs, dı & dĭdī, dĭtūm, ĕrĕ. *To hide, to conceal.* Dōnĕc hŭmō tĕgĕre āc fŏvĕīs ābscōndĕrĕ dīscānt. V. Syn.—Cōndŏ, rĕcōndŏ, ābdŏ, tĕgŏ, ōbtĕgŏ, cēlŏ. Phr.—Tēctōquĕ rĕpōnūnt. Sēcrētī cēlānt cāllēs. Clȳpĕīquĕ sŭb ōrbĕ tĕgūntŭr. Vĭtrĕīsque ābscōndĭtŭr āntrīs. Līgno ōccūltāntŭr Ăchīvī.

Ābsēns, ēntĭs. adj. *Absent, distant.* Īllum aūtem Aēnēās ābsēntem īn prœlĭă pōscĭt. V. Syn.—Rĕmōtŭs, dīstāns, dīsjūnctŭs. Phr.—Sævĭt ĭn ābsēntēs. Īllum ābsēns ābsēntem aūdītquĕ vĭdētquĕ. Ābsēntēm quī rōdĭt ămīcūm. Ēt frūstra ābsēntēm rēspēxĭt ămīcūm.

Ābsĭlĭŏ, īs, ĭlŭī & ĭlĭī, īrĕ. *To leap away from, to spring away, to jump.* Syn.—Sălĭŏ, rĕsĭlĭŏ, ēxsĭlĭŏ, prōsĭlĭŏ. Nīdōsquĕ tĕpēntēs Ābsĭlĭūnt.

Ābsĭmĭlĭs, ĭs, ĕ. *Different.* Syn.—Dīssĭmĭlĭs, haūd sĭmĭlĭs, dīspār, īmpār.

Ābsīnthĭūm, ĭī. n. *Wormwood.* (*See Appendix under list of Trees, etc.*)

Ābsīstŏ, ĭs, stĭtī, ĕrĕ. *To go away, to go forth.* Ābsīstāmŭs, ăĭt, nām lūx ĭnĭmīcă prŏpīnquăt. V. Syn.—Ābscēdŏ, dīscēdŏ, rĕcēdŏ, ăbĕŏ. Phr.—Nēc cūstōs ābsīstĭt līmĭnĕ Jānŭs. Grēssūs rĕmŏvētĕ, prŏfānī. *To escape.* Syn.—Ēxĕŏ, ērūmpŏ, ēxsĭlĭŏ. *To cease from, to desist.* Syn.—Dēsīstŏ, dēsĭnŏ, ābstĭnĕŏ. Phr.—Ābsīstĕ mŏvērī. Nēc vīctī pōssūnt ābsīstĕrĕ fērrō. Āb sīstĕrĕ bēllō.

Ābsŏlūtē. adv. *Perfectly.* Syn.—Pērfēctē, ōptĭmē, ēgrĕgĭē. *Briefly.* Syn.—Paūcīs, brĕvĭtĕr.

Ābsōlvŏ, ĭs, sōlvī, sŏlūtūm, ĕrĕ. *To free from a debt.* Syn.—Sōlvŏ. *To absolve.* Syn.—Dīmīttŏ, līběrŏ. Phr.—Crīmĭnĕ sōlvŏ, ēxĭmŏ. Cūlpā līběrŏ. Cūlpām cōndōnŏ, rĕmīttŏ. *To pay.* Syn.—Sōlvŏ, ēxsōlvŏ, pērsōlvŏ, pēndŏ.

Ābsŏnŭs, ă. ūm. *Discordant.* Sī dīcēntĭs ĕrūnt fōrtūnīs ābsŏnă dīctă. H. Syn.—Dīssŏnŭs. Phr.—Nōn cōnsŏnŭs. Mălĕ sŏnāns. Sŏnō dīscōrs.

Ābsōrbĕō, ēs, bŭī & psī, ptūm, ērĕ. *To engulf, to absorb.* Syn.—Sōrbĕō, ēxsōrbĕō, vŏrō, dēvŏrō, haūrĭō, īngūrgĭtō. Phr.—Ōrĕ hĭāntī ēxcĭpĕrĕ. Ăvĭdām dēmīttĕre ĭn ālvūm. *To devour one's substance* Syn.—Dēcŏquō, hēllŭŏr.

Ābstēmĭŭs, ă, ūm. *Abstemious, one who does not drink wine.* Vīnă fŭgīt gaūdētquĕ mĕrīs ābstēmĭŭs ūndīs. O. Syn.—Sōbrĭŭs. Phr.—Vīnī ābstĭnēns. Ōsŏr Ĭăcchī. Vīnūm ēxōsŭs. Pōtŏr ăquæ. Ābstēmĭă pēctŏră vīnō. *Temperate.* Syn.—Ābstĭnēns, tēmpĕrāns, frūgī.

Ābstērgĕō, ēs, sī, sūm, ērĕ. *To wipe off, to dry, to wipe away.* Syn.—Dētērgĕō, pūrgō, āblŭō, dīlŭō.

Ābstērrĕō, ēs, ŭī, ĭtūm, ērĕ. *To drive away through fear.* Syn.—Dētērrĕō, āvŏcō, ārcĕō, tērrĕō. Phr.—Sāxīs ābstērrēnt tūrrĭbŭs hōstēm. Ābstērrēnt vĭtĭīs.

Ābstĭnēntĭă, æ. f. *Abstinence, temperance.* Syn.—Sōbrĭĕtās, jējūnĭūm. Phr.—Pārcŭs, tĕnŭĭs vīctŭs. Mŏdĭcŭs cĭbŭs. Sōbrĭă mēnsă. Mēns lūxūs ĭnĭmīcă. Pārvō cōntēntă. Pārcī mōrēs. Mŏdĭcæquĕ dăpēs ēt sōbrĭă pōcŭlă.

Ābstĭnĕō, ēs, ŭī, tēntūm, ērĕ. *To abstain from.* Lūdĕrĕ quī nēscīt, cāmpēstrĭbŭs ābstĭnēt ārmīs. H. Syn.—Tēmpĕrō, pārcō, mŏdĕrŏr, mē cōntĭnĕō, fŭgĭō, rĕfŭgĭō. Phr.—Ābstĭnēt ōră cĭbīs. *To prevent.* Syn.—Cŏhĭbĕō, cōntĭnĕō, ārcĕō.

Ābstō, ās, ĭtī, ārĕ. *To stand off from, to be distant.* Syn.—Dīstō, ābsūm, lōngē stō.

Ābstrăhō, ĭs, trāxī, trāctūm, ĕrĕ. *To drag away violently.* Nōn īllūm cūră quĭētĭs Ābstrăhĕre īndĕ pŏtēst. O. Syn.—Dīstrăhō, ābrĭpĭō, āvēllō, dīvēllō, ābdūcō, aūfĕrō. Phr.—Ābstrăhŏr ā pătrĭīs mănĭbŭs. Īn pārtēs ābstrăhŏr.

Ābstrūdō, ĭs, trūsī, trūsūm, ĕrĕ. *To conceal, to dissimulate.* Syn.—Ābdō, ābscōndō, rĕcōndō, ōccūltō, tĕgō, cēlō, īnvōlvō. Phr.—Cæcīs āntrōrum ābstrūsĕrăt ūmbrīs.

Ābsūm, ĕs, fŭī, ēssĕ. *To be absent or away from.* Nūllūm nōmĕn ăbēst, sī sīt prūdēntĭă. J. Syn.—Dīstō, dīsjūngŏr, sūm rĕmōtŭs, dīsjūnctŭs. Phr.—Nūnquam ăbĕrō. Vīr mĭhĭ sēmpĕr ăbēst. Lōngīs īntēr sē pāssĭbŭs ābsūnt. *To be lacking.* Syn.—Dēsūm, dēfĭcĭō. Phr.—Ăbĕrāt plăcĭtæ præsēntĭă fōrmæ. Nĭhĭl ābfŏrĕ crēdūnt.

Ābsūmō, ĭs, sūmpsī, sūmptūm, ĕrĕ. *To consume, to engulf.* Āmbēsās sŭbĭgāt mălīs ābsūmĕrĕ mēnsās. V. Syn.—Cōnsūmō, dēpāscŏr, ābsōrbĕō, vŏrō, dēvŏrō, dēglūtĭō, lĭgūrĭō, cōnfĭcĭō, ēxhaūrĭō. Phr.—Ābsūmĕt hērēs Cæcŭbă dīgnĭŏr. *To destroy.* Syn.—Pēssūmdō, ēxstīnguō, pĕrĭmō, ăbŏlĕō, ēxcīdō.

Ābsūrdē. adv. *Foolishly.* Syn. Stūltē, ĭnēptē, īnsūlsē.

Ābsūrdŭs, ă, ūm. *Absurd, foolish.* Syn.—Stūltŭs, ĭnēptŭs, īnsūlsŭs, ābsŏnŭs.

Ăbūndāns, āntĭs. adj. *Overflowing.* Syn.—Ēxūndāns, ēffūsŭs. *Abundant.* Syn.—Dīvĕs, āfflŭēns, lūxŭrĭāns, plēnŭs, rĕfērtŭs, fĕrāx, fērtĭlĭs, ūbĕr, pīnguĭs.

Ăbūndāntĕr. adv. *Abundantly, sufficiently.* Syn.—Ăbūndē, āffātĭm, cōpĭōsē, lārgē, āfflŭēntĕr, săt, sātĭs, ūbērtĭm.

Ăbūndāntĭă, æ. f. *Abundance.* Syn.—Cōpĭă, ūbērtās, fērtĭlĭtās, lūxŭrĭēs, āfflŭēntĭă. Phr.—Ŏpūm vīs. Prōdĭgą flōrūm lūxŭrĭēs. Bŏnōrūm cŭmŭlŭs.

Ăbūndŏ, ās, āvī, ātūm, ārĕ. *To overflow.* Rūrsŭs ăbūndābăt flŭĭdūs lĭquŏr. V. Syn.—Ēxūndŏ, ēfflŭŏ, ēffūndŏr, ēxspătĭŏr, ēxūbĕrŏ. *To be in abundance.* Syn.—Ēxūbĕrŏ, rĕdūndŏ, lūxŭrĭŏ, āfflŭŏ, cīrcūmflŭŏ. Phr.—Mĭhi ăbūnde ēst.

Ăbūtŏr, ĕrĭs, ūsŭs sūm, ī. *To abuse.* Phr.—Mălĕ, inīquē, īndīgnē, pērvērsē ūtŏr. Īn mălōs, prāvōs ūsūs vērtŏ, ădhĭbĕŏ.

Ăbȳssŭs, ī. f. *Abyss, chasm.* Syn.—Vŏrāgŏ, gūrgĕs, bărăthrūm, hĭātŭs.

Āc. conj. *And.* Syn.—Ātquĕ, ĕt, -quĕ, nēcnōn. (*With a comparative*) *Than, as.* Syn.—Ātquĕ, quām.

Ăcācĭă, æ. f. *Acacia.* (*See Appendix under list of Trees, etc.*)

Ăcānthĭs & Ăcălānthĭs, ĭdĭs. f. *Goldfinch or linnet.* (*See Appendix under list of Birds.*)

Ăcānthŭs, ī. m. *The acanthus.* (*See Appendix under list of Trees, etc.*)

Āccēdŏ, ĭs, cēssī, cēssūm, ĕrĕ. *To approach, to arrive.* Aēnēās cōncūrsu āccēdĕrĕ māgnō Ānthĕă Sērgēstūmquĕ vĭdĕt. V. Syn.—Ādvēntŏ, āpprŏpīnquŏ, ĕŏ, ădĕŏ, āccūrrŏ, īngrĕdĭŏr, sŭbĕŏ. *To go forward.* Syn.—Ĕŏ, ădĕŏ, ādvĕnĭŏ, īngrĕdĭŏr, sūccēdŏ, sŭbĕŏ. *To be added.* Syn.—Ādjūngŏr, āddŏr, ādjĭcĭŏr.

Āccĕlĕrŏ, ās, āvī, ātūm, ārĕ. *To hasten.* Āccĕlĕra, ēt frātrēm, sī quīs mŏdŭs, ērĭpĕ mōrtī. V. Syn.—Ādvŏlŏ, āccūrrŏ, fēstīnŏ, prŏpĕrŏ, āpprŏpĕrŏ. Phr.—Āccĕlĕrārĕ grădūm. Mŏrās rūmpĕrĕ, tōllĕrĕ, pēllĕrĕ. *To hurry another.* Syn.—Cĕlĕrŏ, mātūrŏ, fēstīnŏ.

Āccēndŏ, ĭs, dī, sūm, ĕrĕ. *To burn.* Īllīc sēră rŭbēns āccēndīt lūmĭnă Vēspĕr. V. Syn.—Īnflāmmŏ, sūccēndŏ, ūrŏ. Phr.—Īgnēm, flāmmās, făcēs, tædās sūbdĕrĕ, sūbjĭcĕrĕ, āppōnĕrĕ. Dărĕ īgnĭbŭs. Sūbjēctīs ūrĕrĕ flāmmīs. Fig.—*To inflame, to irritate.* Syn.—Ēxcĭtŏ, ūrgĕŏ, stĭmŭlŏ, hōrtŏr, īnstīgŏ, īmpēllŏ.

Phr.—Seū stĭmŭlīs āccēndăt ĕquūm. Āccēndĕrĕ sēnsūs. Āccēndīt glōrĭă rērūm.

Āccēptŭs, ă, ūm. adj. *Pleasing, acceptable.* Syn.—Prŏbātŭs, grātŭs, jūcūndŭs, āccēptīssĭmŭs.

Āccērsŏ, ĭs, īvī, ītūm, ĕrĕ. *To summon, to invite.* Ēxtēmplō sŏcĭōs prīmūmque āccērsĭt Ăcēstēn. V. Syn.—Āccĭŏ, ādvŏcŏ, ārcēssŏ, ēxcĭŏ, īnvītŏ, vŏcŏ. Phr.—Tōtōque āccērsĭtŭr ōrbĕ. Sŭōs clāmōrĕ vŏcābăt. Cōnvŏcăt hīc āmnēs. *To go and seek something.* Syn.—Quærŏ, pĕtŏ, părŏ. *To hasten someone on.* Syn.—Prŏpĕrŏ, fēstīnŏ, ūrgĕŏ, præcĭpĭtŏ.

Āccēssĭŏ, ōnĭs. f. *Act of approaching.* Syn.—Ādvēntŭs. *Increase.* Syn.—Āccēssŭs, aūgmēntūm, aūctŭs, cŭmŭlŭs, īncrēmēntūm.

Āccēssŭs, ūs. m. *Approach, entrance.* Pōrtŭs ăb āccēssū vēntōrum īmmōtŭs. V. Syn.—Ădĭtŭs, īngrēssŭs. *Arrival.* Syn.—Ādvēntŭs, āppūlsŭs. *Increase.* Syn.—Āccēssĭŏ, aūctūs, aūgmēntūm, īncrēmēntūm.

Āccĭdŏ, ĭs, cĭdī, ĕrĕ. (Cado). *To fall.* Āccĭdĕre īn mēnsās ūt rŏsă mīssă sŏlĕt. O. Syn.—Cădŏ, cōncĭdŏ. *To happen.* Syn.—Ādvĕnĭŏ, ēvĕnĭŏ, āccēdŏ, ōccūrrŏ, fīŏ.

Āccīdŏ, ĭs, cīdī, cīsūm, ĕrĕ. (Cædo). *To cut into, to cut away.* Syn.—Cædŏ, cīrcūmcīdŏ. Fig.—*To ruin.* Syn.—Ābsūmŏ, cōnsūmŏ, īntĕrĭmŏ.

Āccīngŏ, ĭs, xī, ctūm, ĕrĕ. *To girt, to surround.* Lătĕrīque āccīnxĕrăt ēnsēm. V. Syn.—Cīngŏ, præcīngŏ, sūccīngŏ. Phr.—Hīc fērro āccīngōr rūrsŭs. Fīdōque āccīngĭtŭr ēnsĕ.

Āccĭnŏ, ĭs, cĭnŭī, cēntūm, ĕrĕ. *To sing together.* Syn.—Āccāntŏ, āssŏnŏ, cōncĭnŏ.

Āccĭŏ, īs, īvī, ītūm, īrĕ. *To summon.* Sī, Tūrno ēxstīnctō, sŏcĭōs sum āccīrĕ părātŭs. V. Syn.—Ādscīscŏ, ādvŏcŏ, āccērsŏ.

Āccĭpĭŏ, ĭs, cēpī, cēptūm, ĕrĕ. *To take, to receive.* Hīnc scēptra āccĭpĕre ēt prīmōs āttōllĕrĕ fāscēs. V. Syn.—Căpĭŏ, ādmīttŏ, sūmŏ, āssūmŏ, prĕhēndŏ, prēndŏ. Phr.—Căpĕ săcră mănū. Tē grĕmĭo āccĭpĭĕt. Āccĭpĕ dăquĕ fĭdēm. Āccēpīt Fābŭlă prīscă fĭdēm. *To welcome.* Syn.—Ēxcĭpĭŏ, rĕcĭpĭŏ. *To listen.* Syn.—Aūdĭŏ, dīscŏ, cōgnōscŏ. Phr.—Āccĭpĕ nūnc Dănăum īnsĭdĭās.

Āccĭpĭtĕr, trĭs. m. *Hawk.* (*See Appendix under list of Birds.*)

Āccītŭs, ūs. m. *Summons, mandate.* Syn.—Īmpĕrĭūm, jūssūm, māndātūm.

Ācclāmātĭŏ, ōnĭs. f. *Shout, cry of joy.* Syn.—Plaūsŭs, āpplaūsŭs, frĕmĭtŭs.

Ācclāmŏ, ās, āvī, ātūm, ārĕ. *To approve with a shout.* Syn.—Clāmŏ, cōnclāmŏ, rĕclāmŏ, plaūdŏ, āpplaūdŏ. Phr.—Plaūsū dīctă prŏbānt. Lætō clāmōrĕ sălūtānt.

Ācclīnĭs, ĭs, ĕ. *Bent, curved.* Syn.—Ācclīnātŭs, īnclīnātŭs, ācclīvĭs, rĕclīnĭs, īncūmbēns, īnnīxŭs, fūltŭs. Fig.—*Prone to.* Syn.—Prōclīvĭs, prōnŭs, prōpēnsŭs.

Ācclīnŏ, ās, āvī, ātūm, ārĕ. *To bend, to incline.* Cīrcūmspēxĭt Ătȳn, sēque ācclīnāvĭt ăd īllūm. O. Syn.—Īnclīnŏ, rĕclīnŏ, cūrvŏ, flēctŏ.

Āccīvĭs, ĭs, ĕ. *Sloping, bending.* Syn.—Clīvōsŭs, dēclīvĭs, dēvēxŭs, prōclīvĭs.

Āccŏlŏ, ĭs, ŭī, cūltūm, ĕrĕ. *To dwell near.* Āccŏlĭt ēffūsō stāgnāntēm flūmĭnĕ Nīlūm. V. Syn.—Jūxtā hăbĭtŏ, mănĕŏ, cŏlŏ, īncŏlŏ.

Āccōmmŏdātē. adv. *In a suitable manner.* Syn.—Āppŏsĭtē, āptē, cōmmŏdē, cōnvĕnĭēntĕr, dĕcēntĕr.

Āccōmmŏdŏ, ās, āvī, ātūm, ārĕ. *To adjust, to accommodate.* Lătĕrīque Ārgīvum āccōmmŏdăt ēnsēm. V. Syn.—Ādjūngŏ, āptŏ, āpplĭcŏ, ădhĭbĕŏ. Phr.—Clāssem āptēnt tăcĭtī. Clȳpĕōquĕ sĭnīstrām Īnsērtābam āptāns.

Āccōmmŏdŭs, ă, ūm. *Fit, proper, convenient.* Syn.—Cōmmŏdŭs, āccōmmŏdātŭs, āptŭs, ūtĭlĭs, cōngrŭŭs, ĭdōnĕŭs, ōppōrtūnŭs.

Āccrēdŏ, ĭs dĭdī, dĭtūm, ĕrĕ. *To believe.* Syn.—Crēdŏ, fīdŏ, cōnfīdŏ.

Āccrēscŏ, ĭs, crēvī, crētūm, ĕrĕ. *To increase.* Syn.--Crēscŏ, aūgĕŏr.

Āccrētĭŏ, ōnĭs. f. *Increase.* Syn.—Aūgmēntūm, aūctŭs, āccēssŭs, āccēssĭŏ, īncrēmēntūm.

Āccūmbŏ, ĭs, ŭbŭī, ŭbĭtūm, ĕrĕ. *To lie down, to recline.* Tū dās ĕpŭlīs āccūmbĕrĕ dīvūm. V. Syn.—Āccŭbŏ, dīscūmbŏ, rĕcūmbŏ. Phr.—Āccūmbĕrĕ mēnsīs. Ĕpŭlīs āccūmbĕrĕ. Dīscŭbŭērĕ tŏrīs prŏcĕrēs. Strātōquĕ sŭpēr dīscūmbĭtŭr ōstrō.

Āccŭmŭlātē. adv. *Largely.* Syn.—Cŭmŭlātē, lārgē.

Āccŭmŭlŏ, ās, āvī, ātūm, ārĕ. *To accumulate, to heap together.* Syn.—Cōngĕrŏ, āggĕrŏ, ēxāggĕrŏ, ăcērvŏ, cŏăcērvŏ, cōllĭgŏ, cōgŏ. *To overwhelm.* Syn.—Aūgĕŏ, cŭmŭlŏ, ōrnŏ. *To increase. See Augeo.*

Āccūrātē. adv. *Carefully, exactly.* Syn.—Dīlĭgēntĕr, gnāvĭtĕr, sēdŭlō, stŭdĭōsē, sōlērtī cūrā.

Āccūrrŏ, ĭs, cūrrī, cūrsūm, ĕrĕ. *To run towards.* Prīmūsque āccūrrĭt Ăcēstēs. V. Syn.—Ādvŏlŏ, cūrrŏ, āccĕlĕrŏ, prŏpĕrŏ, āpprŏpĕrŏ. Phr.—Cōncūrsu āccēdĕrĕ māgnō. Răpĭdīs āccūrrūnt pāssĭbŭs. Răpĭdō cūrsū ādvŏlăt. Răptīs āccūrrūnt ūndĭquĕ tēlīs.

Āccūrsŭs, ūs. m. *Concourse, arrival.* Syn.—Cōncūrsŭs, ādvēntŭs.

Āccūsātŏr, ōrĭs. m. *Accuser.* Syn.—Dēlātŏr, īndēx. Phr.—Fālsīs īmpŭlĕrĭt crīmĭnĭbŭs.

Ăccūsŏ, ās, āvī, ātūm, ārĕ. *To accuse.* Accūsāssĕ mĭhī, vōbīs dāmnāssĕ dĕcōrum ēst. O. Syn.—Īncūsŏ, īnsĭmŭlŏ, ārgŭŏ, rĕdārgŭŏ. Phr.—Rĕūm ăgŏ, dēfĕrŏ. Crīmĭnĭs, crīmĭnĕ ārgŭŏ. Crīmĭnĭbŭs ŏnĕrārĕ. Scĕlŭs rĕtĕgĕrĕ. Crīmĭnĭbŭsquĕ prĕmūnt vērīs. *To blame, to find fault with.* Syn.—Cārpŏ, rĕprĕhēndŏ, vĭtŭpĕrŏ, crīmĭnŏr. Phr.—Tālĭbŭs īncūsăt.

Ăcēdĭă, æ. f *Laziness, sloth.* Syn.—Īgnāvĭă, ĭnērtĭă, dēsĭdĭă, tædĭūm.

Ăcĕr, ācrĭs, ācrĕ. *Acid, bitter, biting.* Syn.—Ăcĭdŭs, āspĕr, mōrdāx, ămārŭs. Fig.—*Biting, caustic.* Syn.—Mōrdāx, āspĕr, ăcērbŭs. *Eager.* Syn.—Īmpĭgĕr, gnāvŭs. *Shrill-sounding.* Syn.—Ăcūtŭs, ăcērbŭs, sŏnāns. *Dazzling.* Syn.—Vīvĭdŭs, fūlgĭdŭs, flāmmĕŭs. *Strong, vigorous.* Syn.—Vălĭdŭs, rōbūstŭs. Fig.—*Violent.* Syn.—Vĭŏlēntŭs, īngēns, māgnŭs, dūrŭs, grăvĭs.

Ăcĕr, ĕrĭs. n. *Maple tree.* (*See Appendix under list of Trees, etc.*)

Ăcērbē. adv. *Harshly, bitterly.* Syn.—Ăcērbă, grăvĭtĕr, ācrĭŭs. Phr.—Ăcērbă tŭēns. Stābăt ăcērbă frĕmēns. Ăcērbă gĕmēntēm.

Ăcērbĭtās, ātĭs. f. *Greenness of fruit.* Syn.—Ācrĭmōnĭă. Fig.—*Bitterness.* Syn.—Ăcŏr, ăcērbūm. *Affliction.* Syn.—Ăcērbūm.

Ăcērbŏ, ās, āvī, ātūm, ārĕ. *To render bitter, to exasperate.* Ārtĭfĭcĭs scĕlŭs ēt fōrmīdĭnĕ crīmĕn ăcērbăt. V. Syn.—Ēxăcērbŏ, ēxāspĕrŏ, īrrītŏ, ăcŭŏ.

Ăcērbŭs, ă, ūm. *Green, unripe.* Pōmăquĕ crūdēlī vēllĭs ăcērbă mănū. O. Syn.—Ăcĕr, ămārŭs, aūstērŭs, īmmātūrŭs, crūdŭs. *Premature.* Syn.—Īmmātūrŭs, præcōx, prŏpĕrātŭs, fēstīnātŭs. Fig.—*Harsh, severe, hard.* Syn.—Āspĕr, ătrōx, sævŭs, dūrŭs, īmmītĭs, mŏlēstŭs, īnsuāvĭs, sĕvērŭs, trīstĭs. Cāsū cōncūssŭs ăcērbō. Īn rēbŭs ăcērbīs. Pēstĭs ăcērbă bŏūm.

Ăcērvŏ, ās, āvī, ātūm, ārĕ. *To heap together.* Syn.—Cōngĕrŏ, āggĕrŏ, cŏăcērvŏ, cŭmŭlŏ, āccŭmŭlŏ.

Ăcērvŭs, ī. m. *Heap, pile.* Syn.—Āggĕr, cōngĕrĭēs, cōngēstŭs, cŭmŭlŭs, strŭēs. Phr.—Īngēns fārrĭs ăcērvŭs. Cædĭs ăcērvōs.

Ăcētūm, ī. n. *Vinegar.* Syn.—Vīnūm ăcĭdūm. Phr.—Phărĭō mādēns ăcētō. Vĕtĕrĭs nōn pārcŭs ăcētī. Fig.—*Irony.* Syn.—Sătÿră, sălēs. Phr.—Ācrĭă vērbă.

Ăcĭdŭs, ă, ūm. *Acid, bitter.* Syn.—Ăcĕr, ăcērbŭs, āspĕr, mōrdāx.

Ăcĭēs, ēī. f. *Keen edge, point.* Īpsa ăcĭēs fālcĭs nōndūm tēntāndă. V. Syn.—Ăcūmĕn, mūcrŏ, cūspĭs. *Acuteness of mind.* Syn.—Ăcūmĕn, īngĕnĭūm, vīs, sōlērtĭă. *Battle-line.* Syn.—Āgmĕn, ēxērcĭtŭs, lĕgĭŏ, cătērvă, phălānx, mănīplŭs.

Ăcŏnītūm, ī. n. *Aconite, wolfsbane, monksbane.* (*See Appendix under list of Trees, etc.*)

Ăcquĭēscŏ, ĭs, ēvī, ētūm, ĕrĕ. *To repose.* Syn.—Quĭēscŏ, ăccūmbŏ, īnnītŏr. *To acquiesce.* Syn.—Ăssentĭŏr.

Ăcquīrŏ, ĭs, sīvī, sītūm, ĕrĕ. *To acquire, to gain.* Syn.—Ădĭpīscŏr, āssĕquŏr, părŏ, cōmpărŏ, cōnsĕquŏr, cōllĭgŏ, ōbtĭnĕŏ, quærŏ. Phr.—Mĭhĭ părĭŏ. Vōbīs pārtă quĭēs. Aūrō cōncĭlĭātŭr ămŏr. Nĭhĭl ābsquĕ lăbōrĕ părātŭr.

Ăcrĭmōnĭă, æ. f. *Bitterness.* Syn.—Ăcērbūm, ăcērbĭtās.

Ăcrĭtĕr. adv. *Bitterly.* Syn.—Ăcrĕ, ăcērbē. *Lively, strongly.* Syn. —Fōrtĭtĕr, vĕhĕmēntĕr. Phr.—Ăcrī ănĭmō.

Āctă, ōrūm. n. *Deeds, actions.* Sī tămĕn āctă dĕōs nūnqūam mōrtālĭă fāllūnt. O. Syn.—Aūsă, fāctă, gēstă, gēstæ rēs.

Āctĭŏ, ōnĭs. f. *Action, operation.* Syn.—Āctŭs, ŏpŭs, aūsŭs, făcĭnŭs, aūsūm, īncēptūm, īncēptŭs, lăbŏr, āctă, fāctă, gēstă. Phr.—Fāmam ēxtēndĕrĕ fāctīs Hōc vīrtūtĭs ŏpŭs.

Ăcūlĕātŭs, ă, ūm. *Sharp, pointed.* Syn.—Ăspĕr, ăcūmĭnātŭs, ăcūtŭs.

Ăcūlĕŭs, ī. m. *Sting of an insect. In general, any sharp point.* Syn. —Ăcĭēs, ăcūmĕn, cūspĭs, stĭmŭlŭs.

Ăcūmĕn, ĭnĭs. n. *Point.* Syn.—Ăcūlĕŭs, ăcĭēs, cūspĭs. *Keenness of mind.* Syn.—Ăcĭēs, vīs ănĭmī, īngĕnĭūm, sōlērtĭă, săgācĭtās.

Ăcŭŏ, ĭs, ŭī, ūtūm, ĕrĕ. *To sharpen, to file.* Syn.—Ēxăcŭŏ, īnspīcŏ, āspĕrŏ, ēxāspĕrŏ, căcūmĭnŏ. Fig.—*to excite, to irritate.* Syn.—Ēxcĭtŏ, īnstīgŏ, īmpēllŏ, āccēndŏ, īncĭtŏ, stĭmŭlŏ, hōrtŏr.

Ăcūtūm & Ăcūtē. adv. *Sharply, keenly, skilfully.* Syn.—Ărgūtē, săgācĭtĕr, sōlērtĕr, sūbtīlĭtĕr.

Ăd. prep. *To, towards, in the direction of.* Syn.—Vērsŭs, ĭn, prŏpĕ, jūxtā, cīrcā, cīrcūm, ăpŭd, āntĕ, cōrām.

Ădæquŏ, ās, āvī, ātūm, ārĕ. *To equal.* Syn.—Aēquŏ, ēxæquŏ.

Ădaūctŭs, ūs. m. *Increase, augment.* Syn.—Aūgmēntūm, aūctŭs, īncrēmēntūm.

Ădaūgĕŏ, ēs, aūxī, aūctūm, ērĕ. *To increase.* Syn.—Aūgĕŏ, āccŭmŭlŏ, āmplĭfĭcŏr, crēscŏ, aūgēscŏ.

Āddēnsŏ, ās, āvī, ātūm, ārĕ. *To press together, to thicken.* Syn.—Cōgŏ, dēnsō, stīpŏ.

Āddīcŏ, ĭs, dīxī, dīctūm, ĕrĕ. *To sell, to deliver over to another.* Syn.—Vēndŏ, dō, trādŏ, dēdŏ.

Āddŏ, ĭs, dĭdī, dĭtūm, ĕrĕ. *To place upon or near.* Syn.—Ādmŏvĕŏ, īmmīttŏ, īmpōnŏ, īnjĭcĭŏ, ădhĭbĕŏ, āpplĭcŏ, āppōnŏ. *To add.* Syn.—Ādmŏvĕŏ, ădhĭbĕŏ, ādjūngŏ, ādstrŭŏ, ānnēctŏ, āppōnŏ. Phr.—Sŭpĕr, īnsŭpĕr āddŏ. Āddūnt sē sŏcĭōs. Ārdōrēm mēntĭbŭs āddūnt.

Āddūcŏ, ĭs, xī, ctūm, ĕrĕ. *To lead, to conduct.* Syn.—Dūcŏ, ăgŏ, trăhŏ, dēdūcŏ, ādvĕhŏ. Phr.—Nŏctēm dūcēntĭbŭs āstrīs. Quī tē cāsūs āttŭlĕrīnt. Ĕt ăgēntēs frīgŏră vēntŏs. *To attract.* Syn.—Āttrăhŏ, āllĭcĭŏ, āffĕrŏ, īnfĕrŏ.

Ădĕdŏ, ĭs, ēdī, ēsūm, ĕrĕ. *To eat, to gnaw into.* Syn.—Ēxĕdŏ, rōdŏ, cōnsūmŏ, ābsūmŏ.

Ădĕŏ, īs, īvī & ĭī, ĭtūm, īrĕ. *To go towards.* Quīn ădĕās vātēm, prĕcĭbūsque ōrācŭlă pōscās. V. Syn.—Āccēdŏ, cōnvĕnĭŏ, vīsŏ, īnvīsŏ, vīsĭtŏ. *To undertake.* Syn.—Ŏbĕŏ, sŭbĕŏ, sūscĭpĭŏ.

Ădĕō. adv. *So, so much.* Syn.—Tām, ĭtă, sīc.

Ădēps, ĭpĭs. m. *Fat, grease.* Syn.—Ārvīnă, săgīnă, pīnguēdŏ.

Ădhærĕŏ, ēs, sī, sūm, ērĕ. *To be attached to, to cling to.* Frōntĕ tămēn Rhœsī nōn īrrĭtă cūspĭs ădhæsĭt. O. Syn.—Hærĕŏ, ĭnhærĕŏ, ădhærēscŏ, āpplĭcŏr, ādjūngŏr, āffīgŏr.

Ădhĭbĕŏ, ēs, ŭī, ĭtūm, ērĕ. *To employ, to use.* Syn.—Ādmŏvĕŏ, ūtŏr, īndūcŏ, ādjĭcĭŏ.

Ădhīnnĭŏ, īs īvī, ītūm, īrĕ. *To neigh.* Syn.—Hīnnĭŏ, hīnnĭtūm rēddŏ.

Ădhōrtŏr, ārĭs, ātŭs sūm, ārī. *To exhort, to encourage.* Syn.—Hōrtŏr, ēxhōrtŏr, mŏnĕŏ, ādmŏnĕŏ, īmpēllŏ, īncĭtŏ, ēxcĭtŏ.

Ădhūc. adv. *Up to this point.* Syn.—Hāctĕnŭs, ĕtĭāmnūm, ĕtĭāmnūnc, nūnc quŏquĕ.

Ădĭāntūm, ī. n. *The herb maidenhair.* (*See Appendix under list of Trees, etc.*)

Ădĭgŏ, ĭs, ēgī, āctūm, ĕrĕ. *To push, to drive into.* Ēnsēm pēr cōstās ădĭgĭt. V. Syn.—Ăgŏ, īmmīttŏ, sŭbĭgŏ, īmpēllŏ.

Ădĭmŏ, ĭs, ēmī, ēmptūm, ĕrĕ. *To take away, to release.* Nōn īmpūnĕ fĕrēs, ădĭmām tĭbĭ nāmquĕ fīgūrām. O. Syn.—Răpĭŏ, ābrĭpĭŏ, aūfĕrŏ, tōllŏ, pēllŏ, dēpēllŏ, āvēllŏ, ēxtōrquĕŏ.

Ădīmplĕŏ, ēs, ēvī, ētūm, ērĕ. *To fill, fulfil.* Syn.—Cōmplĕŏ, īmplĕŏ, rĕplĕŏ.

Ădĭpīscŏr, ĕrĭs, dēptŭs sūm, ī. *To attain, to obtain.* Syn.—Āssĕquŏr, ācquīrŏ, părŏ, cōmpărŏ, ōbtĭnĕŏ.

Ădĭtŭs, ūs. m. *Approach, arrival.* Syn.—Īngrēssŭs, īntrŏĭtŭs. Phr.—Dēfēndūnt ārmīs ădĭtūs. Fīt vĭă vī; rūmpūnt ădĭtūs. Ădĭtūmquĕ pĕr āvĭă quærĭt.

Ādjăcĕŏ, ēs, ŭī, ērĕ. *To lie near.* Syn.—Āccŭbŏ, āssĭdĕŏ. *To be situated near.* Phr.—Sūm prōxĭmŭs, prŏpĭŏr, vīcīnŭs.

Ādjĭcĭŏ, ĭs, ēcī, ēctūm, ĕrĕ. *To throw or place near.* Cūr vīrŭs ĭn āngueēs Ādjĭcĭs? O. Syn.—Āddŏ, īndŏ, īmmīttŏ, īnfūndŏ. *To attach to.* Syn.—Āpplĭcŏ, ādmŏvĕŏ, ādvērtŏ, ădhĭbĕŏ, āppōnŏ. *To add.* Syn.—Āddŏ, ādjūngŏ, sŭpĕrāddŏ.

Ādjūdĭcŏ, ās, āvī, ātūm, ārĕ. *To award.* Ēt nūnc, sī quĭd ăbēst, Ĭtălīs ādjūdĭcăt ārmīs. H. Syn.—Trĭbŭŏ, āttrĭbŭŏ, āddīcŏ (ĭs).

Ādjūmēntūm, ī. n. *Aid, help, assistance.* Ēssĕ dŭōs jŭvĕnēs fīrma ādjūmēntă părēntĭs. O. Syn.—Aūxĭlĭūm, lĕvāmĕn, sōlāmĕn, sūbsĭdĭūm.

Ādjūngŏ, ĭs, xī, ctūm, ĕrĕ. *To join, to bind, to unite, to attach.* Syn.—Āllĭgŏ, ānnēctŏ, āpplĭcŏ, ădhĭbĕŏ, ādmŏvĕŏ, āddŏ, ādjĭcĭŏ, cōnjūngŏ, sŏcĭŏ. Phr.—Taūrōs ādjūngĭt ărātrō. Sŏcĭūm sūmmīs ādjūngĕrĕ rēbŭs.

Ādjūrŏ, ās, āvī, ātūm, ārĕ. *To swear, to protest with an oath.* Ādjūrō Stўgĭī căpŭt īmplācābĭlĕ fōntĭs. V. Syn.—Jūrŏ, tēstŏr, ōbtēstŏr. Phr.—Ōmnēs tĭbi ādjūrō dĕōs.

Ādjūtŏr, ōrĭs. m. *One who gives help or assistance.* Syn.—Ādmĭnīstĕr, mĭnīstĕr, aūxĭlĭātŏr, faūtŏr, sŏcĭŭs, præsĭdĭūm, aūxĭlĭūm.

Ādjūtrīx, īcĭs. f. *A woman who helps or gives assistance.* Syn.—Sŏcĭă, mĭnīstră, ādmĭnīstră.

Ādjŭvŏ, ās, jūvī, jūtūm, ārĕ. *To aid, to assist.* Quāslĭbĕt īnfīrmās ādjŭvăt īră mănūs. O. Syn.—Sĕcūndŏ, jŭvŏ, făvĕŏ, ādsūm, sūccūrrŏ, āspīrŏ, ŏpēm fĕrŏ. Phr.—Dī nōstra īncœptă sĕcūndēnt! Ēt quōs dĕdĭt, ādjŭvĕt īgnēs! Ādjŭvĕt ēt præsēns īngēntĭbŭs ānnŭăt aūsīs. Ādjūvītquĕ sŭō prōcūmbēns pōndĕrĕ fērrūm.

Ādmĭnĭcŭlūm, ī. n. *Support, prop, stay.* Syn.—Cŏlūmĕn, fūlcīmēntūm, cŏlūmnă, sūbsĭdĭūm.

Ādmĭnīstĕr, trī. m. & Ādmĭnīstră, æ. f. *One who gives assistance or aid.* Syn.—Mĭnīstĕr (tră), ādjūtŏr (trīx), sŏcĭŭs (ă).

Ādmĭnīstrŏ, ās, āvī, ātūm, ārĕ. *To present, to furnish.* Syn.—Mĭnīstrŏ, sūppĕdĭtŏ, sūffĭcĭŏ, præbĕŏ. *To rule, to govern, to manage.* Syn.—Rĕgŏ, cūrŏ, gĕrŏ, gŭbērnŏ.

Ādmīrābĭlĭs, ĭs, ĕ. *Wonderful, astonishing.* Pārcĕ, pŭēr, sæclī dĕcŭs ādmīrābĭlĕ nōstrī. O. Syn.—Mīrābĭlĭs, mīrāndŭs, ādmīrāndŭs, mīrŭs, mīrĭfĭcŭs, spēctābĭlĭs, cōnspĭcŭŭs, ēgrĕgĭŭs, māgnĭfĭcŭs.

Ādmīrābĭlĭtĕr. adv. *In a wonderful, marvellous manner.* Phr.—Mīrūm īn mŏdūm. Mīrīs mŏdīs.

Ādmīrātĭŏ, ōnĭs. f. *Astonishment, wonder.* Syn.—Stŭpŏr.

Ādmīrŏr, ārĭs, ātŭs sūm, ārī. *To wonder at, to be astonished.* Sēd tămĕn ādmīrŏr quō pāctō jūdĭcĭum īllŭd Fūgĕrĭt. H. Syn.—Mīrŏr, dēmīrŏr, ēmīrŏr, stŭpĕŏ, ōbstŭpĕŏ, sūspĭcĭŏ. Phr.—Hīc stŭpĕt āttŏnĭtŭs. Ēmīrābĭtŭr īnsŏlēns. Ōbstŭpŭēre ănĭmī. Āttŏnĭtīs ĭnhĭāns ănĭmīs. Mōtū stŭpĕfāctŭs ăquārūm. Stŭpĕfāctăquĕ cōrdă. Ōbstŭpŭĭt vărĭă cōnfūsŭs ĭmāgĭnĕ rērūm.

Ādmīscĕŏ, ēs, ŭī, stūm & xtūm, ērĕ. *To mingle, to mix.* Prōdĕrĭt ēt tūnsūm gāllæ ādmīscērĕ săpōrēm. V. Syn.—Mīscĕō, cōmmīscĕō, īmmīscĕō, pērmīscĕō.

Ādmīssūm, ī. n. *A fault committed.* Cētĕră sæpĕ tămēn pŏtŭēre ādmīssă nĕgārī. O. Syn.—Cōmmīssūm, dēlīctūm, cūlpă. *See Culpa.*

Ādmīttŏ, ĭs, mīsī, īssūm, ĕrĕ. *To push or send forward.* Syn.—Cōncĭtō, īmpēllō, īmmīttō. *To admit, to receive.* Syn.—Ēxcĭpĭō, rĕcĭpĭō, īndūcŏ, īntrōdūcŏ, īntrōmīttŏ.

Ādmŏdūm. adv. *To a very high degree.* Syn.—Vāldē, mūltūm.

Ādmŏnĕō, ēs, ŭī, ĭtūm, ērĕ. *To warn, to urge.* Ādmŏnĕt ēt māgnā tēstātūr vōcē pĕr ūmbrās. V. Syn.—Mŏnĕō, cōmmŏnĕō, hōrtŏr, suādĕō, jŭbĕō, prǣcĭpĭō.

Ādmŏvĕō, ēs, mōvī, mōtūm, ērĕ. *To conduct.* Āst ŭbĭ dīgrēssūm Sĭcŭlǣ te ādmōvĕrĭt ōrǣ. V. Syn.—Āpplĭcō, āppōnō, ādjĭcĭō, ādjūngŏ.

Ādmūrmŭrŏ, ās, āvī, ātūm, ārĕ. *To murmur applause or blame.* Syn.—Plaūdŏ, āpplaūdŏ, ācclāmŏ, āpprŏbŏ, rĕjĭcĭō. *To make a heavy sound.* Syn.—Mūrmŭrŏ, frĕmŏ.

Ādnŏ, ās, āvī, ātūm, ārĕ. *To swim towards.* Hūc paūcī vēstrīs ādnāvĭmŭs ōrīs. V. Syn.—Ādnătŏ, ādnāvĭgŏ.

Ādnūbĭlŏ, ās, āvī, ātūm, ārĕ. *To obscure.* Syn.—Ōbscūrŏ. Phr.—Nūbĕ, nūbĭbŭs tĕgŏ, cōndŏ, ŏpĕrĭŏ.

Ădŏlĕŏ, ēs, ŭī & ēvī, ădūltūm, ērĕ. *To honor, to burn incense before.* Syn.—Ădōrŏ, hŏnōrŏ, vĕnĕrŏr.

Ădŏlēscēns, ēntĭs. m. & f. *A young boy or girl.* Ĕgo ădŏlēscēns, ĕgo ĕphēbŭs, ĕgŏ pŭĕr. *Cat.* Syn.—Jŭvĕnĭs, ĕphēbŭs, pŭĕr. Phr.—Īntĕgĕr ǣvī. Ăgēns jām trĭă lūstră pŭĕr. Vĭgēns jŭvĕnīlĭbŭs ānnīs. Prīmǣvō flōrĕ jŭvēntǣ. Īnsīgnīs flōrĕ jŭvēntǣ. Fōrmā vĭrĭdīquĕ jŭvēntā. Prīma ǣvī pārtĕ vĭrēns. Prīmī cuī flōrēt tēmpŏrĭs ǣtās. Prīmā spārsŭs, tēctŭs lānūgĭnĕ mālēs. Nēc jŭvĕnīs nēc jām pŭĕr. Jūcūndō flōrĕ jŭvēntǣ. Ōră pŭēr prīmā sīgnāns īntōnsă jŭvēntā.

Ădŏlēscēntĭă, ǣ. f. *Youth.* Rĕgēndă măgĭs ēst fērvĭda ădŏlēscēntĭă. Sen. Syn.—Jŭvēntūs, jŭvēntă, pūbērtās. Phr.—Flōs, vēr ǣtātĭs. Flōs ǣvī. Aēvūm prīmūm. Jŭvēntă prīmă, flōrēns, vĭrĭdĭs. Vērnāntĭs ǣvī pūrpŭră. Aētās mōllĭs ĕt āptă rĕgī.

Ădŏlēscŏ, ĭs, ădŏlēvī, ădūltūm, ĕrĕ. *To grow up.* Mārtĭă tēr sēnōs prōlēs ădŏlēvĕrăt ānnōs. O. Syn.—Aūgĕŏr, crēscŏ, aūgēscŏ, īncrēscŏ. Phr.—Āc dūm prīmă nŏvīs ădŏlēscĭt frōndĭbŭs ǣtās.

Ădŏpĕrĭŏ, īs, ŭī, ŏpērtūm, īrĕ. *To cover, to conceal.* Syn.—Ŏpĕrĭŏ, tĕgŏ, ōbtĕgŏ, vēlŏ, ābdŏ, ābscōndŏ.

Ădōptŏ, ās, āvī, ātūm, ārĕ. *To choose.* Syn.—Ōptŏ, ēlĭgŏ, ādscīscŏ.

Ădŏr, ŏrĭs (ōrĭs). *A grain used in the sacrifices.* Syn.—Fār, frūmēntūm, trītĭcūm.

Ădōrātĭō, ōnĭs. f. *Adoration.* Syn.—Cūltŭs, hŏnŏr.

Ădŏrĭŏr, īrĭs, ōrtŭs sūm, īrī. *To attack.* Syn.—Āggrĕdĭŏr, īnvādŏ.

Ădōrnŏ, ās, āvī, ātūm, ārĕ. *To adorn.* Syn.—Ōrnŏ, ēxōrnŏ, dĕcōrŏ.

Ădōrŏ, ās, āvī, ātūm, ārĕ. *To adore.* Syn.—Cŏlŏ, vĕnĕrŏr, rĕvĕrĕŏr.

Ădrēpŏ, ĭs, psī, ptūm, ĕrĕ. *To glide towards.* Syn.—Īrrēpŏ, ōbrēpŏ, grāssŏr, īllābŏr.

Ădscĭŏ, īs, īvī, ītūm, īrĕ. *To call, to summon.* Syn.—Vŏcŏ, ādvŏcŏ, cōnvŏcŏ, āccērsŏ, āccĭŏ. *To enroll.* Ādjūngŏ, ādscrībŏ.

Ădsūm, ădĕs, ādfŭī, ēssĕ. *To be present.* Syn.—Īntērsūm, ādstŏ, ēxstŏ, ēxīstŏ. *To aid.* Syn.—Jŭvŏ, ādjŭvŏ, aūxĭlĭŏr, sūccūrrŏ.

Ădūlātĭō, ĭōnĭs. f. *Flattery.* Syn.—Āssēntātĭŏ, blāndĭtĭæ, blāndīmēntă.

Ădūlātŏr, ōrĭs. m. *A flatterer.* Syn.—Āssēntātŏr. Phr.—Blāndă lŏquēns. Dōctūs fāllĕrĕ vērbīs.

Ădūlŏ, ās, āvī, ātūm, ārĕ. (*Also a deponent*). *To flatter.* Syn.—Blāndĭŏr, āssēntŏr.

Ădūmbrŏ, ās, āvī, ātūm, ārĕ. *To overshadow, to shade.* Syn.—Ōbscūrŏ, ŏbūmbrŏ. *To trace out with a crayon.* Syn.—Ēffīngŏ, ēxprĭmŏ, dēlīnĕŏ, dēscrībŏ.

Ădūncŭs, ă, ūm. *Bent, curved, twisted.* Rōstrōquę īmmānīs vūltŭr ădūncō. V. Syn.—Ūncŭs, ŏbūncŭs, cūrvŭs, īncūrvŭs, rĕcūrvŭs, flēxŭs, rĕflēxŭs.

Ădūnŏ, ās, āvī, ātūm, ārĕ. *To unite, to assemble.* Syn.—Jūngŏ, cōnjūngŏ, cōgŏ ĭn ūnūm.

Ădūrŏ, ĭs, ūssī, ūstūm, ĕrĕ. *To burn up.* Aūt Bŏrĕæ pĕnĕtrābĭlĕ frīgŭs ădūrăt. V. Syn.—Ūrŏ, ēxūrŏ, sīccŏ, īndūrŏ.

Ădūsquĕ. prep. *As far as, up to.* Syn.—Ūsquĕ ăd, ăd. Adv. *Wholly.* Syn.—Ūsquĕ.

Ădvĕhŏ, ĭs, vēxī, vēctūm, ĕrĕ. *To bring, to carry.* Ādvĕhĭt ūndă rătēs. O. Syn.—Vĕhŏ, dēvĕhŏ, īnvĕhŏ, āddūcŏ, āffĕrŏ.

Ădvēlŏ, ās, āvī, ātūm, ārĕ. *To cover, to conceal.* Vĭrĭdīque ādvēlāt tēmpŏră laūro. V. Syn.—Vēlŏ, tĕgŏ, ābdŏ. *See Tego.*

Ădvĕnă, æ, m. & f., subst. & adj. *A foreigner.* Syn—Ălĭēnĭgĕnă, hōspĕs, ēxtērnŭs, pĕrĕgrīnŭs. Phr.—Mūltōs ādvĕnă tōrsĭt ămŏr. Ādvĕnă grūs. Ādvĕnă quērcŭs.

Ădvĕnĭŏ, īs, vēnī, vēntūm, īrĕ. *To come towards.* Ādvĕnĭăt, vūltūs nēve ēxhōrrēscāt ămīcōs. O. Syn.—Vĕnĭŏ, dēvĕnĭŏ pērvĕnĭŏ, ădĕŏ, ādsūm, āccēdŏ, ādvēntŏ, ādvĕhŏr, āffĕrŏr. Phr.—Ălĭquō grădūm fērrĕ, rĕfērrĕ. Cūrsūm vērtĕrĕ. Ūndĭquĕ cōnflŭĕrĕ.

Cōncūrsū ăccēdĕrĕ māgnō. Dēvēnĕrĕ lŏcōs. Pōrtūs ăccēdĭt Ăvērnī. Jāmquĕ prŏpīnquābānt pōrtīs. Ăd aūrēs Tārdĭūs ădvĕnĭūnt. Tērrāsquĕ cĭtā rătĭs āttĭgĭt aūrā.

Ādvēntĭcĭŭs, ă, ūm. adj. *Foreign.* Syn.—Ādscītŭs, ăccērsītŭs, ălĭēnŭs, ēxtērnŭs, pĕrĕgrīnŭs.

Ādvēntŭs, ūs. m. *Arrival.* Phȳllĭdĭs ādvēntū nōstræ nĕmŭs ōmnĕ vĭrēbĭt. V. Syn.—Ăccēssŭs, āppūlsŭs. Phr.—Ādvēntūmquĕ pĕdūm flātūsque aūdīvĭt ĕquōrūm.

Ādvērsă, ōrūm, n. *Adversity, misfortune.* Sī quāndo ādvērsă vŏcārēnt. V. Syn.—Aērūmnă, cāsŭs, lăbŏr, īnfōrtūnĭūm, clādēs, ēxĭtĭūm. Phr.—Rēs ādvērsæ. Rēs ăcērbæ, ĕgēnæ, dūræ, dŭbĭæ, frāctæ, āfflīctæ. Ādvērsă fōrtūnă. Ādvērsŭs cāsŭs. Sōrs pēssĭmă rērūm. Fōrtūnæ īctūs, tēlă. Ādvērsīs īndŏlŭīssĕ sŭīs. Ēt rēs mĭsĕrābĕrĕ frāctās. Ō pāssī grāvĭōră. Mĭsĕrōs trīstīs fōrtūnă tĕnācĭtĕr ūrgĕt. Me ādvērsă fătīgăt. Trōjæ sūprēmum aūdīrĕ lăbōrēm. Tōtō pătĭōr jāctātŭs īn ōrbĕ. Tū nē cēdĕ mălīs. Fōrtūnă fĕrēnda ēst. Rēbŭs āngūstīs ănĭmōsŭs. Aēquām mĕmēntō rēbŭs īn ārdŭīs Sērvārĕ mēntēm. Gaūdēt pătĭēntĭă dūrīs. Fērrĕ jŭgūm părĭtēr dŏlōsī.

Ādvērsārĭŭs, ă, ūm. *Hostile, opposed to.* Syn.—Cōntrārĭŭs, ādvērsŭs, ōppŏsĭtŭs, īnfēnsŭs, īnfēstŭs, hōstĭs, ĭnĭmīcŭs.

Ādvērsŏr, ārĭs, ātŭs sūm, ārī. *To be opposed to, to resist.* Nōn ādvērsātă pĕtēntī. V. Syn.—Rĕsīstŏ, rĕfrāgŏr, rĕlūctŏr, ōblūctŏr. Phr.—Vīsūsque ōbsīstĕrĕ cōntrā. Frēnīs sæpĕ rĕpūgnăt ĕquŭs. Ēt ĭnēxpūgnābĭlĭs ōbstăt. *See Resisto.*

Ādvērsūm & Ādvērsŭs. prep. *Towards.* Syn.—Vērsŭs, ăd, ĭn. *Against.* Syn.—Cōntrā, ĭn.

Ādvērsŭs, ă, ūm. *Opposed to.* Īntēr se ādvērsī lūctāntūr cōrnĭbŭs hædī. V. Syn.—Cōntrārĭŭs, ōppŏsĭtŭs. Phr.—Gĕnĭbūsque ādvērsæ ōblūctŏr ărēnæ. Dēxtĕr ĭn ādvērsūm nītēns. Īsque ŭbĭ tēndēntem ādvērsūm pēr grāmĭnĕ vīdĭt. Fērrum ādvērsō sūb pēctŏrĕ cōndĭt. *Rival.* Syn.—Ādvērsārĭŭs, ĭnĭmīcŭs, æmŭlŭs, īnfēstŭs.

Ādvērtŏ, ĭs, tī, sūm, ĕrĕ. *To turn towards.* Ōcĭŭs ādvērtūnt prōrās, ūrbīquĕ prŏpīnquānt. V. Syn.—Ōbvērtŏ, cōnvērtŏ, vērtŏ. Phr.—Pĕdēmque ādvērtĕrĕ rīpæ. Ādvērtĭtĭs æquŏrĕ cūrsūm. Nōtæ ādvērtūntŭr ărēnæ. Ādvērtĕrĕ mēntēm.

Ādvĭgĭlŏ, ās, āvī, ātūm, ārĕ. *To watch over.* Syn.—Īnvĭgĭlŏ. cōnsŭlŏ.

Ādvŏcātŭs, ī. m. *A lawyer, patron.* Syn.—Caūsĭdĭcŭs, pătrōnŭs.

Ādvŏcŏ, ās, āvī, ātūm, ārĕ. *To call to oneself, to summon.* Syn.—Vŏcŏ, ăccērsŏ, cōmpēllŏ, cōnvŏcŏ.

Ādvŏlŏ, ās, āvī, ātūm, ārĕ. *To fly towards.* Ādvŏlăt, Haūd ălĭa ēst Tūrnī vĕnĭēntĭs īmāgŏ. V. Syn.—Vŏlŏ. *To run towards.* Syn.—Āccūrrŏ, āccĕlĕrŏ, fēstīnŏ, prŏpĕrŏ, āpprŏpĕrŏ. Phr.—Sēgnēs rūmpĕ mŏrās. Fēstīnātĕ, vĭrī.

Ādvōlvŏ, ĭs, vōlvī, vŏlūtūm, ĕrĕ. *To roll towards.* Ādvōlvĕrĕ fŏcīs ūlmōs īgnīque dĕdērĕ. V. Syn.—Vōlvŏ, sūbvōlvŏ, ādvĕhŏ. Phr.—Vōlvēndō dūcĕrĕ. Mānĭbūs sūbvōlvĕrĕ sāxă.

Ādȳtūm, ī. n. *A sanctuary, or inner part of the temple.* Īsque ădȳtīs hæc trīstĭă dīctă rĕpōrtăt. V. Syn.—Pĕnĕtrālĕ. Phr.—Lŏcūs sēcrētĭŏr ædĭs. Ādȳtī pĕnĕtrālĕ rĕmōtī. Ēx ădȳtō sōrtēs aūdīrĕ prŏfūndō.

Ædēs, ĭs, f. *Temple.* Ēt dĕă mārmŏrĕā cūjūs ĭn ædĕ sŭmŭs. O. Syn.—Tēmplūm, dēlūbrūm. Phr.—Stābăt ĭn ædĕ. *In the plural, a house.* Syn.—Dŏmŭs, tēctūm, lārēs, pĕnātēs, hōspĭtĭūm, sēdēs.

Ædĭfĭcātŏr, ōrĭs. m. *A builder or contractor.* Syn.—Cōnstrūctŏr, ēxstrūctŏr, strūctŏr, cōndĭtŏr.

Ædĭfĭcŏ, ās, āvī, ātūm, ārĕ. *To build, to construct.* Aēdĭfĭcārĕ dŏmōs, lārĭbūs cōnjūngĕrĕ nōstrīs. J. Syn.—Strŭŏ, cōnstrŭŏ, ēxstrŭŏ, cōndŏ, fūndŏ, mōlĭŏr, ērĭgŏ, āttōllŏ, stătŭŏ, cōnstĭtŭŏ. Phr.—Mōlēs, mūrōrūm mōlēs ērĭgĕrĕ, dūcĕrĕ. Cœlō ēdūcĕrĕ. Tēctă lŏcārĕ. Fūndāmēntă, fūndāmĭnă lŏcārĕ. Aēdĭfĭcārĕ căsās. Dædălă fīngĕrĕ tēctă. Tēmplūm dē mārmŏrĕ pōnām. Nōn cœptae āssūrgūnt tūrrēs. Mœnĭă prīmă fūndārĕ. Cīngĕrĕ mūrīs ōppĭdă. Cūm cōndĕrĕt ārcēs. Ārcēmquĕ lŏcārĕ.

Æger, gră, grūm. *Sick.* Ēt mănŭs ōffĭcĭūm lōngĭūs ægră nĕgăt. O. Syn.—Aēgrōtŭs, īnfīrmŭs, īnvălĭdŭs, lānguĭdŭs, lānguēns, mōrbĭdŭs. Mēmbrīs ægĕr. Aēgĕr ēx vūlnĕrĕ. Mōrbō āffēctŭs, āfflīctŭs. Lānguĭdă mēmbră trăhēns. Mōrbī crŭcĭātĭbŭs ūstŭs. Ārtūs īnvălĭdī. Ōssă mōrbō cōllāpsă. Gĕnŭă ægră trăhēns. Fēbrĕ lăbōrāntēs cōrpŏră mōrbō. Hōrrĭdă vūltūm Dēfōrmăt măcĭēs. Aēgēr cōnsĭlĭī. Lūctū mĭsĕrābĭlĭs ægrō. Cūrīs īngēntĭbŭs ægĕr. Aēgră sĕnēctūs. Dējĭcĭt hīnc vūltūs ægēr pŭdŏr. *Difficult, painful.* Syn.—Grăvĭs, dīffĭcĭlĭs.

Aēgrē. adv. *With difficulty.* Syn.—Vīx, dīffĭcĭlĕ. Haūd făcĭlĕ.

Aēgrēscŏ, ĭs, ĕrĕ. *To become ill.* Syn.—Aēgrōtŏ. *To become irritated.* Syn.—Ēxăspĕrŏr, ăcērbŏr. Phr.—Aēgrēscĭt ănĭmŭs. Aēgrēscĭt cūră părēntĭs.

Aēgrĭtūdŏ, ĭnĭs. f. *Illness.* Syn.—Mōrbŭs, lānguŏr. *Anxiety.* Syn.—Cūră, ānxĭĕtās, sōllĭcĭtūdŏ, mœrŏr, ærūmnă.

Aēgrōtŏ, ās, āvī, ātūm, ārĕ. *To be sick.* Quām mĭhĭ dās ægrō, dăbĭs ægrōtārĕ tĭmēntī. H. Syn.—Aēgrēscŏ, dŏlĕŏ, lānguĕŏ, lānguēscŏ. Phr.—Mōrbō, mōrbīs āffĭcī, cōnfĭcī. Ēssĕ mōrbō īmplĭcĭtūm. Aēgrō ēssĕ cōrpŏrĕ. Mōrbŭs mēmbră pŏpŭlātŭr. Sŭbĕūnt mōrbī. Dŏlŏr dēntēs īnvādĭt. Ēxūrĭt vīscĕră fēbrĭs. Ārtūs dēpāscĭtŭr ārĭdă fēbrĭs. Trīstēs īncēssūnt pēctŏră mōrbī. Gĕmĭt mōrbō mŏrĭtūrŭs ĭnērtī. Tērrĭfĭcūs cōrpŏră lānguŏr hăbĕt. Trīstī lānguēbānt cōrpŏră mōrbō. Tūrbăt ăgēns ănĭmām. Cōrpŭs īngēntī lānguōrĕ jăcĕt.

Aēgrōtŭs, ă, ūm. *Sick. See Aeger.*

Aēmŭlŏr, ārĭs, ātŭs sūm, ārī. *To imitate, to follow as a model.* Pīndărūm quīsquīs stŭdĕt æmŭlārī. H. Syn.—Ĭmĭtŏr, sēctŏr. *To dispute with.* Syn.—Cōntēndŏ.

Aēmŭlŭs, ă, ūm. *Imitator, rival.* Syn.—Ĭmĭtātŏr, ĭmĭtātrīx, sēctātŏr. *Envious.* Syn.—Īnvĭdŭs.

Aēnĕŭs, ă, ūm. *Made of bronze.* Syn.—Ăhēnŭs, ăhēnĕŭs, ærĕŭs.

Aēnīgmă, ătĭs, n. *An enigma, puzzle, parable.* Phr.—Aēnīgmătĭs āmbāgēs, lăquĕī. Vērbōrum ōccūltă. Īmplĭcĭtă, īmplēxă, pērplēxă vērbă. Cæcīs vērbīs ōccūltă. Īnvŏlūtă sēntēntĭă.

Aēquālĭs, ĭs, ĕ. *Equal.* Nēc nōn æquālĭs ăb ōmnī Pārtĕ fŏrĕt. O. Syn.—Aēquābĭlĭs, æquŭs, pār, cōmpār, sĭmĭlĭs, părĭlĭs. Phr.—Aēquŭs ŭtērquĕ lăbŏr. Părēs ănĭmīs jŭvĕnēs. Nŭmĕrōquĕ părēs ēt vīrĭbŭs æquī. *Of the same age.* Syn.—Aēquævŭs. Phr.—Pār ætātĕ. Ēx æquālĭbŭs ūnām.

Aēquănĭmĭs, ĭs, ĕ, & Aēquănĭmŭs, ă, ūm. *Even-tempered, calm.* Syn.—Aēquābĭlĭs, cōnstāns, pătĭēns, mŏdĕrātŭs.

Aēquē. adv. *In like manner, equally, just as.* Syn.—Părĭtĕr. Phr.—Haūd sĕcŭs, haūd ălĭtĕr. *Justly, rightly.* Syn.—Jūstē, jūrĕ, mĕrĭtō.

Aēquĭpār, ărĭs. adj. *Equal.* Syn.—Pār, æquŭs, æquālĭs. Phr.—Haūd īmpār.

Aēquĭpărŏ, ās, āvī, ātūm, ārĕ. *To equal.* Nēc călămīs sōlum æquĭpărās, sēd vōcĕ măgīstrūm. V. Syn.—Aēquŏ, ēxæquŏ, ădæquŏ. *To compare.* Syn. Cōmpărŏ, cōnfĕrŏ.

Aēquŏ, ās, āvī, ātūm, ārĕ. *To make things equal.* Sny.—Ădæquŏ, ēxæquŏ. Phr.—Ēt nŭmĕrūm cūm nāvĭbŭs æquăt. Aēquēmŭs pūgnās. Ănĭmōs æquābăt Ŏlȳmpō. Aēquāssēt nōctī lūdūm. *To be equal to.* Syn.—Aēquĭpărŏ. Phr.—Pār, æquālĭs sūm. Mărĕ cœlum æquārĕ vĭdētŭr. Vēntōs æquāntĕ săgīttā. Aēquātquĕ Sĭchæŭs ămōrēm. Quūm prīmūm sūlcōs æquānt sătă. *To imitate.* Syn.—Rĕfĕrŏ, rēddŏ, ĭmĭtŏr.

Aēquŏr, ŏrĭs. n. *Any level surface, a field or plain.* Āt prĭŭs īgnōtūm fērrō quām scīndĭmŭs æquŏr. V. Syn.—Plānĭtĭēs, cāmpŭs. *The sea.* Syn.—Mărĕ, āltūm, prŏfūndūm, frĕtūm, sălūm, pĕlăgŭs, mārmŏr, pōntŭs, ōcĕănŭs. Phr.—Nēptūnĭă ārvă.

Strāta æquālĭtĕr ūndă. Strātūm sĭlēt æquŏr. Ārmātūm scŏpŭlīs æquŏr. Īmmānĭă pōntī æquŏră. Pērvĭă vēlīs Aēquŏră. Lāssātūm flūctĭbŭs æquŏr. Pĕlăgī mĕdĭa ārĕă.

Aēquūm, ī. n. *Justice.* Nōn īllō mĕlĭōr quīsquām nĕc ămāntĭŏr æquī. V. Syn.—Aēquĭtās, jūstĭtĭă, rēctūm.

Aēquŭs, ă, ūm. *Even, level.* Tē cōmĭnŭs æquō Mēcūm crēdĕ sŏlō. V. Syn.—Plānŭs, æquātŭs. *Equal, similar.* Syn.—Aēquālĭs, pār, sĭmĭlĭs. *Tranquil, calm.* Syn.—Plăcĭdŭs, quĭētŭs, lĭbēns. *Just.* Syn.—Jūstŭs. Phr.—Pār ēst. Fās ēt jūră vŏlūnt. *Favorable.* Syn.—Făvēns, prōpĭtĭŭs, sĕcūndŭs, bĕnīgnŭs.

Āēr, āĕrĭs, m. *The air.* Tērră fĕrās cēpīt, vŏlŭcrēs ăgĭtābĭlĭs āēr. O. Syn.—Aēthēr, (*sometimes*) āltūm, aūră, ĭnānĕ, văcŭūm, pŏlŭs, nūbēs, nūbĭlă. Phr.—Āĕrĭs, cœlī, lūmĭnĭs ōræ. Aūræ āĕrĭæ. Āĕrĭī trāctūs. Āĕrĭă plăgă. Ĭnānĭă cœlī. Cœlēstĭă spătĭă. Sĭnĕ nūbĭbŭs āēr. Cœli īn rĕgĭōnĕ sĕrēnā. Āĕrīs īn cāmpīs lātīs. Văcŭūm pĕr ĭnānĕ vŏlūtăt. Tōllūnt īn lūmĭnĭs aūrās. Mănēt sūb Jŏvĕ frīgĭdō. Āĕrĭās tēntāssĕ dŏmōs. Vēctūs pĕr ĭnānĭă cūrrū. Sĭlēt hūmĭdŭs āēr. Grăvĭs īntŏnăt āēr.

Aērĕŭs, ă, ūm. *Bronze.* Mĭcăt ærĕŭs ēnsĭs. V. Syn.—Āhēnŭs, ăhēnĕŭs, ænĕŭs. Phr.—Nēxæ ærĕ trăbēs. Lūcĕ cŏrūscŭs ăhēnā.

Āĕrĭŭs, ă, ūm. *Pertaining to the air, aerial.* Quæ, cūncta āĕrĭī dīscērpūnt īrrĭtă vēntī. Cat. Syn.—Aēthĕrĭŭs, æthĕrĕŭs, sīdĕrĕŭs, cœlēstĭs, sŭpĕrŭs. *Elevated, high.* Syn.—Āltŭs.

Aērūgŏ, ĭnĭs, f. *Copper rust, verdigris.* Syn.—Fērrūgŏ, rūbīgŏ, sĭtŭs. Fig—*Poison.* Syn.—Fēl, vĕnēnūm.

Aērūmnă, æ. f. *Pain, anxiety, trouble.* Trīstĭŏr ēst ĕtĭām præsēns ærūmnă prĭōrĕ. O. Syn.—Lūctŭs, cūră, dŏlŏr, mœrŏr, lăbŏr, ŏnŭs, īnfōrtūnĭūm, ădvērsă.

Aērūmnōsŭs, ă, ūm. *Unhappy, miserable.* Syn.—Īnfēlīx, mĭsĕr, īnfōrtūnātŭs.

Aēs, ærĭs. n. *Bronze, copper, brass.* Phr.—Aērĭs mĕtāllūm, mĕtāllă. Strīdēntĭă tīngūnt Aēră lăcū. Nēxæque ærĕ trăbēs. Fŏrĭbŭs cārdō strīdēbăt ăhēnīs.

Aēscŭlĕŭs, ă, ūm. *Made of Oak.* Vīcĕrăt, æscŭlĕæ căpĭēbăt frōndĭs hŏnōrēm. O. Syn.—Īlĭcĕŭs, īlīgnŭs, īlīgnĕŭs, quērcĕŭs, quērnŭs, rōbŏrĕŭs.

Aēstās, ātĭs. f. *Summer.* Stābăt nūda æstās ēt spīcĕă sērtă gĕrēbăt. V. Syn.—Aēstŭs, cănīcŭlă, Sīrĭŭs. Phr.—Aēstīvī, æstĭfĕrī dĭēs. Aēstīvă tēmpŏră. Sīrĭŭs ārdŏr. Aēstīvŭs ārdŏr. Pārs fērvēntĭŏr ānnī. Călĭdīssĭmă sōlĭbŭs æstās. Jām vĕnĭt æstās. Cūm ārēnt hērbæ. Ūrūntūr grāmĭnă cāmpī. Sōlĕ dĭēs rĕfĕrēntĕ sĭccōs. Lætă tēmpŏră.

Aēstĭfĕr, ĕră, ĕrūm. *Bringing, causing, producing heat.* Syn.—Aēstīvŭs, æstŭōsŭs, fērvĭdŭs.

Aēstĭmŏ, ās, āvī, ātūm, ārĕ. *To esteem, to appreciate.* Syn.—Pēndŏ, pōndĕrŏ. *To judge, to consider.* Syn.—Cēnsĕŏ, jūdĭcŏ, rĕpŭtŏ, pēndŏ, ēxpēndŏ.

Aēstŭŏ, ās, āvī, ātūm, ārĕ. *To burn, to boil.* Syn.—Ārdĕŏ, flāgrŏ, cāndĕŏ, cāndēscŏ, ūrŏr. *To ferment, to seethe.* Syn.—Ēxæstŭŏ, fērvĕŏ, ēffērvēscŏ. *Fig. To be agitated.* Syn.—Āgĭtŏr, jāctŏr, āngŏr, tūrbŏr, trĕpĭdŏ. *To be in doubt, uncertain.* Syn.—Āmbĭgŏ, flūctŭŏ, jāctŏr.

Aēstŭōsŭs, ă, ūm. *Hot.* Syn.—Tōrrĭdŭs, ūstŭs, ădūstŭs. *Boiling.* Syn.—Fērvēns, fērvĭdŭs, īnquĭētŭs.

Aēstŭs, ūs. m. *Heat.* Aēstŭs ĕrāt, māgnūsquĕ lăbōr gĕmĭnāvĕrāt æstūm. O. Syn.—Ārdŏr, călŏr, fērvŏr. Phr.—Aēstŭs hĭūlcāt ăgrōs. Lāssōs æstū fērvēntĕ lăcērtōs. Răpĭdō fēssīs mēssōrĭbŭs æstū. Āspērquĕ sĭti ātque ēxtērrĭtŭs æstū. Tōtōque aūtūmni īncāndŭĭt æstū. Aēstŭs ĕrāt mĕdĭūsquĕ dĭēs. Scīndĭt ăgrōs æstŭs Phœbēīs īgnĭbŭs ārdēns. *Fire. See Ignis. A fever. See Febris. A boiling, heaving, or agitation.* Syn.—Vīs, īmpĕtŭs, ārdŏr, fērvŏr. *Fig.—A commotion of the mind.* Syn.—Cŭpīdŏ, fŭrŏr, īră, răbĭēs. *The swell or surge of the sea.* Phr.—Ūndă rĕcĭprŏcă. Rĕlābēns, ābscēdēns, rĕflŭēns mărĕ. Rĕvŏlūbĭlĭs ūndă. Pōntī rĕcūrsŭs. Ūt mărĕ sōllĭcĭtūm strīdēt rĕflŭēntĭbŭs ūndīs.

Aētās, ātĭs. f. *Age.* Syn.—Ānnī. *See Pueritia, Senectus, Adolescentia, Juventus. Life.* Syn.—Aēvūm, vītă. Phr.—Vītæ tēmpŭs. Cĭtō pĕdĕ fŭgĭēns. Sīngŭlă vērtēns. Cūm mātūra ădŏlēvĕrĭt ætās. Tŭă vītā dīgnĭŏr ætās. Sīngŭlă răpĭdō cūrsū cōntĕrĭt ætās. *An epoch.* Syn.—Sēcŭlūm, sēclūm.

Aētērnĭtās, ātĭs. f. *Eternity.* Phr.—Nēscĭă fīnĭs. Fīnĕ cărēns. Ēxpērs prīncĭpĭī. Aēvūm ætērnūm, pērpĕtŭūm. Pērpĕtŭŭs ævī trāctŭs. Vītă pĕrēnnĭs. Īnnŭmĕrābĭlĭs ānnōrūm sĕrĭēs. Spătĭīs nōn claūdĭtŭr ūllīs. Cuī nĕquĕ prīncĭpĭūm ēst ūnquām nēc fīnĭs. Sēmpĕr ădēst, sēmpērquĕ fŭĭt, sēmpērquĕ mănēbĭt.

Aētērnŏ, ās, āvī, ātūm, ārĕ. *To immortalize.* Phr.—Īmmōrtālĕ, ætērnūm făcĕrĕ, rēddĕrĕ. Aētērnæ mĕmŏrĭæ māndārĕ, trādĕrĕ. Aētērnæ cōmmīttĕrĕ fāmæ. Nēc mōrs mĭhĭ fīnĭēt īrās.

Aētērnūm. adv. *Perpetually, forever.* Sĕdēt, ætērnūmquĕ sĕdēbĭt Īnfēlīx Thēseŭs. V. Syn.—Aētērnō, sēmpĕr, ūsquĕ, pērpĕtŭō. Nūnquām nōn, ōmnī tēmpŏrĕ, dēmptō fīnĕ. Sĭnĕ fīnĕ. *Unceasingly.* Syn.—Āssĭdŭē, sæpĭŭs.

Aētērnŭs, ă, ūm. *Eternal, immortal, perpetual.* Aētērnūm nōstrōs lūctūs ēxtēndĭt ĭn ævūm. O. Syn.—Sēmpĭtērnŭs, pĕrēnnĭs, īmmōrtālĭs, cōntĭnŭŭs, jūgĭs, pērpĕtŭŭs. Phr.—Fīnĕ cărēns. Aērĕ pĕrēnnĭŏr. Mănĕt ætērnūmquĕ mănēbĭt. Nēc mētās rērūm, nēc tēmpŏră pōnŏ. Īmpĕrĭūm sĭnĕ fīnĕ dĕdī. Tēmpŭs ĭn ōmnĕ.

Aēthēr, ĕrĭs. m. *The upper part of the air, the ether.* Crēbrīs mĭcăt īgnĭbŭs æthēr. V. Syn.—Āēr, æthră, ĭnānĕ, cœlūm, aūræ. Phr.—Rŭĭt ārdŭŭs æthēr. Pătŭĭt mĭhĭ pērvĭŭs æthēr. *The heavens.* Syn.—Pŏlŭs, Ŏlȳmpŭs, cœlūm.

Aēthĕrĭŭs, ă, ūm (Aēthĕrĕŭs). *Pertaining to the upper air, ethereal.* Jām mĕdĭum æthĕrĭō cūrsū trājēcĕrăt āxēm. V. Syn.—Āĕrĭŭs, cœlēstĭs, sŭpĕrŭs. Phr.—Aēthĕrĕæ sēdēs. Ārx æthĕrĕă. Aēthĕrĕās tēlūm cōntōrsĭt ĭn aūrās.

Aēthră, æ, f. *The ether or upper air. See Aether.*

Aēvūm, ī. n. *Eternity.* Phr.—Vīvĕt ēxtēntō Prŏcŭleīŭs ævō. *Age* Syn.—Aētās, ānnī. Phr.—Aēvō cōnfēctŭs. Aēvī mātūrŭs. *Life.* Syn.—Vītă, ætās. Phr.—Āngūstī tērmĭnŭs ævī. Spătĭūm mĭhĭ fīnĭăt ævī. Aēvūm prō laūdĕ pācīscī. Aēvī trānscēndĕrĕ mētās. Trādūcĕrĕ lēnĭtĕr ævūm. Brĕve ĕt īrrĕpărābĭlĕ tēmpŭs Ōmnĭbūs ēst ævī. *Epoch.* Syn.—Tēmpŭs, dĭēs, sēclūm, sēcŭlūm.

Āffābĭlĭs, ĭs, ĕ. *Affable.* Nēc vīsū făcĭlĭs, nēc dīctu āffābĭlĭs ūllī. V. Syn.—Cōmĭs, hūmānŭs, ūrbānŭs. Phr.—Āllŏquĭī făcĭlĭs.

Āffăbrē. adv. *With art, artistically.* Syn.—Ēlĕgāntĕr, scītē, pĕrītē, dōctē, sōlērtĕr.

Āffārī, āffātŭs sūm, (*defect. verb.*) *To speak.* Tūm sīc āffāri ēt cūrās hīs dēmĕrĕ dīctīs. V. Syn.—Āllŏquŏr, cōmpēllŏ. Phr.—Dīctīs āggrĕdī. Cōmpēllārĕ vōcĭbŭs.

Āffātĭm. adv. *Abundantly.* Syn.—Ābūndē, lārgē, mūltūm.

Āffēctŏ, ās, āvī, ātūm, ārĕ. *To aspire to.* Cūr ŏpŭs āffēctās, āmbĭtĭōsĕ, nŏvūm? O. Syn.—Āmbĭŏ, aūcŭpŏr, cŭpĭŏ, āppĕtŏ, ēxpĕtŏ, ēxquīrŏ, sĕquŏr, sēctŏr, mōlĭŏr, āggrĕdĭŏr.

Āffēctŭs, ūs. m. *Affection, passion, emotion.* Quōd lĭcĕt, āffēctū tăcĭtō lætārĭs. O. Phr.—Sēnsŭs ănĭmī, pēctŏrĭs, mōtŭs, stŭdĭūm. *Love.* Syn.—Āmŏr, ămīcĭtĭă.

Āffĕrŏ, fērs, āttŭlī, āllātūm, fērrĕ. *To bring to, to carry.* Aūrūm spēctātō nōn quæ mănŭs āffĕrăt aūrūm. Prop. Syn.—Fĕrŏ, dēfĕrŏ, īnfĕrŏ, pōrtŏ, āddūcŏ. *To cause.* Syn.—Fĕrŏ, cōnfĕrŏ, făcĭŏ, ēffĭcĭŏ, trĭbŭŏ, dō, gīgnŏ, părĭŏ. *To announce.* Syn.—Nūntĭŏ.

Āffīgŏ, ĭs, xī, xūm, ĕrĕ. *To fix, to attach.* Cōncrētām pătĭtūr rādīcem āffīgĕrĕ tērræ. V. Syn.—Fīgŏ, īnfīgŏ, āpplĭcŏ, ādnēctŏ, ādjūngŏ.

Āffīngŏ, ĭs, īnxī, īctūm, ĕrĕ. *To add.* Syn.—Ādjūngŏ, ādnēctŏ, ādjĭcĭŏ. *To feign, to pretend.* Syn.—Sĭmŭlŏ, fīngŏ, āssĭmŭlŏ.

Āffīnĭs, ĭs. ĕ. *Neighboring, near.* Syn.—Vīcīnŭs. *Related to.* Syn.—Cōgnātŭs, cōnsānguĭnĕŭs, prŏpīnquŭs. *Resembling.* Syn.—Sĭmĭlĭs, cōnsĭmĭlĭs, prōxĭmŭs.

Āffīrmŏ, ās, āvī, ātūm, ārĕ. *To strengthen, to fortify.* Syn.—Cōnfīrmŏ, fīrmŏ. *To assure.* Syn.—Āssĕrŏ, āssĕvērŏ, jūrŏ.

Āfflātŭs, ūs. m. *A blowing, breathing.* Hōs nĕcăt āfflātū, fūnēsta hōs tābĕ pĕrēdĭt. O. Syn.—Flātŭs, spīrĭtŭs, hālĭtŭs, ănhēlĭtŭs.

Āfflīgŏ, ĭs, xī, ctūm, ĕrĕ. *To overwhelm, to overturn.* Tērræque āfflīxĭt Ăchīllēs. O. Syn.—Prōstērnŏ, dējĭcĭŏ, ēvērtŏ, pēssūmdŏ. Fig.—*To persecute.* Syn.—Āngŏ, vēxŏ, prĕmŏ, ōpprĭmŏ. Phr.—Dŏlōrĭbŭs, mălīs prĕmŏ, cōnfĭcĭŏ. Clādĭbūs īnnŭmĕrīs mĭsĕrām vēxāvĭt. Mē quŏquĕ pēr mūltōs sĭmĭlīs fōrtūnă lăbōrēs Jāctātūm.

Āfflŏ, ās, āvī, ātūm, ārĕ. *To breathe upon.* Fūlmĭnĭs āfflāvīt vēntīs. V. Syn.—Ădhālŏ, spīrŏ, īnspīrŏ. Phr.—Taūrōrum āfflābĭtŭr ōrĕ. Lætōs ŏcŭlīs āfflābăt hŏnōrēs.

Āffluŏ, ĭs, flūxī, flūxūm, ĕrĕ. *To flow towards or upon.* Syn.—Flŭŏ. *To glide towards.* Syn.—Ādrēpŏ, īllābŏr. *To come in a crowd towards.* Syn.—Āccūrrŏ, cōncūrrŏ, cōnvĕnĭŏ. *To have or be in abundance.* Syn.—Ăbūndŏ, rĕdūndŏ, ēxūbĕrŏ, lūxŭrĭŏ.

Ăgĕr, ăgrī. m. *A field.* Ēst āntīquŭs ăgēr, Tūscō mĭhĭ prōxĭmŭs āmnī. V. Syn.—Ăgēllŭs, ārvă, cūltă, jūgĕră, rūră, nĭvālĭă, cāmpŭs, sŏlūm, hŭmŭs, tēllūs. Phr.—Jūgĕră tērræ. Ăgĕr grāmĕn hăbēns. Lætō grāmĭnĕ vērnāns. Cōnsĭtŭs ărbŏrĭbŭs. Ŏpĕrōsī vītĭbŭs ăgrī. Vēstītī grāmĭnĕ cāmpī. Nōn ōmnīs fērt ōmnĭă tēllūs. Ăgĕr mēssĭbŭs ŏnĕrātŭs. Rēddēns sătă lætă. Flāvēntĭă mēssĭbŭs ārvā. Ēxērcĭtă frūgĭbŭs ārvă. Tēllūs frūmēntĭs ŏptĭmă. Dīvĭtĭs ūbĕr ăgrī. Fērtĭlĭs ūbēr cāmpŭs. Prēssō pīnguĭs sūb vŏmĕrĕ tērră. Tēllūs nūnquām mēntītă cŏlōnō. Hūmĭdă mājōrēs hērbās ălĭt. Ūtrăquĕ frūgĭfĕrīs ēst nōbĭlĭs ăgrīs. *Country, region.* Syn.—Tērră, tēllūs, ōræ, ārvă, lĭttŏră, plăgæ, rēgnūm, fīnēs.

Āggĕr, ĕrĭs. m. *A mound.* Īllīdĭtquĕ vădīs ātque āggĕrĕ cīngĭt ărēnæ. V. Syn.—Ăcērvŭs, cŭmŭlŭs, āggēstŭs. Phr.—Āggēstă hŭmŭs. Tērrĕă mōlēs. *An eminence.* Syn.—Tŭmŭlŭs, cōllĭs. *Rampart.* Syn.—Vāllūm, mūnīmĕn, prōpūgnācŭlūm. Phr.—Mūrōrūm āggĕr. Āggĕrĕ fīrmānt mœnĭă.

Āggĕrŏ, ās, āvī, ātūm, ārĕ, & Āggĕrŏ, ĭs, ēssī, ēstūm, ĕrĕ. *To heap up, to pile together.* Præmĭă pūgnæ Āggĕrăt. V. Syn.—Cōngĕrŏ, cŏăcērvŏ, cŭmŭlŏ, āccŭmŭlŏ, strŭŏ, ādstrŭŏ, āgglŏmĕrŏ, cōllĭgŏ.

Āggrăvēscŏ, ĭs, ĕrĕ. *To become, or to be heavy.* Syn.—Grăvŏr, āggrăvŏr, prĕmŏr, dēprĭmŏr, ōpprĭmŏr, ōbrŭŏr.

Āggrăvŏ, ās, āvī, ātūm, ārĕ. *To weigh heavy.* Syn.—Āggrăvēscŏ. Fig.—*To burden, to press down.* Syn.—Grăvŏ, prĕmŏ, ōpprĭmŏ, ŏnĕrŏ, ōbrŭŏ, aūgĕŏ.

Āggrĕdĭŏr, ĕrĭs, grēssŭs sūm, ī. *To go towards.* Tālĭbŭs āggrĕdĭtūr Vĕnĕrēm Sātūrnĭă dīctīs. V. Syn.—Āccēdŏ, ădĕŏ. *To attack.* Syn.—Ădŏrĭŏr, īnvādŏ, lăcēssŏ, ōppūgnŏ, prōvŏcŏ, rŭŏ, īrrŭŏ, īrrūmpŏ, fĕrŏr, īncūrrŏ. Phr.—Dēnsīs īncūrrĭmŭs ārmīs. *To undertake, to commence.* Syn.—Īncĭpĭŏ, ĭnĕŏ, sūscĭpĭŏ, ōrdĭŏr, ădŏrĭŏr, mōlĭŏr.

Āggrĕgŏ, ās, āvī, ātūm, ārĕ. *To gather together.* Syn.—Cōngrĕgŏ, cōgŏ, cōllĭgŏ. Phr.—Īntēr sē cŏĭīssĕ vĭrōs. Mīstæ glŏmĕrāntŭr ĭn ōrbēm.

Āgĭlĭs, ĭs, ĕ. *Nimble, light, agile.* Fēr grēssūs ăgĭlēs mēcum, ēt cŏmĭtārĕ vŏlēntēm. O. Syn.—Ălăcĕr, cĕlĕr, cĭtŭs, ēxpĕdītŭs, gnāvŭs, lĕvĭs, ōcĭŏr, pērnīx, prōmptŭs, vēlōx, vŏlŭcĕr. *Active.* Syn.—Gnāvŭs, īndūstrĭŭs, īmpĭgĕr, ācĕr, ălăcĕr.

Āgĭlĭtās, ātĭs. f. *Agility.* Syn.—Lĕvĭtās, mōbĭlĭtās, vēlōcĭtās.

Āgĭlĭtĕr. adv. *Quickly.* Syn.—Cĭtō, prŏpĕrē, vēlōcĭtĕr, ōcĭŭs. Phr.—Haūd mŏră. Dīctō cĭtĭŭs.

Āgĭtŏ, ās, āvī, ātūm, ārĕ. *To chase, to pursue.* Fūdĭmŭs īnsĭdĭīs tōtāque ăgĭtāvĭmŭs ūrbĕ. V. Syn.—Ăgŏ, pēllŏ, ūrgĕŏ, sĕquŏr, sēctŏr, īnsēctŏr, īnstŏ. Phr.—Tĭmĭdōs ăgĭtāvĭmŭs. Cūrsūquĕ fĕrās ăgĭtābăt Ĭūlŭs. *To conduct or lead.* Syn.—Ăgŏ, dūcŏ. *To agitate, to move.* Syn.—Ăgŏ, jāctŏ, tūrbŏ, vērsŏ. *To meditate.* Syn.—Mĕdĭtŏr.

Āgmĕn, ĭnĭs. n. *Course, march.* Lēnī flŭĭt āgmĭnĕ Tībrĭs. V. Syn.—Cūrsŭs, mōtŭs, āctŭs. *An army on the march, a squadron.* Syn.—Cătērvă, cŏhōrs, ēxērcĭtŭs, lĕgĭŏ, mănīplŭs, mănŭs, phălānx, tūrmă. Phr.—Sūccīnctūm phărĕtrīs āgmĕn. Fūlgēns īnsīgnĭbŭs ārmīs. Dēvōlvĭt mœnĭbŭs āgmĕn. Āgmĭnĕ fāctō, Īnvādūnt hōstēm. *A troop of any kind.* Syn.—Tūrbă, cŏhōrs cătērvă, tūrmă.

Āgnă, æ. f. *Lamb.* Ūtquĕ fŭgĭt vīsōs āgnă nŏvēllă lŭpōs. O. Syn.—Bālāns, bĭdēns, ŏvĭs.

Āgnōscŏ, ĭs, ōvī, ĭtūm, ĕrĕ. *To recognize, to know.* Syn.—Nōscŏ, cōgnōscŏ, scĭŏ, pērspĭcĭŏ. *To confess.* Syn.—Ādmīttŏ, fătĕŏr, cōnfĭtĕŏr.

Āgnŭs, ī. m. *A lamb.* Sæpĕ tĕnēr nōstrīs ăb ŏvīlĭbŭs īmbŭĕt āgnŭs. V. Syn.—Āgnēllŭs, āgnă, bālāns, bĭdēns, ŏvĭs. Phr.—Fœtūs ŏvĭūm tĕnĕrī. Dēpūlsi ā mātrĭbŭs āgnī. Lānĭgĕrī sŏbŏlēs grĕgĭs. Păvĭdōquĕ fŭgācĭŏr āgnō. Tūtī sūb mātrĭbŭs āgnī. Māctāndŭs ăd ārām. Quī sŭō crŭōrĕ sīgnāvĭt ĭtĕr ăd āstră.

Ăgŏ, ĭs, ēgī, āctūm, ĕrĕ. *To drive, to chase.* Syn.—Pēllŏ, ăgĭtŏ, pērsĕquŏr, ūrgĕŏ, īnstŏ. Phr.—Pālāntēs Trōăs ăgēbăt. Ūndĕ sĕrēnās Vēntŭs ăgāt nūbēs. *To lead.* Syn.—Dūcŏ. *To bring, to take along.* Syn.—Ābdūcŏ, aūfĕrŏ, răpĭŏ, ābrĭpĭŏ, tōllŏ. *To trouble.* Syn.—Ăgĭtŏ, tūrbŏ, ēxăgĭtŏ, mŏvĕŏ. *To compel.* Syn.—Cōgŏ, ădĭgŏ, īmpēllŏ, ūrgĕŏ, jŭbĕŏ.

Āgrēstĭs, ĭs, ĕ. *Rural.* Lūdĕrĕ quæ vēllēm călămō pērmīsĭt ăgrēstī. V. Syn.—Rūstĭcŭs, sīlvēstrĭs. *Rustic, rude, uncultivated.* Syn.—Fĕrŭs, īncūltŭs, rūstĭcŭs, sīlvēstrĭs, rŭdĭs. *As a noun, a countryman.* Syn.—Āgrĭcŏlă, rūrĭcŏlă. Phr.—Rūrĭs īncŏlă. Cōllēctōs ārmăt ăgrēstēs.

Āgrĭcŏlă, æ. m. *A farmer.* Syn.—Āgrēstĭs, ărātŏr, cŏlōnŭs, rūrĭcŏlă, rūstĭcŭs, vīllĭcŭs. Phr.—Cūltŏr ăgēllī. Ārvă cŏlēns. Rūrĭs cŏlōnŭs. Cūltōrquĕ vĭrēntĭs ăgēllī. Cūrvī mŏdĕrātŏr ărātrī. Quī tērrām scīndĭt, ēxērcĕt. Rūstĭcă pūbēs. Āgrēstĭs jŭvēntūs. Rūstĭcă tūrbă. Fōrtīs pătĭēnsquĕ lăbōrūm. Ŏpĕrōsă cŏlēntĭbŭs ārvă.

Āgrĭcūltūră, æ. f. *Agriculture. See Ager, Rus, Aro.*

Ăhēnĕŭs, ă, ūm. *Bronze.* Syn.—Ăhēnŭs, ænĕŭs, ærĕŭs. Phr.—Ēt lūcĕ cŏrūscŭs ăhēnā. Fŏrĭbŭs cārdō strīdēbăt ăhēnīs. Fig.—*Inflexible.* Syn.—Dūrŭs, fērrĕŭs.

Ăhēnūm, ī. n. *A bronze caldron or vessel.* Vīrgĕă sūggĕrĭtūr cōstīs ūndāntĭs ăhēnī. V. Syn.—Lĕbēs, ōllă, cācăbŭs. Phr.—Cădŭs ăhēnŭs. Aēs căvūm. Ōrdĭne ăhēnă lŏcānt ălĭī. Ārdēntī dēcōxĭt ăhēnō. Ēt ăhēna ūndāntĭă flāmmīs Ēxpĕdĭūnt.

Āiŏ, ăĭs, ăĭt. *To speak, to affirm.* Syn.—Dīcŏ, īnquām, lŏquŏr, āssĕrŏ, āffīrmŏ. Phr.—Hōc āiēbăt ĕt hōc. Ūt fāma ēst. Dīssĭlŭīssĕ fĕrūnt. Ūt āiūnt. Sīc fātūr lăcrĭmāns.

Ālă, æ. f. *The wing of a bird.* Rādĭt ĭtēr lĭquĭdūm, cĕlĕrēs nĕquĕ cōmmŏvĕt ālās. V. Syn.—Pēnnă, plūmă. Phr.—Ālārūm rēmī. Rēmĭgĭūm ālārūm. Pēnnārūm rēmī. Pēnnārūm vēlă. Hŭmĕrīs āccōmmŏdăt ālās. Āĕrĭīs sūblīmēm sūstŭlĭt ālīs. Īn cœlūm părĭbūs sē sūstŭlĭt ālīs. Pĕdĭbūs cĕlĕr, ēt pērnīcĭbŭs ālīs. Ālās quătĕrĕ. Cīrcūmsŏnăt ālīs. Fĕrĭt æthĕră pēnnīs. Pēnnæ sŏnŭērĕ pĕr aūrās. Sĭmŭl æthĕră vērbĕrăt ālīs. Vēlōcēs ăgĭtăt pēnnīs. Lūdūnt strīdēntĭbŭs ālīs. Vŏlăt īllĕ pĕr āĕră. Lāmbĕrĕ pēnnīs. *The wing of an army.* Syn.—Cōrnū. Phr.—Ĕquĭtūm tūrmæ. Dūm trĕpĭdānt ālæ.

Ălăcĕr, & Ălăcrĭs, ĭs, ĕ. *Quick, prompt, active.* Sīc rŭĭt īn dēnsōs ălăcēr Mēzēntĭŭs hōstēs. V. Syn.—Cĕlĕr, cĭtŭs, lĕvĭs, ēxpĕdītŭs, părātŭs, ācĕr, ăgĭlĭs, prōmptŭs, fēstīnŭs, prŏpĕrŭs. *Gay, joyful.* Syn.—Lætŭs, hĭlărĭs, gaūdēns, ŏvāns, ēxsūltāns. Phr.—Lætĭtĭā ēxsūltāns, lætĭtĭæ plēnŭs.

Ălăpă, æ. f. *A slap or buffet.* Syn.—Cŏlăphŭs. Phr.—Īmpācta īn vūltūs dēxtră. Mūltō majōrĭs ălăpæ mēcūm vēnĕūnt.

Ālātŭs, ă, ūm. *Winged.* Ūt prīmum ālātīs tĕtĭgīt māgālĭă plāntīs. V. Syn.—Ālĭgĕr, pēnnĭgĕr, pēnnātŭs, ālĕs, vŏlāns. Phr.—Ālīs īnstrūctŭs, ōrnātŭs. Ālārūm rēmĭgĭō īnstrūctŭs. Fig.—*Quick, prompt. See Celer.*

Ălaūdă, æ. f. *The lark.* (*See Appendix under list of Birds.*)

Ālbĕō, ēs, ŭī, ērĕ. *To be white.* Cāmpīque īngēntēs ōssĭbŭs ālbēnt. V. Syn.—Ālbĭcō, cāndĕō, cānĕō. Phr.—Cānīs căpīllīs ālbēt căpŭt. Nēc prātă cānīs ālbĭcānt prŭīnīs. Flāmmārūm lōngōs ā tērgo ālbēscĕrĕ trāctūs. Flūctūs frāctīs ālbēscĭt ĭn ūndīs.

Ālbŭs, ă, ūm. *White.* Cāndĭdă pēr sĭlvām cūm fœtū cōncŏlŏr ālbo Prōcŭbŭīt....sūs. V. Syn.—Ālbēscēns, ālbĭcāns, cāndĭdŭs, cānŭs, cāndēscēns, cānēscēns, ārgēntĕŭs, ĕbūrnĕŭs, lāctĕŭs, nĭvĕŭs. Phr.—Cāndōrĕ fūlgēns, dĕcōrŭs, ōrnātŭs, tīnctŭs. Cāndōrĕ nĭvālī. Cāndĭdĭōr cÿcnīs, cÿcnō, nĭvĭbŭs. Cāndĭdă pārtĕ. Lāctĕă cōllă Aūro īnnēctūntŭr. Mārmŏrĕā căpŭt ā cērvīcĕ rĕvūlsūm. *Pale, of an ashen appearance.* Syn.—Pāllĭdŭs, pāllēns, dēcŏlŏr. *Clear, serene.* Syn.—Sĕrēnŭs. Fig.—*Favorable.* Syn.—Faūstŭs.

Ālcēdŏ (Hālcēdŏ), ĭnĭs. f. *The kingfisher.* (*See Appendix under list of Birds.*)

Ālĕă, æ. f. *Dice, or any game of chance.* Nām nĕquĕ mē vīnūm, nēc mē tĕnēt ālĕă fāllāx. O. Phr.—Lūdĭtŭr ālĕă pērnōx. Sī dāmnōsă sĕnēm jŭvăt ālĕă. Nēc tĕnēt īncērtās ālĕă blāndă mānūs. Fig.—*Chance, risk, hazard.* Syn.—Cāsŭs, dīscrīmĕn, pĕrīcŭlūm. Phr.—Ālĕă fātī. Fōrtūnæ lūdī āncĭpĭtēs. Vărĭī cāsūs. Ālĕă grāndĭs ĭnēst.

Ālĕātŏr, ōrĭs. m. *One who plays dice, gamester in general.* Aēdīlēm vŏcăt ūdŭs ālĕātŏr. M. Syn.—Ālĕō, lūsŏr. Phr.—Ālĕæ cŭpĭdŭs. Quēm præcēps ālĕă nūdăt. Mŏvĕt ārmă frĭtīllō. Tālōs ăgĭtārĕ frĭtīllō.

Ālĕs, ĭtĭs. adj. *Winged.* Syn.—Ālātŭs. Fig.—*Quick, nimble, rapid.* Syn.—Cĭtŭs, răpĭdŭs, cĕlĕr, pērnīx, præpĕs, vēlōx. Phr.—Ālĭtĕ vēctūs ĕquō. Ālĭtĕ plūmbō.

Ālĕs, ĭtĭs. m. & f. *A bird.* Aēthĕrĭā quōs lāpsă plăgā Jŏvĭs ālĕs ăpērtō. V. Syn.—Ăvĭs. Phr.—Crīstātŭs ālĕs. Ēxplĭcăt īpsă sŭās ālēs pēnnās. *See Avis.*

Ālgĕō, ēs, ālsī, ālsūm, ērĕ. *To be cold.* Prŏbĭtās laūdātŭr ēt ālgĕt. J. Syn.—Ālgēscō, frīgĕō. Phr.—Frīgŏrĕ rĭgĕō. *See Frigeo.*

Ālgĭdŭs, ă, ūm. *Cold, frozen.* Syn.—Frīgĭdŭs, gĕlĭdŭs.

Ălĭēnō, ās, āvī, ātūm, ārĕ. *To part with, to sell.* Syn.—Ăbălĭēnō, vēndō. Phr.—Ălĭēnūm făcĭō. *To divide.* Syn.—Āmŏvĕō, āvērtō, dīsjūngō, dīstrăhō, sēpărō.

Ălĭēnŭs, ă, ūm. *Belonging to another.* Fērtĭlĭŏr sĕgĕs ēst ălĭēnīs sēmpĕr ĭn ārvīs. O. *A stranger.* Syn.—Ălĭēnĭgĕnă, ēxtērnŭs. *Inconsistent, out of place.* Syn.—Dīscrĕpāns, ăbhōrrēns.

Ālĭfĕr, & Ālĭgĕr, ĕră, ĕrūm. *Winged.* Trānsĭt ĕt ālĭfĕrō tōllĭtŭr āxĕ Cĕrēs. O. Syn.—Ālĕs, ālātŭs, pēnnātŭs.

Ălĭmēntūm, ī. n. *Food, nourishment.* Cōncĭpĭt Īrĭs ăquās, ălĭmēntăquĕ nūbĭbŭs āffērt. O. Syn.—Cĭbŭs, dăpĕs, ēscă, pābŭlūm, nūtrīmēntūm.

Ălĭquāndŏ. *Sometimes.* Syn.—Īntērdūm, nōnnūnquām, quāndōquĕ. *Finally, some day.* Syn.—Tāndēm, dēmūm.

Ălĭquāntūm. adv. *A little, somewhat* Syn.—Ălĭquāntīspĕr, lĕvĭtĕr, nōnnĭhĭl, paūlūm, paūlīspĕr.

Ălĭquĭs, quă, quĭd & quŏd. *Some, someone.* Aūt ălĭquīs lătĕt ērrŏr. V. Syn.—Ūnŭs, quīdām, quĭs, quīspĭām, nōnnūllŭs. Phr.—Sī vīs ēsse ălĭquĭs.

Ălĭtĕr. adv. *Otherwise.* Sēd quĭă nōn ălĭtēr vīrēs dăbĭt ōmnĭbŭs ǣquās. V. Syn.—Ălĭās, sĕcŭs. Phr.—Nōn sīc, nōn ĭtă, ălĭō pāctō. Ălĭā vĭā, rătĭōnĕ. Dīs ălĭtēr vīsūm.

Ālĭūm, ĭī. n. *Garlic, leeks, onions.* (*See Appendix under list of Trees, etc.*)

Ălĭūndĕ. adv. *From another place.* Syn.—Ălĭā ēx pārtĕ.

Ălĭŭs, ălĭă, ălĭŭd. *Another, other, different.* Aūt ălĭūs cāsūs lēctō te āffīxĭt. H. Syn.—Āltĕr, dīvērsŭs, vărĭŭs, nŏvŭs. Phr.—Nōn ĭs, nōn īllĕ, nōn tālĭs. *In the plural, the others.* Syn.—Cētĕrī, rĕlĭquī, ōmnēs.

Āllābŏr, ĕrĭs, lāpsŭs sūm, ī. *To glide towards, to approach, to arrive at.* Seū măre ĭnōffēnsūm crēscēnti āllābĭtŭr ǣstū. V. Syn.—Āccēdŏ, vĕnĭŏ, ādvĕnĭŏ, pērvĕnĭŏ, āffĕrŏr.

Āllăbōrŏ, ās, āvī, ātūm, ārĕ. *To increase by work.* Sīmplĭcī mȳrtō nĭhĭl āllăbōrēs. H. Syn.—Ādjūngŏ, ānnēctō.

Āllāmbŏ, ĭs, ī, ĕrĕ. *To lick, to come in contact with.* Syn.—Lāmbŏ, lībŏ, āttīngŏ.

Āllātrŏ, ās, āvī, ātūm, ārĕ. *To bark at.* Syn.—Lātrŏ. Fig.—*To backbite, to accuse maliciously.* Syn.—Mălĕdīcŏ, cōnvīcĭŏr. Phr.—Mălĕdīctă, cōnvīcĭă fūndŏ, īngĕrŏ. Īngĕnĭūm vĭtĭa āllātrāntĭă quāssānt.

Āllēgŏ, ās, āvī, ātūm, ārĕ. *To send, to depute.* Syn.—Lēgŏ, mīttŏ, māndŏ. *To allege.* Syn.—Āffĕrŏ, rĕfĕrŏ, cĭtŏ, prǣtēndŏ.

Āllĕgŏ, ĭs, lēgī, lēctūm, ĕrĕ. *To choose, to select.* Syn.—Lĕgŏ, dēlĭgŏ, ēlĭgŏ, sēlĭgŏ, ādscrībŏ, āddŏ, ādjūngŏ.

Āllĕvŏ, ās, āvī, ātūm, ārĕ. *To raise up.* Īllĕ crŭōrĕ flŭēns sŭbĭtō tămĕn āllĕvăt ārtūs. O. Syn.—Lĕvŏ, sūblĕvŏ, tŏllŏ, āttŏllŏ, ērĭgŏ. *To relieve.* Nēc vīrĭbŭs āllĕvŏr ūllīs. O. Syn.—Lĕvŏ, sūblĕvŏ, lēnĭŏ, mītĭgŏ, mōllĭŏ, tēmpĕrŏ.

Āllĭcĭŏ, ĭs, ēxī, ēctūm, ĕrĕ. *To entice, to allure, to attract.* Syn.—Pēllĭcĭŏ, īnvītŏ, căpĭŏ, trăhŏ, āttrăhŏ, dūcŏ, īndūcŏ, ēxcĭtŏ.

Āllīdŏ, ĭs, sī, sūm, ĕrĕ. *To dash or strike against.* Syn.—Īllīdŏ, cōllīdŏ, īnfrīngŏ, īmpīngŏ.

Āllĭgŏ, ās, āvī, ātūm, ārĕ. *To bind, to attach to.* Ūncō nōn āllĭgăt ānchŏră mōrsū. V. Syn.—Lĭgŏ, cōllĭgŏ (ās), rĕlĭgŏ, vīncĭŏ, strīngŏ, āstrīngŏ. *To hold, to hinder.* Syn.—Īmpĕdĭŏ, cŏhĭbĕŏ, cŏērcĕŏ. Phr.—Nīlūs nēc rīpīs āllĭgăt āmnēm. Trīstīque ĭnămā- bĭlĭs ūndā Āllĭgăt. *To contract.* Syn.—Strīngŏ, āstrīngŏ, cōn- trăhŏ, āddūcŏ. Phr. Sŏpŏr āllĭgăt āılūs. Vūltum alligăt quæ trīstĭtĭēs? Fig.—*To bind, to oblige.* Syn.—Ōblĭgŏ, vīncĭŏ.

Āllĭnŏ, ĭs, lēvī, lĭtūm, ĕrĕ. *To annoint, to smear, to rub something upon.* Īncōmptīs āllĭnĕt ātrūm Trānsvērsō călămō sīgnūm. H. Syn.—Lĭnŏ, īllĭnŏ, ĭnūngŏ.

Āllŏquĭūm, ĭī. n. *Talk, colloquy.* Aūsŭs ĕs āllŏquĭō sūstĭnŭīssĕ tŭō. O. Syn.—Āllŏcūtĭŏ, cōllŏquĭūm, āffātŭs, sērmŏ, vērbă, vōcēs. Phr.—Frŭĭtūrquĕ dĕōrūm cōllŏquĭō. Lōngīs prōdūcĕrĕ nōctēm Āllŏquĭīs.

Āllŏquŏr, ĕrĭs, cūtŭs sūm, ī. *To speak to someone.* Ēxtrēmā mŏrĭēns tămĕn āllŏquŏr hōrā. V. Syn.—Cōmpēllŏ (ās), āffārī, dīcŏ, lŏquŏr. Phr.—Cōrāmquĕ părēntēm Āllŏquĕrĕ. Dīctīs āffātūr ămīcīs. Prōsĕquĭtūr dīctīs. Vōcēs ōrĕ dăbăt. Tālī fŭgĭēntem ēst vōcĕ sĕcūtŭs. Ād sŭpĕrōs tālĭă vērbă dēdĭt. Sīc prĭŏr ēst īngrēssă Vĕnŭs. Hīs Aēnēān cōmpēllāt vōcĭbŭs ūltrō. Tālĭbŭs āggrĕdĭtūr dīctīs.

Āllūdŏ, ĭs, sī, sūm, ĕrĕ. *To play, to sport.* Syn.—Lūdŏ. *To joke.* Syn.—Jŏcŏr, lūdŏ, rīdĕŏ.

Āllŭŏ, ĭs, ī, ĕrĕ. *To bathe, to wash.* Syn.—Āllābŏr, præflŭŏ, prætēr- flŭŏ, cīrcūmflŭŏ, āllāmbŏ, lăvŏ, prēnătŏ.

Āllŭvĭēs, ēī. f. *An inundation.* Syn.—Āllŭvĭŏ, āllŭvĭūm, ēlŭvĭēs, dīlŭvĭūm, īllŭvĭēs, prōlŭvĭēs. Phr.—Ēlŭvĭē mōns ēst dējēctŭs ĭn æquŏr. Īnfūsō stāgnāntēs æquŏrĕ cāmpī.

Ālmŭs, ă, ūm. *Nourishing, fertile.* Nūtrīt rūră Cērēs ālmăquĕ Faūstĭtās. II. Syn.—Ālēns, fĕrāx, fēcūndŭs, lætŭs, ŏpīmŭs. Phr.—Pārtŭrĭt ālmŭs ăgĕr. Vītĭbŭs ālmīs Āptĭŭs ūbĕr ĕrĭt. Lībĕr ĕt ālmă Cērēs. *Favorable, benignant.* Syn.—Făvēns, fēlīx, faūstŭs. Fig.—*Venerable, august.* Syn.—Sānctŭs, vĕnĕ- rāndŭs.

Ālnŭs, ī. f. *An alder tree.* (*See Appendix under list of Trees, etc.*)

Ălō, ĭs, ălŭī, ălĭtūm & āltūm, ĕrĕ. *To nourish, to bring up.* Bīnōs ălĭt ūbĕrĕ fœtūs. V. Syn.—Pāscō, nūtrĭō, ēdŭcō (ās). Phr.—Ălĭmēntă, dăpēs, pābŭlă, cĭbōs dō, sūffĭcĭō, pōrrĭgō, ōffĕrō, mĭnīstrō. Fērrĕ cĭbūm. Cĭbīs fŏvērĕ. Pārvōs ēdūcĕrĕ nātōs. Ălĭt īră lĕōnēs. Lāctīsque ălĭmēntă dĕdērĕ. (*By extension*) *To produce.* Syn.—Părĭō, gīgnō. Fig.—*To ferment.* Syn.—Nūtrĭō, pāscō, fŏvĕō. *To increase.* Syn.—Aūgĕŏr, crēscō, vĭgĕō.

Ălŏē, ēs. f. *The herb aloe.* (*See Appendix under list of Trees, etc.*)

Āltārĕ, ĭs, n. *An altar.* Bīs sēnōs cuī nōstră dĭēs āltārĭă fūmānt. V. Syn.—Āră. *See Ara.*

Āltē. adv. *High, from on high.* Syn.—Ēxcēlsē, sūblīmĕ, sūrsūm. Phr.—Īn āltūm, īn sūblīmĕ. Āltĭūs īngrĕdĭtŭr. *Deeply.* Syn.—Prŏfūndūm, pĕnĭtŭs.

Āltĕr, ĕră, ĕrūm. *Another.* Syn.—Ălĭŭs. *The second.* Syn.—Sĕcūndŭs, ălĭŭs. *Different.* Syn.—Dīspār, dīssĭmĭlĭs, dīvērsŭs, ălĭŭs, mūtātŭs.

Āltērcŏr, ārĭs, ātŭs sūm, ārī. *To quarrel.* Syn.—Cērtō, cōntēndō, pūgnō.

Āltērnāns, āntĭs. adj. *Alternating.* Syn.—Rĕcĭprŏcŭs. *Hesitating.* Syn.—Āncēps, ānxĭŭs, dŭbĭŭs, īncērtŭs.

Āltērnīs. adv. *Alternately.* Syn.—Vĭcīssīm. Phr.—Pĕr āltērnās vĭcēs. Īn vĭcēm. Pēr vĭcēs. Āltērnā vĭcĕ. Āltērnō tēmpŏrĕ. Āltērnīs vĭcĭbŭs.

Āltērnō, ās, āvī, ātūm, ārĕ. *To alternate.* Syn.—Āltērnīs ăgō, dīcō.

Āltĭlĭs, ĭs. m. & f. *Capon, hen.* (*See Appendix under list of Birds.*)

Āltĭtūdō, ĭnĭs. f. *Height.* Syn.—Ăpēx, vērtēx, fāstīgĭūm, căcūmĕn.

Āltŏr, ōrĭs. m. *A father.* Syn.—Nūtrītŏr, pătĕr, gĕnĭtŏr.

Āltrīx, īcĭs. f. *A mother, nurse.* Syn.—Nūtrīx, mātĕr, părēns, gĕnĭtrīx.

Āltūm, ī. n. *The air, the heavens.* Māiă gĕnĭtūm dēmīsĭt ăb āltō. V. Syn.—Cœlūm, āēr, æthĕr. Phr.—Āltūm nīdīs pĕtĭērĕ rĕlĭctīs. *The sea.* Syn.—Mărĕ.

Āltŭs, ă, ūm. *High, elevated.* Rēgĭă sōlĭs ĕrāt sūblīmĭbŭs āltă cŏlūmnīs. O. Syn.—Ārdŭŭs, āĕrĭŭs, cēlsŭs, ēxcēlsŭs, præcēlsŭs, ēdĭtŭs, ēlātŭs, prōcērŭs, sūblīmĭs, sūmmŭs, sŭprēmŭs. Phr.—Sīdĕră tāngēns. Sūrgēns ĭn āstră. Ērēctŭs ăd sīdĕră. Sīlēx āltīssĭmă vīsū. Ēxcēlsō vērtĭcĕ mōntĭs. Cœlōque ēdūcĕrĕ tēntānt. Āĕrĭī cūrsū pĕtĭt ārdŭă mōntĭs. Ād sīdĕră dūctī. *Tall, in speaking of human beings.* Syn.—Sūblīmĭs, māgnŭs, īngēns. Fig.—*Illustrious, noble.* Syn.—Īnsīgnĭs, nōbĭlĭs, īnclўtŭs. *Proud.* Syn.—Sŭpērbŭs, ēlātŭs, sūblīmĭs, fĕrōx. *Deep.* Syn.—Prŏfūndŭs, īmŭs. Phr.—Āltæ neū crēdĕ pălūdī. Prĕmĭt āltūm cōrdĕ dŏlōrēm. Āltă sĭlēntĭă cōgĭs Rūmpĕrĕ? Mănĕt āltā mēntĕ rĕpōstūm. Mărĕ prŏfūndūm.

Ālveārĕ, ārĭs, Ālvĕārĭūm, ĭī & Ālveārĭă, ōrūm. n. *Beehive*. Seū lēntō fŭĕrīnt ālveārĭă vīmĭnĕ tēxtă. V. Syn.—Ālvĕŭs. Phr.—Cērĕă tēctă, cāstră. Cōrtĭcĭbŭs sūtă căvātīs. Cōrtĭcĭs āntrūm. Ăpūm sēdēs, dŏmŭs, cŭbīlĕ. Ēt flōrĭbŭs hōrrĕă tēxūnt. Dūlcī dīstēndūnt nēctărĕ cēllās. Ēxāmĭnă cōndūnt. Dædălă fīngĕrĕ tēctă.

Ālvĕŭs, ĕī & eī. m. *The bed of a river*. Prōnō răpĭt ālvĕŭs āmnī. V. Phr.—Sŏlĭtārūm līmĕs ăquārūm. Spūmāntīque īncŭbăt ālveō. Īmpŏsĭtās ōrnōs fērt, sūstĭnĕt ālvĕŭs. *The hold of a ship*. Syn.—Nāvĭs, cȳmbă. *Basin*. Syn. Ālvĕŏlŭs.

Ālvŭs, ī. f. *The belly, womb*. Syn.—Vēntĕr, ŭtĕrŭs, īlĭă, vīscĕră.

Ămābĭlĭs, ĭs, ĕ. *Amiable, lovable*. Ŭt ămērĭs, ămābĭlĭs ēstō. O. Syn.—Ămāndŭs, grātŭs, jūcūndŭs, dūlcĭs, suāvĭs, plăcēns. Phr.—Dīgnŭs ămārī. Dīgnāndŭs ămōrĕ. Frōnte ēt mēntĕ bĕnīgnŭs. Quī sĭbĭ cōncĭlĭăt mēntēs. Quī pēctŏră mūlcĕt, āllĭcĭt.

Ămārăcŭs, ī. m., f. & Ămārăcūm, ī. n. *Sweet-marjoram*. (*See Appendix under list of Trees, etc.*)

Ămărānthŭs, ī. m. *The everlasting, a flower that never fades*. (*See Appendix under list of Trees, etc.*)

Ămārĭtĭēs, ēī. f. *Bitterness*. Syn.—Ăcērbĭtās, ămārŏr, ălŏē.

Ămārŏr, ōrĭs. m. *Bitterness*. Syn.—Ămārĭtĭēs, ămārūm. Phr.—Ămārŭs săpŏr.

Ămārŭs, ă, ūm. *Bitter*. Sălĭcēs cārpētĭs ămārās. V. Syn.—Ăcērbŭs. Phr.—Ămārĭŏr hērbīs. *Painful, harsh*. Syn.—Trīstĭs, īngrātŭs, mŏlēstŭs, āspĕr, dūrŭs, īnsuāvĭs, ăcērbŭs. Phr.—Rūmōre āccēnsŭs ămārō. Dīctīs āccēndĭt ămārīs. Ămāră lætō Tēmpĕrēt rīsū.

Āmbāgĕ (abl. sing.) & Āmbāgēs, ūm. f. *Windings, detours*. Dædălŭs īpsĕ dŏlōs tēcti āmbāgēsquĕ rĕsōlvĭt. V. Syn.—Mæāndrŭs, Lăbȳrīnthŭs, gȳrŭs, flēxŭs, sĭnŭs, spīræ, cīrcŭĭtŭs, ērrŏr. Phr.—Rĕmōtæ āmbāgēs. Ōblīquă vĭārūm. Vērbōrūm āmbāgĕ nŏvōrūm.

Āmbĕdŏ, ĭs, ēdī, ēsūm, ĕrĕ. *To gnaw all around*. Syn.—Ābrōdŏ, cīrcūmrōdŏ, cōrrōdŏ.

Āmbĭgŏ, ĭs, ēgī, āctūm, ĕrĕ. *To be in doubt*. Syn.—Dŭbĭtŏ, hærĕŏ, flūctŭŏ. Phr.—Ancēps ănĭmī sūm. *To hesitate*. Syn.—Dŭbĭtŏ. *To dispute*. Syn.—Cōntēndŏ, dīspŭtŏ, cērtŏ.

Āmbĭgŭē. adv. *In a doubtful manner*. Syn.—Dŭbĭē, vărĭē.

Āmbĭgŭŭs, ă, ūm. *Double*. Āgnōvīt prōlem āmbĭgŭām gĕmĭnōsquĕ părēntēs. V. Syn.—Āncēps, gĕmĭnŭs. *Ambiguous, doubtful*. Syn.—Dŭbĭŭs, īncērtŭs. *Treacherous, crafty, deceiving*. Syn.—Fāllāx, pērfĭdŭs, dŏlōsŭs, bĭlīnguĭs. *Uncertain, hesitating*. Syn.—Āncēps, dŭbĭŭs, ānxĭŭs, īncērtŭs, sūspēnsŭs, flūctŭāns.

Āmbĭō, īs, īvī & ĭī, ītūm, īrĕ. *To surround*. Ōrās āmbĭĭt aūrō. V. Syn.—Cīngŏ, cīrcūmdŏ, cīrcūmdūcŏ. *To go around, to make a turn*. Syn.—Cīrcŭmĕŏ, ŏbĕŏ, ŏbāmŭlŏ. *To flow around*. Syn.—Cīrcūmflŭŏ, cīrcūmlābŏr, cōmplēctŏr. Fig.—*To ambition*. Syn.—Āffēctŏ, cāptŏ, sēctŏr, aūcŭpŏr, vēnŏr. *To visit*. Syn.—Āccēdŏ, ădĕŏ.

Āmbĭtĭō, ōnĭs. f. *Ambition, an excessive desire of honors*. Syn.—Āmbĭtŭs, cŭpīdŏ. Phr.—Hŏnōrūm dīră cŭpīdŏ. Āmbĭtĭōnĭs ămŏr. Īmpĕrĭī sĭtĭs. Dŏmĭnāndī vēsānă sĭtĭs. Rēgnāndī dīră cŭpīdŏ. Āvārĭtĭæ fœdīssĭmă nūtrīx. Quæ mōrtālĭă cōrdă tōrquĕt. Āmbĭtĭōnĕ mălā pāllĕt. *Vanity, ostentation*. Syn.—Fāstŭs, sŭpērbĭă. Phr.—Īmmēnsŭs ămōr laūdĭs. Laūdūm ārrēctă cŭpīdŏ. Lūxŭs ĭnānī Āmbĭtĭōnĕ fŭrēns. Vānō splēndĭdă fāstū.

Āmbĭtĭōsŭs, ă, ūm. *Ambitious, eager for honor*. Phr.—Āmbĭtĭōnĕ lăbōrāns, fŭrēns, trĕmēns. Vānīs ĭnhĭāns hŏnōrĭbŭs. Mēndīcŭs hŏnōrūm. Cāptātŏr pŏpŭlārĭs aūræ. Laūdūm māgnō pērcūlsŭs ămōrĕ. Laūdĭs ămōrĕ cāptŭs. Vărĭō jāctātūs laūdĭs ămōrĕ. Quēm laūdĭs ămŏr īncēndĭt, ăgĭt, ēxcĭtăt. Cūjŭs ūrĭt mĭsĕrūm glōrĭă pēctŭs. *Proud, stately*. Syn.—Fāstŭs, vānŭs, sŭpērbŭs. *Affected, pompous*. Syn.—Tŭmĭdŭs, ēlātŭs, ēxquīsītŭs.

Āmbĭtŭs, ūs. m. *Tour, circuit*. Ēt prŏpĕrāntĭs ăquæ pĕr ămœnŏs āmbĭtŭs āgrōs. H. Syn.—Cīrcŭĭtŭs, ōrbĭs, gȳrŭs, flēxŭs, sĭnŭs. Fig.—*Ambition*. Syn.—Āmbĭtĭŏ. *Entreaty, prayer*. Syn.—Vōtūm, prĕcēs, stŭdĭūm.

Āmbŏ, æ, ō. *Both*. Syn.—Dŭŏ, ŭtērquĕ.

Āmbrŏsĭă, æ. f. *Ambrosia, the food of the gods*. Phr.—Āmbrŏsĭæ sūccŭs, cĭbŭs. Dĕōrūm, Dīvūm cĭbŭs.

Āmbŭlācrūm, ī. n. *A private way to walk in, portico, gallery*. Syn.—Ārĕă, pōrtĭcŭs, xȳstūm. Phr.—Trītūm spătĭūm. Sēmĭtă tūtă. Xȳstōrūm īmmēnsī trāctūs. Ārbŏrĭbūs tēctūm grātĭs ĭtĕr.

Āmbŭlātĭŏ, ōnĭs. f. *Walking, a place to walk in*. Syn.—Āmbŭlācrūm.

Āmbŭlŏ, ās, āvī, ātūm, ārĕ. *To walk*. Āmbŭlăt ēt sŭbĭtō fūnŭs mīrātŭr ămīcī. Prop. Syn.—Pĕrāmbŭlŏ, dĕāmbŭlŏ, ĭnāmbŭlŏ, īncēdŏ, spătĭŏr, prōgrĕdĭŏr. Phr.—Ītquĕ rĕdītquĕ vĭām. Pēr tăcĭtūm nĕmūs īrĕ. Ītĕ pĕdēs quōcūnquĕ fĕrēnt. Tālēm sē lætă fĕrēbăt. Grēssūmque ād mœnĭă tēndĭt. Īnstăbĭlī grēssū mētītūr līttŏră cōnjūx.

Āmēns, tĭs. adj. *Foolish, mad, insane.* Ārma āmēns căpĭō, nēc sāt rătĭōnĭs ĭn ārmīs. V. Syn.—Dēmēns, ēxcōrs, vēcōrs, īnsānŭs, mălĕsānŭs, vēsānŭs, dēlīrŭs, lȳmphātŭs, fŭrēns, fŭrĭōsŭs. Phr.—Mēntĭs ĭnŏps. Mēntĕ cāptŭs. Ēxpērs sŭī. Īmpŏs sŭī. Rătĭōnĭs ĕgēns. Rătĭōnĕ cărēns. Cæcā mēntĕ præcēps. Nōn sānō pēctŏrĕ. Quæ vōs dēmēntĭa ădēgĭt? Quæ mēntem īnsānĭă mūtăt? Vīx bĕnĕ sānŭs. Fūgīt mē rătĭŏ. Mēntĕ tūrbātā fĕrŏr.

Āmēntĭă, æ. f. *Madness, folly.* Quæ tānta ănĭmōs āmēntĭă cēpĭt? V. Syn.—Dēmēntĭă, vēcōrdĭă, īnsānĭă, fŭrŏr, dēlīrĭūm. Phr.—Cæcŭs mēntĭs fŭrŏr. Ēffĕră vīs ănĭmī. Mēns dēlīră, īnsānă.

Āmēntūm, ī. n. *Strap or thong to hold a javelin or spear.* Syn.—Lĭgāmĕn, lōrūm, vīncŭlūm, hăbēnă. Phr.—Āmēntăquĕ tōrquēnt.

Ămĭcĭō, īs, ĭcŭī, & īxī, īctūm, īrĕ. *To cover, to clothe.* Syn.—Vēstĭō, vēlō, tēgŏ, īnvōlvŏ, ŏpērĭŏ. Phr.—Ămĭcītūr vītĭbūs ūlmŭs. Fūlvīs ămĭcītŭr ăb ālīs.

Ămīcĭtĭă, æ. f. *Friendship, affection.* Īllŭd ămīcĭtĭæ sānctum āc vĕnĕrābĭlĕ nōmĕn. O. Syn.—Ămŏr, cōncōrdĭă, grātĭă, stŭdĭūm, fĭdēs. Phr.—Fœdŭs ămōrĭs. Ūsŭs ămīcĭtĭæ. Vīncŭlă, vīnclă ămōrĭs. Fœdŭs, nēxŭs ămīcĭtĭæ. Hīs ămŏr ūnŭs ĕrăt. Spēs ănĭmī crēdŭlă mūtŭī.

Ămīctŭs, ūs. m. *A garment, clothing, apparel.* Pūrpŭrĕōs mŏrĭtūră mănū dīscīndĭt ămīctūs. V. Syn.—Ămīcŭlūm, vēstĭs, vēstīmēntūm, tēgmĕn, vēlāmĕn, pāllĭūm, tŏgă. *A veil.* Syn.—Cārbăsŭs, līnūm, pĕplūm, pāllă.

Ămīcŭs, ă, ūm. *Friendly, dear.* Syn.—Cārŭs, dīlēctŭs. *Favorable, propitious.* Syn.—Bĕnīgnŭs, făvēns, faūstŭs, fēlīx, grātŭs, jūcūndŭs, āptŭs. Phr.—Dīctīs āffātŭr ămīcīs. Ămīcă frūgĭbūs æstās.

Ămīcŭs, ī. m. *A friend.* Tŭă mē vīrtūs tĭbĭ fēcĭt ămīcūm. H. Syn.—Cŏmĕs, sŏdālĭs. Phr.—Jūnctūs ămīcĭtĭā. Ōptĭmă vītæ sŭpēllēx. Sānctæ cūltŏr ămīcĭtĭæ. Vērā dūctŭs ămīcĭtĭā. Paūcīs mūnītŭs ămīcīs. Pārs ănĭmī. Pārs ănĭmæ mĕlĭŏr. Ănĭmæ dīmĭdĭūm mĕæ. Ō lūcĕ măgīs dīlēctă sŏrōrī. Dūlcĕ dĕcūs mĕūm. Cūjūs nōtă fĭdēs. Rēbŭs ĭn ādvērsīs cōnstāns. Pēctŏră jūnctă fĭdē.

Ămīttŏ, ĭs, īsī, īssūm, ĕrĕ. *To send away.* Syn.—Mīttŏ, rĕmīttŏ.

To lose. Syn.—Dēmīttŏ, pērdŏ, ābjĭcĭŏ, pōnŏ, spŏlĭŏr, nūdŏr, ēxŭŏr, ēxcŭtĭŏr. Phr.—Jăctūrām făcĭŏ, fĕrŏ, pătĭŏr. Vītam āmīsĭt ĭn ūndīs.

Āmnĭs, ĭs. m. *River.* Scīndĭtŭr īn gĕmĭnās pārtēs cīrcūmflŭŭs āmnĭs. O. Syn.—Flūmĕn, flŭvĭŭs, ūndă. Phr.—Rŭūnt dē mōntĭbŭs āmnēs. Cōncĭtŭs īmbrĭbŭs.

Ămŏ, ās, āvī, ātūm, ārĕ. *To love, to cherish.* Flŭvĭōs dūm pīscĭs ămābĭt. V. Syn.—Dīlĭgŏ, sĕquŏr, sēctŏr, gaūdĕŏ, dēlēctŏr, ōblēctŏr, lætŏr. Phr.—Hōc plăcĕt, ārrīdĕt mĭhĭ. Hōc mē jŭvăt, nōn mĭhĭ īngrātūm ēst, nōn dīsplĭcĕt. Cārūm hăbĕŏ. Ămōrĕ tĕnĕŏr.

Ămœnŭs, ă, ūm. *Pleasant, beautiful.* Dēvēnērĕ lŏcōs lætōs ĕt ămœnă vĭrētă. V. Syn.—Jūcūndŭs, grātŭs, lætŭs. Phr.—Dēlĭcĭīs plēnŭs. Rĕcrĕāns dūlcēdĭnĕ mēntēs. Dīgnŭs ămōrĕ lŏcŭs.

Āmōlĭŏr, īrĭs, ītŭs sūm, īrī. *To remove, to put away.* Syn.—Āmŏvĕŏ, rĕmŏvĕŏ, ārcĕŏ. Phr.—Āvērtĭtĕ pēstēm. Prŏhĭbētĕ nĕfās.

Ămŏr, ōrĭs. m. *Love, affection, esteem.* Aūt mōrs sōllĭcĭtī fīnĭs ămōrĭs ĕrĭt. O. Syn.—Āmīcĭtĭă, cōncōrdĭă, grātĭă, āffēctŭs, stŭdĭūm, cūră. *Love of one's country, parents and children.* Syn.—Pĭĕtās, cārĭtās, āffēctŭs, stŭdĭūm. Phr.—Ămŏr pătrĭæ. Ēt nātī sērvā cōmmūnĭs ămōrēm.

Āmŏvĕŏ, ēs, ōvī, ōtūm, ērĕ. *To set aside, to displace.* Syn.—Rĕmŏvĕŏ, āmōlĭŏr, ārcĕŏ.

Āmphĭthĕātrūm, ī. n. *An amphitheatre.* Ōmnīs Cæsărĕō cēdāt lăbŏr āmphĭthĕātrō. M. Syn.—Ărēnă, căvĕă, cīrcŭs, cŭnĕī.

Āmphŏră, æ. f. *A vase or jar for keeping wine.* Āmphŏră nōn mĕrŭĭt tām prĕtĭōsă mŏrī. M. Syn.—Lăgēnă, quădrāntăl, cădŭs, ĭōtă, œnŏphŏrūm, tēstă, ūrnă, vās.

Āmplēctŏr, ĕrĭs, ēxŭs sūm, ēctī. *To embrace.* Scææque āmplēctōr līmĭnă pōrtæ. V. Syn.—Āmplēxŏr, cōmplēctŏr. Phr.—Cōmplēxū tĕnĕŏ, fŏvĕŏ, cīngŏ, ēxcĭpĭŏ. Dō cīrcūm brāchĭă cōllō. Āmplēxū pĕtŏ. Lăcērtīs, ūlnīs cōmplēctŏr. Cōllō brāchĭă pōnŏ. *To surround.* Syn.—Cīngŏ, āmbĭŏ, cīrcūmdŏ, cōmplēctŏr. *To embrace, to contain.* Syn.—Cōmplēctŏr, īnclūdŏ, cōmprēndŏ, cōntĭnĕŏ. *To choose.* Syn.—Sĕquŏr, ĭnĕŏ.

Āmplēxŭs, ūs. m. *A surrounding or encircling.* Syn.—Āmbĭtŭs, cīrcŭĭtŭs, cīrcŭs. *An embrace.* Syn.—Cōmplēxŭs, ōscŭlă.

Āmplĭfĭcē. adv. *Richly, amply.* Syn.—Āmplē, āmplĭtĕr, lārgē.

Āmplĭfĭcŏ, ās, āvī, ātūm, ārĕ. *To enlarge, to amplify.* Syn.—Aūgĕŏ, ădaūgĕŏ, āmplĭŏ, prōdūcŏ, prōtrăhŏ, dīlātŏ, cŭmŭlŏ, tōllŏ.

Āmplĭō, ās, āvī, ātūm, ārĕ. *To enlarge, to increase. See Amplifico.*

Āmplĭūs. adv. *More, more than.* Āmplĭūs ōbjēctām pāssūs trānsīrĕ pălūdēm. V. Syn.—Măgĭs, plūs, sŭpĕr, īnsŭpĕr, prætĕrĕā. *Longer.* Syn.—Dĭūtĭūs.

Āmplŭs, ă, ūm. *Grand, spacious, ample.* Īllōs pōrtĭcĭbūs rēx āccĭpĭēbāt ĭn āmplīs. V. Syn.—Lātŭs, īngēns, māgnŭs, vāstŭs, spătĭōsŭs. Phr.—Lātē pătēns. *Noble, illustrious.* Syn.—Clārŭs, īnsīgnĭs. *Rich.* Syn.—Prĕtĭōsŭs, ŏpīmŭs, ŏpŭlēntŭs.

Āmpŭtŏ, ās, āvī, ātūm, ārĕ. *To cut, to amputate.* Syn.—Sĕcŏ, ēxsĕcŏ, rĕsĕcŏ, cædŏ, rĕcīdŏ, scīndŏ, ābscīndŏ, rēscīndŏ, ēxcīdŏ. Phr.—Fērrō aūfĕrŏ, sĕcŏ, rĕsĕcŏ. *To prune.* Syn. Pŭtŏ, āt tōndĕŏ, cīrcūmcīdŏ.

Āmy̆gdălă, æ. f. *An almond tree. (See Appendix under list of Trees, etc.)*

Ān. adv. *Whether, or else? (Generally not translated).* Syn.—Ānnĕ, ŭtrūm, nūm, ēcquĭd, nūmquĭd.

Ănădēmă, ătĭs. n. *An ornament for the head.* Syn.—Tænĭă, cŏrōnă, sērtūm.

Ănăs, ătĭs. f. *Duck. (See Appendix under list of Birds.)*

Ănăthēmă, ătĭs. n. *Gift, offering, votive offering.* Syn.—Dōnārĭūm, mūnŭs, dōnūm. Phr.—Mĕmŏrēs tăbēllæ. Vōti ārgūmēntă pŏtēntĭs. Pēndŭlă sīgnă.

Āncēps, ĭtĭs. adj. *Two-headed, two-faced.* Syn.—Dŭplēx. *Doubtful, hesitating, uncertain.* Syn.—Āmbĭgŭŭs, dŭbĭŭs, īncērtŭs, ānxĭŭs.

Ānchŏră, æ. f. *Anchor.* Ātquĕ tĕnāx ūncō clāssēm pĕtĭt ānchŏră rōstrō. V. Syn.—Rĕtĭnācŭlūm. Phr.—Fērrĕŭs dēns, ūncŭs. Ānchŏræ mōrsŭs. Nēxū ānchŏră cūrvō. Ānchŏră dē prōră jăcĭtŭr. Ūncō nōn āllĭgāt ānchŏră mōrsū. Ānchŏră jāctă rătēs tĕnĕāt. Fig.—*Protection.* Syn.—Præsĭdĭūm.

Āncīlĕ, ĭs. n. *A small shield.* Lævāque āncīlĕ gĕrēbăt. V. Syn.—Clȳpĕŭs, scūtūm.

Āncīllă, æ. f. *Maid-servant.* Fāllĭtŭr āncīllæ, dēcĭpĭtūrquĕ lăbŏr. O. Syn.—Fămŭlă, sērvă, mĭnīstră. Phr.—Ŏpĕrum haūd īgnāră Mĭnērvæ.

Ănĕmōnē, ēs & Ănĕmōnă, æ. f. *The anemone. (See Appendix under list of Trees, etc.)*

Ănēthūm, ī. n. *The herb anise. (See Appendix under list of Trees, etc.)*

Ānfrāctŭs, ūs. m. *Detour, circuit.* Ēst cūrvo ānfrāctū vāllēs āccōmmŏdă fraūdī. V. Syn.—Gȳrŭs, cīrcŭĭtŭs.

Āngĕlŭs, ī. m. *Messenger.* Phr.—Cælēstĭs nūntĭŭs. Dīvīnæ mēntĭs īntērprēs. Pēnnātŭs jŭvĕnĭs. Cœlī dēmīssŭs ăb ārcĕ. Cœlēstĕ gĕnŭs.

Āngŏ, ĭs, xī, ĕrĕ. *To suffocate, to strangle.* Cōrrĭpĭt īn nōdūm cōmplēxŭs ĕt āngĭt ĭnhærēns. V. Syn.—Strāngŭlŏ, strīngŏ, sūffōcŏ, cōnstrīngŏ, prĕmŏ, ūrgĕŏ. *To squeeze hard.* Syn.—Prĕmŏ, ārctŏ, cŏārctŏ, cŏērcĕŏ, āngūstŏ. Fig.—*To torment.* Syn.—Crŭcĭŏ, tōrquĕŏ, vēxŏ.

Āngŏr, ōrĭs. m. *Grief, anguish, trouble.* Syn.—Dŏlŏr, mœrŏr, trīstĭtĭă.

Ānguĭs, ĭs. m. *Serpent.* Lătĕt ānguĭs ĭn hērbā. V. Syn.—Drăcŏ, sērpēns, cŏlŭbĕr, hȳdrŭs.

Āngŭlŭs, ī. m. *Angle, corner.* Īnquĕ dŏmō lăcrĭmās āngŭlŭs ōmnĭs hăbĕt. O. Syn.—Rĕcēssŭs.

Āngūstĭæ, ārūm. f. *Defile, narrow pass.* Syn.—Faūcēs. Phr.—Āngūstĭæ vĭārūm. Āngūstī ădĭtūs. Ārctă vĭă. Fig.—*Difficulties, straits.* Syn.—Rēs ārdŭæ, āngūstæ, ĕgēnæ. Āngūstūm tēmpŭs. *Trouble, distress.* Syn.—Āngŏr, mœrĕr, dŏlŏr, ærūmnæ.

Āngūstŏ, ās, āvī, ātūm, ārĕ. *To straiten, to restrain.* Syn.—Ārctŏ, cŏārctŏ, cōmprĭmŏ, strīngŏ.

Āngūstŭs, ă, ūm. *Narrow, strait, close.* Īngēntēs ănĭmōs āngūsto īn pēctŏrĕ vērsānt. V. Syn.—Ārctŭs, ārctātŭs, brĕvĭs, cōntrāctŭs. Phr.—Āngūstōs hăbĕānt ădĭtūs. *Short, brief.* Syn.—Brĕvĭs, ēxĭgŭŭs. *Poor, mean, small.* Syn.—Măcĕr, mĭsĕr, paūpĕr, ĭnōps. *Needy, pinching.* Syn.—Ārctŭs, tĕnŭĭs, dūrŭs, āspĕr, dīffĭcĭlĭs, ārdŭŭs, ĕgēnŭs, āfflīctŭs. Phr.—Rēs āngūstă dŏmī. Mēnsă āngūstă.

Ănhēlāns, āntĭs. adj. *Out of breath.* Syn.—Ănhēlŭs. *Breathing forth.* Syn.—Spīrāns, ēxspīrāns.

Ănhēlĭtŭs, ūs. m. *Breath, vapor, scent.* Ārĭdŭs ē lāssō vĕnĭēbăt ănhēlĭtŭs ōrĕ. O. Syn.—Flātŭs, hālĭtŭs, spīrĭtŭs, spīrāmĕn, ănĭmă. Phr.—Aēthĕrĭs haūstŭs. Vītālĭs aūră. Spīrāmĭnĭs aūræ. Fēssōs quătĭt ægĕr ănhēlĭtŭs ārtūs.

Ănhēlŏ, ās, āvī, ātūm, ārĕ. *To be out of breath, to breathe hard.* Prīncĭpĭō clīvī nōstĕr ănhēlăt ĕquŭs. O. Syn.—Spīrĭtūm, aūrām trăhŏ, dūcŏ. Aūrās cāptŏ, haūrĭŏ. Phr.—Nōn rēspīrārĕ pŏtēstās. Aūræquĕ grăvēs cāptāntŭr hĭātū. Lōngī sūspēndūnt īlĭă flātūs. *To breathe forth.* Syn.—Ēmĭttŏ, spīrŏ, ēxspīrŏ, ēxhālŏ, ēfflŏ.

Ănhēlŭs, ă, ūm. *Short-winded, breathing hard..* Syn.—Ănhēlāns. Phr.—Pēctŭs ănhēlūm. Cūrsū fēstīnŭs ănhēlō. *Breathing.* Syn.—Spīrāns.

Ănĭmă, æ. f. *Air, wind.* Syn.—Aūră, vēntŭs, āĕr, flātŭs. *Breath.* Syn.—Spīrĭtŭs, hālĭtŭs, spīrāmĕn. Phr.—Ănĭmæ aūrārūm lĕvēs. *Soul.* Syn.—Mēns, ănĭmŭs, spīrĭtŭs. Phr.—Fōns vītæ, ŏrīgŏ, prīncĭpĭūm. Pārs nōstrī mĕlĭŏr. Cœlō nātă. Dĕī ĭmāgŏ. Āstrīs dēbĭtă. Nēscĭă fātī, mōrtĕ cărēns. Cōrpŏrĕām mōlēm ăgĭtāns. Dīffūsă pĕr ārtūs. Ēx æthĕrĕ mīssă. *Life.* Syn.—Vītă. Phr.—Ănĭmām ēfflārĕ, rēddĕrĕ, ēffūndĕrĕ, fīnīrĕ, dēpōnĕrĕ, rĕlīnquĕrĕ. Līnquĕrĕ dūlcēs ănĭmās.

Ănĭmādvērtŏ, ĭs, tī, sūm, ĕrĕ. *To notice.* Syn.—Ādvērtŏ, ōbsērvŏ.

Ănĭmăl, ālĭs. n. *Animal.* Prōnăquĕ cūm spēctēnt ănĭmālĭă cētĕră terram. O. Syn.—Ănĭmāns, brūtūm, bēstĭă, bēllŭă, fĕră, pĕcŭs. Phr.—Gĕnŭs ōmnĕ fĕrārūm.

Ănĭmŏ, ās, āvī, ātūm, ārĕ. *To give life to.* Syn.—Vītām dărĕ. Fig.—*To encourage.* Syn.—Āccēndŏ, īncēndŏ, ēxcĭtŏ, cōmmŏvĕŏ, cōmpēllŏ, hōrtŏr.

Ănĭmōsē. adv. *Courageously.* Syn.—Aūdāctĕr, fōrtĭtĕr.

Ănĭmōsŭs, ă, ūm. *Breathing.* Syn.—Spīrāns. *Living.* Syn.—Vīvŭs, spīrāns. *Full of life, animated.* Syn.—Vīvĭdŭs, fērvĭdŭs, ācĕr, vĕhĕmēns. *Courageous.* Syn.—Aūdāx, fōrtĭs, gĕnĕrōsŭs, īmpăvĭdŭs, īntērrĭtŭs, īnvīctŭs, māgnănĭmŭs. Phr.—Præstāns ănĭmī. Ănĭmīs călĭdŭs. Aūctŭs ănĭmō. Rōbŭr ĭnēst ănĭmīs. Rēbŭs āngūstīs ănĭmōsŭs ātquĕ Fōrtĭs.

Ănĭmŭs, ī. m. *The soul, as opposed to the body.* Syn.—Ănĭmă, mēns, spīrĭtŭs. Phr.—Pārs īgnĕă nōstrī æthĕrĕ nātă, dīvīnĭtŭs, ōrtă, nēscĭă mōrtĭs. Dĕī mēns cōnscĭă. *The mind, intelligence.* Syn.—Mēns, pēctŭs, cŏr, īngĕnĭūm, sēnsŭs, rătĭŏ. Phr.—Ănĭmī vīs, vīrēs. *Opinion.* Syn.—Sēnsŭs, sēntēntĭă. *Heart.* Syn.—Pēctŭs, cŏr, mēns, āffēctŭs. *Courage.* Syn.—Pēctŭs, vīs, vīrtūs, rōbŭr, fōrtĭtūdŏ. Phr.—Īpsĕ dŏlōr vīrēs ănĭmō dăbăt. Vīrēs ănĭmūmquĕ mĭnīstrăt. *Desire, wish.* Syn.—Cŭpīdŏ, vŏlūntās, mēns, stŭdĭūm. *Character.* Syn.—Īngĕnĭūm, īndŏlēs, nātūră.

Ānnālēs, ĭūm. m. *History, chronicle.* Sī văcĕt ānnālēs nōstrōrum aūdīrĕ lăbōrūm. V. Syn.—Fāstī, hīstŏrĭă, āctă. Phr.—Prīscī tēmpŏrĭs āctă. Aĕtātīs mŏnŭmēntă vĕtūstæ. Vīctūræ chārtæ. Ānnālēs vōlvĕrĕ prīscōs. Āntīquī mŏnŭmēntă pĕrēnnĭă fāctī.

Ānnēctŏ, ĭs, xŭī, xūm, ĕrĕ. *To attach to.* Aūrĕă cōccĭnĕās ānnēctīt fībŭlă vēstēs. V. Syn.—Nēctŏ, lĭgŏ, āllĭgŏ, vīncĭŏ. *To add.* Syn.—Ādjĭcĭŏ.

Ānnītŏr, ĕrĭs, nīsŭs & nīxŭs sūm, ī. *To lean to or upon.* Syn.—Īnnītŏr. *To strive.* Syn.—Nītŏr, ēnītŏr, cōnŏr, cōntēndŏ, mōlĭŏr, lūctŏr. Phr.—Cōnōr mōlīmĭnĕ māgnō.

Ānnōnă, æ. f. *A year's supply of provisions.* Syn.—Cĭbārĭă, cōmmĕātŭs. Phr.—Ānnōnām īncēndĕrĕ. *Price.* Syn.—Prĕtĭūm. Phr.—Aūgērĕ ānnōnām. Lāxārĕ, lĕvārĕ ānnōnām. Vīlĭs ămīcōrum ēst ānnōnă. Ānnōnă cōnvălēscĭt. Īnfērrĕ cārĭtātēm ānnōnæ.

Ānnōsŭs, ă, ūm. *Full of years, aged.* Ēcce ănŭs īn mĕdĭīs rĕsĭdēns ānnōsă pŭēllīs. O. Syn.—Grāndævŭs, lōngævŭs, āntīquŭs, prīscŭs, vĕtŭs, vĕtūstŭs. Phr.—Aēvō, ānnīs grăvĭs. Aēvī mātūrŭs. Ānnōsă vŏlūmĭnă vātūm.

Ānnŏtō, ās, āvī, ātūm, ārĕ. *To note, to mark.* Syn.—Nŏtō, sīgnō. *To remark, to notice.* Syn.—Nŏtō, ănĭmādvērtō, ōbsērvō.

Ānnŭmĕrō, ās, āvī, ātūm, ārĕ. *To number among, to add to.* Ēt mĭhĭ nōmĕn Tūnc quŏquĕ, cūm vīvĭs ānnŭmĕrārĕr, ĕrăt. O. Syn.—Ādscrībō, āccēnsĕō. Phr.—Īn nŭmĕrūm rĕfĕrō. Īn nŭmĕrō pōnō. Nŭmĕrō āddō. *To count.* Syn.—Nŭmĕrō.

Ānnŭō, ĭs, ī, ĕrĕ. *To nod to, to consent.* Ānnŭĭt, ātquĕ dŏlīs rīsīt Cȳthĕrēă rĕpērtīs. V. Syn.—Āssēntĭō, cōncēdō, prŏbō, cōnsēntĭō. *To grant, to permit.* Syn.—Cōncēdō, trĭbŭō, dō, īndūlgĕō, pērmīttō.

Ānnŭs, ī. m. *Year.* Ātque īn sē sŭă pēr vēstīgĭă vōlvĭtŭr ānnŭs. V. Phr.—Ānnī vĭcēs, tēmpŭs, tēmpŏră. Ānnŭă ōrbĭs. Ānnōrūm sĕrĭēs ēt fŭgă tēmpŏrūm. Tēmpŏră vērtūntŭr Ānnōrūm. Flūmĭnĭs īnstăr Lābĭtŭr. Pōst ălĭquŏt ărīstās, hĭĕmēs. Vōlvēntĭbŭs ānnīs. *Age.* Syn.—Aētās, ævūm. Phr.—Īntĕgĕr ānnōrūm.

Ānnŭŭs, ă, ūm. *Annual, yearly.* Syn.—Sōlēmnĭs. Phr.—Cĕlĕbrābānt ānnŭă fēstă.

Ānsă, æ. f. *Handle.* Ēt grăvĭs āttrītā pēndēbāt cānthărŭs ānsā. V. Syn.—Ānsŭlă. Phr.—Pāndā rŭbĕr ūrcĕŭs ānsā. Ā dĭgĭtīs ēxcĭdĭt ānsă mĕĭs.

Ānsĕr, ĕrĭs. m. *Goose.* (*See Appendix under list of Birds.*)

Āntĕ. adv. *Before.* Syn.—Āntĕā, prĭŭs, ōlīm, quōndām.

Āntĕ. prep. *Before, in the presence of.* Syn.—Cōrām, prō.

Āntĕā. adv. *Before.* Syn.—Āntĕ, prĭŭs, ōlīm, quōndām.

Āntĕcăpĭō, ĭs, cēpī, cēptūm & cāptūm, ĕrĕ. *To take in advance, to anticipate.* Āntĕ lŏcūm căpĭēs ŏcŭlīs. V. Syn.—Ōccŭpō, praĕōccŭpō, āntĭcĭpō, āntĕvĕnĭō, āntĕvērtō.

Āntĕcēdō, ĭs, cēssī, cēssūm, ĕrĕ. *To precede, to go before.* Syn.—Præcēdō, āntĕgrĕdĭŏr, prægrĕdĭŏr, āntĕĕō, praĕĕō, āntĕvĕnĭō, prævĕnĭō, prævērtō. Fig.—*To surpass.* Syn.—Āntĕcēllō, præcēllō, sŭpĕrō, ēmĭnĕō, sŭpĕrēmĭnĕō.

Āntĕcēllō, ĭs, ŭī, ĕrĕ. *To surpass.* Syn.—Ēxcēllō, praĕĕō, vīncō, præstō.

Āntĕŏ, ĕïs, ïvī & iī, ēīrĕ. *To go before, to precede.* Syn.—Praĕĕŏ.
Fig.—*To surpass.* Syn.—Āntĕcēllŏ, vīncŏ, prǣstŏ, sŭpĕrēmïnĕŏ.
Āntĕfĕrŏ, fērs, tŭlī, lātūm, fērrĕ. *To take or bring before.* Phr.—
Āntĕtŭlīt grēssūm. Fig.—*To prefer.* Syn.—Āntĕhăbĕŏ, āntĕ-
pōnŏ, prǣfĕrŏ.
Āntĕpōnŏ, ĭs, pŏsŭī, pŏsĭtūm, ĕrĕ. *To place before, to prefer.* Syn.—
Prǣfĕrŏ, āntĕfĕrŏ, plūrĭs făcĭŏ.
Āntĕquām. adv. *Before.* Syn.—Prĭūsquām.
Āntĕvĕnĭŏ, īs, vēnī, vēntūm, īrĕ. *To come before, to get the start of.*
Syn.—Prǣvĕnĭŏ, āntĕcēdŏ, āntĕgrĕdĭŏr. *To excel.* Syn.—Āntĕ-
cēdŏ, sŭpĕrēmïnĕŏ, ēmïnĕŏ. *See Antecedo.*
Āntĕvērtŏ, ĭs, tī, sūm, ĕrĕ. *To precede, to outstrip.* Syn.—Prǣvērtŏ,
prǣcēdŏ, prǣvĕnĭŏ.
Āntĭcĭpŏ, ās, āvī, ātūm, ārĕ. *To anticipate, to prevent.* Syn.—Ōc-
cŭpŏ, praĕōccŭpŏ, āntĕvērtŏ. Phr.—Prĭŏr ŏccŭpŏ. *To advance
before.* Syn.—Prǣcūrrŏ, āntĕvŏlŏ.
Āntīquĭtās, ātĭs. f. *Antiquity.* Syn.—Vĕtūstās, vĕtĕrēs, prīscī, āntīquī. Phr.—Ūt prīscă gēns mōrtālĭūm. Fāmă mīrātrīx sĕnĭōrĭs
ǣvī.
Āntīquĭtŭs. adv. *Long ago, formerly.* Syn.—Ōlīm.
Āntīquŭs, ă, ūm. *Ancient, old, antique.* Hōspĭtĭs āntīquī sŏlĭtās īn-
trāvĭmŭs ǣdēs. O. Syn.—Prīscŭs, vĕtūstŭs, vĕtŭs, prīstĭnŭs.
Aged, heavy with years. Syn.—Lōngǣvŭs, ānnōsŭs, grāndǣvŭs,
sĕnēx. *Anterior to, preceding.* Syn.—Prīstĭnŭs, prĭŏr, prǣtĕr-
ĭtŭs, ēlāpsŭs. *As a noun, used in the plural. The ancients.*
Syn.—Vĕtĕrēs, mājōrēs, prīscī. Phr.—Prīscī mōrtālēs. Rāncī-
dum ăprum āntīquī laŭdābānt.
Āntīstĕs, ĭtĭs. m. *Priest.* Nōn sĭnĭt īllă sŭī vānās āntīstĭtĭs ūnquām
Ēssĕ prĕcēs. O. Syn.—Săcērdōs, prǣsŭl. Phr.—Săcrōrūm āntīstĕs. Săcrōrūm mōrūmquĕ măgīstĕr. Mītrǣ quĕm săcĕr ōrnăt
hŏnōs. Quĕm săcĕr ōrnăt ăpĕx.
Āntīstĭtă, ǣ. f. *Priestess.* Syn.—Săcērdōs. Phr.—Stābăt ăpŭd să-
crās āntīstĭtă nūmĭnĭs ārās.
Āntīstŏ, ās, āvī, ātūm, ārĕ. *To surpass, to excel.* Syn.—Prǣstŏ, sŭpĕrŏ, prǣcēdŏ, āntĕcēllŏ, āntĕĕŏ.
Āntrūm, ī. n. *Cave, cavern.* Ēt vāstās ăpĕrīt faŭcēs sūb rūpĭbŭs āntrūm. V. Syn.—Căvērnă, spĕcŭs, spēlǣum, spēlūncă, rĕcēssŭs.
Phr.—Mōns căvŭs. Căvă rūpēs. Căvātă sĭlēx. Căvūm sāxūm.
Āntrūm lūcĕ cărēns. Sōlĭs īnāccēssūm rădĭīs. Lōngō spēlūncă
rĕcēssū. Dŏmŭs ātră fĕrārūm. Āntră vĭrēntĭă mūscŏ. Rōrāntĭă
fŏntĭbŭs āntră. Pēndēntĭă pūmĭcĕ tēctă. Scŏpŭlīs pēndēntĭbŭs

āntrūm. Sīlvēstrĭbŭs ābdĭtŭs āntrīs. Sūb tērrā fōdērĕ lărēm. Sūb rūpĕ căvātā. Āntră sŏnānt. Hīc spēlūncă fŭĭt vāstō sūbmōtă rĕcēssū. Ēst spĕcŭs īī mĕdĭō. Vāstōque īmmānĭs hĭātū.

Ānŭlŭs, ī. m. *Ring*. Nĭsĭ fūlsĕrĭt ānŭlŭs īngēns. J. Syn.—Ānēllŭs. Phr.—Dāt dĭgĭtīs gēmmās. Gēmmātō nĭtĕt ānŭlŭs aūrō. Dĭgĭtōs cīrcūmlĭgăt aūrō. *Seal*. Syn.—Sĭgĭllūm, gēmmă.

Ănŭs, ūs. f. *An old woman*. Ēcce ănŭs īn mĕdĭīs rēs8dēns ānnōsă pŭēllīs. O. Syn.—Vĕtŭlă, ănĭcŭlă. Phr.—Grăvĭs ānnīs. Ānnōsă părēns. Cuī frōns rūgīs cōntrāctă. Grāndĭŏr ævō. Īnvălĭdīs ănŭs ēnērvātă lăcērtīs. Quătĭēns vōcĕ trĕmēntĕ căpŭt. Ōră rūgīs ēxărātă. Sūbnīxă băcīllō. *As an adjective*. Syn.—Ānnōsă, lōngævă, vĕtŭs.

Ānxĭĕtās, ātĭs. f. *Anxiety, trouble*. Pērpĕtŭa ānxĭĕtās nēc mēnsæ tēmpŏrĕ cēssăt. J. Syn.—Cūră, sōllĭcĭtūdŏ. Phr.—Ānxĭĕtās ănĭmī. *See Cura.*

Ānxĭŭs, ă, ūm. *Anxious, restless*. Sōllĭcĭtām tĭmŏr ānxĭŭs ūrgĕt. V. Syn.—Āmbĭgŭŭs, ăncēps, dŭbĭŭs, īncērtŭs. Phr.—Ānxĭă fūrtī. Grăvĭdŭs cūrīs. *See Sollicitus.*

Ăpĕr, ăprī. m. *A wild boar*. Fūlmĕn hăbēnt ācrēs īn ădūncīs dēntĭbŭs āprī. O. Syn.—Sūs. Phr.—Dēntĕ mĭnāx. Dēns īmmānĭs ăprī. Ōblīquō dēntĕ tĭmēndŭs ăpĕr. Vūlnĭfĭcōs ăcŭēns dēntēs. Vāstāns rūră cŏlōnīs. Īndŏmĭtūs rēgnābăt ăpĕr. Spūmāntĭs ăprī. Īllĕ rŭĭt spārgītquĕ cănēs. Sānguĭne ĕt īgnĕ mĭcānt ŏcŭlī rĭgĕt hōrrĭdă cērvīx.

Ăpĕrĭŏ, īs, ŭī, ērtūm, īrĕ. *To open*. Nūmĭnĕ claūsa ăpĕrĭt, claūdĭt ăpērtă sŭō. O. Syn.—Rĕsĕrŏ, rĕclūdŏ, pāndŏ, pătĕfăcĭŏ, dīdūcŏ. Phr.—Lāxāt claūstră Sĭnōn. Sŭpĕr fŏrĭbŭs rĕclūsīs. Hōspĭtĭbūs rĕsĕrāns sēcrētă. Jāmquĕ fŏrēs ăpĕrĭt. *To release*. Syn.—Lāxŏ, sōlvŏ, rĕsōlvŏ, rĕlāxŏ. *To unfold, to manifest*. Syn.—Dētĕgŏ, nūdŏ, ēxplĭcŏ. *To show*. Syn.—Pătĕfăcĭŏ, ōstēndŏ, dētĕgŏ.

Ăpērtē. adv. *Openly, plainly*. Syn.—Pălām, mănĭfēstē. *Frankly*. Syn.—Īngĕnŭē, sīncērē.

Ăpērtŭs, ă, ūm. *Open*. Jāmque ădĕo ēxĭĕrāt pōrtīs ĕquĭtātŭs ăpērtīs. V. Syn.—Rĕclūsŭs, pătĕfāctŭs, rĕsĕrātŭs, ădăpērtŭs, pătēns, hĭāns, hĭūlcŭs. *Discovered*. Syn.—Dētēctŭs, nūdātŭs, nūdŭs. *Free, open*. Syn.—Lībĕr, pătēns. *Manifest, clear*. Syn.—Cērtŭs, clārŭs, mănĭfēstŭs. *Frank, open*. Syn.—Cāndĭdŭs, īngĕnŭŭs, sīncērŭs.

Ăpēs (Ăpĭs), ĭs. f. *A bee*. Cēcrŏpĭās īnnātŭs ăpēs ămŏr ūrgĕt hăbēndī. V. Phr.—Ăpūm āgmĕn, ēxāmĕn, ēxērcĭtŭs. Gēns ŏpĭfēx mēllĭs. Nēctărĭs ărtĭfĭcēs. Flōrūm tūrbă răpāx. Stŭdĭōsă cŏhōrs.

Crūră thy̆mō plēnæ. Thy̆mō pāstæ. Mēllĕ grăvĭdæ. Hy̆mēttī pŏpŭlātrīcēs. Cārpĭt ăpīs stŭdĭōsă thy̆mōs. Vērīs pŏpŭlāntŭr ŏpēs. Grātă cārpēntīs thy̆mă pēr lăbōrēm plūrĭmūm. Ēxērcĭtŭs mēllĭfĕr. Pēr cāmpōs vŏlĭtānt. Cōmplĕāt ūt dūlcī sēdŭlă mēllĕ făvōs.

Ăpēx, ĭcĭs. m. *Crest of wool that surmounted the head-dress of the Flamens. Also an omen in the form of a flame at the sacrifices.* Syn.—Crīstă. *Top, summit.* Syn.—Cūlmĕn, căcūmĕn, vērtēx, fāstīgĭūm.

Ăpŏthēcă, æ. f. *Cellar, larder.* Aūt ăpŏthēcă prŏcīs īntācta ēst aūt pĕcŭs. H. Syn.—Cēllă. *Inn, store.* Syn.—Tăbērnă, ōffĭcīnă.

Āppărātŭs, ūs. m. *Apparel, adornment.* Pērsĭcōs ōdī, pŭĕr, āppărātūs. H. Syn.—Părātŭs, pompă.

Āppārĕō, ēs, ŭī, ĭtūm, ērĕ. *To appear, to be seen.* Āppārēnt rārī nāntēs īn gūrgĭtĕ vāstō. V. Syn.—Vĭdĕŏr, cērnŏr, āspĭcĭŏr, cōnspĭcĭŏr. Phr.—Mē ōstēndŏ. Vīsŭs ădēssĕ mĭhĭ. Vīsă mĭhi ānte ŏcŭlōs. *To be evident.* Syn.—Lĭquĕt, pătĕt, ăpērtūm ēst.

Āppărŏ, ās, āvī, ātūm, ārĕ. *To prepare, to make ready.* Īncērtūs quās Jūnŏ fĕrāt, quās āppărĕt īrās. V. Syn.—Părŏ, cōmpărŏ, præpărŏ, ōrnŏ, ădōrnŏ, īnstrŭŏ, āccīngŏ.

Āppēllŏ, ās, āvī, ātūm, ārĕ. *To address, to speak.* Syn.—Cōmpēllŏ. *To declare, to proclaim.* Syn.—Dēclārŏ. *To name.* Syn.—Vŏcŏ, nōmĭnŏ, cōmpēllŏ (ās). Phr.—Nōmĭnĕ clāmŏ. Ēt gēntī nōmēn dĕdĭt. Sīc nōmĭnĕ dīcūnt. Rōmānōs sŭō dē nōmĭnĕ dīcĕt. *To interrupt.* Syn.—Īntērpēllŏ. *To invoke.* Syn.—Īnvŏcŏ, tēstŏr.

Āppēllŏ, ĭs, ŭlī, ūlsūm, ĕrĕ. *To drive or lead towards.* Fēssōs ād līttŏră cūrvă jŭvēncōs Āppŭlĕrām. O. Syn.—Āddūcŏ, ādmŏvĕŏ, ādvĕhŏ. *To touch, to board, to disembark upon.* Syn.—Āppēllŏr, āpplĭcŏr, ādvĕhŏr, ādvērtŏr, āllābŏr. Phr.—Līttŏră nāvĕ tāngŏ. Tēllūrĕ pŏtĭŏr. Pōrtūm tāngŏ, tĕnĕŏ, sŭbĕŏ. Pōrtū cōnsīdŏ, quĭēscŏ. Plēnīs sŭbĭt ōstĭă vēlīs.

Āppēndŏ, ĭs, dī, sūm, ĕrĕ. *To suspend.* Syn.—Sūspēndŏ. Fig.—*To weigh.* Syn.—Pērpēndŏ, pōndĕrŏ.

Āppĕtŏ, ĭs, īvī & ĭī, ītūm, ĕrĕ. *To seek to attain.* Syn.—Pĕtŏ, nītŏr (ĭn), āffēctŏ. *To seize.* Syn.—Prĕhēndŏ, āpprĕhēndŏ. *To attack.* Syn.—Pĕtŏ, īnvādŏ, īmpĕtŏ, āggrĕdĭŏr, ădŏrĭŏr. *To desire.* Syn.—Ēxpĕtŏ, cŭpĭŏ, ōptŏ, ēxōptŏ, pĕrōptŏ. *To approach.* Syn.—Ādvēntŏ, prŏpīnquŏ, īnstŏ. Phr.—Fīŏ prŏpĭŏr.

Āpplĭcŏ, ās, āvī, ātūm, ārĕ. *To attach to, to apply to.* Syn.—Ădhĭbĕŏ. ādmŏvĕŏ, āddŏ, ādjĭcĭŏ, ādjūngŏ, āppōnŏ. *To conduct, to lead towards.* Syn.—Ăgŏ, dūcŏ, āppēllŏ(ĭs).

Āppōnŏ, ĭs, pŏsŭī, pŏsĭtūm, ĕrĕ. *To place near or upon, to add.* Hōc quŏquĕ nēscĭŏ quīd nōstrīs āppōnĕ lĭbēllīs. O. Syn.—Āddŏ, ādmŏvĕŏ, ādjĭcĭŏ, āffīngŏ, ādjūngŏ. *To serve at table.* Syn.—Pōnŏ, āffĕrŏ.

Āpprĕhēndŏ & Āpprēndŏ, ĭs, dī, sūm, ĕrĕ. *To take, to seize.* Syn.—Prĕhēndŏ, prēndŏ, căpĭŏ, cōrrĭpĭŏ, ārrĭpĭŏ.

Āpprīmē. adv. *Very, much, excessively.* Syn.—Vāldē, mūltūm, āpprīmă.

Āpprŏbŏ, ās, āvī, ātūm, ārĕ. *To approve.* Ān vĕrĕār nē nōn āpprŏbĕt īllă Gĕtēs? O. Syn.—Prŏbŏ, laūdŏ, ānnŭŏ, āssēntĭŏr. *To prove.* Syn.—Prŏbŏ.

Āpprŏpĕrŏ, ās, āvī, ātūm, ārĕ. *To hasten, to advance quickly.* Syn.—Prŏpĕrŏ, fēstīnŏ, cĕlĕrŏ, āccĕlĕrŏ, ādvŏlŏ, mātūrŏ. Phr.—Grădūm ūrgĕŏ.

Āpprŏpīnquŏ, ās, āvī, ātūm, ārĕ. *To approach.* Syn.—Prŏpīnquŏ, āccēdŏ, ādvēntŏ, ādvĕnĭŏ. Phr.—Jāmquĕ prŏpīnquābānt pōrtīs.

Āprīcŏr, ārĭs, ātŭs sūm, ārī. *To keep in the sun.* Phr.—Īn āprīcō spătĭŏr, āmbŭlŏ, stō, sĕdĕŏ.

Āprīcŭs, ă, ūm. *Exposed to the sun.* Mītĭs ĭn āprīcīs cŏquĭtūr vīndēmĭă sāxīs. V. Phr.—Sōlī ēxpŏsĭtŭs, ēxpōstŭs, pătēns, ōbnōxĭŭs. Ā vēntīs tūtŭs, dēfēnsŭs. Sōlĕ gaūdēns.

Āptē. adv. *Justly, a propos, aptly.* Syn.—Āccōmmŏdātē, rēctē, bĕnĕ, cōnvĕnĭēntĕr, dĕcēntĕr, ōppōrtūnē, tēmpŏrĕ.

Āptŏ, ās, āvī, ātūm, ārĕ. *To fit, to adjust.* Īntĕrĕā clāssēm vēlīs āptārĕ jŭbēbāt. V. Syn.—Ādāptŏ, āccōmmŏdŏ, cōmpōnŏ, īnstrŭŏ, īntērstrŭŏ, ōrnŏ, părŏ. Phr.—Āptāt sē pūgnæ. Ănĭmōs āptēnt ārmīs. Nērvōque āptārĕ săgīttīs. Āptăt ăd ārmă mănūs. Lătĕrīque āccōmmŏdăt ēnsēm.

Āptŭs, ă, ūm. *Adjusted, attached.* Syn.—Cōnnēxŭs, cōnjūnctŭs, cŏhærēns, āccōmmŏdātŭs. Fig.—*Fit, proper.* Syn.—Cōngrŭŭs, ĭdōnĕŭs, cōmmŏdŭs, āccōmmŏdŭs, ōppōrtūnŭs, hăbĭlĭs, ūtĭlĭs, cōnvĕnĭēns, dĕcēns, bŏnŭs. Phr.—Lŏcŭs āptŭs ĕquīs. Rēmīs āptă pălūs. Aētās mōllĭs ĕt āptă rĕgī. Āptĭŏr ēst mēnsă jŏcō.

Ăpŭd. prep. *At the house of.* Syn.—Īntĕr, ăd. *In the presence of, before.* Syn.—Cōrām, āntĕ. *In.* Syn.—Īntĕr, ĭn. *Near.* Syn.—Jūxtā, prŏpĕ, ăd, cīrcūm, āntĕ.

Ăquă, æ. f. *Water.* Quīd prŏhĭbētĭs ăquās? ūsŭs cōmmūnĭs ăquārum ēst. O. Syn.—Ūndă, hūmŏr, lĭquŏr. Phr.—Sīmplĭcĭs hūmŏr ăquæ. Tērræ cīrcūmflŭŭs hūmŏr. *Spring water.* Syn.—Lўmphă, lătēx, fōns, fōntēs. Phr.—Ăquæ fōns, lāpsŭs. Dēcūrsŭs ăquārūm. Lĭquōrēs gĕlĭdī. Ăquă fōntĭbŭs haūstă. Jūgĭs ăquæ fōns. Sūmmōque haūsīt dē gūrgĭtĕ lўmphās. Ăd ăquæ lēnĕ căpūt sācræ. *River water.* Syn.—Flūmĕn, flŭvĭŭs, flŭēntūm. *Marsh-water.* Syn.—Pălūs, stāgnūm, lăcŭs. Phr.—Lŏcă fœtă pălūstrĭbŭs ūndīs. *Rain-water.* Syn.—Plŭvĭă, īmbĕr. *Sea-water.* Syn.—Mărĕ, Nēptūnŭs, ūndă, flūctŭs, sāl, sălūm. Phr.—Spūmĕă mūrmŭrăt ūndă. Nāvēs āccĭpĭūnt ĭnĭmīcum īmbrēm.

Ăquālĭs, ĭs. m. *Water-pot, vessel, pitcher.* Syn.—Pōcŭlūm, vās.

Ăquĭlă, æ. f. *Eagle.* (*See list of birds in appendix*). *The Roman military standard.* Syn.—Sīgnūm, vēxīllūm.

Ăquĭlŏ, ōnĭs. m. *The north wind.* Frīgĭdŭs ēt sīlvīs ăquĭlō dēcŭssĭt hŏnōrēm. V. Syn.—Bŏrĕās. Phr.—Vīs, răbĭēs, īmpĕtŭs, fŭrŏr, flātŭs, flāmĭnă ăquĭlōnĭs. Ăquĭlōnĭŭs flātŭs. Bŏrĕālĭă flābră. Bīstŏnĭŭs tūrbŏ. Ārmātŭs tūrbĭnĕ. Cōncrētūs grāndĭnĕ pēnnās. Spārgĭt ăb āxĕ nĭvēm. Strīdēns ăquĭlōnĕ prŏcēllă. Hĭĕms ăquĭlōnĭbŭs hōrrĕt.

Ăquŏr, ārĭs, ātŭs sūm, ārī. *To water, to give water to.* Syn.—Ădăquŏ. Phr.—Ăd ăquām, pōtūm dūcŏ. Ăquās, flŭvĭōs mĭnīstrŏ, præbĕŏ.

Ăquōsŭs, ă, ūm. *Watery.* Ĕt ăquōsŭs ālbō Cōrpŏrĕ lānguŏr. H. Syn.—Hūmĭdŭs, ūdŭs. *Clear as water.* Syn.—Pēllūcĭdŭs, vĭtrĕŭs.

Āră, æ. f. *Altar.* Ūt vĕtŭs āccēnsīs īncāndŭĭt īgnĭbŭs āră. O. Syn.—Āltārĕ. Phr.—Tūrĕ călēns. Tūrĕ pĭō rĕdŏlēns. Flāmmīs lūcēns. Fūmāns săcrīs īgnĭbŭs. Mūltō quæ fūmăt ŏdōrĕ. Dărĕ sērtă pĕr ārās. Ārīs īmpōnĕrĕ dōnă. Tūrĕ călēnt āræ. *Refuge, asylum.* Syn.—Ăsȳlūm, pōrtŭs, ārx, pērfŭgĭūm, aūxĭlĭūm.

Ărānĕă, æ. f. *Spider.* Īn fŏrĭbŭs lāxōs sūspēndĭt ărānĕă cāssēs. V. Syn.—Ărānĕŭs, ărānĕŏlŭs, ărānĕŏlă, ărăchnē. Phr.—Īnvīsă Mĭnērvæ. Tĕnŭī stāmēn dē pēctŏrĕ dūcĭt. Īncaūtās fīgĭt ărānĕă mūscās. Āntīquās ēxērcĕt ărānĕă tēlās. *Spider's web.* Syn.—Ărānĕūm.

Ărātŏr, ōrĭs. m. *Ploughman, tiller of the soil.* Rōbūstūs quŏquĕ jām taūrīs jŭgă sōlvĕt ărātŏr. V. Syn.—Rūrĭcŏlă, ăgrĭcŏlă, cŏlōnŭs, vīllĭcŭs. Phr.—Ăgēllī, ăgrī cūltŏr. Præcēptŏr ărāndī. Cūrvī mŏdĕrātŏr ărātrī. Grăvēm dūrō tērrām quī vērtĭt ărātrō.

Ărātrūm, ī. *Plow.* Vōmĭs ĕt īnflēxī prīmūm grăvĕ rōbŭr ărātrī. V. Syn.—Vōmĕr. Phr.—Dēns vōmĕrĭs. Cūrvī pōndŭs ărātrī. Ădūncī vūlnĕra ărātrī. Cūrvī fōrmam āccĭpĭt ūlmŭs ărātrī. Vĕnĭūnt ăd ărātră jŭvēncī.

Ārbĭtĕr, ĭtrī. m. *Judge.* Ārbĭtĕr ēs fōrmæ; cērtāmĭnă sīstĕ dĕārūm. O. Syn.—Jūdēx. Phr.—Quēm pĕnĕs ārbĭtrĭum ēst. Pācĭs āc bēllī mĕdĭŭs. *A witness.* Syn.—Tēstĭs, cōnscĭŭs. *Prince, ruler, master.* Syn.—Mŏdĕrātŏr, rēx, rēctŏr, dŏmĭnŭs. Phr.—Ārbĭtĕr īmpĕrĭī. Mărĭs ărbĭtĕr.

Ārbĭtrĭūm, ĭī. n. *Judgment, decision.* Syn.—Jūdĭcĭūm, dēcrētūm, sēntēntĭă. Phr.—Ārbĭtrĭūm lītĭs trājēcĭt ĭn ōmnēs. *Wish, desire.* Syn.—Lĭbīdŏ, vŏlūntās, nūtŭs.

Ārbĭtrŏr, ārĭs, ātŭs sūm, ārī. *To judge, to think.* Syn.—Jūdĭcŏ, cēnsĕŏ, aūtŭmŏ, crēdŏ, rĕŏr, ēxīstĭmŏ, sēntĭŏ, pŭtŏ.

Ārbŏr & Ārbŏs, ŏrĭs. f. *Tree.* Cīngĭt ĕt āngūstās ārbŏr ŏpācă cŏmās. O. Syn.—Ārbūstūm, ārbūscŭlă, frŭtēx, vīrgūltūm, sīlvă. Phr.—Ārbŏrĭs ūmbră, frōndēs, hōspĭtĭūm, rāmī. Ēxtēndēns lātē sŭă brāchĭă. Rāmĭs dīffūsă. Pătŭlĭs lūxŭrĭōsă cŏmĭs. Ŏpācă cŏmĭs. Frōndĭbŭs ārbŏs Lūxŭrĭăt fēcūndă nŏvĭs. Frūctĭbŭs dĕcōră. Lārgĭs frūctĭbŭs ŏnĕrātă. Ēxcēlsōs tēndēns ăd sīdĕră rāmōs. Tōllēns sē vērtĭce ăd aūrās. Nĭvĕĭs ūbērrĭmă pōmĭs.

Ārbūstūm, ī. n. *Grove of trees, orchard.* Syn.—Ārbŏrētūm, vĭrētūm. Phr.—Lŏcă vīrgūltĭs cōnsĭtă. Lŏcŭs ārbŏrĭbŭs frĕquēns. Rĕsŏnānt ārbūstă cĭcādĭs. *Bush, shrub.* Syn.—Frŭtēx, vīrgūltūm, ārbūscŭlă.

Ārbŭtŭs, ī. f. *The wild strawberry or cherry tree.* (*See Appendix under list of Trees, etc.*)

Ārcă, æ. f. *Box, chest, coffer.* Syn.—Ārcŭlă, căpsă, căpsŭlă, scrīnĭūm. *Coffin.* Syn.—Fĕrĕtrūm.

Ārcānē & Ārcānō. *Secretly.* Syn.—Clām, fūrtīm, lătēntĕr, ōccūltē.

Ārcānūm, ī. n. *Secret, mystery.* Ārcānūm nĕquĕ tū scrūtābĕrĭs ūllĭŭs ūnquăm. H. Syn.—Sēcrētūm, mȳstērĭūm. Phr.—Mēntĭs ăbdĭtă, ōccūltă, lătĕbræ.

Ārcānŭs, ă, ūm. *Secret, mysterious, hidden.* Tē cŏlĕre, ārcānōs ĕtĭăm tĭbĭ crēdĕrĕ sēnsūs. V. Syn.—Cōndĭtŭs, ābscōndĭtŭs, ābstūsŭs, ăbdĭtŭs, lătēns, lătĭtāns, ŏpērtŭs, ădŏpērtŭs, rĕcōndĭtŭs, cæcŭs, ōbdūctŭs, īntĭmŭs, sēcrētŭs, tēctŭs, cēlātŭs, īnvīsŭs. Phr.—Quæ nātūră nĕgāvĭt Vīsĭbŭs hūmānĭs.

Ārcĕŏ, ēs, ŭī, ctūm, ērĕ. *To keep off, to repulse.* Quēm fŭgĭs aūt quĭs tē nōstrĭs āmplēxĭbŭs ārcēt? V. Syn.—Ābārcĕŏ, āmŏvĕŏ, pēllŏ, rĕpēllŏ, prōpēllŏ, prōpūlsŏ, āvērtŏr, āmōlĭŏr, ābstērrĕŏ, prŏhĭbĕŏ, ăbĭgŏ. Phr.—Ārcērī pătrĭă. Præsēpĭbŭs ārcēnt. Trōjānōsque ārcĕăt ūrbĕ. Fīnĭbŭs ārcērĕt. *To restrain, to bind.* Syn.—Cŏērcĕŏ, cŏhĭbĕŏ, cōntĭnĕŏ, īmpĕdĭŏ, rĕprĭmŏ, strīngŏ, cōnstrīngŏ, vīncĭŏ.

Ārcēssītŭs, ūs. m. *Summons.* Syn.—Rŏgātŭs, vŏcātŭs, māndātūm.

Ārcēssŏ, īs, īvī, ītūm, ĕrĕ. *To send for, to summon.* Sī pŏtŭĭt mānēs ārcēssĕrĕ cōnjŭgĭs Ōrpheūs. V. Syn.—Āccĭŏ, āccērsŏ, vŏcŏ, ādvŏcŏ.

Ārchĭtēctŭs, ī. m. *An architect, a master builder.* Syn.—Ārchĭtēctōn, strūctŏr, ædĭfĭcātŏr. Fig.—*Inventor.* Syn.—Māchĭnātŏr, aūctŏr. Phr.—Dŏlī făbrĭcātŏr.

Ārctē. adv. *Straitly, closely.* Syn.—Āngūstē, prēssē.

Ārctŏ, ās, āvī, ātūm, ārĕ. *To crowd, to press close.* Syn.—Āngūstŏ, cōntrăhŏ, cŏārctŏ, prĕmŏ, cōmprĭmŏ, strīngŏ, cōnstrīngŏ. Phr.—Ĭn ārctūm cōnstrīngĕrĕ.

Ārctŭs, ă, ūm. *Straitened, narrow.* Vīnclăquĕ sōpītās āddĭt ĭn ārctă mănūs. O. Syn.—Āngūstŭs, ārctātŭs, cōntrāctŭs, strīctŭs, cōnstrīctŭs, cōmprēssŭs. Phr.—Ĭn ārctūm, ĭn ārctō.

Ārcŭŏ, ās, āvī, ātūm, ārĕ. *To bend like a bow, to arch.* Syn.—Cūrvŏ, īncūrvŏ, cămĕrŏ. Phr.—Ĭn ārcūm sĭnŭŏ, flēctŏ, cūrvŏ.

Ārcŭs, ūs. m. *A bow, hand-bow.* Aūrĕūs ēx hŭmĕrō sŏnăt ārcŭs ĕt ārmă Dĭānæ. V. Syn.—Cōrnū, nērvŭs. Phr.—Flēxĭlĕ cōrnū. Īncērtō dēbĭlĭs ārcū. Nĭtĭdō spēctābĭlĭs ārcū. Ārcū præsīgnĭs ădūncō. Ārcūm tēndĕrĕ, flēctĕrĕ. Ēt spīcŭlă tēndĕrĕ cōrnū. Ārcū cōntēntă părātō. Īntēndūnt ācrēs ārcūs. *Rainbow.* Syn.—Īrĭs. Phr.—Plŭvĭūs dēscrībĭtŭr ārcŭs. Vărĭātă lūcĕ rŭbēns. Īngēns sūb nūbĭbŭs ārcŭs. Prætēxēns pīctā fērrūgĭnĕ cœlūm. *Vault, arch.* Syn.—Fōrnīx, cămĕră.

Ārdĕă, æ. f. *Heron.* (*See Appendix under list of Birds.*)

Ārdēns, ēntĭs. adj. *Inflamed, burning.* Syn.—Āccēnsŭs, īncēnsŭs, īnflāmmātŭs, flăgrāns, tōrrēns, īgnītŭs, fērvēns, fērvĭdŭs, călēns, călĭdŭs. *Brilliant, shining.* Syn.—Īgnĕŭs, rŭtĭlāns, rŭtĭlŭs, cŏrūscŭs, flāmmātŭs, scīntĭllāns. *Eager, impetuous.* Syn.—Ācĕr, īmpĭgĕr. *Furious.* Syn.—Fērvēns, fērvĭdŭs, călēns.

Ārdĕŏ, ēs, sī, sūm, ērĕ. *To burn, to be on fire.* Fērtĭlĭs āccēnsīs mēssĭbŭs ārdĕt ăgĕr. O. Syn.—Ārdēscŏ, ēxārdēscŏ, flăgrŏ, cōnflăgrŏ, āccēndŏr, īncēndŏr, crĕmŏr, ūrŏr, ădūrŏr, fērvĕŏ, æstŭŏ, cāndĕŏ, īncāndēscŏ, īgnēscŏ. Phr.—Flāmmīs, īgnĭbŭs, cōrrĭpĭŏr, ūrŏr, cōnsūmŏr, pĕrĕŏ. Cōnsīdĕre ĭn īgnēs. Flāmmīs crĕpĭtārĕ. Īgnēs ād tēctă fĕrūntŭr. *To shine, to glow.* Syn.—Fūlgĕŏ, mĭcŏ. *To desire.* Syn.—Vŏlŏ, dēsīdĕrŏ, cŭpĭŏ. *To be filled with passion.* Syn.—Ēxārdĕŏ, æstŭŏ, călĕŏ, ūrŏr, īncēndŏr, fŭrŏ, ēxcāndēscŏ.

Ārdēscŏ, ĭs, ĕrĕ. *To take fire.* Syn.—Īnārdēscŏ, īgnēscŏ, īncēndŏr. *See Ardeo.*

Ārdŏr, ōrĭs. m. *Violent heat.* Tērræque ārdōrĕ dĕhīscūnt. V. Syn.—Aēstŭs, călŏr, fērvŏr. Phr.—Īgnĕŭs ārdŏr. Flāmmĕŭs ārdōr sĭlvās ēxēdĕrăt. *Love, affection.* Syn.—Āmŏr. *Desire, longing for.* Syn.—Āmŏr, stŭdĭūm, cŭpīdŏ, vŏlūntās. Phr.—Vīsēndī prīncĭpĭs ārdŏr. Quærēndī nōmĭnĭs ārdŏr. Fŭrĭt ārdŏr ĕdēndī. *Passion.* Syn.—Fērvŏr, călŏr, æstŭs, īmpĕtŭs, vīs, fŭrŏr.

Ārdŭŭs, ă, ūm. *Lofty, high.* Mōns ĭbĭ vērtĭcĭbūs pĕtĭt ārdŭŭs āstră dŭōbŭs. O. Syn.—Āltŭs, cēlsŭs, sūblīmĭs, ābrūptŭs, præcēps, īnvĭŭs. Phr.—Ārdŭă tērrārūm. Ārdŭă pēnnīs Āstră sĕquī. Āmāntēs ārdŭă dūmī. *Difficult.* Syn.—Mŏlēstŭs, grăvĭs, dīffīcĭlĭs, ŏpĕrōsŭs. Phr.—Māgnæ mōlĭs. Rēs ārdŭæ. Nīl mōrtālĭbūs ārdŭum ēst.

Ārĕă, æ. f. *Barn-floor, threshing floor.* Ārĕă cūm prīmīs īngēnti æquāndă cȳlīndrō. Phr.—Crētā sŏlĭtāndă tĕnācī. Aēquātō plāna ārĕă tērgō. Quīdquīd dē Lĭbȳcīs vērrĭtŭr ārĕīs. Crēbrō sŏnăt ārĕă pūlsū. *Smooth surface, a plain.* Syn.—Cāmpŭs, plānĭtĭēs, æquŏr.

Ārĕfăcĭō, ĭs, ēcī, āctūm, ĕrĕ. *To dry.* Syn.—Sīccō, ēxsīccō.

Ārēnă, æ. f. *Sand.* Cōllēctum hūmōrēm bĭbŭlā dīdūcĭt ărēnā. V. Syn.—Săbŭlūm. Phr.—Āggĕr, cŭmŭlŭs ărēnæ. Nŭmĕrō cărēns. Nīmbŭs ărēnæ. Fŭrĭt æstŭs ărēnīs. Zĕphȳrō tūrbāntŭr ărēnæ. *The arena.* Syn.—Āmphĭthĕātrūm, cīrcŭs, căvĕă, ārĕă.

Ārēnōsŭs, ă, ūm. *Sandy.* Līttŭs ărēnōsūm Lĭbȳēs vēntōsquĕ sĕcābăt. V. Phr.—Ărēnīs crēbĕr, strātŭs, ōbdūctŭs, tēctŭs, squālēns.

Ārĕō, ēs, ŭī, ērĕ. *To be dried up, to be parched.* Ārĕt ăgēr, vĭtĭō mŏrĭēns sĭtĭt āĕrĭs hērbă. V. Syn.—Ārēscō, ārĕfīō, sīccŏr, ēxsīccŏr, mārcĕō, ūrŏr, ēxūrŏr. Fig.—*To be dry, to be thirsty.* Syn.—Sĭtĭō.

Ārgēntĕŭs, ă, ūm. *Of or made of silver.* Aūrātīs vŏlĭtāns ārgēntĕŭs ānsĕr Pōrtĭcĭbŭs. V. Phr.—Ārgēntō fāctŭs, grăvĭs, sŏlĭdŭs, mĭcāns. Ārgēntō cælātă bĭpēnnĭs. *Shining like silver.* Syn.—Ālbŭs, cāndĭdŭs, lūcĭdŭs, pēllūcĭdŭs, nĭtĭdŭs, rădĭāns, nĭtēns.

Ārgēntūm, ī. n. *Silver.* Vīlĭŭs ārgēntum ēst aūrō, vīrtūtĭbŭs aūrūm. H. Phr.—Ārgēntī mĕtāllūm. Lĕvĭs ārgēntī lāmĭnă. Ārgēntī vāscŭlă pūrī. Ārgēntō fūlgēbāt ŏpŭs.

Ārgūmēntŏr, ārĭs, ātŭs sūm, ārī. *To dispute, to argue.* Syn.—Rătĭōcĭnŏr, dīspŭtŏ, dīssĕrŏ, prŏbŏ. Phr.—Dōctīs vērbīs dīssĕrŏ, dīscēptŏ.

Ārgūmēntūm, ī. n. *Argument, proof, reasoning.* Syn.—Rătĭō. *Sign, indication.* Syn.—Sīgnūm, īndĭcĭūm, nŏtă. *Subject-matter.* Syn.—Mātĕrĭēs, mātĕrĭă.

Ārgŭō, ĭs, ŭī, ūtūm, ĕrĕ. *To show, to prove.* Dēgĕnĕrēs ănĭmōs tĭmŏr ārgŭĭt. V. Syn.—Īndĭcŏ, mōnstrŏ, ōstēndŏ, prōdŏ, sīgnĭfĭcŏ, dētēgŏ, dēclārŏ. *To blame.* Syn.—Īncrēpŏ, cārpŏ, rĕprĕhēndŏ, dāmnŏ, nŏtŏ. *To accuse.* Syn.—Āccūsŏ, īncūsŏ, īnsĭmŭlŏ, cūlpŏ.

Ārgūtē. adv. *Skilfully, ingeniously.* Syn.—Ācūtē, cāllĭdē.

Ārgūtĭæ, ārūm. f. *Wit, pleasantries.* Syn.—Jŏcī, sălēs. Phr.—Ācūtē dīctă.

Ārgūtŭs, ă, ūm. *Clear, penetrating, piercing.* Hīc ārgūtă săcrā pēndēbĭt fīstŭlă pīnū. V. Syn.—Ăcūtŭs, strīdŭlŭs, sŏnōrŭs, strīdēns. *Melodious.* Syn.—Cănōrŭs, lĭquĭdŭs. *Subtle, ingenious.* Syn.—Ăcūtŭs, īngĕnĭōsŭs, sōlērs, sūbtīlĭs. *Pointed, sharp.* Syn.—Ăcūtŭs, brĕvĭs, ēxīlĭs.

Ārĭdĭtās, ātĭs. f. *Dryness.* Syn.—Sīccĭtās.

Ārĭdŭs, ă, ūm. *Dry, arid.* Ārĭdă, cīrcūm Nūtrīmēntă dĕdĭt. V. Syn.—Ārēns, ārēscēns, sīccŭs, sīccātŭs, hĭūlcŭs, mārcĭdŭs. Phr.—Hūmōrĭs ĕgēns, ĕgēnŭs, ēxpērs. *Burnt, parched.* Syn.—Ārdēns, tōrrĭdŭs, flăgrāns. Fig.—*Poor, miserable.* Syn.—Tĕnŭĭs, ĭnōps, jējūnŭs.

Ărīēs, ărĭĕtĭs & ārĭĕtĭs. m. *A ram.* Ipse ărĭēs ĕtĭām nūnc vēllĕră sīccăt. V. Phr.—Dūx ŏvĭūm. Lānĭgĕrī grĕgĭs dēfēnsŏr. Īnnŏcŭī pĕcŏrĭs tūtēlă. Bēllātōr cōrnūquĕ fĕrōx. *A battering-ram.* Phr.—Māchĭnă bēllĭcă. Vīx murıs tŏlĕrāndă lŭēs. Mūrōs dīsjĭcĭēns. Lăbăt ārĭĕtĕ crēbrō. Ārĭĕtĕ dīssĭlĭūnt mūrī.

Ārĭĕtŏ & Ārĭĕtŏ, ās, āvī, ātūm, ārĕ. *To push or butt like a ram.* Ārĭĕtăt īn pōrtās ēt dūrōs ōbjĭcĕ pōstēs. V. Phr.—Ārĭĕtĕ īmpĕtŏ, vērbĕrŏ, fĕrĭŏ, quătĭŏ, cōncŭtĭŏ.

Ărīstă, æ. f. *The awn or beard of grain, also the grain itself.* Mōllī paŭlātīm flāvēscēt cāmpŭs ărīstā. V. Syn.—Spīcă, cūlmŭs, frūgēs, mēssĭs, sĕgĕs. Phr.—Grăvĭdīs prōcūmbăt cūlmŭs ărīstīs. Cānīs flāvēscīt cūlmŭs ărīstīs. Tĕnŭēs glŏmĕrāntŭr ărīstæ. Zĕphўrō grăcĭlēs vībrāntŭr ărīstæ.

Ārmă, ōrūm. n. *Arms, weapons.* Fŭrŏr ārmă mĭnīstrăt. V. Syn.—Fērrūm, ēnsĭs, glădĭŭs, hāstă, jăcŭlūm, tēlūm. Phr.—Dīră nĕcĭs īnstrūmēntă. Ārmōrūm vīrēs. Īnvīsă mātrĭbŭs ārmă. Cædĕ călēntĭă. Ēnsēs clўpĕīquĕ sŏnānt. Ārma hōrrēndūm sŏnŭērĕ. Ārmōrum īngrŭĭt hōrrŏr. Ārmă cĭtī, fērte ārmă vĭrī. Ārma āmēns căpĭŏ. Rūrsŭs ĭn ārmă fĕrŏr. Cūnctī cŏēāmŭs ĭn ārmă. Ārmă părāte ănĭmīs. Teŭcrūm ārmă quĭēscūnt. Ārmă dēpŏsŭērĕ hŭmĕrīs. *Defensive armor.* Syn.—Clўpĕŭs, lōrīcă, gălĕă. Phr.—Ārmōrūm tūtāmĕn. Cōrpŏrĭs mūnīmĭnă. *War.* Syn.—Bēllūm.

Ārmēntūm, ī, n. *Herd.* Mīllĕ grĕgēs īllī tŏtĭdēmque ārmēntă pĕr hērbās Pāscēbānt. O. Syn.—Bŏvēs, taŭrī, jŭvēncī, văccæ, pĕcŭs. Phr.—Cōrnĭgĕrī grĕgēs. Stăbŭlīs ārmēntă tĕnērĕ. Pāscūntŭr vĭrĭdēs ārmēntă pĕr hērbās.

Ārmĭfĕr, ĕră, ĕrūm. *Bearing arms, warlike.* Syn.—Ārmĭgĕr, ārmĭpŏtēns, ārmĭsŏnŭs, bēllātŏr, bēllātrīx.

Ārmŏ, ās, āvī, ātūm, ārĕ. *To arm, to give arms to.* Tūm quŏquĕ fās nōbīs Teūcrōs ārmārĕ fŭīssĕt. V. Phr.—Ārmīs īndŭŏ, cīngŏ, mūnĭō. Ārmă dō. Īn prœlĭă ārmŏ. Ēnsēs dēxtrīs āptō. Sŏcĭōs sĭmŭl īnstrŭĭt ārmīs. *To furnish.* Syn.—Īnstrŭŏ, mūnĭō. *To equip.* Syn.—Īnstrŭŏ, ōrnŏ, părŏ.

Ārmŏr, ārĭs, ātŭs sūm, ārī. *To arm oneself.* Phr.—Ārmīs īndŭŏr, īnstrŭŏr, mūnĭŏr. Ārmă căpēssŏ, căpĭŏ, sūmŏ. Cīngōr fūlgēntĭbŭs ārmīs. Ārmŏr ĭn prœlĭă. Lătĕrīque āccōmmŏdăt ēnsēm. Spŏlĭīs sē quīsquĕ rĕcēntĭbŭs ārmăt.

Ārŏ, ās, āvī, ātūm, ārĕ. *To labor, to till the fields.* Frūgĭbŭs īnfēlīx ĕă nēc mānsuēscĭt ărāndō. V. Phr.—Tērrām, tēllūrēm, hŭmūm, ārvă, jūgĕră, ăgrūm ărātrō, vōmĕrĕ, rāstrīs, lĭgōnĕ cŏlŏ, sŭbĭgŏ, scīndŏ, prōscīndŏ, vērtŏ, fŏdĭŏ, ēxērcĕŏ. Glēbās frāngŏ. Vōmĕrĕ ăgrūm sūlcārĕ. Rāstrīs tērrām dŏmārĕ. Tērrām vērtēbăt ărātrō. Vălĭdīs tērrām prōscīndĕ jŭvēncīs.

Ārrĭgŏ, ĭs, ēxī, ēctūm, ĕrĕ. *To raise.* Syn.—Ērĭgŏ, sūbrĭgŏ. Phr.—Ārrēxēre ănĭmōs lætī.

Ārrĭpĭŏ, ĭs, ŭī, rēptūm, ĕrĕ. *To seize.* Syn.—Răpĭŏ, sūbrĭpĭŏ, căpĭŏ, prĕhēndŏ, prēndŏ, āpprēndŏ, ōccŭpŏ.

Ārrŏgŏ, ās, āvī, ātūm, ārĕ. *To claim for oneself, to attribute to oneself.* Jūră nĕgēt sĭbĭ nātă, nĭhīl nōn ārrŏgĕt ārmīs. H. Syn.—Vīndĭcŏ, ādscīscŏ, sūmŏ, āssūmŏ. *To give.* Syn.—Āffĕrŏ, trĭbŭŏ, āddŏ.

Ārs, ārtĭs. f. *Art, science.* Quō nōn ārs pĕnētrāt? dīscūnt lăcrĭmārĕ dĕcēntĕr. O. Syn.—Dōctrīnă, scĭēntĭă, dīscĭplīnă, stŭdĭūm. Phr.—Īnvēntrīx ŏpĕrūm. Īngĕnĭī fœtŭs. Nātūræ æmŭlă. Sī lătĕt ārs, prōdēst. *The liberal arts.* Syn.—Stŭdĭă. Phr.—Mūsārum ĕt Ăpōllĭnĭs ārtēs. Stŭdĭī sūccēssŏr ĕt hērēs. Rārās dōtātă pĕr ārtēs. *The mechanical arts.* Syn.—Ārtĭfĭcĭūm, īndūstrĭă, sōlērtĭă. Phr.—Īnŏpī mĭsĕrābĭlĭs ārtĕ. Tāntæ ārtĭs ŏpŭs. *Artifice, ruse, deceit.* Syn.—Fraūs, dŏlŭs. Phr.—Mīllĕ nŏcēndi ārtēs.

Ārtĭcŭlŭs, ī. m. *A joint or knot.* Syn.—Jūnctūră, cōmpāgŏ, cōmpāgēs, nōdŭs.

Ārtĭfēx, ĭcĭs. m. *Workman, artisan.* Ārtĭfĭcūmquĕ mănūs īntēr se ŏpĕrūmquĕ lăbōrēm Mīrātŭr. V. Syn.—Ŏpĭfēx, făbrĭcātŏr. Phr.—Ĭdōnĕŭs ārtī Cuīlĭbĕt. *Inventor.* Syn.—Făbrĭcātŏr, aūctŏr, ŏpĭfēx, caūsă.

Ārtĭfĭcĭōsē. adv. *Artistically, with skill, according to the rules of art.* Phr.—Mūltā ārtĕ. Ārtĕ măgīstrā. Pĕr ārtēm. Mūltā quēm fēcĕrăt ārtĕ. Ārtĕ lăbōrātæ vēstēs. Tāntūs dĕcŏr āffŭĭt ārtī.

Ārtĭfĭcĭūm, ĭī. n. *Art, profession.* Syn.—Ārs. *Skill.* Syn.—Sōlērtĭă. Phr.—Ēgrĕgĭūs lăbŏr ārtĭfĭcĭs.

Ārtūs, ŭūm. m. *Limbs, joints of the body.* Syn.—Mēmbră. Phr.—Cōrpŏrĭs ārtūs. Ēt māgnōs mēmbrōrum ārtūs.

Ārūndĭnōsŭs, ă, ūm. *Full of weeds.* Phr.—Crēbĕr ărūndĭnĭbŭs. Mūltā ărūndĭnĕ crēbĕr, frĕquēns, ŏpērtŭs, tēctŭs, vĭrĭdāns.

Ārūndŏ, ĭnĭs. f. *A reed or cane.* Hīc vĭrĭdēs tĕnĕrā prætēxĭt ărūndĭnĕ rīpās. V. Syn.—Ăvēnă, călămŭs, cānnă. *Shepherd's pipe, flute.* Syn.—Fīstŭlă. *Arrow.* Syn.—Tēlūm, jăcŭlūm, spīcŭlūm, săgīttă. *Pen.* Syn.—Călămŭs.

Ārūspēx, ĭcĭs. m. *Soothsayer, diviner.* Cēnsōre ŏpŭs ēst ăn ărūspĭcĕ nōbīs? J. Syn.—Vātēs, aūgŭr, cōnjēctŏr. Phr.—Fātă cănēns. Vēntūrī præscĭūs ævī. Vēntūrī cērtŭs. Īntērprĕs ăb ēxtīs.

Ārvīnă, æ. f. *Fat, tallow.* Ēt spīcŭlă lūcĭdă tērgūnt Ārvīnā pīnguī. V. Syn.—Ădēps, sēbūm.

Ārvūm, ī. n. *A field, tilled field.* Ēxtērnūm pătrĭō cōntīngăt ămīcĭūs ārvūm. O. Syn.—Ăgĕr, cūltă, sătă, jūgĕră, rūră, sŏlūm, nŏvālĕ, nŏvālĭă, sĕgĕs. Phr.—Ōptĭmă pīnguī Ārva sŏlō. Īmpĕrăt ārvīs. Īnsŭlă nōbĭlĭs ārvīs.

Ārx, ārcĭs. f. *Height, summit.* Īmpĭgĕr ūmbrōsā Pārnāssī cōnstĭtĭt ārcĕ. O. Syn.—Cūlmĕn, vērtēx, căcūmĕn. Cēlsā sĕdēt Aēŏlŭs ārcĕ. *Citadel, fort, fortress.* Syn.—Cāstēllūm, tūrrĭs. Phr.—Ūrbĭs tūtāmĕn, mūnīmĕn, prōpūgnācŭlă. Ēdūctă sūb aūrās. Mōntĭs strūctă jŭgō. Īpsō tūtă lŏcō.

Āscēndŏ, ĭs, dī, sūm, ĕrĕ. *To mount, to ascend.* Scālīs āscēndĕrĕ mūrōs. V. Syn.—Cōnscēndŏ, scāndŏ, āssĭlĭŏ. Phr.—Āscēnsū mōntēm vīncŏ. Nītūntūr grădĭbŭs. Mōntĕ pŏtītŭs. Cūrsū pĕtĭt ārdŭă mōntĭs. Ēvādĕrĕ ād sūmmī fāstīgĭă mōntĭs. Sē tōllĕrĕ sūrsūm.

Āscēnsŭs, ūs. m. *Ascent.* Sūmmī fāstīgĭă tēctī Āscēnsū sŭpĕrŏ. V. Syn.—Cōnscēnsŭs. Phr.—Āscēnsū sŭpĕrārĕ căcūmĕn.

Āscĭă, æ. f. *Axe, hatchet.* Syn.—Bĭpēnnĭs, sĕcūrĭs.

Āscrībŏ, ĭs, psī, ptūm, ĕrĕ. *To write, to add in writing.* Rēstăt ŭt āscrībāt līttĕră nōstră: vălē. O. Syn.—Ānnŭmĕrŏ, īnsĕrŏ, āddŏ. *To attribute to.* Syn.—Āttrĭbŭŏ, āssīgnŏ, trĭbŭŏ, rĕfĕrŏ, īmpōnŏ, īmpŭtŏ, āssĕrŏ.

Āsĭnŭs, ī. m. & Āsĭnă, æ. f. *An ass.* Syn.—Āsēllŭs, āsēllă, aūrītŭlŭs. Phr.—Raūcā vōcĕ rŭdēns. Lēntē grădĭēns. Āssĭdŭō vērbĕrĕ dŏmĭtŭs. Pătĭēns lăbōrūm. Āssuētūs plāgīs. *Clown, blockhead.* Syn.—Caūdēx, stīpĕs, plūmbĕŭs.

Āspēctŭs, ūs. m. *Sight, view.* Ōbstŭpŭīt prīmo āspēctū Sīdōnĭă

Dīdō. V. Syn.—Cōnspēctŭs, ōbtūtŭs, vīsŭs. Phr.—Lætō rīdēt āspēctū. Sīc īstă vĕnūstō Splēndŭĭt āspēctū. Sŭbĭtōque āspēctū tērrĭtŭs hæsĭt. Hōrrēscĭt vīsū sŭbĭtō.

Āspĕr, ĕră, ĕrūm, & Āspră, āsprūm. *Harsh, rude, rough.* Āh tĭbĭ nē tĕnĕrās glăcĭēs sĕcēt āspĕră plāntās. V. Syn.—Scăbĕr. Phr.—Āspĕră gēmmīs. Āspĕră crūră pĭlīs. Āspĕră sāxīs lŏcă. *Bitter to the taste, biting.* Syn.—Ăcērbŭs, ămārŭs, aūstērŭs, īnsuāvĭs. *Rigorous, harsh.* Syn.—Sævŭs, ĭnīquŭs, grăvĭs, dūrŭs, aūstērŭs. *Hard to handle, intractable.* Syn.—Ăcērbŭs, dūrŭs, dīffĭcĭlĭs, fĕrōx. Phr.—Mŏnĭtōrĭbŭs āspĕr. Āspĕr ĕt īmprŏbŭs īrā. Gēns dūra ătque āspĕră cūltū. *Difficult, unpleasant (in speaking of things).* Syn.—Ăcērbŭs, ārdŭŭs, mŏlēstŭs, grăvĭs, īngrātŭs, īnjūcūndŭs.

Āspērgŏ, ĭs, sī, sūm, ĕrĕ. *To sprinkle, to wet, to moisten.* Syn.—Spārgŏ, cōnspērgŏ, rĭgŏ, īrrĭgŏ, pērfūndŏ. Phr.—Pĕcŏrīque āspērgĕrĕ vīrŭs. Quāvīs āspērgĕrĕ cūnctōs.

Āspērgŏ, ĭnĭs. f. *A sprinkling, moistening.* Ōbjēctæ sālsā spūmānt āspērgĭnĕ caūtēs. V. Syn.—Rōs, āspērsŭs. Phr.—Sānguĭs āspērgĭnĕ tīnxĕrāt hērbās.

Āspĕrĭtās, ātĭs. f. *Roughness, rigor.* Syn.—Vīs, vĭŏlēntĭă. Fig.—*Rudeness.* Syn.—Dūrĭtĭă, dūrĭtĭēs, bārbărĭēs.

Āspērnŏr, ārĭs, ātŭs sūm, ārī. *To despise, to contemn.* Nēc Pēlūsĭăcæ cūram āspērnābĕrĕ lēntĭs. V. Syn.—Spērnŏ, tēmnŏ, cōntēmnŏ, dēspĭcĭŏ, fāstīdĭŏ, rēspŭŏ, ābjĭcĭŏ, nēglĕgŏ. Phr.—Nōn cūrŏ. Pārvī, nĭhĭlī dūcŏ, æstĭmŏ, pēndŏ. Sŭpērbō vūltū rēspŭŏ.

Āspĕrŏ, ās, āvī, ātūm, ārĕ. *To render rough.* Phr.—Hĭēms ăquĭlōnĭbŭs āspĕrăt ūndās. Vāllūm Āspĕrăt ăltērnīs sŭdĭbŭs. *To render bitter, to exasperate.* Syn.—Ēxăspĕrŏ, ăcērbŏ, ăcŭŏ, īrrītŏ, āccēndŏ.

Āspērsĭŏ, ōnĭs. f. *A watering, sprinkling.* Syn.—Āspērgŏ, rōs.

Āspĭcĭŏ, ĭs, ēxī, ēctūm, ĕrĕ. *To look, to regard.* Syn.—Vĭdĕŏ, tŭĕŏr, īntŭĕŏr, cērnŏ, cōnspĭcĭŏ, rēspĭcĭŏ, spēctŏ, āspēctŏ. Phr.—Ŏcŭlōs, lūmĭnă vērtŏ, tēndŏ. Ŏcŭlōs, vultūs ădvērtŏ. Ŏcŭlōs fīgŏ, dēfīgŏ. Ŏcŭlīs āspĭcĭŏ. Vīsū lĕgŏ. Ŏcŭlōs ăd mœnĭă tōrsĭt. Vēstīgātque ŏcŭlīs. Vīsūquĕ sĕvērō lūstrŏ. Lōngō sătĭāvīt lūmĭnă vīsū. Ōbsērvāns ŏcŭlīs. Sŏlōque īmmōbĭlĭs hærĕt. Īntēntōs ŏcŭlōs vērtēns. Fig.—*To pay attention to.* Syn.—Rēspĭcĭŏ, rēspēctŏ, āttēndŏ, spēctŏ, cōgĭtŏ, cūrŏ. Phr.—Sī quă pĭōs rēspēctānt nūmĭnă.

Āspīrŏ, ās, āvī, ātūm, ārĕ. *To breathe, to blow upon.* Lēnĭŭs āspīrāns aūră sĕcūndă vĕnĭt. *Cat.* Syn.—Āfflŏ, flō, spīrŏ. *To favor.* Syn.—Ādsūm, făvĕŏ.

Āspĭs, ĭdĭs. f. *An asp, a venomous serpent.* Syn.—Ānguĭs, cŏlŭbĕr, sērpēns. Phr.—Tŭmĭdā cērvīcĕ mĭnāx. Fōrmīdābĭlĭs īctū.

Āspōrtŏ, ās, āvī, ātūm, ārĕ. *To carry away.* Syn.—Aūfĕrŏ, āvĕhŏ.

Āssĕclă, æ. m. *Attendant, page, companion.* Syn.—Cŏmĕs, sŏcĭŭs, sēctātŏr, āssēctātŏr.

Āssēctŏr, ārĭs, ātŭs sūm, ārī. *To accompany.* Syn.—Sĕquŏr, cŏmĭtŏr. Phr.—Cŏmĕs āssēctātŭr ĕūntēm.

Āssēnsŭs, ūs. m. *Assent, consent.* Cōnsŏnăt āssēnsū pŏpŭlī prĕcĭbūsquĕ făvēntūm Rēgĭă. O. Syn.—Āssēnsĭŏ, cōnsēnsŭs, āpprŏbātĭŏ. Phr.—Cūnctīquĕ frĕmēbānt āssēnsū vărĭŏ.

Āssēntĭŏ, īs, sī, sūm, īrĕ & Āssēntĭŏr, īrĭs, sŭs sūm, īrī. *To consent to.* Syn.—Cōnsēntĭŏ, ānnŭŏ, prŏbŏ, āpprŏbŏ.

Āssēntŏr, ārĭs, ātŭs sūm, ārī. *To flatter.* Syn.—Ădūlŏr, blāndĭŏr.

Āssĕquŏr, ĕrĭs, cūtŭs sūm, quī. *To attain, to obtain.* Āssĕquĭtūr trānsītquĕ vĭrūm. O. Syn.—Cōnsĕquŏr, ădĭpīscŏr, ăcquīrŏ, părŏ, cōmpărŏ.

Āssĕr, ĕrĭs. m. *Joist, piece of wood.* Quī sĕquĭtūr, fĕrĭt hīc cŭbĭtō, fĕrĭt āssĕrĕ dūrō. J. Syn.—Tīgnūm, tăbŭlă, āssŭlă, āssĭs, āssērcŭlŭs, āssĭcŭlŭs. Phr.—Cæsa ăbĭēs, sēctæquĕ trăbēs. Sēctāque īntēxūnt ăbĭētĕ cōstās.

Āssĕrŏ, ĭs, ŭī, rtūm, ĕrĕ. *To take or draw to oneself.* Syn.—Ārrĭpĭŏ. *To assure, to affirm.* Syn.—Āssĕvērŏ, affīrmŏ.

Āssĕrŏ, ĭs, ēvī, ĭtūm, ĕrĕ. *To sow, to plant.* Syn.—Sēmĭnŏ, sĕrŏ.

Āssērtŏr, ōrĭs. m. *Liberator, defender.* Syn.—Dēfēnsŏr, tūtēlă, præsĭdĭūm.

Āssērvŏ, ās, āvī, ātūm, ārĕ. *To protect, to guard.* Syn.—Sērvŏ, cōnsērvŏ, tŭĕŏr, cūstōdĭŏ, īnvĭgĭlŏ. Phr.—Prædām āssērvābānt.

Āssĕvērŏ, ās, āvī, ātūm, ārĕ. *To affirm.* Syn.—Āffīrmŏ, āssĕrŏ.

Āssĭdĕŏ, ēs, ēdī, ēssūm, ērĕ & Āssīdŏ, ĭs, sēdī, sēssūm, ĕrĕ. *To sit near.* Syn.—Sĕdĕŏ, cōnsĭdĕŏ, cōnsīdŏ. *To besiege.* Syn.—Ōbsĭdĕŏ.

Āssĭdŭē & Āssĭdŭō. adv. *Continually, frequently.* Syn.—Ūsquĕ, cōntĭnŭō, sēmpĕr.

Āssĭdŭŭs, ă, ūm. *Continual, assiduous.* Īpsă quŏque āssĭdŭō lābūntūr tēmpŏră mōtū. O. Syn.—Cōntĭnŭŭs, pērpĕtŭŭs, pĕrēnnĭs, jūgĭs, crēbĕr, frĕquēns. Phr.—Āssĭdŭā răpĭtūr vērtīgĭnĕ cœlūm.

Āssīgnŏ, ās, āvī, ātūm, ārĕ. *To distribute, to assign.* Cōmpōnūnt āgrōs āssīgnānt, ōppĭdă cōndūnt. H. Syn.—Āscrībŏ, āttrĭbŭŏ, dīvĭdŏ, pārtĭŏr. *To seal.* Syn.—Ōbsīgnŏ, sīgnŏ.

Āssĭlĭŏ, īs, ŭī, īvī & ĭī, ūltūm, īrĕ. *To assail, to jump upon.* Cūm sæpe āssĭlŭĭt dēfēnsæ mœnĭbŭs ūrbĭs. O. Syn.—Āssūltŏ, īnsĭlĭŏ, īrrūmpŏ, īrrŭŏ, īnvādŏ, āggrĕdĭŏr.

Āssĭmĭlĭs, ĭs, ĕ. *Similar, like.* Āssĭmĭlēmquĕ sŭī lōnga āssuētūdĭnĕ fēcĭt. O. Syn.—Sĭmĭlĭs, cōnsĭmĭlĭs.

Āssĭmĭlŏ, ās, āvī, ātūm, ārĕ. *To feign, to counterfeit, to simulate.* Syn.—Sĭmŭlŏ, ĭmĭtŏr, fīngŏ, mēntĭŏr. *To compare.* Syn.—Cōnfĕrŏ, cōmpărŏ, cōmpōnŏ. Phr.—Sīc pārvīs cōmpōnĕrĕ māgnă sŏlēbām.

Āssĭmŭlŏ, ās, āvī, ātūm, ārĕ. *To feign.* Ŏdĭūm cūm cōnjŭgĕ fālsūm Phāsĭăs āssĭmŭlăt. O. Syn.—Sĭmŭlŏ, fīngŏ, cōnfīngŏ, mēntĭŏr.

Āssīstŏ, ĭs, stĭtī, stĭtūm, ĕrĕ. *To stand near, to be present near.* Syn.—Ādsūm, ādstŏ īntērsūm. *To stand.* Syn.—Stō. *To be favorable to.* Syn.—Ādsūm, jŭvŏ, ādjŭvŏ, ānnŭŏ, făvĕŏ.

Āssŏcĭŏ, ās, āvī, ātūm, ārĕ. *To associate with, to join, to accompany.* Syn.—Āddŏ, ādjūngŏ, sŏcĭŏ, cōnsŏcĭŏ, ādnēctŏ, jūngŏ. Phr.—Āssŏcĭăt pāssūs. Āddīt sē cŏmĭtēm. Sŏcĭa āgmĭnă jūngūnt.

Āssŏlĕt. *It is the custom.* Syn.—Sŏlĕt, sŏlĭtūm ēst, mōs, mōrĭs ēst. Phr.—Ūt āssŏlĕt. Quō mōrĕ sŏlēnt.

Āssŏnŏ, ās, ŭī, ĭtūm, ārĕ. *To reecho.* Plāngēntĭbŭs āssŏnăt ēchō. O. Syn.—Rĕsŏnŏ, cōnsŏnŏ, āccĭnŏ, rĕsūltŏ, rēspōndĕŏ. Phr.—Sŏnūm rĕfĕrŏ, rĕmīttŏ, sŏnĭtūm īngĕmĭnŏ.

Āssuēfăcĭŏ, ĭs, ēcī, āctūm, ĕrĕ. *To accustom, to inure.* Syn.—Cōnsuēfăcĭŏ, dŏcĕŏ, ēdŏcĕŏ. Phr.—Mōrēm fēcĕrăt ūsŭs.

Āssuēscŏ, ĭs, ēvī, ētūm, ĕrĕ. *To become accustomed.* Ādĕo īn tĕnĕrīs āssuēscĕrĕ mūltum ēst! V. Syn.—Cōnsuēscŏ, dīscŏ, āssuēfīŏ, cōndīscŏ, sŏlĕŏ. Phr.—Mōrēm dūcŏ. Vōtīs āssuēscĕ vŏcārī. Sŏcĭōrum āssuēscĭtĕ mēnsīs. Ūt mĭhĭ mōs ēst. Sīcūt mĕŭs ēst mōs.

Āssuētūdŏ, ĭnĭs. f. *Custom, habit.* Lāc tĭbĭ cōnsuēscăt; nīl āssuētūdĭnĕ mājŭs. O. Syn.—Cōnsuētūdŏ, ūsŭs, mōs. Phr.—Lōngāque ălĭt āssuētūdĭnĕ flāmmās.

Āssūltŏ, ās, āvī, ātūm, ārĕ. *To assail, to jump upon. See Assilio.*

Āssūmŏ, ĭs, mpsī, mptūm, ĕrĕ. *To take, to choose.* Præsērtīm caūtōs dīgnōs āssūmĕrĕ. H. Syn.—Căpĭŏ, āccĭpĭŏ, dēlĭgŏ. Phr.—Prĭōr nĭsĭ cœnă Săbīnūm Dētĭnĕt, āssūmām.

Āssŭŏ, ĭs, ŭī, ūtūm, ĕrĕ. *To sew on.* Ūnŭs ĕt āltĕr Āssŭĭtūr pānnūs pūrpŭrĕŭs. H. Syn.—Cōnsŭŏ, cōnnēctŏ.

Āssūrgŏ, ĭs, rēxī, rēctūm, ĕrĕ. *To rise.* Sī jŭvĕnēs vĕtŭlō nōn āssūrrēxĕrăt. J. Syn.—Sūrgŏ, cōnsūrgŏ. Phr.—Mē āttōllŏ, tōllŏ. Nōn cœptae āssūrgūnt tūrrēs. Sēptēmque āssūrgĭt ĭn ūlnās.

Āssŭs, ă, ūm. *Roasted, burnt, dried.* Syn.—Āssātŭs, tōrrĭdŭs, sīccŭs.

Āst. conj. *But.* Syn.—Sĕd, ăt, tămĕn, aūtēm, āttămĕn.

Āstŏ & Ādstŏ, ās, ĭtī, ĭtūm, ārĕ. *To stand near.* Vīsi ānte ŏcŭlōs āstārĕ jăcēntĭs. V. Syn.—Stō, ādsūm, āssīstŏ. Phr.—Aēdĭbŭs āstābăt. Ārrēctīsque aūrĭbŭs ādstānt. *To stop.* Syn.—Stō sīstŏ, cōnsīstŏ.

Āstră, ōrūm. n. *Stars, constellations.* Ōrbēm Pēr dŭŏdēnă rĕgīt mūndī sōl aūrĕŭs āstră. V. Syn.—Stēllæ, sīdĕră, sīgnă. Phr.—Īgnēs æthĕriī. Flāmmæ cœlĭvăgæ, sīdĕrĕæ. Rŭtĭlō sīdĕră fīxă pŏlō, spārsă pŏlō. Nōctĕ mĭcāntĭă. Flāmmĕŭs ōrdŏ. Lūmĭnă mūndī. Cœlī mĭcāntĭă āgmĭnă. Pŏlūs dūm sīdĕră pāscĕt. Sīdĕră cœpērūnt tōto ēffērvēscĕrĕ cœlō. Lĭquĭdūm pĕr ĭnānĕ mĭcāntēs.

Āstrīngŏ, ĭs, strīnxī, strīctūm, ĕrĕ. *To bind, to tighten.* Seū dūrāt măgĭs, et venas astringit hiantes. V. Syn.—Strīngŏ, cōnstrīngŏ, lĭgŏ, vīncĭŏ. Phr.—Ārctō nēxū, fīrmīs vīnclīs rĕtĭnĕŏ, cŏērcĕŏ. Fig.—*To force.* Syn.—Ōblĭgŏ, cōgŏ. *To condense with the cold.* Syn.—Cōntrăhŏ, dūrŏ. *See Gelu.*

Āstrūm, ī. n. *Star. See Astra.*

Āstŭr, ŭrĭs. m. *Hawk.* (*See Appendix under list of Birds.*)

Āstŭs, ūs. m. *Ruse, deceit. treachery.* Nōn ārs aūt āstūs bēllī vēl dēxtĕră deērăt. Syn.—Āstūtĭă, fraūs, dŏlŭs, vērsūtĭă, cāllĭdĭtās, fāllācĭă, īnsĭdĭæ.

Āstūtē. adv. *Through a ruse, cunningly, deceitfully.* Syn.—Cāllĭdē, vērsūtē, dŏlōsē. Phr.—Mēntĕ dŏlōsā. Sĭmŭlātā mēntĕ.

Āstūtĭă, æ. f. *Deceit. See Astus.*

Āstūtŭs, ă, ūm. *Skilful, crafty, adroit.* Āstūta īngĕnŭūm vūlpēs ĭmĭtātă lĕōnēs. H. Syn.—Cāllĭdŭs, caūtŭs, vāfĕr, vērsūtŭs, dŏlōsŭs. Phr.—Mūltă mălūs sĭmŭlāns. Cāptēs āstūtŭs ŭbīquĕ.

Āsȳlūm, ī. n. *Asylum, refuge.* Hīnc lūcum īngēntēm quēm Rōmŭlŭs ācĕr ăsȳlūm Rēttŭlĭt. V. Syn.—Pērfŭgĭūm, pōrtŭs, āră, ārx.

Ăt. conj. *But, however.* Syn.—Āst, sĕd, vērūm, āttămĕn, tămĕn. Phr.—Āt vērō, ăt ĕnīm. *At least.* Syn.—Sāltēm.

Ātĕr, ātră, ātrūm. *Black, dark, obscure.* Cālcŭlŭs īmmĭtēm dēmĭttĭtŭr ātĕr ĭn ūrnām. O. Syn.—Nĭgĕr, nĭgrāns, nĭgrēscēns, fūscŭs, fūrvŭs, pĭcĕŭs, cæcŭs, ōbscūrŭs. Phr.—Fūlīgĭnĕ tīnctŭs. Sūb nūbĭbŭs ātrīs. Vōlvĭtŭr ātĕr ŏdŏr. Spēlūncīs ābdĭdĭt ātrīs. Pōntō nōx īncŭbăt ātră. Fig.—*Horrible.* Syn.—Hōrrēndŭs, īmmānĭs, fœdŭs, tūrpĭs. *Sad, mournful.* Syn.—Fūnēstŭs, īnfaūstŭs, dīrŭs, īnfēlīx, trīstĭs.

Āthlētă, æ. m. *Athlete.* Nūnc āthlētārūm stŭdĭīs, nūnc ārsĭt ĕquōrūm. H. Syn.—Pŭgĭl, lūctātŏr, pălæstrĭtă. Phr.—Pōtēns āthlētă lăcērtīs. Ūnctŭs ĭn āthlētæ mōrēm. Pūlchēr sūdōrĕ pălæstræ.

Ātquĕ. conj. *And.* Syn.—Āc, ĕt, -quĕ. *But.* Syn.—Tămĕn, āttămĕn, ăt ĕnīm.

Ātquī. conj. *But, yet.* Syn.—Pōrrō, aūtēm, sĕd, sĕdĕnīm, ăt, āst, vērūm.

Ātrātŭs, ă, ūm. *Blackened, dyed black.* Syn.—Ātĕr. *In the garb of mourning.* Syn.—Pūllātŭs, ātĕr. Phr.—Ātrā, nĭgrā, pūllā vēstĕ īndūtŭs. Pūllō vēlātŭs ămīctū. Cūm vēstĭbŭs ātrīs. Lūctūs īnsīgnĭă gĕrēns. Lūgūbrĭăque īndŭĕ. Mœstī sērvāns lūgūbrĭă lūctūs.

Ātrĭŭm, ĭī. n. *Court-yard, court, hall.* Ātrĭă sērvāntēm pōstīcō fāllĕ clĭēntēm. H. Syn.—Līmĕn, pōrtĭcŭs, vēstĭbŭlŭm. Phr.—Nŏvō Sūblīmĕ rītū mōlĭăr ātrĭŭm. Ātrĭă lōngă pătēscūnt.

Ătrōcĭtās, ātĭs. f. *Cruelty, fierceness.* Syn.—Dūrĭtĭēs, fĕrĭtās, īmmānĭtās.

Ătrōcĭtĕr. adv. *Cruelly.* Syn.—Crūdēlĭtĕr, dūrĭtĕr.

Ătrōx, ōcĭs. adj. *Cruel, fierce.* Syn.—Āspĕr, bārbărŭs, sævŭs, crūdēlĭs, sævŭs, dīrŭs, fĕrŭs, īmmītĭs. *Terrible.* Syn.—Fŭrēns, tērrĭbĭlĭs, mĕtŭēndŭs. *Violent, eager.* Syn.—Vĭŏlēntŭs, ācĕr. *Resolute, inflexible.* Syn.—Fīrmŭs, īncōncūssŭs, fērrĕŭs.

Āttāctŭs, ūs. m. *A soft, gentle touch.* Vōlvĭtŭr āttāctū nūllō. V. Syn.—Tāctŭs, cōntāctŭs.

Āttăgēn, ēnĭs. m. & Āttăgēnă, æ. f. *Grouse, heath-cock, hazel hen.* (*See Appendix under list of Birds.*)

Āttămĕn. conj. *But, however.* Syn.—Tămĕn, ăt, āst, ātquĕ, sĕd, vērūmtămĕn.

Āttēmpĕrŏ, ās, āvī, ātūm, ārĕ. *To make fit, to adjust.* Syn.—Āccōmmŏdŏ, āptŏ.

Āttēndŏ, ĭs, dī, sūm & tūm, ĕrĕ. *To bend the mind to, to regard.* Syn.—Ădhĭbĕŏ, ādvērtŏ, āpplĭcŏ, ādmŏvĕŏ, cōmmŏdŏ (aurem). *To be attentive to.* Syn.—Aūdĭŏ, aūscūltŏ. Phr.—Dīctīs ādvērtĕrĕ mēntēm. Mēntēm ādjĭcĕrĕ. Vōcĭbŭs aūrēs āccōmmŏdārĕ, præbērĕ, āpplĭcārĕ. Dīctă ănĭmīs fīgĕrĕ, dēfīgĕrĕ. Ārrēctīs aūrĭbŭs ādstānt. Făvētĕ līnguīs. *To observe, to take care of.* Syn.—Ādvērtŏ, pērspĭcĭŏ, ōbsērvŏ.

Āttēntŏ, ās, āvī, ātūm, ārĕ. *To attempt.* Syn.—Tēntŏ, ēxpĕrĭŏr, ēxplōrŏ. Phr.—Tāntum aūsi āttēntārĕ nĕfās. *To attack.* Syn.—Āggrĕdĭŏr, īmpĕtŏ, vĭŏlŏ. Phr.—Bēllo āttēntārĕ jŭvēncīs.

Āttēntŭs, ă, ūm. *Attentive.* Vērbă pĕr āttēntām nōn ībūnt Cæsărĭs aūrēm. H. Syn.—Īntēntŭs, ārrēctŭs. Phr.—Ārrēctā mēntĕ. Ārrēctīs aūrĭbŭs ādstānt. Āttēntā mēntĕ sĭlēns. Āttēntīs hærēns ănĭmīs. Hīs ănĭmum ārrēctī dīctīs.

Āttĕnŭātŭs, ă, ūm. *Weakened, feeble.* Syn.—Tĕnŭātŭs, ēxēsŭs, cōnsūmptŭs.

Āttĕnŭŏ, ās, āvī, ātūm, ārĕ. *To cut, to prune.* Nōn fālx āttĕnŭāt frōndātōrum ārbŏrĭs ūmbrām. *Cat.* Syn.—Pŭtŏ, sĕcŏ. *To thin out, to weaken.* Syn.—Mĭnŭŏ, īmmĭnŭŏ, prĕmŏ, dēprĭmŏ, dētrăhŏ. *To wear out.* Syn.—Ēxtĕnŭŏ, tĕnŭŏ, cōnsūmŏ, ēxĕdŏ, pĕrĕdŏ, frāngŏ.

Āttĕrŏ, ĭs, trīvī, trītūm, ĕrĕ. *To wear away, to grind, to rub.* Hōc plūs splēndēscīt quō măgĭs āttĕrĭtŭr. Prop. Syn.—Tĕrŏ, prōtĕrŏ, cōntĕrŏ, īmmĭnŭŏ, āttĕnŭŏ, cōnsūmŏ, ēxĕdŏ. *To trample upon.* Syn.—Cālcŏ, cōncūlcŏ, prōcūlcŏ, cālcĕ prĕmŏ. *To weaken, to destroy.* Syn.—Īmmĭnŭŏ, cōnsūmŏ, āttĕnŭŏ.

Āttēxŏ, ĭs, ŭī, xtūm, ĕrĕ. *To weave.* Syn.—Tēxŏ. *To join to.* Syn.—Ānnēctŏ, āddŏ, ādjūngŏ.

Āttĭnĕŏ, ēs, ŭī, ēntūm, ērĕ. *To hold back, to stay.* Syn.—Tĕnĕŏ, rĕtĭnĕŏ.

Āttĭnĕt. impers. *It concerns, it regards.* Syn.—Pērtĭnĕt, spēctăt, tāngĭt, rēfērt, īntĕrēst.

Āttīngŏ, ĭs, tĭgī, tāctūm, ĕrĕ. *To touch.* Nēc tēlās pōssūnt āttīngĕrĕ pūtrēs. V. Syn.—Tāngŏ, cōntīngŏ, pērtīngŏ. Phr.—Nēc grāmĭnĭs āttĭgĭt hērbām. Quæ nĭhĭl āttīngūnt ād rēm. *To attain to.* Syn.—Āssĕquŏr, āccēdŏ, pērvĕnĭŏ (ăd).

Āttōllŏ, ĭs, ĕrĕ. *To raise, to lift.* Āttōllītquĕ glŏbōs flāmmārum ēt sīdĕră lāmbĭt. V. Syn.—Tōllŏ, ēxtōllŏ, ēffĕrŏ, ērĭgŏ, ēvĕhŏ. Phr.—Ārcēmque āttōllĕrĕ tēctīs. Tēr sēse āttōllēns. Āttōllĭt lūmĭnă cœlō.

Āttŏnŏ, ās, ŭī, ĭtūm, ārĕ. *To astonish, to amaze, to frighten.* Syn.—Pērtūrbŏ, pērcēllŏ, tērrĕŏ.

Āttrăhŏ, ĭs, āxī, āctūm, ĕrĕ. *To draw, to attract.* Dīscĭpŭlōs āttrăhĭt īllă nŏvōs. O. Syn.—Trăhŏ, dūcŏ, āddūcŏ. Phr.—Āttrăhĕ lōră. Āttrăhĭte hūc vīnctūm.

Āttrēctŏ, ās, āvī, ātūm, ārĕ. *To touch, to handle.* Āttrēctārĕ nĕfās, dōnēc mē flūmĭnĕ vīvō Āblŭĕrŏ. V. Syn.—Trāctŏ, pālpŏ, cōntīngŏ, āttēntŏ.

Āttrĭbŭŏ, ĭs, ŭī, ūtūm, ĕrĕ. *To attribute to, to assign to, to give to.* Syn.—Trĭbŭŏ, āddīcŏ, ādscrībŏ, āssīgnŏ.

Aūcēps, cŭpĭs. m. *A fowler, bird-catcher.* Nōn ăvĭs aūcŭpĭbūs mōnstrāt, quā pārtĕ pĕtātŭr. O. Phr.—Vŏlŭcrūm, ăvĭūm vēnātŏr. Fāllĕrĕ dōctŭs ăvēs. Fāllācēs tēndēns lăquĕōs. Quī cāntū dēlūdĭt ăvēs. Lăquĕĭs quōs cāllĭdŭs ābdĭdĭt aūcēps.

Aūctŏr, ōrĭs. m. *Creator, author.* Aūctōrēm frūgūm, tēmpēstātūmquĕ pŏtēntēm. V. Syn.—Crĕātŏr. *Founder.* Syn.—Cōndĭtŏr. Phr.—Ēt Trōjæ Cŷnthĭŭs aūctŏr. *The head of a race.* Syn.—Prīncēps, căpŭt. *Inventor, composer.* Syn.—Īnvēntŏr, rĕpērtŏr. *Cause.* Syn.—Caūsă, rătĭō. *Writer.* Syn.—Scrīptŏr. *A counsellor, persuader.* Syn.—Suāsŏr, hōrtātŏr. Phr.—Aūctŏr ĕgo aūdēndī. Hōrtātŏr ĕt aūctŏr.

Aūctōrĭtās, ātĭs. f. *Authority.* Syn.—Pŏtēntĭă. *Esteem, reputation.* Syn.—Nōmĕn, fāmă. *Weight, credit.* Syn.—Pōndŭs, fĭdēs.

Aūctŭs, ūs. m. *Increase, growth.* Syn.—Aūgmĕn, aūgmēntūm, ădaūctŭs, īncrēmēntūm.

Aūcŭpĭūm, ĭī. n. *Fowling, hunting.* Syn.—Vēnātĭō. Phr.—Ăvĭūm vēnātĭō, vēnātŭs, prædă. Ārs aūcŭpĭs.

Aūcŭpō, ās, āvī, ātūm, ārĕ & Aūcŭpŏr, ārĭs, ātŭs sūm, ārī. *To hunt birds.* Phr.—Ăvēs cāptō, vēnŏr, dēcĭpĭō, fāllō. Vēnātū sĕquŏr. Vŏlŭcrēs nōdōsīs plăgīs dēcĭpĕrĕ. Ăvĭbŭs īnsĭdĭŏr. *To watch, to spy.* Syn.—Vēnŏr, cāptō, aūscūltō.

Aūdācĭă, æ. f. *Boldness, presumption.* Īn aūdācēs nōn ēst aūdācĭă tūtă. O. Syn.—Aūdēntĭă, cōnfīdēntĭă. Phr.—Īmpătĭēns, īndŏcĭlĭs ănĭmŭs. Ārdŏr ănĭmī. Fīdēns ănĭmŭs. Aūdācĭă pērdĭtă. Paūlātīm præcēps aūdācĭă crēvĭt. *Confidence.* Syn.—Fīdūcĭă.

Aūdāctĕr. adv. *Boldly, courageously.* Syn.—Aūdēntĕr, fōrtĭtĕr. Phr.—Aūdācī ănĭmō. Pŏsĭtō, dēpŏsĭtō mĕtū.

Aūdāx, ācĭs. adj. *Bold, confident, resolute.* Quīquĕ pĕdūm cūrsū vălĕt ēt quī vīrĭbŭs aūdāx. V. Syn.—Aūdēns, ācĕr, īmpăvĭdŭs, īmpērtērrĭtŭs, ănĭmōsŭs, fōrtĭs, cæcŭs, præcēps. Phr.—Ănĭmī tĕmĕrārĭŭs. Fīdēns ănĭmī. Spērnāx mōrtĭs. Īmpĭgĕr ād lētūm. Tĭmĕrĕ nēscĭŭs. Ēxpērs tērrōrĭs.

Aūdĕō, ēs, sŭs sūm, ērĕ. *To dare.* Aūdĕo ĕt Aēnĕădūm prōmĭtto ŏccūrrĕrĕ tūrmæ. V. Syn.—Fīdō, cōnfīdō, sūstĭnĕō. Phr.—Nōn mĕtŭō, nōn dŭbĭtō. Ēt tāntās aūdētĭs tōllĕrĕ mōlēs! Aūde, hōspēs, cōntēmnĕre ŏpēs. Flŭvĭōs tēntārĕ mĭnācēs Aūdĕt. *To undertake, to adventure.* Syn.—Tēntŏ, ădŏrĭŏr, āggrĕdĭŏr, mōlĭŏr.

Aūdĭō, īs, īvī & ĭī, ītūm, īrĕ. *To hear.* Ēt văcēt ānnālēs nōstrōrum aūdīrĕ lăbōrūm. V. Syn.—Ēxaūdĭō, ēxcĭpĭō, pērcĭpĭō, sēntĭō. Phr.—Aūrĭbŭs haūrĭō, pērcĭpĭō. Cōncĭpĕre aūrĕ sŏnōs. Tŭbă vērbĕrēt aūrēs. Sŏnūs trĕpĭdās aūrēs fĕrĭt. Vōx aūrēs tĕtĭgĭt. Vōx pērvēnĭt ăd aūrēs. *To hear with attention.* Syn.—Aūscūltō, pērcĭpĭō, ādvērtō, haūrĭō. Phr.—Aūrēs vōcĭbŭs, dīctīs præstō, dō, præbĕō. Dīctīs mēntēm ādjĭcĭō. Bĭbĭt aūrĕ. Ăvĭdām pāndīt rūmōrĭbŭs aūrēm. *To hearken to.* Syn.—Ēxaūdĭō. *To obey.* Syn.—Pārĕō.

Aūdītŏr, ōrĭs. m. *Hearer, disciple.* Ēxcĭtāt aūdītōr stŭdĭūm, laūdātăquĕ vīrtūs Crēscĭt. O. Syn.—Dīscĭpŭlŭs. Phr.—Dēfĭcĭt aūdītŏr.

Aūfĕrō, fērs, ābstŭlī, āblātūm, fērrĕ. *To carry away, to take away.* Hæc tē prīmă dĭēs bēllō dĕdĭt, hæc ĕădem aūfērt. V. Syn.—Tōllō, răpĭō, ābrĭpĭō, ērĭpĭō, dēmō, ădĭmō, ābstrăhō, āvērtō, ēxtōrquĕō. Phr.—Aūfērtĕ mĕtūs. Aūfĕr ăbhīnc lăcrĭmās. Pēnnīs aūfērtŭr. Ūt mē mălŭs ābstŭlĭt ērrŏr! Nōx hūmĭdă cœlūm ābstŭlĭt. Sōmnōs aūfērt tĭmŏr. *To destroy.* Syn.—Tōllō, ōccīdō, dēlĕō. *To gain, to obtain.* Syn.—Cōnsĕquŏr, āssĕquŏr, ōbtĭnĕō, fĕrō. *To stop, to put an end to.* Syn.—Dēsīstō, pārcō, dēsĭnō, mīttō.

Aūgĕō, ēs, xī, ctūm, ērĕ. *To increase, to magnify.* Āt tĭbĭ sūccrēscāt prōlēs, quæ fāctă părēntĭs Aūgĕāt. Tib. Syn.—Ădaūgĕō, āmplĭō, āmplĭfĭcō, āddō, ādstrŭō. Phr.—Rēm strēnŭŭs aūgē. Vīrēs aūxīt fōrtūnă nŏcēndī. Rōbūr flōrēntĭbūs aūxĭmūs ānnīs.

Aūgēscō, ĭs, ĕrĕ. *To grow, to increase in size or stature.* Syn.—Aūgĕŏr, ădaūgĕŏr, ădaūgēscō, āmplĭfĭcŏr, crēscō, cŭmŭlŏr, ădŏlēscō.

Aūgmĕn, ĭnĭs & Aūgmēntūm, ī. n. *Increase.* Syn.—Īncrēmēntūm, aūctŭs, ădaūctŭs. Phr.—Aūgmĭnĕ dōnăt. Pērfēctūm cōrpŏrĭs aūgmĕn.

Aūgŭr, ŭrĭs. m. *A soothsayer, diviner.* Aūgŭrĭbūs Phœbūs, Phœbē vēnāntĭbŭs ādsĭt. O. Syn.—Aūspēx, ărūspēx, vātēs, săcērdōs. Phr.—Ōs fātĭdĭcūm. Præscĭă līnguă. Īntērprēs Dĕūm. Fātă cănēns. Plēnūs Phœbō. Vērī prōvĭdŭs aūgŭr. Săgāx vēntūră vĭdērĕ.

Aūgŭrĭūm, ĭī. n. *Divination, soothsaying.* Dā, pătĕr, aūgŭrĭum, ātque ănĭmīs īllābĕrĕ nōstrīs. V. Syn.—Aūspĭcĭūm, ōmĕn, mōnstrūm. Vātūm præsāgĭă. Cōnjēctūră fŭtūrī. Mēns cōnscĭă vātūm. Vātūm præscĭă līnguă. Dīvīnī mŏnĭtūs.

Aūgŭrō, ās, āvī, ātūm, ārĕ & Aūgŭrŏr, ārĭs, ātŭs sūm, ārī. *To presage, to divine.* Ēt rĕŏr, ēt, sī quīd vērī mēns aūgŭrăt, ōptō. V. Syn.—Prædīcō, vātĭcĭnŏr, cănō. Phr.—Fūtūră ăpērĭō, nūntĭō. *To conjecture, to surmise.* Syn.—Cōnjĭcĭō, præsēntĭō, præsāgĭō.

Aūgūstŭs, ă, ūm. *Consecrated, holy, venerated, majestic.* Syn.—Săcĕr, săcrātŭs, sānctŭs, rēllĭgĭōsŭs, cŏlēndŭs, vĕrēndŭs, vĕnĕrāndŭs.

Aūlă, æ. f. *Hall, court.* Syn.—Ātrĭūm. *A palace.* Syn.—Rēgĭă, pălātĭă (pl.). Phr.—Īllā sē jāctĕt ĭn aūlā. Īntrā līmĭnă sānctĭōrĭs aūlæ. Āltă rēgūm pĕnĕtrālĭă.

Aūlǣă, ōrūm. n. *Tapestry, curtains.* Nōbĭlĭs aūlǣīs pōrtĭcŭs Āttălĭcīs. Prop. Syn.—Tăpētēs. Phr.—Aūrō grăvĭă. Spīrāntĭă sīgnīs. Văriātă fĭgūrīs. Ārtĭfĭcī pērfēctă mănū. Nĭtĭdōs vēlānt aūlǣă pĕnātēs.

Aūră, æ. f. *A gentle breeze.* Aūră pĕtēbātūr mĕdĭō mĭhĭ lēnĭs ĭn ǣstū. O. Syn.—Flābrūm, flāmĕn, flātŭs. Phr.—Aēquŏr sūmmūm strīngĭtŭr aūrā. Vērnāque īncērtĭŏr aūrā. Aūră sĕcūndă vĕnĭt. *Air.* Syn.—Āēr, ǣthēr, cœlūm. Phr.—Aūrās ǣthĕrĕās, āĕrĭās, vītālēs cārpĕrĕ. Īn lūmĭnĭs aūrās sē tōllĕrĕ. Ēxĭt ĭn aūrās. Sī vēscĭtŭr aūrā Aēthĕrĕā. Vērrāntquĕ pĕr aūrās. *The breath.* Syn.—Spīrĭtŭs, hālĭtŭs, flātŭs, ănĭmă. *Odor.* Syn.—Ŏdŏr. *Splendor, brilliancy.* Syn.—Splēndŏr, nĭtŏr, fūlgŏr. Fig.—*Popular favor.* Syn.—Grātĭă, făvŏr, stŭdĭūm.

Aūrāntĭă, ōrūm. n. *Oranges.* (*See Appendix under list of Trees, etc.*)

Aūrātŭs, ă, ūm. *Gilded, plated with gold.* Aūrāta ēst; īpsō tĭbĭ sīt prĕtĭōsĭŏr aūrō. O. Phr.—Āurō ārdēns, fūlgēns, nĭtĭdŭs, nĭtēns, rĕnīdēns. Aūrātō fūlgēbăt Ăpōllĭnĕ pūppēs.

Aūrĕŭs, ă, ūm. *Of gold, golden.* Aūrĕŭs āxĭs ĕrăt, tēmo aūrĕŭs, aūrĕă sūmmǣ Cūrvātūră rŏtǣ. O. Phr.—Aūrō fāctŭs, sŏlĭdŭs, āspĕr, grăvĭs. *Of the color of gold.* Syn.—Aūrĭcŏlŏr. Phr.—Flāvēntēs aūrō spīcǣ. Nōx aūrĕă cīngĭtŭr āstrīs. Bārbǣ cŏlŏr aūrĕŭs.

Aūrĭfŏdīnă, æ. f. *A gold mine.* Phr.—Aūrūm pāllĭdīs ābdĭtūm căvērnīs. Aūreō dīvĕs ūbĕrĕ glēbă. Aūrī vēnǣ. Flāvī sēmĕn mĕtăllī. Vīscĕră tērrǣ prĕtĭōsă. Tēllūs fœtă aūrō. Aūrīquĕ mĕtāllă.

Aūrīgă, æ. m. *Charioteer.* Hīc sĭtŭs ēst Phăĕthōn, cūrrūs aūrīgă pătērnī. O. Syn.—Măgīstĕr. Phr.—Cūrsŏr, rēctŏr ĕquūm. Ĕquōrūm ăgĭtātŏr. Mănĭbūs quī flēctĭt hăbēnās. Ĕquōs frēnīs quī cōntĭnĕt ārctīs. Ēt prōnī dānt lōră.

Aūrĭs, ĭs. f. *The ear.* Tōrquĕt ăb ōbscœ̄nīs jām nūnc sērmōnĭbŭs aūrēm. H. Syn.—Aūrĭcŭlă. Phr.—Aūrēm sūbstrīngĕ lŏquācī. Mĭcăt aūrĭbŭs. Aūrēs dărĕ, ădhĭbērĕ, āpplĭcārĕ.

Aūrōră, æ. f. *The dawn.* Syn.—Tīthōnĭă, Pāllāntĭs, dĭēs, Lūcĭfĕr. Phr.—Lūcĭs nūntĭă. Clārī prǣnūntĭă sōlĭs. Āstră fŭgāns. Dĭēmquĕ rĕdūcĭt. Pūlchră sŭōs Aūrōră cŏlōrēs Ēxplĭcăt. Nŏvō spārgēbăt lūmĭnĕ tērrās. *Personified as a goddess.* (*See Appendix.*)

Aūrūm, ī. n. *The metal gold.* Phr.—Aūrī mĕtāllūm lāmĭnă, pōndŭs. Fūlvūm mĕtāllūm. Flāvă tērrǣ vīscĕră. Māgnī pōndĕrĭs aūrūm. Ārdēbĭt ĭn aūrō. Rēgālī cōnspēctŭs ĭn aūrō.

Aūscūltŏ, ās, āvī, ātūm, ārĕ. *To listen, to hear.* Syn.—Aūdĭŏ, āttēndŏ. Phr.—Dīctīs aūrēs, mēntēm, ănĭmūm, cōrdă ādvērtŏ, ādmŏvĕŏ. *To spy upon.* Syn.—Aūcŭpŏr. *To obey.* Syn.—Ŏbēdĭŏ, pārĕŏ.

Aūspēx, ĭcĭs. m. *A soothsayer, diviner.* Syn.—Aūgŭr, vātēs. *Protector.* Syn.—Dūx, aūctŏr. Phr.—Aūspĭcĕ mūsā. Aūspĭcĭbūs cœptōrum ŏpĕrūm. Aūspĭcĕ Teūcrō. *As an adj. Favorable.* Syn.—Faūstŭs, lætŭs, fēlīx, sĕcūndŭs, făvēns.

Aūspĭcātŭs, ă, ūm. *Lucky, favorable.* Syn.—Faūstŭs, făvēns, fēlīx, prōspĕr, sĕcūndŭs, lætŭs.

Aūspĭcĭūm, ĭī. n. *Divination, consulting the auspices.* Aūspĭcĭō fēlīx tōtŭs ŭt ānnŭs ĕăt. O. Syn.—Aūgŭrĭūm, ōmĕn. Phr.—Ăvĭs æquă, dēxtĕră, sĭnīstră. Vĕtăt aūspĭcĭūm. *Conduct, management, authority.* Syn.—Dūctŭs, ārbĭtrĭūm, nūmĕn.

Aūspĭcŏr, ārĭs, ātŭs sūm, ārī. *To consult the auspices or omens.* Syn.—Aūgŭrŏr, vātĭcĭnŏr. *To commence, to inaugurate.* Syn.—Īnĕŏ, īncĭpĭŏ, ōrdĭŏr.

Aūstĕr, trī. m. *The south wind.* Īntērclūsĭt hĭēms, ēt tērrŭĭt aūstĕr ĕūntēs. V. Syn.—Nŏtŭs, āfrĭcŭs. Phr.—Fūlmĭnĕ pōllēns. Nīgĕr īmbrĭbŭs aūstĕr. Plŭvĭīs vĭŏlēntĭŏr aūstĕr. Sībĭlŭs aūstrī. Crēbĕr prŏcēllīs. Călăbrōque ōbnōxĭŭs aūstrō. Dūx īnquĭētī tūrbĭdŭs Ādrĭæ. Īmmūrmŭrăt aūstĕr. Cōncĭtăt aūstĕr ăquās.

Aūstērĭtās, ātĭs. f. *Harshness, roughness, austerity.* Syn.—Āspĕrĭtās, dūrĭtĭēs, grăvĭtās, sĕvērĭtās.

Aūstērŭs, ă, ūm. *Bitter, sour.* Syn.—Āspĕr, ăcērbŭs, ămārŭs. Fig.—*Rigorous, severe, austere.* Syn.—Āspĕr, tĕtrĭcŭs, rĭgĭdŭs, grăvĭs, sævŭs, īmprŏbŭs.

Aūsūm, ī. n. & Aūsŭs, ūs. m. *A difficult undertaking.* Ādjŭvĕt ēt præsēns īngēntĭbŭs ānnŭăt aūsīs. O. Syn.—Făcĭnŭs, cœptūm. Phr.—Aūdāx făcĭnŭs. Aūdācēs cōmpēscŭĭt aūsūs. Māgnănĭmōs aūsūs ĭmĭtātă părēntūm. Mē nūllă dĭēs tām fōrtĭbŭs aūsīs Dīssĭmĭlem ārgŭĕrĭt.

Aūt. conj. *Or, either.* Syn.—Vĕl, seū, sīvĕ, -vĕ.

Aūtēm. conj. *But, however, moreover.* Syn.—Āst, ăt, sĕd, vērō, vērūm.

Aūtūmnŭs, ī. m. *The season of autumn.* Stābăt ĕt aūtūmnūs cālcātīs sōrdĭdŭs ūvīs. O. Phr.—Pōmīs grăvĭs, grăvĭdŭs. Răcēmīs tēmpŏră cīnctŭs. Răcēmĭfĕrīs cīrcūmdătŭs ūvīs. Ānnŭs pōmĭfĕr. Pūrpŭrĕō vărĭŭs cŏlōrĕ.

Aūtŭmŏ, ās, āvī, ātūm, ārĕ. *To think, to suppose.* Syn.—Cēnsĕŏ, ēxīstĭmŏ, jūdĭcŏ, ŏpīnŏr, pŭtŏ, rĕŏr, sēntĭŏ.

Aūxĭlĭārĭs, ĭs, ĕ. *Coming to aid, auxiliary, subservient.* Cærŭlĕūs frātĕr jŭvăt aūxĭlĭārĭbŭs ūndīs. O. Syn.—Aūxĭlĭātŏr, sŏcĭŭs, fămŭlāns, ādjūtŏr, sĕcūndŭs.

Aūxĭlĭātŏr, ōrĭs. m. *One who brings aid or assistance.* Syn.—Dēfēnsŏr, ādjūtŏr, aūxĭlĭūm, præsĭdĭūm, tūtēlă.

Aūxĭlĭŏr, ārĭs, ātŭs sūm, ārī. *To aid, to help.* Syn.—Ādjŭvŏ, jŭvŏ, ādsūm, sūccūrrŏ, sūblĕvŏ, ŏpĭtŭlŏr, făvĕŏ, prōtĕgŏ, dēfēndŏ, tŭĕŏr, tūtŏr. Phr.—Aūxĭlĭūm, ŏpēm, sūbsĭdĭūm dō, fĕrŏ, præstŏ. Aūxĭlĭō ēssĕ. Dēxtrām mănūm dō, tēndŏ. Nōn ĕrĭt aūxĭlĭō nōbīs. Ībānt sūbsĭdĭō Trōjæ. Āspīrāt prīmō fōrtūnă lăbōrī. Jūngĕrĕ vīrēs. Ŏpēs mīttĕrĕ. Sŏcĭa ārmă jŭvābŏ.

Aūxĭlĭūm, ĭī. n. *Aid, assistance.* Aūxĭlĭūmquĕ vĭæ, vĕtĕrēs tēllūrĕ rĕclūdĭt Thēsaūrōs. V. Syn.—Ādjūmēntūm, præsĭdĭūm, sūbsĭdĭūm, cŏlŭmĕn, tūtāmĕn, lĕvāmĕn, sōlāmĕn, sōlātĭūm. Phr.—Rēbūs sōlāmĕn ĭn ārctīs. Cērtă sălūtĭs Ānchŏră. Pērfŭgĭūm mĭhĭ ĕt pōrtŭs. Stătĭō tūtī plăcĭdīssĭmă pōrtūs. *One who gives assistance.* Syn.—Aūxĭlĭātŏr, ādjūtŏr, dēfēnsŏr, tūtēlă. Phr.—Dŭbĭīs nē dēfĭcĕ rēbŭs. Aūdācĭbŭs ānnŭĕ cœptīs. Fĕr ŏpēm. Nōstrīsquĕ lăbōrĭbŭs ādsīs. Rēbūs sūccūrrĭtĕ læsīs. Lāpsō sūccūrrĕre ămīcō.

Ăvārē. adv. *Greedily, covetously.* Syn.—Ăvĭdē, cŭpĭdē.

Ăvārĭtĭă, æ & Ăvārĭtĭēs, ēī. f. *Avarice, cupidity.* Fērvĕt ăvārĭtĭā mĭsĕrāquĕ cŭpīdĭnĕ pēctŭs. H. Syn.—Cŭpīdŏ. Phr.—Aūrī, nūmmōrūm cŭpīdŏ, fămēs, sĭtĭs. Aūrī cæcŭs ămŏr. Ŏpūm dīră fămēs. Ămŏr īmmŏdĕrātŭs hăbēndī. Tūrpĭs ămōr nūmmī. Trīstĭs ăvārĭtĭæ răbĭēs. Ăvāræ mēntĭs fŭrŏr. Aūrī sācră fămēs. Sĭtĭs īnsătĭābĭlĭs aūrī.

Ăvārŭs, ă, ūm. *Eager, desirous.* Syn.—Cŭpĭdŭs, ăvĭdŭs. *Greedy, avaricious.* Syn.—Cŭpĭdŭs, pārcŭs, ăvĭdŭs. Phr.—Aūrī cæcŭs ămōrĕ. Aūrī quēm dīră cŭpīdŏ Sōllĭcĭtăt. Cuī pēctŭs ăvārĭtĭă fērvĕt. Qui ămōrĕ sĕnēscĭt hăbēndī. Lūcrīquĕ cŭpīdĭnĕ fērvēns. Īntĕr ŏpēs mēndīcŭs ŏpūm. Sēmpĕr ăvārŭs ĕgĕt. Sēmpĕr ĭnōps quīcūnquĕ cŭpĭt.

Ăvē, ăvētō. (*def.*) *All hail, or farewell.* Syn.—Sālvē. Phr.—Jŭbĕŏ sălvĕrĕ. Tē sălūtŏ. Sălūtēm dīcŏ.

Ăvĕhŏ, ĭs, ēxī, ēctūm, ĕrĕ. *To carry away with one.* Syn.—Vĕhŏ, dēvĕhŏ, ābdūcŏ, āspōrtŏ, aūfĕrŏ. Phr.—Quōd pĕlăgo ēt cūrvīs sēcum ĕ că-īnĭs.

Ăvēllŏ, ĭs, vēllī & vūlsī, vūlsūm, ĕrĕ. *To pull or drag away by force.* Fātăle āggrēssī săcrāto ăvēllĕrĕ tēmplō Păllădĭūm. V. Syn.—Vēllŏ, cōnvēllŏ, ābrĭpĭŏ, ābstrăhŏ. Phr.—Ăvēllĭt frōndēs. Ān tĭbĭ māvīs īnsĭdĭās fĭĕrī prĕtĭūmque ăvēllĭĕr.

Ăvēnă, æ. f. *Reed, cane. See Appendix. Flute, shepherd's pipe.* Syn.—Fīstŭlă.

Ăvĕō, ēs, ērĕ. *To desire eagerly.* Syn.—Cŭpĭō, ōptō, ēxōptō.

Ăvērnālĭs, ĭs, ĕ. *Pertaining to the lower regions, to hell.* Syn.—Ăchĕrōntĭcŭs, īnfērnŭs, Tārtărĕŭs.

Āvērsŏr, ārĭs, ātŭs sūm, ārī. *To show aversion for, to turn from.* Cūm fŭgĭās āvērsērīsquĕ pĕtēntēs. O. Syn.—Ōdī, rĕfŭgĭō, hōrrĕō, rēspŭō, āvērtŏr, dētēstŏr, ăbōmĭnŏr, ēxsĕcrŏr.

Āvērsŭs, ă, ūm. *Turned away or back from.* Syn.—Dēvĭŭs, rĕmōtŭs, āmōtŭs. *Opposed to, contrary.* Syn.—Ălĭēnŭs, ĭnĭmīcŭs, īnfēnsŭs. Phr.—Āvērsă dĕæ mēns.

Āvērtō, ĭs, tī, sūm, ĕrĕ. *To turn away, to keep from.* Nēc pōsse Ītălĭă Teūcrōrum āvērtĕrĕ rēgēm. V. Syn.—Pēllō, dēpēllō, prŏhĭbĕō, rĕmŏvĕō, āmŏvĕō, āvŏcō, ārcĕō. Phr.—Dīctīs āvērtĕrĕ cūrās. Fērrōque āvērtĕ dŏlōrēm. Āvērtĭtĕ pēstēm. Dī tālem āvērtĭtĕ cāsūm. *To make a turn backward.* Syn.—Rĕtrăhō. Phr.—Ăgō rĕtrō, rĕtrōrsūm. *To turn oneself backward.* Syn.—Āvērtŏr. Phr.—Sēque ēx ŏcŭlīs āvērtĭt ĕt aūfērt. Sūrdăque āvērtĕrĭs aūrĕ. Tūm prōra āvērtĭt.

Āvērtŏr, ĕrĭs, sŭs sūm, ī. *To be turned away.* Syn.—Āvērsŏr. *To flee.* Syn.—Fŭgĭō, ēffŭgĭō.

Āvĭă, ōrūm. n. *By-paths, hidden ways.* Ădĭtūmquĕ pĕr āvĭă quærĭt. V. Syn.—Dēvĭă, īnvĭă.

Ăvĭdē. adv. *Eagerly.* Syn.—Cŭpĭdē.

Ăvĭdĭtās, ātĭs. f. *Greediness, eagerness.* Syn.—Fămēs, sĭtĭs, cŭpīdō, ārdŏr.

Ăvĭdŭs, ă, ūm. *Eager.* Cōntēmptrīx sŭpĕrūm sævæque ăvĭdīssĭmă cædĭs. V. Syn.—Cŭpĭdŭs, ăvārŭs, ārdēns, cŭpĭēns, ăvēns, sĭtĭēns. *Greedy, ravenous.* Syn.—Gŭlōsŭs, vŏrāx, ĕdāx, ăvārŭs. Phr.—Ăvĭdæ tīgrēs. Ăvĭdō cōnvēllĕrĕ dēntĕ.

Ăvĭs, ĭs. f. *Bird.* Nūnc ăvĭs īn rāmō tēctă lărēmquĕ părăt. O. Syn.—Ālĕs, vŏlŭcrĭs, præpēs. Phr.—Ālĭtŭūm, ālĭgĕrūm gĕnŭs. Vŏlŭcrūm cŏhōrs, āgmĕn, ēxērcĭtŭs, nūbēs. Ālĭtŭūm pēnnātă cŏhōrs. Pēnnĭgĕrī grĕgēs. Vērĭs ălūmnă cŏhōrs. Fig.—*Omen.* Syn.—Ālĕs, ōmĕn, aūspĭcĭūm. Phr.—Ăvēs sĭnīstræ.

Ăvītŭs, ă, ūm. *Ancestral.* Ēt stăbŭla āspēctāns, rēgnīs ēxcēssĭt ăvītīs. V. Syn.—Pătērnŭs, pătrĭŭs, gēntīlĭs. Phr.—Ăvītæ laūdĭs hŏnōrēs. *Ancient, old.* Syn.—Prīscŭs, āntīquŭs, vĕtŭs.

Āvĭŭs, ă, ūm. *Inaccessible, untrodden.* Āvĭă tūm rĕsŏnānt ăvĭbūs vīrgūltă cănōrĭs. V. Syn.—Dēvĭŭs, āvērsŭs, īnvĭŭs, īmpērvĭŭs, ĭnāccēssŭs, ĭnhōspĭtŭs, rĕmōtŭs. Phr.—Plēnŭs āmbāgĭbŭs. Dēcĭpĭēns ērrōrĕ lŏcōrūm, vĭārūm. Ădĭtūquĕ cărēntĭă sāxă.

Āvŏcŏ, ās, āvī, ātūm, ārĕ. *To call off, to alienate, to lead aside.* Syn.—Ābdūcŏ, ābstrăhŏ, āvērtŏ, dētērrĕŏ.

Āvŏlŏ, ās, āvī, ātūm, ārĕ. *To fly off, to hasten off.* Syn.—Aūfĕrŏr, aūfŭgĭŏ, ēvādŏ. Phr.—Răpĭdō cĭtŭs āvŏlăt īmpĕtĕ mīlĕs.

Āvŭs, ī. m. *Grandfather. In the plural, ancestors, elders.* Syn.—Prŏāvī, ătāvī, mājōrēs.

Āxĭs, ĭs, m. *An axle-tree.* Tūm vălĭdō nītēns sūb pōndĕrĕ fāgĭnŭs āxĭs. V. *The wheel.* Syn.—Rŏtă. Phr.—Strīdēnt āxĕ nĭvēs. Vŏlăt vī fērvĭdŭs āxĭs. Āxīs tēmōnĕ rĕvūlsŭs. Pērvŏlăt āxĕ cĭtātō. *The chariot or car.* Syn.—Cūrrŭs. *The poles of the earth.* Syn.—Pŏlŭs. Phr.—Tōtūsque ārdēscĕrĕt āxĭs. Āxĕ sĕrēnō Īntŏnŭĭt. Nūdōquĕ sŭb ǣthĕrĭs āxĕ.

B

Bāccă, æ. f. *Berry, any small fruit of trees.* Sānguĭnĕās ĕbŭlī bāccīs mĭnĭōquĕ rŭbēntēm. V. Phr.—Bāccās frōndēntĭs ăcānthī. Laūrī strīngĕrĕ bāccās. Nūllă mĭhī flōrēt bāccīs fēlīcĭbŭs ārbŏs. *A pearl.* Syn.—Gēmmă, ūnĭŏ. Phr.—Cōnchĕă bāccă mărĭs. Cōnchārūm gērmĭnă. Aūrĕ lĕvēs pēndēnt bāccǣ. Bāccīs ŏnĕrăt cāndēntĭbŭs aūrēs.

Bāccăr, ărĭs. n. *Lady's glove.* (*See Appendix under list of Trees, etc.*)

Bāccātŭs, ă, ūm. *Garnished or set with pearls.* Nōn nĭvĕō rĕtĭnēns bāccāt mōnīlĭă cōllō. V. Syn.—Gēmmātŭs. Phr.—Gēmmīs, bāccīs, dĕcōrŭs, dīvĕs, prĕtĭōsŭs, nĭtēns, īnsīgnĭs, grăvĭs. Rŏtūndĭōrĭbŭs ŏnūstă bāccīs āmbŭlĕt.

Bācchātŭs, ă, ūm. *Raging, furious, in a frenzy.* Syn.—Fŭrēns, fŭrĭōsŭs, īnsānŭs, lȳmphātŭs.

Băcŭlūm, ī. n. & Băcŭlŭs, ī. m. *A stick, club, cane.* Trĕpĭdūmquĕ mĭnīstrō Prǣtēntēs băcŭlō, lūmĭnĭs ōrbŭs, ĭtĕr. O. Syn.—Ārūndŏ, băcīllūm, fūstĭs, scīpĭŏ. Phr.—Īnnīxūs băcŭlō. Băcŭlōque īnnīxŭs ăcērnŏ. Mēmbră lĕvānt băcŭlō. Băcŭlūmquĕ tĕnēns āgrēstĕ sĭnīstrā. Băcŭlūm prĕmĭt īnclīnātă sĕnēctūs.

Bājŭlŏ, ās, āvī, ātūm, ārĕ. *To carry a burden.* Phr.—Hŭmĕrīs fĕrŏ, dēfĕrŏ, gĕrŏ, gēstŏ. Īpsĕ sŭbībo hŭmĕrīs. Sūccēdōque ŏnĕrī.

Bālǣnă, æ. f. *A whale.* Quāntō dēlphīnīs bālǣnă Brĭtānnĭcă mājŏr. J. Syn.—Prīstĭs, cētē. Phr.—Pōntī īmmānĭă cōrpŏră, mōnstră. Īmmānĭs bēllŭă pōntī. Īmmānī cōrpŏrĕ prīstĭs. Māgnā sē mōlĕ mŏvēns. Sūlcāns īngēntī pēctŏrĕ flūctūs.

Bālāns, āntĭs. m. & f. *Sheep, lamb.* Bālāntūmquĕ grĕgēm flūvĭō mērsārĕ sălūbrī. V. Syn.—Ŏvĭs, āgnŭs, lānĭgĕr.

Bălătrŏ, ōnĭs. m. *Vagabond, rogue, rascal.* Mēndīcī, mīmǣ, bălătrōnēs, hŏc gĕnŭs ōmnĕ. H. Syn.—Nēquăm, gănĕŏ.

Bālbŭs, ă, ūm. *One who stammers or stutters, halting.* Quīd, cūm bālbă fĕrīs ānnōsō vērbā pălātō. H. Syn.—Blǣsŭs, bālbūtīēns. Phr.—Līnguā tītŭbāns.

Bālbūtĭŏ, īs, īvī, ītūm, īrĕ. *To stammer, to stutter.* Phr.—Bālbă vērbā rēddŏ, ēdŏ, rĕfĕrŏ. Blǣso ōrĕ lŏquŏr. Līnguā tītŭbāntĕ lŏquŏr. Bālbās dăt ōrĕ lŏquēlās. Dīffĭcīlēs dēdĭt ōrĕ sŏnōs.

Bālīstă, ǣ. f. *A machine for hurling stones or darts in war.* Tōrtăquĕ pēr tĕnĕbrās vălĭdīs bālīstră lăcērtīs. L. Syn.—Cătăpūltă, tōrmēntūm Phr.—Mōlēs āddūctō cōncĭtă nērvō. Bālīstăquĕ pōrtās Cōnfrēgīt sāxō. Strīdēntēs tōrquēt bālīstă mŏlārēs.

Bālnĕūm, ī. n. *A bath, washing place.* Syn.—Thērmǣ. Phr.—Călīdīs sūdāntĭă thērmīs Bālnĕă. Nĭtĭdīs gēmmāntĭă sāxīs Bālnĕă. Nĭtĭdās vărĭō dē mārmŏrĕ thērmās Ēxstrūxĭt.

Bālŏ, ās, āvī, ātūm, ārĕ. *To bleat.* Phr.—Bālātūm dō, ēdŏ, rēddŏ, fūndŏ. Bālātĭbŭs āgrōs īmplĕt. Bālātū caūlās rĕplĕŏ, pērsŏnŏ. Tūtī sūb mātrĭbŭs āgnī Bālātum ēxērcēnt.

Bālsămūm, ī. n. *The balsam tree.* (*See Appendix under list of Trees, etc.*)

Bāltĕŭs, ī. m. & Bāltĕă, ōrūm. n. *A girdle, sword-belt.* Lātō quăm cīrcum āmplēctĭtŭr aūrō Bāltĕŭs. V. Syn.—Cīngŭlūm. Phr.— Lātō bāltĕŭs aūrō. Īmmānĭă pōndĕră bāltĕī. Aūrātō rĕlĭgāns īlĭă bāltĕō. *A cincture or belt in general.* Syn.—Cīngŭlūm, zōnă, nōdŭs.

Bāptīsmă, ătĭs. n. & Bāptīsmŭs, ī. m. (Eccl.) *The sacrament of baptism.* Phr.—Săcrūm lăvācrūm. Ūndă lăvācrī. Ūndă sălūtĭfĕrī flūmĭnĭs. Flūmĭnă bāptīsmī. Fōns săcră. Ūndǣ queīs ănĭmǣ āblūtā sōrdĕ nĭtēnt. Queīs ănĭmī scĕlŭs ēlŭĭtūr, vĕtĕrūmquĕ părēntūm Nōmĭnĕ cōntrāctae ēxcēdūnt cōntāgĭă lābĭs. Vĕtĕrīs cērtă mĕdēlă mălī.

Bāptīzŏ, ās, āvī, ātūm, ārĕ. (Eccl.) *To baptize.* Phr.—Mērgŏ, īmmērgŏ, tīngŏ, āblŭŏ, lăvŏ, pērfūndŏ săcrā bāptīsmătĭs ūndā, săcrō flūmĭnĕ, lūstrālĭbŭs. Săcrō pūrgārĕ lăvācrō. Săcrīs lūstrăt ăquīs. Vēstīgĭă fraūdĭs āblŭĕrĕ bāptīsmătĭs ūndā.

Bărăthrūm, ī. n. *Gulf, pit, a deep place.* Syn.—Hĭātŭs, gūrgĕs. Phr.—Prǣcēps tēllūrĭs hĭātŭs. Tērră dĕhīscēns. Spĕcŭs īngēns. Vāstǣ faūcēs. *A vortex in the sea.* Syn.—Vŏrāgŏ, gūrgĕs, vōrtēx.

Bārbă, ǣ. f. *A beard.* Glăcĭē rĭgĕt hōrrĭdă bārbă. V. Syn.—Lānūgŏ. Phr.—Gĕnās, mālās ōrnāns. Mālīs, gĕnīs īnsērpēns. Īn pēctŭs sōrdĭdă bārbă cădĭt. Sūmmō cădĭt hĭspĭdă mēntō Bārbă. Cānēt bārbă gĕlū. Bārbæ̆ cŏlŏr aūrĕŭs. Grăvīs jŭvĕnī mĭhĭ bārbă sŏnābăt.

Bārbărĭēs, ēī. f. *A savage, rough, uncultivated people.* Syn.—Bārbărī, bārbărĭcī. *Rough, unpolished manner.* Syn.—Rūstĭcĭtās, āspĕrĭtās, fĕrĭtās. *Cruelty.* Syn.—Crūdēlĭtās, fĕrĭtās, īmmānĭtās, sævĭtĭă, sævĭtĭēs.

Bārbărŭs, ă, ūm. *Foreign, outlandish, strange.* Bārbărŭs hīc ĕgŏ sūm, quĭă nōn īntēllĕgŏr īllīs. O. Syn.—Ălĭēnŭs, ălĭēnĭgĕnă, ēxtērnŭs. *Savage, barbarous.* Syn.—Rŭdĭs, rūstĭcŭs, āspĕr, īncūltŭs, fĕrŭs, ăgrēstĭs. Phr.—Gēns dūra ātque āspĕră cūltū. *Cruel.* Syn.—Crūdēlĭs, fĕrŭs, sævŭs, īmmānĭs.

Bārbātŭs, ă, ūm. *Bearded.* Sī jŭvĕnīs vĕtŭlō nōn āssūrrēxĕrăt, ēt sī Bārbātō cuīcūmquĕ pŭĕr. J. Syn.—Bārbĭgĕr. Phr.—Cuī plūrĭmă mēntūm Bārbă tĕgĭt. Bārbātŭs vĭr, sĕnēx.

Bārbĭtŏs, ī. f., Bārbĭtŭs, ī. m. & Bārbĭtŏn, ī. n. *Harp, lute, lyre.* Nōn făcĭt ăd lăcrĭmās bārbĭtŏs ūllă mĕās. O. Syn.—Cĭthără, chĕlỹs, lỹră, tēstūdŏ. Phr.—Ăgĕ, dīc Lătīnūm, bārbĭtĕ, cārmĕn. Hōc gĕnĕre ēt chōrdās, ēt plēctra, ēt bārbĭtă cōndĕ. *See Cithara.*

Băsĭs, ĭs. f. *The base, foot, pedestal of a pillar.* Quōquĕ mĭnūs dŭbĭtēs, stāt băsĭs ōrbă dĕā. O. Syn.—Fūlcrūm, fūlcīmēntūm, fūndāmĕn.

Bĕātē. adv. *Happily.* Syn.—Fēlīcĭtĕr, faūstē, fōrtūnātē. Phr.—Ālĭtĕ dēxtrō. Ōmĭnĕ dēxtrō. Dĕō făvēntĕ. Aūspĭcĭīs fēlīcĭbūs ībăt.

Bĕātĭtūdŏ, ĭnĭs. f. & Bĕātūm, ī. n. *Happiness.* Syn.—Fēlīcĭtās, faūstĭtās, prōspĕrĭtās, prōspĕră (ōrūm), lætă (ōrūm). Phr.—Rēs sĕcūndæ. Mĕlĭōr fōrtūnă sĕcūta ēst. Fātă prōspĕră.

Bĕātŭs, ă, ūm. *Happy, blessed.* Bĕātŭs īllĕ quī prŏcūl nĕgōtĭīs! H. Syn.—Fēlīx, fōrtūnātŭs. Phr.—Ō tērquĕ quătērquĕ bĕātī. Quīd mē lætĭŭs ēst bĕātĭūsvĕ? Pērsārūm rēgĕ bĕātĭŏr. *Rich. See Dives.*

Bēllātŏr, ōrĭs. m. A *warrior.* Pȳgmæūs pārvīs cūrrīt bēllātŏr ĭn ārmīs. J. Syn.—Bēllĭgĕr, mīlĕs. Phr.—Bēllī pĕrītŭs. Bēllō, ārmīs māgnŭs. Sævŭs ĭn ārmīs. Prōmptŭs ăd ārmă. Vĭŏlēntŭs ĭn ārmīs. Vĭr bēllĭpŏtēns. Mārtĕ fĕrōx ēt vīncī nēscĭŭs ārmīs. Ēxpērtī bēllī jŭvĕnēs. Bēllō lēctă jŭvēntūs. Pūgnæ sciēns. Cēdĕrĕ nēscĭŭs. Căpŭt īnsupĕrābĭlĕ bēllō. Ēxpērs tērrōrĭs.

Bēllĭcōsŭs, ă, ūm. *Warlike.* Syn.—Pūgnāx, bēllāx, bēllātŏr, bēllĭgĕr, bēllĭpŏtēns.

Bēllĭs, ĭdĭs. f. *The flower marguerite or white daisy.* (*See Appendix under list of Trees, etc.*)

Bēllō, ās, āvī, ātūm, ārĕ & Bēllŏr, ārĭs, ātŭs sūm, ārī. *To wage war.* Pīctīs bēllāntŭr Ămāzŏnĕs ārmīs. V. Syn.—Bēllĭgĕrŏ, pūgnŏ. Phr.—Ēt nūnc sī bēllārĕ părās. Quŏnĭām prŏhĭbēnt ānnī bēllārĕ, lŏquēndō Pūgnăt. Bēllūm gĕrĕrĕ.

Bēllŭă, æ. f. *A large animal or beast.* Syn.—Fĕră, mōnstrūm. Phr.—Pĕr ŏpācă văgāntēs. Īntēr dēsērtă fĕrārūm. Sānguĭnĕ gaūdēnt.

Bēllūm, ī. n. *War.* Ēt bēllī răbĭēs, ēt ămōr sūccēssĭt hăbēndī. V. Syn.—Prœlĭă, cērtāmĭnă, pūgnă, Mārs, ārmă, mīlĭtĭă. Phr.—Bēllī vīs, fŭrŏr, tūrbŏ. Bēllōrūm flūctūs. Rĭgĭdī cērtāmĭnă Mārtĭs. Dūrī cērtāmĭnă bēllī. Bēllă tŭmēnt. Nūbēs bēllī dūm dētŏnĕt. Nŏvūm cōnsūrgĕrĕ bēllūm. Scĕlĕrāta īnsānĭă bēllī. Bēllă tŏnānt. Bēllă cīvĭcă. Mōtŭs cīvĭcŭs. Īnfāndum āccēndĕrĕ bēllūm. Bēllă cĭērĕ, mŏvērĕ, părārĕ, īnfērrĕ, īndūcĕrĕ. Bēllō lăcēssĕrĕ. Īn ārmă, īn fērrūm rŭĕrĕ Mŏvēnt īn prœlĭă. Mūltă vī prœlĭă mīscēnt. Dŭbĭī Mārtĭs fōrtūnă, pĕrīcŭlă, cērtāmĭnă. Bēllō vĭdŭātă cŏlōnīs Ōppĭdă. Dēsīstĕrĕ bēllō. Cōmpōnĕrĕ fœdĕrĕ bēllūm. Ārmă rĕpōnūnt. Ārmă quĭēscānt. Fīnem īmpŏsŭīt bēllō.

Bēllŭs, ă, ūm. *Pretty, charming.* Hīstŏrĭās bēllās, cārmĭnă bēllă făcĭs. M. Syn.—Vĕnūstŭs, ēlĕgāns, pūlchĕr, fōrmōsŭs, spĕcĭōsŭs. *See Pulcher.*

Bĕnĕ. adv. *Well.* Syn.—Rēctē, prŏbē, pūlchrē, āptē. Phr.—Vīvĭtūr pārvō bĕnĕ. Dēdĕcŏrānt bĕnĕ nātă cūlpæ. *Happily.* Syn.—Fēlīcĭtĕr. *Very, much.* Syn.—Mūltūm, vāldē, lārgē.

Bĕnĕdīcŏ, ĭs, xī, ctūm, ĕrĕ. *To speak well of anyone.* Nēc tĭbĭ cēssārēt dōctūs bĕnĕdīcĕrĕ lēctŏr. O. Syn.—Prædīcŏ(ās), laūdŏ.

Bĕnĕfăcĭŏ, ĭs, ēcī, āctūm, ĕrĕ. *To do well, to do a good turn.* Syn.—Jŭvŏ, ādjŭvŏ, aūxĭlĭŏr. Phr.—Mūnĕră dō, ōffĭcĭă trĭbŭŏ, cōnfĕrŏ. Præclārē făcĭŏ, gĕrŏ.

Bĕnĕfāctūm, ī. n. *A good deed.* Nĕque ĕnīm bĕnĕfāctă mălīgnē Dētrēctārĕ mĕum ēst. O. Syn.—Bĕnĕfĭcĭūm. Phr.—Āctă præclāră, bŏnă. *See Beneficium.*

Bĕnĕfĭcĭūm, ĭī. n. *A benefit, a good turn.* Syn.—Bĕnĕfāctūm, mūnŭs, ōffĭcĭūm, mĕrĭtūm. Phr.—Mūnĕrĭbūs cŭmŭlāt lārgīs. Quāntīs jŭvĕrĭt ōffĭcĭīs.

Bĕnĕfĭcŭs, ă, ūm. *Kind, bountiful, benevolent.* Syn.—Bĕnīgnŭs, bĕnĕvŏlŭs, lārgŭs, lībĕrālĭs, mūnĭfĭcŭs. Phr.—Ō făcĭlēs dărĕ sūmmă dĕōs! Pār dōnīs ārmīsquĕ mănŭs.

Bĕnĕvŏlēntĭă, æ. f. *Benevolence, favor.* Syn.—Stŭdĭūm, ămŏr. Phr.—Ămīcă, prōpēnsă vŏlūntās.

Bĕnĕvŏlŭs, ă, ūm. *Benevolent, kind, well-wishing.* Syn.—Bĕnĕvŏlēns, bĕnīgnŭs, stŭdĭōsŭs, ămīcŭs.

Bĕnīgnē. adv. *Kindly, benevolently.* Syn.—Cōmĭtĕr, ămīcē, mānsuētē. Phr.—Mēntĕ bĕnīgnā. *Generously.* Syn.—Lārgē, mūnĭfĭcē.

Bĕnīgnĭtās, ātĭs. f. *Kindness, benevolence.* Syn.—Bŏnĭtās, lēnĭtās, clēmēntĭă, cōmĭtās, hūmānĭtās.

Bĕnīgnŭs, ă, ūm. *Kind, well-wishing, benevolent.* Āccĭpĭt īn Teūcrōs ănĭmūm mēntēmquĕ bĕnīgnām. V. Syn.—Bŏnŭs, blāndŭs, cōmĭs, hūmānŭs, mānsuētŭs, făcĭlĭs, clēmēns, mītĭs, lēnĭs. *Favorable.* Syn.—Faūstŭs, fēlīx, prōpĭtĭŭs, făvēns, ămīcŭs, sĕcūndŭs, prōspĕr, cōmmŏdŭs, lætŭs, dēxtĕr. *Liberal.* Syn.—Mūnĭfĭcŭs, lārgŭs, fĕrāx, fērtĭlĭs, fēcūndŭs. *Fertile, abundant.* Syn.—Lārgŭs, ăbūndāns, fērtĭlĭs, dīvĕs, ŏpīmŭs, ūbĕr.

Bĕō, ās, āvī, ātūm, ārĕ. *To render happy.* Phr.—Rēddĕrĕ bĕātūm, fēlīcēm. *To enrich.* Syn.—Dītō.

Bēstĭă, æ. f. *Beast, wild animal.* Syn.—Fĕră, jūmēntūm, pĕcŭs, ănĭmăl, bēllŭă, mōnstrūm. Phr.—Pĕcŭs rătĭōnĭs ĕgēns.

Bĭbāx, ācĭs. adj. *A drinker, given to drink.* Syn.—Pōtātŏr, pōtŏr, bĭbŭlŭs, bĭbōsŭs. Phr.—Vīnī ăvĭdŭs.

Bīblĭŏthēcă, æ. f. *A library.* Syn.—Scrīnĭă(ōrūm). Phr.—Dēlūbră mūsārūm. Lŏcă săcră Cămœnīs. Lĭbrōrūm ăcērvŭs, cōpĭă, sŭpēllēx.

Bĭbō, ĭs, ī, ĭtūm, ĕrĕ. *To drink.* Tĕnĕrō lāc bĭbĭt ōrĕ pŭĕr. O. Syn.—Pōtō, haūrĭō. Phr.—Sĭtīm rēstīnguō, ēxplĕō, plācō, lĕvō, prŏhĭbĕō. Āmnēm, ăquām bĭbō, haūrĭō. Pōtăt ăquām gălĕā. Sūmmō tĕnŭs āttĭgĭt ōrĕ. Ēt flūctūs āccĭpĭt ōrĕ. Vīnō īndūlgērĕ. Dĭēm frāngĕrĕ vīnō. Fălērnī sūmĕrĕ pārtēm. Fig. Syn.—Ēbĭbō, cōmbĭbō, haūrĭō. Phr.—Pūgnās bĭbĭt aūrĕ vūlgŭs. Bĭbĕ tālĭă prōnĭs aūrĭbŭs. Bĭbĕrĕ mōrēs pătērnōs.

Bĭbŭlŭs, ă, ūm. *Given to drink, bibulous.* Syn.—Bĭbāx. *That which drinks in or absorbs.* Syn.—Ăvĭdŭs, sĭtĭēns, sīccŭs.

Bīgă, æ. f. *A chariot.* (*Generally used in the plural*). Syn.—Cūrrŭs, bĭjŭgēs, bĭjŭgī. Phr.—Cūrrŭs bĭjŭgŭs, bĭjŭgĭs.

Bīlĭs, ĭs. f. *Bile, bilious humor.* Quī pūrgōr bīlēm sŭb vērnī tēmpŏrĭs hōrām. H. Phr.—Crŏcĕām fēbrīs cŏquĭt ārĭdă bīlēm. Fig.—*Wrath, anger.* Syn.—Īră, īrācūndĭă, stŏmăchŭs. Phr.—Cŏquĭt īllūm bīlĭs ămāră. Ācrī bīlĕ tŭmĕt.

Blāndē. adv. *Flatteringly, agreeably.* Syn.—Suāvĭtĕr, cōmĭtĕr, lēnĭtĕr, bĕnīgnē. Phr.—Cănĭt blāndĭŭs Ōrpheō.

Blāndĭlŏquŭs, ă, ūm. *Courteous, one who speaks sweetly, softly.*

Syn.—Blāndŭs. Phr.—Quĭd vōcĕ blāndĭlŏquā mălă cōnsĭlĭă dīctās. Blāndĭlŏquīs dīctīs, vōcĭbŭs, vērbīs.

Blāndĭŏr, īrĭs, ītŭs sūm, īrī. *To caress, to flatter.* Blāndītūr pŏpŭlūs ūmbrā. O. Syn.—Mūlcĕō, pālpŏ. Fig.—*To flatter.* Syn.—Ădūlŏr, āssēntŏr. Phr.—Blāndĭsŏnīs dīctīs mūlcĕō, dēlīnĭō, căpĭō, fāllŏ, īllăquĕō. Āddŏ, dīcŏ, ădhĭbĕō blāndĭtĭās. Blāndīs vōcĭbŭs ūtŏr. *See Blanditiæ.*

Blāndĭtĭæ, ārūm. f. *Caresses, flatteries.* Mīstăquĕ blāndĭtĭīs pŭĕrīlĭbŭs ōscŭlă jūnxĭt. O. Syn.—Blāndĭmēntă, īllĕcēbræ, dēlīnĭmēntă. Phr.—Blāndă, dūlcīssĭmă, mītīssĭmă, aūrēs mūlcēntĭă vērbă. Blāndæ, mēllītæ vōcēs. Crēbrīs pērjūrĭă nēctĭt blāndĭtĭīs.

Blāndŭs, ă, ūm. *Kind, sweet, gentle.* Blāndīquĕ lĕōnēs Sūbmīsērĕ jŭbās. Syn.—Dūlcĭs, lēnĭs, mānsuētŭs, mītĭs, suāvĭs, grātŭs, jūcūndŭs.

Blătĕrŏ, ās, āvī, ātūm, ārĕ. *To chatter, to babble.* Syn.—Gārrĭŏ.

Bŏnă, ōrūm. n. *Goods, riches.* Hōrūm Sēmpĕr ĕgo ōptārīm paūpērrĭmŭs ēssĕ bŏnōrūm. H. *See Divitiae. Good-fortune. See Felicitas.*

Bŏnĭtās, ātĭs. f. *Goodness, good-will.* Syn.—Mānsuētūdŏ, lēnĭtās, clēmēntĭă. Phr.—Mēns bĕnīgnă. Ănĭmŭs mītĭs, clēmēns. Nŏcŭæ mēns nēscĭă fraūdĭs. Quō mēns īgnāră nŏcēndī. *See Bonus.*

Bŏnūm, ī. n. *A good.* Ēt quĭd sĭt nātūră bŏnī, sūmmūmquĕ quĭd ējŭs. H. *See Rectum. Advantage, interest.* Syn.—Cōmmŏdūm, ūtĭlĭtās. Hūmānīs īllă īnvĭdĕt bŏnīs.

Bŏnŭs, ă, ūm. *Good, excellent.* Īndīgnŏr quāndōquĕ bŏnūs dōrmītăt Hŏmērŭs. H. Syn.—Māgnŭs, clārŭs, dĕcōrŭs, prŏbŭs. *Virtuous.* Syn.—Prŏbŭs, rēctŭs, hŏnēstŭs, pĭŭs, sānctŭs, īntĕgĕr, jūstŭs. Phr.—Fāllĕrĕ nēscĭŭs. Cūltŏr, ămāns æquī. Vĭtĭō cărēns. Īntĕgēr vītæ scĕlĕrīsquĕ pūrŭs. Sĭnĕ crīmĭnĕ vītæ. Sĭnĕ lābĕ. *See Pius. Favorable.* Syn.—Faūstŭs, fēlīx. *Proper.* Syn.—Āptŭs, ĭdōnĕŭs, dōctŭs, pĕrītŭs.

Bŏō, ās, āvī, ātūm, ārĕ. *To bellow, to moo.* Syn.—Mūgĭŏ. *See Reboo.*

Bŏrĕālĭs, ĭs, ĕ. *Northern.* Syn.—Ăquĭlōnĭŭs, ārctōŭs, hўpērbŏrĕŭs.

Bŏrĕās, æ. m. *The north wind, northeast wind.* Nūnc gĕlĭdūs sīccā Bŏrĕās bācchātŭr ăb Ārctō. O. Syn.—Ăquĭlŏ. *See Ventus.*

Bōs, ŏvĭs. m. *Ox, bullock, cow.* Sīvĕ bŏvūm sīve ēst cuī grātĭŏr ūsŭs ĕquōrūm. V. Syn.—Taūrŭs, jŭvēncŭs. Epith.—Cōrnĭgĕr, fĕrōx, tōrvŭs, fĕrŭs, īndŏmĭtŭs. Phr.—Cōrnū, frōntĕ mĭnāx. Cūltŏr ăgrī. Mūgītĭbūs āĕră cōmplēns.

Bŏvīlĕ, ĭs. n. *Steading, stable for oxen.* Syn.—Bŭbīlĕ, stăbŭlūm.

Brāchĭūm, ĭī. n. *Arm.* Īlle īntēr sēsē māgnā vī brāchĭā tōllūnt. V. Syn.—Lăcērtŭs, ūlnæ. Phr.—Īntēntăquĕ brāchĭā rēmīs. Rĕtōrtă tērgō brāchĭă. Sī brāchĭă fōrtĕ rĕmīsĭt. *See Amplector, Lacertus, Ulna.*

Brāctĕă, æ. f. *Gold-leaf.* Sīc lēnī crĕpĭtābāt brāctĕă vēntō. V. Syn.—Lāmĭnă, lāmă, brāctĕŏlă.

Brĕvī. adv. *Shortly.* Syn.—Mōx, mŏdŏ, cĭtŏ, quāmprīmūm, mōmēntō, mātūrē, ōcĭŭs, ēxtēmplō, īlĭcĕt. Phr.—Brĕvī, pārvō, ēxĭgŭō, āngūstō tēmpŏrĕ. Nūllā mŏrā. Haūd mŏră. Mīssā mŏrā. Brĕvī (*or*) īn brĕvī spătĭō. Nēc lōngă mŏrātŭs. Nēc lōngum īn mĕdĭō tēmpŭs.

Brĕvĭs, ĭs, ĕ. *Short, brief.* Vīvĕ mĕmōr quām sīs ævī brĕvĭs. H. Syn.—Āngūstŭs, flūxŭs, cădūcŭs. Phr.—Nōn lōngŭs, nōn dĭūtūrnŭs. Brĕvīs dŏmĭnŭs. Vītæ sūmmă brĕvĭs. Cūram īmpēndĕ brĕvēm.

Brĕvĭtĕr. adv. *Briefly.* Syn.—Paūcīs, brĕvī, cōncīsē, ēxĭgŭē.

Brūmă, æ. f. *The winter soltice, winter.* Brūmă nŏvī prīma ēst vĕtĕrīsquĕ nŏvīssĭmă sōlĭs. O. Phr.—Jām spārsĕrăt Hæmō Brūmă nĭvēs. O. Syn.—Hĭēms, tēmpŭs brūmālĕ. *See Hyems.*

Brūmālĭs, ĭs, ĕ. *Wintry, pertaining to the winter solstice.* Syn.—Hībērnŭs, hĭĕmālĭs.

Brūtūm, ī. n. *Brute, beast.* Syn.—Pĕcŭs. Phr.—Brūtūm pĕcŭs. Brūtă ănĭmālĭă. *See Animal.*

Brūtŭs, ă, ūm. *Stolid, heavy, dull.* Quō brūtă tēllūs ēt văgă flūmĭnă. H. Phr.—Sĭnĕ sēnsū, cărēns sēnsū. *Stupid.* Syn.—Stŏlĭdŭs, stūltŭs, stŭpĭdŭs, hĕbĕs.

Bŭbīlĕ, ĭs. n. *Stable for cows.* Syn.—Bŏvīlĕ. *See Stabulum.*

Būbŏ, ōnĭs. m. (rarely f.). *An owl.* (*See Appendix under list of Birds.*)

Bŭbūlcŭs, ī. m. *Shepherd.* Vēnĭt ĕt ūpĭlĭō tārdī vĕnērĕ bŭbūlcī. V. Syn.—Ārmēntārĭŭs, pāstŏr. Epith. Rūstĭcŭs, dūrŭs, rŭdĭs. Phr.—Ārmēntī, bŏūm cūstōs, măgīstĕr, pāstŏr. *See Pastor.*

Būbŭlŭs, ă, ūm. *Pertaining to an ox or a cow.* Syn.—Bŏvīllŭs, bŏvīnŭs, būcĕrŭs, būcĕrĭŭs, taūrīnŭs.

Būccă, æ. f. *Mouth, cheek.* Quīd caūsae ēst, mĕrĭtō quīn īllīs Jūpĭtĕr āmbās Īrātūs būccās īnflĕt. H. Syn.—Ōs, gĕnæ.

Būccĭnă, æ. f. *Trumpet, horn.* Ūt grăvĭs ōbstrĕpĕrēt mŏdŭlātīs būccĭnă nērvīs. L. Syn.—Tŭbă, cōrnū, clāssĭcūm, lĭtŭŭs. Phr. —Aēs raūcūm. Cōrnū rĕcūrvūm. *See Tuba.*

Būccĭnātŏr, ōrĭs. m. *Trumpeter.* Phr.—Quō nōn præstāntĭŏr āltĕr Aērĕ cĭērĕ vĭrōs. V.

Būccĭnŏ, ās, āvī, ātūm, ārĕ. *To sound the trumpet.* Phr.—Dărĕ sīgnūm ærĕ căvō. Mārtēm accēndĕrĕ cāntū. *See Tuba.*

Būcŏlĭcŭs, ă, ūm. *Bucolic, pastoral.* Būcŏlĭcīs jŭvĕnīs lūsĕrăt āntĕ mŏdīs. O. Syn.—Mænălĭŭs, ăgrēstĭs, pāstōrālĭs, rūstĭcŭs. Phr.—Grăcĭlī mŏdŭlātŭs ăvēnā. Tĕnŭī dēdūctă pŏēmătă fīlō.

Būlbŭs, ī. m. *Onion.* (*See Appendix under list of Trees, etc.*)

Būllĭŏ, īs, īvī, ītūm, īrĕ. *To bubble, to boil.* Dēmērsūs sūmmā nōn būllĭt ĭn ūndā. Pers. Syn.—Ēbūllĭŏ, fērvĕŏ, æstŭŏ. Phr.—Ăēna ūndāntĭă flāmmīs. *See Ferveo.*

Būstūm, ī. n. *Place for burning the dead.* *See Rogus, Cadaver.* *Tomb.* Syn.—Sĕpūlcrūm.

Būxŭs, ī. f. & Būxūm, ī. n. *The box-tree* (*See Appendix under list of Trees, etc.*)

C

Căbāllŭs, ī. m. *Horse.* Syn.—Ĕquŭs, mānnŭs, quădrūpēs. *See Equus.*

Căchīnnŏ, ās, āvī, ātūm, ārĕ & Căchīnnŏr, ārĭs, ātŭs sūm, ārī. *To burst into laughter, to laugh loudly.* Syn.—Rīdĕŏ. Phr.—Căchīnnōs gĕmĭnŏ, tōllŏ. Āttōllŏ rīsūm. Mājōrĕ căchīnnō cōncŭtĭtŭr. *See Rideo.*

Căchīnnŭs, ī. m. *Loud laughter.* Rōmānī tōllēnt ĕquĭtēs pĕdĭtēsquĕ căchīnnūm. H. Syn.—Rīsŭs. Phr.—Rĭgĭdī cēnsūră căchīnnī. *See Risus.*

Căcūmĕn, ĭnĭs. n. *Height, summit.* Nūnc hērbæ, rūptā tēllūrĕ, căcūmĭnă tōllūnt. O. Syn.—Ăpēx, vērtēx. *Tree-top.* Syn.—Cūlmĕn, vērtēx, căpŭt.

Căcūmĭnŏ, ās, āvī, ātūm, ārĕ. *To make sharp, to point.* Syn.—Ăcūmĭnŏ, ăcŭŏ.

Cădāvĕr, ĕrĭs. n. *Body, corpse.* Ūltōrēs răpĭānt tūrpĕ cădāvĕr ĕquī. O. Syn.—Cōrpŭs, trūncŭs, (*sometimes*) fūnŭs. *Epith.* Ēxsānguĕ, ēxănĭmūm, fœdūm, tūrpĕ, crŭēntūm. Phr.—Ārtūs ĭnānēs, ēxsānguēs, ēxănĭmēs. Spŏlĭātūm vītā, lūmĭnĕ cōrpŭs. Cōrpŭs ĭnāne ănĭmæ. Lūcĕ cărēns.

Cădŏ, ĭs, cĕcĭdī, cāsūm, cădĕrĕ. *To fall.* Ēt cădĭt ād pātrĭōs sānguĭnŏlēntă pĕdēs. O. Syn.—Cōncĭdŏ, dēcĭdŏ, ēxcĭdŏ, īncĭdŏ, prōcĭdŏ, lābŏr, cōllābŏr, dēlābŏr, prōlābŏr, rŭŏ, cōrrŭŏ, prōrŭŏ, præcĭpĭtŏ, præcĭpĭtŏr, prōcūmbŏ, stērnŏr, vōlvŏr. Phr.—Ād tērrām, īn præcēps lābŏr, cădŏ. Præcēps ăgŏr, fĕrŏr, īmpēllŏr. Vōlvĭtŭr īn căpŭt. Cōrpŏră dēvōlvūnt ĭn hŭmūm. Prōcūmbĭt hŭmī bōs. *To fail in strength.* Syn.—Fătīscŏ, dēfĭcĭŏ, vīncŏr, sūccūmbŏ, cōllābŏr. Phr.—Cĕcĭdēre ănĭmī.

Cādūcēŭs, ī. & Cādūcēūm, ī. n. *Wand, the famous wand of Mercury.* Syn.—Vīrgă. Phr.—Lēthæūm vīmĕn. Vīrgă pŏtēns. Quā sōmnōs dūcĭt ĕt ārcĕt.

Cădūcŭs, ă, ūm. *About to fall, falling.* Ūtquĕ cădūcīs Pērcūssū crēbrō sāxă căvāntŭ. ĕquīs. O. Syn.—Cădēns, lāpsŭs Phr.—Frōndēs vŏlĭtārĕ cădūcās. Bēllōquĕ cădūcī Dārdănĭdæ. *Fragile, perishable.* Syn.—Flūxŭs, pĕrĭtūrŭs, frăgĭlĭs, lăbāns, brĕvĭs, īnstăbĭlĭs, mūtābĭlĭs. *Vain, fleeting.* Syn.—Ĭnānĭs, īrrĭtŭs, vānŭs, pĕrĭtūrŭs, fŭgāx.

Cădŭs, ī. m. *Great earthen vessel for wine.* Vīnă bŏnūs quæ deīndĕ cădīs ŏnĕrārăt Ăcēstēs. V. Syn.—Dōlĭūm. Phr.—Lўæō plēnŭs. Cōndītă cădīs. *See Urna.*

Cæcātŭs, ă, ūm. *Blinded.* Syn.—Cæcŭs. *See latter.*

Cæcĭtās, ātĭs. f. *Blindness.* Syn.—Tĕnĕbræ, nōx. Phr.—Ēffōssī ŏcŭlī. Ĭnānēs lūmĭnĭs. Lūcĭs ădēmptæ. *Blindness of spirit or heart.* Syn.—Nōx, tĕnĕbræ, ērrŏr. *See Caeco, Caecus.*

Cæcŏ, ās, āvī, ātūm, ārĕ. *To blind.* Sōl ĕtĭām cæcāt, cōntrā sī cērnĕrĕ pērgās. Lr. Syn.—Ēxcæcŏ, ōbcæcŏ. Phr.—Lūmĭnă, ŏcŭlŏs ēffŏdĕrĕ, ērŭĕrĕ, ērĭpĕrĕ, ēlīdĕrĕ, ēxcŭtĕrĕ, gĕnīs ēxpēllĕrĕ, sēdĭbŭs ērŭĕrĕ. Mănū lūmĭnă haūrīrĕ. Lūcĕ ōrbārĕ, prīvārĕ. Lūmĕn ădēmĭt. *See Nox.* Fig.—*To deceive.* Syn.—Ōbcæcŏ, ēxcæcŏ, lўmphŏ. Phr.—Ērrōrēm īnjĭcĭŏ. Sēnsūs ērĭpĭŏ. Cālīgĭnĕ īmmērgŏ, mērgŏ, īnvōlvŏ. *See Caligo.*

Cæcŭs, ă, ūm. *Blind.* Rāptīs lūmĭnĭbūs rĕpēntĕ cæcŭs. M. Syn.—Ēxcæcātŭs, ōbcæcātŭs. Phr.—Ŏcŭlīs cæcŭs. Lūmĭnĭs ēxpērs. Lūmĭnĕ cāssŭs. Pērpĕtŭā dāmnātŭs nōctĕ. Aētērnā nōctĕ, cālīgĭnĕ ŏcŭlōs tēctŭs. Lūmĭnĭbŭs ōrbātŭs. Lūcĕ prīvātŭs. Cuī lūmĕn ădēmptūm. Lūcĕ cărēns. Lūmĭnĕ rāptō. Fig.—*Blinded, deceived.* Syn.—Cæcātŭs, ōbtūsŭs, ōbcæcātŭs, lўmphātŭs, āmēns, dēmēns, īnsānŭs, vēsānŭs. Phr.—Cæcŭs ămōr sŭī. Cæcă fŭtūrī gaūdĭă. Āmēntī cæcă fŭrōrĕ. *Obscure, dark.* Syn.—Ōbscūrŭs, tĕnĕbrōsŭs, ātĕr, cālīgāns. Phr.—Cæcæ tēctă dŏmūs. Cæcæquĕ fŏrēs. Ēt cæcō Mārtĕ rĕsīstūnt. *Unknown.* Syn.—Ōbscūrŭs, tēctŭs, ōccūltŭs, īgnōtŭs, īncōgnĭtŭs, lătēns, ārcānŭs, ābdĭtŭs. *See Abditus.*

Cædēs, ĭs. f. *Massacre, slaughter.* Tūnc cædēs hŏmĭnūm gĕnĕrī, tūnc prœlĭă nātă. Tib. Syn.—Clādēs, fūnĕră, strāgēs. Epith. Dūră, răbĭdă, crŭēntă, mĭsĕră, fœdă, fūnēstă, hōrrĭdă. Phr.—Cædĭs, strāgĭs ăcērvŭs. Mŏrĭēntūm cŭmŭlī, ăcērvī. Māllĕ nĕcĭs. *See Occido, Strages.*

Cædŏ, ĭs, cĕcīdī, cæsūm, cædĕrĕ. *To cut, to amputate.* Hīc vĭrĭdēm dūrā cǣdĕrĕ fālcĕ cŏmām. Tib. *See Amputo, Seco. To strike.* Syn.—Vērbĕrŏ, pērcŭtĭŏ, fĕrĭŏ. *To kill, to sacrifice.* Syn.—Ōccīdŏ, nĕcŏ, ēnĕcŏ, īntĕrĭmŏ, pĕrĭmŏ, trŭcīdŏ, ōbtrūncŏ, īntērfĭcĭŏ, māctŏ. *See Occido, Immolo.*

Cǣlāmĕn, ĭnĭs. n. *Bas-relief.* Syn.—Sīgnă (orum). Phr.—Ōpŭs cǣlātūm.

Cǣlātŭs, ă, ūm. *Chiselled, carved.* Cǣlātūmquĕ nŏvēm Mūsīs ŏpŭs. H. Syn.—Īmprēssŭs. Phr.—Āspĕră sīgnīs.

Cǣlĕbs, ĭbĭs. m. & f. *One who lives in celibacy.* Nīl ăĭt ēssĕ prĭŭs, mĕlĭūs nīl cǣlĭbĕ vītā. H. Syn.—Īnnŭbŭs, īnnūptă. Phr.—Cōnjŭgĭs ēxpērs, īgnārŭs, īnscĭŭs. Cōnnūbĭă vītăt. *See Castus, Virgo.*

Cǣlŏ, ās, āvī, ātūm, ārĕ. *To engrave, to carve.* Quǣ bŏnŭs Eūrўtĭōn mūltō cǣlāvĕrăt aūrō. V. Syn.—Īncīdŏ, scūlpŏ, īmprĭmŏ, cǣdŏ. Phr.—Aērĕ, aūrō, mārmŏrĕ, lăpĭdĕ, līgnō fīngŏ, ēxprĭmŏ, ēffīngŏ, ĭmĭtŏr. Lōngō cǣlāvĕrăt ārgūmēntō. *See Caelatus.*

Cǣlūm, ī. n. *Engraving tool.* Syn.—Scālprūm.

Cǣmēntūm, ī. n. *Rough stone from the quarry.* Nōn sĭlĭcĕ dūrō, strūctĭlĭvĕ cǣmēntō. M. Syn.—Lăpĭs, sāxūm.

Cǣrŭlă, ōrūm. n. *The sea. See Mare.*

Cǣrŭlĕŭs, & Cǣrŭlŭs, ă, ūm. *Azure, blue.* Cǣrŭlĕūs Tībrīs, cœlō grātīssĭmŭs āmnĭs. V. Syn.—Glaūcŭs, cǣsĭŭs, vĭrĭdĭs. *Pertaining to the sea.* Syn.—Aēquŏrĕŭs, mărīnŭs.

Cǣspĕs, ĭtĭs. m. *Turf, sod.* Paūpĕrĭs ēt tŭgŭrī cōngēstūm cǣspĭtĕ cūlmĕn. V. Syn.—Grāmĕn. Phr.—Grāmĭnĕŭs tŏrŭs. Tĕnĕrō cǣspĭtĕ tērră vĭrĕt. Fēcūndīs tēllūs ūbērrĭmă glēbīs.

Cǣstŭs, ūs. m. *The cestus of the boxer.* Cūrsĭbŭs ēt crūdō dēcērtēt Grǣcĭă cǣstū. V. Phr.—Cǣlātăquĕ plūmbō tērgă. Nĭgrāntĭă plūmbō Tēgmĭnă crūdă bŏūm.

Cǣtĕră, & Cētĕră. adv. *As for the rest, but.* Syn.—Cǣtĕrūm, cǣtĕrō. Phr.—Quŏăd, ăd cētĕră.

Călămĭtās, ātĭs. f. *Disaster, loss, calamity.* Syn.—Aērūmnă, cāsŭs, clādēs, īnfōrtūnĭūm, dāmnūm, ēxĭtĭūm. Phr.—Ādvērsī cāsūs. Ādvērsă fōrtūnă. Rēs ārdŭǣ, āfflīctǣ, lāpsǣ. Sōrs ūltĭmă rērūm. Ō pāssī grăvĭōră. *See Malum, Adversa (orum), Fortuna, Infelix.*

Călămĭtōsŭs, ă, ūm. *Harmful, disastrous.* Syn.—Dāmnōsŭs, fūnēstŭs, nōxĭŭs, nŏcŭŭs, ēxĭtĭōsŭs, ēxĭtĭālĭs. *Unhappy.* Syn.—Mĭsĕr, īnfēlīx, ǣrūmnōsŭs, īnfōrtūnātŭs. Phr.—Tōt mălă pērpēssŭs. *See Infelix.*

Călămŭs, ī. m. *Cane, reed.* Cōrpŏrĕ prō nўmphǣ călămōs tĕnŭīs pălūstrēs. O. Syn.—Ărūndŏ, cānnă. *See Arundo.* *Arrow.* Syn.—Săgīttă. *Pen.* Syn.—Ărūndŏ, grăphĭūm, stĭlŭs.

Cătăthŭs, ī. m. *Basket.* Tĭbĭ līlĭă plēnīs Ēccĕ fĕrūnt nȳmphæ cătăthīs. V. Syn.—Cănīstrūm, fīscēllă, fīscĭnă, cōrbĭs, scīrpĕă, scīrpĭcŭlŭs, călăthīscŭs, cīstă, cīstŭlă. Ph:.—Cōntēxtūs vīmĭnĕ jūncī. Vās lēntō vīmĭnĕ tēxtūm.

Cālcăr, ārĭs. n. *Spur.* Seū spūmāntĭs ĕquī fōdĕrēt cālcārĭbŭs ārmōs. V. Syn.—Stĭmŭlŭs. Phr.—Cālx fērrĕă, fērrātă, ærĕă, ærātă. Quō lătŭs ĕquī tūndĭtŭr. Cālcārĭbŭs prĕmĕrĕ, ūrgērĕ, fătīgārĕ.

Cālcĕŭs, ī. m. *Shoe.* Ūt cālcĕūs ōlīm, Sī pĕdĕ mājŏr ĕrĭt sūbvērtēt, sī mĭnŏr, ūrĕt. H. Syn.—Ălūtă, cālcĕāmĕn, sōccŭs. Phr.—Vīnclă pĕdūm. Vīncŭlă plāntæ. Rūptā cālcĕŭs āltēr pēllĕ pătĕt.

Cālcĭtrŏ, ās, āvī, ātūm, ārĕ. *To strike with the heel.* Syn.—Rĕcālcĭtrŏ. *To resist. See Resisto.*

Cālcŏ, ās, āvī, ātūm, ārĕ. *To grind or roll under the feet.* Mīxtāquĕ crŭōr cālcātŭr ărēnā. O. Syn.—Prōcūlcŏ, cōncūlcŏ, tĕrŏ, prōtĕrŏ, cōntĕrŏ, ōbtĕrŏ, īnsūltŏ. Phr.—Cālcĕ tĕrŏ, ōbtĕrŏ. Sūb pĕdĭbūs tĕrŏ. Ātque hōstēm sūbdĭdĕrĭt pĕdĭbūs. Fig.—*To despise. See Contemno.*

Cāldă, æ & Cālĭdă, æ. *Hot water.* Syn.—Cāldæ (ārūm). *See Aqua.*

Cāldŭs, ă, ūm. *Hot, fiery.* Syn.—*See Calda, Ardens.*

Cālĕfăcĭŏ, ĭs, fēcī, fāctūm, făcĕrĕ. *To warm, to grow warm.* Sānguĭnĕ quām lārgō Grāiōs cālĕfēcĕrĭt āmnēs. O. Syn.—Īncālfăcĭŏ, fŏvĕŏ. Phr.—Cālōrēm āddŏ. Cālōrĕ rĕcrĕŏ, fŏvĕŏ. *See Caleo.*

Călēndæ, ārūm. f. *The Calends, the first day of the month.* Phr.—Mēnsīs prīmă dĭēs. *See Mensis.*

Călĕŏ, ēs, ŭī, ērĕ. *To grow warm.* Quāmvīs nōn mŏdĭcō călĕānt spēctācŭlă sōlĕ. M. Syn.—Călĕfīŏ, călēscŏ, īncălēscŏ, æstŭŏ, fērvĕŏ, fērvēscŏ, ārdĕŏ, tĕpĕŏ, tĕpēscŏ. Phr.—Fērvēntī tōrrĕŏr æstū. Rădĭīs sōlārĭbŭs ūrŏr. Sūdŏr pēr mēmbră călĕt. Tūrĕ călēnt āræ. *See Ardeo.*

Călēscŏ, ĭs, ĕrĕ. *To grow warm. See Caleo.*

Călĭdŭs, ă, ūm. *Warm, hot, burning.* Ēt călĭdōs lătĭcēs ēt ăhēna ūndāntĭă flāmmīs. V. Syn.—Călēns, călĕfāctŭs, tĕpēns, tĕpĭdŭs, æstŭōsŭs, ārdēns, ārdēscēns, fērvēns, fērvĭdŭs, fērvēscēns, flāmmĕŭs, īgnītŭs, tōrrĭdŭs. *Ardent, boiling. See Fervidus.*

Cālīgāns, āntĭs. m. f. & n. *Dark, black. See Niger, Obscurus.*

Cālīgĭnōsŭs, ă, ūm. *Dark, black.* Syn.—Cālīgāns, ōbscūrŭs, tĕnĕbrōsŭs, nĭgĕr, ŏpācŭs. *See Obscurus.*

Cālīgŏ, ĭnĭs. f. *Darkness, obscurity.* Trēs ădĕo īncērtōs cæcā cālīgĭnĕ sōlēs Ērrāmūs pĕlăgō. V. Syn.—Nōx, tĕnĕbrǣ, ūmbrǣ, nĕbŭlă. Epith. Āvērnālĭs, cǣcă, trīstĭs, dēnsă, hŏrrēns, hŏrrĭdă. Phr.—Cālīgĭnĕ dēnsŭs ŏpācă. *See Nox, Tenebræ.* Fig. Phr.— Ōccūltă rērūm. Nātūrǣ ārcānă. Cǣcă mēntĭs cālīgŏ.

Cālīgŏ, ās, āvī, ātūm, ārĕ. *To be dark, to be covered with shadows.* Mōrtālēs hĕbĕtāt vīsūs ātque hūmĭdă cīrcūm Cālīgăt. V. Syn.— Ōbscūrŏr. Phr.—Cālīgĭnĕ, nōctĕ, tĕnĕbrīs īnvōlvŏr, ōbdūcŏr, prĕmŏr. Sŭb nōctĕ lătĕŏ, jăcĕŏ. Cālīgāntĕ lătēnt āstră sŭb ǣthĕrĕ. Fig. Syn.—Cǣcŏr, ōbcǣcŏr, cǣcūtĭŏ.

Călīx, ĭcĭs. m. *Cup, vase, chalice.* Prōdīt pērspĭcŭūs nē dŭŏ vīnă călīx. M. Syn.—Pōcŭlūm, pătĕră. *See Poculum.*

Cāllĕŏ, ēs, ŭī, ērĕ. *To be thick-skinned.* Syn.—Īndūrēscŏ *To be experienced, to know perfectly.* Syn.—Scĭŏ, tĕnĕŏ, nōscŏ, nōvī. *See Scio.*

Cāllĭdē. adv. *Skilfully, cunningly. Also in a bad sense, deceitfully.* Syn.—Āstūtē, dŏlōsē.

Cāllĭdĭtās, ātĭs. f. *Skill, shrewdness.* Cōnsĭlĭūm mīrǣ cāllĭdĭtātĭs ĭnĭt. O. Syn.—Īngĕnĭūm, ăcūmĕn, ārs, sōlērtĭă. *See Ingenium. Skill in deceiving.* Syn.—Āstūtĭă, vērsūtĭă, fraūs. *See Dolus.*

Cāllĭdŭs, ă, ūm. *Skilful, adroit.* Cāllĭdŭs ēxcūssō pŏpŭlūm sūs-pēndĕrĕ nāsō. Pers. Syn.—Pĕrītŭs, dōctŭs, sōlērs. Phr.— Vĕtĕrūm jūdēx cāllĭdŭs. Cāllĭdŭs rĕī mīlĭtārĭs. *Deceitful, cun-ning.* Syn.—Āstūtŭs, cătŭs, dŏlōsŭs, sūbdŏlŭs, văfĕr, vērsūtŭs. *See Dolosus, Fallax.*

Cāllĭs, ĭs. m. *Beaten path, way.* Syn.—Sēmĭtă, trāmĕs, vĭă, ĭtĕr. Phr.—Āngūstă vĭārūm. Āngūstǣ faūcēs ădĭtūsquĕ mălīgnī. Sēcrētī cāllēs cēlānt. *See Via.*

Călŏr, ōrĭs. m. *Heat, warmth.* Dīlāpsŭs călŏr ātque īn vēntōs vītā rĕcēssĭt. V. Syn.—Aēstŭs, ārdŏr, fērvŏr. Fig.—*Courage, vivacity.* Syn.—Ārdŏr, ǣstŭs, īmpĕtŭs.

Cālthă, ǣ. f. *The marigold. (See Appendix under list of Trees, etc.)*

Călūmnĭŏr, ārĭs, ātŭs sūm, ārī. *To accuse falsely.* Phr.—Crīmĭnă fīngŏ. Fālsă jăcĭŏ. Fīctīs crīmĭnĭbŭs prĕmŏ, ūrgĕŏ. Fālsō āccūsŏ, ārgŭŏ, īnsĭmŭlŏ. *See Mentior.*

Cālvĕŏ, ēs, ī, ērĕ. *To be bald.* Phr.—Dŏlētquĕ căpĭllōs Jām sŭbĭtō glăbrūm dēstĭtŭĭssĕ căpŭt. *See Calvus.*

Cālvŭs, ă, ūm. *Bald.* Cālvŭs ĕquēs căpĭtī sōlĭtŭs rĕlĭgārĕ căpĭllōs. Syn.—Īncŏmātŭs. Phr.—Cūjŭs (*or*) cuī căpŭt calvŭm, nūdŭm, nūdātūm.

Cālx, cĭs. m. & f. *Heel.* Ūt nĕquĕ cālcĕ lŭpŭs quēmquām, nĕquĕ dēntĕ pĕtīt bōs. H. Syn.—Tālŭs.

Cālx, cĭs. f. *Chalk.* Sāxă vĭdēs prīmūm sōlā cŏălēscĕrĕ cālcĕ. Lr. *The end of the course marked by a chalk line.* Syn.—Fīnĭs, tĕrmĭnŭs.

Cămēlŭs, ī. m. *Camel.* Tōllĕ rĕcēns prīmūs pĭpĕr ē sĭtĭēntĕ cămēlō. Pers. Syn.—Drŏmās. Phr.—Īmmānĭă mēmbră cămēlī.

Cămĕră, æ. f. *Room, vaulted chamber.* Syn.—Ārcŭs, fōrnīx, lăquĕār, tēstūdŏ, lăcūnăr. Phr.—Ēffūlgēnt cămĕræ vărĭō fāstīgĭă vītrō.

Cămĕrŏ, ās, āvī, ātūm, ārĕ. *To bend in the form of a vault.* Phr.—Īn fōrnĭcēm, ĭn ārcūm īncūrvŏ, sĭnŭŏ.

Cămīnŭs, ī. m. *Forge, furnace.* Īmpŏsĭtām rūptīs flāmmam ēxspīrārĕ cămīnīs. V. Syn.—Fōrnāx. Phr.—Cŏquĭtūr dūm māssă cămīnō. *See Fornax.*

Cămœnæ, ārūm. f. *The muses.* *See Musæ (in Appendix).*

Cāmpŭs, ī. m. *Field, camp, place.* Quīquĕ frĕquēns hērbīs ēt fērtĭlĭs ūbĕrĕ cāmpŭs. V. Syn.—Ārvūm, ăgĕr, (*sometimes*) jūgĕră, cūltă. Epith.—Fērtĭlĭs, ămœnŭs, ŏpīmŭs, vĭrĭdĭs. Phr.—Ămœnī dīffūsī jūgĕră cāmpī. Pārtīrī līmĭtĕ cāmpūm. Vēstītī grāmĭnĕ cāmpī. Flāvēscīt cāmpŭs ărīstā. Pēr cāmpōs pāscūntŭr ĕquī. *Plain.* Syn.—Plānĭtĭēs, æquŏr. Phr.—Cāmpōrūm æquŏr. Plānīssĭmă cāmpī Ārĕă. *Battlefield.* Phr.—Cāmpŭs Mārtĭŭs.

Cănālĭs, ĭs. m. *Canal, conduit.* Cūrrēntem īlīgnīs pōtārĕ cănālĭbŭs ūndām. V. Syn.—Tŭbŭs, ālvĕŭs, fīstŭlă. Phr.—Rŭĭt āctă rĕpēntĕ cănālĭbŭs ūndă. Quāntō sē pōrrĭgăt ūndă cănālī. Vĭrĭdēs rĕcrĕārĕ cănālĭbŭs hōrtōs.

Cāndēlă, æ. f. *Candle.* Brĕvĕ lūmēn Cāndēlæ cūjūs dīspēnso ēt tēmpĕrō fīlūm. J. Syn.—Cērĕŭs, fāx, fūnālĕ, (*also*) lāmpăs, lūx, lŭcērnă. Phr.—Trĕmŭlă lūcĕ cŏrūscāns. Sŭō ābsūmĭtŭr īgnĕ. Sēnsīm ā sŭīs flāmmīs pĕrēsă dēfĭcĭt. Ēt nōctēm cāndēlă fŭgăt. *See Lampas, Fax.*

Cāndĕŏ, ēs, ŭī, ērĕ. *To be white.* Hīc fērrātă rĭgēnt, īllīc ārgēntĕă cāndēnt. Syn.—Cāndĭcŏ, cāndēscŏ, cānĕŏ, cānēscŏ, ālbĕŏ, ālbēscŏ, ālbĭcŏ.

Cāndēscŏ, ĭs, ĕrĕ. *To be white.* *See Albeo, Candeo.*

Cāndĭcŏ, ās āvī, ātūm, ārĕ. *To be white.* Syn.—Ālbĭcŏ. *See Candeo.*

Cāndĭdātŭs, ă, ūm. *White, clothed in white.* Syn.—Ālbātŭs, cāndĭdŭs. *A candidate.* Syn.—Pĕtītŏr.

Cāndĭdŭs, ă, ūm. *White.* Cāndĭdă dē nĭgrīs ēt dē cāndēntĭbŭs ātră. O. Syn.—Cāndēns, ālbŭs, ālbēscēns, ālbĭdŭs, ĕbūrnŭs, ĕbūrnĕŭs, lāctĕŭs, nĭvĕŭs, ārgēntĕŭs, cānēns, cānŭs, cānēscēns, cāndēscēns, cāndĭdŭlŭs. Phr.—Cāndōrĕ nĭtēns, fūlgēns, dĕcōrŭs. Cāndĭdĭōr lāctĕ, nĭvĕ, nĭvĭbŭs, cycnō. *See Albus.*

Cāndŏr, ōrĭs. m. *Whiteness.* Cāndŏr ĕrāt quālēm præfērt Lātōnĭă lūnă. Tib. Syn.—Ālbūm. Phr.—Cŏlŏr nĭvĕŭs, ālbŭs, ĕbūrnĕŭs, etc. Nĭvĭs cŏlŏr. Pār nĭtŏr īntāctīs nĭvĭbŭs. Quīppĕ cŏlōr nĭvĭs ēst. Quī cāndōrĕ nĭvēs āntēīrēnt. *See Albus.*

Cānĕō, ēs, ŭī, ērĕ & Cānēscō, ĭs, ĕrĕ. *To be or become white.* Nēc rĕnŏvātŭs ăgēr grăvĭdīs cānēbăt ărīstīs. O. Syn.—Ālbēscō, ālbĭcō. Phr.—Cānēt bārbă gĕlū. Dūm grāmĭnă cānēnt. Fig.—*To whiten with old age.* Tēmpŏrĭbūs gĕmĭnīs cānēbāt spārsă sĕnēctūs. Phr.—Cānīs ālbēscō. Cānīs căpŭt āspērsum ēst căpīllīs. *See Canities, Senesco.*

Cānī, ōrūm. m. *White hairs.* Fālsōs īn tēmpŏră cānōs āddĭt. O. *See Canities.*

Cănīcŭlă, æ. f. *The dog star.* Sīccās īnsānă Cănīcŭlă mēssēs Jāmdūdūm cŏquĭt. Pers. Syn.—Cănĭs, Sīrĭŭs. Phr.—Aēstīvī cănĭs stēllă. Īcărĭūm sīdŭs. Ātrōx hōră cănīcŭlæ.

Cănĭs, ĭs. m. & f. *Dog.* Hīnc cănĭbūs blāndīs răbĭēs vĕnĭt. V. Syn.—Cătŭlŭs. Epith.—Fĭdēlĭs, săgāx, aūdāx. Phr.—Fūrĭbŭs īnvīsŭs. Tūrbă vĭgĭlāns. Cānūm fīdă vīs. *See Latro.*

Cănīstrūm, ī. n. *Basket.* Pūră cŏrōnātīs pōrtābānt sācră cănīstrīs. O. Syn.—Călăthŭs, cīstă, cīstŭlă, fīscĭnă, fīscēllă. Phr.—Cĕrĕrēmquĕ cănīstrīs. Mȳrtōquĕ cănīstră vīnctă. *See Calathus.*

Cānĭtĭēs, ēī. f. *White hairs, beard.* Plūrĭmă mēntō Cānĭtĭēs īncūltă jăcĕt. V. Syn.—Cānī. Phr.—Cānī căpīllī. Cānūm căpŭt. Tēmpŏră cānă. Căpĭtĭs nĭvēs. Frīgĭdă cānĭtĭēs. Spārsī pēr tēmpŏră cānī.

Cānnă, æ. f. *Cane, reed.* Āră vĕtūs stābāt trĕmŭlīs cīrcūmdătă cānīs. O. Syn.—Ărūndŏ, călămŭs, jūncŭs. Phr.—Prætēxēns vĭrĭdīs rīpās. Pĭgrām vēlābāt cānnă pălūdēm. Lōngæ pārvă sŭb ărūndĭnĕ cānnæ. *See Arundo (appendix).*

Cănō, ĭs, cĕcĭnī, cāntūm, ĕrĕ. *To sing.* Nōn cănĭmūs sūrdīs, rēspōndēnt ōmnĭă sīlvæ. V. Syn.—Cāntō, mŏdŭlŏr, cōncĭnō. Phr.—Dō cāntūs, ēxērcĕō. Aēthĕră cāntū mūlcĕō. Fĕrĭo āĕră cāntū. Lætōs ōrĕ cĭērĕ mŏdōs. Mŏdŭlārī cārmĭnĕ vōcĕ. Cāntū fāllĕrĕ cūrās. Nĕmūs cōncēntĭbŭs īmplĕt. Ābsēntēm cāntāt ămīcūm. Dūlcĕ quĕrūntŭr ăvēs. Dūlcĕ sŏnāt cārmĕn. Sīcĭlĭdēs mūsæ paūlō mājōră cănāmŭs. *To celebrate in verse.* Syn.—Cāntō, dīcō, mĕmŏrō, cĕlĕbrō. *See Laudo, Celebro.*

Cănŏr, ōrĭs. m. *Sound of instruments, or of the voice.* Mārtĭŭs īlle ærĭs raūcī cănŏr īncrĕpăt. V. Syn.—Sŏnŭs, sŏnĭtŭs, mŏdī, clāngŏr, cāntŭs. Phr.—Rēs ēst blāndă cănŏr.

Cănōrŭs, ă, ūm. *Harmonious, musical.* Āvĭă tūm rĕsŏnānt ăvĭbūs vīrgūltă cănōrīs. V. Syn.—Sŏnāns, sŏnōrŭs, rĕsŏnāns, ārgūtŭs, dūlcĭs, dūlcĭsŏnāns.

Cāntāmĕn, ĭnĭs. n. *Enchantment.* Ō ŭtĭnām măgĭcæ nōssēm cāntāmĭnă mūsæ. Pr. Syn.—Cāntŭs, īncāntāmēntūm. *See Carmen, Magicus.*

Cāntātōr, ōrĭs. m. *Singer.* Cāntātōr cȳcnūs fūnĕrĭs īpsĕ sŭī. M. Syn.—Cāntŏr.

Cāntātrīx, īcĭs. f. *Singer.* Syn.—Cāntŏr.

Cānthărŭs, ī. m. *Cup.* Ēt grăvĭs āttrītā pēndēbāt cānthărŭs ānsā. V. *See Poculum.*

Cāntĭcūm, ī. n. *Song.* Cāntĭcă quī Nīlī, quī Gādĭtānă sŭsūrrăt. M. Syn.—Cāntŭs, cārmĕn, mĕlŏs.

Cāntĭtŏ, ās, āvī, ātūm, ārĕ. *To sing frequently. See Cano.*

Cāntŏ, ās, āvī, ātūm, ārĕ. *To sing.* Cāntābĭt văcŭŭs cōrām lātrōnĕ vĭātŏr. H. *See Cano.*

Cāntŏr, ōrĭs. m. *Singer.* Syn.—Cāntātŏr.

Cāntŭs, ūs. m. *Song, air, sound of instruments.* Īpsă dŏmūm mūlcēns tĕnĕō Prōsērpĭnă cāntū. Syn.—Cănŏr, cārmĕn, vōx, mĕlŏs, mŏdī, mŏdŭlī, mŏdŭlāmĕn, cōncēntŭs, (*sometimes*) Cămœnă, mūsă. Epith.—Ārgūtŭs, sŏnōrŭs, dūlcĭs, ămœnŭs, lætŭs, grātŭs, rūstĭcŭs, flēbĭlĭs. Phr.—Vōcĭs mŏdŭlāmĕn. Lætūm mūrmŭr. Lĭquĭdæ vōcēs ăvĭum. Vōcĭs jūcūndæ sŏnŭs. *See Cano, Carmen, Musica.*

Cānŭs, ă, ūm. *White.* Cānă lĕgām tĕnĕrā lānūgĭnĕ mālă. V. Syn.—Ālbŭs, cāndēns, cāndĭdŭs, cānēscēns. *See Candidus.*

Căpāx, ācĭs. m. f. & n. *Spacious, vast.* Mūltă căpāx pŏpŭlī cōmmŏdă cīrcŭs hăbĕt. O. Syn.—Āmplŭs, lātŭs, pătēns, spătĭōsŭs, vāstŭs, īngēns.

Căpĕr, rī. m. *Goat.* Nōn ălĭam ōb cūlpām Bācchō căpĕr ōmnĭbŭs ārīs Cædĭtŭr. V. Syn.—Hīrcŭs, (*sometimes*) hædŭs, căprĕŏlŭs. Epith.—Hīrsūtŭs, tōrvŭs, īntōnsŭs. Phr.—Dūx pĕcŏrĭs, căprĭgĕnūm pĕcŭs. Vīrquĕ pătērquĕ grĕgĭs.

Căpēssŏ, ĭs, īvī, ītūm, ĕrĕ. *To take eagerly, to seize. See Capio.*

Căpīllātŭs, ă, ūm. *Covered with hair.* Sīc tē frĕquēntēs aūdĭānt căpīllātī. M. Syn.—Cŏmātŭs, crīnītŭs, īntōnsŭs. Phr.—Cuī căpīllī ĕffūsī, lōngī, dēnsī, flŭēntēs. Căpīllīs hŏrrĭdŭs. Lārgŭs cŏmæ. Cuī căpŭt īntōnsŭs. *See Capillus.*

Căpīllŭs, ī. m. *Hair.* Mōllēs ĭmĭtābĭtŭr ærĕ căpīllōs. H. Syn.—Cæsărĭēs, cŏmă, crīnēs. Epith.—Aūrĕŭs, flāvŭs, nĭgĕr, vĕnūstŭs, lōngŭs. Phr.—Ēt nīgrō crīnĕ dĕcōrŭs. Stĕtĕrūntquĕ cŏmæ. *False hair.* Syn.—Gălērŭs.

Căpĭō, ĭs, cēpī, cāptūm, ĕrĕ. *To take, to seize.* Ārma āmēns căpĭō, nēc sāt rătĭōnĭs ĭn ārmīs. V. Syn.—Căpēssŏ, prĕhēndŏ, prēndŏ, sūmŏ, ārrĭpĭŏ. Phr.—Căpĕ sāxă mănū. *To capture. See Vincio, Captivus. To deceive.* Syn.—Dēcĭpĭŏ, fāllŏ. *To understand.* Syn.—Pērcĭpĭŏ, īntēllĕgŏ, cōmprēndŏ, āssĕquŏr.

Căpīstrūm, ī. n. *Halter.* Aūdĭăt, īnquĕ vĭcēm dēt mōllĭbŭs ōră căpīstrīs. V. Syn.—Frēnūm, hăbēnă, lōrūm, lŭpī, lŭpātă. *See Frenum.*

Căpră, æ. f. *She-goat.* Ēccĕ fĕræ, sāxī dējēctæ vērtĭcĕ, cāpræ. V. Syn.—Căpēllă, căprĕă. *See Caper.*

Cāptīvŭs, ī. m. *Captive, prisoner of war.* Īnfēlīx Stўgĭō dūcōr cāptīvă tўrānnō. Syn.—Cāptŭs. Phr.—Sub jugā mīssŭs. Mănūs pōst tērgă rĕvīnctŭs. Jām nōbīs aūdāx Gērmānĭă sērvĭt.

Cāptŏ, ās, āvī, ātūm, ārĕ. *To try to seize, to seize.* Tūm lăquĕīs cāptārĕ fĕrās ēt fāllĕrĕ vīscō. Syn.—Āppĕtŏ, ĭnhĭŏ, āffēctŏ, nītŏr ĭn, mōlĭŏr.

Cāptŭs, ūs. m. *Understanding, intelligence.* Syn.—Īntēllēctŭs, vīs.

Căpŭt, ĭs. n. *Head.* Cēntūm lūmĭnĭbūs cīnctūm, căpŭt Ārgŭs hăbēbăt. O. Syn.—Vērtēx, cērvīx, frōns, cōllūm, tēmpŏră, căpīllī. Phr.—Rĕdĭmītă laūrō. Prōmīssōs ēffūndēns vērtĭcĕ crīnēs. Fūndĕrĕ lūmĕn ăpēx.

Cārbăsŭs, ī. f. & Cārbăsă, ōrūm. n. *Fine linen; sail.* Flūxă cŏlōrātīs āstrīngūnt cārbăsă gēmmīs. L. Syn.—Ămīctŭs, pāllă; vēlūm, līntĕūm.

Cārbŏ, ōnĭs. m. *Coal, carbon.* Syn.—Prūnă.

Cārcĕr, ĕrĭs. m. *Prison.* Vīdĕrāt īmmēnsām tĕnĕbrōso īn cārcĕrĕ lūcēm. L. Syn.—Cūstōdĭă, claūstră, (*also*) vīncŭlă. Phr.—Sĭnĕ lūcĕ tēctūm, dŏmŭs.

Cārcĕrēs, ūm. m. *Barriers.* Sīgnă tŭbæ dĕdĕrānt, cūm cārcĕrĕ prōnŭs ŭtērquĕ Ēmĭcăt. O. Syn.—Claūstră.

Cārdŏ, ĭnĭs. m. *Hinge.* Ēmōtī prōcūmbūnt cārdĭnĕ pōstēs. V. Epith.—Aērātŭs, fērrātŭs, sŏlĭdŭs, strīdēns. Phr.—Pōstēsque ā cārdĭnĕ vēllĭt.

Cārdŭēlĭs, ĭs. f. *A goldfinch, thistlefinch.* (*See Appendix under list of Birds.*)

Cārē. adv. *Dearly.* Syn.—Māgnī, māgnō. Phr.—Nōn pārvō lŭĭt.

Cărēns, ēntĭs. m. f. & n. *That which is lacking, or in need of.* Vānāquĕ cărēntĭă pōmpā Jūră plăcēnt. L. Syn.—Cāssŭs, ēxpērs, ĕgēns, ēxsōrs, īndĭgŭs, nūdŭs, nūdātŭs, spŏlĭātŭs.

Cărĕŏ, ēs, ŭī, ĭtūm, ērĕ. *To lack, to have need of.* Jāmquĕ pŭdēt vānās fīnĕ cărērĕ prĕcēs. O. Syn.—Ĕgĕō, īndĭgĕŏ, prīvŏr, văcŏ, ēxclūdō̆, dēsīdĕrō̆. Phr.—Sūm ĕgēns, ĕxpērs, ēxsōrs, nūdŭ̄s, īmmūnĭ̄s.

Cărĭēs, ēm, ē. f. (*Other cases not used*). *Rottenness, decay.* Syn.—Sĭtŭ̄s, pŭ̄trō̆r, tābūm (*used only in the ablative*).

Cărīnă, ǣ. f. *Keel.* Pīnĕă cōnjūngēns īnflēxǣ tēctă cărīnǣ. Phr.—Pūppīs vălĭdā fūndātā cărīnā. *Used also for vessel. See Navis.*

Cărĭōsŭ̄s, ă, ūm. *Decayed, rotten.* Syn.—Pŭ̄trĭ̄s. Phr.—Cărĭē ădēsŭ̄s, ēxēsŭ̄s, cōrrūptŭ̄s, vĭtĭātŭ̄s.

Cārĭtās, ātĭ̄s. f. *Dearness. See Penuria.* Fig—*Esteem, affection.* Syn.—Ămō̆r, āffēctŭ̄s, stŭdĭūm. *See Amor, amicitia.*

Cārmĕn, ĭnĭ̄s. n. *Verse, poem, song.* Īllĕ cŏlīt tērrās, īllī mĕă cārmĭnă cūrǣ. V. Syn.—Vērsŭ̄s, mŏdī, nŭmĕrī, mūsă, lȳrā̆. Epith.—Cœ̄lēstĕ, dīvīnūm, dūlcĕ, lēnĕ, cănōrūm, īngĕnĭōsūm. Phr.—Vērbă mŏdŭlāndă fĭdĭbŭ̄s. Mūsārūm gaūdĭă. Phœbī āfflāmĕn. Dūlcĭă mēndācĭă vātūm. Īn pĕdēs vērbă cŏāctă. *To make verses.* Phr.—Vērsūs cănĕrĕ, cōndĕrĕ, dīcĕrĕ, fūndĕrĕ, mŏdŭlārī. Vērsĭbŭ̄s īnclūsa ēst sēntēntĭă.

Cārnĭfēx, ĭcĭ̄s. m. *Executioner.* Cārnĭfĭcī dūrās prǣbŭĭt īllă mănūs. O. Syn.—Tōrtō̆r, līctō̆r. Phr.—Lēgūm vīndēx.

Cārnĭfĭcīnă, ǣ. *The office of executioner. See Supplicium.*

Cărō̆, cārnĭ̄s. f. *Flesh, meat.* Cūrvāt ăpēr lāncēs cārnēm vītāntĭ̄s ĭnērtēm. H. Syn.—Fĕrīnă. Phr.—Sēd mălĕ vīvă căro ēst.

Cārpĭnŭ̄s, ī. f. *The hornbeam, a species of oak or beech.* (*See Appendix under list of Trees, etc.*)

Cārpō̆, ĭ̄s, psī, ptūm, ĕrĕ. *To pluck, to gather, to cull.* Prīmūs vērĕ rŏsam ātque aūtūmnō cārpĕrĕ pōmă. V. Syn.—Lĕgō̆, cōllĭgō̆, mĕtō̆, dēmĕtō̆. *To enjoy.* Syn.—Frŭō̆r. Phr.—Cārpĕ dĭēm. Cārpēbāt sōmnōs.

Cārptīm. adv. *In small portions, at different times.* Syn.—Mĭnūtātīm.

Cārŭ̄s, ă, ūm. *Dear, costly.* Nōn īllās fīxūm cārās ēffēcĕrăt aūrūm. Prop. Fig.—Cārĕ pŭēr, mĕă sōla ēt sērā vŏlūptās. Syn.—Ămātŭ̄s, ămīcŭ̄s, dīlēctŭ̄s, āccēptŭ̄s, grātŭ̄s, dūlcĭ̄s, cārīssĭmŭ̄s. Phr.—Ānte ălĭōs cārŭ̄s. Vītā cārĕ măgĭ̄s. Vītā frātĕr ămābĭlĭō̆r. Ō lūcĕ măgīs dīlēctă sŏrōrī. V.

Căsă, ǣ. f. *Hut, cabin, cottage.* Ātque hŭmĭlēs hăbĭtārĕ căsās ēt fīgĕrĕ sērvōs. V. Syn.—Căsŭlă, tŭgŭrĭūm, māgālĭă, măpālĭă, dŏmŭ̄s. Epith.—Rūstĭcă, ăgrēstĭ̄s, mŏdĭcă, pārvă, vīlĭ̄s. Phr.—Rūstĭcă tēctă. Lărēs āngūstī. Dŏmŭ̄s hŭmĭlĭ̄s. Strāmĭnĕ tēctă dŏmŭ̄s. Dŏmūs sōrdĭdă fūmō.

Cāsĕŭ̄s, ī. m. *Cheese.* Cāndĭdŭs ēlīxǣ mīscētūr cāsĕūs hērbǣ. O. Phr.—Lāctīs māssă cŏāctī. Lāc dēnsūm. Īn nĭvĕās lāc cōgĕrĕ glēbās. Fēcūndī mūnĕră rūrĭ̄s.

Cāssēs, ĭūm. m. *Nets, snares.* Dēcĭdĭt īn cāssēs prædă pĕtītă mĕōs. O. Syn.—Lăqueī, plăgæ, rētĭă. *See Rete.*

Cāssĭs, ĭdĭs. f. *Helmet.* Spīcŭlă cūm pīctīs hærēnt īn cāssĭdĕ pēnnīs. O. Syn.—Cāssĭdă, găleă. Phr.—Tēctī scūtīs ēt cāssĭde ăhēnā Ārmātī. *See Galea.*

Cāssŭs, ă, ūm. *Empty.* Syn.—Ĭnānĭs, văcŭŭs.

Căstănĕă, æ. f. *Chestnut-tree* (*See Appendix*). *Also chestnut, the nut.* Phr.—Căstănĕă nūx.

Cāstē. adv. *Religiously, chastely.* Jūstĭtĭāmquĕ sŭī cāstē plācāssĕ părēntĭs, Īllō quæ tēmplūm pēctŏrĕ sēmpĕr hăbĕt. O. Syn.—Pūrē, pŭdīcē, hŏnēstē.

Cāstēllūm, ī. n. *Fort, fortress.* Aūt mōntānă sĕdet circum cāstēllă sŭb ārmĭs. V. Syn.—Ōppĭdūm, ārx. *See Arx.*

Cāstīgātĭŏ, ōnĭs. f. *Correction, reprimand.* Syn.—Ōbjūrgātĭŏ. *Punishment.* Syn.—Cēnsūră, pœnă.

Cāstīgātŏr, ōrĭs. m. *One who punishes or reprimands.* Cāstīgātōrquĕ mĭnōrūm. H. Syn.—Ōbjūrgātŏr, rĕprĕhēnsŏr, cēnsŏr.

Cāstīgŏ, ās, āvī, ātūm, ārĕ. *To reprimand.* Cāstīgātque aūdītquĕ dŏlōs, sŭbĭgītquĕ fătērī. V. Syn.—Ōbjūrgŏ, īncrĕpŏ. *To punish.* Syn.—Pūnĭŏ, plēctŏ, fĕrĭŏ, mūlctŏ. *To correct a work.* Syn.—Cōrrĭgŏ.

Cāstĭtās, ātĭs. f. *Chastity, purity.* Mĕtŭēns āltĕrĭūs vĭrī Cērtō fœdĕrĕ cāstĭtās. H. Syn.—Pŭdŏr, pŭdīcĭtĭă, vīrgĭnĭtās. Phr.—Cāstă vītă. Cāstī mōrēs. Cāstī jūră pŭdōrĭs. Īntāctūs flōs pŭdīcĭtĭæ. Nūllā rĕpărābĭlĭs ārtĕ. Īngĕnŭæ sīgnă pŭdīcĭtĭæ.

Cāstră, ōrūm. n. *Camp.* Clāssēm quæ lătĕrī cāstrōrum ādjūnctă lătēbăt. V. Syn.—Tēntōrĭă. Phr.—Tēntōrĭă ērēctă. Mūltō rĕfērtă mīlĭtĕ. Īn tūtō lŏcātă lŏcō. Mĕdĭīs īmpŏsĭtă cāmpīs. Cāstră mētārī. Tūtō lŏcō ērĭgĕrĕ, pōnĕrĕ, sīgnārĕ cāstră. Cōnsīdūnt cāstrīs ēt mœnĭă vāllānt. Cāstra ĭnĭmīcă pĕtūnt. *Troops.* Syn.—Āgmĭnă, cătērvæ, tūrmæ, phălāngēs.

Cāstŭs, ă, ūm. *Chaste, pure.* Cāstă pŭdīcĭtĭām sērvāt dŏmŭs. V. Syn.—Pŭdēns, pŭdīcŭs, pūrŭs, hŏnēstŭs, īllībātŭs, īntĕmĕrātŭs. Phr.—Quō nōn ēst cāstĭŏr āltĕr. Nŏcŭīt cuī nūllă vŏlūptās. Nūnquām mōllī lĭbīdĭnĕ vīctŭs. Laūdĕ pŭdīcĭtĭæ cĕlĕbĕr. Ănĭmōque ēt cōrpŏrĕ cāstŭs. Cāstīquĕ mŏdēstĭă vūltūs. Nōn ōblītă pŭdōrĭs.

Cāsŭs, ūs. m. *Fall, downfall.* Tēmpŏrĕ jam ēx īllō cāsūs mĭhĭ cōgnĭtŭs ūrbĭs. V. Syn.—Rŭīnă, lāpsŭs, ēxcĭdĭūm. Phr.—Cēlsæ grăvĭōrĕ cāsū Dēcĭdūnt tūrrēs. Ēvērsæ fūmāntĭă Trōjæ Ēxcĭdĭă. *Misfortune.* Syn.—Clādēs, ēxĭtĭūm, pērnĭcĭēs. Phr.—Dūrī sōlātĭă cāsūs. Dī, tālem āvērtĭtĕ cāsūm! Cāsū cōncūssŭs ăcērbō.

Pēr tāntă pĕrīcŭlă cāsŭs Īnsĕquĭtŭr. *Danger, peril.* Syn.—Dīscrīmĕn, pĕrīcŭlūm. Phr.—Pēr tōt dīscrīmĭnă rērūm. Cāsūs ēvāsĕrăt ōmnēs. Tōt vōlvĕrĕ cāsūs. *Chance, lot.* Syn.—Ālĕă, fōrtūnă, sōrs. Phr.—Īncērtōquĕ flŭūnt mōrtālĭă cāsū. Cāsūs ăbĭēs vīsūră mărīnōs.

Cătē. adv. *Skilfully.* Syn.—Căllĭdē, scītē, sōlērtĕr.

Cătēnă, æ. f. *A chain.* Tāntūm nē rĕlĭgēr dūrā cāptīvă cătēnā. O. Syn.—Vīncŭlūm, vīncŭlă, vīnclūm, vīnclă, cōmpĕdēs, lăquĕŭs, mănĭcæ, nēxŭs, nōdŭs, lōră(ōrūm), lĭgāmĕn, fūnĭs. Phr.—Grăcĭlēs ēx ærĕ cătēnæ. Nēxæ pēr cōllă cătēnæ. Strīdōr fērrī trāctæquĕ cătēnæ. Fērrātæ cōllō sŏnŭērĕ cătēnæ. Vīncītquĕ mănūs pōst tērgă cătēnīs. Fig.—*Ties of tenderness.* Syn.—Vīncŭlă, nēxŭs, nōdŭs. Phr.—Vīncŭla ămīcĭtĭæ.

Cătērvă, æ. f. *Band or troop of soldiers.* Dīffŭgĭūnt ĕquĭtūm tūrmæ pĕdĭtūmquĕ cătērvæ. H. Syn.—Āgmĕn, cŏhōrs, ēxērcĭtŭs, glŏbŭs, lĕgĭŏ, mănĭplŭs, ăcĭēs, mănŭs, phălānx. Phr.—Spūmāntēs cædĕ, fūlgēntēs ærĕ cătērvæ. Flōrēntēs ærĕ cătērvās. *Crowd (in general).* Syn.—Tūrbă. Phr.—Māgnā cŏmĭtāntĕ cătērvā. Stīpāntĕ cătērvā.

Căthĕdră, æ. f. *Chair, seat.* Syn.—Sēllă, sĕdīlĕ, sēdēs, sŏlĭūm.

Cătīnŭs, ī. m. *A large dish or plate.* Syn.—Cătīllŭs, părōpsĭs, dīscŭs, lānx.

Cătŭlŭs, ī. m. *A little dog.* Syn.—Cătēllŭs, cănĭs. Phr.—Cătŭlōrūm blāndă prŏpāgŏ. Sīc cănĭbūs cătŭlōs sĭmĭlēs.

Cătŭs, ă, ūm. *Skilful, adroit.* Fĕrōs, cūltūs hŏmĭnūm rĕcēntūm Vōcĕ fōrmāstī cătŭs. H. Syn.—Căllĭdŭs, caūtŭs, prūdēns, pĕrītŭs, sōlērs. Phr.—Jăcŭlārī caūtŭs. Cătŭs ārtĕ pălæstræ.

Cātŭs, ī. m. *A cat.* Syn.—Cāttă, fēlĭs, ælūrŭs. Phr.—Mūrĭbŭs īnfēnsă. Nātă dŏlīs. Sōmni ĭnĭmīcŭs.

Caūdă, æ. f. *Tail.* Quæque īmā grădĭēns vērrīt vēstīgĭă caūdā. V. Phr.—Hīrtæ lūdībrĭă caūdæ. Mōllī caūdæ vērbĕrĕ.

Caūdēx, ĭcĭs. m. *The trunk of a tree.* Syn.—Trūncŭs, stīpĕs.

Caūlă, æ & Caūlæ, ārūm. f. *The entrance of a sheepfold.* Āc vĕlŭtī plēnō lŭpŭs īnsĭdĭātŭs ŏvīlī Cūm frĕmĭt ād caūlās. V. Syn.—Ŏvīlĕ, stăbŭlūm, sēptă(pl.).

Caūrŭs, ī. (Cōrŭs, ī). m. *The northwest wind.* Sēmpĕr hĭēms, spīrāntēs frīgŏră caūrī. V. Phr.—Vēntŭs ăb ōccāsū flāns, spīrāns. Fĕrĭēns pōntūm, nūbēs glŏmĕrāns. Cœlī fūscātŏr Ēōī. Sīlvām cūm flāmĭnă caūrī pērflānt.

Caūsă, æ. f. *Cause, source, origin.* Ēt caūsās cōgnōscĭtĕ rērūm. Pers. Syn.—Căpŭt, fōns, ŏrīgŏ, prīncĭpĭūm, rādīx, sēmĕn, aūctŏr. Phr.—Tāntī caūsă căpūtquĕ mălī. Hīnc mĭhĭ prīmă mălī lābēs.

Hīnc mĭhĭ prīncĭpĭūm dāmnī. Hīnc īllæ lăcrĭmæ. *Motive, reason, pretext,* Syn.—Rătĭŏ, caūsă. Phr.—Caūsă fŭīt lūctūs. Pĭă caūsă cŏēgĭt. *Process, law-suit.* Syn.—Līs.

Caūsĭdĭcŭs, ī. m. *Lawyer.* Nōn sūm caūsĭdĭcūs, nĕc ămārīs lītĭbŭs āptŭs. M. Syn.—Pătrōnŭs, dēfēnsŏr, āctŏr, ōrātŏr. Phr.—Caūsārūm āctŏr. Ēlŏquĭō præstāns. Fācūndō māxĭmŭs ōrĕ. Fāmă dĕcūsquĕ fŏrī. Sōllĭcĭtī tūtēlă rĕī. Ăgĕrĕ caūsās ēt cōmpōnĕrĕ lītēs. Caūsīs clārŭs ăgēndīs. Lītĭs ămāns. Quī fŏrūm māgnīs clāmōrĭbŭs īmplĕt. Īrās ēt vērbă lŏcāns.

Caūtē. adv. *Prudently.* Syn.—Caūtĭŭs, prūdēntĕr.

Caūtēs, ĭs. f. *Rock, cliff.* Stārĕ vĕl īnsānīs caūtēs ōbnōxĭă vēntīs. Tib. Syn. Rūpēs, scŏpŭlūm, sāxūm, sĭlēx. Phr.—Sālsă spūmānt āspērgĭnĕ caūtēs. Caūtĭbŭs ōbjēctīs rējēctāt cærŭlă.

Caūtŭs, ă, ūm. *Prudent, cautious; skilful.* Īn vērbīs ĕtĭām tĕnŭīs caūtūsquĕ sĕrēndīs. H. Syn.—Prūdēns, prōvĭdŭs, cōnsūltŭs, cīrcūmspēctŭs; pĕrītŭs, săgāx, sōlērs, īngĕnĭōsŭs. Phr.—Caūtūs ădītō. *Cunning, deceitful.* Syn.—Āstūtŭs, dŏlōsŭs, văfĕr, vērsūtŭs, cāllĭdŭs.

Căvĕă, æ. f. *Cave, ditch.* Syn.—Căvŭs, āntrūm, căvērnă, fŏvĕă, fōssă. *Cage.* Syn.—Clāthrī, claūstrūm. *Amphitheatre.* Syn.—Āmpĭthĕātrūm, cīrcŭs, ărēnă.

Căvĕŏ, ēs, cāvī, caūtūm, ērĕ. *To be on one's guard, to take care.* Cōmmīsīssĕ căvēt quōd mōx mūtārĕ lăbōrĕt. H. Syn.—Præcăvĕŏ, ādvērtŏ, vĭdĕŏ, āntĕvĭdĕŏ, prōvĭdĕŏ, prōspĭcĭŏ, vītŏ, fŭgĭŏ, dēclīnŏ. Phr.—Mălūm vītārĕ căvēndō. Aūt hūmānă pārūm cāvīt nātūră. Ēt trīstēs ănĭmī căvērĕ mōrsūs.

Căvērnă, æ. f. *Cave, cavern.* Īnsŏnŭērĕ căvæ gĕmĭtūmquĕ dĕdērĕ căvērnæ. V. Syn.—Āntrūm, lătĕbră, spēlūncă, spĕcŭs. Phr.—Ābrūptīs spĕcŭs ātră căvērnīs. Cūrvīsque īmmūgĭīt Aētnă căvērnīs. Ūmbrōsæ pĕnĭtūs pătŭērĕ căvērnæ. *Lair (of animals).* Syn.—Āntrūm, spĕcŭs.

Căvīllă, æ & Căvīllātĭŏ, ōnĭs. f. *Raillery, wit.* Syn.—Căvīllūm, jŏcātĭŏ, jŏcī, dīctērĭūm, sălēs, scōmmă.

Căvīllŏr, ārĭs, ātŭs sūm, ārī. *To taunt, to jeer, to jest.* Syn.—Rīdĕŏ, īrrīdĕŏ, jŏcŏr, lūdŏ, īllūdŏ. Phr.—Prŏcācĭtĕr īllūdŏ, īrrīdĕŏ. Prŏtērvīs cōnvīcĭīs lăcēssŏ.

Căvŏ, ās, āvī, ātūm, ārĕ. *To hollow out.* Nēc fōrmam āccĭpĭūnt, fērrōquĕ căvāntŭr ăcūtō. V. Syn.—Ēxcăvŏ, fŏdĭŏ, ēffŏdĭŏ. Phr.—Gūttă căvāt lāpĭdēm. Căvātquĕ tēllūrēm. Căvāt ārbŏrĕ līntrēs. Mōllī sāxă căvāntŭr ăquā.

Căvŭs, ă, ūm. *Hollow, hollowed out.* Sūstĭnĕt īmpŏsĭtōs sūmmā căvŭs ālvĕŭs ŭndā. O. Syn.—Căvātŭs, cōncăvŭs, ēffōssŭs, prŏfŭndŭs, āltŭs. Phr.—Dāt sīgnum ǣrĕ căvō. Căvā trăbĕ cŭrrĭmŭs ǣquŏr. Căvīs ēxspēctānt tŭrrĭbŭs hōstēm. *Empty.* Syn.—Ĭnānĭs, văcŭŭs.

Căvŭs, ī. m. *Ditch, trough, cavern.* Syn.—Căvŭm, āntrŭm, căvērnă, fōssă, spĕcŭs, fŏrāmĕn.

Cēdŏ, ĭs, cēssī, cēssŭm, ĕrĕ. *To retire, to go away.* Īllă mănēnt īmmōtă lŏcīs, nĕc ăb ōrdĭnĕ cēdūnt. V. Syn.—Ēxcēdŏ, rĕcēdŏ, cōncēdŏ, ēxĕŏ, ăbĕŏ. Phr.—Cēdēmŭs cāmpīs. Cēdēs cŏēmptīs sāltĭbŭs. Cēssĭt ăb ōrĕ fŭrŏr. Nēc cēdĕrĕ quōquām. *To yield.* Syn.—Cōncēdŏ. Phr.—Cēdĕ Dĕō. Cēdĭt ărēnă pĕdī. *To be inferior to, to yield in dignity.* Syn.—Vīncŏr, sŭpĕrŏr. *To succumb, to be overwhelmed.* Syn.—Vīncŏr, fătīscŏ, dēfĭcĭŏ. Phr.—Nĭmĭō cŏmĭtŭm nē cēdĕ tĭmōrī. Cēdūnt lŭmĭnă sōmnō. Cēdēbāt vīctă pŏtēstās. *To grant.* Syn.—Dō, cōncēdŏ, trĭbŭŏ.

Cĕdrŭs, ī. f. *The cedar tree.* (*See Appendix under list of Trees, etc.*)

Cĕlĕbĕr, ĕbrĭs, ĕbrĕ. *Thronged, frequented.* Cīrcŭs ĕrāt pōmpā cĕlĕbĕr nŭmĕrōquĕ dĕōrŭm. O. Syn.—Frĕquēns, crēbĕr. *Celebrated, illustrious.* Syn.—Clārŭs, prǣclārŭs, īllūstrĭs, īnclȳtŭs, īnsīgnĭs, nōbĭlĭs, nōtŭs, cōnspĭcŭŭs, mĕmŏrātŭs, ēxĭmĭŭs, ēgrĕgĭŭs, laūdātŭs, spēctābĭlĭs, spēctātŭs. Phr.—Cĕlĕbrī fāmā laūdātŭs ĭn ōrbĕ. Fāmā cĕlĕbērrĭmŭs. Fāmā sŭpĕr ǣthĕră nōtŭs. Fāmā īngēns. Fēlīx ǣtērnō nōmĭnĕ. Vīctōrquĕ vĭrŭm vŏlĭtārĕ pĕr ōră. Nōtīssĭmă fāmā Īnsŭlă. *Consecrated.* Syn.—Săcrātŭs, dĭcātŭs, săcĕr.

Cĕlĕbrŏ, ās, āvī, ātŭm, ārĕ. *To frequent, to haunt.* Cūjŭs ĭnaūrātī cĕlĕbrārūnt līmĭnă cūrrūs. Prop. Syn.—Frĕquēntŏ. *To celebrate, to solemnize.* Phr.—Cūnctī lǣtŭm cĕlĕbrēmŭs hŏnōrēm. Fēstōs ālbātūs cĕlĕbrĕt *To praise.* Syn.—Laūdŏ, cănŏ, mĕmŏrŏ, ēffĕrŏ, prǣdĭcŏ.

Cĕlĕr, ĕrĭs, ĕrĕ. *Prompt, rapid, quick.* Īllă vŏlăt, cĕlĕrīque ăd tērrām tūrbĭnĕ fērtŭr. V. Syn.—Cĭtŭs, cōncĭtŭs, cĭtātŭs, fēstīnāns, fēstīnŭs, vēlōx, prǣcēps, răpĭdŭs, lĕvĭs, pērnīx, prǣpĕs, prōmptŭs, vŏlāns, vŏlŭcrĭs. Phr.—Haūd sēgnĭs. Ōcĭŏr eūrō, aūrā, vēntō, săgīttā, fūlmĭnĕ. Pĕdĭbŭs cĕlĕr. Pērnīcĭŏr ālĭtĕ vēntō. Fig. Syn.—Gnāvŭs, īmpĭgĕr, ăgĭlĭs, ălăcĕr. *Joyful, exuberant.* Syn.—Ācĕr, fērvĭdŭs, ălăcĕr, prǣcēps.

Cĕlĕrĭtās, ātĭs. f. *Quickness.* Syn.—Vēlōcĭtās, lĕvĭtās.

Cĕlĕrĭtĕr. adv. *Quickly.* Syn.—Cĭtŏ, cōnfēstīm, ēxtēmplō, ōcĭŭs, prōmptē, prŏpĕrē, lĕvĭtĕr. Phr.—Haūd mŏră.

Cĕlĕrŏ, ās, āvī, ātūm, ārĕ. *To hasten, to hurry.* Sēd cĕlĕrārĕ fŭgam īn sīlvās, ēt fīdĕrĕ nōctī. V. Syn.—Āccĕlĕrŏ, fēstīnŏ, mātūrŏ, prŏpĕrŏ. Phr.—Īnde ălĭæ cĕlĕrānt cūrsūs. Īllă vīām cĕlĕrāns.

Cēllă, æ. f. *Cellar, larder.* Syn.—Ăpŏthēcă, cēllārĭūm. *Cell, small chamber.* Syn.—Cēllŭlă.

Cēlŏ, ās, āvī, ātūm, ārĕ. *To conceal.* Sēd bĕnĕ cēlētūr, bĕnĕ sī cēlābĭtŭr īndēx. O. Syn.—Ābdŏ, ābscōndŏ, tĕgŏ, ōbtĕgŏ, ōccŭlŏ, ōccūltŏ. Phr.—Vūltūm mănĭbūs cēlārĕ. Cēlāntŭr ărūndĭnĕ fōssæ. Nēc sē pŏtŭĭt cēlārĕ tĕnēbrīs. Grānūm sūb cōrtĭcĕ cēlānt. *To keep silent about.* Syn.—Tĕgŏ, dīssĭmŭlŏ, sĭlĕŏ, tăcĕŏ, prĕmŏ.

Cēlsŭs, ă, ūm. *High, elevated.* Fĕrĭūntquĕ cēlsōs fūlgŭră mōntēs. H. Syn.—Ēxcēlsŭs, præcēlsŭs, āltŭs, ărdŭŭs, sūblīmĭs. Phr.—Cēlso ē vērtĭcĕ mōntĭs. Stāns cēlsa īn pūppī. Cēlsum īn cōrnŭă cērvūm. *Haughty.* Syn.—Sŭpērbŭs.

Cēnsĕŏ, ēs, ŭī, ūm, ērĕ. *To esteem, to consider, to judge.* Quām scĭt ŭtērquĕ lĭbēns, cēnsēbo, ēxērcĕăt ārtēm. H. Syn.—Ārbĭtrŏr, ēxīstĭmŏ, jūdĭcŏ, pŭtŏ, rĕŏr, sēntĭŏ. *To decree.* Syn.—Ŏpīnŏr, dēcērnŏ, jŭbĕŏ.

Cēnsŏr, ōrĭs. m. *A censor, a Roman magistrate.* Syn.—Mōrūm măgīstĕr, ārbĭtĕr, jūdēx. *A critic, censurer.* Syn.—Cāstīgātŏr, ōbjūrgātŏr, rĕprĕhēnsŏr.

Cēnsŭs, ūs. m. *A census, enumeration.* Syn.—Cēnsĭŏ, rĕcēnsŭs. *The valuation of a man's estate, one's property, wealth.* Syn.—Bŏnă, ŏpēs, rĕdĭtŭs, rēs. Phr.—Dāt cēnsūs hŏnōrēs. Cēnsūs aūgērĕ pātērnōs.

Cēntūmvĭrī, ōrūm. m. *The Centumviri, Roman magistrates.* Phr.—Cēntūm jūdĭcēs. Cēntēnŭs jūdēx.

Cēră, æ. f. *Wax.* Hīnc ārtĕ rĕcēntēs Ēxcūdūnt cērās. V. Phr.—Ārtĕ lăbōrātă. Rĕdŏlēns thȳmūm. Ādmōtō călōrĕ lĭquēns. Călōrĭs īmpătĭēns. Hȳmēttĭă sōlĕ Cēră rĕmōllēscĭt.

Cĕrăsŭs, ī. f. *The cherry tree. (See Appendix under list of Trees, etc.)*

Cērātŭs, ă, ūm. *Waxed, smeared with wax.* Phr.—Cērā ōblĭtŭs, ūnctŭs.

Cĕrĕbrōsŭs, ă, ūm. *Headstrong.* Syn.—Stŏmăchōsŭs.

Cĕrĕbrūm, ī. n. *The brain, the head.* Ōssăquĕ dīspērgīt cĕrĕbrō pērmīxtă crŭēntō. V. Spārsōque īnfēctă cĕrĕbrō. V. Fig.—*The head, mind, reason. See Caput, Mens.*

Cērĕŭs, ă, ūm. *Waxen, smeared with wax.* Syn.—Cērātŭs. Fig.—*Flexible, pliable.* Syn.—Mōllĭs, dūctĭlĭs, trāctābĭlĭs, tĕnĕr, flēxĭlĭs, flēxĭbĭlĭs.

Cērĕŭs, ī. m. *A wax taper.* Syn.—Cāndēlă, fūnālĭă, lŭcērnă. Phr.—Trĕmŭlā lūcĕ cŏrūscāns. Ērĭpĭēs nōctēm. Vīncēns tĕnĕbrās.

Cērnŏ, ĭs, crēvī, crētūm, ĕrĕ. *To separate.* Prōtĭnŭs īnnŭmĕrīs ōmnĭă cērnĕ căvīs. O. Syn.—Ēxcērnŏ, sēpārŏ, dīvĭdŏ. *To see distinctly.* Syn.—Vĭdĕŏ, āspĭcĭŏ, cōnspĭcĭŏ, pērspĭcĭŏ, īntŭĕŏr. Phr.—Lūmĭnĕ, ŏcŭlīs lūstrŏ, pērlūstrŏ. Cērnĕrĕ ăcūtē, ăcūtūm. *To decide.* Syn.—Dēcērnŏ.

Cērnŭŭs, ă, ūm. *Stooping, bending.* Īmplĭcăt, ējēctōque īncūmbīt cērnŭŭs ārmō. V. Syn.—Ācclīvĭs, prōnŭs, prǣcēps.

Cērtāmĕn, ĭnĭs. n. *Conflict, battle.* Aēquō gĕrĭtūr cērtāmĭnĕ bēllūm. L. Syn.—Bēllūm, Mārs, prœlĭūm, pūgnă. Phr.—Dūrī, rĭgĭdī cērtāmĭnă Mārtĭs. Pūgna āspĕră sūrgĭt. Prŏcŭl ā cērtāmĭnĕ pūgnă. *Effort, attempt.* Syn.—Ārdŏr, cōnātŭs, cōnāmĕn, īmpētŭs. *A game, or exercise.* Syn.—Lūdī.

Cērtātīm. adv. *With rivalry, earnestly, eagerly.* Phr.—Pārī ārdōrĕ. Ănĭmīs, stŭdĭīs cērtāntĭbŭs ōmnēs.

Cērtātĭŏ, ōnĭs. f. *Combat. See Certamen.*

Cērtātŭs, ūs. m. *Struggle, combat.* Syn.—Cērtāmĕn, cērtātĭŏ.

Cērtē & Cērtō. adv. *Certainly, assuredly.* Syn.—Ēquĭdēm, nǣ, prŏfēctō, vērē. Phr.—Vēră lŏquŏr.

Cērtŏ, ās, āvī, ātūm, ārĕ. *To strive, to contest, to fight.* Tāntūmque ănĭmīs cērtātĭs ĭnīquīs. V. Syn.—Dēcērtŏ, cōnflīgŏ, cōngrĕdĭŏr, dīmĭcŏ, pūgnŏ, cērnŏ, dēcērnŏ. Phr.—Cērtāmĕn ĭnīrĕ. Pūgnām cōmmīttĕrĕ. Dēcērnĕrĕ fērrō. Cōnfērrĕ mănūs. Tēntārĕ pĕrīcŭlă bēllī. Vāstō cērtāmĭnĕ tēndūnt. *To dispute, to argue.* Syn.—Cōntēndŏ.

Cērtŭs, ă, ūm. *Certain.* Rĕquĭēs ĕă cērtă lăbōrūm. V. Syn.—Clārŭs, mănĭfēstŭs, īndŭbĭtātŭs. Phr.—Nōn dŭbĭŭs, nōn īncērtŭs. Nōn īnfĭtĭāndŭs. Aūspĭcĭīs mănĭfēstă fĭdēs. Dĕī cērtīssĭmă prōlēs. *Worthy of trust, faithful.* Syn.—Vērŭs, vērāx, fĭdēlĭs, fīdŭs. Phr.—Nōn mēndāx, nōn fāllāx. *Resolute, courageous.* Syn.—Fīrmŭs, fōrtĭs, fīdēns, aūdāx. *Fixed, determined.* Syn.—Fīxŭs, īmmōtŭs, fīrmŭs, stăbĭlĭs, rătŭs.

Cērvīx, īcĭs. f. *The neck.* Īt crŭŏr, īnque hŭmĕrōs cērvīx cōllāpsă rĕcūmbĭt. V. Syn.—Cōllūm. Phr.—Rŏsĕā cērvīcĕ rĕfūlsĭt. Mārmŏrĕā căpŭt ā cērvīcĕ rĕvūlsūm. Fig.—*Pride.* Syn.—Sŭpērbĭă.

Cērvŭs, ī. m. *A stag.* Cērvī cœlō căpĭta āltă fĕrēntēs Cōrnĭbŭs ărbŏrĕīs. V. Syn.—Cērvă. Phr.—Pērnīx fĕră. Cēlsŭs, sūrgēns īn cōrnŭă. Rāmōsa ēxtōllēns cōrnŭă. Cĕlĕrēs pĕr āvĭă cērvī. Dēfēndūnt cōrnŭă cērvūm.

Cēssŏ, ās, āvī, ātūm, ārĕ. *To cease, to be at ease.* Ēt sī quīd cēssārĕ pŏtēs, rĕquĭēscĕ sŭb ūmbrā. V. Syn.—Quĭēscŏ, văcŏ, ōtĭŏr. Phr.—Rētĭă cēssānt. Cīrcŭs ădhūc cēssăt. *To discontinue.* Syn.—Dēsĭnŏ, sīstŏ, ābsīstŏ, dēsīstŏ. Phr.—Ŏpŭs īntērmīttĕrĕ, sīstĕrĕ. Īncœptō dēsīstĕrĕ. *To delay.* Syn.—Mŏrŏr.

Ceū. adv. *As, just as.* Syn.—Ŭtī, ŭt, vĕlŭt, vĕlŭtī, sīcŭt, quăsĭ, tāmquām.

Chærĕphy̆lūm, ī. n. *The herb chervil.* (*See Appendix under list of Trees, etc.*)

Chăly̆bs, y̆bĭs. m. *Steel.* Phr.—Chăly̆bĭs mĕtāllūm, māssă, lāmĭnă.

Chărāctēr, ērĭs. m. *Character, sign.* Syn.—Nŏtă, sīgnūm, īnsīgnĕ, fōrmă.

Chārtă, æ. f. *Paper.* Syn.—Păpy̆rŭs. Phr.—Scrībĕre ĭn āvērsā chārtā.

Chlămy̆s, y̆dĭs. f. *An upper garment of wool.* Syn.—Ămīctŭs, tŭnĭcă, vēstĭs.

Chōrdă, æ. f. *The string of an instrument.* Rīdētūr chōrdā quī sēmpĕr ŏbērrăt ĕādēm. H. Syn.—Nērvŭs, fĭdēs (ĭūm). Phr.—Sŏcĭāndă chōrdīs. Īmpēllĕrĕ pōllĭcĕ chōrdās. Chōrdă sŏnūm rēddĭt. Prætēntăt pōllĭcĕ chōrdās.

Chŏrĕă, æ. f. & Chŏrĕæ, ārūm. f. *Dance.* Syn.—Chŏrŭs. Phr.—Īndūlgērĕ chŏrēīs. Ēxērcērĕ chŏrĕās. Mŏvērĕ ăd nŭmĕrūm. Tērrām, hŭmūm quătĕrĕ, tūndĕrĕ.

Chŏrŭs, ī. m. *A company of dancers.* Syn.—Chŏrĕă. Phr.—Ēxērcēt Dīānă chŏrōs. Īnquĕ chŏrī lūdūnt spĕcĭēm. *An assembly.* Syn.—Cœtŭs, cōncĭlĭūm, tūrbă.

Chry̆sānthĕmūm, ī. n. *The chrysanthemum.* (*See Appendix under list of Trees, etc.*)

Cĭbŭs, ī. m. *Food, nourishment.* Nōn dŏmŭs āptă sătĭs, nōn hīc cĭbŭs ūtĭlĭs ægrō. O. Syn.—Ēscă, ălĭmēntūm, nūtrīmēntūm, pābŭlūm, dăpēs, ĕpŭlæ. Phr.—Rĕfĭcĭēns vīrēs, cōrpŏră. Mœstōs ēxhĭlărāns ănĭmōs. Fig. Syn.—Ălĭmēntūm, nūtrīmēntūm, pābŭlūm.

Cĭcādă, æ. f. *Grasshopper.* Ēt cāntū quĕrŭlæ rūmpēnt ārbūstă cĭcādæ. V. Phr.—Ēbrĭă rōrĕ. Cœlī rōrĭfĕrīs ēbrĭă lăcrĭmĭs. Brūmæ sēcūră fŭtūræ.

Cĭcātrīx, īcĭs. f. *Wound, scar.* Vūlnŭs ĭn āntīquūm rĕdĭīt mălĕ fīrmă cĭcātrīx. O. Syn.—Vūlnŭs. Phr.—Sīgnāta īn frōntĕ cĭcātrīx. Vūlnĕrĭs īnflīctī vēstīgĭă.

Cĭcĕr, ĕrĭs. n. *Chick-pea.* Nĕque īllĕ Sēpŏsĭtī cĭcĕrĭs nēc lōngae īnvīdĭt ăvēnæ. H. Syn.—Cĭcērcŭlă. Phr.—Tēllūrĭs ĕdāx.

Cĭchŏrēūm, ī. n. *Chicory or succory.* (*See Appendix under list of Trees, etc.*)

Cĭcōnĭă, ǣ. f. *Stork.* (*See Appendix under list of Birds.*)

Cĭcŭr, ŭrĭs. m., f., & n. *Tame, domestic.* Syn.—Cĭcŭrātŭs, dŏmēstĭcŭs, mānsuētŭs, mānsuēfāctŭs.

Cĭcŭrŏ, ās, āvī, ātūm, ārĕ. *To tame.* Syn.—Lēnĭŏ, mānsuēfăcĭŏ, mītĭgŏ. *See Mansuefacio.*

Cĭcūtă, ǣ. f. *Hemlock, used as a poison. See Venenum.*

Cĭĕŏ, ēs, cīvī, & cĭī, cĭtūm, cĭēre. *To arouse, to move.* Īmō Nēreūs cĭēt ǣquŏră fūndō. V. Syn.—Mŏvĕŏ, cōmmŏvĕŏ, cōncĭtŏ, ēxcĭtŏ, āccēndŏ, cōncŭtĭŏ, stĭmŭlŏ. Phr.—Aērĕ cĭērĕ vĭrōs. Cĭērĕ flētūs.

Cīnctŭs, ūs. m. *Girdle.* Syn.—Cīngŭlūm, zōnă.

Cīngŏ, ĭs, cīnxī, cīnctūm, ĕrĕ. *To gird, to bind.* Cīngōr fūlgēntĭbūs ārmīs. V. Syn.—Cīrcūmcīngŏ, præ̆cīngŏ, ārmŏ. Phr.—Nĕc ăcūtō cīngĭmŭr ēnsĕ. *See Armor. To crown.* Syn.—Cŏrōnŏ. *To surround.* Syn.—Āmbĭŏ, cīrcūmdŏ, cīrcūmcīngŏ, āmplēctŏr, cōmplēctŏr, claūdŏ, īnclūdŏ, sēpĭŏ, cŏrōnŏ. Phr.—Nīgrā nĕmŭs ābiētĕ cīngūnt. Ūndĭquĕ cīrcūm Fūndĭmŭr. Īnfērt sē sēptūs nĕbŭlā. *See Circumdo.*

Cīngŭlūm, ī. n. *Cincture, girdle.* Aūrĕă sūbnēctēns ēxsērtǣ cīngŭlă māmmǣ. V. Syn.—Zōnă, bāltĕŭs. Phr.—Prĕtĭōsăquĕ cīngŭlă gēmmīs. Aūrĕă būllīs Cīngūlă. *See Balteus, Zona.*

Cĭnĭs, ĕrĭs. m. *Ashes.* Ēffœ̄tōs cĭnĕrem īmmūndūm jāctārĕ pĕr āgrōs. V. Phr.—Cāndĕt ĭn īgnĕ cĭnĭs. Cĭnĕrēmquĕ fŏcō dīmōvĭt. Cĭnĕrī lātĕt ōbrŭtŭs īgnĭs. *Ashes of the dead.* Syn.—Mānēs, rēllĭquĭæ, ōssă. Phr.—Āccĭpĭāt cĭnĕrēs tērrā pătērnă.

Cīnnămŏn, ī. n. *The cinnamon tree.* (*See Appendix under list of Trees, etc.*)

Cīrcā. prep. *Around, around about.* Ēt cīrcā rēgem ātque īpsa ād prǣtōrĭă dēnsǣ Mīscēntŭr. V. Syn.—Cīrcūm, jūxtā, prŏpĕ. *As an adverb.* Syn.—Cīrcūm, jūxtā, prŏpĕ.

Cīrcĭtĕr. prep. & adv. *Roundabout, near.* Syn.—Cīrcā, ăd, sŭb, fĕrĕ, fērmē.

Cīrcŭĭtŭs, ūs. m. *Circuit, tour.* Sæ̆văquĕ cīrcŭĭtū cūrvāntēm brăchĭă lōngō. O. Syn.—Āmbĭtŭs, cīrcŭlŭs, gȳrŭs, ōrbĭs. Phr.—Mōllēs ădĭtūs pēr dēvĭă flēxō Cīrcŭĭtū pĕtĭt. *Detour.* Syn.—Cīrcĭtĭŏ, āmbāgēs.

Cīrcŭlŭs, ī. m. *Circle.* Ŭbĭ cīrcŭlūs āxīm Ūltĭmūs ēxtrēmūm spătĭōquĕ brĕvīssĭmŭs āmbĭt. O. Syn.—Cīrclŭs, ōrbĭs, zōnă. *A gathering, society.* Syn.—Cœ̄tŭs, cŏrōnă.

Cīrcūm. prep. & adv. *Around.* Syn.—Cīrcā, jūxtā, prŏpĕ.

Cīrcŭmăgŏ, ăgĭs, ēgī, āctūm, ăgĕrĕ. *To turn around.* Nīl ŏpŭs ēst tē cīrcŭmăgī. H. Syn.—Cīrcūmdūcŏ, cīrcūmfĕrŏ, cīrcūmvōlvŏ, cōnvērtŏ. Phr.—Dĕūs cīrcūm căpŭt ēgĭt hŏnēstūm.

Cīrcūmcīdŏ, dĭs, dī, sūm, ĕrĕ. *To cut around.* Ēt cīrcūmcīdās ăcĭēm sōlāmquĕ rĕlīnquās. Lr. Syn.—Āmpŭtŏ, cīrcūmsĕcŏ. *To cut off.* Syn.—Rĕsĕcŏ, dētrăhŏ.

Cīrcūmcīngŏ, ĭs, xī, ctūm, ĕrĕ. *To surround.* Syn.—Cīrcūmdŏ. *See Circumdo.*

Cīrcūmclaūdŏ, ĭs, sī, sūm, ĕrĕ. *To shut in. See Cingo, Claudo.*

Cīrcūmdŏ, ās, dĕdī, dătūm, dărĕ. *To shut in, or around.* Sēptēmque ūnă sĭbī mūrō cīrcūmdĕdĭt ārcēs. V. Syn.—Āmbĭŏ, cīngŏ, cīrcūmcīngŏ, cīrcūmvāllŏ, claūdŏ, īnclūdŏ, cŏrōnŏ, ŏbĕŏ, sēpĭŏ. Phr.—Īgnī cīrcūmdărĕ mūrōs. Cīrcūmdătă cōllă cătēnīs.

Cīrcŭmĕŏ, īs, īvī, ĭtūm, īrĕ. *To go around.* Mōrĕ lŭpī claūsās cīrcŭmĕūntĭs ŏvēs. O. Syn.—Ērrŏ, lūstrŏ, pērlūstrŏ, ŏbĕŏ, ŏbāmbŭlŏ, pĕrăgrŏ. *To surround. See Cingo.*

Cīrcūmfĕrŏ, fērs, tŭlī, lātūm, fērrĕ. *To carry around.* Cīrcūmfērre ŏcŭlōs spēctāndīs rēbŭs. Syn.—Vōlvŏ, tōrquĕŏ. Phr.—Pārtēs cōnvērtĕre ĭn ōmnēs. Tēr sŏcĭōs pūrā cīrcūmtŭlĭt ūndā. *To publish.* Syn.—Prædĭcŏ, dīctĭtŏ.

Cīrcūmflēctŏ, ctĭs, xī, xūm, tĕrĕ. *To turn around, to describe a circle.* Ūndĕ rĕvērtī Scīrēnt ēt lōngōs ŭbĭ cīrcūmflēctĕrĕ cūrsūs. V. *See Flecto.*

Cīrcūmflŭŏ, ĭs, ūxī, ūxūm, ĕrĕ. *To flow around.* Cōcȳtūsquĕ sīnū lābēns cīrcūmflŭĭt ātrō. V. Syn.—Āllŭŏ, cīrcūmlŭŏ, cīrcūmfūndŏr, cīrcūmlābŏr. *To surround.* Syn.—Cīngŏ.

Cīrcūmfūndŏ, ĭs, fūdī, fūsūm, ĕrĕ. *To spread around, to expand.* Tūm dēmūm tērrīs quās cīrcūmfūdĕrăt ātră Tēmpēstās Stȳgĭæ tāndēm fūgērĕ tĕnēbræ. *See Fundo.*

Cīrcūmlĭgŏ, ās, āvī, ātūm, ārĕ. *To bind around.* Īmplĭcăt ātque hăbĭlēm mĕdĭæ cīrcūmlĭgăt hāstæ. V. *See Ligo.*

Cīrcūmlĭnŏ, ĭs, lēvī, lĭtūm, lĭnĕrĕ. *To smear around, to cover.* Phr.—Mūscō cīrcūmlĭtă sāxă.

Cīrcūmquāquĕ. adv. *On every side.* Syn.—Ūndĭquĕ, ūndĕquāquĕ.

Cīrcūmrētĭŏ, īs, īvī, ītūm, īrĕ. *To surround with nets.* Syn.—Īmplĭcŏ, īmpĕdĭŏ.

Cīrcūmscrībŏ, ĭs, scrīpsī, ptūm, ĕrĕ. *To write around, to trace. To limit.* Syn.—Fīnĭŏ, līmĭtŏ. Phr.—Prĕmēns stīvām, dēsīgnāt mœnĭă sūlcō.

Cīrcūmsīstŏ, ĭs, stĭtī, stĭtūm, ĕrĕ. *To surround.* Syn.—Cīngŏ, Cīrcūmdŏ.

Cīrcūmspēctŭs, ă, ūm. *Circumspect, careful.* Syn.—Caūtŭs, prūdēns. *See Prudens.*

Cīrcūmspĭcĭō, ĭs, spēxī, spēctūm, ĕrĕ. *To look around, to cast one's eyes on every side.* Cōnstĭtĭt ātque ŏcŭlīs Phrўgĭa āgmĭnă cīrcūmspēxĭt. V. Syn.—Cīrcūmspēctŏ. Phr.—Ŏcŭlōs hūc īllūc pēr sīngŭlă vōlvŏ. Ŏcŭlĭs lŭstrŏ, pĕrērrŏ. Hūc ōră fĕrēbăt ĕt īllūc. Ōmnĭă ōbsērvāns. Dūm vērsăt ĭn ōmnĭă vūltūs. Hūc īllūc vōlvēns.

Cīrcūmstŏ, ās, stĕtī, stătūm, ārĕ. *To stand around.* Cīrcūmstānt ănĭmæ dēxtrā lævāquĕ frĕquēntēs. V. Syn.—Cīrcūmsīstŏ, āmbĭŏ, cīngŏ. Phr.—Stō cīrcūm. Sævūs cīrcūmstĕtĭt hōrrŏr.

Cīrcūmvāllŏ, ās, āvī, ātūm, ārĕ. *To surround.* Quīppe ăcĭēm dēnsō cīrcūmvāllāvĕrăt ōrbĕ. Syn.—Vāllŏ, ōbvāllŏ, cīngŏ, āmbĭŏ, īnclūdŏ, mūnĭŏ, ŏbĕŏ. *See Vallo.*

Cīrcūmvĕhŏ, ĭs, vēxī, vēctūm, ĕrĕ. *To transport around.* Vīx cīrcūmvĕhĭmūr spārsæ dīspēndĭă rūpīs. Syn.—Cīrcūmvēctŏr, pērcūrrŏ, pērlūstrŏ.

Cīrcūmvĕnĭŏ, īs, vēnī, vēntūm, īrĕ. *To envelop, to surround.* Tēr quătĕr ārdēntī tērgō cīrcūmvĕnĭt āngŭĭs. V. Syn.—Cīrcūmdŏ, cīrcŭmĕŏ, āmbĭŏ, cīngŏ, ōbsĭdĕŏ. *To deceive.* Syn.—Dēcĭpĭŏ.

Cīrcŭs, ī. m. *Circle.* Hīnc tĭbĭ cīrcūs ĕrīt sēmpēr vērtēntĭbūs ānnīs. Syn.—Cīrcŭlŭs, ōrbĭs. *Circus.* Syn.—Căvĕă, āmphĭthĕātrūm, cŭnĕī, ărēnă. *See Amphitheatrum.*

Cĭs. prep. *On this side (of anything).* Syn.—Cĭtrā.

Cĭtĕrĭŏr, ŭs, ōris. m. *That which is nearer.* Syn.—Prŏpĭŏr, prŏpīnquĭŏr, vīcīnĭŏr.

Cĭthără, æ. f. *Harp, lute.* Nēc stŭdĭō cĭthăræ, nēc mūsæ dēdĭtūs ūllī. H. Syn.—Bārbĭtŭs, fĭdēs, lўră, plēctrūm, tēstūdŏ. Phr.—Cĭthăræ nērvī, cāntŭs, cōncēntŭs, sŏnŭs, strĕpĭtŭs, mŏdī. Cūrārūm dūlcĕ lĕvāmĕn. Dūlcēs rēddīt pōllĭcĕ tāctă sŏnōs. Īmbēllī cĭthără cārmĭnă dīvĭdēs. *See Lyra, Fides, Plectrum.*

Cĭthărœdŭs, ī. m. *Harpist, minstrel.* Ēt cĭthărœdŭs Rīdētūr chōrdā quī sēmpĕr ŏbērrăt ĕādēm. H. Syn.—Cĭthărīstă, fĭdĭcĕn, lўrĭcĕn. Phr.—Cĭthărām pūlsāns. Nērvōs pūlsārĕ pĕrītŭs. Stŭdĭō cĭthăræ dēdĭtŭs. Cĭthăræ pŏtēns. Plēctră mŏvēns. Īmpēllēns pōllĭcĕ. Frētūs cĭthără.

Cĭtŏ. adv. *Quickly, promptly.* Nēc cĭtŏ crēdĭdĕrīs quāntūm cĭtŏ crēdĕrĕ lædăt. O. Syn.—Cōnfēstīm, cōntĭnŭō, ēxtēmplō, mōx, prōtĭnŭs, rĕpēntĕ, sŭbĭtō, prŏpĕrē, ōcĭŭs. Phr.—Haūd mŏră. *See* Brĕvī.

Cĭtŏ, ās, āvī, ātūm, ārĕ. *To excite, to arouse, to push, to animate.*

Ād frēnă cĭtāvĭt ŏlōrēs. *See Incito. To make come.* Syn.—Cĭĕŏ, vŏcŏ. *To mention.* Syn.—Mĕmŏrŏ, rĕfĕrŏ.

Cĭtrā. prep. *On this side of.* Nēc vīrtūs cĭtrā gĕnŭs ēst. O. Syn.—Cĭs. *Before.* Syn.—Āntĕ.

Cĭtrŭs, ī. f. *The citron tree.* (*See Appendix under list of Trees, etc.*)

Cīvĭcŭs, ă, ūm. *Pertaining to a citizen.* Cīvĭcă prō trĕpĭdīs cūm tŭlĭt ārmă rĕīs. O. Phr.—Seū cīvĭcă jūră Rēspōndērĕ părās. *Civil.* Syn.—Cīvīlĭs.

Cīvīlĭs, ĭs, ĕ. *Pertaining to a citizen.* Syn.—Cīvĭcŭs, ūrbānŭs.

Cīvĭs, ĭs. m. *Citizen.* Quīs fŭrŏr ō cīvēs, quæ tāntă lĭcēntĭă fērrī? Syn.—Īncŏla.

Cīvĭtās, ātĭs. f. *State, city.* Tū cīvĭtātēm quīs dĕcĕāt stătŭs Cūrās. H. Syn.—Ūrbs. *See Urbs.*

Clādēs, ĭs. f. *Misfortune, loss, destruction.* Īnque īpsōs sævă mĕdēntēs Ērūmpīt clādēs. O. Syn.—Cāsŭs, ēxĭtĭūm, pēstĭs, pērnĭcĭēs. *See Exitium, Calamitas. Slaughter.* Syn.—Cædēs.

Clām. adv. *Secretly.* Clām fērro īncaūtūm sŭpĕrāt sēcūrŭs ămōrūm Gērmānæ. V. Syn.—Clāncŭlūm, fūrtīm, lătēntĕr, ōccūltē, sēcrētō, tăcĭtē. Phr.—Rēmōtō tēstĕ. Īn ōccūltō. Ōccūltā fraūdĕ.

Clāmŏ, ās, āvī, ātūm, ārĕ. *To cry out, to speak loud.* Clāmābīs căpĭtī vīnă sŭbēssĕ mĕō. Pr. Syn.—Cōnclāmŏ, vōcĭfĕrŏr. Phr.—Cœlūm, aūrās, vōcĭbŭs, clāmōrĕ īmplĕō, rĕplĕō. Clāmōrēm dō. Clāmōre īncēndūnt cœlūm. Nēc vōci īræquĕ pĕpērcĭt. *See Clamor.*

Clāmŏr, ōrĭs. m. *Shout, cry.* Naūtĭcŭs ēxŏrĭtūr văriō cērtāmĭnĕ clāmŏr. V. Syn.—Vōx, clāmĭtātĭŏ, sŏnŭs, sŏnĭtŭs, frĕmĭtŭs, strĕpĭtŭs; (*Of grief*), plāngōr, ŭlŭlātŭs, lāmēntūm, quēstŭs, gĕmĭtŭs, mūgītŭs. Phr.—Sūblātŭs ăd æthĕră clāmŏr. Vōcēsquĕ rĕpēntĕ prŏfūsæ. Tūm vēro īngĕmĭnāt clāmŏr. Cœlūm clāmōrĕ mīscētŭr. Īt clāmōr cœlō.

Clāndēstīnŭs, ă, ūm. *Secret, clandestine.* Ēt clāndēstīnīs sūrgēntĭă fraūdĭbŭs ārmă. Syn.—Ārcānŭs, ōccūltŭs, sēcrētŭs, cæcŭs, ŏpērtŭs.

Clāngŏr, ōrĭs. m. *Sound of the trumpet.* Tўrrhēnūsquĕ tŭbæ mūgīrĕ pĕr æthĕră clāngŏr. V. Syn.—Sŏnŭs, sŏnĭtŭs, strĕpĭtŭs. Phr.—Raūcūs strīdēntī mūrmŭrĕ clāngŏr Īncrĕpŭĭt. Sŏnĭpēs mōtūs clāngōrĕ tŭbārūm. *See Tuba.*

Clārē. adv. *Clearly.* Pēnsĭŏ tē cōrām pĕtĭtūr clārēquĕ pălāmquĕ. M. Syn.—Ăpērtē, plānē, lĭquĭdō, mănĭfēstō, cōnspĭcŭē.

Clārĕō, ēs, ŭī, ērĕ. *To be clear, to shine.* Clārĕăt Āndrŏmĕdēs sīgnūm. Cic. Syn.—Splēndĕō, lūcĕō, pătĕō, āppārĕō, clārēscŏ, īnclārēscŏ, īnnōtēscŏ, ēnĭtĕō.

Clārēscŏ, ĭs, ĕrĕ. *See Clareo.*

Clārĭtās, ātĭs. f. *Clearness, splendor.* Syn.—Splēndŏr, lūx, lūmĕn. Fig. Syn.—Fāmă, hŏnŏr, nōmĕn.

Clārŏ, ās, āvī, ātūm, ārĕ. *To illuminate, to make clear.* Mītĭs, ĭtēr lōngæ̅ clārāvīt līmĭtĕ flāmmæ̅. Syn.—Īllūmĭnŏ, īllūstrŏ.

Clārŭs, ă, ūm. *Bright, clear, brilliant.* Syn.—Lūcĭdŭs, pēllūcĭdŭs, nĭtĭdŭs, splēndĭdŭs. *Famous.* Syn.—Īllūstrĭs, īnsīgnĭs.

Clāssĭs, ĭs. f. *Fleet.* Clāssĭbŭs, hīc lŏcŭs; hīc ăcĭē cērtārĕ sŏlēbānt. V. Syn.—Rătēs, nāvēs, pūppēs, rōstră. Phr.—Fērtūr cĭtă gūrgĭtĕ clāssĭs. Lătēt sūb clāssĭbŭs æ̅quŏr. Clāssēmquĕ rĕlātām nūntĭō. *See Navis.*

Clāthrŭs, ī. m. *Bars, barriers.* Syn.—Cāncēllī, claūstră, crātēs, sēptă, rĕpāgŭlă.

Claūdŏ, ĭs, sī, sūm, ĕrĕ. *To shut, to close* Claūdĭtĕ jām rīvōs pŭĕrī sāt prātă bĭbērūnt. V. Syn.—Ōcclūdŏ, præ̅clūdŏ, īntērclūdŏ, ōbsĕrŏ, ōbstrŭŏ. Phr.—Pōstĭbŭs sĕrām ōbdŏ. Fērro ēt cōmpāgĭbŭs ārctīs.

Claūdŭs, ă, ūm. *Lame.* Pārs, vūlnĕrĕ claūdă, rĕtēntăt Nēxāntēm nōdīs. V. Syn.—Claūdĭcāns, tĭtŭbāns. Phr.—Brĕvĭŏr pĕdĕ. Pĕdĕ claūdō īncēdēns. Quī grēssūm trăhĭt īmpărēm.

Claūstrūm, ī. n. *Enclosure, cloister.* Claūstrăquĕ cūstōdēm pācīs cŏhĭbēntĭă Jānūm. H. Syn.—Fŏrēs, vālvæ̅, ŏbēx, sēptă. Phr.—Claūsæ̅ fŏrēs. Ōbstāntĭă rūmpĕrĕ claūstră.

Clāvĭs, ĭs. f. *Key.* Nēc prŏhĭbēnt clāvēs ēt cănĭs īpsĕ tăcĕt. Tib. Phr.—Pōrtās rĕsĕrāns, pāndēns, rĕclūdēns. Sēnsīt jānŭă clāvēm.

Clāvŭs, ī. m. *Nail.* Āspĕr ĕt ōbtūsā cūspĭdĕ clāvŭs ĕrĭt. Phr.—Clāvum īnfīgŏ. Clāvīs fīgŏ. *The tiller.* Syn.—Gŭbērnācŭlūm, gŭbērnāclūm, tēmŏ, mŏdĕrāmĕn, rĕgĭmĕn, hăbēnæ̅. *See Gubernator.*

Clēmēns, ēntĭs. adj. *Kind.* Prīmō clēmēntĭŏr æ̅vō. Syn.—Bĕnīgnŭs, bŏnŭs, cōmĭs, ēxōrābĭlĭs, făcĭlĭs, mōllĭs, hūmānŭs, īndūlgēns, lēnĭs, mānsuētŭs, mītĭs. Phr.—Pĭgĕr ād pœ̅nās. Vĕnĭæ̅ părātŭs. Lēnĭs ĭn mĭsĕrōs. Prĕcĭbūs nūnquam īmplācābĭlĭs.

Clēmēntĕr. adv. *Kindly.* Syn.—Bĕnīgnē, plăcĭdē, lēnĭtĕr. *Calmly.* Syn.—Plăcĭtĕr, mōllĭtĕr, lēnĭtĕr.

Clēmēntĭă, æ̅. f. *Kindness.* Ēmōllīt gēntēs clēmēntĭă cœ̅lī. L. Syn.—Bĕnīgnĭtās, bŏnĭtās, mānsuētūdŏ. Phr.—Mītĭs ănĭmŭs. Pācĭs ămāns.

Clĭēns, ēntĭs. m. *Client.* Pūlsātūsvĕ părēns ēt fraūs īnnēxă clĭēntī. V. Phr.—Cūltōrūm tūrbă tŭōrūm. Ūltrā līmĭtēs clĭēntūm. *Client of a lawyer.* Syn.—Cūltŏr.

Clĭēntēlă, æ. f. *Patronage, protection.* Syn.—Pătrōcĭnĭūm, tūtēlă.

Clīvōsŭs, ă, ūm. *Hilly ,steep.* Syn.—Prærūptŭs, ārdŭŭs, dēclīvĭs, ăcclīvĭs.

Clīvŭs, ī. m. *Hill.* Syn.—Clīvŭlŭs, cōllĭs. *See Collis.*

Clŏācă, æ. f. *Sewer, cloaca.* Phr.—Lŏcŭs sēntīnārūm.

Clȳpĕŭs, ī. m. *Shield.* Ōppŏsŭī mōlēm clȳpĕī tēxīquĕ jăcēntēm. O. Syn.—Aēgĭs, pārmă, pēltă, scūtūm, ūmbŏ, cētră. Phr.—Clȳpĕī ōrbĭs. Aērātūm tēgmĕn. Aērĕ mūnītŭs. Sævō fūlgōrĕ mĭcāns. Clȳpĕūs sŏnăt ærĕūs hāstīs.

Cŏăcērvŏ, ās, āvī, ātūm, ārĕ. *To heap up.* Ēt cŏăcērvātīs ārdēbānt cōrpŏră mēmbrīs. Syn.—Ăcērvŏ, āggĕrŏ, cōngĕrŏ, cŭmŭlŏ, ăccŭmŭlŏ, cōllĭgŏ. *See Aggero.*

Cŏălēscŏ, ĭs, ŭī, ĭtūm, ĕrĕ. *To grow together, to unite.* Suādĕt ēt īnfūsūs tĕnĕrōs cŏălēscĕrĕ fētūs. Phr.—Ūnā, sĭmŭl crēscŏ. Syn.—Cŏĕŏ, jūngŏr, cōnjūngŏr, cŏhærĕŏ, cōncrēscŏ.

Cŏārgŭŏ, ĭs, ŭī, ūtūm, ĕrĕ. *To convince.* Syn.—Cōnvīncŏ.

Cōccūm, ī. n. *The berry of the scarlet oak. Scarlet hue.* Syn.—Mūrēx, ōstrūm, pūrpŭră. Phr.—Cōccō vēlātă rŭbēntī. Ārdēntī rădĭābāt Scīpĭŏ cōccō.

Cōdēx, ĭcĭs. m. *Trunk of a tree.* Syn.—Caūdēx, trūncŭs. *Tablet, testament.* Syn.—Tăbŭlă, lĭbĕr, chārtă.

Cœlēstĭs, ĭs, ĕ. *Divine, celestial.* Tāntæne ănĭmīs cœlēstĭbŭs īræ? V. Syn.—Āĕrĭŭs, æthĕrĭŭs, sīdĕrĕŭs, sŭpĕrŭs, dīvīnŭs. *See Coelum.*

Cœlĭcōlæ, ārūm. m. *The inhabitants of Heaven.* Ōmnēs cœlĭcŏlās ōmnēs sŭpĕra āltă tĕnēntēs. V. Syn.—Cœlēstēs, cœlĭtēs, dĭī, dīvī, sŭpĕrī. Phr.—Quī cœlēstēs aūrās, sŭpĕrās dŏmōs, cœlī tēctă īncŏlūnt. *See Deus.*

Cœlĭtēs, ūm. m. *The inhabitants of heaven. See Coelicolae.*

Cœlĭtŭs. adv. *From on high.* Syn.—Cœlō, ē cœlō, dīvīnĭtŭs.

Cœlūm, ī. n. *Heaven.* Quāntŭs ăd æthĕrĕūm cœlō cōnspēctŭs Ŏlȳmpūm. V. Syn.—Aēthēr, āstră, sīdĕră, pŏlŭs, āxĭs, Ŏlȳmpŭs. Phr.—Cœlēstĕ sŏlūm. Ōræ cœlēstēs, āĕrĭæ. Cœlī āxĭs. Aēthĕrĕūs vērtēx. Stēllīs ārdēns lūcēntĭbŭs æthēr. Mūndī flāmmĕă tēctă. Pŏlūs dūm sīdĕră pāscĕt. Sūb cœlī tēgmĭnĕ. Tēr cœlō clārŭs ăb āltō Īntŏnŭīt Pătĕr. Ēt cœtū cīnxērĕ pŏlūm. Līmĕn Ŏlȳmpī. Cœlēstĭă tēmplă. Cœlēstĭs aūlă.

Cœnă, æ. f. *Feast, supper.* Ō nōctēs cœnæquĕ dĕūm quĭbŭs īpsĕ mĕīquĕ Āntĕ lărēm prŏprĭūm vēscŏr. H. Phr.—Mūltō splēndĭdă lūxū. *See Convivium.*

Cœnātĭŏ, ĭōnĭs. f. *Dining-room.* Syn.—Cœnācŭlūm, trīclīnĭūm.

Cœnŏ, ās, āvī, ātūm, ārĕ. *To sup, to dine.* Sæpĕ trĭbūs lēctīs vĭdĕās cœnārĕ quătērnōs. H. *See Convivium.*

Cœnūm, ī. n. *Mud, dirt.* Syn.—Līmŭs, lŭtūm, sōrdēs.

Cŏĕŏ, īs, īvī & ĭī, ĭtūm, īrĕ. *To join, to unite.* Syn.—Jūngŏr, cŏălēscŏ. *To assemble.* Syn.—Cōnvĕnĭŏ, cōncūrrŏ.

Cœpī, īstī, cœptūm, īssĕ. *To commence.* Dīmĭdĭūm cœptī quī bĕnĕ cœpĭt hăbĕt. O. Phr.—Plăcĭdō sīc pēctŏrĕ cœpĭt. *See Incipio.*

Cœptŏ, ās, āvī, ātūm, ārĕ. *To commence, to undertake. See Incipio.*

Cœptūm, ī. n. *Undertaking.* Āt trĕpĭda ēt cœptīs īmmānĭbŭs ēffĕră Dīdō. V. Syn.—Īncēptūm, aūsūm, prōpŏsĭtūm, cōnsĭlĭūm, ōrsă. Phr.—Vānīque īnsānĭă cœptī. Cœptă tĕnē. Dī, cœptīs āspīrātĕ mĕīs.

Cŏērcĕŏ, ēs, ŭī, ĭtūm, ērĕ. *To encompass, to enclose.* Vīttă cŏērcŭĕrāt nēglēctōs ālbă căpīllōs. O. Syn.—Cōntĭnĕŏ, rĕtĭnĕŏ, cŏhĭbĕŏ, cōnstrīngŏ, prĕmŏ, īnclūdŏ. *To check.* Syn.—Cŏhĭbĕŏ, frēnŏ, rĕfrēnŏ, rĕprĭmŏ. *To correct.* Syn.—Ēmēndŏ.

Cœtŭs, ūs. m. *Gathering, assembly.* Syn.—Cōncĭlĭūm, cōnsēssŭs, cōnvēntŭs, cŏrōnă, chŏrŭs, āgmĕn, tūrbă, frĕquēntĭă, glŏbŭs, grēx. *See Turba.*

Cōgĭtātĭŏ, ōnĭs. f. *Thought.* Syn.—Cōgĭtātūm, cōnsĭlĭūm, mēns, sēntēntĭă, mĕdĭtātă(ōrūm).

Cōgĭtŏ, ās, āvī, ātūm, ārĕ. *To think, to reflect.* Cōgĭtăt ēt dŭbĭum ēst. O. Syn.—Pŭtŏ, rĕpŭtŏ, ăgĭtŏ. Phr.—Ănĭmō, cōrdĕ ăgĭtŏ, vōlvŏ, vērsŏ, rĕvōlvŏ. Ănĭmō ōccūrrĭt. Vĕnĭt ĭn mēntēm. Ōmnĭă sēcūm vērsāntī. *To plan, to design.* Syn.—Mĕdĭtŏr, părŏ, mōlĭŏr, ăgĭtŏ. Phr.—Jām sūspēndĭă sævă cōgĭtābās.

Cōgnātĭŏ, ōnĭs. f. *Relationship.* Cāră dărēt sōlēmnĕ tĭbī cōgnātĭŏ mūnŭs. M. Syn.—Āffīnĭtās, cōnsānguĭnĭtās.

Cōgnātŭs, ă, ūm. *Related.* Hīc ŭbĭ cōgnātōrum ŏpĭbūs cūrīsquĕ rĕfēctŭs. H. Syn.—Āffīnĭs, prŏpīnquŭs, cōnsānguĭnĕŭs. Phr.—Sānguĭnĕ jūnctŭs.

Cōgnĭtĭŏ, ōnĭs. f. *Knowledge.* Syn.—Nōtĭŏ, nōtĭtĭă.

Cōgnĭtŏr, ōrĭs. m. *One who has knowledge.* Syn.—Scĭēns, dōctŭs, pĕrītŭs.

Cōgnōmĕn, ĭnĭs. n. *Surname.* Drūsŭs ĭn hīs mĕrŭĭt quōndām cōgnōmĭnă tērrīs. O. Syn.—Cōgnōmēntūm. *See Nomen.*

Cōgnōscŏ, ĭs, nōvī, nĭtūm, ĕrĕ. *To know, to recognize.* Fēlīx quī pŏtŭĭt rērūm cōgnōscĕrĕ caūsās. V. Syn.—Nōscŏ, nōvī, scĭŏ, pērcĭpĭŏ, īntēllĕgŏ. Phr.—Ēt cōgnōscēntī sĭmĭlĭs. *To learn.* Syn.—Aūdĭŏ, dīscŏ, ăccĭpĭŏ, rēscĭŏ.

Cōgŏ, ĭs, cŏēgī, cŏāctūm, ĕrĕ. *To force, to compel.* Syn.—Ădĭgŏ, sŭbĭgŏ, cōmpēllŏ. *To amass.* Syn.—Cōllĭgŏ, āccŭmŭlŏ. *To assemble.* Syn.—Cōngrĕgŏ, cōnvŏcŏ, cōmpēllŏ, ăgŏ, cōllĭgŏ, cōntrăhŏ, cōndūcŏ. Phr.—Tītўrĕ cōgĕ pĕcŭs. Sŏcĭōs ād līttŏră cōgānt. Ōmnēs ĕōdēm cōgĭmŭr.

Cŏhærĕŏ, ēs, sī, sūm, ērĕ. *To hold together.* Syn.—Cŏhærēscŏ, hærĕŏ, ădhærēscŏ, ānnēctŏr, cōnnēctōr, cōnjūngŏr.

Cŏhĭbĕŏ, ēs, ŭī, ĭtūm, ērĕ. *To retain.* Nōn pŏtŭīt fōrtēs aūrō cŏhĭbērĕ lăcērtōs. O. Syn.—Tĕnĕŏ, rĕtĭnĕŏ, cŏērcĕŏ, rēstrīngŏ, cōnstrīngŏ. *See Vincio. To check.* Syn.—Īnhĭbĕŏ, ārcĕŏ, cŏērcĕŏ, cōmpēscŏ, cōmprĭmŏ, rĕprĭmŏ, frēnŏ, rĕfrēnŏ, cōntĭnĕŏ, tĕnĕŏ, rĕtĭnĕŏ. *See Freno.*

Cŏhors, ōrtĭs. f. *Cohort, company of soldiers.* Ībăt ĭn ærātās nūllō tērrōrĕ cŏhōrtēs. Syn.—Ăcĭēs, āgmĕn, lĕgĭŏ, mănŭs, mănĭplŭs, phălānx. Phr.—Pīlīs ārmātă. Fŭrĭātă cŏhōrs. *See Acies. Crowd.* Syn.—Cătērvă, tūrbă, āgmĕn. *See Turba.*

Cŏlăphŭs, ī. m. *Buffet.* Syn.—Ălăpă, īctŭs. Phr.—Ōbjūrgāt pŭĕrūm cŏlăphīs. Dūrĭōrī mănū pūlsārĕ gĕnās.

Cōllābŏr, ĕrĭs, lāpsŭs sūm, ī. *To fall.* Syn.—Lābŏr, cădŏ, cōncĭdŏ. *See Cado.*

Cōllēgĭūm, ĭī. n. *Association, company.* Syn.—Cœtŭs, cōnvēntŭs.

Cōllīdŏ, ĭs, īsī, īsūm, ĕrĕ. *To break against.* Ānŭlŭs ūt fīāt prīmō cōllīdĭtŭr aūrūm. O. Syn.—Āttĕrŏ, cōntĕrŏ, īmpīngŏ, īllīdŏ, cōnfrīngŏ.

Cōllĭgŏ, ās, āvī, ātūm, ārĕ. *To bind, to unite.* Ānsăquĕ cōmprēssōs cōllĭgăt ārctă pĕdēs. Tib. Syn.—Lĭgŏ, āllĭgŏ, cōnstrīngŏ, vīncĭŏ, rĕvīncĭŏ. *See Vincio.*

Cōllĭgŏ, ĭs, ēgī, ēctūm, ĕrĕ. *To gather together.* Cōllĭgĕre ārmă jŭbēt vălĭdīsque īncūmbĕrĕ rēmīs. V. Syn.—Cōgŏ, lĕgŏ, cōngĕrŏ, āggĕrŏ, cōngrĕgŏ. Phr.—Plŭvĭām nōx cōllĭgĭt. Īrām cōllĭgĭt ēt pōnīt tĕmĕrĕ. Flōrēs cārpēbānt. Tōndērĕ, dēcērpĕrĕ, mĕtĕrĕ, cōllĭgĕrĕ rŏsās.

Cōllĭnŏ, ĭs, ēvī, ĭtūm, ĕrĕ. *To besmear.* Syn.—Ōblĭnŏ, lĭnŏ. Fig.—*To stain.* Syn.—Fœdŏ, măcŭlŏ.

Cōllĭs, ĭs. m. *Hill.* Lĭbēr pāmpĭnĕās īnvīdīt cōllĭbŭs ŭvās. V. Syn.—Clīvŭs, jŭgūm, tŭmŭlŭs, ăpēx, vērtēx. Phr.—Frōndōsō vērtĭcĕ cōllĭs. Mōllĭtĕr āssūrgēns cōllĭs. *See Mons.*

Cōllŏcŏ, ās, āvī, ātūm, ārĕ. *To put, to place.* Hīc jŭvĕnem īn lătĕbrīs āvērsum ā lūmĭnĕ Nўmphă Cōllŏcăt. V. Syn.—Pōnŏ, dēpōnŏ, cōmpōnŏ, stătŭŏ, cōnstĭtŭŏ.

Cōllŏquĭūm, ĭī. n. *Conversation.* Nām mĭsĕrīs nēc flērĕ quĭdem aūt lēnīrĕ dŏlōrĕ Cōllŏquĭīs īmpūnĕ lĭcēt. Syn.—Āllŏquĭūm, cōngrēssŭs, sērmŏ. Phr.—Hāc vĭcĕ sērmōnūm. *See Colloquor.*

Cōllŏquŏr, quĕrĭs, cūtŭs sūm, quī. *To speak, to converse.* Vĭdēbīt, cōllŏquētŭr, ădĕrĭt ūna īn ūnīs ǣdĭbŭs. Ter. Syn.—Āllŏquŏr, āffārī, cōnfābŭlŏr. Phr.—Aūdīre ēt rēddĕrĕ vōcēs. Vărĭō nōctēm sērmōnĕ trăhēbăt. *See Loquor.*

Cōllūcĕō, ēs, ūxī, ērĕ. *To shine brilliantly.* Mœnĭă cōllūcēnt flāmmīs. V. Syn.—Cŏrūscŏ, rĕfūlgĕŏ. *See Luceo, splendeo.*

Cōllūdŏ, ĭs, ūsī, ūsūm, ĕrĕ. *To play together.* Aūt sūmmā nāntēs īn ăquā cōllūdĕrĕ plūmās. V. *See Ludo.*

Cōllūm, ī. n. *Neck.* Īlle ŭbĭ cōmplēxu Aēnēǣ cōllōquĕ pĕpēndĭt. V. Syn.—Cērvīx. Phr.—Cōllă tĕgēntĕ cŏmā. Pārvīs āddūxīt cōllă lăcērtīs. O.

Cōllūstrŏ, ās, āvī, ātūm, ārĕ. *To shine. See Illustro.*

Cŏlŏ, ĭs, ŭī, cūltūm, ĕrĕ. *To cultivate the ground. See Ager, Aro. To adore, to honor.* Syn.—Ădōrŏ, vĕnĕrŏr, rĕvĕrĕŏr, hŏnōrŏ. *To celebrate.* Syn.—Cĕlĕbrŏ. *To dwell.* Syn.—Īncŏlŏ, hăbĭtŏ.

Cŏlōnŭs, ī. m. *Laborer, farmer.* Dūră lăcērtōsī fŏdĭēbānt ārvă cŏlōnī. O. Syn.—Ărātŏr, ăgrēstĭs, āgrĭcŏlă, cūltŏr, rūstĭcŭs, vīllĭcŭs. *See Agricola. Inhabitant.* Syn.—Īncŏlă, cīvĭs.

Cŏlŏr, ōrĭs. m. *Color.* Sītnĕ cŏlōr prŏprĭūs rērūm lūcīsquĕ rĕpūlsū Ēlūdānt ăcĭēm. L. Phr.—Cŏlŏr pūnĭcĕǣ flōrĕ prĭōr rŏsǣ. Rēbūs nōx ābstŭlĭt ātră cŏlōrēm. Nĭmĭūm nē crēdĕ cŏlōrī. *Paint.* Syn.—Pīgmēntūm.

Cŏlōrŏ, ās, āvī, ātūm, ārĕ. *To color, to paint.* Quōs Aūrōră sŭīs rūbră cŏlōrăt ĕquīs. Pr. Syn.—Pīngŏ, tīngŏ. Phr.—Cŏlōrēm dō, īndūcŏ. Cŏlōrĕ fūcŏ, mĕdĭcŏ, sătŭrŏ, īnfĭcĭŏ, dīstīnguŏ, dĕcōrŏ.

Cŏlŭbĕr, ŭbrī. m. *Snake.* Syn.—Ānguĭs, sērpēns, drăcŏ. *See Serpens.*

Cŏlūmbă, ǣ. f. *Dove, pigeon.* (*See Appendix under list of Birds.*)

Cŏlŭmĕn, ĭnĭs. n. *Support.* Syn.—Fūlcrūm, cŏlūmnă, tūtēlă, tūtămĕn, prǣsĭdĭūm, aūxĭlĭūm. Phr.—Tū cŏlŭmēn vītǣ. Cŏlŭmēnquĕ rērūm.

Cŏlūmnă, ǣ. f. *Column, pillar.* Syn.—Cŏlŭmĕn, fūlcrūm. Phr.—Nāvālī sūrgēntēs ǣrĕ cŏlūmnǣ. Cēlsīs sūggēstă thĕātră cŏlūmnīs.

Cŏlŭs, ī & ūs. m. & f. *Distaff.* Ēt cŏlŭs ēt fūsūs dĭgĭtīs cĕcĭdērĕ rĕmīssīs. O. Phr.—Nōn īllă cŏlō călăthīsvĕ Mĭnērvǣ Āssuētă. *See Neo.*

Cŏmă, ǣ. f. *Hair.* Fōrmōsǣ pĕrĭērĕ cŏmǣ, quās vēllēt Ăpōllŏ. O. Syn.—Cǣsărĭēs, căpīllī, crīnēs. *See Capillus. Head. See Caput.*

Cŏmātŭs, ă, ūm. *One who has much hair.* Cālvūs quūm fŭĕrīs, ĕrīs cŏmātŭs. M. Syn.—Căpīllātŭs, crīnītŭs. Phr.—Cæsărĭē, căpīllīs ōrnātŭr, dĕcōrŭs. *See Capillus.*

Cōmbĭbŏ, ĭs, bĭbī, bĭbĭtūm, ĕrĕ. *To drink, to imbibe.* Sīc mŏdŏ cōmbĭbĭtūr, tēctō mŏdŏ gūrgĭtĕ lāpsŭs Rēddĭtūr Ārgŏlĭcīs īngēns Ĕrăsīnŭs ĭn ārvīs. O. Syn.—Bĭbŏ, ādbĭbŏ, ēbĭbŏ, haūrĭŏ. Phr.—Āră crŭōrēm Cōmbĭbĕrāt. Cōmbĭbĭt ōs măcŭlās. *To be penetrated with.* Syn.—Sōrbĕŏ, ābsōrbĕŏ.

Cōmbĭbŏ, ōnĭs. m. *Drinking companion.* Syn.—Cōmpōtŏr. Phr.—Mēnsæ sŏcĭŭs, cŏmĕs.

Cōmbūrŏ, rĭs, ssī, stūm, rĕrĕ. *To burn up.* Syn.—Ūrŏ, ădūrŏ, ēxūrŏ, crĕmŏ. Phr.—Flāmmīs ābsūmŏ. *See Uro, Incendo.*

Cŏmĕdŏ, ĕdĭs, & ēs, ēdī, ēsūm, ĕrĕ & ēssĕ. *To eat.* Hæc pōrcīs hŏdĭē cŏmĕdēndă rĕlīnquēs. H. Syn.—Ĕdŏ, māndŏ, māndūcŏ, pāscŏ, ābsūmŏ. *See Edo.* Fig.—*To devour with the eyes.* Syn.—Vŏrŏ, dēvŏrŏ, haūrĭŏ.

Cŏmĕs, ĭtĭs. m. & f. *Companion.* Tū tĭbĭ dūx cŏmĭtī, tū cŏmĕs īpsă dŭcī. Tib. Syn.—Cŏmĭtāns, cŏmĭtātŭs, sŏcĭūs, sŏdālĭs, sŏcĭātŭs. Phr.—Ēxsĭlĭī cŏmĭtēm quærĭs. *See Comitor, Socius.*

Cŏmētă, æ & Cŏmētēs, æ. m. *Comet.* Nēc dīrī tŏtĭēs ārsērĕ cŏmētæ. V. Phr.—Stēllă cŏmāns, crīnītă. Clārō ārdōrĕ trĕmŭlŭs. Ēxĭtĭālĕ mĭcāns. Stēllă făcēm dūcēns. Fāx dīră cŏmētæ.

Cōmĭcŭs, ă, ūm. *Comic, pertaining to comedy.* Vērsĭbŭs ēxpōnī trăgĭcīs rēs cōmĭcă nōn vūlt. H. Phr.—Āc prŏpĕ sōccō dīgnīs cārmĭnĭbŭs.

Cōmĭnŭs. adv. *Near at hand.* Cōmĭnŭs ēnsĕ fĕrīt, jăcŭlō cădĭt ēmĭnŭs īpsĕ. O. Syn.—Prŏpĕ, prŏpĭŭs.

Cōmĭs, ĭs, ĕ. *Polite, affable.* Hīc tĭbĭ cōmĭs ĕt ūrbānŭs lībērquĕ vĭdētŭr. H. Syn.—Bĕnīgnŭs, blāndŭs, cōmmŏdŭs, făcĭlĭs, hūmānŭs, lēnĭs, mānsuētŭs, mītĭs, plăcĭdŭs, ūrbānŭs, cīvīlĭs. Phr.—Mītĕ īngĕnĭūm. Ădĭtū clēmēns. *See Benignus, Clemens.*

Cōmĭtās, ātĭs. f. *Affability, politeness.* Syn.—Bĕnīgnĭtās, hūmānĭtās, ūrbānĭtās. *See Bonitas.*

Cŏmĭtātŭs, ūs. m. *Following, suite.* Syn.—Cœtŭs, cătērvă, cŏhōrs, cŏmĭtēs. *See Turba.*

Cōmĭtĕr. adv. *Politely.* Syn.—Bĕnīgnē, hūmānē.

Cŏmĭtĭūm, ĭī. n. *Public assembly.* Syn.—Cœtŭs, cōnsēssŭs, cōnvēntŭs, cōncĭlĭūm.

Cŏmĭtŏr, ārĭs, ātŭs sūm, ārī. *To accompany, to follow.* Ēt nōstrō cŏmĭtātĕ grădūs, ĕt ĭn ārdŭă mōntĭs Ītĕ sĭmŭl. O. Syn.—Sĕquŏr, stīpŏ. Phr.—Cŏmĕs sūm. Cŏmĕs vĕnĭŏ. Mē sŏcĭūm āddŏ.

Īpsĕ cŏmēs Nīsō grădĭtŭr. Tĭbī cŏmĕs īrĕ rĕcūsŏ. Āddĭdĕrāt sēsē sŏcĭūm.

Cōmmăcŭlŏ, ās, āvī, ātūm, ārĕ. *To stain.* Syn.—Fœdŏ, īnquĭnŏ, măcŭlŏ. *See Maculo.*

Cōmmĕdĭtŏr, ārĭs, ātŭs sūm, ārī. *To meditate. See Meditor.*

Cōmmēndŏ, ās, āvī, ātūm, ārĕ. *To entrust.* Nātōs cōmmēndānt cūræ nūmĭnĭbūsquĕ tŭīs. O. Syn.—Crēdŏ, cōmmīttŏ, trādŏ.

Cōmmēntūm, ī. n. *Lie.* Syn.—Mēndācĭūm, fābŭlă, fīctĭŏ. Phr.—Fīctă vērbă, fīctæ rēs.

Cōmmĭnīscŏr, scĕrĭs, mēntŭs sūm, mĭnīscī. *To contrive.* Pōst hæc căchīnnāns Cōmmĭnīscĭtūr lībrōs. M. Syn.—Cōmmēntŏr, fīngŏ, ēxcōgĭtŏ, īnvĕnĭŏ. *See Fingo.*

Cōmmĭnŭŏ, ŭĭs, ŭī, ūtūm, ŭĕrĕ. *To break.* Syn.—Frāngŏ. *To diminish, to enfeeble.* Syn.—Mĭnŭŏ, īmmĭnŭŏ, frāngŏ, dēbĭlĭtŏ. *See Debilito. To move.* Syn.—Flēctŏ, plācŏ, mŏvĕŏ, vīncŏ.

Cōmmīssūm, ī. n. *A fault.* Pōst mĭhĭ nōn sĭmĭlī pœnā cōmmīssă lŭētĭs. V. Syn.—Dēlīctūm, ērrātūm, crīmĕn, ādmīssūm, cūlpă. *Secret.* Syn.—Ārcānūm.

Cōmmīttŏ, ĭs, mīsī, mīssūm, ĕrĕ. *To join. See Jungo. To entrust to.* Syn.—Crēdŏ, trādŏ, māndŏ, cōmmēndŏ, mīttŏ. *To commit.* Syn.—Ādmīttŏ, făcĭŏ, pătrŏ.

Cōmmŏdē. adv. *Conveniently, easily.* Syn.—Āptē, bĕnĕ, rēctē, dĕcēntĕr. *Kindly.* Syn.—Cōmĭtĕr, bĕnīgnē.

Cōmmŏdĭtās, ātĭs. f. *A favorable occasion.* Syn.—Ōccāsĭŏ. Phr.—Āptă, ōppōrtūnă, cōmmŏdă tēmpŏră.

Cōmmŏdŏ, ās, āvī, ātūm, ārĕ. *To lend with good will.* Syn.—Præbĕŏ, ădhĭbĕŏ, sūffĭcĭŏ, dō, lārgĭŏr.

Cōmmŏdūm, ī. n. *Utility, profit.* Syn.—Ūtĭlĭtās, bŏnūm, frūctŭs, ēmŏlŭmēntūm.

Cōmmŏdŭs, ă, ūm. *Fit, proper.* Syn.—Āccōmmŏdŭs, āptŭs, ĭdōnĕŭs, cōnvĕnĭēns, ōppōrtūnŭs, tēmpēstīvŭs, ūtĭlĭs. Phr.—Mēquĕ lŏcō plēctī cōmmŏdĭōrĕ vĕlĭt. O.

Cōmmōlĭŏr, īrĭs, ītŭs sūm, īrī. *To contrive, to prepare.* Cūm cōmmōlīrī tēmpēstās fūlmĭnă cœptăt. Syn.—Mōlĭŏr, nītŏr, ādnītŏr, cōnnītŏr. *See Molior.*

Cōmmŏvĕŏ, ēs, mōvī, mōtūm, ērĕ. *To move, to agitate.* Rādĭt ĭtēr lĭquĭdūm, cĕlĕrēs nĕquĕ cōmmŏvĕt ālās. V. Syn.—Mŏvĕŏ, pērmŏvĕŏ, ăgŏ, ăgĭtŏ, pēllŏ, quătĭŏ. Phr.—Cōmmōrūnt æquŏră vēntī. *To excite.* Syn.—Ēxcĭtŏ, cĭĕŏ, ēxcĭĕŏ. *To disturb, to trouble.* Syn.—Āffĭcĭŏ, mŏvĕŏ, pērtūrbŏ, ăgĭtŏ, īmpēllŏ, pērcēllŏ.

Cōmmūnĭcŏ, ās, āvī, ātūm, ārĕ. *To communicate.* Āt sŭă Tȳdīdēs mēcūm cōmmūnĭcāt āctă. O. Syn.—Cōmmīttŏ, crēdŏ, īmpērtĭŏr. Phr.—Pārtĭcĭpēm făcĭŏ, sŏcĭūm ādvŏcŏ, mĭhĭ ādjūngŏ, ĭn pārtēm rĕī vŏcŏ.

Cōmmūnĭs, ĭs, ĕ. *Common.* Quīd prŏhĭbētĭs ăquās? ūsūs cōmmūnĭs ăquārum ēst. O. Phr.—Īn mĕdĭūm pŏsĭtŭs. Īn cōmmūnĕ dătŭs. Sēnsū cōmmūnī plānē cărĕt. Ūnă sălūs āmbōbŭs ĕrĭt.

Cōmmūnĭtās, ātĭs. f. *Society, community.* Syn.—Cōmmūnĭŏ, sŏcĭĕtās. Phr.—Ĕōsdēm hăbērĕ pĕnātēs. *See Communis, Societas.*

Cōmmūnĭtĕr. adv. *Commonly.* Syn.—Părĭtĕr. *Equally.* Syn.—Aēquālĭtĕr, æquē, părĭtĕr.

Cōmŏ, ĭs, psī, ptūm, ĕrĕ. *To arrange, to set in order, to comb.* Cōmat vīrgĭnĕās hāstă rĕcūrvă cŏmās. O. Syn.—Pēctŏ, dēpēctŏ. *See Pecto.*

Cōmœ̄dĭă, æ. f. *Comedy.* Īntērdūm tămĕn ēt vōcēm cōmœ̄dĭă tōllĭt. H. Syn.—Sŏccŭs.

Cōmœ̄dŭs, ī. m. *Actor, comedian.* Syn.—Mīmŭs, āctŏr, hīstrĭŏ.

Cŏmōsŭs, ă, ūm. *Hairy.* Cālvūs cŏmōsā frōntĕ nūdō cōrpŏrĕ. Phaed. Syn.—Căpīllātŭs, crīnītŭs, īntōnsŭs, cŏmātŭs. *See Capillus.*

Cōmpāgēs, ĭs & Cōmpāgŏ, ĭnĭs. f. *A joining, joint.* Ēffĭcĭēns hŭmĭlēm lăpĭdūm cōmpāgĭbŭs ārcūm. O. Syn.—Cōmmīssūră, jūnctūră, nēxŭs, vīncŭlūm. Phr.—Dūrā vīnctōs cōmpāgĕ tĕnēbānt. Lāxīs lătĕrūm cōmpāgĭbŭs. *See Vinculum.*

Cōmpăr, ărĭs. m., f. & n. *Equal, alike.* *See Par.* *Companion.* Syn.—Sŏcĭŭs, cōnjūnx.

Cōmpārĕŏ, ēs, ŭī, ērĕ. *To appear, to be seen.* Syn.—Āppārĕŏ, vĭdĕŏr.

Cōmpărŏ, ās, āvī, ātūm, ārĕ. *To prepare.* Ēt călĭdām fēssō cōmpărăt ūxŏr ăquām. Tib. *See Paro.* *To be prepared.* Syn.—Părŏ, āppărŏ, mōlĭŏr. *To acquire.* *See Acquiro.* *To assemble together.* Syn.—Cōllĭgŏ, cōgŏ, cōngĕrŏ. *To compare.* Syn.—Cōmpōnŏ, cōnfĕrŏ, æquŏ, cŏæquŏ, ēxæquŏ, æquĭpărŏ, āptŏ, āssĭmĭlŏ, cōmmīttŏ.

Cōmpēllŏ, ās, āvī, ātūm, ārĕ. *To speak.* Ūltrō vērbīs cōmpēllăt ămīcīs. V. Syn.—Āllŏquŏr, āppēllŏ, āffārī. Phr.—Dīctīs āggrĕdĭŏr. Mūltō cōmpēllăt hŏnōrĕ. *See Alloquor.*

Cōmpēllŏ, ĭs, ŭlī, ūlsūm, ĕrĕ. *To push, to chase, to drive.* Hædōrūmquĕ grĕgēm vĭrĭdī cōmpēllĕre hĭbīscō. V. Syn.—Īmpēllŏ, pēllŏ, ăbĭgŏ, trūdŏ, ūrgĕŏ, ăgŏ. *To force.* Syn.—Cōgŏ, ădĭgŏ, sŭbĭgŏ.

Cōmpēnsŏ, ās, āvī, ātūm, ārĕ. *To reckon, to balance, to weigh.* Tōt tămĕn āmīssīs tē cōmpēnsāvĭmŭs ūnūm. O. Syn.—Pēnsŏ, rĕpēnsŏ, ǽquŏ.

Cōmpĕrĭŏ, īs, ĕrī, ērtūm, īrĕ. *To discover, to find out.* Cōmpĕrĭt īnvĭdĭām sūprēmō fīnĕ dŏmārī. H. Syn.—Cōgnōscŏ, nōvī, aŭdĭŏ, dīscŏ, scĭŏ, rēscīscŏ.

Cōmpĕdēs, ūm. f. *Shackles.* Īmplĭcĭtī cŏhĭbēnt fērrātǽ cōmpĕdĭs ōrbēs. O. Syn.—Vīncŭlă, lăquĕŭs. *See Vinculum.*

Cōmpēscŏ, ĭs, ŭī, ĭtūm, ĕrĕ. *To stop, to check.* Syn.—Cŏērcĕŏ, cŏhĭbĕŏ, cōmprĭmŏ, cōntĭnĕŏ, rĕtĭnĕŏ, frēnŏ, rĕfrēnŏ. Phr.—Cōmpēscĕrĕ flūmĭnă rīpīs. Cōmpēscĭtŭr īră lĕōnūm. *To cut off.* Syn.—Āmpŭtŏ, rĕcīdŏ, rēscīndŏ.

Cōmpĕtŏ, ĭs, īvī & ĭī, ītūm, ĕrĕ. *To agree with, to be fitting.* Syn.—Cōngrŭŏ, cōnvĕnĭŏ, dĕcĕŏ.

Cōmpīngŏ, ĭs, ēgī, āctūm, ĕrĕ. *To push with violence.* Syn.—Ădĭgŏ, cōmpēllŏ, dētrūdŏ. *To join.* Syn.—Jūngŏ (*which see*).

Cōmpĭtūm, ī. n. *Cross-road.* Syn.—Trĭvĭūm, quādrĭvĭūm, plătĕă, vīcŭs. Phr.—Rūmōr pēr cōmpĭtă mānăt. Īn tērnās cōmpĭtă sēctă vĭās. *See Via.*

Cōmplăcĕŏ, ēs, ŭī, ĭtūm, ērĕ. *To please. See Placeo.*

Cōmplēctŏr, ĕrĭs, xŭs sūm, ctī. *To embrace. See Amplector. To love.* Syn.—Cŏlŏ, dīlĭgŏ (*which see*). *To shut in, to surround.* Syn.—Āmplēctŏr, cōmprĕhēndŏ, cōmprēndŏ, cōntĭnĕŏ, căpĭŏ. *See Cingo, Circumdo.*

Cōmplĕŏ, ēs, ēvī, ētūm, ērĕ. *To fill.* Lūnǽ sē cōrnŭă lūmĭnĕ cōmplēnt. V. Syn.—Īmplĕŏ, rĕplĕŏ, ădīmplĕŏ. Phr.—Lātē lŏcă mīlĭtĕ cōmplēnt. Cōmplētĕ sĕdīlĭă pātrēs. *To accomplish.* Syn.—Ābsōlvŏ, cōnfĭcĭŏ, pērfĭcĭŏ, fīnĭŏ, pĕrăgŏ.

Cōmplēxŭs, ūs. m. *Embrace. See Amplexus.*

Cōmplūrēs, ēs, ă. *Several.* Syn.—Mūltī, pērmūltī, plūrēs, plūrĭmī.

Cōmpōnŏ, ĭs, ŏsŭī, ĭtūm, ĕrĕ. *To put together.* Cōmpōnēns mănībūsquĕ mănūs ātque ōrĭbŭs ōră. V. Syn.—Cōmmīttŏ, jūngŏ, cōnjūngŏ. *To arrange.* Syn.—Āptŏ, fīngŏ, fōrmŏ, īnfōrmŏ, ōrdĭnŏ. Phr.—Cōmpōnĕrĕ crīnēs.

Cōmprĕhēndŏ, ĭs, dī, sūm, ĕrĕ. *To take, to seize.* Syn.—Āpprĕhēndŏ, āpprēndŏ, căpĭŏ, răpĭŏ, ārrĭpĭŏ. *To shut in.* Syn.—Cōmplēctŏr, āmplēctŏr, căpĭŏ, cōntĭnĕŏ. *To comprehend.* Syn.—Īntēllĕgŏ, āssĕquŏr, cōncĭpĭŏ.

Cōmprĭmŏ, ĭs, ēssī, ēssūm, ĕrĕ. *To press, to shut together.* Syn.—Prĕmŏ, strīngŏ, cōnstrīngŏ, ārctŏ. *To hold back, to check.* Syn.—Cŏērcĕŏ, cŏhĭbĕŏ, cōmpēscŏ, sīstŏ, rĕtārdŏ, rĕtĭnĕŏ.

Cōmprŏbŏ, ās, āvī, ātūm, ārĕ. *To approve.* Syn.—Prŏbŏ, āpprŏbŏ, laŭdŏ.

Cōmpŭtŏ, ās, āvī, ātūm, ārĕ. *To calculate, to compute.* Syn.—Nŭmĕrŏ, rĕcēnsĕō, rĕpŭtŏ.

Cōnātŭs, ūs. m. *Effort.* Īn mĕdĭīs cōnātĭbŭs ǣgrī Sŭccĭdĭmŭs. V. Syn.—Cōnāmĕn, cōnātă (ōrūm), mōlīmĕn, lūctāmĕn, nīsŭs, vīs. *Enterprise.* Syn.—Īncēptūm, cœptūm, aūsūm, tēntāmĕn, ōrsă (pl.).

Cōncăvŏ, ās, āvī, ātūm, ārĕ. *To hollow out.* Ēst lŏcŭs īn gĕmĭnōs ŭbĭ brāchĭă cōncăvăt ārcūs Scōrpĭŭs. O. Syn.—Căvŏ, ēxcăvŏ, flēctŏ, īnflēctŏ, sĭnŭŏ.

Cōncăvŭs, ă, ūm. *Hollow.* Syn.—Căvŭs, căvātŭs, ēxcăvātŭs, īmŭs, prŏfūndŭs. *See Cavus.*

Cōncēdŏ, dĭs, ssī, ssūm, ĕrĕ. *To retire, to yield.* Cūm Zĕphўrīs sī cōncēdēs ĕt hĭrūndĭnĕ prīmā. H. Syn.—Ăbĕō. *To permit.* Syn.—Pērmīttŏ, dō, trĭbŭō, lārgĭŏr. Phr.—Lūdūm pŭĕrīs cōncēdĕrĕ. Plūs trĭbŭīt quām mōrtālī cōncēdĕrĕ pār ēst. Cōncēssūm mūnĕrĕ dīvum.

Cōncĕlĕbrŏ, ās, āvī, ātūm, ārĕ. *To frequent.* Syn.—Cĕlĕbrŏ, frĕquēntŏ. *To solemnize.* *See Celebro.*

Cōncēntŭs, ūs. m. *Harmony.* Tūnc vŏlŭcrēs lǣtīs cōncēntĭbŭs āĕră mūlcēnt. V. Phr.—Cōncōrs cāntŭs. Vōcūm dīscōrdĭă cōncōrs. Rĕsŏnāt cōncēntŭs ĭn aūrās. *See Cantus.*

Cōnchă, ǣ. f. *Mussel, mussel-shell.* Ēbrĭă Bāiānō vēnī mŏdŏ cōnchă Lŭcrīnō. Syn.—Cōnchўlĭūm. Phr.—Īmplĭcĭtă tēstǣ. *Trumpet.* Syn.—Tŭbă.

Cōnchўlĭūm, ĭī. n. *Mussel, mussel-shell.* Syn.—Cōnchă.

Cōncĭdŏ, ĭs, dī, ĕrĕ. *To fall.* Īpsĕ grăvīs, grăvĭtērque ād tērrām pōndĕrĕ vāstō Cōncĭdĭt. V. *See Cado.* *To die.* *See Morior.*

Cōncĭlĭŏ, ās, āvī, ātūm, ārĕ. *To unite, to join.* Ōmnĭă quǣ sūrsūm cūm cōncĭlĭāntŭr ĭn āltō. *See Jungo.* *To procure.* Syn.—Āffĕrŏ, părŏ, cōmpărŏ.

Cōncĭlĭūm, ĭī. n. *Council, assembly.* Syn.—Cœtŭs, cōnvēntŭs, cŏrōnă, cōnsēssŭs. *See Convoco.*

Cōncīnnē. adv. *Proportionately, elegantly.* Syn.—Lĕpĭdē, vĕnūstē, dĕcēntĕr.

Cōncīnnŏ, ās, āvī, ātūm, ārĕ. *To arrange, to prepare.* Syn.—Părŏ, cōmpărŏ, strŭŏ, făcĭŏ, ēffĭcĭŏ.

Cōncĭnŏ, ĭs, ŭī, cēntūm, ĕrĕ. *To sing together.* Ād vădă Mǣāndrī cōncĭnĭt ālbŭs ŏlŏr. O. Syn.—Cănŏ, āccĭnŏ. Phr.—Cōncēntūm ēdŏ, cāntū rēspōndĕrĕ. *See Cano.*

Cōncĭōnātŏr, ōrĭs. m. *Orator.* Syn.—Ōrātŏr.

Cōncĭpĭŏ, ĭs, ēpī, ēptūm, ĕrĕ. *To conceive, to bring forth. See*

Genero. To receive. Syn.—Căpĭō, āccĭpĭō, dūcŏ, trăhŏ, rĕcĭpĭō, răpĭō, ādmīttō. Phr.—Cōncĭpĭt īrās. *To meditate.* Syn.—Mĕdĭtŏr, ăgĭtŏ, vōlvŏ, vērsŏr, mōlĭŏr.

Cōncĭtŏ, ās, āvī, ātūm, ārĕ. *To arouse, to excite.* Āt mălŭs īntērprēs pŏpŭlī mĭhĭ cōncĭtăt īrām. O. Syn.—Ēxcĭtŏ, īncĭtŏ, ăgŏ, mŏvĕŏ, īmpēllŏ, ăcŭŏ, stĭmŭlŏ, īnstīgŏ, īncēndŏ. Phr.—Cōncĭtăt Eūrŭs ăquās. Quæ vōs dēmēntĭă, dīxī, Cōncĭtăt? *See Excito.*

Cōnclāmŏ, ās, āvī, ātūm, ārĕ. *To cry out.* Syn.—Clāmŏ, ēxclāmŏ, vōcĭfĕrŏr, vŏcŏ, īnvŏcŏ. *See Invoco. To resound.* Syn.—Rĕsŏnŏ.

Cōnclāvĕ, ĭs. n. *Room.* Cūrrĕrĕ pēr tōtūm păvĭdī cōnclāvĕ. H. Syn.—Cămĕră, cŭbīcŭlūm, cēllă. Phr.—Dŏmūs īntĭmă, sēcrētă (pl.).

Cōnclūdŏ, ĭs, sī, sūm, ĕrĕ. *To shut in, to enclose.* Pārs ōptārĕ lŏcūm tēcto ēt cōnclūdĕrĕ sūlcō. V. Syn.—Claūdŏ, īnclūdŏ, āmplēctŏr, cōmplēctŏr. Phr.—Cōnclūdĕrĕ fōllĭbŭs aūrās. Pōrtŭs cōnclūdĭtŭr ūrbĕ. *See Claudo.*

Cōncōrdĭă, æ. f. *Harmony, concord.* Quĭd mĭhĭ, sī tāntō fēlīx cōncōrdĭă bēllō Ēxstĭtĕrĭt? Prop. Syn.—Pāx, ămīcĭtĭă, fœdŭs. Phr.—Cōncōrdēs ănĭmī. Sēnsūs ūnănĭmēs. Cōntrārĭă lītī. *See Amicitia.*

Cōncōrs, dĭs. m., f. & n. *Of the same mind, agreeing.* Syn.—Ūnănĭmĭs, ūnănĭmŭs, cōnsŏnŭs.

Cōncrēdŏ, ĭs, dĭdī, dĭtūm, ĕrĕ. *To entrust.* Vēl quĭbŭs ōbsēssōs pōssīt cōncrēdĕrĕ mūrōs. V. Syn.—Crēdŏ, cōmmīttō, māndŏ, cōmmēndŏ. Phr.—Vītām cōncrēdĕrĕ vēntīs. Ēt cuī cōncrēdĕrĕ nūgās. *See Confido.*

Cōncrĕmŏ, ās, āvī, ātūm, ārĕ. *To burn.* Syn.—Ădūrŏ, cōmbūrŏ, crĕmŏ, īncēndŏ. *See Uro.*

Cōncrĕpŏ, ās, ŭī, ĭtūm, ārĕ. *To rattle, to crash.* Cȳmbălă Thēbānō cōncrĕpŭērĕ Dĕō. Prop. Syn.—Crĕpŏ, crĕpĭtŏ, strĕpŏ, strĕpĭtŏ, strīdĕŏ. *To resound.* Syn.—Pērsŏnŏ, pūlsŏ, quătĭŏ.

Cōncrēscŏ, ĭs, ēvī, ētūm, ĕrĕ. *To grow together.* Ŭt hīs ēxōrdĭă prīmīs Ōmnĭa ĕt īpsĕ tĕnēr mūndī cōncrēvĕrĭt ōrbĭs. V. Syn.—Cŏĕŏ, cŏălēscŏ, cōgŏr, dēnsŏr, cōndēnsŏr, īndūrēscŏ, īndūrŏr.

Cōncūlcŏ, ās, āvī, ātūm, ārĕ. *To trample under foot.* Ērĭgĭtŭr, pĕdĭbūsquĕ vĭrūm cōncūlcăt ĕquīnīs. O. Syn.—Cālcŏ, prōcūlcŏ, tĕrŏ, āttĕrŏ, cōntĕrŏ, prōtĕrŏ. *See Calco.*

Cōncŭpĭŏ, ĭs, īvī & ĭī, ītūm, ĕrĕ. *To desire strongly.* Āt sī quĭd ūnquām tālĕ cōncŭpīvĕrĭt. H. Syn.—Cŭpĭŏ, pĕtŏ, āppĕtŏ, ōptŏ, pĕrōptŏ. *See Cupio.*

Cōncūrrŏ, ĭs, rrī, rsūm, ĕrĕ. *To run together.* Sēd glŏmĕrārĕ mănūm bēllo, ēt cōncūrrĕre ĭn ārcēm. V. Syn.—Cōncūrsŏ, āccūrrŏ, ādvŏlŏ, cōnvŏlŏ, cŏĕŏ, cōnflŭŏ. Phr.—Cōncūrsu āccēdĕrĕ māgnō. Cōncūrrūnt trĕpĭdæ cŏmĭtēs. *To fight. See Pugno.* Phr.—Aūdētquĕ vĭrīs cōncūrrĕrĕ vīrgŏ. Aūsūs cōncūrrĕrĕ cōmĭnŭs hōstī. *To clash together.* Syn.—Īmpīngŏr, cōnflīgŏ.

Cōncūrsŭs, ūs. m. *Concourse, gathering.* Quīd vūlt cōncūrsŭs ăd āmnēm? V. Syn.—Āccūrsŭs. *See Turba. Shock.* Syn.—Cōnflīctŭs.

Cōncūssŭs, ūs. m. *Shock. See Motus.*

Cōncŭtĭŏ, ĭs, ūssī, ūssūm, ĕrĕ. *To shake, to agitate.* Aēgĭdă cōncŭtĕrēt dēxtrā, nīmbōsquĕ cĭĕrĕt. V. Syn.—Quătĭŏ, ăgĭtŏ, jāctŏ, mŏvĕŏ, cōmmŏvĕŏ. Phr.—Nūtū cōncŭtĭt ōrbēm. Cōncŭtĭt ōssă mĕtŭs. Mēns cōncūssă mĕtū.

Cōndēmnŏ, ās, āvī, ātūm, ārĕ. *To condemn. See Damno.*

Cōndēnsŭs, ă, ūm. *Pressed close together.* Nātæ nēquīcquam āltārĭă cīrcūm cōndēnsæ. V. *See Densus.*

Cōndīcŏ, ĭs, xī, ctūm, ĕrĕ. *To agree to, to promise.* Syn.—Īndīcŏ, cōnstĭtŭŏ. Phr.—Vīctōrī laūdēm cuīdām pȳctae ūt scrībĕrĕt. *See Promitto.*

Cōndīmēntūm, ī. n. *Seasoning.* Syn.—Cōndītĭŏ, cōndītūră.

Cōndĭŏ, īs, īvī & ĭī, ītūm, īrĕ. *To season.* Ēt quādrīngēntīs nūmmīs cōndīrĕ gĕlōsūm. J. Phr.—Cōndīmēntīs, suāvī săpōrĕ tēmpĕrŏ. Cōndīmēntă mīscĕŏ, ădhĭbĕŏ.

Cōndīscŏ, ĭs, dĭdĭcī, ĕrĕ. *To learn with someone.* Ā tĕnĕrīs crīmēn cōndīscĭtŭr ānnīs. Syn.—Dīscŏ, āssuēscŏ. *See Disco.*

Cōndĭtĭŏ, ōnĭs. f. *Condition.* Āccĭpe ĕt hōc mūnūs cōndĭtĭōnĕ mălā. O. Syn.—Lēx, pāctūm, prōmīssūm. Phr.—Āccĭpĕ sūb cērtā cōndĭtĭōnĕ prĕcēs. *Fortune, lot.* Syn.—Fōrtūnă, sōrs, stătŭs. *Manner, fashion.* Syn.—Rătĭŏ, Mŏdŭs.

Cōndĭtŏr, ōrĭs. m. *Founder, author.* Syn.—Ēxstrūctŏr, fūndātŏr, făbrĭcātŏr, crĕātŏr, aūctŏr, mōlītŏr. Phr.—Ō stēllĭfĕrī cōndĭtŏr ōrbĭs. *Historian.* Syn.—Scrīptŏr.

Cōndŏ, ĭs, ĭdī, ĭtūm, ĕrĕ. *To conceal.* Syn.—Ābscōndŏ, rĕcōndŏ, ābdŏ, ōccŭlŏ, ōccūltŏ, tĕgŏ, ōbtĕgŏ. Phr.—Claūsūmquĕ căvā tē cōndĕrĕ tērrā. V. Ŭbĭ cœlūm cōndĭdĭt ūmbrā Jūpĭtĕr. Tĕnĕbrīs cōndēntĭă nūbĭlă cœlūm. *To bury.* Syn.—Sĕpĕlĭŏ. *To build.* Syn.—Aēdĭfĭcŏ, fūndŏ. *To write.* Syn.—Scrībŏ. *See Carmen.*

Cōndŏlĕŏ, ēs, ŭī, ērĕ. *To grieve.* Āt sī cōndŏlŭĭt tēntātūm frīgŏrĕ cōrpŭs. H. Syn.—Dŏlĕŏ, īndŏlĕŏ. *See Doleo.*

Cōndōnŏ, ās, āvī, ātūm, ārĕ. *To give.* Syn.—Lārgĭŏr. *See Dono. To pardon.* Syn.—Ignōscŏ, pārcŏ, rĕmīttŏ. *See Parco.*

Cōndūcĭt. Impers. *It is becoming.* Quōd nōn prōpŏsĭtō cōndūcăt ĕt hærĕăt āptē. H. Syn.—Cōnvĕnĭt, ēxpĕdĭt, prōdēst, ūtĭlĕ ēst.

Cōndūcŏ, ĭs, xī, ctūm, ĕrĕ. *To lead together. See Duco. To reassemble.* Syn.—Cōllĭgŏ, cōntrăhŏ, cōgŏ, cōngrĕgŏ.

Cōnfĕrŏ, fērs, tŭlī, lātūm, fērrĕ. *To carry, to bring together.* Syn.—Syn.—Fĕrŏ, āffĕrŏ, cōngĕrŏ. *To transport.* Syn.—Trānsfĕrŏ, fĕrŏ, vērtŏ.

Cōnfērtē & Cōnfērtĭm. adv. *In close rank.* Phr.—Cōnfērtō, dēnsātō āgmĭnĕ.

Cōnfēstĭm. adv. *Straightway, immediately.* Syn.—Cōntĭnŭō, sŭbĭtō, stătĭm.

Cōnfĭcĭŏ, ĭs, ēcī, ēctūm, ĕrĕ. *To execute, to do.* Sēd nōs īmmēnsūm spătĭīs, cōnfēcĭmŭs æquŏr. V. Syn.—Făcĭŏ, ēffĭcĭŏ, pērfĭcĭŏ, pĕrăgŏ, pătrŏ, pērpĕtrŏ, ābsōlvŏ, ēxsĕquŏr. *To exhaust.* Syn.—Ēxhaŭrĭŏ, ābsūmŏ, dēcŏquŏr. *To destroy.* Syn.—Dēlĕŏ, dēstrŭŏ, ābsūmŏ. *To overwhelm.* Syn.—Prĕmŏ, stērnŏ, afflīgŏ.

Cōnfīdēntĕr. adv. *Confidently.* Syn.—Cōnfīdēntĭŭs, aūdāctĭŭs.

Cōnfīdēntĭă, æ. f. *Confidence.* Syn.—Fīdūcĭă. *Impudence.* Syn.—Aūdācĭă.

Cōnfīdŏ, ĭs, sŭs sūm, ĕrĕ. *To trust, to rely on.* Dēsĭnăt ēlātīs quīsquām cōnfīdĕrĕ rēbŭs. Syn.—Fīdŏ, crēdŏ, cōncrēdŏ. Phr.—Mē cōmmīttŏ. Cōnfīdĕ fĭgūræ. *See Fido.*

Cōnfīgŏ, ĭs, xī, xūm, ĕrĕ. *To pierce.* Nīl pŭĕrī făcĭūnt, īpsām cōnfīgĭtĕ mātrēm. J. Syn.—Fīgŏ, trānsfīgŏ, fŏdĭŏ, cōnfŏdĭŏ.

Cōnfīngŏ, ĭs, nxī, ctūm, ĕrĕ. *To invent.* Syn.—Fīngŏ, ēxcōgĭtŏ, cōmmēntŏr, cōmmĭnīscŏr. *See Fingo.*

Cōnfīrmŏ, ās, āvī, ātūm, ārĕ. *To strengthen.* Syn.—Fīrmŏ, cōrrōbŏrŏ. *To encourage.* Syn.—Rĕfĭcĭŏ, rĕcrĕŏ, fīrmŏ, ērĭgŏ. Phr.—Ănĭmūm, ănĭmōs āddō. Prīncēps cōnfīrmăt ĭtūrōs. *To assure.* Syn.—Āffīrmŏ, āssĕrŏ, āssĕvērŏ.

Cōnfĭtĕŏr, ērĭs, ēssŭs sūm, ērī. *To confess, to avow.* Ēt scĕlĕrīs nŭmĕrōs cōnfĭtĕārĕ tŭī. O. *See Fateor.*

Cōnflăgrŏ, ās, āvī, ātūm, ārĕ. *To burn.* Syn.—Flăgrŏ, ārdĕŏ, ārdēscŏ, ēxārdēscŏ, cōmbūrŏr, crĕmŏr, īncēndŏr.

Cōnflīgŏ, ĭs, xī, ctūm, ĕrĕ. *To fight.* Tōt sĭmŭl ābjēctīs pōssēt cōnflīgĕrĕ rēbŭs. Syn.—Cōngrĕdĭŏr, cōncūrrŏ, cērtŏ, dēcērtŏ, dīmĭcŏ, pūgnŏ, lūctŏr. *See Certo, Pugno, Luctor.*

Cōnflŏ, ās, āvī, ātūm, ārĕ. *To forge.* Syn.—Făbrĭcŏr, făbrĭcŏ, cūdŏ, ēxcūdŏ, fīngŏ, cōnfĭcĭŏ. Fig.—*To excite.* Syn.—Ēxcĭtŏ, ēxcĭĕŏ, cōncĭĕŏ.

Cōnflŭŏ, ĭs, ūxī, ūxŭm, ĕrĕ. *To flow together.* Syn.—Afflŭŏ, cŏĕŏ, cōncūrrŏ, cōnvĕnĭŏ.

Cōnfŏdĭŏ, ĭs, ŏdī, ŏssŭm, ĕrĕ. *To dig.* Syn.—Fŏdĭŏ, pērfŏdĭŏ. *To pierce with a weapon.* Syn.—Fŏdĭŏ, pērfŏdĭŏ, trānsfŏdĭŏ, ēffŏdĭŏ, pērfŏrŏ, ăpĕrĭŏ, rĕclūdŏ, pērfrīngŏ, rūmpŏ, pērrūmpŏ, pērcŭtĭŏ, fĕrĭŏ, trānsĭgŏ, trānsădĭgŏ, trānsvērbĕrŏ, haūrĭŏ. *See Vulnero.*

Cōnfōrmŏ, ās, āvī, ātŭm, ārĕ. *To form, to fashion.* Syn.—Fōrmŏ, īnfōrmŏ, cōmpōnŏ, fĭgūrŏ, cōnflŏ, fīngŏ.

Cōnfrăgōsŭs, ă, ūm. *Rugged, uneven.* Syn.—Āspĕr, scăbĕr, pĕtrōsŭs, lăpĭdōsŭs, sălĕbrōsŭs, scrūpĕŭs, ĭnŭccēssŭs, ĭnvĭŭs. *See Saxosus.*

Cōnfŭgĭum, ĭī. n. *Refuge, retreat.* Syn.—Āsylŭm, pērfŭgĭŭm. Phr.—Quī mĭhĭ cōnfŭgĭŭm, quī mĭhĭ pōrtŭs ĕrās. *See Perfugium, Auxilium.*

Cōnfūndŏ, ĭs, ūdī, ūsŭm, ĕrĕ. *To confound, to mingle.* Sĭcŭlīs cōnfūndĭtŭr ūndīs. V. Syn.—Mīscĕŏ, pērmīscĕŏ. Phr.—Nāmquĕ dĭēs cōnfūndĭt ĭtĕr. Cōnfūndĕrĕ sācră prŏfānīs. Īmpĕrĭŭm, prōmīssă, prĕcēs cōnfūndĭt ĭn ūnŭm. *To disfigure.* Syn.—Fœdŏ (*which see*). *To trouble.* Syn.—Tūrbŏ (*which see*).

Cōnfūtŏ, ās, āvī, ātŭm, ārĕ. *To refute.* Syn.—Rĕfūtŏ, rĕfēllŏ, cŏārgŭŏ.

Cōngĕlŏ, ās, āvī, ātŭm, ārĕ. *To freeze, to harden.* Pēctŏră naūtīs Cōngĕlăt hībērnī vūltūs Jŏvĭs. V. Syn.—Gĕlŏ. Phr.—Lătĭcēs sŭōs cōngĕlăt āmnĭs. *To become thick or hard.* Syn.—Īndūrēscŏ, rĭgēscŏ, gĕlŏr.

Cōngĕmŏ, ĭs, ŭī, ĭtŭm, ĕrĕ. *To weep together.* Quīd mōrtēm cōngĕmĭs ēt flēs? L. Syn.—Gĕmŏ, lūgĕŏ, ādgĕmŏ, ĭngĕmŏ, ĭndŏlĕŏ. Phr.—Nūm flētū ĭngĕmŭĭt nōstrŏ? Aūt dŏlŭĭt mĭsĕrāns ĭnŏpēm. Nōstrōs lĭcĕăt cōnfūndĕrĕ flētūs. *See Gemo.*

Cōngĕrĭēs, ĭēī. f. *Heap, mass.* Cōngĕrĭēm sĕcŭĭt, sēctāmquĕ īn mēmbră rĕdēgĭt. O. Syn.—Cōngēstŭs, cŭmŭlŭs, strŭēs, ăcērvŭs.

Cōngĕrŏ, ĭs, ēssī, ēstŭm, ĕrĕ. *To heap together, to form a mass.* Syn.—Āggĕrŏ, ăcērvŏ, cŏăcērvŏ, āccŭmŭlŏ, glŏmĕrŏ, āgglŏmĕrŏ, cōnglŏmĕrŏ, strŭŏ, ēxstrŭŏ, cōllĭgŏ, cōgŏ, cōngrĕgŏ. *See Aggero.*

Cōngrĕdĭŏr, ĕrĭs, ēssŭs sŭm, ĕdī. *To march together.* Nēc pĕdĕ cōngrēssōs æquŏ, nēc tēlă fĕrēntēs Īnsĕquĭtŭr. V. *To meet anyone.* Syn.—Cōnvĕnĭŏ, ădĕŏ, cŏĕŏ, āllŏquŏr. *To fight. See Pugno.*

Cōngrĕgātīm. adv. *Together, by squadrons.* Syn.—Tūrmātīm, ūnā sĭmŭl.

Cōngrĕgŏ, ās, āvī, ātūm, ārĕ. *To collect together, to gather.* Syn.—Āggrĕgŏ, cōgŏ, cōllĭgŏ, cōntrăhŏ, glŏmĕrŏ.

Cōngrŭŏ, ĭs, ŭī, ĕrĕ. *To unite together.* Syn.—Cōnvĕnĭŏ, cŏĕŏ, cōngrĕgŏ. *To agree.* Syn.—Cōnvĕnĭŏ, cōnsēntĭŏ, cōnsŏnŏ, quădrŏ.

Cōngrŭŭs, ă, ūm. *Conformable, suitable.* Syn.—Cōnvĕnĭēns, āptŭs, ĭdōnĕŭs, pār.

Cōnjēctūră, æ. f. *Interpretation of dreams.* Syn.—Aūgŭrĭūm, dīvīnātĭŏ, vātĭcĭnĭūm, ŏpīnĭŏ, sūspĭcĭŏ.

Cōnjĭcĭŏ, ĭs, jēcī, jēctūm, ĕrĕ. *To throw, to hurl.* Tēlăquĕ cōnjĭcĭūnt prōtūrbāntque ēmĭnŭs hōstēm. V. Syn.—Jăcĭŏ, īnjĭcĭŏ, īnfĕrŏ, mīttŏ, īmmīttŏ, tōrquĕŏ. Phr.—Ēt grāndĭă cōnjĭcĕ sāxă. Sēsē Cōnjĭcĭt īn lătĕbrās. Ābsēntī sæpĕ quĕrēlās Cōnjĭcĭt. *To interpret a dream.* Syn.—Aūgŭrŏr, vātĭcĭnŏr, cōnjēctŏ, dīvīnŏ, prævĭdĕŏ, prænōscŏ, præsēntĭŏ, sūspĭcŏr.

Cōnjŭgālĭs, ĭs, ĕ. *Pertaining to marriage.* Syn.—Jŭgālĭs, cōnnŭbĭālĭs, mărītālĭs, sŏcĭālĭs, mărītŭs.

Cōnjŭgĭūm, ĭī. n. *Marriage.* Cōnjŭgĭūm vŏcăt, hōc prætēxīt nōmĭnĕ cūlpām. V. Syn.—Cōnnŭbĭūm, hўmĕnæī. Phr.—Tædæ jŭgālēs. Cōnjŭgĭī făcēs. Cōnnŭbĭālĕ jŭgūm. Jŭgālĭă vīncŭlă. Mărītūm fœdŭs.

Cōnjŭgŏ, ās, āvī, ātūm, ārĕ. *To place under the same yoke, to unite.* Syn.—Jŭgŏ, cōllĭgŏ, jūngŏ, cōnjūngŏ.

Cōnjŭgŭs, ă, ūm. *That which is united, husband, wife.* Syn.—Vĭr, cōnjūx, mărītŭs, ūxŏr.

Cōnjūngŏ, ĭs, xī, ctūm, ĕrĕ. *To join, to unite.* Pān prīmūs călămōs cērā cōnjūngĕrĕ plūrēs Īnstĭtŭĭt. V. Syn.—Jūngŏ, ādjūngŏ, nēctŏ, ădnēctŏ, cōpŭlŏ. Phr.—Ăvĭdī cōnjūngĕrĕ dēxtrās ārdēbānt.

Cōnjūrātĭŏ, ōnĭs. f. *Conspiracy.* Syn.—Cŏĭtĭŏ, cōnspīrātĭŏ.

Cōnjūrŏ, ās, āvī, ātūm, ārĕ. *To swear together.* Quæ jūrāt, mēns ēst: nīl cōnjūrāvĭmŭs īllă. V. *See Juro. To conspire.* Syn.—Cōnspīrŏ. *To make an alliance.* Syn.—Cōnspīrŏ, cōnvĕnĭŏ, cōnsēntĭŏ.

Cōnjūx, ŭgĭs. m. *Husband.* Heū! Quīs tē cāsūs dējēctām cōnjŭgĕ tāntō Ēxcĭpĭt? V. Syn.—Mărītŭs, vĭr, spōnsŭs. *See Maritus, Conjugium. Wife.* Syn.—Spōnsă, ūxŏr. *See Uxor.*

Cōnnēctŏ, ĭs, xī & xŭī, xūm, ĕrĕ. *To unite, to join.* Syn.—Nēctŏ, ădnēctŏ, jūngŏ, ādjūngŏ, cōnjūngŏ, āllĭgŏ, cōllĭgŏ, cōmpōnŏ. *See Jungo.*

Cōnnītŏr, ĕrĭs, sŭs & xŭs sūm, ī. *To strive together.* Hāstīs cōnnīxi īncūrrūnt. V. Syn.—Nītŏr, īnnītŏr, cōnŏr. Phr.—Tōtō cōrpŏrĕ cōnnīxŭs. *See Nitor.*

Cōnŏr, ārĭs, ātŭs sūm, ārī. *To attempt something.* Mōllĭtĕr īmprēssō cōnŏr ădīrĕ tŏrō. Prop. Syn.—Nītŏr, ādnītŏr, cōnnītŏr, ēnītŏr, ōbnītŏr, tēndŏ, cōntēndŏ, īncūmbŏ, mōlĭŏr, lūctŏr, ăggrĕdĭŏr. Phr.—Cōnātūs ēdĕrĕ. Vīrĭbŭs ēnītī. Cōnārī plūrĭmă frūstrā. Sūmmīs ādnīxūs vīrĭbŭs.

Cōnquĕrŏr, ĕrĕrĭs, ēstŭs sūm, ĕrī. *To complain.* Sēd quĭd ĕgo īgnārīs nēquīcquām cōnquĕrŏr aūrīs? *Cat.*. Syn.—Quĕrŏr. Phr.—Quĕrēlās, quēstūs ēdŏ, fūndŏ, ēffūndŏ, prōmŏ, prōfĕrŏ. *See Queror.*

Cōnquīrŏ, ĭs, sīvī & sĭī, sītūm, ĕrĕ. *To seek, to investigate.* Nōn īllīs stŭdĭūm vūlgō cōnquīrĕre ămāntēs. Prop. Syn.—Vēstīgŏ, īnvēstīgŏ, scrūtŏr. *See Quæro.*

Cōnsānguĭnĕŭs, ă, ūm. *Related to, relative.* Ēt cōnsānguĭnĕō lăcrīmāns cōmmēndăt Ăcēstæ. V. Syn.—Āffīnĭs, cōgnātŭs, prŏpīnquŭs. Phr.—Sāngĭnĕ jūnctŭs. Cōnsānguĭnĭtātĕ prŏpīnquŭs. Cōnsōrs gĕnĕrĭs. Ā stīrpĕ jūnctŭs. Cōgnātō sānguĭnĕ vīnctŭs. Sānguĭnĕ ĕōdēm nātŭs, ōrtŭs. Sānguĭne ăb ūnō dūcēns.

Cōnsānguĭnĭtās, ātĭs. f. *Relationship.* Īllī mē cŏmĭtem ēt cōnsānguĭnĭtātĕ prŏpīnquūm. V. Syn.—Āffīnĭtās, cōgnātĭō. Phr.—Āffīnĭă vīncŭlă. Gĕnĕrĭs cōnsōrtĭă. *See Consanguineus.*

Cōnscēndŏ, ĭs, dī, sūm, ĕrĕ. *To mount.* Cōnscēndēbăt ĕquōs, pătrĭō mūcrōnĕ rĕlīctō. O. Syn.—Scāndŏ, āscēndŏ. *See Ascendo.*

Cōnscĭēntĭă, æ. f. *Conscience.* Nōn tămĕn ērĭpĭēt laūdīs cōnscĭēntĭām. Phaed. Phr.—Cōnscĭă mēns. Ănĭmūs cōnscĭŭs. Mēns cōnscĭă făctī. Cōnscĭă pēctŏră. Tēstĭs dŏmēstĭcŭs. Āssĭdŭŭs ĭn pēctŏrĕ tēstĭs. Hăbĭtāns sŭb āltō pēctŏrĕ tēstĭs.

Cōnscīndŏ, ĭs, ĭdī, īssūm, ĕrĕ. *To tear down.* Syn.—Scīndŏ, dīscērpŏ, lăcĕrŏ, dīlănĭŏ.

Cōnscĭŏ, īs, īvī, ītūm, īrĕ. *To feel oneself at fault.* Phr.—Cūlpæ cōnscĭŭs sūm.

Cōnscīscŏ, ĭs, īvī, ītūm, ĕrĕ. *To decree publicly.* Syn.—Dēcērnŏ, stătŭŏ.

Cōnscĭŭs, ă, ūm. *Having common knowledge with some one.* Cōnscĭŭs īn cūlpā nōn scĕlŭs ēssĕ sŭā. O. Syn.—Cōnscĭēns. Phr.—Săcrī sĭbī cōnscĭă făctī. *Witness.* Syn.—Tēstĭs, ārbĭtĕr, ārbĭtră. Phr.—Āt nūmĭnă cōnscĭă vērī. Cōnscĭă sīdĕră tēstŏr.

Cōnscrīptŭs, ī. m. *Roman Senator.* Syn.—Sĕnātŏr, pătrēs cōnscrīptī.

Cōnsĕcrŏ, ās, āvī, ātūm, ārĕ. *To consecrate, to dedicate.* Syn.—

Săcrŏ, dĭcŏ, dēdĭcŏ, āddĭcŏ, vŏvĕŏ. Phr.—Sūrgēnt tēmplă tŭō dēdĭtă nōmĭnī.

Cōnsēnsŭs, ūs. m. *Agreement, concord.* Syn.—Āssēnsŭs, cōncōrdĭă. Phr.—Cōncōrdēs ănĭmī. *See Concordia.*

Cōnsēntānĕŭs, ă, ūm. *Agreeable, conformable.* Ūndă mărīs tĕpĭdī nōn cōnsēntānĕă brūmǣ. Syn.—Cōnsēntĭēns, cōnvĕnĭēns, āptŭs, cōncōrs, cōngrŭŭs, æ̆quŭs, pār.

Cōnsēntĭŏ, īs, sī, sūm, īrĕ. *To agree with.* Cōnsēntīrĕ sŭīs stŭdĭīs quī crēdĭdĕrīt tē. H. Syn.—Āssēntĭŏ, āssēntĭŏr, ānnŭŏ. Phr.—Mēns ōmnĭbŭs ūna ēst. Ōmnĭbŭs īdem ănĭmŭs.

Cōnsĕquŏr, ĕrĭs, sĕcūtŭs sūm, quī. *To follow closely upon.* Gўās quēm deīndĕ Clŏānthŭs Cōnsĕquĭtūr mĕlĭōr rēmīs. V. Syn.—Īnstŏ, ūrgĕŏ. *See Sequor. To acquire, to obtain.* Syn.—Ācquīrŏ, ădĭpīscŏr, āssĕquŏr, părŏ, cōmpărŏ, ōbtĭnĕŏ. *See Acquiro.*

Cōnsĕrŏ, ĭs, ēvī, ĭtūm, ĕrĕ. *To sow, to plant.* Syn.—Sĕrŏ, īnsĕrŏ, sēmĭnŏ, plāntŏ. *See Sero.*

Cōnsĕrŏ, ĭs, ĕrŭī, ērtūm, ĕrĕ. *To mingle, to join together.* Quīd nōctī cōnsĕrŭīssĕ dĭēm? O. Syn.—Mīscĕŏ, cōnjūngŏ, cōnnēctŏ. *See Jungo.*

Cōnsērvŏ, ās, āvī, ātūm, ārĕ. *To preserve.* Phr.—Cōnsērvābăt ŏpēs hŭmĭlīs căsă. Syn.—Sērvŏ, āssērvŏ, tŭĕŏr, tūtŏr. *See Servo*

Cōnsĭdĕŏ, ēs, ēdī, ēssūm, ērĕ. *To sit together.* Fōrtĕ sŭb ārgūtā cōnsēdĕrăt īlĭcĕ Dăphnĭs. V. Syn.—Āssĭdĕŏ, cōnsīdŏ, āssīdŏ. *To stop, to delay.* Syn.—Mŏrŏr, cōmmŏrŏr, cōnsīstŏ, cōnsīdŏ.

Cōnsīdĕrŏ, ās, āvī, ātūm, ārĕ. *To regard with attention.* Aūt lātūm pīctǣ vēstīs cōnsīdĕrăt aūrūm. J. Syn.—Cōntēmplŏr, tŭĕŏr. *To reflect.* Syn.—Rĕpŭtŏ, cōgĭtŏ, mĕdĭtŏr, ēxpēndŏ, pōndĕrŏ.

Cōnsīdŏ, ĭs, ēdī, ēssūm, ĕrĕ. *To sit, to recline.* Dīvī cōnsīdūnt tēctīs bĭpătēntĭbŭs. V. Syn.—Cōnsĭdĕŏ, sĕdĕŏ, sīdŏ. *To fall.* Syn.—Dēsīdŏ, fătīscŏ, prōlābŏr, ēvērtŏr, cŏrrŭŏ. Phr.—Tōtāmquĕ vĭdēmŭs Cōnsēdīsse ūrbēm lūctū. *To be calm.* Syn.—Pōnŏ, quĭēscŏ, sēdŏr.

Cōnsĭlĭūm, ĭī. n. *Advice.* Cōnsĭlĭūm nōbīs rēsquĕ lŏcūsquĕ dăbūnt. O. Syn.—Mŏnĭtŭs, mŏnĭtūm, ādmŏnĭtŭs.

Cōnsīstŏ, ĭs, stĭtī, stĭtūm, ĕrĕ. *To stop.* Cōnstĭtĭt Ānchīsā sătŭs, ēt vēstīgĭă prēssĭt. V. Syn.—Stō, sīstŏ, sūbsīstŏ. Phr.—Cōnsīstĕrĕ cōntrā. Tēr frīgŏrĕ cōnstĭtĭt Īstĕr. *To stand.* Syn.—Stō. *To exist.* Syn.—Cōnstŏ, ēxstŏ, ēxsīstŏ, sūm.

Cōnsōlŏr, ārĭs, ātŭs sūm, ārī. *To console.* Syn.—Sōlŏr, lĕvŏ.

Cōnsŏnŏ, ās, ŭī, ĭtūm, ārĕ. *To sound in unison.* Syn.—Sŏnŏ, pērsŏnŏ, rĕsŏnŏ. Fig.—*To be in harmony.* Syn.—Cōnsēntĭŏ, cōnvĕnĭŏ, cōngrŭŏ, cōncōrdŏ, quădrŏ.

Cōnsŏnŭs, ă, ūm. *Harmonious.* Trāctāt ĭnaūrātæ cōnsŏnă fīlă lўræ. O. Syn.—Cōncōrs. *Suitable.* Syn.—Cōnsēntānĕŭs, cōncōrs, cōnvĕnĭēns, cōngrŭŭs, āptŭs.

Cōnsōrs, ōrtĭs. *Companion.* Syn.—Sŏcĭŭs, cŏmĕs, pārtĭcēps. Phr.—Cōnsōrs pătrĭæquĕ lўræquĕ. Sŏcĭūsquĕ lăbōrĭs.

Cōnsōrtĭūm, ĭī. n. *Community, participation in.* Nām tē lōngă mănēnt nōstrī cōnsōrtĭă mūndī. Phr.—Sŏcĭă vītă. Sŏcĭă fātă. Sŏcĭŭs lăbŏr.

Cōnspēctŭs, ūs. m. *Sight, view.* Vīx ē cōnspēctū Sĭcŭlæ tēllūrĭs ĭn āltūm Vēlă dăbānt. V. Syn.—Āspēctŭs, vīsŭs. Phr.—Sēque ēx ŏcŭlĭs āvērtĭt ēt aūfērt.

Cōnspērgŏ, ĭs, sī, sūm, ĕrĕ. *To scatter around.* Ānnī Tēmpŏră cōnspērgūnt vĭrĭdāntēs flōrĭbūs hērbās. L. Syn.—Spārgŏ, fūndŏ. *See Spargo. To water.* Syn.—Spārgŏ, āspērgŏ, pērfūndŏ, īrrōrŏ, rĭgŏ, hūmēctŏ, mădĕfăcĭŏ.

Cōnspĭcĭŏ, ĭs, spēxī, spēctūm, ĕrĕ. *To look, to see.* Mœnĭă cōnspĭcĭo ātque ādvērsō fōrnĭcĕ pōrtās. V. Syn.—Cōnspĭcŏr, āspĭcĭŏ, vĭdĕŏ, īntŭĕŏr. Phr.—Vĭrĭdīque īn lĭttŏrĕ cōnspĭcĭtūr sūs. *See Aspicio.*

Cōnspĭcŭŭs, ă, ūm. *That which is easily perceived.* Syn.—Cōnspēctŭs, cōnspĭcĭēndŭs, spēctābĭlĭs, īnsīgnĭs. *Distinguished.* Syn.—Clārŭs, præclārŭs, ēgrĕgĭŭs, nōbĭlĭs.

Cōnspīrŏ, ās, āvī, ātūm, ārĕ. *To breathe together.* Syn.—Cōnsŏnŏ. *To conspire.* Syn.—Cōnjūrŏ, cōnsēntĭŏ. *To agree.* Cōnvĕnĭŏ, cōnjūrŏ, cōncōrdŏ.

Cōnspŭŏ, ĭs, ŭī, ūtūm, ĕrĕ. *To spit upon.* Syn.—Spŭŏ, ēxspŭŏ.

Cōnstāns, āntĭs. adj. *Fixed, constant.* Āt cōntrā mēllĭs cōnstāntĭŏr ēst nātūră. L. Syn.—Stăbĭlĭs, īdēm, ūnŭs. *Firm.* Syn.—Fīrmŭs, īmmōtŭs, īmmōbĭlĭs, īncōncūssŭs, cērtŭs, stăbĭlĭs, īmmūtābĭlĭs. Phr.—Mēns nēscĭă flēctī. Ănĭmūs cōnstāntĭŏr ānnīs. Cōnstāns ĭn ămīcĭtĭă. Nĕquĕ mē sēntēntĭă vērtĭt. Stāt cūnctīs īmmōtă mĭnĭs. Nūllă dĭēs tām fōrtĭbŭs aūsīs Dīssĭmĭlem ārgŭĕrĭt.

Cōnstāntĕr. adv. *Constantly.* Dī quōs ēxpĕrĭōr nĭmĭūm cōnstāntĕr ĭnīquōs. O. Syn.—Āssĭdŭē, ūsquĕ, sēmpĕr.

Cōnstāntĭă, æ. f. *Constancy, firmness.* Syn.—Rōbŭr. Phr.—Ănĭnŭs fīrmŭs, cōnstāns, īmmōbĭlĭs, īmmōtŭs. Mēns nēscĭă flēctī. *See Constans, Fortitudo.*

Cōnstăt. impers. *It is certain.* Pătĕt, cērtūm, (*or*) mănĭfēstūm ēst, lĭquĕt.

Cōnstērnŏ, ĭs, strāvī, strātūm, ĕrĕ. *To strew around, to scatter.* Syn.—Stērnŏ, prōstērnŏ, cōnspērgŏ. Phr.—Tērrām cōnstērnĕrĕ tērgō. Cōnstērnūntūr mīlĭtĕ cāmpī. *See Sterno.*

Cōnstĭtŭŏ, ĭs, ŭī, ūtūm, ĕrĕ. *To place, to establish.* Cōnstĭtŭūnt taūrum ānte ārās. V. Syn.—Pōnŏ, stătŭŏ, lŏcŏ. *To build.* Syn.—Stătŭŏ, pōnŏ, ǣdĭfĭcŏ, ērĭgŏ, strŭŏ. Phr.—Cōnstĭtŭĕrĕ pўrās. Ūrbēm cōnstĭtŭĕrĕ. *To resolve, to decree.* Syn.—Stătŭŏ, dēcērnŏ, vŏlŏ, sāncĭŏ.

Cōnstŏ, ās, stĭtī, stĭtūm & stātūm, ārĕ. *To be together, to stand together.* Syn.—Cōnsīstŏ, cōnflŏr. *To persevere.* Syn.—Pērstŏ, mănĕŏ, pērmănĕŏ, dūrŏ. *To agree with. See Convenio. To cost.* Syn.—Vēndŏr, vēnĕŏ, ĕmŏr.

Cōnstrīngŏ, ĭs, īnxī, īctūm, ĕrĕ. *To bind.* Brĕvĭs ēxpĕdītōs zōnā cōnstrīngĭt sĭnūs. Sen. Syn.—Strīngŏ, āstrīngŏ, lĭgŏ, ārctŏ, cŏārctŏ, cōmprĭmŏ. *See Vincio.* Fig.—*To force, to reduce.* Syn.—Cōgŏ, ădĭgŏ, rĕdĭgŏ.

Cōnstrŭŏ, ĭs, ūxī, ūctūm, ĕrĕ. *To build, to construct.* Nīdūm sĭbĭ cōnstrŭĭt ōrĕ. O. Syn.—Āggĕrŏ, strŭŏ. Phr.—Mēnsǣ cōnstrūctǣ dăpĕ mūltĭplĭcī.

Cōnsuēfăcĭŏ, ĭs, fēcī, fāctūm, ĕrĕ. *To accustom.* Syn.—Āssuēfăcĭŏ.

Cōnsuēscŏ, ĭs, ēvī, ētūm, ĕrĕ. *To be accustomed to.* Syn.—Āssuēscŏ.

Cōnsuētūdŏ, ĭnĭs. f. *Custom, habit.* Cōnsuētūdō mălī; tĕnēt īnsānābĭlĕ mūltōs. J. Syn.—Āssuētūdŏ, mōs, ūsŭs. Phr.—Nīl cōnsuētūdĭnĕ mājŭs.

Cōnsŭl, ŭlĭs. m. *Consul, Roman magistrate.* Sī fōrtūnă vŏlēt, fīēs dē rhētŏrĕ cōnsŭl. J. Phr.—Ūrbĭs rēctŏr. Sūmmă tĕnēns. Quī jūstĭs mŏdĕrātūr lēgĭbŭs ūrbēm. Ānnŭă jūră căpĭt. *See Consulatus.*

Cōnsŭlātŭs, ūs. m. *Consulship.* Syn.—Fāscēs, sĕcūrēs. Phr.—Cōnsŭlĭs mūnŭs, pŏtēstās, jūs. Cōnsŭlĭs īmpĕrĭūm.

Cōnsŭlŏ, ĭs, ŭī, ūltūm, ĕrĕ. *To consult, to ask advice.* Phœbīque ōrăcŭlă sūpplēx Cōnsŭlĭt. V. Syn.—Īntērrŏgŏ, scīscĭtŏr, scītŏr, quǣrŏ. Phr.—Cōnsĭlĭūm pĕtŏ, căpĭŏ. Cōnsĭlĭīs ūtŏr. Spĕcŭlūm cōnsŭlăt āntĕ sŭūm. *To deliberate.* Syn.—Dēlībĕrŏ, trāctŏ, ăgŏ. *To watch over, to take care of.* Syn.—Prōvĭdĕŏ, prōspĭcĭŏ, căvĕŏ, cūrŏ.

Cōnsūltē. adv. *Prudently.* Syn.—Prūdēntĕr, cautē.

Cōnsūltō. adv. *By design.* Syn.—Cōnsĭlĭō.

Cōnsūltūm, ī. n. *Resolution, decree.* Syn.—Dēcrētūm, stătūtūm.

Cōnsūmmŏ, ās, āvī, ātūm, ārĕ. *To achieve, to consummate.* Syn.—Nōndūm lĭtāstī, nātĕ; cōnsūmmā săcrūm. Syn.—Ābsōlvŏ, pĕrăgŏ, cōnfĭcĭŏ, pērfĭcĭŏ. *See Finio.*

Cōnsūmŏ, ĭs, psī, ptūm, ĕrĕ. *To consume.* Āccīsīs cōgēt dăpĭbūs cōnsūmĕrĕ mēnsās. V. Syn.—Ābsūmŏ, ēxhaūrĭŏ, cōnfĭcĭŏ. *To use up, to destroy.* Syn.—Ābsūmŏ, ĕdŏ, pĕrĕdŏ, dēstrŭŏ. *See Perdo, Exedo. To satisfy.* Syn.—Ēxplĕŏ, sătĭŏ.

Cōnsūrgŏ, ĭs, sūrrēxī, rēctūm, ĕrĕ. *To rise together.* Cūnctīquĕ rĕlīctīs Cōnsūrgūnt mēnsīs. V. Syn.—Sūrgŏ.

Cōntāctŭs, ūs. m. *Touch, contact.* Syn.—Tāctŭs.

Cōntāgēs, ĭs, Cōntāgĭŏ, ōnĭs, f. & Cōntāgĭūm, ĭī. n. *Contagion.* Quæ cōntāgĕ sŭā pāllōrĭbŭs ōmnĭă pīngānt. Syn.—Lŭēs, pēstĭs. Phr.—Grēx tōtŭs ĭn āgrō Ūnīūs scăbĭē pĕrĭt. Scĕlĕrūm cōntagiă.

Cōntāmĭnŏ, ās, āvī, ātūm, ārĕ. *To soil, to corrupt.* Sīc īntērpŏsĭtūs vīllō cōntāmĭnăt ūnctō. M. Syn.—Fœdŏ, īnquĭnŏ, cŏīnquĭnŏ, pōllŭŏ, īnfĭcĭŏ, cōntĕmĕrŏ. *See Polluo.*

Cōntĕgŏ, ĭs, ēxī, ēctūm, ĕrĕ. *To cover, to conceal.* Aūt ĕgō Tænărĭă cōntĕgăr ēxsŭl hŭmō. O. Syn.—Tĕgŏ, ōbtĕgŏ, cōndŏ, ābscōndŏ, ŏpĕrĭŏ.

Cōntĕmĕrŏ, ās, āvī, ātūm, ārĕ. *To corrupt. See Contamino.*

Cōntēmnŏ, ĭs, psī, ptūm, ĕrĕ. *To scorn, to despise.* Cōntēmnūntquĕ făvōs ēt frīgĭdă tēctă rĕlīnquūnt. V. Syn.—Tēmnŏ, spērnŏ, āspērnŏr, dēspĭcĭŏ, fāstīdĭŏ, rēsp..ŏ, dēspēctŏ, cōncūlcŏ, ābjĭcĭŏ. rĕjĭcĭŏ, nēglĭgŏ. Phr.—Pārvī, nĭhĭlī dūcŏ, făcĭŏ, æstĭmŏ, pēndŏ. Nōn (*or*) nĭhĭl cūrŏ. Cōntēmnĕrĕ fāmæ mūrmŭră. *See Aspernor.*

Cōntēmplātŭs, ūs. m. *Sight, view.* Syn.—Vīsŭs, īntŭĭtŭs, āspēctŭs, cōnspēctŭs.

Cōntēmplŏr, ārĭs, ātŭs sūm, ārī. *To contemplate, to consider.* Syn. —Āspĭcĭŏ, īntŭĕŏr, cōnsīdĕrŏ.

Cōntēmptŏr, ōrĭs. m. *One who despises.* Syn.—Sprētŏr.

Cōntēmptŭs, ūs. m. *Contempt.* Syn.—Fāstīdĭūm. Phr.—Mēntēm cōntēmptū nĕcĭs ārmăt. Sŭpērbă pătī fāstīdĭă.

Cōntēndŏ, ĭs, dī, sūm & tūm, ĕrĕ. *To stretch.* Syn.—Tēndŏ, īntēndŏ. Phr.—Īlĭă rīsū cōntēndĕrĕ. Nōn ūt cōntēndĕrēt ārcūm. *To strive.* Syn.—Cōnŏr, nītŏr. *To maintain.* Syn.—Āffīrmŏ, āssĕrŏ.

Cōntēntē. adv. *With an effort.* Syn.—Ēnīxē.

Cōntēntĭŏ, ōnĭs. f. *Dispute, strife.* Syn.—Līs, rīxă.

Cōntēntŭs, ă, ūm. *Happy, contented.* Syn.—Lætŭs, fēlīx. Phr.—Cōntēntūs vīvĕrĕ pārvō. Hāc gălĕā cōntēntŭs ăbītō. Mēns plăcĭdā cōntēntă quĭētĕ.

Cōntĕrŏ, ĭs, trīvī, trītūm, ĕrĕ. *To rub away.* Sĕd ōmnĕ līmēn cōntĕrīs sălūtātŏr. M. Syn.—Tĕrŏ, āttĕrŏ, prōtĕrŏ, cōmmĭnŭō. Phr.—Vīvācīs cōrnŭă cērvī cōntĕrĕ. *To consume, to destroy.* Syn.—Ābsūmō, cōnsūmŏ, cōnfĭcĭŏ, ēxhaūrĭŏ.

Cōntĕxŏ, ĭs, xŭī, xtūm, ĕrĕ. *To join together.* Ūt cūm cōntēxūnt ămărānthīs ālbă pŭēllæ Lĭlĭă. Tib. Syn.—Nēctŏ, cōnnēctŏ, lĭgŏ, cōnsŭŏ, jūngŏ, cōmpīngŏ. Phr.—Cōntēxĕrĕ vīllōs.

Cōntĭcĕŏ, ēs, ŭī, ērĕ. *To be silent.* Cōntĭcŭēre ōmnēs īntēntīque ōră tĕnēbānt. V. Syn.—Tăcĕŏ, rĕtĭcĕŏ. Phr.—Cōntĭcŭīstĭs ăvēs. *See Sileo.*

Cōntĭgŭŭs, ă, ŭm. *Touching.* Hūnc ŭbĭ cōntĭgŭūm mīssæ fŏrĕ crēdĭdĭt hāstæ. V. Syn.—Prŏpīnquŭs, prŏpĭŏr, prōxĭmŭs, vīcīnŭs, cōntērmĭnŭs, jūnctŭs, cōnjūnctŭs.

Cōntĭnēntĕr. adv. *Continually.* Syn.—Cōntĭnŭō, āssĭdŭē, pērpĕtŭō. *With restraint.* Syn.—Mŏdēstē.

Cōntĭnēntĭă, æ. f. *Restraint, abstinence.* Syn.—Ābstĭnēntĭă. *See Castitas.*

Cōntĭnĕŏ, ēs, ŭī, ēntūm, ērĕ. *To hold.* Syn.—Īnclūdŏ, cōmplēctŏr, tĕnĕŏ, căpĭŏ. *To restrain.* Syn.—Mŏrŏ, dētĭnĕŏ, īmpĕdĭŏ, rĕtĭnĕŏ. *To restrain.* Syn.—Ābstĭnĕŏ, tēmpĕrŏ(ab).

Cōntīngŏ, ĭs, ĭgī, āctūm, ĕrĕ. *To touch.* Syn.—Tāngŏ, āttrēctŏ. *To attain.* Syn.—Āttīngŏ, āssĕquŏr.

Cōntĭnŭŏ, ās, āvī, ātūm, ārĕ. *To continue.* Syn.—Pērgŏ, pērsĕvērŏ. Phr.—Nōn ābsīstŏ. Nōn dēsīstŏ, cēssŏ, dēsĭnŏ.

Cōntĭnŭō. adv. *Continually.* Syn.—Sēmpĕr, prōtĭnŭs. *Straightway.* Syn.—Āctūtūm, cōnfēstĭm, ēxtēmplō, īlĭcēt, īlĭcō, mōx, rĕpēntĕ, sŭbĭtō, prōtĭnŭs. Phr.—Haūd mŏră. Mŏră nūllă.

Cōntĭnŭŭs, ă, ūm. *Continued, continuous.* Syn.—Cōntĭnŭātŭs, cōntĭnēns. *Continual.* Syn.—Pĕrēnnĭs, jūgĭs, pērpĕtŭŭs, āssĭdŭŭs, ætērnŭs.

Cōntōrquĕŏ, ēs, tōrsī, tōrtūm, ērĕ. *To twist, to turn.* Cōntōrsĭt lævās prōrām Pălĭnūrŭs ăd ūndās. V. Syn.—Tōrquĕŏ, īntōrquĕŏ, flēctŏ, īnflēctŏ. *To hurl.* Syn.—Tōrquĕŏ, īnjĭcĭŏ, jăcŭlŏr, vĭbrŏ, ēmīttŏ. *See Jaculor.*

Cōntrā. prep. *Against.* Ītălĭām cōntrā Tĭbĕrīnăquĕ lōngē Ōstĭă. V. Syn.—Ādvērsŭs, ĭn.

Cōntrā. adv. *To the contrary.* Cōntrā nōn nūlla ēst ŏlĕīs cūltūră. V. Syn.—Vērūm, vērō, aūtēm.

Cōntrădīcŏ, ĭs, īxī, īctūm, ĕrĕ. *To contradict.* Syn.—Ādvērsŏr, ōblŏquŏr, rĕpūgnŏ, rĕsīstŏ.

Cōntrăhŏ, ĭs, āxī, āctūm, ĕrĕ. *To draw together, to narrow.* Īpsĕ tĭbī jām brāchĭă cōntrăhĭt ārdēns Scōrpĭŭs. V. Syn.—Ārctŏ, āngūstŏ, prĕmŏ, strīngŏ, cŏārctŏ, āddūcŏ. Phr.—Cōntrăhes vēntō nĭmĭūm sĕcūndō tūrgĭdā vēlā. Ănĭmŭs fōrmīdĭnĕ dīvūm Cōntrăhĭtŭr. *To assemble, to unite.* Syn.—Cōllĭgŏ, cōgŏ, cōngrĕgŏ, cōnvŏcŏ.

Cōntrārĭŭs, ă, ūm. *Opposed to.* Scīndĭtŭr īncērtūm stŭdĭa īn cōntrārĭă vūlgŭs. V. Syn.—Ādvērsārĭŭs, ādvērsŭs, ōppŏsĭtŭs, ĭnĭmīcŭs, pūgnāns.

Cōntrĕmīscŏ, ĭs, ĕrĕ, & Cōntrĕmŏ, ĭs, ŭī, ĕrĕ. *To tremble.* Cōntrĕmŭīt nĕmŭs, ēt sīlvae īntŏnŭērĕ prŏfūndæ. V. Syn.—Trĕmŏ, īntrĕmŏ. *To fear. See Timeo.*

Cōntrĭbŭŏ, ĭs, ŭī, ūtūm, ĕrĕ. *To contribute.* Syn.—Cōnfĕrŏ, trĭbŭŏ.

Cōntrōvērsĭă, æ. f. *Dispute.* Syn.—Āltērcātĭŏ, cōntēntĭŏ, jūrgĭūm, līs, rīxă.

Cōntrōvērsŭs, ă, ūm. *Disputed.* Syn.—Āmbĭgŭŭs, āncēps, dŭbĭŭs īncērtŭs.

Cōntŭĕŏr, ērĭs, ĭtŭs sūm, ērī. *To regard. See Aspicio.*

Cōntŭmācĭă, æ. f. *Obstinacy.* Syn.—Pērtĭnācĭă, sŭpērbĭă. *Arrogance.* Syn.—Ārrŏgāntĭă, fāstŭs, sŭpērbĭă.

Cōntŭmāx, ācĭs. adj. *Rebellious.* Syn.—Rĕbēllĭs, īndŏcĭlĭs, sŭpērbŭs, pērtĭnāx.

Cōntŭmēlĭă, æ. f. *Insult, injury.* Syn.—Īnjūrĭă, prŏbrūm, ōpprŏbrĭūm, cōnvīcĭūm, dēdĕcŭs. Phr.—Fāctīs īmmītĭbŭs āddĭt Vērbă sŭpērbă fĕrōx. Pŭdĕt hæc ōpprōbrĭă dīcī.

Cōntūndŏ, ĭs, ŭdī, ūsūm, ĕrĕ. *To break, to bruise.* Syn.—Tūndŏ, ōbtĕrŏ, frāngŏ, cōmmĭnŭŏ. *To check, to repress.* Syn.—Dŏmŏ, sŭbĭgŏ, frāngŏ, rĕtūndŏ.

Cōntūrbŏ, ās, āvī, ātūm, ārĕ. *To trouble, to disturb.* Syn.—Tūrbŏ, cōntūrbŏ, mīscĕŏ, cōmmīscĕŏ, cōnfūndŏ. *See Turbo.*

Cōntŭs, ī. m. *Pole.* Īpsĕ rătēm cōntō sŭbĭgĭt. V. Phr.—Dūrīs hōstēs dētrūdĕrĕ cōntīs.

Cōnvēctŏ, ās, āvī, ātūm, ārĕ. *To transport.* Syn.—Vĕhŏ, vēctŏ, trānspōrtŏ.

Cōnvēllŏ, ĭs, ēllī & ūlsī, ūlsūm, ĕrĕ. *To uproot.* Vīncĕrĕ nēc dūrō pŏtĕrīs cōnvēllĕrĕ fērrō. V. Syn.—Vēllŏ, āvēllŏ, ēvēllŏ, rĕvēllŏ. Phr.—Ăvĭdōquĕ dăpēs cōnvēllĕrĕ dēntĕ. Ā tērrā cōnvēllĕrĕ fūnēm. Vērbīs cōnvēllĕrĕ pēctŭs. *See Frango, Moveo.*

Cōnvĕnĭēntĕr. adv. *Conformably.* Syn.—Āptē, dĕcēntĕr.

Cōnvĕnĭēntĭă, æ. f. *Conformity, concord.* Syn.—Cōnsēnsŭs, cōncōrdĭă.

Cōnvĕnĭŏ, īs, vēnī, vēntūm, īrĕ. *To assemble.* Cōnvĕnĭūnt, quĭbŭs aūt ŏdĭūm crūdēlĕ tўrānnī. V. Syn.—Cŏĕŏ, cōngrĕdĭŏr, cōnflŭŏ, cōncūrrŏ. Phr.—Bŏnī quŏnĭām cōnvēnĭmŭs āmbŏ. Īntēr sē cŏīssĕ vĭrōs. Ūndĭquĕ cōllēctī cŏēūnt. *To agree.* Syn.—Cōnsŏnŏ, cōnsēntĭŏ, cōngrŭŏ.

Cōnvēntūm, ī. n. *Compact.* Cōnvēntūm tămĕn ēt pāctum ēt spōnsālĭă nōstrā Tēmpēstātĕ părās. J. Syn.—Pāctūm, cōnvēntŭs, fœdŭs.

Cōnvēntŭs, ūs. m. *Assembly, agreement.* Syn.—Cœtŭs, cōncĭlĭūm, tūrbă, frĕquēntĭă, cōnsēssŭs.

Cōnvērtŏ, ĭs, tī, sūm, ĕrĕ. *To turn.* Īn mē cōnvērtĭtĕ fērrūm. V. Syn.—Vērtŏ. *To change.* Syn.—Vērtŏ, mūtŏ, cōmmūtŏ.

Cōnvēxŭs, ă, ūm. *Convex, curved.* Syn.—Cūrvŭs. *Hollow.* Syn.—Căvŭs, cōncăvŭs, cūrvŭs.

Cōnvīcĭūm, ĭī. n. *Injury, insult.* Tūm pŭĕrī naūtīs, pŭĕrīs cōnvīcĭă naūtæ Īngĕrĕrĕ. H. Syn.—Mălĕdīctūm, prŏbrūm, ōpprŏbrĭūm. Phr.—Līnguæ cōnvīcĭă, jūrgĭă, vērbĕră. Līnguă mălă, āspĕră, prŏtērvă. Āmāræ prœlĭă līnguæ. Tūrpĭă dīctă. Cōnvīcĭă fūndĕrĕ. Prŏbrīs ŏnĕrārĕ. Āddīt cōnvīcĭă fāctō. *Reproach.* Syn.—Ōbjūrgātĭŏ.

Cōncīncŏ, ĭs, īcī, īctūm, ĕrĕ. *To convince.* Syn.—Cŏārgŭŏ. Phr.—Cōnvīncĕrĕ fālsī. *To prove.* Syn.—Ēvīncŏ, ōstēndŏ, prŏbŏ, ārgŭŏ.

Cōnvīvă, æ. m. *Guest.* Trēs mĭhĭ cōnvīvæ prŏpĕ dīssēntīrĕ vĭdēntŭr. H. Syn.—Cōnvīctŏr, cōmpōtŏr, cōmbĭbŏ, sŏdālĭs. Phr.—Mēnsæ sŏcĭŭs. Tū dās ĕpŭlīs āccūmbĕrĕ dīvūm. Tŏrīs jūssī dīscūmbĕrĕ pīctīs.

Cōnvīvātŏr, ōrĭs. m. *Host.* Syn.—Hōspĕs, caūpŏ, hōspĭtă, mēnsæ pătĕr.

Cōnvīvĭūm, ĭī. n. *Feast.* Syn.—Ĕpŭlæ, dăpēs mēnsæ, cœnă. Phr.—Ēxplēnt cōnvīvĭă dīctīs.

Cōnvīvŏ, ĭs, xī, ctūm, ĕrĕ. *To live together.* Nōn cōnvīvĕrĕ, nēc vĭdērĕ sāltēm. M. Phr.—Sĭmŭl, ūnā vīvŏ, dēgŏ, ævūm, vītām trādūcŏ.

Cōnvīvŏr, ārĭs, ātŭs sūm, ārī. *To feast.* Quōd cōnvīvārīs sĭnĕ mē tām sæpĕ, Lŭpērcĕ. M. Syn.—Ĕpŭlŏr, cœnŏ. Phr.—Cōnvīvĭă ăgĭtŏ, cĕlĕbrŏ, cūrŏ, ĭnĕŏ, făcĭŏ, dūcŏ. Dăpēs īnstĭtŭĕrĕ. Ĕpŭlīs văcārĕ. *See Convivium.*

Cōnvŏcŏ, ās, āvī, ātūm, ārĕ. *To call together.* Cōnvŏcāt āltērnōs ād sŭă fēstă dĕōs. O. Syn.—Vŏcŏ, ādvŏcŏ, āccērsŏ, āccĭŏ, cōngrĕgŏ.

Cōnvōlvŏ, ĭs, vī, ŏlūtūm, ĕrĕ. *To roll together.* Syn.—Cōgŏ, cōllĭgŏ, cōntrăhŏ. *To envelop.* Syn.—Īnvōlvŏ.

Cŏŏpĕrĭŏ, īs, ŭī, ērtūm, īrĕ. *To cover.* Syn.—Ŏpĕrĭŏ, tĕgŏ, cōntĕgŏ, ōbtĕgŏ, ōccūltŏ. *See Abscondo, Tego, Abditus.*

Cŏŏrĭŏr, īrĭs, ōrtŭs sūm, īrī. *To rise.* Sē vēntīs cōmmīsĕrăt ūndă cŏōrtīs. O. *See Orior.*

Cōpĭă, æ. f. *Abundance.* Quōd cŭpĭō mēcum ēst, ĭnŏpēm mē cōpĭă fēcĭt. O. Syn.—Ăbūndāntĭă, ūbērtās, vīs, ăcērvŭs, nŭmĕrŭs. Phr.—Vītæ cōpĭă dēfŭĭt īllīs. Quōd sī nōn ēssēt făcĭlīs tĭbĭ cōpĭă. Fāstīdĭōsām dēsĕrĕ cōpĭām.

Cōpĭæ, ārūm. f. *Forces.* Syn.—Āgmĕn, ēxērcĭtŭs.

Cōpŭlă, æ. f. *Knot.* Lūctāntēm frūstrā cōpŭlă dūră tĕnēt. O. Syn.—Vīncŭlūm, lĭgāmĕn, nĕxŭs.

Cŏquŏ, ĭs, ōxī, ōctūm, ĕrĕ. *To cook.* Īndĕ cĭbūm cŏquĕre ēt flāmmæ mōllīrĕ văpōrĕ Sōl dŏcŭĭt. L. Syn.—Cōncŏquŏ, īncŏquŏ, pērcŏquŏ. Phr.—Īgnĕ, flāmmīs tōrrērĕ. Dŏmārĕ fērvēntĭbŭs ūndīs. Vīncĕrĕ flāmmā. Ātrā vērsārĕ făvīllā. Aūt hūmānā pālām cŏquăt ēxtă.

Cŏr, cōrdĭs. n. *Heart.* Mōrbĭdă vīs īn cōr mœstūm cōnflūxĕrăt ægrīs. L. Syn.—Præcōrdĭă. Phr.—Pūlsāntūr trĕpĭdī cōrdĕ. Pērfĭdă cōrdă. Fig.—*Courage.* Syn.—Ănĭmŭs, pēctŭs. Phr.—Pācem īndīgnāntĭă cōrdă. Bēllō trĕpĭdāntĭă cōrdă. Nēscĭă vīncī Pēctŏră. Nūnc pēctŏrĕ fīrmō.

Cōrām. prep. *In the presence of.* Nē pŭĕrōs cōrām pŏpŭlō Mēdēă trŭcīdēt. H. Syn.—Āntĕ. Phr.—Īn ŏcŭlīs, īn cōnspēctū. Ānte ŏcŭlōs, ōră. Ād cōnspēctūm. Sŭb ōră.

Cōrdātē. adv. *Wisely, sensibly.* Syn.—Prūdēntĕr, săpĭēntĕr, cātē, scītē.

Cōrdātŭs, ă, ūm. *Judicious.* Āt tē cuī săpĭēns fŭĭt ēt cōrdātă jŭvēntūs. M. Syn.—Prūdēns, săpĭēns, scītŭs, sōlērs, săgāx, cătŭs.

Cōrnīcŭlă, æ. f. *Jackdaw, or little crow.* (*See Appendix under list of Birds.*)

Cōrnĭgĕr, ă, ūm. *Horned.* Cōrnĭgĕr Hēspĕrĭdūm flŭvĭūs rēgnātŏr ăquārūm. V. Syn.—Cōrnūtŭs. Phr.—Gĕrēns cōrnŭă. **Cōrnĭbŭs īnstrūctŭs.** Frōns hædō prīmīs tūrgĭdă cōrnĭbŭs.

Cōrnīx, īcĭs. f. *Crow.* (*See Appendix under list of Birds.*)

Cōrnū. n. indecl. *Horn.* Ēt dūctūs cōrnū stābāt săcĕr hīrcŭs ăd ārām. V. Phr.—Nātūm frōntī. Īn tērgă rēcūrvūm. Cuī frōns āspĕră cōrnū. Īn cōrnŭă cēlsŭs. Sūmmīs vīx cōrnĭbŭs ēxstānt.

Cōrnŭs, ī. f. *The cornel tree.* (*See Appendix under list of Trees, etc.*)

Cŏrōnă, æ. f. *Crown, diadem.* Pālam ēt gēmmĭfĕræ dōnum ēxĭtĭālĕ cŏrōnæ. V. Syn.—Dĭădēmă. Phr.—Dŭplĭcēm gēmmīs aūrōquĕ cŏrōnām. Tēmpŏră cīngēns, ōrnāns. Cŏrōnă căpŭt āmbĭt. *Garland of flowers.* Syn.—Sērtūm, cŏrōllă, flōrēs. Phr.—Nēxæ phy̆ly̆rā cŏrōnæ. Cŏrōnām tĕnĕrō pōllĭcĕ. Fūsæ pēr cōllă cŏrōnæ. *See Corono, Sertum.*

Cŏrōnŏ, ās, āvī, ātūm, ārĕ. *To crown.* Tē dŭŏ dīvērsā dŏmĭnī dē pārtĕ cŏrōnānt. O. Phr.—Cŏrōnā căpŭt, tēmpŏră, crīnēs, căpīllōs, cŏmām, frōntēm ōrnŏ. Cŏrōnā cīngŏ, vīncĭŏ, īmplĭcŏ. Cīngŏ flōrĕ căpŭt. Frōndēntī tēmpŏră rāmọ Īmplĭcăt. Mĕrĭtōs ōrnāt dĭădēmătĕ crīnēs.

Cōrpŭlēntŭs, ă, ūm. *Heavy, fat.* Syn.—Pīnguĭs, crāssŭs, ŏbēsŭs. Phr.—Ŏbēsī cōrpŏrĭs. Ăbūndāns cōrpŏrĭs ēxĭgŭŭsque ănĭmī.

Cōrpŭs, ŏrĭs. n. *Body.* Mājŏr ĭn ēxĭgŭō rēgnābāt cōrpŏrĕ vīrtūs. Syn.—Mēmbră, ārtūs. Phr.—Cōrpŏrĭs ārtūs, mēmbră. Ănĭmæ cārcĕr. Cōrpŏrĕă mōlēs. Cōmpāgēs mēmbrōrūm. Cōrpūs dēmīttĕrĕ mōrtī. Dēlēctă vīrūm cōrpŏră. Māgnō cōntūsă lăbōrĕ. *Dead body.* Phr.—Cōrpūs cāssum ănĭmā. Cōrpŭs ĭnāne anĭmæ. Cōrpŏră lūcĕ cărēntūm.

Cōrrādŏ, ĭs, sī, sūm, ĕrĕ. *To rake together.* Syn.—Rādŏ, ābrādŏ, cōllĭgŏ.

Cōrrēptē. adv. *Briefly.* Syn.—Brĕvĭtĕr, prēssē.

Cōrrĭgŏ, ĭs, ēxī, ēctūm, ĕrĕ. *To make straight, to better.* Tŭă cōrrĭgĕ vōtă. H. Syn.—Ēmēndŏ, mūtŏ. *To correct.* Syn.—Ēmēndŏ, cāstīgŏ, pŏlĭŏ, ēxpŏlĭŏ, līmŏ. Phr.—Ērrātă ēxpūngŏ. Līmām ădhĭbĕŏ. Mēndīs pūrgŏ, ēxpūngŏ. Ăd īncūdēm rĕvŏcārĕ lĭbēllūm. Īncūdī rēddĕrĕ vērsūs. Cōrrēxī sūb tē cēnsōrĕ lĭbēllōs.

Cōrrĭpĭŏ, ĭs, ŭī, ēptūm, ĕrĕ. *To seize, to take.* Ārcūmquĕ mănū, cĕlĕrēsquĕ săgīttās Cōrrĭpŭĭt. V. Syn.—Căpĭŏ, ārrĭpĭŏ, prĕhēndŏ. *To reprehend.* Syn.—Rĕdārgŭŏ, cāstīgŏ, ōbjūrgŏ.

Cōrrōbŏrŏ, ās, āvī, ātūm, ārĕ. *To strengthen.* Syn.—Rōbŏrŏ, fīrmŏ.

Cōrrōdŏ, ĭs, sī, sūm, ĕrĕ. *To gnaw.* Syn.—Rōdŏ, ārrōdŏ, cīrcūmrōdŏ, ĕdŏ, ēxĕdŏ.

Cōrrūmpŏ, ĭs, rūpī, rūptūm, ĕrĕ. *To break.* Mĭhĭ cōrrūpīt dēntēs. Plaut. *To corrupt.* Syn.—Fœ̄dŏ, cōntāmĭnŏ, vĭtĭŏ, pōllŭŏ, īnfĭcĭŏ, pērdŏ, pēssūmdŏ. Phr.—Cōrrūmpĕrĕ fēbrĭbŭs ārtūs. Cōrrūmpĕrĕ dēntĭbŭs ūnguēs. Pĕcŏrīque āspērgĕrĕ vīrŭs. *See Polluo.*

Cŏrūscŏ, ās, āvī, ātūm, ārĕ. *To be in movement, to be agitated.* Syn.—Trĕpĭdŏ, ăgĭtŏr, mŏvĕŏr, trĕmŏ. *To shine.* Syn.—Splēndĕŏ, splēndēscŏ, rēsplēndĕŏ, fūlgĕŏ, rĕfūlgĕŏ, mĭcŏ, rădĭŏ. Phr.—Lūcēm dō, spārgŏ, fūndŏ, vĭbrŏ. Lūcēm sūb nūbĭlă jāctŏ. Fūlgōrĕ cŏrūscānt. *See Luceo.*

Cŏrūscŭs, ă, ūm. *Trembling.* Syn.—Trĕmŭlŭs. *Shining, brilliant.* Syn.—Cŏrūscāns, splēndĭdŭs, splēndēns, fūlgēns, fūlgĭdŭs, ārdēns, rŭtĭlāns, rŭtĭlŭs, mĭcāns, rădĭāns.

Cōrvŭs, ī. m. *A raven.* (*See Appendix under list of Birds.*)

Cŏrўlŭs, ī. f. *The hazel tree.* (*See Appendix under list of Trees, etc.*)

Cōs, cōtĭs. f. *Whetstone.* Fūngār vĭcĕ cōtĭs, ăcūtūm Rēddĕrĕ quæ fērrūm vălĕt, ēxsōrs īpsă sĕcāndī. H. Phr.—Cōte ăcūīt tēlūm. Sŭbĭgūnt īn cōtĕ sĕcūrēs. Cōtĕ nŏvāt nīgrās rūbīgĭnĕ fālcēs. *Stone.* Syn.—Sāxūm, sĭlēx, caūtēs, rūpēs.

Cōstă, æ. f. *Side.* Sæpe ŏlĭō tārdī cōstās ăgĭtātŏr ăsēllī Vīlĭbŭs aūt ŏnĕrēt pōmīs. V. Syn.—Lătŭs. Phr.—Cōstārūm crātēs, ōssă. Lătĕrūm, pēctŏrĭs crātēs. Frĭcāt ārbŏrĕ cōstās. Tērgŏră dīrĭpĭūnt cōstīs. Cōstīs spūmāntĭs ăhēnī.

Cŏthūrnātŭs, ă, ūm. *Wearing the buskin. Pertaining to tragedy.* Syn.—Trăgĭcŭs, hērōĭcŭs, grāndĭlŏquŭs.

Cŏthūrnŭs, ī. m. *Buskin.* Pūrpŭrĕōque āltē sūrās vīncīrĕ cŏthūrnō. V. *Tragedy.* Syn.—Trăgœdĭă. Phr.—Māgnūmquĕ lŏquī nītīquĕ cŏthūrnō. *See Tragoedia.*

Cŏtūrnīx, īcĭs. f. *A quail.* (*See Appendix under list of Birds.*)

Crābrŏ, ōnĭs. m. *Hornet.* Prēssŭs hŭmō bēllātŏr ĕquūs crābrōnĭs ŏrīgo ēst. O. Syn.—Vēspă, fūcŭs.

Crās. adv. *Tomorrow.* Quīd sīt fŭtūrūm crās fŭgĕ quærĕrĕ. H. Phr.—Crāstĭnă lūx, aūrōră, dĭēs. Lūx āltĕră. Lūx sĕquēns. Sēd cūm lūx āltĕră vēnĭt. Quīd crāstĭnă vōlvĕrĭt ætās Scīrĕ nĕfās hŏmĭnī.

Crāssŭs, ă, ūm. *Thick, dense, solid.* Syn.—Spīssŭs, dēnsŭs, dēnsātŭs, pīnguĭs. Phr.—Crāssăquĕ cōnvĕnĭānt lĭquĭdīs. Crāssās gūrgĭtĕ vōlvĭt ăquās. *Stout, fat.* Syn.—Pīnguĭs, ŏbēsŭs, āmplŭs, prōcērŭs, īngēns.

Crāstĭnŭs, ă, ūm. *Pertaining to the morrow.* Syn.—Pōstĕrŭs, prōxĭmŭs. *See Cras.*

Crātēr, ērĭs. m. *Mixing bowl for wine, goblet, cup.* Īndūlgēnt vīno, ēt vērtūnt crātērăs ăhēnōs. V. Syn.—Crātēră, călĭx, scȳphŭs, pătĕră, cārchēsĭūm, pōcŭlūm. Phr.—Căpāx ūrnæ. Aūrō sŏlĭdŭs. Sīgnīs āspĕr, īmprēssŭs. Gēstāt crātēră cŏrūscūm. Īmplēvĭt crātēră mĕrō. *See Poculum.*

Crātēră, æ. f. *Mixing bowl. See Crater.*

Crātēs, ĭs. f. *Frame.* Phr.—Sīccīs tērgă sŭīs rāră pēndēntĭă crātĕ. *Shield.* Syn.—Clȳpĕŭs.

Crĕātŏr, ōrĭs. m. *Creator, maker.* Īllĕ crĕātōr rērūm. L. Syn.—Aūctŏr, cōndĭtŏr, ŏpĭfēx.

Crēbĕr, ră, rūm. *Frequent.* Nēc tām crēbĕr ăgēns hĭĕmēm rŭĭt æquŏrĕ tūrbŏ. V. Syn.—Frĕquēns, spīssŭs, mūltŭs, plūrĭmŭs, rĕpĕtītŭs. Phr.—Crēbērquĕ prŏcēllīs Āfrĭcŭs. Ērrāt tēmpŏră cīrcūm Crēbră mănŭs. Crēbrīsquĕ bĭpēnnĭbŭs īnstānt. Crēbrĭŭs āgmĕn ĕrĭt.

Crēbrēscŏ, ĭs, bŭī. *To increase, to redouble.* Syn.—Īncrēbrēscŏ, crēscŏ, aūgēscŏ, aūgĕŏr.

Crēbrō. adv. *Frequently*. Syn.—Sæpĕ, sæpĭŭs, frĕquēntĕr, crēbră.

Crēdĭbĭlĭs, ĭs, ĕ. *Credible, worthy of belief*. Crēdĭbĭle ēst īpsōs cōnsŭlŭīssĕ dĕōs. Syn.—Prŏbābĭlĭs, vērīsĭmĭlĭs. Phr.—Crēdī, fīdē dīgnŭs. Fĭdēm haūd sŭpĕrāns. Fĭdē nōn mājŏr. Cuī crēdĕrĕ fās ēst. Vīx crēdĕrĕ pōssēs. *See Fides.*

Crēdŏ, ĭs, dĭdī, dĭtūm, ĕrĕ. *To believe*. Īd cĭnĕrem aūt mānēs crēdĭs cūrārĕ sĕpūltōs. V. Syn.—Ārbĭtrŏr, rĕŏr, ĕxīstĭmŏ, pŭtŏ. Phr.—Sūm rătŭs ēssĕ fĕrām. Jāmquĕ dĭēs, nī fāllŏr, ădēst. Ōmnĭă prō vērīs crēdām. Quī vītā bĕnĕ crēdăt ĕmī, quō tēndĭs, hŏnōrēm. Aūt ūllă pŭtātĭs Dōnă cărērĕ dŏlīs Dănăūm? Fĭdēm dō, ăddŏ, ădhĭbĕŏ. Crēdĭtĕ dīcēntī.

Crĕmŏ, ās, āvī, ātūm, ārĕ. *To burn*. Āltĭūs ēgrēssūs cœlēstĭă sīgnă crĕmābĭs. O. Syn.—Ūrŏ, cōmbūrŏ, ēxūrŏ, ădūrŏ. Phr.—Num īncēnsă crĕmāvĭt Trōjă vĭrōs? Flāmmā crĕpĭtāntĕ crĕmārī. *See Uro.*

Crĕŏ, ās, āvī, ātūm, ārĕ. *To create, to produce*. Syn.—Prōcrĕŏ, gīgnŏ, gĕnĕrŏ, părĭŏ, prōdūcŏ, ēdŏ. Phr.—Fōrtēs crĕāntūr fōrtĭbŭs. Māgnīque īmmēnsă crĕāvĭt.

Crĕpĭdă, æ. f. *Sandal*. Syn.—Sŏlĕă, sāndălĭūm.

Crĕpĭtŏ, ās, āvī, ātūm, ārĕ. *To rattle, to creak*. Syn.—Crĕpŏ, pērcrĕpŏ, sŏnŏ, strīdĕŏ, strĕpĭtŏ.

Crĕpĭtŭs, ūs. m. *Creaking, rattling*. Cāssĭs ĕt īnvērsō crĕpĭtūm dĕdĭt aūrĕă fūndō. J. Syn.—Sŏnŭs, sŏnĭtŭs, strĕpĭtŭs, frăgŏr. *See Sonitus.*

Crĕpŏ, ās, ŭī, ĭtūm, ārĕ. *To rattle, to make a sound*. Syn.—Crĕpĭtŏ, pērcrĕpŏ, sŏnŏ, strīdĕŏ. Phr.—Dēntēs crĕpŭērĕ rĕtēctī.

Crĕpūscŭlūm, ī. n. *Twilight*. Pāstŏr ŏvēs sătŭrās ād prīmă crĕpūscŭlă lūstrăt. O. Phr.—Dŭbĭæquĕ crĕpūscŭlă nōctĭs. Ēxtrēmă pĕrāctæ pārs lūcĭs. Nōx prīmă. Nōctēm dūcēntĭbŭs āstrīs. Īn nōctēm vērgēntĕ dĭĕ. Nōctĕ sīc mīxtā sŏlĕt Præbērĕ lūmēn prīmŭs aūt sērūs dĭēs. *See Diluculum, Aurora, Nox, Vesper.*

Crēscŏ, ĭs, vī, ētūm, ĕrĕ. *To increase*. Syn.—Āccrēscŏ, cōncrēscŏ, īncrēscŏ, aūgēscŏ, aūgĕŏr, ădaūgĕŏr, ēxtēndŏr, ēxtōllŏr. Phr.—Aūgmĭnă sūmŏ. Căvă flūmĭnă crēscūnt Cūm sŏnĭtū. Aēquŏr crēscĭt ăquīs. Mœnĭă crēscūnt.

Crīmĕn, ĭnĭs. n. *Crime*. Crīmĭnĭs īnjūstī tūrpĭă sīgnă pătī. O. Syn.—Cūlpă, āccūsātĭŏ. Phr.—Crīmĭnĭbūs tērrērĕ nŏvīs. Vītāsque ēt crīmĭnă dīscĭt. *Wrong*. Syn.—Scĕlŭs, făcĭnŭs, nĕfās, flāgĭtĭūm, nōxă, dēlīctūm, pēccātūm.

Crīmĭnōsŭs, ă, ūm. *Injurious*. Syn.—Prŏbrōsŭs, cōntŭmēlĭōsŭs.

Crīnēs, ĭūm. f. *Hair*. Dūlcīs cōmpŏsĭtīs spīrāvĭt crīnĭbŭs aūră. V. Syn.—Căpīllī, cŏmă, cæsărĭēs.

Crīnītŭs, ă, ūm. *Hairy.* Syn.—Căpīllātŭs.

Crīspŏr, ārĭs, ātŭs, sūm, ārī. *To be agitated.* Syn.—Ūndŏ, flūctŭŏ.

Crīspŭs, ă, ūm. *Curly, curled.* Syn.—Cūrvŭs, cūrvātŭs. *Agitated.* Syn.—Crīspāns, crīspātŭs, trĕmŭlŭs.

Crīstă, æ. f. *Top of the head, used generally of a rooster, sometimes of a man's head.* Syn.—Ăpēx, cōrnū. Phr.—Mānāntēs sānguĭnĕ crīstæ. Āltō vērtĭcĕ crīstă trĕmēns. Dĕcŭs crīstārūm sŭpērbūm.

Crŏcēŭs, ă, ūm. *Saffron.* Nōnnĕ vĭdēs crŏcēōs ūt Tmōlŭs ŏdōrēs Mīttĭt? V. Syn.—Crŏcĭnŭs. *Saffron colored.* Syn.—Crŏcĭnŭs, flāvŭs, lūtēŭs, lūtĕŏlŭs, rŭtĭlŭs. Phr.—Crŏcī cōntrāctă cŏlōrĕ.

Crŏcŭs, ī. m. *The saffron.* (*See Appendix under list of Trees, etc.*)

Crŭcĭātŭs, ūs. m. *Suffering.* Lătĕrīs crŭcĭātĭbŭs ūrŏr. O. Syn.—Tōrmēntūm, dŏlŏr, pœnă. *See Poena.*

Crŭcĭfīgŏ, ās, āvī, ātūm, ārĕ. *To crucify.* Phr.—Mēmbră crŭcī āffīgŏ, sūffīgŏ, īn trăbĕ fīgŏ. Īn crŭcēm tōllŏ. Īnfāmī sūspēndĕrĕ līgnō. Sūpplĭcĭō crŭcĭs fīnīrĕ lăbōrēs. *See Crux.*

Crŭcĭŏ, ās, āvī, ātūm, ārĕ. *To torment.* Quāntūm sīc crŭcĭāt lūmĭnă vēstră dŏlŏr. Pr. Syn.—Dīscrŭcĭŏ, ēxcrŭcĭŏ, āngŏ, tōrquĕŏ, māctŏ. Fig. Syn.—Āfflīgŏ, vēxŏ, prĕmŏ, cōnfĭcĭŏ. Phr.—Clādĭbŭs īnnŭmĕrīs vēxārĕ, tōrquērĕ.

Crūdēlĭs, ĭs, ĕ. *Cruel.* Crūdēlĭs mātēr măgĭs, ān pŭĕr īmprŏbŭs īllĕ? V. Syn.—Ăcērbŭs, āspĕr, ātrōx, bārbărŭs, dīrŭs, dūrŭs, sævŭs, īmmītĭs, fĕrŭs, ēffĕrŭs, fŭrēns, trūx, trŭcŭlēntŭs, īnclēmēns, īmmānĭs, īmprŏbŭs. Phr.—Āspĕr ĕt īmprŏbŭs īră. Flēctī nēscĭŭs. Pēctŏră sævă. Sānguĭnĕ gaūdēns. Sævītquĕ jŭvēntūs. Īn dūrō stāt cōrdĕ sĭlēx.

Crūdēlĭtās, ātĭs. f. *Cruelty.* Crūdēlĭtātĕ nōn mĕtū mōrtĭs trĕmēns. Syn.—Sævĭtĭă, sævĭtĭēs, ăcērbĭtās, āspĕrĭtās, ātrōcĭtās, bārbărĭēs, dūrĭtĭēs, fĕrĭtās, īmmānĭtās, īnclēmēntĭă. Phr.—Mēns crŭŏrĭs, sævă. Sānguĭnĕă sĭtĭs. Crūdēlēs aūsūs.

Crūdēlĭtĕr adv. *Cruelly.* Crūdēli ōffĭcĭō nĭmĭūm crūdēlĭtĕr ūtī. M. Syn.—Bārbărē, ātrōcĭtĕr, īmmānĭtĕr, rĭgĭdē. *Violently.* Syn.—Vĭŏlēntĕr, vĕhĕmentĕr.

Crūdēscŏ, ĭs, ŭī, ĕrĕ. *To become bitter.* Syn.—Rĕcrūdēscŏ, īngrăvēscŏ, aūgĕŏr, crēscŏ, īrrītŏr, āccēndŏr, stĭmŭlŏr. Phr.—Dējēctă crūdēscīt pūgnă Cămīllā. Crūdēscūnt īræ.

Crūdŭs, ă, ūm. *Raw.* Phr.—Nōn cōctūm. Ēssĕ nĕgās cōctūm lĕpŏrēm. *Unripe.* Syn.—Ăcērbŭs, īmmātūrŭs. *Young, vigorous.* Syn.—Fīrmŭs, vĕgĕtŭs, rōbūstŭs, vĭgēns. *Unpolished.* Syn.—Āspĕr, scābĕr, dūrŭs.

Crŭēntŏ, ās, āvī, ātūm, ārĕ. *To make bloody.* Syn.—Crŭōrĕ, sānguĭnĕ spārgŏ, cōnspērgŏ, ĭmbŭŏ, pōllŭŏ, tūrpŏ.

Crŭēntŭs, ă, ūm. *Bloody.* Tȳdīdēs mūlta vastābăt cǣdĕ crŭēntŭs. V. Syn.—Crŭēntātŭs, sānguĭnĕŭs, sānguĭnŏlēntŭs. Phr.—Sānguĭnĕ mădēns. Ātrō tĕpĕfāctă crŭōrĕ mādĕt. Stĕtĭt ōrĕ crŭēntō. Rōrāntēs sānguĭnĕ crīstās. Spūmās ăgĭt ōrĕ crŭēntās.

Crŭmēnă ǣ. f. *Pouch, purse.* Ēt mūndūs vīctūs nōn dēfīcĭēntĕ crŭmēnā. H. Syn.—Mārsūpĭūm, sāccŭlŭs, lŏcŭlī.

Crŭŏr, ōrĭs. m. *Blood.* Vīrgĭnĕŭmque āltē bĭbĕt āctă crŭōrēm Hāstă. V. Syn.—Sānguĭs, sănĭēs, tābŏ (abl.). Phr.—Sānguĭnĕŭs, crŭēntŭs rōs, ĭmbĕr, rīvŭs, flūmĕn. Ēffūsŭs sānguĭs. Ātrō sānguĭnĕ gŭttǣ. *See Cruentus.*

Crūstă, ǣ. f. *Crust, bark.* Syn.—Cōrtēx.

Crūstūm, ī. n. *Cake.* Syn.—Crūstŭlūm, bēllārĭă, cŭpēdĭă (ǣ & ōrūm).

Crūx, ŭcĭs. f. *Cross.* Syn.—Trābs, līgnūm, trūncŭs, stīpĕs, ārbŏr, rōbŭr, pătĭbŭlūm. Phr.—Crŭcĭs fērālĕ līgnūm. Ārbŏr īnfēlīx. Trābs fūnēstă. Fātālĕ rōbŭr. *See Crucifigo.*

Crȳstāllŭs, ī. f. *Crystal.* Phr.—Lĭquĭdī mīrācŭlă sāxī. Mīră sĭlēx mīrūsquĕ lătēx. Prōdĭgĭōsă sĭlēx.

Cŭbīcŭlūm, ī. n. *Sleeping-room.* Syn.—Thălămŭs, cŭbīlĕ.

Cŭbīlĕ, ĭs. n. *Bed.* Syn.—Lēctŭs, tŏrŭs, thălămŭs, strātūm. *See Lectus, thalamus.*

Cŭbĭtūm, ī. n. & Cŭbĭtŭs, ī. m. *Elbow.* Tēr sēse āttōllēns cŭbĭtōque īnnīxă lĕvāvĭt. V. Phr.—Sŭppŏsĭtō cērvīcem īnnīxă lăcērtō.

Cŭbŏ, ās, ŭī, ĭtūm, ārĕ. *To rest, to take a sleep.* Ēt tĭmĕt īn văcŭ͞c sōlă cŭbārĕ tŏrō. O. Syn.—Īncŭbŏ rĕcŭbŏ, rĕcūmbŏ, jăcĕŏ, stērnŏr, quĭēscŏ, rĕquĭēscŏ. Phr.—Mēmbră lēctō pōnĕrĕ. Sōmnō jăcĕŏ. Sōmnō mē stērnŏ. Lēctūm pĕtŏ.

Cŭcŭlŭs (Cŭcūllŭs), ī. m. *A cuckoo.* (*See Appendix under list of Birds.*)

Cūdŏ, dĭs, dī, sūm, ĕrĕ. *To forge.* Mūlcĭbĕr Aētnǣīs fūlmēn cūdēbăt ĭn āntrīs. V. Syn.—Ēxcūdŏ, prōcūdŏ, făbrĭcŏ. Phr.—Fērrūm īgnĕ mōllĭŏ. Fōrnācĕ cŏquŏ, cūdĕ dĭffīngŏ. Dūrūm prōcūdĭt ărātŏr. *See Procudo.*

Cūlcĭtă & Cūlcĭtră, ǣ. f. *Bed.* Syn.—Lēctŭlŭs, pūlvīnŭs. Phr.—Mōllī tŭmĕāt tĭbĭ cūlcĭtră plūmā. *See Cubile, lectus.*

Cŭlēx, ĭcĭs. m. *Gnat.* Phr.—Pōndĕrĕ vēl cŭlĭcĭs lĕvĭŏr fāmāquĕ fĕrētŭr.

Cŭlīnă, ǣ. f. *Kitchen.* Cāptūm tē nīdōrĕ sŭǣ pŭtăt īllĕ cŭlīnǣ. J. Syn.—Cŏquīnă.

Cūlmĕn, ĭnĭs. n. *Top, summit, height.* Ārdŭă tūrrĭgĕrǣ sūrgēnt īn cūlmĭnă rīpæ. Syn.—Căcūmĕn, ăpēx, fāstīgĭūm, tēctūm, tēctă. Phr.—Ēvādo ād sūmmī fāstīgĭă cūlmĭnĭs. *See Cacumen.*

Cūlmŭs, ī. m. *Stalk.* Rōmŭlĕōquĕ rĕcēns hōrrēbāt rēgĭă cūlmō. V. Syn.—Ăvēnă, călămŭs, stĭpŭlă, pălĕă. Phr.—Sūrgēntēs cūlmi īn sĕgĕtēm. Nē grăvĭdīs prōcūmbāt cūlmŭs ărīstīs. V. Tūrgēscūnt lāctēntĭbŭs hōrdĕă cūlmīs.

Cūlpă, æ. f. *Fault.* Pœnă pŏtēst pōnī, cūlpă pĕrēnnĭs ĕrĭt. O. Syn.—Dēlīctūm, nōxă, pēccātūm, ādmīssūm, cōmmīssūm, ērrātūm, ērrŏr, scĕlŭs, flāgĭtĭūm, pĭācŭlūm. Phr.—Lŭĭmūs mĭsĕrāndæ crīmĭnă cūlpæ. Ŏpērtæ cōnscĭă cūlpæ cūnctă căvĕt. Tăcĭtā sūdānt præcōrdĭă cūlpā. Sūccūmbĕrĕ cūlpæ. *See Crimen, Scelus, Pecco.*

Cūlpŏ, ās, āvī, ātūm, ārĕ. *To blame, to accuse.* Rēspōndēt; cūlpātŭr ăb hīs, laūdātŭr ăb īllīs. H. Syn..—Āccūsŏ, īncūsŏ, īnsĭmŭlŏ, ārgŭŏ, rĕdārgŭŏ, rĕprĕhēndŏ, crīmĭnŏr, ōbjūrgŏ, cārpŏ, dāmnŏ, īncrĕpŏ. *See Accuso.*

Cūltē. adv. *Elegantly.* Syn.—Ōrnātē, cōncīnnē, cōncīnnĭtĕr.

Cūltĕr, trī. m. *Knife.* Mōrĕ sŭpērvăcŭām cūltrīs ābrūmpĕrĕ cārnēm. J. Syn.—Cūltēllŭs, fērrūm. Phr.—Călĭdō tīnctūrūs sānguĭnĕ cūltrōs. Fīxō vūlnĕrā cūltrō. Lōngī mūcrōnem ādmīttĕrĕ cūltrī.

Cūltŭs, ūs. m. *Culture, labor.* Syn.—Cūltūră. Phr.—Pātrĭōs cūltūsque hăbĭtūsquĕ lŏcōrūm. Nūllō tāntūm jāctāt sē Mœsĭā cūltū. *Education.* Syn.—Dīscĭplīnă. *Manners.* Syn.—Hăbĭtŭs, mōrēs, vītă.

Cūm. prep. *With.* Phr.—Ūnā cūm. Nōn sĭnĕ.

Cūm (*more correct than* Quūm), conj. *When.* Syn.—Quāndŏ, pōstquām, quāndōquĕ, ŭt, ŭbĭ, dūm, quŏtĭēs. Phr.—Quō tēmpŏrĕ. Sī fōrtĕ. Sī quāndŏ. *Since.* Syn.—Quāndŏ, ŭt, quŏnĭām, sĭquĭdēm.

Cŭmŭlātīm. adv. *Abundantly, copiously.* Syn.—Cŭmŭlātē, ăcērvātīm.

Cŭmŭlŏ, ās, āvī, ātūm, ārĕ. *To heap together.* Quī mălĕ cōngēstōs aūrō cŭmŭlābāt ăcērvōs. Syn.—Āccŭmŭlŏ, ăcērvŏ, cŏăcērvŏ, āggĕrŏ, cōngĕrŏ, cōgŏ, cōllĭgŏ, cōmpōnŏ, cōngrĕgŏ. Phr.—Dīvĭtĭās cŭmŭlārĕ cădūcās.

Cŭmŭlŭs, ī. m. *Mass, heap.* Īnsĕquĭtūr cŭmŭlōsquĕ rŭīt mălĕ pīnguĭs ărēnæ. V. Syn.—Ăcērvŭs, cōngĕrĭēs, strŭēs, āggĕr, cōpĭă, vīs. Phr.—Īngēns fārrĭs ăcērvŭs. Aērĭs ăcērvŭs ēt aūrī. Īnsĕquĭtūr cŭmŭlō prærūptŭs ăquāe mōns.

Cūnābŭlă, ōrūm. n. *Cradle.* Syn.—Īncūnābŭlă, cūnæ.

Cūnæ, ārūm. f. *Cradle.* Ēt tĕnĕr īn cūnīs fīlĭŭs ægĕr ĕrĭt. O. Syn.—Cūnābŭlă, īncūnābŭlă. Fig.—*Infancy.* *See Infantia.*

Cūnctāntĕr. adv. *Hesitatingly, slowly.* Syn.—Sēgnĭtĕr, tārdē, lēntē.

Cūnctātŏr, ōrĭs. m. *One who delays.* Syn.—Cūnctāns, cūnctābŭndŭs, dīlātŏr.

Cūnctŏr, ārĭs, ātŭs sūm, ārī. *To delay.* Cūnctātūrquĕ mĕtū tēlūmque īnstārĕ trĕmīscĭt. V. Syn.—Mŏrŏr, hærĕō, sūbsīstō.

Cūnctŭs, ă, ūm. *Whole.* Cūnctŭs ŏb Ītălĭām tērrārūm claūdĭtŭr ōrbĭs. V. Syn.—Ōmnĭs, quīsquĕ, ūnūsquīsquĕ, sīngŭlī. Phr.—Ēt cūnctă tērrārūm sŭbāctă.

Cŭnĕŭs, ī. m. *Wedge.* Nām prīmī cŭnĕīs scīndēbānt fīssĭlĕ līgnūm. V. Phr.—Fīndĭtŭr īn sŏlĭdūm cŭnĕīs vĭă. Cŭnĕīs gĕmĭt rōbŭr ădāctīs. *Wedge of troops in battle.* Syn.—Ăcĭēs.

Cŭpēdĭă, æ. f. & Cŭpēdĭă, ōrūm. n. *Sweetmeats.* Syn.—Crūstŭlă, bēllārĭă, dūlcĭă.

Cŭpĭdē. adv. *Eagerly.* Syn.—Ăvĭdē, vĕhĕmēntĕr, ārdēntĕr, stŭdĭōsē. Phr.—Ăvĭdā mēntĕ.

Cŭpīdŏ, ĭnĭs. f. *Desire, passion.* Crēvērūnt ĕt ŏpēs ĕt ŏpūm fŭrĭōsă cŭpīdŏ. O. Syn.—Ārdŏr, lĭbīdŏ, ămŏr, stŭdĭūm. Phr.—Laūdūmque īmmēnsă cŭpīdŏ. Ēxăgĭtāns ănĭmūm. Sĭtĭs ārdēscĭt hăbēndī. Sŭă cuīquĕ dĕūs fĭt dīră cŭpīdŏ. Quæ lūcīs mĭsĕrīs tām dīră cŭpīdŏ? *See Libido, Ambitio.*

Cŭpĭdŭs, ă, ūm. *Desirous.* Ēt rĕvŏcāt cŭpĭdās ālĕă sæpĕ mănūs. O. Syn.—Ăvĭdŭs, ăvārŭs, ămāns, cŭpĭēns, ōptāns, āppĕtēns, flăgrāns, stŭdĭōsŭs. Phr.—Cŭpīdĭnĕ cāptŭs, dūctŭs, tāctŭs, æstŭāns. Cŭpĭdūsquĕ crŭōrĭs lŭpŭs.

Cŭpĭŏ, ĭs, īvī & ĭī, ītūm, ĕrĕ. *To desire, to wish.* Cŭpĭo ōmnĭă quæ tū vīs. Plaut. Syn.—Pĕtŏ, āppĕtŏ, ēxpĕtŏ, ōptŏ, ēxōptŏ, ăvĕŏ, pērcŭpĭŏ, cōncŭpĭŏ, cōncŭpīscŏ, dēsīdĕrŏ, vŏlŏ, ārdĕŏ, flăgrŏ, quærŏ, rĕquīrŏ, āmbĭŏ, āspīrŏ, āffēctŏ, stŭdĕŏ. Phr.—Mĭhĭ plăcĕt, ārrīdĕt, cōrdī ēst. Mēns ăgĭtăt mĭhĭ. Mēns ēst. Ārdēnt ănĭmī. Quōd vōtīs ōptāstĭs ădēst. Hăbēs quōd tōtā mēntĕ pĕtīstī. Hōc ĕrăt īn vōtīs. *See Volo.*

Cŭprēssŭs, ī, & ūs. f. *A cypress tree.* (*See Appendix under list of Trees, etc.*)

Cūr. adv. *Why.* Cūr nōn īpsă vĕnīt cūr hæc cērtāmĭnă vītăt? O. Syn.—Quĭānām, quĭd, ūndĕ, cūrnām, ūndĕnām, quārē. Phr.—Quā, quānām caūsā. Quīd caūsae ēst? Quĭd ĭtă? Quæ caūsă sĕrēnōs Fœdāvĭt vūltūs? Quæ rătĭo ēst, īnquĭs?

Cūră, æ. f. *Care.* Jām tum ācēr cūrās vĕnĭēntem ēxtēndĭt ĭn ānnūm Āgrĭcŏlă. V. Syn.—Stŭdĭūm, lăbōr, īndūstrĭă, ŏpĕră, sēdŭlĭtās. Phr.—Cūrīs ăcŭēns mōrtālĭă cōrdă. Fōrtĭŏr ōbstăt Cūră dŭcĭs. Ō cūrās hŏmĭnūm! Ō mĭhĭ cūrārūm prĕtĭūm! *Affection.* Syn.—Ămŏr, stŭdĭūm. Phr.—Pŭĕr īrĕ părāt, mĕă māxĭmă cūră. Raūcæ, tŭă cūră, pălūmbēs.

Cūrĭă, æ. f. *Senate-house.* Syn.—Aūlă, sĕnātŭs.

Cūrŏ, ās, āvī, ātūm, ārĕ. *To care for, to pay attention to.* Nēmpe ūt cūrēntūr rēcte hæc? Ter. Syn.—Cōnsŭlŏ, īnvĭgĭlŏ. Phr.—Cūrām sūscĭpĭŏ. Ŏpĕrām dō. Nōn nēglĕgŏ. Rēm cūræ hăbĕŏ. Cūrās īmpēndŏ. Īntēndĕrĕ cūrās. Īllī sūnt ōmnĭă cūræ. Nēc tĭbĭ cūră cănūm fŭĕrīt pōstrēmă.

Cūrrĭcŭlūm, ī. n. *Course.* Sūnt quōs cūrrĭcŭlō pūlvĕrem Ŏlȳmpĭcūm Cōllēgīssĕ jŭvăt. H. Syn.—Stădĭūm, spătĭă, cīrcŭs, cūrsŭs, cāmpŭs, æquŏr. Phr.—Gȳrō cūrrĕ, pŏētă, tŭō. *Revolution of the stars.* Syn.—Cūrsŭs, ĭtĕr.

Cūrrŏ, ĭs, cŭcūrrī, cūrsūm, ĕrĕ. *To run.* Nūnc hūc, nūnc īllūc, ēt ŭtrōquĕ sĭne ordĭne cūrrŏ. Syn.—Dēcūrrŏ, āccūrrŏ, fēstīnŏ, prŏpĕrŏ, āccĕlĕrŏ, fĕrŏr, aūfĕrŏr, ābrĭpĭŏr, rŭŏ, fŭgĭŏ, vŏlŏ, ādvŏlŏ. Phr.—Mē prōrĭpĭŏ. Cūrsū fĕrŏr. Præcĭpĭtēs cūrsūs răpĭŏ. Fērt īmpĕtŭs īpsĕ vŏlāntēm. Fŭgĭt ōcĭŏr Eūrō. Răpĭdīquĕ fĕrūntŭr Ād mūrōs. Lĭttŏră cūrsū Fīdă pĕtūnt.

Cūrrŭs, ūs. m. *Chariot.* Prōsĕquăr ēt cūrrūs ūtrōque ā līttŏre ŏvāntēs. Pr. Syn.—Bĭjŭgī, bĭjŭgēs, quădrīgæ, quădrĭjŭgī, rhēdă, plaūstrūm, āxĭs, tēmŏ, rŏtă, ĕquī. Phr.—Spŏlĭīs ŏnĕrātōs Cæsărĭs āxēs. Vēstīgĭă cūrrūs. Sīstĭt ĕquōs. Cūrrū fĕrŏr. Vĕhăr ālĭtĕ cūrrū. Cūrrūm ăgĭtārĕ. Stĭmŭlābăt ĭn æquŏrĕ cūrrūm. Sūb jŭgă cōgĭt ĕquōs. Cœlōque īnvēctŭs ăpērtō Flēctĭt ĕquōs.

Cūrsīm. adv. *Hastily.* Syn.—Ŏbĭtĕr, cūrsū, cĭtŏ, prŏpĕrē, prŏpĕrāntĕr.

Cūrsŭs, ūs. m. *Course.* Īnde ălĭōs ĭnĕūnt cūrsūs ălĭōsquĕ rĕcūrsūs Ādvērsīs spătĭīs. V. Syn.—Stădĭūm, spătĭūm, cūrrĭcŭlūm, cīrcŭs, cāmpŭs, æquŏr. Phr.—Cōncĭtŭs grădŭs. Jāmque hōs cūrsū, jām prætĕrĭt īllōs. *Route, way.* Syn.—Ĭtĕr, vĭă.

Cūrtŭs, ă, ūm. *Short.* Syn.—Brĕvĭs, ēxĭgŭŭs, pārvŭs. Phr.—Nūnc mĭhĭ cūrtō Īrĕ lĭbēt mūlō. Sīc cūrtă pĕcūnĭă crēscĕt.

Cūrvāmĕn, ĭnĭs. n. *A curving, vaulting.* Syn.—Flēxŭs, sĭnŭs, cīrcŭs, ānfrāctŭs. Phr.—Sĕquĭtūr pătrĭæ cūrvāmĭnă rīpæ. Prēssō cūrvāmĭnĕ flēctī Īncĭpĭt.

Cūrvātūră, æ. f. *A curving.* Aūrĕă sūmmæ Cūrvātūră rŏtæ. O. Syn.—Cūrvāmĕn, flēxŭs, ōrbĭs, gȳrŭs.

Cūrvŏ, ās, āvī, ātūm, ārĕ. *To bend, to curve.* Pōrtŭs ăb Ēōō flūctū cūrvātŭr ĭn ārcūm. V. Syn.—Īncūrvŏ, rĕcūrvŏ, flēctŏ, īnflēctŏ, sĭnŭŏ, īnclīnŏ, tōrquĕŏ, īntōrquĕŏ. Phr.—Vēntīquĕ lăbōrānt Tōt cūrvārĕ sĭnūs. Māgnā vī flēxă dŏmātŭr Īn būrīm. Dōnēc cūrvātă cŏīrēnt Īntēr sē căpĭtă. Nūx rāmōs cūrvābĭt ŏlēntēs.

Cūrvŭs, ă, ūm. *Bent, curved.* Nēc vēnīt tārdō cūrvă sĕnēctă pĕdĕ. Tib. Syn.—Cūrvātŭs, rĕcūrvŭs, rĕcūrvātŭs, īncūrvŭs, flēxŭs, īnflēxŭs, sĭnŭātŭs, sĭnŭōsŭs, ōblīquŭs, tōrtŭs, īntōrtŭs, rĕtōrtŭs. Phr.—Cūrvātūs cōrpŏrĕ tōtō.

Cūspĭs, ĭdĭs. f. *Point, especially of a spear.* Dăt ăcūtæ cūspĭdĭs hāstām. O. Syn.—Mūcrŏ, ăcĭēs, ăcūmĕn. Phr.—Ēt ăcūtā cūspĭdĕ cōntos. Fig.—*An arrow, weapon.* Syn.—Fērrūm, hāstă, spīcŭlūm, ēnsĭs, tēlūm.

Cūstōdĭă, æ. f. *A watching, care.* Pūpīllī quōs dūră prĕmīt cūstōdĭă mātrūm. H. Syn.—Tūtēlă, vĭgĭlāntĭă. Phr.—Nĭhĭl īnvītæ prōdēst cūstōdĭă sōlērs. Fīdă cănūm cūstōdĭă. *Guard, sentinel.* Syn.—Ēxcŭbĭæ, vĭgĭlĭæ, vĭgĭlēs, præsĭdĭūm. Phr.—Pōrtārūm vĭgĭlēs. Vĭgĭlum ēxcŭbĭæ. Nōctēm cūstōdĭă dūcĭt Īnsōmnēm lūdō. Ădĭtūs cūstōdĭă sērvāt. Fŭgām cūstōdĭă claūdĭt. Ōmnēmque ădĭtūm cūstōdĕ cŏrōnăt.

Cūstōdĭŏ, īs, īvī, & ĭī, ītūm, īrĕ. *To guard, to watch.* Cūstōdīte ănĭmās ēt nūllī crēdĭtĕ mēnsæ. J. Syn.—Sērvŏ, āssērvŏ, cōnsērvŏ, tŭĕŏr, tūtŏr, tĕgŏ, prōtĕgŏ, dēfēndŏ.

Cūstōs, ōdĭs. m. *Guard.* Cūstōs ēs paūpĕrĭs hōrtī. V. Syn.—Tūtŏr, dēfēnsŏr, tūtēlă, cūstōdĭă, præsĭdĭūm. Phr.—Vĭgĭlāns īn līmĭnĕ. Fīdūsque ād līmĭnă cūstōs. Cæsīs sūmmæ cūstōdĭbŭs ārcĭs. Cūstōdūm trānsīrĕ mănūs. *See Custodia.*

Cŭtĭs, ĭs, f. *Skin.* Īn cŭtĕ cūrāndā plūs æquo ŏpĕrātă jŭvēntūs. H. Syn.—Pēllĭs. Phr.—Āddūcītquĕ cŭtēm măcĭēs. Ārmāvīt nātūră cŭtēm. Bĕnĕ cūrātā cŭtĕ nĭtĭdŭs.

Cyănŭs, ī. m. *Turquoise, lapis lazuli.* Phr.—Gēmmă cærŭlĕă. Pūrpŭrĕŭs lăpĭs. Cyănŭs mĭcāns.

Cyăthŭs, ī. m. *Cup.* Cārdĭăcō nūnquām cyăthūm mīssūrŭs ămīcō. J. Syn.—Pōcŭlūm, călīx, crātēr, pătĕră, scўphŭs. *See Poculum.*

Cўclĭcŭs, ī. *Cycle. As an adj.* Nēc sīc īncĭpĭās ŭt scrīptōr cўclĭcŭs ōlĭm. H.

Cўcnŭs, ī. m. *A swan.* (*See list of Birds in Appendix.*)

Cўmbă, æ. f. *Bark, skiff.* Ēt fērrūgĭnĕā sūbvēctāt cōrpŏră cўmbā. V. Syn.—Nāvĭcŭlă, nāvĭgĭūm, lēmbŭs, līntĕr, phăsēlŭs, scăphă. *See Navis.*

Cўmbălūm, ī. n. *Cymbal.* Tīnnītūsquĕ cĭe, ēt mātrīs quătĕ cўmbălă cīrcūm. V. Phr.—Raūcōs fūndēns sŏnōs. Cўmbălă pūlsārĕ, fĕrīrĕ, quătĕrĕ, pērcŭtĕrĕ. Ēt căvă cўmbălă pūlsānt. Crĕpĭtāntĭăque æră.

D

Dāctўlŭs, ī. m. *Dactyl, a foot in verse, consisting of one long and two short syllables.* Phr.—Spōndæō cŏmĭtāntĕ dāctўlōquĕ. Pēs hērōĭcŭs. Nŭmĕrŭs hērōĭcŭs.

Dāmnŏ, ās, āvī, ātūm, ārĕ. *To condemn.* Ābsōlvēs hŏmĭnem ēt scĕlĕrĭs dāmnābĭs ĕūndēm. J. Syn.—Cōndēmnŏ, mūlctŏ. Phr.—Dūcĕrĕ dīgnūm sūpplĭcĭō. Vĭtĭō nīgrūm præfīgĕrĕ thētă. Dēdĕ nĕcī. *To blame, to accuse.* Syn.—Rĕdārgŭŏ, quĕrŏr, cūlpŏ, īncūsŏ, īncrĕpŏ, nŏtŏ, ārgŭŏ. Phr.—Dāmnārĕ mŏrās. Scĕlĕrĭs crīmĭnĕ dāmnăt ăvōs.

Dāmnōsŭs, ă, ūm. *Hurtful.* Dāmnōsūs pĕcŏrī cūrrĭs, dāmnōsĭŏr āgrīs. O. Syn.—Nŏcēns, īncōmmŏdŭs, fūnēstŭs, ĭnĭmīcŭs, ēxĭtĭōsŭs, ēxĭtĭālĭs, pērnĭcĭōsŭs. *See Noceo.*

Dāmnūm, ī. n. *Loss, damage.* Syn.—Dētrīmēntūm, jāctūră, ærūmnă, clādēs, mălūm, īncōmmŏdūm, ēxĭtĭūm, pērnĭcĭēs. Phr.—Līnguă fŭĭt dāmnō. Āccēdēns īn dāmnă pŭdŏr. Dāmnă mĭnus cōnsuētă mŏvēnt. Nēc pērdĭtă cūrēnt. *See Malum, Pernicies.*

Dăpēs, ūm. f. *Feast, banquet.* Syn.—Ĕpŭlæ, fērcŭlūm, cĭbŭs, ēscă, mēnsă, cœnă. Phr.—Īllōs dăpĭbūs sōlātūr ŏpīmīs. Dăpēs ăvĭdō cōnvēllĕrĕ dēntĕ. Nōn Sĭcŭlæ dăpēs Dūlcem ēlăbōrābūnt săpōrēm. *See Cibus, Convivium, Epulæ.*

Dăphnē, ēs. f. *A laurel tree.* (*See Appendix under list of Trees, etc.*)

Dāpsĭlĭs, ĭs, ĕ. *Rich, sumptuous.* Syn.—Laūtŭs, ŏpīmŭs, dăpālĭs, ăbūndāns, māgnĭfĭcŭs.

Dāpsĭlĭtĕr. adv. *Abundantly, sumptuously.* Syn.—Dāpsĭlĕ, laūtē, māgnĭfĭcē.

Dătŏr, ōrĭs. m. *One who gives.* Syn.—Dōnātŏr, lārgītŏr. Phr.—Ādsīt lætĭtĭæ Bācchūs dătŏr.

Daūlĭăs (ālĕs), ădĭs. f. *A nightingale.* (*See Appendix under list of Birds.*)

Dē. prep. *From, away from.* Dē cœlō tāctās mĕmĭnī prædīcĕrĕ quērcūs. V. Syn.—Ē, ēx, ăb. *According to.* Syn.—Prō, ēx, ăd, sĕcūndūm, jŭxtā.

Dĕă, æ. f. *Goddess.* Quāttŭŏr hīs ārās ālta ād dēlūbră Dĕārūm Cōnstĭtŭĕ. V. Syn.—Dīvă, nūmĕn. *See Deus.*

Dĕāmbŭlŏ, ās, āvī, ātūm, ārĕ. *To walk.* Syn.—Āmbŭlŏ, īncēdŏ, spătĭŏr. *See Ambulo.*

Dēbēllŏ, ās, āvī, ātūm, ārĕ. *To fight, to conquer.* Syn.—Dŏmŏ, sŭbĭgŏ, sŭpĕrŏ, vīncŏ. Phr.—Bēllō cōntūndŏ, frāngŏ, stērnŏ, vīncŏ. *See Vinco.*

Dēbĭlĭs, ĭs, ĕ. *Weak.* Cōrpŏră dēbĭlĭbūs nītūntūr sīstĕrĕ mēmbrīs. Syn.—Īnvălĭdŭs, īnfīrmŭs, ĭnērs, īmbēllĭs, īmbēcīllĭs, ēnērvĭs, ēlūmbĭs, mōllĭs, tĕnĕr, frăgĭlĭs, ēffœtŭs, dēbĭlĭtātŭs, fēssŭs, dēfēssŭs, lāssŭs, ēxhaūstŭs, dēfĭcĭēns, lānguēns, lānguĭdŭs, ægĕr. Phr.—Sĭnĕ vīrĭbŭs. Rōbŏrĭs ēxpērs. Rōbŏrĕ dēfēctŭs. Vīrĭbŭs āmīssīs. Aēgrē lānguĭdă mēmbră trăhēns.

Dēbĭlĭtās, ātĭs. f. *Weakness.* Syn.—Īnfīrmĭtās, lānguŏr, īnfrāctæ vīrēs. *See Languor, Senectus.*

Dēbĭlĭtŏ, ās, āvī, ātūm, ārĕ. *To weaken.* Dēbĭlĭtāt vīrēs ănĭmī mūtātquĕ vĭgōrēm. V. Syn.—Īnfīrmŏ, ēnērvŏ, frāngŏ. Phr.—Vĭgōrēm, vīrēs tōllŏ, frāngŏ.

Dēcēdŏ, ĭs, cēssī, cēssūm, ĕrĕ. *To go, depart.* Gnōssĭăque ārdēntīs dēcēdāt stēllă Cŏrōnæ. V. Syn.—Cēdŏ, dīscēdŏ, ēxcēdŏ, rĕcēdŏ, ăbĕŏ, ēxĕŏ, mĭgrŏ. Phr.—Ăbĭtūmquĕ părābăt. Ēmēnsō cūm jām dēcēdĕt Ŏlўmpō. *To yield to.* Syn.—Cēdŏ.

Dĕcēm. *Ten.* Syn.—Dēnī. Phr.—Bīs quīnquĕ. Bīs quīnī. Bīs quīnōs sĭlĕt īllĕ dĭēs.

Dĕcēmbĕr, rĭs. m. *December.* Phr.—Mēnsĭs ūltĭmŭs ānnī. Mēnsĭs dĕcĭmŭs. Quō cānēnt Bŏrĕālĭbŭs ārvă prŭīnīs. Gĕlĭdō trĕmĕrēm cūm mēnsĕ Dĕcēmbrī.

Dĕcēmvĭrī, ōrūm. m. *Decemvirs, Roman magistrates.* Phr.—Măgīstrātŭs Rōmānŭs.

Dĕcēns, ēntĭs. adj. *Becoming, befitting.* Plăcĭdōquĕ dĕcēns rĕvĕrēntĭă vūltū. O. Syn.—Āptŭs, cōngrŭŭs, cōngrŭēns, cōnsŏnŭs, cōnvĕnĭēns. *Beautiful.* Syn.—Dĕcōrŭs, fōrmōsŭs.

Dĕcēntĕr. adv. *Becomingly.* Syn.—Cōnvĕnĭēntĕr, āptē, rēctē, bĕnĕ. *Gracefully.* Syn.—Dĕcōrē, āptē, ēlĕgāntĕr, pūlchrē.

Dēcērnŏ, ĭs, crēvī, crētūm, ĕrĕ. *To decree.* Nūnc prō Cæsărĭbūs sŭpĕrīs dēcērnĕrĕ grātēs. O. Syn.—Stătŭŏ, cōnstĭtŭŏ, sāncĭŏ. *To judge.* Syn.—Jūdĭcŏ.

Dēcērpŏ, ĭs, sī, ptūm, ĕrĕ. *To detach with the hand.* Āddūctō pōmūm dēcērpĕrĕ rāmō. O. Syn.—Lĕgŏ, cōllĭgŏ, cārpŏ, ēxcērpŏ, dētrăhŏ, āvēllŏ. Phr.—Nŏvōs dēcērpĕrĕ flōrēs.

Dēcērtŏ, ās, āvī, ātūm, ārĕ. *To fight.* Īn ūltĭmā bēllō dēcērtārĕ plăcĕt. O. Syn.—Cērtŏ, cōnflīgŏ, cōngrĕdĭŏr, dīmĭcŏ, pūgnŏ, prœlĭŏr. Phr.—Āgmĭnă dēcērtānt bēllō. *See Bellum.*

Dĕcĕt. impers. *It is becoming.* Quīs fīnīs stāndī? quō mē dĕcĕt ūsquĕ tĕnērī? V. Syn.—Cōnvĕnĭt, quădrăt, cōngrŭĭt, jŭvăt, ēxpĕdĭt. Phr.—Ēst pār, āptūm, cōnvĕnĭēns, cōnsēntānĕūm, æquūm. Pūlchrum ēt dĕcōrum ēst. Tūm dĕcŭĭt cūm scēptră dăbās. Nēc tĭbĭ quīd lĭcĕāt sēd quīd fēcīssĕ dĕcēbĭt, Ōccūrrăt.

Dēcīdŏ, ĭs, cīdī, cīsūm, ĕrĕ. *To cut.* Ārbŏrĭbūs frōndēs dēcīdĕrĕ fālcĕ nŏvēllās. V. Syn.—Sĕcŏ, rĕsĕcŏ, scīndŏ, ābscīndŏ. *See Scindo.*

Dēcĭdŏ, ĭs, cĭdī, ĕrĕ. *To fall down.* Dēcĭdĭt īn cāssēs prædă pĕtītă mĕōs. O. Syn.—Cădŏ, cōncĭdŏ, ēxcĭdŏ, lābŏr, dēlābŏr, prōlābŏr, rŭŏ, præcĭpĭtŏ. Phr.—Ēxcēlsæ grăvĭōrĕ cāsū dēcĭdūnt tūrrēs. Dēcĭdĭt ēxănĭmĭs. Sī dēcĭdĭt īmbĕr. Fig.—Ūrbīsquĕ pŏtēstās Dēcĭdĭt. *To be forgotten.* Syn.—Ēxcĭdŏ, lābŏr, ēlābŏr, dēflŭŏ.

Dēcīdŭŭs, ă, ūm. *Cut.* Syn.—Cǣdŭŭs, cǣsŭs.

Dēcĭdŭŭs, ă, ūm. *Fallen, about to fall.* Syn.—Cădēns, lāpsŭs, cădūcŭs, flūxŭs, lăbāns.

Dĕcĭmŭs, ă, ūm. *Tenth.* Syn.—Dēnŭs.

Dēcĭpĭŏ, ĭs, cēpī, ēptūm, ĕrĕ. *To deceive.* Nām nĕquĕ dēcĭpĭtūr rătĭō nēc dēcĭpĭt ūnquām. Syn.—Lūdŏ, dēlūdŏ, ēlūdŏ, lūdĭfĭcŏ, lūdĭfĭcŏr, fāllŏ, frūstrŏr, cīrcŭmĕŏ, cīrcūmvĕnĭŏ, căpĭŏ. Phr.—Dŏlīs, āstū, fraūdĭbŭs, ārtĭbŭs cāptŏ, căpĭŏ, īnnēctŏ, vīncĭŏ. Fraūdĭbŭs āmbĭŏ. Fraūdĕ pĕtŏ. Ārtēs dŏlōsās ădhĭbĕŏ. Dŏlōsīs ārtĭbŭs ūtŏr. Dŏlōs nēctĕrĕ. Īnsĭdĭīs dēlūdĕrĕ mēntēs. Sĭmŭlātā mēntĕ lŏquī. Prōmīssīs dūcĕrĕ ămāntēm. Aūt fraūs īnnēxă clĭēntī. *See Fallax.*

Dēclāmŏ, ās, āvī, ātūm, ārĕ. *To declaim.* Syn.—Rĕcĭtŏ. *To cry out against.* Syn.—Mălĕdīcŏ.

Dēclārŏ, ās, āvī, ātūm, ārĕ. *To declare.* Vīctōrēm māgnā prǣcōnĭs vōcĕ Clŏānthūm Dēclārăt. V. Syn.—Dēnūntĭŏ, prōclāmŏ. *To show, to manifest.* Syn.—Īndĭcŏ, sīgnĭfĭcŏ, ăpĕrĭŏ, mănĭfēstŏ, nūntĭŏ, ēxplĭcŏ, ēxprōmŏ, vūlgŏ, dīvūlgŏ. *See Ostendo.*

Dēclīnŏ, ās, āvī, ātūm, ārĕ. *To turn away.* Dēclīnāmŭs ĭtēm mōtūs, nēc tēmpŏrĕ cērtō. L. Syn.—Dēflēctŏ, flēctŏ, āvērtŏ, dēmŏvĕŏ. *To avoid.* Syn.—Vītŏ. *To go away from.* Syn.—Dēflēctŏr, āvērtŏr, rĕcēdŏ, ăbĕŏ.

Dēclīvĭs, ĭs, ĕ. *Inclined.* Stēllă Lȳcāŏnĭām vērgīt prōclīvĭs ăd ārctŏn. O. Syn.—Prōclīvĭs, dēvēxŭs, īnclīnātŭs, īnflēxŭs, prōnŭs, dēscēndēns, prǣcēps, ăcclīvĭs, clīvōsŭs. Phr.—Dēclīvĭs ŏlȳmpŭs. Nātās rīpīs dēclīvĭbŭs ūmbrās.

Dēcŏlŏr, ōrĭs. adj. *Discolored.* Syn.—Dēcŏlōrātŭs. *Pale.* Syn.—Syn.—Pāllēns, pāllĭdŭs, ēxsānguĭs.

Dēcŏquŏ, ĭs, ōxī, ōctūm, ĕrĕ. *To cook. See Coquo. To burn.* Syn.—Ūrŏ, ēxĕdŏ. Fig.—*To devour.* Syn.—Dēvŏrŏ. *To ruin, to consume.* Syn.—Cōncŏquŏ, prŏfūndŏ, ābsūmŏ, cōnsūmŏ, pērdŏ, ēffūndŏ, prōdĭgŏ, dīspērdŏ, lĭgūrĭŏ, dēvŏrŏ, ēxhaūrĭŏ, dīssĭpŏ.

Dĕcŏr, ōrĭs. m. *Beauty, grace.* Mīră dĕcōrĕ pĭō sērvābāt nātă pĕnātēs. Syn.—Dĕcŭs, hŏnŏr, grātĭă, fōrmă, pūlchrĭtūdŏ, vĕnūstās, spĕcĭēs. *See Forma.*

Dĕcōrē. adv. *Elegantly.* Syn.—Pūlchrē, ōrnātē.

Dĕcŏrŏ, ās, āvī, ātūm, ārĕ. *To adorn.* Ābsēntī fĕrăt īnfĕrĭās dĕcŏrētquĕ sĕpūlcrō. V. Syn.—Ōrnŏ. Phr.—Dĕcŏrāntquĕ sŭpēr fūlgēntĭbŭs ārmīs. Ēt sērtīs dĕcŏrārĕ cŏmās. *To honor.* Syn.—Hŏnestŏ, cŏhŏnēstŏ, cĕlĕbrŏ, laūdŏ.

Dĕcōrŭs, ă, ūm. *Becoming, fitting.* Ān fālsō crīmĭnĕ tūrpĕ Āccūsāssĕ mĭhī, vōbīs dāmnāssĕ dĕcōrum ēst. O. Syn.—Cōnvĕnĭēns, āptŭs. *Beautiful.* Syn.—Pūlchĕr, fōrmōsŭs, cōnspĭcŭŭs, cōnspĭcĭēndŭs, vĕnūstŭs, cōncīnnŭs. *Adorned.* Syn.—Dĕcŏrātŭs, ōrnātŭs, īnsīgnĭs.

Dēcrēscŏ, ĭs, vī, ētūm, ĕrĕ. *To decrease.* Syn.—Mĭnŭŏr, īmmĭnŭŏr; (*sometimes*) lānguēscŏ, dēflăgrŏ, dēfērvĕŏ.

Dēcrētūm, ī. n. *Decree.* Syn.—Cōnsūltūm, scītūm, sēntēntĭă. Phr.—Pătrūmquĕ Prōspĕrēs dēcrētă sŭpēr jŭgāndīs Fēmĭnīs.

Dēcūmbŏ, ĭs, ŭbŭī, ŭbĭtūm, ĕrĕ. *To lie down, to recline.* Tē sŭmŭs ōblītī dēcŭbŭīssĕ sĕnēm. Syn.—Cŭbŏ, rĕcŭbŏ, rĕcūmbŏ, āccūmbŏ, jăcĕŏ, quĭēscŏ, rĕquĭēscŏ. *See Cubo, Jaceo.*

Dēcūrrŏ, ĭs, cūrrī, rsūm, ĕrĕ. *To run down.* Ā tē dēcūrrĭt ād mĕōs haūstūs lĭquŏr. Phaed. Syn.—Cūrrŏ, rŭŏ, prǣcĭpĭtŏ, dēscēndŏ. Phr.—Cĭtō dēcūrrĭt trāmĭtĕ vīrgŏ. Ēffūsō dēcūrrĕrĕ pāssū. Dēcūrrērĕ rŏgōs. *To run through, to finish.* Syn.—Pērcūrrŏ, ēxsĕquŏr, cōnfĭcĭŏ.

Dēcūrsŭs, ūs. m. *Running, course.* Syn.—Cūrsŭs, īncūrsŭs, īmpĕtŭs, lāpsŭs. Phr.—Māgnūs dēcūrsŭs ăquārūm.

Dĕcŭs, ŏrĭs. n. *Ornament, decoration.* Ībăt ĕrātquĕ dĕcūs pōmpǣ cŏmĭtūmquĕ sŭōrūm. O. Syn.—Dĕcŏr, dĕcŏrāmĕn, ōrnātŭs. Phr.—Vĕtĕrūm dĕcŏra āltă părēntūm. Scēnīs dĕcŏra āltă fŭtūrīs. Rēgĭūm căpĭtī dĕcŭs. *Glory, honor.* Syn.—Laūs, hŏnŏr, glōrĭă, splēndŏr, nōmĕn. Phr.—Dĕcūs āddĭtĕ dīvīs. Tū dĕcūs ōmnĕ tŭīs. Dĕcūs ēt tūtāmĕn ĭn ārmīs. Nēc mĭnĭmūm mĕrŭērĕ dĕcŭs.

Dēcŭtĭŏ, ĭs, ūssī, ūssūm, ĕrĕ. *To shake down, to throw off.* Aūt ērrāns būcŭlă cāmpō Dēcŭtĭăt rōrem ēt sūrgēntēs āttĕrăt hērbās. V. Syn.—Ēxcŭtĭŏ, ējĭcĭŏ, dētūrbŏ. Phr.—Sīlvīs hŏnōrēm dēcŭtĭt Dĕcēmbĕr.

Dēdĕcĕt. impers. *It is unbecoming.* Ādmōvīquĕ prĕcēs quārūm mē dēdĕcĕt ūsŭs. O. Syn.—Nōn dĕcĕt, nōn cōnvĕnĭt.

Dēdĕcŭs, ŏrĭs. m. *Dishonor, infamy.* Īllĕ nŏtăt vĕtĕrēs ēt lōngī dēdĕcŭs ǣvī Ābstŭlĭt. O. Syn.—Prŏbrūm, ōpprŏbrĭūm, īgnōmĭnĭă, īnfāmĭă, lābēs, măcŭlă, nŏtă, stīgmă. Phr.—Fāmǣ lābēs. Nōn ĕgŏ dēdĕcŏrī tĭbĭ sūm. *See Infamia.*

Dēdĭcŏ, ās, āvī, ātūm, ārĕ. *To dedicate, to consecrate.* Syn.—Dĭcŏ (ās), săcrŏ, cōnsĕcrŏ, vŏvĕŏ, dēvŏvĕŏ, ōffĕrŏ. *See Consecro.*

Dēdīgnŏr, ārĭs, ātŭs sūm, ārī. *To disdain.* Īs mē nēc cŏmĭtēm, nēc dēdīgnātŭr ămīcūm. O. Syn.—Āspērnŏr, rēspŭŏ, fāstīdĭŏ, cōntēmnŏ.

Dēdŏ, ĭs, ĭdī, ĭtūm, ĕrĕ. *To deliver.* Dēdātūr cŭpĭdō jāmdūdūm nūptă mărītō. *Cat.* Syn.—Dō, trādŏ, āddīcŏ, trĭbŭŏ. Phr.—Dēdĕ nĕcī.

Dēdūcŏ, ĭs, dūxī, dūctūm, ĕrĕ. *To conduct from.* Mēmnŏnĭĭs dēdūcēns āgmĭnă rēgnīs. L. Syn.—Dūcŏ. Phr.—Mē dēdūxĭt ĭn Hēllēs. *To lead down.* Syn.—Dētrăhŏ, dēvōlvŏ, ăgŏ (præcĭpĭtēm). —cārmĕn. *To compose verses. See Scribo. To chase away.* Syn.—Āmŏvĕŏ, ăbĭgŏ, ēxĭmŏ, ēxpēllŏ, āvērtŏ.

Dĕērrŏ, ās, āvī, ātūm, ārĕ. *To wander from the way.* Syn. Ērrŏ, ăbērrŏ, dēflēctŏ, dēvĭŏ. *See Erro.*

Dēfēctŭs, ūs. m. *Defect.* Dēfēctūs sōlĭs vărĭōs lūnæquĕ lăbōrēs. V. Syn.—Cărēntĭă, ĕgēstās.

Dēfēndŏ, ĭs, dī, sūm, ĕrĕ. *To defend.* Āssuētī lōngō dēfēndĕrĕ bēllō. V. Syn.—Dēfēnsŏ, tŭĕŏr, tūtŏr, tĕgŏ, prōtĕgŏ, cūstōdĭŏ, aūxĭlĭŏr, sērvŏ, prōpūgnŏ. Phr.—Sūm tūtēlă. Fīnēs cūstōdĕ tŭērī. Prō Trōjā stābăt Ăpōllŏ. Hæc ără tŭēbĭtŭr ōmnēs. *See Auxilior. To repulse.* Syn.—Ārcĕŏ.

Dēfēnsŏr, ōrĭs. m. *Defender.* Nōn tāli aūxĭlĭō, nēc dēfēnsōrĭbŭs ĭstĭs Tēmpŭs ĕgĕt. V. Syn.—Pătrōnŭs, prōpūgnātŏr, sērvātŏr, tūtŏr, aūxĭlĭātŏr, tūtāmĕn, tūtēlă, cūstōs, cūstōdĭă, cŏlūmĕn, præsĭdĭūm, aūxĭlĭūm. Phr.—Rērūm cērtă sălūs. Īnsīgnĕ mæstĭs præsĭdĭūm rĕĭs. Dī quōrūm sūb nūmĭnĕ Trōja ēst. Ītălĭæ præsēns tūtēlă. Nātĕ, mĕæ vīrēs, mĕă māgnă pŏtēntĭă.

Dēfĕrŏ, fērs, tŭlī, lātūm, fērrĕ. *To bring, to carry.* Nātōs ād flūmĭnă prīmūm Dēfĕrĭmŭs. V. *See Fero, Porto.*

Dēfērvĕŏ, ēs, bŭī, ērĕ. *To boil.* Syn.—Dēfērvēscŏ, rĕfrīgēscŏ, rĕsīdŏ.

Dēfēssŭs, ă, ūm. *Tired out, wearied.* Pāndĭtĕ dēfēssīs hōspĭtă fānă vĭrīs. Prop. Syn.—Fēssŭs, dēfătīgātŭs, lāssŭs, dēbĭlĭtātŭs, ēnērvātŭs, frāctŭs, ēxhaūstŭs, lānguēns, lānguēscēns, lānguĭdŭs. *See Fessus.*

Dēfĭcĭŏ, ĭs, fēcī, fēctūm, ĕrĕ. *To lack, to be wanting.* Nōctĭs lēntūs nōn dēfĭcĭt hūmŏr. V. Syn.—Cărĕŏ, ēgĕŏ. *To lack strength.* Syn.—Lānguĕŏ, frāngŏr, ēxhaūrĭŏr, dēbĭlĭtŏr, cēssŏ, sūccĭdŏ. Phr.—Dēfĭcĭūnt ād cœptă. *To abandon.* Syn.—Dēsĕrŏ, dēstĭtŭŏ, rĕcēdŏ. *To revolt.* Syn.—Dēflēctŏ, dēscīscŏ.

Dēfīgŏ, ĭs, xī, xūm, ĕrĕ. *To fix, to plant.* Dēfīgūnt tēllūre hāstās ēt scūtă rĕclīnānt. V. Syn.—Fīgŏ, īnfīgŏ. Phr.—Tērræ dēfīgĭtŭr ărbōs. Spīcŭlă dēfīgūnt crābrōnēs.

Dēfīnĭō, īs, īvī & ĭī, ītūm, īrĕ. *To limit.* Ēt cērtō dēfīnīt līmĭtĕ cāmpōs. Syn.—Fīnĭō, tērmĭnŏ, dētērmĭnŏ, dēscrībŏ, cīrcūmscrībŏ, līmĭtŏ. *To prescribe.* Syn.—Dētērmĭnŏ, stătŭŏ, cōnstĭtŭŏ.

Dēflăgrŏ, ās, āvī, ātūm, ārĕ. *To burn.* Răpĭdō cūm dēflăgrăt īgnĕ. Lr. Syn.—Flăgrŏ, ārdĕŏ, ārdēscŏ, ēxārdēscŏ, ūrŏr, cōmbūrŏr, ēxūrŏr.

Dēflēctŏ, ĭs, xī, xūm, ĕrĕ. *To bend.* Quĭd răpĭdūm dēflēctĭs ĭtĕr? L. Syn.—Flēctŏ, tōrquĕŏ, dētōrquĕŏ. *To turn away from.* Syn.—Āvērtŏ, āmŏvĕŏ, ārcĕŏ. *To wander.* Syn.—Dēvĭŏ, ăbērrŏ.

Dēflĕŏ, ēs, ēvī, ētūm, ērĕ. *To weep.* Grăvĭbūs cōgōr dēflērĕ quĕrēlīs. Pr. Syn.—Flĕŏ, dēplōrŏ, lūgĕŏ, plāngŏ, lāmēntŏr. Phr.—Vānōs dēflērĕ lăbōrēs. *See Lacrimo.*

Dēflŭŏ, ĭs, ūxī, ūxūm, ĕrĕ. *To flow down.* Ēxĭgŭā dēflŭĭt ūndă mŏrā. O. Syn.—Flŭŏ, lābŏr. *To escape.* Syn.—Ēxcĭdŏ, lābŏr, ēlābŏr. *To fall.* Syn.—Cădŏ, ēxcĭdŏ. *To fall into disuse.* Syn.—Cădŏ, īntērcĭdŏ, ăbŏlĕŏr, ēxŏlĕŏ.

Dēfŏdĭŏ, ĭs, fōdī, fōssūm, ĕrĕ. *To dig.* Syn.—Fŏdĭŏ. *To bury.* Syn.—Īnfŏdĭŏ, ōbrŭŏ.

Dēfōrmĭs, ĭs, ĕ. *Deformed.* Sērmōnum īndŏctī, făcĭēm dēfōrmĭs ămīcī. H. Syn.—Īnfōrmĭs, tūrpĭs. Phr.—Fōrmā cărēns. Āspēctū hōrrĭdŭs. Hōrrēndūs vīsū. Quō nōn ēst tūrpĭŏr āltĕr. Nāmque ălĭæ tūrpēs hōrrēnt. *Dirty.* Syn.—Fœdŭs, squālĭdŭs, squālēns, tētĕr, ātĕr. Phr.—Cōcȳtī dēfōrmĭs ărūndŏ. Fœdŭs āspēctū. Ōbscūrīsquĕ gĕnīs tūrpĭs.

Dēfōrmŏ, ās, āvī, ātūm, ārĕ. *To form, to fashion.* Mārmŏră prīmā dēfōrmātă mănū. M. Syn.—Ēffīngŏ, fĭgūrŏ. *To disfigure.* Syn.—Tūrpŏ, dētūrpŏ, fœdŏ. Phr.—Hōrrĭdă vūltūm dēfōrmăt măcĭēs.

Dēgĕnĕr, ĕrĭs. m. & f. *Degenerate, unworthy of one's race.* Sī mē dēgĕnĕrī strāvīssēnt fātă sūb hōstĕ. L. Syn.—Dēgĕnĕrāns, mūtātŭs, īndīgnŭs, dētĕrĭŏr. Phr.—Pătrĭī nōmĭnĭs, vīrtūtĭs. ăvītæ īmmĕmŏr, haūd mĕmŏr, ōblītūs. Dēdĕcūs ēgrĕgĭī gĕnĕrĭs. Dēgĕnĕrēs ănĭmōs tĭmŏr ārgŭĭt. *See Ignavus.*

Dēgĕnĕrŏ, ās, āvī, ātūm, ārĕ. *To degenerate.* Dēgĕnĕrăt, pālmæ vĕtĕrūmque ōblītŭs hŏnōrēm. O. Syn.—Sūm dēgĕnĕr, dēscīscŏ, mūtŏr. Phr.—Ā vīrtūtĕ pătērnā dēfĭcērĕ. Vīrtūtī nōn rēspōndērĕ pătērnæ. Dēgĕnĕrēs āffērre ănĭmōs. Āvōrum īndīgnum ēssĕ. *See Degener.*

Dēgŏ, ĭs, ī, ĕrĕ. *To spend one's life.* Tēmpŏre ĭn āntĕāctō cūm pūlchrē dēgĕrĕt ǣvūm. Lr. Syn.—Ăgŏ, ăgĭtō, ēxĭgŏ, dūcŏ, vīvŏ. Phr.—Dīgnām Dīs dēgĕrĕ vītām. Āltĕrĭūs sūb nūtū dēgĭtūr ǣtās.

Dēgūstŏ, ās, āvī, ātūm, ārĕ. *To taste.* Cĕlĕrī dēgūstāt sīngŭlă sēnsū. Syn.—Gūstŏ, lībŏ, dēlībŏ.

Dĕhīnc. adv. *Henceforth.* Ūt spĕcĭōsă dĕhīnc mīrācŭlă prōmăt. H. Syn.—Dĕīndĕ, deīndĕ, dĕĭn, deīn, ēxīn, pōstĕā.

Dĕhīscŏ, ĭs, ĕrĕ. *To yawn.* Sēd mĭhĭ vēl tēllūs ōptēm prĭūs īmă dĕhīscăt. V. Syn.—Hĭŏ, hīscŏ, dīscēdŏ, dīdūcŏr, ăpĕrĭŏr, fīndŏr, lāxŏr, pătĕfīŏ, pătĕŏ, dīssĭlĭŏ. Phr.—Vāstō tēllūs dīscēdĭt. Dĕhīscĭt Cōnvūlsūm rēmīs ǣquŏr. Tērrǣque ārdōrĕ dĕhīscūnt. Rīmīs cȳmbă dĕhīscĭt.

Dĕhōrtŏr, ārĭs, ātūs sūm, ārī. *To dissuade.* Syn.—Dīssuādĕŏ, dētērrĕŏ, āvŏcŏ, āvērtŏ.

Dĕĭn, Dĕīncēps, Dĕīndĕ & Deīn, Deīncēps, Deīndĕ. *Again, in the second place.* Syn.—Ēxīn, ēxīndĕ, dĕhīnc, dehīnc, pōst, pōsthāc.

Dējĭcĭŏ, ĭs, jēcī, jēctūm, ĕrĕ. *To hurl down.* Gĕnĭtōr quǣ plūrĭmă cœ̄lō Dējĭcĭt īn tērrās. V. Syn.—Mīttŏ, jăcŭlŏr, stērnŏ, prōstērnŏ, dīrŭŏ, ēvērtŏ, dētūrbŏ. Phr.—Stērnĕre hŭmī. Sŏlō tērrǣ ēffūndĕrĕ. *See Everto. To chase.* Syn.—Dēpēllŏ, ēxpēllŏ, ēxtūrbŏ, dētrūdŏ, pēllŏ.

Dēlābŏr, ĕrĭs, lāpsūs sūm, ī. *To fall.* Syn.—Lābŏr, dēfĕrŏr, dēscēndŏ. *To fall from on high.* Syn.—Lābŏr, cădŏ, dēcĭdŏ, dēflŭŏ.

Dēlēctŏ, ās, āvī, ātūm, ārĕ. *To give delight.* Quēm plūs nĭmĭō dēlēctāvērĕ sĕcūndō. H. Syn.—Ōblēctŏ, rĕcrĕŏ, jŭvŏ, rĕlāxŏ, mūlcĕŏ, pērmūlcĕŏ, plăcĕŏ, ārrīdĕŏ. Phr.—Gaūdĭă āffĕrŏ. Lǣtĭtĭă pērfūndŏ, īmplĕŏ. *See Gaudium.*

Dēlĕŏ, ēs, ēvī, ētūm, ērĕ. *To destroy.* Dēlērĕ pĕdūm vēstīgĭă caūdā. Syn.—Ēxpūngŏ, ābstērgĕŏ, ōblītĕrŏ, ōblīnŏ, rādŏ, tōllŏ. *To correct.* Syn.—Cōrrĭgŏ, ēmēndŏ. *To destroy totally.* Syn.—Ăbŏlĕŏ, dēstrŭŏ, dīrŭŏ, ēvērtŏ, pērdŏ, tōllŏ, pēssūmdŏ, ēxstīnguŏ. Phr.—Māssĭlĭām dēlērĕ văcăt. Tēmpūs dēlēvĭt ămōrēm. *See Everto.*

Dēlībĕrŏ, ās, āvī, ātūm, ārĕ. *To deliberate.* Scīt quĭd īn Ārsăcĭā Păcŏrūs dēlībĕrĕt aūlā. M. Syn.—Cōnsŭlŏ, cōnsūltŏ, vōlvŏ, vērsŏ, ăgĭtŏ, mĕdĭtŏr. *See Statuo.*

Dēlĭcātūs, ă, ūm. *Delicious, charming.* Cēlsǣ cūlmĭnă dēlĭcātă vīllǣ. M. Syn.—Ămœ̄nūs, grātūs, dūlcĭs, suāvĭs. *Tender.* Syn. Tĕnĕr, mōllĭs. *Fastidious.* Syn.—Fāstīdĭōsūs, sŭpērbūs. *Given to pleasure.* Phr.—Dēlĭcĭīs dēdĭtūs, lūxŭrĭāns. Mōllĭtĭē, lūxū sŏlūtūs, flŭēns.

Dēlĭcĭă, ǣ. f. *Delight, pleasure.* Syn.—Gaūdĭă, vŏlŭptās. Phr.—
Dūlcĭă vītǣ. Lūxū cărēntēs dēlĭcĭǣ. Dēlĭcĭīs īmplēre ănĭmōs.
Dēlĭcĭīs lūxŭrĭārĕ nŏvīs. *See Voluptas. Softness.* Syn.—
Mōllĭtĭēs, lūxŭs.

Dēlīctūm, ī. n. *Fault, offense.* Syn.—Ādmīssūm, cūlpă, ērrŏr, ērrātūm, nŏxă, pĭācŭlūm. Phr.—Quī nŏstră sătīs dēlīctă pĭābĭt. Prō
dēlīctīs hŏstĭă blāndă fŭĭt. *See Culpa, Peccatum.*

Dēlĭgŏ, ĭs, ēgī, ēctūm, ĕrĕ. *To pick, to pluck.* Ēt prīmām tĕnŭī
dēlĭgĕre ūngŭĕ rŏsām. O. Syn.—Lĕgŏ, cōllĭgŏ, cārpŏ, dēcērpŏ.
See Carpo. To choose. See Eligo.

Dēlīnīmēntūm, ī. n. *Caress.* Syn.—Blāndĭtĭǣ, blāndīmēntă, īllĕ-
cĕbrǣ.

Dēlīnĭŏ, īs, īvī & ĭī, ītūm, īrĕ. *To flatter, to charm.* Syn.—Lēnĭŏ,
sōlŏr, mūlcĕŏ, pērmūlcĕŏ, blāndĭŏr.

Dēlīnquŏ, ĭs, īquī, īctūm, ĕrĕ. *To commit a fault.* Mājūs pēccātum
ēst, paŭlūm dēlīquĭt ămīcŭs. H. Syn.—Pēccŏ, ērrŏ. *See Erro.*

Dēlīrŏ, ās, āvī, ātūm, ārĕ. *To be in delirium.* Syn.—Dēsĭpĭŏ, īnsānĭŏ. *See Amens.*

Dēlīrŭs, ă, ūm. *Delirious.* Prǣtŭlĕrīm scrīptōr dēlīrŭs ĭnērsquĕ
vĭdērī. H. Syn.—Dēmēns, stūltŭs, īnsānŭs, lȳmphātŭs. Phr.—
Dēlīrŭs ĕt āmēns. Dēlīrăquĕ fătŭr. *See Amens.*

Dēlĭtĕŏ, ēs, ŭī, ērĕ. *To be concealed.* Vīpĕră dēlĭtŭĭt, cǣlūmque
ēxtērrĭtă fūgĭt. V. Syn.—Lătĕŏ, lătĭtŏ, ābdŏr, ābscōndŏr, ōccūltŏr, ŏpĕrĭŏr. *See Lateo.*

Dēlūbrūm, ī. n. *Shrine, temple.* Ād dēlūbră vĕnīt, mōnstrātās ēxcĭtăt ārās. V. Syn.—Fānūm, tēmplūm, ǣdēs. Phr.—Āltă
dĕōrūm dēlūbră. Dēlūbrăquĕ dītĭă dōnīs. Sŭpĕrūm dēlūbră
văpōrānt. *See Templum.*

Dēlūdŏ, ĭs, dī, sūm, ĕrĕ. *To deceive, to fool.* Aūt quǣ sōpītōs
dēlūdūnt sōmnĭă sēnsūs. V. Syn.—Lūdŏ, īllūdŏ, fāllŏ, dēcĭpĭŏ,
cīrcūmvĕnĭŏ. Phr.—Cōrvūm dēlūdĭt hĭāntēm. Tēllūs dēlūdĭt
ărāntēs. *See Decipio, Fallo.*

Dēmēns, ēntĭs. adj. *Foolish.* Dēmēns ēt cāntū vŏcăt īn cērtāmĭnă
dīvōs. V. Syn.—Āmēns, īnsānŭs, mălĕsānŭs, vēsānŭs, vēcōrs,
lȳmpātŭs, dēlīrŭs. Phr.—Tĭmĭdūm dēmēntĭă sōmnĭă tērrēnt.
Mēntĕ cărērĕ. Sǣvĭt ĭnōps ănĭmī. *See Amens, stultus.*

Dēmēntĕr. adv. *Foolishly.* Syn.—Stūltē, īnsānē.

Dēmēntĭă, ǣ. f. *Foolishness, madness.* Cūm sŭbĭta īncaūtūm
dēmēntĭă cēpĭt ămāntēm. V. Syn.—Āmēntĭă, īnsānĭă, fŭrŏr,
stūltĭtĭă. Phr.—Dēmēns, āmēns ănĭmŭs. Quǣ tānta īnsānĭă
cīvēs? Scĕlĕrāta īnsānĭă bēllī. Fŭrōrnĕ cǣcŭs, ān răpĭt vīs
ācrĭŏr? *See Amens.*

Dēmĕrĕŏ, ēs, ŭī, ĭtūm, ērĕ. *To gain something, to merit.* Syn.— Dēvīncĭŏ, ōbstrīngŏ.

Dēmērgŏ, ĭs, ērsī, sūm, ĕrĕ. *To submerge.* Dūm lĭcĕt, ōbscœnām pōntō dēmērgĭtĕ pūppīm. O. Syn.—Mērgŏ, ĭmmērgŏ, dēmērgŏ, dēmĭttŏ, ōbrŭŏ.

Dēmĕtŏ, ĭs, ēssŭī, ēssŭm, ĕrĕ. *To gather the harvest.* Sōlĕ sŭb ārdēntī flāvēntĭă dēmĭtĭt ārvă. Cat. *See Meto. To cull.* Syn.— Cārpŏ, lĕgŏ, cōllĭgŏ.

Dēmĭgrŏ, ās, āvī, ātūm, ārĕ. *To change one's dwelling, to go away.* Pătrĭīs quī dēmĭgrāvĕrĭt ōrīs. Syn.—Mĭgrŏ, ăbĕŏ, ēxĕŏ, dīscēdŏ, rĕcēdŏ, ēvādŏ. *See Abeo.*

Dēmĭttŏ, ĭs, mīsī, mīssum, ĕrĕ. *To send down.* Plūsquĕ cŭpīt quō plūră sŭām dēmĭttĭt ĭn ālvūm. Syn.—Mīttŏ, ĭmmīttŏ. Phr.— Quī lārgŭm cœlō dēmĭttĭtĭs ĭmbrēm. *To lower.* Lāssōvĕ pāpāvĕră cōllō Dēmīsērĕ căpŭt. Syn.—Dējĭcĭŏ, īnclīnŏ, pōnŏ. *To lose courage.* Syn.—Ābjĭcĭŏ, dējĭcĭŏ, pōnŏ, dēspōndĕŏ.

Dēmŏ, ĭs, psī, ptūm, ĕrĕ. *To take away.* Ēxĭgŭūm plēnō dē mărĕ dēmăt ăquæ. O. Syn.—Ādĭmŏ, tōllŏ, aūfĕrŏ, dētrăhŏ, ērĭpĭŏ, āmŏvĕŏ, ēxŭŏ. Phr.—Dēmĕ sŭpērcĭlĭō nūbēm. Dē grĕmĭō pāllĭă dēmĕ tŭō.

Dēmōlĭŏr, īrĭs, ītŭs sūm, īrī. *To demolish.* Syn.—Dētūrbŏ, dējĭcĭŏ.

Dēmōnstrŏ, ās, āvī, ātūm, ārĕ. *To show.* Syn.—Dēclārŏ, ōstēndŏ.

Dēmŏvĕŏ, ēs, ōvī, ōtūm, ērĕ. *To displace.* Syn.—Āmŏvĕŏ, ārcĕŏ. Phr.—Nĭhīl lūcrō tē dēmŏvĕt.

Dēmūm. adv. *Finally.* Syn.—Tāndēm, dēnĭquĕ, pōstrēmō.

Dēnĕgŏ, ās, āvī, ātūm, ārĕ. *To deny.* Āmnīs tĭbĭ dēnĕgăt ūndās. O. Syn.—Nĕgŏ, ăbnĕgŏ, ābnŭŏ, rĕnŭŏ, rĕcūsŏ. *See Abnego.*

Dēnī, æ, ă. *Ten.* Syn.—Dĕcēm. Phr.—Bīs quīnquĕ.

Dēnĭquĕ. adv. *Finally.* Syn.—Dēmūm, pōstrēmō.

Dēnōmĭnŏ, ās, āvī, ātūm, ārĕ. *To name.* Quāndo ēt prĭōrēs hīnc Lămĭās fĕrūnt Dēnōmĭnātōs. H. Syn.—Āppēllŏ, dīcŏ, nōmĭnŏ. Phr.—Ĭmpōnĕrĕ nōmĕn.

Dēnŏtŏ, ās, āvī, ātūm, ārĕ. *To designate.* Quĭă pēr gāllīnăm dēnŏtāvīt fēmĭnās. Phaed. Syn.—Sīgnĭfĭcŏ, īndĭcŏ.

Dēns, dēntĭs. m. *Tooth.* Dēntĭbŭs īnfrēndēns gĕmĭtū nēmŭs ōmnĕ rēplēbăt. O. Phr.—Ōssă ōrīs. Māgnīs īnsīgnĭă dēntĭbŭs ōră. Dēntēs crēpŭĕrĕ rĕtēctī. Dăpēs ĭvĭdō cōnvēllĕrĕ dēntĕ. Dēntēmque īn dēntĕ fătīgăt. Lāssō dēntĕ pĭgĕr.

Dēnsĕŏ, ēs, ī, ērĕ & Dēnsŏ, ās, āvī, ātūm, ārĕ. *To condense.* Ēt Jūppĭtĕr hūmĭdŭs Aūstrīs Dēnsĕt, ĕrānt quæ rāră mŏdo ēt quæ dēnsă rĕlāxăt. V. Syn.—Cōndēnsĕŏ, āddēnsĕŏ, āddēnsŏ, cōgŏ. *To put close together.* Syn.—Stīpŏ, cōgŏ, spīssŏ.

Dēnsŭs, ă, ūm. *Thick, condensed.* Dēnsă măgīs Cĕrĕrī rārīssĭmă quǣquĕ Lȳǣō Tērră făvĕt. V. Syn.—Spīssŭs, dēnsātŭs, cōmprēssŭs, cōmpāctŭs, cŏāctŭs, cōncrētŭs. Phr.—Dēnsĭŏr āĕrĕ tēllūs. Dēnsă frīgŏrĭs āspĕrĭtās. Dēnsīs tēxīt sŭă nūbĭbŭs ōră. *Pressed close together.* Syn.—Cōnfērtŭs, cōndēnsŭs. Phr.—Dēnsīs īncŭrrĭmŭs ārmīs. Dēnsǣque īn mōntĭbŭs ūmbrǣ. Dēnsīssĭmŭs īmbĕr. Mīllĕ răpīt dēnsōs ăcĭē. *Numerous.* Syn.—Frĕquēns, crēbĕr, mūltŭs, plūrĭmŭs.

Dēnūdŏ, ās, āvī, ātūm, ārĕ. *To denude.* Syn.—Nūdŏ, ēxŭŏ, spŏlĭŏ. *See Nudo.*

Dēnūntĭŏ, ās, āvī, ātūm, ārĕ. *To announce, to declare.* Trīstēs dēnūntĭăt īrās. V. Syn.—Nūntĭŏ, sīgnĭfĭcŏ, dēclārŏ, īndĭcŏ, prǣdĭcŏ. *See Nuntio.*

Dēnŭŏ. adv. *Anew.* Syn.—Rūrsŭs, rūrsūm, ĭtĕrūm.

Dĕōrsūm. adv. *Downward.* Syn.—Ăd īmūm. Īn īmūm (*or*) īmă.

Dēpāscŏr, ĕrĭs, stŭs sūm, ī. *To eat, to consume.* Nēc quădrŭpēs dēnsās dēpāscĭtŭr āspĕră sīlvās. Tib. Syn.—Pāscŏr, cārpŏ, dētōndĕŏ, dēmētŏ.

Dēpēllŏ, ĭs, ŭlī, ūlsūm, ĕrĕ. *To expel.* Cūrās dēpēllĕrĕ vīnō. Tib. Syn.—Pēllŏ, ēxpēllŏ, rēpēllŏ, prōpēllŏ, prōpūlsŏ, dējĭcĭŏ, dētūrbŏ, ēxtūrbŏ, ăbĭgŏ, āmŏvĕŏ, ārcĕŏ. Phr.—Caūsām dēpēllĕrĕ lētī. Quām mōrtēm frātrī dēpŭlĭt, īpsă tŭlĭt.

Dēpēndĕŏ, ēs, dī, sūm, ērĕ. *To hang.* Dēpēndēnt lȳchnī lăquĕārĭbŭs aūreīs. V. Syn.—Pēndĕŏ.

Dēpēndŏ, ĭs, dī, sūm, ĕrĕ. *To pay.* Māllēm fēlīcĭbŭs ārmīs Dēpēndīssĕ căpŭt. L. *See Solvo, Pendo.*

Dēpērdŏ, ĭs, ĭdī, ĭtūm, ĕrĕ. *To lose.* Ēt mēmbrātīm vītālēm dēpērdĕrĕ sēnsūm. L. Syn.—Pērdŏ, āmīttŏ. Phr.—Bŏnām dēpērdĕrĕ fāmām. Ūsūm līnguǣ dēpērdĕrĕ.

Dēpĕrĕŏ, īs, īvī & ĭī, ĭtūm, īrĕ. *To perish.* Dĕcōr lăcrĭmīs dēpĕrĭt. O. Syn.—Pērĕŏ, dīspĕrĕŏ, īntĕrĕŏ, ōccĭdŏ.

Dēplōrŏ, ās, āvī, ātūm, ārĕ. *To weep.* Stērnūntūr sĕgĕtēs ēt dēplōrātă cŏlōnī Vōtă jăcēnt. V. Syn.—Flĕŏ, dēflĕŏ, lūgĕŏ, dŏlĕŏ, gĕmŏ, plāngŏ. Phr.—Dēplōrātǣ līmĕn ădīrĕ dŏmūs. *See Fleo.*

Dēpōnŏ, ĭs, pŏsŭī, pŏsĭtūm, ĕrĕ. *To put down.* Ārmăquĕ dēpŏsŭēre hŭmĕrīs. *To entrust, to place in one's care.* Syn.—Crēdŏ, cōncrēdŏ, cōmmīttŏ. *To give up.* Syn.—Pōnŏ, ābjĭcĭŏ, ēxŭŏ, rĕlīnquŏ, mīttŏ.

Dēpŏpŭlŏr, ārĭs, ātŭs sūm, ārī. *To ravage, to devastate.* Fūrtīs āssuētŭs ĭnūltīs Dēpŏpŭlārĕ grĕgēs. Syn.—Pŏpŭlŏr, dēprǣdŏr, vāstŏ.

Dēpōrtō, ās, āvī, ātūm, ārĕ. *To transport.* Cūrvă te ĭn Hērcŭlĕūm dēpōrtānt ēssĕdă Tībŭr. Pr. Syn.—Fĕrŏ, trānsfĕrŏ, dēvĕhŏ.
Dēpōscŏ, ĭs, pŏpōscī, ĭtūm, ĕrĕ. *To ask.* Aūt prĭŭs īnfēctō dēpōscīt prǣmĭă cūrsū. Pr. Syn.—Pōscŏ, ēxpōscŏ, rĕpōscŏ, rĕquīrŏ, pĕtŏ, pōstŭlŏ. Phr.—Vōtīs dēpōscĕrĕ pūgnām. *See Posco.*
Dēprāvŏ, ās, āvī, ātūm, ārĕ. *To corrupt.* Nē grăvĭs ārtĭcŭlūs dēprāvāt pōndĕrĕ mōlēs. Syn.—Cōrrūmpŏ, vĭtĭŏ.
Dēprĕcŏr, ārĭs, ātŭs sūm, ārī. *To pray earnestly.* Hōc sŭpĕrōs, hōc tē quŏquĕ dēprĕcŏr, hōspĕs. V. *See Precor. To refuse.* Syn.—Rĕcūsŏ, ābnŭŏ.
Dēprĕhēndŏ, ĭs, dī, sūm, ĕrĕ. *To take, to seize.* Īmprōvīsŭs ădēs; dēprēndēs tūtŭs ĭnērmēm. O. (*The syncopated form is used generally in verse as in the quotation*). Syn.—Ōpprĭmŏ, ōccŭpŏ, căpĭŏ, ēxcĭpĭŏ. Phr.—Dēprēndĭt ĭn ǣquŏrĕ nāvēm Aūstĕr. Tĭbĭ, Tāntălĕ, nūllǣ dēprēndūntŭr ăquǣ. *To recognize.* Syn.—Āgnōscŏ, cōmpĕrĭŏ, dētĕgŏ, īnvĕnĭŏ.
Dēprĭmŏ, ĭs, prēssī, sūm, ĕrĕ. *To press down.* Ēt nē dēprĭmĕrēt flūctūsvĕ lăpīsvĕ cărīnām. V. Syn.—Prĕmŏ, cōmprĭmŏ, āfflīgŏ, āttĕrŏ, cōntĕrŏ, prōtĕrŏ, dējĭcĭŏ, dēmīttŏ, dēpēllŏ, dēmērgŏ.
Dēprōmŏ, ĭs, psī, ptūm, ĕrĕ. *To bring forth.* Ūltrīcēm phărĕtrā dēprōmĕ săgīttām. V. Syn.—Prōmŏ, ēxprōmŏ, ērŭŏ, ēxtrăhŏ, ēxsĕrŏ, prōfĕrŏ. Phr.—Dēprōmĕrĕ Cǣcŭbūm Cēllīs ăvītīs. *To publish.* Syn.—Ēdŏ, ēmīttŏ, prōfĕrŏ. *See Edo.*
Dēprŏpĕrŏ, ās, āvī, ātūm, ārĕ. *To hasten.* Quĭs ūdō dēprŏpĕrāre ăpĭō cŏrōnās Cūrātvĕ myrtō? H. Syn.—Prŏpĕrŏ, fēstīnŏ.
Dēpūgnŏ, ās, āvī, ātūm, ārē. *To fight.* Nōn mĕă māgnănĭmō dēpūgnāt tēssĕră tālō. M. Syn.—Lūctŏr, ōbnītŏr. Phr.—Dēpūgnāt mōrtī jŭvĕnĭs. *See Pugno.*
Dēpŭtŏ, ās, āvī, ātūm, ārĕ. *To cut.* Nōn mĭhĭ fālx nĭmĭās Sātūrnĭă dēpŭtāt ūmbrās. O. Syn.—Pŭtŏ, āmpŭtŏ, rĕsĕcŏ. *To esteem.* Syn.—Pŭtŏ, cēnsĕŏ, ǣstĭmŏ, jūdĭcŏ.
Dērīdĕŏ, ēs, dī, sūm, ērĕ. *To laugh at.* Dērīdēnt stŏlĭdī vērbă Lătīnă Gĕtǣ. O. Syn.—Rīdĕŏ, īrrīdĕŏ, lūdŏ, īllūdŏ. Phr.—Rīsū, căchīnnō, sălĭbŭs, jŏcīs ēxcĭpĕrĕ, lăcēssĕrĕ, ōbstrĕpĕrĕ. Tōllĕrĕ căchīnnūm. *See Irrideo.*
Dērĭpĭŏ, ĭs, pŭī, ēptūm, ĕrĕ. *To tear down.* Cōlăquĕ prǣlōrūm fūmōsīs dērĭpĕ tēctīs. V. Syn.—Răpĭŏ, dīrĭpĭŏ, ērĭpĭŏ, dētrăhŏ, dēdūcŏ, dēmīttŏ, ābrĭpĭŏ. Phr.—Vēlāmĭnă Prōcnē Dērĭpĭt ēx hŭmĕrīs. Pēctŏrĕ vēstēm Dērĭpŭĭt.
Dērīsŭs, ūs. m. *Derision.* Syn.—Rīsŭs, jŏcŭs, lūdĭbrĭūm.
Dērīvŏ, ās, āvī, ātūm, ārĕ. *To draw off water.* Fig.—*To turn.* Syn.—Āvērtŏ.

Dērŏgŏ, ās, āvī, ātūm, ārĕ. *To abrogate.* Syn.—Ābrŏgŏ, dētrăhŏ, aūfĕrŏ, ădĭmŏ.

Dēsăcrŏ, ās, āvī, ātūm, ārĕ. *To consecrate.* Syn.—Săcrŏ, cōnsĕcrŏ.

Dēsævĭŏ, īs, ĭī, ītūm, īrĕ. *To rage.* Sīc tōto Aēnēās dēsævīt pēctŏrĕ. V. Dēsævĭt ĭn ōmnēs. *See Saevio. To be appeased.* Syn.—Dēfērvĕŏ, rĕsīdŏ, cădŏ, mītēscŏ, mītĭgŏr, plăcŏr.

Dēscēndŏ, ĭs, dī, sūm, ĕrĕ. *To descend.* Aūt fūlvūm dēscēndĕrĕ mōntĕ lĕōnēm. V. Syn.—Lābŏr, dēlābŏr, īllābŏr, dēmīttŏr, dēsĭlĭŏ, dēfĕrŏr, dēflŭŏ (*of waters*). Phr.—Ād tērrām fĕrŏr, vōlvŏr, īllābŏr. Ĕrĕbī dēscēndĭt ăd ūmbrās. Īn mărĕ dēscēndīt Tĭbrĭs. Dēmīssūm lāpsī pēr fūnēm. *To penetrate into.* Syn.—Pĕnĕtrŏ.

Dēscīscŏ, ĭs, īvī, ītūm, ĕrĕ. *To withdraw.* Syn.—Dīscēdŏ, dēsĕrŏ. *See these words.*

Dēscrībŏ, ĭs, psī, ptūm, ĕrĕ. *To describe.* Aūt plŭvĭūs dēscrībĭtŭr ārcŭs. H. Syn.—Dēpīngŏ, pīngŏ, ădūmbrŏ, ēffīngŏ, dēlĭnĕŏ. *To write.* Syn.—Scrībŏ, ēxărŏ, scūlpŏ, īnscūlpŏ. *To brand.* Syn.—Dēsīgnŏ, nŏtŏ.

Dēsĕcŏ, ās, ŭī, ēctūm, ārĕ. *To cut.* Syn.—Sĕcŏ, scīndŏ, præcīdŏ.

Dēsĕrŏ, ĭs, ŭī, ērtūm, ĕrĕ. *To abandon.* Hānc quŏquĕ dēsĕrĭmūs sēdēm, paūcīsquĕ rĕlīctīs, Vēlă dămŭs. V. Syn.—Līnquŏ, rĕlīnquŏ, fŭgĭŏ, dīscēdŏ. *See Relinquo.* Phr.—Vīrtūtīsquĕ vĭām dēsĕrĭt ārdŭæ. Mūltă vŏlēntēm Dīcĕrĕ dēsĕrŭĭt. *To abandon a work.* Syn.—Līnquŏ, rĕlīnquŏ, ŏmīttŏ, dīmīttŏ, nēglĕgŏ, prætērmīttŏ, ābjĭcĭŏ. *To betray.* Syn.—Dēscīscŏ, dēfĭcĭŏ, dēstĭtŭŏ, prōdŏ, līnquŏ, rĕlīnquŏ, dīscēdŏ. *See Prodo.*

Dēsērtă, ōrūm. n. *Desert.* Sēd mē Pārnāssī dēsērtă pĕr ārdŭă mōntĭs Rāptăt ămŏr. V. Syn.—Sōlĭtūdŏ, rĕcēssŭs, āvĭă. Phr. Dēsērtă tēllūs, tērră, ōră, lŏcă, līttŏră. Īgnōtæ lătĕbræ. Rūs văcŭūm.

Dēsīdĕrĭūm, ĭī. n. *Desire, wish.* Aūt ălĭæ cūjūs dēsīdĕrĭum īnsīdĕāt rē. Lr. Syn.—Cŭpīdŏ, vōtūm. *Regret.* Syn.—Mœstĭtĭă, mœrŏr, lūctŭs. Phr.—Quīs dēsīdĕrĭō sīt pŭdŏr aūt mŏdŭs Tām cārī căpĭtĭs? Quærīt pātrĭă Cæsărēm.

Dēsīdĕrŏ, ās, āvī, ātūm, ārĕ. *To wish, to desire.* Tū quĭd ĕgo ēt pŏpŭlūs mēcūm dēsīdĕrēt aūdī. H. Syn.—Cŭpĭŏ, ōptŏ, ēxōptŏ, quærŏ, vŏlŏ, lĭbĕt, plăcĕt. Phr.—Cōrdī ēst. Dēsīdĕrāntēm quīd sătĭs ēst. *See Cupio. To regret.* Syn.—Lūgĕŏ, dēflĕŏ, flĕŏ, quĕrŏr.

Dēsĭdĭă, æ. f. *Laziness.* Syn.—Īgnāvĭă, ĭnērtĭă, pĭgrĭtĭă, sōcōrdĭă, sēgnĭtĭēs, ōtĭūm, tōrpŏr, vĕtērnūm. Phr.—Vītānda ēst īmprŏbă Sīrēn Dēsĭdĭă. *See Pigritia.*

Dēsĭdĭōsŭs, ă, ūm. *Lazy.* Syn.—Dēsĕs, ĭnērs, pĭgĕr, sēgnĭs, sōcōrs. Phr.—Dēsĭdĭā tārdŭs. Cuī sūnt dēsĭdĭæ cōrdī. Hōrrĭdŭs āltēr dēsĭdĭā.

Dēsīdŏ, ĭs, ēdī, ĕrĕ. *To settle down.* Cūr vădă dēsīdānt ēt rīpă cŏērcĕăt ūndās? Syn.—Rĕsīdŏ, cōnsīdŏ, sūccūmbŏ, cōllābŏr. Phr.—Vāstō dēsēdĭt hĭātū.

Dēsīgnŏ, ās, āvī, ātūm, ārĕ. *To mark out, to design.* Īpse hŭmĭlī dēsīgnāt mœnĭă fōssā. V. Syn.—Dēscrībŏ, dēfīnĭŏ, nŏtŏ. *To show.* Syn.—Sīgnŏ, mōnstrŏ, ōstēndŏ, īndĭcŏ.

Dēsĭlĭŏ, īs, ĭī & ŭī, ūltūm, īrĕ. *To jump down.* Dēsĭlŭīt Tūrnūs bĭjŭgīs, pĕdĕs āppārăt īrĕ. V. Syn.—Ēxsĭlĭŏ, dēscēndŏ, præcĭpĭtŏ, rŭŏ. Phr.—Aēthĕrĕ dēsĭlŭīt Jūnŏ. Dēsĭlĭt ē cūrrū.

Dēsĭnŏ, ĭs, īvī & ĭī, ĭtūm, ĕrĕ. *To cease, to finish.* Ātque ūt vīvāmūs vīvĕrĕ dēsĭnĭmŭs. Syn.—Dēsīstŏ, ābsīstŏ, cēssŏ, ābstĭnĕŏ, mīttŏ, ŏmīttŏ, fīnĭŏ. Phr.—Hīc fīnīs fāndī. Fīnēm dĕdĭt ōrĕ lŏquēndī. Lūsŭs hăbēt fīnēm.

Dēsīstŏ, ĭs, stĭtī, stĭtūm, ĕrĕ. *To stop, to desist.* Īn prīmō dēstĭtĭt ōrĕ sŏnŭs. O. Syn.—Cēssŏ, dēfĭcĭŏ. *To give up.* Syn.—Ābsīstŏ, rĕlīnquŏ, ŏmīttŏ, dēsĕrŏ.

Dēspērŏ, ās, āvī, ātūm, ārĕ. *To despair.* Prōxĭmŭs huīc grădŭs ēst bĕnĕ dēspērārĕ sălūtēm. O. Syn.—Dīffīdŏ, spēm pōnŏ. Phr.—Mē spēs dēstĭtŭĭt. Ănĭmō cădŏ. Spē ēxcĭdŏ. Ănĭmūm dēspōndĕŏ, pērdŏ. Nēc spēs ūllă fŭgæ. Hīc pōssĕ frŭī dēspērăt.

Dēspĭcĭŏ, ĭs, ēxī, ēctūm, ĕrĕ. *To look down upon.* Dē vērtĭcĕ mōntĭs Dēspĭcĕre īn vāllēs. O. Syn.—Dēspēctŏ, īmmĭnĕŏ. Fig.—*To despise.* Syn.—Spērnŏ, āspērnŏr, tēmnŏ, cōntēmnŏ, rēspŭŏ, fāstīdĭŏ, pōsthăbĕŏ, nēglĕgŏ. Phr.—Nōn cūrŏ. Frōntĕ sŭpērbā dēspĭcĭt. Dēspĭcĭt īrrīsūm vūltū. *See Aspernor, Contemno.*

Dēspŭŏ, ĭs, ŭī, ūtūm, ĕrĕ. *To spit.* Fig.—*To reject.* Syn.—Rēspŭŏ, rējĭcĭŏ, fāstīdĭŏ.

Dēstĭnŏ, ās, āvī, ātūm, ārĕ. *To fix, to determine.* Cōmpŏsĭtō rūmpĭt, vōcem ēt mē dēstĭnăt āræ. V. Syn.—Āssīgnŏ, trĭbŭŏ, āttrĭbŭŏ, dēvŏvĕŏ, āddīcŏ, dĭcŏ, sērvŏ, rĕsērvŏ. *To plan, to meditate.* Syn.—Mōlĭŏr, mĕdĭtŏr, părŏ. *To choose.* Syn.—Præfīnĭŏ, præstĭtŭŏ, ēlĭgŏ. *To intend.* Syn.—Stătŭŏ, cōnstĭtŭŏ, cōgĭtŏ, părŏ.

Dēstĭtŭŏ, ĭs, ŭī, tūtūm, ĕrĕ. *To abandon.* Nēc spēs dēstĭtŭăt sēd frūgūm sēmpĕr ăcērvōs Præbĕăt. J. Syn.—Dēsĕrŏ, līnquŏ, rĕlīnquŏ. Phr.—Spē dēstĭtŭī. Pōmă dēstĭtŭūnt fămēm. Mēntēm jām vērbă părātām Dēstĭtŭūnt.

Dēstrīngŏ, ĭs, nxī, īctūm, ĕrĕ. *To grasp, to pluck.* Aūt sūmmās dēstrīnge ēx ārbŏrĕ plāntās. V. Syn.—Cārpŏ, vēllŏ. *To wound slightly.* Syn.—Pērstrīngŏ, lædŏ Fig.—*To censure.* Syn.—Lædŏ, cārpŏ, mōrdĕŏ, lăcĕrŏ.

Dēstrŭŏ, ĭs, ūxī, ūctūm, ĕrĕ. *To destroy.* Mĕă Pȳgmălĭōn dūm mœnĭă frātĕr Dēstrŭăt. V. Syn.—Dīrŭŏ, ērŭŏ, pērdŏ, dēlĕŏ.

Dēsūm, ĕs, fŭī, ēssĕ. *To be lacking, to be absent.* Syn.—Dēfĭcĭŏ, ābsūm, dēsīdĕrŏ.

Dētĕgŏ, ĭs, ēxī, ēctūm, ĕrĕ. *To uncover.* Lăcĕrōs ārtūs ēt grāndĭă dētĕgĭt ōssă. O. Syn.—Rĕtĕgŏ, nūdŏ, ăpĕrĭŏ, pāndŏ, pătĕfăcĭŏ, ōstēndŏ. *See Ostendo.* *To reveal.* Syn.—Rĕtĕgŏ, ăpĕrĭŏ, ōstēndŏ, mōnstrŏ, nūdŏ, dēnūdŏ, pătĕfăcĭŏ, mănĭfēstŏ, rĕsĕrŏ, pāndŏ, prōdŏ, īndĭcŏ, tēstŏr, ārgŭŏ, dēclārŏ, dēmōnstrŏ, vūlgŏ, dīvūlgŏ, sīgnĭfĭcŏ, ēxprōmŏ, rĕvēllŏ, rĕsīgnŏ, ēxsĕrŏ. Phr.—Sŭb aūrās fĕrŏ. Īn ăpērtūm ēffĕrŏ. Lătĕbrīs ēdūcŏ. Īndĭcĭūm făcĭĕt.

Dētērgĕŏ, ēs, ērĕ & Dētērgŏ, ĭs, sī, sūm, ĕrĕ. *To clean, to wipe.* Dētērgūnt stămĭnĕ flētūs. Syn.—Tērgŏ, ābstērgŏ, ēlŭŏ, mūndŏ, pūrgŏ. Phr.—Dētērsīt lăcrĭmās. *To take away.* Syn.—Dēmŏ, ădĭmŏ.

Dētĕrĭŏr, ōrĭs. *Mean, inferior.* Syn.—Pējŏr, vĭtĭōsĭŏr.

Dētērmĭnŏ, ās, āvī, ātūm, ārĕ. *To limit.* Syn.—Tērmĭnŏ, dēfīnĭŏ.

Dētĕrŏ, ĭs, trīvī, trītūm, ĕrĕ. *To rub away.* Dētĕrĕt īnvălĭdōs ēt vĭă lōngă pĕdēs. Tib. Syn.—Tĕrŏ, āttĕrŏ, cōntĕrŏ, ābsūmŏ. *To efface.* Syn.—Tōllŏ, dēlĕŏ. *To weaken.* Syn.—Mĭnŭŏ, dēprĭmŏ, ēlĕvŏ.

Dētērrĕŏ, ēs, ŭī, ĭtūm, ērĕ. *To dissuade.* Cædĭbŭs ēt vīctū fœdō (sīlvēstrēs hŏmĭnēs) dētērrŭĭt Ōrpheūs. H. Syn.—Dĕhōrtŏr, āvŏcŏ, rĕvŏcŏ, āmŏvĕŏ, dēdūcŏ, ābdūcŏ, āvērtŏ, āmōlĭŏr, dīssuādĕŏ, dēprĕcŏr. Phr.—Ā fāctō tĭmŏr āvŏcăt. Ălĭquīsque ēx ōmnĭbŭs aūdĕt Dētērrērĕ nĕfās. Īncēptō dēsīstĕrĕ cōgĭt. Quīppĕ vĕtōr fātīs. *To drive away.* Syn.—Dēpēllŏ, rĕpēllŏ, ēxpēllŏ.

Dētēstābĭlĭs, ĭs, ĕ. *Hateful.* Nōn ĕrĭt ūllūm Ēxēmplum īn nōstrō tām dētēstābĭlĕ sēxū. J. Syn.—Dētēstāndŭs, ēxsĕcrābĭlĭs, ēxsĕcrāndŭs, hōrrēndŭs, īnfāndŭs.

Dētēstŏr, ārĭs, ātŭs sūm, ārī. *To curse.* Syn.—Ăbōmĭnŏr, ăbhōrrĕŏ, ēxsĕcrŏr, āvērsŏr. *See Imprecor.*

Dētĭnĕŏ, ēs, ŭī, ēntūm, ērĕ. *To hold, to restrain.* Sēd mē māgnă dĕūm gĕnĭtrīx hīs dētĭnĕt ōrīs. V. Syn.—Tĕnĕŏ, rĕtĭnĕŏ, mŏrŏr, dēmŏrŏr, rĕmŏrŏr, căpĭŏ.

Dētōrquĕŏ, ēs, sī, sūm, ērĕ. *To bend, to twist.* Ārdŭă tōrquēnt Cōrnŭă, dētōrquēntquĕ; fĕrūnt sŭă flāmĭnă clāssēm. V. Syn.—

Dēflēctŏ, āvērtŏ. Phr.—Ŏcŭlōs dētōrquĕt ăd ūndās. Lūmēn dētōrquĕt ăb īllā.

Dētrăhŏ, ĭs, xī, ctūm, ĕrĕ. *To take away.* Dētŭlĕrăt fāscēs īndīgnō dētrăhĕt īdēm. H. Syn.—Aūfĕrŏ, tōllŏ, dēmŏ, ădĭmŏ, ērĭpĭŏ, sūbdūcŏ, spŏlĭŏ, ēxŭŏ, nūdŏ. *To pluck.* Syn.—Dēcērpŏ.

Dētrēctŏ, ās, āvī, ātūm, ārĕ. *To reject, to refuse.* Dūctŭs ăb ārmēntō taūrūs dētrēctăt ărātrūm. O. Syn.—Ābnŭŏ, rĕcūsŏ, dēclīnŏ, dēnĕgŏ, fŭgĭŏ, rĕfŭgĭŏ, rēspŭŏ, īndīgnŏr. Phr.—Aūt jŭgă dētrēctāns (vacca). Dētrēctārĕ fŭrōrĕ Mīlĭtĭām fīctō.

Dētrīmēntūm, ī. n. *Loss, damage.* Syn.—Dāmnūm, jāctūră, īncōmmŏdūm.

Dētrūdŏ, ĭs, sī, sūm, ĕrĕ. *To push down.* Sŭpĕrīsquĕ Jŏvēm dētrūdĕrĕ rēgnīs. V. Syn.—Dējĭcĭŏ, dētūrbŏ, ēxtūrbŏ, dēvōlvŏ. Phr.—Nūnc dūrō cōntrārĭă pēctŏră cōntō Dētrūdīt mūrīs. *To drive.* Syn.—Ēvēllŏ, rĕvēllŏ, pēllŏ, dēpēllŏ, ējĭcĭŏ. *See Pello.*

Dētūrbŏ, ās, āvī, ātūm, ārĕ. *To drive away with violence.* Īn mărĕ præcĭpĭtēm pūppī dētūrbăt ăb āltā. V. Syn.—Ēxtūrbŏ, dējĭcĭŏ, dētrūdŏ, dēpēllŏ. Phr.—Āgmĭnă dētūrbāt glădĭō. Căpūt dētūrbāt tērræ. *See Dejicio.*

Dĕŭs, ī. m. *God.* Rēgēs ĭn īpsōs īmpĕrĭum ēst Dĕī Cūnctă sŭpērcĭlĭō mŏvēntĭs. H. Syn.—Nūmĕn, dŏmĭnŭs, crĕātŏr. Phr.—Pătĕr ōmnĭpŏtēns. Rērūm gĕnĭtŏr. Cœlī tērræquĕ crĕātŏr. Rēgnātŏr Ŏlўmpī. Quī sīdĕră tōrquĕt. Quī nūtū cōncŭtĭt ōrbēm. Quī mărĕ, quī tērrās, quī cœlūm nūmĭnĕ cōmplĕt.

Dēvĕhŏ, ĭs, ēxī, ēctūm, ĕrĕ. *To carry, to transport.* Trāns æquŏră mērcēs Dēvĕhĭt. Syn.—Vĕhŏ, dēfĕrŏ, fĕrŏ, trānspōrtŏ, cōnvēctŏ. Phr.—Nūnc ād tŭă dēvĕhŏr āstrā.

Dēvĕnĭŏ, īs, vēnī, vēntūm, īrĕ. *To arrive.* Dēvēnērĕ lŏcōs lætōs ēt ămœnă vĭrētă. V. Syn.—Vĕnĭŏ, pērvĕnĭŏ, ādvĕnĭŏ, āccēdŏ. Phr.—Dēvĕnĭt īn Scўthĭām.

Dēvērtŏ, ĭs, tī, sūm, ĕrĕ. *To turn.* Vēntūră pŏtēs dēvērtĕrĕ cūrsū. L. Syn.—Dēflēctŏ, āvērtŏ. *See Averto.*

Dēvīncĭŏ, īs, īnxī, īnctūm, īrĕ. *To bind.* Syn.—Vīncĭŏ. Fig. Syn.—Ōblĭgŏ, ōbstrīngŏ, dēmĕrĕŏ.

Dēvĭŭs, ă, ūm. *Out of the way.* Pēr dēvĭă lūstră văgāntēs Ōrĕ trăhēbāt ăquās. O. Syn.—Āvĭŭs, rĕdūctŭs, rĕmōtŭs. *Wanderer.* Syn.—Ērrāns, ăbērrāns, văgŭs. Phr.—Īgnārōsquĕ vĭæ. Āvĭă cūrsū dūm sĕquŏr. Sīve ērrōrĕ vĭæ. Nēc vōs vĭă fāllĭt ĕūntēs.

Dēvōlvŏ, ĭs, vī, vŏlūtūm, ĕrĕ. *To roll down.* Cōrpŏră dēvōlvūnt īn hŭmūm. O. Syn.—Vōlvŏ, dēmīttŏ, dējĭcĭŏ. Phr.—Dūm mōllĭă pēnsă Dēvōlvūnt fūsīs.

Dēvŏrŏ, ās, āvī, ātūm, ārĕ. *To devour.* Prōlēm dēvŏrăt īmmērsām vīscĕrĭbūsquĕ tĕnĕt. O. Syn.—Vŏrŏ. *To engulf.* Syn.—Haūrĭŏ, ābsōrbĕŏ. Phr.—Ūnctă dēvŏrārĕ pātrĭmōnĭă.

Dēvŏvĕŏ, ēs, ōvī, ōtūm, ērĕ. *To vow, to consecrate.* Sŭpĕrōs quōrūm sē dēvŏvĕt ārīs. V. Syn.—Vŏvĕŏ, săcrŏ, cōnsĕcrŏ, dĭcŏ, āddīcŏ, ōffĕrŏ, dēstĭnŏ. Phr.—Mē dēstĭnăt āræ̆. Dīs Ītălīs vōtum īmmōrtālĕ săcrābăt. Nātām prō mūtā dēvŏvĕt āgnā. *To curse.* Syn.—Īmprĕcŏr.

Dēxtĕr, ĕră, ĕrūm & Dēxtră, trūm. *Right.* Īn pārtĕ sĭnīstrā Ōppŏsŭēre ăcĭēm nām dēxtĕră cīngĭtŭr āmnī. V. Syn.—Dēxtĕrĭŏr. Fig.—*Dexterous.* Syn.—Cāllĭdŭs, īndūstrĭŭs, īngĕnĭōsŭs, săgāx, sōlērs. *Propitious.* Syn.—Faūstŭs, fēlīx, fōrtūnātŭs, præ̆sēns, prōspĕr, sĕcūndŭs. *Opportune.* Syn.—Āptŭs, cōmmŏdŭs, ōppōrtūnŭs.

Dēxtĕră & Dĕxtră, æ̆. f. *The right hand.* Dēxtĕră crūdēlīs quæ̆ mē frātrēmquĕ nĕcāvĭt. O. Syn.—Mănŭs. Phr.—Cūr dēxtræ̆ jūngĕrĕ dēxtrām nōn dătŭr. Jūncta ēst mĭhī fœ̆dĕrĕ **dēxtră.** Ād fœ̆dĕră jūngĕrĕ dēxtrām.

Dēxtĕrē & Dēxtrē. adv. *Adroitly.* Syn.—Pĕrītē, sōlērtĕr.

Dēxtĕrĭtās, ātĭs. f. *Skill.* Syn.—Sōlērtĭă, īndūstrĭă, cāllĭdĭtās.

Dĭădēmă, ătĭs. n. *Diadem.* Dīgnĭŏr ēst scēptro ēt rēgnī dĭădēmătĕ vīrtūs. M. Syn.—Cŏrōnă. Phr.—Rēgĭs īnsīgnĕ. Frōntīs dĕcŭs. Īmpŏsĭtūm căpĭtī. Gēmmīs dĭădēmă cŏrūscāns. Cuī frōns dĭădēmă cŏrūscāns.

Dĭcŏ, ās, āvī, ātūm, ārĕ. *To dedicate, to consecrate.* Dēĭŏpēām Cōnnūbĭō jūngām stăbĭlī prŏprĭāmquĕ dĭcābŏ. V. Syn.—Dēdĭcŏ, săcrŏ, cōnsĕcrŏ, vŏvĕŏ, dēvŏvĕŏ, āddīcŏ, dēstĭnŏ. Phr.—Tēmplă dĭcātă dĕīs. Cōncēptăquĕ vōtă dĭcābānt.

Dīcŏ, īs, īxī, īctūm, ĕrĕ. *To say, to speak.* Dīcĕrĕt ; hæ̆c mĕă sūnt, vĕtĕrēs, mīgrātĕ cŏlōnī. V. Syn.—Lŏquŏr, ēlŏquŏr, fārī, prŏfārī, ēffārī, mĕmŏrŏ, rĕfĕrŏ, ēdīssĕrŏ, ēdŏ. Phr.—Dīctă dărĕ. Ēffūndĕrĕ pēctŏrĕ vōcēs. Fūndo ōrĕ lŏquēlās. Vōcĕ sĭlēntĭă rūmpŏ. Tālĭă vōcĕ rĕfērt. Ōrĕ sŏnōs ēdŏ. *To relate.* Syn.—Mĕmŏrŏ, nārrŏ, ēnārrŏ, rĕfĕrŏ, pāndŏ.

Dīctūm, ī. n. *Word.* Tālĭbŭs āggrĕdĭtūr Vĕnĕrēm Sātūrnĭă dīctīs. V. Syn.—Vērbūm, sērmŏ. Phr.—Ēt mūtŭă dīctă rĕfērrĕ. Īntēr sē dīctă cŏhæ̆rēnt. Cūm fāctīs cōmpōnĕrĕ dīctă. *Written work.* Syn.—Scrīptă, ŏpŭs.

Dīdūcŏ, īs, xī, ctūm, ĕrĕ. *To divide.* Tūm vēro īn cūrās ănĭmūs dīdūcĭtŭr ōmnēs. V. Syn.—Dīvĭdŏ, dĭrĭmŏ, dīstrăhŏ, dīvēllŏ, sēpărŏ, ăpĕrĭŏ. Phr.—Āssem īn cēntūm pārtēs dīdūcĕrĕ. Cōntĭnŭām dīdūxĭt hŭmūm. Vēstēm dīdūxĭt ăb ōrĕ. Īmmānī faūcēs dīdūcĭt hĭātū.

Dĭēs, ēī. m. & f. *Day.* Nōn ūllī pāstōs īllīs ēgērĕ dĭēbŭs. V. Syn.—Lūx, sōl. Phr.—Dĭūrnūm tēmpŭs. Dĭūrnī mŏră tēmpŏrĭs. Hōræ dĭūrnæ. Ēxspēctātă dĭēs ădĕrăt. Quĭbŭs ūltĭmŭs ēssĕt Īllĕ dĭēs. Dĭēs ŏrĭēns. Sōlēs hībērnī. Vĕnĭēntĕ dĭē. Sīvĕ dĭēm dūcīt sōl. Vōlvēndă dĭēs ēn āttŭlĭt ūltrō.

Dīffĕrŏ, ērs, īstŭlī, īlātūm, ērrĕ. *To scatter.* Mĕtĭum īn dīvērsă quădrīgæ Dīstŭlĕrānt. V. Syn.—Dīsjĭcĭŏ, dīssĭpŏ, spārgŏ, dīspērgŏ, dīstrăhŏ, dīscērpŏ, dīrĭpĭŏ, dīvēllŏ. Phr.—Lātē dīffērrĕ făvīllām. *To toss about.* Syn.—Ăgĭtŏr, jăctŏr, dīstrăhŏr. *To spread abroad.* Syn.—Vūlgŏ, dīvūlgŏ, spārgŏ, nūntĭŏ. *To delay.* Syn.—Cūnctŏr, mŏrŏr, rĕmīttŏ, prōcrāstĭnŏ, prōtrăhŏ, prōdūcŏ, prōrŏgŏ. Phr.—Cārōs nē dīffĕr ămīcōs. Nēc tē vĕntūrās dīffĕr ĭn hōrās. *To differ.* Syn.—Dīscrĕpŏ, dīstŏ.

Dīffĭcĭlĭs, ĭs, ĕ. *Difficult.* Dīffĭcĭle ēst, fătĕŏr, sēd tēndĭt ĭn ārdŭă vīrtūs. O. Syn.—Ārdŭŭs, ŏpĕrōsŭs, grăvĭs. Phr.—Tē sĭnĕ nīl āltūm mēns īnchŏăt. Nīl mōrtālĭbŭs ārdŭum ēst. Dūrŭs ŭtērquĕ lăbŏr. Ārdŭă prīmă vĭa ēst. *Hard to please, morose.* Syn.—Āspĕr, grăvĭs, mŏlēstŭs, mōrōsŭs, quĕrŭlŭs. *Ungovernable.* Syn.—Dūrŭs, āspĕr, fērrĕŭs.

Dīffĭcūltās, ātĭs. f. *Difficulty.* Syn.—Lăbŏr, mōlēs, nĕgōtĭūm. Phr.—Hōc ŏpŭs, hīc lăbŏr ēst. Nēc māgnūs prŏhĭbērĕ lăbŏr. Tāntæ mōlĭs ĕrăt Rōmānām cōndĕrĕ gēntēm.

Dīffĭcūltĕr. adv. *With difficulty.* Syn.—Dīffĭcĭlĕ, ægrē, vīx.

Dīffīdŏ, ĭs, sŭs sūm, ĕrĕ. *To mistrust.* Heū nĭmĭūm făcĭlēs læsīs dīffīdĕrĕ rēbŭs. Phr.—Nōn fīdŏ. Nōn cōnfīdŏ. Cūm jām dīffīdĕrĕt ārmīs. Deērātnĕ tĭbī fīdūcĭă nōstră. *To despair. See Despero.*

Dīffīngŏ, ĭs, īnxī, īctūm, ĕrĕ. *To change.* Īncŭdĕ dīffīngās rĕtūsum īn Māssăgĕtās Ărăbāsquĕ fērrūm. H. *See Muto.*

Dīfflŭŏ, ĭs, ūxī, ūxūm, ĕrĕ. *To flow in different directions.* Quāssātīs ūndĭquĕ vāsīs Dīfflŭĕre hūmōrēm. L. Syn.—Flŭŏ, ēfflŭŏ. Fig.—*To waste away.* Syn.—Tābēscŏ, lānguĕŏ, dīssōlvŏr.

Dīffŭgĭŏ, ĭs, ūgī, ĕrĕ. *To fly in different directions.* Dīffūgērĕ nĭvēs, rĕdĕūnt jām grāmĭnă cāmpīs. H. Syn.—Fŭgĭŏ. Phr.—Dīffŭgĭmŭs vīsu ēxsānguēs. *See Fugio.*

Dīffūndŏ, ĭs, ūdī, ūsūm, ĕrĕ. *To expand.* Ūndāntīque ănĭmām dīffūndĭt ĭn ārmă crŭōrĕ. V. Syn.—Fūndŏ, ēffūndŏ, prŏfūndŏ, spārgŏ, dīspērgŏ, dīssĭpŏ. Phr.—Aēstīvās plătănūs dīffūdĕrăt ūmbrās. Dĕdĕrātquĕ cŏmām dīffūndĕrĕ vēntīs. Fig.—Dīffūndĭmŭs īrām. *To rejoice.* Syn.—Rĕcrĕŏ, hĭlărŏ.

Dīffūsē. adv. *Diffusely.* Lătŭs hōc tērræ dīffūsĭŭs ēxplĭcăt āgrōs. Syn.—Lātē.

Dīgĕrŏ, ĕrĭs, ēssī, stūm, ĕrĕ. *To distribute.* Quām mĕrŭīt pœnām sōlūs, dīgēssīt ĭn ōmnēs. O. Syn.—Dīffĕrŏ, dīstrĭbŭŏ, dīvĭdŏ. *To arrange.* Syn.—Dīspōnŏ, ōrdĭnŏ, rĕgŏ, cōnstĭtŭŏ. *To consume.* Syn.—Cōnsūmŏ, ābsūmŏ, dīssĭpŏ.

Dĭgĭtŭs, ī. m. *Finger.* Ēt dĭgĭtōs dĭgĭtīs, ēt frōntēm frōntĕ prĕmēbām. O. Syn.—Pōllēx, ārtĭcŭlī. Phr.—Aūrōrǣ vīncīs dĭgĭtōs. Dĭgĭtīs īntēndīt mōllĭbŭs ārcūm.

Dīglădĭŏr, ārĭs, ātŭs sūm, ārī. *To fight.* Syn.—Pūgnŏ, prǣlĭŏr, cērtŏ, dēcērtŏ. *To dispute.* Syn.—Cōntēndŏ, rīxŏr.

Dīgnē, adv. *Worthily.* Vĕtĕrūm dīgnē vĕnĕrōr cūm scrīptă vĭrōrūm. O. Syn.—Jūstē, mĕrĭtō.

Dīgnĭtās, ātĭs. f. *Honor, merit.* Syn.—Vīrtūs, dĕcŭs, hŏnōs. *Dignity.* Syn.—Hŏnŏr, mūnŭs, măgĭstrātŭs. Phr.—Sūmēndă tĭbī fāstīgĭă jūrĭs. *See Auctoritas, Fama.*

Dīgnŏr, ārĭs, ātŭs sūm, ārī. *To judge worthy.* Haŭd ĕquĭdēm tālī mē dīgnŏr hŏnōrĕ. V. Syn.—Dīgnūm cēnsĕŏ, hăbĕŏ, dīcŏ, pŭtŏ. Phr.—Nūllā tămĕn ălĭtĕ vērtī dīgnātŭr. Hūnc vĕnĭă dīgnārĕ lĭbēllūm. *To deign.* Syn.—Nōn rĕcūsŏ, nōn dētrēctŏ.

Dīgnōscŏ, ĭs, ōvī, ĕrĕ. *To discern.* Nōn quī cīvēm dīgnōscĕrēt hōstĕ. H. Syn.—Dīscērnŏ, dīstīnguŏ. Phr.—Cūrvō dīgnōscĕrĕ rēctūm.

Dīgnŭs, ă, ūm. *Worthy.* Sī tē dīgnă mănēt dīvīnī glōrĭă rūrĭs. V. Syn.—Mĕrĭtŭs, prōmĕrĭtŭs, dēbĭtŭs, jūstŭs, pār. Phr.—Nōn īndīgnŭs. Dīgnŭs ămārī. Mūltō dīgnŭs hŏnōrĕ. Sī crēdĕrĕ dīgnum ēst. Dīgnăquĕ vērbă jŏcō. Dīc ălĭquĭd dīgnūm prōmīssīs.

Dīgrĕdĭŏr, ĕrĭs, ēssŭs sūm, ī. *To retire.* Hōs ĕgŏ dīgrĕdĭēns lăcrĭmīs āffābŏr ŏbōrtīs. V. Syn.—Ăbĕŏ, ēxĕŏ, dīscēdŏ, rĕcēdŏ. *See Abeo.* Fig.—*To digress.* Syn.—Dīscēdŏ, ēxcūrrŏ.

Dīgrēssŭs, ūs. m. *Departure.* Syn.—Dīscēssŭs, ăbĭtŭs.

Dīlābŏr, ĕrĭs, psŭs sūm, ī. *To glide apart, to go to pieces.* Prǣcēps sānguĭnĕō dīlābĭtŭr īgnĕ cŏmētēs. Syn.—Lābŏr, ēlābŏr, dīfflŭŏ, sōlvŏ, cōnsūmŏr, ābsūmŏr.

Dīlăcĕrŏ, ās, āvī, ātūm, ārĕ. *To tear, to rend.* Dīlăcĕrāndă fĕrīs dăbŏr ālĭtĭbūsquĕ Prǣdă. Cat. Syn.—Lăcĕrŏ, dīscērpŏ.

Dīlăpĭdŏ, ās, āvī, ātūm, ārĕ. *To stone, to put to death by stoning.* *See Lapido.* *To scatter.* Syn.—Dīssĭpŏ, dīspērdŏ, ābsūmŏ.

Dīlātŏ, ās, āvī, ātūm, ārĕ. *To spread out.* Ipsăquĕ dīlātānt pătŭlōs cônvīcĭă rīctūs. O. Syn.—Dīstēndŏ, prōtēndŏ, ēxtēndŏ.

Dīlĭgēns, ēntĭs. adj. *Diligent, attentive.* Quēm sī tērsĕrĭs aūrĕ dīlĭgēntī. M. Syn.—Īmpĭgĕr, ācĕr, ălăcĕr, gnāvŭs, vĭgĭl, sēdŭlŭs, āttēntŭs, stŭdĭōsŭs, īndūstrĭōsŭs. Phr.—Haŭd sēgnĭs. Sēgnĭtĭēm fŭgĭēns. Quĭētīs īmpătĭēns. Dēsĭdĭam ēxōsŭs. Ōtĭă dētēstāns. Mūltǣ sēdŭlĭtātĭs hŏmŏ. *See Alacer.*

Dīlĭgēntĕr. adv. *Diligently.* Ō quām, Rēgŭlĕ, dīlĭgēntĕr ērrās. M. Syn.—Sēdŭlō, gnāvĭtĕr, ācrĭtĕr, āssĭdŭē, stŭdĭōsē. Phr.—Haŭd sēgnĭŭs.

Dīlĭgēntĭă, ǣ. f. *Diligence, attention.* Cūrāte hǣc, stūltī, māgnā dīlĭgēntĭā. Sen. Syn.—Cūră, sēdŭlĭtās, īndūstrĭă, stŭdĭūm, lăbŏr. Phr.—Ōmnĭă vīncēns.

Dīlĭgŏ, ĭs, ēxī, ēctūm, ĕrĕ. *To love.* Dīlĭgĭtūr nēmō, nĭsĭ cuī fōrtūnā sĕcūnda ēst. O. Syn.—Ămŏ. Phr.—Frātērnō mōrĕ sŏdālēs Dīlĭgĕrĕ. *See Amo.*

Dīlūcĕŏ, ēs, xī, ērĕ. *To shine, to be clear.* Syn.—Lūcĕŏ, īllūcĕŏ. *See Luceo.*

Dīlūcĭdē. adv. *Clearly.* Syn.—Clārē, pērspĭcŭē.

Dīlūcĭdŭs, ă, ūm. *Clear, luminous.* Ēt rērūm dīlūcĭdŭs ōrdŏ. Syn.—Lūcĭdŭs, clārŭs, nĭtĭdŭs, pērspĭcŭŭs, cōnspĭcŭŭs, mănĭfēstŭs.

Dīlūcŭlūm, ī. n. *Dawn.* Syn.—Crĕpūscŭlūm, aūrōră, mānĕ. Phr.—Lūx prīmă. Ūt prīmūm lūx ālmă dăta ēst. Jām nōctĕ pūlsā dŭbĭŭs ēffūlsĭt dĭēs. Vīx sūmmōs spārgēbāt lūmĭnĕ mōntēs Ōrtă dĭēs.

Dīlŭŏ, ĭs, ŭī, ūtūm, ĕrĕ. *To wash away, to dissolve.* Dīlŭĭt ēt lăcrĭmīs mœrēns ūnguēntă prŏfūsīs. O. Syn.—Āblŭŏ, ēlŭŏ, lăvŏ, ābstērgŏ. *To mingle, to dilute.* Syn.—Mīscĕŏ, tēmpĕrŏ, lĭquĕfăcĭŏ.

Dīlŭvĭūm, ĭī. n. *Flood, inundation.* Hōrrēndāmquĕ cūltĭs Dīlŭvĭēm mĕdĭtātŭr ăgrīs. H. Syn.—Ēlŭvĭēs. Phr.—Ūltrīcēs ūndǣ. Īt strāgēs fātālĭs ăquǣ. Sŭpĕrānt nūnc flūmĭnă rīpās.

Dīmĭcŏ, ās, āvī, ātūm, ārĕ. *To fight.* Ēt glădĭīs ĕt ăcūtā dīmĭcĕt hāstā. O. Syn.—Cērtŏ, dēcērtŏ, cōngrĕdĭŏr, cōnflīgŏ, pūgnŏ. Phr.—Bēllūm gĕrŏ.

Dīmĭnŭŏ, ĭs, ŭī, ūtūm, ĕrĕ. *To break in pieces.* Syn.—Cōmmĭnŭŏ, frāngŏ. *To diminish.* Syn.—Dēmĭnŭŏ, mĭnŭŏ.

Dīmīttŏ, ĭs, mīsī, īssūm, ĕrĕ. *To send in different directions.* Pēr līttŏră cērtōs dīmīttām. V. Syn.—Mīttŏ. *To dismiss.* Syn.—Mīttŏ. *To renounce, to give up.* Syn.—Ŏmīttŏ, dēpōnŏ, mīttŏ.

Dīmŏvĕŏ, ēs, ōvī, ōtūm, ērĕ. *To move aside, to separate.* Aēthĕrĕ sē mīttĭt, spīrāntēs dīmŏvĭt aūrās. V. Syn.—Rĕmŏvĕŏ, pēllŏ, ārcĕŏ, dēpēllŏ. Phr.—Īncūrvō tērrām dīmōvĭt ărātrō.

Dīnŭmĕrŏ, ās, āvī, ātūm, ārĕ. *To number.* Tēmpŏră dīnŭmĕrāns. V. Syn.—Nŭmĕrŏ, ēnŭmĕrŏ, rĕcēnsĕŏ, pērcēnsĕŏ.

Dīrē. adv. *In a terrible manner.* Syn.—Dīrūm, dīră, hōrrĭfĭcē. Phr.—Dīră frĕmēntūm Ūt vīdērĕ.

Dīrĭgŏ, ĭs, ēxī, ēctūm, ĕrĕ. *To direct.* Hūc ădēs ēt cœptūm dīrĭgĕ, Cæsăr, ĭtĕr. O. Syn.—Rĕgŏ, ōrdĭnŏ, cōmpōnŏ, dīspōnŏ. Phr.—Īn mĕdĭō dīrĭgĕ vēlă frĕtō. Dīrēxēre ăcĭēs.

Dĭrĭmŏ, ĭs, ēmī, ēmptūm, ĕrĕ. *To separate, to divide.* Ēt quī cærŭlĕūm dĭrĭmēbāt Nērĕă Dēlphīn. O. Syn.—Sēpărŏ, dīvĭdŏ. Phr.—Pērtēntāt crīmĭnă Mīnōs Ēt jūstīs dĭrĭmīt sōntēs. *See Separo.*

Dīrĭpĭŏ, ĭs, ĭpŭī, ēptūm, ĕrĕ. *To tear apart.* Cūm cōnstērnātīs dīrĭpĕrērĭs ĕquīs. O. Syn.—Dīffĕrŏ, dīstrăhŏ, dīscērpŏ. Phr.—Dīrĭpĭēntquĕ rătēs ălĭī nāvālĭbŭs. Dīrĭpĭūnt tērgŏră cōstīs. *To pillage.* Syn.—Răpĭŏ, prædŏr, dēprædŏr, pŏpŭlŏr, vāstŏ, aūfĕrŏ. Phr.—Dīrĭpĭūntquĕ dăpēs.

Dīrŭŏ, ĭs, ŭī, ŭtūm, ĕrĕ. *To overthrow.* Dīrŭĭt, ædĭfĭcāt, mūtāt quādrātă rŏtūndīs. H. Syn.—Dēstrŭŏ, sūbrŭŏ, ēvērtŏ, vērtŏ, pērdŏ, dējĭcĭŏ. *See Verto.*

Dīrŭs, ă, ūm. *Cruel, terrible, fearful.* Cūstōdēs lēctī, Phœnīx ēt dīrūs Ŭlȳssēs. V. Syn.—Crūdēlĭs, ătrox, sævŭs, trūx, īmmītĭs, īnfēnsŭs, ĭnĭmīcŭs, īnfēstŭs, mĕtŭēndŭs, hōrrēndŭs. Phr.—Ānte ŏcŭlōs mōrs dīră văgātŭr. Dīrī mēns cōnscĭă fāctī. Quæ mēns tām dīră? *Hideous.* Syn.—Fœdŭs, hōrrĭdŭs. *Unpropitious.* Syn.—Īnfaūstŭs, īnfēlīx, lævŭs, īmpōrtūnŭs.

Dīscēdŏ, ĭs, ēssī, ēssūm, ĕrĕ. *To depart.* Īnfūsūmquĕ jŭbēt pŏpŭlūm dīscēdĕrĕ cīrcō. V. Syn.—Cēdŏ, dēcēdŏ, rĕcēdŏ, ăbĕŏ, ēxĕŏ, mĭgrŏ. Phr.—Dīscēdĭt īn aūrās.

Dīscēptŏ, ās, āvī, ātūm, ārĕ. *To dispute.* Dīscēptēntque ārmīs, tērrārum ŭtĕr īmpĕrĕt ōrbī. Syn.—Cērtŏ, dēcērtŏ, cōntēndŏ, dīspŭtŏ.

Dīscērnŏ, ĭs, crēvī, crētūm, ĕrĕ. *To separate.* Syn.—Dīvĭdŏ, dīscrīmĭnŏ, dīstīnguŏ, sēpărŏ, dĭrĭmŏ. *To distinguish.* Syn.—Dīstīnguŏ, dīscrīmĭnŏ, dīgnōscŏ, īntērnōscŏ.

Dīscērpŏ, ĭs, sī, tūm, ĕrĕ. *To tear in pieces.* Īn pārvās pārtēs dīscērpĭtŭr aūrūm. Lr. Syn.—Dīscīndŏ, dīssĕcŏ, dīffĕrŏ, dīlăcĕrŏ, dīlănĭŏ. *To disperse.* Syn.—Dīssĭpŏ, dīsjĭcĭŏ.

Dīscīndŏ, ĭs, ĭdī, īssūm, ĕrĕ. *To cut, to tear open.* Dīscīndĭtŭr æquē Īn mūltās pārtēs. Lr. Syn.—Dīvĭdŏ, scīndŏ, ābscīndŏ, dīvēllŏ, dīlăcĕrŏ.

Dīscīngŏ, ĭs, xī, ctūm, ĕrĕ. *To ungird, to disarm.* Syn.—Ēxārmŏ, vīncŏ.

Dīscĭplīnă, æ. f. *Science, course of instruction.* Dōctŏr ămārŭs ĕnīm dīscēntī sēmpĕr ĕphēbō, Nēc dūlcĭs ūllī dīscĭplīna īnfāntĭæ. Syn.—Ārs, dōctrīnă, scĭēntĭă. *Conduct.* Syn.—Rēgŭlă, mōs. Phr.—Vītæ rătĭŏ, mŏdŭs, nōrmă.

Dīscĭpŭlŭs, ī. m. *Pupil.* Dūc ăgĕ dīscĭpŭlōs ād mĕă tēmplă tŭōs. O. Syn.—Aūdītŏr.

Dīsclūdŏ, ĭs, sī, sūm, ĕrĕ. *To separate.* Tūm dūrārĕ sŏlum ēt dīsclūdĕrĕ Nērĕă pōntō. V. Syn.—Sēpărŏ, dĭrĭmŏ. *To open.* Syn.—Ăpĕrĭŏ, fīndŏ.

Dīscŏ, ĭs, dĭdĭcī, ĕrĕ. *To learn.* Dīscĕrēt ūndĕ prĕcēs, vātēm nī Mūsă dĕdīssĕt. H. Syn.—Āddīscŏ, ēdīscŏ, pērdīscŏ, cōgnōscŏ, pērcĭpĭŏ, nōvī, dŏcĕŏr, ērŭdĭŏr. Phr.—Ārtĭbŭs īngĕnŭīs văcŏ. Mūsās cŏlŏ. Stŭdĭīs īntēndĕrĕ mēntēm. Mūsīs sērvīrĕ. Dīscĕ mĕo ēxēmplō. Vĕnĭēndī dīscĕrĕ caūsās.

Dīscŏlŏr, ōrĭs. adj. *Varicolored.* Dīscŏlŏr ūnde aūrī pēr rāmōs aūră rĕfūlsĭt. V. Phr.—Vărĭīs flōrēt vĭă dīscŏlŏr ārmĭs. Pĕlăgō nēc dīscŏlŏr āmnīs. Fig.—*Different.* Syn.—Dīssĭmĭlĭs, dīvērsŭs, dīspār, dīscōrs.

Dīscōnvĕnĭŏ, īs, ēnī, ēntūm, īrĕ. *To disagree.* Vītæ dīscōnvĕnĭt ōrdĭnĕ tōtō. H. Syn.—Dīscōrdŏ, dīssĭdĕŏ, dīscrĕpŏ.

Dīscōrdĭă, æ. f. *Discord, dissension.* Ēxŏrĭtūr trĕpĭdōs īntēr dīscōrdĭă cīvēs. V. Syn.—Dīssēnsĭŏ, dīssĭdĭūm, cērtāmĕn, cōntēntĭŏ, rīxă, līs, pūgnă, prœlĭūm, sēdĭtĭŏ, tŭmūltŭs. Phr.—Stŭdĭă dīscōrdĭă, cōntrārĭă. Dīscōrdēs ănĭmī. Ēgīt flāgrāns dīscōrdĭă cīvēs. Sŏcĭīsquĕ cŏmēs dīscōrdĭă rēgnīs. *See Seditio.*

Dīscōrdŏ, ās, āvī, ātūm, ārĕ. *To disagree.* Quāntūm pārcūs dīscōrdēt ăvārō. H. Syn.—Dīssĭdĕŏ, dīscōnvĕnĭŏ, dīscrĕpŏ, dīssēntĭŏ, pūgnŏ, ōbstŏ. Phr.—Rūpērĕ fĭdēm. Tōt dīscōrdāntĭă rītū Cōrdă vĭrūm.

Dīscōrs, ōrdĭs. adj. *Disagreeing, inharmonious.* Ēxtĭmŭī nē vōs ăgĕrēt vēsānĭă dīscōrs. H. Syn.—Dīscōrdāns, pūgnāns, īnfēnsŭs, ĭnĭmīcŭs, ōppŏsĭtŭs, ādvērsŭs, cōntrārĭŭs. Phr.—Prŏcŭl dīscōrdĭbŭs ārmīs. Dīscōrdĭă sēnsĭt Pēctŏră. *Different.* Syn.—Dīscōrdāns, ābsŏnŭs, dīssŏnŭs, dīspār, ōppŏsĭtŭs. Phr.—Nōn cōngrŭŭs.

Dīscrĕpŏ, ās, ŭī, ĭtūm, ārĕ. *To disagree.* Mĕdĭō nē dīscrĕpĕt īmūm. H. Syn.—Dīssēntĭŏ, dīssĭdĕŏ, dīffĕrŏ, pūgnŏ, rĕpūgnŏ, ābscēdŏ, dīscēdŏ, rĕcēdŏ, dīstŏ, dīscōrdŏ, dīscōnvĕnĭŏ. Phr.—Sūm dīssĭmĭlĭs, dīscōrs, dīssŏnŭs, dīspār. Nēc mūltūm dīscrĕpĕt ætās.

Dīscrīmĕn, ĭnĭs. n. *Division, separation.* Mĭnĭmūm quōs īntĕr ĕt hōstēm Dīscrīmēn mūrōs, pōrtăquĕ claūsă făcĭt. O. Syn.—Īntērvāllūm, spătĭūm, dīstāntĭă. *Distinction.* Syn.—Dīstīnctĭŏ, crĭsĭs. *See Periculum.*

Dīscrīmĭnŏ, ās, āvī, ātūm, ārĕ. *To separate.* Quāntŭs ăb Ārctōīs dīscrīmĭnăt æthĕră plaūstrīs Ānguĭs. Syn.—Sēpărŏ, dīvĭdŏ, dīstīnguŏ. *To vary.* Syn.—Vărĭŏ, dīstīnguŏ, dīvĭdŏ.

Dīscrŭcĭŏ, ās, āvī, ātūm, ārĕ. *To torment.* Syn.—Crŭcĭŏ, tōrquĕŏ, vēxŏ, stĭmŭlŏ.

Dīscūmbŏ, ĭs, ŭbŭī, ŭbĭtūm, ĕrĕ. *To recline (at a feast).* Syn.—Āccūmbŏ.

Dīscūrrŏ, ĭs, rī, ūrsūm, ĕrĕ. *To run about.* Īlĭcĕt īn mūrōs tōtā dīscūrrĭtŭr ūrbĕ. V. Syn.—Văgŏr, dīvăgŏr, ēxspătĭŏr. Phr.—Ōllī Dīscūrrērĕ părēs. Mēns dīscūrrĭt ŭtrōquĕ.

Dīscŭs, ī. m. *Discus.* Āĕră sī mīssō văcŭūm jăcŭlābĕrĕ dīscō. O. Phr.—Dīscī mīssĭlĕ pōndŭs. Splēndĭdă Spārtānī pōndĕră dīscī.

Dīscŭtĭŏ, ĭs, ūssī, ūssūm, ĕrĕ. *To disperse, to rend.* Māgnōquĕ frăgōrĕ Dīscūssīt trābs āctă căpŭt. Syn.—Ēxcŭtĭŏ, dīsjĭcĭŏ. *To dissipate.* Syn.—Dīmŏvĕŏ, dīspēllŏ, āmŏvĕŏ, ārcĕŏ, aŭfĕrŏ, fŭgŏ. Phr.—Mōrtĕ tŭā dīscūssă fĭdēs.

Dĭsērtŭs, ă, ūm. *Eloquent.* Īn caŭsā făcĭlī cuīvīs lĭcĕt ēssĕ dĭsērtō. O. Syn.—Fācūndŭs, ēlŏquēns. Phr.—Dĭsērtūs lĕpōrum ēt făcētĭārūm. Dīctă tĭbī plēnō vērbă dĭsērtā fŏrō.

Dīsjĭcĭŏ, ĭs, ēcī, ēctūm, ĕrĕ. *To disperse, to scatter.* Frōntēm Dīsjĭcĭt ēt spārsō lātĕ rĭgăt ārmă crŭōrĕ. V. Syn.—Spārgŏ, dīspērgŏ, dīssĭpŏ, dīffūndŏ, dīffĕrŏ. *To destroy.* Syn.—Dīstūrbŏ, dīssōlvŏ, ēvērtŏ, rūmpŏ.

Dīsjūngŏ, ĭs, nxī, nctūm, ĕrĕ. *To separate.* Ĭtălīs lōngē dīsjūngĭmŭr ōrīs. V. Syn.—Ābjūngŏ, dīssŏcĭŏ, dīvĭdŏ, sēpărŏ, āvēllŏ, dīvēllŏ.

Dīspāndŏ, ĭs, (), ānsūm & ēssūm, ĕrĕ. *To expand, to extend.* Vēstēs dīspānsæ īn sōlĕ sĕrēscūnt. L. Syn.—Pāndŏ, ēxplĭcŏ.

Dīspār, ărĭs. adj. *Unequal, different.* Ēst mĭhĭ dīspărĭbūs sēptēm cōmpāctă cĭcūtīs Fīstŭlă. V. Syn.—Ĭnæquŭs, īmpār, dīspărĭlĭs, ĭnæquālĭs. *See Dissimilis.*

Dīspēllŏ, ĭs, ŭlī, ūlsūm, ĕrĕ. *To chase away, to dissipate.* Aērātā dīspēllēns æquŏră prōrā. Syn.—Pēllŏ, ēxpēllŏ, fŭgŏ, dīscŭtĭŏ, dīsjĭcĭŏ.

Dīspēndĭūm, ĭī. n. *Expense.* Sĭnĕ sūmptū, sĭnĕ dīspēndĭō. Ter. Syn.—Īmpēnsă, sūmptŭs. *Loss.* Syn.—Dāmnūm, jāctūră.

Dīspēnsŏ, ās, āvī, ātūm, ārĕ. *To distribute.* Tūnc quæ dīspēnsānt mōrtālĭă fātă sŏrōrēs. O. Syn.—Dīstrĭbŭŏ, pārtĭŏr, dīspērtĭŏ, dīvĭdŏ.

Dīspērdŏ, ĭs, ĭdī, ĭtūm, ĕrĕ. *To destroy.* Strīdēntī mĭsĕrūm stĭpŭlā dīspērdĕrĕ cārmĕn. V. Syn.—Pērdŏ.

Dīspērgŏ, ĭs, sī, sūm, ĕrĕ. *To scatter.* Ōssăquĕ dīspērgĭt cĕrĕbrō pērmīxtă crŭēntō. V. Syn.—Spārgŏ, dīssēmĭnŏ, dīffūndŏ, dīffĕrŏ, dīsjĭcĭŏ. Phr.—Vītām dīspērgĭt īn aŭrās. Dīspērsa īmmīttīt sīlvīs īncēndĭă pāstŏr.

Dīspērtĭŏ, īs, īrĕ, & Dīspērtĭŏr, īrĭs, ītŭs sūm, īrī. *To distribute.* Dīspērtītŭr ŭt hōrrŏr ĕt īncŭtĭt īndĕ tĭmōrēm. L. Syn.—Pārtĭŏr, dīvĭdŏ, dīstrĭbŭŏ.

Dīspĭcĭŏ, ĭs, ēxī, ēctūm, ĕrĕ. *To look around.* Lĕvēs ērēctŭs ĭn aūrās Dīspĭcĭt ōmnĕ nĕmŭs. O. Syn.—Cīrcūmspĭcĭŏ.

Dīsplĭcĕŏ, ēs, ŭī, ĭtūm, ērĕ. *To displease.* Nēc mĭhĭ dīsplĭcĕāt măcŭlīs īnsīgnĭs ĕt ālbō. V. Syn.—Sōrdĕŏ, lædŏ, ōffēndŏ, nōn plăcĕŏ. Phr.—Nōn ārrīdĕŏ, sūm ŏdĭōsŭs, īngrātŭs, īnvīsŭs, īnjūcūndŭs, mŏlēstŭs, grăvĭs. Sōrdēnt tĭbĭ mūnĕră nōstră. Dūmquĕ tĭbi ēst ŏdĭō mĕă fīstŭlă. Aūrĭbŭs īngrātūm cārmĕn. Ŏcŭlōs ōffēndĭt ĕt aūrēs.

Dīspŏlĭŏ, ās, āvī, ātūm, ārĕ. *To despoil.* Sæpĕ tămēn prŏprĭīs dīspŏlĭātŭr hŏmŏ. Pr. Nōn sīc prātă nŏvō vērĕ dĕcēntĭă Aēstātīs călĭdæ dīspŏlĭāt văpŏr. Sen. Syn.—Spŏlĭŏ.

Dīspōnŏ, ĭs, ŏsŭī, ŏsĭtūm, ĕrĕ. *To dispose, to set in order.* Plēnăque ŏdōrātī dīspōnūnt pōcŭlă Bācchī. O. Syn.—Cōmpōnŏ, ōrdĭnŏ, dīgĕrŏ, dīstrĭbŭŏ.

Dīspŭtŏ, ās, āvī, ātūm, ārĕ. *To dispute, to discuss.* Quŏd ōptĭmūm sīt cōnvīvĭūm dīspŭtăt. M. Syn.—Dīssĕrŏ, ăgĭtŏ, dīscēptŏ, trāctŏ.

Dīsquīrŏ, ĭs, sīvī, sītūm, rĕrĕ. *To inquire after.* Syn.—Quærŏ, īnquīrŏ, scrūtŏr, īnvēstīgŏ.

Dīsrūmpŏ, ĭs, ūpī, ūptūm, ĕrĕ. *To break.* Syn.—Rūmpŏ.

Dīssĕcŏ, ās, ŭī, ārĕ. *To cut open, to cut to pieces.* Nēc tāntă tŭōs vĭŏlēntĭă nērvōs Dīssĕcĕt. Syn.—Sĕcŏ, scīndŏ, dīscīndŏ, dīscērpŏ, dīvĭdŏ, lăcĕrŏ.

Dīssēmĭnŏ, ās, āvī, ātūm, ārĕ. *To scatter broadcast.* Syn.—Sēmĭnŏ, spārgŏ, dīspērgŏ, dīffūndŏ, (*sometimes*) vūlgŏ, dīvūlgŏ.

Dīssēnsĭŏ, ōnĭs. f. & Dīssēnsŭs, ūs. m. *Dissension.* Syn.—Dīscōrdĭă, dīssĭdĭūm. Phr.—Ūrbēm scīndūnt dīssēnsū vărĭō. *See Discordia.*

Dīssēntĭŏ, īs, sī, sūm, īrĕ. *To disagree.* Trēs mĭhĭ cōnvīvæ prŏpĕ dīssēntīrĕ vĭdēntŭr. H. Syn.—Dīssĭdĕŏ, dīscrĕpŏ, dīscōrdŏ. Phr.—Dīssēnsērĕ dĕæ.

Dīssēpĭŏ, īs, sī, tūm, īrĕ. *To divide, separate.* Vīx ĕă līmĭtĭbūs dīssēpsĕrăt ōmnĭă cērtīs. O. Syn.—Dīscērnŏ, dīscrīmĭnŏ, sēpărŏ, dīstīnguŏ. Phr.—Bĕnĕ dīssēptī fœdĕră mūndī Trāxĭt ĭn ūnūm Thēssălă pīnŭs.

Dīssĕrŏ, ĕrĭs, ĕrŭī, ērtūm, ĕrĕ. *To discuss.* Sēd cūr nōn pŏtĭūs vērbīs quæ dīssĕrĭs ūsū Ēxpĕrĭŏr? Syn.—Dīspŭtŏ, dīscēptŏ, pūgnŏ.

Dīssĭdĕō, ēs, ēdī, ēssūm, ērĕ. *To be seated apart or away from.* Ōmnem ĕquĭdēm scēptrīs tērrām quæ lībĕră nōstrīs Dīssĭdĕt ēxtērnām rĕŏr. *See Disto. To disagree.* Syn.—Dīssēntĭŏ, dīscōrdŏ, dīscrĕpŏ, dīstŏ, rĕpūgnŏ. Phr.—Mātrĭs ăb īngĕnĭō dīssĭdĕt. *See Discors.*

Dīssĭlĭŏ, īs, ĭī & ŭī, ūltūm, īrĕ. *To leap apart, to burst forth.* Dīssĭlĭt ōmnĕ sŏlūm, pĕnĕtrātque īn Tārtără rīmīs Lūmĕn. O. **Syn.—Dīssūltŏ, dīscēdŏ, dĕhīscŏ, fīndŏr, dīsrūmpŏr.** Phr.—Aērăquĕ dīssĭlĭūnt. *See Rumpo.*

Dīssĭmĭlĭs, ĭs, ĕ. ***Unlike, different.*** Nōs quŏquĕ dīssĭmĭlī cērtāmĭnă mēntĕ sŭbīmŭs. O. Syn.—Ābsĭmĭlĭs, dīspār, dīspărĭlĭs, dīvērsŭs, ălĭŭs, dīstāns, dīscrĕpāns, dīscōnvĕnĭēns. Phr.—Nōn sĭmĭlĭs. Nōn īdēm. *Unfit.* Mē nūllă dĭēs tām fōrtĭbŭs aūsīs Dīssĭmĭlem ārgŭĕrĭt. Syn.—Dēgĕnĕr.

Dīssĭmŭlŏ, ās, āvī, ātūm, ārĕ. *To dissemble.* Dīssĭmŭlāre ĕtĭām spērāstī, pērfĭdĕ, tāntūm Pōssĕ nĕfās. V. Syn.—Sĭmŭlŏ, fīngŏ, cēlŏ, tĕgŏ, ōccūltŏ, fāllŏ, mēntĭŏr. Phr.—Sĭmŭlātā mēntĕ lŏquī. Trīstī fīngĕrĕ mēntĕ jŏcūm. Īmĭtārī gaūdĭă fālsă. Mūltă mălūs sĭmŭlāns.

Dīssĭpŏ, ās, āvī, ātūm, ārĕ. *To disperse, to scatter.* Fūlmĭnĕō cĕlĕrēs dīssĭpăt ōrĕ cănēs. O. Syn.—Spārgŏ, dīspērgŏ, dīspēllŏ, dīsjĭcĭŏ, fŭgŏ. Phr.—Dīssĭpăt ūmbrās. Dīssĭpătŭr īn aūrās.

Dīssĭtŭs, ă, ūm. *Spread out.* Syn.—Dīffūsŭs. *Separated.* Syn.—Dīsjūnctŭs, dīvīsŭs, sējūnctŭs, dīssŏcĭātŭs, dīstāns, rĕmōtŭs.

Dīssŏcĭŏ, ās, āvī, ātūm, ārĕ. *To separate.* Syn.—Dīsjūngŏ, sēpărŏ, dīvĭdŏ.

Dīssōlvŏ, ĭs, vī, ŏlūtūm, ĕrĕ. *To dissolve.* Nūbĭlă dīssōlvīt Phœbŭs. Syn.—Sōlvŏ, rĕsōlvŏ, lāxŏ, rĕlāxŏ, frāngŏ, dīlŭŏ, rĕmīttŏ.

Dīssŏnŏ, ās, ŭī, ĭtūm, ārĕ. *To disagree.* Syn.—Dīscrĕpŏ, dīscōrdŏ, dīssēntĭŏ.

Dīssŏnŭs, ă, ūm. *Discordant.* Syn.—Ābsŏnŭs, dīscōrs, ābsĭmĭlĭs. Phr.—Nōn cōnsŏnŭs. *See Discors.*

Dīssuādĕō, ēs, sī, sūm, ērĕ. *To dissuade.* Hīnc dīssuādĕt ămōr, vīctūs pŭdŏr ēssĕt ămōrĕ. O. Syn.—Dĕhōrtŏr, dētērrĕō, ābdūcŏ, āvērtŏ, āvŏcŏ.

Dīstāns, āntĭs. adj. *Distant.* Aēquālī spătĭō dīstāntĭbŭs īllīs. O. Syn.—Dīsjūnctŭs, dīssĭtŭs, rĕmōtŭs, dīssŏcĭātŭs. *Different.* Stŭdĭīsquĕ făvōr dīstāntĭbŭs ārdĕt. Syn.—Vărĭŭs, dīvērsŭs, dīspār, dīscōnvĕnĭēns.

Dīstāntĭă, æ. f. *Distance, interval.* Syn.—Spătĭūm, īntērvāllūm, dīscrīmĕn.

Dīstēndŏ, ĭs, dī, sūm & tūm, ĕrĕ. *To extend.* Dīstēndĕrĕ brāchĭă. O. Syn.—Tēndŏ. *To fill.* Syn.—Dīstēntŏ, implĕŏ, cōmplĕŏ. Fig.—*To divide.* Syn.—Dīvĭdŏ, dīstrăhŏ.

Dīstērmĭnŏ, ās, āvī, ātūm, ārĕ. *To divide, to separate.* Syn.—Dīvĭdŏ, sēpărŏ.

Dīstĭnĕŏ, ēs, ŭī, ēntūm, ērĕ. *To retain.* Ēt mărĕ quōd lātē tērrārūm dīstĭnĕt ōrās. Lr. Syn.—Tĕnĕŏ, dētĭnĕŏ, rĕtĭnĕŏ, mŏrŏr, cŏērcĕŏ, ōccŭpŏ. Phr.—Dūm dīstĭnĕt hōstēm Āggēr mūrōrūm.

Dīstīnguŏ, ĭs, xī, ctūm, ĕrĕ. *To divide, to separate.* Sēd dŭŏ sūnt, quæ nōs dīstīnguūnt, mīllĭă pāssūm. M. Syn.—Dīvĭdŏ, sēpărŏ, dīscrīmĭnŏ, sējūngŏ, dīstērmĭnŏ. *To vary.* Syn.—Vărĭŏ, dīscrīmĭnŏ. *To distinguish. See Discerno.*

Dīstŏ, ās, ārĕ. *To be apart.* Nĭmĭūm dīstārĕ cărīnās Jām quĕrĭtŭr. H. Syn.—Ābsūm, sēpărŏr, sēmŏvĕŏr, sējūngŏr. Phr.—Sūm rĕmōtŭs, dīvīsŭs. Nēc lōngō dīstāt cūrsū. Nēc nōs mărĕ sēpărăt īngēns. *To be different.* Syn.—Dīscrĕpŏ, dīffĕrŏ, dīssŏnŏ, dīscōnvĕnĭŏ, ābsūm, rĕcēdŏ.

Dīstrăhŏ, ĭs, xī, ctūm, ĕrĕ. *To pull apart, to pull away.* Syn.—Dīvēllŏ, dīdūcŏ, ābstrăhŏ, dīscīndŏ, dīscērpŏ. *To separate.* Syn.—Sēpărŏ, sējūngŏ, dīsjūngŏ.

Dīstrĭbŭŏ, ĭs, ŭī, ūtūm, ĕrĕ. *To distribute.* Dīstrĭbŭēndă pĭōs hŏmĭnūm māndāvĭt ĭn ūsūs. Syn.—Dīvĭdŏ, pārtĭŏr, dīspērtĭŏr.

Dīstrīngŏ, ĭs, nxī, ictūm, ĕrĕ. *To bind. See Stringo.*

Dīstūrbŏ, ās, āvī, ātūm, ārĕ. *To overthrow, to demolish.* Tūm fūlmĭnă mīttăt ēt ædēs Sæpĕ sŭās dīstūrbēt. L. Syn.—Dīrŭŏ, dīsjĭcĭŏ. *See Everto. To put in disorder. See Turbo.*

Dītēscŏ, ĭs, ĕrĕ. *To become rich.* Sīvĕ fĕrās īntērfīcĕre ēt dītēscĕrĕ prædā. Lr. Syn.—Dītŏr, lŏcŭplētŏr. Phr.—Dīvēs, lŏcŭplēs, ŏpŭlēntŭs fīŏ. Ŏpēs, dīvĭtĭās părŏ, cōmpărŏ, cŏăcērvŏ. Rēm făcĭŏ. Rēm strŭŏ. Sīc āltă pĕcūnĭă crēscĕt.

Dītŏ, ās, āvī, ātūm, ārĕ. *To enrich.* Suēvĕrăt īnnŭmĕrās hŏmĭnūm dītārĕ cătērvās. Syn.—Lŏcŭplētŏ. Phr.—Dīvĭtĭīs, ŏpĭbŭs, fōrtūnīs aūgĕŏ, cŭmŭlŏ.

Dĭū. adv. *Long time.* Syn.—Lōngē, lōngūm, lōngĭŭs. Phr.—Pēr lōngūm. Mūltōs ānnōs, dĭēs, lōngūm tēmpŭs.

Dĭūm, ĭī, & Dīvūm, ī. n. *Air.* Nēc mĭhĭ tūm mōllēs sūb dīō cārpĕrĕ sōmnōs. V. Syn.—Āēr, æthēr.

Dĭūrnŭs, ă, ūm. *Lasting for a day.* Phr.—Īmplēsse ætātīs fātă dĭūrnă sŭæ. Dūrātquĕ dĭēm.

Dĭŭs, ă, ūm. *Godlike.* Sī tămĕn īn dīō quōndām cōncrētă prŏfūndō Spūmă fŭī. O. Syn.—Dīvīnŭs, cœlēstĭs, dīvŭs.

Dīvēllŏ, ĭs, ūlsī, ūlsūm, ĕrĕ. *To snatch apart, to separate.* Nēquīcquām tēndīt mănĭbūs dīvēllĕrĕ nōdōs. V. Syn.—Dīstrăhŏ, ābstrăhŏ, āvēllŏ, dīsjūngŏ. Phr.—Dīvēllĭmŭr īndĕ. Dīvēllĕrĕ sōmnōs. Fig. Syn.—Ădĭmŏ, ēxcŭtĭŏ, ābrūmpŏ.

Dīvērsōrĭūm, ĭī. n. *Inn.* Syn.—Hōspĭtĭūm.

Dīvērsŭs, ă, ūm. *Turned in different directions.* Quō tāntūm dīvērsŭs ăbīs? V. Phr.—Dīvērsōs ŭbĭ sēnsĭt ĕquōs. Ōbrŭĕ pūppēs, Aūt ăgĕ dīvērsās. *Different.* Syn.—Dīssĭmĭlĭs, dīspār, cōntrārĭŭs, etc. Phr.—Rūrsum ē dīvērsō cœlī. Plēbs hăbĭtăt dīvērsă lŏcīs. *Hostile.* Syn.—Āvērsŭs, ādvērsŭs, dīvīsŭs, ŏppŏsĭtŭs.

Dīvērtŏ, ĭs, tī, sūm, ĕrĕ. *To turn away from.* Cāstălĭăm mōllī dīvērtĭtŭr ōrbĭtă clīvō. V. Phr.—Dē, ēx vĭā dēflēctŏ. Ālĭō ĭtĕr flēctŏ, fĕrŏ, ălĭō fĕrŏr. *To have recourse to.* Syn.—Cōnvērtŏr, cōnfŭgĭŏ.

Dīvĕs, ĭtĭs. adj. *Rich.* Dīvĭtĭs aūdīta ēst cuī nōn ŏpŭlēntĭă Crœsī? O. Syn.—Lŏcŭplēs, dīs, ŏpŭlēntŭs, dītīssĭmŭs, prædīvĕs, bĕātŭs. Phr.—Dīvĕs ŏpūm, aūrī. Dīvĭtĭīs, ŏpĭbŭs ăbūndāns. Bĕnĕ nūmmātŭs. Aūrī cōngēstō pōndĕrĕ dīvĕs. Āttălĭcīs pōllēns ŏpĭbŭs. *Precious.* Syn.—Prĕtĭōsŭs, laūtŭs. *Abundant.* Fēcūndŭs, ūbĕr.

Dīvĭdŏ, ĭs, īsī, īsūm, ĕrĕ. *To divide, to share.* Dīvĭdĭmūs mūrōs ēt mœnĭă pāndĭmŭs ūrbĭs. V. Syn.—Dīsjūngŏ, dīstrăhŏ, dīstīnguŏ, sēpărŏ. Phr.—Pārs īn frūstă sĕcānt. Ābjūnctīs dīssŏcĭāmŭr ăquīs. *To distribute.* Syn.—Dīstrĭbŭŏ, pārtĭŏr, dīspērtĭŏr. Phr.—Sŏcĭōs pārtītŭr ĭn ōmnēs. Vīnă Dīvĭdĭt.

Dīvīnĭtŭs. adv. *Divinely.* Haūd ĕquĭdēm crēdō, quĭă sīt dīvīnĭtŭs īllīs Īngĕnĭūm. V. Syn.—Cœlĭtŭs. Phr.—Ēx Dĕō, dīvīnō, cœlēstī nūmĭnĕ, mūnĕrĕ. Ē nĭhĭlō gīgnī dīvīnĭtŭs.

Dīvīnŏ, ās, āvī, ātūm, ārĕ. *To divine, to forecast the future.* Dīvīnāre ĕtĕnīm māgnūs mĭhĭ dōnăt Āpōllŏ. H. Syn.—Vātĭcĭnŏr, prædīcŏ, præsāgĭŏ, aūgŭrŏr. *To conjecture.* Syn.—Cōnjĭcĭŏ, aūgŭrŏ, præsēntĭŏ.

Dīvīnŭs, ă, ūm. *Divine, heavenly.* Lūdĭt ĭn hūmānīs dīvīnă pŏtēntĭă rēbŭs. O. Syn.—Dīvŭs, æthĕrĭŭs, cœlēstĭs. Phr.—Cœlō dēmīssŭs ăb āltō. Cœlēstī nātŭs ŏrĭgĭnĕ. Dīvīnā stīrpĕ crĕātŭs, sătŭs, crētŭs. Dīvūm cērtīssĭmă prōlēs.

Dīvĭtĭæ, ārūm. f. *Riches.* Nīl Dīvĭtĭīs pŏtĕrūnt rēgālēs āddĕrĕ mājŭs. H. Syn.—Ŏpēs, fōrtūnæ, gāzæ, thēsaūrī, aūrūm, ārgēntūm, pĕcūnĭă, nūmmī, bŏnă, cēnsŭs, ŏpŭlēntĭă. Phr.—Cēnsūs īngēntēs. Rēgālēs gāzæ. Aēs cōngēstūm. Māgnum īngēns ārgēntī pōndŭs ĕt aūrī. Ēt Trōĭă gāză pĕr ūndās. Sī rēs āmplă dŏmī. *See Pecunia.*

Dīvōrtĭūm, ĭī. *Detour.* Syn.—Flēxŭs, dīvērtĭcŭlūm. *Divorce.* Syn.—Dīscĭdĭūm, dīscēssĭŏ.

Dīvŭs, ī. m. *God.* Syn.—Dĕŭs, nūmĕn.

Dō, ās, ĕdī, ătūm, ărĕ. *To give.* Vītăquĕ māncĭpĭō nūllī dătŭr, ōmnĭbŭs ūsū. Lr. Syn.—Dōnŏ, præbĕŏ, trĭbŭŏ, lārgĭŏr, īmpērtĭŏr, trādŏ, mĭnīstrŏ, sūffĭcĭŏ, sŭppĕdĭtŏ, cōmmŏdŏ, præstŏ. Phr.—Mūnĕrĕ dōnŏ. Dōnō dărĕ. Dăbĭtūr, Trōjānĕ, quŏd ōptās. Sōl quŏquĕ dīgnă dăbĭt. *To grant.* Syn.—Cōncēdŏ, ānnŭŏ, pērmīttŏ, trĭbŭŏ. Phr.—Tĭbĭ dī quæcūnquĕ prĕcērĭs. Sī dānt ĕă mœnĭă Pārcæ. Rērūm dĕdĭt ēssĕ măgīstrōs. *To make.* Syn.—Ēffĭcĭŏ, ēdŏ.

Dŏcĕŏ, ēs, ŭī, ōctūm, ērĕ. *To teach.* Ēxpĕdĭam ēt paūcīs ănĭmōs ādvērtĕ, dŏcēbŏ. V. Syn.—Ēdŏcĕŏ, ērŭdĭŏ, īnstĭtŭŏ, īnfōrmŏ, præcĭpĭŏ. Phr.—Ārtĭbŭs īnstĭtŭŏ, īnstrŭŏ. Præcēptă trādŏ. Ēxēmplō mūltă dŏcērĕ. *To indicate.* Syn.—Ōstēndŏ, īndĭcŏ, mōnstrŏ, ăpĕrĭŏ, pāndŏ.

Dŏcĭlĭs, ĭs, ĕ. *Teachable, docile.* Pērcĭpĭānt ănĭmī dŏcĭlēs tĕnĕātquĕ fĭdēlēs. H. Syn.—Căpāx, āptŭs. Phr.—Cērĕŭs īn vĭtĭūm flēctī. Prāvī dŏcĭlĭs. Mŏnĭtīs aūrēs ādvērtĕrĕ.

Dōctē. adv. *In a learned manner.* Syn.—Scītē, pĕrītē, bĕnĕ.

Dōctĭlŏquŭs, ă, ūm. *Eloquent.* Syn.—Dōctŭs, ēlŏquēns, fācūndŭs, dĭsērtŭs.

Dōctŏr, ōrĭs. m. *Teacher, master.* Syn.—Măgīstĕr, præcēptŏr. Phr.—Pŭĕrīs dānt crūstŭlă blāndī Dōctōrēs. *See Magister.*

Dōctrīnă, æ. f. *Teaching.* Dōctrīnæ prĕtĭūm trīstĕ măgīstĕr hăbĕt. O. Syn.—Dīscĭplīnă, cūltŭs, præcēptă. *Learning.* Syn.—Ārs, dīscĭplīnă, scĭēntĭă.

Dŏcŭmēntūm, ī. n. *Teaching, proof.* Syn.—Mŏnĭtūm, præcēptūm, præscrīptūm, dōctrīnă, ārgūmēntūm.

Dŏlēntĕr. adv. *Sorrowfully, sadly.* Pōst Phăĕtōntēōs vīdīssĕ dŏlēntĭŭs īgnēs. O. Syn.—Mœstē. Phr.—Cūm gĕmĭtū.

Dŏlĕŏ, ēs, ŭī, ĭtūm, ērĕ. *To grieve, to suffer pain.* Vūlnĕră nōn ălĭtēr quăm mŏdŏ fāctă dŏlēnt. O. Syn.—Crŭcĭŏr, īndŏlĕŏ, mœrĕŏ, gĕmŏ, īngĕmŏ, lūgĕŏ. Phr.—Dŏlōrĕ, dŏlōrĭbŭs ūrŏr, crŭcĭŏr, vēxŏr, āngŏr, ăgĭtŏr, prĕmŏr, tōrquĕŏr, cōnfĭcĭŏr, ēxērcĕŏr. Īndūlgērĕ dŏlōrī. Mœrōrī văcārĕ. Grăvēs haūrīrĕ dŏlōrēs. Ō pāssī grăvĭōră! Tăcĭtūm nūtrīt sūb pēctŏrĕ vūlnŭs. *To bewail.* Syn.—Gĕmŏ, īngĕmŏ, dēflĕŏ. *See Queror.*

Dōlĭūm, ĭī. n. *Cask.* Dūmmŏdŏ pūrpŭrĕō spūmēnt mĭhĭ dōlĭă Bācchō. Pr. Syn.—Cădŭs, vās, āmphŏră, dĭōtă. Phr.—Dōlĭă quāssă nŏvăt. Tŭām vīncānt dōlĭă fūsă sĭtĭm. Pīnguī spūmāntĭă dōlĭă mūstō.

Dŏlŏr, ōrĭs. m. *Sorrow, suffering.* Fŭrĭt īmă dŏlōr dēlāpsŭs ăd ōssă. V. Syn.—Crŭcĭātŭs. *Suffering of the mind.* Syn.—Āngŏr, mœrŏr, crŭcĭātŭs, ærūmnă, trīstĭtĭă, lūctŭs, cūră. Phr.—Quĭēte ĭnĭmīcŭs. Lōngī tōrmēntă dŏlōrĭs. Ăcūti īn cōrdĕ dŏlōrēs. Stĕtĭt ācrī fīxă dŏlōrĕ. Dŏlŏr ēxcĭtăt īrās. Ēxārsĭt jŭvĕnī dŏlŏr ōssĭbŭs īngēns. Īnfāndūm, rēgīnă, jŭbēs rĕnŏvārĕ dŏlōrēm.

Dŏlōsē. adv. *Deceitfully.* Syn.—Āstūtē.

Dŏlōsŭs, ă, ūm. *Crafty, deceitful.* Syn.—Fāllāx, āstūtŭs, cāllĭdŭs, văfĕr, sūbdŏlŭs, pērfĭdŭs. Phr.—Dŏlī făbrĭcātŏr. Dŏlīs āptīssĭmă tēllūs. Dŏlīs īnstrūctŭs ĕt ārtĕ Pĕlāsgā. *See Fallax.*

Dŏlŭs, ī. m. *Deceit, guile.* Dŏlŭs ān vīrtūs, quĭs ĭn hōstĕ rĕquīrăt? V. Syn.—Āstŭs, āstūtĭă, fraŭs, fāllācĭă, īnsĭdĭæ, ārs, cāllĭdĭtās, pēllācĭă, pērfĭdĭă, lăquĕī. Phr.—Mēns sĭmŭlātă. Ārs sūbdŏlă. Crīmĭnă fraŭdĭs. Pŭtātĭs Dōnă cărērĕ dŏlīs. *See Fraus, Decipio.*

Dŏmēstĭcŭs, ă, ūm. *Pertaining to the family.* Īlle ĕgŏ cōnvīctōr dēnsōquĕ dŏmēstĭcŭs ūsū. O. Phr.—Lūctūsquĕ dŏmēstĭcŭs aŭgĕt. *Pertaining to one's country.* Syn.—Pătrĭŭs, gēntīlĭs. Phr.—Cĕlĕbrārĕ dŏmēstĭcă fāctă.

Dŏmĭnātĭŏ, ĭōnĭs. f. *Rule, domination.* Syn.—Dŏmĭnātŭs, dŏmĭnĭūm, īmpĕrĭūm, rēgnūm, dĭtĭŏ, pŏtēstās. .

Dŏmĭnŏr, ārĭs, ātŭs sūm, ārī. *To rule over.* Hīc dŏmŭs Aēnēæ cūnctīs dŏmĭnābĭtŭr ōrīs. V. Syn.—Īmpĕrŏ, rĕgŏ, rēgnŏ, gŭbērnŏ, præsūm, mŏdĕrŏr. Phr.—Īmpĕrĭō tĕnĕŏ, prĕmŏ. Īmpĕrĭī frēnă tĕnĕŏ. Jūră dăbūnt. Stĕrĭlēs dŏmĭnāntŭr ăvēnæ.

Dŏmĭnŭs, ī. m. *Lord, master.* Rōmānōs rērūm dŏmĭnōs. V. Syn.—Hĕrŭs, dŏmĭnātŏr, rēctŏr, rēx, dūx, tўrānnŭs, ārbĭtĕr, mŏdĕrātŏr. *See Rex.*

Dŏmĭtŏ, ās, ārĕ. *To tame.* Ēt prēnsōs dŏmĭtārĕ bŏvēs. V. Syn.—Dŏmŏ, sŭbĭgŏ, vīncŏ. Phr.—Dŏmĭtānt īn pūlvĕrĕ cūrrūs. Dŏmĭtārĕ fŭrōrēs.

Dŏmĭtŏr, ōrĭs. m. *Tamer.* Quīd tĭbĭ dē tētrĭcō rĕfĕrām dŏmĭtōrĕ Chĭmēræ? O. Syn.—Dŏmātŏr, vīctŏr, dēbēllātŏr, trĭūmphātŏr. Phr.—Hŏmĭnūm dŏmĭtōr, dŏmĭtōrquĕ fĕrārūm. Cūrārūm dŏmĭtōr sōmnŭs.

Dŏmŏ, ās, ŭī, ĭtūm, ārĕ. *To subdue.* Nōn ānnī dŏmŭērĕ dĕcēm, nōn mīllĕ cărīnæ. V. Syn.—Vīncŏ, sŭbĭgŏ, sŭpĕrŏ, dēbēllŏ, dŏmĭtŏ, frēnŏ, cōmpēscŏ. Phr.—Cōmpēscĕrĕ frēnō. Sūb jŭgă mīttĕrĕ.

Dŏmūncŭlă, æ. f. *Little house, hut.* Syn.—Aēdĭcŭlæ, căsă, tŭgŭrĭūm.

Dŏmŭs, ūs. f. *House.* Nūllī cērtă dŏmūs, lūcīs hăbĭtāmŭs ŏpācĭs. V. Syn.—Aēdēs, ātrĭă, aūlă, tēctūm, tēctă, līmĕn, līmĭnă, sēdēs, pĕnātēs, lār, lărēs, fŏcī, pĕnĕtrālĭă, hōspĭtĭūm. Phr.—Fŏrĭbūs dŏmŭs āltă sŭpērbīs. Phrȳgĭīs īnnīxă, fūltă cŏlūmnīs. Dŏmūs rēgālī splēndĭdă lūxū. Rīdĕt ārgēntō dŏmŭs. Sēptă, tēctă dŏmōrūm. Līmĭnă sēdĭs. Tēctīs sūccēdĭtĕ nōstrīs. Pērvēntum ād līmĭnă sēdĭs.

Dōnĕc. adv. *Until.* Cōgĕrĕ dōnĕc ŏvēs stăbŭlīs, nūmĕrūmquĕ rĕfērrĕ Jūssĭt. V. Syn.—Dūm, quāmdĭū, quŏăd, quoād (*one syllable*). *As long as.* Syn.—Dūm, quāmdĭū.

Dōnŏ, ās, āvī, ātūm, ārĕ. *To give, to present with.* Quēm pătĕr īpsĕ dĕūm scēptrī dōnāvĭt hŏnōrī. V. Syn.—Ōrnŏ, aūgĕŏ, dō, trĭbŭŏ, trādŏ, lārgĭŏr, īmpērtĭŏr. Phr.—Dōnō dărĕ. Mūnĕrĭbŭs ōrnārĕ. Hūnc prōmīssō mūnĕrĕ dōnăt. Mūnĕrĭbūs cŭmŭlăt măgnīs. Prǣstāntī mūnĕrĕ dōnăt.

Dōnūm, ī. n. *Gift.* Ēt cūr nōn ălĭīs ĕădēm dărĕ dōnă lĭcēbĭt. Syn.—Mūnŭs, dătūm, mūnūscŭlūm. Phr.—Dōna aūrō grăvĭă. Ēxĭgŭī brĕvĕ dōnūm tēmpŏrĭs. Dĕdĕrăt mŏnūmēntum ēt pīgnŭs ămōrĭs.

Dōrmĭŏ, īs, īvī & ĭī, ītūm, īrĕ. *To sleep.* Īn nĭvĕ Lūcānā dōrmīs ŏcrĕātŭs. H. Syn.—Dōrmītŏ, quĭēscŏ, rĕquĭēscŏ. Phr.—Sōmnūm, sŏpōrēm cārpŏ, căpĭŏ, pĕtŏ. Ŏcŭlīs īndūlgĕŏ. Sōmnō frŭŏr. Quĭētī sūccūmbŏ. Dō nōctēm sōmnō. Sōmnō cōrpŏră lāxŏ. Sōmnŭs ŏcŭlōs vīncĭt. Dēmīttĕrĕ mēmbră quĭētī. Nōx ēst dătă cētĕră sōmnō. Sōmnō fāllĕrĕ cūrās.

Dōrsūm, ī. n. *Back.* Gȳrōsquĕ dĕdērĕ Īmpŏsĭtī dōrsō. Syn.—Tērgūm.

Dōtŏ, ās, āvī, ātūm, ārĕ. *To provide with a dowry, to endow.* Sānguĭnĕ Trōjāno ēt Rŭtŭlō dōtābĕrĕ, Vīrgŏ. V. Phr.—Īn dōtēm dō, trĭbŭŏ, cōnfĕrŏ. Dōtĕ dōnŏ. Ēt tōtō dōtāndă mărī.

Drăcŏ, ōnĭs. m. *Dragon, serpent.* Syn.—Sērpēns, ānguĭs.

Dŭbĭē. adv. *In a doubtful manner.* Nēc dŭbĭē vīrēs quās hǣc hăbĕt īnsŭlă. O. Syn—Āmbĭgŭē, ōbscūrē. *Hesitatingly.* Tĭmĭdē, dŭbĭtāntĕr.

Dŭbĭtāntĕr. adv. *Hesitatingly.* Syn.—Dŭbĭē, tĭmĭdē, păvĭdē.

Dŭbĭtŏ, ās, āvī, ātūm, ārĕ. *To doubt.* Sǣpĕ tămēn dŭbĭtăt, mĕtŭītquĕ mĭsērrĭmă fāllī. O. Syn.—Āmbĭgŏ, flūctŭŏ, hǣsĭtŏ. Phr.—Dŭbĭŭs sūm. Īn dŭbĭō sūm, vērsŏr. Ănĭmō īncērtō pēndĕŏ. Mēns tĭtŭbăt. Ănĭmūs stăt īncērtŭs. Mēns dŭbĭīs pērcūssă păvĕt. Dŭbĭa ēst sēntēntĭă nōbīs. *To hesitate.* Syn.—Mŏrŏr, cūnctŏr, tĭmĕŏ. *To meditate.* Syn.—Cōgĭtŏ, vōlvŏ, mĕdĭtŏr.

Dŭbĭūm, ĭī. n. *Doubt.* Spēs tămĕn īn dŭbĭo ēst. O. Syn.—Dŭbĭtātĭŏ. Phr.—Ēst ĭn āmbĭgŭō. Nōn bĕnĕ cōmpērtūm. Nōn lĭquĕt. Scīrĕ nĕfās.

Dŭbĭŭs, ă, ūm. *Doubtful.* Sæpĕ mĭhī dŭbĭām trāxīt sēntēntĭă mēntēm. Syn.—Āmbĭgŭŭs, āncēps, īncērtŭs, ānxĭŭs, vărĭŭs, sūspēnsŭs, dŭbĭtāns, āltērnāns. Phr.—Ănĭmī dŭbĭŭs. Cōnsĭlĭī ĭnōps. Mēntĕ lăbāns. Īncērtūs quō fātă fĕrānt. Spēmquĕ mĕtūmque īntēr dŭbĭī. *See Dubito.*

Dūcŏ, ĭs, xī, ctūm, ĕrĕ. *To lead, to conduct.* Jām Cўthĕrēă chŏrōs dūcīt Vĕnŭs. H. Syn.—Ăgŏ, rĕgŏ, prǣsūm, praĕĕŏ. Phr.—Dūx, prǣvĭŭs sūm, īncēdŏ. Quā tē dūcīt vĭă, dīrĭgĕ grēssūm. Rērum ōrdĭnĕ dūcăr. *To pass (one's life).* Syn.—Ăgŏ, dēgŏ, cōnsūmŏ, trādūcŏ, tĕrŏ. *To draw forth.* Syn.—Trăhŏ, ēdūcŏ. *To charm.* Syn.—Căpĭŏ, trăhŏ, mūlcĕŏ, īmpēllŏ.

Dūdūm. adv. *For a long time.* Syn.—Prīdēm. Phr.—Jām dūdūm. Jām prīdēm. Jām dĭū. Ēx lōngō.

Dŭēllūm, ī. n. *War.* Grǣcĭă bārbărĭē lēntō cōllīsă dŭēllō. H. Syn.—Bēllūm, pūgnă, cērtāmĕn. *See Bellum.*

Dūlcĕ. adv. *Sweetly.* Syn.—Suāvĕ, suāvĭtĕr.

Dūlcēdŏ, ĭnĭs. f. *Sweetness, charm.* Nēscĭŏ quā prǣtēr sŏlĭtūm dūlcēdĭnĕ lǣtī. V. Syn.—Suāvĭtās, dēlĭcĭǣ, gaūdĭūm, vŏlūptās. *See Voluptas.*

Dūlcĭs, ĭs, ĕ. *Sweet, agreeable.* Ōrĕ fĕrūnt dūlcēm nīdīs īmmītĭbŭs ēscām. V. Syn.—Suāvĭs, mītĭs, blāndŭs, mēllĕŭs, mēllītŭs, nēctărĕŭs, āmbrŏsĭŭs. Phr.—Dūlcēs ā fōntĭbŭs ūndǣ. Dūlcĕ mălūm. Thўmō mĭhĭ dūlcĭŏr Hўblǣ. *Friendly.* Syn.—Cārŭs, grātŭs, jūcūndŭs, dīlēctŭs, ămīcŭs, plăcēns.

Dūlcĭsŏnŭs, ă, ūm. *Sweetly-sounding.* Dūlcĭsŏnūm quătĭtūr fĭdĭbūs dūm pēctĭnĕ mūrmŭr. Syn.—Blāndĭsŏnŭs, dūlcĭs, suāvĭs, cănōrŭs.

Dūm. conj. *While.* Syn.—Quāndŏ, cūm, dŏnĕc, quāmdĭū. *Until.* Syn.—Dōnĕc, quŏăd. *Provided that.* Syn.—Dūmmŏdŏ.

Dūmētūm, ī. n. *Thicket, thornbush.* Tērcēntūm nĭvĕī tōndēnt dūmētă jŭvēncī. V. Syn.—Spīnētūm, rŭbētūm. Phr.—Dūmōsă lŏcă. Lŏcŭs, sāltŭs, mōns spīnīs āspĕr, hōrrēns, cōnsĭtŭs. *See Dumosus, Spina.*

Dūmmŏdŏ. conj. *Provided that.* Syn.—Dūm, mŏdŏ, ŭt, sī.

Dūmōsŭs, ă, ūm. *Covered with thornbushes.* Dūmōsā pēndērĕ prŏcūl dē rūpĕ vĭdēbŏ. V. Syn.—Spīnĭfĕr, spīnōsŭs. Phr.—Dūmīs, spīnīs, rŭbīs, sēntĭbŭs, vĕprĭbŭs āspĕr, hōrrēns, plēnŭs, dēnsŭs, ōbsĭtŭs. Sīlvēstrĭbŭs hōrrĭdă dūmīs.

Dūmŭs, ī. m. *Thornbush, brambles.* Pēr jŭgă, pēr sīlvās, dūmōs ēt săxă văgātŭs. O. Syn.—Dūmētūm, rŭbŭs, sēntēs, spīnǣ, vĕprēs. Phr.—Ămāntēs ārdŭă dūmī. Āspĕră dūmīs Rūră tēnēnt. Spīssīs ārcānă cŭbīlĭă dūmīs. Dūmīsquĕ sĭlēntĭbŭs ērrăt. Ăcūtīs āspĕrī vēprēs rŭbīs.

Dūntāxăt. adv. *Only.* Dēnĭquĕ sīt quōdvīs sīmplēx dūntāxăt ĕt ūnūm. H. Syn.—Sōlūm, tāntūm, tāntūmmŏdŏ.

Dŭŏ, æ, ŏ. *Two.* Jūpĭtĕr, īpsĕ dŭās æquāto ēxāmĭnĕ lāncēs Sūstĭnĕt. V. Syn.—Āmbŏ, bīnī, gĕmĭnī, dŭplēx. Phr.—Ūnŭs ĕt āltĕr. Pīngĕ dŭōs ānguēs. Sī dŭŏ prætĕrĕā tālēs Īdæă tŭlīssĕt Tērră vĭrōs.

Dŭplēx, ĭcĭs. adj. *Double, of two kinds.* Dŭplĭcēm gēmmīs aūrōquĕ cŏrōnām. V. Syn.—Gĕmĭnŭs, dŭplŭs. *Two.* Syn.—Gĕmĭnī, bīnī, dŭŏ, āmbŏ. Phr.—Īræ caūsă dŭplēx. Dŭplĭcēs tēndēns ād sīdĕră pālmās.

Dŭplĭcŏ, ās, āvī, ātūm, ārĕ. *To double, redouble.* Mōbĭlĭtās dŭplĭcātŭr ĕt īmpĕtŭs īllĕ grăvēscĭt. Lr. Syn.—Āddŭplĭcŏ, cōndŭplĭcŏ, gĕmĭnŏ, cōngĕmĭnŏ, ĭtĕrŏ. *To fold into two parts.* Syn.—Flēctŏ, cūrvŏ, īncūrvŏ.

Dūrābĭlĭs, ĭs, ĕ. *Lasting.* Quōd cărĕt āltērnā rĕquĭē, dūrābĭlĕ nōn ēst. O. Syn.—Dĭūtūrnŭs, fīrmŭs, mānsūrŭs, stăbĭlĭs, cōnstāns. Phr.—Dĭū dūrāns, mănēns, stāns. Mūltōs pĕr ānnōs mănēns, mānsūrŭs.

Dūrē. adv. *Harshly.* Syn.—Grăvĭtĕr, dūrĭtĕr.

Dūrēscŏ, ĭs, ĕrĕ. *To become hardened.* Syn.—Īndūrēscŏ, ōbdūrēscŏ, dūrŏr, īndūrŏr, rĭgĕŏ, rĭgēscŏ, āstrīngŏr, cōncrēscŏ. *See Gelo.*

Dūrĭtĭă, æ, & Dūrĭtĭēs, ēī. f. *Hardness.* Syn.—Rĭgŏr, sævĭtĭă.

Dūrŏ, ās, āvī, ātūm, ārĕ. *To harden.* Syn.—Īndūrŏ, āstrīngŏ, cōnstrīngŏ, prĕmŏ, fīrmŏ. *To persist.* Syn.—Mănĕŏ, stō, pērstŏ, pērmănĕŏ, ēdūrŏ. *To endure.* Syn.—Fĕrŏ, pērfĕrŏ, sūstĭnĕŏ, tŏlĕrŏ.

Dūrŭs, ă, ūm. *Hard.* Syn.—Rĭgĭdŭs, ēdūrŭs, sŏlĭdŭs, āspĕr, ădămāntĭnŭs, fērrĕŭs, ænĕŭs, mārmŏrĕŭs. *Cruel.* Syn.—Crūdēlĭs, mōrōsŭs. *Painful.* Syn.—Grăvĭs, ŏpĕrōsŭs, dīffĭcĭlĭs.

E

Ē or Ēx. prep. *Out of, away from.* Syn.—Ā, ăb, dē. *On account of.* Syn.—Ōb, prōptĕr.

Ēātĕnŭs. adv. *So far.* Syn.—Hāctĕnŭs.

Ēbrĭĕtās, ātĭs. f. *Drunkness.* Syn.—Crāpŭlă, tēmŭlēntĭă, (*sometimes*) vīnūm. Phr.—Cōpĭă Bācchī. Īmmŏdĭcūm vīnūm. Cōrpŏrĭs rōbŭr frāngēns. Fēcūndă mălōrūm. Rīxārūm caūsă. Sānæ mēntī īnĭmīcă. Mălă ārcānī cūstōs. *See Vinum.*

Ēbrĭŭs, ă, ūm. *Inebriated.* Syn.—Tēmŭlēntŭs. Phr.—Vīnō mădēns, mădĕfāctŭs. Mălĕ sōbrĭŭs. Ēbrĭŭs āc pĕtŭlāns. Pōtŭs ĕt ēxlēx. Mēmbră dĕō vīctŭs. Mūltīs ūrgērĕ cŭlūllīs, ēt tōrquērĕ mĕrō.

Ĕbŭr, ŏrĭs. n. *Ivory.* Īndūm sānguĭnĕō vĕlŭtī vĭŏlāvĕrĭt ōstrō Sī quĭs ĕbŭr. V. Syn.—Ĕlĕphāntŭs. Phr.—Dēns Īndŭs, Īndĭcŭs, ĕbūrnŭs. Quālĕ pĕr ārtēm lūcĕt ĕbŭr.

Ĕbūrnĕŭs, & Ĕbūrnŭs, ă, ūm. *Made of ivory.* Ōppĭdă tūrrītīs cīngāntŭr ĕbūrnĕă mūrīs. O. Syn.—Ĕlĕphāntĭnŭs. Fig.—Ĕbūrnĕă cōllă.

Ēccĕ. adv. *Behold.* Ēccĕ Dĭōnæī prōcēssīt Cæsărĭs āstrūm. V. Syn.—Ēn. Phr.—Ēcce aūtēm. Ēn aūtēm. Ēn āspĭcĕ. Ēn ēccĕ.

Ēchō, ūs. f. *Echo.* (*From the nymph Echo*). Phr.—Rĕdĭtūrăquĕ rūpĭbŭs ēchō. Īngĕmĭnāns vōcēs. Vōcĭs ĭmāgŏ. Vōx rĕpērcūssă. Vōx rĕsŏnă. Fōntĭbŭs ātque āntrīs gaūdēns. Vōx rĕdĭēns ādvērsīs cōllĭbŭs īctă. Pūlsæ rĕfĕrūnt ād sīdĕră vāllēs.

Ēclīpsĭs, ĭs. f. *Eclipse.* Syn.—Dēfēctŭs, dēlĭquĭūm, lăbōrēs. Phr.—Dēfēctūs sōlīs vărĭōs lūnæquĕ lăbōrēs. Sōl nĭgrō ămĭctū, ātră cālīgĭnĕ, nĭgrō vēlāmĭnĕ ōbdūcĭtŭr, tĕgĭtŭr. Căpŭt ōccŭlĭt. Ōră tĕgĭt. Phœbūs cālīgĭnĕ mērgĭtŭr ātrā. Nām cūr lūnă quĕāt tērrām sēclūdĕrĕ sōlĭs Lūmĭnĕ?

Ēclŏgă, æ. f. *Eclogue, pastoral poem.* Syn.—Ĭdȳllĭūm, Būcŏlĭcūm. Phr.—Pāstōrālĕ, ăgrēstĕ cārmĕn, pŏēmă. Dēdūctūm dīcĕrĕ cārmĕn.

Ēcquāndŏ. adv. *Ever.* (*Generally in a question*). Syn.—Ūnquāmnĕ, ăn, ēn ūnquām.

Ĕdācĭtās, ātĭs. f. *Great hunger.* Gŭla ēst fĕrīnă, sēd sōcōrs ĕdācĭtās. Syn.—Vŏrācĭtās, īnglŭvĭēs, gŭlă. *See Fames.*

Ĕdāx, ācĭs. adj. *Greedy, gluttonous.* Syn.—Vŏrāx, hēllŭŏ, lūrcŏ. *See Gulosus. Eager.* Syn.—Răpāx, ăvĭdŭs, răbĭdŭs.

Ēdīcŏ, ĭs, īxī, īctūm, ĕrĕ. *To ordain, command.* Ārmārī Vōlscōrum ēdīcĕ mănīplīs. V. Syn.—Jŭbĕŏ, præcĭpĭŏ, māndŏ. *To issue a decree.* Syn.—Dēnūntĭŏ, prædīcŏ (as).

Ēdīctūm, ī. n. *Edict, decree.* Syn.—Jūssūm, māndātūm, dēcrētūm, lēx, plăcĭtūm, præscrīptūm. *See Jussum, Lex.*

Ēdīscŏ, ĭs, ĭdĭcī, ĕrĕ. *To learn.* Aūdĭīt Eūrōtās jūssītque ēdīscĕrĕ laūrōs. V. Syn.—Dīscŏ, āddīscŏ, pērdīscŏ, pērcĭpĭŏ. Phr.—Nōn hæc ārtēs cōntēntă pătērnās Ēdĭdĭcīssĕ fŭĭt. *See Disco.*

Ēdīssĕrŏ, ĕrĭs, ŭī, ērtūm, ĕrĕ. *To explain.* Mĭhĭque hæc ēdīssĕrĕ vērā rŏgāntī. V. Syn.—Ĕlŏquŏr, ēxplĭcŏ, ēnārrŏ.

Ĕdŏ, ĭs, & ēs, ĕdĭt & ēst, ēdī, ēsūm, ĕdĕrĕ, & ēssĕ. *To eat.* Prīămĭdēs Hĕlĕnēn ăvĭdē sī spēctĕt ĕdēntēm. O. Syn.—Cŏmĕdŏ, māndūcŏ, vēscŏr, pāscŏr. Phr.—Ĕpŭlīs, dăpĭbŭs, cĭbīs fāmēm pēllŏ, sŏlŏr, ēxplĕŏ, ārcĕŏ. Mēmbră, cōrpŭs cĭbō, ĕpŭlīs fŏvĕŏ, rĕpărŏ. Dăpĭbūs pāscŏr. Fŭrĭt ārdŏr ĕdēndī. Pōstquam ĕpŭlīs ēxēmptă fămēs. Mĭsĕrōs mōrsū dēpāscĭtŭr ărtūs. *See Fames.*

Ēdŏ, ĭs, ĭdī, ĭtūm, ĕrĕ. *To produce.* Ēt pĕcŭs āntĕ dĭēm pārtūs ēdēbăt ăcērbōs. O. Syn.—Părĭŏ, gīgnŏ, ēdūcŏ. Phr.—Ēdĭdĭt īnnŭmĕrās spĕcĭēs. *To publish.* Syn.—Prōmŏ, ēxprōmŏ, ēmīttŏ, prōfĕrŏ, ēffĕrŏ. *To speak.* Syn.—Ēmĭttŏ, ēlŏquŏr, dīcŏ. *To raise.* Syn.—Ēffĕrŏ, āttōllŏ, ērĭgŏ, ēdūcŏ (ĭs).

Ēdŏmŏ, ās, ŭī, ĭtūm, ārĕ. *To conquer.* Syn.—Dŏmŏ, dŏmĭtŏ, vīncŏ, sŭpĕrŏ, sŭbĭgŏ.

Ēdŭcŏ, ās, āvī, ātūm, ārĕ. *To cultivate, to nourish.* Nōn ăgĕr hīc pōmūm, nōn dūlcēs ēdŭcăt ūvās. O. Syn.—Ālŏ, ēdūcŏ. Phr.—Fēlīcĭbŭs ēdŭcăt hōrtīs. Tērră mălōs hŏmĭnēs nūnc ēdŭcăt. *To instruct.* Syn.—Īnstĭtŭŏ, īnfōrmŏ, ēdŏcĕŏ, ērŭdĭŏ.

Ēdūcō, ĭs, xī, ctūm, ĕrĕ. *To lead forth.* Syn.—Ēxtrăhŏ, ēffĕrŏ, ēmīttŏ, ēxpĕdĭŏ.

Ēffārĭs (*from the verb* Effor *which is not used*), ātŭs sūm, ārī. *To speak.* Syn.—Fārī, prŏfārī, lŏquŏr, dīcŏ, āiŏ, ēlŏquŏr. Phr.—Sīc ōre ēffātŭs ămīco ēst.

Ēffēmĭnŏ, ās, āvī, ātūm, ārĕ. *To weaken, to enervate.* Ōstēntātŭr ănūs, tĭtŭlūmque ēffēmĭnăt ānnī. Syn.—Ēnērvŏ, mōllĭŏ, ēmōllĭŏ, dēbĭlĭtŏ, sōlvŏ, frāngŏ.

Ēffĕrŏ, fērs, ēxtŭlī, ēlātūm, fērrĕ. *To bring or carry forth.* Lōngō căpŭt ēxtŭlĭt āntrō. O. Phr.—Ēxtŭlĭt ēnsēm. Ădȳtīs ēffērt pĕnĕtrālĭbŭs īgnēm.

Ēffĕrŏ, ās, āvī, ātūm, ārĕ. *To render savage.* Syn.—Ăcērbŏ, īrrītŏ.

Ēffērvĕŏ, ēs, bŭī, ērĕ & ĕrĕ. *To boil.* Quŏtĭēs Cȳclōpum ēffērvĕre ĭn āgrōs Vīdĭmŭs ūndāntēm rūptīs fōrnācĭbŭs Aētnām. V. Syn.—Fērvĕŏ, æstŭŏ, ēxæstŭŏ, ērūmpŏ.

Ēffĭcāx, ācĭs. adj. *Powerful, efficacious.* Syn.—Pŏtēns, præstāns, pōllēns, ŏpĕrōsŭs, ŭtĭlĭs.

Ēffĭcĭŏ, ĭs, ēcī, ēctūm, ĕrĕ. *To make, to accomplish.* Īnsŭlă pōrtūm Ēffĭcĭt ōbjēctū lătĕrūm. V. Syn.—Făcĭŏ, præstŏ, ăgŏ, dō, ēdŏ, părĭŏ, pērfĭcĭŏ, pĕrăgŏ, ēxsĕquŏr.

Ēffĭgĭēs, ĭēī. f. *Image, statue.* Ēffĭgĭēs hăbĭtūm nōtī mūtāvĕrăt ōrĭs. L. Syn.—Ĭmāgŏ, sĭmŭlācrūm, spĕcĭēs, sīgnūm. Phr.—Ēffĭgĭēs săcræ Dīvūm. Ēffĭgĭēmquĕ tŏrō lŏcăt.

Ēffīngŏ, ĭs, nxī, ictūm, ĕrĕ. *To represent, to express.* Bīs cōnātŭs ĕrăt cāsūs ēffīngĕre ĭn aūrō. V. Syn.—Ēxprĭmŏ, fīngŏ, fōrmŏ, īnfōrmŏ, rēddŏ.

Ēfflāgĭtŏ, ās, āvī, ātūm, ārĕ. *To ask persistently.* Nōtūmque ēfflāgĭtāt ēnsēm. V. Syn.—Flāgĭtŏ, pĕtŏ, pōscŏ, ēxpōscŏ, rŏgĭtŏ, pōstŭlŏ.

Ēfflŏ, ās, āvī, ātūm, ārĕ. *To breathe.* Quōs īn pēctŏre hăbēnt, quōs ōre'ēt nārĭbūs ēfflānt. O. Syn.—Ēxhālŏ, ēxspīrŏ, ēmīttŏ, mīttŏ, rēddŏ. Phr.—Vītam ēfflāvĭt ănhēlō Pēctŏrĕ.

Ēfflōrĕŏ, ēs, ŭī, ērĕ. *To flourish.* Līlĭă nēc nōstrīs ēfflōrēnt tālĭă cāmpīs. *See Floreo.*

Ēfflŭŏ, ĭs, ūxī, ūxūm, ĕrĕ. *To flow. See Fluo. To escape.* Syn.—Ēlābŏr, lābŏr, ēxcĭdŏ. *To disappear.* Syn.—Ăbĕŏ, cēdŏ, rĕcēdŏ, ēvānēscŏ, fŭgĭŏ.

Ēffŏdĭŏ, ĭs, ōdī, ōssūm, ĕrĕ. *To dig.* Hīc pōrtūs ălĭi ēffŏdĭūnt. V. Syn.—Fŏdĭŏ, ērŭŏ, ēvēllŏ, ēxtrăhŏ, ēgĕrŏ.

Ēffœtŭs, ă, ūm. *Worn out.* Syn.—Fēssŭs, dēfēssŭs, dēbĭlĭs, īnfīrmŭs, īnvălĭdŭs, ægĕr, frāctŭs.

Ēffrīngŏ, ĭs, ēgī, āctūm, ĕrĕ. *To break.* Ēffrēgĭt ēccĕ līmĕn īnfērnī Jŏvĭs. Sen. *See Frango.*

Ēffŭgĭŏ, ĭs, ūgī, ĕrĕ. *To escape.* Ēffŭgĭmūs scŏpŭlōs Ĭthăcæ Lāērtĭă rēgnă. V. Syn.—Fŭgĭŏ, ēvādŏ, ēlābŏr, dēclīnŏ, vītŏ, dēvītŏ, ēvītŏ.

Ēffŭgĭūm, ĭī. n. *Flight, escape.* Quōs īllī fōrs ād pœnās ōb nōstră rĕpōscēnt. V. Syn.—Fŭgă, ăbĭtŭs, ēxĭtŭs.

Ēffūlgĕŏ, ēs, sī, ērĕ & ĕrĕ. *To shine.* Īpsīque īn pūppĭbūs aūrō Dūctōrēs lōnge ēffūlgēnt. V. Syn.—Fūlgĕŏ, ēlūcĕŏ, mĭcŏ, ēmĭcŏ, cŏrūscŏ, splēndĕŏ. Phr.—Ēffūlgēns Lælĭūs ōstrō. *See Fulgeo.*

Ēffūndŏ, ĭs, ūdī, ūsūm, ĕrĕ. *To spread out, to pour.* Cūmque ănĭmă crŭŏr ēst ēffūsŭs ĭn aūrās. O. Syn.—Fūndŏ, prŏfūndŏ, ēmīttŏ, spārgŏ. Phr.—Pēctŏrĕ quēstŭs. Tālīque ēffūndĭtŭr īrā. *To lose.* Syn.—Ābsūmŏ, āmīttŏ.

Ēffūtĭŏ, īs, īvī & ĭī, ītūm, īrĕ. *To babble, to speak lightly.* Ēffūtīrĕ lĕvēs īndīgnă trăgœdĭă vērsūs. H. Syn—Gārrĭŏ. Phr.—Tĕmĕrĕ dīcŏ. Īnānĭă vērbă fūndŏ, prōfĕrŏ.

Ĕgēnŭs, ă, ūm. *Needing, wanting, needy.* Ōmnĭbūs ēxhaūstōs jām cāsĭbūs, ōmnĭum ĕgēnōs. V. Syn.—Cărēns, ĕgēns, cāssŭs, nūdŭs, īndĭgēns, īndĭgŭs, ĭnōps, ōrbātŭs, ōrbŭs, nūdātŭs, ēxsōrs, ēxpērs.

Ĕgĕŏ, ēs, ŭī, ērĕ. *To be in need of.* Syn.—Īndĭgĕŏ, pōscŏ, pōstŭlŏ, rĕquīrŏ, rĕpōscŏ. *To lack. See Careo.*

Ēgĕrŏ, ĕrĭs, ēssī, ēstūm, ĕrĕ. *To cast out, to reject.* Rĕsĕrātō pēctŏrĕ dīrās Ēgĕrĕre īndĕ dăpēs. Syn.—Ēxtrăhŏ, ēxpēllŏ, ējĭcĭŏ, ējēctŏ, rējēctŏ, ēffūndŏ, ēmīttŏ, ērŭŏ, vŏmŏ, ērūctŏ, ēxāntlŏ. *To carry away.* Syn.—Ēffĕrŏ.

Ĕgēstās, ātĭs. f. *Want, poverty.* Dūrĭs ūrgēns īn rēbŭs ĕgēstās. V. Syn.—Īnŏpĭă, pēnūrĭă, paūpērtās, paūpĕrĭēs. Phr.—Tūrpĭs ĕgēstās. Ācrĭs ĕgēstās. Lōngæ dīra ōbsĭdĭōnĭs ĕgēstās. Rēs āngūstă dŏmī.

Ĕgŏ, mĕī. pers. pron. *I, myself.* Īlle ĕgŏ quī quōndām grăcĭlī mŏdŭlātŭs ăvēnā. V. Syn.—Ĕgŏmĕt, īpsĕ, nōs. Phr.—Īpse ĕgŏ. Īpsĕ ĕgŏmĕt.

Ēgrĕdĭŏr, ĕrĭs, ēssŭs sūm, ī. *To go forth, to go out.* Ēgrĕdĭtŭr fērrōquĕ mănūs ārmātă bĭdēntī. V. Syn.—Ābscēdŏ, ēxcēdŏ, ēxĕŏ, ăbĕŏ. Phr.—Grēssūs rĕmŏvētĕ prŏfānī. Pĕdēm sī fōrtĕ tŭlīssĕt. Rŭūnt portīs. Sē līmĭnĕ prōfērt. *See Abeo.*

Ēgrĕgĭē. adv. *Excellently, perfectly.* Syn.—Bĕnĕ, āptē, rēctē, laūtē, pērfēctē, prǣclārē.

Ēgrĕgĭŭs, ă, ūm. *Excellent, remarkable.* Āddĕ tŏt ēgrĕgĭās ūrbēs ŏpĕrūmquĕ lăbōrēm. V. Syn.—Ēxĭmĭŭs, ēxēllēns, prǣstāns, cōnspĭcŭŭs, īnsīgnĭs. Phr.—Pĭĕtātĕ vĕl ārmīs Ēgrĕgĭŭs. Ēgrĕgĭūm fōrmā jŭvĕnēm. *Fine, noble.* Syn.—Nōbĭlĭs, dĕcōrŭs, pūlchĕr, prǣstāns.

Ēheū. interj. *Alas!* Ēheū fŭgācēs Pōstŭmĕ, Pōstŭmĕ! H. Syn.—Heū, prōh, heī.

Ēiă. interj. *Come now.* Ēia ăgĕ, rūmpĕ mŏrās. V. Syn.—Āgĕ, ăgĕdūm.

Ējĭcĭŏ, ĭs, ēcī, ēctūm, ĕrĕ. *To cast out, to reject.* Spūmās ējēcĭt ăhēnō Īgnĭs. O. Syn.—Ējēctŏ, ēgĕrŏ, ēmīttŏ, ēffūndŏ, ēxspŭŏ, ăgŏ, dējĭcĭŏ, ēxpēllŏ, ēxtrūdŏ, dētrūdŏ.

Ējŭlŏ, ās, āvī, ātūm, ārĕ. *To lament.* Syn.—Lāmēntŏr, ŭlŭlŏ, lūgĕŏ, flĕŏ, vōcĭfĕrŏr, gĕmŏ, dēplōrŏ. *See Fleo, Queror.*

Ēlābŏr, ĕrĭs, āpsŭs sūm, ī. *To slip by, to escape.* Māxĭmŭs hīc flēxū sĭnŭōso ēlābĭtŭr ānguĭs. V. Syn.—Ēffŭgĭŏ, ēvādŏ, ēxcēdŏ, ēxcĭdŏ, dēclīnŏ, vītŏ.

Ēlăbōrŏ, ās, āvī, ātūm, ārĕ. *To labor hard, to strive hard for.* Nōn Sĭcŭlǣ dăpēs Dūlcem ēlăbōrābūnt săpōrēm. H. Syn.—Ēxcŏlŏ, ēxpŏlĭŏ, cūrŏ.

Ēlĕgāns, āntĭs. adj. *Choice, fine, elegant.* Nēc sānē nĭmĭs ēlĕgāntĕ līnguā. Cat. Syn.—Cōncīnnŭs, pŏlītŭs, ēxcūltŭs, ōrnātŭs, vĕnūstŭs.

Ēlĕgāntĭă, ǣ. f. *Elegance, grace.* Syn.—Cūltŭs, ōrnātŭs, dĕcŏr, grātĭă, vĕnūstās, lĕpŏr.

Ĕlĕgĭă, ǣ. f. *Elegy.* Syn.—Ĕlĕgēĭă, ĕlĕgīdĭŏn (n.), ĕlĕgī (m.). Phr.—Flēbĭlĕ cărmĕn. Lūgŭbrēs mŏdī. Īmpărēs nŭmĕrī. Cūltīs aūt ĕlēgĭă cŏmīs. Neū mĭsĕrābĭlēs Dēcāntēs ĕlĕgōs. Præcĭpĕ lūgŭbrēs Cāntūs. Quīs tămĕn ēxĭgŭōs ĕlĕgōs ēmīsĕrĭt aūctŏr. Vērsĭbŭs īmpărĭtĕr jūnctīs.

Ĕlĕmēntă, ōrūm. n. *Elements.* Syn.—Prīncĭpĭă, prīmōrdĭă, sēmĭnă, cōrpūscŭlă, pārtĭcŭlæ.

Ĕlĕphās, āntĭs, & Ĕlĕphāntŭs, ī. m. *Elephant.* Sīc Lĭbўcūs dēnsīs ĕlĕphās ōpprēssŭs ăb ārmīs. L. Syn.—Bārrŭs, bēllŭă. Phr.—Bēllŭă, fĕră Gætūlă, Lĭbўcă. Tūrrītō bēllŭă dōrsō. Bēllāntĭă mōnstră.

Ēlĕvŏ, ās, āvī, ātūm, ārĕ. *To elevate.* Ēlĕvăt hūnc plūmā, squāmīs hūnc fābŭlă vēstĭt. Syn.—Lĕvŏ, tōllŏ, ēxtōllŏ. *To weaken.* Syn.—Dēprĭmŏ, āttĕnŭŏ, dētrăhŏ, cārpŏ, mĭnŭŏ, īmmĭnŭŏ.

Ēlĭcĭŏ, ĭs, ŭī, ĭtūm, ĕrĕ. *To draw out, to allure.* Syn.—Trăhŏ, ēxtrăhŏ, ēdūcŏ, dēdūcŏ, ērŭŏ, ēxprōmŏ.

Ēlīdŏ, ĭs, sī, sūm, ĕrĕ. *To strike, to drive out.* Cōmplēxōs ŭtĭnām Sўmplēgădĕs ēlīsīssēnt. O. Syn.—Frāngŏ, ērŭŏ, pēllŏ.

Ēlĭgŏ, ĭs, ēgī, ēctūm, ĕrĕ. *To elect, to choose.* Pūgnāndī tēmpŏră mēcūm Ēlĭgĭt Ātrīdēs. O. Syn.—Lĕgŏ, dēlĭgŏ, sēlĭgŏ, ōptŏ. Phr.—Ĕquōs nŭmĕrō pătĕr ēlĭgĭt ōmnī. Cōrpŏră præcĭpŭē mātrūm lĕgăt.

Ēlīmĭnŏ, ās, āvī, ātūm, ārĕ. *To make go out, to chase.* Syn.—Ējĭcĭŏ, ēxpēllŏ, ēxclūdŏ.

Ēlīmŏ, ās, āvī, ātūm, ārĕ. *To polish.* Grăcĭlēs ēx ærĕ cătēnās Ēlīmăt. O. Syn.—Pŏlĭŏ, ēxpŏlĭŏ, pērpŏlĭŏ.

Ēlŏquēns, ēntĭs. adj. *Eloquent.* Syn.—Fācūndŭs, dĭsērtŭs, dōctĭlŏquŭs. Phr.—Ēlŏquĭō pōllēns. Flēxănĭmō sērmōnĕ pŏtēns. Fāndī pĕrītŭs. Līnguā bŏnŭs. Pōllēns flūmĭnĕ līnguæ. *See Eloquentia.*

Ēlŏquēntĭă, æ. f. *Eloquence.* Cĕlĕbrātă vărĭē cūjŭs ēlŏquēntĭă Dŏmī fŏrīsquĕ clārŭĭt. Syn.—Ēlŏquĭūm, fācūndĭă. Phr.—Dīcēndī vīs. Ēlŏquĭī nĭtŏr. Tōrrēns dīcēndī cōpĭă. Glōrĭă fāndī. Ōrīs fācūndĭă cūltī.

Ēlūcĕŏ, ēs, xī, ērĕ. *To shine.* Ēlūcēnt ălĭae ēt fūlgōrĕ cŏrūscānt. V. Syn.—Lūcĕŏ, rĕlūcĕŏ, ēnĭtĕŏ, ēmĭcŏ. *To be distinguished.* Syn.—Ēmĭnĕŏ, ēxcēllŏ, ēnĭtĕŏ.

Ēlūdŏ, ĭs, sī, sūm, ĕrĕ. *To avoid.* Īllĕ cĭtō mōtū răpĭdōs ēlūdĕrĕ cæstūs. *See Vito. To deceive.* Syn.—Dēcĭpĭŏ, fāllŏ.

Ēlŭŏ, ĭs, ŭī, ūtūm, ĕrĕ. *To wash. See Lavo. To efface.* Syn.—Āblŭŏ, dēlĕŏ.

Ēlŭvĭēs, ēī. f. *Deluge.* Ēlŭvĭē mōns ēst dēdūctŭs ĭn æquŏr. O. Syn.—Dīlŭvĭūm, dīlŭvĭēs.

Ēmānŏ, ās, āvī, ātūm, ārĕ. *To flow forth.* Syn.—Mānŏ, ēfflŭŏ.

Ēmēndŏ, ās, āvī, ātūm, ārĕ. *To amend, to correct.* Cūltŭs ĕt īn pōmīs sūccōs ēmēndăt ăcērbōs. O. Syn.—Cōrrĭgŏ, cāstīgŏ.

Ēmēntĭŏr, īrĭs, ītŭs sūm, īrī. *To feign, to pretend.* Syn.—Mēntĭŏr, fīngŏ, cōnfīngŏ, sĭmŭlŏ.

Ēmērgŏ, ĭs, sī, sūm, ĕrĕ. *To emerge.* Syn.—Ēvādŏ, sūrgŏ, ēxsūrgŏ, ēxĕŏ, ēxstŏ, ēxŏrĭŏr, ŏrĭŏr.

Ēmĭcŏ, ās, ŭī, ātūm, ārĕ. *To spring forth, to dart forth.* Pēr mīllĕ fŏrāmĭnă sānguĭs Ēmĭcŭĭt. O. Syn.—Ēxsĭlĭŏ, fĕrŏr, rŭŏ, ērūmpŏ, prōvŏlŏ. *To shine. See Fulgeo.*

Ēmĭgrŏ, ās, āvī, ātūm, ārĕ. *To emigrate.* Tū, dūctōr pŏpŭlī lōnge ēmīgrāntĭs Ăpōllŏ. Syn.—Mĭgrŏ, dēmĭgrŏ, dīscēdŏ, ēxcēdŏ, ēxĕŏ, ēxsŭlŏ. Phr.—Pătrĭāque ēxcēdĕrĕ tērrā.

Ēmĭnĕŏ, ēs, ŭī, ērĕ. *To stand forth.* Fēlīx ĭn ăpērtīs ēmĭnĕt ārvīs ārbōs. O. Syn.—Ēxstŏ, sŭpĕrŏ, sŭpĕrēmĭnĕŏ, āssūrgŏ. Fig.—*To excel.* Syn.—Prǣstŏ, ēxcēllŏ.

Ēmĭnŭs. adv. *From afar off.* Ādvĕnĭt ēt rĭgĭdā Drўŏpēn fĕrĭt ēmĭnŭs hāstā. V. Syn.—Lōngē, lōngĭŭs, prŏcŭl.

Ēmīttŏ, ĭs, īsī, īssūm, ĕrĕ. *To send forth, to send out.* Ēmīttītquĕ Nŏtūm: mădĭdīs Nŏtŭs ādvŏlăt ālīs. O. Syn.—Mīttŏ. *To hurl.* Syn.—Mīttŏ, jăcĕŏ, tōrquĕŏ, cōnjĭcĭŏ.

Ĕmŏ, ĭs, ēmī, ēmptūm, ĕrĕ. *To buy.* Ōmnĭă, Cāstŏr, ĕmīs, sīc fīĕt ŭt ōmnĭă vēndās. M. Syn.—Părŏ, cōmpărŏ, mērcŏr.

Ēmōllĭŏ, īs, īvī & ĭī, ītūm, īrĕ. *To soften, to soothe.* Syn.—Mōllĭŏ, plācŏ, mītĭgŏ, mūlcĕŏ. Phr.—Ēmōllīt gēntēs clēmēntĭă cœlī.

Ēmŏlŭmēntūm, ī. n. *Profit, gain.* Prǣmĭă nūnc ălĭa ātque ēmŏlŭmēntă dŏcēmŭs. J. Syn.—Lŭcrūm, cōmmŏdūm, ūtĭlĭtās, bŏnūm.

Ēmŏvĕŏ, ēs, ōvī, ōtūm, ērĕ. *To move from its place.* Syn.—Mŏvĕŏ, ēmōlĭŏr, ēdūcŏ, sūbdūcŏ. Phr.—Ēmōtī cārdĭnĕ pōstēs.

Ēn. adv. *Behold.* Hōs tĭbĭ dānt călămōs, ēn āccĭpĕ, Mūsǣ. V. Syn.—Ēccĕ.

Ēnārrŏ, ās, āvī, ātūm, ārĕ. *To relate.* Syn.—Nārrŏ, dīcŏ.

Ēnērvŏ, ās, āvī, ātūm, ārĕ. *To weaken.* Syn.—Dēbĭlĭtŏ, mōllĭŏ, frāngŏ, ēffēmĭnŏ. Phr.—Ēnērvānt ănĭmōs cĭthărǣ.

Ĕnĭm. conj. *For.* Syn.—Nām, nāmquĕ, ĕtĕnĭm, quīppĕ.

Ēnĭtĕŏ, ēs, ŭī, ērĕ. *To shine.* Ēt quāntūm făcĭlēs ēnĭtŭērĕ dĕǣ. Tib. Syn.—Nĭtĕŏ.

Ēnōdĭs, ĭs, ĕ. *Without knots.* Āt rūrsūm ēnōdēs rĕsĕcāntŭr. V. Syn.—Lǣvĭs, lǣvĭgātŭs. Phr.—Nōdīs cărēns.

Ēnōrmĭs, ĭs, ĕ. *Enormous, immense.* Syn.—Īmmānĭs, īmmēnsŭs, pōrtēntōsŭs. *Irregular.* Syn.—Ābnōrmĭs.

Ēnsĭs, ĭs. m. *Sword.* Vāgīna ērĭpĭt ēnsēm Fūlmĭnĕūm. V. Syn.—Glădĭŭs, fērrūm, mūcrŏ, cūspĭs. Phr.—Glădĭī mūcrŏ. Fērri ăcĭēs. Hŭmĕrō sĭmŭl ēxŭĭt ēnsēm. Rēctō glădĭūm mūcrōnĕ tĕnēntēm. Mĭcăt ǣrĕŭs ēnsĭs.

Ēnŭclĕō, ās, āvī, ātūm, ārĕ. *To take out the kernel.* Fig.—*To explain.* Syn.—Ēxpōnŏ, pāndŏ, ēxplĭcŏ, ēnārrŏ, ăpĕrĭŏ, ēnōdŏ.

Ēnŭmĕrŏ, ās, āvī, ātūm, ārĕ. *To enumerate.* Ēnŭmĕrăt mīlēs vūlnĕră, pāstŏr ŏvēs. Pr. Syn.—Nŭmĕrŏ, dīnŭmĕrŏ, pērcēnsĕŏ, rĕcēnsĕŏ.

Ēnūntĭŏ, ās, āvī, ātūm, ārĕ. *To announce.* Syn.—Dīcŏ, prōfĕrŏ, ēlŏquŏr, ēxprĭmŏ, prōnūntĭŏ.

Ĕŏ, īs, īvī, ĭtūm, īrĕ. *To go.* Deīnde ĕŏ dōrmītūm, nōn sōllĭcĭtūs mĭhĭ quōd crās. H. Syn.—Īncēdŏ, prōcēdŏ, grădĭŏr, īngrĕdĭŏr, prōgrĕdĭŏr, tēndŏ, vādŏ, prŏfĭcīscŏr, fĕrŏr, pērgŏ, pĕtŏ, ădĕŏ. Phr.—Vĭām tēndŏ, cārpŏ. Ĭtēr tĕnĕŏ. Grēssūm tēndŏ. Grēssūs īnfĕrŏ. Pĕdēm fĕrŏ. Quĭbūs vēnīstĭs ăb ōrīs. Quōvĕ tĕnētĭs ĭtĕr.

Ĕpĭgrāmmă, ătĭs. n. *Epigram, epitaph.* Dō tĭbĭ naūmăchĭām, tū dās ĕpĭgrāmmătă nōbīs. M. Syn.—Cārmĕn, tĭtŭlŭs, īnscrīptĭŏ, ēlŏgĭūm. Phr.—Sāxūm nōmĭnĕ sīgnātūm. Nōmĭnă sāxo īncīsă. Tŭmŭlō sŭpĕrāddĭtă vērbă.

Ĕpīstŏlă, ǣ. f. *Letter, epistle.* Ānxĭă prǣcĭpĭtī vēnīssĕt ĕpīstŏlă pēnnā. J. Syn.—Lĭttĕrǣ, scrīptūm, ĕpīstŏlĭūm, chārtă, lĭbēllŭs, tăbēllǣ. Phr.—Mūtă vōx ābsēntĭūm. Scrīptō mīssă sălūs. *See Litterae.*

Ĕpŭlǣ, ārūm. f. *Viands, food.* Tūrgĭdŭs hīc ĕpŭlīs ātque ālbō vēntrĕ lăvātŭr. Pers. Syn.—Dăpēs, cĭbŭs, ēscă, pābŭlūm. *See Cibus.*

Ĕquĕs, ĭtĭs. m. *Horseman.* Trēs ĕquĭtūm nŭmĕrō tūrmǣ. V. Phr.—Frēnātŏr ĕquōrūm. Ĕquōrūm dūctŏr. Flēctĕrĕ dōctūs ĕquōs. Frēnātīs lūcēnt ĭn ĕquīs. *See Equito.*

Ĕquĭdēm. adv. *Indeed, truly.* Syn.—Nǣ, cērtē, sānē.

Ĕquĭtātŭs, ūs. m. *Cavalry.* Jāmque ădĕo ēxĭĕrăt pōrtīs ĕquĭtātŭs ăpērtīs. V. Syn.—Ĕquĭtēs, tūrmǣ, ālǣ. Phr.—Ālĭpĕdēs tūrmǣ. Quīsquĕ mĕrēbăt ĕquō.

Ĕquĭtŏ, ās, āvī, ātūm, ārĕ. *To ride horseback.* Tēr cīrcum āstāntēm lǣvōs ĕquĭtāvĭt ĭn ōrbēs. V. Phr.—Ĕquō ūtŏr, vĕhŏr, vēctŏr. Ĕquūm ăgĭtŏ. Ĕquī ōră frēnīs tōrquĕŏ. Dōrsō fērtŭr ĕquī.

Ĕquŭs, ī. m. *Horse.* Hīnc bēllātŏr ĕquīs cāmpō sēse ārdŭŭs īnfērt. V. Syn.—Cōrnĭpēs, quădrŭpēs, sŏnĭpēs, căbāllŭs, mānnŭs. Phr.—Frēnă rĕcūsāns. Āspĕr frēnă pătī. Cārpĕrĕ grāmĕn ĕquōs. Ād tērrām dēflūxĭt ĕquīs.

Ērādīcŏ, ās, āvī, ātūm, ārĕ. *To uproot.* Dī te ērādīcēnt, ĭtă mē mĭsĕrām tērrĭtās. Ter. Syn.—Ērŭŏ, ēvēllŏ, ēxstīrpŏ.

Ērādŏ, ĭs, sī, sūm, ĕrĕ. *To strike out, to destroy.* Syn.—Rādŏ, ēxpūngŏ, ēvēllŏ.

Ērgā. prep. *Towards.* Syn.—Vērsŭs, ĭn, ăd.

Ērgāstŭlūm, ī. n. *Prison.* Syn.—Cārcĕr.

Ērgŏ. adv. *Therefore.* Fōrtūnātĕ sĕnēx, ērgō tŭă rūră mănēbūnt. V. Syn.—Ĭgĭtŭr, ĭtăquĕ, ĭtă, ĭdĕō, quārē, īdcīrcō, quāprōptĕr, quōcīrcā.

Ērĭgŏ, ĭs, ēxī, ēctūm, ĕrĕ. *To set up, to raise.* Ātquĕ sōlō prōcērās ērĭgĭt ālnōs. V. Syn.—Tōllŏ, āttōllŏ, ēxtōllŏ, ēffĕrŏ, ēvĕhŏ, ēxcĭtŏ, ēdūcŏ, rĕlĕvŏ. Phr.—Ād cœlūm dūcŏ. Ād sīdĕră tōllĕrĕ pālmās. Cœlōque āttōllĕrĕ mōlēm. *To reanimate.* Syn.—Tōllŏ, ēffĕrŏ.

Ērĭpĭŏ, ĭs, ŭī, ēptūm, ĕrĕ. *To snatch away, to tear away.* Ērĭpĭt hærēntēs ādvērsō līttŏrĕ nāvēs. H. Syn.—Răpĭŏ, ābrĭpĭŏ, prærĭpĭŏ, tōllŏ, ădĭmŏ, ēxtōrquĕŏ, dētrăhŏ, sūbdūcŏ, āmŏvĕŏ, prīvŏ, spŏlĭŏ, nūdŏ, ēxŭŏ. Phr.—Ērĭpĕ lētō. Mōrtālēs ērĭpĭām fōrmām. Ērĭpĭūnt tĕnĕbræ lūcēm.

Ērŏgĭtŏ, ās, āvī, ātūm, ārĕ. *To ask earnestly.* Mīrātŭs ĕquūm, nōmēnquĕ dĕcūsquĕ Ērŏgĭtăt. Syn.—Rŏgŏ, rŏgĭtŏ, ēfflāgĭtŏ.

Ērŏgŏ, ās, āvī, ātūm, ārĕ. *To give.* Syn.—Dō, dōnŏ, lārgĭŏr, trĭbŭŏ, dīstrĭbŭŏ, īmpērtĭŏr.

Ērrŏ, ās, āvī, ātūm, ārĕ. *To wander.* Mīllĕ mĕæ Sĭcŭlīs ērrānt īn mōntĭbŭs āgnæ. V. Syn.—Ăbērrŏ, pĕrērrŏ, dīscūrrŏ, văgŏr. Phr.—Ērrăt ĭn ārmīs. *To err.* Syn.—Dēcĭpĭŏ, fāllŏr, ŏbērrŏ.

Ērrŏr, ōrĭs. m. *A wandering about.* Pālāntēs ērrōr cērtō dē trāmĭtĕ pēllĭt. H. Syn.—Flēxŭs, āmbāgēs, mæāndĕr, fāllācĭă.

Ērŭbēscŏ, ĭs, ŭī, ĕrĕ. *To grow red.* Sāxăquĕ rōrātīs ērŭbŭīssĕ rŏsīs. O. Syn.—Rŭbĕŏ. *To be ashamed.* Syn.—Rŭbĕŏ.

Ērūctŏ, ās, āvī, ātūm, ārĕ. *To belch forth.* Syn.—Ējēctŏ, ējĭcĭŏ, vŏmŏ, ēvŏmŏ. *See Ejicio.*

Ērūmpŏ, ĭs, rūpī, ūptūm, ĕrĕ. *To break forth.* Ērūmpūnt pōrtīs, cōncūrrĭtŭr. V. Syn.—Rŭŏ, præcĭpĭtŏ, ēxsĭlĭŏ, ēxĕŏ, ēlūctŏr. Phr.—Stўgĭīs ērūmpĕrĕ nītŏr ăb ōrīs. O. Ērūmpĕrĕ nūbēm Ārdēbānt.

Ērŭŏ, ĭs, ŭī, ŭtūm, ĕrĕ. *To dig out.* Āntīquāsquĕ dŏmōs ăvĭūm cūm stīrpĭbŭs īmīs Ērŭĭt. V. Syn.—Ērādīcŏ, ēxstīrpŏ, ēvēllŏ. *To bring forth to light.* Syn.—Ēffĕrŏ, pāndŏ, ēxsĕrŏ, dētĕgŏ, ēmīttŏ.

Ērvūm, ī. n. *A kind of pulse like the vetch.* (*See Appendix under list of Trees, etc.*)

Ēscă, æ. f. *Food, nourishment.* Mĕmŏr īllĭŭs ēscæ Quæ sīmplēx ōlīm tĭbī sēdĕrĭt. H. Syn.—Cĭbŭs, ălĭmēntūm, nūtrīmēntūm, ĕpŭlæ, pābŭlūm.

Ēssĕdūm, ī. n. *Gallic war-chariot. See Currus.*

Ēsŭrĭō, īs, īvī & ĭī, ītūm, īrĕ. *To be hungry.* Syn.—Fămē prĕmŏr, cōnfĭcĭŏr. Phr.—Cōllēctă fătīgăt ĕdēndī Ēx lōngō răbĭēs. V. Lēntā dēpĕrĭt īllĕ fămē. *See Fames.*

Ĕt. conj. *And.* Syn.—Āc, ătquĕ, -quĕ. Phr.—Nēc nōn, nēc nōn ĕt. Rēmō cūm frātrĕ Quĭrīnŭs. *Also.* Syn.—Ĕtĭăm, quŏquĕ.

Ĕtĕnĭm. conj. *For.* Syn.—Ĕnĭm, năm, nāmquĕ, quīppĕ.

Ĕtĭăm. conj. *Even, also.* Syn.—Āc, ĕt, quŏquĕ, părĭtĕr, quīn, īmmō, sŭpĕr, īnsŭpĕr.

Ētsī. conj. *Although.* Syn.—Lĭcĕt, quămvīs, quămquăm.

Eūgĕ. interj. *Fine! Well done!* Syn.—Bĕnĕ, pūlchrē, rēctē, prŏbē.

Ēvādŏ, ĭs, sī, sūm, ĕrĕ. *To escape.* Ēxsŭpĕrātquĕ jŭgūm sīlvăque ēvādĭt ŏpācă. V. Syn.—Fŭgĭŏ, aūfŭgĭŏ, ēxcēdŏ, ēxĕŏ, ērūmpŏ.

Ēvălĕŏ, ēs, ŭī, ērĕ. *To be able.* Āt nōn Dārdănĭæ mĕdĭcārī cūspĭdĭs īctūm Ēvălŭĭt. V. Syn.—Pōssūm, vălĕŏ. *See Possum.*

Ēvānēscŏ, ĭs, ŭī, ĕrĕ. *To vanish.* Ēt prŏcŭl īn tĕnŭem ēx ŏcŭlīs ēvānŭĭt aūrăm. V. Syn.—Vānēscŏ, ăbĕŏ, rĕcēdŏ, dīscēdŏ, fŭgĭŏ, īntērcĭdŏ. Phr.—Ŏcŭlōs fŭgĭŏ. Tĕnĕbrīs mē cōndŏ. Ēx ŏcŭlīs fŭgĭŏ. Spīssīs nōctīs sē cōndĭdĭt ūmbrīs. Tĕnŭēsquĕ rĕcēssĭt īn aūrās.

Ēvĕhŏ, ĭs, ēxī, ēctūm, ĕrĕ. *To carry.* Īn pĕlăgūs răpĭdīs ēvĕhĭt āmnĭs ăquīs. Tib. Syn.—Vĕhŏ, ēffĕrŏ, prōmŏvĕŏ. *To raise up. See Extollo.*

Ēvēllŏ, ĭs, ēllī & ūlsī, ūlsūm, ĕrĕ. *To tear out.* Nēquīcquăm cænō cŭpĭēns ēvēllĕrĕ plāntăm. H. Syn.—Vēllŏ, cōnvēllŏ, āvēllŏ, rĕvēllŏ, ēffŏdĭŏ, ērŭŏ, ēxstīrpŏ, ēxtrăhŏ. Phr.—Rādīcĭbŭs ērŭtă pīnŭs Cōncĭdĭt. Tēlūmque ālta āb rādīcĕ rĕvēllĭt. Rūptīs rādīcĭbŭs ārbŏr Vēllĭtŭr. Tēlăquĕ cōnfīxīs cērtănt ēvēllĕrĕ mēmbrīs.

Ēvĕnĭŏ, īs, ēnī, ēntūm, īrĕ. *To go out of.* Syn.—Ēxstŏ, ēmērgŏ. *To happen.* Syn.—Fīŏ, cōntīngŏ, ōbtīngŏ, āccĭdŏ. Phr.—Nōn hæc sĭnĕ nūmĭnĕ Dīvūm Ēvĕnĭūnt. *It happens (impers).* Syn.—Fĭt, āccĭdĭt, cōntīngĭt, ōbtīngĭt.

Ēvēntŭs, ūs. m. *Event, result.* Quīsquĭs ăb ēvēntū fāctă nŏtāndă pŭtăt. O. Syn.—Cāsŭs, sōrs, ēxĭtĭūm, ēffēctŭs, fōrtūnă. Phr.—Īncērtī rērum ēvēntūs. Ēvēntūs bēllī vărĭōs.

Ēvērtŏ, ĭs, tī, sūm, ĕrĕ. *To overturn, to destroy.* Aūt tēmpēstīvăm sīlvīs ēvērtĕrĕ pīnūm. V. Syn.—Vērtŏ, sūbvērtŏ, dēstrŭŏ, dīrŭŏ, ērŭŏ, prōrŭŏ, sūbrŭŏ, ēxcĭdŏ, āccĭdŏ, dēmōlĭŏr, ēxscīndŏ, stērnŏ, prōstērnŏ, quătĭŏ, cōncŭtĭŏ, dējĭcĭŏ, dētūrbŏ, ēxtūrbŏ, pērdŏ, pēssūmdŏ, frāngŏ, āfflīgŏ. Phr.—Aēquārĕ sŏlō. Ēvērtēre ăb hŭmō mœnĭă. Præcĭpĭtēmquĕ dĕdĭt tŭrrīm. Stērnītque ā cūlmĭnĕ Trōjām. Hās ēvērtĭt ŏpēs.

Ēvĭgĭlŏ, ās, āvī, ātŭm, ārĕ. *To watch.* Ēt dŭcĕ stānt ăcĭēs ēvĭgĭlāntĕ sŭō. Cat. Syn.—Vĭgĭlŏ.

Ēvīncŏ, ĭs, īcī, īctŭm, ĕrĕ. *To conquer. See Vinco. To convince.* Syn.—Prŏbŏ, dēmōnstrŏ.

Ēvītābĭlĭs, ĭs, ĕ. *Avoidable.* Frēnă dăbāt; dāntem ēvītābĭlĕ tēlŭm Cōnsĕquĭtŭr. O. Syn.—Vītābĭlĭs, ēlūctābĭlĭs.

Ēvŏcŏ, ās, āvī, ātŭm, ārĕ. *To call forth, to summon.* Ănĭmās hāc ēvŏcăt Ōrcō Mērcŭrĭŭs. V. Syn.—Vŏcŏ, āccērsŏ, cĭĕŏ, āccĭŏ, ēxcĭŏ, ēxcĭtŏ, ēxsŭscĭtŏ. Phr.—Ăvōs ătăvōsquĕ sĕpūlcrīs Ēvŏcăt. Mānēsquĕ sĕpūlcrīs Ēlĭcĭt. *See Resuscito.*

Ēvŏlŏ, ās, āvī, ātŭm, ārĕ. *To fly away.* Mădĭdīs Nŏtŭs ēvŏlăt ālīs. Syn.—Vŏlŏ, ēffŭgĭŏ, ēxĕŏ, ērūmpŏ. *See Fugio.*

Ēvōlvŏ, ĭs, vī, & ŏlŭī, ŏlūtŭm, ĕrĕ. *To roll out, to roll forth.* Nūdīs ēvōlvūnt sāxă lăcērtīs. L. Syn.—Vōlvŏ, prōvōlvŏ, dēvōlvŏ, dējĭcĭŏ, dētūrbŏ. Phr.—Jāctāsque ēvōlvĕrĕ sīlvās. *To relate, to set forth.* Syn.—Ēxplĭcŏ, ēxpōnŏ, pāndŏ, rĕtĕgŏ, ăpĕrĭŏ, ēxprōmŏ, ēdŏ. *See Narro. To draw out.* Syn.—Ērŭŏ, ēlĭcĭŏ, ēxtrăhŏ, ēdūcŏ, ēxprōmŏ, ēxcŭtĭŏ, ēxtrūdŏ. *To meditate.* Syn.—Vōlvŏ, mĕdĭtŏr.

Ēvŏmŏ, ĭs, ŭī, ĭtŭm, ĕrĕ. *To vomit forth.* Syn.—Vŏmŏ, ēgĕrŏ, ērūctŏ, ēmīttŏ, ējĭcĭŏ.

Ēxăcŭŏ, ĭs, ŭī, ūtŭm, ĕrĕ. *To sharpen.* Ēxăcŭūnt ălĭī vāllōs. V. Phr.—Dēntēsquĕ Săbēllĭcŭs ēxăcŭĭt sŭs. Spīcŭlăque ēxăcŭūnt rōstrīs. *See Acuo. To excite.* Syn.—Ēxcĭtŏ, āccēndŏ.

Ēxæquŏ, ās, āvī, ātŭm, ārĕ. *To render smooth. To render equal.* Syn.—Aēquŏ, ădæquŏ. *To resemble.* Syn.—Aēquŏ, æquĭpărŏ, āccēdŏ. *See Similis.*

Ēxăgĭtŏ, ās, āvī, ātŭm, ārĕ. *To pursue.* Ēxăgĭtānt ēt lār ēt tūrbă Dĭānĭă fūrēs. O. Syn.—Ăgĭtŏ, ăgŏ, īnsĕquŏr, sēctŏr, īnsēctŏr, ūrgĕŏ, īnstŏ, pērsĕquŏr. Phr.—Ēxăgĭtārĕ fĕrās. *To torment.* Syn.—Ăgĭtŏ, jāctŏ, īnsēctŏr, ēxērcĕŏ, vēxŏ, tūrbŏ.

Ēxāmĕn, ĭnĭs. n. *Swarm of bees.* Ūt cūm prīmă nŏvī dūcēnt ēxāmĭnă rēgēs. V. Syn.—Āgmĕn. Phr.—Făvīs ēmīssă jŭvēntūs. Pēndĕt ĕt ēxāmēn rāmō frōndēntĕ. Āpēs ēxāmĭnă cōndēnt. Īncērtă vŏlānt cælōque ēxāmĭnă lūdūnt.

Ēxāmĭnŏ, ās, āvī, ātŭm, ārĕ. *To examine, to weigh.* Tēmpŭs ĕrăt quō Lībră părēs ēxāmĭnăt hōrās. L. Syn.—Lībrŏ, pōndĕrŏ, æquŏ, ēxæquŏ.

Ēxănĭmātŭs, ă, ūm. *Out of breath.* Ēxănĭmātă sĕquēns īmpīngĕrĕt āgmĭnă mūrīs. V. Syn.—Ănhēlŭs, ănhēlāns, ēxănĭmĭs.

Ēxănĭmŭs, ă, ūm. *Inanimate.* Ēxănĭmūmque aūrō cōrpūs vēndēbăt Ăchīllēs. V. Syn.—Ēxsānguĭs, mōrtŭŭs. *Half-dead with fright.* Syn.—Sēmiănĭmĭs, āmēns. Phr.—Ēxănĭmēs trĕpĭdārĕ.

Ēxănĭmō, ās, āvī, ātūm, ārĕ. *To deprive of life.* Syn.—Ēnĕcō. *See Occido.*

Ēxārdĕō, ēs, sī, sūm, ērĕ. *To take fire, to burn.* Īlĭŏn ēxārsĭt tōtūmque ābscēssĭt ĭn īgnēs. V. Fig. Syn.—Ārdĕō, ārdēscō, ēxārdēscō, īnflāmmŏr. Phr.—Dŏlŏr ēxārsĭt ĭn īmīs Ōssĭbŭs.

Ēxārmō, ās, āvī, ātūm, ārĕ. *To disarm.* Ēxārmātquĕ dŭcēm. Phr.—Ārmă dētrăhō, răpĭō, aūfĕrō. Ārmīs nūdō, ēxŭō, spŏlĭō.

Ēxaūdĭō, īs, īvī & ĭī, ītūm, īrĕ. *To hear.* Hīnc ēxaūdīrĕ vŏcēs ēt sævă sŏnārĕ Vērbĕră. V. *See Audio. To listen to prayers.* Phr.—Sūpplĭcĭs ēxaūdīrĕ prĕcāntĭs. Ānnŭō vōtīs. Aūdĭō prĕcāntēm. Aūrēs præbērĕ prĕcāntī. Prĕcēs ēxcĭpĭō.

Ēxcæcō, ās, āvī, ātūm, ārĕ. *To blind. See Caeco. To obstruct.* Syn.—Ōbstrŭō, præclūdō, claūdō, ōbtūrō.

Ēxcēdō, ĭs, ssī, ssūm, ĕrĕ. *To go out, to depart.* Sī jŭbĕāt pătrĭā dāmnātum ēxcēdĕrĕ tērrā. M. Syn.—Ăbĕō, dīscēdō, rĕcēdō, fŭgĭō, ēgrĕdĭŏr, līnquō, rĕlīnquō, dēsĕrō. Pătrĭāque ēxcēdĕrĕ suādĕt. Rēgnīs ēxcēssĭt ăvītīs. *To die. See Morior. To surpass.* Syn.—Vīncō, sŭpĕrō.

Ēxcēllō, ĭs, ŭī, ĕrĕ. *To excel, to surpass.* Ōmnĭbūs ōrnātūm vŏlŭīsti ēxcēllĕrĕ rēbŭs. Lr. Syn.—Sŭpĕrō, ēxsŭpĕrō, ēmĭnĕō, sŭpĕrēmĭnĕō, præstō, prætĕrĕō. *See Supero.*

Ēxcērnō, ĭs, crēvī, crētūm, ĕrĕ. *To separate.* Jāmque īnde ēxcērnĕrĕ pārvōs. Syn.—Sēcērnō, sēpărō, sēlĭgō.

Ēxcērpō, ĭs, sī, tūm, ĕrĕ. *To extract.* Quīd? cūm Pīcēnīs ēxcērpēns sēmĭnă pōmīs Gaūdēs? H. Syn.—Cōllĭgō, dēlĭgō, dēcērpō. *To except.* Syn.—Ēxcĭpĭō.

Ēxcĭdĭūm, ĭī. n. *Ruin, destruction.* Hīc pĕtĭt ēxcĭdĭīs ūrbēm mĭsĕrōsquĕ pĕnātēs. V. Syn.—Rŭīnă, clādēs, cāsŭs, pērnĭcĭēs. *See Clades, Ruina, Everto.*

Ēxcĭdō, ĭs, ī, ĕrĕ. *To fall.* Ēxcĭdĭt, ēt mĭsĕrō vōxquĕ cŏlōrquĕ fŭgĭt. O. Syn.—Cădō, dēcĭdō, lābŏr, cōllābŏr, prōcūmbō, dēfĭcĭō. Phr.—Ēxcĭdĕrāt cūrrū. Fūlmĭnă cœlō Ēxcĭdĕrānt. Sŭbĭtōquĕ dŏlōrĕ Cōllāpsūs cĕcĭdĭt. Ēxcĭdĭt ōrĕ nĕfās. *To escape.* Syn.—Ēxĕō, ăbĕō, ēlābŏr, fŭgĭō, ēffŭgĭō.

Ēxcīdō, ĭs, dī, sūm, ĕrĕ. *To cut.* Cŏlūmnās Rūpĭbūs ēxcīdūnt, scēnīs dĕcŏra āltă fŭtūrīs. V. Syn.—Cædō. *To destroy. See Caedo.*

Ēxcĭĕō, ēs, īvī, ĭtūm, ērĕ & Ēxcĭō, īs, īvī, ītūm, īrĕ. *To summon forth.* Fōrtĕ sŭēm lătēbrīs vēstīgĭă cērtă sĕcūtī, Ēxcīvērĕ cănēs. O. Syn.—Ēxtrūdō, ēxtūrbō, ēvŏcō. *To excite.* Syn.—Cōmmŏvĕō, cōncĭtō.

Excĭpĭŏ, ĭs, ēpī, ēptūm, ĕrĕ. *To take from, to draw from.* Quēmne ĕgo ēxcēpi ēx mărī? Plaut. Syn.—Ēdūcŏ, ēxtrăhŏ. *To receive.* Syn.—Āccĭpĭŏ, căpĭŏ. *To except.* Syn.—Ēxcērpŏ, sēpōnŏ, dētrăhŏ, subtrăhŏ, ēxĭmŏ, dēmŏ.

Excĭtŏ, ās, āvī, ātūm, ārĕ. *To call out. See Voco. To arouse. See Expergefacio. To provoke.* Syn.—Prōvŏcŏ, sūscĭtŏ, mŏvĕŏ, cĭĕŏ. *To animate.* Syn.—Incĭtŏ, cōncĭtŏ, sūscĭtŏ, ēxsūscĭtŏ, ădhōrtŏr, āccēndŏ, ăcŭŏ, cōmmŏvĕŏ, stĭmŭlŏ.

Exclūdŏ, ĭs, sī, sūm, ĕrĕ. *To exclude.* Āstră fŭgātĕ, prēcōr, tōtōque ēxclūdĭtĕ cœlō. Syn.—Ārcĕŏ, prŏhĭbĕŏ, ējĭcĭŏ, ēxpēllŏ. Phr.— Ēxclūdĭt sānōs Hĕlĭcōnĕ pŏētās. H. Quōs nōn dŭbĭtās ēxclūdĕrĕ tēmplō.

Excōgĭtŏ, ās, āvī, ātūm, ārĕ. *To think.* Ēxcōgĭtāvĭt hŏmŏ săgāx ĕt ăstutŭs. M. Syn.—Cōgĭtŏ, mĕdĭtŏr, fīngŏ, īnvĕnĭŏ.

Excŏquŏ, ĭs, ōxī, ōctūm, ĕrĕ. *To cook.* Ēxcŏquĭtūr flāmmīs scŏpŭlŭs. Syn.—Cŏquŏ. pērcŏquŏ.

Excōrs, ōrdĭs. adj. *Foolish, silly.* Syn.—Āmēns, stūltŭs.

Excŭbĭæ, ārūm. f. *Guard, watch.* Intĕrĕā vĭgĭlum ēxcŭbĭīs ōbsīdĕrĕ pōrtās Cūră dătŭs. V. Syn.—Cūstōdĭă, cūstōdēs, vĭgĭlēs. Phr.— Fīdūsque ād līmĭnă cūstōs Pōnĭtŭr. In stătĭōnĕ mănēbānt ēxcŭbĭæ. *See Custodia.*

Excŭbĭtŏr, ōrĭs. m. *Sentinel, guard.* Syn.—Cūstōs, ēxcŭbĭæ, vĭgĭlēs, cūstōdĭă.

Excŭbŏ, ās, ŭī, ĭtūm, ārĕ. *To be on guard.* Syn.—Pērnōctŏ, vĭgĭlŏ. Phr.—Vēstĭbŭlum īnsōmnēs sērvānt. Sŭccēdūnt sērvāntquĕ vĭcēs. Cōmmūnī pōrtām stătĭōnĕ tĕnēbānt. Dīscūrrūnt vărĭāntquĕ vĭcēs. Mūrōs quī mīlĭtĕ sērvēnt.

Excūdŏ, ĭs, dī, sūm, ĕrĕ. *To strike out.* Āc prīmūm sĭlĭcī scīntīllam ēxcūdĭt Āchātēs. V. Syn.—Ēlĭcĭŏ, ēxcŭtĭŏ, ēxtūndŏ. *To forge.* Syn.—Cūdŏ, prōcūdŏ. Fig.—*To compose.* Syn.—Cōmpōnŏ, ēlūcŭbrŏ, fīngŏ.

Excūrrŏ, ĭs, rī, rsūm, ĕrĕ. *To make sorties, to run forth.* Syn.— Incūrrŏ, ēxcūrsŏ, văgŏr.

Excūsābĭlĭs, ĭs, ĕ. *Excusable.* Syn.—Ēxcūsāndŭs. Phr.—Vĕnĭā dĭgnŭs.

Excūsŏ, ās, āvī, ātūm, ārĕ. *To excuse.* Quā pŏtĕs ēxcūsā, nĕc ămīcī dēsĕrĕ caūsām. O. Phr.—Crīmĭnĕ, cūlpā pūrgŏ, lībĕrŏ, ēxĭmŏ. Vērbīs dēfēndŏ. Ēxcūsāt crīmēn lăcrĭmīs. Cūlpām prætēxĭt hŏnēstō nōmĭnĕ. Ērgŏ dĕīs frātrīquĕ mŏrās ēxcūsăt. Dīcĕrĕ ēxcūsāntĭă vērbă.

Excŭtĭŏ, ĭs, ūssī, ūssūm, ĕrĕ. *To strike out, to stamp out.* Dē crīnĭbŭs ēxcŭtĭt īgnēm. O. Syn.—Dējĭcĭŏ, dēcŭtĭŏ, ējĭcĭŏ, ēxtūrbŏ.

Phr.—Scēptrīs ēxcŭtĭērĕ sŭīs. Ēxcŭtĭāt Teūcrŏs vāllō. *To agi-*
tate. Syn.—Quătĭŏ, quāssŏ, cōncŭtĭŏ, jāctŏ. *To hurl.* Syn.—
Jăcŭlŏr, mīttŏ, ēmīttŏ, cōntōrquĕŏ. *To drive away.* Syn.—
Ārcĕŏ, dēpēllŏ, āvērtŏ, ējĭcĭŏ.

Ēxĕcrābĭlĭs, & Ēxsĕcrābĭlĭs, ĭs, ĕ. *Accursed.* Syn.—Ēxsĕcrāndŭs,
dētēstāndŭs, ăbōmĭnāndŭs, ēxsĕcrātŭs, hōrrēndŭs.

Ēxĕcrŏr & Ēxsĕcrŏr, ārĭs, ātŭs sūm, ārī. *To curse.* Ēt tērram āltrī-
cēm sævi ēxsēcrāmŭr Ŭlȳssĭs. V. Syn.—Dētēstŏr, ăbōmĭnŏr,
dēvŏvĕŏ. Phr.—Dīrīs dēvŏvĕŏ. Dīrīs ŏnĕrŏ. Căpĭtī dīră cănŏ.
Dīră prĕcŏr. Vērbă ēxsēcrāntĭă ēdŏ.

Ēxĕdŏ, ĭs, ēdī, ēsūm, ĕrĕ. *To eat.* Mĭsĕrābĭlĕ tūrpēs Ēxĕdērĕ căpŭt
tĭnĕæ. Syn.—Ēdŏ, ădĕdŏ, rōdŏ, cōrrōdŏ, pāscŏr, dēpāscŏr. *To*
devour, to ruin. Syn.—Ēdŏ, pĕrĕdŏ, ābsūmŏ, cōnsūmŏ, cārpŏ,
rōdŏ, dēpāscŏr, cōnfĭcĭŏ, cŏquŏ, mācĕrŏ, pērdŏ, dēstrŭŏ, āttĕrŏ,
ēvērtŏ. Phr.—Sīlvās ēxĕdĕrăt ārdŏr Flāmmĕŭs. Mŏnŭmēntă
Mūltă vĕtūstās ēxĕdīt. Mŏrs lēntă jăcēntĭs ēxĕdīt pŭĕrīlĕ dĕcŭs.

Ēxēmplăr, ārĭs. n. *Model.* Ūtĭlĕ prŏpŏsŭīt nōbīs ēxēmplăr Ŭlȳssēm.
H. Syn.—Ēxēmplūm, ĭmāgŏ, spĕcĭēs. Phr.—Vōs ēxēmplārĭă
Græcă Nōctūrnā vērsātĕ mănū.

Ēxēmplūm, ī. n. *Model, type.* Syn.—Ēxēmplăr, ēxēmplārĕ, spĕcĭmĕn. Phr.—Præbēre ēxēmplūm. Hæc ēxēmplă dăbăt.

Ēxĕŏ, īs, īvī & ĭī, ĭtūm, īrĕ. *To go out.* Quāmvīs mūltă mĕīs ēxīrēt
vīctĭmă sēptĭs. V. Syn.—Ēgrĕdĭŏr, ēvādŏ, ēxcēdŏ, ăbĕŏ, ābcēdŏ, dīscēdŏ, ēxsĭlĭŏ, ērūmpŏ, prōrūmpŏ, rŭŏ, ēxcūrrŏ, ēvŏlŏ.
Mĕ pĕdēm ēffĕrŏ. Mĕ prōrĭpĭŏ. Ēxcēssēre ădȳtĭs ōmnēs. Quā
grēssum ēxtŭlĕrām rĕpĕtŏ. Āgmĭnă sē fūndŭnt pōrtīs. Cĕlĕrēm
quō răpīs tēctīs pĕdēm. Quŏtĭēs dē līmĭnĕ mŏvĕrăt ūnūm Prō-
tŭlĕrātquĕ pĕdēm. Spīrĭtŭs ēxĭt ĭn aūrās.

Ēxĕquĭæ & Ēxsĕquĭæ, ārūm. f. *Funeral rites.* Præclārīquĕ dŏcēnt
Fūnĕrĭs ēxsĕquĭæ. O. Syn.—Fūnŭs, fūnĕră, sŭprēmă, fūnĕrĭs
hŏnŏr. Phr.—Ēxsĕquĭālĭs hŏnōs. Rītĕ sŏlūtīs Ēxsĕquĭīs. Mītĭ-
bŭs ēxsĕquĭīs ădĕs. *See Funus.*

Ēxĕquŏr, ĕrĭs, ĕcūtŭs sūm, ī. *To execute, to accomplish.* Jūssă
tămēn dīvum ēxsĕquĭtūr clāssēmquĕ rĕvīsĭt. V. Syn.—Cōnfĭcĭŏ, făcēssŏ, ăgŏ, pĕrăgŏ, ābsōlvŏ, īmplĕŏ. Phr.—Īmpĕrĭūm
cĕlĕr ēxsĕquĭtŭr. Prŏpēre ēxsĕquĭtūr præcēptă Sĭbȳllæ.

Ēxērcĕŏ, ēs, ŭī, ĭtūm, ĕrĕ. *To exercise.* Quăm sĭt ŭtērquĕ lĭbēns
cēnsēbo ēxērcĕăt ārtēm. H. Syn.—Prōfĭtĕŏr, cŏlŏ, fūngŏr. *To*
agitate, to torment. Syn.—Vēxŏ, prĕmŏ, ūrgĕŏ, fătīgŏ, īnsēctŏr, īnsĕquŏr, jāctŏ.

Ēxērcĭtŭs, ūs. m. *Army.* Jāmque ōmnīs cāmpīs ēxērcĭtŭs ībăt
ăpērtīs. V. Syn.—Ăcĭēs, āgmĕn, cŏhōrs, phălānx, tūrmă, cōpĭæ,

lĕgĭō, mănīplŭs, mănŭs, ārmātī, mīlĕs, mīlĭtĕs. Phr.—Dēnsīs ăcĭēs stīpātā cătērvīs. Fūlgēntēs ǣrĕ cătērvās. Ăcĭēs stĕtĭt ōrdĭnĕ cērtō. Dēsuētăquĕ bēllō Āgmĭna ĭn ārmă vŏcăt. *See Agmen, Acies.*

Ēxĕrŏ & Ēxsĕrŏ, ĭs, ŭī, ērtūm, ĕrĕ. *To thrust out.* Tū nāntī prōtēndĕ mănūm, tū, Pīsŏ, lătēntēm Ēxsĕrĕ. L. Syn.—Ēxsērtŏ, ēdūcŏ, prōmŏ, ēxprōmŏ, ōstēndŏ, nūdŏ, dētĕgŏ. Phr.—Ēxsĕrĭt ēnsēm.

Ēxhālŏ, ās, āvī, ātūm, ārĕ. *To breathe out.* Quǣ tĕnŭem ēxhālăt nĕbŭlām fūmōsquĕ vŏlŭcrēs. V. Syn.—Hālŏ, spīrŏ, ēxspīrŏ, sūspīrŏ, ēffūndŏ, ēmīttŏ, mīttŏ.

Ēxhaūrĭŏ, īs, sī, stūm, īrĕ. *To exhaust, to empty.* Syn.—Haūrĭō, ēxsīccŏ, ēbĭbŏ. *To sustain to the end.* Syn.—Pērpĕtĭŏr, ēxāntlŏ, dēfūngŏr.

Ēxhĭbĕŏ, ēs, ŭī, ĭtūm, ērĕ. *To exhibit.* Ēxhĭbĕāt vūltūs nōxquĕ dĭēsquĕ tŭōs. O. Syn.—Ōstēndŏ, ēdŏ, prōdŏ, prōferŏ. *To render.* Syn.—Făcĭŏ, ēffĭcĭŏ, rēddŏ.

Ēxhĭlărŏ, ās, āvī, ātūm, ārĕ. *To rejoice.* Ēxhĭlărēnt īpsōs gaūdĭă nōstră Dĕōs. M. Syn.—Hĭlărŏ, ōblēctŏ, rĕcrĕŏ. *See Hilaro.*

Ēxhōrrĕŏ, ēs, ŭī, ērĕ. *To shudder.* Syn.—Hōrrĕŏ, frĕmŏ, rĭgĕŏ, ēxhōrrēscŏ, ōbrĭgĕŏ, rĭgēscŏ. *To fear. See Timeo.*

Ēxhōrtŏr, ārĭs, ātŭs sūm, ārī. *To urge, to encourage.* Ēt nōmĭnĕ quēmquĕ vŏcāndō Ēxhōrtātŭr ĕquōs. O. Syn.—Hōrtŏr, ădhōrtŏr, āccēndŏ, ăcŭŏ, ēxcĭtŏ, cōncĭtŏ, īncĭtŏ. *See Hortor.*

Ēxĭgŏ, ĭs, ēgī, āctūm, ĕrĕ. *To drive out, to drive away.* Aūt ēxĭgĭt ūmbĕr Nārĕ săgāx ē cōllĕ fĕrās. Syn.—Āgŏ, ăbĭgŏ, dēpēllŏ, ējĭcĭŏ. Phr.—Ēxĭgĭt ē strātīs cōrpŭs. *To excite.* Syn.—Āgŏ, īmpēllŏ, pēllŏ. *To pass, to traverse.* Syn.—Āgŏ, dēgŏ, trānsĭgŏ, dūcŏ, trādūcŏ. *To pierce.* Syn.—Trānsfīgŏ, trānsfŏdĭŏ, trānsădĭgŏ.

Ēxĭgŭŭs, ă, ūm. *Little, feeble, small.* Ēt quāmvīs īgni ēxĭgŭō prŏpĕrātā mădērēnt. V. Syn.—Pārvŭs, mŏdĭcŭs, hŭmĭlĭs, ēxīlĭs, grăcĭlĭs, tĕnŭĭs, brĕvĭs, āngūstŭs.

Ēxĭlĭŏ, & Ēxsĭlĭŏ, īs, ŭī & ĭī, ūltūm, īrĕ. *To leap, to jump.* Syn.—Sălĭŏ, prōsĭlĭŏ, ēmĭcŏ. *To leave hastily.* Syn.—Prōsĭlĭŏ, rŭŏ, ērūmpŏ, prǣcĭpĭtŏ.

Ēxīlĭs, ĭs, ĕ. *Small, thin, narrow.* Syn.—Grăcĭlĭs, tĕnŭĭs, ēxĭgŭŭs, āngūstŭs, măcĕr. Phr.—Dŏmŭs ēxīlīs Plūtōnĭă.

Ēxĭlĭūm & Ēxsĭlĭūm, ĭī. n. *Exile.* Ēxsĭlĭōquĕ dŏmōs ēt dūlcĭă līmĭnă līnquūnt. V. Syn.—Fŭgă. Phr.—Mĭsĕrō mĭhĭ dēmūm Ēxsĭlĭum īnfēlīx. Pătrĭăque ēxcēdĕrĕ suādĕt. Nōs pătrĭām fŭgĭmŭs. *See Exul.*

Ēxĭmĭē. adv. *Excellently.* Syn.—Ēgrĕgĭē. *See Bene.*

Ēxĭmĭŭs, ă, ūm. *Superior, remarkable.* Quāttŭŏr ēxĭmĭōs prǣstāntī cōrpŏrĕ taūrōs. V. Syn.—Ēgrĕgĭŭs, ēxcēllēns, īnsīgnĭs, prǣstāns, prǣclārŭs. *See Egregius.*

Ēxĭmŏ, ĭs, ēmī, ēmptūm, ĕrĕ. *To take away.* Ēxĭmĭt īpsă dĭēs ōmnēs dē cōrpŏrĕ mēndās. O. Syn.—Aūfĕrŏ, ērĭpĭŏ, tōllŏ, dēmŏ. *To deprive.* Syn.—Ădĭmŏ, ērĭpĭŏ, nūdŏ, spŏlĭŏ, prīvŏ. *To deliver.* Syn.—Lībĕrŏ, sōlvŏ, sūbdūcŏ, ēxpĕdĭŏ.

Ēxīn, Ēxīndĕ. adv. *Thence.* Syn.—Deīn, deīndĕ, hīnc, īndĕ. *See Deinde.*

Ēxīstŏ, & Ēxsīstŏ, ĭs, stĭtī, stĭtūm, ĕrĕ. *To stand forth, to appear.* Īn lūcem ēxsīstūnt prīmōrdĭă rērūm. Lr. Syn.—Ēxstŏ, ēxĕŏ, prōdĕŏ, ēmĭnĕŏ, ēxŏrĭŏr, sūrgŏ, ēxsūrgŏ, āppārĕŏ, ēmērgŏ. Phr.—Ēxsīstĭt tōtō cōrpŏrĕ sūdŏr. *To exist.* Syn.—Sūm, ēxstŏ.

Ēxĭtĭālĭs, ĭs, ĕ, & Ēxĭtĭōsŭs, ă, ūm. *Fatal, deadly.* Syn.—Fātālĭs, fūnēstŭs.

Ēxĭtĭūm, ĭī. n. *Ruin, destruction.* Ēxĭtĭūm Trōjǣ nōstrīque ōrbātŏr, Ăchīllēs. O. Syn.—Pērnĭcĭēs, clādēs, rŭīnă. Phr.—Āgrīs tēmpēstās tŭlĭt ēxĭtĭūm. Ūnă dĭēs dăbĭt ēxĭtĭō.

Ēxĭtŭs, ūs. m. *Exit.* Syn.—Ăbĭtŭs, dīscēssŭs, rĕcēssŭs, ēffŭgĭūm, ĭtĕr. *Result.* Syn.—Cāsŭs, ēvēntŭs, sūccēssŭs, rēs. Phr.—Ēxĭtŭs āctă prŏbăt. Ēxĭtŭs aūspĭcĭō grăvĭŏr. Ēxĭtŭs āccēssĭt vērbīs. *Death. See Mors.*

Ēxŏlĕŏ, ēs, ēvī, ētūm, ērĕ. *To become obsolete.* Syn.—Ōbsŏlēscŏ, ăbŏlĕŏr, āntīquŏr, cădŏ.

Ēxŏnĕrŏ, ās, āvī, ātūm, ārĕ. *To relieve of one's burden.* Pōssŭmŭs īmpŏsĭtīs căpŭt ēxŏnĕrārĕ tĕnēbrīs. O. Syn.—Lĕvŏ, sūblĕvŏ. Phr.—Ŏnŭs dēpōnŏ, lībĕrŏ. Cōrpūs pōndĕrĕ sōlvŏ.

Ēxōptābĭlĭs, ĭs, ĕ. *Desirable.* Syn.—Ōptābĭlĭs, ōptāndŭs, ēxōptāndŭs.

Ēxōptŏ, ās, āvī, ātūm, ārĕ. *To desire earnestly.* Syn.—Ōptŏ, pĕrōptŏ, pērcŭpĭŏ, ēxpĕtŏ. *See Cupio.*

Ēxōrdĭŏr, īrĭs, sŭs sūm, īrī. *To commence.* Syn.—Ōrdĭŏr, īncĭpĭŏ, sūscĭpĭŏ, āggrĕdĭŏr, aūspĭcŏr, īnchŏŏ.

Ēxōrdĭūm, ĭī. n. *Beginning.* Ēxpĕdĭam ēt prīmǣ rĕvŏcābo ēxōrdĭă pūgnǣ. V. Syn.—Ēxōrsŭs, ēxōrsă, prīncĭpĭūm, īngrēssŭs, ŏrīgŏ.

Ēxōrĭŏr, īrĭs, rtŭs sūm, īrī. *To be born, to appear.* Syn.—Ŏrĭŏr, nāscŏr, ēxsūrgŏ, sūrgŏ. *See Orior.*

Ēxōrŏ, ās, āvī, ātūm, ārĕ. *To beseech earnestly, to obtain by prayer.* Syn.—Ōrŏ, plācŏ, sēdŏ, flēctŏ. *See Precor.*

Ēxpāllĕō, ēs, ŭī, ērĕ. *To grow pale. See Palleo. To fear.* Syn.—Fōrmīdō, ēxpăvĕō.

Ēxpāndŏ, ĭs, dī, ānsūm & āssūm, ĕrĕ. *To expand, to extend.* Syn.—Pāndŏ, ēxplĭcŏ, ēxtēndŏ, ăpĕrĭŏ, ēffūndŏ, spārgŏ.

Ēxpĕdĭŏ, īs, īvī & ĭī, ītūm, īrĕ. *To deliver from.* Nōn mōrtīs lăquĕīs ēxpĕdĭēs căpŭt. H. Syn.—Ēxĭmŏ, lībĕrŏ, sōlvŏ, sūbdūcŏ. *To explain.* Syn.—Pāndŏ, ēxplĭcŏ. Phr.—Ēxpĕdĭānt dīctīs. Prōmptĭŭs ēxpĕdĭām.

Ēxpĕdĭt. impers. *It is better, convenient.* Syn.—Prōdēst, cōndūcĭt. Phr.—Ūtĭlĕ ēst.

Ēxpēllŏ, ĭs, ŭlī, ūlsūm, ĕrĕ. *To expel, to chase.* Syn.—Pēllŏ, ējĭcĭŏ, dējĭcĭŏ, ēxĭgŏ, ăbĭgŏ, ārcĕŏ, dētūrbŏ. *See Pello.*

Ēxpēndŏ, ĭs, dī, sūm, ĕrĕ. *To weigh.* Ēxpēnde Hānnĭbălēm: quōt lībrās īn dŭce sūmmō Īnvĕnĭēs? J. Syn.—Pēndŏ, pōndĕrŏ, ēxāmĭnŏ. *See Pondero. To examine.* Syn.—Pēndŏ, pērpēndŏ, pōndĕrŏ, æstĭmŏ, ēxāmĭnŏ, ēxquīrŏ, dīscŭtĭŏ, ēxcŭtĭŏ, ēxĭgŏ. Phr.—Ōmnēs ēxpēndĕrĕ cāsūs. Mĕrĭtīs ēxpēndĕrĕ caūsām. *To pay.* Syn.—Pēndŏ, lŭŏ, sōlvŏ. Phr.—Scĕlŭs ēxpēndīssĕ mĕrēntēm Lāŏcŏōntă fĕrūnt.

Ēxpērgēfăcĭŏ, ĭs, ēcī, āctūm, ĕrĕ. *To awake.* Ēxpērgēfāctīquĕ sĕquūntŭr ĭnānĭă sæpĕ. L. Syn.—Ēxcĭtŏ, sūscĭtŏ. Phr.—Sōmnūm, sōpōrēm ădĭmŏ, ērīpĭŏ, fŭgŏ, tūrbŏ. Sōmnō ēxcĭĕŏ, ēxcĭŏ. Sōmnōs ābrūmpīt cūră sălūbrēs. Ōrtă dĭēs sōpītās ēxcĭtăt ūrbēs. Ēxcŭtĭām sōmnōs.

Ēxpĕrĭēntĭă, æ. f. *Experience.* Āpĭbūs quānta ēxpĕrĭēntĭă pārcīs. V. Syn.—Ūsŭs. Phr.—Cōgnĭtă rēs ūsū. Rēs ōbsērvātă cōlōnīs. Rērum ēxpĕrĭēntĭă dōctă. *See Usus, Prudentia.*

Ēxpĕrĭmēntūm, ī. n. *Trial.* Syn.—Tēntāmĕn, tēntāmēntūm, ēxpĕrĭēntĭă, pĕrīcŭlūm.

Ēxpĕrĭŏr, īrĭs, ērtŭs sūm, īrī. *To prove, to experience.* Syn.—Tēntŏ, ēxplōrŏ, ădĕŏ, sŭbĕŏ. Phr.—Īrĕ pĕr īnvītās ēxpĕrĭēmŭr ăquās. Tūrnum ēxpĕrĭātŭr ĭn ārmīs. *To obtain.* Syn.—Tēntŏ, āggrĕdĭŏr.

Ēxpērs, tĭs. adj. *Inexperienced.* Syn.—Rŭdĭs, īgnārŭs, ĭnēxpērtŭs, īnscĭŭs. *Lacking.* Syn.—Cărēns, ĕgēns, ĭnōps, ēxsōrs. Phr.—Ēxpērs ūndæquĕ cĭbīquĕ.

Ēxpĕtŏ, ĭs, īvī & ĭī, ītūm, ĕrĕ. *To desire earnestly.* Syn.—Ōptŏ, ārdĕŏ, cŭpĭŏ. *To seek.* Syn.—Ārcēssŏ, quærŏ.

Ēxpīlŏ, ās, āvī, ātūm, ārĕ. *To pillage.* Īpsum ēxpīlāvīt nūmĕn ād lūmēn sŭūm. Phaed. Syn.—Dīrĭpĭŏ, spŏlĭŏ, prædŏr. *See Praedor.*

Ēxpĭō, ās, āvī, ātūm, ārĕ. *To expiate.* Dĭgĭto ēt lūstrālĭbūs āntĕ sălīvīs Ēxpĭăt. Pers. Syn.—Pĭō, pūrgŏ, āblŭŏ, dēlĕō. Phr.—Cuī dăbīt pārtēs scĕlŭs ēxpĭāndī Jūpĭtĕr. H. *See Pio, Purgo.*

Ēxplĕō, ēs, ēvī, ētūm, ērĕ. *To fill, to complete.* Dūm scrībo, ēxplēvī tōtās cērās quăttŭŏr. Plaut. Syn.—Īmplĕō. *To accomplish.* Syn.—Ābsōlvŏ, cōnfĭcĭŏ, pērfĭcĭŏ, pĕrăgŏ. *To content, to satiate.* Syn.—Sătĭō, sătŭrō.

Ēxplĭcŏ, ās, āvī, ātūm, ārĕ, & ŭī, ĭtūm, ārĕ. *To unfold, to develop.* Syn.—Pāndŏ, ēvōlvŏ, ēxpāndŏ, dīffūndŏ. *To bring forth.* Syn.—Prōmŏ, ēxpĕdĭō, dēprōmŏ. *To relate.* Syn.—Pāndŏ, ēvōlvŏ, ēnārrŏ, ăpĕrĭŏ, ēxpĕdĭŏ, ēnōdŏ, ēnŭclĕō, ēxplānŏ.

Ēxplōdŏ, ĭs, sī, sūm, ĕrĕ. *To drive off with a noise.* Fig.—*To hiss.* Syn.—Rēspŭŏ, īmprŏbŏ, sībĭlŏ.

Ēxplōrātŏr, ōrĭs. m. *Explorer, scout, spy.* Syn.—Spĕcŭlātŏr.

Ēxplōrŏ, ās, āvī, ātūm, ārĕ. *To examine.* Fīnēs ēt līttŏră gēntĭs Dīvērsi ēxplōrānt. V. Syn.—Īnquīrŏ, lūstrŏ, rīmŏr, scrūtŏr, ŏbsērvŏ. Phr.—Ēxīrĕ lŏcōsquĕ Ēxplōrārĕ nŏvōs. Dēxtĕră mōtū Cæcum ĭtĕr ēxplōrăt. *To spy upon.* Syn.—Spĕcŭlŏr, cīrcūmspĭcĭō, quærŏ. *To attempt.* Syn.—Tēntŏ, ēxpĕrĭŏr.

Ēxpŏlĭō, īs, īvī & ĭī, īrĕ. *To polish, to embellish.* Syn.—Pŏlĭō, pērpŏlĭō, ēxcŏlŏ, ēxōrnŏ.

Ēxpōnŏ, ĭs, ŏsŭī, ĭtūm, ĕrĕ. *To set out, to set before.* Ēxpŏsŭīt mĕă mē pŏpŭlō fōrtūnă vĭdēndūm. O. Syn.—Ōbjĭcĭō, prōpōnŏ, præbĕō, ēffĕrŏ. *To explain.* Syn.—Ēxplĭcŏ, ēnārrŏ, ēxplānŏ, pāndŏ, prōfĕrŏ, ēlŏquŏr, ēxprōmŏ. Phr.—Vērām vērbīs ēxpōnĕrĕ caūsām. Ērrōrēs ēxpŏsŭītquĕ sŭōs.

Ēxpōrtŏ, ās, āvī, ātūm, ārĕ. *To carry away, to transport.* Tūm cōrpŏră lūcĕ cărēntūm Ēxpōrtānt tēctīs. O. Syn.—Ēffĕrŏ, aūfĕrŏ, ēdūcŏ, ābdūcŏ.

Ēxpōscŏ, ĭs, pŏpōscī, ĭtūm, ĕrĕ. *To ask earnestly.* Sēd vōtīs prĕcĭbūsquĕ jŭbēnt ēxpōscĕrĕ pācēm. V. Syn.—Pōscŏ, pĕtŏ, flāgĭtŏ. Phr.—Pōscĕre ŏpēm. Īlĭăcōs aūdīrĕ lăbōrēs Ēxpōscĭt. *See Peto.*

Ēxprĭmŏ, ĭs, ēssī, ēssūm, ĕrĕ. *To press forth.* Ūtquĕ lĭquōr rārī sūb pōndĕrĕ crībrī Mānăt ĕt ēxprĭmĭtūr pēr dēnsă fŏrāmĭnă sūccŭs. O. Syn.—Ēlĭcĭŏ, ēdūcŏ, ēxtrăhŏ, ēxtōrquĕō. Phr.—Mădĭdās ēxprĭmĭt īmbrĕ cŏmās. *To express.* Syn.—Ēffīngŏ, ĭmĭtŏr. *To announce.* Syn.—Ēlŏquŏr.

Ēxprŏbrŏ, ās, āvī, ātūm, ārĕ. *To reproach.* Ēst ălĭquam īngrātō mĕrĭtum ēxprōbrārĕ vŏlūptās. O. Syn.—Ōbjĭcĭŏ, ōbjēctŏ, ōppōnŏ. *See Culpo.*

Ēxprōmŏ, ĭs, psī, ptūm, ĕrĕ. *To bring forth.* Dūlcēs Mūsārum ēxprōmĕrĕ fœtūs. Cat. Syn.—Prōmŏ, ēdūcŏ, ēffĕrŏ, prōfĕrŏ, ēdŏ. Phr.—Mœstās ēxprōmĕrĕ vōcēs. Ēxprōmĕrĕ mēntĕ quĕrēlās.

Ēxpūgnŏ, ās, āvī, ātūm, ārĕ. *To take by assault.* Mē dūcĕ, Dārdănĭūs Spārtam ēxpūgnāvĭt. V. Syn.—Vīncŏ, ēvīncŏ, sŭpĕrŏ, dēbēllŏ, ŏccŭpŏ. Phr.—Sēd dūm pērrūmpĕrĕ pōrtās ōbsĭdĭōnĕ părăt. *To take by force.* Syn.—Ēlĭcĭŏ, ēxtōrquĕŏ.

Ēxpūngŏ, ĭs, xī, ctūm, ĕrĕ. *To efface.* Pūpīllūmve ŭtĭnām, quēm prōxĭmŭs hērēs Īmpēllo, ēxpūngām! Pērs. Syn.—Dēlĕŏ, rādŏ, tōllŏ. *See Deleo.*

Ēxquīrŏ, ĭs, sīvī, sītūm, ĕrĕ. *To seek.* Ēxquīrītque aūdītquĕ vĭrūm mŏnŭmēntă prĭōrūm. V. Syn.—Quærŏ cōnquīrŏ, īnquīrŏ, rĕquīrŏ. Phr.—Ūmbrōsam ēxquīrĕrĕ vāllēm. Lŏcūm sĭmĭlem ēxquīrūnt. *See Quaero. To demand.* Syn.—Ōrŏ, pōscŏ, rŏgŏ, flāgĭtŏ, ēfflāgĭtŏ, ēxpōstŭlŏ.

Ēxsāngŭĭs, ĭs, ĕ. *Bloodless.* Ītŭr ĭn ēxsānguēm pŏpŭlūm bēllīquĕ jăcēntĭs Rēllĭquĭās. Phr.—Sānguĭnĕ cărēns. *Dead.* Syn.—Ēxănĭmĭs, mōrtŭŭs. *Pale with fright.* Syn.—Pāllēns, pāllĭdŭs, sēmiănĭmĭs. *Feeble.* Syn.—Frāctŭs, ēffētŭs.

Ēxsătĭŏ, ās, āvī, ātūm, ārĕ. *To satisfy, to satiate.* Mūltōquĕ crŭōrĕ Ēxsătĭātĕ, vĭrī, plēnōs rūbīgĭnĭs ēnsēs. Syn.—Sătŭrŏ, sătĭŏ, ēxplĕŏ.

Ēxscīndŏ, ĭs, ĭdī, īssūm, ĕrĕ. *To cut down.* Præcĭpŭūs sĕd ĕnīm lăbŏr ēst ēxscīndĕrĕ dēxtrā Ōppŏsĭtās rūpēs. Syn.—Sĕcŏ, scīndŏ. Phr.—Gēntem ēxscīndĕrĕ fērrŏ.

Ēxsĕcŏ, ās, ŭī, ēctūm, ārĕ. *To cut.* Syn.—Sĕcŏ, scīndŏ, ēxscīndŏ. *To retrench.* Syn.—Dētrăhŏ, tōllŏ, sūbdūcŏ.

Ēxsōlvŏ, ĭs, vī, ŏlūtūm, ĕrĕ. *To unbind, to deliver.* Ēxsōlvĭt glăcĭēm nōdōsquĕ rĕlāxăt. Lr. Syn.—Sōlvŏ, līběrŏ, ēxpĕdĭŏ. Phr.—Ēxsōlvĕrĕ nēxūs. Tōtō paūlātim ēxsōlvĭt sē cōrpŏrĕ. Mēque hīs ēxsōlvĭtĕ cūrīs. Ēxsōlvĭt prōmīssă.

Ēxsōrs, ōrtĭs. adj. *Having no share in, deprived of.* Syn.—Ēxpērs, cărēns, ĕgēns. *Extraordinary.* Syn.—Īnsīgnĭs, ēxĭmĭŭs, præstāns.

Ēxspătĭŏr, ārĭs, ātŭs sūm, ārī. *To extend out, to wander from side to side.* Syn.—Spătĭŏr, ērrŏ, văgŏr, dīvăgŏr, ēxcūrrŏ, ēffūndŏr, dīffūndŏr.

Ēxspēctŏ, ās, āvī, ātūm, ārĕ. *To expect.* Ārmātīquĕ căvīs ēxspēctānt tūrrĭbŭs hōstēm. V. Syn.—Ōppĕrĭŏr, mănĕŏ. *To delay.* Syn.—Mănĕŏ, mŏrŏr, cūnctŏr, hærĕŏ. Phr.—Sīstĕ grădūm. Quæ tāntæ tĕnŭērĕ mŏræ? Pārvī tēmpŏrĭs āddĕ mŏrām. *To hope. See Spero.*

Ēxspīrŏ, ās, āvī, ātūm, ārĕ. *To breathe out.* Sānguĭnĭs ēxspīrāns călĭdūm dē pēctŏrĕ flūmĕn. Lr. Syn.—Ēxhālŏ, ēxsībĭlŏ. *To die.* Syn.—Ănĭmām, vītām ēxhālŏ. *See Morior.*

Ēxstīnguŏ, ĭs, xī, ctūm, ĕrĕ. *To extinguish.* Paūlātim ēxstīnguĭtŭr īgnĭs. O. Syn.—Rēstīnguŏ. Phr.—Flāmmās, īgnēs, lūcēm ūndā flūctĭbŭs sŭpĕrŏ, dŏmŏ. Gĕlĭdĭs rēstīnguĕrĕ fōntĭbŭs īgnēs. Nēc flāmmās sŭpĕrānt ūndæ̆. *To destroy.* Syn.—Ăbŏlĕŏ, dēlĕŏ, dēstrŭŏ.

Ēxstīrpŏ, ās, āvī, ātūm, ārĕ. *To uproot.* Syn.—Ērādīcŏ, ērŭŏ, ēxtūrbŏ, āvēllŏ. *To snatch away.* Syn.—Vēllŏ, āvēllŏ, ēvēllŏ.

Ēxstŏ, ās, stĭtī, ārĕ. *To stand out.* Tōrpēnt mōlĕ nŏva, ēt sūmmīs vīx cōrnĭbŭs ēxstānt. V. Syn.—Ēmĭnĕŏ. *To survive.* Syn.—Sŭpērstŏ. *To exist.* Syn.—Ēxsīstŏ, vīvŏ, sūm.

Ēxstrŭŏ, ĭs, ūxī, ūctūm, ĕrĕ. *To build.* Pūlchrāmque ūxōrĭūs ūrbēm Ēxstrŭĭs. V. Syn.—Aēdĭfĭcŏ. *To accumulate.* Syn.—Strŭŏ, āggĕrŏ.

Ēxsūdŏ, ās, āvī, ātūm, ārĕ. *To perspire.* Ēxsūdăt ĭnūtĭlĭs hūmŏr. V. Syn.—Sūdŏ, stīllŏ, ēxstīllŏ.

Ēxsŭpĕrābĭlĭs, ĭs, ĕ. *Surmountable.* Syn.—Sŭpĕrābĭlĭs, dŏmābĭlĭs.

Ēxsŭpĕrŏ, ās, āvī, ātūm, ārĕ. *To surpass.* Syn.—Sŭpĕrŏ, sŭpērēmĭnĕŏ. *To pass over.* Syn.—Trānsmīttŏ, trānscūrrŏ, trājĭcĭŏ. *To conquer.* Syn.—Sŭpĕrŏ, præ̆stŏ, vīncŏ.

Ēxtă, ōrūm. n. *Entrails.* Lāncĭbŭs ēt pāndīs fūmāntĭă rēddĭmŭs ēxtă. V. Syn.—Vīscĕră, fĭbræ̆. *See Viscera.*

Ēxtābēscŏ, ĭs, ŭī, ĕrĕ. *To waste away.* Rĕfūgēre ŏcŭlī; cōrpūs măcĭe ēxtābŭĭt. Syn.—Tābĕŏ, tābēscŏ, mārcēscŏ. Phr.—Tābĕ cōnfĭcĭŏr, ēxĕdŏr. *To grow old. See Senesco.*

Ēxtēmplō. adv. *Straightway.* Syn.—Stătīm.

Ēxtēndŏ, ĭs, dī, sūm, ĕrĕ. *To extend.* Ēxtēndĭtŭr ūnā Hōrrĭdă pēr lātōs ăcĭēs Vūlcānĭă cāmpōs. V. Syn.—Pāndŏ, ēxpāndŏ, prōtēndŏ, ēffūndŏ, dīffūndŏ, ēxplĭcŏ, pōrrĭgŏ, prōfĕrŏ, prōdūcŏ, dīlātŏ. Fig. Syn.—Prŏpāgŏ, dīffūndŏ. *To prolong.* Syn.—Prōfĕrŏ, prōdūcŏ, prōtrăhŏ. *To augment.* Syn.—Aūgĕŏ, āmplĭfĭcŏ.

Ēxtĕnŭŏ, ās, āvī, ātūm, ārĕ. *To weaken, to diminish.* Quōd pŏtĕs, ēxtĕnŭā fōrtī mălā cōrdĕ fĕrēndō. O. Syn.—Tĕnŭŏ, āttĕnŭŏ, mĭnŭŏ, īmmĭnŭŏ.

Ēxtĕrĭŏr, ŭs, ōrĭs. adj. *Exterior, outside.* Syn.—Ēxtērnŭs, ēxtĕrŭs.

Ēxtērmĭnŏ, ās, āvī, ātūm, ārĕ. *To banish.* Syn.—Ēxpēllŏ, āmāndŏ, rĕlēgŏ. *See Expello.*

Ēxtērnŭs, ă, ūm. *External, foreign, strange.* Ārcēbātquĕ sŭīs ēxtērnōs fīnĭbŭs ōmnēs. O. Syn.—Ēxtĕrŭs, ălĭēnŭs, ēxtrānĕŭs, bărbărŭs, pĕrĕgrīnŭs, ălĭēnĭgĕnă, ādvĕnă. Phr.—Ēxtērna ā sēdĕ prŏfēctŭs. Gĕnĕrōs ēxtērnīs āffōre ăb ōrīs.

Ēxtĕrŏ, ĭs, trīvī, trītūm, ĕrĕ. *To rub off, to trample upon.* Syn.—Tĕrŏ, cālcŏ. *To break.* Syn.—Frāngŏ, cōmmĭnŭŏ.

Ēxtōllŏ, ĭs, tŭlī, ēlātūm, tōllĕrĕ. *To raise up, to elevate.* Tōrvōs ēxtōllĭt ăd æthĕră vūltūs. O. Syn.—Tōllŏ, āttōllŏ, ēffĕrŏ, ēdūcŏ, ērĭgŏ, ēvĕhŏ. *To praise. See Laudo.*

Ēxtōrquĕŏ, ēs, sī, tūm, ērĕ. *To snatch by force.* Syn.—Răpĭŏ, ērĭpĭŏ, aūfĕrŏ, ēlĭcĭŏ.

Ēxtrăhŏ, ĭs, āxī, āctūm, ĕrĕ. *To draw out of.* Vīvūm pŭĕrum ēxtrăhăt ālvō. H. Syn.—Prōmŏ, ēxprōmŏ, ēdūcŏ, ēlĭcĭŏ.

Ēxtrēmō & Ēxtrēmūm. adv. *For the last time, finally.* Syn.—Sŭprēmūm. Phr.—Ēxtrēmā jām īn mōrtĕ. Ēxtrēma hōrā.

Ēxtrēmŭs, ă, ūm. *Last.* Īlĭăcī cĭnĕrēs ēt flāmma ēxtrēmă mĕōrūm. V. Syn.—Ūltĭmŭs, sŭpremŭs, nŏvīssĭmŭs. Phr.—Ēxtrēmōs pŭdĕāt rĕdīissĕ. Dūrārĕ ĭn ēxtrēmūm. Fig.—Ēxtrēmă pătī.

Ēxtrīcŏ, ās, āvī, ātūm, ārĕ. *To draw out, to extricate.* Ēxtrīcātă dēnsīs Cērvă plăgīs. H. Syn.—Ēxpĕdĭŏ, sōlvŏ, lībĕrŏ.

Ēxtrūdŏ, ĭs, sī, sūm, ĕrĕ. *To push out, to thrust out.* Mē nūnc ēxtrūsīsti ēx ædĭbŭs. Plaut. Syn.—Ējĭcĭŏ, ēxpēllŏ, dētrūdŏ, dētūrbŏ.

Ēxtūndŏ, ĭs, ŭdī, ūsūm, ĕrĕ. *To beat out.* Ăsĭnŭs, ūt vīdĭt fĕrūm īmpūnĕ lædī, cālcĭbūs frōntem ēxtŭdĭt. Phaed. Syn.—Ēlĭcĭŏ, ēxcŭtĭŏ, ēxpēllŏ, ēxtūrbŏ. *To forge.* Syn.—Cūdŏ.

Ēxŭl (Ēxsŭl), ŭlĭs. m. *Exile.* Ēxsŭl ăb ōctāvā Mărĭūs bĭbĭt, ēt frŭĭtūr Dīs Īrātīs. J. Syn.—Ēxtōrrĭs, ējēctŭs, pūlsŭs, ēxpūlsŭs, ēxtūrbātŭs, rĕlēgātŭs. Phr.—Pătrĭā pūlsŭs, cărēns. Pătrĭīs pūlsŭs. Pătrĭā cēdĕrĕ. Pătrĭīs ēxŭl ăb ōrīs. Fātō prŏfŭgŭs. *See Exilium.*

Ēxūlcĕrŏ, ās, āvī, ātūm, ārĕ. *To render sore.* (*Transf.*) *To aggravate.* Syn.—Ēxăcērbŏ, ēxăspĕrŏ, īrrītŏ.

Ēxŭlŏ (Ēxsŭlŏ), ās, āvī, ātūm, ārĕ. *To be exiled.* Phr.—Pătrĭīs ēxpēllŏr ăb ōrīs. Phr.—Pătrĭăm līnquŏ, fŭgĭŏ. Pătrĭā ārcĕŏr, ējĭcĭŏr. Prŏfŭgŭs ērrŏ. Īgnōtā cōnstĭtĭt ēxsŭl hŭmō.

Ēxūltŏ (Ēxsūltŏ), ās, āvī, ātūm, ārĕ. *To leap up.* Syn.—Ēxsĭlĭŏ, sūbsĭlĭŏ, ēmĭcŏ. Fig.—*See Gestio, Laetor, Superbio.*

Ēxūndŏ, ās, āvī, ātūm, ārĕ. *To inundate.* Prærūptum ēxūndāt pĕlăgŭs. Syn.—Ēfflŭŏ, ēffūndŏr, ēxspătĭŏr, ēxcūrrŏ, ēvăgŏr.

Ēxŭŏ, ĭs, ŭī, ūtūm, ĕrĕ. *To take off.* Syn.—Pōnŏ, dēpōnŏ, rējĭcĭŏ, mīttŏ, nūdŏ, dēmīttŏ. Phr.—Vēstēm nūdŏ, dēpōnŏ. Ēx hŭmĕrīs vēstēm răpĭŏ. *To despoil.* Syn.—Spŏlĭŏ, nūdŏ, ērĭpĭŏ, dētrăhŏ, ădĭmŏ. *See Nudo.*

Ēxūrŏ, ĭs, ssī, stūm, ĕrĕ. *To burn.* Īnfēstum ēlŭĭtūr scĕlŭs aūt ēxūrĭtūr īgnī. V. Syn.—Ūrŏ, ădūrŏ, cōmbūrŏ, crĕmŏ. Phr.—

Pīctās ēxūrĕ cărīnās. Ēxūssīt fœ̄dē pūppēs. *To dry up.* Syn.—Ūrŏ, sīccŏ, ēxhaūrĭŏ. *See Sicco, Siccitas.*

Ēxŭvĭæ̅, ārūm. f. *Spoils.* Hǣc ārma ēxŭvĭāsquĕ vĭrī tŭă quērcŭs hăbēbĭt. Syn.—Spŏlĭă, prǣdă, trŏpǣūm. Phr.—Bēllōrum ēxŭvĭǣ. Rĕdĭt ēxŭvĭās īndūtŭs Ăchīllĭs. Dāt Nīsō Mnēstheūs pēllem hōrrēntīsquĕ lĕōnĭs Ēxŭvĭās. *See Tropaeum, Spolia, Praeda.*

F

Fābēllă, æ̅. f. *Fable, story.* Scrīptōrēs aūtēm nārrārĕ pŭtārĕt ăsēllō Fābēllām sūrdō. H. Syn.—Fābŭlă. *See Fabula.*

Făbĕr, făbrī. m. *Workman.* Cum făbĕr īncērtūs scāmnūm făcĕrētnĕ Prĭāpūm, Mālŭĭt ēssĕ dĕūm. H. Syn.—Făbrĭcātŏr, ŏpĭfēx, ārtĭfēx. Phr.—Īngēntī mōlīmĭnĕ vīrēs Ēxērcēns vălĭdās. Mūltō cōnāmĭnĕ nītēns. Făbĕr ūnŭs ĕt ūnguēs Ēxprĭmĕt.

Făbrĭcātŏr, ōrĭs. m. *Workman, architect.* Ĕt īpsĕ dŏlī făbrĭcātŏr Ĕpēŭs. V. Syn.—Făbĕr, ārtĭfēx, ŏpĭfēx, strūctŏr, ēxstrūctŏr. *See Conditor.*

Făbrĭcŏ (also dep.), ās, āvī, ātūm, ārĕ. *To make, to forge.* Pūgnābānt ārmīs quǣ pōst făbrĭcāvĕrăt. H. Syn.—Cūdŏ, prōcūdŏ, ēxcūdŏ, făcĭŏ, cōnfĭcĭŏ, pērfĭcĭŏ, cōndŏ, mōlĭŏr. *To construct.* Syn.—Aēdĭfĭcŏ, ēxstrŭŏ.

Fābŭlă, æ̅. f. *Tale, story, fable.* Hǣc fŭĭt īn tōtō nōtīssĭmă fābŭlă cœ̄lō. O. Syn.—Sērmŏ, rūmŏr. Phr.—Fābŭlă fīās. Pĕr ūrbēm fābŭlă quāntă fŭī! Fābŭlă nārrābōr fămŭlīs. *See Fama.*

Făcēssŏ, ĭs, ī & īvī, ītūm, ĕrĕ. *To do eagerly, to accomplish.* Īmpĕrĭō lǣtī pārēnt āc jūssă făcēssūnt. V. Syn.—Făcĭŏ, ēffĭcĭŏ, pĕrăgŏ, ēxsĕquŏr. Phr.—Mātrīs māndātă făcēssĭt. Ē cœ̄lo ēmōtǣ tērrāquĕ rĕpēntĕ făcēssūnt.

Făcētē. adv. *Wittily, humorously.* Syn.—Lĕpĭdē, sālsē, fēstīvē, ūrbānē, ārgūtē.

Făcētĭǣ, ārūm. f. *Wit, sallies.* Syn.—Jŏcī, sălēs, dīctērĭă.

Făcētŭs, ă, ūm. *Elegant, in good taste.* Mōlle ātquĕ făcētūm Vērgĭlĭo ānnŭĕrūnt gaūdēntēs rūrĕ Cămœ̄nǣ. H. Syn.—Ēlĕgāns, lĕpĭdŭs. *Humorous, witty.* Syn.—Lĕpĭdŭs, sālsŭs, ārgūtŭs, jŏcōsŭs, fēstīvŭs, ūrbānŭs. *Amiable.* Syn.—Cōmĭs, blāndŭs.

Făcĭēs, ēī. f. *Face.* Ēt prēssum īn făcĭē dĭgĭtīs ēxtēndĕrĕ pānēm. J. Syn.—Ōs, ōră, frōns, vūltŭs. Phr.—Ēt făcĭēm taūrō prŏpĭŏr. Făcĭēmquĕ dĕǣ vēstēsquĕ rĕpōnĭt. *See Vultus. Body.* Syn.—Cōrpŭs, fōrmă, spĕcĭēs. *Aspect.* Syn.—Fōrmă, spĕcĭēs, fĭgūră, ĭmāgŏ, vīsŭs, āspēctŭs.

Făcĭlĕ, făcĭlĭtĕr. adv. *Easily.* Syn.—Pērfăcĭlĕ. Phr.—Haūd (*or*) nōn aēgrē.

Făcĭlĭs, ĭs, ĕ. *Easy.* Fūndĭt hŭmō făcĭlēm vīctūm jūstīssĭmă tēllūs. V. Syn.—Ōbvĭŭs, prōnŭs. Phr.—Haūd dīffĭcĭlĭs, nōn ŏpĕrōsŭs, nōn ărdŭŭs. Făcĭlĭs jăctūră sĕpūlcri ēst. *Docile, flexible.* Syn.—Cērĕŭs, flēxĭbĭlĭs, mōllĭs, trāctābĭlĭs, dŏcĭlĭs.

Făcĭnŭs, ŏrĭs. n. *Action, deed (good or bad).* Syn.—Āctūm, făctūm, ŏpŭs. *Crime.* Syn.—Scĕlŭs, cūlpă, crīmĕn.

Făcĭō, ĭs, fēcī, āctūm, ĕrĕ. *To do, to act, to make.* Nīmbōrūmquĕ făcĭs tēmpēstātūmquĕ pŏtēntēm. V. Syn.—Ēffĭcĭō, pērfĭcĭō, cōnfĭcĭō, ăgŏ, pĕrăgŏ, ēxsĕquŏr, mōlĭŏr, ŏpĕrŏr, pătrŏ, pērpĕtrŏ. Phr.—Ūlcīscōr făcĭōquĕ nĕfās. Quīd făcĭăt lætās sĕgĕtēs. Ēt mē fēcērĕ pŏētām Pĭĕrĭdēs. *To execute.* Syn.—Cōnfĭcĭō, fīngŏ, făbrĭcŏ, ēffīngŏ. *To esteem. See Aostimo.*

Făctūm, ī. n. *Deed, action.* Syn.—Āctūm, făcĭnŭs, rēs. *Bad action. See Scelus. Work.* Syn.—Ŏpŭs, lăbŏr.

Făcūltās, ātĭs. f. *Force, virtue.* Syn.—Vīs, vīrtūs, pŏtēntĭă. *Faculty, power.* Syn.—Pŏtēstās, cōpĭă, ōccāsĭō, vĕnĭă.

Fācūndĭă, æ. f. *Eloquence. See Eloquentia.* Phr.—Fācūndă vīs. Dīcēndī prōnă făcūltās.

Fāgŭs, ī. f. *A beech tree.* (*See Appendix under list of Trees, etc.*)

Fālcātŭs, ă, ūm. *Curved like a scythe. See Curvus. Scythebearing.* Phr.—Fālcĭbŭs īnstrūctŭs, ārmātŭs, ōrnātŭs.

Fālcŏ, ōnĭs. m. *A falcon.* (*See Appendix under list of Birds.*)

Fāllācĭă, æ. f. *Ruse, trickery.* Vērum ŭbĭ nūllă fŭgām rĕpĕrīt fāllācĭă. V. Syn.—Āstŭs, āstūtĭă, dŏlŭs, fraūs, căllĭdĭtās, ărtēs, īnsĭdĭæ. Phr.—Ārs sūbdŏlă. Mēndācī tēctă cŏlōrĕ. *See Dolus.*

Fāllācĭtĕr. adv. *Deceitfully.* Syn.—Āstū, dŏlō, dŏlōsē. *See Astute.*

Fāllāx, ācĭs. adj. *Deceitful, treacherous.* Nōstrăquĕ fāllācī vĕnĕrātūs nūmĭnă vūltŭr. Cat. Syn.—Dŏlōsŭs, pērfĭdŭs, āstūtŭs, vērsūtŭs, căllĭdŭs, văfĕr, sūbdŏlŭs, mēndāx, pēllāx, fīctŭs, fālsŭs, īnsĭdĭōsŭs. Phr.—Blāndō căllĭdŭs ōrĕ. Fāllĕrĕ dōctŭs. Mūltă mălūs sĭmŭlāns. Căllĭdă fīngĕrĕ dōctŭs. Ănĭmī sūb vūlpĕ lătēntĭs.

Fāllŏ, ĭs, fĕfēllī, fālsūm, ĕrĕ. *To deceive.* Tūtă frĕquēnsquĕ vĭa ēst pĕr ămīcī fāllĕrĕ nōmĕn. O. Syn.—Dēcĭpĭō, lūdŏ, dēlūdŏ, căpĭŏ. Phr.—Dŏlĭs, āstū cāptārĕ. Mē fraūdĕ pĕtēbās. *See Decipio.*

Fālx, fālcĭs. f. *Scythe, sickle.* Phr.—Fālcĭs cūrvāmĕn. Fālcĭs ăcĭēs. Cūrvūs Sātūrnī dēns.

Fāmă, æ. f. *Report.* Syn.—Rūmŏr, sērmŏ, fābŭlă, nūntĭŭs. Phr.—Fāmă rērūm Aūră rūmōrĭs. Quīdquīd fāmă cănĭt. Quīsquĕ păvēndō Dāt vīrēs fāmæ. *Reputation, fame.* Syn.—Dĕcŭs, glōrĭă, nōmĕn, laūs, hŏnŏr. Phr.—Vŏlŭcrĭs præcōnĭă fāmæ. Fāmāmquĕ fŏvēmŭs ĭnānēm. Aēmŭlă fāmă lăbōrĭs Hērcŭlĕī. Mĭnŭīt præsēntĭă fāmām.

Fămēlĭcŭs, ă, ūm. *Hungry, famished.* Nōctĕ bŏvēs mācrī lāssōquĕ fămēlĭcă cōllō Ārmēntă. J. Syn.—Īmpāstŭs, jējūnŭs, ēsŭrĭēns, ăvĭdŭs. Phr.—Fămē cōnfēctŭs. Jējūnīs dēntĭbŭs ācĕr. Pāllĭdă sēmpĕr Ōră fămē.

Fămēs, ĭs. f. *Hunger.* Ēt mĕtŭs, ēt mălĕsuādă fămēs, ēt tūrpĭs ĕgēstās. V. Syn.—Ēsŭrĭēs, jējūnĭă. Phr.—Ārdŏr ĕdēndī. Jējūnă cŭpīdŏ. Mōrtĭs ălūmnă fămēs. Ōmnĕ pĕrīclūm dōctă sŭbīrĕ fămēs. Trīstī mŏrĭēntĭă tōrpēnt Mēmbră fămē. Cōllēctă fătīgăt ĕdēndī Ēx lōngō răbĭēs. Pāllĭdă jējūnō sævĭăt ōrĕ fămēs.

Fămĭlĭă, æ. f. *Family, house, race.* Pătēr fămĭlĭæ vērŭs ēst Quĭrīnālĭs. M. Syn.—Dŏmŭs, gēns, stīrps, gĕnŭs. *Servants of a house.* Syn.—Fămŭlī, sērvī.

Fămĭlĭārĭs, ĭs, ĕ. *Domestic, pertaining to the family.* Ĕgŏ lār sūm fămĭlĭārĭs ēx hāc fămĭlĭā. Plaut. Syn.—Dŏmēstĭcŭs, prīvātŭs.

Fāmōsŭs, ă, ūm. *Famous, celebrated.* Syn.—Clārŭs, præclārŭs, īnclȳtŭs, cĕlĕbĕr, īnsīgnĭs, nōbĭlĭs. Phr.—Īnsīgnīs fāma ēt fēlīcĭbŭs ārmīs. Nōtĭssĭmă fāmā Īnsŭlā.

Fămŭlă, æ. f. *Maid-servant.* Syn.—Āncīllă, mĭnīstră, sērvă *See Ancilla, Famulus.*

Fămŭlātŭs, ūs. m. *Servitude, service.* Syn.—Sērvĭtūs, sērvĭtĭūm.

Fămŭlŏr, ārĭs, ātŭs sūm, ārī. *To serve, to be in service.* Quæ tĭbī jūcūndō fămŭlārēr sērvă lăbōrĕ. Cat. Syn.—Sērvĭŏ, mĭnīstrŏ. *To be a slave to.* Syn.—Pārĕŏ, sērvĭŏ, ōbsĕquŏr.

Fămŭlŭs, ī. m. *Servant.* Vōs fămŭlī, quæ dīcam ănĭmīs ādvērtĭtĕ vēstrīs. V. Syn.—Mĭnīstĕr, sērvŭs, pŭĕr. *See Servus. Slave.* Syn.—Sērvŭs.

Fānūm, ī. n. *Temple.* Fānă tămēn vĕtĕrēs īllīs claūsērĕ dĭēbŭs. O. Syn.—Tēmplūm, dēlūbrūm.

Fār, fārrĭs. n. *Wheat.* Āt sī trītĭcĕam īn mēssēm, rōbūstăquĕ fārră Ēxērcēbĭs hŭmūm. V. Syn.—Ădŏr, frūmēntūm, trītĭcūm, frūgēs.

Fārī, fārĭs, fātŭs sūm. (*The first person of the present is not used*). *To speak.* Syn.—Ēffārī, prŏfārī, lŏquī. Phr.—Tālĭă fātŭr. Tĭbī fābŏr ĕnīm. Vīx ĕă fātŭs ĕrăt. Fāndī dōctīssĭmă.

Fās. indecl. *Right, justice.* Quīppe ĕtĭām fēstīs quædam ēxērcērĕ dĭēbūs Fās ēt jūră sĭnūnt. V. Syn.—Jūs, jūstĭtĭă, æquūm, jūstūm, lĭcĭtūm. Phr.—Fās ōmne ābrūmpĭt. Fās ēst. Fās ēst dīcĕrĕ.

Fāstī, ōrūm. m. *Fasti, Roman calendar.* Tēr quătĕr ēvōlvī sīgnāntēs tēmpŏră fāstōs. O. Syn.—Ānnālēs, mŏnŭmēntă, āctă, hīstŏrĭă.

Fāstīdĭŏ, īs, īvī & ĭī, ītūm, īrĕ. *To disdain, to reject.* Syn.—Āspērnŏr, dēdīgnŏr, spērnŏ, āvērsŏr, rēspŭŏ, rējĭcĭŏ, rĕfŭgĭŏ. Phr.—Ōmnĭă fāstīdīt prætēr pāvōnēm. H.

Fāstīdĭōsŭs, ă, ūm. *Disdainful.* Syn.—Cōntēmptŏr, spērnāx, sŭpērbŭs. *Disgusting.* Syn.—Grăvĭs, mŏlēstŭs.

Fāstīdĭūm, ĭī. n. *Disgust.* Syn.—Cōntēmptŭs, tædĭūm.

Fāstīgĭūm, ĭī. n. *Top, summit.* Cūjŭs ĕbūr nĭtĭdūm fāstīgĭă sūmmă tĕgēbăt. O. Syn.—Āpēx, căcūmĕn, cūlmĕn, vērtēx, căpŭt. Phr.—Ēt fāstīgĭă sūspĭcĭt ūrbĭs. Sūmmī fāstīgĭă tēctī. *See Cacumen.*

Fāstōsŭs, ă, ūm. *Proud, disdainful.* Syn.—Fāstīdĭōsŭs, sŭpērbŭs. Phr.—Fāstū tŭmēns. Cālcāt fāstōsă clĭēntēm. Fāstū tūrgĭdŭs āltō.

Fāstŭs, ūs. m. *Pride.* Fāstŭs ĭnēst pūlchrīs, sĕquĭtūrquĕ sŭpērbĭă fōrmām. O. Syn.—Sŭpērbĭă, tŭmŏr, fastidiūm. *See Superbia.*

Fātālĭs ĭs, ĕ. *Fatal, destined.* Quīd sī fātālēs jām nūnc ēxplēvĭmŭs ānnōs? Tib. Syn.—Cērtŭs, rătŭs, præscrīptŭs. *Deadly.* Phr.—Scāndĭt fātālĭs māchĭnă mūrōs. Tēlūm fātālĕ cŏrūscăt. Tērrārūm fātālĕ mălūm. *See Funestus.*

Fătĕŏr, ērĭs, fāssŭs sūm, ērī. *To avow, to confess.* Lĭtĕră cēlātōs ārcānă fătēbĭtŭr īgnēs. O. Syn.—Cōnfĭtĕŏr, āgnōscŏ, cōncēdŏ. Phr.—Nōn nĕgŏ. Nōn īnfĭtĭŏr. *To uncover, to unfold.* Syn.—Prōdŏ, dētĕgŏ, ōstēndŏ, ăpĕrĭŏ, tēstŏr.

Fātĭcănŭs, Fātĭcĭnŭs, fātĭdĭcŭs, ī. m. *Prophet, soothsayer.* Syn.—Prænūntĭŭs, præsāgŭs. *See Vates, Oraculum.*

Fătīgŏ, ās, āvī, ātūm, ārĕ. *To tire out.* Quādrŭpĕdēmquĕ cĭtūm fērrātā cālcĕ fătīgăt. V. Syn.—Lāssŏ, dēlāssŏ, frāngŏ, prĕmŏ, ūrgĕŏ, ēxērcĕŏ, ăgŏ, ăgĭtŏ. Phr.—Jāctāndō mēmbră fătīgăt. Quōs mūltă fătīgānt prœlĭă Sæpe ĕtĭām cūrsū quătĭūnt ēt sōlĕ fătīgānt.

Fātūm, ī. n. *Fate, destiny, lot.* Nēscĭă mēns hŏmĭnūm fātī sōrtīsquĕ fŭtūræ. V. Syn.—Sōrs, fōrtūnă, Pārcæ, Dĕŭs, Dīī. Phr.—Fātī lēx. Nūllī mūtābĭlĕ fātūm. Dīvūm dēcrētă. Sōrs ōmnĭă vērsăt. Sīc vōlvĕrĕ Pārcās. Mănēnt īmmōtă tŭōrūm fātă tĭbī. Quīppĕ vĕtōr fātīs. Nī fātă rĕsīstūnt.

Fătŭŭs, ă, ūm. *Foolish.* Syn.—Īnsūlsŭs, stūltŭs.

Faūx, faūcĭs (*generally plural*). f. *Jaws, gullet, throat.* Vīx ĕquĭdēm faūcēs hæc īpsa īn vērbă rĕsōlvŏ. O. Syn.—Gūttŭr, ōs, ōră. *Narrow passage.* Syn.—Āngūstĭæ. Phr.—Faūcĭbŭs Orcī.

Faūstŭs, ă, ūm. *Favorable, happy.* Īnquĕ părūm faūstō cārmĭnĕ dōctă fŭī. O. Syn.—Fēlīx, bĕātŭs, fōrtūnātŭs.

Faūtŏr, ōrĭs. m. & Faūtrīx, īcĭs. f. *Patron, protector.* Faūtŏr ŭtrōquĕ tŭūm laūdābĭt pōllĭcĕ lūdūm. H. Syn.—Āmīcŭs, dēfēnsŏr, ādjūtŏr, tūtŏr, făvēns, pătrōnŭs.

Făvĕō, ēs, fāvī, faūtūm, ērĕ. *To favor.* Cāstă, făvē, Lūcīnă. V. Syn.—Ādsūm, āspīrŏ, ānnŭō, sĕcūndō, ādjŭvŏ, fŏvĕō, jŭvŏ, prōtēgŏ, tŭĕŏr, rēspĭcĭŏ. Phr.—Ādsīs, ō Tĕgĕææ făvēns. Ādsīs, ō plăcĭdūsquĕ jŭvēs. Ādsīs, ō pĕdĕ Dīvă sĕcūndō.

Făvīllă, æ. f. *Glowing ashes.* Mīxtă bĭbūnt mōllēs lăcrĭmīs ūnguēntă făvīllæ. O. Syn.—Cĭnĭs. Phr.—Vīnō bĭbŭlām lāvērĕ făvīllām. *See Cinis. Flame, spark.* Syn.—Scīntīllă. *See Ignis.*

Făvŏr, ōrĭs. m. *Favor, grace.* Syn.—Ămŏr, stŭdĭūm, grātĭă. Phr.—Aūră pŏpŭlārĭs. *Applause.* Syn.—Plaūsŭs, frĕmĭtŭs.

Făvŭs, ī. m. *Honey-comb.* Crātēs sōlvērĕ făvōrūm. V. Syn.—Mēl, cēllæ, cēră. Phr.—Spūmāntĭă cōgĕrĕ prēssīs Mēllă făvīs. Ēxprēssīs mēllă lĭquātă făvīs. Prīmă făvī pōnūnt fūndāmĭnă. *See Mel.*

Fāx, făcĭs. f. *Torch.* Ātque ōmnīs făcĭbūs pūbēs āccīngĭtŭr ātrīs. V. Syn.—Tædă, fūnālĕ, lāmpăs, lūmĕn, cērĕŭs. Phr.—Pĭcĕă tædă. Flāmmĭfĕræque ārdēnt pīnūs. Āccēnsās vēntĭlăt aūră făcēs. Fērtĕ făcēs īn tēctă. Jāmquĕ făcēs ēt sāxă vŏlānt. *The light of the sun.* Syn.—Lūx, jŭbăr, lūmĕn, flāmmă, īgnĭs.

Fĕbrĭs, ĭs. f. *Fever.* Nēc călĭdæ cĭtĭūs dēcēdūnt cōrpŏrĕ fēbrēs. Phr.—Cōrpŏrĭs ārdŏr. Fĕbrĭs īmpĕtŭs. Dīrīs ūrēns fērvōrĭbŭs ārtūs. Dēdūcĕrĕ cōrpŏrĕ fēbrēs. Ēt nŏvă fēbrĭūm Tērrīs īncŭbŭīt cŏhōrs.

Fēcūndŭs, ă, ūm. *Fertile.* Āt sī nōn fŭĕrīt tēllūs fēcūndă. V. Syn.—Fĕrāx, fērtĭlĭs. Fig.—*Abundant.* Syn.—Plēnŭs, ăbūndāns, fērtĭlĭs, fĕrāx.

Fēl, fēllĭs. n. *Gall, venom.* Ōmnĭă vīpĕrĕō spīcŭlă fēllĕ lĭnūnt. O. Syn.—Vīrŭs, vĕnēnūm. Phr.—Fēllĕ vĕnēnī ārmātă săgīttă. *See Venenum. Bitterness.* Syn.—Āmārŏr, ămārĭtĭēs.

Fēlīcĭtās, ātĭs. f. *Happiness, good fortune.* Ō nūllă lōngī tēmpŏrīs fēlīcĭtās! Sen. Syn.—Faūstĭtās, prōspĕrĭtās, prōspĕră (ōrūm), lætă. Phr.—Fōrtūnă fēlīx. Fātă prōspĕră. Mĕlĭŏr fōrtūna ēst. Nūnquām lætīs crēdĕrĕ rēbŭs. Vūltūm sērvāt fōrtūnă bĕnīgnūm.

Fēlīcĭtĕr. adv. *Happily.* Nām spīrāt trăgĭcūm sătĭs, ēt fēlīcĭtĕr aūdĕt. H. Syn.—Bĕātē, faūstē, fōrtūnātē. Phr.—Ālĭtĕ dēxtrō. Ōmĭnĕ dēxtrō. Aūspĭcĭō faūstō. Īmplērĕ sŭōs fēlīcĭtĕr ānnōs.

Fēlĭs & Fēlēs, ĭs. m. & f. *Cat.* Fēlĕ sŏrōr Phœbī, nĭvĕā Sātūrnĕā văccā. O. Syn.—Aēlūrŭs.

Fēlīx, īcĭs. adj. *Happy.* Fēlīx quī pŏtŭīt rērūm cōgnōscĕrĕ caūsās. V. Syn.—Bĕātŭs, fōrtūnātŭs. Phr.—Quō nōn fēlīcĭŏr āltĕr. Ēt fēlīcīssĭmă mātrūm. Cuī vūltū rīdēt fōrtūnă sĕrēnō. Cuī fōrtūnă sĕrēna ēst. Ōmnĭă Dī cuī vōtă sĕcūndānt. Ō tērquĕ bĕātī! Ō fēlīx ūna ānte ălĭās. Nēmŏ mălūs fēlīx. *See Felicitas.* *Favorable, propitious.* Syn.—Prōspĕr, faūstŭs, sĕcūndŭs. *Proper, useful.* Syn.—Āptŭs, ĭdōnĕŭs, ūtĭlĭs, ōppōrtūnŭs, præsēns.

Fēmĭnă, æ. f. *Woman.* Quōt scĕlĕrātă gĕrīt fēmĭnă mēntĕ dŏlōs! O. Syn.—Mŭlĭĕr. Phr.—Mŭlĭĕbrĕ, fēmĭnĕūm gĕnŭs. Īmbēllĭs sēxŭs. Vărĭum ēt mūtābĭlĕ sēmpĕr Fēmĭnă. Nōtūmquĕ fŭrēns quīd fēmĭnă pōssīt.

Fēmĭnĕŭs, ă, ūm. *Pertaining to woman.* Ēt dē fēmĭnĕō rĕpărāta ēst fēmĭnă jāctū. O. Syn.—Mŭlĭĕbrĭs. *Effeminate.* Syn.—Īmbēllĭs, īgnāvŭs.

Fēnĕrātŏr, ōrĭs. m. *Usurer.* Hæc ŭbĭ lŏcutus fenerātŏr Alphĭŭs. H. Phr.—Fēnŭs ăvārum ēxērcēns. Ūsūræ lŭcrūm quærēns, lŭcră cāptāns, lŭcrīs ĭnhĭāns. *See Fenero.*

Fēnĕrō, ās, āvī, ātūm, ārĕ. (*Also used as a deponent*). *To lend money at interest.* Hæc săpĭt hæc ōmnēs fēnĕrāt ūnă dĕōs. M. Phr.—Dō fēnŏrī, ĭn ūsūrām ēxērcĕō. Fēnŏrĕ lŭcrūm quærō. Īn fēnŭs căpĭō.

Fĕnēstră, æ. f. *Window.* Bĭfōrēs īntrābāt lūnă fĕnēstrās. O. Phr.—Āltæ cālīgāntēsquĕ fĕnēstræ. Lūnă pĕr īnsērtās fūndēbāt plēnă fĕnēstrās.

Fēnūm, ī. n. *Hay.* Sēd tūtă fēnō cūrsŏr ōvă pōrtābăt. M. Syn.—Hērbă, grāmĕn.

Fēnŭs, ŏrĭs. n. *Usury, interest.* Ūsūră vŏrāx, ăvĭdūmque īn tēmpŏrĕ fēnŭs. L. Syn.—Ūsūră, lŭcrūm, quæstŭs. See *Fenero.*

Fĕră, æ. f. *Wild beast.* Ītŭr ĭn āntīquām sīlvām stăbŭla āltă fĕrārūm. V. Syn.—Fĕrŭs, bēllŭă, mōnstrūm. Phr.—Mōntĭvăgūm fĕrārūm gĕnŭs. Ārmēntă fĕrārūm. Īntēr dēsērtă fĕrārūm.

Fērālĭs, ĭs, ĕ. *Pertaining to funerals, funereal.* Sōlăquĕ cūlmĭnĭbūs fērālī cārmĭnĕ būbō Vīsă quĕrī. V. Syn.—Fūnĕrĕŭs, fūnĕbrĭs, lūgŭbrĭs. Phr.—Fērālēs āntĕ cŭprēssōs. *Fatal.* Syn.—Fātālĭs, fūnēstŭs, dīrŭs, ēxĭtĭālĭs. *See Funestus.*

Fērcŭlūm, ī. n. *A dish or mess of food.* Mūltăquĕ dē māgnā sŭpĕrēssēnt fērcŭlă cœnā. H. Syn.—Ĕpŭlæ, dăpēs, ēscă, cĭbŭs. Phr.—Nūllĭs ōrnātă măcēllĭs Fērcŭlă. *See Cibus.*

Fĕrē. adv. *Almost.*. Jāmquĕ fĕrē sīccō sūbdūctæ līttŏrĕ pūppēs. V. Syn.—Fērmē, prŏpĕ, pēnĕ. *Generally.* Syn.—Vūlgō, plērūmquĕ, fērmē, sæpĭŭs.

Fĕrĕtrūm, ī. n. *Bier.* Mōllĕ fĕrētrūm Ārbŭtĕīs tēxūnt vīrgīs ēt vīmĭnĕ quērnō. V. Syn.—Căpŭlŭs, ārcă, sāndăpĭlă. Phr.—Plēbēiī fūnĕrĭs ārcă. Dūrō pŏsŭērūnt mēmbră fĕrētrō.

Fērĭæ, ārūm. f. *Festal days.* Lōngās, ō ŭtĭnām, dūx bŏnĕ, fērĭās Præstēs Hēspĕrĭæ. H. Syn.—Fēstă, (*sometimes*) ōtĭă. *See Festum.*

Fĕrĭŏ, īs, īrĕ. *To strike, to beat.* Ōccūrsārĕ căprō, cōrnū fĕrĭt īllĕ, căvētō. V. Cædŏ, pērcŭtĭŏ, vērbĕrŏ, pūlsŏ; (*with the foot*) tĕrŏ, prōtĕrŏ, cālcŏ. Phr.—Mănū pērcŭtĭŏ. Mănĭbŭs īnsĕquŏr. Taūrūs fĕrĭt ūncīs cōrnĭbŭs hōstēm. Ūt cālcĕ fĕrītŭr ăsēllī. Īngēns ā vērtĭcĕ pōntŭs Īn pūppīm fĕrĭt. Sūblīmī fĕrĭām sīdĕră vērtĭcĕ.

Fĕrĭtās, ātĭs. f. *Wildness, fierceness.* Quāmquĕ lŭpī sævæ plūs fĕrĭtātĭs hăbēnt. O. Syn.—Bārbărĭēs, rĭgŏr, āspĕrĭtās. Phr.—Nēque īpsĕ mănūs fĕrĭtātĕ dĕdīssĕt. *See Barbaries.*

Fērmē. adv. *Almost.* Syn.—Fĕrē, pēnĕ, prŏpĕ. *Generally.* Syn.—plērūmquĕ, vūlgō, sæpĕ, sæpĭŭs.

Fĕrŏ, fērs, tŭlī, lātūm, fērrĕ. *To carry, to bear.* Aēthĕrĭūm quī fērt cērvīcĭbŭs āxēm. O. Syn.—Pōrtŏ, tōllŏ, gĕrŏ, gēstŏ. Phr.—Pēplūmquĕ fĕrēbānt. Mōllī cŏmĭtūm cērvīcĕ fĕrētŭr. Īllă phărētrām Fērt hŭmĕrō. *See Porto. To endure.* Syn.—Tŏlĕrŏ, pătĭŏr, pērpĕtĭŏr, sūstĭnĕŏ, sŭbĕŏ, pērfĕrŏ. Phr.—Pēccātō dāmnă tŭlērĕ sŭō. *To produce.* Syn.—Prōfĕrŏ, crĕŏ, gīgnŏ, părĭŏ, ēdŏ. *To give.* Syn.—Dō, trĭbŭŏ, āffĕrŏ.

Fĕrōcĭtās, ātĭs. f. *Fierceness.* Syn.—Fĕrĭtās. *See Feritas.*

Fĕrōcĭŏ, īs, īrĕ. *To rage, to be ungovernable.* Syn.—Ēffĕrŏr, sævĭŏ, bācchŏr. *See Furo.*

Fĕrōcĭtĕr. adv. *Proudly.* Syn—Sŭpērbē. *Cruelly.* Syn.—Crūdēlĭtĕr, īmmānĭtĕr.

Fĕrōx, ōcĭs. adj. *Fierce, ungovernable.* Stāt sŏnĭpēs ēt frēnă fĕrōx spūmāntĭă māndĭt. V. Syn.—Fĕrŭs, āspĕr, īndŏmĭtŭs. Phr.—Fĕrōcī vīrtūtĕ. *Bold, intrepid.* Syn.—Aūdāx, fīdēns, ācĕr, īmpăvĭdŭs. Phr.—Bēllo ĕrāt īllĕ fĕrōx. *Cruel.* Syn.—Fĕrŭs, ēffĕrŭs, bārbărŭs, ătrōx, crūdēlĭs, tōrvŭs, trūx, trŭcŭlēntŭs.

Fērrĕŭs, ă, ūm. *Iron.* Īt tōtō tūrbĭdă cœlō Tēmpēstās tēlōrum āc fērrĕŭs īngrŭĭt īmbĕr. V. Phr.—Fērrĕă tēlōrūm sĕgĕs. Ăgĕr hōrrēt fērrĕŭs hāstīs. Dēcrētă sŏrōrūm fērrĕă. Fērrĕă ætās. *Cold, hardened.* Syn.—Dūrŭs. *Of the color of iron.* Syn.—Fērrūgĭnĕŭs, ātĕr.

Fērrūgŏ, ĭnĭs. f. *Iron-rust.* Syn.—Rūbīgŏ.

Fērrūm, ī. n. *Iron.* Āst hŏmĭnī fērrūm lētāle īn cōtĕ nĕfāndā Prōdūxīssĕ părum ēst. J. Syn.—Chălȳbs. Phr.—Fērrī rĭgŏr, rōbŭr. Fērrūm dūm mōllĭăt īgnĭs. Fig.—*Sword.* Syn.—Glădĭŭs.

Fērtĭlĭs, ĭs, ĕ. *Fertile.* Fērtĭlĭŏr sĕgĕs ēst ălĭēnīs sēmpĕr ĭn ārvīs. O. Syn.—Fēcūndŭs, fĕrāx, ăbūndāns, dīvĕs, lætŭs, ŏpīmŭs, ūbĕr, fēlīx, lūxŭrĭāns. Phr.—Frūgĭbŭs ūbĕr. Bācchī Cĕrĕrīsquĕ fĕrāx. Tēllūs dītīssĭmă. Cāmpūs frūmēntīs ūtĭlĭs. Ăgĕr mēssĭbŭs ŏnĕrātŭs. *See Abundantia.*

Fērtĭlĭtās, ātĭs. f. *Fertility.* Syn.—Cōpĭă, fēcūndĭtās, fĕrācĭtās, ūbērtās, ăbūndāntĭă. Phr.—Dīvĭtĭs ūbĕr ăgrī. Tēllūrĭs ālmæ lætă sĭnūm bĕāns. *See Abundantia.*

Fĕrŭs, ă, ūm. *Wild, savage.* Prīmă fĕrōs hăbĭtūs hŏmĭnī dētrāxĭt. O. Syn.—Āspĕr, ăgrēstĭs, īndŏmĭtŭs. Phr.—Īndŏmĭtă cērvīcĕ fĕrŭs. *Cruel.* Syn.—Sævŭs, bārbărŭs, crūdēlĭs, īmmānĭs, īmmītĭs, trŭcŭlēntŭs. *See Crudelis.*

Fĕrŭs, ī. m. *Wild beast.* *See Fera.*

Fērvĕō, ēs, bŭī, ērĕ & ĕrĕ. *To grow warm, or hot.* Cōncāvă līttŏreī fervēbānt brāchĭă cāncrī. O. Syn.—Fērvēscŏ, ārdĕō, ēxārdĕō, călĕō, ūrŏr, āccēndŏr. Phr.—Fērvēt līnguă mĕrō. *To boil.* Syn.—Aēstŭō, ēxæstŭō, būllĭō, ēbūllĭō. Fig.—*To become angry.* Syn.—Aēstŭō, ăgĭtŏr, mŏvĕŏr, tūrbŏr.

Fērvēscŏ, ĭs, ĕrĕ. *To begin to grow warm.* Syn.—Călēscŏ, īncălēscŏ, ārdēscŏ, āccēndŏr.

Fērvĭdŭs, ă, ūm. *Hot, boiling, burning.* Vŏlāt vī fērvĭdŭs āxĭs. V. Syn.—Fērvēns, ārdēns, æstŭāns, īgnĕŭs, călĭdŭs. Phr.—Ēt cŭmŭlānt āltōs fērvĭdă mūstă lăcūs. Mētăquĕ fērvĭdīs Ēvītātă rŏtīs. *Agitated.* Syn.—Aēstŭāns, æstŭōsŭs, fērvēns, ăgĭtātŭs, cōmmōtŭs, tūrbātŭs. *Fiery.* Syn.—Fērvēns, ārdēns, flăgrāns, īncēnsŭs, sūccēnsŭs, călĭdŭs, călēns.

Fērvŏr, ōrĭs. m. *Great heat, ardor.* Tūm prīmūm sīccīs āēr fērvōrĭbŭs ūstŭs Cāndŭīt. O. Syn.—Ārdŏr, æstŭs, călŏr. Phr.—Mĕdĭīs fērvōrĭbŭs ācrĭŏr īnstăt. Īncēndītque āĕră fērvŏr Aēstīvŭs. *See Aestas, calor.*

Fēssŭs, ă, ūm. *Tired, weary.* Āccĭpĭt ēt fēssōs ŏpĭbūs sōlātŭr ămīcīs. V. Syn.—Dēfēssŭs, lāssŭs, fătīgātŭs, frāctŭs, lānguēns, lānguĭdŭs, vīctŭs, dēfĭcĭēns, ēffētŭs, ēxhaūstŭs. Phr.—Răpĭdō fēssīs mēssōrĭbŭs æstū. Mĭhī vōx fēssă lŏquēndō. Fēssī rērūm.

Fēstīnŏ, ās, āvī, ātūm, ārĕ. *To hasten.* Fēstīnātĕ vĭrī; Nām quæ tām sēră mŏrātŭr Sēgnĭtĭēs. V. Syn.—Cĕlĕrŏ, āccĕlĕrŏ, prŏpĕrŏ, āpprŏpĕrŏ, ādvŏlŏ, prōvŏlŏ, mātūrŏ, præcĭpĭtŏ, cūrrŏ, āccūrrŏ, prōsĭlĭō, vŏlŏ. Phr.—Răpĭdīs pāssĭbŭs fĕrŏr. Mŏrās pēllŏ. Āccĕlĕrārĕ grădūm. Mātūrātĕ fŭgām. Īn mē mŏră nōn ĕrĭt ūllă. Haūd mŏră. Dīctō cĭtĭūs tŭmĭda æquŏră plācăt. *To hasten on a work.* Syn.—Prŏpĕrŏ, mātūrŏ, cĕlĕrŏ, āccĕlĕrŏ, prĕmŏ, ūrgĕŏ, īnstŏ, āccĕlĕrŏ.

Fēstīnŭs, ă, ūm. *Prompt, quick.* Syn.—Cĭtŭs, cōncĭtŭs, cĭtātŭs, lĕvĭs, pērnīx, prŏpĕrŭs, prŏpĕrāns, răpĭdŭs, vēlōx, vŏlŭcĕr.

Fēstīvē. adv. *Agreeably, pleasantly.* Syn.—Făcētē, ūrbānē, lĕpĭdē.

Fēstīvŭs, ă, ŭm. *Agreeable, joyous, pleasant.* Syn.—Fēstŭs, lætŭs, hĭlărĭs, jŏcōsŭs, lĕpĭdŭs, ūrbānŭs, făcētŭs.

Fēstŭm, ī. n. *Feast-day.* Fōrtĕ Jŏvī Phœbŭs fēstŭm sōlēmnĕ părābăt. O. Phr.—Dĭēs fēstŭs (*or*) fēstă. Fēstīvă dĭēs, lūx. Sōllēmnĭă săcră. Dĭēs dĕō săcĕr. Īmmūnēs ŏpĕrŭm dĭēs. Sēcŭlō fēstās rĕfĕrēntĕ lūcēs. Fēstă dĭē pĕrăgēndă săcră.

Fētĭdŭs, ă, ŭm. *Ill-smelling.* Syn.—Fētēns, pūtēns, pūtĭdŭs, grăvĭs, grăvĕŏlēns, pēstĭfĕr, tētĕr, vīrōsŭs.

Fĭbră, æ. f. *Entrails.* Syn.—Ēxtă, vīscĕră.

Fībŭlă, æ. f. *Buckle, brooch.* Aūrĕă pūrpŭrĕām sūbnēctĭt fībŭlă vēstēm. V. Phr.—Tĕrĕtī fībŭlă gēmmā. Sūmmām mōrdēbăt fībŭlă vēstēm. Huĭc strīngĭt ĕbūrnĕă vēstēm Fībŭlă.

Fīcēdŭlă, æ. f. *A figpecker, becafico.* (*See Appendix under list of Birds.*)

Fīctĭlĕ, ĭs. n. *Earthen vessel.* Nūllīs ăcōnītă bĭbūntŭr Fīctĭlĭbŭs. J. Syn.—Fīglīnă, tēstă, fĭdēlĭă. Phr.—Fīctĭlĭă pōcŭlă, vāsă. Sămĭă tēstă.

Fīctĭlĭs, ĭs, ĕ. *Earthen, made of clay.* Fīctĭlĭbūs crēvērĕ Dĭīs hæc aūrĕă tēmplă. Pr. Syn.—Fīglīnŭs, lūtĕŭs. Pōcŭlă fāctă lūtō.

Fīctŭm, ī. n. *Falsehood.* Tām fīctī prāvīquĕ tĕnāx quām nūntĭă vērī. V. Syn.—Mēndācĭŭm, cōmmēntŭm. *See Mendacium.*

Fĭdēlĭă, æ. f. *Earthen vessel.* Rēspōndēt nōn cōctă fĭdēlĭă līmō. Pers. Syn.—Tēstă, fīglīnŭm, fīctĭlĕ. *See Fictile.*

Fĭdēlĭs, ĭs, ĕ. *Faithful.* Īlle hăbŭĭt fīdāmquĕ mănŭm sŏcĭōsquĕ fĭdēlēs. O. Syn.—Fīdŭs, cōnstāns. Phr.—Fĭdē nōtŭs, clārŭs. Hŏmŏ fĭdēlī mēntĕ. Pācĕ prŏbātă fĭdēs. Cōnstāntī jŭvĕnīs fĭdē. Făcĭlĭs tĕmĕrārĕ fĭdēm. Quī mūtārĕ fĭdēm nēscĭt. Pēctŏră nēscĭă fraūdŭm. *See Constans.*

Fĭdēlĭtĕr. adv. *Faithfully.* Syn.—Fĭdē, cōnstāntĕr.

Fĭdēs, ĕī. f. *Faith, trust.* Cānă fĭdēs ēt Vēstă, Rĕmō cūm frātrĕ Quĭrīnŭs. V. Phr.—Hæsūră sŭīs tēmpŭs ĭn ōmnĕ fĭdēs. Hæccĭnĕ vēstră fĭdēs? Ēn dēxtră fĭdēsquĕ! Ēn hæc prōmīssă fĭdēs ēst! *See Fidelis. Virtue.* Syn.—Īnnŏcēntĭă, vīrtūs. *See Innocentia. Word of honor, oath.* Syn.—Jūsjūrāndŭm, jūrāmēntŭm, săcrāmēntŭm.

Fĭdēs, dĭs. f. *Lyre.* Syn.—Cĭthără, chĕlȳs, bārbĭtŭs, lȳră, tēstūdŏ. *The chords of a musical instrument.* Syn.—Chōrdæ, fīlă, nērvī. *To play on the lyre.* Phr.—Fĭdēs, chōrdās pūlsŏ, tēndŏ. Fīlă lȳræ mĕdĭtŏr. Cănōrĭs fĭdĭbŭs rĕsŏnānt. Lēsbōŭm tēndĕrĕ bārbĭtŏn.

Fĭdĭcĕn, ĭnĭs. m. *Harpist, player on the lyre.* Rōmānæ fĭdĭcĕn lȳræ. H. Syn.—Cĭthărīstă, cĭthărœdŭs.

Fīdŏ, ĭs, sŭs sŭm, ĕrĕ. *To trust in.* Heū, nĭhĭl īnvītīs fās quēmquām fīdĕrĕ dīvīs. V. Syn.—Cōnfīdŏ, crēdŏ, cōncrēdŏ. Phr.—Fĭdēm hăbĕŏ. Mē hăbĕt fīdūcĭă. Nĭmĭūm nē crēdĕ jŭvēntæ. Nūnquām lætīs crēdĕrĕ rēbŭs.

Fīdūcĭă, æ. f. *Faith, confidence.* Tāntănĕ vōs gĕnĕrīs tĕnŭīt fīdūcĭă vēstrī? V. Syn.—Fĭdēs, cōnfīdēntĭă, aūdācĭă, aūsŭs. Phr.—Quæ sīt fīdūcĭă cāptō. Nōn aūdācī cēssīt fīdūcĭă Tūrnō. Quō sīt fīdūcĭă mājŏr Mūnĕrĭs. *See Audacia.*

Fīdŭs, ă, ūm. *Faithful.* Fōrtūnātă, dŏmūs, mŏdŏ sīt tĭbĭ fīdŭs ămīcŭs. Prop. Syn.—Fĭdēlĭs. Phr.—Fīdīs ŏffēndăr ămīcīs. Fīdusque ād līmĭnă cūstōs. Rēx ō fīdīssĭmă Teūcrūm. *Sure.* Syn.—Tūtŭs, ămīcŭs, fĭdēlĭs.

Fīgŏ, ĭs, xī, xūm, ĕrĕ. *To fix, to nail, to attach.* Vĕrūbūsquĕ trĕmēntĭă fīgūnt Tērgŏră. V. Syn.—Āffīgŏ, dēfīgŏ, īnfīgŏ, præfīgŏ. Phr.—Īnĭmīcăquĕ nōmĭnă fīgī. *To suspend.* Syn.—Sūspēndŏ, āffīgŏ.

Fĭgŭlŭs, ī. m. *Potter.* Syn.—Fīctŏr. Phr.—Ārgīllæ făbrĭcātŏr. Tēstārum ŏpĭfēx. Lŭtĕūm ŏpŭs fīngĕrĕ dōctŭs. *See Artifex.*

Fĭgūră, æ. f. *Figure, form.* Īndŭĭt īgnōtās hŏmĭnūm cōnvērsă fĭgūrās. O. Syn.—Fōrmă, spĕcĭēs, ĭmāgŏ, făcĭēs, sĭmŭlācrūm. Phr.—Mūltĭgĕnīs vărĭātă fĭgūrīs. Sīgnātūr cērā fĭgūrīs. *The body.* Syn.—Vūltŭs, ōs, făcĭēs, fōrmă, cōrpŭs, vīsŭs, āspēctŭs. *Shadow. See Simulacrum.*

Fĭgūrŏ, ās, āvī, ātūm, ārĕ. *To form, to fashion.* Ōs tĕnĕrūm pŭĕrī bālbūmquĕ pŏētă fĭgūrăt. H. Syn.—Fōrmŏ, fīngŏ, ēffīngŏ. *To represent.* Syn.—Fīngŏ, ēffīngŏ, ĭmĭtŏr.

Fīlĭă, æ. f. *Daughter.* Sōlă dŏmūm tāntās sērvābĭt fīlĭă sēdēs. V. Syn.—Nātă, prōlēs, sŏbŏlēs, fīlĭŏlă. Phr.—Fōrmā præstāntĕ pŭēllās. Mātrĕ pūlchrā fīlĭă pūlchrĭŏr. *See Virgo.*

Fīlĭŭs, ĭī. m. *Son.* Fīlĭŭs huīc fātō dīvūm prōlēsquĕ vĭrīlĭs Nūllă fŭĭt. V. Syn.—Nātŭs, prōlēs, prōgĕnĭēs, sŏbŏlēs. Phr.—Māscŭlă prōlēs. Părēntīs spēs. Cūrārum ēt sĕnĭī dūlcĕ lĕvāmĕn. Spēs fīrmă părēntĭs. Quō sānguĭnĕ crētŭs.

Fīlūm, ī. n. *Thread.* Pūrpŭrĕāsquĕ nŏtās fīlīs īntēxŭĭt ālbīs. O. Syn.—Stāmĕn, līnūm. Phr.—Stāmēn fīlī. Lēntūm fīlīs īmmīttĭtŭr aūrūm. Lĕvī dēdūcēns pōllĭcĕ fīlūm. *Strings of a lyre.* Syn.—Chōrdæ, nērvī.

Fīmbrĭă, æ. f. *Fringe, border.* Fīmbrĭă sāltēm vīx āttāctă Dĕī mōrbīs mĕdĕātūr ăcērbīs. Syn.—Lăcīnĭă, īnstĭtă, līmbŭs, ōră, cīrrŭs.

Fīndŏ, ĭs, ĭdī, īssūm, ĕrĕ. *To split, to cleave.* Nām prīmī cŭnĕīs fīndēbānt fīssĭlĕ līgnūm. V. Syn.—Dīffīndŏ, ēffīndŏ, scīndŏ, prōscīndŏ, sĕcŏ, dīvĭdŏ, sēpărŏ. Phr.—Fīndĭtŭr īn sŏlĭdūm cŭnĕīs vĭă. Pārtēs ŭbī sē vĭă fīndĭt ĭn āmbās. Frĕtă fīndĕrĕ clāssĕ. *See Scindo.*

Fīnēs, ĭūm. m. *End, limit, boundaries.* Fīnĭbŭs ōmnēs Prōsĭlŭērĕ sŭīs. V. Syn.—Cōnfīnĭă, tērmĭnī, līmĭtēs. Phr.—Fīnĭtĭmī ăgrī. Vīcīnă tēllūs. Lātē fīnēs cūstōdĕ tŭērī. Dētrūdĕrĕ fīnĭbŭs hōstēs. Jūrĭs trānscēndĕrĕ fīnēs.

Fīngŏ, ĭs, nxī, ctūm, ĕrĕ. *To make, to forge.* Mūlcēre āltērnōs ēt cōrpŏră fīngĕrĕ līnguā. V. Syn.—Făcĭŏ, ēffīngŏ, fōrmŏ, fĭgūrŏ, īnfōrmŏ, cōmpōnŏ, strŭŏ, pōnŏ. Phr.—Ēt Dædălă fīngĕrĕ tēctă. Ēt mēllă tĕnācĭă fīngūnt. *To instruct.* Syn.—Īnstĭtŭŏ, īnfōrmŏ, fōrmŏ. *To persuade.* Syn.—Trāctŏ, flēctŏ. *To imagine, to invent.* Syn.—Părŏ, strŭŏ, mōlĭŏr, ēxcōgĭtŏ, mĕdĭtŏr. *To pretend.* Syn.—Sĭmŭlŏ.

Fīnĭŏ, īs, īvī & ĭī, ītūm, īrĕ. *To finish, to end.* Syn.—Ābsōlvŏ, cōnfĭcĭŏ, pērfĭcĭŏ, cōnclūdŏ, ēxĭgŏ, pĕrăgŏ, īmplĕŏ, cōmplĕŏ, ēxplĕŏ. Phr.—Fīnēm făcĭŏ, dō. Mŏdūm stătŭŏ. Ād fīnēm pērdūcĕrĕ. Ēxtrēmām mănūm āddĕrĕ. Fīnēm dĕdĭt ōrĕ lŏquēndī. Prīmă mĕī pārs ēst ēxāctă lăbōrĭs.

Fīnĭs, ĭs. m. & f. *End.* Syn.—Ēxĭtŭs, tērmĭnŭs, mētă, līmĕs. Phr.—Jām fīnĭs ĕrăt. Quīs scĕlĕrūm mŏdŭs ēst. Īmpĕrĭūm sĭnĕ fīnĕ dĕdī. Fīnĭs ădēst.

Fīnĭtĭmŭs, ă, ūm. *Near, neighboring.* Hīc ĕgŏ fīnĭtĭmīs quāmvīs cīrcūmsŏnĕr ārmīs. O. Syn.—Vīcīnŭs, prōxĭmŭs, prŏpīnquŭs, cōntērmĭnŭs, āccŏlă.

Fĭŏ, fīs, āctŭs sūm, ĭĕrī. *To be made.* (*The passive of Facio*). *See Facio.*

Fīrmāmĕn, ĭnĭs. n. *Rest, support.* Pōrrĭgĭtūr rādīx lōngī fīrmāmĭnĕ trūncī. O. Syn.—Cŏlŭmĕn, fūlcrūm, fūlcīmĕn, fūlcīmēntūm.

Fīrmĭtās, ātĭs, & Fīrmĭtūdŏ, ĭnĭs. f. *Firmness, force, vigor.* Syn.—Rōbŭr, vīs, cōnstāntĭă.

Fīrmĭtĕr. adv. *Firmly.* Syn.—Īmmōtē, sŏlĭdē, vălĭdē, cōnstāntĕr, fōrtĭtĕr.

Fīrmŏ, ās, āvī, ātūm, ārĕ. *To strengthen.* Sēd nōn ūllă măgīs vīrēs īndūstrĭă fīrmăt. V. Syn.—Cōnfīrmŏ, rōbŏrŏ, cōrrōbŏrŏ, mūnĭŏ, stăbĭlĭŏ. *To assure.* Syn.—Cōnfīrmŏ, ērĭgŏ, ēxtōllŏ.

Fīrmŭs, ă, ūm. *Firm, solid.* Ēt fīrmō pōplĭtĕ nōndūm Cōnstĭtĭt. O. Syn.—Fīxŭs, stăbĭlĭs, sŏlĭdŭs, vălĭdŭs, īmmōtŭs, īmmōbĭlĭs.

Fīstŭlă, æ. f. *Tube, pipe. See Canalis. Flute.* Quēm mĕă cārmĭnĭbūs mĕrŭīssēt fīstŭlă cāprūm. Syn.—Ărūndŏ, ăvēnă, būxŭs, călămŭs, cānnă, tībĭă, cĭcūtă. Phr.—Ārgūtă ărūndŏ. Cănōră būxŭs. Tĭbĭ fīstŭlă cērā Jūnctă fŭĭt. Sūspīrāt mōtōs ĭn ărūndĭnĕ vēntōs. Cārmēn grăcĭlī mŏdŭlātŭs ăvēnā.

Flābrūm, ī. n. *Blast of wind.* Syn.—Flāmĕn, flātŭs, aūră, vēntŭs. Phr.—Mōntēsquĕ sŭprēmōs Sīlvĭfrăgīs vēxāt flābrīs. Pĕtŭlāntĭbŭs īncĭtă flābrīs.

Flăgēllŏ, ās, āvī, ātūm, ārĕ. *To whip.* Syn.—Cædŏ, pērcŭtĭŏ, vērbĕrŏ. Phr.—Flăgēllō ĕquōs ēxcĭtŏ. Ūrgĕt ĕnīm stĭmŭlīs aūrīgă crŭēntīs. *See Verbero.*

Flăgēllūm, ī. n. *Whip.* Sīc tĭbĭ dē Fŭrĭīs scīndāt lătŭs ūnă flăgēllō. O. Syn.—Lōrūm, flăgrūm, vīrgă, scŭtĭcă, vērbĕr, vērbĕră.

Flāgĭtĭūm, ĭī. n. *Crime.* Pōssĕt ĕt īn tāntō vīvĕrĕ flāgĭtĭō. Pr. Syn.—Scĕlŭs, măcŭlă, īnfāmĭă, ōpprŏbrĭūm, dēdĕcŭs. *See Scelus, Infamia.*

Flāgĭtŏ, ās, āvī, ātūm, ārĕ. *To ask. See Peto.*

Flăgrŏ, ās, āvī, ātūm, ārĕ. *To burn.* Flāgrābānt sānctī scĕlĕrātīs īgnĭbŭs īgnēs. O. Syn.—Dēflăgrŏ, ārdĕŏ, ēxārdēscŏ, āccēndŏr, ūrŏr. *To desire. See Cupio.*

Flāmĕn, ĭnĭs. n. *Blast, wind.* Ōbvĭăque ādvērsās vībrābānt flāmĭnă vēstēs. O. Syn.—Flābră, flātŭs, aūră, spīrĭtŭs, vēntŭs.

Flāmĕn, ĭnĭs. m. *High-priest.* Syn.—Āntīstĕs, săcērdōs.

Flāmmă, æ. f. *Flame.* Īn sĕgĕtēm vĕlŭtī cūm flāmmă fŭrēntĭbŭs Aūstrīs Īncĭdĭt. V. *See Ignis.* Phr.—Ēxsŭpĕrānt flāmmæ. Flāmmās ād cūlmĭnă jāctăt. Mœnĭă cōllūcēnt flāmmīs. Cōrrĭpŭĭt trĕmŭlīs āltārĭă flāmmīs Īgnĭs ĕdāx. *Fire.* Syn.—Īgnĭs, Vūlcānŭs.

Flāmmĕŭs, ă, ūm. *Inflamed.* Syn.—Flāmmātŭs, flāmmāns, flāmmĭfĕr, flāmmĭvŏmŭs, īgnĕŭs, īgnĭfĕr, īgnĭvŏmŭs, īgnītŭs, āccēnsŭs, flăgrāns, ārdēns, călĭdŭs, cāndēns.

Flātŭs, ūs. m. *Wind.* Ēt mădĭdīs Eūrī rĕsŏlūtæ flātĭbŭs Ālpēs. L. Syn.—Flābră, flāmĕn, vēntŭs, aūră, spīrĭtŭs. Phr.—Āspīrāns prōpēllĭt cārbăsă flātŭs. *Breath.* Syn.—Spīrĭtŭs, ănhēlĭtŭs, ănĭmă, spīrāmĕn.

Flāvĕŏ, ēs, ērĕ, & Flāvēscŏ, ĭs, ĕrĕ. *To be or to become yellow.* Seū flāvēnt; plăcŭĭt crŏcĕĭs aūrōră căpīllīs. O. Phr.—Flāvēntĭbŭs ărvīs. Flāvūm cŏlōrēm dūcŏ, trăhŏ, cōncĭpĭŏ, sūmŏ, cōntrăhŏ, īndŭŏ.

Flāvŭs, ă, ūm. *Yellow.* Flāvăquĕ dē rūbrō prōmĕrĕ mēllă cădō. M. Syn.—Flāvēns, flāvēscēns, aūrĕŭs, crŏcĕŭs, lūtĕŭs. Phr.—Cūm flāvīs mēssōrem īndūcĕrĕt ārvīs. Flāvāquĕ căpŭt nēctēntŭr ŏlīvā.

Flēbĭlĭs, ĭs, ĕ. *Tearful, mournful.* Nēc jăcēām claūsām flēbĭlĭs āntĕ dŏmūm. Tib. Syn.—Lăcrĭmābĭlĭs, lāmēntābĭlĭs, flēndŭs, dēflēndŭs, lūgēndŭs. Phr.—Nūllī flēbĭlĭŏr quām tĭbĭ Vērgĭlī. Sad. Syn.—Lūgŭbrĭs, mœstŭs, trīstĭs, fūnēstŭs, mĭsĕrābĭlĭs.

Flēbĭlĕ & Flēbĭlĭtĕr. *In a tearful manner.* Syn.—Mœstūm, lūgŭbrĕ, fērālĕ.

Flēctŏ, ĭs, xī, xūm, ĕrĕ. *To bend, to turn.* Flēctĕre ĭtēr sŏcĭīs tērræque ādvērtĕrĕ prōrām Īmpĕrăt. V. Syn.—Īnflēctŏ, rĕflēctŏ, cūrvŏ, īncūrvŏ, tōrquĕŏ, cōntōrquĕŏ, vērtŏ, cōnvērtŏ. Phr.—Gȳrō brĕvĭōrĕ flēctī. Flēctĕ vĭām vēlīs. Flēctĭt hăbēnās. Quæ sēse ād fœdĕră flēctĭt. Flēctĭt ĕquōs. *To appease.* Syn.—Ēxōrŏ, mītĭgŏ, mōllĭŏ, mŏvĕŏ, plācŏ, vīncŏ. *See Placo.*

Flĕŏ, ēs, ēvī, ētūm, ērĕ. *To weep.* Sī vīs mē flērĕ, dŏlēndum ēst Prīmum īpsī tĭbĭ. H. *See Lacrimo. To mourn.* Syn.—Lūgĕŏ, dēflĕŏ, sūspīrŏ. *See Queror.*

Flēxĭbĭlĭs & Flēxĭlĭs, ĭs, ĕ. *Flexible.* Nōbīs flēxĭbĭlēs cūrvāntŭr Ăpōllĭnĭs ārcūs. O. Syn.—Lēntŭs, făcĭlĭs. Phr.—Cūrvābĭt flēxĭlĕ cōrnū.

Flēxŭs, ūs. m. *Bend, detour.* Māxĭmŭs hīc flēxū sĭnŭōso ēlābĭtŭr ānguĭs. V. Syn.—Flēxūră, gȳrŭs, sĭnŭs, spīră, cīrcŭĭtŭs, cūrvātūră, ōrbēs (pl).

Flō, ās, āvī, ātūm, ārĕ. *To blow.* Īnflēxō tĭbĭă cōrnū flābĭt. O. Syn.—Āfflŏ, pērflŏ, spīrŏ, āspīrŏ. Phr.—Flātūs mīttŏ, īngĕmĭnŏ. *See Ventus.*

Flōrĕŏ, ēs, ŭī, ērĕ. *To flourish.* Vērnăt hŭmūs flōrētque, ēt mōllĭă pābŭlă sūrgūnt. O. Phr.—Flōrēs īndŭŏ, fūndŏ, nūdŏ, ēxplĭcŏ, spārgŏ, fĕrŏ, gĕrŏ, mĭnīstrŏ. Flōrĭbŭs īndŭŏr. Spīrānt ārvă crŏcĕīs vēstītū flōrĭbŭs. Dĕcŏrāntūr flōrĭbŭs āgrī. Fūndĭt hŭmūs flōrēs.

Flōrēscŏ, ĭs, ĕrĕ. *To begin to flourish. See Floreo.*

Flōs, ōrĭs, m. *Flower.* Flōrĕ sĕmēl læsō pĕrĕūnt vĭcĭæquĕ făbæquĕ. V. Syn.—Flōscŭlŭs. Phr.—Prātōrūm, hōrtōrūm hŏnōs, dĕcŭs. Vērĭs ŏpēs. Flōs prātă ēxhĭlărāns. Quī dūlcēm lātē dīffūndĭt hŏnōrēm. Flōs dāns lūmĭnă prātīs. Pīctāquĕ dīssĭmĭlī flōrĕ nĭtēbăt hŭmŭs.

Flūctŭŏ, ās, āvī, ātūm, ārĕ. *To be tossed about, to undulate.* Syn.—Aēstŭŏ, fērvĕŏ, āgĭtŏr, jāctŏr, cōmmŏvĕŏr. *See Fluctus, Aestus. To be uncertain.* Syn.—Dŭbĭtŏ, flŭĭtŏ, jāctŏr, āmbĭgŏ.

Flūctŭs, ūs. m. *Wave.* Quām mūltī Lĭbȳcō vōlvūntŭr mārmŏrĕ flūctūs. V. Syn.—Aēstŭs, ūndă. Phr.—Spūmæ sălĭs. Ūndă tŭmēns. Īngēns mōlēs ăquæ. Prærūptŭs ăquæ mōns. Īngēns pōntŭs. Mărīs frăgŏr. Tāntās aūdētīs tōllĕrĕ mōlēs!

Flŭĭdŭs, ă, ūm. *Liquid, flowing.* Lūmĭnĭs ēffōssī flŭĭdūm lăvĭt īndĕ crŭōrēm. V. Syn.—Flŭēns, dēflŭēns, prōflŭēns, lĭquĭdŭs.

Flūmĕn, ĭnĭs. n. *River.* Ĕt quī prīmă bĭbĭt dēprēnsī flūmĭnă Nīlī. M. Syn.—Āmnĭs, flŭvĭŭs. *Stream, course.* Syn.—Flŭēntūm, lāpsŭs, cūrsŭs, dēcūrsŭs.

Flŭŏ, ĭs, ūxī, ūxŭm, ĕrĕ. *To flow.* Ŭbĭ Lȳdĭŭs ārvă Īntĕr ŏpīmä vĭrūm lēnī flŭĭt āgmĭnĕ Tĭbrĭs. V. Syn.—Mānŏ, prōflŭŏ, dēflŭŏ, ēfflŭŏ, īnflŭŏ, dēcūrrŏ, lābŏr, dēlābŏr, fĕrŏr, vōlvŏr, ĕŏ. Phr.—Āquās vōlvŏ. Pĕr sĭlvām vōlvĭtŭr āmnĭs. Īt mărĕ prōrŭptūm.

Flŭvĭŭs, ĭī. (*gen. pl.* flūvĭōrūm) m. *River.* Prōlŭĭt īnsānō cōntōrquēns vōrtĭcĕ sĭlvās Flūvĭōrūm rēx Ērĭdănŭs, V. Syn.—Flumĕn, flŭēntă, āmnĭs, tōrrēns, rīvŭs. Phr.—Cūrsŭs ăquārūm. Cĕlĕrēs ăquărūm lāpsŭs. Pĕr prātă vĭrēntĭă cūrrēns. Īn mărĕ dēcūrrēns. Mĕdĭām sūlcāns tērrām. Dēclīvī flūmĭnă cūrsū. Flŭvĭōs tēntārĕ tĕnācēs.

Fŏcŭs, ī. m. *Fire-place.* Āt fŏcŭs ā flāmmīs ēt quŏd fŏvĕt ōmnĭă dīctŭs. O. Syn.—Fŏcŭlŭs, cămīnŭs, ĭgnĭs. Phr.—Līgnĭs fŏcūm ēxstrŭĕrĕ. Līgnă sŭpĕr fŏcō Lārgē rĕpōnēns. Āssĭdŭŏ lūcĕăt īgnĕ fŏcŭs. Răpĭāntquĕ fŏcīs pĕnĕtrālĭbŭs īgnēm. *The Lares.* Syn.—Lărēs, pĕnātēs. *Fire. See Ignis.*

Fŏdĭcŏ, ās, āvī, ātūm, ārĕ. *To pierce.* Syn.—Fŏdĭŏ, trānsfŏdĭŏ, pūngŏ, tūndŏ.

Fŏdīnă, æ. f. *Metal mine.* Phr.—Vēnă mĕtāllĭfĕră. Mĕtāllī ærĭs, aŭrī, ārgēntī. Ābdĭtă tērrīs lāmnă. Tēllūs fœtă mĕtāllīs. Hŭmūs gĕnĕrōsă mĕtāllīs.

Fŏdĭŏ, ĭs, ōdī, ōssūm, ĕrĕ. *To dig.* Dūră lăcērtōsī fŏdĭēbānt ārvă cŏlōnī. O. Syn.—Ēffŏdĭŏ, dēfŏdĭŏ, căvŏ, ēxcăvŏ, pērfŏrŏ, ērŭŏ. Vĕtĕrēs tēllūrĕ rĕclūdĭt Thēsaŭrōs. *To pierce.* Syn.—Fŏdĭcŏ, pūngŏ, ūrgĕŏ, prĕmŏ.

Fœdŏ, ās, āvī, ātūm, ārĕ. *To stain, to spoil.* Quæ caŭsa īndīgnă sĕrēnōs Fœdāvĭt vūltūs? V. Syn.—Măcŭlŏ, cōmmăcŭlŏ, īnquĭnŏ, cŏīnquĭnŏ, pōllŭŏ, tūrpŏ, dētūrpŏ, tĕmĕrŏ, vĭŏlŏ. *See Polluo. To mutilate.* Syn.—Lăcĕrŏ.

Fœdŭs, ă, ūm. *Horrible, hideous.* Hæc pāssĭm Dĕă fœdă vĭrūm dĭffūndĭt ĭn ōră. V. Syn.—Tūrpĭs, dēfōrmĭs. *Hideous, disgusting.* Syn.—Sōrdĭdŭs, fœdātŭs, ōbscœnŭs, īmpūrŭs, īmmūndŭs, spūrcŭs, ātĕr, tūrpĭs. *Infamous. See Turpis.*

Fœdŭs, ĕrĭs. n. *Alliance.* Mūltă Jŏvem ēt læsī tēstātūs fœdĕrĭs ārās. V. Syn.—Pāctŭm, cōncōrdĭă, (*sometimes*) ămĭcĭtĭă, dēxtră, dēxtræ. Phr.—Lēx fœdĕrĭs. Fīrmātæ pācīs lēgēs. Dēxtræ dătæ. Pīgnŏră pācĭs. Fœdŭs ămĭcĭtĭæ. Pācĭs īnvĭŏlābĭlĕ pīgnŭs. Fœdŭs ĭnĕō. Fœdĕră pāngō. Pācĕm fœdĕrĕ jūngō. Dēxtræ cōnjūngĕrĕ dēxtrām. Fœdĕrĕ pāctō. Fāllĕrĕ dēxtrās. Cōnfūndĕrĕ fœdŭs.

Fŏlĭūm, ĭī. n. *Leaf*. Āt sī lūxŭrĭă fŏlĭōrum ēxūbĕrăt ūmbră. V. Syn.—Frōns. Phr.—Ārbŏrĭs dĕcŭs, hŏnōs. Āt spīssæ nĕmŏrūm cŏmæ. Nēxă cŏmām fŏlĭīs.

Fōllĭs, ĭs & Fōllēs, ĭūm. m. *Bellows*. Ālĭī taūrīnīs fōllĭbŭs aūrās Āccĭpĭūnt rēddūntquĕ. V. Phr.—Vēntōsæ pēllēs. Vēntōsæ pēllīs spīrāmĭnă. Ūtrēs vēntōrūm plēnī.

Fōmēntūm, ī. n. *Poultice*. Syn.—Lēnīmĕn, lĕvāmĕn, mĕdēlă.

Fōmĕs, ĭtĭs. m. *Tinder*. Nūtrīmēntă dĕdīt răpŭītque īn fōmĭtĕ flāmmām. V. Phr.—Līgnūm sīccūm, ārĭdūm. Pābŭlă flāmmæ.

Fōns, fōntĭs m. *Fountain*. Dēsĭlĭt ē sāxō quĕrŭlīs fōns gārrŭlŭs ūndīs. O. Syn.—Lȳmphă, lătēx, ăquă, ūndă. Phr.—Fōns ăquæ. Fōntĭs ăquæ. Fōntānī lătĭcēs. Scătēns rīvŭlŭs. Fōns lārgŭs ăquæ. Ăquæ lēnĕ căpūt săcræ. Lȳmphă fŭgāx trĕpĭdārĕ rīvō.

Fŏrāmĕn, ĭnĭs. n. *Hole, cavity*. Īdem ĕgŏ cūm sŭbĭī cōnvēxă fŏrāmĭnă tērræ. O. Syn.—Mĕātŭs, căvŭs, hĭātŭs, rīmă, fĭssūră, spīrāmēntūm, ēxĭtŭs. Phr.—Sīmplēxquĕ fŏrāmĭnĕ paūcō. Āngūstōs hăbĕānt ădĭtūs.

Fŏrēs, ĭūm & Fŏrĭs, ĭs. f. *Door*. Dīffĭcĭlēs mōtō cārdĭnĕ pāndĕ fŏrēs. O. Syn.—Jānŭă, vālvæ, līmĕn, pōstēs, ōstĭūm, ădĭtŭs, vēstĭbŭlūm. Phr.—Fŏrĭbūs cārdō strīdēbăt ăhēnīs. Īmpŭlĭt ăcrī Tūm vălĭdās strīdōrĕ fŏrēs.

Fŏrīnsĕcŭs, Fŏrīs. adv. *Outside*. Syn.—Ēxtrā, ēxtĕrĭŭs.

Fōrmă, æ. f. *Form, figure*. Cœpĕrĭt ēt rērūm paūlātīm sūmĕrĕ fōrmās. V. Syn.—Fĭgūră, ēffĭgĭēs, ĭmāgŏ, făcĭēs, spĕcĭēs. Phr. —Fōrmās ūnūs vērtēbăr ĭn ōmnēs. Fōrmam āccĭpĭt ūlmŭs ărātrī. *Plan, design*. Syn.—Ēxēmplăr, tȳpŭs. *Face*. Syn.—Spĕcĭēs, făcĭēs, fĭgūră, ōs, sĭmŭlācrūm, cōrpŭs. *Species*. Syn.—Spĕcĭēs, gĕnŭs, făcĭēs, fĭgūră. *Beauty*. Syn.—Pūlchrĭtūdŏ, dĕcŏr, vĕnūstās, nĭtŏr, grātĭă. Phr.—Grātĭă fōrmæ. Ēxĭmĭūm fōrmæ dĕcŭs. Dĕcōrŭs cŏlŏr. Fōrmă sĭne ārtĕ dĕcēns. *Shadow, spectre*. Syn.—Ūmbră, spĕcĭēs, lārvă, sĭmŭlācrūm.

Fōrmīcă, æ. f. *Ant*. Pārvŭlă nam ēxēmplo ēst māgnī fōrmīcă lăbōrĭs. H. Phr.—Prōvĭdă bēstĭă. Pārcūm gĕnŭs. Fārrīs pŏpŭlātrīx tūrbă. Pătĭēns fōrmīcă lăbōrūm. Hĭēmīs mĕmŏr.

Fōrmīdābĭlĭs, ĭs, ĕ. *Formidable*. Syn.—Fōrmīdāndŭs, hōrrēndŭs, hōrrĭbĭlĭs, mĕtŭēndŭs, tērrĭbĭlĭs, tĭmēndŭs, trĕmēndŭs.

Fōrmīdŏ, ās, āvī, ātūm, ārĕ. *To fear*. Syn.—Rĕfōrmīdŏ, mĕtŭŏ, păvĕŏ, tĭmĕŏ, pērtĭmēscŏ. *See Timeo*.

Fōrmīdŏ, ĭnĭs. f. *Fear.* Tū nĭhĭl ādmīttēs īn tē fōrmīdĭnĕ pœnæ. H. Syn.—Păvŏr, mĕtŭs, tĭmŏr, hōrrŏr, trĕmŏr. Phr.—Fōrmīdĭnĕ tōrpēns. Păvĭdūs fōrmīdĭnĕ pœnæ. Pērcūlsă nŏvā mēntēm fōrmīdĭnĕ.

Fōrmŏ, ās, āvī, ātūm, ārĕ. *To form, to fashion.* Rōmŭlŭs ætērnæ nōndūm fōrmāvĕrăt ūrbĭs Mœnĭă. Tib. Syn.—Ēffōrmŏ, fīngŏ, ēffīngŏ, fĭgūrŏ, cōmpōnŏ, cōndŏ, strŭŏ. Phr.—Lāpsōs fōrmārĕ căpīllōs. *See Fingo. To instruct.* Syn.—Īnfōrmŏ, ērŭdĭŏ, ēdŏcĕŏ, ēxcŏlŏ, īnstĭtŭŏ, īnstrŭŏ.

Fōrmōsŭs, ă, ūm. *Beautiful.* Fōrmōsī pĕcŏrĭs cūstōs fōrmōsĭŏr īpsĕ. V. Syn.—Pūlchĕr, dĕcōrŭs, vĕnūstŭs, spĕcĭōsŭs. *Shining, bright.* Syn.—Pūlchĕr, rīdēns, nĭtēns, nĭtĭdŭs, cāndĭdŭs.

Fōrmŭlă, æ. f. *Rule, principle.* Syn.—Rēgŭlă, nōrmă.

Fornāx, ācĭs. f. *Furnace.* Vūlnĭfĭcūsquĕ Chălybs vāstā fōrnācĕ lĭquēscĭt. V. Syn.—Fōrnācŭlă, fŏcŭs, cămīnŭs. Phr.—Lōngō fōrnāx īncāndŭĭt æstū. Fōrnācĕ căpācī Īgnĕā vīs fŭrĭt. Fōrnācĭbŭs īgnĭs ănhēlăt.

Fōrnĭcātŭs, ă, ūm. *Vaulted.* Syn.—Cămĕrātŭs, cūrvātŭs.

Fōrnīx, ĭcĭs. m. *Vault, arch.* Syn.—Ārcŭs, cămĕră, tēstūdŏ, thŏlŭs.

Fōrs, fōrtĭs. f. *Fortune, chance.* Fōrtĕ sŭā Lĭbycīs tēmpēstās āppŭlĭt ōrīs. V. Syn.—Fōrtūnă, cāsŭs, fātūm, sōrs. Phr.—Fōrs īncērtă văgātŭr. Seū rătĭō dĕdĕrīt seū fōrs ōbjēcĕrĭt. *See Fortuna.*

Fōrsăn, Fōrsĭtăn, Fōrtāssĕ, Fōrtāssĭs. adv. *Perhaps.*

Fōrtĕ. adv. *By chance.* Syn.—Fōrtŭĭtō.

Fōrtĭs, ĭs, ĕ. *Strong.* Hīc lăbŏr hīnc laūdēm fōrtēs spērātĕ cŏlōnī. V. Syn.—Rōbūstŭs, vălĭdŭs. Phr.—Vīrĭbŭs īnsīgnĭs, pŏtēns. Fōrtī fīdĭs ĕquō. Fōrtēs ăd ărātră jŭvēncōs. *Solid, firm.* Syn.—Fīrmŭs, sŏlĭdŭs, vălĭdŭs. *Large.* Syn.—Īmmānĭs, īngēns, māgnŭs. *Brave.* Syn.—Ănĭmōsŭs, strēnŭŭs, aūdāx, māgnănĭmŭs, gĕnĕrōsŭs, īnvīctŭs, īmpăvĭdŭs, fīdēns, fīrmŭs, cōnstāns, fĕrōx. Phr.—Bēllō īnvīctŭs. Ārmīs ācĕr. Căpŭt īnsŭpĕrābĭlĕ bēllō. Vīrtūtĕ præstāns. Fōrtĭs īn ārmīs. Vīr fōrtĭs ăd ārmă.

Fōrtĭtĕr. adv. *Strongly.* Syn.—Vălĭdē, fīrmĭtĕr, ācrĭtĕr, vĕhĕmēntĕr. *Bravely.* Syn.—Ănĭmōsē, gĕnĕrōsē, cōnstāntĕr, ācrĭtĕr, aūdāctĕr.

Fōrtĭtūdŏ, ĭnĭs. f. *Courage.* Syn.—Vīrtūs, ănĭmŭs, rōbŭr, cōnstāntĭă, aūdācĭă, fīdūcĭă. Phr.—Fōrtĕ pēctŭs. Fōrtīssĭmă cōrdă. Fōrtĭs mănŭs. Fōrtĭă aūsă. Stāre ănĭmīs. *See Fortis, Virtus.*

Fōrtŭĭtō. adv. *By chance.* Syn.—Cāsū, fōrtĕ, fōrtūnā.

Fōrtūnă, æ. f. *Fortune*. Syn.—Sōrs, fātūm. Phr.—Fōrtūnæ nūmĕn. Fōrtūnă nūnquām sīstĭt ĭn ĕōdēm grădū. Fōrtūnă sævō lætă nĕgōtĭō. Ūt cāsūs fōrtūnă rŏtăt! Āspĕră fātă. Trīstēs cāsūs. Rēs āfflīctæ. Rēs ādvērsă. Dūm fōrtūnă fŭĭt. *See Felicitas.*

Fōrtūnātē. adv. *Happily*. Syn.—Bĕātē, faūtē, fēlīcĭtĕr. *See Feliciter.*

Fōrtūnātŭs, ă, ūm. *Fortunate, happy*. Fōrtūnātŭs ĕt īllĕ dĕōs quī nōvĭt ăgrēstēs. V. Syn.—Fēlīx, bĕātŭs. Phr.—Dĕōs ēxpērtŭs ămīcōs. Blānda ūtēns fōrtūnā. Fōrtūnātă dŏmŭs.

Fōrtūnŏ, ās, āvī, ātūm, ārĕ. *To render happy*. Syn.—Prōspĕrŏ, sĕcūndŏ.

Fŏrūm, ī. n. *Forum, market*. Syn.—Ārĕă, plătĕă, cōmpĭtūm, măcēllūm. *Place where justice was administered*. Syn.—Rōstră. Phr.—Jūdĭcĭālĭă claūstră. Jūrĭs trĭbūnāl. *See Tribunal.*

Fōssă, æ. f. *Ditch*. Syn.—Fŏvĕă, lăcūnă, scrōbs. *Redoubt*. Syn.—Vāllūm. Phr.—Fōssārūmquĕ mōræ. Ēt fōssās āggĕrĕ cōmplēnt. *See Vallo.*

Fŏvĕŏ, ēs, fōvī, fōtūm, ērĕ. *To warm, to keep warm*. Syn.—Călĕfăcĭŏ, cālfăcĭŏ, tĕpĕfăcĭŏ. *To nourish*. Syn.—Ălŏ, pāscŏ, nūtrĭŏ. *To protect*. Syn.—Cŏlŏ, tŭĕŏr, făvĕŏ.

Frăgĭlĭs, ĭs, ĕ. *Easily broken*. Jām frăgĭlēs pŏtĕram ā tērrā cōntīngĕrĕ rāmōs. V. Syn.—Tĕnĕr, īnsŏlĭdŭs. *Perishable*. Syn.—Tĕnŭĭs, dēbĭlĭs, īnfīrmŭs.

Frăgŏr, ōrĭs. m. *Crash, noise*. Īndĕ frăgōrĕ grăvī strĕpĭtūs lŏcă prōxĭmă tērrĕt. O. Syn.—Sŏnŭs, strĕpĭtŭs, strīdŏr, mūrmŭr. Phr.—Tērrĭfĭcūm tēllūs dĕdĭt īctă frăgōrēm. Rĕbŏānt mōntānă frăgōrĕ. Dāt sīlvă frăgōrēm. Cœlūm tŏnăt ōmnĕ frăgōrĕ.

Frăgōsŭs, ă, ūm. *Crashing, roaring*. Syn.—Sŏnōrŭs, sŏnāns, raūcŭs, strīdēns, clāmōsŭs. *Rough*. Syn.—Āspĕr, prærūptŭs.

Frāgrŏ, ās, āvī, ātūm, ārĕ. *To give forth an odor*. Frāgrāvĭt ōrĕ quōd rŏsārĭūm Pæstī. M. Syn.—Ŏlĕŏ, rĕdŏlĕŏ, hālŏ, spīrŏ. Phr.—Āssȳrĭō frāgrăt ŏdōrĕ dŏmŭs. Frāgrăt ăcērbŭs ŏdŏr.

Frāgūm, ī. n. *Strawberry*. (*See Appendix under list of Trees, etc.*)

Frāngŏ, ĭs, ēgī, āctūm, ĕrĕ. *To break, to bruise*. Āc vĕlŭt ūrsŭs Ōbjēctōs căvĕæ vălŭĭt sī frāngĕrĕ clāthrōs. H. Syn.—Īnfrīngŏ, cōnfrīngŏ, pērfrīngŏ, rĕfrīngŏ, rūmpŏ, pērrūmpŏ, cōmmĭnŭŏ, cōntūndŏ, ēlīdŏ, dīssŏlvŏ, dīsjĭcĭŏ. Phr.—Ēt frūgēs frāngĕrĕ sāxō. Frāngūntūr rēmī. Vĕtŭs ūt nōn frēgĕrĭt ætās. *To violate an alliance*. Syn.—Rūmpŏ, rēscīndŏ, ēvērtŏ, vĭŏlŏ. *To weaken*. Syn.—Īnfrīngŏ, vīncŏ, lăbĕfāctŏ, stērnŏ, cōrrūmpŏ.

Frātĕr, rĭs. m. *Brother.* Frātĕr ŭt Aēnēās pĕlăgō tŭŭs ōmnĭă cīrcūm. V. Syn.—Gērmānŭs. Phr.—Gērmānă prŏpāgŏ, prōlēs. Pār nōbĭlĕ frātrūm. Glōrĭă mātrĭs.

Frātērnŭs, ă, ūm. *Fraternal.* Frātērnō prīmī mădŭērūnt sānguĭnĕ mūrī. L. Syn.—Gērmānŭs. Phr.—Frātērnŭs ămŏr. Frātērnă fĭdēs. Frātērnūm dūlcĕ sŏdālĭtĭūm. Frātērnūm rūmpĕrĕ fœdŭs.

Fraūdŏ, ās, āvī, ātūm, ārĕ. *To deceive.* Syn.—Dēcĭpĭŏ, fāllŏ. *To frustrate.* Syn.—Frūstrŏr.

Fraūs, fraūdĭs. f. *Fraud, deceit. See Astus, Dolus.* Phr.—Crīmĭnă fraūdĭs. Āstūtă mōlīmĭnă. Pŭdīcā Fāllĕrĕ fraūdĕ prŏcōs. Īgnēm fraūdĕ mălā gēntĭbŭs īntŭlĭt. Fraūdĕ pĕrĭt vīrtūs. Fraūs ēst cōncēssă rĕpēllĕrĕ fraūdēm.

Frāxĭnŭs, ī. f. *An ash tree.* (*See Appendix under list of Trees, etc.*)

Frĕmĕbūndŭs, ă, ūm. *Growling, murmuring.* Syn.—Frĕmēns, frēndēns.

Frĕmĭtŭs, ūs. m. *Growling, murmuring.* Ēt răbĭdī frĕmĭtūs ēt mūrmŭră māgnă mĭnārūm. L. *Applause.* Syn.—Plaūsŭs, frĕmŏr, făvŏr, mūrmŭr. Phr.—Cīrcūmstānt frĕmĭtū dēnsō. Clāmōre ēxcĭpĭūnt sŏcĭī frĕmĭtūquĕ sĕquūntŭr. *Great noise.* Syn.—Strĕpĭtŭs, frăgŏr. Phr.—Strīdēns mūrmŭr. *See Sonitus.*

Frĕmŏ, ĭs, ŭī, ĭtūm, ĕrĕ. *To murmur, to roar, to growl.* Frĕmĭt æquŏrĕ tōtō Īnsūltāns sŏnĭpēs. V. Syn.—Īnfrĕmŏ, frēndĕŏ, frēndŏ. Phr.—Frĕmĭt hōrrĭdŭs ōrĕ crŭēntō. Māgnōquĕ dŏlōrĕ frĕmēbānt. *To applaud.* Syn.—Āpplaūdŏ, mūrmŭrŏ. Phr.—Mūrmŭrĕ mīxtō Tūrbă frĕmĭt. Cūnctī sĭmŭl ōrĕ frĕmēbānt. Māgnō cīrcūm clāmōrĕ frĕmēbānt. Lætĭtĭāquĕ frĕmūnt, ănĭmōsque ād sīdĕră tōllūnt.

Frēndĕŏ, ēs, ĕrĕ & Frēndŏ, ĭs, ĕrĕ. *To gnash the teeth.* Syn.—Īnfrēndĕŏ, frĕmŏ. Phr.—Dēntĭbŭs frēndĕŏ. Dēntĕ mĭnārī. Dēntĭbŭs īncŭtĭō dēntēs. Prōdīt cōllīsīs dēntĭbŭs īrās. Mĭnācī mūrmŭrĕ frēndŏ.

Frēnŏ, ās, āvī, ātūm, ārĕ. *To check, to bridle.* Mōllĭă pūrpŭrĕīs frēnābās ōră căpīstrīs. O. Syn.—Īnfrēnŏ. Phr.—Frēnūm, frēnă, frēnōs dŏ, āddŏ, īnjĭcĭŏ. Frēnīs, hăbēnīs flēctŏ, tōrquĕŏ, dŏmŏ. Ād frēnă cōgŏ. Frēnīs scīt flēctĕrĕ mōllĭbŭs ōră. Lōră tĕnērĕ mănū. Nēc frēnă rĕmīttĭt. Fig.—*To check.* Syn.—Cŏērcĕŏ, cōmpēscŏ, cōntĭnĕŏ, dŏmŏ, sŭbĭgŏ, prĕmŏ, mŏdĕrŏr. Phr.—Frēnābām cōrdĕ dŏlōrēs. Ăvĭdās spēs frēnārĕ. Jūstĭtĭāquĕ dĕdīt gēntēs frēnārĕ sŭpērbās. Īmpĕrĭō prĕmĭt.

Frēnūm, ī. n. Frēnī & Frēnă, ōrūm. *Rein, bridle.* Stāt sŏnĭpēs ēt frēnă fĕrōx spūmāntĭă māndĭt. V. Syn.—Lŭpī, lŭpātă (ōrūm), căpīstrūm, lōră, vīncŭlă, hăbēnæ, rĕtĭnācŭlūm. Phr.—Frēnōrūm hăbēnæ. Mŏdĕrāmĕn ĕquōrūm. Frēnum āccĭpĭŏ. Frēno āssuēscŏ. Fig.—Lāxāt frēnōs pŏpŭlīs fŭrēntĭbŭs. Īmpĕrĭī mŏdĕrārī frēnă. Ănĭmūm frēnīs cōmpēscĕrĕ.

Frĕquēns, ēntĭs. adj. *Numerous, crowded.* Tūtă frĕquēnsquĕ vĭa ēst. O. Syn.—Trītŭs, cĕlĕbĕr, cĕlĕbrātŭs. Phr.—Ūrbs pŏpŭlīs frĕquēns. *Abounding in.* Syn.—Plēnŭs, rĕfērtŭs, crēbĕr, ăbūndāns. *Assiduous, eager.* Syn.—Crēbĕr, āssĭdŭŭs.

Frĕquēntĕr. adv. *Frequently, often.* Syn.—Crēbrō, sæpĕ, āssĭdŭē, cōntĭnŭō, plērūmquĕ, vūlgō, frĕquēns (adj.).

Frĕquēntĭă, æ. f. *Crowd.* Syn.—Mūltĭtūdŏ, tūrbă, cōpĭă. Phr.—Tūrbă frĕquēns.

Frĕquēntŏ, ās, āvī, ātūm, ārĕ. *To be present in great numbers.* Syn.—Cĕlĕbrŏ, cōnvĕnĭŏ, cŏēŏ, cōnflŭŏ. Phr.—Tēmplă frĕquēntārī dĕcĕt. Sæpe ădĕŏ. Frĕquēns ădĕŏ. *To repeat.* Syn.—Ĭtĕrŏ, īngĕmĭnŏ.

Frĕtūm, ī. n. *Strait.* Nāvĭfrăgūmquĕ frĕtūm gĕmĭnō quōd līttŏrĕ prēssūm. O. Syn.—Faŭcēs. Phr.—Cæco ūndāns æstū. Frĕmēntĭs īră frĕtī. Crēbrīs frĕtă cōnsĭtă tērrīs. *Sea. See Mare.*

Frētŭs, ă, ūm. *Relying on.* Syn.—Fīdēns, fīsŭs, cōnfīsŭs, nīxŭs, fūltŭs, fĕrōx.

Frĭcŏ, ās, ŭī, ĭctūm, ārĕ. *To rub.* Syn.—Āffrĭcŏ, pērfrĭcŏ. Phr.—Frĭcăt ărbŏrĕ cōstās.

Frīgĕŏ, ēs, ērĕ. *To be cold.* Quāmvīs cærŭlĕō sīccūs Jŏvĕ frīgĕăt æthēr. Syn.—Ālgĕŏ, frīgēscŏ. Phr.—Frīgŏrĕ cōrrĭpĭŏr. Frīgūs mēmbra hăbĕt. Frīgūs dūcŏ. *See Frigus.* Fig.—*See Langueo.*

Frīgĭdŭs, ă, ūm. *Cold.* Frīgĭdūs īn prātīs cāntāndō rūmpĭtŭr ānguĭs. V. Syn.—Frīgēns, ālgēns, ālgĭdŭs, gĕlĭdŭs. Phr.—Gĕlū, frīgŏrĕ strīctŭs. Glăcĭālī cōnstrīctūs frīgŏrĕ. *Languishing.* Syn.—Lānguĭdŭs, ĭnērs, lānguēns, frīgēns, gĕlĭdŭs, ēffœtŭs, dēbĭlĭs.

Frīgŭs, ŏrĭs. n. *Cold, coldness.* Frīgŏrĭbūs pārto āgrĭcŏlæ plērūmquĕ frŭūntŭr. V. Syn.—Gĕlū, hĭēms. Phr.—Frīgŏrĭs āspĕrĭtās, vīs. Frīgĭdūs hōrrŏr. Frīgŏră mĭnŭūnt zĕphÿrī.

Frīngīllă, Frīgīllă & Frīnguīllă, æ. f. *Chaffinch.* (*See Appendix under list of Birds.*)

Frōndĕŏ, ēs, ŭī, ērĕ. *To send forth leaves.* Dīcās āddūctūm prŏpĭūs frōndērĕ Tărēntūm. H. Phr.—Frōndēs fūndŏ, ēffūndŏ. Frōndĭbūs īndŭŏr. Frōndĕ vĭrērĕ nŏvā. Sīlvă cŏmās tōllĭt.

Frōndēscŏ, ĕrĕ. *To begin to send forth leaves. See Frondeo.*

Frōndĕŭs, Frōndōsŭs & Frōndĭfĕr, ă, ūm. *Leafy.* Ăquās dūlcēs ēt frōndĕă sēmpĕr Tēctă pĕtūnt. V. Syn.—Frōndēns, ūmbrōsŭs, cŏmāns, ŏpācŭs, pătŭlŭs. Phr.—Frōndĭbŭs, fŏlĭīs ŏpērtŭs. Lūxŭrĭāns cŏmīs. Frōndōsă rĕdūcĭtŭr æstās.

Frōns, dĭs. f. *Leaf, foliage.* Mōllīquĕ flŭēntēm Frōndĕ prĕmīt crīnēm. V. Syn.—Fŏlĭūm, rāmī. Phr.—Ārbŏrĕæ cŏmæ. Ārbŏrĕī crīnēs. Frōndēntĭă hōspĭtĭă.

Frōns, tĭs. f. *Brow.* Ēt mĕdĭām fērrō gĕmĭna īntĕr tēmpŏră frōntēm Dīvĭdĭt. V. Phr.—Frōns āspĕră cōrnū. Prīmīs frōns tūrgĭdă cōrnĭbŭs. Frōntĕ fĕrīt tērrām. Grăvēm rĕmīttĕrĕ frōntēm. *Face.* Syn.—Ōs, făcĭēs, vūltŭs. Phr.—Spēm frōntĕ sĕrēnăt. Mœstă frōntĕ quĕrī.

Frūctŭs, ūs. m. *Fruit.* Frūctĭbŭs īmmēnsīs ăvĭdōs sătĭārĕ cŏlōnōs. V. Syn.—Frūgēs, pōmă. Phr.—Pēndēntēs ārbŏrĕ frūctūs. Fœtūs ārbŏrĕ dēmptī. *Revenue.* Syn.—Prōvēntŭs, rĕdĭtŭs. Fig. Syn.—Quæstŭs, cōmmŏdūm, lŭcrūm, ūtĭlĭtās.

Frūgālĭŏr, ĭūs, ōrĭs. *Frugal, industrious.* Syn.—Frūgī, sōbrĭŭs, pārcŭs, tēmpĕrāns, ābstĭnēns. Phr.—Bŏnæ frūgĭs, pārvō cōntēntŭs, bĕātŭs. Cĭbī pārcŭs. Tĕnŭī vīctū cōntēntŭs.

Frūgālĭtās, ātĭs. f. *Frugality.* Syn.—Sōbrĭĕtās. *See Abstinentia.*

Frūgēs, ūm. *Fruits of the earth.* Ēt mĕdĭō tōstās æstū tĕrĭt ārĕă frūgēs. V. Syn.—Sĕgĕs, mēssĭs, frūmēntūm, Cĕrēs. Phr.—Cĕrĕālĭă dōnă. Mūnĕră tērræ. Rūrĭs ŏpēs.

Frūmēntūm, ī. n. *Grain, corn.* Sī quĭs ăd īngēntēm frūmēntī sēmpĕr ăcērvūm Pōrrēctūs vĭgĭlēt. H. Syn.—Frūgēs, fār, trītĭcūm, Cĕrēs, mēssĭs, sĕgĕs.

Frŭŏr, ĕrĭs, frūctŭs & frŭĭtŭs sūm, ī. *To enjoy.* Nēc frŭĭtūr sōmnō vĭgĭlāntĭbŭs ēxcĭtă cūrīs. O. Syn.—Pērfrŭŏr, pŏtĭŏr, ūtŏr, tĕnĕō, pōssĭdĕō, hăbĕō, gaūdĕō. Phr.—Frŭī părātŭs. Frŭĭtūrquĕ Dĕōrūm cōllŏquĭō.

Frūstrā. adv. *In vain.* Nē quĭd ĭnēxpērtūm frūstrā mŏrĭtūră rĕlīnquăt. V. Syn.—Īncāssūm, nēquīcquām, ĭnānĕ, ĭnūtĭlĭtĕr. Phr.—Vānō cōnāmĭnĕ. Mōlīmĭnĕ cāssō. Īnānī cōnātū. Quīd jŭvăt? Ŏpĕrām pērdŏ. Sūccēssūm Dĕă dīră nĕgăt. Sūdēt mūltūm frūstrāquĕ lăbōrĕt.

Frūstrŏr, ārĭs, ātŭs sūm, ārī. *To frustrate.* Nēc spē frūstrābŏr ĭnānī. Syn.—Fraūdŏ, fāllŏ, dēcĭpĭŏ. *See Decipio.*

Frŭtēx, ĭcĭs. m. *Bush, shrub.* Nēc pārvī frŭtĭcēs īrām mĕrŭērĕ Tŏnāntĭs. Syn.—Vīrgūltūm, ārbūstūm, ārbūscŭlă.

Fūcŏ, ās, āvī, ātūm, ārĕ. *To color, to tint.* Ālbă nĕc Āssÿrĭō fūcātūr lānă vĕnēnō. V. Syn.—Īnfūcŏ, īnfĭcĭŏ, tīngŏ, cŏlōrŏ. Phr.—Nātūrālĕ dĕcūs fīctæ nōn cōmmŏdăt ārtī.

Fūcŭs, ī. m. *Red color.* Syn.—Mĕdĭcāmĕn, cŏlŏr, vĕnēnūm. *Rouge.* Syn.—Cērūssă, mĭnĭūm, pīgmēntūm.

Fŭgă, ǣ. f. *Flight.* Ūt tēmpŏră tāndēm Fūrtīvæ̆ plăcŭērĕ fŭgæ̆. L. Phr.—Fŭgæ̆ cūrsŭs. Præ̆cēps dīscēssŭs. Nēc spēs ūllă fŭgæ̆. Dīmīttĕ fŭgām. Ăpĕrīrĕ fŭgām. *See Exsilium.*

Fŭgāx, ācĭs. adj. *Fleeing, fleeting.* Cōnvērsīsquĕ fŭgāx aūfērtŭr hăbēnīs. V. Syn.—Fŭgĭēns, fŭgĭtīvŭs, prŏfŭgŭs. Phr.—Ād fŭgām pĕdĕ fērvĭdŭs. Sī fōrtĕ fŭgācēm cōnspēxīt căprĕām. Fŭgācĭŏr aūră. Quīd lăbōrāt Lȳmphă fŭgāx trĕpĭdārĕ rīvō? *Fleeting, short-lived.* Syn.—Fŭgĭēns, fŭgĭtīvŭs, cădūcŭs, răpĭdŭs, flūxŭs, brĕvĭs.

Fŭgĭŏ, ĭs, fūgī, fŭgĭtūm, ĕrĕ. *To fly.* Nōn fŭgĭs hīnc præ̆cēps, dūm præ̆cĭpĭtārĕ pŏtēstās. V. Syn.—Aūfŭgĭŏ, ēffŭgĭŏ, dīffŭgĭŏ, fŭgĭtŏ, cēdŏ, rĕcēdŏ. Phr.—Fŭgām căpĭŏ, mātūrŏ. Fŭgā ăbĕŏ. Ārvă pĕtŏ. Fŭgā tērgă dŏ. Fŭgĭt īlĭcĕt ōcĭŏr Eūrō. Ārdĕt ăbīrĕ fŭgā. Dīffŭgĭūnt quōcūnque ăgĭt ērrŏr. Fŭgam īntēndūnt ād mœ̄nĭă.

Fŭgŏ, ās, āvī, ātūm, ārĕ. *To put to flight.* Trāns pōntēm fŭgăt, ēt tērrīs īmmīttĭt ăprīcīs. V. Syn.—Pēllŏ, ēxpēllŏ, rĕpēllŏ, ăbĭgŏ, prōpūlsŏ. Phr.—Īn fŭgām dō. Dărĕ tērgă cōgŏ. *See Pello.*

Fūlcīmĕn, ĭnĭs & Fūlcīmēntūm, ī. n. *Support, rest.* Tērră pĭlæ̆ sĭmĭlĭs, nūllō fūlcīmĭnĕ nīxă. O. Syn.—Fūlmēntūm, fūltūră, fīrmāmĕn, cŏlūmĕn.

Fūlcĭŏ, īs, fūlsī, ūltūm, īrĕ. *To support.* Ātlāntīs dūrī cœ̄lūm quī vērtĭcĕ fūlcĭt. V. Syn.—Sūffūlcĭŏ, fĕrŏ, sūstĭnĕŏ, sūstēntŏ.

Fūlgĕŏ, ēs, sī, gērĕ. *To shine.* Pīctă nĕc īndūctō fūlgēbāt pārmă pȳrōpō. Pr. Syn.—Ēffūlgĕŏ, rĕfūlgĕŏ, lūcĕŏ, nĭtĕŏ, splēndĕŏ, cŏrūscŏ, mĭcŏ, ārdĕŏ, rădĭŏ, īrrădĭŏ. Phr.—Rŏsæ̆ fūlgēnt īntēr sŭă lĭlĭă. Ēt grātūm nātīs sīdūs fūlgērĕ. Fūlgēt gēmmă tŏrīs. *See Luceo.*

Fūlgĭdŭs, ă, ūm. *Bright, brilliant.* Fūlgĭdă præ̆sērtīm cūm cērnĕrĕ sæ̆pĕ nĕquīmŭs. Lr. Syn.—Fūlgēns, lūcĭdŭs, cŏrūscŭs, rŭtĭlŭs, mĭcāns.

Fūlgŏr, ōrĭs. m. *Brilliancy, splendor.* Măcŭlōsŭs ĕt aūrō Squāmam īncēndēbāt fūlgŏr. V. Syn.—Lūx, nĭtŏr, splēndŏr. Phr.—Mĭcăt īgnĕŭs ōrĕ Fūlgŏr. Āttōllīt nĭtĭdīs pēctūs fūlgōrĭbŭs. Ēlūcēnt ălĭae ēt fūlgōrĕ cŏrūscānt. *See Nitor, Splendor.*

Fūlgŭr, ŭrĭs. n. *Brightness, splendor.* Nām præ̆tēr pĕlăgī cāsūs ēt fūlgŭrĭs īctūm. J. Syn.—Fūlgŏr, (*sometimes*) īgnēs, flāmmæ̆. Phr.—Fūlmĭnĭs īgnēs. Lūx nūntĭă fūlmĭnĭs.

Fūlgŭrŏ, ās, ārĕ. *To give forth light.* Phr.—Fūlgŭr jăcĭŏ, vĭbrŏ, ēxcŭtĭŏ, ēmīttŏ, spārgŏ. Jăcŭlāri ē nūbĭbŭs īgnēs. *See Fulgur.*

Fŭlĭcă, æ. f. *A coot.* (*See list of Birds in Appendix.*)

Fūlmĕn, ĭnĭs. n. *Lightning, thunderbolt.* Āddĭdĭt ēt tŏnĭtrūs ĕt ĭnēvītābĭlĕ fūlmĕn. O. Syn.—Tŏnĭtrū, fūlgŭr. Phr.—Fūlmĭnĭs īgnēs, īctŭs, īră. Jŏvĭs īgnĕă tēlă. Haūd ĭmĭtābĭlĕ fūlmēn. Fūlmĭnă mīssă pŏlō. Tōtō Jŏvĕ fūlmĕn ădāctūm. *See Fulmino.*

Fūlmĭnŏ, ās, āvī, ātūm, ārĕ. *To thunder.* Īngēntēs quērcūs, ānnōsās fūlmĭnăt ōrnōs. Syn.—Fūlmĭnĕ āfflŏ, dīsjĭcĭŏ. Phr.—Fūlmĭnă mīttŏ. Fūlmĕn ābrūptō mīttĕrĕ cœlō. Mīssō pērfrēgĭt Ŏlўmpūm fūlmĭnĕ. Īnquĕ Jŏvĭs mīssĭlĕ fūlmĕn ĕrăt.

Fūlvŭs, ă, um. *Tawny, yellow, brown.* Ātque īllī stēllātŭs ĭăspĭdĕ fūlvā Ēnsĭs ĕrăt. V. Syn.—Flāvŭs, rūfŭs, aūrĕŭs, crŏcĕŭs, rŭtĭlŭs. Phr.—Fūlvūm spēctātŭr ĭn īgnĭbŭs aūrūm. Fūlvāquĕ căpūt nēctēntŭr ŏlīvā. Fūlvā pūgnās dē nūbĕ tŭēntēm.

Fūmŏ, ās, āvī, ātūm, ārĕ. *To smoke.* Tūră dăbānt tĕpĭdūsquĕ crŭŏr fūmābăt ăd ārās. V. Phr.—Fūmūm, fūmōs dŏ, mīttŏ, vŏmŏ. Cœlūm sūbtēxĕrĕ fūmō. Īgnĭbŭs ātrĭă fūmānt. Pĭcĕūm fērt fūmĭdă lūmĕn Tædă. *See Fumus.*

Fūmōsŭs, ă, ūm. *Smoky.* Syn.—Fūmāns, fūmĭdŭs.

Fūmŭs, ī. m. *Smoke.* Săxă vĭdēs mīstōque ŭndāntēm tūrbĭnĕ fūmūm. V. Syn.—Cālīgŏ, văpŏr, (*sometimes*) nūbēs, nĕbŭlă, făvīllă. Phr.—Fūmĕŭs văpŏr. Fūmī nūbēs. Ātræ pĭcĕā cālīgĭnĕ nūbēs. Vŏlāt văpŏr ātĕr ăd aūrās.

Fūnālĕ, ĭs. n. *Torch.* Ēt nōctēm flāmmīs fūnālĭă vīncūnt. V. Syn.—Fāx, tædă, lўchnŭs, lāmpăs. Phr.—Lāmpădĭbŭs dēnsūm răpŭĭt fūnālĕ cŏrūscīs.

Fūndĭtŭs. adv. *From the ground, from the very foundations.* Fūndĭtŭs āvēllūnt pōstēs. V. Syn.—Rādīcĭtŭs, fūndō. Phr.—Ā sēdĭbŭs īmīs. Ā rādīcĭbŭs īmīs. Ā cūlmĭnĕ sūmmō. *Entirely.* Syn.—Pĕnĭtŭs, prōrsŭs, ōmnīnō.

Fūndŏ, ās, āvī, ātūm, ārĕ. *To found, to establish.* Tūm vīcīna āstrīs Ĕrўcīno īn vērtĭcĕ sēdēs Fūndātŭr Vĕnĕri Īdălĭæ. V. Syn.—Cōndŏ, pōnŏ, cōnstĭtŭŏ, stătŭŏ, ædĭfĭcŏ, strŭŏ, ēxstrŭŏ, mōlĭŏr. Phr.—Fūndāmēntă pōnŏ. Mūrōs ăb īmō dēdūcŏ. Mūrōs jăcĭŏ. Fūndāmēntă lŏcānt ălĭī.

Fūndŏ, ĭs, fūdī, fūsūm, ĕrĕ. *To pour, to pour out.* Syn.—Cōnflŏ, ēffūndŏ, spārgŏ. Phr.—Vīnă lĭquēntĭă fūndām. *To spread around.* Syn.—Prŏfūndŏ, dīffūndŏ, mīttŏ, ēmīttŏ, spārgŏ, dīspērgŏ. *To extend.* Syn.—Ēxtēndŏ, pāndŏ, ēxplĭcŏ. *To put to flight.* Syn.—Fŭgŏ, dīssĭpŏ.

Fūnĕbrĭs, ĭs, ĕ, & Fūnĕrĕŭs, ă, ūm. *Pertaining to a funeral, mournful, lugubrious.* Syn.—Fērālĭs, fūnēstŭs, lūgŭbrĭs, flēbĭlĭs, mœstŭs, trīstĭs.

Fūnĕrŏ, ās, āvī, ātūm, ārĕ. *To bury, to perform the funeral rites.* Syn.—Cōndŏ, tŭmŭlŏ, sĕpĕlĭŏ.

Fūnēstŭs, ă, ūm. *Pertaining to a funeral. See Funebris. Mournful, dreadful.* Syn.—Lētālĭs, fātālĭs, ēxĭtĭālĭs, ēxĭtĭōsŭs, ēxĭtĭābĭlĭs, fātĭfĕr, mōrtĭfĕr, lētĭfĕr, grăvĭs, lūctĭfĭcŭs, dīrŭs.

Fūngŏr, ĕrĭs, fūnctŭs sūm, ī. *To fulfil the office of.* Ămīcī mūnĕrĕ fūngī. H. Syn.—Dēfūngŏr, pērfūngŏr, ēffĭcĭŏ præstŏ, ēxsĕquŏr, ēxērcĕŏ, ŏbĕŏ. Phr.—Ōffĭcĭō fūngī pĭĕtātĭs. Fūngōr vĭcĕ cōtĭs.

Fūngŭs, ī. m. *Mushroom.* (*See Appendix under list of Trees, etc.*)

Fūnĭs, ĭs. m. *Rope, cable.* Nēc tĭbĭ Tȳrrhēnā fūnīs sōlvātŭr ărēnā. Pr. Syn.—Rēstĭs, vīncŭlūm, vīnclūm, (*sometimes*) lōrūm, rĕtĭnăcŭlă. Phr.—Vīncŭlă līnī. Stūpĕă vīncŭlă. Tōrtūm līnūm.

Fūnŭs, ĕrĭs. n. *Death, violent death.* Ābstŭlĭt ātră dĭēs ēt fūnĕrĕ mērsĭt ăcērbō. V. Syn.—Nēx. *Obsequies.* Syn.—Ēxsĕquĭæ, jūstă, sŭprēmă, dēbĭtă. Phr.—Fūnĕbrĭs pōmpă. Pōmpă flēbĭlĭs. Sŭprēmŭs hŏnōs. Fūnĕrĭs ēxsĕquĭæ. Rītĕ sŏlūtīs ēxsĕquĭīs. *See Exequiæ.*

Fūr, fūrĭs. m. *Thief.* Cāllĭdŭs ēffrāctā nūmmōs fūr aūfĕrĕt ārcā. M. Syn.—Lătrŏ, prædŏ, (*sometimes*) prædātŏr, spŏlĭātŏr, rāptŏr, ērēptŏr, ăbāctŏr. Phr.—Nūmmōrūm spŏlĭātŏr. Fūrtōrūm dōctŭs. Fūrtum īngĕnĭōsŭs ăd ōmnĕ. Fūrēs, ăvĭdūm gĕnŭs. Fūr nōctĕ lătēns. *See Prædor.*

Fŭrĭbūndŭs, ă, ūm. *Raging, furious.* Pāssīs fŭrĭbūndă căpīllīs Ēvŏlăt. O. Syn.—Fŭrĭōsŭs, fŭrēns.

Fŭrĭŏ, ās, āvī, ātūm, ārĕ. *To enrage.* Quæ sŏlēt mātrēs fŭrĭārĕ. H. Syn.—Lȳmphŏ, ēxstērnŏ. Phr.—Īn fŭrĭās, īn fŭrōrēm ăgŏ, īmpēllŏ, cōncĭtŏ. Fŭrōrĕ cōncĭtŏ. Ābstŭlīt mēntēm fŭrŏr.

Fŭrĭōsŭs, ă, ūm. *Raging, furious.* Nēmpĕ tŭō, fŭrĭōsĕ; mĕō, sēd nōn fŭrĭōsŭs. H. Syn.—Fŭrēns, fŭrĭātŭs, fŭrĭbūndŭs, lȳmphātŭs, dēlīrŭs, īnsānŭs, āmēns, dēmēns. Phr.—Fŭrōrĕ, fŭrĭīs ăccēnsŭs. Īmmŏdĭcōs gēstāns īn cōrdĕ fŭrōrēs. Āmēntī fŭrōrĕ cæcŭs. Răbĭē stĭmŭlātă. Āctă fŭrōrĕ grăvī. Cædĕ fŭrēns. Fŭrĭīs mēns ēffĕră.

Fŭrŏ, ĭs, ĕrĕ. *To be in a rage.* Īmmēnsām sĭnĕ mōrĕ fŭrīt lȳmphātă pĕr ūrbēm. V. Syn.—Īnsānĭŏ, dēlīrŏ, lȳmphŏr, bācchŏr. Phr.—Fŭrōre ăccēndŏr. Cæco īnsānīrĕ fŭrōrĕ. Mēntĕ fŭrōrēs cōncĭpĭŏ. Ārdēt fŭrōrĕ pēctŭs. Quæ mēntem īnsānĭă mūtăt? Dēlīrăt līnguăquĕ mēnsquĕ.

Fŭrŏr, ōrĭs. m. *Madness, fury, rage.* Jāmquĕ făcēs ēt sāxă vŏlānt, fŭrŏr ārmă mĭnīstrăt. V. Syn.—Fŭrĭæ, răbĭēs, īnsānĭă, dēmēntĭă, vēsānĭă, dēlīrĭă. Phr.—Fŭrōrĭs stĭmŭlī. Mălă mēns. Fŭrĭātă mēns. Ănĭmi ēffĕră vīs. Nēscĭŭs rĕgī fŭrŏr. Frēnī īmpătĭēns. Ēxpērs cōnsĭlĭī.

Fūrŏr, ārĭs, ātŭs sūm, ārī. *To steal.* Syn.—Răpĭŏ, sūbdūcŏ, sūbrĭpĭŏ, sūbtrăhŏ, cōmpīlŏ, āvērtŏ, tōllŏ, aūfĕrŏ, prædŏr. Phr.—Ādmīttĕrĕ fūrtūm. Vīvĕrĕ rāptō. Jŏcōsō cōndĕrĕ fūrtō.

Fūrtīm. adv. *Stealthily.* Syn.—Clām, ārcānō.

Fūrtīvŭs, ă, ūm. *Stolen.* Mŏvĕāt cōrnīcŭlă rīsūm Fūrtīvīs nūdātă cŏlōrĭbŭs. H. Syn.—Rāptŭs, sūbrēptŭs. Phr.—Āmōtæ pēr dŏlūm bŏvēs. Pōst īgnem æthĕrĕā dŏmō Sūbdūctūm. *Secret. See Arcanus.*

Fūrtūm, ī. n. *Theft.* Seū quĭs ăpūd Sŭpĕrōs fūrtō lætātŭs ĭnānī. V. Syn.—Prædă, răpīnă, rāptūm, lătrōcĭnĭūm. Phr.—Fūrtī crīmĕn. Dīrī sōlērtĭă fūrtī. Vīvĭtŭr ēx rāptō. *Secret. See Abditum.*

Fūrvŭs, ă, ūm. *Dark, obscure.* Syn.—Ātĕr, nĭgĕr, fūscŭs. *See Niger.*

Fūscŏ, ās, āvī, ātūm, ārĕ. *To darken.* Fūscāndī cūră cŏlōrĭs. O. Syn.—Īnfūscŏ. Phr.—Fūscāntŭr cōrpŏră. Lānūgĭnĕ mālă Fūscāntĕ.

Fūscŭs, ă, ūm. *Dark.* Nōx rŭĭt ēt fūscīs tēllūrem āmplēctĭtŭr ālīs. Syn.—Sūbnĭgĕr, nĭgrāns, ōbscūrŭs.

Fūsē. adv. *At length, widely, diffusely.* Syn.—Lātē, plēnē, cōpĭōsē.

Fūstĭs, ĭs. m. *Stick, club.* Syn.—Băcŭlŭs, stīpēs. Phr.—Fūste ăpĕrīrĕ căpŭt. Ăgĕrĕ fōrmīdĭnĕ fūstĭs. *See Baculum.*

Fūtĭlĭs, ĭs, ĕ. *Brittle, fragile.* Mūcrō, glăcĭēs ceū fūtĭlĭs, īctū Dīssĭlŭĭt. V. *See Fragilis. Vain, useless.* Syn.—Īnānĭs, īrrĭtŭs, lĕvĭs, vānŭs.

Fŭtūrūm, ī. n. *The future.* Quīd sīt fŭtūrūm crās fŭgĕ quærĕrĕ. H. Syn.—Vēntūrūm, vēntūră. Phr.—Vēntūrūm tēmpŭs. Pōstĕră sæcŭlă, sēclă. Vēntūrī tēmpŏrĭs ætās. Fŭtūrī cāsūs. Prūdēns fŭtūrī. *See Posteritas.*

G

Gălĕă, æ. f. *Helmet, casque.* Tūm gălĕām Mēssāpi hăbĭlēm crīstīsquĕ dĕcōrām Īndŭĭt. V. Syn.—Cāssĭs, cāssĭdă. Phr.—Aēs căvūm. Fērrātŭs ăpēx. Căpĭtĭs ārmă. Aērĕ rĭgēns. Īn gălĕā fōrmōsŭs ĕrăt. Aērĕ căpūt fūlgēns.

Gălĕātŭs, ă, ūm. *Armed with a helmet.* Quēm præstārĕ pŏtēst mŭlĭĕr gălĕātă pŭdōrēm. J. Phr.—Gălĕā ārmātŭs. Crīstīs căpĭta āltă cŏrūscīs.

Gālgŭlŭs, ī. m. & Gālbŭlă, æ. f. *Witwall or thrush.* (*See Appendix under list of Birds.*)

Gāllīnă, æ. f. *A hen.* (*See Appendix under list of Birds.*)

Gāllŭs, ī. m. *Cock, rooster.* (*See Appendix under list of Birds.*)

Gārrŭlĭtās, ātĭs. f. *Chattering, babble.* Raūcăquĕ gārrŭlĭtās, stŭdĭūmque īmmānĕ lŏquēndī. O. Syn.—Lŏquācĭtās. Phr.—Gārrŭlĭtās līnguæ. Gārrŭlă līnguă. Līnguæ prūrīgŏ. Vērbīs prŏcācĭbŭs ārdēns. Lŏquācĭs mūrmŭră līnguæ.

Gārrŭlŭs, ă, ūm. *Babbler, chatterer.* Gārrŭlă quām tīgnīs nīdūm sūspēndăt hĭrūndŏ. V. Syn.—Lŏquāx, strīdŭlŭs, strīdēns, vērbōsŭs, mūltĭlŏquŭs, vānĭlŏquŭs.

Gaūdĕŏ, ēs, gāvīsŭs sūm, ērĕ. *To rejoice.* Ēxcĭpĭūnt plaūsū sŏcĭōs, gaūdēntquĕ tŭēntēs. V. Syn.—Lætŏr, ŏvŏ, ēxsūltŏ, gēstĭŏ, ēxhĭlărŏ. Phr.—Gaūdĭă cōncĭpĭŏ, ăgĭtŏ, ēxsĭlĭŏ. Lætĭtĭā pērfūndŏr, ēxsūltŏ. Lætīs vōcĭbŭs tēstātŭr. Lætōs dīffūndĕrĕ vūltūs. Hĭlărī mēntĕ gaūdĭă cārpĕrĕ. Tōtō pēctŏrĕ lætārī. Tăcĭtām pērtēntānt gaūdĭă mēntēm. Dŭbĭē gaūdēt fāllīquĕ vĕrētŭr. Gaūdĕt hĭāns īmmānĕ. *See Lætus. To take pleasure in.* Syn.—Dēlēctŏr, ōblēctŏr, căpĭŏr, dūcŏr, ămŏ. Phr.—Rēs mē jŭvăt. Mĭhĭ plăcĕt, ārrīdĕt. Sānguĭnĕ gaūdĕt. Rēbūs gaūdērĕ nŏvīs.

Gaūdĭūm, ĭī. n. *Joy.* Gaūdĭă prīncĭpĭūm nōstrī sūnt sæpĕ dŏlōrĭs. O. Syn.—Lætĭtĭă, vŏlūptās. Phr.—Ēxhĭlărāns ănĭmōs. Lætĭtĭæ sīgnă. Vūltūs hĭlărēs. Ēt mălă mēntĭs gaūdĭă. Nōn vītæ gaūdĭă quærŏ. Gaūdĭă nēc rĕtĭnēt Rhœtŭs.

Gāză, æ. f. *Wealth, riches.* Dīgnĕ Mĭdæ Crœsīquĕ bŏnīs ēt Pērsĭdĕ găză. Syn.—Thēsaūrŭs, ŏpēs, pĕcūnĭă, dīvĭtĭæ. Phr.—Ŏpŭlēntă sŭpēllēx. Ŏpūm cŭmŭlŭs. Bĕātæ Ărăbūm gāzæ. *See Divitiæ.*

Gĕlĭdŭs, ă, ūm. *Cold, frozen.* Vērĕ nŏvō gĕlĭdūs cānīs cūm mōntĭbŭs hūmŏr Līquĭtŭr. V. *See Gelo.* Phr.—Gĕlĭdūsquĕ cŏīt fōrmīdĭnĕ sānguĭs. Āstrīctūm gĕlĭdō frīgŏrĕ pēctŭs.

Gĕlŏ, ās, āvī, ātūm, ārĕ. *To freeze.* Vūltūsquĕ gĕlāssēnt Pērsĕōs ādvērsī. L. Syn.—Cōngĕlŏ, cōnglăcĭŏ, glăcĭŏ, dūrŏ, īndūrŏ, āstrīngŏ. Phr.—Gĕlū āstrīngŏ. (*In the passive*) *To be frozen.* Syn.—Dūrēscŏ, īndūrēscŏ, āstrīngŏr, rĭgĕŏ, cŏĕŏ, cōngĕlŏ. Phr.—Gĕlū, glăcĭē cōncrēscŏ, īndūrēscŏ, rīgĕŏ, hōrrĕŏ. Glăcĭē rĭgĕt hōrrĭdă bārbă. Pāllĕt ădūstă gĕlū. Cūm glăcĭē brūmă rĭgēntĕ vĕnĭt.

Gĕlū. n. *indecl. Cold, frost.* Prīmō brūmă gĕlū sīccīsque Ăquĭlōnĭbŭs hōrrēns. V. Syn.—Glăcĭēs, frīgŭs, (*by extension*) brūmă, hĭēms, prŭīnă. Phr.—Ārctō frīgĭdă brūmă gĕlū. Cōncrētūm frīgŭs. Tērră cōncrētă gĕlū. Hōrrĭdă cānō brūmă gĕlū. *See Hiems.*

Gĕmēllī, ōrūm. m. *Twins.* Syn.—Gĕmĭnī. Phr.—Gĕmĭnŭs pārtŭs. Prōlēs gĕmĭnă.

Gĕmĭnī, ōrūm. m. *Twins.* Syn.—Gĕmēllī. *The Constellation.* Phr. Clāră, gĕmĭnī, sīgnă. Gērmānīquĕ părēs.

Gĕmĭnŏ, ās, āvī, ātūm, ārĕ. *To double.* Jāmquĕ dĕcēm vītæ frātēr gĕmĭnāvĕrăt ānnōs. O. Syn.—Īngĕmĭnŏ, cōngĕmĭnŏ, dŭplĭcŏ, cōndŭplĭcŏ, rĕpĕtŏ, ĭtĕrŏ, rĕnŏvŏ.

Gĕmĭnŭs, ă, ūm. *Double.* Syn.—Dŭplēx. *Two.* Syn.—Bīnī, dŭŏ, ŭtērquĕ, āmbŏ.

Gĕmĭtŭs, ūs. m. *Groan.* Aūdĭĭt Ālcīdēs jŭvĕnēm, māgnūmquĕ sŭb īmō Cōrdĕ prĕmīt gĕmĭtūm. V. Syn.—Lūctŭs, sūspīrĭă (pl), plānctŭs, plāngŏr, lāmēntūm, flētūs, querelă, quēstŭs, ŭlŭlātŭs, clāmŏr. Phr.—Gĕmĭtūs lăcrĭmābĭlĭs īmō Aūdītūr tŭmŭlō. Aēdēs clāmōrĕ rĕsūltānt. Āttŏnĭtō gĕmĭtūs ā cōrdĕ pĕtītōs. Hīnc ēxaūdīrī gĕmĭtūs. *See Gemo.*

Gēmmă, æ. f. *Gem, precious stone.* Quālĭs gēmmă mĭcāt fūlvūm quæ dīvĭdĭt aūrūm. V. Syn.—Lăpīllŭs, lăpĭs. Phr.—Rŭbrī mūnĕră Pōntī. Īndī dōnă mărĭs. Pĕlăgī dōnă rŭbēntĭs. Gēmmă nĭtĭdō fūlgōrĕ. Mīrō cāndōrĕ cŏrūscāns. Clārī lăpĭdēs. Grăvēm gēmmīs pătĕrām. *Bud, shoot.* Syn.—Ŏcŭlŭs, sūrcŭlŭs, nōdŭs, ārtĭcŭlŭs.

Gĕmŏ, ĭs, ŭī, ĭtūm, ĕrĕ. *To groan.* Ēt gĕmŭĭt, gĕmĭtūs vērbă părēntĭs ĕrānt. O. Syn.—Īngĕmŏ, gĕmīscŏ, sūspīrŏ, quĕrŏr, lāmēntŏr. Phr.—Pēctŏre ăb īmō dō gĕmĭtūm. Quēstū pēctŏră rūmpŏ. Cōnsūrgūnt gĕmĭtū. Dāt gĕmĭtūs fīctōs. Fīt gĕmĭtŭs. Mūltă gĕmēns. *See Lacrimo, Queror. To deplore.* Syn.—Dŏlĕŏ, quĕrŏr, dēplōrŏ, īndŏlĕŏ, īngĕmŏ.

Gĕnĕr, ĕrī. m. *Son-in-law.* Quīs gĕnĕr hīc plăcŭīt cēnsū mĭnŏr ātquĕ pŭēllæ Sārcĭnŭlīs īmpār? J. Phr.—Gĕnĕrōs ēxtērnīs āffŏre ăb ōrīs. Quōs gĕnĕrōs vŏcĕt. Gĕnĕrūm mĭhĭ, fīlĭă, dēbēs.

Gĕnĕrŏ, ās, āvī, ātūm, ārĕ. *To bring forth, to produce.* Syn.—Prōgĕnĕrŏ, gīgnŏ, prōgīgnŏ, crĕŏ, prōdūcŏ, părĭŏ.

Gĕnĕrōsē. adv. *Nobly, generously.* Syn.—Fōrtĭtĕr, ănĭmōsē.

Gĕnĕrōsŭs, ă, ūm. *Of noble birth.* Nēmō gĕnĕrōsĭŏr ēst tē. H. Phr.—Nōbĭlī gĕnĕr. *Noble, courageous.* Syn.—Aūdāx, ănĭmōsŭs, fōrtĭs, māgnănĭmŭs, strēnŭŭs, īmpăvĭdŭs, īntērrĭtŭs. Phr.—Vīrtūtĕ pŏtēns, præstāns. Vīr fōrtī pēctŏrĕ. *See Animosus.*

Gĕnĭālĭs, ĭs, ĕ. *Joyous.* Nūnc ĕlĕgī mōllēs, gĕnĭālīs mūsă, vălētĕ. O. Syn.—Fēstŭs, fēstīvŭs, lætŭs, laūtŭs, hĭlărĭs.

Gĕnīstă, æ. f. *The broom-plant.* (*See Appendix under list of Trees, etc.*)

Gĕnĭtŏr, ōrĭs. m. *Father*. Syn.—Gĕnĕrātŏr, prōgĕnĭtŏr, sătŏr, părēns, pătĕr, aūctŏr.

Gĕnĭtrīx, īcĭs. f. *Mother*. Syn.—Părēns, mātĕr. *See Mater*.

Gēns, tĭs. f. *Nation*. Nēc pŭĕr Īlĭăcā quīsquām dē gēntĕ Lătīnōs Īn tāntūm spē tōllĕt ăvōs. V. Syn.—Pŏpŭlŭs, nātĭŏ. Phr.—Gēns dūra ātque āspĕră cūltū. Gēns ēffrēnă vĭrūm. Gēntēs frēnārĕ sŭpērbās. *Race, family*. Syn.—Gĕnŭs, sānguĭs, stīrps, prōlēs, prŏpāgŏ.

Gĕnū. (*indecl. in sing.*, pl. gĕnŭă & gēnuă) n. *Knee*. Īmprēssōquĕ gĕnū nītēns, tērrae āpplĭcăt īpsūm. V. Syn.—Pŏplĕs. Phr.—Rĭgĭdō nīxūs gĕnū. Īllūm gĕnŭa ǣgră trăhēntēm dūcūnt. Gĕnŭă flēctŏ. Īncĭdĭt ăd tērrām dŭplĭcātī pōplĭtĕ. Gĕnĭbūs sūpplēx ādvōlvī. Sūbmīssō pŏplĭtĕ.

Gĕnŭīnŭs, ă, ūm. *Natural, true*. Syn.—Nātīvŭs, nātūrālĭs, vērŭs, sīncērŭs, gērmānŭs.

Gĕnŭs, ĕrĭs. n. *Race, species*. Syn.—Gēns. Phr.—Ūnde hŏmĭnūm gĕnŭs ēt pĕcŭdēs. Gĕnŭs īrrītābĭlĕ vātūm. Gĕnŭs ōmne ănĭmāntūm. *Family*. Syn.—Gēns, ōrtŭs, ŏrīgŏ, stīrps, sānguĭs, prōlēs, prŏpāgŏ, prōgĕnĭēs, dŏmŭs. Phr.—Gēntĭs hŏnōs. Ōrtūs nōbĭlĕ prīncĭpĭūm. Āb Jŏvĕ prīncĭpĭūm gĕnĕrĭs.

Gērmĕn, ĭnĭs. n. *Bud, root*. Syn.—Sūrcŭlŭs, frŭtēx, pālmĕs, gēmmă.

Gērmĭnŏ, ās, āvī, ātūm, ārĕ. *To put forth buds, or roots*. Syn.—Prōgērmĭnŏ, gēmmŏ, pūbēscŏ, pūllŭlŏ, ădŏlēscŏ, frŭtĭcŏ. Phr.—Gērmĭnă, gēmmās fūndŏ, ēxplĭcŏ. Gērmĭnĕ pūbĕŏ. Rāmīs vĭrĕŏ.

Gĕrŏ, ĭs, gēssī, gēstūm, ĕrĕ. *To carry*. Quō fērrūm, quīdve hǣc gĕrĭtĭs tēla īrrĭtă dēxtrīs? V. Syn.—Gēstŏ, fĕrŏ, pōrtŏ. *To administer*. Syn.—Trāctŏ, cūrŏ, ăgŏ, ēxsĕquŏr.

Gēstĭŏ, īs, īvī & ĭī, ītūm, īrĕ. *To desire greatly*. Ēt stŭdĭo īncāssūm vĭdĕās gēstīrĕ lăvāndī. V. Syn.—Cŭpĭŏ, ārdĕŏ, glīscŏ. Phr.—Cūm părĭbūs gēstīt cōllūdĕrĕ. *To rejoice*. Syn.—Ēxsūltŏ, lǣtŏr, gaūdĕŏ.

Gēstŏ, ās, āvī, ātūm, ārĕ. *To carry*. Syn.—Gĕrŏ, fĕrŏ, pōrtŏ.

Gēstŭs, ūs. m. *Movement, gesture*. Syn.—Mōtŭs. Phr.—Hŭmĕrīs brāchĭă mōtă sŭīs. Īllă plăcēt gēstū. Mōtūs dŏcērī gaūdēt Īōnĭcōs.

Gīgnŏ, ĭs, gĕnŭī, gĕnĭtūm, ĕrĕ. *To bring forth*. Quǣnām tē gĕnŭīt sōlā sūb rūpĕ lĕǣnă? Syn.—Gĕnĕrŏ, ēdŏ, crĕŏ, prōcrĕŏ, părĭŏ, prōgĕnĕrŏ, pārtŭrĭŏ, ēnītŏr, prōdūcŏ, prōgīgnŏ. Phr.—Quǣ tē tām lǣtă tŭlērūnt sǣcŭlă. *To cause*. Syn.—Părĭŏ, āffĕrŏ, ēffĭcĭŏ, ēdŏ, prōdūcŏ.

Glăcĭālĭs, ĭs, ĕ. *Cold, icy.* Ēt glăcĭālĭs hĭēms cānōs hīrsūtă căpīllōs. O. Syn.—Ālgĭdŭs, gĕlĭdŭs, frīgĭdŭs, prŭīnōsŭs. *See Frigidus.*

Glăcĭēs, ēī. f. *Ice.* Āh! tĭbĭ nē glăcĭēs tĕnĕrās sĕcĕt āspĕră plāntās! V. Phr.—Ūndă gĕlū cōncrētă. Gĕlū cōncrētūs lătēx. Crūstă lūbrĭcă. Quæ frīgŏrĕ cōnstĭtĭt ūndă. Stāt glăcĭēs ĭnērs.

Glădĭātŏr, ōrĭs. m. *Gladiator.* Lūstrāvītquĕ fŭgā mĕdĭām glădĭātŏr ărēnām. J. Syn.—Pŭgĭl, lūctātŏr, lănīstă. Phr.—Mēdĭă pūgnāt glădĭātŏr ărēnā. Fātālĭs ărēnæ mūnĕră.

Glădĭŭs, ĭī. m. *Sword.* Nēscĭĕrīnt prīmī glădĭōs ēxcūdĕrĕ fābrī. J. Syn.—Ēnsĭs, fērrūm, mūcrŏ, cūspĭs, ăcĭēs. Phr.—Pārs glădĭōs strīngūnt mănĭbŭs. Frīgĭdŭs īndĕ Stat glădĭŭs. Īrĕ pĕr īgnēs ēt glădĭōs.

Glaūcŭs, ă, ūm. *Blue, azure.* Ārdēntēs ŏcŭlōs īntōrsĭt lūmĭnĕ glaūcō. V. Syn.—Cærŭlŭs, cærŭlĕŭs, vĭrĭdĭs.

Glēbă, æ. f. *Clump of earth.* Līquĭtŭr ēt zĕphy̆rō pūtrĭs sē glēbă rĕsōlvĭt. V. Phr.—Dītēs sĭnĕ vōmĕrĕ glēbæ. Ūbĕrĕ glēbæ Tērră fĕrāx. Pŏtēns tērrĭs ātque ūbĕrĕ glēbæ. Glēbās vērsārĕ lĭgōnĭbŭs. Vērtēntēs vōmĕrĕ glēbās.

Glīscŏ, ĭs, ĕrĕ. *To increase, to extend.* Haūd āccēnsō glīscĭt vĭŏlēntĭă Tūrnō. V. Syn.—Crēscŏ, āccrēscŏ, aūgēscŏ, aūgĕŏr, grăvēscŏ, īnvălēscŏ. *To desire. See Cupio.*

Glŏbŭs, ī. m. *Ball, sphere.* Syn.—Sphæră, ōrbĭs.

Glŏmĕrŏ, ās, āvī, ātūm, ārĕ. *To roll together.* Syn.—Āgglŏmĕrŏ, cōnglŏmĕrŏ. *To gather together, to collect.* Syn.—Āgglŏmĕrŏ, cōnglŏmĕrŏ, cōllĭgŏ, cōntrăhŏ, cōnvĕhŏ, dēnsĕŏ, āccŭmŭlŏ, āggĕrŏ. Phr.—Sēd bēllō glŏmĕrārĕ mănūm. Tūm sē glŏmĕrānt, rētrōquĕ rĕsīdūnt. Nĭgrō glŏmĕrārī pūlvĕrĕ nūbēm. Hīnc ātque hīnc glŏmĕrāntŭr Ŏrēădĕs.

Glōrĭă, æ. f. *Glory, honor.* Ō dĕcŭs ātque ævī glōrĭă rāră tŭī! O. Syn.—Laūs, hŏnŏr, dĕcŭs, fāmă, nōmĕn, splēndŏr. Phr.—Nōmĕn īmmōrtālĕ. Īnclӯtă fāmă. Nēscĭă mōrtĭs. Glōrĭă sēră vĕnĭt. *Ornament.* Syn.—Hŏnŏr, dĕcŭs, grātĭă.

Glōrĭŏr, ārĭs, ātŭs sūm, ārī. *To boast.* Syn.—Ōstēntŏ, jāctĭtŏ, vēndĭtŏ, ēffĕrŏ. Phr.—Vērbīs ēxtōllĕrĕ gēstă sŭpērbīs. Fāctă fērrĕ pŏlō, ĭn āstră.

Glōrĭōsŭs, ă, ūm. *Honorable, glorious.* Syn.—Hŏnēstŭs, dĕcōrŭs, pūlchĕr.

Gnārŭs, ă, ūm. *Knowing.* Syn.—Dōctŭs, ēxpērtŭs, scĭēns, pĕrītŭs, prūdēns, sōlērs.

Gnāvĭtĕr. adv. *Actively.* Syn.—Aūdāctĕr fōrtĭtĕr, strēnŭē. *Carefully.* Syn.—Sōlērtĕr, stŭdĭōsē.

Gnāvŭs, ă, ūm. *Diligent, active.* Gnāvūs mānĕ fŏrum ēt vēspērtīnūs pĕtĕ tēctūm. H. Syn.—Īmpĭgĕr, strēnŭŭs, ălăcĕr, dīlĭgēns, prōmptŭs, fēstīnŭs, cĕlĕr. *See Diligens.*

Grăbātŭs, ī. m. *Couch, bed, a poor man's bed.* Syn.—Cŭbīlĕ, tŏrŭs, strātă (ōrūm), lēctŭs. *See Lectus.*

Grăcĭlĭs, ĭs, ĕ. *Thin, slender.* Syn.—Ēxīlĭs, tĕnŭĭs, pārvŭs, ēxĭgŭŭs, măcĭlēntŭs.

Grădātīm. adv. *Gradually.* Syn.—Sēnsĭm, paūlātīm, pĕdĕtēntīm. Phr.—Pēr grădūs.

Grădĭŏr, ĕrĭs, grēssŭs sūm, grădī. *To step, to walk.* Īpse ūnō grădĭtūr cŏmĭtātŭs Ăchātĕ. V. Syn.—Īngrĕdĭŏr, āmbŭlō, ĕō, īncēdō, vādō. Phr.—Fērrĕ grădūm. Grēssūm flēctō, dīrĭgō. Āccĕlĕrārĕ grădūm. Cōnfērrĕ grădūm.

Grădŭs, ūs. m. *Step.* Sēd rĕvŏcārĕ grădūm sŭpĕrāsque ēvādĕre ăd aūrās. V. Syn.—Grēssŭs, pāssŭs, īncēssŭs, pēs, vēstīgĭă.

Grāmĕn, ĭnĭs. n. *Grass, sward.* Rōscĭdă mōbĭlĭbūs lāmbēbānt grāmĭnă rīvīs Ērrāntēs lўmphæ. Syn.—Hērbă, cæspĕs. Phr.—Hērbæ grāmĭnĕæ. Grāmĭnĕūs cæspĕs. Tērræ grāmĭnă īnjūssă. Hērbōsō vĭrĭdēs, vērnāntēs grāmĭnĕ cāmpī. Vĭrĭdī sē grāmĭnĕ tēllūs Vēstĭt.

Grāmĭnōsŭs, Grāmĭnĕŭs, ă, ūm. *Grassy.* Syn.—Hērbōsŭs, hērbĭdŭs.

Grāndævŭs, ă, ūm. *Aged.* Ēt quā vēctŭs Ăbās ēt quā grāndævŭs Ălēthēs. V. Syn.—Lōngævŭs, ānnōsŭs. Phr.—Grāndĭŏr ævō. Grāndĭs nātū. Aēvō mātūrŭs. *See Senex.*

Grāndĭlŏquŭs, ă, ūm. *Speaking grandly, grandiloquent.* Syn.—Māgnĭlŏquŭs, ēlātŭs.

Grāndĭnăt. *Impers. It hails.* Phr.—Grāndŏ plŭĭt. Grāndŏ cūlmĭnă lædĭt. Cūlmĭnă grāndĭnĕ crēbrā Īctă sŏnānt. Īn tēctīs crĕpĭtāns sălĭt hōrrĭdă grāndŏ. Tāntā quătĭtūr nēc grāndĭnĕ Sўrtĭs. Grāndĭnĕ nīmbī Præcĭpĭtānt.

Grāndĭs, ĭs, ĕ. *Great, large.* Syn.—Māgnŭs, vāstŭs, lārgŭs, āmplŭs, īngēns, prōcērŭs. *Sublime.* Syn.—Sūblīmĭs, grāndĭlŏquŭs.

Grāndŏ, ĭnĭs. f. *Hail.* Hīs ĕgŏ nīgrāntēm cōmmīxtā grāndĭnĕ nīmbūm Dēsŭpĕr īnfūndām. V. Phr.—Grāndĭnĭs īmbĕr. Nīx īndūrātă. Nīmbī mūltā grāndĭnĕ mīxtī.

Grāssātŏr, ōrĭs. m. *Highway robber, thief.* Syn.—Prædŏ, prædātŏr, lătrŏ.

Grāssŏr, ārĭs, ātŭs sūm, ārī. *To go, to advance. See Cedo, Progredior. To rob.* Syn.—Lătrōcĭnŏr, prædŏr. *To attack.* Syn.—Īnvādŏ, glīscŏ, īrrūmpŏ, īmpĕtŏ, īrrŭŏ, ădŏrĭŏr.

Grātē. adv. *Pleasantly, agreeably.* Syn.—Jūcūndē, lĭbēntĕr.

Grātĭă, æ. f. *Grace, benefit.* Syn.—Făvŏr, dōnūm, mūnŭs, ōffĭcĭūm. *Beauty.* Syn.—Lĕpŏr, vĕnūstās, pūlchrĭtūdŏ, dĕcŏr. *Friendship.* Syn.—Ămŏr, stŭdĭūm, cōncōrdĭă. *Gratitude. Syn.*—Grātēs.

Grātĭs. adv. *Freely.* Syn.—Grātŭītō, ūltrō.

Grātŭlŏr, ārĭs, ātŭs sūm, ārī. *To congratulate.* Tōtā tĭbĭ mēntĕ mĭhīquĕ Grātŭlŏr īngĕnĭūm nōn lătŭīssĕ tŭūm. O. Syn.—Grātŏr, cōngrātŭlŏr, plaūdŏ, prŏbŏ. Phr.—Gaūdĭă vērbīs prōdŏ. Lætĭtĭæ dărĕ sīgnă sŭæ. *See Plaudo.*

Grātŭs, ă, ūm. *Agreeable, pleasing.* Grātă sŭpērvĕnĭēt quæ nōn spērābĭtŭr hōră. H. Syn.—Ăccēptŭs, ămātŭs, ămīcŭs, dīlēctŭs, ārrīdēns, dūlcĭs, jūcūndŭs, plăcēns. Phr.—Aēstīvā grātĭŏr ūmbrā. Tūrnō grātīssĭmŭs aūgŭr.

Grăvĭdŭs, ă, ūm. *Heavy.* Syn.—Grăvĭs, ŏnūstŭs, ŏnĕrātŭs.

Grăvĭs, ĭs, ĕ. *Heavy.* Nām grăvĭs īmbēllēs āttĕrĭt hāstă mănūs. O. Syn.—Ŏnĕrōsŭs, pōndĕrōsŭs. Phr.—Nōn lĕvĭs. Pōndŭs hăbēntĭă. Vōmĕrĕ tērrās īnvērtīssĕ grăvēs. Īnfēstō vōlvēbānt pōndĕrĕ sāxă. Dēcĭdūnt cāsū grăvĭōrĕ tūrrēs. *Oppressed, weighed down.* Syn.—Grăvātŭs, tārdŭs, lānguēns, prēssŭs, ōpprēssŭs. *Important.* Syn.—Māgnŭs, īngēns, grāndĭs. *Hurtful.* Syn.—Nōxĭŭs, nŏcēns, īmpōrtūnŭs, īncōmmŏdŭs, dāmnōsŭs. *Painful.* Syn.—Ăcērbŭs, mŏlēstŭs, trīstĭs, dūrŭs, āspĕr.

Grăvĭtās, ātĭs. f. *Weight.* Īgnāvā nĕquĕūnt grăvĭtātĕ mŏvērī. O. Syn.—Pōndŭs, ŏnŭs, mōlēs. *Gravity.* Syn.—Aūstērĭtās, sĕvērĭtās, mājēstās, pōndŭs, sŭpērcĭlĭūm, tētrĭcĭtās. Phr.—Vūltŭs grăvĭs. Frōns mājēstātĕ vĕrēndă. Vūltū grăvĭtās īmmōtă sĕrēnō. Sŭpĕrāt grăvĭtātĕ Cătōnēm. *Importance.* Syn.—Pōndŭs, mōmēntūm.

Grăvĭtĕr. adv. *Heavily.* Syn.—Dūrē, dūrĭtĕr. *Violently.* Syn.—Ăcrĭtĕr, vĕhĕmēntĕr, mūltūm. *Irritably.* Syn.—Aēgrē, grăvātē, īndīgnē, āspĕrē, mŏlēstē.

Grăvŏ, ās, āvī, ātūm, ārĕ. *To load, to burden.* Syn.—Prægrăvŏ, ŏnĕrŏ, prĕmŏ, ōpprĭmŏ, ōbrŭŏ. *To aggravate.* Syn.—Lædŏ, ōffēndŏ.

Grĕmĭūm, ĭī. n. *Lap.* Ūt cūm tē grĕmĭo āccĭpĭēt lætīssĭmă Dīdō. V. Syn.—Sĭnŭs, pēctŭs, (*sometimes*) cōmplēxŭs.

Grēssŭs, ūs. m. *Step, course.* Sūbsĕquĭtūr, prēssōquĕ lĕgĭt vēstīgĭă grēssū. O. Syn.—Grădŭs, īncēssŭs, īngrēssŭs. Phr.—Tēndĭt ăd līmĭnă grēssūm.

Grēx, grĕgĭs. m. *Flock.* Dūx grĕgĭs īpsĕ căpēr deērrāvĕrăt. V. Syn.—Pĕcŭs, pĕcŭdēs, pĕcŏră, pĕcŭārĭă. Phr.—Pĕcŭdūm grēx, tūrbă.

Grūs & Grŭĭs, ĭs. f. *A crane.* (*See Appendix under list of Birds.*)

Gŭbērnācŭlūm & Gŭbērnāclūm, ī. n. *Helm, rudder.* Īpsĕ gŭbērnāclō rēctōr sŭbĭt īpsĕ măgīstĕr. V. Syn.—Clāvŭs, tēmŏ, mŏdĕrāmĕn, rĕgĭmĕn, hăbēnæ. Phr.—Clāvŭs nāvĭs. Cūrvæ mŏdĕrāmĭnă pūppĭs.

Gŭbērnātŏr, ōrĭs. m. *Pilot.* Īpsĕ gŭbērnātōr pūppī Pălĭnūrŭs ăb āltā. V. Syn.—Nāvĭtă, naūclērŭs, rēctŏr, mŏdĕrātŏr, măgīstĕr. Phr.—Nāvĭs măgīstĕr. Dŏmĭtŏr frĕtī. Quī rĕgĭt ārtĕ rătēm. Quī vēntīs īmpĕrăt. Dōctūs frēnārĕ rătēm.

Gŭbērnŏ, ās, āvī, ātūm, ārĕ. *To steer, to guide.* Syn.—Rĕgŏ, dīrĭgŏ, mŏdĕrŏr, dūcŏ, īmpĕrŏ.

Gŭlă, æ. f. *Throat.* Gŭlæquĕ crēdēns cōllī lōngĭtūdĭnēm. Phaed. Syn.—Faūcēs, gūttŭr. *Mouth.* Syn.—Ōs, pălātūm. *Gluttony.* Syn.—Īnglŭvĭēs, vēntĕr, ĕdācĭtās, vŏrācĭtās. Phr.—Īmprŏbă vēntrĭs īnglŭvĭēs. Vēntrĭs ārdŏr. Mălĕ mōrātūs vēntĕr. *See Fames.*

Gŭlōsŭs, ă, ūm. *Greedy, a gourmand.* Nōn ēst, Tūccă, sătĭs quŏd ēs gŭlōsŭs. M. Syn.—Hēllŭŏ, lūrcŏ, cŏmĕdŏ, gūrgĕs, gŭlă. Gŭlæ dēdĭtŭs. Īnsătĭābĭlĭs ōrĕ. Nōn dāns frēnă gŭlæ. Vēntrĭs cŭpīdĭnĕ vīctŭs.

Gūrgĕs, ĭtĭs. m. *Whirlpool, abyss.* Āppārēnt rărī nāntēs īn gūrgĭtĕ vāstō. V. Syn.—Vŏrāgŏ, bărăthrūm, hĭātŭs, vōrtēx. Phr.—Spūmōsī gūrgĭtĭs æstŭs, vōrtēx. Frĕtī spūmāntĭs hĭātŭs. Spūmĕās rŏtāns ăquās. Vāstā vŏrāgĭnĕ gūrgĕs.

Gūstŏ, ās, āvī, ātūm, ārĕ. *To taste.* Prĭūsquām Pābŭlă gūstāssēnt Trōjæ. V. Syn.—Dēgūstŏ, lībŏ, dēlībŏ. Phr.—Gūstū āttīngŏ. Ēscās gūstārĕ pălātō. *To experience.* Syn.—Ēxpĕrĭŏr, tēntŏ.

Gūstŭs, ūs. m. *Taste.* Syn.—Pălātūm, săpŏr.

Gūttă, æ. f. *Drop.* Gūttă căvāt lăpĭdēm, nōn vī, sēd sæpĕ cădēndō. O. Syn.—Stīllă, gūttŭlă. Phr.—Rōs ēxĭgŭŭs. Tĕnŭĭs ăquæ lĭquŏr. Grāndēs ībūnt pēr vīmĭnă gūttæ.

Gūttŭr, ŭrĭs. n. *Windpipe, throat.* Īllĕ fāmē răbĭdā trĭă gūttŭră pāndēns. V. Syn.—Gŭlă, faūcēs, ōs, jŭgŭlūm. *Voice, song.* Syn.—Ōs, vōx, cāntŭs. Phr.—Vōcĭs ĭtĕr.

Gūttŭs, ī. m. *Jar, jug used in the sacrifices.* Syn.—Ūrcĕŭs, ūrcĕŏlŭs.

Gȳrŭs, ī. m. *Circle, circular course.* Syn.—Ōrbĭs, cīrcŭĭtŭs, cīrcŭlŭs āmbĭtŭs, ārcŭs, flēxŭs. Phr.—Īn gȳrūm flēctĕrĕ. Īn ōrbēm vērtĕrĕ. *Fold.* Syn.—Nēxŭs, vŏlūmĕn, spīră, ōrbĭs, flēxŭs. Phr.—Pĕr īmmēnsōs sĭnŭārĕ vŏlūmĭnă gȳrōs. Īn gȳrōs īrĕ.

H

Hăbēnă, æ. f. *Rein, bridle.* Cūm răpĭdum ēffūsīs rĕgĕrēt sūblīmĭs hăbēnīs Cōrnĭpĕdēm. Syn.—Lōrūm, frēnūm, rĕtĭnācŭlūm, căpīstrūm. Phr.—Mŏdĕrāmĕn ĕquōrūm. Frēnōrum hăbēnæ. Lōră tĕnērĕ mănū. Hăbēnās mănĭbŭs rĕgĕrĕ. Frēnă lāxārĕ. Līběr hăbēnīs ĕquŭs.

Hăbĕŏ, ēs, ŭī, ĭtūm, ērĕ. *To have, to hold.* Nīl tĭbĭ quōd dēmūs mājŭs hăbēmŭs, ăĭt. O. Syn.—Pōssĭdĕŏ, tĕnĕŏ. Phr.—Ēst mĭhĭ, nōbīs. Pĕnĕs mē ēst. Nōn cărĕŏ. Mĭhi īn prōmptu ēst. *To dwell. See Habito. To esteem.* Syn.—Dūcŏ, făcĭŏ, pēndŏ, æstĭmŏ.

Hăbĭlĭs, ĭs, ĕ. *Suitable, proper.* Syn.—Āptŭs, āccōmmŏdŭs, ĭdōnĕŭs. *Fit, convenient.* Syn.—Dĕcēns, āptŭs, āccōmmŏdŭs.

Hăbĭtacŭlūm, ī. n. *Habitation, dwelling.* Syn.—Sēdēs, ædēs, dŏmŭs.

Hăbĭtŏ, ās, āvī, ātūm, ārĕ. *To dwell, to inhabit.* Nūllī cērtă dŏmūs, lūcīs hăbĭtāmŭs ŏpācīs. V. Syn.—Cŏlŏ, īncŏlŏ, tĕnĕŏ, hăbĕŏ, frĕquēntŏ, mănĕŏ, rĕsĭdĕŏ, sĕdĕŏ, cōmmŏrŏr, mŏrŏr. Phr.—Sēdēm pŏsŭī. Mĭhĭ sēdēs ēst. Tўrĭī tĕnŭērĕ cŏlōnī. Hŭmĭlēs hăbĭtārĕ căsās.

Hăbĭtŭs, ūs. m. *Appearance, exterior.* Vīrgĭnĭs ōs hăbĭtūmquĕ gĕrēns ēt vīrgĭnĭs ārmă. V. Syn.—Vūltŭs, ōs, fōrmă, făcĭēs, spĕcĭēs, vīsŭs, āspēctŭs. Phr.—Hăbĭtūm mūtāvĕrĭt ōrĭs. Stătŭs ēst vūltūsquĕ dīsērtī. *See Vultus.*

Hāctĕnŭs. adv. *Up to this point.* Syn.—Ădhūc. Phr.—Hūc ūsquĕ.

Hædŭs, ī. m. *Young goat, kid.* Ūt cănĭbūs cătŭlōs sĭmĭlēs, sīc mātrĭbŭs hædōs nōrām. V. Syn.—Hædŭlŭs. Phr.—Căpēllæ fœtŭs. Pĕtŭlāns mōlli hædŭs ĭn hērbā. Cuī frōns prīmīs tūrgĭdă cōrnĭbŭs.

Hærēdĭtās, ātĭs. f. *Heritage.* Hærēdĭtātīs tĭbĭ trĕcēntă vēnīssĕ. M. Syn.—Pătrĭmōnĭūm, pătrĭs ŏpēs, bŏnă, fōrtūnă, prædĭă.

Hærĕŏ, ēs, sī, sūm, ērĕ. *To cling to, to hang to.* Syn.—Ădhærĕŏ, cŏhærĕŏ, ĭnhærĕŏ, hærēscŏ, mănĕŏ, jūngŏ. Phr.—Hærēnt pārĭētĭbūs scālæ. Tērgō vŏlŭcrēs hæsērĕ săgīttæ. Hæsĭt ĭn āmplēxū. *To hesitate.* Syn.—Hæsĭtŏ, dŭbĭtŏ, flūctŭŏ, mănĕŏ, cōnsīstŏ, sūbsīstŏ, rĕsīstŏ, stō. Phr.—Līngua hærēt mĕtū.

Hærēs (Hērēs), ēdĭs. m. *Heir.* Pārcŭs ŏb hērēdīs cūrām nĭmĭūmquĕ sĕvērŭs Āssĭdēt īnsānō. H. Phr.—Spēs pătrĭs. Ăvītī nōmĭnĭs hērēs.

Hālĭtŭs, ūs. m. *Breath.* Ēxtrēmūs sī quĭs sŭpĕr hālĭtŭs ērrăt. V. Syn.—Spīrĭtŭs, ănhēlĭtŭs. Phr.—Mălĕ ŏdōrātī ănhēlĭtŭs ōrĭs. *See Vapor, Odor.*

Hālŏ, ās, āvī, ātūm, ārĕ. *To breathe, to exhale.* Īnvītēnt crŏcēīs hālāntēs faūcĭbŭs hōrtī. V. Syn.—Spīrŏ, ēxhālŏ, ŏlĕŏ, rĕdŏlĕŏ.

Hāmŭs, ī. m. *Hook.* Cūrvōs dĕdĭt ūnguĭbŭs hāmōs. O. Syn.—Hāmŭlŭs, ūncŭs, ūncĭnŭs. Phr.—Pīscārĭūs ūncŭs. Hāmātă līnĕă.

Hārmŏnĭă, æ. f. *Harmony, concord.* Hārmŏnĭām Grāiī quām dīcūnt. Lr. Syn.—Cōncōrdĭă. *Melody.* Syn.—Cōncēntŭs, mĕlŏs. Phr.—Cōncōrs dīscōrdĭă vōcūm. Cōnsŏnă fēstīvī mŏdŭlāmĭnă cāntūs. *See Musica.*

Hāstă, æ. f. *Spear, javelin.* Dēfīgūnt tēllūre hāstās āc scūtă rĕclīnānt. V. Syn.—Lāncĕă, pīlūm, hāstīlĕ, cūspĭs, fērrūm, mīssĭlĕ, jăcŭlūm, spīcŭlūm, tēlūm, (*sometimes*) ăbĭēs, frāxĭnŭs, pīnŭs. Phr.—Aērātæ cūspĭdĭs hāstă. Sānguĭnĕā mănŭs hōrrĕăt hāstā. Ārmātquĕ cŏrūscă Hāstă mănūm. Dēnsīsquĕ vĭrūm sĕgĕs hōrrŭĭt hāstīs.

Hāstīlĕ, ĭs. n. *Shaft of a spear.* Phr.—Præfīxo hāstīlĭă fērrō. Tēlum īngēns ārbŏrĕūm. Hāstīlĭs vīrgă, stīpĕs. Ārmātă fērrō cōrnŭs. Tōrquēns hāstīlĕ lăcērtō.

Haūdquāquām. adv. *By no means.* Syn.—Mĭnĭmē, nēquāquām.

Haūrĭŏ, īs, sī, stūm, īrĕ. *To draw out, to exhaust.* Ād ūndām Prōcēssīt, sūmmōque haūsīt dē gūrgĭtĕ lȳmphās. V. Syn.—Trăhŏ, dūcŏ, ēxtrăhŏ, ēdūcŏ, ēgĕrŏ. *See Bibo. To exhaust, to consume.* Syn.—Sōrbĕŏ, ābsōrbĕŏ, ēxhaūrĭŏ. Phr.—Haūsĭt ŏpēs pătrĭās. *To tire out.* Syn.—Cōnfĭcĭŏ, ēxhaūrĭŏ, quătĭŏ.

Hēbdŏmăs, ădĭs & Hēbdŏmădă, æ. f. *The seventh day, week. See Dies.*

Hĕbĕŏ, ēs, ērĕ. *To grow dull, blunt.* Sānguĭs hĕbēt, frīgēntque ēffœtae īn cōrpŏrĕ vīrēs. V. Syn.—Hĕbĕtŏr, tōrpĕŏ, dēfĭcĭŏ, cōnsīdŏ, fătīscŏ.

Hĕbĕs, ĕtĭs. adj. *Dull, heavy, inactive.* Jāmque hĕbēs ēt crāssō nōn āspēr sānguĭnĕ mūcrŏ. L. Syn.—Hĕbēns, hĕbēscēns, hĕbĕtātŭs, ōbtūsŭs, rĕtūsŭs, stŏlĭdŭs, stūpĭdŭs, bārdŭs.

Hĕbĕtŏ, ās, āvī, ātūm, ārĕ. *To dull.* Syn.—Ōbtūndŏ, rĕtūndŏ. Fig.—*To enfeeble. See Debilito.*

Hĕcătōmbē, ēs. f. *Hecatomb.* Phr.—Cēntēnă cōllă sūbmīttūnt bŏvēs. *See Sacrifico.*

Hĕdĕră, æ. f. *Ivy.* Ūtquĕ sŏlēnt hĕdĕræ lōngōs īntēxĕrĕ trūncōs. O. Phr.—Frōndēntēs bāccīs hĕdĕræ. Frōndĕ sĕquācī rōbŏră līgāns. Dōctārūm prœmĭă frōntĭūm. Nōbĭlĭs cŏrōnă vātūm. Hĕdĕră fōrmōsĭŏr ālbā. (*See Appendix.*)

Hĕră, æ. f. *Mistress of the house.* Syn.—Dŏmĭnă, dŏmĭnātrīx, rēgīnă.

Hērbă, æ. f. *Grass, herb.* Quīquĕ frĕquēns hērbīs ēt fērtĭlĭs ūbĕrĕ cāmpīs. V. Syn.—Grāmĕn, cæspĕs. Phr.—Grāmĭnĭs hērbă. Vīvāx cæspĭtĕ grāmĕn. Grāmĭnĕă hŭmŭs. Grāmĭnĕŭs tŏrŭs. Mīxtīs rĕdŏlēntēs flōrĭbŭs hērbæ. Făcĭlĭs quærēntĭbŭs hērbă. Tēllūs gēmmāntēs ēxplĭcăt hērbās.

Hērbĭfĕr, ĕră, ĕrūm. *Grassy.* Prætĕrĭt ēt rīpās, hērbĭfĕr Ācĭ, tŭās. O. Syn.—Hērbĭdŭs, hērbōsŭs. Phr.—Hērbīs fœtŭs. Hērbōsă pāscŭă. Vĭrĭdīssĭmă grāmĭnĕ rīpă. Vĭrĭdī cæspĭtĕ mōllĭs hŭmŭs.

Hĕrī. adv. *Yesterday.* Syn.—Hĕrĕ. Phr.—Hēstērnā dĭē, lūcĕ.

Hērōs, ōĭs. m. *Hero, demigod.* Phr.—Vīrtūte ēt ārmīs nōbĭlĭs. Vīrĭbŭs īnvīctŭs. Māgnănĭmī prŏcĕrēs. Īnsīgnēs ēt pāce hērōās ēt ārmīs.

Heū. interj. *Alas!* Syn.—Heī. Phr.—Heī mĭhĭ.

Hĭātŭs, ūs. m. *Opening.* Nē pătĕăt, lātōquĕ sŏlūm rĕtĕgātŭr hĭātū. O. Syn.—Gūrgĕs, bărăthrūm, vŏrāgŏ, ōs. Phr.—Vāstæ faūcēs. Īmmānēs pāndĭt hĭātūs. Ūndă dĕhīscēns. *See Gurges.*

Hīc. adv. *Here.* Syn.—Ĭbĭ, īllīc. *Then.* Syn.—Tūm, tūnc.

Hĭlărĭs, ĭs, ĕ. *Joyful.* Ōdērūnt hĭlărēm trīstēs, trīstēmquĕ jŏcōsī. H. Syn.—Lætŭs, gaūdēns, ălăcĕr, ŏvāns, lĕpĭdŭs, jŏcōsŭs, făcētŭs. Phr.—Lætĭtĭā pērfūsŭs. Ēxsūltāns ănĭmīs. Gaūdĭă cōncĭpĭēns. Pēnsă mănū dūcūnt hĭlărēs. *See Gaudeo, Lætus.*

Hĭlărĭtās, ātĭs. f. *Joy.* Syn.—Gaūdĭūm, lætĭtĭă, ălăcrĭtās. Phr.—Lætă mēns. Fēstīvūm īngĕnĭūm.

Hĭlărŏ, ās, āvī, ātūm, ārĕ. *To rejoice.* Hōs ŭbĭ făcūndō tŭă vōx hĭlărāvĕrĭt ōrĕ. O. Syn.—Ēxhĭlărŏ, lætĭfĭcŏ, ōblēctŏ, rĕcrĕŏ.

Hīnc. adv. *Hence.* Syn.—Īndĕ, ĭdĕō, hōc.

Hĭŏ, ās, āvī, ātūm, ārĕ. *To stand open, to gape.* Tērræ vēnās āstrīngĭt hĭāntēs. V. Syn.—Hīscŏ, dĕhīscŏ, ōscĭtŏ, pătĕŏ, ăpĕrĭŏr, fīndŏr, scīndŏr.

Hīrcŭs, ī. m. *Goat.* Cārmĭnĕ quī trăgĭcō vīlēm cērtāvĭt ŏb hīrcūm. H. Syn.—Căpĕr, hīrcŭlŭs, hædŭs. Phr.—Dūx pĕcŏrĭs. Vīrquĕ pătērquĕ grĕgĭs. Dūxquĕ grĕgĭs.

Hīrsūtŭs, ă, ūm. & Hīrtŭs, ă, ūm. *Hairy, shaggy.* Hīrsūtūmquĕ sŭpērcĭlĭūm, prōmīssăquĕ bārbă. V. Syn.—Hīspĭdŭs, hōrrĭdŭs, pĭlōsŭs, sētōsŭs, vīllōsŭs. Phr.—Vīllīs āspĕr. Crīstāque hīrsūtŭs ĕquīnā.

Hīrūndŏ, ĭnĭs. f. *Swallow.* (*See Appendix under list of Birds.*)

Hīspĭdŭs, ă, ūm. *Rough, shaggy.* Cuī lătĕrūm tĕnŭs hīspĭdă mēntō Frōns hŏmĭnēm præfērt. V. Syn.—Hīrsūtŭs, hīspĭdōsŭs, hōrrēns, āspĕr, rĭgēns.

Hīstŏrĭă, æ. f. *History.* Pārs ĕrĭt hīstŏrĭæ, tōtōquĕ lĕgētŭr ĭn ōrbē. O. Syn.—Ānnālēs, fāstī, mŏnŭmēntă. Phr.—Vĕtĕrūm scrīptă, mŏnŭmēntă. Hīstŏrĭæ fāmă. Aētātīs mŏnŭmēntă vĕtūstæ. Prīscī tēmpŏrĭs făctă, āctă.

Hīstŏrĭcŭs, ī. m. *Historian.* Quīs dăbĭt hīstŏrĭcō, quāntūm dărĕt āctă lĕgēntī. J. Phr.—Cōndĭtŏr hīstŏrĭæ. Hīstŏrĭārūm scrīptŏr. Ōblīvĭōsī tēmpŏrĭs vīndēx. Vĕtĕrīs nōn īnscĭŭs ævī.

Hīstrĭŏ, ōnĭs. m. *Actor.* Pāllēbāt chŏrŭs ōmnĭs hīstrĭōnūm. Syn.—Mīmŭs, lūdĭŏ, lūdĭŭs, āctŏr, cōmœdŭs. Phr.—Mŏvēns rīsūs. Vēstĭbŭs ēt vūltū rīdĭcŭlŭs.

Hĭūlcŭs, ă, ūm. *Gaping, open.* Hōc ŭbi hĭūlcă sĭtī fīndĭt Cănĭs æstĭfĕr ārvă. V. Syn.—Hĭāns, dĕhīscēns, pătēns, pătŭlŭs, ăpērtŭs, rīmōsŭs, fīssŭs, fătīscēns.

Hŏdĭē. adv. *Today.* Quōd nōn ēst hŏdĭē, crās mĭnŭs āptŭs ĕrĭt. O. Syn.—Nūnc. Phr.—Hōc dĭē. Hŏdĭērnā lūcĕ. Hŏdĭērnō lūmĭnĕ.

Hŏmĭcīdă, æ. m. *Homicide, murderer.* Sī fūr dīsplĭcĕāt Vērrī, si hŏmĭcīdă Mĭlōnī. J. Syn.—Sīcārĭŭs, īntērfēctŏr. Phr.—Aūctŏr, ārtĭfēx lētī. Rēgīs cædĕ nŏcēns.

Hŏmŏ, ĭnĭs. m. *Man.* Ēt quŏtă pārs hŏmŏ sĭt tērrāī tōtĭŭs ūnŭs. Lr. Syn.—Vĭr, ădŏlēscēns, jŭvĕnĭs. Phr.—Gēns hūmānă, hŏmĭnūm. Mōrtālĕ gĕnŭs. Vīs hūmānă. Tērrĕă prōlēs. Hŏmĭnūm cōrpŏră. Vīx sūnt hŏmĭnēs hōc nōmĭnĕ dīgnī. Quōd gĕnŭs hōc hŏmĭnūm.

Hŏnēstās, ātĭs. f. *Honesty, honor.* Syn.—Hŏnēstūm, vīrtūs, dĕcŏr. Phr.—Hŏnēstī glōrĭă. Dĕcŭs ănĭmī. *See Probitas, Justitia.*

Hŏnēstē. adv. *Honorably.* Tūm quŏquĕ jām mŏrĭēns, nē nōn prōcūmbăt hŏnēstē Rēspĭcĭt. O. Syn.—Dĕcōrē, pūlchrē, bĕnĕ, rēctē, dĕcēntĕr, cōnvĕnĭēntĕr.

Hŏnēstŭs, ă, ūm. *Honored, distinguished.* Syn.—Hŏnōrātŭs, hŏnōrŭs. *Honorable, praiseworthy.* Syn.—Dĕcōrŭs, laūdāndŭs, laūdābĭlĭs, pūlchĕr, ēgrĕgĭŭs. Phr.—Īpsō pūlchră lŏcō vūlnĕră. *Honest.* Syn.—Prŏbŭs, bŏnŭs, pĭŭs.

Hŏnŏr & Hŏnōs, ōrĭs. m. *Honor.* Sīc hŏnŏr ēt nōmēn dīvīnīs vātĭbŭs ātquĕ Cārmĭnĭbūs vēnĭt. H. Syn.—Glōrĭă, laūs, cūltŭs, rĕvĕrēntĭă, fāmă, dĕcŭs, nōmĕn. Phr.—Hŏnōrĭs tĭtŭlī. Nōmĭnĭs glōrĭă. Nōmĕn īngēns. Haūd ĕquĭdēm tālī mē dīgnŏr hŏnōrē. Fālsŭs hŏnōr jŭvăt. *See Gloria, Nomen.*

Hŏnōrābĭlĭs, ĭs, ĕ. *Honorable.* Syn.—Hŏnōrāndŭs, cŏlēndŭs, laūdābĭlĭs, hŏnēstŭs. Phr.—Hŏnōrĕ dīgnŭs.

Hŏnōrŏ, ās, āvī, ātūm, ārĕ. *To honor.* Cūm quō cōnsĕnŭĭt, mīlĕs hŏnōrăt ĕquūm. M. Syn.—Hŏnēstŏ, cŏlŏ, vĕnĕrŏr. Phr.—Hŏnōrĕ prōsĕquŏr. Hŏnōrēs rēddŏ. Mīrō quŏd hŏnōrĕ cŏlēbăt.

Hŏnōrŭs, ă, ūm. *Honorable.* Syn.—Hŏnēstŭs, dĕcōrŭs, pūlchĕr. Phr.—Nōn īndĕcŏr, nōn īndĕcōrŭs, nōn ĭnhŏnēstŭs. *See Honestus.*

Hōră, ǣ. f. *Hour, time.* Grātă sŭpērvĕnĭēt quǣ nōn spērābĭtŭr hōră. H. Phr.—Hōrǣ mŏră, pūnctūm, spătĭŭm, mōmēntūm, tēmpŭs. Īntērvāllă dĭēī. Fŭgĭēns frēnō nōn rĕmŏrāntĕ. Ālmūm quǣ răpĭt hōră dĭēm. Vŏlăt āmbĭgŭīs mōbĭlĭs ālīs Hōră.

Hōrrēndŭs, ă, ūm. *Horrible.* Clāmōrēs sĭmŭl hōrrēndōs ād sīdĕră tōllĭt. V. *See Horridus. Worthy of reverence.* Syn.—Vĕrēndŭs, hōrrēns.

Hōrrĕŏ, ēs, ŭī, ērĕ. *To shudder at, to be afraid.* Syn.—Hōrrēscŏ, ēxhōrrēscŏ, ĭnhōrrĕŏ, pĕrhōrrĕŏ, păvĕŏ, rĕfōrmīdŏ, tĭmĕŏ, trĕmŏ. Phr.—Prǣcōrdĭă pēllĭt, ōccŭpăt hōrrŏr. Hōrrĕt ădhūc ănĭmŭs. Frīgĭdŭs hōrrōr mēmbră quătĭt. Cōr pĕpŭlĭt hōrrŏr. Nēc mōrtem hōrrēmŭε.

Hōrrĕŭm, ī. n. *Barn, storehouse.* Īllĭŭs īmmēnsǣ rūpērūnt hōrrĕă mēssēs. V. Syn.—Grānārĭă. Phr.—Mēssĭs ŭbī plūrĭmă. Ŭbī cōndĭtă mēssĭs. Frūmēntī, frūgūm cōmpŏsĭtī ăcērvī.

Hōrrĭdŭs, ă, ūm. *Bristling.* Sīlvă fŭīt lātē dūmīs ātque īlĭcĕ nĭgrā Hōrrĭdă. V. Syn.—Āspĕr, hīrsūtŭs, hōrrēns, hīrtŭs, hīspĭdŭs, rĭgĭdŭs, rĭgēns. Phr.—Glăcĭē hōrrĭdă bārbă. Lŏcă sīlvēstrĭbŭs hōrrĭdă dūmīs. *Uncultivated.* Syn.—Rŭdĭs, īncūltŭs, squālĭdŭs. *Hideous.* Syn.—Hōrrēns, dēfōrmĭs. *Terrible.* Syn.—Hōrrĭbĭlĭs, hōrrēndŭs, hōrrĭfĭcŭs, hōrrĭfĕr, mĕtŭēndŭs, tērrĭbĭlĭs, tērrĭfĭcŭs, fōrmīdābĭlĭs, fōrmīdāndŭs.

Hōrrŏr, ōrĭs. m. *Fear.* Syn.—Păvŏr, trĕmŏr, fōrmīdŏ.

Hōrtātĭŏ, ōnĭs. f. *Encouragement.* Syn.—Hōrtāmĕn, hōrtāmēntūm, hŏrtātŭs, mŏnĭtŭs, īmpŭlsŭs, stĭmŭlī. Phr.—Hōrtāntĭă dīctă. Mōtūrǣ prōclĭă vōcēs.

Hōrtātŏr, ōrĭs. m. *An exhorter.* Hōrtātōr scĕlĕrum Aĕŏlĭdēs. V. Syn.—Suāsŏr, īmpūlsŏr, aūctŏr, mŏnĭtŏr, stĭmŭlātŏr. Phr.— Hōrtātōr pūgnǣ. Aūctŏr ĕgo aūdēndī. Nōn sī mĭhī Jūpĭtĕr aūctŏr Spōndĕăt.

Hōrtŏr, ārĭs, ātŭs sūm, ārī. *To encourage.* Ārmātās hŏmĭnum ēst prǣsēns hōrtātă cătērvās. Cat. Syn.—Ēxhōrtŏr, ădhōrtŏr, ăcŭŏ, ēxăcŭŏ, stĭmŭlŏ, ēxstĭmŭlŏ, āccēndŏ, īncēndŏ, īnflāmmŏ, īnstīgŏ, pēllŏ, īmpēllŏ, cōncĭtŏ, īncĭtŏ, ēxcĭtŏ, sūscĭtŏ, mŏnĕŏ, ādmŏnĕŏ, suādĕŏ. Phr.—Hōrtāndō ēxcĭtŏ. Hōrtātĭbŭs īnstīgŏ. Vērbīs vīrtūtem āccēndŏ. Stĭmŭlīs vīrēs sūscĭtŏ. Dīctīs cōnfīrmăt ĭtūrōs.

Hōrtŭs, ī. m. *Garden.* Hōrtŭs ŭbĭ ēt tēctŏ vīcīnŭs jūgĭs ăquǣ fōns. H. Syn.—Pōmārĭŭm, vĭrētūm, vĭrĭdārĭŭm. Phr.—Ămœnă vĭrētă. Hōrtōrūm sēptă hērbĭs, flōrĭbŭs, frūctĭbŭs. Cōnsĭtŭs ārbŏrĭbŭs. Rūrĭs ămœnī dēlĭcĭǣ. Flōrūm gĕmmīs cōllūcēns. Nĭtĭdīs gēmmāns flōrĭbŭs. Mōbĭlĭbŭs pōmārĭă rīvīs.

Hōspĕs, ĭtĭs. m. *Guest, stranger*. Vīvĭtŭr ēx rāptō; nōn hōspĕs ăb hōspĭtĕ tūtŭs. O. Syn.—Ādvĕnă, pĕrĕgrīnŭs. Phr.—Nŏvŭs hīc nōstrīs sūccēssīt sēdĭbŭs hōspĕs. *Host*. Phr.—Sūccīnctŭs cūrsĭtăt hōspĕs.

Hōspĭtĭŭm, ĭī. n. *Hospitality*. Hōspĭtĭum āntīquŭm Trōjæ sŏcĭōsquĕ Pĕnātēs. V. Phr.—Hōspĭtĭī tēctă. Tēllūs, dŏmŭs hōspĭtă. Hōspĭtĭī jūră. Hōspĭtĭs ōffĭcĭūm. Vĕrĕōr quō sē Jūnōnĭă vērtānt Hōspĭtĭă. Hōspĭtĭō prŏhĭbēmŭr ărēnæ. Īndūlge hōspĭtĭō. Nōstrīs sūccēdĕ pĕnātĭbŭs.

Hōspĭtŭs, ă, ūm. *Stranger*. Nēc plăcĭdōs pōrtūs hōspĭtă nāvĭs hăbĕt. O. Syn.—Pĕrĕgrīnŭs, hōspĕs, ēxtērnŭs. Phr.—Bēllum, ō tērra hōspĭtă, pōrtās. Ăvĭs hōspĭtă.

Hōstĭă, æ. f. *Victim*. Hōstĭbŭs ē vīctīs hōstĭă nōmĕn hăbĕt. O. Syn.—Vīctĭmă, pĭăcŭlūm, (*sometimes*) hŏnŏr, hŏnōrēs, ēxtă.

Hōstīlĭs, ĭs, ĕ. *Hostile*. Syn.—Ādvērsŭs, ĭnĭmīcŭs, īnfēnsŭs, īnfēstŭs, hōstĭcŭs.

Hōstīlĭtĕr. adv. *In a hostile manner*. Syn.—Crūdēlĭtĕr, sævē, īnfēstē.

Hōstĭs, ĭs. m. *Enemy*. Dŏlŭs ān vīrtūs, quĭs ĭn hōstĕ rĕquīrāt? V. Phr.—Hōstīlēs ănĭmī. Tūrbă, gēns, mănŭs ĭnĭmīcă. Hōstĭs cædĕ nŏcēns. Flēctī nēscĭŭs. Ārmă cōntrārĭă. Hōstĭcă tūrbă. Hōstĭs hăbēt mūrōs.

Hūc. adv. *Hither*. Hūc ădĕs, ō fōrmōsĕ pŭĕr? V. Syn.—Īllūc, īllō.

Hūmānē. adv. *Humanly, like a human being*. Syn.—Hūmānĭtŭs, hūmānĭtĕr.

Hūmānĭtās, ātĭs. f. *Humanity*. Syn.—Hūmānă nātūră. *Kindness, politeness*. Syn.—Cōmĭtās, bĕnīgnĭtās, bŏnĭtās.

Hūmānĭtĕr. adv. *Kindly*. Syn.—Hūmānē, bĕnīgnē, clēmēntĕr, lēnĭtĕr, cōmĭtĕr.

Hūmānŭs, ă, ūm. *Human*. Nōn hæc hūmānīs ŏpĭbūs, nōn ārtĕ măgīstrā. V. Syn.—Mōrtālĭs. *Kind*. Syn.—Cōmĭs, ūrbānŭs, mītĭs, āffābĭlĭs, bĕnīgnŭs.

Hūmēctŏ, ās, āvī, ātūm, ārĕ. *To wet, to moisten, to water*. Quā nĭgĕr hūmēctāt flāvēntĭă cūltă Gălēsŭs. V. Syn.—Rĭgŏ, īrrĭgŏ, īrrōrŏ. Phr.—Lăcrĭmīs hūmēctēnt ōră gĕnāsquĕ. Scātĕbrīsque ārēntĭă tēmpĕrāt arvă.

Hŭmĕrŭs, ī. m. *Shoulder*. Āxem hŭmĕrō tōrquēt stēllīs ārdēntĭbŭs āptūm. V. Syn. (*By extens.*)—Cērvīx, cōllūm, cōllă, dōrsūm, tērgūm, scăpŭlæ. Phr.—Īstă dĕcēnt hŭmĕrōs gēstāmĭnă nōstrōs. Hŭmĕrōs ād vūlnĕră dūrāt. Sūblīmĕ rĕfērrēm Hīs hŭmĕrīs cŏrpŭs.

Hŭmī. adv. *On the ground.* Syn.—Tērrā, tēllūrĕ, ărēnā. Phr.—Prōcūmbĭt hŭmī bōs. Cōrpŏră fūndăt hŭmī. Prēssĭt hŭmī nītēns. Īn nūdā tēllūrĕ jăcēns. Sēdĭt hŭmō nūdā.

Hŭmĭlĭs, ĭs, ĕ. *Low.* Ātque hŭmĭlēs hăbĭtārĕ căsās. V. Syn.—Dēmīssŭs, dēprēssŭs, jăcēns. Phr.—Hŭmĭlēsquĕ mўrīcæ. Hŭmĭlīquĕ vŏlātū. *Of low birth.* Syn.—Vīlĭs, īnfĭmŭs, ōbscūrŭs, īgnōtŭs, īnglōrĭŭs, cōntēmptŭs. *Humble, modest.* Syn.—Mŏdēstŭs, sūbmīssŭs, dējēctŭs, sūpplēx. Phr.—Cōntēmptŏr hŏnōrūm.

Hŭmŏ, ās, āvī, ātūm, ārĕ. *To bury, to inter.* Quīsquĕ sŭūm prō rē cōnsōrtēm mœstūs hŭmābăt. L. Syn.—Sĕpĕlĭŏ, tŭmŭlŏ. Phr.—Hŭmō, tērræ māndŏ. *See Sepelio.*

Hūmŏr, ōrĭs m. *Liquid, fluid.* Syn. Lĭquŏr. *Water.* Syn.—Ăquă, lĭquŏr, rōs, ūndă, lătēx. *Dew.* Syn.—Văpŏr, rōs.

Hŭmŭs, ī. f. *Ground.* Spārgĭte hŭmūm fŏlĭīs. Īndūcĭtĕ fōntĭbŭs ūmbrās. V. Syn.—Tērră, tēllūs, sŏlūm, ăgĕr, cāmpŭs. Phr.—Pīnguĭs hŭmūs dūlcīque ūlĭgĭnĕ lætă. *See Ager, Terra.*

Hўăcīnthŭs & Hўăcīnthŏs, ī. m. *The hyacinth.* (*See Appendix under list of Trees, etc.*)

Hўdră, æ. *Water-snake.* Syn.—Ēxcĕtră, Ĕchīdnă, sērpēns, ānguĭs. Phr.—Bēllŭă Lērnæ.

Hўĕmālĭs & Hĭĕmālĭs, ĭs, ĕ. *Wintry.* Syn.—Hībērnŭs, brūmālĭs, Bŏrĕālĭs, Hўpērbŏrĕŭs, Ăquĭlōnĭŭs, ăquōsŭs, plŭvĭālĭs, frīgĭdŭs, gĕlĭdŭs, glăcĭālĭs.

Hўĕmŏ & Hĭĕmŏ, ās, āvī, ātūm, ārĕ. *To pass the winter.* Syn.—Hībērnŏ. Phr.—Hĭĕmēm trānsĭgŏ. Hībērnă căstră lŏcŏ.

Hўĕms & Hĭēms, ĕmĭs. f. *Winter.* Ēt glăcĭālĭs hĭēms Ăquĭlōnĭbŭs āspĕrăt ūndās. V. Syn.—Brūmă, Dĕcēmbĕr, frīgŭs, glăcĭēs, gĕlū, nix, prŭīnă. Phr.—Hībērnūm, hĭĕmālĕ tēmpŭs. Hĭĕmĭs vīs. Frīgŏră brūmæ. Brūmæ hōrrŏr. Hībērnæ mĭnæ. Frīgĭdă tēmpŏră. Frīgĭdŭs ānnŭs. Ădŏpērtă gĕlū. *See Frigus, Gelu.*

Hўpērbŏrĕŭs, ă, ūm. *Northern.* Tālĭs hўpērbŏrĕō sēptēm sūbjēctă Trĭōnī Gēns ēffrēnă vĭrūm. V. Syn.—Ăquĭlōnĭŭs, Ārctōŭs, Bŏrĕālĭs, glăcĭālĭs.

Hўssōpŭs, ī. m. *The herb hyssop.* (*See Appendix under list of Trees, etc.*)

I

Ĭāmbēŭs & Ĭāmbĭcŭs, ă, ūm. *Iambic.* Syn.—Trĭmĕtrŭs, sēnārĭŭs.

Ĭbĭ. adv. *There.* Aūt ĭbĭ flāvă sĕrēs mūtātō sīdĕrĕ fārră. V. Syn.—Hīc, īllīc.

Ībĭs, ĭs & ĭdĭs. f. *The ibis.* (*See Appendix under list of Birds.*)

Ĭcŏ, ĭs, īcī, īctūm, ĕrĕ. *To strike.* Ēmĭcăt īn pārtēm sānguīs, ūnde īcĭmŭr īctū. Lr. Syn.—Fĕrĭŏ, cædŏ, pērcŭtĭŏ, vērbĕrŏ. Phr.—Căpŭt īcĕrĕ tēlīs.

Īctŭs, ūs. m. *Blow.* Vāstīs trĕmĭt īctĭbŭs ærĕă pūppĭs. V. Syn.—Īmpūlsŭs, (*by exten.*) plāgă, vērbĕr, vūlnŭs. Phr.—Crēbrō īctū pērcŭtĭŏ, cōntūndŏ. Pŏtēntĭŭs īctū Fūlmĭnĕō. Vĕhĕmēntī pērcŭlĭt īctū. Īctĭbŭs ærā sŏnānt. Vērbĕrăt īctĭbŭs aūrās. *See Percutio.*

Īdcīrcō. conj. *Therefore.* Syn.—Ĭdĕō. *See Ideo.*

Īdēm, ĕădēm, ĭdēm. *The same.* Ămŏr ōmnĭbŭs īdēm. V. Syn.—Sĭmĭlĭs, pār. Phr.—Ūnŭs ĕt īdēm. Nōn ălĭŭs. Sēdĭbŭs hærĕt ĭn īsdēm.

Ĭdĕō. conj. *Therefore.* Nōn ĭdĕō dēbēt pĕlăgō sē crēdĕrĕ. O. Syn.—Īdcīrcō, prōptĕrĕā, hīnc, īndĕ, hōc. Phr.—Nōn ălĭam ōb cūlpām.

Īdŏlūm & Īdŏlŏn, ī. n. *Statue, idol.* Syn.—Sĭmŭlācrūm. Phr.—Ĭnānĭs ĭmāgŏ. Ĭnānĕ sīgnūm. Prŏfānă ēffĭgĭēs. Ĭnānĭă dīvūm Nūmĭnă. Vānī nūmĕn ĭnānĕ Jŏvĭs.

Ĭdōnĕŭs, ă, ūm. *Suitable.* Sī făcĭs ūt pătrĭæ sĭt ĭdōnĕŭs, ūtĭlĭs āgrīs. J. Syn.—Āptŭs, cōmmŏdŭs, ōppōrtūnŭs, ūtĭlĭs, cōnvĕnĭēns, cōngrŭŭs. Phr.—Ĭdōnĕŭs ārmīs. Dărĕ pōndŭs ĭdōnĕă fūmō.

Ĭgĭtŭr. conj. *Therefore, thus.* Syn.—Ērgŏ, ĭtăquĕ.

Īgnārŭs, ă, ūm. *Ignorant.* Mīrātūr rērūmque īgnārŭs ĭmāgĭnĕ pēndĕt. V. Syn.—Īnscĭŭs, nēscĭŭs, īndōctŭs, rŭdĭs. *Imprudent.* Syn.—Īmprūdēns, īgnōrāns. *Forgetful.* Syn.—Īmmĕmŏr, ōblĭtŭs.

Īgnāvĭă, æ. f. *Sloth, laziness.* Tȳrrhēnī, quæ tānta ănĭmīs īgnāvĭă vēnĭt? V. Syn.—Dēsĭdĭă, ĭnērtĭă, sōcōrdĭă, vĕtērnūm, sēgnĭtĭēs, pĭgrĭtĭă. Phr.—Fŭgĭēns pērīclă. Sōmnīque īgnāvĭă mātĕr. Tōrpēns dēmīssō vūltū.

Īgnāvŭs, ă, ūm. *Lazy.* Īgnāvūm fūcōs pĕcŭs ā præsēpĭbŭs ārcĕt. V. Syn.—Pĭgĕr, ĭnērs, dēsĕs, dēsĭdĭōsŭs, tōrpēns. *Cowardly.* Syn.—Sēgnĭs, ĭnērs, ēnērvĭs, īmbēllĭs, tĭmĭdŭs, dēgĕnĕr. Phr.—Vīrtūtĭs ēxpērs. Mălĕ fōrtĭs. Ād fātă sēgnĭs. *See Timidus.*

Īgnēscŏ, ĭs, ĕrĕ. *To take fire.* Īgnēscūnt īrae, ēt dūrīs dŏlŏr ōssĭbŭs ārdĕt. V. Syn.—Ārdēscŏ, ēxārdēscŏ, īncēndŏr, īnflāmmŏr. Phr—Īgnēscūnt ănĭmīs dīscōrdĭbŭs īræ. Īgnēscūnt sānguĭnĕ vūltŭs.

Īgnĕŭs, ă, ūm. *Fiery.* Cærŭlĕŭs plŭvĭām dēnūntĭăt, īgnĕŭs Eūrōs. V. Syn.—Īgnĭfĕr, īgnītŭs, īgnĭvŏmŭs, ārdēns, ēxārdēns, cāndēns, fērvēns, flāmmātŭs, flāmmĕŭs, flāmmĭfĕr. Phr.—Īgnĕ rŭbēns. Aēstās īgnĕă. *Burning*. Syn.—Călēns, călĭdŭs, fērvĭdŭs, tōrrĭdŭs. *See Ardens.*

Īgnĭs, ĭs. m. *Fire*. Vōlvĭtŭr īgnĭs ĕdāx sūmma ăd vēstīgĭă vēntō. V. Syn.—Vūlcānŭs, Mūlcĭbĕr, flāmmă, īncēndĭă. Phr.—Īgnĭs ārbŏr. Īgnĕă vīs. Īgnĕŭs ārdŏr. Sūppŏsĭtūs cĭnĕrī dŏlōsō. Lĭquĭdī cŏlŏr aūrĕŭs īgnĭs. Vūlcānĭă pēstĭs. Pĭcĕō vōrtĭcĕ ūndāns. Sēmĭnă flāmmæ vōlvēns. Sævа īncēndĭă vōlvĭt. *See Flamma, Incendium.*

Īgnōbĭlĭs, ĭs, ĕ. *Unknown*. Sōlŭs ŭbi īn sīlvīs Ītălīs īgnōbĭlĭs aēvūm Ēxĭgĭt. V. Syn.—Īgnōtŭs, ōbscūrŭs, īnglōrĭŭs, lătēns. Phr.—Hŏmŏ sĭnĕ nōmĭnĕ. Nōn ēst īgnōbĭlĕ cārmĕn. Stŭdĭīs flōrēntem īgnōbĭlĭs ōtī. *Lowly born*. Syn.—Vīlĭs, ābjēctŭs, ōbscūrŭs, hŭmĭlĭs, dēspēctŭs. Phr.—Sĭnĕ gēntĕ. Sĭnĕ nōmĭnĕ. Īmā plēbĕ. Plēbēiō sānguĭnĕ nātŭs. Cuī sĭnĕ lūcĕ gĕnŭs. Hŭmĭlī dē plēbĕ părēntēs. Nūllīs mājōrĭbŭs ōrtŭs. Īgnōtā dē stīrpĕ nĕpōtūm.

Īgnōmĭnĭă, æ. f. *Ignominy*. Syn.—Īnfāmĭă, dēdĕcŭs, măcŭlă, lābēs, prŏbrūm.

Īgnōmĭnĭōsŭs, ă, ūm. *Shameful*. Syn.—Īnfāmĭs, prŏbrōsŭs. *See Turpis.*

Īgnōrāntĭă, æ. f. *Ignorance*. Prætĕrĭtæ vĕnĭām dăbĭt īgnōrāntĭă cūlpæ. O. Syn.—Īnscītĭă, īmpĕrītĭă.

Īgnōrŏ, ās, āvī, ātūm, ārĕ. *To be ignorant of*. Năīdĕs īgnōrānt, īgnōrăt ĕt Īnăchŭs īpsĕ. O. Syn.—Nēscĭŏ. Phr.—Mē lătĕt. Sūm nēscĭŭs. Haūd īgnārŭs ĕrām. Nēc lătŭērĕ dŏlī frātrēm Jūnōnĭs. Mūltăquĕ mē fŭgĭūnt. Quīs Trōjæ nēscĭăt ūrbēm?

Īgnōscŏ, ĭs, vī, tūm, ĕrĕ. *To pardon*. Syn.—Pārcŏ, īndūlgĕŏ, cōndōnŏ. Phr.—Dō vĕnĭām. *See Parco.*

Īgnōtŭs, ă, ūm. *Unknown*. Quōd lătĕt īgnōtum ēst; īgnōtī nūllă cŭpīdŏ. O. Syn.—Īncōgnĭtŭs, īncōmpērtŭs, ābdĭtŭs, ārcānŭs, lătēns. Phr.—Īgnōtīs ērrārĕ lŏcīs. Īgnōta īn vēstĕ vĭrōs. *Unheard of*. Syn.—Nŏvŭs, īnsŏlĭtŭs, mīrŭs.

Īlēx, ĭcĭs. f. *The ilex, one of the species of oak.* (*See Appendix under list of Trees, etc.*)

Īllăbĕfāctŭs, ă, ūm. *Unshaken*. Quæ sēmpēr mănĕānt īllăbĕfāctă prĕcŏr (vincula). O. Syn.—Īntĕgĕr, īncōncūssŭs, fīrmŭs, īnvĭŏlātŭs.

Īllābŏr, ĕrĭs, psŭs sūm, bī. *To glide into*. Syn.—Sŭbĕŏ, pĕnĕtrŏ, īnsĭnŭŏ. *To fall upon*. Syn.—Īncĭdŏ, rŭŏ.

Īllăcrĭmābĭlĭs, ĭs, ĕ. *Pitiless, inexorable*. Nōn Ămīcĕ, plācēs īllăcrĭmābĭlēm Plūtōnă. H. Syn.—Dūrŭs, ĭnēxōrābĭlĭs.

Īllætābĭlĭs, ĭs, ĕ. *Sad*. Syn.—Ĭnămœnŭs, īnjūcūndŭs, ĭnāmābĭlĭs. *See Tristis.*

Īllăquĕō, ās, āvī, ātūm, ārĕ. *To ensnare.* Syn.—Īrrĕtĭō, cīrcūmrĕtĭō, īllĭgō, īntrīcō, īnvōlvō.

Īllĕ, īllă, īllŭd. *This, that.* Syn.—Hīc, ĭs, īpsĕ.

Īllĕcĕbræ, ārūm. f. *Charms, attractiveness.* Īllĕcĕbrīs ĕrăt ēt grātā nŏvĭtātĕ mŏrāndŭs. H. Syn.—Lēnōcĭnĭūm, blāndĭtĭæ, īnvītāmēntă, īrrītāmēntă, stĭmŭlŭs.

Īllĕcĕbrōsŭs, ă, ūm. *Attractive.* Syn.—Blāndŭs, fāllāx.

Īllĕpĭdē. adv. *Ungracefully.* Syn.—Ĭnēptē, īnsūlsē, ĭnūrbānē.

Īllĕpĭdŭs, ă, ūm. *Ungraceful.* Syn.—Ĭnēptŭs, īnsūlsŭs, ĭnūrbānŭs, īnvĕnūstŭs.

Īllĭcĭtŭs, ă, ūm. *Forbidden.* Syn.—Vĕtĭtŭs, ĭnīquŭs. Phr.—Nōn lĭcĭtŭs. *See Nefas.*

Īllīdō, ĭs, sī, sūm, ĕrĕ. *To strike, to dash against.* Īllīdĭtquĕ vădīs ātque āggĕrĕ cīngĭt ărēnæ. V. Syn.—Āllīdō, cōllīdō, īmpīngō, īnfrīngō, cōntĕrō, ōbtĕrō, ōffēndō. *See Frango.*

Īllĭgō, ās, āvī, ātūm, ārĕ. *To bind.* Sūmmă pĕdūm prŏpĕrē plāntārĭbŭs īllĭgăt ālīs. Syn.—Lĭgō, āllĭgō, vīncĭō, īmplĭcō, īllăquĕō, īnnēctō.

Īllĭmĭs, ĭs, ĕ. *Free from mud, clear.* Syn.—Pūrŭs, līmpĭdŭs, pēllūcĭdŭs. *See Limpidus.*

Īllīnc. adv. *Thence.* Syn.—Īndĕ, hīnc, īstīnc.

Īllĭnō, ĭs, lēvī, lĭtūm, ĕrĕ. *To smear, to daub.* Hīc ŏcŭlīs ĕgŏ nīgră mĕīs cōllȳrĭă līppŭs Īllĭnĕrĕ. H. Syn.—Lĭnō, ōblĭnō, cīrcūmlĭnō, ūngō, ĭnūngō.

Īllō. adv. *Thither.* Syn.—Ĕō, hūc, īllūc.

Īllūcĕō, ēs, xī, ērĕ & Īllūcēscō, ĭs, ĕrĕ. *To shine, to give light.* Īllūcērĕ sŏlēt māgnīs ēt fērrĕ trĭūmphōs. Syn.—Lūcĕō, īrrădĭō. Phr.—Nōn ălĭōs īllūxīssĕ dĭēs. *See Luceo.*

Īllūdō, ĭs, sī, sūm, ĕrĕ. *To play with, to sport with.* Sī quīd dătūr ōtī, Īllūdō chārtīs. *See Ludo. To mock.* Syn.—Lūdō, dēlūdō, rīdĕō, īrrīdĕō.

Īllūmĭnō, ās, āvī, ātūm, ārĕ. *To illuminate.* Syn.—Īllūstrō, cōllūstrō, īrrădĭō. Phr.—Lūmĕn dō, præbĕō, fĕrō. Lūmĭnĕ rĕplĕō. Lūcĕ tĕnĕbrās pēllĕrĕ. Nōctēm flāmmīs fūnālĭă vīncūnt. Cōllūcēnt īgnĭbŭs ædēs.

Īllūstrĭs, ĭs, ĕ. *Clear.* Syn.—Clārŭs, lūcĭdŭs, cŏrūscŭs. *Illustrious.* Syn.—Clārŭs, cōnspĭcŭŭs, cĕlĕbĕr, īnclȳtŭs, nōbĭlĭs. *See Celeber.*

Īllūstrō, ās, āvī, ātūm, ārĕ. *To enlighten, to give light. See Illumino. To render famous.* Syn.—Nōbĭlĭtō, dĕcŏrō, īnsīgnĭō.

Īllŭvĭēs, ĭēī. f. *Dirt, mud.* Syn.—Cōllŭvĭēs, sōrdēs, pædŏr, squālŏr.

Ĭmāgĭnŏr, ārĭs, ātŭs sūm, ārī. *To imagine.* Syn.—Fīngō, ēffīngō, ēxcōgĭtō. Phr.—Ănĭmō cōncĭpĭō.

Ĭmāgŏ, ĭnĭs. f. *Resemblance.* Jāmquĕ dĕūs pŏsĭtā fāllācĭs ĭmāgĭnĕ Taūrī. O. Syn.—Fōrmă, spĕcĭēs, fĭgūră, sĭmŭlācrūm, sĭmŭlāmĕn. *Image, statue.* Syn.—Ēxēmplăr, spĕcĭēs, ēffĭgĭēs, fĭgūră, sĭmŭlācrūm, stătŭă, sīgnūm. *Vision.* Syn.—Sĭmŭlācrūm, fōrmă.

Īmbēllĭs, ĭs, ĕ. *Feeble, weak.* Trēs sŭmŭs īmbēllēs nŭmĕrō, sĭnĕ vīrĭbŭs. V. Syn.—Dēbĭlĭs, mōllĭs, frāctŭs, ĭnērs, īgnāvŭs, sēgnĭs, pĭgĕr. Phr.—Īmbēllī cĭthără cārmĭnă dīvĭdēs. Cuī tōrpēnt īnfrāctae ād prœlĭă vīrēs. *See Debilis, Iners.*

Īmbĕr, brĭs. m. *Rain.* Aūt āctūm cœlō māgnīs ăquĭlōnĭbŭs īmbrēm. V. Syn.—Plŭvĭă, nīmbŭs, (*sometimes*) nūbēs, nūbĭlă. Phr.—Rŭĭt æthĕrĕ tōtō Tūrbĭdŭs īmbĕr ăquæ. Āgmĕn ăquārūm. Cœlestĭs hūmŏr. Ēffūsī rūmpūntūr nūbĭbŭs īmbrēs. Quōd nōn īmbĕr ĕdāx Pōssīt dīrŭĕrĕ. *See Pluvia.*

Īmbērbĭs, ĭs, ĕ. *Beardless, young.* Īmbērbīs jŭvĕnīs tāndēm cūstōdĕ rĕmōtō. H. Syn.—Īmpūbĭs, īmpūbĕr, īntōnsŭs. Phr.—Dūm nūllā tĕnĕrī sōrdēnt lānūgĭnĕ vūltūs. M. *See Adolescens.*

Īmbĭbŏ, ĭs, bī, bĭtūm, ĕrĕ. *To drink.* Īmbĭbĕrāt dīrūm spārgēns pēr rūră crŭōrēm. Syn.—Bĭbŏ, cōmbĭbŏ, haūrĭŏ.

Īmbrēx, ĭcĭs. m. *Hollow tile.* Syn.—Tēgŭlă, lătĕr.

Īmbrĭfĕr, ĕră, ĕrūm. *Rain-bringing.* Vēntūram ādmīttāt īmbrĭfĕr ārcŭs ăquām. Tib. Syn.—Plŭvĭŭs, plŭvĭālĭs, nīmbōsŭs, mădĭdŭs, mădēns. Phr.—Nīmbīs grăvātŭs. Īmbrĭbŭs hōrrēns. Quīs trăhăt īmbrĭfĕrās nūbēs.

Īmbŭŏ, ĭs, ŭī, ūtūm, ĕrĕ. *To moisten, to steep.* Īllĭŭs ārām Sæpĕ tĕnĕr nōstrīs ăb ŏvīlĭbŭs īmbŭĕt āgnŭs. V. Syn.—Rĭgŏ, īrrĭgŏ, mădĕfăcĭŏ, tīngŏ, pērfūndŏ. Phr.—Sānguīs nŏvŭs īmbŭĭt ārmă. *To instruct.* Syn.—Dŏcĕŏ.

Ĭmĭtŏr, ārĭs, ātŭs sūm, ārī. *To imitate.* Ēxprĭmĕt ēt mōllēs ĭmĭtābĭtŭr ærĕ căpīllōs. H. Syn.—Aēmŭlŏr, ēffīngŏ, ēxprĭmŏ, sĭmŭlŏ, āssĭmŭlŏ. Phr.—Ĭmĭtāndō sĕquŏr, āssĕquŏr, æquŏ, ēxprĭmŏ. Vēstĭgĭă sĕquŏr. Ēxēmplīs sēsē mĕlĭōrĭbŭs āddĭt.

Īmmānĕ. adv. ***Excessively.*** **Syn.—Īmmŏdĭcē, īmmēnsūm.** ***Cruelly, horribly.*** Syn.—Īmmānĭtĕr, crūdēlĭtĕr, hōrrēndūm.

Īmmānĭs, ĭs, ĕ. *Extraordinary, immense.* Quō mōlem hānc īmmānĭs ĕquī stătŭĕrĕ? V. Syn.—Grāndĭs, māgnŭs, prōcērŭs, āmplŭs, māxĭmŭs, īngēns, īmmēnsŭs, vāstŭs. Phr.—Tĕnĕt īlle īmmānĭă săxă. Pŏsŭĭtque īmmānĭă tēmplă. *Terrible, frightful.* Syn.—Hōrrēndŭs. *Cruel.* Syn.—Bārbărŭs, sævŭs, dīrŭs, crūdēlĭs, fĕrŭs, ĭnhūmānŭs, īmmītĭs.

Īmmēnsŭs, ă, ūm. *Vast, immense.* Syn.—Īngēns, īmmānĭs, vāstŭs, īnfīnītŭs.

Īmmērgŏ, īs, sī, sūm, ĕrĕ. *To plunge into.* Spārgĭtĕ me īn flūctūs, vāstōque īmmērgĭtĕ pōntō. V. Syn.—Mērgŏ, sūbmērgŏ, dēmērgŏ, ōbrŭŏ. Phr.—Pĕlăgō præcĭpĭtō. Īn frĕtūm prōjĭcĭō. Præcĭpĭtem īn mărĕ dētūrbŏ.

Īmmĕrĭtŭs, ă, ūm. *Undeserving.* Syn.—Īmmĕrēns, īnsōns, īndīgnŭs.

Īmmĭgrŏ, ās, āvī, ātūm, ārĕ. *To remove into.* Syn.—Mĭgrŏ, cōmmĭgrŏ, ăbĕŏ.

Īmmĭnĕŏ, ēs, ŭī, ērĕ. *To hang over.* Hīc cāndĭdă pōpŭlŭs āntrō Īmmĭnĕt. V. Syn.—Īmpēndĕŏ, īncūmbŏ. *To threaten.* Syn.—Īnstŏ, īngrŭŏ, ūrgĕŏ. *To be near.* Syn.—Īnstŏ, āpprŏpĕrŏ, prŏpīnquŏ. Phr.—Fīŏ prŏpĭŏr.

Īmmīscĕŏ, ēs, ŭī, ērĕ. *To mingle.* Syn.—Mīscĕŏ, ādmīscĕŏ, cōmmīscĕŏ, pērmīscĕŏ, cōnfūndŏ. Phr.—Īmmīscērĕ mănūs mănĭbŭs.

Īmmītĭs, ĭs, ĕ. *Pitiless.* Ōrĕ fĕrūnt dūlcēm nīdīs īmmītĭbŭs ēscām. V. Syn.—Bārbărŭs, crūdēlĭs, dīrŭs, fĕrŭs, ĭnhūmānŭs. Phr.—Īmmītĭă fāctă.

Īmmīttŏ, ĭs, īsī, īssūm, ĕrĕ. *To send in, to cast into.* Tȳrrhēnūsquĕ frĕtīs īmmīttĭtŭr æstŭs Ăvērnīs. V. Syn.—Mīttŏ, īmpēllŏ, īnjĭcĭŏ, īnfĕrŏ. Phr.—Lēntūm fīlīs īmmīttĭtŭr aūrūm. *To loosen.* Syn.—Lāxŏ, pērmīttŏ, ēffūndŏ.

Īmmōbĭlĭs, ĭs, ĕ. *Firm, immovable.* Căpĭtōli īmmōbĭlĕ sāxūm. V. Syn.—Īmmōtŭs, īncōncūssŭs, stăbĭlĭs, hærēns, fīxŭs. Phr.—Pĕlăgī rūpēs īmmōtă rĕsīstĭt. Mōlĕ sŭā stăt. Sōlōque īmmōbĭlĕ hærĕt. Clāvōque āffīxŭs ĕt hærēns.

Īmmŏdĕrātŭs, ă, ūm. *Unrestrained, lawless.* Rēs īmmŏdĕrātă cŭpīdo ēst. O. Syn.—Īmmŏdēstŭs, īmmŏdĭcŭs, īntēmpĕrāns, ēffrēnĭs, īnfrēnĭs, ēxlēx, præcēps, nĭmĭŭs. *Excessive.* Syn.—Īmmŏdĭcŭs, nĭmĭŭs.

Īmmŏdĭcŭs, ă, ūm. *Immoderate, excessive.* Syn.—Nĭmĭŭs, īmmānĭs, īngēns.

Īmmŏlŏ, ās, āvī, ātūm, ārĕ. *To sacrifice.* Syn.—Māctŏ, cædŏ. *See Sacrifico.*

Īmmōrtālĭs, ĭs, ĕ. *Immortal, eternal.* Mōrtālīnĕ mănū fāctae īmmōrtālĕ cărīnæ Jūs hăbĕānt? V. Syn.—Aētērnŭs, pĕrēnnĭs, pērpĕtŭŭs. Phr.—Mōrtĕ cărēns. Mōrtĭs, nĕcĭs ēxpērs, nēscĭŭs. Īmmūnīs fātī. Fūnĕrĭs ēxpērs. Mŏrī nēscĭŭs. Nūllō pĕrĭtūrŭs ævō. **Cuī mōrtĭs ădēmpta ēst Cōndĭtĭō. Fātō măjŏr.** ***Immortal.*** (*in fame*). Syn.—Aētērnŭs, pĕrēnnĭs, pērpĕtŭŭs, vīctūrŭs, mānsūrŭs, ĭnēxstīnctŭs, īndēlēbĭlĭs. Phr.—Aētērnō nōmĭnĕ fēlīx. Aētērnūmquĕ tĕnēt pēr sæcŭlă nōmĕn. Dīgnūm laūdĕ vĭrūm Mūsă vĕtăt mŏrī. Nōn ōmnīs mŏrĭăr, mūltăquĕ părs mĕī Vītābĭt Lĭbĭtīnām. Nōmēnque ĕrĭt īndēlēbĭlĕ vēstrūm.

Īmmōrtālĭtās, ātĭs. f. *Immortality*. Phr.—Tēmpŭs ǣtērnūm, īmmōrtālĕ, pērpĕtŭūm, mansūrūm. Vītă īmmōrtālĭs. Īmmūnĭs lētī. Jūs īmmōrtālĕ. Stāt sĭnĕ mōrtĕ dĕcŭs.

Īmmūndŭs, ă, ūm. *Dirty, unclean*. Nēc pĭgĕr īmmūndō pērfūndĭs lĭttŏră cœ̄nō. H. Syn.—Fœ̄dŭs, sōrdĭdŭs, squālĭdŭs, spūrcŭs, īmpūrŭs, tūrpĭs.

Īmmūnĭs, ĭs, ĕ. *Free, exempt*. Nūllūm pāssă jŭgūm, cūrvīque īmmūnĭs ărātrī. O. Syn.—Ēxpērs, lībĕr, văcŭŭs, văcāns, sŏlūtŭs. Phr.—Īmmūnēs ŏpĕrūm fămŭlǣ. Sōlŭs īmmūnĭs mĕtū.

Īmmūtŏ, ās, āvī, ātūm, ārĕ. *To change*. Syn.—Mūtŏ, pērmūtŏ.

Īmpār, ărĭs. adj. *Unequal*. Aūt āspēr crābro īmpărĭbūs se īmmīscŭĭt ārmīs. V. Syn.—Īnæ̆quālĭs, dissimilĭs. Phr.—Nōn pār, nōn ǣquŭs. *Inconstant*. Syn.—Īnæ̆quālĭs, vărĭŭs, īncōnstāns, mūtābĭlĭs.

Īmpăvĭdŭs, ă, ūm. *Intrepid*. Īmpăvĭdūm fĕrĭēnt rŭīnǣ. H. Syn.—Īntrĕpĭdŭs, īntērrĭtŭs, īmpērtērrĭtŭs, aūdāx, fōrtĭs. *See Fortis*.

Īmpĕdĭŏ, īs, īvī & ĭī, ītūm, īrĕ. *To hinder, to prevent*. Eūrўălūm tĕnĕbræ̆ rāmōrum ŏnĕrōsăquĕ præ̆dă īmpĕdĭūnt. Syn.—Prŏhĭbĕŏ, ĭnhĭbĕŏ, vĕtŏ, ōbstŏ, ōbsūm, ōbsīstŏ, rĕsīstŏ. Phr.—Ārcēre ădĭtū. Quīppĕ vĕtōr fātīs. Fāta ōbstānt. Hōspĭtĭō prŏhĭbēmŭr ărēnǣ. Sūccēssūm Dĕă dīră nĕgăt. Prīmăquĕ vĕtānt cōnsīstĕrĕ tērrā.

Īmpēllŏ, ĭs, ŭlī, ūlsūm, ĕrĕ. *To drive, to set in motion*. Hōc gĕrĭtūr, Zĕphўrīs prīmum īmpēllēntĭbūs ūndās. V. Syn.—Cōncĭtŏ, ūrgĕŏ, prĕmŏ, ăgŏ, īncĭtŏ, mŏvĕŏ, cōmmŏvĕŏ. *To drive towards*. Syn.—Īmmīttŏ, ēmīttŏ, īnjĭcĭŏ, cōmpēllŏ, īntrūdŏ. *To strike*. Syn.—Ēxcĭtŏ, vērbĕrŏ, pērcŭtĭŏ, fĕrĭŏ, quătĭŏ, mŏvĕŏ, pērcēllŏ.

Īmpēndŏ, ĭs, dī, sūm, ĕrĕ. *To expend*. Syn.—Ēxpēndŏ. *To consume*. Syn.—Cōnsūmŏ, īnsūmŏ, cōnfĕrŏ, cōllŏcŏ, āddŏ, dō, āddīcŏ. Phr.—Īmpēndĕrĕ cūrām, lăbōrēm.

Īmpĕnĕtrābĭlĭs, ĭs, ĕ. *Impenetrable*. Syn.—Īmpērvĭŭs, īnvĭŭs, ĭnāccēssŭs. *Hidden*. Syn.—Ārcānŭs, ābdĭtŭs.

Īmpēnsă, æ̆. f. *Expense*. Māgnārūm nēc pārcŭs ŏpūm gĕmĭnārĕ prŏfūndās Dīstŭlĭt īmpēnsās. Syn.—Īmpēndĭūm, īmpēnsūm, sūmptŭs.

Īmpēnsē. adv. *At great cost*. Phr.—Māgnō sūmptū, īmpēnsā. *Much*. Syn.—Vāldē, gnāvĭtĕr. *See Multum*.

Īmpĕrātŏr, ōrĭs. m. *Leader, general*. Syn.—Dūx, prīncēps. Phr.—Cūstōs rērūm. Prīmŭs ĭn ārmīs. *King, emperor*. Syn.—Prīncēps. Phr.—Ōrbĭs mŏdĕrātŏr. Rēctŏr īmpĕrĭī. Rērūm cūstōs, dŏmĭnŭs. Rēgnātōr rērūm pŏtēns.

Īmpērfēctŭs, ă, ūm. *Imperfect, unfinished.* Syn.—Īnfēctŭs, ĭnēxplētŭs.

Īmpĕrĭōsŭs, ă, ūm. *Powerful.* Syn.—Pŏtēns. *Imperious, haughty.* Syn.—Sŭpērbŭs, īmpĕrĭō dūrŭs.

Īmpĕrītŭs, ă, ūm. *Ignorant.* Syn.—Īndōctŭs, īgnārŭs, rŭdĭs.

Īmpĕrĭūm, ĭī. n. *Authority, power.* Cōnsŭlĭs īmpĕrĭum hīc prīmūs sævāsquĕ sĕcūrēs Āccĭpĭĕt. V. Syn.—Jūs, pŏtēstās. *Control, rule.* Syn.—Dĭtĭō, pŏtēstās, rēgnūm, jūs, **dŏmĭnātĭō, dŏmĭnātŭs,** mŏdĕrāmĕn, scēptrūm. Phr.—Īmpĕrĭī jūs, pŏtēstās, dĕcŭs. Īmpĕrĭī pōndŭs. Rērūm sūmmă pŏtēstās. Dī quĭbŭs īmpĕrĭum hōc stētĕrăt. Ūndārūm tērræquĕ pŏtēns.

Īmpĕrŏ, ās, āvī, ātūm, ārĕ. ***To command, to order.*** **Rēx īmpĕrāvĭt,** īnstĭtīt vīrtūs mĭhĭ. Sen. Syn.—Īmpĕrĭtō, ēdīcŏ, jŭbĕō, māndŏ, præcĭpĭō, præscrībŏ. *To govern.* Syn.—Dŏmĭnŏr, īmpĕrĭtō, rēgnŏ, præsūm, rĕgŏ, mŏdĕrŏr. Phr.—Īmpĕrĭūm tĕnĕō. Rēgnūm hăbĕō. Īmpĕrĭī clāvūm, frēnūm, hăbēnās hăbērĕ. Pŏpŭlĭs jūra īmpōnŏ. Māgnās rēgnārĕ pĕr ūrbēs. Tōtūm sūb lēgēs mīttĕrĕt ōrbēm. Vīctīs dŏmĭnābĭtŭr Ārgīs. Quī tērrām, mărĕ tēmpĕrăt.

Īmpērtērrĭtŭs, ă, ūm. *Fearless.* Syn.—Īntērrĭtŭs, īmpăvĭdŭs. *See Audax, Fortis.*

Īmpērtĭō, īs, īvī & ĭī, ītūm, īrĕ. *To share with, to impart.* Syn.—Dō, trĭbŭō, præbĕō, lārgĭŏr, ēlārgĭŏr.

Īmpĕtrŏ, ās, āvī, ātūm, ārĕ. *To obtain.* Īmpĕtrăt ēt pācem ēt lŏcŭplētēm frūgĭbŭs ānnūm. H. Syn.—Ōbtĭnĕō, cōnsĕquŏr, ēxōrŏ. *See Obtineo.*

Īmpĕtŭs, ūs. m. *Attack.* Pōst ŭbĭ cōmmōvīt vīs ējŭs ēt **īmpĕtŭs** ācĕr. Lr. Syn.—Īncūrsŭs, īctŭs. Phr.—Sŭbĭtō rŭīt īmpĕtĕ præcēps. Fŭrĭt īmpĕtŭs Aētnæ. *Violence.* Syn.—Vīs, vĭŏlēntĭă, mōtŭs.

Īmpĭĕtās, ātĭs. f. *Impiety.* Sŏcĭāsquĕ sŏrōrēs īmpĭĕtātĭs hăbĕt. O. Phr.—Mēns īmpĭă. Īmpĭŭs aūsŭs. Īmpĭŭs ērrŏr. Īmpĭĕtās sēcūră dĕī. Ōmnĕ scĕlŭs aūsă. Rŭēns īn vĕtĭtūm nĕfās. Āssuētă tēmnĕrĕ dīvōs. *Unnatural.* Syn.—Īmprŏbĭtās, nēquĭtĭă, crūdēlĭtās. *See latter.*

Īmpĭgĕr, gră, grūm. *Diligent, active.* Īmpĭgĕr ēxtrēmōs cūrrīt mērcātŏr ăd Īndōs. H. Syn.—Ācĕr, gnāvŭs, strēnŭŭs. *See Gnavus, Diligens.*

Īmpīngŏ, ĭs, ēgī, āctūm, ĕrĕ. ***To strike, to push against.*** Syn.—Īmpēllŏ, īncŭtĭō, īnjĭcĭō, īllīdŏ. ***To force upon by violence.*** Ōbtrūdŏ, īnjĭcĭō, īnfĕrŏ.

Īmpĭŭs, ă, ūm. *Impious.* Pāllădĭs aūxĭlĭīs sēmpēr stĕtĭt; īmpĭŭs ēx quō Tȳdīdēs. V. Syn.—Nĕfāndŭs, nĕfārĭŭs, săcrĭlĕgŭs, scĕlĕrātŭs, scĕlēstŭs. Phr.—Dĕī, sŭpĕrūm cōntēmptŏr Quēm īmpĭŭs ābstŭlĭt ērrŏr. Pĕr ōmnĕ Fāsquĕ nĕfāsquĕ rŭĭt. Læsĭt īmpĭă līnguă dĕōs.

Īmplācābĭlĭs, ĭs, ĕ. *Implacable.* Ēffĭcĕ sīt nōbīs nōn īmplācābĭlĭs īră. O. Syn.—Īmplācātŭs, īmmītĭs, īllăcrĭmābĭlĭs, ĭnēxōrābĭlĭs. Phr.—Īndŏcĭlĭs flēctī. Prĕcĭbūs mānsuēscĕrĕ nēscĭŭs. Mēns īmmōtă mănĕt.

Īmplĕŏ, ēs, ēvī, ētūm, ērĕ. *To fill.* Īmplēntūr fōssae, ēt căvă flūmĭnă crēscūnt. V. Syn.—Cōmplĕŏ, ēxplĕŏ, rĕplĕŏ, cŭmŭlō. Phr.—Īmplēvītquĕ mĕrō pătĕrām. Vēntīs īmplēvīt vēlă sĕcūndīs. Īmplēvīt clāmōrĕ lŏcūm. *To fulfil a duty.* Syn.—Præstō, ēxsĕquŏr, fūngŏr.

Īmplĭcŏ, ās, āvī, ātūm, ārĕ. *To envelope, to embarrass.* Īmplĭcăt ēt mĭsĕrōs mōrsū dēpāscĭtŭr ārtūs. V. Syn.—Īmpĕdĭŏ, īnnēctŏ, īntēxŏ, īnvōlvŏ, īrrētĭŏ, cīrcūmrētĭŏ, īllăquĕŏ, īntrīcŏ, vīncĭŏ, rĕlĭgŏ. Phr.—Crīnem īmplĭcăt aūrō. **Brāchĭă cōllō Īmplĭcŭĭt.**

Īmplōrŏ, ās, āvī, ātūm, ārĕ. *To implore help.* Tūm dēmūm pātrem īmplōrānt, ēt nōmĕn ĭnānī Vōcĕ cĭēnt. Syn.—Īnvŏcŏ, ōbtēstŏr, ēxpōscŏ, prĕcŏr, tēstŏr, āppēllŏ. Phr.—Īmplōrāntquĕ dĕōs. Māgnōque īmplōrānt nūmĭnă quēstū.

Īmpōnŏ, ĭs, ŏsŭī, ŏsĭtūm, ĕrĕ. *To put upon.* Vīdīt tūrĭcrĕmīs cūm dōna īmpōnĕrēt ārīs. V. Syn.—Sŭpērpōnŏ, āddŏ, sŭpĕrāddŏ, ādstrŭŏ, āggĕrŏ, cŭmŭlŏ, strŭŏ, ŏnĕrŏ. Phr.—Īmpōnĕrĕ mōntĭbŭs ārcēs. Mōlēmque ēt mōntēs īnsŭpĕr āltōs Īmpŏsŭĭt. Īmpōnĕrĕ fīnēm cūrīs. *To place away in.* Syn.—Īnfĕrŏ, dēpōnŏ, rĕpōnŏ.

Īmpōrtūnŭs, ă, ūm. *Sinister, ill-omened.* Nōctĕ sĕdēns sērā cănĭt īmpōrtūnĕ pĕr ūmbrās. V. Syn.—Īnfaūstŭs, fūnēstŭs, īnfēstŭs. *Disagreeable.* Syn.—Grăvĭs, mŏlēstŭs, īnfēstŭs, ĭnĭmīcŭs, īncōmmŏdŭs, nŏcēns, nŏcŭŭs, nōxĭŭs, dāmnōsŭs.

Īmpōssĭbĭlĭs, ĭs, ĕ. (*rare*). *Impossible.* Syn.—Vĕtĭtŭs. Phr.—Quōd fĭĕrī nĕquĭt. Quōd vīrēs sŭpĕrăt. Vīrĭbŭs mājŭs. Fĭĕrī nūllā quōd rătĭōnĕ pŏtēst. Quīdquīd cōrrĭgĕre ēst nĕfās. Prĭus flūctūs pŏtĕrīs sīccārĕ mărīnōs.

Īmpŏtēns, tĭs. adj. *Powerless, feeble.* Syn.—Īmbēcīllŭs, īnfīrmŭs, dēbĭlĭs, īnvălĭdŭs. *Violent, uncontrolled.* Syn.—Īmpŏs, īnsānŭs, dēmēns, āmēns, fŭrēns, vĭŏlēntŭs.

Īmprĕcŏr, ārĭs, ātŭs sūm, ārī. *To curse.* Phr.—Dīră prĕcŏr. Dīrīs ăgŏ. Dīrās prĕcēs mīttŏ. Măla ōmnĭă pōscŏ. Mălă mūltă prĕcŏr.

Imprīmīs & In prīmīs. adv. *Principally.* Syn.—Cūmprīmīs, præsērtīm, præcīpŭē, māxĭmē.

Imprĭmŏ, ĭs, ēssī, ēssūm, ĕrĕ. *To print, to mark, to sign.* Syn.—Sīgnŏ, ōbsīgnŏ, fīgŏ, īnfīgŏ.

Imprŏbĭtās, ātĭs. f. *Meanness, wickedness.* Syn.—Scĕlŭs, īmpĭĕtās, nēquĭtĭă, sævĭtĭă.

Imprŏbŏ, ās, āvī, ātūm, ārĕ. *To condemn.* Syn.—Dāmnŏ, ārgŭŏ, cūlpŏ.

Imprŏbŭs, ă, ūm. *Bad.* Mōllĭbŭs īn prātīs āltē flōs īmprŏbŭs ēxstăt. Syn.—Mălŭs, mălīgnŭs, scĕlēstŭs, nēquām, prāvŭs, pērvērsŭs, nĕfārĭŭs, ĭnīquŭs. *Obstinate.* Syn.—Tĕnāx, pērtĭnāx, āssĭdŭŭs.

Imprŏpĕrātŭs & Imprŏpĕrŭs, ă, ūm. *Slow, without haste.* Syn.—Lēntŭs, tārdŭs.

Imprōvĭdŭs, ă, ūm. *Not anticipating, improvident.* Imprōvĭdă pēctŏră tūrbăt. V. Syn.—Incaūtŭs, īmprūdēns. Phr.—Sŭbĭtī cāsūs īmprŏvĭdŭs.

Imprōvīsŭs, ă, ūm. *Unforeseen.* Imprōvīsŭs ăĭt; cōrām quēm qærĭtĭs, ādsūm. V. Syn.—Inŏpīnŭs, ĭnŏpīnātŭs, ĭnēxspēctātŭs, īnspērātŭs, rĕpēntīnŭs, sŭbĭtŭs, rĕpēns, nŏvŭs. Phr.—Nōn (*or*) haūd ēxspēctātŭs. Vīs īmprōvīsă lētī.

Imprūdēns, ēntĭs. adj. *Imprudent.* Nūnquam īmprūdēntĭbŭs īmbĕr Ōbfŭĭt. V. Syn.—Imprōvĭdŭs, īncaūtŭs. *Ignorant.* Syn.—Inscĭŭs, nēscĭŭs, īgnārŭs, rŭdĭs.

Impŭdēns, ēntĭs. adj. *Impudent, bold.* Impŭdēns līquī pătrĭōs pēnātēs. H. Syn.—Invĕrēcūndŭs, aūdāx, īmpŭdīcŭs, prŏcāx, prŏtērvŭs. Phr.—Pŭdōrĕ, pŭdōrēm ēxūtŭs. Vīr pērfrīctæ frōntĭs. Cuī nūllŭs ĭn ōrĕ pŭdŏr. Cūjŭs ēxsŭlăt ōrĕ pŭdŏr. Pŭdōrĭs ēxpērs. Cūjūs fūgĭt ăb ōrĕ pŭdŏr.

Impŭdēntĕr. adv. *Boldly, without shame.* Syn.—Prŏcācĭtĕr, prŏtērvē, aūdāctĕr.

Impŭdēntĭă, æ. f. *Boldness.* Syn.—Invĕrēcūndĭă, aūdācĭă, prŏtērvĭă.

Impŭdīcŭs, ă, ūm. *Immodest, unchaste.* Nĕc īmpŭdīcă Cōlchĭs īntŭlĭt pĕdēm. H. Syn.—Impūrŭs, lāscīvŭs, lĭbīdĭnōsŭs, flāgĭtĭōsŭs, ōbscœnŭs, īmprŏbŭs, nēquām, prŏtērvŭs, īgnōmĭnĭōsŭs, tūrpĭs, īnfāmĭs.

Impūgnŏ, ās, āvī, ātūm, ārĕ. *To attack.* Syn.—Aggrĕdĭŏr, cārpŏ.

Impūnĭtās, ātĭs. f. *Impunity.* Syn.—Lĭcēntĭă, vĕnĭă.

Impūrŭs, ă, ūm. *Impure.* Syn.—Fœdŭs, īmmūndŭs, ōbscœnŭs, sōrdĭdŭs, spūrcŭs, tūrpĭs.

Impŭtŏ, ās, āvī, ātūm, ārĕ. *To impute, to attribute to.* Syn.—Trĭbŭŏ, āttrĭbŭŏ.

Īmŭs, ă, ūm. *Lowest.* Grăvĭtēr gĕmĭtūs īmō dē pēctŏrĕ dūcēns. V. Syn.—Īnfĭmŭs, prŏfūndŭs, īntĭmŭs, āltŭs, dēmīssŭs. Phr.—Īmă pĕdĭs. Īmă pĕtĭt. Tēllūrĕ sŭb īmā. *The last, the lowest in rank.* Syn.—Hŭmĭlĭs, ūltĭmŭs, īnfĭmŭs.

Ĭn. prep. *In.* Syn.—Īntrā. *Into, towards.* Syn.—Ērgā, ăd, īntrā. *Against.* Syn.—Ādvērsŭs, cōntrā.

Ĭnāccēssŭs, ă, ūm *Inaccessible.* Syn.—Īnvĭŭs, īmpērvĭŭs, ĭnhōspĭtŭs.

Ĭnămābĭlĭs, ĭs, ĕ. *Displeasing, odious.* Syn.—Īnjūcūndŭs, ĭnămœnŭs, īllætābĭlĭs, īngrātŭs, hōrrĭdŭs, īnvīsŭs, ŏdĭōsŭs, mŏlēstŭs.

Ĭnāmbĭtĭōsŭs, ă, ūm. *Humble.* Syn.—Mŏdēstŭs, hŭmĭlĭs.

Ĭnămœnŭs, ă, ūm. *Displeasing.* Syn.—Mœstŭs, trīstĭs.

Ĭnānĕ, ĭs. n. *A vacuum.* Syn.—Văcŭūm. Phr.—Lōngūm pĕr ĭnānĕ sĕcūtŭs. Cĕlĕrī rāptūs pĕr ĭnānĭă vēntō. *As an adverb.* Syn.—Frūstrā.

Ĭnānĭs, ĭs, ĕ. *Empty.* Pērquĕ dŏmōs Dītĭs văcŭās ĕt ĭnānĭă rēgnă. V. Syn.—Văcŭŭs, văcŭātŭs. *In need. See Pauper. Vain, useless.* Syn.—Vānŭs, īrrĭtŭs, cāssŭs, fūtĭlĭs. Phr.—Ŏpĕrām quī sūmĭt ĭnānēm. Caūsās nēquīcquām nēctĭs ĭnānēs. Dŏlī frāngūntŭr ĭnānēs.

Ĭnārdēscŏ, ĭs, ĕrĕ. *To be inflamed.* Syn.—Ārdĕŏ, ĭnārdĕŏ, īncēndŏr, īncāndĕŏ, īncāndēscŏ.

Ĭnāssuētŭs, ă, ūm. *Unaccustomed.* Syn.—Īnsuētŭs, īncōnsuētŭs.

Ĭnaūdāx, ācĭs. adj. *Timid.* Syn.—Tĭmĭdŭs, īgnāvŭs.

Ĭnaūgŭrŏ, ās, āvī, ātūm, ārĕ. *To consecrate.* Syn.—Săcrŏ, cōnsĕcrŏ.

Ĭnaūrŏ, ās, āvī, ātūm, ārĕ. *To gild.* Phr.—Aūrō dĕcŏrŏ, ōrnŏ, ēxōrnŏ, dĭtŏ, īllūstrŏ, tĕgŏ, ōbdūcŏ, īllĭnŏ.

Ĭnaūspĭcātŭs, ă, ūm. *Unfavorable, under evil auspices.* Syn.—Lævŭs, sĭnīstĕr, īnfaūstŭs, īnfēlīx. Phr.—Nōn aūspĭcātŭs.

Īncălēscŏ, ĭs, ŭī, ĕrĕ. *To become warm.* Syn.—Călĕfīŏ, ĭnārdēscŏ, īnflāmmŏr. Fig.—*To be animated.* Syn.—Călĕfīŏ.

Īncāndēscŏ, ĭs, ŭī, ĕrĕ. *To catch fire.* Syn.—Īnārdēscŏ, īncălēscŏ, īgnēscŏ, īncēndŏr, īnflāmmŏr, flăgrŏ.

Īncānēscŏ, ĭs, ŭī, ĕrĕ. *To whiten.* Syn.—Cānēscŏ, ālbēscŏ, ālbĭcŏ.

Īncāntāmēntūm, ī. n. *Enchantment, charm.* Syn.—Cāntāmĕn, fāscĭnūm, cārmĕn. Phr.—Măgĭcūm mĭnīstĕrĭūm. Thēssālī cāntūs. Ārs Cīrcæă.

Īncaūtŭs, ă, ūm. *Incautious.* Syn.—Īncōnsūltŭs, īmprōvĭdŭs, īmprūdēns, ĭnŏpīnāns, īmpărātŭs. Phr.—Nĕc ŏpīnŭs, nĕc ŏpīnāns. Īncaūtă fŭtūrī.

Īncēdŏ, ĭs, ēssī, ēssūm, ĕrĕ. *To go, to advance.* Āst ĕgŏ quæ dīvum īncēdō rēgīnă. V. Syn.—Ĕŏ, vādŏ, āmbŭlŏ, grădĭŏr, īngrĕdĭŏr.

Phr.—Grēssūm fĕrō. Vēstīgĭă flēctō. Grēssū gaūdēns īncēdĭt Iūlī. Pāssūque īncēdĭt ĭnērtī.

Īncēndĭūm, ĭī. n. *Fire.* Prŏpĭūsque æstūs īncēndĭă vōlvūnt. V. Syn.—Īgnĭs, flāmmă, Vūlcānŭs. Phr.—Vūlcānĭă pēstĭs. Īgnĕă tēmpēstās. Dānt clāra īncēndĭă lūcēm. Ōmnĕ mĭhī vīsūm cōnsīdĕre ĭn īgnēs Īlĭūm. *See Ardeo, Ignis.*

Īncēndŏ, ĭs, dī, sūm, ĕrĕ. *To burn.* Frăgĭlēs īncēndĕ bĭtūmĭnĕ laūrōs. V. Syn.—Āccēndŏ, sūccēndŏ, crĕmŏ, ūrŏ, ădūrŏ, cōmbūrŏ, ēxūrŏ, īnflāmmŏ. Fig.—*To inflame.*

Īncērtē, Īncērtō, Īncērtūm. adv. *With uncertainty, doubtfully.* Syn.—Āmbĭgŭē, dŭbĭē.

Īncērtŭs, ă, ūm. *Uncertain.* Īncērtī quō fātă fĕrānt, ŭbĭ sīstĕrĕ dētŭr. V. Syn.—Āncēps, āmbĭgŭŭs, dŭbĭŭs, dŭbĭtāns, ānxĭŭs. Phr.—Nōn cērtŭs. *Unstable.* Syn.—Văgŭs, ērrāns, tĭtŭbāns, īnstăbĭlĭs, flŭĭtāns, mōbĭlĭs, lĕvĭs.

Īncēssŏ, ĭs, ī & īvī, ĕrĕ. *To attack.* Syn.—Lăcēssŏ, prōvŏcŏ, āggrĕdĭŏr.

Īncēssŭs, ūs. m. *Gait, walk.* Syn.—Grēssŭs, grădŭs, hăbĭtŭs.

Īncēstŏ, ās, āvī, ātūm, ārĕ. *To corrupt.* Syn.—Pōllŭŏ, vĭŏlŏ, cōrrūmpŏ.

Īnchŏŏ, ās, āvī, ātūm, ārĕ. *To lay the foundation of, to commence.* Syn.—Īncĭpĭŏ, āggrĕdĭŏr, mōlĭŏr.

Īncĭdŏ, ĭs, ī, ĕrĕ. *To fall.* Īncĭdĭt īn cāssēs prædă pĕtītă mĕōs. O. Syn.—Cădŏ, dēcĭdŏ, lābŏr. *To arrive by chance.* Syn.—Ādvĕnĭŏ, sŭpērvĕnĭŏ, ōbjĭcĭŏr.

Īncīdŏ, ĭs, dī, sūm, ĕrĕ. *To cut.* Ātquĕ mălā vītēs īncīdĕrĕ fālcĕ nŏvēllās. V. Syn.—Cædŏ, præcīdŏ, scīndŏ, sĕcŏ, āmpŭtŏ. *To interrupt.* Syn.—Ābrūmpŏ, īntērrūmpŏ. *To engrave.* Syn.—Cælŏ, scūlpŏ, īmprĭmŏ, īnscrībŏ. Phr.—Lēgēs īncīdĕrĕ līgnō.

Īncĭpĭŏ, ĭs, ēpī, ēptūm, ĕrĕ. *To commence.* Cūm prīmă quĭēs mōrtālĭbŭs ægrīs Īncĭpĭt. V. Syn.—Nāscŏr, ŏrĭŏr, sūrgŏ, ōrdĭŏr, īnchŏŏ, āggrĕdĭŏr, cœpī, ĭnĕŏ, sūscĭpĭŏ, īnstĭtŭŏ.

Īncĭtŏ, ās, āvī, ātūm, ārĕ. *To incite.* Stĭmŭlīs haūd mōllĭbŭs īncĭtāt īrās. V. Syn.—Cōncĭtŏ, ēxcĭtŏ, sūscĭtŏ, ăcŭŏ, īncēndŏ, cŏhōrtŏr, stĭmŭlŏ, ūrgĕŏ, īmpēllŏ, ăgŏ.

Īncĭtŭs, ă, ūm. *Rapid, violent.* Syn.—Cōncĭtŭs, cōncĭtātŭs, cĭtŭs, cĕlĕr, vĭŏlēntŭs.

Īnclēmēntĭă, æ. f. *Rigor, harshness.* Ēt lăbŏr ēt dūræ răpĭt īnclēmēntĭă mōrtĭs. V. Syn.—Sævĭtĭēs, sævĭtĭă, āspĕrĭtās, rĭgŏr.

Īnclīnŏ, ās, āvī, ātūm, ārĕ. *To incline, to bend.* Syn.—Cūrvŏ, īncūrvŏ, īnflēctŏ, dēflēctŏ, flēctŏ, dēmīttŏ.

Īnclūdŏ, ĭs, sī, sūm, ĕrĕ. *To enclose.* Mūltĭplĭcīquĕ dŏmo ēt cæcīs īnclūdĕrĕ tēctīs. O. Syn.—Claūdŏ, cōnclūdŏ, ābdŏ, ōbsĕrŏ, īnsĕrŏ, īntrūdŏ. Phr.—Īnclūdūnt cæcō lătĕrī. *To surround.* Syn.—Āmbĭŏ, cīrcūmdŏ, cīngŏ, sēpĭŏ, āmplēctŏr.

Īnclÿtŭs, ă, ūm. *Famous, illustrious.* Īnclÿtă bēllō Mœnĭă Dārdănĭdūm. Syn.—Clārŭs, cĕlĕbĕr, īllūstrĭs, nōbĭlĭs. Phr.—Gēns tĭtŭlīs īnclÿtă. *See Celeber.*

Īncœptūm, ī. n. *Beginning, undertaking.* Dī nōstra īncœptă sĕcūndēnt. V. Syn.—Cœptūm, ōrsă, ēxōrsă, aūsŭs, aūsă.

Īncōgnĭtŭs, ă, ūm. *Unknown. See Ignotus. Unperceived.* Syn.—Īnāspēctŭs, īnvīsŭs, cæcŭs, ōbscūrŭs, lătēns.

Īncŏlŏ, ĭs, ŏlŭī, ūltūm, ĕrĕ. *To inhabit.* Sīc vĕtĕrīs sēdēs īncŏlŭīstĭs ăvī. Tib. Syn.—Cŏlŏ, hăbĭtŏ, mănĕŏ.

Īncŏlŭmĭs, ĭs, ĕ. *Safe and sound.* Īncŏlŭmēm Pāllāntă mĭhī sī fātă rĕsērvānt. V. Syn.—Sōspĕs, tūtŭs, sānŭs, īllæsŭs, īntĕgĕr, sērvātŭs, vīvŭs, sŭpērstĕs. Phr.—Rĕge īncŏlŭmī, mēns ōmnĭbŭs ūnă. Vīrtūtem īncŏlŭmem ŏdĭmŭs.

Īncōmmŏdūm, ī. n. *Inconvenience.* Syn.—Mălūm. *Misfortune.* Syn.—Mălūm, dētrīmēntūm.

Īncōmmŏdŭs, ă, ūm. *Inconvenient.* Syn.—Mŏlēstŭs, īmpōrtūnŭs, ĭnĭmīcŭs, ŏdĭōsŭs, īnvīsŭs, grăvĭs.

Īncōnstāns, āntĭs. adj. *Inconstant, fickle.* Syn.—Lĕvĭs, īnstăbĭlĭs, mōbĭlĭs, mūtābĭlĭs, vŏlūbĭlĭs, mūltĭvŏlŭs. Phr.—Āncēps ănĭmō. Ănĭmō lĕvī. Mōbĭlĭōr vēntō. Sĭbĭ nōn cōnstāns. Īmpār sĭbĭ. Nīl dŭbĭō plăcĕt.

Īncōnstāntĭă, æ. f. *Fickleness.* Syn.—Lĕvĭtās, mōbĭlĭtās. Phr.—Mēns īnstăbĭlĭs. Văgī ērrōrēs.

Īncōnsūltŭs, ă, ūm. *Unadvised.* Phr.—Sĭnĕ cōnsĭlĭō. Ābsquĕ rătĭōnĕ. *Imprudent, rash.* Syn.—Cæcŭs, lĕvĭs, tĕmĕrārĭŭs, præcēps, īmprūdēns, īncaūtŭs, īncōgĭtāns.

Īncōrrūptŭs, ă, ūm. *Incorrupt.* Jūstĭtĭæ sŏrŏr īncōrrūptă fĭdēs. H. Syn.—Īntĕmĕrātŭs, īnvĭŏlātŭs, īntĕgĕr, pūrŭs, sānŭs, sīncērŭs.

Īncrēbrēscŏ, ĭs, bŭī, ĕrĕ. *To increase.* Syn.—Crēbrēscŏ, crēscŏ. aūgĕŏr.

Īncrēdĭbĭlĭs, ĭs, ĕ. *Incredible.* Phr.—Fĭdē mājŏr. Fĭdem ēxcēdēns. Hōc crēdī nĕfās. Crēdĕrĕ quĭs pōssĭt? Sī crēdĕrĕ dīgnūm. Nĭsĭ vātĭbŭs ōmnēs Ērĭpĭēndă fĭdēs.

Īncrēmēntūm, ī. n. *Increase.* Syn.—Āccēssĭŏ, aūgmĕn, aūgmēntūm, aūctŭs.

Īncrĕpŏ, ās, ŭī, ĭtūm, ārĕ. *To make a sound, to sound.* Pōllĭcĭtĭs frăgĭlēs īncrĕpŭērĕ mănūs. Pr. Syn.—Crĕpŏ, sŏnŏ, strĕpŏ, īnstrĕpŏ. *To strike with a noise.* Syn.—Īmpēllŏ, fĕrĭŏ, pūlsŏ, īncŭtĭō, pērcŭtĭō. *To reproach.* Syn.—Ārgŭō, cāstīgŏ, ōbjūrgŏ, īncūsŏ, cūlpŏ.

Īncŭbŏ, ās, ŭī, ĭtūm, ārĕ. *To recline upon. See Incumbo.* Fig.—*To cover.*

Īncūltŭs, ă, ūm. *Uncultivated.* Syn.—Ĭnărātŭs. Phr.—Rāstrō īntāctŭs. Nūllīs tēllūs saūcĭă vōmĕrĭbŭs. *Neglected.* Syn.—Īncōmptŭs, īncōmpŏsĭtŭs, īncōncīnnŭs, ĭnōrnātŭs, hōrrĭdŭs, squālēns, squālĭdŭs, nēglēctŭs.

Īncūmbŏ, ĭs, ŭbŭī, ŭbĭtūm, ĕrĕ. *To recline upon.* Syn.—Īncŭbŏ, jăcĕō, stērnŏr. *To lean upon.* Syn.—Īnnītŏr, nītŏr, fūlcĭŏr. *To push upon.* Syn.—Rŭō, īrrŭō, īncūrrŏ, præcĭpĭtŏ. *To apply oneself to.* Syn.—Stŭdĕō, īnvĭgĭlō, cūrŏ, īntēndŏ, văcŏ.

Īncūrrŏ, ĭs, rrī, ūrsūm, ĕrĕ. *To run towards, to throw oneself upon.* Pēctŏrĕ nēc nūdō strīctōs īncūrrĭs ĭn ēnsēs. M. Syn.—Īncūrsŏ, īrrŭō, īrrūmpŏ, fĕrŏr.

Īncūsŏ, ās, āvī, ātūm, ārĕ. *To accuse, to complain of.* Quēm nōn īncūsāvi āmēns hŏmĭnūmquĕ Dĕūmquĕ? V. Syn.—Ārgŭō, dāmnŏ, cūlpŏ, īncrĕpŏ.

Īncūstōdītŭs, ă, ūm. *Unguarded.* Syn.—Īndēfēnsŭs, īntūtŭs, dēsērtŭs, pătēns. Phr.—Mălĕ tūtŭs.

Īncŭtĭō, ĭs, ūssī, ūssūm, ĕrĕ. *To strike.* Syn.—Īnflīgŏ, īmpīngŏ. Fig.—Syn. Īmmīttŏ, īnjĭcĭō, īnfĕrŏ, āffĕrŏ. *To strike the lyre.* Syn.—Pūlsŏ, īmpēllŏ.

Īndĕ. adv. *Thence.* Syn.—Īllīnc, hīnc. *Then.* Syn.—Dĕīndĕ. *Therefore.* Syn.—Hīnc, ĭdĕō. Phr.—Ēx hōc.

Īndēbĭtŭs, ă, ūm. *Undeserved.* Syn.—Īmmĕrĭtŭs, īndīgnŭs. Phr.—Nōn dēbĭtŭs. Nōn jūstŭs.

Īndĕcōrĭs, ĭs, ĕ & Īndĕcōrŭs, ă, ūm. *Shameful, inglorious.* Nōn ĕrĭmūs rēgno īndĕcōrēs. V. Syn.—Ĭnhŏnēstŭs, īnglōrĭŭs, dēfōrmĭs, tūrpĭs.

Īndēlībātŭs, ă, ūm. *Untouched, inviolate.* Syn.—Īllībātŭs, īntāctŭs, īntĕgĕr.

Īndĭcĭūm, ĭī. n. *Sign, mark.* Īndĭcĭūm mōrēs nōbĭlĭtātĭs hăbēnt. O. Syn.—Īndēx, sīgnūm, ārgūmēntūm, nŏtă, īnsīgnĕ, spĕcĭmĕn.

Īndĭcŏ, ās, āvī, ātūm, ārĕ. *To indicate, to show.* Īndĭcăt ēt nōmēn līttĕră păctă tŭūm. Tib. Syn.—Ăpĕrĭŏ, mōnstrŏ, ōstēndŏ, sīgnĭfĭcŏ.

Īndīcŏ, ĭs, īxī, īctūm, ĕrĕ. *To declare, to make known.* Syn.—Ēdīcŏ, dēnūntĭŏ, dēclārŏ.

Īndĭgĕŏ, ēs, ŭī, ērĕ. *To need, to lack.* Syn.—Ĕgĕŏ, cărĕŏ, rĕquīrŏ. Phr.—Ŏpŭs ēst, ŏpŭs hăbĕŏ.

Īndīgnŏr, ārĭs, ātŭs sūm, ārī. *To be indignant.* Syn.—Īrāscŏr, sūccēnsĕō.

Īndīgnŭs, ă, ūm. *Unworthy.* Pērcŭtĭt īndīgnōs clārō plāngōrĕ lăcērtōs. O. Syn.—Īmmĕrĭtŭs, īmmĕrēns. *Cruel.* Syn.—Tūrpĭs, crūdēlĭs.

Īndĭgŭs, ă, ūm. *Needy.* Syn.—Ĕgēns, īndĭgēns, ĭnōps. *See Egenus.*

Īndīscrētŭs, ă, ūm. *Indistinct.* Syn.—Īndīstīnctŭs. *That which cannot be distinguished.* Syn.—Īndīstīnctŭs, sĭmīllĭmŭs.

Īndīstrīctŭs, ă, ūm. *Unharmed, intact.* Syn.—Īllæsŭs, īntāctŭs, īntĕgĕr.

Īndŏ, ĭs, ĭdī, ĭtūm, ĕrĕ. *To put within.* Syn.—Īnsĕrŏ, īmmīttŏ, īntrūdŏ. *To add.* Syn. Āddŏ, īmpōnŏ.

Īndŏcĭlĭs, ĭs, ĕ. *Uncivilized.* Syn.—Rŭdĭs, ăgrēstĭs, fĕrŭs, āspĕr.

Īndōctŭs, ă, ūm. *Ignorant.* Nōn tu īn trĭvĭīs, īndōctĕ, sōlēbās Strīdēntī mĭsĕrūm stĭpŭlā dīspērdĕrĕ cārmĕn? V. Syn.—Īgnārŭs, īmpĕrĭtŭs, rŭdĭs. Phr.—Ārtĭs, dōctrīnæ ēxpērs. Ārtĕ rŭdĭs. Cuī nūllīs ārtĭbŭs īmbūtūm pēctŭs. Quī dūlcĕ nēctăr Pēgăsēī fōntĭs nōn haŭsĭt. *Unlearned.* Syn.—Īndŏcĭlĭs, rŭdĭs, nēscĭŭs.

Īndŏlēs, ĭs. f. *Natural character.* Quīd pĭŭs Aēnēās tāntā dăbĭt īndŏlĕ dīgnūm? V. Syn.—Īngĕnĭūm, nātūră, mōrēs, mēns, ănĭmŭs, pēctŭs, cŏr.

Īndŏlēscŏ, ĭs, lŭī ĕrĕ. *To groan, to grieve.* Īndŏlŭīt, quōd nōn mĕlĭōră pĕtīssĕt. O. Syn.—Dŏlĕŏ, īngĕmŏ.

Īndŏmĭtŭs, ă, ūm. *Unconquerable.* Nātĕ, quĭs īndŏmĭtās tāntūs dŏlŏr ēxcĭtăt īrās? V. Syn.—Īnvīctŭs, īnsŭpĕrābĭlĭs, āspĕr, īndŏcĭlĭs, īnfrēnĭs. Phr.—Nōn āntĕ dŏmābĭlĭs. Nūllā dŏmābĭlĭs ārtĕ. Rĕgī nēscĭŭs. Nēscĭŭs ōrĕ rĕgī. *Immoderate.* Syn.—Ēffrēnĭs, ēffūsŭs, vĕhĕmēns, vĭŏlēntŭs.

Īndūcŏ, ĭs, xī, ctūm, ĕrĕ. *To introduce, to lead in.* Deīndĕ sătīs flŭvĭum īndūcĭt rīvōsquĕ sĕquēntēs. V. Syn.—Āddūcŏ, ādmīttŏ, īmmīttŏ, īntrōdūcŏ.

Īndūlgēntĭă, æ. f. *Indulgence.* Dēxtĕră præcĭpŭē căpĭt īndūlgēntĭă mēntēs. O. Syn.—Lēnĭtās, clēmēntĭă.

Īndūlgĕŏ, ēs, sī, sūm, ērĕ. *To grant, to permit.* Syn.—Cōncēdŏ. *To favor.* Syn.—Făvĕŏ, plăcĕŏ. *To pardon.* Syn.—Pārcŏ, cōndōnŏ, īgnōscŏ. *To apply oneself to.* Syn.—Īnsērvĭŏ, īncūmbŏ. Phr.—Mē dō, mē trādŏ.

Īndŭŏ, ĭs, ŭī, ūtūm, ĕrĕ. *To put on.* Syn.—Īndūcŏ, cīrcūmdŏ, vēstĭŏ, āmīcĭŏ, ŏpĕrĭŏ, tĕgŏ, āccīngŏr.

Īndūrēscŏ, ĭs, ŭī, ĕrĕ. *To harden.* Syn.—Dūrēscŏ, īndūrŏr, rĭgēscŏ.

Īndūrŏ, ās, āvī, ātūm, ārĕ. *To harden, to freeze.* Syn.—Āstrīngŏ, prĕmŏ, gĕlŏ. *See Gelo.*

Indūstrĭă, æ. f. *Application, industry.* Sĕd nōn ūllă măgīs vīrēs īndūstrĭă fīrmăt. V. Syn.—Īngĕnĭūm, cūră, lăbŏr, ārs, sōlērtĭă, dēxtĕrĭtās. *See Labor.*

Īndūstrĭŭs, ă, ūm. *Active, laborious.* Syn.—Ācĕr, strēnŭŭs, gnāvŭs, vĭgĭl, īmpĭgĕr. *Industrious.* Syn.—Dēxtĕr, īngĕnĭōsŭs, săgāx, sōlērs, căllĭdŭs.

Ĭnēbrĭŏ, ās, āvī, ātūm, ārĕ. *To intoxicate.* Ēt mĭsĕrām vīnōsŭs ĭnēbrĭĕt aūrēm. J. Phr.—Vīnō ōbrŭŏ, mērgŏ. *Pass., To be intoxicated.* Phr.—Vīnō īmplĕŏr. Vīnō sōlvŏr, sĕpĕlĭŏr.

Ĭnēlūctābĭlĭs, ĭs, ĕ. *Inevitable.* Syn.—Īnvĭctŭs, īnsŭpĕrābĭlĭs, ĭnēvītābĭlĭs.

Ĭnĕŏ, īs, īvī & ĭī, ĭtūm, īrĕ. *To enter.* Syn.—Īntrŏ, sŭbĕŏ, īngrĕdĭŏr. Phr.—Ĭnīrĕ sēdēs lūcĭdās. Vītæ līmĕn ĭnĭt. *To attack.* Syn.—Īmpĕtŏ, īnvādŏ, āggrĕdĭŏr, īrrŭŏ. *To undertake.* Syn.—Sūscĭpĭŏ, āggrĕdĭŏr.

Ĭnēptē. adv. *Foolishly.* Syn.—Stūltē, stŏlĭdē, īnsūlsē.

Ĭnēptŭs, ă, ūm. *Foolish.* Syn.—Īnsūlsŭs, fătŭŭs, stūltŭs, stŏlĭdŭs, hĕbĕs.

Ĭnērmĭs, ĭs, ĕ & Ĭnērmŭs, ă, ūm. *Unarmed.* Ārcădĭo īnfēlīx tēlō dăt pēctŭs ĭnērmūm. V. Syn.—Nūdŭs, ēxārmātŭs. Phr.—Ārmīs nūdŭs, ēxūtŭs, spŏlĭātŭs. Nūllīs ārmīs tēctŭs, dēfēnsŭs. Tēlō vĭdŭŭs.

Ĭnērs, ērtĭs, adj. *Inactive.* Lībērtās quæ sēră tămēn rēspēxĭt ĭnērtēm. V. Syn.—Pĭgĕr, tārdŭs, nōn strēnŭŭs.

Ĭnērtĭă, æ. f. *Sloth, inertia.* Mōllĭs ĭnērtĭă cūr tāntām dīffūdĕrĭt īmīs Ōblīvĭōnēm sēnsĭbŭs. H. Syn.—Dēsĭdĭă, īgnāvĭă, sēgnĭtĭēs. Phr.—Nē vīncăt ĭnērtĭă mēntēs.

Ĭnēvītābĭlĭs, ĭs, ĕ. *Inevitable.* Syn.—Ĭnēlūctābĭlĭs. Phr.—Nōn ēvītābĭlĭs, nōn fŭgĭēndŭs, nōn vītāndŭs, nōn dēclīnāndŭs.

Ĭnēxōrābĭlĭs, ĭs, ĕ. *Inexorable.* Syn.—Īmplācābĭlĭs, dūrŭs, īmmītĭs, rĭgĭdŭs. Phr.—Nōn ēxōrābĭlĭs, nōn ēxōrātŭs. Īndŏcĭlĭs flēctī. Vīctĭmă nīl mĭsĕrāntĭs Ōrcī.

Ĭnēxplētŭs, ă, ūm. *Insatiable.* Syn.—Īnsătŭrātŭs, īnsătĭātŭs, ĭnēxsătŭrābĭlĭs, īmplācātŭs, ĭnēxplēbĭlĭs.

Ĭnēxpūgnābĭlĭs, ĭs, ĕ. *Impregnable.* Syn.—Īnsŭpĕrābĭlĭs, īndŏmĭtŭs, īnvīctŭs.

Īnfāmĭă, æ. f. *Infamy, dishonor.* Fālsŭs hŏnōr jŭvăt ēt mēndāx īnfāmĭă tērrĕt. H. Syn.—Dēdĕcŭs, prŏbrūm, ōpprŏbrĭūm, īgnōmĭnĭă. Phr.—Tūrpĭs, īnfāmĭs nŏtă. Fāmă mălă. Fāmă sĭnīstră. Fāmæ jăctūră pŭdīcæ.

Īnfāmĭs, ĭs, ĕ. *Infamous, base.* Hūnc īnfāmĭs ămōr vērsīs dărĕ tērgă cărīnīs Jūssĭt. Pr. Syn.—Fāmōsŭs, ĭnhŏnēstŭs, tūrpĭs, prŏbrōsŭs. Phr.—Ōpprŏbrĭō tāctŭs. Quēm măcŭlōsa īnfāmĭă læsĭt.

Īnfāmŏ, ās, āvī, ātūm, ārĕ. *To defame.* Dēsĭnĕ mītem ănĭmām vāno īnfāmārĕ tĭmōrĕ. O. Syn.—Dēdĕcŏrŏ, dīffĕrŏ. Phr.—Prŏbrō măcŭlŏ. Fāmām ērĭpĭŏ, tōllŏ. Nōmĕn ōbscūrŏ.

Īnfāndŭs, ă, ūm. *Unspeakable, awful.* Syn.—Nĕfāndŭs, īndīgnŭs, fœdŭs, crūdēlĭs.

Īnfāns, tĭs. m. & f. *Speechless.* Syn.—Mūtŭs. *Infant.* Syn.—Īnfāntŭlŭs, pārvŭlŭs, pŭĕr, fīlĭŏlŭs, fīlĭŏlă. Phr.—Pŭēr lāctēns. Jăcēns sĭnĕ vīrĭbŭs īnfāns. Vīx ōrtă prōlēs. Stāntēs īn līmĭnĕ vītæ.

Īnfāntĭă, æ. *Infancy.* Syn.—Cunæ, incūnābŭlă. Phr.—Infāntĭs ætās. Prīmūm ævūm.

Īnfaūstŭs, ă, ūm. *Unhappy, fatal.* Quāre ăgĭte ēt mēcum īnfaūstās ēxūrĭtĕ pūppēs. V. Syn.—Īnaūspĭcātŭs, lævŭs, sĭnīstĕr, īnfēlīx, mălŭs, trīstĭs. Phr.—Nōn dēxtĕr. Bēlla īnfaūstă gĕrūnt.

Īnfēlīx, īcĭs. adj. *Unhappy, miserable.* Quōsdam īnfēlīcēs āstrīs dāmnāvĭt ĭnīquīs. Pr. Syn.—Mĭsĕr, īnfōrtūnātŭs, ærūmnōsŭs. Phr.—Īnfēlīx ănĭmī. Fōrtūnă ĭnīquă. Fātīs ĭnīquīs vēxātŭs. Fātīs ăcērbīs āctŭs. Quēm Jŏvĭs īră prĕmĭt. Tērquĕ quătērquĕ mĭsĕr. Tōt mălă pērpēssŭs. Fōrtūnă rĕcēssĭt.

Īnfĕrī, ōrūm. m. *Hell, Hades.* Syn.—Īnfērnŭs, Īnfērnī, Īnfērnă, Ōrcŭs, Ăvērnŭs, Ăvērnă, Tārtărŭs, Tārtără, Cōcȳtŭs, Stȳx, Ăchĕrōn. Phr.—Īnfērnæ sēdēs. Stȳgĭă dŏmŭs. Cæca ōstĭă Dītĭs. Ūmbrārūm dŏmŭs, lŏcŭs. Aētērnæ cālīgĭnĭs ūmbræ. *See Appendix.*

Īnfĕrŏ, fērs, tŭlī, lātūm, fērrĕ. *To bring into.* Īnfĕrĭmŭs tĕpĭdō spūmāntĭă cȳmbĭă lāctĕ. V. Syn.—Dēfĕrŏ, fĕrŏ, īndūcŏ, īnvĕhŏ, dēvĕhŏ, īmpōrtŏ. *To cause, to inspire.* Syn.—Āffĕrŏ, īnjĭcĭŏ, īmmīttŏ, īncŭtĭŏ.

Īnfĕrŭs, ă, ūm. *Low.* Syn.—Īnfērnŭs, īnfĕrĭŏr, īmŭs, hŭmĭlĭs, īnfĭmŭs.

Īnfēstē. adv. *In a hostile manner.* Syn.—Hōstīlĭtĕr, sævē, crūdēlĭtĕr. Phr.—Īnfēstō ănĭmō, īnfēstā mēntĕ.

Īnfēstŏ, ās, āvī, ātūm, ārĕ. *To render dangerous.* Syn.—Ēxăgĭtŏ, tōrquĕŏ, vēxŏ.

Īnfēstŭs, ă, ūm. *Hostile.* Syn.—Īnfēnsŭs, hōstīlĭs, ĭnĭmīcŭs, ăcērbŭs, ĭnīquŭs, sævŭs, mŏlēstŭs, nōxĭŭs, dāmnōsŭs, ēxĭtĭōsŭs, ēxĭtĭālĭs.

Īnfĭcĭŏ, ĭs, ēcī, ēctūm, ĕrĕ. *To tint, to dye.* Syn.—Tīngŏ, īmbŭŏ. *To soil.* Syn.—Tīngŏ, īmbŭŏ, pōllŭŏ. *To infect, to poison.* Syn.—Cōrrūmpŏ, vĭtĭŏ, dēprāvŏ, pōllŭŏ, tĕmĕrŏ.

Īnfĭcĭŏr, ārĭs, ātŭs sūm, ārī. *To deny.* Syn.—Nĕgŏ, dēnĕgŏ, pērnĕgŏ, ābnŭŏ.

Īnfĭdēlĭs, ĭs, ĕ, & Īnfīdŭs, ă, ūm. *Faithless.* Syn.—Pērfĭdŭs, mălĕfīdŭs, fāllāx. Phr.—Quī fĭdēm vĭŏlăt.

Īnfīgŏ, ĭs, xī, xūm, ĕrĕ. *To fix to, to attach to.* Syn.—Fīgŏ, āffīgŏ, cōnfīgŏ, dēfīgŏ, īmpīngŏ.

Īnfīnītŭs, ă, ūm. *Infinite.* Syn.—Pĕrēnnĭs, pērpĕtŭŭs, īmmēnsŭs. Phr.—Sĭnĕ līmĭtĕ, fīnĭs ēxpērs.

Īnfīrmŏ, ās, āvī, ātūm, ārĕ. *To weaken.* Syn.—Dēbĭlĭtŏ, ēnērvŏ, frāngŏ, īnfrīngŏ, āttĕnŭŏ, sōlvŏ, cōnfĭcĭŏ. Phr.—Vīrēs, rōbŭr mĭnŭŏ, frāngŏ.

Īnfīrmŭs, ă, ūm. *Weak, sick.* Lōngĭŏr īnfīrmūm nē lāssĕt ĕpistŏlă cōrpŭs. O. Syn.—Dēbĭlĭs, ēnērvĭs, frāctŭs, īnvălĭdŭs. Phr.—Vīrĭbŭs dēfēctŭs, ēnērvĭs, ēffœtŭs. Īnvălĭdæ mănūs. Īnānēs lăcērtī.

Īnflāmmŏ, ās, āvī, ātūm, ārĕ. *To inflame.* Syn.—Īncēndŏ, cōmbūrŏ. *To excite. See Excito.*

Īnflēctŏ, ĭs, xī, xūm, ĕrĕ. *To bend.* Cōllă căve īnflēctās ād sūmmum ōblīquă thĕātrūm. Pr. Syn.—Flēctŏ, cūrvŏ, īncūrvŏ.

Īnflīgŏ, īs, xī, ctūm, ĕrĕ. *To strike.* Syn.—Īnfĕrŏ, īmpīngŏ, īncŭtĭŏ, īmprĭmŏ, īmmīttŏ.

Īnfŏdĭŏ, ĭs, fōdī, fōssūm, ĕrĕ. *To dig.* Syn.—Fŏdĭŏ, dēfŏdĭŏ, ōbrŭŏ. *To bury.* Syn.—Cōndŏ, rĕcōndŏ.

Īnfōrmŏ, ās, āvī, ātūm, ārĕ. *To form.* Īngēntem īnfōrmānt clÿpĕūm. V. Syn.—Fīngŏ, ēffīngŏ, fīgūrŏ. *To instruct.* Syn.—Ērŭdĭŏ, īmbŭŏ.

Īnfōrtūnĭūm, ĭī. n. *Misfortune.* Tūnc tŭă me īnfōrtūnĭă lædēnt. H. Syn.—Aērūmnă, ærūmnæ, ādvērsă, mălūm, mălă, cāsŭs. Phr.—Ādvērsă fōrtūnă. Rēs āfflīctæ. Trīstēs cāsūs.

Īnfrĕmŏ, ĭs, ŭī, ĕrĕ. *To groan.* Syn.—Frĕmŏ, frēndĕŏ, īnfrēndĕŏ.

Īnfrēnĭs, ĭs, ĕ & Īnfrēnŭs, ă, ūm.—*Unchecked.* Syn.—Ēffrēnĭs, īnfrēnātŭs, īndŏmĭtŭs, īndŏcĭlĭs. Phr.—Frēnōrūm nēscĭŭs. Frēnō nōn rĕmŏrāntĕ. Frēnīs sŏlūtŭs.

Īnfrīngŏ, ĭs, ēgī, āctūm, ĕrĕ. *To break. See Frango.* Fig.—*To weaken.* Syn.—Āttĕnŭŏ, īnfīrmŏ, īmmĭnŭŏ.

Īnfrōns, dĭs & Īnfrōndĭs, ĭs, ĕ. *Leafless.* Syn.—Nūdŭs. Phr.—Frōndĕ, frōndĭs hŏnōrĕ cărēns, spŏlĭātŭs, ēxūtŭs.

Īnfūndŏ, ĭs, ūdī, ūsūm, ĕrĕ. *To pour over, or into.* Syn.—Fūndŏ, īnstīllŏ, īngĕrŏ, īmmīttŏ, īnjĭcĭŏ, sŭpērfūndŏ, cīrcūmfūndŏ, spārgŏ, īnspērgŏ. Fig.—*To instil principles.* Syn.—Īncūlcŏ, īnstīllŏ, īngĕrŏ.

Īnfūscŏ, ās, āvī, ātūm, ārĕ. *To blacken, to stain.* Sūmmăquĕ jējūnā sănĭe īnfūscātŭr ărēnă. V. Syn.—Ōbscūrŏ, fœdŏ, măcŭlŏ.

Īngĕmĭnŏ, ās, āvī, ātūm, ārĕ. *To redouble.* Nūnc dēxtra īngĕmĭnāns ictūs, nūnc īllĕ sĭnīstrā. V. Syn.—Gĕmĭnŏ, cōngĕmĭnŏ, ĭtĕrŏ, dŭplĭcŏ. *To repeat.* Syn.—Gĕmĭnŏ, ĭtĕrŏ, īntĕgrŏ.

Īngĕmīscŏ, ĭs, ĕrĕ & Īngĕmŏ, ĭs, ŭī, ĕrĕ. *To groan.* Īngĕmĭt ēt dŭplĭcēs tēndēns ād līttŏră pālmās. V. Syn.—Gĕmŏ, dŏlĕŏ, īndŏlĕŏ, dēflĕŏ.

Īngĕnĭōsŭs, ă, ūm. *Skilful.* Syn.—Sūbtīlĭs, săgāx, sōlērs, cāllĭdŭs. Phr.—Īngĕnĭō prædĭtŭs. Īngĕnĭī ārtĕ pŏtēns. Cuī mēns sōlērs ĭn ārtĭbŭs. Cuī īngĕnĭī vēnă bĕnīgna ēst.

Īngĕnĭum, ĭī. n. *Nature, character.* Syn.—Nātūră. *Talent.* Syn.—Mēns, ănĭmŭs, ăcūmĕn, spīrĭtŭs. Phr.—Īngĕnĭī ăcĭēs. Mēntĭs ăcūmĕn. Īngĕnĭūm dōcta ārtĕ pŏlītūm.

Īngēns, tĭs. adj. *Great.* Syn.—Māgnŭs. *Extended, large.* Syn.—Māgnŭs, īmmēnsŭs, vāstŭs, lātŭs, pătēns.

Īngĕnŭŭs, ă, ūm. *Natural.* Syn.—Nātīvŭs, nātūrālĭs. *Honest.* Syn.—Līběrālĭs, hŏnēstŭs, nōbĭlĭs, prŏbŭs. *Chaste, modest.* Syn.—Cāndĭdŭs, vĕrēcūndŭs, mŏdēstŭs, cāstŭs, hŏnēstŭs.

Īngĕrŏ, ĕrĭs, ēssī, ēstūm, ĕrĕ. *To throw upon, or into.* Syn.—Īnjĭcĭŏ, īnfĕrŏ, īntrūdŏ, īmmīttŏ, īmpōnŏ, īncŭtĭŏ, īnfūndŏ. *To heap up.* Syn.—Āggĕrŏ, āccŭmŭlŏ, āddŏ.

Īnglŭvĭēs, ēī. f. *Stomach.* Syn.—Vēntĕr, gŭlă.

Īngrātŭs, ă, ūm. *Disagreeable.* Sēd quĭd ĕgo hæc aūtēm nēquīcquam īngrātă rĕvōlvŏ? V. Syn.—Īnjūcūndŭs, mŏlēstŭs, īnvīsŭs, ĭnămātŭs, ĭnămœnŭs, īllætābĭlĭs, grăvĭs, īnsuāvĭs, nōn plăcĭtŭs. *Ungrateful.* Syn.—Īmmĕmŏr. Phr.—Nōn grātŭs. Mălĕ grātŭs. Mĕrĭtōrūm īmmĕmŏr. Īmmĕmŏr ănĭmŭs. Īngrātă mēns. Īn ămīcōs mălĕ grātŭs.

Īngrăvēscŏ, ĭs, ĕrĕ. *To become heavy.* Syn.—Grăvēscŏ, grăvŏr. *To become more violent.* Syn.—Grăvēscŏ, ægrēscŏ, crūdēscŏ, glīscŏ.

Īngrăvŏ, ās, āvī, ātūm, are. *To overburden.* Syn.—Grăvŏ, prĕmŏ, ōpprĭmŏ, ōbrŭŏ. *To aggravate.* Syn.—Āggrăvŏ, ŏnĕrŏ, ăcērbŏ.

Īngrĕdĭŏr, ĕrĭs, ēssŭs sūm, ī. *To enter.* Syn.—Ēntrŏ, ĭnĕŏ. *To proceed.* Syn.—Ĕŏ, īncēdŏ.

Īngrŭŏ, ĭs, ī, ĕrĕ. *To be suspended over.* Syn.—Īmmĭnĕŏ. *To be about to burst upon.* Syn.—Īrrŭŏ, īrrūmpŏ, īmmĭnĕŏ, ūrgĕŏ, īnstŏ.

Īngūrgĭtŏ, ās, āvī, ātūm, ārĕ. *To engulf.* Syn.—Vŏrŏ, dēvŏrŏ, ābsōrbĕŏ.

Īnhĭbĕŏ, ēs, ŭī, ĭtūm, ērĕ. *To prevent.* Syn.—Cŏhĭbĕŏ, prŏhĭbĕŏ.

Ĭnhŏnēstŏ, ās, āvī, ātūm, ārĕ. *To dishonor.* Syn.—Dēdĕcŏrŏ, fœ̄dŏ, pōllŭŏ, măcŭlŏ, īnfāmŏ.

Ĭnhŏnēstŭs, ă, ūm. *Dishonorable.* Ēxĭtŭs hīc nōbīs nōn ĭnhŏnēstŭs ĕrĭt. Pr. Syn.—Tūrpĭs, pŭdēndŭs, prŏbrōsŭs, īnfāmĭs, īndĕcŏr, īndĕcōrŭs, īnglōrĭŭs, īgnōbĭlĭs.

Ĭnhōrrĕŏ, ēs, ŭī, ērĕ. *To bristle.* Syn.—Hōrrĕŏ, rĭgĕŏ, rĭgēscŏ. *To shudder at.* Syn.—Cŏhōrrĕŏ, ēxhōrrĕŏ.

Ĭnhōspĭtālĭs, ĭs, ĕ. *Inhospitable.* Sīvĕ fāctūrūs (iter) pĕr ĭnhōspĭtālēm Caūcăsūm. H. Syn.—Ĭnāccēssŭs, īnvĭŭs, īncūltŭs.

Ĭnhŭmātŭs, ă, ūm. *Unburied.* Ĭntĕrĕā sŏcĭōs ĭnhŭmātăquĕ cōrpŏră tērræ̆ Māndēmŭs. V. Syn.—Ĭnsĕpūltŭs, īntŭmŭlātŭs, īncōndĭtŭs. Phr.—Tŭmŭlō, sĕpūlcrō, mōrtĭs hŏnōrĕ cărēns. Sĭne hŏnōrĕ sĕpūlcrī. Ōssă cărēntĭă būstĭs. Jăcĕt īngēns lĭttŏrĕ trūncŭs.

Ĭnĭmīcĭtĭă, æ̅. f. *Enmity, hatred.* Syn.—Ŏdĭūm, sĭmūltās, dĭscōrdĭă, dĭssĭdĭūm.

Ĭnĭmīcŭs, ă, ūm. *Hostile.* Gēns ĭnĭmīcă mĭhī Tȳrrhēnūm nāvĭgăt æ̅quŏr. V. Syn.—Ādvērsŭs, ŏppŏsĭtŭs, cōntrārĭŭs, īnfēstŭs, īnfēnsŭs. Phr.—Īnfēnsō pēctŏrĕ fātŭr. Ĭnĭmīcŭs pōntĭbŭs āmnĭs. Āccĭpĭūnt ĭnĭmīcum īmbrēm.

Ĭnīquĭtās, ātĭs. f. *Injustice.* Syn.—Īnjūstĭtĭă, īnjūrĭă, īnjūstūm, ĭnīquūm, nēquĭtĭēs, nēquĭtĭă, fraūs, nĕfās, scĕlŭs. Phr.—Ĭbĭ fās ŭbĭ māxĭmă mērcēs.

Ĭnīquŭs, ă, ūm. *Unequal.* Syn.—Īmpār. *Too narrow.* Syn.—Āngūstŭs, āngūstĭŏr, ārctŭs. *Unfavorable.* Syn.—Īnfēnsŭs, īnfēstŭs, ādvērsŭs, ălĭēnŭs, ĭnĭmīcŭs, īnfaūstŭs, dīrŭs, īrātŭs, dāmnōsŭs.

Ĭnĭtĭūm, ĭī. n. *Beginning.* Syn.—Ēxōrdĭūm, ēxōrsūm, ēxōrsŭs, prīmōrdĭūm, īngrēssŭs, ŏrīgŏ, prīncĭpĭūm.

Ĭnjĭcĭŏ, ĭs, ēcī, ēctūm, ĕrĕ. *To throw upon, or into.* Syn.—Jăcĭŏ, mīttŏ, īmmīttŏ, īnfĕrŏ.

Ĭnjūrĭă, æ̅. f. *Injustice.* Syn.—Īnjūstūm, ĭnīquūm. *Wrong.* Syn.—Nōxă, dāmnūm.

Ĭnjūrĭōsŭs & Ĭnjūrĭŭs, ă, ūm. *Harmful.* Syn.—Ĭnīquŭs, ĭnĭmīcŭs, īnfēnsŭs, dāmnōsŭs, nŏcīvŭs, nŏcŭŭs, nōxĭŭs.

Īnjūstŭs, ă, ūm. *Excessive.* Īnjūstō sūb fāscĕ vĭām cūm carpĭt. V. Syn.—Ĭnīquŭs, īmpār, nĭmĭŭs, īmmŏdĭcŭs. *Unjust.* Syn.—Ĭnīquŭs. Phr.—Aēquī, jūrĭs, jūstĭtĭæ̆, rēctī cōntēmptŏr. Fraūdĭs ămāns. Īnjūstă tĕnēbāt rēgnă.

Īnnătŏ, ās, āvī, ātūm, ārĕ. *To swim.* Syn.—Sŭpērnătŏ, nătŏ, flŭĭtŏ, flūctŭŏ.

Īnnēctŏ, ĭs, xŭī, xūm, ĕrĕ. *To bind or attach to.* Syn.—Ādnēctŏ, cōnnēctŏ, īllĭgŏ, cīrcūmlĭgŏ, nōdŏ, vīncĭŏ.

Īnnītŏr, ĕrĭs, xŭs & sŭs sūm, tī. *To bend down upon.* Syn.—Īncūmbŏ, nītŏr, fūlcĭŏr.

Īnnŏcēns, ēntĭs. adj. *Harmless.* Syn.—Īnnŏcŭŭs, īnnōxĭŭs. Phr.—Sĭnĕ nōxā lūcĕ bĭbūntŭr. *Innocent.* Syn.—Īnsōns, īnnŏcŭŭs, īnnōxĭŭs, īntĕgĕr, īmmĕrĭtŭs, sānctŭs, pūrŭs, pĭŭs, hŏnēstŭs, prŏbŭs. Phr.—Crīmĭnĭs, nōxæ ēxpērs. Nūllĭŭs nōxæ rĕŭs. Mōrūm lābĕ cărēns. Cuī căstæ mōrēs. Rēctŭs ănĭmŭs. Cuī mēns cōnscĭă rēcti ēst.

Īnnŏcēntĭă, æ. f. *Innocence.* Frōntĭs pŭdōrēm, cōrdĭs īnnŏcēntĭām Syn.—Īntĕgrĭtās, sānctĭtās, prŏbĭtās. Phr—Vīta īncūlpātă fĭdēsquĕ. Īnsōns ănĭmŭs. Īnnŏcŭī mōrēs.

Īnnŏcŭŭs, ă, ūm. *Harmless.* Syn.—Īnnŏcēns, īnnōxĭŭs.

Īnnŭmĕrābĭlĭs, ĭs, ĕ. *Innumerable.* Syn.—Plūrĭmŭs, frĕquēns. Phr.—Nŭmĕrō īnfīnītŭs. Cuī deēst nŭmĕrŭs. Nŭmĕrō cōpĭă mājŏr ĕrăt. Īnnŭmĕrābĭlĭs ānnōrūm sĕrĭēs.

Īnōps, ŏpĭs. adj. Tūrpĭs ĭnōpsquĕ sĭmūl mĭsĕrābĭlĕ trānsĭgĭt ævūm. O. Syn.—Ēgēns, ĕgēnŭs, īndĭgŭs, paŭpĕr. Phr.—Vērsūs ĭnŏpēs rērūm.

Īnquĭēs, ētĭs & Īnquĭētŭs, ă, ūm. *Restless, agitated.* Syn.—Īrrĕquĭētŭs, tūrbĭdŭs, sōllĭcĭtŭs, īmplăcĭdŭs, ăgĭtātŭs, mōtŭs, tūrbŭlēntŭs, mōbĭlĭs. Phr.—Īmpătĭēns mŏræ.

Īnquĭnŏ, ās, āvī, ātūm, ārĕ. *To stain, to pollute.* Syn.—Cŏīnquĭnŏ, fœdŏ, tĕmĕrŏ, īnfĭcĭŏ, cōntămĭnŏ, pōllŭŏ, măcŭlŏ.

Īnsānē. adv. *Foolishly.* Syn.—Stūltē, dēmēntĕr, īnsĭpĭēntĕr. *Excessively.* Syn.—Īmmŏdĭcē, vĕhĕmēntĕr, vāldē, pērdĭtē.

Īnsānĭă, æ. f. *Madness, folly.* Syn.—Āmēntĭă, dēmēntĭă, fŭrŏr, dēlīrĭūm. *Passion, rage.* Syn.—Fŭrŏr, ămŏr, răbĭēs.

Īnsānĭŏ, īs, īvī & ĭī, ītūm, īrĕ. *To become foolish, or mad.* Syn.—Dēsĭpĭŏ, fŭrŏ, lȳmphŏr, bācchŏr, dēlīrŏ. Phr.—Quæ mēntem īnsānĭă mūtăt? Mēntĕ cărērĕ pŭtānt.

Īnsānŭs, ă, ūm. *Mad, furious.* Syn.—Vēsānŭs, mălĕsānŭs, vēcōrs, āmēns, dēmēns, fŭrēns, fŭrĭōsŭs. *Immoderate.* Syn.—Īmmŏdĭcŭs, vĭŏlēntŭs, īngēns, vĕhĕmēns, īmmānĭs.

Īnscĭtŭs, ă, ūm. *Ignorant.* Syn.—Īgnārŭs, īndōctŭs, rŭdĭs, stūltŭs.

Īnscrībŏ, ĭs, psī, ptūm, ĕrĕ. *To write upon.* Ūt nōstrūm tāntĭs īnscrībām nōmĕn ĭn āctīs. Tib. Syn.—Scrībŏ, īncīdŏ, nŏtŏ. *To trace, to mark.* Syn.—Īmprĭmŏ, sīgnŏ, īnscūlpŏ.

Īnsēctŏr, ārĭs, ātŭs sūm, ārī. *To pursue.* Syn.—Sēctŏr, cōnsēctŏr, sĕquŏr, īnsĕquŏr, pērsĕquŏr. *To torment.* Syn.—Vēxŏ, vērsŏ, īnsĕquŏr, ēxērcĕŏ, fătīgŏ.

Īnsĕquŏr, ĕrĭs, cūtŭs sūm, ī. *To follow, to pursue.* Syn.—Sĕquŏr, cōnsĕquŏr, īnsēctŏr, īnstŏ, ūrgĕŏ, ăgĭtŏ. *To persecute.* Syn.—Īnsēctŏr, pērsĕquŏr, ūrgĕŏ, lăcēssŏ, fătīgŏ.

Īnsĕrŏ, ĕrĭs, ēvī, ĭtūm, ĕrĕrĕ. *To graft.* Syn.—Īnŏcŭlŏ. Phr.—Īnsĕrĕ nūnc, Mĕlĭbœĕ, pĭrōs.

Īnsĕrŏ, ĕrĭs, ĕrŭī, ērtūm, ĕrĕrĕ. *To insert, to place in.* Syn.—Īnsērtŏ, īmmīttŏ, īnsĭnŭŏ, mīscĕŏ, īmmīscĕŏ. *To enroll.* Syn.—Ādscrībŏ, āddŏ, ānnŭmĕrŏ.

Īnsērvĭŏ, īs, ĭī, ītūm, īrĕ. *To be a slave to. See Servio. To be occupied with.* Syn.—Īnvĭgĭlŏ, cūrŏ, stŭdĕŏ.

Īnsĭdĭæ, ārūm. f. *Snares, ambuscade.* Nūllae hīc īnsĭdĭæ tālēs ābsīstĕ mŏvērī. V. Syn.—Dŏlī, fraūs, fraūdēs, lăquĕī. Phr.—Fāllēndī vĭæ.

Īnsĭdĭŏr, ārĭs, ātŭs sūm, ārī. *To lay snares.* Phr.—Īnsĭdĭās pōnŏ, īnstrŭŏ, mĕdĭtŏr, lŏcŏ, cōmpărŏ. Dŏlōs, rētĭă, lăquĕōs, plăgās nēctŏ. Ōccūltās lătĕbrās fērro ōbsĭdĕŏ. Īn sīlvīs ārmīs īnsĭdĕŏ. Sĕdĕt ēnsĕ rĕpōstō Ābdĭtŭs.

Īnsĭdĭōsŭs, ă, ūm. *Insidious, perfidious.* Syn.—Īnsĭdĭāns, pērfĭdŭs, dŏlōsŭs.

Īnsīgnĕ, ĭs. n. *Mark, sign.* Mūtēmūs clўpĕōs, Dănăūmque īnsīgnĭă nōbīs Āptēmŭs. Syn.—Sīgnūm, nŏtă, īndĭcĭūm, dĕcŭs, ōrnātŭs, ōrnāmēntūm.

Īnsīgnĭŏ, īs, īvī & ĭī, ītūm, īrĕ. *To render remarkable.* Clўpĕum aūro īnsīgnābăt. V. Syn.—Īllūstrŏ, dĕcŏrŏ, cōndĕcŏrŏ, ōrnŏ, ēxōrnŏ.

Īnsīgnĭs, ĭs, ĕ. *Remarkable, noticeable.* Īpsī pēr mĕdĭās ăcĭēs īnsīgnĭbŭs ālīs. V. Syn.—Clārŭs, cōnspĭcŭŭs, spēctābĭlĭs, nĭtēns, cōnspĭcĭēndŭs, ēgrĕgĭŭs, ēxĭmĭŭs, īnclўtŭs, īllūstrĭs, nōbĭlĭs, præstāns, cĕlĕbĕr. Phr.—Ōstrōque īnsīgnĭs ĕt aūrō. Mūltāque īnsīgnēm rĕddĭdĭt ārtĕ.

Īnsĭlĭŏ, īs, ŭī & ĭī, ūltūm, īrĕ. *To jump into or upon.* Syn.—Īrrŭŏ, sălĭŏ, ēmĭcŏ.

Īnsĭmŭlŏ, ās, āvī, ātūm, ārĕ. *To accuse.* Crīmĭnĭbūs fālsīs īnsĭmŭlārĕ vĭrūm. O. Syn.—Āccūsŏ, crīmĭnŏr, ārgŭŏ.

Īnsĭnŭŏ, ās, āvī, ātūm, ārĕ. *To introduce into.* Syn.—Īndŏ, īndūcŏ, īnsĕrŏ, īmmīttŏ, īnfūndŏ. *To insinuate, to penetrate.* Syn.—Īnsĭnŭŏr, pĕnĕtrŏ, sŭbĕŏ, pērmĕŏ, īntrŏ, īrrēpŏ, īnfūndŏr, īllābŏr.

Īnsīstŏ, ĭs, stĭtī, stĭtūm, ĕrĕ. *To hold firm.* Răpĭdīsquĕ rŏtīs īnsīstĕrĕ vīctŏr. V. Syn.—Cōnsīstŏ, īnnītŏr, nītŏr.

Īnsŏlēns, ēntĭs. adj. *Unaccustomed.* Syn.—Īnsuētŭs, īnsŏlĭtŭs, īnēxpērtŭs. *Arrogant. See Superbus.*

Īnsŏlĭtŭs, ă, ūm. *Unaccustomed.* Præbēnt īnsŏlĭtās ād jŭgă cūrvă jŭbās. O. Syn.—Īnsuētŭs, īnsŏlēns, ĭnāssuētŭs. *Extraordinary.* Syn.—Īnsuētŭs, ĭnaūdītŭs, ĭnēxpērtŭs, īntēntātŭs, mīrŭs, nŏvŭs.

Īnsōmnĭs, ĭs, ĕ. *Sleepless.* Nōctēm cūstōdĭă dūcĭt Īnsōmnēm. V. Syn.—Vĭgĭl, pērvĭgĭl, vĭgĭlāns, īnsōpītŭs, pērnōx. Phr.—Sōmni ĭnōps, ēxpērs, īmmĕmŏr, ĭgnārŭs. Nĕque ĕnīm mēmbrīs dāt cūră quĭētēm.

Īnsōmnĭūm, ĭī. n. *Dream, vision.* Syn.—Sōmnĭūm, vīsūm.

Īnsŏnŏ, ās, ŭī, ārĕ. *To sound, to make a noise.* Īnsŏnŭērĕ căvæ, gĕmĭtūmquĕ dĕdērĕ căvērnæ. V. Syn.—Sŏnŏ, rĕsŏnŏ, pērsŏnŏ, pērstrĕpŏ.

Īnspĭcĭŏ, ĭs, ēxī, ēctūm, ĕrĕ. *To regard, to examine* Syn.—Rēspĭcĭŏ, spectŏ, inspectŏ, intŭĕŏr.

Īnspīrŏ, ās, āvī, ātūm, ārĕ. *To breathe into.* Ōccūltum īnspīrēs ĭgnēm fāllāsquĕ vĕnēnō. V. Syn.—Āfflŏ, īmmīttŏ, īnsĭnŭŏ, īnfūndŏ. *To inspire. See Afflo.*

Īnstăr. adv. *Like, just as.* Syn.—Sīcŭt, ŭt, vĕlŭt, vĕlŭtī, lŏcō, rītū, mōrĕ.

Īnstaūrŏ, ās, āvī, ātūm, ārĕ. *To restore.* Syn.—Rēstaūrŏ, rĕfĭcĭŏ, rēstĭtŭŏ, rĕpărŏ, rĕnŏvŏ, rĕdīntĕgrŏ, părŏ, cĕlĕbrŏ.

Īnstīgŏ, ās, āvī, ātūm, ārĕ. *To instigate, to excite.* Fērtŭr ĕquō, vărĭīsque īnstīgāt vōcĭbŭs ālās. V. Syn.—Īncĭtŏ, cōncĭtŏ, īmpēllŏ, hōrtŏr, ăcŭŏ, ēxăcŭŏ. Phr.—Īnstīgāntĕ dĕō.

Īnstĭtŭŏ, ĭs, ŭī, ūtūm, ĕrĕ. *To commence, to undertake.* Āmphŏră cœpĭt Īnstĭtŭī; cūrrēntĕ rŏtā cūr ūrcĕŭs ēxĭt? H. Syn.—Īncĭpĭŏ, āggrĕdĭŏr, sūscĭpĭŏ, ĭnĕŏ, īnchŏŏ, mōlĭŏr. *To establish, to construct.* Syn.—Stătŭŏ, cōnstĭtŭŏ, pōnŏ, strŭŏ, īnstrŭŏ, părŏ, īnstaūrŏ.

Īnstŏ, ās, ĭtī, ārĕ. *To press, to pursue.* Trĕpĭdāntī fērvĭdŭs īnstăt. V. Syn.—Īnsīstŏ, ūrgĕŏ, prĕmŏ, pērsĕquŏr, sĕquŏr. Phr.—Īnstāt vī pătrĭā Pўrrhŭs. Dūm nītĭtŭr ăcĕr ĕt īnstăt. *To threaten.* Syn.—Īmmĭnĕŏ, īmpēndĕŏ, mĭnĭtŏr. *To insist upon.* Syn.—Īnsīstŏ, văcŏ, īncūmbŏ, īnsūdŏ.

Īnstrūmēntūm, ī. n. *Instrument.* Syn.—Ārmă.

Īnstrŭŏ, ĭs, ūxī, ūctūm, ĕrĕ. *To furnish.* Syn.—Ōrnŏ, ārmŏ. *To prepare, to dispose.* Syn.—Strŭŏ, cōllŏcŏ, pōnŏ, dīspōnŏ, cōmpōnŏ, ōrdĭnŏ, părŏ, āppărŏ.

Īnsūdŏ, ās, āvī, ātūm, ārĕ. *To perspire over.* Syn.—Sūdŏ. Fig.—*To apply oneself with energy.* Syn.—Sūdŏ, dēsūdŏ, īnstŏ, īncūmbŏ.

Īnsuētŭs, ă, ūm. *Unaccustomed.* Ārcădās īnsuētōs ăcĭēs īnfērrĕ pĕdēstrēs. V. Syn.—Īnsŏlĭtŭs, īnsŏlēns, ĭnāssuētŭs, īncōnsuētŭs, ĭnēxpērtŭs, rŭdĭs, ĭgnārŭs, nēscĭŭs.

Īnsŭlă, æ. f. *Island.* Phr.—Tēllūs ăquīs, æquŏrĕ, pōntō, mărī cīnctă, claūsă, cīrcūmdătă. Tērră flūmĭnĕ āmbītă, cīrcūmvāllātă. Mĕdĭō jăcĕt īnsŭlă pōntō. Sēntīt hŭmūs sūccīnctă sălō.

Īnsūlsŭs, ă, ūm. *Tasteless.* Syn.—Īnsĭpĭdŭs, fătŭŭs, ĭnērs. Fig.—*Foolish.* Syn.—Fătŭŭs, ĭnēptŭs.

Īnsūm, ĕs, fŭī, ēssĕ. *To be present.* Syn.—Sūm, ădsūm, vērsŏr.

Īnsūmŏ, ĭs, psī, ptūm, ĕrĕ. *To take. See Sumo. To expend.* Syn.—Īmpēndŏ, cōnsūmŏ, ūtŏr.

Īnsŭpĕr. adv. *Above.* Syn.—Sŭpĕr, sŭprā. *Besides.* Syn.—Sŭpĕr, ădhūc, ūltrā, ūltĕrĭŭs, prætĕrĕā. (prep.) *Above. See Super.*

Īnsŭpĕrābĭlĭs, ĭs, ĕ. *Insurmountable.* Hīnc Gētūlae ūrbēs, gĕnŭs īnsŭpĕrābĭlĕ bēllō. V. Syn.—Īnēxpūgnābĭlĭs, īndŏmĭtŭs, īnvīctŭs.

Īnsūrgŏ, ĭs, rēxī, rēctūm, ĕrĕ. *To attack.* Syn.—Sūrgŏ, cōnsūrgŏ, āggrĕdĭŏr. *See Aggredior.*

Īntĕgĕr, gră, grūm. *Whole, entire.* Syn.—Īntāctŭs, tōtŭs, sŏlĭdŭs, īllībātŭs, īntēntātŭs, ĭnāttĕnŭātŭs. Phr.—Nōn tĭbĭ sūnt īntĕgră līntĕă. *Fresh, vigorous.* Syn.—Vălēns, vălĭdŭs, vĕgĕtŭs, fīrmŭs, rōbūstŭs. *Virtuous, innocent.* Syn.—Īnnŏcēns, īncōrrūptŭs, cāstŭs.

Īntĕgrŏ, ās, āvī, ātūm, ārĕ. *To renew, to recommence.* Rāmōquĕ sĕdēns mĭsĕrābĭlĕ cārmĕn Īntĕgrăt. V. Syn.—Īnstaūrŏ, rĕnŏvŏ, rĕpărŏ, rĕfĭcĭŏ, ĭtĕrŏ, gĕmĭnŏ, īngĕmĭnŏ.

Īntēllēctŭs, ūs. m. *Intelligence.* Syn.—Mēns, ănĭmŭs, rătĭŏ.

Īntēllĕgŏ, ĭs, ēxī, ēctūm, ĕrĕ. *To understand.* Bārbărŭs hīc ĕgŏ sūm, quĭă nōn īntēllĕgŏr īllīs. O. Syn.—Căpĭŏ, pērcĭpĭŏ, cōncĭpĭŏ, cōgnōscŏ, āgnōscŏ. Phr.—Ănĭmō pērcĭpĭŏ. Mēntĕ cōmplēctī. Ănĭmō īnfīgĕrĕ.

Īntēmpĕrāns, ntĭs. adj. *Intemperate, immoderate.* Syn.—Īntēmpĕrātŭs, īmmŏdĕrātŭs, īncōntĭnēns, īmmŏdēstŭs, ēffrēnŭs, īmpŭdīcŭs.

Īntēndŏ, ĭs, dī, ĕrĕ. *To stretch.* Ārcum īntēndēbăt Ăpōllŏ. V. Syn.—Tēndŏ, cōntēndŏ. *To direct one's attention towards.* Syn.—Ădhĭbĕŏ, āpplĭcŏ, ādvērtŏ, ādjĭcĭŏ, ādmŏvĕŏ, dīrĭgŏ.

Īntĕpĕŏ, ēs, ŭī, ērĕ. *To grow warm.* Syn.—Tĕpĕŏ, tĕpēscŏ, īntĕpēscŏ, tĕpĕfīŏ, călēscŏ, īncălēscŏ.

Īntērcēdŏ, ĭs, ssī, ssūm, ĕrĕ. *To come between.* Syn.—Īncĭdŏ, īntērcĭdŏ, sŭpērvĕnĭŏ, īntērvĕnĭŏ.

Īntērcĭdŏ, ĭs, ī, ĕrĕ. *To fall, to perish.* Syn.—Cădŏ, īntĕrĕŏ, pĕrĕŏ, ăbĕŏ, ăbŏlēscŏ.

Īntērcīdŏ, ĭs, dī, sūm, ĕrĕ. *To cut through.* Syn.—Cædŏ, scīndŏ, sĕcŏ, dīvĭdŏ.

Īntērcĭpĭō, ĭs, ēpī, ēptūm, ĕrĕ. *To intercept.* Syn.—Ēxcĭpĭō, ŏpprĭmō. *To destroy.* Syn.—Īntērfĭcĭō, ŏpprĭmō, ēvērtō, ērŭō. *To make way with.* Syn.—Sūbdūcō, sūbrĭpĭō, ērĭpĭō.

Īntērdīcō, ĭs, xī, ctūm, ĕrĕ. *To interdict, to forbid.* Īllă sŭām vŏcăt hănc, cuī quŏndăm rēgĭă Jūnō Ōrbe īntērdīxĭt. O. Syn.—Vĕtō, prŏhĭbĕō, īntērclūdō.

Īntērdĭū. adv. *During the day.* Syn.—Dĭē, lūcĕ. Phr.—Īn lūcĕ dĭūrnā.

Īntērdūm. adv. *Sometimes.* Syn.—Ălĭquāndō, nōnnūnquăm, quāndōquĕ, sæpĕ.

Īntĕrĕā. adv. *Meanwhile.* Syn.—Īntĕrĭm, tūm. Phr.—Hæc īntĕr.

Īntĕrĕō, īs, īvī & ĭī, ĭtūm, īrĕ. *To perish.* Īntĕrĭt ēt cūrvīs frūstra dēfēnsă lătēbrīs Vīpĕră. V. Syn.—Pĕrĕō. *See Pereo.*

Īntērfĭcĭō, ĭs, ēcī, ēctūm, ĕrĕ. *To kill, to destroy.* Fēr stăbŭlīs ĭnĭmīcum ĭgnem ătque īntērfĭcĕ mēssēs. V. Syn.—Pĕrĭmō, dīrŭō, ăbŏlĕō, ēvērtō, ērŭō, nĕcō, ēnĕcō, īntĕrĭmō. *See Occīdo.*

Īntērflŭō, ĭs, ŭī, ūxūm, ĕrĕ. *To flow between.* Syn.—Īntērlŭō, īntērlăbŏr.

Īntĕrĭmō, ĭs, ēmī, ēmptūm, ĕrĕ. *To destroy.* Syn.—Ŏpprĭmō, sūpprĭmō, pērdō, īntērfĭcĭō, īntērcĭpĭō. *To kill. See Occīdo.*

Īntĕrĭŏr, ŭs. *Inner, retired.* Syn.—Īntērnŭs, īntĭmŭs, īmŭs, rĕmōtŭs.

Īntērjĭcĭō, ĭs, ēcī, ēctūm, ĕrĕ. *To place between.* Syn.—Īntērpōnō, īntērsĕrō.

Īntērlūcĕō, ēs, xī, ērĕ. *To shine between.* Syn.—Īntērmĭcō, īntērnĭtĕō.

Īntērmĭnātŭs, ă, ūm. *Unending.* Syn.—Īntērmĭnŭs, īnfīnītŭs, īmmēnsŭs.

Īntērpēllō, ās, avī, ātūm, ārĕ. *To interrupt.* Īntērpēllāndī lŏcŭs hīc ĕrăt. H. Syn.—Īntērfārī, īntērlŏquŏr, īntērrūmpō.

Īntērpōnō, ĭs, ŏsŭī, ŏsĭtūm, ĕrĕ. *To interpose.* Syn.—Īntērjĭcĭō, īntērsĕrō, īntērmīscĕō, mīscĕō.

Īntērrĭtŭs, ă, ūm. *Unterrified.* Brāchĭăque ād sŭpĕrās īntērrĭtŭs ēxtŭlĭt aūrās. V. Syn.—Īmpērtērrĭtŭs, īmpăvĭdŭs, īntrĕpĭdŭs. Phr.—Nōn tērrĭtŭs. Tĭmōrĭs ēxpērs. Mētū īmmūnĭs. Nīl mētŭēns. Fōrmīdĭnĕ nūllā. *See Audax.*

Īntērrŏgō, ās, āvī, ātūm, ārĕ. *To ask.* Syn.—Quærō, īnquīrō, scīscĭtŏr, scītŏr, pērcōntŏr, rŏgō, rŏgĭtō, rĕquīrō. Phr.—Vĕnĭēndī quærĕrĕ caūsās. Mūltă sŭpēr Prĭămō rŏgĭtāns. Naūtās rŏgĭtārĕ cĭtātōs.

Īntērrūmpō, ĭs, ūpī, ūptūm, ĕrĕ. *To interrupt.* Syn.—Ābrūmpō, īntērcĭpĭō, tūrbō, īntērlŏquŏr.

Īntērsĕrŏ, ĭs, sēvī, sĭtūm, ĕrĕ. *To plant among.* Syn.—Īntērpōnŏ, īmmīscĕŏ, mīscĕŏ.

Īntērsĕrŏ, ĭs, ĕrŭī, ērtūm, ĕrĕ. *To insert among.* Syn.—Īntērmīscĕŏ, īntērjĭcĭŏ, mīscĕŏ, īmmīscĕŏ.

Īntērsūm, ĕs, fŭī, ēssĕ. *To be present.* Lætŭs īntērsīs pŏpŭlō Quĭrīnī. H. Syn.—Ādsūm. Phr.—Præsēns sūm. Impers. *It matters.* Syn.—Prōdēst, rēfērt.

Īntērvāllūm, ī. n. *Interval.* Prōxĭmŭs huīc, lōngō sēd prōxĭmŭs īntērvāllō. V. Syn.—Īntērstĭtĭūm, spătĭūm.

Īntērvĕnĭŏ, īs, vēnī, vēntūm, īrĕ. *To come upon.* Syn.—Ādsūm, īntērcēdŏ, sŭpērvĕnĭŏ, ōccūrrŏ. *To oppose.* Syn.—Ōbstŏ. *See Obsto.*

Īntēstīnŭs, ă, ūm. *Internal, inward.* Syn.—Īntĕrĭŏr, īntĭmŭs, īntērnŭs. *Domestic, civil.* Syn.—Dŏmēstĭcŭs, cīvīlĭs.

Īntēxŏ, ĭs, ŭī, tūm, ĕrĕ. *To weave into.* Īllă tĭbī lætīs īntēxīt vītĭbŭs ūlmōs. V. Syn.—Tēxŏ, īnnēctŏ, īmpĕdĭŏ, īntērsĕrŏ, īmplĭcŏ.

Īntrā. prep. *In, among.* Syn.—Īntĕr, ĭn, īntrōrsūm. *Within the space of.* Syn.—Pĕr, īntĕr.

Īntrăctābĭlĭs, ĭs, ĕ. *Unconquerable.* Syn.—Āspĕr, fĕrōx, īndŏmĭtŭs. *Harsh, severe.* Syn.—Sævŭs, āspĕr, dīrŭs, ācĕr, ĭnīquŭs.

Īntrĕmīscŏ & Īntrĕmŏ, ĭs, ŭī, ĕrĕ. *To tremble.* Pāllŭĭt ēt sŭbĭtō gĕnŭa īntrĕmŭērĕ tĭmōrĕ. O. Syn.—Trĕmīscŏ, trĕpĭdŏ. *See Tremo.*

Īntrŏ, ās, āvī, ātūm, ārĕ. *To enter.* Jāmquĕ, căpūt rērūm, Rōmānam īntrāvĕrăt ūrbēm. O. Syn.—Īngrĕdĭŏr, ĭnĕŏ, sŭbĕŏ, īntrŏĕŏ, īntrōgrĕdĭŏr, sūccēdŏ, pĕnētrŏ. Phr.—Pĕdēm īnfĕrŏ. Vēstīgĭă, pĕdēs fĕrŏ. Fŏrĭbŭs mē īnfĕrŏ.

Īntrōdūcŏ, ĭs, xī, ctūm, ĕrĕ. *To introduce, to lead into.* Syn.—Ādmīttŏ, īntrōmīttŏ, īndūcŏ.

Īntrŏĕŏ, īs, īvī, ĭtūm, īrĕ. *To enter.* Syn.—Īngrĕdĭŏr, īntrŏ.

Īntrŏĭtŭs, ūs. m. *Entrance.* Syn.—Īngrēssŭs. *Approach.* Syn.—Ădĭtŭs, līmĕn. *Exordium.* Syn.—Ēxōrdĭūm.

Īntŭĕŏr, ērĭs, ĭtŭs sūm, ērī. *To regard.* Syn.—Cērnŏ, vĭdĕŏ, īnspĭcĭŏ, spēctŏ, cōntēmplŏr. Phr.—Vūltūs, ŏcŭlōs, lūmĭnă fīgŏ ĭn. Ŏcŭlīs lūstrŏ, ōbsērvŏ. *See Aspicio.*

Īntŭmĕŏ, ēs, ŭī, ērĕ. *To swell.* Syn.—Īntŭmēscŏ, tŭmĕŏ, tŭmĕfīŏ, īnflŏr. Fig.—*To become angry. See Irascor.*

Īntŭs. adv. *Within.* Syn.—Īntrā, īntĕrĭŭs, īntrīnsĕcŭs, īntrōrsūm.

Īnūndātĭŏ, ōnĭs. f. *Inundation.* Syn.—Dīlŭvĭūm, ēlŭvĭēs. Phr.—Ēdĭtă cœlō prōlŭvĭēs. Ēlŭvĭēs fātālĭs ăquæ. Ēxcūrrīt rīpās. Flŭvĭōs rūptīs īmmīttĕrĕ rīpīs.

Ĭnūndō, ās, āvī, ātūm, ārĕ. *To inundate.* Syn.—Mădĕfăcĭō. *To overflow with.* Syn.—Ēxūndō, ēffūndŏr, dīfflŭō, flŭō, nătō, mānō, mădĕō.

Ĭnūrō, ĭs, ūssī, ūstūm, ĕrĕ. *To brand.* Syn.—Īmprĭmō, nŏtō, īnscrībō.

Ĭnūtĭlĭs, ĭs, ĕ. *Useless.* Syn.—Cāssŭs, ĭnānĭs, īrrĭtŭs, vānŭs, fūtĭlĭs.

Īnvādō, ĭs, sī, sūm, ĕrĕ. *To march upon, to attack.* Īnvādūnt ūrbēm sōmnō vīnōquĕ sĕpūltām. V. Syn.—Ădŏrĭŏr, āggrĕdĭŏr, ōccŭpō, īmpĕtō, īncūrrō, īrrŭō, fĕrŏr, īnvŏlō, īnsĭlĭō, īrrūmpō. Phr.—Fōrti ănĭmo īn hōstēs tēndĕrĕ. Īn hōstēs īrrŭĕrĕ. Īrrŭĭmūs fērrō. Dēnsōs prōrūmpĭt ĭn hōstēs. Mĕdĭīs se īmmīscŭĭt ārmīs. *To undertake.* Syn.—Āggrĕdĭŏr, sūscĭpĭō, ĭnĕō, tēntō, mōlĭŏr.

Īnvălĕō, ēs, ŭī, ērĕ. *To strengthen oneself.* Īnvălŭĭt, vīrēsquĕ nŏvās ēt rōbŏră sūmpsĭt. O. Syn.—Īnvălēscō, vĭgēscō, cōrrōbŏrŏr. Phr.—Vīrēs sūmō.

Īnvălĭdŭs, ă, ūm. *Weak, infirm.* Syn.—Dēbĭlĭs, dēbĭlĭtātŭs, īnfīrmŭs, īmbēcīllĭs.

Īnvĕhō, ĭs, ēxī, ēctūm, ĕrĕ. *To transport. See Fero, Veho.* (*In passive*) *To attack.* Syn.—Īnsēctŏr, ūrgĕō, īncrĕpō.

Īnvĕnĭō, īs, vēnī, ēntūm, īrĕ. *To find.* Ēt quōs nōn hăbŭĭt, sūb nūbĭbŭs īnvĕnĭt īgnēs. O. Syn.—Rĕpĕrĭō, rēppĕrĭō, nāncīscŏr, cōmpĕrĭō, īncĭdō, ōccūrrō.

Īnvēntŏr, ōrĭs. m. *Inventor, author.* Syn.—Aŭctŏr, rĕpērtŏr, commēntŏr, ārtĭfēx, ŏpĭfēx.

Īnvĕnūstŭs, ă, ūm. *Ungraceful.* Syn.—Incōmptŭs, īllĕpĭdŭs, ĭnūrbānŭs, tūrpĭs.

Īnvērgō, ĭs, ĕrĕ. *To pour over.* Syn.—Fūndō, īnfūndō.

Īnvēstīgō, ās, āvī, ātūm, ārĕ. *To investigate.* Syn.—Vēstīgō, īndāgō, quærō, īnquīrō, scrūtŏr.

Īnvĭcēm. adv. *Mutually, in turn.* Syn.—Vĭcīssīm, āltērnīs, mūtŭō. Phr—Īntēr sē. Īnquĕ vĭcēs ĕquĭtānt.

Īnvīctŭs, ă, ūm. *Unconquerable.* Dīs quāmquām gĕnĭti ātque īnvīctī vīrībŭs ēssēnt. V. Syn.—Īndŏmĭtŭs, īnfrāctŭs, īnsŭpĕrābĭlĭs, ĭnēxpūgnābĭlĭs, ĭnēxsŭpĕrābĭlĭs. Phr.—Nōndūm dŏmĭtŭs. Nūllā vī, ārtĕ sŭpĕrābĭlĭs. Vīrībŭs īnvīctŭs. Căpŭt īnsŭpĕrābĭlĕ bēllō. Īnvīctūs Rōmānō Mārtĕ Brĭtānnŭs. *Indefatigable.* Syn.—Dūrŭs, īmpĭgĕr, īndēfēssŭs, ācĕr.

Īnvĭdĕō, ēs, īdī, īsūm, ērĕ. *To envy.* Cōncēdĭt laŭdem, ēt părībūs nōn īnvĭdĕt ārmīs. V. Syn.—Aēmŭlŏr, līvĕō, līvēscō. Phr.—Līvōrĕ, răbĭē, īnvĭdĭā cōnfĭcĭŏr, vēxŏr, ăgĭtŏr. Ălĭēnīs bŏnīs mœrĕō. Līvŏr ĕdāx præcōrdĭā rōdĭt.

Īnvĭdĭă, æ. f. *Envy, jealousy.* Īnvĭdĭă Sĭcŭlī nōn īnvēnērĕ tўrānnī Tōrmēntūm mājŭs. H. Syn.—Līvŏr. Phr.—Īnvĭdĭæ līvŏr. Īnvĭdă līnguă. Īngēntĭă fāctă rōdĭt. Răbĭēm līvōrĭs ăcērbī nūllă pŏtēst plācārĕ dĭēs.

Īnvĭdĭōsŭs, ă, ūm. *Envious.* Tēmpŭs ĕdāx rērūm, tūque īnvĭdĭōsă vĕtūstās. O. Syn.—Īnvĭdŭs. *Odious, revolting.* Syn.—Īndīgnŭs, fœdŭs, hōrrēndŭs.

Īnvĭdŭs, ă, ūm. *Jealous, envious.* Īnvĭdŭs āltĕrĭŭs rēbūs mācrēscĭt ŏpīmīs. H. Syn.—Īnvĭdĭōsŭs, æmŭlŭs, līvĭdŭs. Phr.—Cuī nŏcēns vīrŭs īnspīrăt līvŏr. Nĭmĭăque ærūgĭnĕ cāptŭs.

Īnvĭŏlābĭlĭs, ĭs, ĕ. *Inviolable, sacred.* Syn.—Săcĕr, vĕnĕrāndŭs, vĕrēndŭs.

Īnvĭŏlātŭs, ă, ūm. *Inviolate.* Syn.—Īntĕgĕr, īntāctŭs, īntĕmĕrātŭs, īncōrrūptŭs, īllæsŭs.

Īnvīsŏ, ĭs, ī, sūm, ĕrĕ. *To visit.* Syn.—Vīsŏ, ădĕŏ, cōnvĕnĭŏ, lūstrŏ, pērlūstrŏ.

Īnvīsŭs, ă, ūm. *Unseen.* Ābdĭdĕrāt sēse ātque ārīs īnvīsă sĕdēbăt. V. Syn.—Ĭnāspēctŭs, ĭnŏbsērvātŭs, ōccūltŭs, ābdĭtŭs, lătēns. *Disagreeable.* Syn.—Ŏdĭōsŭs, īnvĭdĭōsŭs, mŏlēstŭs, grăvĭs, īmpōrtūnŭs, dētēstātŭs.

Īnvītŏ, ās, āvī, ātūm, ārĕ. *To invite.* Āccĭpĭt Aēnēān sŏlĭōque īnvītăt ăcērnō. V. Syn.—Vŏcŏ, ādvŏcŏ. *To excite.* Syn.—Vŏcŏ, prōvŏcŏ, īnstīgŏ, trăhŏ, āllĭcĭŏ, īllĭcĭŏ, pēllĭcĭŏ, sōllĭcĭtŏ, suādĕŏ, īmpēllŏ, hōrtŏr.

Īnvītŭs, ă, ūm. *Unwilling.* Īnvītŭs, rēgīnă, tŭō dē līttŏrĕ cēssī. V. Syn.—Cŏāctŭs, nōlēns, rĕpūgnāns, rĕlūctāns. Phr.—Nōn lĭbēns. Nōn ūltrō. Nōn sĭnĕ vī. Vīs trăhĭt īnvītām. Vīm tŭlĭt īnvītæ. Ītălĭām nōn spōntĕ sĕquŏr.

Īnvĭŭs, ă, ūm. *Inaccessible.* Lōngă prŏcŭl lōngīs vĭă dīvĭdĭt īnvĭă tērrīs. V. Syn.—Īmpērvĭŭs, ĭnāccēssŭs, īmpĕnĕtrābĭlĭs, ĭnăpērtŭs, ĭnhōspĭtŭs, dĭffĭcĭlĭs, īnsŭpĕrābĭlĭs, ārdŭŭs. Phr.—Āspĕr āccēssū. Nōn pērvĭŭs. Nōn ădĕūndŭs. Mărĭa īnvĭă Teūcrīs.

Īnvŏcŏ, ās, āvī, ātūm, ārĕ. *To call upon for aid.* Īnvŏcăt ēt dŭplĭcēs Cœlōque Ĕrĕbōquĕ părēntēs. V. Syn.—Rŏgŏ, prĕcŏr, īmplōrŏ, pōscŏ, ēxpōscŏ, ōbtēstŏr.

Īnvŏlŏ, ās, āvī, ātūm, ārĕ. *To fly upon.* Syn.—Īnsĭlĭŏ, īmpĕtŏ, īnvādŏ, īrrŭŏ.

Īnvōlvŏ, ĭs, ī, ŏlūtūm, ĕrĕ. *To roll into, to envelop.* Īnvōlvēns ūmbrā māgnā tērrāmquĕ pŏlūmquĕ. V. Syn.—Īmplĭcŏ, cīngŏ, cīrcūmdŏ, āmbĭŏ, ābscōndŏ, ābdŏ, tēgŏ, cōmprēndŏ, āmplēctŏr.

Īră, æ. f. *Wrath.* Cāndĭdă pāx hŏmĭnēs, trūx dĕcĕt īră fĕrās. O. Syn.—Bīlĭs, stŏmăchŭs, dŏlŏr, fŭrŏr, răbĭēs, vĭŏlēntĭă, īrācūndĭă, ănĭmī. Phr.—Īræ stĭmŭlī. Īrārum æstŭs. Fāx īræ. Mēntĭs fŭrĭæ. Īrātūs dŏlŏr. Fŭrōrĭs cŏmĕs. Īră călĕt.

Īrācŭndŭs, ă, ūm. *Wrathful.* Īrācŭndăquĕ mēns făcĭle ēffērvēscĭt ĭn īrās. Syn.—Stŏmăchōsŭs, īrrītābĭlĭs, călĭdŭs. Phr.—Īn īrām prōmptŭs. Īmmŏdĭcŭs īræ.

Īrāscŏr, ārĭs, rātŭs sūm, ārī. *To become angry.* Nēc cuīquam īrāscī prŏpĭŭsque ăccēdĕrĕ vīrtūs. V. Syn.—Sŭccēnsĕŏ, īndīgnŏr, stŏmăchŏr, ēxcāndēscŏ, ēxārdĕŏ, fŭrŏ, sævĭŏ, æstŭŏ. Phr.—Īrā flăgrŏ, ārdĕŏ. Īră mēntēm, ănĭmūm ăgĭtăt, mŏvĕt. Īrās cōncĭpĭŏ. Mēns īrā tŭmĕt. Cæcō fŭrōrĕ īnsānĭŏ. Flūctŭăt īră.

Īrātŭs, ă, ūm. *Angry.* Jām vĕnĭt īrātūs nĭmĭūm, nĭmĭūmquĕ sĕvērŭs. Tib. Syn.—Fŭrēns, răbĭdŭs, īndīgnāns, īndīgnātŭs, fŭrĭōsŭs, flāmmātŭs, īrrītātŭs, cōmmōtŭs, āccēnsŭs, īrācŭndŭs. Phr.—Īrā pērcĭtŭs, flăgrāns, āccēnsŭs. Fŭrēns ănĭmīs. Īræ nōn pătĭēns. Ūltro īmplācābĭlĭs ārdĕt.

Īrĭs, ĭdĭs. f. *Rainbow.* Phr.—Cœlēstĭs, plŭvĭŭs ārcŭs. *See Appendix.*

Īrĭs, ĭdĭs. f. *The iris.* (*See Appendix under list of Trees, etc.*)

Īrrădĭŏ, ās, āvī, ātūm, ārĕ. *To illuminate.* Syn.—Rădĭŏ, īllūcĕŏ, īllūmĭnŏ, īllūstrŏ.

Īrrēpŏ, ĭs, sī, tūm, ĕrĕ. *To creep into.* Syn.—Īrrēptŏ, īnsĭnŭŏ, īnsĭnŭŏr. *See Repo.*

Īrrĕquĭēs, ētĭs & Īrrĕquĭētŭs, ă, ūm. *Continued.* Syn.—Cōntĭnŭŭs, āssĭdŭŭs. *Restless.* Syn.—Īnquĭētŭs, tūrbŭlēntŭs, sōllĭcĭtŭs, pērvĭgĭl, īnsōmnĭs.

Īrrētĭŏ, īs, īvī & ĭī, ītūm, īrĕ. *To ensnare.* Syn.—Īmplĭcŏ, īllăquĕŏ, īntrīcŏ. Phr.—Īn rētĭă mīttŏ. Rētĭbŭs căpĭŏ, īnvōlvŏ.

Īrrīdĕŏ, ēs, sī, sūm, ērĕ. *To mock, to ridicule.* Syn.—Rīdĕŏ, dērīdĕŏ, īllūdŏ, īnsūltŏ, jŏcŏr, căvīllŏr, lūdĭfĭcŏr. Phr.—Rīsū, căchīnnō, jŏcīs ēxcĭpĭŏ. Īn rīsūm vērtŏ. Cērtānt īllūdĕrĕ căptō.

Īrrĭgŏ, ās, āvī, ātūm, ārĕ. *To water.* Syn.—Rĭgŏ, āspērgŏ, hūmēctŏ, īrrōrŏ.

Īrrītŏ, ās, āvī, ātūm, ārĕ. *To irritate, to provoke.* Īrrītātquĕ vĭrūm tēlīs āc vōcĕ lăcēssĭt. V. Syn.—Prōvŏcŏ, lăcēssŏ, ēxāspĕrŏ. Phr.—Ăd īrām prŏvŏcŏ. Īrās ăcŭŏ.

Īrrĭtŭs, ă, ūm. *Vain, useless.* Tēlă mănū mĭsĕrī jăctābānt īrrĭtă Teŭcrī. V. Syn.—Vānŭs, cāssŭs, ĭnānĭs, ĭnūtĭlĭs.

Īrrŭŏ, ĭs, ŭī, ĕrĕ. *To rush upon.* Īrrŭĭmūs, dēnsīs ēt cīrcūmfūndĭmŭr ārmīs. V. Syn.—Rŭŏ, īncūrrŏ, īrrūmpŏ, īnsĭlĭŏ, prōsĭlĭŏ, præcĭpĭtŏ, fĕrŏr, īnvādŏ, āggrĕdĭŏr, īmpĕtŏ, ădŏrĭŏr, īngrŭŏ. Phr.—Mē fĕrŏ. Sē dĕdĭt īn mĕdĭās ăcĭēs. Răpĭdō fērtŭr īmpĕtĕ mīlĕs.

Īs, ĕă, ĭd. *This, that.* Syn.—Hīc, īstĕ, īllĕ.

Īsthīc. adv. *There.* Syn.—Hīc, īllīc.

Īsthīnc. adv. *Thence.* Syn.—Hīnc, īndĕ, īllīnc.

Ĭtă adv. *Thus.* Syn.—Sīc. Phr.—Nōn ălĭtĕr, haūd sĕcŭs, nōn sĕcŭs. *So, of such a kind.* Syn.—Sīc, ădĕō, tām, tāntūm.

Ĭtăquĕ. conj. *Therefore.* Syn.—Ērgŏ, ĭgĭtŭr, quārē, quāprōptĕr, ĭdĕō, īdcīrcō.

Ĭtēm. adv. *Also, likewise.* Syn.—Aēquē, părĭtĕr, ĭtĭdēm, prætĕrĕā, īnsŭpĕr, ădhūc, rūrsŭs, rūrsūm, ĭtĕrūm.

Ĭtĕr, ĭtĭnĕrĭs. n. *Route, journey.* Vīrtūs nĕgātā tēntăt ĭtĕr vĭā. H. Syn.—Vĭă, sēmĭtă, cāllĭs, trāmĕs, ădĭtŭs. Phr.—Vīcĭt ĭtĕr dūrūm pĭĕtās. Ĭtĕr ăd nāvēs tēndēbăt.

Ĭtĕrŏ, ās, āvī, ātūm, ārĕ. *To recommence.* Crās īngēns ĭtĕrābĭmŭs æquŏr. H. Syn.—Gĕmĭnŏ, īngĕmĭnŏ, dŭplĭcŏ, īntĕgrŏ, rĕdīntĕgrŏ, rĕpĕtŏ.

Ĭtĕrūm. adv. *Again, anew.* Syn.—Rūrsūm, rūrsŭs, īnsŭpĕr, ădhūc, dēnŭō, sæpĕ.

Ĭtĭdēm. adv. *Likewise.* Syn.—Ĭtēm, sīc, æquē, părĭtĕr.

J

Jăcĕŏ, ēs, ŭī, ērĕ. *To lie, to recline.* Hārum ēffūltūs tērgō strātīsquĕ jăcēbăt Vēllĕrĭbŭs. V. Syn.—Cŭbŏ, rĕcŭbŏ, īncŭbŏ, rĕcūmbŏ, prōcūmbŏ, dīscūmbŏ, stērnŏr, prōstērnŏr, ēxtēndŏ, quĭēscŏ, rĕquĭēscŏ, rĕsĭdĕŏ. Phr.—Mēmbră, cōrpŭs stērnĕrĕ, pōnĕrĕ, ēxtēndĕrĕ. Dēfēssă cōmpōnĕrĕ mēmbră. Vĭrĭdī mēmbră sŭb ărbŭtō strātŭs. Cōrpŏră fūsă jăcēnt. *To be situated.* Syn.—Ādjăcĕŏ, āccŭbŏ, sūbjăcĕŏ. Phr.—Sūm sĭtŭs, pŏsĭtŭs. *To be cast down.* Syn.—Āfflīgŏr, stērnŏr.

Jăcĭŏ, ĭs, jēcī, jāctūm, ĕrĕ. *To throw, to hurl.* Syn.—Jāctŏ, cōnjĭcĭŏ, prōjĭcĭŏ, ējĭcĭŏ, mīttŏ, ēmīttŏ, fūndŏ, ēffūndŏ, spārgŏ.

Jāctāntĭă, æ. f. *Boasting, display.* Syn.—Jāctātĭŏ, fāstŭs, ōstēntātĭŏ. *See Superbia.*

Jāctŏ, ās, āvī, ātūm, ārĕ. *To throw. See Jacio, Jaculor. To agitate.* Syn.—Ăgĭtŏ, mŏvĕŏ, ăgŏ, īmpēllŏ, quătĭŏ, quāssŏ. *To boast.* Syn.—Jāctĭtŏ, ōstēntŏ, prædĭcŏ, ēffĕrŏ, laūdŏ.

Jăcŭlŏr, ārĭs, ātŭs sūm, ārī. *To hurl, to throw.* Syn.—Ējăcŭlŏr, jăcĭŏ, jāctŏ, cōnjĭcĭŏ, īnjĭcĭŏ, tōrquĕŏ, īntōrquĕŏ, cōntōrquĕŏ, mīttŏ, ēmīttŏ, vĭbrŏ, spārgŏ, ēxcŭtĭŏ, fūndŏ, ēffūndŏ. Phr.—Tēlūm, hāstām, jăcŭlūm vĭbrŏ. Mīssĭlĭbŭs, tēlīs stērnŏ, trānsfŏdĭŏ. *To strike.* Syn.—Fĕrĭŏ, pērcŭtĭŏ, vūlnĕrŏ, fīgŏ, fŏdĭŏ, trānsfŏdĭŏ. *See Vulnero.*

Jăcŭlūm, ī. n. *Javelin, dart.* Nĕque ĕnīm jăcŭlō vītam īllĕ dĕdīssĕt. V. Syn.—Tēlūm, spīcŭlūm, hāstă, mīssĭlĕ, săgīttă.

Jām. adv. *Now.* Syn.—Nūnc, ĕō tēmpŏrĕ. *Soon.* Syn.—Jāmjām, mōx, prŏpĕ, pēnĕ, fĕrē.

Jānŭă, æ. f. *Door.* Ōmnĭs hăbēt gĕmĭnās hīnc ātque hīnc jānŭă frōntēs. O. Syn.—Pōrtă, līmĕn, ōstĭūm, fŏrēs, pōstēs, vālvæ, vēstĭbŭlūm, ădĭtŭs, īngrēssŭs. Phr.—Līmĭnă pōrtæ. Tēctī līmĕn. Pōrtārum īngēntĭă claūstră.

Jējūnŏ, ās, āvī, ātūm, ārĕ. *To fast.* Phr.—Cĭbīs ābstĭnĕō, mē fraūdŏ. Ĭnŏpī vīctū cōrpŭs āttĕrĕrĕ. Tĕnŭī cĭbō mēmbră dŏmārĕ.

Jējūnŭs, ă, ūm. *Fasting.* Syn.—Īmpāstŭs, ēsŭrĭēns, fămēlĭcŭs. Phr.—Ĭnōps cĭbī. Ēxpērs ūndæquĕ cĭbīquĕ. Cĕrĕrĭs sĭnĕ mūnĕrĕ.

Jŏcŏr, arĭs, ātŭs sūm, ārī. *To joke.* Quŏtĭēs vŏlŭit fōrtūnă jŏcārī. H. Syn.—Rīdĕŏ, īrrīdĕŏ, lūdŏ, īllūdŏ, căvīllŏr. Īncŏlŭmī grăvĭtātĕ jŏcūm tēntāvĭt.

Jŏcōsŭs, ă, ūm. *Humorous, merry.* Sī mĕă mātĕrĭæ rēspōndēt mūsă jŏcōsæ. O. Syn.—Ărgūtŭs, fēstīvŭs, lĕpĭdŭs.

Jŏcŭs, ī. m. *Joke, jest.* Hīstŏrĭæ tūrpēs īnsĕrŭīssĕ jŏcōs. O. Syn.—Lūdŭs, lūsŭs, rīsŭs, lūdĭcrūm, sălēs, căvīllŭs, scōmmă. Phr.—Āptăquĕ vērbă jŏcō. Plēnă jŏcī. Āccēdēnt sĭnĕ fēllĕ jŏcī.

Jŭbă, æ. f. *Mane of an animal.* Dēnsă jŭba ēt dēxtrō jăctātă rĕcūmbĭt ĭn ărmō. V. Syn.—Cŏmă, crīnĭs. Phr.—Cŏmāntĭă cōllă. Jŭbīsquĕ cŏmāntēs Ēxcŭtĭt īllĕ tŏrōs.

Jŭbăr, ărĭs. n. *Morning star. See Aurora, Dies. Light in general.* Syn.—Lūx, lūmĕn, splēndŏr, fūlgŏr, rădĭī, fāx.

Jŭbĕō, ēs, ūssī, ūssūm, ērĕ. *To order, to command.* Seū Trōās fĭĕrī jŭbĕās, Teūcrōsquĕ vŏcārī. V. Syn.—Īmpĕrŏ, māndŏ, præcĭpĭŏ, ēdīcŏ, præscrībŏ, vŏlŏ. Phr.—Dō jūssă. Bēllă jŭbērĕ. *See Impero.*

Jūcūndŭs, ă, ūm. *Pleasant, agreeable.* Syn.—Grātŭs, āccēptŭs, plăcēns, ămœnŭs, blāndŭs, dūlcĭs, suāvĭs, lætŭs, fēstīvŭs. *Happy.* Syn.—Lætŭs, fēlīx. *Kind.* Syn.—Suāvĭs, cōmĭs, făcĭlĭs, bĕnīgnŭs.

Jūdēx, ĭcĭs. m. *Judge.* Syn.—Ārbĭtĕr, quæsītŏr, cōgnĭtŏr. Phr.—Lĭtĭs ārbĭtĕr. Jūrĭs, jūstĭtĭæ præsēs. Lēgūm vīndēx. Quō nōn jūstĭŏr āltĕr. Vīndēx ăvāræ fraūdĭs.

Jūdĭcĭūm, ĭī. n. *Judgment.* Mānēt āltā mēntĕ rĕpōstūm Jūdĭcĭūm Părĭdĭs. V. Syn.—Ārbĭtrĭūm, sēntēntĭă. Phr.—Jūdĭcĭs ōffĭcĭūm fŏrī. Jūrĭs, lēgĭs vīndĭctă. *Advice.* Syn.—Sēntēntĭă, ŏpīnĭŏ. *Taste, judgment.* Syn.—Mēns, ăcūmĕn, cōnsĭlĭūm, rătĭŏ.

Jūdĭcŏ, ās, āvī, ātūm, ārĕ. *To judge.* Phr.—Jūs ēxērcĕŏ, dīcŏ. Jūră dō. Lĭtēs cōmpōnŏ. Jūdĭcĭūm stătŭŏ, dēcērnŏ. Lēgūm mŏdĕrātŭr hăbēnās. *To decide.* Syn.—Dījūdĭcŏ, stătŭŏ, dēcērnŏ, æstĭmŏ, ārbĭtrŏr, cēnsĕŏ, sēntĭŏ, ēxīstĭmŏ.

Jūgĭs, ĭs, ĕ. *Continual, perpetual.* Hōrtŭs ŭbi ēt tēctō vīcīnŭs jūgĭs ăquæ fōns. H. Syn.—Pērpĕtŭŭs, pĕrēnnĭs, āssĭdŭŭs, cōntĭnŭŭs.

Jŭgŏ, ās, āvī, ātūm, ārĕ. *To put under the yoke.* Syn.—Cōllă jŭgō sūbdĕrĕ, sūbmīttĕrĕ, sūppōnĕrĕ. Sūb jŭgă cōgĕrĕ, vŏcārĕ, dūcĕrĕ, mīttĕrĕ. Plaūstrō, ărātrō ādjūngĕrĕ.

Jŭgŭlŏ, ās, āvī, ātūm, ārĕ. *To strangle.* Ūt jŭgŭlēnt hŏmĭnēs, sūrgūnt dē nōctĕ lătrōnēs. H. Phr.—Ēnsĕ, glădĭō, fērrō jŭgŭlŏ, jŭgŭlūm rĕclūdŏ. Jŭgŭlō fērrūm, glădĭūm tīngŏ, ādmŏvĕŏ, cōndŏ.

Jŭgŭlūm, ī. n. *Throat.* Syn.—Cōllūm, faūcēs, gūttŭr.

Jŭgūm, ī. n. *Yoke.* Prīmă jŭgīs taūrōs sūppōnĕrĕ cōllă cŏēgĭt. O. Phr.—Jŭgūm fērrĕ, sŭbīrĕ, pătī. Sūb jŭgă īrĕ. Jŭgūm cōllō fērrĕ. Cōllă jŭgō sūbtrăhĕrĕ. Nūllūm bōs pāssă jŭgūm. Jŭgūm sōlvĕrĕ. Jūngĕrĕ taūrōs. *A chain of mountains.* Syn.—Ăpēx, cūlmĕn, căcūmĕn.

Jūnctūră, æ. f. *A joining.* Tāntūm sĕrĭēs jūnctūrăquă pōllĕt Cāllĭdă. H. Syn.—Cōmmīssūră, vīncŭlūm, vīnclūm, nēxŭs.

Jūncŭs, ī. m. *Rush, bulrush.* Līmōsōquĕ pălūs ōbdūcāt pāscŭă jūncō. V. Syn.—Ărūndŏ, scīrpŭs.

Jūngŏ, ĭs, ūnxī, ūnctūm, ĕrĕ. *To join.* Jūngĭmŭs hōspĭtĭō dēxtrās ēt tēctă sŭbīmŭs. V. Syn.—Ādjūngŏ, cōnjūngŏ, nēctŏ, ādnēctŏ, cōnnēctŏ, lĭgŏ, āllĭgŏ, cōpŭlŏ, cōmmīttŏ, āddŏ, ādmŏvĕŏ, ādjĭcĭŏ, āpplĭcŏ, mīscĕŏ.

Jūnĭpĕrŭs, ī. f. *The juniper tree.* (*See Appendix under list of Trees, etc.*)

Jūrgĭūm, ĭī. n. *Dispute, quarrel.* Jūrgĭă præcĭpŭē vīnō stĭmŭlātă căvētō. O. Syn.—Rīxă, līs, pūgnă, dīscōrdĭă, cērtămĕn, cōntēntĭŏ.

Jūrgŏ, ās, āvī, ātūm, ārĕ. *To dispute.* Syn.—Āltērcŏr, cērtŏ, cōntēndŏ, lītĭgŏ, rīxŏr.

Jūrīscōnsūltŭs, ī. m. *Lawyer.* Phr.—Jūrĭs īntērprēs, prūdēns, scĭēns, præsĭdĭūm fŏrī. Cōnsūltŭs jūrĭs. Jūrĕ mădēns.

Jūrŏ, ās, āvī, ātūm, ārĕ. *To swear an oath.* Nōn ĕgŏ jūrāvī, lēgī jūrāntĭă vērbă. O. Syn.—Ādjūrŏ, tēstŏr, āttēstŏr.

Jūs, ūrĭs n. *Right, justice.* Syn.—Aēquūm, rēctūm, jūstūm, jūstĭtĭă, æquĭtās. *Law.* Syn. Lēx.—*Authority, power.* Syn.—Pŏtēstās, īmpĕrĭūm, vīs.

Jūsjūrāndūm, jūrīsjūrāndī. n. *Oath.* Syn.—Jūrāndūm, jūrāmēntūm, săcrāmēntūm, fĭdēs.

Jūssūm, ī. n. *Order.* Syn.—Īmpĕrĭūm, māndātūm, prǣcēptūm.

Jūstē. adv. *Rightly.* Syn.—Jūrĕ, mĕrĭtō.

Jūstĭtĭă, æ. f. *Justice.* Jūstĭtĭā vīrēs tēmpĕrāt īllĕ sŭās. O. Syn.—Jūs, æquūm, jūstūm, rēctūm, fĭdēs, æquĭtās. Phr.—Jūrĭs ămŏr. Rēctī rĕvĕrēntĭă. Mēns sĭbĭ cōnscĭă rēctī.

Jūstŭs, ă, ūm. *Just.* Syn.—Aēquŭs, rēctŭs, pĭŭs, sānctŭs. Phr.—Jūstĭtĭæ, jūrĭs, æquī ămāns, cūltŏr, cūstōs. Jūstĭtĭæ tĕnāx. Quō nōn jūstĭŏr āltĕr. *See Jus.*

Jŭvēncă, æ. f. *Heifer.* Syn.—Jŭvencŭlă, bōs, būcŭlă, vĭtŭlă, vāccă.

Jŭvĕnīlĭs, ĭs, ĕ. *Youthful.* Syn.—Īntĕgĕr, vĕgĕtŭs. Phr.—Jŭvĕnīlĭbŭs āctă lăcērtīs. Căpŭt īntōnsīs jŭvĕnīlĕ căpīllīs. Vĭtĭūm jŭvĕnīlĕ.

Jŭvĕnĭs, ĭs. m. *Youth.* Mōx, jŭvĕnēs, ăgĭtātĕ jŏcōs. Pers. Syn.—Pūbĕr, ădŏlēscēns, ĕphēbŭs. Phr.—Jŭvēntā, flōrĕ jŭvēntæ fīdēns, aūdāx. Īnsīgnīs prīmævō cōrpŏrĕ. Aētātĭs flōrĕ vĭrēns. Vĭgēns prīmævō flōrĕ jŭvēntæ. Vălĭdīs ārdēns ănĭmīs. Flōrēntĕ jŭvēntā fērvĭdŭs.

Jŭvēntūs, ūtĭs. f. *Youth, adolescence.* Ēt pătĭēns ŏpĕrūm pārvōque āssuētă jŭvēntūs. V. Syn.—Jŭvēntă, pūbērtās. Phr.—Jŭvĕnīlĭs ætās. Aēvūm vĭrĭdĕ. Jŭvēntæ ēgrĕgĭūm dĕcŭs. Pārs mĕlĭōr vītæ. Aētātĭs brĕvĕ vēr. Mōllĭs ĕt āptă căpī, rĕgī. Īmpūbĕ cōrpŭs. Mēmbră dĕcōră jŭvēntæ.

Jŭvŏ, ās, jūvī, jūtūm, ārĕ. *To aid, to assist.* Aūxĭlĭō tūtōs dīmīttam ŏpĭbūsquĕ jŭvābŏ. V. Syn.—Ădjŭvŏ, aūxĭlĭŏr. Phr.—Nĕque īllōs jūvĕrĭs aūxĭlĭō. Jūvīt fācūndĭă caūsām. *To please.* Syn.—Rĕcrĕŏ, dēlēctŏ, ōblēctŏ, plăcĕŏ.

Jūxtā. adv. *Hard by, close to.* Syn.—Prŏpĕ. Phr.—Nōn (*or*) haūd prŏcŭl. prep. Syn.—Ăd, prŏpĕ, prōptĕr, sĕcūndūm. *Equally.* Syn.—Aēquē, părĭtĕr.

L

Lăbĕfăcĭŏ, ĭs, ēcī, āctūm, ĕrĕ & Lăbĕfāctŏ, ās, āvī, ātūm, ārĕ. *To shake, to break.* Syn.—Quătĭŏ, cōncŭtĭŏ, quăssŏ, rūmpŏ, cōnvēllŏ, dīssōlvŏ, sūbvērtŏ, ērŭŏ, dīrŭŏ, dīstūrbŏ.

Lābēs, ĭs. f. *Ruin, fall.* Syn.—Rŭīnă, clādēs, ēxĭtĭūm, cāsŭs, pērnĭcĭēs. *Pest.* Syn.—Pēstĭs, lŭēs, cōntāgĭŏ. *Stain.* Syn.—Măcŭlă, nŏtă, sōrdēs, nævŭs. Fig.—*Infamy.* Syn.—Dēdĕcŭs, īnfāmĭă.

Lābŏ, ās, ārĕ. *To totter.* Pōstquam ēxplōrātūm sătĭs ēst lŏcă nūllă lăbārĕ. O. Syn.—Lăbāscŏ, nūtŏ, văcīllŏ, fătīscŏ.

Lābŏr, ĕrĭs, psŭs sūm, bī. *To fall.* Præcĭpĭtēs cœlō lābī. V. Syn.—Prōlābŏr, cădŏ, cōncĭdŏ, prōcĭdŏ. *To glide along.* Syn.—Ēŏ, dēcūrrŏ, fĕrŏr. *To escape, to get rid of.* Syn.—Ēxcĭdŏ, ēffluŏ.

Lăbŏr, ōrĭs. m. *Labor, work.* Nēc tĭbĭ quī vĕnĭēnt făcĭēs ĕrĭt ūnă lăbōrūm. V. Syn.—Ŏpĕră, ŏpŭs. Phr.—Lăbōrĭs ŏnŭs. Ŏpĕrūm lăbōrēs. Lăbŏr ōmnĭă vīncĭt. Sĕrĭēs īmmēnsă lăbōrūm. Hōc ŏpŭs hīc lăbŏr ēst. Lēnīmēn dūlcĕ lăbōrūm. Dūlcĭs ĕrăt mērcēdĕ lăbŏr. *Enterprise, undertaking.* Syn.—Īncēptūm, aūsūm, aūsŭs, cōnātŭs, ōrsă. *Disaster, reverse.* Syn.—Călămĭtās, pĕrīclūm.

Lăbōrĭfĕr, ĕră, ĕrūm. *Bearing toil.* Syn.—Gnāvŭs, strēnŭŭs, īmpĭgĕr. Phr.—Lăbōrĭs pătĭēns.

Lăbōrĭōsŭs, ă, ūm. *Full of toil, laborious.* Syn.—Dūrŭs, lăbōrĭfĕr, gnāvŭs, īmpĭgĕr. Phr.—Plēnă lăbōrūm.

Lăbōrŏ, ās, āvī, ātūm, ārĕ. *To work, to labor.* Syn.—Ŏpĕrŏr. Phr.—Lăbōrī văcŏ, īndūlgĕŏ, īncūmbŏ, mē dō. Ŏpĕrī īnstŏ. Lăbōrēm sŭbĕŏ. Lăbōrĕ mēmbră dūrŏ, ēxērcĕŏ. Mē lăbŏr ēxērcĕt. *To be fatigued or ill.* Syn.—Aēgrōtŏ, dŏlĕŏ, āngŏr, vēxŏr, ōpprĭmŏr, prĕmŏr, crŭcĭŏr.

Lăbrūm, ī. n. *Lip.* Syn.—Lăbĭūm, lăbēllūm, ōs. Phr.—Rŏsĕŭs pīngīt mōllĭă lābră nĭtŏr. Lābră mŏvēt mĕtŭēns aūdīrī. *Edge or rim of a vessel.* Syn.—Mārgŏ, ōră. *Basin.* Syn.—Lĕbĕs, ăhēnūm, cădŭs, lăcŭs.

Lābrūscă, æ. f. *The wild vine.* Āspĭce ŭt āntrūm Sȳlvēstrĭs rārĭs spārsĭt lābrūscă răcēmĭs. V. Syn.—Vītĭs, œnānthĭnūm.

Lāc, lāctĭs. n. *Milk.* Ēt sălĭs ōccūltūm rĕfĕrūnt īn lāctĕ săpōrēm. V. Phr.—Lāctĭs, lāctĕŭs hūmŏr. Cōpĭă lāctĭs. Lāctĭs ălĭmēntă. Cŏāgŭlă lāctĭs.

Lăcĕr & Lăcĕrŭs, ă, ūm. *Torn to pieces.* Syn.—Lăcĕrātŭs, dīlăcĕrātŭs, lănĭātŭs, dīlănĭātŭs, dīscērptŭs, scīssŭs, dīscīssŭs, mŭtĭlŭs.

Lăcĕrŏ, ās, āvī, ātūm, ārĕ. *To tear to pieces.* Lōrīcāmquĕ mănū vălĭdā lăcĕrārĕ rĕvūlsām. V. Syn.—Dīlăcĕrŏ, lănĭŏ, dīlănĭŏ, sĕcŏ, dīssĕcŏ, scīndŏ, ābscīndŏ, cōnscīndŏ, dīscīndŏ, dīscērpŏ, frāngŏ, rūmpŏ, dīsrūmpŏ, cōmmĭnŭŏ, vēllŏ, dīvēllŏ, dīvĭdŏ, mŭtĭlŏ, fœdŏ. Phr.—Fērrō, dēntĕ răbĭdō sĕcārĕ īn pārtēs. Ūnguĭbŭs fœdārĕ. *To torment.* Syn.—Crŭcĭŏ, dīscrŭcĭŏ, vēxŏ, āngŏ, tōrquĕŏ.

Lăcērtōsŭs, ă, ūm. *Strong, vigorous.* Syn.—Tŏrōsŭs, nērvōsŭs, rōbūstŭs, vălĭdŭs.

Lăcērtŭs, ī. m. *Nerve, muscle.* Syn.—Tŏrŭs, nērvŭs.

Lăcēssŏ, ĭs, īvī & ĭī, ītūm, ĕrĕ. *To provoke, to excite.* Syn.—Tēntŏ, sōllĭcĭtŏ, mŏvĕŏ. *To attack.* Syn.—Prōvŏcŏ, āggrĕdĭŏr. *To strike.* Syn.—Pērcŭtĭŏ, fĕrĭŏ, pūlsŏ.

Lăcrĭmābĭlĭs, ĭs, ĕ. *Lamentable, deplorable.* Syn.—Flēbĭlĭs, lăcrĭmāndŭs, dēflēndŭs, flēndŭs, mĭsĕrāndŭs, mĭsĕrābĭlĭs, lăcrĭmōsŭs.

Lăcrĭmæ, ārūm. f. *Tears.* Ēt lăcrĭmās cērnēns īn sīngŭlă vērbă cădēntēs. O. Syn.—Lăcrĭmŭlæ, flētŭs, gūttæ, gĕmĭtŭs, plōrātŭs, lūctŭs. Phr.—Lăcrĭmārūm flūxŭs. Tĕpĭdŭs rōs. Mœstae īmbĕr ăquæ. Mōrĕ nĭvĭs sōlĕ mădēntĭs. Pĕr ōră vŏlūtæ. Lăcrĭmās rĕtĭnērĕ, sūpprĭmĕrĕ. Flētĭbŭs pārcŏ. Gĕnās tērgērĕ. Quĭs tēmpĕrĕt lăcrĭmās?

Lăcrĭmŏ, ās, āvī, ātūm, ārĕ & Lăcrĭmŏr, ārĭs, ātŭs sūm, ārī. *To weep.* Īt lăcrĭmāns gūttīsque hūmēctāt grāndĭbŭs ōră. V. Syn.—Īllăcrĭmŏ, flĕŏ, dēflĕŏ, plōrŏ, lūgĕŏ, gĕmŏ, plāngŏ, lāmēntŏr. Phr.—Lăcrĭmās dō, fūndŏ. Īre īn lăcrĭmās. Īn flētum ērūmpĕrĕ. Lăcrĭmæ mănānt, flŭūnt. Lăcrĭmās ēffūdĭt. Lăcrĭmīs spārgūnt rōrāntĭbŭs ōră. Nēc mŏdŭs ēst lăcrĭmīs.

Lăcrimōsŭs, ă, ūm. *Tearful, shedding tears.* Syn.—Lăcrĭmāns, īllăcrĭmāns, flēns, dēflēns, lūgēns. Phr.—Cūm lăcrĭmīs, cūm flētū. Lăcrĭmīs, flētū mădēns, rōrāns. Mădĭdīs gĕnīs. Lăcrĭmīs ŏcŭlōs sūffūsă nĭtēntēs.

Lāctĕŭs, ă, ūm. *Milky.* Syn.—Lāctĕŏlŭs. *Milkwhite.* Syn.—Lāctĕŏlŭs, nĭvĕŭs, ālbŭs, cāndēns, cāndĭdŭs, ĕbūrnĕŭs.

Lāctūcă, æ. f. *Lettuce.* (*See Appendix under list of Trees, etc.*)

Lăcŭs, ūs. m. *Lake, any body of water.* Līmōsōquĕ lăcū pēr nōctem ōbscūrŭs ĭn ūlvā Dēlĭtŭī. V. Syn.—Pălūs, stāgnūm. Phr.—Stāgnāns ăquă. Stāgnă tăcēntĭs ăquæ. Līmōsŭs gūrgĕs.

Lædŏ, ĭs, sī, sūm, ĕrĕ. *To hurt, to do harm to.* Tĕnĕrōs lædūnt jŭgă prīmă jŭvēncōs. V. Syn.—Vūlnĕrŏ, vĭŏlŏ, saūcĭŏ, ōffēndŏ. *To corrupt.* Syn.—Vĭŏlŏ, pōllŭŏ, cōrrūmpŏ, fœdŏ. *To offend.* Syn.—Ōffēndŏ, lăcēssŏ, īmpĕtŏ, cārpŏ.

Lætĭfĭcŏ, ās, āvī, ātūm, ārĕ. *To rejoice.* Syn.—Hĭlărŏ, ēxhĭlărŏ, rĕcrĕŏ, dēlēctŏ. *See Delecto, Gaudium.*

Lætĭtĭă, æ. f. *Joy.* Syn.—Gaūdĭūm. *See Gaudium.*

Lætŏr, ārĭs, ātŭs sūm, ārī. *To rejoice.* Lætātūr gĕmĭnā vōtōrūm sōrtĕ mărītŭs. M. Syn.—Gaūdĕŏ, ēxsūltŏ. *See Gaudeo.*

Lætŭs, ă, ūm. *Joyful.* Dōnă præsēntīs răpĕ lætŭs hōræ. H. Syn.—Hĭlărĭs, ălăcĕr, ŏvāns, gaūdēns, ēxsūltāns, lætātŭs, gāvīsŭs. Phr.—Jūstō lætĭŏr. Ănĭmīs ēxsūltāns, gāvīsŭs. Lætŭs ĭn ādvērsīs. Mēns ēbrĭă gaūdĭō. *See Gaudeo, Hilaris. Prosperous.* Syn.—Faūstŭs, fēlīx, sĕcūndŭs.

Lævĭs & Lēvĭs, ĭs, ĕ. *Smooth, polished.* Tāndem īntēr pătĕrās āc lævĭă pōcŭlă sērpēns. V. Syn.—Plānŭs, pŏlītŭs, lævātŭs, nĭtĭdŭs.

Lævŭs, ă, ūm. *Left.* Lævōs ĕquĭtāvĭt ĭn ōrbēs. V. Syn.—Sĭnīstĕr. *Sinister, inauspicious.* Syn.—Ādvērsŭs, īnfaūstŭs.

Lăgēnă, æ. f. *Earthen jar or bottle.* Syn.—Āmphŏră, lăgūncŭlă.

Lāmbŏ, ĭs, ī, ĕrĕ. *To lick.* Sībĭlă lāmbēbānt līnguīs vībrāntĭbŭs ōră. V. Syn.—Āllāmbŏ, līngŏ. *To touch lightly.* Syn.—Āllāmbŏ, āttīngŏ, tāngŏ, dēlībŏ.

Lāmēntābĭlĭs, ĭs, ĕ. *Deplorable, lamentable.* Syn.—Flēbĭlĭs, quĕrŭlŭs, quĕrĭbūndŭs, gĕmĭbūndŭs, lūctĭsŏnŭs.

Lāmēntātĭŏ, ōnĭs. f., Lāmēntūm, ī & Lāmēntă, ōrūm. n. *Weeping.* Syn.—Lūctŭs, flētŭs, plānctŭs, gĕmĭtŭs, quēstŭs.

Lāmēntŏr, ārĭs, ātŭs sūm, ārī. *To weep.* Cūm lāmēntāmūr nōn āppārērĕ lăbōrēs. H. Syn.—Quĕrŏr, cōnquĕrŏr, plōrŏ, lūgĕŏ, flĕŏ, gĕmŏ, īngĕmŏ, plāngŏ.

Lāmpăs, ădĭs. f. *Torch.* Lāmpădĭbūs dēnsūm răpŭīt fūnālĕ cŏrūscīs. O. Syn.—Lŭcērnă, lȳchnŭs, fāx, fūnālĕ, flāmmă. Phr.—Flāmmă vĭgĭl. Īgnēs nōctūrnī. Trĕmŭlā lūcĕ cŏrūscānt.

Lānă, æ. f. *Wool.* Āntĕ pĕdēs cālăthī lānăquĕ mōllĭs ĕrānt. O. Syn.—Vēllŭs. Phr.—Lānæ vēllĕră, stāmĭnă. Mōllēs vīllī. Nĭvĕūm lānæ mūnŭs. Lānā sŭă fīlă sĕquēntĕ.

Lāncĭnŏ, ās, āvī, ātūm, ārĕ. *To pierce.* Syn.—Stĭmŭlŏ, pūngŏ. *See Pungo. To dissipate.* Syn.—Dīstrăhŏ, lăcĕrŏ.

Lānguĕŏ, ēs, ŭī, ērĕ. *To be feeble.* Lānguēnt ēxhaūstō rōbŏrĕ vīrēs. V. Syn.—Ēlānguĕŏ, lānguēscŏ, tōrpĕŏ, dēfĭcĭŏ, mārcĕŏ, frāngŏr, dēbĭlĭtŏr, sūccĭdŏ, fătīscŏ, lābŏr, cōllābŏr. Phr.—Mēmbră tōrpŏr hăbĕt. Cōrpŏră lānguŏr hăbĕt. Īngēntī lānguōrĕ jăcēt cōrpŭs. Sĭnĕ vīrĭbŭs ægrūm.

Lānguēscŏ, ĭs, ĕrĕ. *To lose strength.* Syn.—Tōrpēscŏ, mārcēscŏ, frāngŏr. *See Langueo.*

Lānguĭdŭs, ă, ūm. *Weak, fatigued.* Syn.—Lānguēns, ēlānguĭdŭs, tōrpēns, dēbĭlĭs, dēbĭlĭtātŭs, īnfīrmŭs, īnvălĭdŭs, frāctŭs, fēssŭs, ægĕr. Phr.—Dēfēctă vīrĭbŭs. Mōllī lānguōrĕ sŏlūtŭs.

Lānguŏr, ōrĭs. m. *Weakness, torpor.* Heī mĭhĭ! pērpĕtŭūs cōrpŏră lānguŏr hăbĕt. O. Syn.—Tōrpŏr, dēbĭlĭtās.

Lănĭŏ, ās, āvī, ātūm, ārĕ. *To rend in pieces, to tear.* Syn.—Lăcĕrŏ, dīlăcĕrŏ, dīscērpŏ, dīssĕcŏ, dīvēllŏ.

Lānx, cĭs. f. *Plate, basin.* Lāncĭbŭs ēt pāndīs fūmāntĭă rēddĭmŭs ēxtă. V. Syn.—Scŭtŭlă, cătīnŭs, părōpsĭs, pătĭnă. *The scale of a balance.* Syn.—Bĭlānx, lībră, stătēră, trŭtĭnă.

Lăpĭdŏ, ās, āvī, ātūm, ārĕ. *To stone.* Phr.—Lăpĭdĭbŭs, sāxīs, sāxōrūm grāndĭnĕ, lăpĭdūm īmbrĕ lăcēssŏ, pĕtŏ, īnsēctŏr, ōpprĭmŏ, ōbrŭŏ. Lăpĭdēs jăcĭŏ. Īnflīgūnt vūlnĕră sāxīs. Īmmīssīs sāxīs.

Lăpĭdōsŭs, ă, ūm. *Rocky.* Syn.—Sāxōsŭs, pĕtrōsŭs, scrūpĕŭs. Phr. —Sāxīs āspĕr, frĕquēns.

Lăpĭs, ĭdĭs. m. *Stone.* Syn.—Sāxūm, sĭlēx. *Precious stone.* Syn.—Gēmmă, lăpīllŭs.

Lāpsŭs, ūs. m. *Fall.* Nĭmĭōquĕ grăvēs sūb pōndĕrĕ lāpsŭs. L. Syn.—Cāsŭs, rŭīnă.

Lăquĕār, ārĭs. n. *Panel in a ceiling.* Syn.—Lăquĕārĭūm, lăcūnăr. Phr.—Lăquĕātă tēctă. Cōnnēxæ trăbēs. Trăbēs aūrō nĭtĭdæ. Dēpēndēnt lychnī lăquĕārĭbŭs aūreīs.

Lăquĕŭs, ī. m. *Noose, snare.* Ēt lăquĕīs cāptārĕ fĕrās. V. Syn.—Vīncŭlūm, rētĕ. *Deceit.* Syn.—Fraūs, dŏlŭs, īnsĭdĭæ.

Lārgē & Lārgĭtĕr. adv. *Largely, amply.* Līgnă sŭpēr fŏcō lārgē rĕpōnēns. H. Syn.—Ăbūndē, mūltūm, ūbērtĭm, mūnĭfĭcē. Phr.—Lārgā mănū. Mănĭbūs plēnīs. Pōtūs lārgĭūs æquō.

Lārgĭŏr, īrĭs, ītŭs sūm, īrī. *To bestow lavishly.* Quīd sīt lārgīrī, quīd sīt dōnārĕ dŏcēbŏ. M. Syn.—Dōnŏ, īmpērtĭŏ, īmpērtĭŏr, trĭbŭŏ.

Lārgītŏr, ōrĭs. m. *Lavish giver.* Syn.—Dătŏr, dōnātŏr.

Lāscīvŭs, ă, ūm. *Sportive, playful (in a good sense).* Syn.—Ēxsūltāns, lūdēns, ălăcĕr, pĕtŭlāns. *Dissolute.* Syn.—Mōllĭs, prŏcāx, īmpŭdīcŭs.

Lāssŏ, ās, āvī, ātūm, ārĕ. *To weary, to tire out.* Mē lăbŏr īnsŏlĭtūs lāssāvĕrăt. O. Syn.—Fătīgŏ, frāngŏ, cōnfĭcĭŏ.

Lāssŭs, ă, ūm. *Tired, fatigued.* Hīc pŭĕr ēt stŭdĭō vēnāndī lāssŭs ĕt æstū. O. Syn.—Lāssātŭs, fătīgātŭs, fēssŭs, dēfēssŭs. Phr.—Vĭā, lăbōrĕ frāctŭs, cōnfēctŭs. *Sick.* Syn.—Aēgĕr, lānguĭdŭs.

Lătĕbræ, ārūm. f. *Hiding place.* Syn.—Lătĭbŭlūm, āntrūm, căvērnă, spĕcŭs, spēlūncă, spēlæūm, rĕcēssŭs, sĭnŭs, ūmbră, tĕnĕbræ. Phr.—Lătĕbrōsă dŏmŭs.

Lătĕbrōsŭs, ă, ūm. *Full of hiding places, retired.* Syn.—Lătēns, ōccūltŭs, ābdĭtŭs, rĕdūctŭs, ārcānŭs, cæcŭs, ōbscūrŭs, tĕnĕbrōsŭs.

Lătēntĕr, adv. *Secretly.* Syn.—Fūrtīm, clām, ōccūltē, sēcrētō.

Lătĕŏ, ēs, ŭī, ērĕ. *To be concealed, to lie hidden.* Sprētă lătēt sīlvīs pŭdĭbūndăquĕ frōndĭbŭs ōră Prōtĕgĭt. O. Syn.—Lătĭtŏ, lătēscŏ, dēlĭtēscŏ, ābdŏr, ābscōndŏr, ōccūltŏr, tĕgŏr, cēlŏr. Phr.—Lătĕbrīs ābscōndŏ, cōndŏ. Ōccūltē lătĕŏ. Lătĕbrās quærŏ. Sēse ābdĭdĭt ūmbrīs.

Lătēx, ĭcĭs. m. *Water, liquid.* Syn.—Ăquă, hūmŏr, lĭquŏr. *See Fons, Aqua.*

Lătrŏ, ās, āvī, ātūm, ārĕ. *To bark.* Cērvīnām pēllēm lātrāvĭt ĭn aūlā. H. Syn.—Āllătrŏ. Phr.—Lătrātūs tōllĕre ĭn aūrās. Aūrās, æthĕră, cāmpōs lătrātĭbŭs īmplĕŏ, cĭĕŏ. Nōctūrnōs ŭlŭlāssĕ cănēs.

Lātrŏ, ōnĭs. m. *Robber.* Syn.—Fūr, prædŏ, grāssātŏr.

Lātrōcĭnĭūm, ĭī. n. *Brigandage.* Syn.—Prædă, răpīnă.

Lātŭs, ă, ūm. *Broad, wide.* Lātīs aūdāx Hīspānĭă tērrīs Tib. Syn.—Āmplŭs, pătēns, pătŭlŭs, spătĭōsŭs, vāstŭs, īngēns, dīffūsŭs, ēffūsŭs, māgnŭs, māxĭmŭs. Phr.—Lātē ēxtēnsŭs, ēffūsŭs, dīffūsŭs.

Lătŭs, ĕrĭs, n. *Side, flank.* Lătĕrīque ăccōmmŏdăt ēnsēm. V. Syn.—Cōstæ̆.

Laūdābĭlĭs, ĭs, ĕ. *Praiseworthy.* Nātūră fĭĕrĕt laūdābĭlĕ cārmĕn ăn ārtĕ Quæ̆sītum ēst. H. Syn.—Laūdāndŭs, mĕmŏrāndŭs, cĕlĕbrāndŭs, mĕmŏrābĭlĭs, ēgrĕgĭŭs. Phr.—Lōngā laūdĕ cănēndŭs. Plēnūm laūdĭs ŏpŭs. Laūdĕ fĕrēndŭs. Laūdārī dīgnŭs. Cuī dēbĭtă laūs īngēns.

Laūdātŏr, ōrĭs. m. *Praiser.* Syn.—Laūdāns, præ̆cō.

Laūdŏ, ās, āvī, ātūm, ārĕ. *To praise.* Aūt spŏlĭīs ĕgŏ jām rāptīs laūdābŏr ŏpīmīs. V. Syn.—Cĕlĕbrŏ, præ̆dĭcŏ, ēxtōllŏ, jāctŏ. Phr.—Laūdĕ, laūdĭbŭs ēffĕrŏ, ēxtōllŏ, cŭmŭlŏ, dĕcŏrŏ. Hŏnōrēm trĭbŭŏ. Teūcrōs īnsīgnī laūdĕ fĕrēbăt. Fĕrēnt ăd sīdĕră nōmĕn.

Laūrŭs, ī. f. *Laurel.* Ītĕ trĭūmphālēs cīrcūm mĕă tēmpŏră laūrī. O. Syn.—Laūrĕă. Phr—Laūrī frōndēs. Phœ̄bī dĕcŭs. Laūrī pērpĕtŭūm dĕcŭs. Săcră cŏmāns. Laūrō dēvīnctŭs ăgrēstī. *The laurel or bay tree. See Appendix.*

Laūs, laūdĭs. f. *Praise.* Syn.—Præ̆cōnĭūm, laūdātĭŏ. *Glory.* Syn.—Glōrĭă, dĕcŭs, fāmă, nōmĕn, hŏnŏr. Phr.—Nēscĭă mōrtĭs. Laūs nūllūm pĕrĭtūră pĕr æ̆vūm. Laūdĕ pŏtēns. Crēscĕrĕ laūdĕ pŏstĕrā. *See Fama, Nomen.*

Lăvŏ, ās, āvī, ātūm, ārĕ & Lăvŏ, ĭs, lāvī, lōtūm & laūtūm, ĕrĕ. *To bathe.* Cōrpūsquĕ lăvānt frīgēntĭs ēt ūnguūnt. V. Syn.—Āblŭŏ, ēlŭŏ, ābstērgĕŏ, ābstērgŏ, tērgĕŏ, pūrgŏ, mūndŏ. *To dissolve.* Syn.—Ēlŭŏ, dīlŭŏ, mērgŏ.

Lāxŏ, ās, āvī, ātūm, ārĕ. *To open.* Syn.—Sōlvŏ, ăpĕrĭŏ, pāndŏ, rĕsĕrŏ, dīdūcŏ, rĕlāxŏ, dīlātŏ. Phr.—Lāxăt claūstră Sĭnōn. *To loosen, to release.* Syn.—Rĕlāxŏ, sōlvŏ, rĕmīttŏ. *To lengthen.* Syn.—Prōdūcŏ, prōtrăhŏ, ēxtēndŏ.

Lāxŭs, ă, ūm. *Large, ample, spacious.* Syn.—Lātŭs, āmplŭs. *Loosened, relaxed.* Syn.—Rĕmīssŭs, lāxātŭs, sŏlūtŭs, rĕlāxātŭs.

Lĕbēs, ētĭs. m. *Bronze cauldron, kettle.* Syn.—Ăhēnūm, ōllă, cācăbŭs.

Lēctīcă, æ̆. f. *Litter.* Syn.—Lēctīcŭlă, sēllă, hēxăphŏrūm.

Lēctŭs, ī. m. *Bed.* Syn.—Thălămŭs, tŏrūs, cŭbīlĕ, lēctŭlŭs, strātūm fūlcrūm, spōndă. Phr.—Strātă tŏrīs fūlgēntĭbŭs. Strātă mōllĭă lēctī. Lūcēnt aūrĕă fūlcră tŏrīs.

Lēgātŭs, ī. m. *Legate, ambassador.* Syn.—Ōrātŏr. Phr.—Pācĭs āc bēllī nūntĭŭs. Ōrātŏr ĭn fœ̄dĕră mīssŭs. Ŏlīvā insignĭs. Pāllădĭs ārbŏrĕ tēctŭs.

Lēgĭfĕr, ĕră, ĕrŭm. *Legislator, lawgiver.* Syn.—Lēgīslātŏr, lēgŭm lātŏr. Phr.—Quī lēgēs fērt, dīcĭt, īndīcĭt, stătŭĭt. Quī lēgĕ cŏērcĕt. Prīmŭs quī lēgĭbŭs ūrbēm Fūndāvĭt. Cōmpōnĕrĕ lēgĭbŭs ōrbem.

Lĕgĭŏ, ōnĭs. f. *Legion.* Syn.—Cătērvă, cŏhōrs, phălānx, mănīplŭs, āgmĕn, ăcĭēs, tūrmă. *See Exercitus.*

Lēgĭtĭmŭs, ă, ŭm. *Lawful, according to rule.* Syn.—Aēquŭs, jūstŭs, rătŭs, fīxŭs, cērtŭs, sōlēmnĭs, lĭcĭtŭs, cōncēssŭs.

Lĕgŏ, ĭs, lēgī, lēctŭm, ĕrĕ. *To read.* Syn.—Lēctĭtŏ, pērlĕgŏ, vōlvŏ, ēvōlvŏ. Phr.—Ŏcŭlīs lūstrŏ, pērlūstrŏ. Vĕtĕrŭm vōlvēns mŏnŭmēntă vĭrōrŭm. Quæ dīgnă lĕgī sūnt.

Lĕmŭrēs, ŭm. m. *Shades, spirits.* Syn.—Lārvæ, ūmbræ, spēctră, sĭmŭlācră, mānēs. *See Spectrum.*

Lēnīmĕn, ĭnĭs. n. *Solace.* Ēt mĭhĭ sōllĭcĭtō lēnīmēn dūlcĕ sĕnēctæ. O. Syn.—Lĕvāmĕn, sōlāmĕn, sōlātĭŭm, fōmēntŭm, mĕdēlă, rĕmĕdĭŭm.

Lēnĭŏ, īs, īvī & ĭī, ītŭm, īrĕ. *To soften, to soothe.* Syn.—Mītĭgŏ, mūlcĕŏ, sēdŏ, fŏvĕŏ, mĭnŭŏ. Phr.—Fĕrōs lēnīrĕ lăbōrēs. Nŏvă rēs ōblātă tĭmōrēm Lēnĭĭt. Rĕquĭē lēnīrĕ dŏlōrēs. *To appease.* Syn.—Plācŏ, flēctŏ.

Lēnĭs, ĭs, ĕ. *Gentle, mild.* Syn.—Mītĭs, mōllĭs, clēmēns, bĕnīgnŭs, blāndŭs, plăcĭdŭs, quĭētŭs. *Kind, sweet in disposition.* Syn.—Bŏnŭs, bĕnīgnŭs, blāndŭs, cōmĭs, hūmānŭs, mānsuētŭs, mītĭs, clēmēns, īndūlgēns, făcĭlĭs, mōllĭs, plăcĭdŭs. Phr.—Lēnĭs ĭn hōstēm. Nōn lēnĭs prĕcĭbŭs fātă rĕclūdĕrĕ.

Lēnĭtās, ātĭs. f. *Sweetness, kindness.* Syn.—Clēmēntĭă, īndūlgēntĭă, cōmĭtās.

Lēnĭtĕr. adv. *Sweetly, gently.* Syn.—Lēnĕ, blāndē, plăcĭdē, bĕnīgnē, clēmēntĕr. *With good will.* Syn.—Plăcĭdē, bĕnīgnē, bĕnīgnĭŭs, cōmĭtĕr.

Lēns, lēntĭs. f. *Lentils.* (*See Appendix under list of Trees, etc.*)

Lēntē. adv. *Slowly.* Syn.—Tārdē, cūnctāntĕr, sēgnĭtĕr, rĕmīssē, īgnāvē. Phr.—Nōn cĕlĕrī, lēntō, tārdō grădū, pĕdĕ. Dēsĭdĕ pāssū.

Lēntēscŏ, ĭs, ĕrĕ. *To become soft, to become supple.* Syn.—Mōllĭŏr, flēctŏr. Fig.—*To soften, to be appeased.* Syn.—Lēnĭŏr, plācŏr, mītĭgŏr, mĭnŭŏr.

Lēntŏ, ās, āvī, ātŭm, ārĕ. *To bend. See Flecto.* Fig.—*To relent.* Syn.—Lēnĭŏr, plācŏr.

Lēntŭs, ă, ūm. *Pliable, flexible.* Seū lēntō fŭĕrīnt ālveārĭă vīmĭnĕ tēxtă. V. Syn.—Tĕnĕr, flēxĭlĭs, flēxĭbĭlĭs. Phr.—Lēntă sălīx. Vērbĕră lēntă pătī. Fig.—*Slow.* Syn.—Tārdŭs, pĭgĕr, ĭnērs, sēgnĭs, lānguĭdŭs, īgnāvŭs, rĕmīssŭs, dēsĕs, tōrpēns. *Indifferent.* Syn.—Plăcĭdŭs, īmmōtŭs, trānquīllŭs, æquŭs, pătĭēns.

Lĕŏ, ōnĭs. m. *Lion.* Īmpĕtŭs ēt fūlvīs ēt vāstă lĕōnĭbŭs īră. O. Phr.—Fĕrārūm rēx. Sīlvārūm dŏmĭnŭs. Vīrĭbŭs aūdāx. Gĕnŭs ācrĕ lĕōnūm.

Lĕpĭdē. adv. *Agreeably, rightfully, skilfully.* Syn.—Rēctē, pūlchrē, bĕnĕ; ūrbānē, jūcūndē, fēstīvē, făcētē.

Lĕpĭdŭs, ă, ūm. *Amiable, agreeable.* Scīmŭs ĭnūrbānō lĕpĭdūm sēcērnĕrĕ dīctūm. H. Syn.—Ārgūtŭs, făcētŭs, fēstīvŭs, jŏcōsŭs, ūrbānŭs, vĕnūstŭs, jūcūndŭs.

Lĕpŏr & Lĕpōs, ōrĭs. m. *Grace, refinement.* Syn.—Vĕnūstās, grātĭă, dĕcŏr, dĕcŭs, fēstīvĭtās, ūrbānĭtās, jŏcī, sălēs.

Lētālĭs, ĭs, ĕ. *Deadly.* Hærēt lătĕrī lētālĭs ărūndŏ. V. Syn.—Lētĭfĕr, ēxĭtĭōsŭs, ēxĭtĭālĭs, fātālĭs, fūnēstŭs. Phr.—Quā fātă cĕlērrĭmă. Quāque ēst vĭă prōxĭmă lētō.

Leūcŏĭŏn & Leūcŏĭūm, ī. n. *The white violet.* (*See Appendix under list of Trees, etc.*)

Lĕvāmĕn, ĭnĭs. n. *Solace.* Syn.—Lĕvāmēntūm, lēnīmĕn, sōlātĭūm.

Lĕvĭs, ĭs, ĕ. *Light.* Phr.—Grăvĭtātĕ cărēns. Ēxpērs grăvĭtātĭs. Sĭnĕ pōndĕrĕ. Nīl grăvĭtātĭs. *Nimble.* Syn.—Ăgĭlĭs, ălăcĕr, cĕlĕr. *Fickle.* Syn.—Mōbĭlĭs, īncōnstāns, mūtābĭlĭs, īnstābĭlĭs.

Lĕvĭtās, ātĭs. f. *Lightness, quickness. See Celeritas. Inconstancy.* Syn.—Īncōnstāntĭă, mōbĭlĭtās.

Lĕvĭtĕr. adv. *Lightly.* Syn.—Mōllĭtĕr. *Superficially.* Syn.—Brĕvĭtĕr, ŏbĭtĕr, strīctūm. *Rashly.* Syn.—Tĕmĕrĕ, īncōnsūltē.

Lĕvŏ, ās, āvī, ātūm, ārĕ. *To raise, to elevate.* Tēr sēse āttōllēns cŭbĭtōque īnnīxă lĕvāvĭt. V. Syn.—Sūblĕvŏ, tōllŏ, āttōllŏ, ērĭgŏ. *To get rid of.* Syn.—Ēxōnĕrŏ, dētrăhŏ, ădĭmŏ. *To charm.* Syn.—Lēnĭŏ, jŭvŏ, sōlŏr, mūlcĕŏ, rĕcrĕŏ.

Lēx, lēgĭs. f. *Law, right.* Ōppĭdă mōlīrī, lēgēs īncīdĕrĕ līgnō. H. Syn.—Jūs, jūră, ēdīctūm, dēcrētūm, scītūm, plăcĭtūm, mōs. Phr.—Lēgūm jūră, jūssă, dēcrētă. Fās ēt jūră. Lēgūm mŏdĕrāmĕn. Vĭdŭātæ jūdĭcĕ lēgēs. Pērrūmpĕrĕ lēgēs.

Lĭbēntĕr. adv. *Gladly, freely.* Syn.—Lŭbēntĕr, ūltrō, spōntĕ. Phr.—Lĭbēntī ănĭmō.

Lĭbĕr, lĭbrī. m. *Book.* Syn.—Lĭbēllŭs, scrīptūm, vŏlūmĕn, chārtæ, cōdēx, ŏpŭs. Phr.—Lĭbrōs cōmpōnĕrĕ, ēdĕrĕ, prōfērrĕ īn lūcēm. Cārmĭnă fāmæ trādĕrĕ.

Lībĕr, ĕră, ĕrūm. *Free.* Syn.—Īmmūnĭs, ēxpĕdītŭs, lībĕrātŭs, sŏlūtŭs. Phr.—Lībērtātĕ, lībērtātĭs jūrĕ frŭēns, gaūdēns. Sērvĭtĭō lībĕr. Vīnclīs sŏlūtŭs. Lībērquĕ lăbōrūm. Plūs æquō lībĕr. *Lawless, unchecked.* Syn.—Prŏcāx, pĕtŭlāns, ēffrēnŭs, aūdāx.

Lībĕrālĭs, ĭs, ĕ. *Noble, worthy of a free man.* Syn.—Īngĕnŭŭs, lībĕr. *Liberal, generous.* Syn.—Lārgŭs, bĕnĕfĭcŭs, mūnĭfĭcŭs, prŏfūsŭs, bĕnīgnŭs. Phr.—Nōn ăvārŭs. Nōn pārcŭs. Prōdĭgŭs æris. Prōdĭgă dēxtră.

Lībĕrālĭtās, ātĭs. f. *Liberality.* Syn.—Mūnĭfĭcēntĭă, īndūlgēntĭă. Phr.—Mūnĭfĭcă nātūră.

Lībĕrō, ās, āvī, ātūm, ārĕ. *To free.* Syn.—Ēxĭmŏ, sōlvŏ, vīndĭcŏ. Phr.—Vīnclīs, jŭgō ēxĭmŏ, ērĭpĭŏ. Sērvĭlĭă vĭncŭlă sōlvŏ. Sērvĭtĭī tūrpĕ jŭgum aūfĕrŏ. Sērvĭtĭō rĕdĭmŏ. *See Solvo.*

Lībērtās, ātĭs. f. *Liberty.* Phr.—Lībērtātĭs hŏnōs. Lībĕră cōndĭtĭŏ. Vītæ lībĕrĭōrĭs ămŏr. *Liberty to speak, act, etc.* Syn.—Vĕnĭă, făcūltās, cōpĭă, lĭcēntĭă.

Lĭbēt, lĭbŭĭt, ērĕ. *It pleases.* Syn.—Lŭbēt, jŭvăt, plăcēt. Phr.—Lĭbīdŏ ēst. Ēst ănĭmŭs. Fērt ĭtă cōrdĕ vŏlūntās.

Lĭbīdŏ, ĭnĭs. f. *Desire, caprice.* Syn.—Ārbĭtrĭūm, vŏlūntās, cŭpīdŏ. *Passion, unbridled desires.* Syn.—Cŭpīdŏ, fŭrŏr, răbĭēs, īmpĕtŭs, ārdŏr.

Lībŏ, ās, āvī, ātūm, ārĕ. *To taste.* Vīna ĕgŏ lībārăm, sŏcĕrō lībātă prŏpīnŏ. O. Syn.—Dēlībŏ, gūstŏ, dēgūstŏ, prægūstŏ. *To diminish, to take away.* Syn.—Ădĭmŏ, dētrăhŏ, tōllŏ, dēmŏ.

Lībră, æ. f. *Pound-weight.* Syn.—Ās. *Balance.* Syn.—Lānx, trŭtĭnă, stătēră, bĭlānx, ēxāmĕn.

Lībrŏ, ās, āvī, ātūm, ārĕ. *To balance.* Syn.—Ēxāmĭnŏ, pēndŏ, āppēndŏ, æquŏ, sūstĭnĕŏ, sūspēndŏ. *To share.* Syn.—Aēquŏ, dīvĭdŏ, pārtĭŏr. *To brandish.* Syn.—Ăgĭtŏ, vĭbrŏ, tōrquĕŏ, īntōrquĕŏ, jăcŭlŏr.

Lĭcēntĕr. adv. *Freely, immoderately.* Syn.—Aūdāctĕr, īmmŏdĭcē, sŏlūtē.

Lĭcēntĭă, æ. f. *Permission, faculty.* Syn.—Lībērtās, vĕnĭă, făcūltās, pŏtēstās, cōpĭă. *License.* Syn.—Lībērtās, lĭbīdŏ. Phr.—Lībĕră frēnīs. Sŏlūtă lēgĭbŭs. Scĕlĕrātă aūdācĭă.

Lĭcēt, ŭĭt, ērĕ. *It is permitted.* Syn.—Dătŭr, pērmīttĭtŭr, cōncēdĭtŭr. Phr.—Fās ēst. Jūră sĭnūnt. Nīl vĕtăt, prŏhĭbēt.

Lĭcēt. conj. *Although.* Syn.—Ētsī, tămētsī, quāmvīs, quāmquām. *See Quamvis.*

Līgnūm, ī. n. *Wood.* Nām prīmī cŭnĕīs scīndēbānt fīssĭlĕ līgnūm. V. Syn.—Stīpĕs, rōbŭr, sŭdĕs, trābs, ārbŏr, sīlvă, trūncŭs.

Lĭgō, ās, āvī, ātŭm, ārĕ. *To bind.* Cōrrĭpĭŭnt spīrīsquĕ lĭgānt īngĕntĭbŭs. V. Syn.—Āllĭgō, rĕlĭgō, vīncĭō, rĕvīncĭō, nēctō, ādnēctō, cōnnēctō, strīngō, cōnstrīngō.

Lĭgūrĭō, īs, īvī & ĭī, ītŭm, īrĕ. *To eat ravenously.* Syn.—Āblĭgūrĭō, vŏrō, dēvŏrō, sōrbĕō, ābsōrbĕō, hēllŭŏr, ābsūmō.

Lĭgūstrŭm, ī. n. *The privet, a plant.* (*See Appendix under list of Trees, etc.*)

Lĭlĭŭm, ĭī. n. *The lily.* (*See Appendix under list of Trees, etc.*)

Līmĕn, ĭnĭs. n. *Threshold of a door.* Aērĕă cuī grădĭbŭs sūrgēbānt līmĭnă. V. Syn.—Ōstĭŭm, pōrtă, jānŭă, vālvæ, pōstēs, fŏrēs, ădĭtŭs, vēstĭbŭlŭm. Phr.—Līmĭnă prīmă dŏmūs. Līmĭnĕ sŭbmŏvĕŏr. Fig.—*Threshold of life. See Initium.*

Līmĕs, ĭtĭs. m. *Path, way.* Jām pătēt āttrītūs sŏlĭtārŭm līmĕs ăquārŭm. O. Syn.—Trāmĕs, sēmĭtă. *Limit.* Syn.—Fīnĭs, mētă, tērmĭnŭs.

Līmō, ās, āvī, ātŭm, ārĕ. *To file, to polish.* Phr.—Līmā tĕrō, āttĕrō, cōntĕrō, pŏlĭō, ēxpŏlĭō, pērpŏlĭō, lævĭgō, dŏlō. Fig.—*To polish up a writing.*

Līmpĭdŭs, ă, ŭm. *Clear, limpid.* Ērŭmpīt pĕr ăgrōs vāstīs fōns līmpĭdŭs āntrīs. O. Syn.—Lūcĭdŭs, pēllūcĭdŭs, nĭtĭdŭs, pūrŭs, lĭquĭdŭs, clārŭs, īllīmĭs, ārgēntĕŭs, vĭtrĕŭs, crȳstāllĭnŭs.

Līmŭs, ī. m. *Mud.* Syn.—Fæx, cœnŭm, lŭtŭm.

Līnĕă, æ. f. *Line, stroke of a pen or pencil.* Fig.—*Limit.* Syn.—Mētă, tērmĭnŭs, fīnĭs, līmĕs. *String, cord.* Syn.—Fūnĭs, rēstĭs, fūnĭcŭlŭs. *Fishing-line.* Syn.—Līnŭm, ărūndō.

Līnguă, æ. f. *Tongue.* Phr.—Līnguæ dēfēcĕrăt hūmŏr. Faūcēs āspĕră līnguă prĕmĭt. Fērvēt līnguă mĕrō. Līnguīs mĭcăt ōrĕ trĭsūlcīs. *Speech, voice.* Syn.—Vōx, ōs, vōcēs, vērbă, dīctă, sŏnŭs. *Discourse.* Syn.—Ēlŏquĭŭm, fācūndĭă.

Lĭnĭō, īs, īrĕ & Lĭnō, ĭs, lēvī, lĭtŭm, ĕrĕ. *To smear with, to annoint with.* Syn.—Īllĭnō, āllĭnō, pērlĭnō, ūngō, ĭnūngō, tīngō. *To soil.* Syn.—Īnfĭcĭō, cōllĭnō, fœdō.

Līnquō, ĭs, lĭquī, lĭctŭm, ĕrĕ. *To leave.* Sĭmŭl hīs dīctīs līnquēbăt hăbēnās. V. Syn.—Rĕlīnquō, dēsĕrō. *To remit, to give up.* Syn.—Pērmīttō, rĕlīnquō, trādō.

Līnŭm, ī. n. *Flax.* (*See Appendix under list of Trees, etc.*)

Lĭquĕfăcĭō, ĭs, ēcī, āctŭm, ĕrĕ. *To melt.* Syn.—Lĭquō, ēlĭquō, sōlvō, rĕsōlvō, dīssōlvō, mōllĭō.

Lĭquĕfīō, īs, fāctŭs sŭm, ĭĕrī. *To become liquid.* Syn.—Cōllĭquēscō, lĭquŏr, sōlvŏr, dīssōlvŏr, rĕsōlvŏr, mōllĭŏr, rĕmōllĭŏr. Phr.—Īn ăquās sōlvŏr. Nĭvĭbŭs dē mōntĭbŭs sŏlūtīs. Vīctæ sōlĕ tĕpēntĕ nĭvēs.

Lĭquĕt. impers. *It is clear.* Syn.—Pătĕt, cōnstăt. Phr.—Cērtūm ēst. Clārūm, mănĭfēstūm ēst.

Lĭquĭdē & Lĭquĭdō. adv. *Clearly.* Syn.—Clārē, ăpērtē.

Lĭquĭdŭs, ă, ūm. *Liquid, fluid.* Syn.—Lĭquātŭs, lĭquēns, lĭquĕfāctŭs, flŭĭdŭs, flūxŭs, dēflŭŭs, hūmĭdŭs, sŏlūtŭs, rĕsŏlūtŭs. Phr.—Aūt cūm līquēntĭă mēllă Stīpānt. Ēt vīnă līquēntĭă fūndām. *Clear (in speaking of the voice).* Syn.—Pūrŭs, clārŭs, mōllĭs, flŭēns, făcĭlĭs, cănōrŭs.

Līs, lītĭs. f. *Process, law-suit.* Īnsĕquĕrĭs tămĕn hūnc, ēt lītĕ mŏrārĭs ĭnīquā. H. Syn.—Lītigĭūm, cōntēntĭŏ, rīxă, āltērcātĭŏ, dīscōrdĭă, cōntrŏvērsĭă, dīssĭdĭūm, jūrgĭūm, pūgnă, cērtāmĕn. Phr.—Nŏvās īncīdĕrĕ lītēs. Pērdĕrĕ lītēm. Ērĭpĕre ātrīs lītĭbŭs īmplĭcĭtūm. Ăd ārmă fōrī.

Lĭtāmĕn, ĭnĭs. n. *Sacrifice, offering.* Syn.—Lībāmĕn, lĭtātĭŏ.

Lītĭgŏ, ās, āvī, ātūm, ārĕ. *To plead a case, to sue.* Syn.—Dīscēptŏ, cōntēndŏ, rīxŏr, jūrgŏ, jūrgŏr, āltērcŏr, cērtŏ, pūgnŏ. Phr.—Lītēs ēxērcĕŏ. Lītĕ cōntēndŏ. Bēllō fŏrēnsī cōntēndĕrĕ. Fŏrō sī rēs cērtābĭtŭr ōlīm.

Lĭtŏ, ās, āvī, ātūm, ārĕ. *To make an offering, a sacrifice.* Sānguĭnĕ quærēndī rĕdĭtūs, ănĭmāquĕ lĭtāndūm Ārgŏlĭcā. V. Syn.—Ōffĕrŏ, māctŏ, săcrĭfĭcŏ.

Lĭttĕră, æ. f. *Letter of the alphabet.* Syn.—Lĭttĕrŭlă, nŏtæ, sīgnūm. *In the plural a letter, epistle.* Syn.—Ĕpīstŏlă, scrīptūm, ĕpīstŏlĭūm, chārtă, lĭbēllŭs, tăbēllæ. Phr.—Lĭttĕrās scrībĕrĕ. Scrīptō mīttĕrĕ sălūtēm. Scrībĕrĕ sălūtēm.

Lĭttŭs, ŏrĭs. n. *Shore.* Quā mōllĭbŭs ūndīs Lĭttŏrĭs īncūrvī bĭbŭlām lăvĭt æquŏr ărēnām. L. Syn.—Āctă (æ), ōră, ărēnă. Phr.—Lĭttŏrĭs ōră. Lĭttŏrĕæ ărēnæ. Hōspĭtĭūm ărēnæ. Nĭmĭūm prĕmēndō Lĭttŭs ĭnīquūm. Tōrquēre ăd lĭttŏră clāvūm.

Lŏcŏ, ās, āvī, ātūm, ārĕ. *To put, to place.* Āltă thĕātrī fūndāmēntă lŏcānt. V. Syn.—Cōllŏcŏ, pōnŏ, rĕpōnŏ, stătŭŏ, cōnstĭtŭŏ. Phr.—Grāmĭnĕōquĕ vĭrōs lŏcăt īpsĕ sĕdīlĕ. *To let.* Syn.—Cōndūcŏ.

Lŏcŭplēs, ētĭs. adj. *Rich.* Aēquē paūpĕrĭbūs prōdēst lŏcŭplētĭbŭs æquē. H. Syn.—Dīvĕs, ŏpŭlēntŭs. *Fertile, abundant.* Syn.—Dīvĕs, ăbūndāns.

Lŏcŭs, ī. m. *Place.* Hīc lŏcŭs ūrbĭs ĕrĭt. V. Syn.—Spătĭūm, sēdēs. *Situation.* Syn.—Sĭtŭs. *Country.* Syn.—Sēdēs, rĕgĭŏ, tērră, ōræ. *Condition, rank.* Syn.—Cōndĭtĭŏ, fōrtūnă, sōrs, stătŭs, grădŭs. *Occasion.* Syn.—Tēmpŭs, ōccāsĭŏ. Abl. *In the place of.* Syn.—Vĭcĕ, prō.

Lŏlĭūm, ĭī. n. *Cockle.* (*See Appendix under list of Trees, etc.*)

Lōngævŭs, ă, ūm *Aged*. Syn.—Grāndævŭs, ānnōsŭs, sĕnēx, sĕnĭŏr.

Lōngē. adv. *Afar*. Syn.—Prŏcŭl. *From afar*. Syn.—Prŏcŭl, ēmĭnŭs.

Lōngīnquŭs, ă, ūm. *Far off, distant*. Lōngīnquō rĕfĕrām lāssŭs ăb ōrbĕ pĕdēm. O. Syn.—Rĕmōtŭs, dīssĭtŭs, dīstāns, dīsjūnctŭs, rĕpōstŭs. *Stranger*. Syn.—Ēxtĕrŭs, pĕrĕgrīnŭs.

Lōngūm. adv. *A long time*. Syn.—Lōngē, dĭū. Phr.—Lōngō tēmpŏrĕ.

Lōngŭs, ă, ūm. *Long*. Flāmmārūm lōngōs ā tērgo ālbēscĕrĕ trāctūs. V. Syn.—Ōblōngŭs, prōdūctŭs, prōlīxŭs, ēxcūrrēns, pătēns, īmmēnsŭs. Phr.—Lōngūm pēr vāllūm pāscĭtŭr āgmĕn. Lōngĭŏr ānnō. Nōn lōnga ēst fābŭlă. Sĕrĭēs lōngīssimă rērūm.

Lŏquācĭtās, ātĭs. f. *Talkativeness, loquacity*. Syn.—Gārrŭlĭtās. Phr.—Līnguă lŏquāx. Gārrŭlă līnguā. Lārgă fāndī cōpĭă.

Lŏquācĭtĕr. adv. *Garrulously*. Syn.—Vērbōsē, fūsĭŭs.

Lŏquāx, ācĭs. adj. *Talkative*. Syn.—Vērbōsŭs, gārrŭlŭs, mūltĭlŏquŭs. Phr.—Ēdēns mīllĕ sŏnōs. Vărĭās ĭtĕrāns vōcēs. Vānīs īmplēt sērmōnĭbŭs aūrēs. Mĕlĭŏr cōntēndĕrĕ līnguā.

Lŏquŏr, ĕrĭs, cūtŭs sūm, ī. *To speak*. Grāiīs dĕdĭt ōrĕ rŏtūndō Mūsă lŏquī. H. Syn.—Ēlŏquŏr, dīcŏ, fārī. Phr.—Vērbă mīttŏ, făcĭŏ, fūndŏ, ēdŏ, prōmŏ. Vōcēm dō. Pēctŏrĕ, ōrĕ vōcēs rĕfĕrŏ. Dūlcĕ lŏquī. Sīc ōre ēffātŭs ămīco ēst. Hæc ŭbĭ dīctă. Sŏlĭō sīc īnfĭt ăb āltō. Trăhĭt dē pēctŏrĕ vōcēm. Tālĭă vōcĕ rĕfērt. Sīc mĕmŏrăt. Tālĭă pērstābăt mĕmŏrāns. Aūdīre ēt rēddĕrĕ vōcēs. Sīc ōre ēffātă. Hæc ēffūdĭt pēctŏrĕ dīctă. Fīnēm dĕdĭt ōrĕ lŏquēndī. Nēc plūra ēffātŭs.

Lōrūm, ī. n. *Strap, thong, bond. See Vinculum. Whip*. Syn.—Hăbēnă, flăgēllūm, flăgrūm, scŭtĭcă.

Lūbrĭcŭs, ă, ūm. *Slipping, gliding by*. Syn.—Lābĭlĭs, mōbĭlĭs, lævĭs, fŭgĭēns, flūxŭs, fāllēns, fāllāx.

Lūcĕŏ, ēs, lūxī, ērĕ. *To shine, to give forth light*. Ūt mĭhĭ pērpĕtŭō lūcĕāt īgnĕ fŏcŭs. Tib. Syn.—Cōllūcĕŏ, ēlūcĕŏ, īllūcĕŏ, rĕlūcĕŏ, fūlgĕŏ, ēffūlgĕŏ, nĭtĕŏ, splēndĕŏ, cŏrūscŏ, rădĭŏ. Phr.—Lūcēm spārgŏ, ēmīttŏ. Rădĭōs spārgŏ. Lūcĕ cŏrūscŏ. Īn lūcĕ rĕfūlsĭt. Lōngō dāt līmĭtĕ lūcēm. Dāt clāra īncēndĭă lūcēm. *See Lumen, Splendeo*.

Lūcērnă, æ. f. *Torch, lamp*. Syn.—Lȳchnŭs, tēstă, lāmpăs, lūmĕn, flāmmă, fāx, fūnālĕ. *See Lampas*.

Lūcĭdŭs, ă, ūm. *Clear, brilliant*. Hædōrūmquĕ dĭēs sērvāndi ēt lūcĭdŭs ānguĭs. V. Syn.—Lūcēns, nĭtĭdŭs, nĭtēns, clārŭs. Phr.—Lūcēntēs aūrō tŭnĭcæ. Ēt spīcŭlă lūcĭdă tērgēnt. Tōtĭs lūcēm spārgēntĭă rīpīs. Fig. Syn.—Clārŭs.

Lŭcrōsŭs, ă, ūm. *Lucrative.* Syn.—Quæstŭōsŭs, ūtĭlĭs, cōmmŏdŭs.

Lŭcrūm, ī. n. *Gain, profit.* Spērnĕ lŭcrūm; vēxāt mēntēs vēsānă lĭbīdŏ. Tib. Syn.—Quæstŭs, cōmmŏdūm, ēmŏlŭmēntūm. Phr.—Ăvāro īncūmbĕrĕ lūcrō. Āppōne īn lūcrūm. Īn lūcro ēst quæ dătŭr hōră mĭhĭ. Lŭcrī fēcĭt. Īmpĭŭs lŭcrī fŭrŏr.

Lūctă, æ. f. *Struggle.* Syn.—Lūctātĭŏ, pălæstră, lūctāmĕn, lūctātŭs, cērtāmĕn, pūgnă. *See Palæstra, Luctor.*

Lūctāmĕn, ĭnĭs. n. *Struggle. See Lucta. Effort.* Syn.—Cōnātŭs, nīsŭs. *See Conatus.*

Lūctŏr, ārĭs, ātŭs sūm, ārī. *To struggle.* Ēt jām cōntŭlĕrānt ārctō lūctāntĭă nēxū Pēctŏră pēctŏrĭbŭs. O. Phr.—Cōrpŭs ēxērcĕŏ pălæstrā. Cōntēndŏ, cērtŏ lūctā. Īndūlgĕŏ pălæstrā. Pūgnām ĭnĕŏ, ēxērcĕŏ. *To fight in single combat.* Syn.—Cērtŏ, dēcērtŏ, cōntēndŏ, ōblūctŏr, cōllūctŏr.

Lūctŭōsŭs, ă, ūm. *Sad, deplorable.* Syn.—Flēbĭlĭs, lūgŭbrĭs, lūgēns, mœstŭs, trīstĭs, mĭsĕr, īnfēlīx, fērālĭs, fūnēstŭs.

Lūctŭs, ūs. m. *Grief, sorrow.* Quæ sōlă lĕvābās Mātērnōs lūctūs. O. Syn.—Dŏlŏr, mœrŏr, āngŏr, cūră, flētŭs, gĕmĭtŭs, quĕrēlæ, quēstŭs, lăcrĭmæ, plānctŭs, ējūlātŭs, lāmēntūm.

Lūdĭbrĭūm, ĭī. n. *Sport, joke.* Syn.—Lūdŭs, jŏcŭs. Phr.—Lūdībrĭă vēntīs.

Lūdĭcĕr & Lūdĭcrŭs, ă, ūm. *Jocose.* Syn.—Jŏcōsŭs, jŏcŭlārĭs, fēstīvŭs, lūsōrĭŭs.

Lūdĭcrūm, ī. n. *Spectacle, play.* Syn.—Lūdī, spēctācŭlă. *Amusement, play.* Syn.—Jŏcŭs, lūdŭs, ōblēctātĭŏ, ōblēctāmĕn, gaūdĭūm.

Lūdĭfĭcŏ, ās, āvī, ātūm, ārĕ. *To deceive, to dupe.* Syn.—Īllūdŏ, dēcĭpĭŏ, fāllŏ.

Lūdŏ, ĭs, lūsī, lūsūm, ĕrĕ. *To play.* Syn.—Cōllūdŏ. Phr.—Lūdō văcŏ, īndūlgĕŏ. Lūdōs ēxērcĕŏ. Mēntēm, ănĭmūm, cōrpŭs lāxŏ, rĕcrĕŏ. Tēmpŭs lūdō trăhŏ. Nōctī lūdum æquārĕ. Īn lūcēm lūdūm fērrĕ. *To abuse, to deceive.* Syn.—Dēlūdŏ, fāllŏ, īllūdŏ, lūdĭfĭcŏr.

Lūdŭs, ī. m. *Play.* Lūdŭs ĕnīm gĕnŭĭt trĕpĭdūm cērtāmĕn ĕt īrās. H. Syn.—Lūsŭs. Phr.—Lūdī dūlcēdŏ, gaūdĭă. *Distraction.* Syn.—Lūsŭs, lūdĭcră, gaūdĭă. *Joke.* Syn.—Jŏcŭs, sălēs. *Spectacle.* Syn.—Spēctācŭlă, lūdĭcră.

Lŭēs, ĭs. f. *Contagion, corruption.* Syn.—Pēstĭs, cōntāgēs, cōntāgĭŏ, cōntāgĭă (ōrūm). (*In general*) *A pest.* Syn.—Pēstĭs, ēxĭtĭūm.

Lūgĕŏ, ēs, lūxī, ctūm, ērĕ. *To grieve, to mourn, to be afflicted.* Dīssĭmĭlīsquĕ sŭī frātrēm lūgēbăt ădēmptūm. O. Syn.—Flĕŏ, plōrŏ, lăcrĭmŏ, dŏlĕŏ, gĕmŏ, quĕrŏr, lāmēntŏr, plāngŏ. Phr.—Lūctĭbŭs īndūlgĕŏ. Īn lūctūm mē sōlvŏ. Lūctū vūltūs cōndŏ. Quīd tāntō tūrbāntūr mœnĭă lūctū.

Lūgŭbrĭs, ĭs, ĕ. *Mournful, deplorable.* Syn.—Flēbĭlĭs, lūctŭōsŭs, lāmēntābĭlĭs, trīstĭs, mœstŭs, fūnĕbrĭs, īnfaūstŭs, lūctĭfĭcŭs.

Lūmĕn, ĭnĭs. n. *Light.* Pāscūntūr īgnēs nōctūrni, ēt lūmĭnă fūndūnt. V. Syn.—Lūx, jŭbăr, fāx, nĭtŏr, fūlgŏr, splēndŏr. Phr.—Lūmĭnĭs dĕcŏr, nĭtŏr, splēndŏr. Lūcĭdŭs nĭtŏr. Clārā lūcĕ cŏrūscūm. Dĭūrnī īgnēs. Rŭtĭlō scīntīllāt lūmĭnĕ lāmpăs. Splēndēt lūrĭdă tērrīs. Lūmĭnă præbēbăt. *Star. See Astrum. Eye. See Oculus.*

Lūnă, æ. f. *Moon.* Nōx ĕrăt ēt cœlō fūlgēbāt lūnă sĕrēnō. Syn.—Cȳnthĭă, Dĭānă, Lātōnă. Phr.—Nōctĭs sīdŭs, jŭbăr. Lūnæ vūltūs, făcĭēs, cōrnŭă, cūrrŭs. Lūnæ rădĭāntĭs ĭmāgŏ. Lūcēm sōlĭs dē lūmĭnĕ dūcēns. Tăcĭtæ pĕr ămīcă sĭlēntĭă Lūnæ. Phœbī sŏrŏr. Nĭvĕĭs īnvēctă bīgīs. Īgnēs cūrvātī lūnæ nŏvūm rĕfĕrēntĭs ōrtūm. Lūnă dēcrēscēns.

Lŭŏ, ĭs, ī, ĕrĕ. *To bathe. See Lavo. To pay, to satisfy.* Syn.—Sōlvŏ, ēxsōlvŏ, pērsōlvŏ, pēndŏ, pĭŏ. Phr.—Mōrtĕ lŭēt mĕrĭtā. Lŭĭmūs pērjūrĭă Trōjæ.

Lŭpīnŭs, ī. m. *Lupin, a kind of pulse.* (*See Appendix under list of Trees, etc.*)

Lŭpŭs, ī. m. *Wolf.* Tōrvă lĕænă lŭpūm sĕquĭtūr lŭpŭs īpsĕ căpēllām. V. Phr.—Pĕcŏrūm, ŏvĭūm hōstĭs. Ārmēntīs īnfēstŭs. Ŏvĭūm prædŏ vŏrāx. Gĕnŭs ēxĭtĭālĕ lŭpōrūm. Flāmmāntĭă lūmĭnă tōrquēns. Lŭpŭs ōrĕ crŭēntō.

Lūscĭnĭă, æ. f. *The nightingale.* (*See Appendix under list of Birds.*)

Lūstrŏ, ās, āvī, ātūm, ārĕ. *To purify a place.* Syn.—Pĭŏ, ēxpĭŏ, pūrgŏ. *To wander around.* Syn.—Pērlūstrŏ, āmbĭŏ, cīrcŭmĕŏ, ŏbĕŏ, pērcūrrŏ, pĕrăgrŏ, pĕrērrŏ. *To review, to examine.* Syn.—Pērlūstrŏ, īnvīsŏ, ădĕŏ, cīrcūmspĭcĭŏ, spēctŏ, ēxāmĭnŏ.

Lūsŭs, ūs. m. *Joke, jest.* Syn.—Lūdŭs, jŏcŭs. *See Ludus, Jocus.*

Lūtĕŭs, ă, ūm. *Saffron, yellow.* Syn.—Lūtĕŏlŭs, crŏcĕŭs.

Lŭtĕŭs, ă, ūm. *Muddy.* Syn.—Lŭtōsŭs. *Smeared as with mud.* Syn.—Īllĭtŭs, ōblĭtŭs, lŭtātŭs.

Lŭtŏ, ās, āvī, ātūm, ārĕ. *To smear.* Syn.—Īllĭnŏ, ōblĭnŏ.

Lŭtūm, ī. n. *Mud.* Syn.—Cœnūm, līmŭs, sōrdēs, fēx, īllŭvĭēs.

Lūx, lūcĭs. f. *Light.* Nŏvă lūx ŏcŭlīs āffūlsĭt. V. Syn.—Lūmĕn, splēndŏr. *See Lumen.* Phr.—Lūx sōlīs cŏmĕs. Fīlĭă sōlĭs. Lūcĭs nĭtŏr. Ūt prīmūm lūx ālmă dăta ēst. *Glory, honor.* Syn.—Lūmĕn, splēndŏr, dĕcŭs. Phr.—Lūx pătrĭæ. Ō lūx Dārdănĭæ.

Lūxŭrĭōsŭs, ă, ūm. *Abundant, luxurious.* Syn.—Lūxŭrĭāns. *One who loves luxury.* Syn.—Prōdĭgŭs, ēffūsŭs. Phr.—Lūxūs ămāns. Lūxū sŏlūtŭs. Mēns cīrcūmflŭă lūxū. Lātē mūltō spēctābĭlĭs aūrō.

Lūxŭs, ūs. m. *Luxury, abundance.* Syn.—Lūxŭrĭă, lūxŭrĭēs, pōmpă, fāstŭs, părātŭs, ŏpŭlēntĭă, dēlĭcĭæ. Phr.—Pērsĭcŭs āppărātŭs. Pŏpŭlātŏr ŏpūm. Quēm sēmpēr cŏmĭtātŭr ĕgēstās. Fāmi āffīnĭs ăvāræ. Rēgālī splēndĭdă lūxū Ātrĭă. *Sloth, inaction.* Syn.—Īgnāvĭă, mōllĭtĭēs, sēgnĭtĭēs.

Lȳmphātŭs, ă, ūm. *Delirious, mad.* Syn.—Dēmēns, āmēns, īnsānŭs, fŭrēns, fŭrĭōsŭs, răbĭdŭs, ēxstērnātŭs. Phr.—Lȳmphātō trĕpĭdārĕ mĕtū. Lȳmphātā mēntĕ fŭrēbānt.

Lȳră, æ. f. *Lyre.* Ēt movėt aūrātæ pōllĭcĕ fīlă lȳræ. O. Syn.—Bārbĭtŏn, chĕly̆s, cĭthără, fĭdēs (ĭūm), tēstūdŏ. *See Cithara, Fides. Poetry in general.* Syn.—Cārmĕn, mŏdŭs.

Lȳrĭcŭs, ă, ūm. *Lyric.* Quōd sī mē lȳrĭcīs vātĭbŭs īnsĕrēs. H. Syn.—Pīndărĭcŭs.

M

Măcĕr, măcră, măcrūm. *Thin, lean, slender.* Ēheū! quām pīnguī măcĕr ēst mĭhĭ taūrŭs ĭn ārvō. V. Syn.—Măcĭlēntŭs, grăcĭlĭs, grăcĭlēntŭs, (*sometimes*) līgnĕŭs, ōssĕŭs, ārĭdŭs.

Mācĕrŏ, ās, āvī, ātūm, ārĕ. *To render supple by immersing in water.* Fig.—*To weaken, to enfeeble.* Syn.—Āttĕrŏ, ēxtĕnŭŏ, ēxĕdŏ, cōnfĭcĭŏ, tābĕfăcĭŏ.

Măcēscŏ & Măcrēscŏ, ĭs, ĕrĕ. *To become thin, slender.* Syn.—Mācĕrŏr, tābēscŏ, ēxĕdŏr, cōnsūmŏr.

Māchĭnă, æ. f. *Work, construction.* Syn.—Ŏpŭs. Phr.—Ŏpĕrūm strūctūră. Mōlēs ēxstrūctă. *Machine in general.* Syn.—Īnstrūmēntūm. *Engine of war.* Syn.—Mōlēs, bālīstă, ărĭēs, vīnĕă, tōrmēntūm. Phr.—Fœtă ārmīs. Mūrīs mĕtŭēndă. Mœnĭă cōncŭtĭēns. Sāxă rŏtāns.

Māchĭnŏr, ārĭs, ātŭs sūm, ārī. *To invent.* Syn.—Făbrĭcŏ, făbrĭcŏr, strŭŏ, ēxstrŭŏ, mōlĭŏr, ēxcōgĭtŏ, mĕdĭtŏr, īnvĕnĭŏ, cōmmĭnīscŏr.

Māctŏ, ās, āvī, ātūm, ārĕ. *To sacrifice.* Sōlēmnēs taūrum īngēntēm māctābăt ăd ārās. V. Syn.—Īmmŏlŏ, săcrĭfĭcŏ. *See Sacrifico. To slay. See Occīdo.*

Măcŭlă, æ. f. *Stain.* Syn.—Nŏtă, lābēs, (*sometimes*) lĭtūră. Fig.—Syn.—Dēdĕcŭs, īnfāmĭă, prŏbrūm. *Mistake in a work.* Syn.—Mēndūm, ērrŏr.

Măcŭlŏ, ās, āvī, ātūm, ārĕ. *To tint.* Syn.—Dīstīnguŏ, vărĭŏ, pīngŏ. *To soil.* Syn.—Cōmmăcŭlŏ, īnquĭnŏ, cŏīnquĭnŏ, cōntămĭnŏ, fœdŏ, pōllŭŏ, īnfĭcĭŏ. Phr.—Măcŭlīs āspērgŏ, lĭnŏ, īllĭnŏ. Lābē īnfĭcĭŏ. Lābēm īnfĕrŏ. Ēt tērrām tābō măcŭlānt. *To corrupt.* Syn.—Vĭtĭŏ, cōrrūmpŏ.

Măcŭlōsŭs, ă, ūm. *Stained.* Ātquĕ nŏtīs lōngām măcŭlōsūs grāndĭbūs ālvūm. V. Syn.—Măcŭlātŭs, vărĭŭs, vărĭātŭs, gūttātŭs. Phr.—Măcŭlīs āspērsŭs. Bōs măcŭlīs īnsīgnĭs. *Soiled.* Syn.—Tīnctŭs, īmbūtŭs, fœdātŭs.

Mădĕfăcĭŏ, ĭs, fēcī, fāctūm, ĕrĕ. *To moisten, to steep.* Vĭrĭdēsquĕ sŭpēr mădĕfēcĕrăt hērbās. V. Syn.—Hūmēctŏ, īrrĭgŏ, rĭgŏ, īrrōrŏ, pērfūndŏ, āblŭŏ, ĭnūndŏ, īmbŭŏ, ūngŏ. Phr.—Ăquā spārgŏ, tīngŏ. *Pass. To be moist.* Syn.—Mădēscŏ, īmmădĕŏ, hūmēctŏr.

Mădĕŏ, ēs, ŭī, ērĕ. *To be moist.* Syn.—Īmmădĕŏ, mădēscŏ, mădĕfīŏ, hūmēctŏr, hūmĕŏ, ūvēscŏ, rĭgŏr, īrrĭgŏr, pērfūndŏr, īmbŭŏr, tīngŏr, spārgŏr, āspērgŏr, ūngŏr, sūdŏ, mānŏ, dīfflŭŏ, flŭŏ, ĭnūndŏ. Phr.—Sūm hūmĭdŭs, mădĭdŭs. Ăquā mădĕŏ. Mădēnt īmbrĕ gĕnæ. *To be intoxicated. See Ebrius.*

Mădĭdŭs, ă, ūm. *Moist, immersed, wet.* Dūm sĕdĕt ēt sīccāt mădĭdās īn līttŏrĕ pēnnās. J. Syn.—Mădēns, mădĕfāctŭs, hūmēns, hūmĭdŭs, ūdŭs, ūvĭdŭs, rĭgātŭs, īrrĭgŭŭs, rōrāns, spārsŭs, āspērsŭs, pērfūsŭs, rēspērsŭs, flŭēns, ūnctŭs. Phr.—Ūdŭs ăquīs. Ăquā pērfūsŭs. Mădĭdīs Nŏtŭs ēvŏlăt ālīs. Mădĭdāquĕ flŭēns īn vēstĕ Mĕnœtēs. *Tinted.* Syn.—Tīnctŭs.

Măgă, æ. f. *Magician, witch.* Syn.—Sāgă, vĕnēfĭcă, īncāntātrīx, Thēssălă. Phr.—Thēssălă ănŭs. Măgĭcō pŏtēns sāgă mĭnīstĕrĭō. Măgĭcā ārtĕ pŏtēns. Cīrcææ ārtĭs pĕrītă. Măgĭcī dōctă mĭnīstră dŏlī. Măgĭcās āccīngĭĕr ārtēs.

Măgīă, æ. f. (*rare*). *Magic.* Syn.—Cāntŭs, cārmĕn, īncāntāmēntūm, īncāntātĭŏ, vĕnēfĭcĭūm. Phr.—Ārs măgĭcă. Măgĭcūm mĭnīstĕrĭūm. Măgĭcă līnguă. Măgĭcă aūxĭlĭă. Măgĭcă fraūs. Vērbă nōxĭă. Hērbārūm vīrtūs. Pōcŭlă Cīrcæă.

Măgĭcŭs, ă, ūm. *Magic, magical.* Hīc măgĭcōs āffērt cāntūs, hīc Thēssălă vēndĭt. J. Syn.—Măgŭs, Mēdēŭs, Aēæŭs, Cīrcæŭs, Thēssălŭs, Thēssălĭcŭs.

Măgĭs. adv. *More.* Ō lūcĕ măgīs dīlēctă sŏrōrī. V. Syn.—Plūs, āmplĭŭs, măgĕ (*archaic*). Phr.—Măgĭs ēt măgĭs hōrrōr crēscĭt. Tĕnŭēmquĕ măgīs măgĭs āĕră cārpūnt. *Rather.* Syn.—Pŏtĭŭs.

Măgīstĕr, trī. m. *Master, teacher.* Ūt pŭĕrūm sævō crēdās dīctātă măgīstrō Rēddĕrĕ. H. Syn.—Dōctŏr, præcēptŏr. Phr.—Prīmæ cūstōs rēctōrquĕ jŭvēntæ. Cūltōrque ănĭmī mōrūmquĕ măgīstĕr.

Jŭvēntǣ rēctŏr, mŏdĕrātŏr. Cuī dŏcēndī mūnŭs ĕt ōffĭcĭūm. Rŭdēs ănĭmōs prǣcēptīs dŏcēns, īnstĭtŭēns. Tĕnĕrām pūbēm mŏdĕrāns. Dōctrīnā ēxērcēns.

Măgīstĕrĭūm, ĭī. n. *Teaching*. Syn.—Mŏdĕrāmĕn, prǣcēptūm, dūctŭs.

Măgīstrātŭs, ūs. m. *Magistrate*. Jūră măgīstrātūsquĕ lĕgūnt sānctūmquĕ sĕnātūm. V. Syn.—Mŏdĕrātŏr, rēctŏr, jūdēx, prǣsĕs. Phr.—Cuī crēdĭtă ēst īmpĕrāndī pŏtēstās. Cuī īmpĕrĭī cōmmīssă pŏtēstās. Cuī pŏpŭli īncūmbīt cūră rĕgēndī. Jūră dăt. *The office of magistrate*. Syn.—Mūnŭs, fāscēs.

Māgnĭfĭcē. adv. *Magnificently, splendidly*. Syn.—Laūtē, splēndĭdē, ēgrĕgĭē.

Māgnĭfĭcŭs, ă, ūm. *Magnificent*. I, nūnc, māgnĭfĭcōs vīctōr mōlīrĕ trĭūmphōs. O. Syn.—Rēgĭŭs, laūtŭs, splēndĭdŭs, rēgĭfĭcŭs, sŭpērbŭs. *Glorious, honorable*. Syn.—Pūlchĕr, dĕcōrŭs, laūdāndŭs, ēgrĕgĭŭs.

Māgnĭlŏquŭs, ă, ūm. *Clear, sublime*. Syn.—Grāndĭlŏquŭs, grāndĭs, ēlātŭs, sūblīmĭs. *Boastful*. Syn.—Tŭmĭdŭs, tūrgĭdŭs, vānĭlŏquŭs.

Māgnŏpĕrĕ. adv. *Greatly*. Syn.—Vāldē, mūltūm.

Māgnŭs, ă, ūm. *Great*. Ōppĭdăque ĕt māgnōs ēvōlvĕrĕ cōrpŏrĕ mōntēs. O. Syn.—Īmmānĭs, lātŭs. *Powerful*. Syn.—Ēgrĕgĭŭs, ēxcēllēns, prǣstāns, pŏtēns, āmplŭs, sūmmŭs, māxĭmŭs, īngēns. Fig. Syn.—Āltŭs, sūblīmĭs, ēlātŭs, īngēns.

Mājēstās, ātĭs. f. *Majesty, dignity*. Nōn bĕnĕ cōnvĕnĭūnt nĕc ĭn ūnā sēdĕ mŏrāntŭr Mājēstās. O. Syn.—Grăvĭtās, dīgnĭtās, dĕcŏr, dĕcŭs, splēndŏr. Phr.—Ōrĭs hŏnōs. Aūgūstă grăvĭtās. Rēgĭŭs fāstŭs. Rēgālĭs ĭmāgŏ. Splēndōrĕ pērcēllēns. Tăcĭtō vĕnĕrābĭlĭs ōrĕ.

Mălĕ. adv. *Badly*. Syn.—Prāvē, pērvērsē, vĭtĭōsē, pērpĕrām. Phr.—Nōn bĕnĕ. Vērsūs mălĕ nātī. Jūs mălĕ cōndītūm. *Unhappily*. Syn.—Mĭsĕrē, īnfēlīcĭtĕr. *Meanly, wickedly*. Syn.—Īmprŏbē, nēquĭtĕr, mălīgnē.

Mălēdīcŏ, ĭs, xī, ctūm, ĕrĕ. *To curse*. Nēc sē māgnănĭmō sēntīt mălĕdīcĕre Ăchīllī. O. Syn.—Cārpŏ, lǣdŏ, lăcĕrŏ, dētrăhŏ, ōbtrēctŏ.

Mălēdīctūm, ī. n. *Injury, calumny*. Cōnvīcĭūm, ōpprŏbrĭūm, prŏbrūm. Phr.—Dīră vērbĕră līnguǣ. Līnguǣ vĕnēnūm. Mŏlēstǣ vōcēs.

Mălēdīcŭs, ă, ūm. *Slanderous, one who speaks ill of another*. Syn.—Mălĕdīcēns, ōbtrēctātŏr. Phr.—Līnguă prŏcāx, īnvĭdă, līvĭdă.

Mălĕfĭcŭs, ă, ūm. *Wicked*. Syn.—Mălŭs, īmprŏbŭs, nŏcēns, nōxĭŭs.

Mălĕfīdŭs, ă, ūm. *Treacherous, untrustworthy*. Nōn tāntūm sĭnŭs ēt stătĭō mălĕfīdă cărīnīs. V. Syn.—Īnfīdŭs, sūspēctŭs, dŭbĭŭs. Phr.—Nōn fīdŭs, părūm, nōn sătĭs fīdŭs.

Mălĕsānŭs, ă, ūm. *Unsound. See Sanus. Foolish.* Syn.—Īnsānŭs, vēsānŭs, āmēns, dēmēns.

Mălĕvŏlŭs, ă, ūm. *Inimical, malevolent.* Syn.—Ĭnĭmīcŭs, īnfēnsŭs, īnfēstŭs, īnvĭdŭs.

Mălīgnĭtās, ātĭs. f. *Avarice, meanness. See Avaritia. Hostility.* Syn.—Mălĭtĭă, īmprŏbĭtās, īnvĭdĭă.

Mălīgnŭs, ă, ūm. *Feeble, slight.* Syn.—Tĕnŭĭs, ēxĭgŭŭs, pārvŭs, dēbĭlĭs. *Malicious, mean.* Syn.—Īmprŏbŭs, īnvĭdŭs, mălŭs, ōblīquŭs. *Hostile to.* Syn.—Ĭnĭmīcŭs, īnfēstŭs.

Mălĭtĭă, æ. f. *Malice.* Syn.—Nēquĭtĭă, īmprŏbĭtās.

Mālŏ, māvīs, mālŭī, māllĕ. *To prefer.* Syn.—Āntĕfĕrŏ, āntĕpōnŏ. Phr.—Sătĭŭs hăbĕŏ, dūcŏ. Mĭhĭ sătĭŭs ēst, vĭdētŭr. Ōptŏ pŏtĭŭs.

Mălūm, ī. n. *Ill, pain, torment.* Aūt Dĕŭs īllĕ mălīs hŏmĭnūm mītēscĕrĕ dīscăt. V. Syn.—Dŏlŏr, ærūmnă, lăbŏr. Phr.—Mălōrūm sĕrĭēs, tūrbă, cŭmŭlŭs. Mūltă mălōrūm. Prīmă mĭhī lābēs. Tū nē cēdĕ mălīs. *Damage, loss.* Syn.—Pēstĭs, lŭēs, pērnĭcĭēs, ēxĭtĭūm. *Crime. See Scelus.*

Mālūm, ī. n. *An apple. See Pomum.*

Mālŭs, ī. f. *An apple-tree.* (*See Appendix under list of Trees, etc.*)

Mălŭs, ă, ūm. *Bad.* Syn.—Īmprŏbŭs, prāvŭs, pērvērsŭs, mălīgnŭs, nēquām, scĕlēstŭs, scĕlĕrātŭs, nŏcēns. Phr.—Nēmŏ mălūs fēlīx. Mălă mēntīs gaūdĭă. *Dangerous.* Syn.—Nŏcēns, nŏxĭŭs, dāmnōsŭs, fūnēstŭs.

Mālŭs, ī. m. *Mast.* Phr.—Ārbŏr mālī. Naūtĭcă pīnŭs. Vēlĭfĕră pīnŭs, ārbŏr, ăbĭēs. Vēlĭfĕrī rōbŏră mālī. Rĭgĭdō pēndēntĭă līntĕă mālō. Mālūs cĕlĕrī saūcĭūs Āfrĭcō.

Mālvă, æ. f. *The herb mallows.* (*See Appendix under list of Trees, etc.*)

Māmmă, æ. f. *Breast.* Syn.—Mămīllă, māmmŭlă, ūbĕr, păpīllă.

Māndātūm, ī. n. *Command, commission.* Syn.—Jūssūm, jūssŭs, īmpĕrĭūm, præcēptūm. Phr.—Fērrĕ jŭbēt māndātă. Dēfēr mĕă dīctă.

Māndŏ, ās, āvī, ātūm, ārĕ. *To entrust.* Īnfēlīx Prĭămūs fūrtīm māndārăt ălēndūm. V. Syn.—Dō, cōmmēndŏ, trādŏ, cōmmīttŏ, crēdŏ. Phr.—Fŏlĭīs nē cārmĭnă māndă. Māndăt ărēnæ Sēmĭnă. *To recommend, to order.* Syn.—Īmpĕrŏ, jŭbĕŏ, præscrībŏ.

Māndŏ, ĭs, dī, sūm, ĕrĕ. *To eat, to bite.* Syn.—Māndūcŏ, ĕdŏ, cŏmĕdŏ.

Māndūcŏ, ās, āvī, ātūm, ārĕ. *To eat.* Syn.—Māndŏ, pāscŏr, dēpāscŏr, ĕdŏ. Phr.—Dēntĭbŭs cōnfĭcĭŏ. Frāngĕrĕ mōrsū.

Mānĕ. indecl. n. *Morning.* Cārpāmūs dūm mānĕ nŏvūm, dūm grāmĭnă cānēnt. V. Syn.—Aūrōră, dīlūcŭlūm, Lūcĭfĕr. Phr.—Mātūtīnūm tēmpŭs. Mātūtīnæ hōræ. Mātūtīnŭs sōl. Sōl ŏrĭēns. Dĭēs ŏrĭēns. Ŏrĭēntĭă lūmĭnă sōlĭs. Pārs prīmă dĭēī.

Mānĕ. adv. *In the morning.* Phr.—Mānĕ nŏvō. Prīmā, nŏvā lūcĕ. Rĕdĕūntĕ dĭē. Vĕnĭentĕ sōlĕ. Aūrōrā sūrgēntĕ. Sōlĕ nŏvō. Cōnsūmptā nōctĕ. Tĕnĕbrīs rĕmōtīs. Pūlsīs mānĕ tĕnĕbrīs.

Mănĕŏ, ēs, mānsī, mānsūm, ērĕ. *To remain.* Īn quā nēc Bŏrĕās īpsĕ mănērĕ vĕlĭt. M. Syn.—Mŏrŏr, cōmmŏrŏr, vērsŏr, hăbĭtŏ, īncŏlŏ. *To persist.* Syn.—Pērmănĕŏ, rĕmănĕŏ, hærĕŏ, stŏ, pērstŏ, pērsīstŏ, rēstŏ, rĕsīstŏ. *To be reserved for.* Syn.—Sērvŏr, rĕsērvŏr, āddīcŏr, dēvŏvĕŏr.

Mānēs, ĭūm, m. pl. *Souls of the dead.* Sī pŏtŭīt mānēs ărcēssĕrĕ cōnjŭgĭs Ŏrpheūs. V. Phr.—Ūmbræ sĭlēntēs. Tĕnŭēs sĭnĕ cōrpŏrĕ vītæ.

Mănĭfēstŏ, ās, āvī, ātūm, ārĕ. *To manifest, to put in evidence.* Syn.—Ăpĕrĭŏ, dēclārŏ, pătĕfăcĭŏ, pāndŏ. *See Ostendo.*

Mănĭfēstŭs, ă, ūm. *Clear, apparent.* Ēt nē cērtă fŏrēnt mănĭfēstæ sīgnă răpīnæ. Pr. Syn.—Ăpērtŭs, clārŭs, cōnspĭcŭŭs, ēvĭdēns, cērtŭs, īndŭbĭtātŭs, nōtŭs, cōgnĭtŭs. Phr.—Tūm vērō mănĭfēstă fĭdēs. Mănĭfēstăquĕ nūmĭnĭs īră. Mănĭfēstă nĕgārĕ.

Mănĭpŭlŭs & Mănĭplŭs, ī. m. *Troop, battalion.* Syn.—Cŏhōrs, āgmĕn, cătērvă, tūrmă. *See Exercitus.*

Mānŏ, ās, āvī, ātūm, ārĕ. *To flow.* Sēmpĕr ăbūndāre ēt lătīcēs mānārĕ pĕrēnnēs. O. Syn.—Stīllŏ, flŭŏ, dēflŭŏ. Phr.—Ăquæ mānānt dē flūmĭnĕ. Mēllă căvā mānānt ēx īlĭcĕ.

Mānsuēfăcĭŏ, ĭs, ēcī, āctūm, ĕrĕ. *To soften, to soothe, to tame.* Syn.—Dŏmŏ, flēctŏ, dŏmĭtŏ, mōllĭŏ, lēnĭŏ. Phr.—Mānsuētūm rēddŏ, ēffĭcĭŏ. Pārērĕ cōgŏ. Cōrdă dŏmānt. (*In the pass.*) *To be tamed.* Syn.—Dŏmŏr, mītēscŏ, mōllĭŏr, lēnĭŏr, flēctŏr, mītīgŏr. Phr.—Fĕrĭtātēm, răbĭēm ēxŭŏ, dēpōnŏ.

Mānsuētŭs, ă, ūm. *Tamed.* Syn.—Mītĭs, dŏmĭtŭs, mānsuēfāctŭs. *Sweet, good.* Syn.—Mītĭs, bĕnīgnŭs, āffābĭlĭs, clēmēns, cōmĭs, făcĭlĭs, hūmānŭs, lēnĭs, mītĭs.

Mănūmīttŏ, (*or*) Mănū mīttŏ & Mănū ēmīttŏ, ĭs, ĕrĕ. *To set free a slave.* Syn.—Lībĕrŏ, vīndĭcŏ. Phr.—Īn lībērtātēm vīndĭcŏ. Lībĕrūm ēssĕ jŭbĕŏ.

Mănŭs, ūs. f. *Hand.* Ēt jăcēt īn grĕmĭō lānguĭdă fāctă mănŭs. O. Syn.—Dēxtră, dēxtĕră, pālmă, sĭnīstră, lævă, dĭgĭtī, pūgnŭs.

Phr.—Lăbōrĭbŭs āptă. Āssuētă bēllō. Jūngĕ mănūs. Īmmīscēntquĕ mănūs mănĭbŭs. Vīx rĕtĭnērĕ mănūm. *Troop, band. See Turba, Exercitus.*

Māppă, æ. f. *Napkin.* Syn.—Māntīlĕ, gaūsăpĕ.

Mārcĭdŭs, ă, ūm. *Putrid, decayed.* Syn.—Mārcēns, flāccĭdŭs, pūtrĭdŭs, vĭētŭs.

Mărĕ, ĭs. n. *Sea.* Vāstūm mărĭs æquŏr ărāndūm. V. Syn.—Aēquŏr, pōntŭs, pĕlăgŭs, āltūm, prŏfūndūm, frĕtūm, sălūm, mārmŏr, cærŭlă, ūndæ, ăquæ, flūctūs, gūrgĕs, ōcĕănŭs, Nēptūnŭs. Phr.—Pĕlăgī vădă. Aēquŏrĭs ūndæ. Ăquæ sālsæ. Mărĭs trāctŭs. Cāmpŭs ăquārūm. Mūltum īlle ēt tērrīs jāctātŭs ĕt āltō. Pāx pĕlăgī. Viă tūtă mărĭs. Jăcēt sĭnĕ mūrmŭrĕ pōntŭs. Mărĕ vēntīs răpĭdīs ăgĭtātūm. Flūctĭbŭs hōrrēns. Fīt sŏnĭtūs spūmāntĕ sălō.

Mārgărītă, æ. f. *Pearl.* Syn.—Ūnĭŏ, gēmmă. *See Gemma.*

Mārgŏ, ĭnĭs. m. *Border, edge.* Īmŭs ĭn ēxtrēmō mārgĭnĕ fūndŭs hăbēt. O. Syn.—Crĕpīdŏ, ōră. Phr.—Sĭnŭs ēxtrēmŭs. Sūmmă crĕpīdŏ.

Mărīscă, æ. f. *A large kind of fig.* (*See Appendix under list of Trees, etc.*)

Mărītŭs, ī. m. *Husband.* Syn.—Vĭr, spōnsŭs, cōnjūx. Phr.—Jŭgālĭs cōnsōrs vīnclī. *The male of animals.* Syn.—Vĭr, mās, māscŭlŭs.

Mărītŭs, ă, ūm. adj. *Conjugal, marital.* Syn.—Mărītālĭs, cōnjŭgālĭs, sŏcĭālĭs.

Mārmŏr, ŏrĭs. n. *Marble.* Prætĕrĕā fŭĭt īn tēctīs dē mārmŏrĕ tēmplūm. V. Phr.—Părĭŭs lăpĭs. Phrўgĭūm sāxūm. Lўbĭcŭs sĭlēx. Mārmŏrĕŭs nĭtŏr. *Sea. See Mare.*

Mārrŭbĭūm, ĭī. n. *Hore-hound.* (*See Appendix under list of Trees, etc.*)

Mārtĭŭs, ă, ūm. *Warlike.* Syn.—Bēllĭcŭs, bēllĭcōsŭs, bēllāx, Māvōrtĭŭs.

Māssă, æ. f. *Mass, block.* Syn.—Mōlēs, pōndŭs.

Mātĕr, trĭs. f. *Mother.* Īncĭpĕ, pārvĕ pŭēr, rīsū cōgnōscĕrĕ mātrēm. V. Syn.—Gĕnĭtrīx, părēns, mātērcŭlă. Phr.—Stŭdĭōsă prōlĭs. Ōblīvīscī nēscĭă prōlĭs. Fēlīcīssĭmă mātrūm.

Mātūrātē. adv. *Promptly.* Syn.—Cōnfēstĭm, ōcĭŭs.

Mātūrŏ, ās, āvī, ātūm, ārĕ. *To ripen.* Syn.—Cŏquŏ, cōncŏquŏ. *To hasten, to accelerate.* Syn.—Āccĕlĕrŏ, prŏpĕrŏ, fēstīnŏ, ūrgĕŏ.

Mātūrŭs, ă, ūm. *Ripe.* Mātūrīs ālbēscīt mēssĭs ărīstīs. O. Syn.—Mītĭs, cōctŭs, cōncōctŭs. *Before the time, in good season.* Syn.—Prŏpĕrātŭs, fēstīnātŭs, prēmātūrŭs, præcōx, ăcērbŭs.

Māxĭmē. adv. *Greatly, very.* Syn.—Vāldē, mūltūm, īmprīmīs.

Mĕātŭs, ūs. m. *Passage, course.* Syn.—Cūrsŭs, ĭtĕr, lāpsŭs.

Mĕdĕŏr, ērĭs, ērī. *To remedy, to cure.* Scīrĕ pŏtēstātēs hērbārum ūsūmquĕ mĕdēndī. V. Syn.—Mĕdĭcŏr, mĕdĭcŏ, cūrŏ, sānŏ. Phr.—Mĕdĭcīnām, fōmēntă āffĕrŏ, ădhĭbĕŏ. Fĕrŏ mĕdĭcām ŏpēm. Mōrbūm mĕdĭcāmĭnĕ pēllŏ, lēnĭŏ, vīncŏ. Cōrpŏră mōrbīs lĕvārĕ.

Mĕdĭcāmĕn, ĭnĭs. n. *Remedy, medicine.* Syn.—Mĕdĭcāmēntūm, mĕdĭcātŭs, mĕdĭcīnă, rĕmĕdĭūm, mĕdēlă, phārmăcūm, fōmēntūm. Phr.—Hērbæ mĕdĭcæ. Hērbārūm sūccŭs. Mĕdĭcæ lȳmphæ. Vīs mĕdĭcæ ŏpŭs. Ēxpēllēns mōrbōs.

Mĕdĭcīnă, æ. f. *The art of curing, healing.* Phr.—Ārs mĕdĭcă. Ārtēs Ăpōllĭnĭs. Pæŏnĭă cūră. Ūsŭs mĕdēndī. *Remedy. See Medicamen.*

Mĕdĭcŭs, ī. m. *Doctor.* Sæpe ălĭquēm sōlērs mĕdĭcōrūm cūră rĕlīquĭt. O. Syn.—Mĕdēns. Phr.—Ārtēm dōctūs Pæŏnĭām. Ārtĕ Ăpōllĭnĕā pŏtēns, pĕrītŭs. Ārtĭs mĕdĭcæ pĕrītŭs. Pĕrītūs ĭn ārtĕ mĕdēndī. Dōctūs dēpēllĕrĕ mōrbōs.

Mĕdĭtŏr, ārĭs, ātŭs sūm, ārī. *To meditate.* Quōcīrcā căpĕre āntĕ dŏlīs ēt cīngĕrĕ flāmmā Rēgīnām mĕdĭtŏr. V. Syn.—Cōgĭtŏ, rĕpŭtŏ, mōlĭŏr, părŏ. Phr.—Mēntĕ vōlvŏ, vērsŏ, ăgĭtŏ. *To write verses. See Cano.*

Mēl, mēllĭs. n. *Honey.* Stīllābānt īlĭcĕ mēllă. O. Syn.—Făvŭs. Phr.—Nēctăr ăpūm. Mūnĕră mēllĭs. Lĭquŏr hȳblæŭs. Dūlcĭs ăpūm lăbŏr. Mēllĭs ŏpŭs. Prēssīs cŏāctă făvīs. Ēxprēssă făvīs. Cērĕă dōnă thȳmī rĕdŏlēntĭă rōrĕ. Mēllă căvā mānānt ēx īlĭcĕ. Frīgŏrĕ mēllă Cōgĭt.

Mĕlĕāgrĭs, ĭdĭs. f. *Turkey or guinea-hen.* (*See Appendix under list of Birds.*)

Mĕlīsphȳllūm, ī. n. *The balm-gentle, apiastrum.* (*See Appendix under list of Trees, etc.*)

Mĕlĭŭs. adv. *Better.* Syn.—Rēctĭŭs, āptĭŭs, pūlchrĭŭs, dōctĭŭs. *Rather.* Syn.—Pŏtĭŭs.

Mēllĭfĭcŏ, ās, āvī, ātūm, ārĕ. *To make honey.* Sīc vōs nōn nōbīs mēllĭfĭcātĭs ăpēs. V. Syn.—Mēl cōnfĭcĭŏ, fīngŏ, cōgŏ, fīgŏ, stīpŏ. Phr.—Cērĕă rēgnă rĕfīgūnt. Cōgĕrĕ mēllă făvīs. *See Mel.*

Mĕlŏs. n. indecl. *Melody, chant.* Rēgīnă lōngūm, Căllĭŏpē, mĕlŏs. H. Syn.—Cāntŭs, mŏdī, mŏdŭlī, mŏdŭlāmĕn. *See Cantus.*

Mēmbră, ōrūm. n. *Members.* Syn.—Ārtūs. Phr.—Hīc mēmbrīs ēt mōlĕ vălēns. Ăccōmmŏdă bēllīs Mēmbră.

Mēmbrānă, æ. f. *Membrane, skin.* Syn.—Pēllĭcŭlă, pēllĭs, cŭtĭs. *Skin of a serpent.* Syn.—Ēxŭvĭæ, pēllĭs.

Mĕmĭnī, īssĕ. *To remember.* Lōngōs Cāntāndō mĕmĭnī pŭĕrūm mē cōndĕrĕ sōlēs. V. Syn.—Cōmmĕmĭnī, rĕcōrdŏr, rĕmĭnīscŏr. Phr.—Sūm mĕmŏr, nōn īmmĕmŏr. Mĕmŏr vīvŏ. Pēctŏrĕ tĕnĕŏ. Mĕmŏrĭā tĕnĕŏ. Hæc ănĭmō hærēnt. Sūb cōrdĕ rĕfĕrŏ. Mēntĕ rĕpōnŏ. Rēs nōn ănĭmō ēxcĭdĭt. Fōrsăn ĕt hæc ōlīm mĕmĭnīssĕ jŭvābĭt. Vīvĕ mĕmōr nōstrī. Nārrārĕ mĕmēntō. Pārs ēst mĕmĭnīssĕ dŏlōrĭs. Hōc tĭbĭ dīctūm Tōllĕ mĕmŏr.

Mĕmŏr, ŏrĭs. adj. *Mindful.* Quīquĕ sŭī mĕmŏrēs ălĭōs fēcērĕ mĕrēndō. V. Syn.—Īnōblītŭs. Phr.—Nōn īmmĕmŏr, nōn ōblītŭs. Haūd īmmĕmŏr ūnquām. Vĕtĕrūm nōn īmmĕmŏr īllĕ părēntūm. *See Memini.*

Mĕmŏrābĭlĭs, ĭs, ĕ. *Memorable.* Ēt sī nūllūm mĕmŏrābĭlĕ nōmĕn Fēmĭnĕa īn pœna ēst. V. Syn.—Mĕmŏrāndŭs, ēgrĕgĭŭs, nōbĭlĭs.

Mĕmŏrŏ, ās, āvī, ātūm, ārĕ. *To recall, to relate.* Ēt mĕmĭnīstĭs ĕnīm, Dīvae, ēt mĕmŏrārĕ pŏtēstĭs. V. Syn.—Cōmmĕmŏrŏ, nārrŏ, rĕfĕrŏ.

Mēndācĭūm, ĭī. n. *Lie.* Nēc vōs dēcĭpĭānt blāndæ mēndācĭă līnguæ. O. Syn.—Cōmmēntūm. Phr.—Fīctŭs, fīctĭtĭŭs, sĭmŭlātŭs sērmŏ. Fīctă, fāllācĭă vērbă. Fīctæ vōcēs. Fālsæ pērjūrĭă līnguæ.

Mēndāx, ācĭs. adj. *Lying.* Syn.—Fāllāx, vānŭs, fālsŭs, pērfĭdŭs, dŭplēx, bĭlīnguĭs, sūbdŏlŭs, fālsĭlŏquŭs, sĭmŭlātŏr, pērjūrŭs. Phr.—Fāndī fīctŏr. Mēntīrī, fāllĕrĕ dōctŭs. Ōrĕ fālsō dēcĭpĭēns. Līnguă fāllāx, mēndāx. Ōs pērjūrūm.

Mēndīcŏ, ās, āvī, ātūm, ārĕ. *To beg.* Syn.—Ēmēndīcŏ. Phr.—Stĭpēm cōrrŏgŏ. Aĕră rŏgŏ. Pārvæ stĭpĭs æră rŏgŏ. Prĕcĭbŭs cĭbūm, ălĭmēntă rŏgŏ.

Mēndīcŭs, ă, ūm. *In want, needy.* Syn.—Paūpĕr, ĕgēns, ĕgēnŭs, ĭnŏps.

Mēns, mēntĭs. f. *Mind, spirit.* Syn.—Ănĭmŭs. *Intelligence.* Syn.—Ănĭmŭs, rătĭŏ. Phr.—Cæcă fŭtūrī Mēns hŏmĭnūm. Cōnscĭă mēns fāctī sĭbĭ. Mēns tămĕn ūt rĕdĭĭt. *Heart.* Syn.—Ănĭmŭs, pēctŭs, cŏr. *Thought, design.* Syn.—Ănĭmŭs, sēntēntĭă, cōnsĭlĭūm, vŏlūntās.

Mēnsă, æ. f. *Table.* Hūnc pĕdĕ cōnvūlsō mēnsæ Pēllæŭs ăcērnæ. O. Fig.—*Feast, repast.* Syn.—Cœnă, ĕpŭlæ, cōnvīvĭă, dăpēs. Phr.—Īnstrūctă cĭbīs. Ĕpŭlīs ŏnĕrātă. Laūtīs cĭbīs splēndĭdă. Īnstrŭĕrĕ mēnsās. Ēxstrūctæ dăpĭbūs mēnsæ. *See Convivium.*

Mēnsĭs, ĭs. m. *Month.* Trīgīntă māgnōs vōlvēndīs mēnsĭbŭs ōrbēs Īmpĕrĭo ēxplēbĭt. V. Syn.—Călēndæ. Phr.—Mēnstrŭŭs cūrsŭs. Mēnstrŭūm tēmpŭs. Lūnæ cūrsŭs. Mŏră mēnstrŭă. Īncĭpĭūnt māgnī prōcēdĕrĕ mēnsēs. Prīmīs ā mēnsĭbŭs ānnī. Mēnsĭbŭs ēxāctīs.

Mēntă, æ. f. *Mint.* (*See Appendix under list of Trees, etc.*)

Mēntĭŏr, īrĭs, tītŭs sūm, īrī. *To lie.* Āt nōn īllĕ, sătūm quō tē mēntīrĭs, Ăchīllēs. V. Syn.—Fīngŏ, cōmmĭnīscŏr. Phr.—Fālsă dīcŏ, mĕmŏrŏ. Fīctă vērbă prōfĕrŏ. Nōn vēră lŏquŏr. Āddīt mēndācĭă cūlpæ. Mēndācēs rēddĭt ăb ōrĕ sŏnōs. Mēndācī fāllĕrĕ līnguā.

Mērcātŏr, ōrĭs. m. *Merchant.* Īmpĭgĕr ēxtrēmōs cūrrīt mērcātŏr ăd Īndōs. H. Syn.—Ēmptŏr, vēndĭtŏr, īnstĭtŏr, mērcāns, nĕgōtĭātŏr. Phr.—Lŭcrī cŭpĭdŭs. Lŭcrīs dīvĭtĭīs ĭnhĭāns. Lŭcrī spē dūctŭs. Īndŏcĭlīs paūpĕrĭēm pătī. Pēr mărĕ paūpĕrĭēm fŭgĭēns.

Mērcēs, ēdĭs. f. *Price of work, salary.* Mērcēdĕ dĭūrnā Cōndūctūm pāvĭt. H. Syn.—Prĕtĭūm. Phr.—Mērcēdem ŏpĕrĭs nĕgăt. Dūlcĭs ĕrāt mērcēdĕ lăbŏr. *Reward.* Syn.—Præmĭūm, prĕtĭūm. *Punishment. See Poena.*

Mĕrĕŏ, ēs, ŭī, ĭtūm, ērĕ. *To merit, to deserve.* Prædă sĭt hæc īllīs quōrūm mĕrŭērĕ lăbōrēs. Prop. Syn.—Mĕrĕŏr (*used as a deponent*), prōmĕrĕŏr, cōmmĕrĕŏ, ēmĕrĕŏ. Phr.—Sūm dīgnŭs. *To win a reward.* Syn.—Părŏ, cōmpărŏ, rĕfĕrŏ. *To serve a campaign.* Syn.—Mīlĭtŏ. Phr.—Cāstră sĕquŏr. Īn cāstrīs mĕrĕŏ. Aērĕ mĕrēns pārvō.

Mērgŏ, ĭs, sī, sūm, ĕrĕ. *To immerge, to plunge into.* Nēc mē Dĕŭs æquŏrĕ mērsĭt. V. Syn.—Īmmērgŏ, dēmērgŏ, sūbmērgŏ, mērsŏ, īmmērsŏ, lăvŏ, āblŭŏ, tīngŏ. Phr.—Ăquīs āblŭŏ, spārgŏ. Īn ăquās præcĭpĭtŏ, prōjĭcĭŏ, īmmīttŏ. Ăquīs prĕmŏ. Sēse īn flŭvĭūm sāltū dĕdĭt. Fig. Syn.—Ōbrŭŏ, ōpprĭmŏ, āfflīgŏ.

Mērgŭs, ī. m. *A cormorant.* (*See Appendix under list of Birds.*)

Mĕrīdĭēs, ēī. m. *Mid-day.* Īnclīnārĕ mĕrīdĭēm Sēntīs. H. Phr.—Mĕdĭŭs dĭēs. Sōl āltīssĭmŭs. Mĕdĭūs sōlīs cūrsŭs. Cūm fērvĕt Ōlȳmpō. Mĕdĭō cūm Phœbŭs ĭn āxe ēst. Mĕdĭās sōlĕ tĕnēntĕ vĭās. Īn mĕdĭūm sūrgēntĕ dĭē.

Mĕrĭtō. adv. *Deservedly.* Ō dĕcŭs, ō fāmæ mĕrĭtō pārs māxĭmă nōstræ. V. Syn.—Jūrĕ, dīgnē, jūstē; (*sometimes*) bĕnĕ, āptē, dĕcēntĕr, cōnvĕnĭēntĕr. Phr.—Ēx mĕrĭtō. Haūd īmmĕrĭtō. Jūre āc mĕrĭtō. Nōn mălĕ.

Mĕrōps, ŏpĭs. m. *The bee-eater.* (*See Appendix under list of Birds.*)

Mĕrŭlă, æ. f. *Blackbird.* (*See Appendix under list of Birds.*)

Mĕrŭs, ă, ūm. *Sole, alone.* Syn.—Sōlŭs. *Pure, unmixed.* Syn.—Sīncērŭs, pūrŭs.

Mēssĭs, ĭs. f. *Harvest.* Āt sī trītĭcēam īn mēssēm rōbūstăquĕ fārră Ēxērcēbĭs hŭmūm. V. Syn.—Frūgēs, Cĕrēs, sĕgĕs, ărīstæ̆, spīcæ̆, sătă, frūmēntūm. Phr.—Cĕrĕālĭă dōnă. Mātūræ̆ sĕgĕtēs. Tērræ̆, tēllūrĭs ŏpēs. Sĕgĕtūm mūnŭs. Mātūrīs ărīstīs ālbēscēns. Tĕrĕt ārĕă mēssēs. *Wheat.* Syn.—Frūmēntūm, frūgēs, grānă.

Mētă, æ̆. f. *Goal, term, turn.* Syn.—Līmĕs, tērmĭnŭs, fīnĭs. Phr.—Fērvĭdīs ēvītātă rŏtīs. Ādmīssā mētă tĕrēndă rŏtā. Mētām trīvĕrīt rŏtă.

Mĕtāllĭfĕr, ĕră, ĕrūm. *Rich in metals.* Syn.—Mĕtāllī fĕrāx, dīvĕs, fēcūndŭs.

Mĕtāllūm, ī. n. *Metal.* Phr.—Mĕtāllī māssă, pōndĕră. Mĕtāllōrūm vīs īngēns, īmīs rĕcōndĭtă tērræ̆ vīscĕrĭbŭs. Fūlvī vāstă mĕtāllī cōngĕrĭēs.

Mĕtămōrphōsĭs, ĭs & ĕōs. f. *Change, metamorphosis.* Phr.—Vărĭæ̆ spĕcĭēs. Vērsæ̆, vărĭātæ̆ fĭgūræ̆. Nŏvă fōrmă. Mūtātă cōrpŏră. Nŏvī vūltūs. Mūtātī ārtūs. Vērsæ̆ sōlātĭă fōrmæ̆.

Mētĭŏr, īrĭs, mēnsŭs sūm, īrī. *To measure.* Syn.—Dīmētĭŏr, mētŏr. *To distribute. See Distribuo. To measure with the eye.* Syn.—Lūstrŏ, pērcūrrŏ, cīrcūmspĭcĭŏ. *To appreciate.* Syn.—Pōndĕrŏ, ēxpēndŏ, æ̆stĭmŏ.

Mĕtŏ, ĭs, mēssŭī, mēssūm, ĕrĕ. *To harvest.* Syn.—Dēmĕtŏ. Phr.—Mēssēm, ărīstās, frūgēs sūccīdŏ, tōndĕŏ, cōllĭgŏ, cārpŏ. Fālcĕ rĕsĕcŏ, mĕtŏ. Tērrām frūgĭbŭs stērnŏ. Cæ̆dĭtĕ mēssēs. *To cut (in general). See Cædo. To gather (in general).* Syn.—Lĕgŏ, cōllĭgŏ, cārpŏ. *To devastate.* Syn.—Dēmĕtŏ, stērnŏ, dējĭcĭŏ, pŏpŭlŏr.

Mĕtŭŏ, ĭs, ī, ĕrĕ. *To fear.* Syn.—Tĭmĕŏ, vĕrĕŏr, păvĕŏ, fōrmīdŏ, hōrrĕŏ.

Mĕtŭs, ūs. m. *Fear.* Ōmnĭă sōllĭcĭtī sūnt lŏcă plēnă mĕtūs. O. Syn.—Tĭmŏr, păvŏr, fōrmīdŏ, tērrŏr. Phr.—Cūrā ācrĭŏr ōmnī. Spēmquĕ mĕtūmque īntēr dŭbĭī. Præ̆cĭpĭtēs mĕtŭs ācĕr ăgĭt. Mĕtŭs īncŭbăt āmēns. Dīrĭgŭērĕ mĕtū. Cōmmōtă mĕtū mēns.

Mĕŭs, ă, ūm. *Mine.* Syn.—Nōstĕr.

Mĭcŏ, ās, ŭī, ārĕ. *To be stirred, to be agitated.* Syn.—Cŏrūscŏ, mŏvĕŏr, ăgĭtŏr, trĕpĭdŏ, sălĭŏ, sūbsĭlĭŏ, sūbsūltŏ. *To shine, to glitter.* Syn.—Cŏrūscŏ, fūlgĕŏ, rĕfūlgĕŏ, nĭtēscŏ, splēndĕŏ, splēndēscŏ, rădĭŏ, īrrădĭŏ, fūlgŭrŏ.

Mĭgrŏ, ās, āvī, ātūm, ārĕ. *To migrate, to move.* Syn.—Dēmĭgrŏ, ēmĭgrŏ, cōmmĭgrŏ, dīscēdŏ, ābscēdŏ, ăbĕŏ, ēxĕŏ. *To change.* Syn.—Mūtŏr.

Mīlĕs, ĭtĭs. m. *Soldier.* Mīlēs nŭmĕrō præ̆stāntĭŏr ōmnī. O. Syn.—Bēllātŏr, vĭr; (*in the plural*) ārmātī, ārmĭgĕrī, bēllĭgĕrī, pūgnantes. Phr.—Dūrī mīlēs Mārtĭs. Hōrrĭdă cāstră sĕquēns. Sūmptīs ănĭmōsŭs ārmīs. Ācĕr ĭn ārmīs. Bēllĭcă tūrbă. Māvōrtĭă pūbēs. Mūltōs cāstră jŭvānt.

Mīlĭtārĭs, ĭs, ĕ. *Military, warlike.* Syn.—Mārtĭŭs, bēllĭcŭs, cāstrēnsĭs.

Mīlĭtĭă, æ. f. *Military service.* Mīlĭtĭæ quāmquām pĭgĕr ēt mălŭs, ūtĭlĭs ūrbī. H. Syn.—Bēllūm, ārmă, cāstră, stīpēndĭă. Phr.—Ārs bēllĭcă. Mārtĭs ŏpŭs. Mīlĭtĭæ lăbŏr, ōffĭcĭūm, prǣmĭă, tēmpŭs. *War. See Bellum.*

Mīlĭtō, ās, āvī, ātūm, ārĕ. *To go to war.* Ēt mīlĭtāvī nōn sĭnĕ glōrĭā. H. Syn.—Mĕrĕō, bēllō. Phr.—Ārmă gĕrō. Gĕrō Mārtĭs ŏpŭs. Ārmă, cāstră sĕquŏr. Stīpēndĭă, ǣră mĕrĕō. Mīlĭtĭām sŭbĕō. Mīlĭtĭæ lăbōrem sŭbĕō. Pĕrīcŭlă Mārtĭs ēxpĕrĭŏr.

Mĭlĭūm, ĭī. n. *Millet.* (*See Appendix under list of Trees, etc.*)

Mīllĕ. indecl. (pl. mīllĭă, ĭūm.) *Thousand.* Mīllĕ mĕǣ Sĭcŭlīs ērrānt īn mōntĭbŭs āgnǣ. V. Syn.—Bīs quīngēntī. Cēntēnī dĕcĭēs. *A thousand, that is, any large, indefinite number.* Syn.—Īnnŭmĕrī, crēbrī, dēnsī, etc.

Mīllĭēs. adv. *A thousand times.* Syn.—Crēbrō, sǣpĭŭs.

Mīlŭŭs & Mīlvŭs, ī. m. *The kite, a bird of the falcon species.* (*See Appendix under list of Birds.*)

Mĭnǣ, ārūm. f. *Threats.* Nūllae īn frōntĕ mĭnǣ nēc fōrmīdābĭlĕ lūmĕn. O. Phr.—Mĭnācĭă, mĭnāntĭă, mĭnĭtāntĭă, āspĕră, plēnă mĭnārūm vērbă. Vōx mĭnāns. Tŭmĭdǣ vōcēs. Vērbōrūm fūlmĭnă.

Mĭnāx, ācĭs. adj. *Threatening.* Syn.—Mĭnāns, mĭnĭtāns, trūx. Phr.—Vūltū tōrvă mĭnācī. Mĭnās vūltū, ōrĕ gĕrēns. Quās gĕrĭt ōrĕ mĭnās. *Frightful.* Syn.—Trūx, hōrrēndŭs, āspĕr, sǣvŭs, ătrōx, mĕtŭēndŭs, tērrĭbĭlĭs.

Mĭnĭmē. adv. *By no means.* Syn.—Nēquāquām, nōn, nĭhĭl, nīl, mĭnĭmūm. Phr.—Nūllō mŏdō, quām mĭnĭmūm.

Mĭnīstĕr, trī. m. *Servant.* Nĕquĕ tē mĭnīstrūm dēdĕcēt mȳrtŭs. H. Syn.—Mĭnīstră, fămŭlŭs, sērvŭs, sătēllĕs. Phr.—Tăcĭtīquĕ sĕdēnt ād jūssă mĭnīstrī. *One who serves as an instrument.* Syn.—Fămŭlŭs, fămŭlāns, ādjūtŏr, ădjūtrīx, aūxĭlĭāns.

Mĭnīstĕrĭūm, ĭī. n. *Office.* Mēquĕ mĭnīstĕrĭo scĕlĕrīsque ārtīsquĕ rĕmōvī. O. Syn.—Ōffĭcĭūm, mūnŭs, mūnĭă, ŏpĕră, pārtēs.

Mĭnīstrō, ās, āvī, ātūm, ārĕ. *To serve.* Syn.—Fămŭlŏr. *To furnish.* Syn.—Prǣbĕō, sūffĭcĭō, sūppĕdĭtō, dō, sūggĕrō. *To execute.* Syn.—Gĕrō, ēxsĕquŏr, făcēssō, trāctō, ăgō.

Mĭnŏr, ārĭs, ātŭs sūm, ārī. *To threaten.* Syn.—Mĭnĭtŏr, cōmmĭnĭtŏr. Phr.—Mĭnās īntēntō, jāctō. Mĭnīs īnstō. Ōrĕ mĭnācī mĕtūm īncŭtĭō. Spīrăt ăb ōrĕ mĭnās.

Mĭnŭŏ, ĭs, ŭī, ūtūm, ĕrĕ. *To break, to smash to pieces. See Frango. To diminish.* Syn.—Dēmĭnŭŏ, īmmĭnŭŏ, āttĕnŭŏ, ēxtĕnŭŏ, dēbĭlĭtŏ, dētrăhŏ, dēmŏ, ădĭmŏ, tōllŏ. *To weaken.* Syn.—Dēbĭlĭtŏ, frāngŏ, ēxhaŭrĭŏ.

Mĭnŭs. adv. *Less.* Phr.—Nōn tām. *In nowise.* Syn.—Părūm, mălĕ, mĭnĭmē, nōn. *Unless.* Syn.—Ēxcēptō, ēxcēptā.

Mĭnūtē. adv. *In small bits.* Syn.—Mĭnūtātīm, mĭnūtīm, mēmbrātīm, pārtĭcŭlātīm.

Mīrābĭlĭs, ĭs, ĕ. *Wonderful, admirable.* Syn.—Mīrŭs, mīrāndŭs, ādmīrābĭlĭs, ādmīrāndŭs, mīrĭfĭcŭs. Phr.—Mīrābĭlĕ dīctū.

Mīrābūndŭs, ă, ūm. *Filled with admiration.* Syn.—Ōbstŭpēns, mīrāns, ādmīrāns, stŭpĕfāctŭs, ōbstŭpĕfāctŭs.

Mīrācŭlūm, ī. n. *Miracle, marvel.* Ōmnĭă trānsfōrmāt sēse īn mīrācŭlă rērūm. V. Syn.—Pōrtēntūm, prōdĭgĭūm, sīgnūm, mōnstrūm. Phr.—Mīrābĭlĕ fāctūm. Dīctū mīrābĭlĕ mōnstrūm. Mīrācŭlă rērūm. Rēs mīrāndă. Rēs nōn ūllīs cōgnĭtă.

Mīrĭfĭcē. adv. *Marvellously.* Syn.—Mīrē, mīrābĭlĭtĕr. Phr.—Mīrīs mŏdīs. Mīrĭfĭcīs mŏdīs.

Mīrŏr, ārĭs, ātŭs sūm, ārī. *To wonder at, to be astonished.* Ōbstŭpĕt āc mōlēm tăcĭtē mīrātŭr. V. Syn.—Ādmīrŏr, dēmīrŏr, sūspĭcĭŏ, stŭpĕŏ, ōbstŭpĕŏ, hĭŏ, ĭnhĭŏ. Phr.—Āttŏnĭtūs stŭpĕŏ. Ōbstŭpŭīt vīsū. Dōnūm stŭpĕt ēxĭtĭālĕ Mĭnērvæ̆.

Mīrŭs, ă, ūm. *Surprising, wonderful.* Quī sē crēdēbāt mīrōs aŭdīrĕ trăgœ̆dōs. H. Syn.—Mīrāndŭs, mīrābĭlĭs, ādmīrāndŭs, ādmīrābĭlĭs, mīrĭfĭcŭs, stŭpēndŭs, nŏvŭs, īnsŏlĭtŭs, ĭnaŭdītŭs, īmmānĭs, īngēns, pōrtēntōsŭs, prōdĭgĭōsŭs.

Mīscĕŏ, ēs, ŭī, stūm & xtūm, ērĕ. *To mix, to mingle.* Aūfĭdĭūs fōrtī mīscēbāt mēllă Fălērnō. H. Syn.—Ādmīscĕŏ, īmmīscĕŏ, pērmīscĕŏ, cōmmīscĕŏ, īntērmīscĕŏ, tēmpĕrŏ, sŏcĭŏ, cōnsŏcĭŏ, jūngŏ, cōnjūngŏ, ādjūngŏ, īnsĕrŏ, āddŏ, ādjĭcĭŏ, īnfūndŏ. *To stir up trouble, to embroil.* Syn.—Cōnfūndŏ, pērmīscĕŏ, tūrbŏ.

Mĭsĕr, ĕră, ĕrūm. *Miserable, unhappy.* Sūm mĭsĕr, hæ̆c brĕvĭs ēst nōstrōrūm sūmmă mălōrūm. O. Syn.—Aērūmnōsŭs, īnfēlīx, īnfōrtūnātŭs, āfflīctŭs. Ō mĭsĕrās hŏmĭnūm mēntēs! Fōrtūnă mĭsērrĭmă nōstra ēst. Quām mĭsĕrūm nēscīrĕ mŏrī.

Mĭsĕrābĭlĭs, ĭs, ĕ. *Pitiable.* Sīsquĕ mĭhī sēmpēr, nēc sĭs mĭsĕrābĭlĭs ūllī. O. Syn.—Mĭsĕrāndŭs. Phr.—Āt nūnc mĭsĕrāndă vĕl hōstī. Mĭsĕrābĭlĕ cārmĕn Īntĕgrăt. Gĕnūs mĭsĕrābĭlĕ lētī. *See Lacrimabilis.*

Mĭsĕrābĭlĭtĕr. adv. *Miserably, pitiably.* Syn.—Mĭsĕrābĭlĕ, mĭsĕrē, flēbĭlĭtĕr, flēbĭlĕ.

Mĭsĕrĭă, ǣ. f. *Misery, wretchedness.* Syn. -Aērŭmnă, călămĭtās, īnfŏrtūnĭŭm, mălūm. Phr.—Mĭsĕră sŏrs. Rēs mĭsĕrǣ. Rēs afflictǣ. Mĭsĕrǣ īncōmmŏdă vītǣ. Sŏrs ŭltĭmă rērūm. Dūrīs ŭrgēns, prĕmēns īn rēbŭs ĕgēstās.
Mĭsĕrĭcōrs, cōrdĭs. adj. *Merciful.* Syn.—Clēmēns, bĕnīgnŭs, prō-pĭtĭŭs, mītĭs, pĭŭs. *See Clemens.*
Mĭsĕrŏr, ārĭs, ātŭs sūm, ārī. *To pity.* Cōntūsōsque ănĭmōs, ēt rēs mĭsĕrābĕrĕ frāctās. V. Syn.—Dŏlĕŏ, indŏlĕŏ, tāngŏr, mŏvĕŏr, rēspĭcĭŏ. Phr.—Vĭcēm ĭnīquām dŏlĕŏ. Mălĭs, flētĭbŭs, lăcrĭmīs tāngŏr, flēctŏr, mŏvĕŏr. Sē mītēm prǣbĕrĕ. Jăcēntēm ǣquīs āspĭcĕrĕ ŏcŭlīs. Mĭsĕrīs aūxĭlĭum fĕrŏ. Nēc tē mĭsĕrēt nātīquĕ tŭĭquĕ. Mĭsĕrīs sūccūrrĕrĕ dĭscŏ.
Mītĭgŏ, ās, āvī, ātūm, ārĕ. *To ripen. See Maturo. To soften, to tame.* Syn.—Dŏmŏ, mōllĭŏ, plācŏ. *To calm.* Syn.—Lēnĭŏ, mōl-lĭŏ, plācŏ, sēdŏ.
Mītĭs, ĭs, ĕ. *Sweet to the taste, ripe.* Cuī tū lāctĕ făvōs ēt mītī dīlŭĕ bācchō. V. Syn.—Dūlcĭs, suāvĭs. *Pleasant, kind.* Syn.— Lēnĭs, plăcĭdŭs, clēmēns, făcĭlĭs, mānsuētŭs, cōmĭs, bĕnīgnŭs. Phr.—Făcĭlĭs vūltūquĕ sĕrēnŭs. Cōmĭs ēt ūrbānŭs. Cuī mīte īngĕnĭum. Plăcĭdī mōrēs. *Easy to bear.* Syn.—Lēnĭs, lĕvĭs.
Mīttŏ, ĭs, mīsī, mīssūm, ĕrĕ. *To send.* Syn.—Lēgŏ. *To exile.* Syn.— Ējĭcĭŏ, āblēgŏ, āmāndŏ, rĕlēgŏ. *To abandon.* Syn.—Dīmīttŏ. *To push towards.* Syn.—Īmmīttŏ, ăgŏ, īmpēllŏ. *To chase away.* Syn.—Pēllŏ, dēpēllŏ, ābjĭcĭŏ, pōnŏ, dēpōnŏ. *To cease from.* Syn.—Ŏmīttŏ, dēsĭnŏ, pārcŏ, ābsīstŏ.
Mōbĭlĭs, ĭs, ĕ. *Light, movable.* Syn.—Lĕvĭs, vŏlūbĭlĭs, mūtābĭlĭs. *Inconstant.* Syn.—Īncōnstāns, vărĭŭs, īrrĕquĭētŭs, īncērtŭs, dŭbĭŭs, lūbrĭcŭs.
Mōbĭlĭtās, ātĭs. f. *Fickleness.* Mōbĭlĭtātĕ vĭgēt, vīrēsque ācquīrĭt ĕūndō. V. Syn.—Lĕvĭtās, īncōnstāntĭă, īnstăbĭlĭtās.
Mŏdĕrāmĕn, ĭnĭs. n. *Rule, control.* Syn.—Rĕgĭmĕn, dūctŭs, īm-pĕrĭum, hăbēnǣ.
Mŏdĕrātŏr, ōrĭs. m. *One who governs, guides, directs.* Syn.— Rēctŏr, gŭbērnātŏr, dūx, prǣsĕs, măgĭstĕr, aūrīgă.
Mŏdĕrŏr, ārĭs, ātŭs sūm, ārī. *To moderate, to hold in check.* Syn.— Ēmŏdĕrŏr, tēmpĕrŏ, cōntĭnĕŏ, rĕtĭnĕŏ, cŏērcĕŏ, cŏhĭbĕŏ, īnhĭbĕŏ, cōmpēscŏ, cōmprĭmŏ, rĕprĭmŏ, frēnŏ, rĕfrēnŏ. Phr.—Pōne īrǣ frēnă mŏdūmquĕ. *To guide.* Syn.—Rĕgŏ, gŭbērnŏ.
Mŏdēstē. adv. *With moderation.* Syn.—Mŏdĕrāntĕr, mŏdĭcē, pārcē. *Modestly.* Syn.—Vĕrēcūndē, pŭdīcē, pŭdēntĕr.
Mŏdēstĭă, ǣ. f. *Modesty.* Syn.—Pŭdŏr. Phr.—Hŏnēstī prǣclāră mŏdēstĭă vūltūs. Cāstī vūltūs. Tĕnĕră frŏns. Mŏdēstă făcĭēs.

Ōs vĕrēcūndūm. *Moderation.* Syn.—Mŏdĕrātĭŏ, mŏdŭs, tēm-pĕrāntĭă, ābstĭnēntĭă.

Mŏdēstŭs, ă, ūm. *Modest.* Nēc pŭdĕāt cōrām vērbă mŏdēstă lŏquī. O. Syn.—Vĕrēcūndŭs, pŭdēns, pŭdĭbūndŭs, pŭdīcŭs. Phr.—Plēnŭs pŭdōrĭs. Ŏcŭlōs dējēctă dĕcōrōs. Vūltūs blāndē dēmīssā mŏdēstōs. *Temperate.* Syn.—Mŏdĕrātŭs. Phr.—Cōntēntūs mŏdīcō. Vōtī mŏdĭcŭs. Cūltū mŏdĭcŭs. *Peaceful.* Syn.—Plăcĭdŭs, trānquīllŭs, quĭētŭs.

Mŏdī, ōrūm. m. *Feet, measures used in poetry, therefore verses.* Ēt sēnsīt vărĭōs quāmvīs dīvērsă sŏnārēnt, Cōncōrdārĕ mŏdōs. O. Syn.—Nŭmĕrī, mŏdŭlāmĕn, cāntŭs, cārmĕn, mĕlŏs. Phr.—Māgnă mŏdīs tĕnŭārĕ pārvīs. *See Cantus, Carmen.*

Mŏdĭcē. adv. *With moderation.* Syn.—Mŏdĭcūm, mŏdĕrātē, mŏdēstē, pārcē, mĕdĭŏcrĭtĕr.

Mŏdĭcŭs, ă, ūm. *Moderate.* Syn.—Mŏdēstŭs. *Slight.* Syn.—Mĕdĭŏcrĭs, ēxĭgŭŭs, pārvŭs, tĕnŭĭs.

Mŏdŏ. adv. *Lately.* Syn.—Nŭpĕr, rĕcēns, jām. *Now. See Nunc. Only.* Syn.—Tāntūm, tāntūmmŏdŏ. Mŏdŏ nōn, *all but.* Syn.—Tāntūm nōn, fĕrē, pēnĕ, prŏpĕ, fērmē. *Provided that.* Syn.—Dūmmŏdŏ, sī, dūm.

Mŏdŭlāmĕn, ĭnĭs. n. *Harmonious song, harmony.* Syn.—Mŏdŭlātĭŏ, mŏdŭlātŭs, mŏdī, mĕlŏs, cāntŭs, cārmĕn, cōncēntŭs, mŏdŭlī.

Mŏdŭlŏr, ārĭs, ātŭs sūm, ārī. *To sing according to time, to play on an instrument.* Syn.—Ēmŏdŭlŏr, cănŏ, cōncĭnŏ, cāntŏ.

Mŏdŭs, ī. m. *Mode, fashion, manner.* Syn.—Rătĭŏ, vĭă. *Moderation.* Syn.—Mŏdēstĭă, mŏdĕrātĭŏ. *End, limit.* Syn.—Fīnĭs, tērmĭnŭs. *See these words.*

Mœnĭă, ĭūm. n. *City-wall, fortification.* Syn.—Mūrī, āggĕr, mūnīmēntă, mūnīmĭnă, prŏpūgnācŭlă. Phr.—Mūrōrūm āggĕr. Ūrbĭs mœnĭă. Mœnĭbŭs āssĭlīīt mīlĕs.

Mœrĕŏ, ēs, ŭī, ērĕ. *To grieve, to be sad.* Sōlă dŏmō mœrēt văcŭā. V. Syn.—Dŏlĕŏ, īndŏlĕŏ, gĕmŏ, lūgĕŏ.

Mœrŏr, ōrĭs. m. *Grief, sorrow.* Aūt ăd hŭmūm mœrōrĕ grăvī dēdūcĭt ĕt āngĭt. H. Syn.—Mœstĭtĭă, dŏlŏr, āngŏr, lūctŭs, trīstĭtĭă. Phr.—Vīta īn mœrōrĕ jăcēbĭt. Mœrōrem ē pēctŏrĕ dēmĕt.

Mœstŭs, ă, ūm. *Sad, sorrowful.* Āltĕr ăb āltĕrĭūs fūnĕrĕ mœstŭs ĕrăt. O. Syn.—Mœrēns, dŏlēns, lūctū ŏpprēssŭs, cōnfēctŭs, ægĕr, pērcĭtŭs. Phr.—Stĕtĭt ācrī fīxă dŏlōrĕ. Tăcĭtă mœstīssĭmŭs īrā.

Mōlēs, ĭs. f. *Mass.* Ārdĕăt ĕt mūndī mōlēs ŏpĕrōsă lăbōrĕt. O. Syn.—Māssă, pōndŭs, ŏnŭs, ăcērvŭs, cŭmŭlŭs. Phr.—Mōlĭs ŏnŭs. Pōndŭs ĭnērs. Tōrpēnt mōlĕ nŏvā. *Difficult burden.* Syn.—Lăbŏr, ŏpŭs, pōndŭs. Phr.—Tāntæ mōlĭs ĕrāt Rōmānām cōndĕrĕ gēntēm.

Mŏlēstē. adv. *With difficulty.* Syn.—Aēgrē, grăvĭtĕr, īndīgnē, ĭnīquē.

Mŏlēstĭă, æ. f. *Heaviness of mind, oppression.* Syn.—Cūră, lăbŏr, nĕgōtĭŭm, īncōmmŏdūm.

Mŏlēstŭs, ă, ūm. *Disagreeable, burdensome.* Syn.—Dūrŭs, grăvĭs, īncōmmŏdŭs, īmpōrtūnŭs, ŏdĭōsŭs, īnvīsŭs, īngrātŭs, īnjūcūndŭs, dĭffĭcĭlĭs, ŏpĕrōsŭs.

Mōlīmĕn, ĭnĭs. n. *Effort.* Māgnă tĕnēnt īllūd nūmēn mōlīmĭnă rĕrūm. O. Syn.—Mōlīmēntūm, cōnāmĕn, cōnātŭs, nīsŭs.

Mōlĭŏr, īrĭs, ītŭs sūm, īrī. *To construct.* Ērgo ăvĭdūs mūrōs ōptātæ mōlĭŏr ūrbĭs. V. Syn.—Ādmōlĭŏr, strŭŏ, ædĭfĭcŏ. *To strive.* Syn.—Nītŏr, ēnītŏr, tēntŏ. *To plan.* Syn.—Părŏ, vōlvŏ, ăgĭtŏ, vērsŏ, āggrĕdĭŏr, mĕdĭtŏr, strŭŏ, cŏgĭtŏ.

Mōlītŏr, ōrĭs. m. *Constructor, contractor.* Syn.—Aūctŏr, făbrĭcātŏr, ŏpĭfēx.

Mōllēscŏ, ĭs, ĕrĕ. *To become soft.* Syn.—Mōllĭŏr, rĕmōllēscŏ, lĭquēscŏ, lĭquĕfīŏ, sōlvŏr, tābēscŏ. *To become effeminate.* Syn.—Ēnērvŏr, frāngŏr, sōlvŏr, lānguēscŏ. Phr.—Dēlĭcĭīs dīffluŏ, sōlvŏr.

Mōllĭŏ, īs, īvī & ĭī, ītūm, īrĕ. *To soften, to soothe.* Phr.—Mōllēm, tĕnĕrūm ēffĭcĭŏ. Dūrĭtĭēm, rĭgōrēm dēmŏ, tōllŏ. (*In speaking of men*) *To appease one's wrath.* Syn.—Lēnĭŏ, mānsuēfăcĭŏ, flēctŏ, plăcŏ.

Mōllĭs, ĭs, ĕ. *Soft, tender.* Syn.—Tĕnĕr, mōllĭcŭlŭs, lēntŭs. *Flexible.* Syn.—Făcĭlĭs, flēxĭlĭs, flēxĭbĭlĭs, lēntŭs. *Effeminate.* Syn.—Tĕnĕr, īmbēllĭs, dēbĭlĭs, ĭnērs, lānguĭdŭs, frāctŭs, dīscīnctŭs. *Sweet, kind.* Syn.—Rĕmīssŭs, lēnĭs, mītĭs, mānsuētŭs. *Tractable.* Syn.—Făcĭlĭs, trāctābĭlĭs, cērĕŭs.

Mōllĭtĕr. adv. *Softly.* Syn.—Mōllĕ, plăcĭdē. Fig.—*Kindly.* Lēnĭtĕr, clēmēntĕr, bĕnīgnē. *Agreeably.* Syn.—Jūcūndē, grātē.

Mōllĭtĭă, æ. f. *Luxury.* Syn.—Lūxŭs, mōllĭtĭēs, lūxŭrĭă, lūxŭrĭēs, ĭnērtĭă, dēlĭcĭæ.

Mŏlŏ, ĭs, ŭī, ĭtūm, ĕrĕ. *To grind.* Syn.—Ēmŏlŏ, cōmmŏlŏ, pērmŏlŏ. Phr.—Mŏlā, sāxō tĕrŏ, ōbtĕrŏ, āttĕrŏ. Cĕrĕrĭs frūgēs āspĕră sāxă tĕnēnt.

Mōmēntūm, ī. n. *Force, impulse.* Syn.—Mōtŭs, vīs. *Weight.* Syn.—Vīs, pōndŭs. *Moment of time.* Phr.—Tēmpŏrĭs, hōræ mōmēntūm, pūnctūm. Tēmpŭs ēxĭgŭūm. Brĕvĕ spătĭūm. Pārvă mŏră. Mŏră pārvŭlă.

Mŏnēdŭlă, æ. f. *Jackdaw.* (*See Appendix under list of Birds.*)

Mŏnĕō, ēs, ŭī, ĭtūm, ērĕ. *To warn.* Hæc sūnt quæ nōstrā lĭcĕāt tē vōcĕ mŏnērī. V. Syn.—Ādmŏnĕō, cōmmŏnĕō, mōnstrō, īndĭcō, nūntĭō, dŏcĕō, suādĕō, hōrtŏr, præcĭpĭō. Phr.—Scīt sē nōn fālsă mŏnērī. Crēbrō sērmōnĕ mŏnērĕ. *To remonstrate.* Syn.—Rĕprĕhēndō, īncrĕpō, cāstīgō.

Mŏnētă, æ. f. *Money.* Syn.—Nūmmŭs, nŭmīsmă, pĕcūnĭă.

Mŏnīlĕ, ĭs. n. *Collar, necklace.* Dāt dĭgĭtīs gēmmās, dāt lōngă mŏnīlĭă cōllō. O. Syn.—Tōrquēs, tōrquĭs, cīrcŭlŭs. Phr.—Bāccātŭs, gēmmātŭs cīrcŭlŭs. Tōrtĭlĕ cōllō dĕcŭs. Gēmmīs cōntēxtă tōrquēs.

Mŏnĭtŏr, ōrĭs. m. *Advisor.* Hæc ĕgŏ sī, mŏnĭtōr, mŏnĭtūs prĭŭs īpsĕ fŭīssēm. O. Syn.—Ādmŏnĭtŏr, suāsŏr, aūctŏr, hōrtātŏr. *One who reprehends.* Syn.—Cēnsŏr, cāstīgātŏr.

Mŏnĭtūm, ī. n. *Advice.* Syn.—Mŏnĭtŭs, hōrtātŭs, hōrtāmĕn, præcēptūm, cōnsĭlĭūm, māndātūm, jūssŭs.

Mōns, tĭs. m. *Mountain.* Rŭūnt dē mōntĭbŭs āmnēs. V. Syn.—Cōllĭs, jŭgūm, vērtēx, cūlmĕn, căcūmĕn, fāstīgĭă, rūpēs, ārcēs, sāxūm. Phr.—Mōntĭs vērtēx. Fāstīgĭă mōntĭs. Ārdŭă mōlēs. Mōntīs sūblīmĕ căcūmĕn. Frōndōsō vērtĭcĕ mōntēs. Sŭpĕrās sē tōllēns ĭn aūrās. Sīdĕră vērtĭcĕ tāngēns. Tōllēns ăd āstră căpŭt. Nūbĭbŭs īnsērtāns āltīs căpŭt. Mōns quī sūrgĭt ĭn āĕră. Ŏpērtī ārbŏrĕ mōntēs. Fig.—*Mass.* Syn.—Cŭmŭlŭs, ăcērvŭs, mōlēs.

Mōnstrō, ās, āvī, ātūm, ārĕ. *To show.* Tālĭă mōnstrābāt rĕlēgēns ērrātă rĕtrōrsūm. V. Syn.—Cōmmōnstrō, dēmōnstrō, ōstēndō, īndĭcō (ās). Phr.—Ūt sī cæcŭs ĭtĕr mōnstrārĕ vĕlĭt. *To uncover. See Detego. To teach. See Doceo.*

Mōnstrūm, ī. n. *Wonder, prodigy.* Hōrrēndum āc dīctū vĭdĕō mīrābĭlĕ mōnstrūm. V. Syn.—Ōstēntūm, pōrtēntūm, prōdĭgĭūm. *Monster.* Syn.—Pōrtēntūm, bēllŭă.

Mōntōsŭs, ă, ūm. *Mountainous.* Syn.—Mōntānŭs, scŏpŭlōsŭs, sāxōsŭs, ārdŭŭs, ābrūptŭs, jŭgōsŭs, clīvōsŭs.

Mŏnŭmēntūm, ī. n. *Pledge, sign, remembrance.* Āccĭpe ĕt hæc, mănŭūm tĭbĭ quæ mŏnŭmēntă mĕārūm Sīnt, pŭĕr. V. Syn.—Pīgnŭs, sīgnūm, nŏtă, īndĭcĭūm, mnēmŏsȳnŏn. Phr.—Mŏnŭmēntum ēt pīgnŭs ămōrĭs. Mŏnŭmēntum ærĕ pĕrēnnĭŭs. *History.* Syn.—Ānnālēs, fāstī, hīstŏrĭă.

Mŏră, æ. f. *Delay.* Trōjă cădēt, sĕd ĕrīt nōstrī mŏră lōngă lăbōrĭs. O. Phr.—Mŏræ spătĭūm. Nēc mŏră, nēc rĕquĭēs. Nōn ēst mŏră līběră nōbīs. Īn mē mŏră nōn ĕrĭt ūllă.

Mōrbĭdŭs, ă, ūm. *Unhealthy.* Syn.—Nŏcēns, grăvĭs, pēstĭfĕr, mălŭs, mălīgnŭs.

Mōrbŭs, ī. m. *Disease, sickness.* Mōrbōrūm quŏquĕ tē caūsās ēt sīgnă dŏcēbŏ. V. Syn.—Lānguŏr, fĕbrĭs, lŭēs, pēstĭs, mălūm, dŏlŏr. Phr.—Mōrbī vīs. Trīstĕ mălūm. Mōrbōrūm vīncŭlă. Cōrpŏră āttĕrēns. Cœpīt crūdēscĕrĕ mōrbŭs.

Mōrdāx, ācĭs. adj. *Cutting, piquant.* Syn.—Ăcūtŭs. Fig.—*Caustic.* Syn.—Ămārŭs, ăcērbŭs, ăcĕr, āspĕr.

Mōrdĕŏ, ēs, mŏmōrdī, mōrsūm, ērĕ. *To bite.* Mōrdēbītquĕ tŭōs sōrdĭdă prǣdă cănēs. O. Syn.—Ādmōrdĕŏ. Phr.—Mōrsūs īnfĕrŏ. Mōrsū ărrĭpĭŏ. Dēntēs fīgĕrĕ. Mĭsĕrōs mōrsū dēpāscĭtŭr artus. *To attach to.* Syn.—Rĕtĭnĕō, āstrīngō, cōnstrīngō, nēctŏ, līgŏ, āllĭgŏ. *To wound.* Syn.—Lǣdŏ, ūrŏ, nŏcĕŏ. *To torment.* Syn.—Rĕmōrdĕŏ, crŭcĭŏ, āngŏ, cārpŏ, āfflīgŏ.

Mŏrĭbūndŭs, ă, ūm. *Dying.* Ēxcūssūs cūrrū mŏrĭbūndūs vōlvĭtŭr ăgrīs. V. Syn.—Sēmiănĭmĭs, mŏrĭēns. Phr.—Mōrtī, lētō vīcīnŭs. Jām mōrtĕ sŭb īpsā. Ēxtrēmā jām īn mōrtĕ lānguēscēns. Līnquēns vītām. Mĕdĭo īn dīscrīmĭnĕ mōrtĭs. Lŭctātŭr mōrtī.

Mōrĭgĕrŭs, ă, ūm. *Complaisant.* Syn.—Ōbsĕquĭōsŭs, īndūlgēns.

Mŏrĭŏr, mŏrĕrĭs, mōrtŭŭs sūm, mŏrī. *To die.* Syn.—Ēmŏrĭŏr, cădŏ, ŏbĕŏ, ōccūmbŏ, ōccĭdŏ, īntĕrĕŏ, ēxspīrŏ. Phr.—Ănĭmām rēddŏ. Vītām fūndŏ. Ē vītā ēxĕŏ. Mōrtēm ŏbĕŏ. Mōrtī ōccūmbŏ. Lūmēn vītālĕ dēsĕrŏ. Ĕŏ sŭb ūmbrās. Sŭprēmūm ĭtĕr cārpĕrĕ. *To die by a violent death.* Syn.—Pĕrĕŏ, dīspĕrĕŏ, cădŏ, ōccĭdŏ, cǣdŏr, ōccīdŏr, pĕrĭmŏr, māctŏr, stĕrnŏr, jŭgŭlŏr, cōnfŏdĭŏr. Phr.—Nĕcī ōccūmbŏ. Ēnsĕ jăcĕŏ. Vūlnĕrĕ cădŏ. Pūrpŭrĕām vŏmĭt īlle ănĭmām. Bēllō, Mārtĕ cădŏ.

Mŏrŏr, ārĭs, ātŭs sūm, ārī. *To delay, to remain.* Aūlĭdĕ tē fāma ēst vēntō rĕtĭnēntĕ mŏrārī. V. Syn.—Dēmŏrŏr, īmmŏrŏr, cūnctŏr, cēssŏ, hǣrĕŏ, sūbsīstŏ, cōnsīstŏ. Phr.—Mŏrās nēctŏ. Grădūm, grēssūm, cūrsūm sīstŏ, cōntĭnĕŏ, cōmprĭmŏ. Fīgŏ pĕdēm. Haūd mūltă mŏrātŭs. *To hesitate.* Syn.—Tārdŏ, dŭbĭtŏ, rĕfŭgĭŏ. *To dwell.* Syn.—Mănĕŏ, vērsŏr. *To retard.* Syn.—Rĕmŏrŏr, tārdŏ, rĕtārdŏ, dētĭnĕŏ, rĕtĭnĕŏ, tĕnĕŏ, īmpĕdĭŏ, sīstŏ, ĭnhĭbĕŏ, dīffĕrŏ.

Mōrs, mōrtĭs. f. *Death.* Tūm brĕvĭŏr dīrǣ mōrtĭs ăpērtă vĭa ēst. Tib. Syn.—Fūnŭs, lētūm, īntĕrĭtŭs, fātūm, nēx, ŏbĭtŭs, ēxĭtŭs. Phr.—Ēxtrēmūs dĭēs. Lētī vīs. Ātră dĭēs. Tērmĭnŭs ǣvī. Quēm mōrtĭs tĭmŭĭt grădūm. Mōrtĭs ĭmāgŏ.

Mōrtālĭs, ĭs, ĕ. *Mortal, doomed to die.* Syn.—Pĕrĭtūrŭs, cădūcŭs. Phr.—Mōrtī dēbĭtŭs. Ōbnōxĭŭs mōrtī.

Mōrŭs, ī. f. *A mulberry-tree.* (*See Appendix under list of Trees, etc.*)

Mōs, mōrĭs. m. *Custom, habit.* Īllum ădĕō plăcŭīsse ăpĭbūs mīrābĕrĕ mōrēm. V. Syn.—Ūsŭs, āssuētūdŏ, cōnsuētūdŏ. Phr.—Prīscō dēdūctŭs ăb ævō. Tēmpūs pĕr ōmnĕ dēdūctŭs. Mōs ĕrăt āntīquīs. *Nature, character.* Syn.—Nātūră, īngĕnĭūm, īndŏlēs, hăbĭtŭs.

Mōtŭs, ŭs. m. *Movement.* Sæpĕ pĕr āssĭdŭōs lānguēnt mĕă brāchĭă mōtūs. O. Syn.—Pūlsŭs, īmpūlsŭs, īmpĕtŭs, āctŭs, jāctātŭs. *Sentiment.* Syn.—Sēnsŭs, āffēctŭs.

Mŏvĕŏ, ēs, mōvī, mōtūm, ērĕ. *To move.* Tālī rēmĭgĭō nāvīs sē tārdă mŏvēbăt. V. Syn.—Cōmmŏvĕŏ, pērmŏvĕŏ, mōtŏ, ăgŏ, ăgĭtŏ, pēllŏ, īmpēllŏ, quătĭŏ, quāssŏ, cōncŭtĭŏ, cĭĕŏ. *To dance. See Salto. To excite.* Syn.—Cĭĕŏ, ēxcĭtŏ, prōvŏcŏ, īmpēllŏ, lăcēssŏ, āccēndŏ. *To persuade.* Syn.—Pērmŏvĕŏ, tāngŏ, flēctŏ, āllĭcĭŏ, vīncŏ. *To medidate.* Syn.—Vōlvŏ, vērsŏ, ăgĭtŏ, mōlĭŏr, āggrĕdĭŏr, sūscĭpĭŏ.

Mōx. adv. *Soon.* Syn.—Mŏdŏ, cĭtŏ, cōnfēstīm, īlĭcĕt, ōcĭŭs, prŏpĕrē, brĕvī, jāmjām.

Mūcrŏ, ōnĭs. m. *Point.* Syn.—Ăcūmĕn. *The point of a sword.* Syn.—Ăcĭēs, cūspĭs.

Mūgĭŏ, īs, īvī & ĭī, ītūm, īrĕ. *To bellow.* Syn.—Īmmūgĭŏ. Phr.—Mūgītūs ēdŏ, dō, cĭĕŏ. Mūgītĭbŭs aūrās, ăgrōs īmplĕŏ. Mōrĕ bŏvīs gĕmŏ. Sŏnānt sīlvæ mūgītĭbŭs āltæ. *To reecho.* Syn.—Īmmūgĭŏ, rĕbŏŏ, pērsŏnŏ.

Mūlcĕŏ, ēs, lsī, lsūm, ērĕ. *To caress.* Syn.—Pērmūlcĕŏ, ădūlŏr, blāndĭŏr. Fig.—*To charm.* Syn.—Dēmūlcĕŏ, pērmūlcĕŏ, dēlīnĭŏ, lēnĭŏ, mītĭgŏ, mōllĭŏ, flēctŏ, ōblēctŏ, rĕcrĕŏ, rĕfĭcĭŏ, fŏvĕŏ, dēlēctŏ, āllĭcĭŏ.

Mūlctŏ, ās, āvī, ātūm, ārĕ. *To punish.* Syn.—Cāstīgŏ, dāmnŏ, plēctŏ.

Mūlgĕŏ, ēs, lsī, lsūm, ērĕ. *To milk.* Phr.—Ūbĕră prēmŏ, prēssŏ, sīccŏ, ēxsīccŏ. Mūlgēndō lāc ēxprĭmŏ. Dīstēntă sīccă ūbĕră.

Mŭlĭĕbrĭs, ĭs, ĕ. *Effeminate, womanlike.* Syn.—Fēmĭnĕŭs, īmbēllĭs, dēbĭlĭs.

Mŭlĭĕr, ĕrĭs. f. *Woman.* Syn.—Fēmĭnă. *Spouse. See Uxor.*

Mūltĭcŏlŏr, ōrĭs. adj. *Many-colored.* Syn.—Vērsĭcŏlŏr, vărĭŭs. Phr.—Vărĭō cŏlōrĕ mĭcāns. Īnsīgnīs vărĭō splēndōrĕ cŏlōrūm. Vărĭīs dĕcŏrātă cŏlōrĭbŭs.

Mūltĭplēx, ĭcĭs. adj. *Of several kinds.* Syn.—Vărĭŭs, dīvērsŭs, mūltŭs, mūltĭmŏdŭs.

Mūltĭtūdŏ, ĭnĭs. f. *Multitude.* Syn.—Tūrbă, cătērvă, cōpĭă, vīs, nŭmĕrŭs, frĕquēntĭă, cœtŭs.

Mūltūm. adv. *Much, very.* Syn.—Mūltă, vāldē, plūrĭmūm, ăbūndē, lārgē. Phr.—Haūd mĕdĭŏcrĭtĕr. Haūd lĕvĭtĕr.

Mūltŭs, ă, ūm. *Many, much, abundant.* Syn.—Ăbūndāns, frĕquēns, crēbĕr, plūrĭmŭs, nŭmĕrōsŭs, īnnŭmĕrŭs, mūltĭplēx, lōngŭs, māgnŭs, īngēns, dēnsŭs, īnfīnītŭs. Phr.—Nōn paūcŭs. Haūd mŏdĭcŭs.

Mūndŭs, ă, ūm. *Neat, clean.* Syn.—Nĭtĭdŭs, tērsŭs, pŏlītŭs, laūtŭs, cūltŭs, pūrŭs. Phr.—Lābĕ, măcŭlīs cărēns, nōn sōrdĭdŭs. Nūllīs sōrdĭbŭs hōrrēns, squālēns.

Mūndŭs, ī. m. *The world.* Syn.—Ōrbĭs. Phr.—Mūndī făbrĭcă, māchĭnă, mōlēs. Tērrārūm ōrbĭs. Ŏpūs mīrābĭlĕ mūndī. Māxĭmŭs ōrbĭs. Aētērnī gĕnĭtōrĭs ŏpŭs. *The world, that is, the people in it.* Syn.—Ōrbĭs, gēntēs, pŏpŭlī.

Mūnĭă, ōrūm. n. *Charge, function, duty.* Syn.—Mūnŭs, pārtēs, ōffĭcĭūm.

Mūnĭfĭcŏ, ās, āvī, ātūm, ārĕ. *To present lavishly.* Syn.—Mūnĕrŏ, lārgĭŏr.

Mūnīmēntūm, ī. n. *Fortification, defense.* Syn.—Vāllūm, āggĕr, prōpūgnācŭlă, mūrŭs.

Mūnĭŏ, īs, īvī & ĭī, ītūm, īrĕ. *To fortify.* Lōngām mūltā vī mūnĭĕt Ālbām. V. Syn.—Fīrmŏ, vāllŏ, sēpĭŏ, dēfēndŏ, tĕgŏ, prōtĕgŏ. Phr.—Mūnīmĭnĕ, āggĕrĕ, mūrō claūdŏ, cīrcūmdŏ, īnstrŭŏ. Prōpūgnācŭlă bēllō Tūtă părānt.

Mūnŭs, ĕrĭs. n. *Gift, present.* Quīcūnquĕ tērræ mūnĕrĕ vēscĭmŭr. H. Syn.—Dōnūm, mūnūscŭlūm. Phr.—Mūnūs mūnĕrĕ pēnsăt. Pīnguī dōnātūs mūnĕrĕ. *Duty, charge.* Syn.—Ōffĭcĭūm, mūnĭă, pārtēs.

Mūrmŭr, ŭrĭs. n. *Murmur, sound in general.* Āspĭcĕ, vēntōsī cĕcĭdērūnt mūrmŭrĭs aūræ. V. Syn.—Sŏnŭs, sŏnĭtŭs, sŭsūrrŭs, frĕmĭtŭs. Phr.—Sŭsūrrŭs, mūrmŭr mōllēs sōmnōs īnvītăt, suādĕt. Dūlcĕ mūrmŭr suādĕt. Claūsō fĭt gūrgĭtĕ mūrmŭr. Strĕpĭt ōmnĭs mūrmŭrĕ cāmpŭs. Māgnō mīscērī mūrmŭrĕ cœlūm. Trĕmĭt ōmnĭs mūrmŭre Ōlўmpŭs.

Mūrmŭrŏ, ās, āvī, ātūm, ārĕ. *To murmur, to make a low sound.* Syn.—Īmmūrmŭrŏ, sŭsūrrŏ, sŏnŏ, frĕmŏ. Phr.—Mūrmŭr, strĕpĭtūm dō, ēdŏ, cĭĕŏ, tōllŏ. Aūrās, æthĕră mūrmŭrĕ cōmplĕŏ, rĕplĕŏ. Īnānĭă mūrmŭră mīscēnt. *To speak in a low voice.* Syn.—Sŭsūrrŏ, īmmūrmŭrŏ, ōbmūrmŭrŏ, mūssŏ, mūtĭŏ.

Mūrŭs, ī. m. *City wall, wall in general.* Dīvĭdĭmūs mūrōs ēt mœnĭă pāndĭmŭs ūrbĭs. V. Syn.—Mœnĭă, āggĕr, mōlēs, vāllūm, prōpūgnācŭlūm, mūnīmĕn, mūnīmēntūm. Phr.—Mūrōrūm āggĕr. Mūnīmēn mūrālĕ. Fāstīgĭă mūrī. Cīrcūmdătă mœnĭă mūrō *Wall of a house.* Syn.—Părĭēs. *See Paries.* Fig.—*Fortification, defense.* Syn.—Præsĭdĭūm, mūnīmĕn, tūtāmĕn, tūtēlă, clўpĕŭs.

Mūs, mūrĭs. m. *Rat.* Syn.—Mūscŭlŭs, sōrēx. Phr.—Fēlī dūlcīssĭmă prædă. Frūgūm dīră lŭēs. Ōmnĭă cōrrōdēns.

Mūsĭcă, æ. f. *Music.* Syn.—Mĕlŏs, cāntŭs. Phr.—Ārs mūsĭcă. Ārs cănēndī. Ārs Phœbēă. Dūlcĭbŭs mŏdīs mŏvēns, dēlēctāns. Ănĭmōs mūlcēns. Cūrīs ānxĭă cōrdă lĕvāns. Nŭmĕrī dūlcĭsŏnī. *Poetry. See Carmen.*

Mūtābĭlĭs, ĭs, ĕ. *Changeable.* Sēd flēctī pŏtĕrĭt, mēns ēst mūtābĭlĭs īllī. Tib. Syn.—Mōbĭlĭs, īnstăbĭlĭs, vărĭābĭlĭs, īncērtŭs, īncōnstāns, lĕvĭs. Phr.—Mūtārī făcĭlĭs. Vūltū mūtābĭlĭs. Mūtābĭlĕ pēctŭs. Vērbō mūtāntŭr ămāntēs.

Mūtābĭlĭtās, ātĭs. f. *Fickleness, constancy.* Syn.—Mōbĭlĭtās, īncōnstāntĭă, lĕvĭtās.

Mūtātĭŏ, ōnĭs. f. *Change.* Syn.—Cōnvērsĭŏ, cōmmūtātĭŏ, pērmūtātĭŏ, mōtŭs.

Mŭtĭlŏ, ās, āvī, ātūm, ārĕ. *To mutilate, to cut.* Syn.—Trūncŏ, ābscīndŏ, āmpŭtŏ. *See Lacero.*

Mūtŏ, ās, āvī, ātūm, ārĕ. *To displace.* Ēt quŏtĭēs fēssūm mūtāt lătŭs. V. Syn.—Mŏvĕŏ, ăgŏ, trānsfĕrŏ. *To change.* Syn.—Cōmmūtŏ, īmmūtŏ, vērtŏ, cōnvērtŏ, nŏvŏ, rĕnŏvŏ, īnnŏvŏ, vărĭŏ. (*In the passive*) *To vary, to change.* Syn.—Vērtŏr, cōnvērtŏr, trānsfōrmŏr, ăbĕŏ, trānsĕŏ, fīŏ. Phr.—Nŏvām fōrmām, fĭgūrām, spĕcĭēm īndŭŏ, sūmŏ, căpĭŏ. Nūllă tĕnēnt vĕtĕrīs vēstīgĭă fōrmæ. Īn spĕcĭēm trānslātă nŏvām. Īn făcĭēm cōnvērsă.

Mūtŭō. adv. *Mutually, reciprocally.* Syn.—Mūtŭē, mūtŭă, āltērnūm, āltērnīs, īnvĭcēm.

Mūtŭs, ă, ūm. *Mute, silent.* Plēctră dŏlōrĕ tăcēnt; mūtă dŏlōrĕ lўră ēst. O. Syn.—Ēlīnguĭs, īnfāns. Phr.—Lŏquī nēscĭŭs. Ēxpērs lŏquēlæ. Vōcĕ cărēns. Ōră quĭdēm sēd mūtă gĕrēns. *Calm.* Syn.—Sĭlēns, plăcĭdŭs, trānquīllŭs.

Mўrīcă, æ. f. *The tamarisk.* (*See Appendix under list of Trees, etc.*)

Mўrrhă (Mūrră), æ. f. *The myrrh-tree.* (*See Appendix under list of Trees, etc.*)

Mўstērĭă, ōrūm. n. *Mystery.* Syn.—Săcră, ārcānă. Phr.—Săcră mўstĭcă. Ārcānă săcră. Rēs săcræ. Săcrārūm pĕnētrālĭă rērūm.

N

Nænĭă, æ. f. *Funeral chant.* Ābsīnt īnānī fūnĕrĕ nænĭæ. H. Syn.—Nænĭæ (pl.), quĕrēlă. Phr.—Flēbĭlĕ, fērālĕ, fūnĕrĕūm cārmĕn. Fūnĕbrēs quĕrēlæ. Lūgŭbrēs cāntūs.

Nām. conj. *For.* Syn.—Ĕnīm, ĕtĕnīm, quīppĕ, nēmpĕ, sĭquĭdēm, nīmīrūm.

Nāncīscŏr, ĕrĭs, nāctŭs sūm, īscī. *To discover.* Syn.—Īnvĕnĭŏ, rĕpĕrĭŏ. *To obtain.* Syn.—Ōbtĭnĕŏ, ăcquīrŏ, cōmpărŏ, cōnsĕquŏr, āssĕquŏr.

Nārcīssŭs, ī. m. *The daffodil.* (*See Appendix under list of Trees, etc.*)

Nārdŭs, ī. f. & Nārdūm, ī. n. *Nard.* (*See Appendix under list of Trees, etc.*)

Nārĭs, ĭs & Nārēs, ĭūm. f. *Nose.* Īnquĕ căvā nūllūs stēt tĭbĭ nārĕ pĭlŭs. O. Syn.—Nāsŭs. Phr.—Quā nārĭs frōntī cōmmīttĭtŭr. Spīrāmĭnă nārĭs ădūncæ. Nārēs ā frōntĕ rĕmīssæ.

Nārrŏ, ās, āvī, ātūm, ārĕ. *To relate.* Hīc ĕtĭam īnvēntūm Prĭămō nārrābĭs Ăchīllēm. V. Syn.—Ēnārrŏ, rĕnārrŏ, mĕmŏrŏ, cōmmĕmŏrŏ, rĕfĕrŏ, ēxpōnŏ, dīcŏ, pāndŏ, ăpĕrĭŏ, ēvōlvŏ, ēxplĭcŏ, ēlŏquŏr, rĕcēnsĕŏ, ēxpĕdĭŏ, rĕtēxŏ. Phr.—Paūcă tĭbi ēxpĕdĭam ē mūltīs. Tōtām rem ōrdĭnĕ pāndām. Tēmpŏră nārrāndō fāllĕrĕ. Tālĭă pērstābāt mĕmŏrāns. Quīd mājōră sĕquăr?

Nāscŏr, ĕrĭs, nātŭs sūm, nāscī. *To be born.* Syn.—Ēnāscŏr, ŏrĭŏr, gīgnŏr, crĕŏr, gĕnĕrŏr. Phr.—Āccĭpĭŏ vītām. Vītām īngrĕdĭŏr. Ād lūmĭnĭs aūrās ēmīttŏr. Ēdŏr ĭn lūcēm. Vītālĕ lūmĕn prīmūm āspĭcĭŏ. *To arise.* Syn.—Sūrgŏ, ŏrĭŏr, ēxŏrĭŏr, āppārĕŏ, vĕnĭŏ, ādsūm.

Nāstūrtĭūm, ĭī. n. *A kind of cress.* (*See Appendix under list of Trees, etc.*)

Nāsŭs, ī. m. *Nose.* Syn.—Nārĭs, nārēs. Phr.—Rōrāntēm frīgŏrĕ nāsūm. Vĭgĭlāntī stērtĕrĕ nāsō. *Discernment, taste.* Syn.—Nārĭs, ăcūmĕn.

Nātĭŏ, ōnĭs. f. *Nation, people.* Syn.—Gēns, pŏpŭlŭs, gĕnŭs.

Nătŏ, ās, āvī, ātūm, ārĕ. *To swim.* Vīs, pŭtŏ, cūm lībrō, Mārcĕ, nătārĕ tŭō. M. Syn.—Nō, īnnŏ, īnnătŏ, dēnătŏ. Phr.—Ăquās, ūndās, æquŏră nătŏ, īnnŏ. Ăquās pēctŏrĕ pūlsŏ, fĕrĭŏ. Pĕr ăquās fĕrŏr. Rēmĭgŏ sŭb ūndās. Sĕcō spūmāntēm pēctŏrĕ pōntūm.

Nātūră, æ. f. *Nature.* Rērūmquĕ nŏvātrīx Ēx ălĭīs ălĭās rĕpărāt nātūră fĭgūrās. O. Syn.—Vīs nātūrālĭs. Vīs nātūræ. Phr.—

Rērūm nātūră. Rērūm părēns. Rērūm nātūră crĕātrīx. *Quality, characteristic.* Syn.—Īngĕnĭūm, vīs, vīrtūs.

Nātūrālĭs, ĭs, ĕ. *Natural.* Syn.—Nātīvŭs. *Innate, inborn.* Syn.—Nātīvŭs, īnsĭtŭs, īnnātŭs, īndĭtŭs, īngĕnĭtŭs, īngĕnĕrātŭs, gĕnŭīnŭs.

Nātŭs, ī. m. *Son.* Syn.—Fīlĭŭs, prōlēs, pōstĕrī.

Naūfrăgĭūm, ĭī n. *Shipwreck.* Phr.—Trīstĭs jāctūră naūfrăgĭī. Naūfrăgĭūm făcĭŏ, pătĭŏr. Gūrgĭtĕ jāctŏ. Īmmērgŏr ăquīs. Nāvĕ frāctā. Spūmāntĭbŭs æquŏrĭs ūndīs ōbrŭŏr. Mēdĭō jāctātūr gūrgĭtĕ nāvĭs. Dīsjēctæ tōto æquŏrĕ clāssēs.

Naūtă, æ. m. *Sailor.* Naūtæquĕ pĕr ōmnĕ Aūdācēs mărĕ quī cūrrūnt. H. Syn.—Nāvĭtă, rēmēx. Phr.—Naūtĭcă pūbēs. Quī rēmōs ăgĭtăt. Pĕlăgō vŏlĭtāns. Aēquŏră vīncēns. Aēquŏră cærŭlă vērrēns.

Nāvĭgŏ, ās, āvī, ātūm, ārĕ. *To sail.* Gēns ĭnĭmīcă mĭhī Tȳrrhēnūm nāvĭgăt æquŏr. V. Phr.—Nāvĭgŏ æquŏr. Vēntō nāvĭgŏ. Aēquŏrĕ cūrrŏ. Vēlă făcĭŏ. Vĭās mărĭs, ĭtĕr vēlīs tēntŏ. Vădă, æquŏr sūlcŏ, ărŏ, sēcŏ. Pūppĕ vĭām făcĭām. Pēr cærŭlă fĕrŏr. Īn āltūm vēlă dăbānt.

Nāvĭs, ĭs. f. *Boat, vessel.* Quæquĕ pĕr ādvērsās nāvīs cĭtă dūcĭtŭr ūndās. O. Syn.—Nāvĭgĭūm, rătĭs, bĭrēmĭs, trĭrēmĭs, lĭbūrnă, lēmbŭs, cȳmbă, līntĕr, clāssĭs, cărīnă, prōră, pūppĭs, pīnŭs, ăbĭēs. Phr.—Pīnĕă tēctă. Pōntĭcă pīnŭs. Crēdĭtă vēntīs. Jāctātă pĕr æquŏr. Quæ vāstī sēcăt æquŏră pōntī. Nāvēm sōlvŏ. Cărīnæ vīncŭlă lāxŏ. Ōstĭă tāngŏ.

Nāvĭtă, æ. m. *Sailor.* Ātque ōmnīs nāvĭtă pōntō Hūmĭdă vēlă lĕgĭt. V. Syn.—Naūtă, nāvĭgātŏr. *Pilot.* Syn.—Gŭbērnātŏr, măgīstĕr, rēctŏr, mŏdĕrātŏr, naūclērŭs. Phr.—Nāvĭs măgīstĕr. Nāvālĭs cūrsūs ārbĭtĕr. Nāvēm quī tēmpĕrăt. Quī nāvēm rĕgĭt.

Nē. conj. & adv. *No, not. A negative conjunction introducing clauses of prohibition.* Syn.—Nōlī, căvē, pārcĕ, ŏmīttĕ (*all with the infinitive*).

Nĕ. *Enclitic* (*not translated*). Syn.—Nūm, ăn, ŭtrūm?

Nĕbŭlă, æ. f. *Mist, vapor.* Ēt mūltō nĕbŭlæ cīrcūm (gradientes) Dĕă fūdĭt ămīctū. V. Syn.—Văpŏr, nūbēs, nīmbŭs, cālīgŏ.

Nĕbŭlōsŭs, ă, ūm. *Misty, cloudy.* Syn.—Nūbĭlŭs, nīmbōsŭs, ōbscūrŭs, ŏpācŭs, tĕnĕbrōsŭs, cālīgāns.

Nĕc. conj. *Not, either.* Syn.—Nĕquĕ, nōn, nōn....aūt. *Not even.* Syn.—Nē....quĭdēm, nĕc īpsĕ, nōn īpsĕ.

Nĕcdūm. adv. *Not yet.* Syn.—Nōndūm. Phr.—Nōn dūm, nōn ădhūc, nĕque ădhūc.

Něcēssārĭŭs, ă, ūm. *Necessary, inevitable.* Syn. Īnēlūctābĭlĭs, īnēvītābĭlĭs.

Něcēssĭtās, ātĭs. f. *Need. See Egestas. Destiny, fate.* Syn.—Fātūm. Phr.—Vīs nēscĭă flēctī. Nūllīs āstrīctă lēgĭbŭs.

Nēctŏ, ĭs, nēxŭī, nēxūm, ĕrĕ. *To weave, to bind.* Syn.—Cōnnēctŏ, lĭgŏ, cōllĭgŏ, vīncĭŏ, nōdŏ, strīngŏ, cōnstrīngŏ, cōnjūngŏ. Fig.—Syn.—Īnnēctŏ, strŭŏ.

Něfāndŭs, ă, ūm. *Unspeakable, horrible.* Syn.—Īnfāndŭs, hōrrēndŭs, nĕfārĭŭs, scĕlĕrātŭs, scĕlēstŭs, īmpĭŭs.

Něfās. indecl. n. *Wrong, crime.* Syn.—Scĕlŭs, crīmĕn, flāgĭtĭūm. *Prodigy.* Syn.—Īnfāndūm, mōnstrūm.

Něglĕgēntĭă, æ. f. *Negligence.* Syn.—Dēsĭdĭă, īncūrĭă, īnērtĭă, īgnāvĭă, pĭgrĭtĭēs.

Nēglĕgŏ, ĭs, ēxī, ēctūm, ĕrĕ. *To neglect, to have no care for.* Syn.—Āspērnŏr, spērnŏ, tēmnŏ, cōntēmnŏ, dēspĭcĭŏ. Phr.—Nōn cūrŏ. Părūm cūrŏ.

Něgŏ, ās, āvī, ātūm, ārĕ. *To deny.* Īpsĕ fătēbāntūr sēd rēddĕrĕ pōssĕ nĕgābăt. V. Syn.—Ābnĕgŏ, dēnĕgŏ, pērnĕgŏ, īnfĭcĭŏr, ābnŭŏ, rĕnŭŏ. Phr.—Āiŏ nōn. Mănĭfēstă nĕgārĕ.

Něgōtĭūm, ĭī. n. *Business, occupation.* Syn.—Rēs, ŏpŭs, ŏpĕră, lăbŏr, cūră, mūnŭs, prōvīncĭă. Phr.—Ălĭēnă nĕgōtĭă cūrŏ.

Nēmŏ, ĭnĭs. m. *No one.* Vīndīctā Nēmŏ măgīs gaūdēt quām fēmĭnă. J. Syn.—Nūllŭs. Phr.—Nōn ūllŭs, nōn quīsquām. Nēc quēmquām fŭgĭŏ.

Nēmpĕ. adv. *Forsooth, assuredly.* Syn.—Scīlĭcĕt, vĭdēlĭcĕt, nīmīrūm, quīppĕ, ĕnīm, sānē.

Němŭs, ŏrĭs. n. *Wood, forest.* Nĕmūs sēclūsum īn vāllĕ rĕdūctā. V. Syn.—Sīlvă, sāltŭs, lūcŭs. Phr.—Nĕmŏrūm jām claūdĭtĕ sāltūs.

Něŏ, ēs, nēvī, nētūm, ērĕ. *To spin.* Phr.—Vērsō pōllĭcĕ fūsūm. Lānām, fīlă, stāmĭnă, vēllĕră nĕŏ, trăhŏ, dūcŏ, dēdūcŏ, tōrquĕŏ. Pēnsă trăhŏ. Dĭgĭtīs ŏpŭs sŭbĭgŏ.

Nēquām. indecl. adj. *Worthless, vile.* Syn.—Īmprŏbŭs, mălŭs, flāgĭtĭōsŭs, scĕlēstŭs.

Nēquāquām. adv. *By no means.* Syn.—Haūdquāquām, mĭnĭmē.

Něquĕŏ, īs, īvī & ĭī, ĭtūm, īrĕ. *To be unable.* Syn.—Vĕtŏr, īmpĕdĭŏr, prŏhĭbĕŏr. Phr.—Nōn quĕŏ, nōn pōssūm, nōn vălĕŏ, nōn ēvălĕŏ. Haūd sūm pŏtĭs. Haūd ŏpŭs ēst mĕæ̆. Mĭhĭ nōn fās ēst. Nōn lĭcĕt. Īmpăr sūm. Mĭhī nūllă pŏtēstās. Nōn dătŭr făcūltās. Haūd mĭhĭ sūffĭcĭūnt vīrēs.

Nequĭtĭă, æ. f. *Meanness, injustice.* Syn.—Īmprŏbĭtās, scĕlŭs, īmpĭĕtās, sævĭtĭă.

Nĕscĭŏ, īs, īvī & ĭī, ītūm, īrĕ. *To be ignorant.* Nĕscĭŏ quīs tĕnĕrōs ŏcŭlūs mĭhĭ fāscĭnăt āgnŏs. V. Syn.—Īgnōrŏ. Phr.—Sūm nĕscĭŭs, īnscĭŭs, īgnārŭs, rŭdĭs. Mē fŭgĭt. Hăbĕŏ īgnōtūm. Nōn mĭhĭ cōmpērtum ēst.

Nĕscĭŭs, ă, ūm. *Ignorant.* Nĕscĭă mēns hŏmĭnūm fātī, sōrtīsquĕ fŭtūrǣ. V. Syn.—Īgnārŭs, nĕscĭēns, īgnōrāns, rŭdĭs. *Unaccustomed to.* Syn.—Īgnārŭs, īndŏcĭlĭs, rŭdĭs, īnsuētŭs, ĭnāssuētŭs.

Nĕx, nĕcĭs. f. *Violent death.* Quām nĕcĭs ārtĭfĭcēs ārtĕ pĕrīrĕ sŭā. O. Syn.—Mōrs, fūnŭs, lētūm, cǣdēs.

Nī. conj. *Unless.* Syn.—Nĭsĭ, sī nōn.

Nīdĭfĭcŏ, ās, āvī, ātūm, ārĕ. *To build a nest.* Sīc vōs nōn vōbīs nīdĭfĭcātĭs, ăvēs. V. Syn.—Nīdūm, nīdōs ǣdĭfĭcŏ, lŏcŏ, strŭŏ, fīngŏ, sūspēndŏ. Pārvă cŭbīlĭă, dŏmūm sūspēndŏ. Lŭtĕōs lărēs fīgŏ. Căsām cēlsā sūb trăbĕ fīgŏ.

Nīdŭs, ī. m. *Nest.* Cuī dŏmŭs ēt dūlcēs lătĕbrōso īn pūmĭcĕ nīdī. V. Syn.—Nīdŭlŭs, cŭbīlĭă, tēctă, dŏmŭs, lărēs, pĕnātēs. Phr.— Ăvĭūm cŭbīlĭă. Lŭtĕūm ŏpŭs. Rāmōsă hōspĭtĭă. Frōndōsă dŏmŭs. Nīdŭs āltā ārbŏrĕ pēndŭlŭs.

Nĭgĕr, gră, grūm. *Black.* Ēt nīgrām māctābĭs ŏvēm, lūcūmquĕ rĕvīsēs. V. Syn.—Nĭgrāns, ātĕr, fūscŭs, fūrvŭs, pūllŭs, pĭcĕŭs, ōbscūrŭs, nōctĭcŏlŏr. Phr.—Cālĭgĭnĕ tīnctŭs. Ātrō cŏlōrĕ īmbūtŭs. Pĭcĕ nīgrĭŏr ātrā. *Black-skinned.* Syn.—Fūscŭs, ātĕr, ūstŭs, ădūstŭs, pĕrūstŭs, pĭcĕŭs, nōctĭcŏlŏr. Phr.—Sōlĕ ūstŭs. Ădūstō cōrpŏrĕ. Tīnctŭs cŏlōrĕ nōctĭs. *Mean.* Syn.—Ātĕr, tētĕr, līvĭdŭs, mălīgnŭs, mălŭs.

Nĭgrēscŏ, ĭs, ĕrĕ. *To become black.* Syn.—Nĭgrĕŏ. Phr.—Nĭgrōrēm, nĭgrūm cŏlōrēm dūcŏ, trăhŏ. Nĭgrēdĭnĕ, nĭgrō cŏlōrĕ īnfĭcĭŏr. *To become obscure.* Syn.—Ōbscūrŏr, ĭnhōrrēscŏ.

Nĭgrŏ, ās, āvī, ātūm, ārĕ. *To blacken.* Syn.—Fūscŏ, īnfūscŏ. Phr.— Ātrō cŏlōrĕ īnfĭcĭŏ, īmbŭŏ.

Nĭhĭl. n. indecl. *Nothing.* Syn.—Nīl, nĭhĭlūm. Phr.—Nōn quīdquām. Rēs nūllă. *As an adv.* Syn.—Mĭnĭmē, nēquāquām.

Nĭhĭlōmĭnŭs. adv. *None the less.* Phr.—Nĭhĭlō sēcĭŭs. Nōn sēcĭŭs. Nōn mĭnŭs.

Nīmbōsŭs, ă, ūm. *Stormy, rainy.* Syn.—Ĭmbrĭfĕr, plŭvĭālĭs, plŭvĭŭs, plŭvĭōsŭs, nūbĭfĕr, prŏcēllōsŭs.

Nīmbŭs, ī. m. *Rain-storm.* Syn.—Ĭmbĕr, plŭvĭă, prŏcēllă. *Cloud of dust.* Syn.—Nūbēs, glŏbŭs, tūrbŏ.

Nīmīrūm. adv. *To be sure, certainly.* Syn.—Nēmpĕ, quīppĕ, sānĕ, scīlĭcĕt, vĭdēlĭcĕt.

Nĭmĭs. adv. *Too much.* Syn.—Nĭmĭum, ĭmmŏdĕrātē, ĭmmŏdĭcē. Phr.—Ēxtrā mŏdūm. Prǣtĕr, sŭprā mŏdūm. Nĭmĭŏ plūs. Plūs ǣquō, plūs jūstō.

Nĭmĭŭs, ă, ūm. *Too great, excessive.* Syn.—Īmmŏdĕrātŭs, īmmŏdĭcŭs, mājŏr. Phr.—Mŏdūm ēxcēdēns. Nĭmĭs māgnŭs. Aēquō, jūstō mājŏr.

Nīngĭt. impers. *It is snowing.* Phr.—Nīx cœlō cĕcĭdĭt. Jām spārsĕrăt Hæmō Brūmă nĭvēs. Spārsĭt ĭn ārvă nĭvēs.

Nĭsĭ. conj. *Unless.* Syn.—Nī, sī nōn, nĭsī sī. *Except.* Syn.—Prætĕr, ēxcēptŭs.

Nĭtĕō, ēs, ŭi, erē. *To shine, to be brilliant.* Ēt nĭtēt īndūctō cāndĭdă bārbă gĕlū. O. Syn.—Splēndĕō, lūcĕō, fūlgĕō. Phr.—Cāndĭdă ōră nĭtēnt. Nĭtēt dīffūsō lūmĭnĕ cœlūm.

Nĭtĭdŭs, ă, ūm. *Shining brilliant.* Syn.—Nĭtēns, splēndēns, lūcēns, lūcĭdŭs, splēndĭdŭs. Phr.—Ārĭes nĭtĭdĭssĭmŭs aūrō. Crīnĕ nĭtēns. Nĭtĭdās ōstēndĕ cŏlūmnās. *Polished.* Syn.—Lævĭs, pŏlītŭs. *Shining with the freshness of youth.* Syn.—Nĭtēns, flōrēns. *Healthy, sleek.* Syn.—Nĭtēns, pīnguĭs, ŏpīmŭs, laūtŭs. *Rich, opulent.* Syn.—Laūtŭs, splēndĭdŭs, ŏpŭlēntŭs, dīvĕs.

Nĭtŏr, ōrĭs. m. *Splendor.* Ēt nĭtŏr īn tăcĭtā lūcĕ dĭūrnŭs ĕrăt. O. Syn.—Lūx, lūmĕn, splēndŏr. Phr.—Nĭtŏr īgnĕŭs ōrĭs. Nūllūs tōtā nĭtŏr īn cŭtĕ.

Nītŏr, ĕrĭs, sŭs sūm & xŭs sūm, tī. *To strive.* Nĭtĭmŭr īn vĕtĭtūm sēmpēr, cŭpĭmūsquĕ nĕgātă. O. Syn.—Ādnītŏr, cōnnītŏr, ēnītŏr, cōnŏr, cōntēndō, lăbōrŏ, mōlĭŏr. *To lean upon.* Syn.—Īnnītŏr, īncūmbō, fūlcĭŏr, sūstĭnĕŏr.

Nĭvālĭs, ĭs, ĕ. *Snowy.* Syn.—Nĭvōsŭs, nĭvĕŭs, nīnguĭdŭs, glăcĭālĭs, gĕlĭdŭs.

Nĭvĕŭs, ă, ūm. *Snowy. See Nivalis. White as snow.* Syn.—Nĭvālĭs, ālbŭs, cāndēns, cāndĭdŭs, cānŭs, lāctĕŭs, ĕbūrnŭs.

Nĭvōsŭs, ă, ūm. *Snowy. See Nivalis, Niveus.*

Nīx, nĭvĭs. f. *Snow.* Nĭvēs mōllĭt ăquātĭcŭs Aūstĕr. O. Syn.—Prŭīnă. Phr.—Nĭvĕŭs hūmŏr. Gĕlĭdŭs hūmŏr. Nĭvĕī flōccī. Nĭvĕă vēllĕră. Nīx æmŭlă lānæ. Cōncrētŭs īmbĕr. Cœlō dēlāpsă, īn cāmpōs dēscēndēns. Tēctă tĕgēns. Āgrōs ālbō vēllĕrĕ īndŭēns. Nīx ācrī gĕlū. Nĭvĭbŭs aūctă. Cūm nīx āltă jăcĕt. Vĭdēs ŭt āltā stēt nĭvĕ cāndĭdūm.

Nōbĭlĭs, ĭs, ĕ. *Well-known.* Syn.—Nōtŭs. *Famous.* Syn.—Clārŭs, cĕlĕbĕr, ēgrĕgĭŭs, ēxĭmĭŭs, īllūstrĭs, īnsīgnĭs, īnclўtŭs. *Of noble birth.* Syn.—Gĕnĕrōsŭs. Phr.—Nōbĭlĭtātĕ părēns. Ōrtū nōbĭlĭs. Gĕnĕrōsī sānguĭnĭs. Præclārā stīrpĕ. Nōbĭlī ā sānguĭnĕ. Trōjāno ā sānguĭnĕ clārŭs.

Nōbĭlĭtās, ātĭs. f. *Fame. See Fama. Nobility.* Syn.—Stēmmătă, gĕnŭs, nōmĕn, prŏăvī. Phr.—Gĕnĕrĭs, nōmĭnĭs āntīquĭtās, vĕtūstās, fāmă, glōrĭă. Nōbĭlĭtātĭs hŏnōs. Nōbĭlĕ stēmmă. Nōn ōbscūră dŏmŭs. Āmpla ē sānguĭnĕ prīscō. *Nobility of character.* Phr.—Gĕnĕrōsŭs ănĭmŭs. Mēns ēxcēlsă, sūblīmĭs. Sēnsūs āltī. Pēctŭs nōbĭlĕ.

Nōbĭlĭtātŭs, ă, ūm. *Celebrated.* Syn.—Nōbĭlĭs, cĕlĕbrātŭs, īnsīgnītŭs.

Nŏcĕō, ēs, ŭī, ĭtūm, ērĕ. *To harm.* Nōctĕ nŏcēnt pōtæ̆, sĭnĕ nōxā lūcĕ bĭbūntŭr. O. Syn.—Lædō, ōbsūm, ōffĭcĭō. Phr.—Dāmnō sūm. Dāmnūm, dētrīmēntūm āffĕrō, īmpōrtō. Līnguă fŭĭt dāmnō. Nŏcŭīt tĕmĕrārĭă vīrtūs. Haūd īgnāră nŏcēndī. Mīllĕ nŏcēndi ārtēs.

Nōctŭă, æ. f. *The owl.* (*See Appendix under list of Birds.*)

Nōdō, ās, āvī, ātūm, ārĕ. *To bind, to twist into a knot.* Cuī phărĕtra ēx aūrō, crīnēs nōdāntŭr ĭn aūrūm. V. Syn.—Īnnōdō, lĭgō, nēctō, īnnēctō, nēxō, vīncĭō, rĕvīncĭō. Phr.—Īn nōdōs făcĭō. Nōdīs īmplĭcō.

Nōdŭs, ī. m. *Knot.* Nēctĕ trĭbūs nōdīs tērnōs, Ămărȳllĭ, cŏlōrēs. V. Syn.—Lĭgāmĕn, nēxŭs, vīncŭlŭm, vīnclūm. Phr.—Mănĭbūs nōdōs dīvēllĕrĕ tēntăt. Nōdōs mănū dīdūcĕrĕ.

Nōlō, nōn vīs, nōlŭī, nōllĕ. *To be unwilling.* Syn.—Ābnŭō, nĕgō, rĕcūsō, dētrēctō, ōbstō, rĕpūgnō, rĕfŭgĭō, āvērsŏr. Phr.—Nōn plăcĕt. Īnvītā Mĭnērvā.

Nōmĕn, ĭnĭs. n. *Name.* Phr.—Ăvītī nōmĭnĭs hærēs. Dēdūctūm nōmĕn ăb Āncō. Nōtūs mĭhĭ nōmĭnĕ tāntūm. Rōmānam ēxtīnguĕrĕ nōmĕn. *Reputation, fame.* Syn.—Fāmă, hŏnŏr, glōrĭă, dĕcŭs, laūs, tĭtŭlŭs. *Race.* Syn.—Gĕnŭs, gēns, stīrps. *Title of a book.* Syn.—Tĭtŭlŭs.

Nōmĭnō, ās, āvī, ātūm, ārĕ. *To name.* Syn.—Dīcō, vŏcō, āppēllō, nūncŭpō. Phr.—Nōmĕn dō, āddō, trĭbŭō. Nōmĭnĕ dīcō. Sīc īllōs nōmĭnĕ dīcūnt.

Nōn. adv. *Not.* Syn.—Haūd, nĕc, nĕquĕ, haūdquāquām, nēquāquām, nēquīcquām, nĭhĭl, nīl, mĭnĭmē, nūsquām, mĭnŭs, mălĕ.

Nōnāgīntă. *Ninety.* Syn.—Nōngīntă, nŏvēm dēnī.

Nōndūm. adv. *Not yet.* Syn.—Nōndūm ĕtĭām, nĕquĕ ădhūc, nōn ădhūc, nōn hāctĕnŭs.

Nōrmă, æ. f. *Rule.* Syn.—Rēgŭlă, lēx.

Nōscō, ĭs, nōvī, nōtūm, ĕrĕ. *To know.* Nūllăquĕ mōrtālēs, prætēr sŭă līttŏră, nōrānt. O. Syn.—Cōgnōscō, scĭō. *To recognize.* Syn.—Āgnōscō, nōscĭtō.

Nŏtă, æ. f. *Mark, sign.* Syn.—Sīgnūm, īnsīgnĕ, ārgūmēntūm, īndĭcĭūm, vēstīgĭūm. Phr.—Nŏtām sĭnĕ vūlnĕrĕ fēcĭt. Fīgĕrĕ dēntĕ nŏtās. Nōndūm dē pēctŏrĕ cædĭs Ēxcēssērĕ nŏtæ. *Stain.* Syn.—Lābēs, măcŭlă.

Nōtēscŏ, ĭs, nōtŭī, ĕrĕ. *To become known.* Syn.—Īnnōtēscŏ, nōscŏr, vūlgŏr, ăpĕrĭŏr, cōmpĕrĭŏr. Phr.—Nōtūm, pălām fĭt. Īn nōtĭtĭām vĕnĭt. *To become celebrated.* Syn.—Īnnōtēscŏ, clārēscŏ, īnclārēscŏ, nōtŭs fīŏ.

Nŏtŏ, ās, āvī, ātūm, ārĕ. *To mark, to sign.* Sīgnŏ, īnsīgnĭŏ, dīstīnguŏ, dēsīgnŏ. *To stain.* Syn.—Măcŭlŏ. *To remark, to notice.* Syn.—Ădnŏtŏ, ōbsērvŏ.

Nŏtŭs, ī. m. *South-wind.* Syn.—Aūstĕr, Āfrĭcŭs. Phr.—Mădĭdīs Nŏtŭs ēvŏlăt ālīs. Mădĭdūs tĕpĭdō sībĭlăt ōrĕ Nŏtŭs. Trīstīquĕ rŏsārĭă pāllēnt Ūstă Nŏtō.

Nŏvēllŭs, ă, ūm. *New, young.* Syn.—Nŏvŭs, tĕnĕr, tĕnēllŭs, rĕcēns.

Nŏvīssĭmŭs, ă, ūm. *Last.* Syn.—Extrēmŭs, ūltĭmŭs, pōstrēmŭs. Phr.—Hōră nŏvīssĭmă.

Nŏvŏ, ās, āvī, ātūm, ārĕ. *To renew.* Vōtă Sērvātī făcĭmūs mĕrĭtōsquĕ nŏvāmŭs hŏnōrēs. V. Syn.—Īnnŏvŏ, rĕnŏvŏ, īnstaūrŏ, rĕfĭcĭŏ, rĕpărŏ.

Nŏvŭs, ă, ūm. *New.* Syn.—Rĕcēns. *Renewed.* Syn.—Nŏvātŭs, rĕnāscēns, īnstaūrātŭs. *Unknown.* Syn.—Īgnōtŭs, īnsuētŭs, īnsŏlĭtŭs, ĭnaūdĭtŭs, mīrŭs.

Nōx, nōctĭs. f. *Night.* Nōx ātră căvā cīrcūmvŏlăt ūmbrā. V. Syn.—Tĕnĕbræ, cālīgŏ. Phr.—Nōctĭs, nōctūrnūm tēmpŭs. Ōbscūræ nōctĭs ĭmāgŏ. Lătĕbrōsæ tēmpŏră nōctĭs. Plăcĭdūm sōmnī tēmpŭs. Nōx ăccōmmŏdă fraūdī. Lūdō dūcĕrĕ nōctēm. Nōctēm dūcēntĭbŭs āstrīs. Dĭēm nōx ābstŭlĭt ātră. Nōctĕ sŭpēr mĕdĭā. Cæcā cālīgĭnĕ nōctĭs. Sōlĕ lătēntĕ. Cūm sōl ōcĕănō sŭbēst. Cœlūm nōx ātră tĕnĕt. Sĭnĕ sīdĕrĕ nōctēs. Tēllūs ābscōndĭtŭr ūmbrīs. Ēt nōctĕ tĕgūntŭr ŏpācā.

Nōxă, æ. f. *Damage, loss.* Syn.—Dāmnūm, mălūm. *Fault.* Syn.—Cūlpă, dēlĭctūm.

Nōxĭŭs, ă, ūm. *Hurtful.* Syn.—Nŏcĭtūrŭs, nŏcīvŭs, nŏcēns, nŏcŭŭs, dāmnōsŭs, ĭnĭmīcŭs, īnfēstŭs, pērnĭcĭōsŭs, grăvĭs, īncōmmŏdŭs, īmpōrtūnŭs, ēxĭtĭōsŭs, ēxĭtĭālĭs, fūnēstŭs, trīstĭs.

Nūbēs, ĭs. f. *Cloud.* Ōbscūrāmquĕ trăhī vēntō mīrābĕrĕ nūbēm. V. Syn.—Nĕbŭlă, nīmbŭs, nūbĭlă, nūbēcŭlă. Phr.—Tūrbŏ pĭcĕŭs. Cālīgŏ pĭcĕă. Cœlūm ōbscūrō ămĭctū. Īmbrĕ grăvĭdă. Cōndĭtă nūbĕ dĭēs. Nūbĕ căvā spĕcŭlāntŭr ămĭctī. *Cloud of dust.* Syn.—Nĕbŭlă, nīmbŭs, glŏbŭs, tūrbŏ.

Nūbĭlŭs, ă, ūm. *Cloudy.* Syn.—Nĕbŭlōsŭs, nīmbōsŭs, ātĕr, nĭgĕr, nĭgrāns, ōbscūrŭs, cālīgĭnōsŭs, tĕnĕbrōsŭs, cæcŭs, ŏpācŭs, pĭcĕŭs. Phr.—Nūbĭbŭs, nīmbīs dēnsīs, grăvĭs, spīssīs. Cālīgĭnĕ dēnsŭs.

Nūdŏ, ās, āvī, ātūm, ārĕ. *To disrobe.* Syn.—Dēnūdŏ, ēxŭŏ. *To despoil.* Syn.—Spŏlĭŏ. *To expose.* Syn.—Dētĕgŏ, pāndŏ, ăpĕrĭŏ.

Nūdŭs, ă, ūm. *Naked.* Syn.—Nūdātŭs, ēxūtŭs, spŏlĭātŭs, dētēctŭs. Phr.—Tēgmĭnĭs ēxpērs. Vēstĕ cărēns. Nūdŭs mēmbră. Pŏsĭtā vēstĕ. Pŏsĭtō vēlāmĭnĕ nūdŭs. Nūdă gĕnū. *Discovered.* Syn.—Nūdātŭs, ĭnŏpērtŭs, ăpērtŭs, dētēctŭs. *Despoiled.* Syn.—Nūdātŭs, spŏlĭātŭs, cărēns. *Without ornament.* Syn.—Sīmplēx.

Nūgātŏr, ōrĭs. m. *Trifler.* Syn.—Nūgāx, cēssātŏr, mēndāx, vānĭlŏquŭs, gārrŭlŭs, ĭnēptŭs, lŏquāx.

Nūgŏr, ārĭs, ātŭs sūm, ārī. *To trifle.* Syn.—Ōtĭŏr, lāscīvĭŏ.

Nūm. adv. *Introducing a question that supposes a negative answer, (not to be translated).* Syn.—Nūmquĭd, nōnnĕ, ăn, ānnĕ.

Nūmĕn, ĭnĭs. n. *Divine will.* Phr.—Dĕī, dīvīnŭs nūtŭs. Dīvīnă vīs, pŏtēstās, vŏlūntās. Dĕī nōn vĭŏlābĭlĕ nūmĕn. Sūpplēx tŭă nūmĭnă pōscŏ. Mĕō sĭnĕ nūmĭnĕ.

Nŭmĕrŏ, ās, āvī, ātūm, ārĕ. *To count, to enumerate.* Syn.—Ēnŭmĕrŏ, dīnŭmĕrŏ, cēnsĕŏ, pērcēnsĕŏ, rĕcēnsĕŏ, cōmpŭtŏ, sūppŭtŏ. Phr.—Nŭmĕrō cōmprēndŏ. Bīsquĕ dĭē nŭmĕrānt āmbō pĕcŭs. Nŭmĕrūmquĕ rĕfērrĕ. Nŭmĕrūm cūm nāvĭbŭs æquăt. *To possess.* Syn.—Hăbĕŏ, pōssĭdĕŏ. *To estimate.* Syn.—Cēnsĕŏ, ānnŭmĕrŏ, æstĭmŏ.

Nŭmĕrōsŭs, ă, ūm. *Numerous.* Īn tĕnĕbrīs nŭmĕrōsōs pōnĕrĕ grēssūs. O. Syn.—Plūrĭmŭs, frĕquēns, mūltŭs, mūltĭplēx, dēnsŭs, cōnfērtŭs.

Nŭmĕrŭs, ī. m. *Number, crowd.* Syn.—Vīs, mūltĭtūdŏ, tūrbă, āgmĕn. Phr.—Ēxplēbō nŭmĕrūm. *Rank.* Syn.—Ōrdŏ. *Rhyme, metre, verse.* Syn.—Mĕtrūm, cārmĕn, mŏdŭs, mŏdī. Phr.—Nŭmĕrī lēgĕ sŏlūtī.

Nŭmīsmă, ătĭs. n. *Piece of money.* Syn.—Aēs, nūmmŭs, mŏnētă.

Nūmŭs & Nūmmŭs, ī. m. *Piece of money.* Syn.—Nŭmīsmă, pĕcūnĭă, mŏnētă, dēnārĭŭs, sēstērtĭŭs, aūrĕŭs, aūrĕŏlŭs. Phr.—Sūmmă nūmmōrūm. Nūmmōrum ēffūndĕrĕ sāccōs. Crēscĭt ămōr nūmmī

Nūnc. adv. *Now.* Syn.—Jāmmŏdŏ, jām nūnc, jāmjām, hōc tēmpŏrĕ, præsēntī tēmpŏrĕ.

Nūncŭpŏ, ās, āvī, ātūm, ārĕ. *To call, to name.* Syn.—Dīcŏ, nōmĭnŏ, vŏcŏ, vŏcĭtŏ.

Nūnquām. adv. *Never.* Syn.—Nōn ūnquām. Nūllō tēmpŏrĕ. Nūllō ĭn ævō.

Nūntĭŏ, ās, āvī, ātūm, ārĕ. *To announce.* Dūm sācră sĕcūndūs ărūspēx nūntĭĕt. V. Syn.—Ānnūntĭŏ, dēnūntĭŏ, rĕnūntĭŏ, rĕfĕrŏ, dēfĕrŏ, rĕpōrtŏ, mŏnĕŏ, sīgnĭfĭcŏ, īndĭcŏ, nārrŏ. Phr.—Māndātă rĕfērrĕ. Nūntĭă rĕfērrĕ.

Nūntĭŭs, ĭī. m. *Message, news.* Syn.—Nūntĭūm, rūmŏr, fāmă.

Nūntĭŭs, ĭī. m. *Messenger.* Dīxĕrāt ēt vēlōx jām nūntĭūs āstră tĕnēbāt. Phr.—Sērmōnūm măgīstĕr. Quī dīctă, fāctă, māndātă dēfērt, rĕfērt. Quī vărĭās ītquĕ rĕdītquĕ vĭās. Crēbērquĕ rĕcūrrīt nūntĭŭs. Rĕfĕrēs ērgo hæc.

Nūpĕr. adv. *Lately.* Syn.—Rĕcēns, mŏdŏ. Phr.—Nōn (*or*) haūd prīdēm, nōn ĭtă prīdēm, nēc dūdūm.

Nūptĭæ, ārūm. f. *Nuptials, marriage.* Syn.—Hўmĕnæŭs, cōnjŭgĭūm, cōnnŭbĭūm, nūptŭs. Phr.—Săcră jŭgālĭă, cōnnŭbĭālĭă, nūptĭālĭă. Jŭgālēs tædæ. Thălămī fœdūs sŏcĭālĕ. Nūptĭās cĕlĕbrārĕ.

Nūptĭālĭs, ĭs, ĕ. *Nuptial.* Syn.—Cōnnŭbĭālĭs, cōnjŭgĭālĭs, jŭgālĭs.

Nūtŏ, ās, āvī, ātūm, ārĕ. *To nod.* Āttōllūnt căpĭta ēt sūblīmī vērtĭcĕ nūtant. V. *To totter.* Syn.—Lăbŏ, lăbāscŏ, tĭtŭbŏ, văcīllŏ, mŏvĕŏr, ăgĭtŏr. Phr.—Rŭīnām, lāpsūm mĭnŏr. Īn rŭīnām tēndŏ. *To incline.* Syn.—Flūctŭŏ, văcīllŏ, tĭtŭbŏ.

Nūtrĭŏ, īs, īvī & ĭī, ītūm, īrĕ. *To nourish.* Nūtrĭĕrāt Lўcĭă, părĭbūsque ōrnāvĕrāt ārmīs. V. Syn.—Ălŏ, pāscŏ, ēdūcŏ, fŏvĕŏ. Phr.—Ălĭmēntă dō. Dăpĭbŭs, cĭbīs fŏvĕŏ. Dăpĭbūs mēmbră fŏvĕt.

Nūtrīx, īcĭs. f. *Nurse.* Īndĕ lŭpæ fūlvō nūtrīcīs tēgmĭnĕ lætŭs. V. Syn.—Āltrīx, nūtrīcŭlă. Phr.—Pŭĕrī fīdīssĭmă cūstōs.

Nūtŭs, ī. m. *Nod.* Syn.—Nŏtæ, sīgnă. Phr.—Vūltūs sīgnūm. Căpĭtīs gēstŭs. Nūtū tōtūm trĕmĕfēcĭt Ŏlўmpūm. *Wish, will.* Syn.—Vŏlūntās, ārbĭtrĭūm, nūmĕn.

O

Ŏb. prep. *Before.* Syn.—Āntĕ, præ. *On account of.* Syn.—Prōptĕr, caūsă, ērgō, grātĭă.

Ŏbāmbŭlŏ, ās, āvī, ātūm, ārĕ. *To walk around.* Syn.—Ŏbĕŏ, cīrcŭmĕŏ, cīrcŭmāmbŭlŏ, īncēdŏ, cīrcūmvōlvŏ, spătĭŏr.

Ōbcæcŏ, ās, āvī, ātūm, ārĕ. *To blind.* Syn.—Cæcŏ, ēxcæcŏ.

Ōbdūcŏ, ĭs, xī, ctūm, ĕrĕ. *To cover, to place around.* Ēt sĕgĕtēm dēnsīs ōbdūcūnt sēntĭbŭs hērbæ. V. Syn.—Cōndŏ, tĕgŏ, cōntĕgŏ, ŏpĕrĭŏ, ōccūltŏ.

Ōbdūrēscŏ, ĭs, ŭī, ĕrĕ. *To become hardened.* Syn.—Īndūrēscŏ, īndūrŏr, dūrēscŏ, rĭgēscŏ.

Ōbdūrŏ, ās, āvī, ātūm, ārĕ. *To persist.* Syn.—Dūrŏ, īndūrēscŏ.

Ŏbēdĭŏ, īs, īvī & ĭī, ītūm, īrĕ. *To obey.* Syn.—Pārĕŏ, ōbtēmpĕrŏ, sĕquŏr, ōbsĕquŏr, aūdĭŏ. Phr.—Jūssă, māndātă, præcēptă căpēssŏ, pērfĭcĭŏ. Mŏnĭtīs pārĕŏ. Nōn sĕcŭs āc jūssī făcĭūnt. Jūssă vĭrī făcĭūnt. Quō dūră vŏcăt fōrtūnă, sĕquāmŭr.

Ŏbĕŏ, īs, īvī & ĭī, ĭtūm, īrĕ. *To go in front of, to oppose.* Syn.—Īncūrrŏ, ōccūrrŏ, īntērvĕnĭŏ, ōbjĭcĭŏr. *To go around.* Syn.—Cīrcŭmĕŏ, ŏbāmbŭlŏ, lūstrŏ, pĕrērrŏ, pērlūstrŏ, pērcūrrŏ, ŏbērrŏ, pērvăgŏr, mētĭŏr, pērmētĭŏr. *To visit.* Syn.—Ădĕŏ, vīsŏ, īnvīsŏ. *To exercise.* Syn.—Ădĕŏ, pĕrăgŏ, pērfĭcĭŏ, ēxsĕquŏr. *To die. See Morior.*

Ŏbēsŭs, ă, ūm. *Fat, stout.* Syn.—Pīnguĭs, ŏpīmŭs, crāssŭs.

Ŏbēx, ĭcĭs (ōbjĭcĭs). m. *Obstacle.* Syn.—Ōbstācŭlūm, īmpĕdīmēntūm, rĕpāgŭlūm, mŏră. Phr.—Ōppŏsĭtă mōlēs. Ōbjĭcĕ fīrmō claūdūntūr pōrtæ. *Dike, mole.* Syn.—Mōlēs.

Ōbjĭcĭŏ, ĭs, jēcī, jēctūm, ĕrĕ. *To place in front of, to oppose.* Ōbjĭcĭūnt ĕquĭtēs sēse ād dīvōrtĭă nōtă. V. Syn.—Ōppōnŏ, īntērjĭcĭŏ, ōbjēctŏ. Phr.—Ōbjĭcĭūnt clўpĕōs ād tēlă. *To offer, to present.* Syn.—Ōffĕrŏ, pōrrĭgŏ, āffĕrŏ, ēxhĭbĕŏ. *To expose.* Syn.—Ōbjēctŏ, ēxpōnŏ, prōjĭcĭŏ.

Ōbjūrgātĭŏ, ōnĭs. f. *Reprimand.* Syn.—Cāstīgātĭŏ, rĕprĕhēnsĭŏ, īncūsātĭŏ, īnsēctātĭŏ. Phr.—Dīctă, vērbă sĕvēră, ămāră, āspĕră, dūră. Sĕvēræ vōcēs. Vōx plēnă mĭnārūm.

Ōbjūrgŏ, ās, āvī, ātūm, ārĕ. *To reprimand.* Syn.—Ārgŭŏ, īncrĕpŏ, īncūsŏ, rĕprĕhēndŏ, cāstīgŏ. Phr.—Vērbīs cāstīgŏ, īnsēctŏr. Sĕvērīs vōcĭbŭs īnvĕhŏr.

Ōblēctŏ, ās, āvī, ātūm, ārĕ. *To please, to delight.* Ōblēctānt dūlcī mē cārmĭnĕ. Cat. Syn.—Dēlēctŏ, rĕcrĕŏ, jŭvŏ.

Ōblĭgŏ, ās, āvī, ātūm, ārĕ. *To bind around.* Syn.—Lĭgŏ, cīrcūmlĭgŏ, cōnstrīngŏ, ōbstrīngŏ, ōbnēctŏ. Fig.—*To oblige, to bind.* Syn.—Dēvīncĭŏ, ōbstrīngŏ.

Ōblĭnŏ, ĭs, īvī & ēvī, ĭtūm, ĭnĕrĕ. *To smear, to soil.* Cīrcūmlĭnŏ, īllĭnŏ, ĭnūngŏ, īmbŭŏ, īnfĭcĭŏ, tīngŏ, ōbdūcŏ.

Ōblīquŏ, ās, āvī, ātūm, ārĕ. *To turn, to bend in another direction.* Ōblīquātquĕ sĭnūs īn vēntum āc tālĭă fātŭr. V. Syn.—Flēctŏ, īnflēctŏ, tōrquĕŏ. Phr.—Īn ōblīquūm flēctŏ. Păvēntēs ōblīquāvĭt ĕquōs.

Ōblīquŭs, ă, ūm. *Oblique, crosswise.* Syn.—Trānsvērsŭs. *Bending, tortuous.* Syn.—Sĭnŭōsŭs, flēxŭs, cūrvātŭs, tōrtŭs. Fig.—*Jealous.* Syn.—Līmŭs, trānsvērsŭs, īnvĭdŭs, īnvĭdĭōsŭs.

Ōblĭtĕrŏ, ās, āvī, ātūm, ārĕ. *To efface.* Syn.—Ăbŏlĕŏ, dēlĕŏ.

Ōblīvīscŏr, ĕrĭs, blītŭs sūm, vīscī. *To forget.* Syn.—Dēdīscŏ. Phr.—Nōn mĕmĭnī, nōn rĕcōrdŏr. Mē fŭgĭt. Sūm īmmĕmŏr. Ănĭmō, pēctŏrĕ dēcĭdĭt. Ēlāpsum ēst ēx ănĭmō. Ēx ănĭmō dēlērĕ. Caūsae īrārūm, sævīquĕ dŏlōrēs Ēxcĭdĕrānt ănĭmō.

Ōblŏquŏr, ĕrĭs, cūtŭs sūm, quī. *To contradict.* Syn.—Ădvērsŏr, cōntrādīcŏ, ōbsīstŏ. *To interrupt.* Syn.—Ōbstrĕpŏ, īntĕrpēllŏ. *To speak, to sing. See Loquor, Cano.*

Ōbmūrmŭrŏ, ās, āvī, ātūm, ārĕ. *To murmur against.* Syn.—Ōbstrĕpŏ, rĕmūrmŭrŏ. Phr.—Cōntrā mūrmŭrŏ.

Ōbmūtēscŏ, ĭs, mūtŭī, ĕrĕ. *To remain silent.* Prēssōque ōbmūtŭĭt ōrĕ. Syn.—Mūtēscŏ, īmmūtēscŏ, sĭlĕŏ, tăcĕŏ, ōbtĭcĕŏ, cōntĭcēscŏ, rĕtĭcĕŏ. Phr.—Vōcēm dŏlōrĕ, mĕtū prĕmŏ, rĕprĭmŏ. Āspēctu ōbmūtŭĭt āmēns. Vōx faūcĭbŭs hæsĭt. Līnguām sŭā vērbā rĕlīnquūnt. Mĕdĭăque īn vōcĕ rĕsīstĭt.

Ōbnītŏr, ĕrĭs, nīsŭs & nīxŭs sūm, nītī. *To resist.* Nēc nōs ōbnītī cōntrā, nēc tēndĕrĕ tāntūm. V. Syn.—Rĕnītŏr, ōbsīstŏ, ōblūctŏr. Phr.—Cōntrā nītŏr.

Ōbnōxĭŭs, ă, ūm. *Culpable, faulty.* Tūrpī mēns ēst ōbnōxĭă cūlpæ. O. *See Noxius. Exposed to.* Syn.—Ēxpŏsĭtŭs, ōbjēctŭs, ōbvĭŭs. *Submissive.* Syn.—Sūbmīssŭs, dēmīssŭs, sūpplēx, sūbjēctŭs, sūbdĭtŭs.

Ŏbŏrĭŏr, īrĭs, ōrtŭs sūm, ŏrīrī. *To arise, to begin to appear.* Īnde ŭbĭ sōl rădĭīs tērrām dīmōvĭt ŏbōrtīs. L. Syn.—Ŏrĭŏr, ēxsūrgŏ, nāscŏr, āppārĕŏ. Phr.—Lăcrĭmīs āffātŭr ŏbōrtĭs.

Ōbrēpŏ, ĭs, sī, tūm, ĕrĕ. *To creep up, to approach stealthily.* Ăd ōptātōs ōbrēpĕre hŏnōrēs. H. Syn.—Rēpŏ, ādrēpŏ, īrrēpŏ. Phr.—Tăcĭtē, sēnsīm ādrēpŏ.

Ōbrŭŏ, ĭs, ŭī, ŭtūm, ĕrĕ. *To cover with earth.* Syn.—Dēfŏdĭŏ, īnfŏdĭŏ, cōndŏ, rĕcōndŏ. *To cover. See Tego. To engulf. See Mergo. To overwhelm.* Syn.—Prĕmŏ, ōpprĭmŏ, cōnfĭcĭŏ.

Ōbscœnŭs, ă, ūm. Ill-omened. Syn.—Īnfaūstŭs. *Unclean.* Syn.—Īmmūndŭs, fœdŭs, tūrpĭs, sōrdĭdŭs. *Obscene.* Syn.—Īmpūrŭs, īncēstŭs, spūrcŭs, flāgĭtĭōsŭs.

Ōbscūrŏ, ās, āvī, ātūm, ārĕ. *To obscure.* Syn.—Īnōbscūrŏ, īnūmbrŏ, ŏbūmbrŏ, ōbnūbĭlŏ, ŏpācŏ, cōndŏ, tĕgŏ, ōccūltŏ, ōbrŭŏ. Phr.—Tĕnĕbrīs cōndŏ. Dĭēm sūbtēxŏ. Nōctĕ, cālīgĭnĕ īnvōlvŏ. Tĕnĕbrās īngĕmĭnŏ.

Ōbscūrŭs, ă, ūm. *Obscure, dark.* Syn.—Ātĕr, nĭgĕr, nĭgrāns, cālīgāns, cālīgĭnōsŭs, nūbĭlŭs, ŏpācŭs, pĭcĕŭs, ūmbrōsŭs, spīssŭs, dēnsŭs, hōrrēns. Phr.—Tĕnĕbrīs, cālīgĭnĕ dēnsŭs. Cālīgĭnĕ dēnsŭs ŏpācā. Lūcĭs ēt Phœbi īnscĭŭs. Nōx sĭnĕ sīdĕrĕ. Sōlĕ cărēns. Vīsă sŭb ōbscūrūm nōctĭs. *Unknown.* Syn.—Īgnōtŭs, īgnōrātŭs. *Difficult to comprehend.* Syn.—Ābdĭtŭs, īncērtŭs, āmbĭgŭŭs, cæcŭs, pērplēxŭs, īmplēxŭs. *Lowly, obscure.* Syn.—Hŭmĭlĭs, tĕnŭĭs, īgnōbĭlĭs.

Ōbsĕcrŏ, ās, āvī, ātūm, ārĕ. *To beseech, to pray.* Syn.—Ōbtēstŏr, prĕcŏr, ōrŏ, rŏgŏ.

Ōbsĕquĭōsŭs, ă, ūm. *Obsequious, complaisant.* Syn.—Ōbsĕquēns, ōbnōxĭŭs, sūbmīssŭs, ōffĭcĭōsŭs, mōrĭgĕrŭs, īndūlgēns, fămŭlāns.

Ōbsĕquĭūm, ĭī. n. *Indulgence.* Syn.—Făcĭlĭtās, īndūlgēntĭă.

Ōbsĕquŏr, ĕrĭs, ĕcūtŭs sūm, sĕquī. *To obey.* Syn.—Ŏbēdĭŏ, ōbsĕcūndŏ, pārĕŏ, ōbtēmpĕrŏ, cēdŏ, īndūlgĕŏ, fămŭlŏr, īnsērvĭŏ, făvĕŏ.

Ōbsērvāntĭă, æ. f. *Regard, consideration.* Syn.—Hŏnŏr, vĕnĕrātĭŏ.

Ōbsērvŏ, ās, āvī, ātūm, ārĕ. *To observe.* Syn.—Sērvŏ, nŏtŏ, ēxplōrŏ, spĕcŭlōr, tŭĕŏr, cōntēmplŏr. Phr.—Āttēntīs ŏcŭlīs lūstrŏ, cōntēmplŏr.

Ōbsĕs, ĭdĭs. m. *Hostage.* Syn.—Præs, vās, pīgnŭs, spōnsŏr.

Ōbsĭdĕŏ, ēs, ēdī, ēssūm, ēre & Ōbsīdŏ, ĭs, ēdī, ēssūm, ĕrĕ. *To besiege.* Syn.—Ōppūgnŏ. Phr.—Ōbsĭdĭōnĕ, ōbsĭdĭō mūrōs, mœnĭă prĕmŏ, cīngŏ, claūdŏ. Mīlĭtĕ cīngo ūrbēm. Pŏsĭtīs cāstrīs cīngo ūrbēm. Mūrīs āgmĭnă ādmŏvĕŏ. Pōrtīs ādstŏ. Ĭtălōs ōbsīdĕrĕ fīnēs. *To take, to hold.* Syn.—Tĕnĕŏ, ōbtĭnĕŏ, ōccŭpŏ. *To oppose.* Syn.—Ōbstŏ.

Ōbsĭdĭŏ, ōnĭs. f. *Siege.* Syn.—Ōbsĭdĭūm, ōppūgnātĭŏ.

Ōbsīstŏ, ĭs, stĭtī, ĕrĕ. *To stand in front.* Syn.—Ōbsĭdĕŏ, cōnsīstŏ, mănĕŏ, stō. *To oppose.* Syn.—Ōbstŏ. Phr.—Ōbsīstĕrĕ vēntīs. Fŭgĭēnti ōbsīstĕrĕ.

Ōbsŏlētŭs, ă, ūm. *Old, superannuated.* Syn.—Dēsuētŭs, vĕtŭs. *See Vetus. Dull. See Sordidus.*

Ōbstĭnātŭs, ă, ūm. *Obstinate, inflexible.* Syn.—Cōnstāns, fīrmŭs, dūrātŭs, pērtĭnāx, pērvĭcāx, īndŏcĭlĭs. Phr.—Flēctī nēscĭŭs. Prōpŏsĭtī nĭmĭūm tĕnāx. Cuī ōbstĭnātă, ōbdūrātă mēns. Pēctŭs ōbdūrātūm. Cuī dūră sŭpērbĭă.

Ōbstŏ, ās, ĭtī, ārĕ. *To oppose, to stand in front.* Ōbstĭtĭt īn mĕdĭā cāndĭdă tūrbă vĭā. O. Syn.—Ōbsīstŏ, ōbsĭdĕŏ. Phr.—Stō, cōnsīstŏ āntĕ, cōntrā. *To resist.* Syn.—Ōbsıstŏ, rĕnītŏr, ōbnītŏr, rĕlūctŏr, rĕsīstŏ, īmpĕdĭŏ, vĕtŏ, mŏrŏr. Phr.—Dŏlŏr ārtĭbŭs ōbstăt. *To contrast.* Syn.—Dīscrĕpŏ, dīscōrdŏ, pūgnŏ.

Ōbstrīngŏ, ĭs, īnxī, īctūm, ĕrĕ. *To bind tightly.* Syn.—Ādstrīngŏ, cōnstrīngŏ, dēvīncĭŏ, ōblĭgŏ. *To bind one with a promise.* Syn.—Ōblĭgŏ, dēvīncĭŏ.

Ōbstrŭŏ, ĭs, ūxī, ūctūm, ĕrĕ. *To block up, to barricade.* Syn.—Ōbtūrŏ, ōbsĕrŏ, præclūdŏ.

Ōbstŭpĕŏ, ēs, ŭī, ērĕ. *To be amazed.* Ōbstŭpŭīt prīmo āspēctū Sīdōnĭă Dīdō. V. Syn.—Ōbstŭpēscŏ, stŭpēscŏ, mīrŏr. Phr.—Ōbstŭpŭēre ănĭmī.

Ōbtĕgō̆, ĭs, xī, ēctūm, ĕrĕ. *To cover, to conceal.* Syn.—Cōntĕgō̆, ŏpĕrĭō̆, tĕgō̆.

Ōbtēndō̆, ĭs, dī, sūm, ĕrĕ. *To present before.* Prōquĕ vĭrō nĕbŭlam ēt vēntōs ōbtēndĕre ĭnānēs. V. Syn.—Ōbjĭcĭō̆, ōppōnō̆, prætēndō̆. *To pretend. See Prætendo.*

Ōbtĕrō̆, ĭs, trīvī, trītūm, ĕrĕ. *To bruise, to crush to pieces.* Syn.—Āttĕrō̆, cōntĕrō̆, tĕrō̆, cōncūlcō̆, ēlīdō̆. *To crush under foot. See Calco.*

Ōbtēstō̆r, ārĭs, ātŭs sūm, ārī. *To implore.* Īpsum ōbtēstēmūr, vĕnĭāmquĕ rŏgēmŭs ăb īpsō. V. Syn.—Ōbsĕcrō̆, īmplōrō̆, ōrō̆, rŏgō̆, prĕcō̆r. *To call to witness.* Syn.—Tēstō̆r.

Ōbtĭnĕō̆, ēs, ŭī, tentum, ērĕ. *To take, to hold.* Syn. Tĕnĕō̆, ōccŭpō̆, hăbĕō̆, pōssĭdĕō̆. *To obtain.* Syn.—Āssĕquō̆r, cōnsĕquō̆r, ădĭpīscō̆r, īmpĕtrō̆, ăcquīrō̆.

Ōbtīngĭt. impers. *It happens.* Syn.—Ādvĕnĭt, ōbvĕnĭt, cōntīngĭt, ăccĭdĭt.

Ōbtrēctō̆, ās, āvī, ātūm, ārĕ. *To speak enviously.* Syn.—Dētrăhō̆, cārpō̆, īnsēctō̆r, călūmnĭō̆r, mălĕdīcō̆.

Ōbtrūncō̆, ās, āvī, ātūm, ārĕ. *To behead.* Ēxcĭpĭt īncaūtūm pătrĭāsque ōbtrūncăt ăd ārās. V. Syn.—Trūncō̆, dētrūncō̆. Phr.—Căpŭt, cōllūm, cērvīcēm ēnsĕ, fērrō, glădĭō cædō̆, rĕcīdō̆. Căpŭt ā cērvīcĕ rĕvēllō̆. Căpŭt ēx hŭmĕrīs aūfĕrō̆. Fērrōquĕ sĕcăt pēndēntĭă cōllō. Ābscīssă dŭōrūm sūspēndīt căpĭtă. Īmpĭūm fērrō dēmĕtĭt căpŭt. Căpŭt ēnsĕ rŏtārĕ.

Ōbtūrō̆, ās, āvī, ātūm, ārĕ. *To close, to stop up.* Syn.—Ōbstrŭō̆, fērrō dēmĕtīt căpŭt. Căpŭt ēnsĕ rŏtārĕ.

Ōbtūtŭs, ūs. m. *Look, regard.* Syn.—Āspēctŭs, vīsŭs. Phr.—Dēfīxa ōbtūtū tĕnĕt ōră. Ōbtūtū tăcĭtō stĕtĭt.

Ŏbūmbrō̆, ās, āvī, ātūm, ārĕ. *To shadow, to darken.* Pālmăquĕ vēstĭbŭlum aūt īngēns ŏlĕāstĕr ŏbūmbrĕt. V. Syn.—Ūmbrō̆, ĭnūmbrō̆, ōbtĕgō̆, ōbscūrō̆. *To disguise.* Syn.—Cēlō̆, tĕgō̆, dīssĭmŭlō̆.

Ōbvērsō̆r, ārĭs, ātŭs sūm, ārī. *To present oneself before.* Syn.—Sūccūrrō̆, ōccūrrō̆, sŭbĕō̆.

Ōbvērtō̆, ĭs, tī, sūm, ĕrĕ. *To turn towards.* Ōbvērtūnt pĕlăgō prōrās. V. Syn.—Ōppōnō̆, ōbjĭcĭō̆.

Ōbvĭŭs, ă, ūm. *That which comes or goes in front of.* Haūd mĭnŭs Aēnēās tōrtūs lĕgĭt ōbvĭŭs ōrbēs. V. Syn.—Ōccūrrēns. Ōbvĭŭs (*or*) ōbvĭăm ĕō̆. *To meet, to go to meet.* Phr.—Ōbvĭŭs prōcēdō̆, ăccēdō̆, prōdĕō̆, vĕnĭō̆, ōccūrrō̆. Vĕnĭēntī ōccūrrō̆. Ōbvĭŭs ārdēntī sēsē tŭlĭt. Sēsē tŭlĭt ōbvĭă sīlvā.

Ōccāsĭō, ōnĭs. f. *Opportunity, occasion.* Răpĭāmŭs, ămīcī, Ōccāsĭōnēm dē dĭē. H. Syn.—Ānsă, fōrtūnă. Phr.—Cōmmŏdūm, ōppōrtūnūm, āptūm, ĭdōnĕūm, dēxtrūm tēmpŭs. Ōccāsĭō fūrtīm lābĭtŭr. Cāptō tēmpŏrĕ. Vĕnĭt ēcce ōptābĭlĕ tēmpŭs. Brĕvĭs ēst ōccāsĭō lūcrī.

Ōccāsŭs, ūs. m. *Downfall, ruin.* Syn.—Clādēs, rŭīnă. *Sunset.* Phr.—Sōlĭs ŏbĭtŭs. Sōl ōccĭdēns.

Ōccĭdŏ, ĭs, ĭdī, āsūm, ĕrĕ. *To fall.* Syn.—Cădŏ. *To die.* Syn.—Ōccūmbŏ, īntĕrĕŏ, pĕrĕŏ.

Ōccīdŏ, ĭs, īdī, īsūm, ĕrĕ. *To kill.* Vēndĕrĕ cūm pōssīs cāptīvum ōccīdĕrĕ nōlī. H. Syn.—Cædŏ, nĕcŏ, ēnĕcŏ, pĕrĭmŏ, īntĕrĭmŏ, īntērfĭcĭŏ, trŭcīdŏ, ōbtrūncŏ, jŭgŭlŏ, măctŏ, ēxtīnguŏ, cōnfŏdĭŏ, stērnŏ, ōpprĭmŏ. Phr.—Vītām, ănĭmām tōllŏ, aūfĕrŏ. Vītā, lūmĭnĕ spŏlĭŏ, prīvŏ. Nĕcī, mōrtī dō, trādŏ. Lētō ēxtīnguŏ. Lētō dărĕ. Sŭb Ōrcūm dēmīttŏ. Mănūm tīngŏ cædĕ. Ēnsēm pēctŏrĕ cōndŏ. Cōrpŏră fūndĭt hŭmī.

Ōcclūdŏ, ĭs, sī, sūm, ĕrĕ. *To shut, to close.* Syn.—Claūdŏ, prǣclūdŏ, ōbstrŭŏ.

Ōccŭbŏ, ās, ŭī, ĭtūm, ārĕ. *To fall, to die.* Syn.—Ōccūmbŏ, cădŏ, mŏrĭŏr.

Ōccŭlŏ, ĭs, ŭlŭī, ūltūm, ĕrĕ. *To hide, to conceal.* Spārgĕ fĭmō pīngui ēt mūltā mĕmŏr ōccŭlĕ tērrā. V. Syn.—Cōndŏ, ābscōndŏ, rĕcōndŏ, tĕgŏ, cōntĕgŏ, ōbtĕgŏ, ōbdūcŏ, ōccūltŏ, ōcclūdŏ, ābstrūdŏ, cēlŏ, ŏpĕrĭŏ, vēlŏ. Phr.—Dēnsīs ūmbrīs, tĕnĕbrīs ōbvēlŏ, claūdŏ, ōbvōlvŏ. Cæcīs lătĕbrīs cōmmīttĕrĕ. Tērrā ābdĕrĕ. Căvā sē cōndĕrĕ tērrā.

Ōccūltē. adv. *Secretly.* adv. Syn.—Clām, fūrtīm, lătēntĕr.

Ōccūltŭs, ă, ūm. *Hidden.* Syn.—Ōccūltātŭs, ābdĭtŭs, cōndĭtŭs, ābscōndĭtŭs, tēctŭs, cōntēctŭs, lătēns, ŏpācŭs, lătĕbrōsŭs. Phr.—Lătĕbrīs, ūmbrīs ōbtēctŭs, dēfēnsŭs. Cæcīs ōbscūrīs lătĕbrīs.

Ōccūmbŏ, ĭs, ŭbŭī, ĭtūm, ĕrĕ. *To fall, to die.* Syn.—Ōccĭdŏ, ōccŭbŏ, cădŏ, mŏrĭŏr.

Ōccŭpātĭŏ, ōnĭs. f. *Occupation, task.* Syn.—Nĕgōtĭūm, cūră, lăbŏr, mūnŭs, ŏpĕră, ŏpŭs.

Ōccŭpŏ, ās, āvī, ātūm, ārĕ. *To get possession of, to take.* Ōccŭpăt Aēnēās ădĭtūm cūstōdĕ sĕpūltō. V. Syn.—Īnvādŏ, cōrrĭpĭŏ, āggrĕdĭŏr, căpĭŏ, tĕnĕŏ, prĕhēndŏ. *To prevent.* Syn.—Prǣvērtŏ, āntĕcăpĭŏ, praĕōccŭpŏ, āntĭcĭpŏ, āntĕvērtŏ.

Ōccūrrŏ, ĭs, ī, sūm, ĕrĕ. *To run towards, to meet.* Nē quā scīrĕ dŏlōs, mĕdĭŭsve ōccūrrĕrĕ pōssĭt. V. Syn.—Ōccūrsŏ, ōbvērsŏr, ōffēndŏ, īncĭdŏ. Phr.—Ūltro ōccūrrāmŭs ăd ūndām. Tālĭbŭs ōccūrrīt dīctīs. *To occur to the mind.* Syn.—Sūccūrrŏ, sŭbĕŏ, ōbvērsŏr, ōbjĭcĭŏr, ădsūm.

Ōcĭŏr, ōrĭs. adj. *Quicker, fleeter.* Ēt fūlmĭnĭs ōcĭŏr ālīs. V. Syn.—Lĕvĭŏr, pērnīcĭŏr, vēlōcĭŏr.

Ōcĭŭs. adv. *More quickly.* Syn.—Cĭtĭŭs, vēlōcĭŭs, lĕvĭŭs.

Ŏcŭlŭs, ī. m. *Eye.* Ārdēntēs ŏcŭlōs īntōrsīt lūmĭnĕ glaūcō. V. Syn.——Lūmĭnă, vīsŭs, ăcĭēs, ōrbes, ŏcēllī. Phr.—Ŏcŭlōrūm ōrbēs, lūx. Ŏcŭlōrum ăcĭēs cōntēntă. Gĕmĭnūm frōntĭs sīdŭs. Vĭgĭlēs sūb frōntĕ mĭnīstrī. Ārdēntēs sīdĕrĭs īnstăr. Ŏcŭlī sūffēctī sānguĭnĕ. Sīc ŏcŭlōs, sīc ōră fĕrēbăt.

Ōdă, æ. f. *Ode, song.* Syn.—Cārmĕn, cāntŭs. Phr.—Aēŏlĭūm cārmĕn.

Ōdī, ōdīstī, ōdĭt, īssĕ. *To hate.* Syn.—Dētēstŏr, āvērsŏr, ăbhōrrĕŏ, ăbōmĭnŏr ēxsĕcrŏr, fŭgĭŏ, rĕfŭgĭŏ, spērnŏ, āspērnŏr, rēspŭŏ, fāstīdĭŏ. Phr.—Ŏdĭō hăbĕŏ. Ŏdĭō īnsĕquŏr, ūrgĕŏ. Mĭhĭ īnvīsūm ēst. Gĕnŭs ōmne ēxērcēre ŏdĭīs. Fās ōdīssĕ vĭrōs. Fŭrĭālĭtĕr ōdĭt.

Ŏdĭōsŭs, ă, ūm. *Hated, detested.* Syn.—Īnvīsŭs, īnfēnsŭs, īnvĭdĭōsŭs, dētēstāndŭs, dētēstātŭs.

Ŏdĭūm, ĭī. n. *Hatred.* Cōnvĕnĭūnt quĭbŭs aūt ŏdĭūm crūdēlĕ tўrānnī Aūt mĕtŭs ācĕr ĕrăt. V. Syn.—Sĭmūltās, īnvĭdĭă, īră, răbĭēs, fŭrŏr. Phr.—Ŏdĭī sīgnă. Hōstīlĭs ănĭmŭs. Ĭnĭmīcă mēns. Cōrdă āspĕră.

Ŏdŏr, ōrĭs. m. *Odor, smell.* Syn.—Hālĭtŭs, aūră, spīrāmĕn. Phr.—Nōtō nārēs cōntīngĭt ŏdōrĕ. Ŏdōră, suāvĭs, dūlcĭs aūră. Mūlcēns aūrās.

Ŏdōrŏ, ās, āvī, ātūm, ārĕ. *To give a fragrance to.* Syn.—Ĭnŏdōrŏ, sūffĭŏ. Phr.—Ŏdōrĕ pērfūndŏ, rĕplĕŏ. Ŏdōrēm mīttŏ.

Ŏdōrŏr, ārĭs, ātŭs sūm, ārī. *To smell.* Syn.—Ōlfăcĭŏ, ōlfāctŏ. Phr—Ŏdōrēm haūrĭŏ, pērcĭpĭŏ, sēntĭŏ. Ŏdŏr ăd nārēs fērtŭr. Nārēs cōntīngĭt. Fig.—*To suspect.* Syn.—Sŭbŏdōrŏr, præsēntĭŏ.

Ŏdōrŭs, ă, ūm. *Odorous, redolent.* Syn.—Ŏdōrātŭs, ŏdōrĭfĕr, frăgrāns, rĕdŏlēns. Phr.—Bĕnĕ ŏlēns. Suāvĕ ŏlēns. Suāvĭtĕr hālāns.

Ōffēndŏ, ĭs, dī, sūm, ĕrĕ. *To strike, to dash against.* Īn quĭbŭs ōffēndīt naūfrăgă nāvĭs, ăquās. O. Syn.—Īmpīngŏ, īmpīngŏr, ōffēnsŏ, īllīdŏ, āllīdŏ. *To meet on the way.* Syn.—Īnvĕnĭŏ, rĕpĕrĭŏ, īncĭdŏ, īncūrrŏ. *To offend. See Lædo.*

Ōffēnsă, æ. f. *Shock, crash.* Syn.—Ōccūrsŭs, ōffēnsŭs, īllīsŭs. *Injury, wrong.* Syn.—Ōffēnsĭŏ, īnjūrĭă.

Ōffĕrŏ, fērs, ōbtŭlī, ōblātūm, fērrĕ. *To offer, to present.* Bĕne ēst cuī dĕŭs ōbtŭlĭt Pārcă, quōd sătĭs ēst mănū. H. Syn.—Dō, præbĕŏ, dēfĕrŏ, ēxhĭbĕŏ, prōpōnŏ. Phr.—Dūm pācī mĕdĭūm se ōffērt. Sēsē mĕlĭōrĭbŭs ōffērt. *To expose.* Syn.—Ōbjĭcĭŏ, ōbjēctŏ.

Ōffĭcĭŏ, ĭs, fēcī, fēctūm, ĕrĕ. *To oppose.* Syn.—Ōbstŏ, ōbsūm, īmpĕdĭŏ, nŏcĕŏ.

Ōffĭcĭōsŭs, ă, ūm. *Obliging.* Nōn ūltrā quāmvīs ōffĭcĭōsŭs ĕrŏ. O. Syn.—Ōbsĕquĭōsŭs, sōllĭcĭtŭs, cōmĭs, sēdŭlŭs, bĕnīgnŭs, fămŭlāns. Phr.—Īn ōffĭcĭūm, ăd ōbsĕquĭūm prōnŭs. Ōffĭcĭī stŭdĭōsŭs. Ōffĭcĭōsă mēns. Cuī cōmĕ īngĕnĭūm.

Ōffĭcĭūm, ĭī. n. *Duty, office.* Dēfŭĭt offĭcĭō Părĭdĭs præsēntĭă trīstī. O. Syn.—Mūnŭs, mĭnīstĕrĭūm, mūnĭă, pārtēs, vĭcēs, prōvīncĭă. Phr.—Mīlĭtĭs ōffĭcĭūm. Ōffĭcĭīs fūngī vērnālĭtĕr.

Ŏlĕă, æ. f. *Olive tree.* (*See Appendix*). *Olive, the fruit.* Syn.—Ŏlīvă, bāccă.

Ŏlĕācĕŭs, ă, ūm. *Of the olive tree, of the olive.* Syn.—Ŏlĕārĭs, ŏlĕāgĭnŭs, ŏlĕāgĭnĕŭs, ŏlĕārĭŭs.

Ŏlĕāstĕr, trī. m. *The wild olive.* (*See Appendix under list of Trees, etc.*)

Ŏlĕŏ, ēs, ŭī, ĭtūm, ērĕ. *To give forth an odor.* Cōnsŭlŭĭt nārēs ăn ŏlērent æră Cŏrīnthūm. M. Syn.—Hālŏ, spīrŏ, rĕdŏlĕŏ, frăgrŏ. Phr.—Ŏdōrēm mīttŏ, ēmīttŏ, fūndŏ, dīffūndŏ, spīrŏ, āfflŏ, spārgŏ. Dŏmūm aūrās ŏdōrĕ, ŏdōrĭbŭs pērfūndŏ, īmplĕŏ, rĕplĕŏ, spārgŏ. Bĕnĕ, suāvĕ, suāvĭtĕr ŏlĕŏ, rĕdŏlĕŏ. Grātō ŏdōrĕ frăgrŏ. Suāvēs spīrăt ŏdōrēs. Crŏcĕīs hālāntēs flōrĭbŭs hōrtī. Sērtīsquĕ rĕcēntĭbŭs hālānt. Ārăbĭcō spīrăt ŏdōrĕ rŏgŭs. *To give forth a bad odor.* Syn.—Fœtĕŏ, pūtĕŏ. Phr.—Mălĕ, grăvĕ, grăvĭtĕr ŏlĕŏ, rĕdŏlĕŏ. Grăvī ŏdōrĕ spīrŏ. Fūnēstūm pĕr āĕră vīrŭs spārgŏ. Vōlvĭtŭr ātĕr ŏdōr tēctīs.

Ŏlĕūm, ī. n. *Olive oil.* Scīntīllāre ŏlĕum ēt pūtrēs cōncrēscĕrĕ fūngōs. V. Syn.—Ŏlīvūm, Pāllăs. Phr.—Ŏlīvī, ŏlĕī, pīnguĭs hūmŏr, lĭquŏr, lătēx, sūccŭs. Pāllădĭŭs lĭquŏr. Pāllădĭī lătĭcēs. Pīnguĭs ŏlīvæ sūccŭs. Pāllădĭs, ŏlīvæ dōnūm, mūnŭs. Hŭmĕrō ŏlĕō pērfūsă nĭtēscĭt.

Ōlfăcĭŏ, ĭs, fēcī, fāctūm, ĕrĕ. *To smell out, to scent.* Syn.—Ōlfāctŏ, ŏdōrŏr. Phr.—Nārĕ, nārĭbŭs ŏdōrēm pērcĭpĕrĕ, haūrīrĕ. Fig.—*To suspect.* Syn.—Ŏdōrŏr, sŭbŏdōrŏr, sūspĭcŏr.

Ŏlĭdŭs, ă, ūm. *That which has a strong smell, fetid.* Syn.—Ŏlēns, grăvĕ (*or*) măleŏlēns, fœtĭdŭs, grăvĭs. Phr.—Ŏlĭdūmquĕ vĕtērnūm.

Ōlīm. adv. *Formerly.* Syn.—Quōndām. Phr.—Prīscīs, āntīquīs tēmpŏrĭbŭs, sēclīs. Tēmpŏrĕ prætĕrĭtō, ætātĕ mājōrūm. Ăpŭd ăvōs, vĕtĕrēs, prĭōrēs. *Some day, in the future.* Syn.—Quōndām, ălĭquāndō. Phr.—Tēmpŭs ĕrĭt, vĕnĭĕt, cūm.

Ŏlĭtŏr, ōrĭs. m. *Gardener.* Syn.—Hōrtŭlānŭs. Phr.—Hōrtī, ŏlĕrūm cūstōs, cūltŏr. Ŏlĭtōrĭs ăgēns mērcēdĕ căbāllūm.

Ŏlīvă, æ. f. *Olive.* Syn.—Ŏlĕă.

Ōllă, æ. f. *A pot (either of clay or metal).* Syn.—Ăhēnūm, lĕbēs, ōllŭlă. Phr.—Aērĕ prĭōr fūsa ēst, āltĕră fīctă lŭtō. *See Ahenum.*

Ŏlŏr, ōrĭs. m. *Swan.* (*See Appendix under list of Birds.*)

Ōmĕn, ĭnĭs. n. *Omen, augury.* Sērăquĕ tērrĭfĭcī cĕcĭnērūnt ōmĭnă vātēs. V. Syn.—Aūgŭrĭūm, aūspĭcĭūm, sīgnūm, pōrtēntūm, mōnstrūm. Phr.—Dĕōrūm, Dīvūm, Sŭpĕrūm mŏnĭtūs. Faūstă sīgnă. Trīstĭă cœlō mōnstră. Ōmĭnĕ quō fīrmāns ănĭmūm. Dīvīnō cĕcĭnērūnt ōmĭnĕ Pārcæ. Mălūm Mārs tŭŭs ōmĕn hăbĕt. Ōmĭnĕ bŏnō. Faūstīs ăvĭbŭs, aūspĭcĭīs aūgŭrĭīs. Nūmĭnĕ dēxtrō. Īnfaūstīs ăvĭbŭs, aūgŭrĭīs. Trīstĕ pĕr aūgŭrĭūm. Rūmōrĕ sĭnīstrō.

Ōmĭnŏr, ārĭs, ātŭs sūm, ārī. *To give forth omens, to foretell.* Syn.—Aūgŭrŏr, pōrtēndŏ, cōnjĭcĭŏ.

Ŏmīttŏ, ĭs, īsī, īssūm, ĕrĕ. *To omit, to leave, to abandon.* Plērăquĕ dīffĕrăt, ēt præsēns īn tēmpŭs ŏmīttăt. H. Syn.—Mīttŏ, prætērmīttŏ, dīmīttŏ, līnquŏ, rĕlīnquŏ, dēpōnŏ, ādjĭcĭŏ, nēglĕgŏ, spērnŏ. *To cease from.* Syn.—Dēsĭnŏ.

Ōmnīnō. adv. *Wholly, entirely.* Syn.—Prōrsŭs, plānē, pĕnĭtŭs, fūndĭtŭs.

Ōmnĭs, ĭs, ĕ. *All, every.* Syn.—Quīsquĕ, cūnctŭs. Phr.—Nūllŭs nōn. Tēmpŭs ĭn ōmnĕ. *All, everyone.* Syn.—Quīsquĕ, ūnūsquīsquĕ, cūnctī, ūnĭvērsī.

Ŏnĕrŏ, ās, āvī, ātūm, ārĕ. *To load, to burden.* Syn.—Grăvŏ, prægrăvŏ, prĕmŏ, ōpprĭmŏ, ūrgĕŏ, fătīgŏ. Phr.—Hŭmĕrīs, cērvīcĭbŭs pōndŭs, ŏnŭs īnjĭcĭŏ, īmpōnŏ. Hŭmĕrōs pōndĕrĕ, mōlĕ prĕmŏ. *To cover.* Syn.—Tĕgŏ, cōndŏ, ōbrŭŏ. *To overburden.* Syn.—Prĕmŏ, āffĭcĭŏ, cōnfĭcĭŏ. *To fatigue.* Syn.—Grăvŏ, fătīgŏ, cōnfĭcĭŏ.

Ŏnĕrōsŭs, ă, ūm. *Heavy, burdensome.* Syn.—Grăvĭs, prægrăvĭs, ŏnĕrāns, pōndĕrōsŭs. Phr.—Māgnī pōndĕrĭs. Īngēntī pōndĕrĕ.

Ŏnŭs, ĕrĭs. n. *Burden, weight.* Syn.—Pōndŭs, mōlēs, sārcĭnă, fāscĭs, grăvāmĕn. Phr.—Ŏnĕrōsă mōlēs. Fāscĭs ŏnĕrōsŭs. Mēmbră grăvāns. Pōndŭs ĭnīquūm. Vīx fĕrēndă.

Ŏnūstŭs, ă, ūm. *Laden.* Hūnc tu ōlīm cœlō spŏlĭīs Ŏrĭēntĭs ŏnūstūm Ăccĭpĭēs. V. Syn.—Ŏnĕrātŭs, grăvātŭs, grăvĭs. Phr.—Pōndĕrĕ prēssŭs. Sūb pōndĕre ĭnīquō gĕmēns. Grăvĕ ŏnūs vīx fērt.

Ŏpācŏ, ās, āvī, ātūm, ārĕ. *To darken, to shadow.* Nūnc āltæ frōndēs ēt rāmī mātrĭs ŏpācānt. V. Syn.—Ŏbūmbrŏ, ōbscūrŏ, tĕgŏ, cōntĕgŏ, ŏpĕrĭŏ, vēstĭŏ.

Ŏpācŭs, ă, ūm. *Dark, obscure.* Dēfēnsī tĕnĕbrīs ēt dōnō nōctĭs ŏpācæ. V. Syn.—Ūmbrōsŭs, ōbscūrŭs, tēctŭs, ŏpērtŭs, dēnsŭs. Phr.—Lūcĭs hăbĭtāmŭs ŏpācīs. Pĕr ŏpācă lŏcōrūm. Ŏpācă quĭēs.

Ŏpĕră, æ. f. *Work, trouble.* Syn.—Lăbŏr, ŏpŭs, cūră, stŭdĭūm. Phr.—Īnānem ŏpĕrām sūmĕrĕ. Īnfēlix ŏpĕrām pērdās. *Duty, function.* Syn.—Mūnŭs, pārtēs.

Ŏpĕrĭŏ, īs, ŭī, ērtūm, īrĕ. *To cover.* Nōx ŏpĕrīt tērrās. V. Syn.—Tĕgŏ, cōntĕgŏ, īnvōlvŏ, vēlŏ, cōndŏ, ābscōndŏ. Phr.—Frōndĕ dŏmōs ŏpĕrīrĕ. Ŏpĕrīt sŏpŏr.

Ŏpĕrŏr, ārĭs, ātŭs sūm, ārī. *To work.* Āddĕ quŏd ōrnāndīs īlla ēst ŏpĕrātă căpīllīs. O. Syn.—Lăbōrŏ, īncūmbŏ. Phr.—Ŏpĕrī, lăbōrī văcŏ, mănūm ădhĭbĕŏ, ādmŏvĕŏ. Stŭdĭīs ŏpĕrātă Mĭnērvæ.

Ŏpĕrōsŭs, ă, ūm. *Painful, arduous.* Cūr vāllĕ pērmūtēm Săbīnā Dīvĭtĭās ŏpĕrōsĭōrēs? H. Syn.—Dīffĭcĭlĭs, ārdŭŭs. Phr.—Mūndī mōlēs ŏpĕrōsă lăbōrăt. *Efficacious.* Syn.—Præsēns, ūtĭlĭs, pŏtēns, præstāns, pōllēns.

Ŏpēs, ŏpūm. f. *Riches.* Cōndĭt ŏpēs ălĭŭs dēfēssōque īncŭbăt aūrō. V. Syn.—Bŏnă, dīvĭtĭæ, fōrtūnæ. Phr.—Īntĕr ŏpēs ĭnŏps.

Ŏpĭfĕr, ă, ūm. *Propitious.* Syn.—Ādjūtŏr, aūxĭlĭātŏr, præsēns, sĕcūndŭs.

Ŏpīmŭs, ă, ūm. *Rich, abundant, fertile.* Ēxstrŭĭmūsquĕ tŏrōs, dăpĭbūsque ĕpŭlāmŭr ŏpīmīs. V. Syn.—Pīnguĭs, ăbūndāns, fērtĭlĭs, laūtŭs, lārgŭs, dīvĕs, ŏpŭlēntŭs. Phr.—Ārva īntĕr ŏpīmă vĭrūm.

Ŏpīnĭŏ, ōnĭs. f. *Opinion.* Syn.—Jūdĭcĭūm, sēntēntĭă, mēns, ănĭmŭs, cōnsĭlĭūm.

Ŏpīnŏr, ārĭs, ātŭs sūm, ārī. *To think, to judge.* Syn.—Ārbĭtrŏr, aūtŭmŏ, cēnsĕŏ, ēxīstĭmŏ, jūdĭcŏ, pŭtŏ, rĕŏr, sēntĭŏ.

Ŏpōrtēt. impers. *It is necessary.* Syn.—Dĕcēt, cōnvĕnĭt, jŭvăt, ēxpĕdĭt. Phr.—Ŏpŭs ēst. Nĕcēssĕ ēst. Aēquūm ēst.

Ōppĕtŏ, ĭs, tĭī, tītūm, ĕrĕ. *To go towards.* Syn.—Īncūrrŏ, ŏbĕŏ, sŭbĕŏ, pătĭŏr, fĕrŏ.

Ŏppĭdūm, ī. n. *Town.* Syn.—Ūrbs, cāstēllūm.

Ōppōnŏ, ĭs, pŏsŭī, pŏsĭtūm, ĕrĕ. *To offer.* Syn.—Ōffĕrŏ, præbĕŏ, pōrrĭgŏ. *To oppose.* Syn.—Ōbjĭcĭŏ, ōbjēctŏ.

Ōppōrtūnē. adv. *At an opportune time.* Syn.—Cōmmŏdē, ōptātō, tēmpēstīvē, tēmpŏrĕ. Phr.—Īn tēmpŏrĕ, ĭn īpsō tēmpŏrĕ.

Ōppōrtūnĭtās, ātĭs. f. *Opportunity.* Syn.—Cōmmŏdĭtās, ūtĭlĭtās, ōccāsĭŏ, tēmpŭs.

Ōppōrtūnŭs, ă, ūm. *Favorable, opportune.* Syn.—Cōmmŏdŭs, ăccōmmŏdŭs, tēmpēstīvŭs, āptŭs, ĭdōnĕŭs, ūtĭlĭs, faūstŭs.

Ōpprĭmŏ, ĭs, ēssī, ēssūm, ĕrĕ. *To kill. See Occido. To suffocate.* Syn.—Prĕmŏ, cōmprĭmŏ, sūffōcŏ. *To silence.* Syn.—Prĕmŏ, cōmprĭmŏ, sūpprĭmŏ.

Ōpprŏbrĭūm, ĭī. n. *Disgrace.* Syn.—Prŏbrūm, dēdĕcŭs, lābēs, īnjūrĭă, īnfāmĭă, īgnōmĭnĭă.

Ōppūgnŏ, ās, āvī, ātūm, ārĕ. *To besiege, to fight.* Syn.—Īmpūgnŏ, īnvādŏ, āggrĕdĭŏr, īmpĕtŏ, lăcēssŏ.

Ōps, ŏpĭs (*nomin. not used*). f. *Power, means, resources.* Grātēs pērsōlvĕrĕ dīgnās Nōn ŏpĭs ēst nōstræ. V. Syn.—Vīs, făcūltās, pŏtēstās. *Strength.* Syn.—Ŏpēs, vīrēs. *Aid.* Syn.—Aūxĭlĭūm.

Ōptābĭlĭs, ĭs, ĕ. *Desirable.* Syn.—Ōptāndŭs, ēxōptāndŭs, ēxōptābĭlĭs.

Ōptĭmātēs, ūm. m. *Nobles, aristocrats, first men in the state.* Syn.—Prŏcĕrēs, prīmī, prīmōrēs, prīncĭpēs.

Ōptŏ, ās, āvī, ātūm, ārĕ. *To choose. See Eligo. To desire.* Syn.—Ēxōptŏ, pĕrōptŏ, ăvĕŏ, ārdĕŏ, cŭpĭŏ.

Ŏpŭlēntŭs, ă, ūm. *Rich.* Tēmplūm Cōndēbāt dōnīs ŏpŭlēntum ēt mūnĕrĕ dīvæ. V. Phr.—Dīvĕs ŏpūm. Ŏpĭbŭs ăbūndāns. Thēsaūrīs Ărăbūm ŏpŭlēntĭŏr. Mēns ŏpŭlēntĭŏr aūrō. *See Dives.*

Ŏpŭs, ĕrĭs. n. *Work.* Syn.—Ŏpĕră, lăbŏr, cūră, nĕgōtĭūm. Phr.—Ŏpĕrūm lăbōrēs. Āccīngūnt ŏpĕrī. Hōc ŏpŭs, hīc lăbŏr ēst. Fērvĕt ŏpŭs.

Ōră, æ. f. *Shore.* Syn.—Mārgŏ. *Frontier.* Syn.—Fīnēs, lŏcŭs, plăgă.

Ōrācŭlūm, ī. n. *Oracle.* Syn.—Ōrāclūm. Phr.—Dĕōrūm, Dīvūm jūssă. Fātālĭă rēspōnsă. Cœlēstēs mŏnĭtūs. Ōrācŭlă vātūm. Rēspōnsă sĕcūtī. Īn dŭbĭīs rēspōnsă pĕtūnt. Phœbīque ōrācŭlă sūpplēx Cōnsŭlĭt. Quærĕrĕ sōrtēs.

Ōrātĭŏ, ōnĭs. f. *Speech, discourse.* Syn.—Sērmŏ, dīctă, vērbă.

Ōrātŏr, ōrĭs. m. *Orator.* Phr.—Ănĭmō līnguāquĕ dĭsērtŭs. Māxĭmŭs ēlŏquĭō. Pōllēns flūmĭnĕ līnguæ. Fāndī dŏctīssĭmŭs. *Ambassador.* Syn.—Lēgātŭs.

Ōrbĭs, ĭs. m. *Circle.* Syn.—Cīrcŭlŭs. *Wheel.* Syn.—Rŏtă. *Ring.* Syn.—Ānŭlŭs. *World.* Syn.—Tērră, mūndŭs. *Region.* Syn.—Trāctŭs, rĕgĭŏ, ōră, tēllūs. *Orbit.* Syn.—Cīrcŭlŭs, cūrsŭs.

Ōrdĭnŏ, ās, āvī, ātūm, ārĕ. *To arrange, to ordain.* Ēx hāc lūcĕ Mæcænās mĕŭs āfflŭēntēs Ōrdĭnāt ānnōs. H. Syn.—Cōmpōnŏ, dīspōnŏ, dīgĕrŏ, īnstrŭŏ. Phr.—Ōrdĭnĕ, ĭn ōrdĭnĕ pōnŏ, stătŭŏ.

Ōrdĭŏr, īrĭs, sŭs sūm, īrī. *To commence.* Syn.—Ēxōrdĭŏr, āggrĕdĭŏr, īnchŏŏ, īncĭpĭŏ.

Ōrdŏ, ĭnĭs. m. *Order, arrangement.* Īllă mănēnt īmmōtă lŏcīs, nĕque ăb ōrdĭnĕ cēdūnt. V. Syn.—Lŏcŭs. Phr.—Ēx ōrdĭnĕ. *Successively.* Syn.—Vĭcīssīm, sīngŭlī. *Rank, condition.* Syn.—Cōndĭtĭŏ.

Ōrīgŏ, ĭnĭs. f. *Origin.* Ō quām dē tĕnŭī Rōmānŭs ŏrīgĭnĕ crēvĭt. O. Syn.—Ōrtŭs, ēxōrdĭūm, prīmōrdĭūm, ĭnĭtĭūm, ōrsŭs, prīncĭpĭūm, sēmĕn, cūnābŭlă. *Family, race.* Syn.—Stīrps, gĕnŭs, ōrtŭs, sānguĭs, gēns, sēmĕn, dŏmŭs, nātālēs. *Cause.* Syn.—Caūsă, fōns, căpŭt, aūctŏr.

Ŏrĭŏr, ĕrĭs, ōrtŭs sūm, ŏrīrī. *To arise.* Cūm sŭbĭtūm dīctūque ŏrĭtūr mīrābĭlĕ mōnstrūm. V. Syn.—Ēxŏrĭŏr, ŏbŏrĭŏr, sŭbŏrĭŏr, nāscŏr, ēnāscŏr, prōcēdŏ, ēxĕŏ, prōdĕŏ, vĕnĭŏ, ēxsūrgŏ. Phr.—Ŏrĭtūrquĕ mĭsērrĭmă cædēs. Prōspĕră lūx ŏrĭtŭr.

Ŏrĭūndŭs, ă, ūm. *Descended, sprung from.* Syn.—Ōrtŭs, gĕnĭtŭs, nātŭs, sătŭs, crētŭs.

Ōrnātŭs, ūs. m. *Preparations, arrangements.* Syn.—Părātŭs. *Adornment, decorations.* Syn.—Ōrnāmēntūm, dĕcŏrāmĕn, cūltŭs, dĕcŏr, dĕcŭs, hŏnŏr, hŏnōs, īnsīgnĕ.

Ōrnŏ, ās, āvī, ātūm, ārĕ. *To prepare.* Syn.—Părŏ. *To adorn.* Syn.—Ădōrnŏ, ēxōrnŏ, dĕcŏrŏ, hŏnēstŏ, īnsīgnĭŏ, īnstrŭŏ, cŏlŏ, ēxcŏlŏ.

Ōrnŭs, ī. f. *The wild ash.* (*See Appendix under list of Trees, etc.*)

Ōrŏ, ās, āvī, ātūm, ārĕ. *To speak, to say.* Syn.—Dīcŏ. *To pray, to beseech.* Syn.—Prĕcŏr, ōbtēstŏr, rŏgŏ. Phr.—Sūpplĭcĭbŭs vērbīs āffārī. Fūndĕrĕ prĕcēs. Prĕcāntĭă vērbă dīcĕrĕ. Vōcĕ prĕcārī. Īn vōtă vŏcārĕ. Vōtīs prōsĕquī. Sūpplĭcĕ vōcĕ ōbtēstārī. Aūxĭlĭō vŏcārĕ. Āntĕ pĕdēs sūpplēx vōlvŏr. Pācem ōrārĕ mănū.

Ōs, ōrĭs. n. *Mouth.* Syn. (*with regard to* **animals**).—Faūcēs, gŭlă, gūttŭr, mālæ, rīctŭs, dēntēs. *Speech, tongue.* Syn.—Līnguă, vōx, sŏnŭs, vērbă, sērmŏ, lŏquēlă. Phr.—Ōrĕ făvēte ōmnēs. Dŏlŏr ōră rĕprēssĭt. Īntŏnăt ōrĕ. Ōrĕ prĕmīt rēspōnsă.

Ŏs, ŏssĭs. n. *Bone.* Phr.—Ŏssĕă cōmpāgēs. Ŏssă sŭīs āstrīctă nērvīs. Dūră sŭb īctū Ŏssă sŏnānt. *Remains, body.* Syn.—Cĭnĕrēs, rĕlĭquĭæ.

Ōscŭlŏr, ārĭs, ātŭs sūm, ārī. *To kiss.* Syn.—Bāsĭŏ, suāvĭŏr, āmplēctŏr. Phr.—Ōscŭlă dō. Ōs ōrī, lābră lābrīs ādmŏvĕŏ. Ōscŭlă ōrĕ ōccŭpŏ. Ōscŭlăque ōrĕ lĕgĕt.

Ōscŭlūm, ī. n. *Kiss.* Syn.—Bāsĭūm, suāvĭūm, suāvĭŏlūm, āmplēxŭs. Phr.—Ōscŭlă ōrĕ, lābrīs, lăbēllīs jūnctă, mīxtă. Rŏsĕīs jūnctă lăbēllīs Ōscŭlă. Mēllĕ suāvĭŭs ōscŭlūm.

Ōsŏr, ōrĭs. m. *One who hates, an enemy.* Syn.—Ōsŭs, ēxōsŭs, pĕrōsŭs, īnfēnsŭs, ĭnĭmīcŭs, hōstĭs.

Ōstēndŏ, ĭs, dī, sūm, ĕrĕ. *To show.* Ōstēndēnt tērrīs hūnc tāntūm fātă, nĕque ūltrā Ēssĕ sĭnēnt. V. Syn.—Ōstēntŏ, mōnstrŏ, mănĭfēstŏ, pāndŏ, dētĕgŏ, ăpĕrĭŏ, ēxprōmŏ, ēxpōnŏ, ēffĕrŏ, pătĕfăcĭŏ. Phr.—Īn lūcēm trăhŏ. Lătĕbrīs ēdūcŏ. Īn mĕdĭūm dō. Sŭōs ōstēndĕrĕ mōrēs.

Ōstēntŏ, ās, āvī, ātūm, ārĕ. *To show. See Ostendo. To boast.* Syn.—Jāctŏ, jactitŏ, prædicŏ, vendĭtŏ, glōrĭŏr.

Ōstĭūm, ĭī. n. *Door.* Quō lātī dūcūnt ădĭtūs cēntum, ōstĭă cēntūm. V. Syn.—Jānŭă, fŏrēs, līmĕn, ădĭtŭs, pōrtă.

Ōstrūm, ī. n. *Purple-dye.* Syn.—Mūrēx, cōccŭs, pūrpŭră.

Ōtĭŏr, ārĭs, ātŭs sūm, ārī. *To be at ease.* Syn.—Văcŏ, fērĭŏr, quĭēscŏ. Phr.—Nīl ăgŏ. Ōtĭă dūcŏ. Īn ōtĭă sōlvŏr. Ōtĭă vītæ Dēsĭdĭōsă sĕquŏr. Vītām pĕr ōtĭă dūcŏ.

Ōtĭōsŭs, ă, ūm. *At ease, inactive.* Syn.—Văcŭŭs, dēsĕs, rĕsĕs, fērĭātŭs, sēgnĭs, ĭnērs, dēsĭdĭōsŭs. Phr.—Cūrīs līběr. Ōtĭă dūcēns. Dēsĭdĭă lānguēns. Ŏpĕrūm sŏlūtŭs. Īmmūnĭs ŏpĕrūm.

Ōtĭūm, ĭī. n. *Ease, sloth.* Syn.—Īgnāvĭă, ĭnērtĭă, dēsĭdĭă, lānguŏr, tōrpŏr, sēgnĭtĭēs, vĕtērnūm. Phr.—Vītă sēgnĭs. Lūxŭs ĭnērs. Dēsĭdĭs ōtĭă vītæ. Īgnāvă quĭēs. *Rest, leisure.* Syn.—Quĭēs, rĕquĭēs, fērĭæ.

Ŏvīlĕ, ĭs. n. *Sheep-fold.* Īncūstōdītūm cāptăt ŏvīlĕ lŭpŭs. O. Syn.—Caūlă, stăbŭlūm, sēptă (ōrūm). Phr.—Plēnō lŭpŭs īnsĭdĭātŭs ŏvīlī. Cīrcūmgĕmĭt ūrsŭs ŏvīlĕ.

Ŏvĭs, ĭs. f. *Sheep.* Dĕcŏri ēst ŏvĭbūs sŭă lānă. O. Syn.—Āgnă, bālāns, bĭdēns, pĕcŭs (ŭdĭs). Phr.—Mōllĕ pĕcŭs. Lānĭgĕrī grĕgēs. Mītĭs bālāntūm grēx. Cāmpōs bālāntībŭs īmplēns. Īnnŏcŭæ pĕcŭdēs. Āvĭdīs prædă pĕtītă lŭpīs. Pătĭēns īnjūrĭæ. Cōgĕre ŏvēs stăbŭlīs.

Ŏvŏ, ās, āvī, ātūm, ārĕ. *To receive the honors of a triumph.* Syn.—Trĭūmphŏ. Fig.—*To be triumphant with joy, to feel proud.* Syn.—Trĭūmphŏ, lætŏr, gaūdĕŏ, ēxsūltŏ. Phr.—Dīctīs pārēmŭs ŏvāntēs. Pĕr ūrbēm ībăt ŏvāns.

Ŏvūm, ī. n. *Egg.* Phr.—Gāllīnæ fœtŭs. Gāllīnæ dĭūrnă dōnă, mūnĕră. Ŏvī ālbūmĕn, tēstă.

P

Pābŭlŏr, ārĭs, ātŭs sūm, ārī. *To forage.* Syn.—Frūmēntŏr. Phr.—Pābŭlă cārpŏ, lĕgŏ, cōllĭgŏ, quærŏ, cūrŏ.

Pābŭlūm, ī. n. *Fodder.* Syn.—Pāscŭă, pāstŭs, frūmēntūm. *Nourishment.* Syn.—Nūtrīmēntūm, ălĭmēntūm, cĭbŭs, ēscă.

Pācĭfĭcŭs, ă, ūm. *Peaceful.* Syn.—Lēnĭs, mītĭs, plăcĭdŭs, trānquīllŭs. Phr.—Pācĭs ămāns. Ēgrĕgĭæ cūstōs fīdīssĭmă pacĭs. Pācĕ Cĕrēs læta ēst.

Păcīscŏr, ĕrĭs, pāctŭs sūm, păcīscī. *To come to an agreement, to make a compact.* Syn.—Cōnvĕnĭŏ, cōnstĭtŭŏ, stătŭŏ, pāngŏ. *To promise.* Syn.—Prōmīttŏ, spōndĕŏ.

Pācŏ, ās, āvī, ātūm, ārĕ. *To pacify, to appease.* Syn.—Plācŏ, cōmpōnŏ, lēnĭŏ.

Pāctūm, ī. n. *Compact.* Syn.—Fœdŭs, cōnvēntūm, cōndĭtĭŏ, lēx. Phr.—Pāctă fĭdēs. Pāctă plăcēnt.

Pălæstră, æ. f. *Wrestling.* Ēxērcēnt pătrĭās, ŏlĕō lābēntĕ, pălæstrās. V. Syn.—Lŭctă, gȳmnăs, pălē. Phr.—Pălæstræ cērtāmĕn, mōs, ŏpŭs. Cērtāmĭnă dūră pălæstræ. *Place or school for wrestling.* Syn.—Gȳmnăsĭūm.

Pălām. adv. *Openly.* Syn.—Mănĭfēstē, ăpērtē, cōrām. Phr.—Īn ŏcŭlĭs, īn cōnspēctū. Ānte ōră. Lūcĕ pălām. Cōrām pŏpŭlō. Īn ăpērtā lūcĕ.

Pălĕă, æ. f. *Straw.* Syn.—Cūlmŭs, stĭpŭlă. Phr.—Stĭpŭlæ sĕgĕs. Pălĕæ cūlmī. Vēntō jāctātă.

Pāllă, æ. f. *Long robe.* Syn.—Īnstĭtă, stŏlă. Phr.—Pāllā spēctābĭlĭs aūreā. Tȳrĭā prōcēdĕrĕ pāllā. Vērrĭt hŭmūm. Vēstīgĭă vērrĕrĕ pāllā.

Pāllĕŏ, ēs, ŭī, ērĕ. *To be pale.* Syn.—Pāllēscŏ, ēxpāllēscŏ. Phr.—Pāllŏr ōră ōccŭpăt. Ōrĕ cŏlōr fŭgĭt. Ōrī pāllŏr ĭnēst. Ēxsānguī cŏlōrĕ pāllĕŏ. Cŏlŏr ōră rĕlīquĭt. Cuī tōto ēst nūllŭs ĭn ōrĕ cŏlŏr. *To become weak.* Syn.—Īmpāllēscŏ, tābēscŏ, īntābēscŏ, cōnfĭcĭŏr, ēxĕdŏr.

Pāllĭdŭs, ă, ūm. *Pale.* Ēt pāllĭdă sēmpĕr Ōră fămē. V. Syn.—Pāllēns, dēcŏlŏr, ālbŭs, ēxsānguĭs, pāllĭdŭlŭs. Phr.—Pāllōrĕ dēfōrmĭs. Ōră Părĭō mārmŏrĕ, sāxō pāllĭdĭōră gĕrēns. *Livid, lifeless.* Syn.—Ālbŭs, līvĭdŭs, lūrĭdŭs, ēxsānguĭs.

Pāllŏr, ōrĭs. m. *Pallor.* Phr.—Cŏlōr sĭnĕ sānguĭnĕ. *See Pallidus.*

Pālmă, æ. f. *Palm.* Phr.—Căcūmĭnĕ pālmæ. Pālmārūm dīvĕs. *Sign of victory.* Syn.—Vīctōrĭă. Phr.—Īnsīgnĕ vīctōrĭæ. Vīctōrūm dĕcŭs, laŭs, hŏnŏr, glōrĭă. Ēlĭădūm pālmæ. Dōnēt vĭrĭdī mĕă cārmĭnă pālmā. *Palm of the hand.* Syn.—Vŏlă, mănŭs.

Pālŏr, ārĭs, ātŭs sūm, ārī. *To wander.* Syn.—Ērrō, vāgŏr. Phr.—Pāssīm, sĭnĕ ōrdĭnĕ, sĭnĕ lēgĕ fĕrŏr. Pĕr ārvă văgŏr.

Pālpĭtŏ, ās, āvī, ātūm, ārĕ. *To tremble, to pant.* Syn.—Trĕmŏ, trĕpĭdŏ, sīngūltŏ, mĭcŏ.

Pālpŏ, ās, āvī, ātūm, ārĕ. *To flatter.* Syn.—Plaūdŏ, tāngŏ, trāctŏ, āttrēctŏ. *See Adulor.*

Pălūmbēs, ĭs f. & Pălūmbŭs, ī. m. *A wood-pigeon, ring-dove.* (*See Appendix under list of Birds.*)

Pălūs, ūdĭs. f. *Marsh, swamp.* Līmōsōquĕ pălūs ōbdūcāt pāscŭă jūncō. V. Syn.—Lăcŭs, stāgnūm. Phr.—Ăquă, ūndă stāgnāns. Hūmŏr ĭnērs. Pălūdĭs vŏrāgŏ.

Pālŭs, ī. m. *Stake, prop, support.* Hīc dŏcŭīt tĕnĕrām pālīs ādjūngĕrĕ vītēm. Tib. Syn.—Sŭdēs, stīpĕs, trūncŭs, vāllŭs.

Pāndŏ, ĭs, dī, pānsūm & pāssūm, ĕrĕ. *To open.* Syn.—Ăpĕrĭŏ, rĕsĕrŏ, pătĕfăcĭŏ. Fig.—*To unveil.* Syn.—Dētĕgŏ.

Pāndŭs, ă, ūm. *Bent, curved.* Lāncĭbŭs ēt pāndīs fūmāntĭă rēddĭmŭs ēxtă. V. Syn.—Cūrvŭs, īncūrvŭs, rĕpāndŭs.

Pāngŏ, ĭs, pĕpĭgī & pānxī, pāctūm, ĕrĕ. *To fix, to drive in.* Syn.—Fīgŏ, dēfīgŏ. *To make a compact. See Paciscor.*

Pānĭs, ĭs. m. *Bread.* Syn.—Cĕrēs. Phr.—Cĕrĕālēs ŏpēs. Dōnă lăbōrātæ Cĕrĕrĭs. Mānū mōllītă. Īgnĕ tōstă Cĕrēs. Cĕrĕālĭă dōnă. Cĕrĕrēmquĕ cănīstrīs Ēxpĕdĭūnt.

Păpāvĕr, ĕrĭs. n. *The poppy.* (*See Appendix under list of Trees, etc.*)

Păpȳrŭs, ī. m., f. & Păpȳrūm, ī. n. *Papyrus.* (*See Appendix under list of Trees, etc.*)

Pār, părĭs. adj. *Equal, alike.* Syn.—Cōmpār, părĭlĭs, cōmpărĭlĭs, æquālĭs, sĭmĭlĭs, cōnsĭmĭlĭs, īdēm, ūnŭs. Phr.—Pār ămŏr ēst īllīs. *Capable of.* Syn.—Căpāx, āptŭs, ĭdōnĕŭs, sūffĭcĭēns. Phr.—Nōn īmpār.

Părābĭlĭs, ĭs, ĕ. *Easily procured.* Syn.—Ōbvĭŭs, făcĭlĭs. Phr.—Părātū, īnvēntū făcĭlĭs.

Părātŭs, ūs. m. *Preparation.* Syn.—Āppărātŭs. *Ornament, luxury.* Syn.—Cūltŭs, ōrnatŭs, lūxŭs, āppărātŭs.

Pārcē. adv. *Frugally.* Syn.—Frūgālĭtĕr, mŏdĭcē, pērpārcē, ēxĭgŭē, sīmplĭcĭtĕr. *With restraint, modesty.* Syn.—Mŏdĕrātē, mŏdēstē, mŏdĭcē.

Pārcĭmōnĭă, æ. f. *Parsimony.* Syn.—Frūgālĭtās, sīmplĭcĭtās. Phr.—Pārcūs rērūm ūsŭs. Pārcă īmpēnsă. Mŏdĕrātĭŏ sūmptūs.

Pārcŏ, ĭs, pārsī & pĕpērcī, pārsūm, & pārctūm, ĕrĕ. *To use sparingly.* Phr.—Mŏdĕrātē, mŏdĕrātĭŭs, pārcĭŭs ūtŏr. Pārcĕ fŭtūrō. *To pardon.* Syn.—Īgnōscŏ, īndūlgĕŏ, rĕmīttŏ, cōndōnŏ. Phr.—Nōxām rĕmīttŏ. Vĕnĭām dō. Vĕnĭām cōncēdĕrĕ cūlpǣ. Īndūlgē vĕnĭām pŭĕrīs.

Pārcŭs, ă, ūm. *Economical.* Tāmquām pārcŭs hŏmo ēt rērūm tūtēlă sŭārūm. H. Syn.—Ābstĭnēns, frūgī. *Parsimonious.* Syn.—Ăvārŭs. *Small, scanty.* Syn.—Pārvŭs, ēxĭgŭŭs, mŏdĭcŭs, tĕnŭĭs, mălīgnŭs.

Părēns, tĭs. m. & f. *Father, mother.* Syn.—Pătĕr, mātĕr, aūctŏr. Phr.—Sānguĭnĭs, gĕnĕrĭs aūctōrēs. Rērūmquĕ părēns.

Pārĕŏ, ēs, ŭī, ērĕ. *To obey.* Syn.—Ōbsĕquŏr, aūscūltŏ. Phr.—Mōrēm gĕrŏ. Rēgĭs īmpĕrĭūm, lēgēs, jūssă pătī.

Părĭēs, ĕtĭs (dat. & abl. pl. Pārĭĕtĭbŭs). m. *A wall.* Syn.—Mūrŭs, mācĕrĭă. Phr.—Quām fīxām părĭēs īllōs sērvābăt ĭn ūsūs. Hærēnt pārĭĕtĭbūs scālǣ.

Părĭŏ, ĭs, pĕpĕrī, pārtūm, ĕrĕ. *To give birth.* Syn.—Pārtŭrĭŏ, gīgnŏ, gĕnĕrŏ, prŏcrĕŏ, ēnītŏr. Phr.—Prōlēm ēdūcŏ. *To cause, to bring forth.* Syn.—Āffĕrŏ, dō, ēdŏ, gīgnŏ, părŏ, sūffĭcĭŏ, præbĕŏ.

Părĭtĕr. adv. *Likewise, equally.* Syn.—Aēquē, æquālĭtĕr. Phr.—Nōn sĕcŭs. Nōn mĭnŭs. Nōn ălĭtĕr. *At the same time.* Syn.—Sĭmŭl, ūnā.

Pără, ās, āvī, ātūm, ārĕ. *To prepare, to make ready.* Tū mœnĭă māgnīs Māgnă pără. V. Syn.—Āppărŏ, cōmpărŏ, præpărŏ, īnstrŭŏ, īnstĭtŭŏ, ōrnŏ. *To dispose one's companions.* Syn.—Āppărŏ, āccēndŏ, ērĭgŏ. *To make oneself ready.* Syn.—Āppărŏ, āccīngŏr, mĕdĭtŏr, mōlĭŏr, cōgĭtŏ.

Pārs, pārtĭs. f. *Part, portion.* Pārtēs ŭbĭ sē vĭă fīndĭt ĭn āmbās. V. Syn.—Pōrtĭŏ, pārtĭcŭlă, ălĭquĭd, nōnnĭhĭl. Phr.—Pārs ē mōntĕ rĕvūlsă. Pārtēs vēlātĕ tĕgēndās. Pārs ūltĭmă vītǣ. *Region.* Syn.—Rĕgĭŏ, lŏcŭs.

Pārtēs, ĭūm. f. *Charge, office, function.* Jŭvĕnī pārtēs māndārĕ sĕnīlēs. H. Syn.—Mūnĭă, mūnŭs, ōffĭcĭūm. *Faction, party.* Syn.—Caūsă, sīgnă, cāstră.

Pārtĭcēps, ĭpĭs. adj. *Sharer, participant, associate.* Syn.—Cōmpŏs, cōnsōrs, sŏcĭŭs, cōnscĭŭs. Phr.—Nōn ēxpērs, nōn ēxsōrs.

Pārtĭcĭpŏ, ās, āvī, ātūm, ārĕ. *To take part in, to share.* Phr.—Īn pārtēm, īn cōnsōrtĭă vĕnĭŏ. Pārtēm căpĭŏ, hăbĕŏ. Sūm pārtĭcēps. Nōn sūm ēxpērs. *To share with.* Syn.—Cōmmūnĭcŏ, īmpērtĭŏr, trādŏ. Phr.—Īn pārtēm vŏcŏ.

Pārtĭŏr, īrĭs, ītŭs sūm, īrī. *To divide among.* Hīnc pōrtūm pĕtĭt ēt sŏcĭōs pārtītŭr ĭn ōmnēs. V. Syn.—Dīvĭdŏ, dīstrĭbŭŏ, īmpērtĭŏr.

Phr.—Īn pārtēs sēpărŏ, dīvĭdŏ. Pārtĭbŭs æquābăt jūstīs. Mēcūm pārtīrĕ lăbōrēm. Pārtīrī līmĭtĕ cāmpūm.

Pārtŭrĭŏ, īs, īvī & ĭī, ītūm, īrĕ. *To give birth to, to bring forth.* Syn.—Părĭŏ, ēdŏ, gīgnŏ, gĕnĕrŏ, prōgĕnĕrŏ, ēnītŏr, cōnnītŏr, dēpōnŏ. Phr.—Sūb lūmĭnĭs aūrās ēdŏ. Gĕmĭnām pārtū dăbĭt Īlĭă prōlēm.

Părūm. adv. *Little.* Syn.—Paūlūm, paūlō, paūlŭlūm, lĕvĭtĕr, mŏdĭcūm, ēxĭgŭūm, pārcē, mĕdĭŏcrĭtĕr, mĭnŭs. Phr.—Nōn, haūd mūltūm.

Părūmpĕr. adv. *For a little while.* Syn—Paūlīspĕr, ălĭquāntūm, ălĭquā.

Pārvŭs, ă, ūm. *Little.* Sæpe ŏcŭlōs, mĕmĭnī, tīngēbām pārvŭs ŏlīvō. Pers. Syn.—Pārvŭlŭs, pŭsīllŭs, ēxĭgŭŭs, brĕvĭs, mĭnĭmŭs, tĕnĕr, tĕnēllŭs.

Pāscŏ, ĭs, pāvī, pāstūm, ĕrĕ. *To pasture.* Phr.—Ād pāscŭă dūcŏ. Stăbŭlīs ēdūcŏ. Ād pāstūm ēdūcŏ. Hērbās, pābŭlă præbĕŏ, sūppĕdĭtŏ. Pāscēntēs sērvārĕ grĕgēs. *To nourish.* Syn.—Ălŏ, nūtrĭŏ. *To feed upon, to browse.* Syn.—Pāscŏr, pābŭlŏr, ĕdŏ, vēscŏr. Phr.—Grāmĕn, hērbās, pābŭlă cārpŏ. Pāscŭă pĕtŏ. Tōndēnt dūmētă jŭvēncī.

Pāscŭă, ōrūm. n. *Pasturage.* Quīd tĭbī pāstōrēs Lĭbўæ, quīd pāscŭă vērsū Prōsĕquăr? V. Syn.—Pābŭlă, pāstŭs, hērbă, grāmĕn, prātă, vīrgūltă, dūmētă. Phr.—Vĭrĭdāntĭă lātē. Hūmēntĭă prātă. Pīnguĭă prātă. Vĭrĭdīssĭmă grāmĭnĕ rīpă.

Pāssĕr, ĕrĭs. m. *A sparrow.* (*See Appendix under list of Birds.*)

Pāssīm. adv. *Here and there.* Syn.—Ŭbĭquĕ, quōcūnquĕ, ūndĭquĕ. Phr.—Hīc īllīc, hūc īllūc, hīnc īllīnc. Sĭnĕ ōrdĭnĕ, sĭnĕ lēgĕ.

Pāssŭs, ūs. m. *Step, gait, pace.* Sĕquĭtūrquĕ pătrēm nōn pāssĭbŭs æquīs. V. Syn.—Grēssŭs, grădŭs, īngrēssŭs, pēs. Phr.—Īncēssĭt pāssū dē vūlnĕrĕ tārdō.

Pāstŏr, ōrĭs. m. *Pastor, shepherd.* Nām sæpe īncaūtīs pāstōrĭbŭs ēxcĭdĭt īgnĭs. V. Syn.—Ārmēntārĭŭs, ūpĭlĭŏ, būbūlcŭs. Phr.—Grĕgĭs, pĕcŏrĭs dūx, cūstōs, măgīstĕr. Ŏvēs īn pāscŭă dūcēns. Gaūdēt pāscĕre ŏvēs īn grāmĭnĕ lætō.

Pāstŭs, ūs. m. *Pasturage.* Syn.—Pāscŭă, pābŭlă, prātă, grāmĭnă.

Pătĕfăcĭŏ, ĭs, fēcī, fāctūm, ĕrĕ. *To open.* Syn.—Ăpĕrĭŏ, pāndŏ, rĕsĕrŏ. *To discover, to bring to light.* Syn.—Dētĕgŏ, īllūstrŏ.

Pătēllă, æ. f. *Plate, dish used in the sacrifices.* Syn.—Pătĕră, părōpsĭs, lānx, cătīllŭs.

Pătĕŏ, ēs, ŭī, ērĕ. *To be open.* Syn.—Pătēscŏ, pătĕfīŏ, ăpĕrĭŏr, rĕsĕrŏr, rĕclūdŏr, pāndŏr.

Pătĕr, pătrĭs. m. *Father.* Nātum ānte ōră pătrīs, pātrēmque ōbtrūncăt ăd ārās. V. Syn.—Părēns, gĕnĭtŏr, sătŏr, crĕātŏr. Phr.—Sānguĭnĭs aūctŏr.

Pătēscŏ, ĭs, ĕrĕ. *To be open. See Pateo. To be discovered, to be unveiled.* Syn.—Pătĕfīŏ, pătĕŏ, dētēgŏr, ăpĕrĭŏr, rĕclūdŏr, pāndŏr, nūdŏr, ōstēndŏr, mōnstrŏr, prōdŏr, āppārĕŏ.

Pătĭēntĕr. adv. *Patiently.* Syn.—Plăcĭdē, fōrtĭtĕr, cōnstāntĕr. Phr.—Mēntĕ æquā, plăcĭdā, cōmpŏsĭtā. Pătĭēntī ănĭmō. Īnvīctā mēntĕ. Pēctŏrĕ fōrtī.

Pătĭēntĭă, æ. f. *Patience, fortitude.* Syn.—Cōnstāntĭă. Phr.—Īnfrāctă mălīs. Prōmptă pătī. Cēdĕrĕ nēscĭă. Plăcĭdō vūltū. Lĕvĭŭs fĭt pătĭēntĭā. Gaūdēt pătĭēntĭă dūrīs.

Pătĭŏr, ĕrĭs, pāssŭs sūm, pătī. *To suffer, to endure.* Syn.—Pērpĕtĭŏr, fĕrŏ, pērfĕrŏ, sŭbĕŏ, sūstĭnĕŏ, tŏlĕrŏ. Phr.—Aēquā mēntĕ pătī. Fērrĕ cāsūs pătĭēntĕr ăcērbōs. Fērrĕ mălūm. Ēxhaūrīrĕ pĕrīcŭlă. Aēquām rēbūs ĭn ărdŭīs Sērvārĕ mēntēm. Prœlĭă dūră pătī. Ō pāssī grăvĭōră. *To allow.* Syn.—Pērmīttŏ, sĭnŏ, cōncēdŏ, ānnŭŏ, vŏlŏ.

Pătrĭă, æ. f. *Fatherland, country.* Lūcēm rēddĕ tŭæ, dūx bŏnĕ, pātrĭæ. H. Phr.—Pătrĭæ sēdēs, līmĭnă. Pătrĭă tēllūs. Pătrĭūm sŏlūm. Pătrĭæ līmĭnă sēdĭs. Tērră āltrīx. Pătrĭōs ēxcēdĕrĕ mūrōs.

Pătrĭmōnĭūm, ĭī. n. *Patrimony.* Syn.—Cēnsŭs, ŏpēs, dīvĭtĭæ, rēs. Phr.—Bŏnă ăvītă. Pătrĭæ ŏpēs. Cēnsūs aūgērĕ pătērnōs. Crēscūnt pătrĭmōnĭă.

Pătrĭŭs, ă, ūm. *Paternal.* Syn.—Ăvītŭs, pătērnŭs. Phr.—Pătrĭs, pătrūm, mājōrūm, ăvōrūm rēs. *Innate, natural.* Syn.—Nātīvŭs, īngĕnĭtŭs, īnnātŭs, gēntīlĭs.

Pătrŏ, ās, āvī, ātūm, ārĕ. *To execute, to accomplish.* Syn.—Pērpĕtrŏ, pērfĭcĭŏ, cōnfĭcĭŏ. *To do.* Syn.—Făcĭŏ, ăgŏ, ādmīttŏ.

Pătrōcĭnĭūm, ĭī. n. *Protection.* Syn.—Præsĭdĭūm, tūtēlă.

Pătrōcĭnŏr, ārĭs, ātŭs sūm, ārī. *To protect.* Syn.—Tŭĕŏr, tūtŏr, tēgŏ, prōtēgŏ.

Pătrōnŭs, ī. m. *Patron.* Cūjūs fōrtūnæ, quō sīt pătrĕ, quōvĕ pătrōnō? H. Syn.—Tūtŏr, dēfēnsŏr, cūstōs, præsĭdĭūm, tūtēlă. *Lawyer.* Syn.—Caūsĭdĭcŭs, ōrātŏr.

Pătŭlŭs, ă, ūm. *Open, spreading, extended.* Pătŭlæ sūb tēgmĭnĕ făgī. V. Syn.—Pătēns, ăpērtŭs, dīffūsŭs, lātŭs.

Paūlātīm. adv. *Little by little.* Syn.—Sēnsīm, pĕdĕtēntīm.

Paūlīspĕr. adv. *For a little while.* Syn.—Ălĭquāntūm, părūmpĕr.

Paūpĕr, ĕrĭs. adj. *Poor.* Paūpĕr ĕnīm nōn ēst, cuī rērūm sūppĕtĭt ūsŭs. H. Syn.—Ĕgēns, ĕgēnŭs, mĭsĕr, paūpērrĭmŭs, īndĭgŭs, ĭnōps, mēndīcŭs. Phr.—Paūpērtātĕ prēssŭs. Quī vītām ĭnŏpēm ăgĭt. Nūdŭs ŏpūm. Pānnīs ōbsĭtŭs. Ĭnōps rērūm. *Wretched.* Syn.—Ēxĭgŭŭs, pārvŭs, hŭmĭlĭs, mŏdĭcŭs, tĕnŭĭs, vīlĭs. *Sterile.* Syn.—Stĕrĭlĭs, jējūnŭs, măcĕr.

Paūpĕrŏ, ās, āvī, ātūm, ārĕ. *To impoverish, to render poor.* Syn.—Nūdŏ, dēnūdŏ, ēxŭŏ, spŏlĭŏ.

Paūpērtās, ātĭs. f. *Poverty.* Ēt lărĭs ēt fūndī paūpērtās īmpŭlĭt aūdāx, Ūt vērsūs făcĕrēm. H. Syn.—Paūpĕrĭēs, ĕgēstās, ĭnŏpĭă, pēnūrĭă, īndĭgēntĭă. Phr.—Rēs pārvă, āngūstă. Tĕnŭĭs fōrtūnă. Rēbŭs ĭnĭmīcă sĕcūndīs. Frīgēns ēt sĭnĕ lūcĕ fŏcŭs. Āngūstām paūpĕrĭēm pătī. Rēs āngūstă dŏmī.

Păveŏ, ēs, pāvī, ērĕ. *To be afraid.* Cōr păvĕt ādmŏnĭtū tĕmĕrātæ sānguĭnĕ nōctĭs. O. Syn.—Tĭmĕŏ, mĕtŭŏ, vĕrĕŏr, fōrmīdŏ, rĕfōrmīdŏ, hōrrĕŏ, trĕpĭdŏ.

Păvĭdē. adv. *Timidly.* Syn.—Tĭmĭdē, sēgnĭtĕr, īgnāvē.

Păvĭdŭs, ă, ūm. *Timid, frightened.* Stānt păvĭdae īn mūrīs mātrēs. V. Syn.—Păvĕfāctŭs, tĭmĭdŭs, trĕpĭdŭs, tērrĭtŭs, ēxtērrĭtŭs, āttŏnĭtŭs.

Păvīmēntūm, ī. n. *Pavement.* Syn.—Strātūm, sŏlūm. Phr.—Ēt mĕrō Tīngēt păvīmēntūm.

Pāvŏ, ōnĭs. m. *A peacock.* (*See Appendix under list of Birds.*)

Păvŏr, ōrĭs. m. *Fear.* Syn.—Tĭmŏr, mĕtŭs, tērrŏr. Phr.—Păvōr ōccŭpăt īllūm. Cōrdă păvōr pūlsāns. Pēr gēntēs hŭmĭlīs strāvīt păvŏr. Tōrpēt tēlīs pērfīxă păvōrĭs.

Pax, ācĭs. f. *Peace.* Pāx Cĕrĕrēm nūtrīt, pācĭs ălūmnă Cĕrēs. O. Syn.—Cōncōrdĭă, fœdŭs, ămīcĭtĭă. Phr.—Pācĭs, ămīcĭtĭæ fœdŭs. Īnvĭŏlābĭlĕ pīgnŭs. Mūsārūm nūtrīx. Ūnă trĭūmphīs pŏtĭŏr. Pācĭs īmpōnĕrĕ mōrēm. Pācēm făcĭŏ, ĭnĕŏ. Ārmă pōnŏ, dēpōnŏ. Pācĕ frŭŏr. Pācĕ quĭētă Tēllūs.

Pēccātŏr, ōrĭs. m. *Sinner.* Syn.—Nŏcēns, sōns, rĕŭs, pēccāns. Phr.—Scĕlĕrĭs ādmīssī rĕŭs. Aēquī cōntēmptŏr. Trānsĭlĭēns jūssă vĕrēndă Dĕī. Pēccātī lābĕ nŏtātŭs. Cōnscĭă mēns prāvī.

Pēccātūm, ī. n. *Fault, crime.* Syn.—Cūlpă, dēlīctūm, ādmīssūm, ērrŏr, ērrātūm, mălūm, nōxă, vĭtĭūm, flāgĭtĭūm, pĭăcŭlūm, făcĭnŭs, scĕlŭs. Phr.—Aūsă nĕfāndă. Fāctūm tūrpĕ.

Pēccŏ, ās, āvī, ātūm, ārĕ. *To commit a fault, to err.* Ōdērūnt pēccārĕ bŏnī vīrtūtĭs ămōrĕ. H. Syn.—Dēlīnquŏ, ērrŏ. Phr.—Crīmĕn, scĕlŭs, nĕfās ādmīttŏ, cōmmīttŏ, sūscĭpĭŏ. Mē crīmĭnĕ īmplĭcŏ. Fās ōmnĕ ābrūmpŏ. Sūccūmbĕrĕ cūlpæ.

Pēctŏ, ĭs, pēxī & pēxŭī, pēxūm, ĕrĕ. *To comb.* Pēctēbātquĕ fĕrūm, pūrōque īn fōntĕ lăvābăt. V. Syn.—Dēpēctŏ, cōmŏ, cōmpōnŏ, ōrnŏ. Phr.—Crīnēs, cŏmām cōmpōnŏ, fīngŏ. Cōllă cŏmāntĭă pēctūnt.

Pēctŭs, ŏrĭs. n. *Breast, bosom.* Syn.—Sĭnŭs. Phr.—Āfflīxērĕ sōlō pēctŏră. Pēctūs lāxāvĭt ămīctū. Rūpīt pēctŏrĕ vōcēm. Fig.—*Heart, soul.* Syn.—Cŏr, ănĭmŭs, mēns, prǣcōrdĭă. *Courage.* Syn.—Ănĭmŭs, fōrtĭtūdŏ.

Pĕcūnĭă, æ. f. *Money.* Syn.—Mŏnētă, nūmmī, æs, aūrūm, ārgēntūm. Fig.—*Riches, wealth.* Syn.—Dīvĭtĭæ, ŏpēs. Phr.—Vĭtĭōrūm mātĕr. Vĭtĭī fēcūndă părēns. Ād sē cūnctă dūcēns.

Pĕcūnĭōsŭs, ă, ūm. *Wealthy.* Syn.—Ŏpūlēntŭs, dīvĕs, nūmmātŭs. *Profitable.* Syn.—Frūctŭōsŭs, lŭcrōsŭs.

Pĕdĕs, ĭtĭs. m. *Pedestrian.* Syn.—Pĕdēstĕr. *Infantryman.* Syn.—Pĕdĭtātŭs, mīlĕs.

Pĕlăgŭs, ī. n. *Sea, high sea.* Syn.—Āltūm, prŏfūndūm, mărĕ.

Pēllĭcĭŏ, ĭs, ēxī, ēctūm, ĕrĕ. *To allure, to seduce.* Syn.—Āllĭcĭŏ, āllēctŏ, prōlĭcĭtŏ, dēlīnĭŏ, dūcŏ, trăhŏ.

Pēllĭs, ĭs. f. *Skin, hide.* Ārĕt Pēllĭs ĕt ād tāctūm trāctāntī dūră rĕsīstĭt. V. Syn.—Cŭtĭs, tēgmĕn, vēlāmĕn, cŏrĭūm, vēllŭs. Phr.—Sētīs hōrrēns. Pēllĭs dēnsă pĭlĭs. Pēllem hōrrēntīsquĕ lĕōnĭs Ēxŭvĭās. Īnstērnōr pēllĕ lĕōnĭs.

Pēllŏ, ĭs, pĕpŭlī, pūlsūm, ĕrĕ. *To strike, to shake.* Nēc pŭdĕāt pĕpŭlīssĕ lўrām. O. Syn.—Īmpēllŏ, pūlsŏ, quătĭŏ, fĕrĭŏ, pērcŭtĭŏ, mŏvĕŏ. *To push, to drive.* Syn.—Dēpēllŏ, prōpēllŏ, pūlsŏ, prōpūlsŏ, dētūrbŏ, ēxtūrbŏ, dētrūdŏ, ējĭcĭŏ, ārcĕŏ, ēlīmĭnŏ, fŭgŏ.

Pēllūcĕŏ, ēs, ūxī, ērĕ. *To be transparent.* Syn.—Pērlūcĕŏ, trānslūcĕŏ, rĕlūcĕŏ, lūcĕŏ.

Pēllūcĭdŭs, ă, ūm. *Clear, transparent.* Pūrāquĕ măgīs pēllūcĭdă gēmmā. O. Syn.—Pēllūcēns, trānslūcĭdŭs, clārŭs, rĕlūcēns, līmpĭdŭs, pērspĭcŭŭs, lūcĭdŭs.

Pēltă, æ. f. *A small shield.* Dūcĭt Ămāzŏnĭdūm lūnātīs āgmĭnă pēltīs. V. Syn.—Pārmă, clўpĕŭs, scūtūm, ūmbŏ.

Pēlvĭs, ĭs. f. *Basin.* Syn.—Cătīnŭs, ăhēnūm.

Pĕnātēs, ūm. m. *Household-gods.* Syn.—Lărēs. Phr.—Dī, dīvī pĕnātēs. Dī pătrĭī. (*By extension*) *House, home.* Syn.—Dŏmŭs.

Pēndĕŏ, ēs, pĕpēndī, ērĕ. *To hang, to be suspended.* Syn.—Dēpēndĕŏ, sūspēndŏr. Phr.—Hī sūmmo īn flūctū pēndēnt. Pēndērĕ dē rūpĕ. *To hesitate.* Syn.—Hærĕŏ, hæsĭtŏ, dŭbĭtŏ. Phr.—Sūm dŭbĭŭs, sūspēnsŭs. Sūm īncērtŭs. *To depend.* Syn.—Dēpēndĕŏ.

Pēndŏ, ĭs, pĕpēndī, pēnsūm, ĕrĕ. *To weigh.* Syn.—Ēxpēndŏ, pōndĕrŏ, pēnsŏ, ēxāmĭnŏ, pērpēndŏ. *To pay.* Syn.—Sōlvŏ, ēxsōlvŏ, pērsōlvŏ.

Pēndŭlŭs, ă, ūm. *Hanging, suspended.* Syn.—Pēndēns, sūspēnsŭs.

Pēnĕ. adv. *Almost.* Syn.—Fērmē, fĕrē, prŏpĕ.

Pĕnĕtrābĭlĭs, ĭs, ĕ. *Penetrating, piercing.* Āspĭcĕ nūm măgĕ sīt nōstrūm pĕnĕtrābĭlĕ tēlūm. V. Syn.—Ăcūtŭs, ācĕr, praĕăcūtŭs.

Pĕnĕtrālĕ, ĭs. n. *The inner, most retired part of the house.* Syn.—Rĕcēssŭs, lătĕbræ, īntĕrĭōră. Phr.—Lŏcŭs ābdĭtŭs. Tēctūm pĕnĕtrālĕ. Dŏmŭs īntĕrĭŏr.

Pĕnĕtrālĭs, ĭs, ĕ. *Inner, retired.* Syn.—Īntĕrĭŏr, īmŭs, īntĭmŭs, rĕmōtŭs, rĕcōndĭtŭs, sēcrētŭs, ārcānŭs.

Pĕnĕtrŏ, ās, āvī, ātūm, ārĕ. *To penetrate, to pierce.* Īllȳrĭcōs pĕnĕtrārĕ sĭnūs ātque īntĭmă tūtŭs Rēgnă Lĭbūrnōrūm. V. Syn.—Pērmĕŏ, pērvādŏ, sŭbĕŏ, īrrēpŏ, īllābŏr, īnsĭnŭŏ.

Pēnnă, æ. f. *Wing.* Syn.—Ālă. *Pen.* Syn.—Stȳlŭs, grăphĭūm, ărūndŏ.

Pēnsĭlĭs, ĭs, ĕ. *Hung, suspended.* Syn.—Pēndēns, pēndŭlŭs, sūspēnsŭs.

Pēnsŏ, ās, āvī, ātūm, ārĕ. *To weigh.* Syn.—Pēnsĭtŏ, pēndŏ, ēxpēndŏ, pērpēndŏ, pōndĕrŏ, trŭtĭnŏ.

Pēnsūm, ī. n. *Task.* Syn.—Ŏpŭs, lăbŏr, mūnŭs.

Pēnūrĭă, æ. f. *Want, need.* Syn.—Ĕgēstās, ĭnŏpĭă. Phr.—Rēs ĕgēnæ.

Pĕnŭs, ūs. m. & f. & Pĕnūm, ī. n. *Store of provisions.* Fămŭlī quĭbŭs ōrdĭnĕ lōngō Cūră pĕnūm strŭĕrĕ. V. Syn.—Vīctŭs, cĭbŭs, ălĭmēntă, cĭbārĭă, ānnōnă. Phr.—Dăpēs, ĕpŭlæ cōndĭtæ. Dăpūm, cĭbōrūm ăcērvŭs, cŭmŭlŭs.

Pĕr. prep. *Through, among.* Syn.—Īntĕr, ĭn.

Pĕrăgrŏ, ās, āvī, ātūm, ārĕ. *To go through.* Syn.—Lūstrŏ, pērlūstrŏ, ŏbĕŏ, pĕrērrŏ, pērcūrrŏ. *To walk through, to traverse.* Syn.—Ŏbāmbŭlŏ, ŏbĕŏ, pĕrērrŏ.

Pērcēllŏ, ĭs, cŭlī, cūlsūm, ĕrĕ. *To strike violently.* Pērcŭlĭt ēt fūlvā mŏrĭbūndum ēxtēndĭt ărēnā. V. Syn.—Fĕrĭŏ, pērcŭtĭŏ, āfflīgŏ, stērnŏ, prōstērnŏ, dējĭcĭŏ, prōrŭŏ. Fig.—*To move, to trouble.* Syn.—Tērrĕŏ, mŏvĕŏ.

Pērcēnsĕŏ, ēs, ŭī, ērĕ. *To review.* Syn.—Pērlĕgŏ, pērsĕquŏr. *To visit.* Syn.—Pĕrăgrŏ, pērlūstrŏ.

Pērcĭĕŏ, ēs, īvī, ĭtūm, ērĕ. *To excite.* Syn.—Ēxcĭĕŏ, pērmŏvĕŏ, pērcēllŏ.

Pērcĭpĭŏ, ĭs, cēpī, cēptūm, ĕrĕ. *To cull, to gather.* Syn.—Căpĭŏ, cārpŏ, lĕgŏ, cōllĭgŏ, sūmŏ, frŭŏr, pŏtĭŏr. *To comprehend.*

Syn.—Căpĭō, cōncĭpĭō, īntēllĕgō, cōmprĕhēndō, dīscō, aūdĭō, sēntĭō.

Pērcōntŏr, ārĭs, ātŭs sūm, ārī. *To inquire, to procure information.* Syn.—Scītŏr, scīscĭtŏr, quærō, īnquīrō, rŏgō, īntērrŏgō, rŏgĭtō.

Pērcūrrō, ĭs, cūrrī, cūrsūm, ĕrĕ. *To run, to rush through.* Syn.—Pērcūrsō, pĕrērrō, pērlūstrō, lūstrō, cōllūstrō, ŏbĕō, pērlĕgō, pērvăgŏr, pērlābŏr, trājĭcĭō, pērvŏlō.

Pērcūssŏr, ōrĭs. m. *Murderer.* Syn.—Ōccīsŏr, pĕrēmptŏr, īntērfēctŏr.

Pērcŭtĭō, ĭs, cūssī, cūssūm, ĕrĕ. *To strike.* Pērcŭtĭtūrquĕ căpūt cōnvērsæ vērbĕrĕ vīrgæ. O. Syn.—Fĕrĭō, pūlsō, tūndō. *To excite the mind.* Syn.—Pērcēllō, āffĭcĭō, tāngō, mŏvĕō.

Pērdīx, īcĭs. m. & f. *A partridge.* (*See Appendix under list of Birds.*)

Pērdō, ĭs, dĭdī, dĭtūm, ĕrĕ. *To destroy, to ruin.* Syn.—Pēssūmdō, dēstrŭō, pĕrĭmō, ēxstīnguō, pērvērtō, prōflīgō. *To lose.* Syn.—Āmīttō. Phr.—Jāctūrām făcĭō. Dāmnūm pătĭŏr.

Pērdūcō, ĭs, xī, ctūm, ĕrĕ. *To conduct, to lead through.* Syn.—Dūcō, āddūcō, ăgō. *To carry.* Syn.—Dūcō, fĕrō. *To annoint.* Syn.—Pērfūndō, ūngō, līnō.

Pērdūrō, ās, āvī, ātūm, ārĕ. *To last.* Syn.—Dūrō, pērstō, mănĕō, pērmănĕō.

Pĕrĕdō, ĭs, ēdī, ēsūm, ĕrĕ. *To eat, to consume.* Syn.—Ĕdō, cōnsūmō, ēxĕdō.

Pĕrĕgrĭnŏr, ārĭs ātŭs sūm, ārī. *To voyage abroad.* Phr.—Pĕrĕgrē ĕō. Pĕrĕgrīnās tērrās lūstrō, ădĕō, īnvīsō. Lōngīnquă pĕtō.

Pĕrĕgrīnŭs, ă, ūm. *Foreign.* Syn.—Ēxtērnŭs, ēxtrānĕŭs, ălĭēnŭs, lōngīnquŭs, rĕmōtŭs. *Stranger, voyager.* Syn.—Hōspĕs, ădvĕnă, vĭātŏr, ēxtērnŭs.

Pĕrēnnĭs, ĭs, ĕ. *Perpetual.* Cārmĭnă quām trĭbŭēnt, fāmă pĕrēnnĭs ĕrĭt. O. Syn.—Aētērnŭs, jūgĭs, cōntĭnŭŭs, āssĭdŭŭs, pērpĕtŭŭs, īmmōrtālĭs, īnfīnītŭs, ĭnēxstīnctŭs, stăbĭlĭs. Phr.—Nōn pĕrĭtūrŭs. Nūllō pĕrĭtūrŭs ævō. Fīnĕ cărēns. Īmmūnĭs fātī. Mŏnŭmēntum ærĕ pĕrēnnĭŭs.

Pĕrĕō, īs, īvī & ĭī, ĭtūm, īrĕ. *To perish.* Syn.—Dīspĕrĕō, īntĕrĕō, cădō, ōccĭdō, ōccūmbō, cædŏr, stērnŏr, ābsūmŏr, jŭgŭlŏr. Phr.—Lētūm ōppĕtō. Lētō cădō. Mĕrĭtā mōrtĕ pĕrīrĕ.

Pĕrērrō, ās, āvī, ātūm, ārĕ. *To wander, to run about.* Syn.—Ŏbērrō, pērcūrrō, ădĕō, lūstrō, pērlūstrō.

Pērfĭcĭō, ĭs, fēcī, fēctūm, ĕrĕ. *To accomplish.* Quæ rīte īncœptă părāvī Pērfĭcĕre ēst ănĭmŭs. V. Syn.—Cōnfĭcĭō, ăbsōlvō, pĕrăgō, ēxĭgō, ēxplĕō, ēxsĕquŏr. Phr.—Fīnēm, mŏdūm făcĭō, pōnŏ, impōnŏ. Ăd fīnēm pērdūcŏ. *To instruct.* Syn.—Ērŭdĭŏ, ēdŏcēŏ, pŏlĭŏ, pērpŏlĭŏ, dŏcēŏ.

Pērfĭdĭă, æ. f. *Treachery, perfidy.* Pērfĭdĭæ cŭmŭlūm fālsīs pērjūrĭă vērbīs. O. Syn.—Fraūs, dŏlŭs, fāllācĭă. Phr.—Pērfĭdă mēns. Pērfĭdă cōrdă. Fīctūm pēctŭs. Līnguæ pērjūrĭă.

Pērfĭdŭs, ă, ūm. *Treacherous.* Dīssĭmŭlāre ĕtĭām spērāstī pērfĭdĕ, tāntūm Pōssĕ nĕfās? V. Syn.—Pērfĭdĭōsŭs, īnfīdŭs, mălĕfīdŭs, dŏlōsŭs, fāllāx, sūbdŏlŭs, fālsŭs, vānŭs, mēndāx, pērjūrŭs. Phr.—Vīr plēnŭs pērjūrĭæ. Īn pērjūrĭă nātŭs. Fĭdēm vĭŏlāns. Dŏlī mĕdĭtātŏr. Fraūdēs īn pēctŏrĕ vērsăt. Quī fœdĕră rūmpĭt. Frōnti nulla fides.

Pērfīnĭŏ, īs, īvī & ĭī, ītūm, īrĕ. *To finish.* Syn.—Pērfĭcĭŏ, ăbsōlvŏ, fīnĭŏ.

Pērflŭŏ, ĭs, flūxī, xūm, ĕrĕ. *To flow through.* Syn.—Pērmĕŏ, pērmānŏ. *To escape, to be lost.* Syn.—Ēfflŭŏ, ēxcĭdŏ, lābŏr, ēlābŏr, vānēscŏ, ēvānēscŏ, pĕrĕŏ.

Pērfŏdĭŏ, ĭs, fōdī, fōssūm, ĕrĕ. *To pierce.* Syn.—Fŏdĭŏ, cōnfŏdĭŏ, trānsfŏdĭŏ, ăpĕrĭŏ.

Pērfŏrŏ, ās, āvī, ātūm, ārĕ. *To pierce through and through.* Syn.—Fŏrŏ, fŏdĭŏ, pērfŏdĭŏ, tĕrĕbrŏ, ăpĕrĭŏ.

Pērfŭgĭūm, ĭī. n. *Refuge, asylum.* Syn.—Pōrtŭs, ăsȳlūm, ără, sōlātĭūm, spēs.

Pērfūndŏ, ĭs, fūdī, fūsūm, ĕrĕ. *To pour over, to water.* Syn.—Spārgŏ, āspērgŏ, rĭgŏ, īrrĭgŏ, īrrōrŏ.

Pērgŏ, ĭs, pērrēxī, rēctūm, ĕrĕ. *To pursue one's way.* Pērgĕ mŏdo, ātque hīnc tē rēgīnae ăd līmĭnă pērfĕr. V. Syn.—Ĕŏ, tēndŏ, vādŏ. *To continue.* Syn.—Pērsĕvērŏ, pērstŏ, pērsīstŏ, cōntĭnŭŏ. Phr.—Nōn cēssŏ. Nōn dēfĭcĭŏ. Cœptīs ĭnhærĕŏ. Prōpŏsĭtūm ūrgērĕ.

Pērgrāndĭs, ĭs, ĕ. *Very large.* Syn.—Māxĭmŭs, īngēns, pērmāgnŭs.

Pĕrhĭbĕŏ, ēs, ŭī, ĭtūm, ērĕ. *To speak, to assure.* Sī mŏdŏ, quēm pĕrhĭbēs, pătĕr ēst Thȳmbræŭs Ăpōllŏ. V. Syn.—Dīcŏ, nārrŏ, rĕfĕrŏ, mĕmŏrŏ, cōmmĕmŏrŏ, āssĕrŏ, āffīrmŏ.

Pĕrīclĭtŏr, ārĭs, ātŭs sūm, ārī. *To be exposed to danger.* Phr.—Īn pĕrīclūm vĕnĭŏ. Īn dīscrīmĭnĕ vērsŏr. Īnsĭdĭīs hŏmĭnūm lăbōrŏ. Pĕrīclă ŭbīquĕ sūrgūnt.

Pĕrīclūm & Pĕrīcŭlūm, ī. n. *Danger.* Syn.—Dīscrīmĕn, ālĕă, cāsŭs, sōrs, fōrtūnă, fātūm. Phr.—Dŭbĭī cāsūs. Dŭbĭă sōrs. Dŭbĭă rēs. Dīscrīmĭnă rērūm. Āncēps fōrtūnă. Pĕrīclă tēntŏ. Fātă lăcēssŏ.

Pĕrĭmō, ĭs, ēmī, ēmptūm, ĕrĕ. *To destroy.* Aūt sŭbĭtī pĕrĭmūnt īmbrēs. V. Syn.—Ēxstīnguŏ, pērdŏ. *To kill.* Syn.—Cǣdŏ, īntĕrĭmŏ, īntērfĭcĭŏ.

Pĕrīndĕ. adv. *Likewise, equally.* Syn.—Părĭtĕr, ǣquē, sīc. Phr.—Nōn sĕcŭs āc.

Pĕrītĭă, ǣ. f. *Skill, experience.* Syn.—Scĭēntĭă, ārs, prūdēntĭă, īngĕnĭūm, sōlērtĭă, ăcūmĕn.

Pĕrītŭs, ă, ūm. *Skilled.* Sōlī cāntārĕ pĕrītī. V. Syn.—Dōctŭs, scĭēns, prūdēns, gnārŭs, cāllĭdŭs. Phr.—Haūd īgnārŭs, rŭdĭs.

Pērjūrŭs, ă, ūm. *Deceiving, false.* Syn.—Mēndāx, fāllāx, pērfĭdŭs, dŏlōsŭs.

Pērmănĕŏ, ēs, mānsī, mānsūm, ērĕ. *To remain.* Syn.—Mănĕŏ, pērstŏ, pērsīstŏ.

Pērmānŏ, ās, āvī, ātūm, ārĕ. *To expand.* Syn.—Mānŏ, īnflŭŏ, pērflŭŏ, pērvādŏ, pērmĕŏ. *To transpire, to be divulged.* Syn.—Pērvādŏ, vūlgŏ, mānŏ.

Pērmĕŏ, ās, āvī, ātūm, ārĕ. *To penetrate, to traverse, to run through.* Syn.—Pērlābŏr, pērmānŏ, pērflŭŏ, pērvādŏ, pĕnĕtrŏ, sŭbĕŏ, pērcūrrŏ, ŏbĕŏ, pĕrērrŏ, pērmētĭŏr, pērlūstrŏ.

Pērmīttŏ, ĭs, mīsī, mīssūm, ĕrĕ. *To send along or through.* Syn.—Mīttŏ, īmmīttŏ, jăcĭŏ, cōnjĭcĭŏ. *To permit, to grant.* Syn.—Cōncēdŏ, dō, trĭbŭŏ, īndūlgĕŏ, pătĭŏr, sĭnŏ, ānnŭŏ, ādmīttŏ. Phr.—Vĕnĭām, lĭcēntĭām dō, trĭbŭŏ. Nōn vĕtŏ, nōn ōbstŏ. Cūr nōn dătŭr. Nūmĭnă sī quă sĭnūnt. *To abandon.* Syn.—Rĕlīnquŏ, trādŏ.

Pērmŏvĕŏ, ēs, mōvī, mōtūm, ērĕ. *To agitate strongly.* Syn.—Mŏvĕŏ, ăgĭtŏ.

Pērmūlcĕŏ, ēs, mūlsī sūm, ērĕ. *To flatter.* Syn.—Mūlcĕŏ. *To soothe, to calm.* Syn.—Mītĭgŏ, mōllĭŏ, lēnĭŏ, plācŏ.

Pērnĭcĭēs, ēī. f. *Ruin.* Syn.—Clādēs, dāmnūm, mălūm, ēxĭtĭūm, rŭīnă.

Pērnĭcĭōsŭs, ă, ūm. *Harmful.* Nūmĭnă cūltōrī pērnĭcĭōsă sŭō. O. Syn.—Dāmnōsŭs, ēxĭtĭōsŭs, ēxĭtĭālĭs, ēxĭtĭābĭlĭs, fātālĭs.

Pērnīcĭtĕr. adv. *Quickly.* Syn.—Lĕvĭtĕr, ōcĭŭs, prŏpĕrē.

Pērnīx, īcĭs. adj. *Quick, prompt.* Syn.—Cĕlĕr, cĭtŭs, prǣpĕs, vēlōx.

Pērnōctŏ, ās, āvī, ātūm, ārĕ. *To pass the night.* Phr.—Nōctēm ăgŏ, dūcŏ. Nōctĕ, nōctū, pēr nōctēm mănĕŏ.

Pērnōtēscŏ, ĭs, ŭī, ĕrĕ. *To become noted.* Syn.—Vūlgŏr, pērlābŏr, pērcrēbrēscŏ.

Pērpĕtŭŭs, ă, ūm. *Perpetual, uninterrupted.* Syn.—Cōntĭnŭŭs, pĕrēnnĭs, jūgĭs, āssĭdŭŭs.

Pērplēxŭs, ă, ūm. *Involved, interwoven.* Syn.—Īmplĭcĭtŭs, īnvŏlūtŭs, pērplĭcātŭs. Fig.—*Obscure, enigmatic.* Syn.—Ōbscūrŭs, ānceps, dŭbĭŭs.

Pērpŏlĭŏ, īs, īvī & ĭī, ītūm, īrĕ. *To polish.* Syn.—Pŏlĭŏ, ēxpŏlĭŏ. Fig.—*To render perfect.* Syn.—Ābsōlvŏ, pērfĭcĭŏ.

Pērrūmpŏ, ĭs, ūpī, ūptūm, ĕrĕ. *To break in pieces.* Syn.—Rūmpŏ, frāngŏ, cōrrūmpŏ.

Pērsĕquŏr, ĕrĭs, cūtŭs sūm, quī. *To pursue.* Syn.—Īnsĕquŏr, īnsēctŏr, cōnsēctŏr, ūrgĕŏ, īnstŏ, prĕmŏ, ēxērcĕŏ. *To work continually.* Syn.—Īnsēctŏr, ēxērcĕŏ. *To seek out.* Syn.—Sĕquŏr, quærŏ. *To continue to speak.* Syn.—Pērgŏ.

Pērsĭcŭs, ī. f. *A peach-tree.* (*See Appendix under list of Trees, etc.*)

Pērsĭdĕŏ, ēs, sēdī, sēssūm, ērĕ. *To remain, to stay permanently.* Syn.—Pērstŏ, stō, mănĕŏ, pērmănĕŏ. *To penetrate.* Syn.—Pĕnĕtrŏ, pērmĕŏ.

Pērsīstŏ, ĭs, stĭtī, ĕrĕ. *To persist.* Syn.—Pērstŏ, pērsĕvērŏ.

Pērsōlvŏ, ĭs, sōlvī, sŏlūtūm, ĕrĕ. *To pay in full.* Quŏd hăbŭī sūmmūm, prĕtĭūm pērsōlvī tĭbĭ. Ter. Syn.—Sōlvŏ, pēndŏ, rēddŏ. Phr.—Pērsōlvĕrĕ vōtă, hŏnōrēm, præmĭă.

Pērsōnă, æ. f. *Mask.* Syn.—Lārvă. Fig.—*Deceit, appearance.* Syn.—Spĕcĭēs, fūcŭs, pēllĭs. *Role.* Syn.—Pārtēs, āctŏr.

Pērsŏnŏ, ās, ŭī, ĭtūm, ārĕ. *To resound.* Sōlēmnī tībĭă cāntū Pērsŏnăt. O. Syn.—Sŏnŏ, rĕsŏnŏ, īnsŏnŏ, rĕbŏŏ, rĕmūgĭŏ. Phr.—Sŏnūm ēdŏ, īngĕmĭnŏ, ēmīttŏ.

Pērspĭcĭŏ, ĭs, ēxī, ēctūm, ĕrĕ. *To see through, to examine attentively.* Syn.—Īnspĭcĭŏ, īntrōspĭcĭŏ, pērvĭdĕŏ, pērnōscŏ. Phr.—Vĭgĭlī pērspēxĕrăt ōmnĭă cūrā.

Pērspĭcŭē. adv. *Clearly.* Syn.—Clārē, mănĭfēstō.

Pērspĭcŭŭs, ă, ūm. *Clear, transparent.* Syn.—Pēllūcĭdŭs, vĭtrĕŭs, līmpĭdŭs, nĭtĭdŭs. Fig.—*Clear, evident, plain.* Syn.—Clārŭs, ăpērtŭs, mănĭfēstŭs.

Pērstŏ, ās, ĭtī, ārĕ. *To remain firm.* Syn.—Pērmănĕŏ, hærĕŏ, īnsīstŏ, mănĕŏ, pērsĭdĕŏ. Phr.—Pērstăt ĭn ōrĕ pŭdŏr. Fig.—*To persist.* Syn.—Pērsīstŏ, pērsĕvērŏ. Phr.—Mēns ĕădēm pērstăt mĭhĭ. Pērstăt hĭēms.

Pērstrĕpŏ, ĭs, ŭī, ĕrĕ. *To make a great noise.* Syn.—Strĕpŏ, strĕpĭtŏ.

Pērsuādĕŏ, ēs, sī, sūm, ērĕ. *To persuade.* Nēc tĭbĭ jām prūdēns quīsquām pērsuādĕăt aūctŏr. V. Syn.—Suādĕŏ, pēllŏ, īmpēllŏ, īndūcŏ, pērvīncŏ, vīncŏ. Phr.—Īn mēntēm īndūcŏ. Fĭdēm făcĭŏ. Pērsuādēntĭă vērbă.

Pērtĭnācĭă, æ. f. *Obstinacy.* Syn.—Pērvĭcācĭă, ōbstĭnātĭō. Phr.—Mēns ōbfīrmātă. Tĕnāx sēntēntĭă. Mēns īmmōtă. Nēscĭă flēctī.

Pērtĭnāx, ācĭs. adj. *Obstinate.* Lūdum īnsŏlēntēm lūdĕrĕ pērtĭnāx. H. Syn.—Ōbstĭnātŭs, pērvĭcāx, tĕnāx, īmmōtŭs, īmmōbĭlĭs. Phr.—Flēctī nēscĭŭs. Mēns īmmōtă mănĕt. Quēm prōpŏsĭtūm nōn pĭgĕt.

Pērtĭnĕō, ēs, ŭī, ērĕ. *To pertain to, to have reference to* (*impersonally*). Syn.—Āttĭnĕt, spēctăt, cōnvĕnĭt, tāngĭt.

Pērtūrbŏ, ās, āvī, ātūm, ārĕ. *To trouble, to disturb.* Syn.—Tūrbŏ, cōmmŏvĕō, cōnfūndŏ, mīscĕō, pērmīscĕŏ.

Pĕrūrŏ, ĭs, ūssī, ūstūm, ĕrĕ. *To consume.* Syn.—Ūrŏ, ēxūrŏ.

Pērvādŏ, ĭs, sī, sūm, ĕrĕ. *To spread around.* Syn.—Pērlābŏr, pērcūrrŏ. *To attain.* Syn.—Āttīngŏ, āssĕquŏr, āccēdŏ (ad).

Pērvăgŏr, ārĭs, ātŭs sūm, ārī. *To wander around.* Syn.—Văgŏr, ērrŏ, pērcūrrŏ.

Pērvĕnĭō, īs, ēnī, ēntūm, ĕnīrĕ. *To arrive.* Sī fōrtĕ tŭās pērvēnĭt ăd aūrēs Bēlīdæ nōmēn Pălămœdĭs. V. Syn.—Vĕnĭō, dēvĕnĭō, āccēdŏ, tāngŏ, āttīngŏ, pērtīngŏ, tĕnĕō, sŭbĕō, pērvādŏ, āllābŏr.

Pērvērtŏ, ĭs, tī, sūm, ĕrĕ. *To turn, to overturn.* Syn.—Īnvērtŏ, sūbvērtŏ, ēvērtŏ.

Pērvĭgĭl, ĭlĭs. adj. *Ever watchful.* Syn.—Vĭgĭl, vĭgĭlāns, ācĕr, sēdŭlŭs,

Pērvĭgĭlŏ, ās, āvī, ātūm, ārĕ. *To watch continually.* Syn.—Āgŏ, dūcŏ, trādūcŏ.

Pērvĭŭs, ă, ūm. *Open, accessible.* Syn.—Āpērtŭs, pătēns, pĕnĕtrābĭlĭs. Phr.—Nōn (*or*) haūd īmpērvĭŭs. Quō ēst ădĭtŭs. Quō pĕnĕtrārĕ dătŭr.

Pēs, pĕdĭs. m. *Foot.* Syn.—Plāntă, (*sometimes*) vēstīgĭă. Phr.—Fīgēns vēstīgĭă. Āptăquĕ fōrmă pĕdĭs. Mōllī pĕdĕ fūltă. Īncērtō pĕdĕ fērtŭr. *Measure of verse.* Syn.—Mĕtrūm, nŭmĕrŭs.

Pēssūmdŏ, ās, dĕdī, ătūm, ărĕ. *To ruin, to destroy.* Nōn mĭhĭ quærēntī pēssūmdărĕ cūnctă pĕtītūm. O. Syn.—Pērdŏ, tōllŏ, ēvērtŏ, dēstrŭō, ēxtīnguŏ, dēlĕō, ăbŏlĕō, dējĭcĭō.

Pēstĭfĕr, ĕră, ĕrūm. *Pestilential, contagious.* Mīttūnt pēstĭfĕrōs æstūs ēt tētră vĕnēnă. V. Syn.—Cōrrūptŭs, lētālĭs, pēstĭlēns, vĭtĭātŭs. Phr.—Pēstĭfĕrās ăpĕrīt faūcēs.

Pēstĭs, ĭs. f. *Pest.* Quīd pēstem ēvādĕrĕ bēllī Jūvĭt. V. Syn.—Pēstĭlēntĭă, clādēs, pērnĭcĭēs. Phr.—Dī, tālēm tērrīs āvērtĭtĕ pēstēm. Īn pārtēm quæ pēstĕ cărĕt. *Disease, contagion.* Syn.—Lŭēs, cōntāgĭō, cōntāgĭă, tābēs. Phr.—Dīră lŭēs. Lētĭfĕr æstŭs.

Cœlī mōrbŭs. Pĕr ōmnĭă vīscĕră sērpēns. Sævō vĭŏlēntă vĕnēnō. Vĭdŭāns ūrbēs.

Pĕtŏ, ĭs, īvī & ĭī, ītūm, ĕrĕ. *To direct one's steps towards.* Syn.—Ĕŏ, tēndŏ, ădĕŏ. *To seek.* Syn.—Quærŏ. *To ask.* Syn.—Pōstŭlŏ, pōscŏ, dēpōscŏ, ēxpōscŏ, quærŏ, rŏgŏ, flāgĭtŏ.

Pĕtră, æ. f. *Rock.* Syn.—Sāxūm, rūpēs, sĭlēx, caūtēs, scŏpŭlŭs.

Phălānx, gĭs. f. *Phalanx.* Ōccĭdĭs, Ārgīvæ quēm nōn pŏtŭĕrĕ phălāngēs Stērnĕrĕ. V. Syn.—Āgmĕn, cŏhōrs, lĕgĭŏ, mănīplŭs, cătērvă.

Phāntāsmă, ătĭs. n. *Phantom, vision.* Syn.—Vīsūm, spēctrūm, sĭmŭlăcrūm, fōrmă, spĕcĭēs, ĭmāgŏ. Phr.—Tăcĭtæ nōctĭs ĭmāgŏ.

Phărĕtră, æ. f. *Quiver.* Phr.—Săgīttĭs plēnă. Pūlsāns tērgă. Ēx hŭmĕrō sŏnāns. Īllă phărētrām fērt hŭmĕrŏ.

Phāsĭānŭs, ī. m. *A pheasant.* (*See Appendix under list of Birds.*)

Phĭlŏmēlă, æ. f. *A nightingale.* (*See Appendix under list of Birds.*)

Phœnīcŏptĕrŭs, ī. m. *A flamingo.* (*See Appendix under list of Birds.*)

Phœnīx, īcĭs. m. *The phoenix, a mythical bird of Arabia.* (*See Appendix under list of Birds.*)

Pĭcĕă, æ. f. *The pitch-pine.* (*See Appendix under list of Trees, etc.*)

Pīctūră, æ. f. *Picture.* Ūt pīctūră pŏēsĭs ĕrĭt. H. Syn.—Tăbŭlă. *A painted picture.* Phr.—Tăbēllă, tăbŭlă pīctă. Pīctæ ēffĭgĭēs. Pīctă ĭmāgŏ.

Pīctūrātŭs, ă, ūm. *Painted, embroidered with colors.* Syn.—Pīctŭs, vărĭŭs, dīstīnctŭs, nĭtĭdŭs, fūlgēns.

Pīcŭs, ī. m. *A woodpecker.* (*See Appendix under list of Birds.*)

Pĭĕtās, ātĭs. f. *Piety.* Syn.—Rĕlīgĭŏ. Phr.—Pĭĕtātĭs hŏnōs. Pĭă fāctă. Pĭă vīrtūs. Vīctă jăcēt pĭĕtās. *Justice, virtue.* Syn.—Fĭdēs, vīrtūs, jūstĭtĭă. *Affection for one's family.* Syn.—Āmŏr, stŭdĭūm, āffēctŭs, cārĭtās.

Pĭgĕr, pĭgra, pĭgrūm. *Lazy, negligent.* Nūnquām pīgră fŭīt nōstrīs tŭă grātĭă rēbŭs. O. Syn.—Dēsĕs, dēsĭdĭōsŭs, ĭnērs, sēgnĭs, lēntŭs, īgnāvŭs, lānguĭdŭs, sōcōrs, vēcōrs. Phr.—Tūrpī dēsĭdĭă tārdŭs. Grăvī tōrpēns vĕtērnō. Cuī pūlchrūm īn mĕdĭōs dōrmīrĕ dĭēs. *Slow in speaking.* Syn.—Ĭnērs, sēgnĭs, īgnāvŭs, īmmōtŭs, īmmōbĭlĭs.

Pĭgĕt, ŭĭt, ērĕ. *It disgusts, it displeases.* Syn.—Tædĕt, pænĭtĕt, grăvŏr.

Pīgnĕrŏ, ās, āvī, ātūm, ārĕ. *To engage, to pledge.* Syn.—Ōppīgnĕrŏ, ōppōnŏ. Phr.—Pīgnŭs, pīgnŏră dō.

Pĭgrē. adv. *Slowly, nonchalantly.* Syn.—Cūnctāntĕr, lēntē, sēgnĭtĕr, gĕlĭdē.

Pĭgrĭtĭă, æ. f. *Laziness, negligence.* Syn.—Pĭgrĭtĭēs, dēsĭdĭă, sēgnĭtĭēs, īgnāvĭă, lānguŏr, ōtĭŭm, sōcōrdĭă, tōrpŏr, vĕtērnŭs. Phr.—Fœdă ănĭmī rūbīgŏ. Fŭgĭēns lăbōrēs. Ēxōsă lăbōrūm.

Pīngŏ, ĭs, īnxī, īctūm, ĕrĕ. *To paint.* Syn.—Dēpīngŏ, ădūmbrŏ, ēffīngŏ. Phr.—Cŏlōrĭbŭs, pīctīs tăbŭlīs (*or*) fĭgūrīs ĭmĭtŏr, ēxprĭmŏ, ēffīngŏ. *To color.* Syn.—Cŏlōrŏ, tīngŏ, īnfĭcĭŏ, īndūcŏ. *To spread over.* Syn.—Dīstīnguŏ, vărĭŏ, spārgŏ, dīscrīmĭnŏ.

Pīnguēdŏ, ĭnĭs. f. *Fatness.* Syn.—Ădēps, pīnguĕ.

Pīnguĭs, ĭs, ĕ. *Fat, stout.* Syn.—Ŏbēsŭs, ŏpīmŭs, crāssŭs, pērpāstŭs, ŏpīmātŭs, săgīnātŭs. Phr.—Cōrpŏrĕ pīnguĭs. Pīnguī tēntŭs ŏmāsō. *Stupid, dull.* Syn.—Rŭdĭs, hĕbĕs, tārdŭs, ŏbēsŭs, ōbtūsŭs, crāssŭs. Phr.—Pīnguī Mĭnērvā.

Pīnŭs, ī & ūs. f. *A pine-tree.* (*See Appendix under list of Trees, etc.*)

Pĭŏ, ās, āvī, ātūm, ārĕ. *To expiate, to purify.* Ēffĭgĭēm stătŭērĕ nĕfās quæ trīstĕ pĭārĕt. V. Syn.—Ēxpĭŏ, lŭŏ, lūstrŏ, pūrgŏ. Phr.—Cūlpām mĭsĕrōrūm mōrtĕ pĭābūnt. Ārās tūrĕ pĭānt.

Pĭrŭs, ī. f. *A pear-tree.* (*See Appendix under list of Trees, etc.*)

Pīscātŏr, ōrĭs. m. *Fisherman.* Phr.—Aēquŏrĕŭs pīscātŏr. Mŏdĕrātŏr ărūndĭnĭs. Lĕvēs hāmōs jāctāns. Paūpĕrēm vītām ăgēns. Pīscātōr fĕrāt æquŏrūm răpīnās.

Pīscĭs, ĭs. m. *Fish.* Cēssērūnt nĭtĭdīs hăbĭtāndæ pīscĭbŭs ūndæ. O. Syn.—Pīscĭcŭlŭs. Phr.—Gēns squāmĭgĕră. Gĕnŭs, pĕcŭs æquŏrĕūm. Āgmĭnă mūtă. Nătāntūm gĕnŭs ōmnĕ. Nāntēs sūb gūrgĭtĕ vāstō. Mărĭs īmmēnsă prōlēs. Īncŏlæ mărĭs.

Pīscŏr, ārĭs, ātŭs sūm, ārī. *To fish.* Phr.—Fāllĕrĕ, prædārī călămō pīscēs. Ărūndĭnĕ pīscēs cāptārĕ. Pīscĭbŭs īnsĭdĭārī. Rētĭbŭs jāctīs călămō dūcĕrĕ.

Pĭŭs, ă, ūm. *Pious, just, virtuous.* Syn.—Rĕlĭgĭōsŭs, jūstŭs, sānctŭs, æquŭs, cāstŭs, prŏbŭs, pūrŭs. Phr.—Pĭĕtātĕ ēgrĕgĭŭs. Pĭĕtātĭs ămāns. Sĭnĕ crīmĭnĕ vīvēns. Īntĕgēr vītæ. *Respectful, dutiful.* Syn.—Rĕvĕrēns. Phr.—Īnsīgnīs pĭĕtātĕ. *Favorable.* Syn.—Bŏnŭs, bĕnīgnŭs, mītĭs.

Plācābĭlĭs, ĭs, ĕ. *Easy to appease.* Syn.—Ēxōrābĭlĭs, mītĭs, clēmēns, plăcĭdŭs. Phr.—Vĕnĭæ părātŭs. Plācārī, flēctī pătĭēns. Dŏcĭlĭs prĕcĭbŭs.

Plăcĕŏ, ēs, ŭī, ĭtūm, ērĕ. *To please.* Nūllă plăcērĕ dĭū nēc vīvĕrĕ cārmĭnă pōssūnt. H. Syn.—Ārrīdĕŏ, prŏbŏr, dēlēctŏ, ōblēctŏ, jŭvŏ. Phr.—Ācceptŭs, grātŭs, jūcūndŭs, dūlcĭs sūm. Mĕă plăcŭērūnt ōtĭă mēntī. Placet. *impers. It seems good to me.* Syn.—Stăt, lĭbĕt, jŭvăt, sēdĕt. Phr.—Ēst ănĭmŭs, vŏlūntās. Fērt ĭtă cōrdĕ vŏlūntās. Sīc plăcĭtūm. Dīs ălĭtēr vīsūm.

Plăcĭdē. adv. *Peaceably.* Syn.—Lēnĭtĕr, quĭētē, trānquīllē.

Plăcĭdŭs, ă, ūm. *Peaceful, calm.* Sēdĭbŭs ūt sāltēm plăcĭdīs īn mōrtĕ quĭēscām. V. Syn.—Quĭētŭs, mītĭs, trānquīllŭs, pācātŭs. *Gentle, meek.* Syn.—Mītĭs, lēnĭs, făcĭlĭs. *Favorable.* Syn.—Făvēns, bĕnīgnŭs.

Plācŏ, ās, āvī, ātūm, ārĕ. *To appease.* Mūnĕră, crēdĕ mĭhī, plācānt hŏmĭnēsquĕ dĕōsquĕ. O. Syn.—Lēnĭŏ, mītĭgŏ, mōllĭŏ, mūlcĕŏ, pērmūlcĕŏ, flēctŏ, sēdŏ, tēmpĕrŏ, dēlīnĭŏ, mŏdĕrŏr, ēxōrŏ, mŏvĕŏ, pērmŏvĕŏ, tāngŏ, vīncŏ, frāngŏ. Phr.—Tŭmĭdās īrās flēctŏ. Īrām mītĭgŏ. Prĕcĭbŭs, lăcrĭmīs lēnĭŏ. Mānsuēscĕrĕ cōrdă. Plăcĭtūm rēddĕrĕ. Tēmpĕrăt īrās.

Plăgă, æ. f. *Wound.* Syn.—Īctŭs, vūlnŭs.

Plānctŭs, ūs. m. *Weeping, lamentation.* Syn.—Plāngŏr, lāmēntūm, lūctŭs, ējūlātŭs, dŏlŏr, gĕmĭtŭs.

Plānē. adv. *Wholly, entirely.* Syn.—Ōmnīnō, prōrsŭs.

Plāngŏ, ĭs, xī, ctūm, ĕrĕ. *To strike.* Syn.—Fĕrĭŏ, vērbĕrŏ, quătĭŏ, pērcŭtĭŏ. *To weep.* Syn.—Dŏlĕŏ, lăcrĭmŏ. Phr.—Pēctŭs, pēctŏră mănĭbŭs fĕrĭŏ. Plānctĭbŭs īncēssŏ. Crēbrō īctū cōntūndŏ. Pāssōs lănĭārĕ căpīllōs. Vērbĕrăt ōră mănū.

Plāngŏr, ōrĭs. m. *Weeping.* Syn.—Plānctŭs, gĕmĭtŭs, ŭlŭlātŭs.

Plānĭtĭēs, ēī. f. *Level surface.* Syn.—Aēquŏr, ārĕă, plānūm. *Plain.* Syn.—Cāmpŭs, æquŏr. Phr.—Cāmpŭs ăpērtŭs. Ăpērtă lŏcōrūm. Plānīssĭmă cāmpī Ārĕă.

Plāntă, æ. f. *Sprout, shoot.* Syn.—Ărbŏr, stīrps, sūrcŭlŭs, pālmĕs. Phr.—Pārvō dē sēmĭnĕ sūrgēns. *Plant.* Syn.—Hērbă.

Plānŭs, ă, ūm. *Plane, level.* Syn.—Aēquŭs, æquālĭs. Phr.—Quī cădĭt īn plānō. *Clear, evident.* Syn.—Ēvĭdēns, mănĭfēstŭs.

Plătănŭs, ī. f. *A plane-tree.* (*See Appendix under list of Trees, etc.*)

Plaūdŏ, ĭs, sī, sūm, ĕrĕ. *To strike, to beat.* Syn.—Fĕrĭŏ, pērcŭtĭŏ. *To applaud.* Syn.—Āpplaūdŏ, cīrcūmplaūdŏ. Phr.—Mănĭbŭs plaūdŏ. Plaūsūm dō. Plaūsĭbŭs prŏbŏ. Lætĭtĭā plaūsūquĕ frĕmŏ. Āttōllūnt plaūsūs. Cōncūrrĭt dēxtĕră lævæ.

Plaūstrūm, ī. n. *Chariot.* Syn.—Plaūstēllūm, cūrrŭs, āxĭs. Phr.—Fērtūr plaūstrō prædă trĕmēntī. Grăvĭbūs jŭgă dūcĕrĕ plaūstrīs.

Plaūsŭs, ūs. m. *Applause.* Syn.—Clāmŏr, mūrmŭr, frĕmĭtŭs, āssēnsŭs, făvŏr. Phr.—Stŭdĭūm pŏpŭlārĕ. Făvēntūm frĕmĭtŭs. Āccēnsŭs făvŏr. Plaūsūquĕ vŏlăt frĕmĭtūquĕ sĕcūndō.

Plēbēiŭs, ă, ūm. *Belonging to the lower class.* Ēt dărĕ plēbēiō cōrpŭs ĭnānĕ rŏgŏ. O. Syn.—Īgnōbĭlĭs, īnfĭmŭs, vūlgārĭs.

Plēbs, plēbĭs. f. *The lower class.* Syn.—Plēbēcŭlă, vūlgŭs, tūrbă, pŏpēllŭs. Phr.—Fæx plēbĭs. Sēdĭtĭōnĭs ămāns. Rēbŭs ămīcă nŏvāndīs. Tūrbă stŏlĭdă īncūltæ plēbĭs.

Plēctŏ, ĭs, ĕrĕ. *To strike, to punish.* Syn.—Vērbĕrŏ, cædŏ, mūlctŏ, pūnĭŏ, cāstīgŏ.

Plēctrūm, ī. n. *Quill, plectrum for musical instruments.* Syn.—Pēctĕn, ēbŭr. Phr.—Tēntāt cārmĭnă plēctrō. Plēctrō mŏdŭlātŭs ĕbūrnō. Fig.—*For poetry.* Syn.—Cĭthără, cārmĕn.

Plēnē. adv. *Fully, entirely.* Syn.—Cŭmŭlātē, ōmnīnō, prōrsŭs, plānē.

Plēnŭs, ă, ūm. *Full.* Pārs ĕpŭlīs ŏnĕrānt mēnsās, ēt plēnă rĕpōnūnt Pōcŭlă. V. Syn.—Cŭmŭlātŭs, cōnfērtŭs, rĕplētŭs, āffluēns, rĕfērtŭs, frĕquēns, ăbūndāns, lūxŭrĭāns. Phr.—Plēnō sŭbĭt ōstĭă vēlō. Plēnōs sānguĭnĕ rīvōs. *Satisfied.* Syn.—Sătŭr, sătĭātŭs, ēxsătĭātŭs, ēxsătŭrātŭs. *Proud.* Syn.—Tŭmĭdŭs, īnflātŭs, sŭpērbŭs.

Plērīquĕ, æquĕ, ăquĕ. *The most, the majority.* Syn.—Mūltī, pērmūltī, plūrĭmī. Phr.—Nōn paūcī. Māxĭmă, mājŏr pārs.

Plērūmquĕ. adv. *Generally.* Syn.—Sæpĕ, sæpĭŭs, vūlgō.

Plĭcŏ, ās, āvī, ātūm, ārĕ. *To bend, to fold.* Nēxāntēm nōdōs sēque īn sŭă mēmbră plĭcāntēm. V. Syn.—Cōmplĭcŏ, rĕplĭcŏ, cōllĭgŏ, īntōrquĕŏ, cōnvōlvŏ, flēctŏ, īnflēctŏ, cōntrăhŏ. Phr.—Īn gȳrūm, nēxūs, nōdōs dūcŏ. Nōdōs nēctŏ. Īnflēctūnt īmmēnsă vŏlūmĭnĕ tērgă.

Plōrātŭs, ūs. m. *Weeping, lamentation.* Syn.—Flētŭs, lăcrĭmæ, lūctŭs.

Plōrŏ, ās, āvī, ātūm, ārĕ. *To weep.* Plōrātūr lăcrĭmīs āmīssă pĕcūnĭă vērĭs. J. Syn.—Flĕŏ, lăcrĭmŏr, lūgĕŏ.

Plŭĭt, ĕrĕ. *It rains.* Phr.—Plŭvĭă, īmbĕr cădĭt, cœlō dēscēndĭt, rŭĭt, præcĭpĭtăt. Dūm plŭĭt īn tērrīs. Jūpĭtĕr īmbrĭbŭs rĭgăt ārvă. Cœlō dēmĭttĭtŭr īmbĕr. Dēnsīssĭmŭs īmbĕr īngĕmĭnăt. Nūbēs sē sōlvĭt ĭn īmbrēm. Nĕquĕ pārtŭrĭt īmbrēs pērpĕtŭōs.

Plūrēs, ră, ĭŭm. *Several, many.* Syn.—Mūltī, plūrĭmī, frĕquēntēs. Phr.—Nŭmĕrōsă mănŭs, cŏhōrs. Īngēntī ădstāntĕ cŏrōnā. Māgnā cŏmĭtāntĕ cătērvā. Āgmĭnĕ lōngō.

Plūrĭmūm. adv. *Very much.* Syn.—Mūltūm, vāldē.

Plūs. adv. *Much, more.* Syn.—Măgĭs, măgĕ, āmplĭŭs.

Plŭvĭă, æ. f. *Rain.* Syn.—Īmbĕr, nīmbŭs. Phr.—Plŭvĭŭs īmbĕr. Cœlēstĭs hūmŏr. Cœlēstēs ăquæ.

Plŭvĭālĭs, ĭs, ĕ. *Rainy.* Vērĕ mădēnt ūdō tērrae ăc plŭvĭālĭbŭs aūstrīs. V. Phr.—Nīmbīs grăvātŭs. Aūstrālĭbŭs hūmĭdă nīmbīs.

Pōcŭlūm, ī. n. *Cup.* Syn.—Crātĕr, crātēră, cārchēsĭūm, pătĕră, scўphŭs, călīx, cўăthŭs. Phr.—Pōcŭlă vălĭdō spūmāntĭă Bācchō. Pērfēcta ārgēntō. Āspĕră sīgnīs. Căpācēs vīnă grăvānt pătĕrās.

Pŏēmă, ătĭs. n. *Poem. See Carmen.*

Pœnă, æ. f. *Pain, punishment.* Dīstŭlĕrātquĕ grăvēs ĭn ĭdōnĕă tēmpŏră pœnās. O. Syn.—Sūpplĭcĭūm, crŭcĭātŭs, tōrmēntūm, pĭācŭlūm, pĭāmĕn. Phr.—Pœnă scĕlĕrūm vīndēx. Crīmĭnĭs ūltrīx. Gĕnŭs mĭsĕrābĭlĕ pœnæ. Pœnārūm gĕnŭs ōmnĕ. Pœnă mĭnōr mĕrĭtō.

Pœnĭtēntĭă, æ. f. *Repentance.* Syn.—Mĕtănœă, dŏlŏr. Phr.—Crīmĭnĭs ādmīssī dŏlŏr. Īn melius vītām cōmmūtāns. Hōrrēscēns crīmĭnă vītæ prætĕrĭtæ.

Pœnĭtĕt, ŭĭt, ērĕ. *It repents me, I am sorry.* Syn.—Pĭgĕt, dŏlĕō.

Pŏēsĭs, ĭs & ĕŏs, & Pŏētĭcă, æ. f. *Poetry. See Carmen.* Phr.—Āpōllĭnĭs ārs, ārtēs, stŭdĭūm, stŭdĭă. Dūlcēs mūsæ. Pŏēsĭs blāndă pŏtēstās.

Pŏētă, æ. m. *Poet.* Syn.—Vātēs. Phr.—Phœbī săcērdōs. Pīĕrĭdūm cōmĕs. Āfflātūs nūmĭnĕ Phœbī. Fēlīcī cārmĭnĕ clārŭs. Laūrō cīnctŭs. Mūsīs dĭcātŭs.

Pŏētĭcă, ă, ūm. *Poetic.* Syn.—Āpōllĭnĕŭs, Phœbēŭs, Pārnāssĭŭs, Cāstălĭŭs.

Pŏlĭŏ, īs, īvī, ītūm, īrĕ. *To polish.* Syn.—Ēxpŏlĭŏ, pērpŏlĭŏ, lævŏ, lævĭgŏ, plānŏ, rādŏ, ābrādŏ. Fig.—*To perfect, to polish.* Syn.—Ēxpŏlĭŏ. Phr.—Cāstīgārĕ ăd ūnguēm.

Pōllĕŏ, ēs, ērĕ. *To have strength, to have power.* Syn.—Vălĕŏ, pōssūm, præstŏ.

Pōllĭcĕŏr, ērĭs, ĭtŭs sūm, ērī. *To promise.* Syn.—Pōllĭcĭtŏr, prōmĭttŏ, spōndĕŏ. *See Promitto.*

Pōllŭŏ, ĭs, ŭī, ūtūm, ĕrĕ. *To corrupt, to pollute.* Syn.—Fœdŏ, măcŭlŏ, cōmmăcŭlŏ, īnquĭnŏ, cŏīnquĭnŏ, cōntāmĭnŏ, cōntĕmĕrŏ, cōrrūmpŏ, īnfĭcĭŏ, tūrpŏ, vĭŏlŏ. Phr.—Măcŭlām, lābēm, īnjĭcĭŏ. Lābĕ rēspērgŏ. Fig. Syn.—Lædŏ, tĕmĕrŏ, cōrrūmpŏ, vĭŏlŏ, frāngŏ.

Pōmpă, æ. f. *Cortege, procession.* Syn.—Trĭūmphŭs.

Pōmūm, ī. n. *Fruit.* Syn.—Frūctŭs. Phr.—Ārbŏrĕī fœtūs. Ārbŏrĭs ŏpēs. Aūtūmnī mūnĕră. Mōtīs rāmīs cădēns. Prĕmēns pōndĕrĕ rāmōs. *Apple.* Syn.—Mālūm.

Pōndĕrŏ, ās, āvī, ātūm, ārĕ. *To weigh.* Syn.—Pēndŏ, āppēndŏ, ēxpēndŏ, lībrŏ, ēxāmĭnŏ. Fig.—*To weigh, to examine.* Syn.—Ēxāmĭnŏ, ēxpēndŏ, pērpēndŏ, ēxcŭtĭŏ, dīscŭtĭŏ, æstĭmŏ.

Pōndŭs, ĕrĭs. n. *Weight.* Syn.—Ŏnŭs, grăvĭtās, sārcĭnă, mōlēs. Phr.—Mōlēs ŏnĕrōsă. Pōndĕrĕ grăvŏ. Vīx trāctābĭlĕ pōndŭs. *Burden.* Syn.—Ŏnŭs, īncōmmŏdŭm. *Weight, gravity.* Syn.—Mōmēntūm, vīs, aūctōrĭtās.

Pōnĕ. adv. *Behind.* Syn.—Pōst. Phr.—Ā tērgō. Pōst tērgă. Pōnĕ sĕquēns. Pārs cētĕră pōntūm Pōnĕ lĕgĭt.

Pōnŏ, ĭs, ŏsŭī, ĭtūm, ĕrĕ. *To put, to place.* Prīmă făvīs pōnūnt fūndāmĭnă. V. Syn.—Dēpōnŏ, rĕpōnŏ, lōcŏ, cōllŏcŏ, stătŭŏ, cōnstĭtŭŏ. *To raise, to build.* Syn.—Cōndŏ, stătŭŏ, cōnstĭtŭŏ, ǣdĭfĭcŏ, ērĭgŏ, ēxstrŭŏ. *To leave, to renounce.* Syn.—Dēpōnŏ, rĕlīnquŏ, mīttŏ, ŏmīttŏ, ēxŭŏ, pēllŏ. Phr.—Pōnĭtĕ cōrdĕ mĕtūm. *To execute.* Syn.—Pērfĭcĭŏ, fīngŏ, ēffīngŏ.

Pōns, pōntĭs. m. *Bridge.* Sāxĕŭs īngēntī quēm pōns āmplēctĭtŭr ārcū. L. Phr.—Pōntĭs ārcŭs, fōrnīx, cūrvāmĕn, cūrvāmĭnă. Āmnēm jūngĕrĕ pōntĕ. Rĕvēllĕrĕ pōntēs.

Pōntĭfēx, ĭcĭs. m. *Priest, high-priest.* Syn.—Āntīstĕs, săcērdōs, prǣsŭl. Phr.—Săcrōrūm āntīstĕs. Vīttīs īnsīgnĭs. Pūră īn vēstĕ rĕfūlgēns. Frōndĕ vīctŭs.

Pŏpīnă, ǣ. f. *Small inn.* Syn.—Caūpōnă, tăbērnă.

Pōplĕs, ĭtĭs. m. *Knee.* Syn.—Gĕnū. Phr.—Vĕnĕrārī pōplĭtĕ cūrvō. Dēfēctō pōplĭtĕ lābēns. Sūspēnsō pōplĭtĕ trānsĭt.

Pŏpŭlārĭs, ĭs, ĕ. *Popular, belonging to the people.* Syn.—Plēbēiŭs, plēbēĭŭs, cīvīlĭs, pūblĭcŭs.

Pŏpŭlŏ, ās, āvī, ātūm, ārĕ & Pŏpŭlŏr, ārĭs, ātŭs sūm, ārī. *To devastate.* Fērrō Lĭbycōs pŏpŭlārĕ pĕnātēs. V. Syn.—Dēpŏpŭlŏr, vāstŏ, dēvāstŏ, dīrĭpĭŏ, prǣdŏr. Fig. Syn.—Ābsūmŏ, pĕrĭmŏ, pērdŏ, pēssūmdŏ.

Pŏpŭlŭs, ī. m. *People, nation.* Hīnc pŏpŭlūm lātē rēgēm bēllōquĕ sŭpērbūm. V. Syn.—Gēns, nātĭŏ. Phr.—Gĕnŭs ūndĕ Lătīnūm. Māvōrtĭă tēllūs. Rōmānă prŏpāgŏ. *The common people.* Syn.—Cīvēs, plēbs, plēbēs, vūlgŭs.

Pōpŭlŭs, ī. f. *A poplar-tree.* (*See Appendix under list of Trees, etc.*)

Pōrcă, ǣ. f. *Sow.* Syn.—Scrōfă, sūs.

Pōrcŭs, ī. m. *Hog, pig.* Syn.—Sūs, pōrcēllŭs, pōrcŭlŭs. Phr.—Īmmūndō sē flūmĭnĕ vōlvēns. Lŭtō sē vŏlūtāns. Gaūdēns cœ̄no īmmūndāquĕ pălūdĕ.

Pōrrĭgŏ, ĭs, rēxī, rēctūm, ĕrĕ. *To stretch out, to spread out.* Syn.—Ēxpōrrĭgŏ, tēndŏ, īntēndŏ, ēxtēndŏ, prōtēndŏ, prōfĕrŏ, prōdūcŏ. Phr.—Flōrēs ād cāndĭdă pōrrĭgĭt ōră. *To lay low.* Syn.—Ēxtēndŏ, stērnŏ, ēvērtŏ, dējĭcĭŏ. *To offer.* Syn.—Tēndŏ, prōtēndŏ, ōffĕrŏ, prǣbĕŏ.

Pōrrō. adv. *Afar off.* Syn.—Lōngē. *In turn.* Syn.—Deīndĕ, deīncēps, prætĕrĕā, ūltrā. *Therefore.* Syn.—Ātquī, ĭgĭtŭr, ērgō.

Pōrtă, æ. f. *Gate, door.* Sūnt quĭbŭs ăd pōrtās cĕcĭdīt cūstōdĭă sōrtī. V. Syn.—Vālvæ, līmĕn, pōstēs, claūstră. Phr.—Fērrātæ rōbŏră pōrtæ. Claūsæ mūnīmĭnă pōrtæ. Īpso īn līmĭnĕ pōrtæ. Pōrtīs bĭpătēntĭbŭs ādsūnt. *Door, or approach in general.* Syn.—Jānŭă, vālvæ, fŏrēs, pōstēs, līmĕn, līmĭnă, ōstĭūm, ădĭtŭs.

Pōrtēndŏ, ĭs, dī, sūm, ĕrĕ. *To announce, to foretell.* Syn.—Mōnstrŏ, ōmĭnŏr, præsāgĭŏ, aūgŭrŏ, aūgŭrŏr, præmōnstrŏ, ōstēndŏ, dēnūntĭŏ, nūntĭŏ, sīgnĭfĭcŏ, prædīcŏ, cănŏ, præcĭnŏ.

Pōrtēntōsŭs, ă, ūm. *Portentous, prodigious, monstrous.* Syn.—Prōdigiosŭs, mīrābĭlĭs, mōnstrōsŭs.

Pōrtēntūm, ī. n. *Portent, prodigy.* Syn.—Prōdĭgĭūm, ōstēntūm, mōnstrūm, ōmĕn.

Pōrtĭcŭs, ūs. m. *Gallery, porch, portico.* Syn.—Āmbŭlācrūm, āmbŭlātĭŏ, ātrĭūm. Phr.—Īnnīxă cŏlūmnīs. Părĭīs nĭtēt fūltă, cŏlūmnīs. Spătĭōsă tĕrētŭr Pōrtĭcŭs.

Pōrtŏ, ās, āvī, ātūm, ārĕ. *To carry.* Syn.—Gĕrŏ, gēstŏ, fĕrŏ, ēffĕrŏ, vĕhŏ, vēctŏ, bājŭlŏ, sūstĭnĕŏ, tōllŏ. Phr.—Dōrsō, cērvīcĕ, tērgō pōrtŏ. Sūccēdō ŏnĕrī. Ŏnŭs sŭbĕŏ. Fērt hŭmĕrīs.

Pōrtŭs, ūs. m. *Port, harbor.* Syn.—Stătĭŏ, ōstĭă, rīpă, sĭnŭs. Phr.—Stătĭō tūtīssĭmă naūtīs. Sēdēs grātīssĭmă naūtīs. Hōspĭtă tēllūs. Tāngĕrĕ pōrtās. Dēlāti īn pōrtūs.

Pōscŏ, ĭs, pŏpōscī, ĕrĕ. *To ask, to demand.* Dīvūmquĕ sĭbī pōscēbăt hŏnōrēm. V. Syn.—Dēpōscŏ, ēxpōscŏ, pĕtŏ, pōstŭlŏ, ēxpōstŭlŏ, rĕquīrŏ. Phr.—Pōscĭt ĕquōs. Nīl pōscĭmŭs ūltrā. *To seek earnestly.* Syn.—Pĕtŏ, pōstŭlŏ, rŏgŏ, flāgĭtŏ, ēfflāgĭtŏ, ēxpōscŏ, ōrŏ, prĕcŏr.

Pōssĭdĕŏ, ēs, sēdī, sēssūm, ērĕ. *To possess.* Ēt văcŭūm Zĕphÿrī pōssĭdĕt aūră nĕmŭs. Pr. Syn.—Tĕnĕŏ, hăbĕŏ, ōbtĭnĕŏ, ōccŭpŏ, frŭŏr, pŏtĭŏr.

Pōssūm, pŏtĕs, pŏtŭī, pōssĕ. *To be able.* Syn.—Quĕŏ, vălĕŏ, ēvălĕŏ, lĭcĕt. Phr.—Fās ēst, pŏtĭs sūm. Mĭhĭ dătŭr. Ēst ŏpĭs mĕæ. Ēst mĭhĭ cōpĭă, făcūltās, pŏtēstās. Nōn ŏpĭs ēst nostræ.

Pōstĕā. adv. *Afterwards.* Syn.—Pōst, deīn, deīndĕ, tūm, prætĕrĕā, īndĕ, ēxīndĕ. Phr.—Pōst hæc.

Pōstĕrĭtās, ātĭs. f. *Posterity.* Syn.—Pōstĕrī, vēntūrī, mĭnōrēs, nĕpōtēs, pōstgĕnĭtī. Phr.—Pōstĕră ætās, gēns. Mĕmŏrī ævō.

Pōstĕrŭs, ă, ūm. *That which comes after.* Syn.—Sĕquēns, vēntūrŭs.

Pōsthăbĕŏ, ēs, ŭī, ĭtūm, ērĕ. *To esteem less.* Syn.—Pōstpōnŏ, pōstfĕrŏ.

Pōsthāc. adv. *Henceforth, for the future.* Syn.—Pōst, pōstĕā, deīncēps, deīndĕ, ēxīndĕ.

Pōstquām. conj. *After.* Syn.—Pōstĕāquām, ŭbĭ, pōstŭbĭ, cūm, sĭmŭl. Phr.—Sĭmŭl āc, sĭmŭl ŭt, sĭmŭl ātquĕ.

Pōstrēmō. adv. *Finally.* Syn.—Dēnĭquĕ, dēmūm, tāndēm.

Pōstrēmŭs, ă, ūm. *Last.* Syn.—Ēxtrēmŭs, ūltĭmŭs, nŏvīssĭmŭs, sŭprēmŭs.

Pŏtēns, ēntĭs. adj. *Powerful.* Syn.—Vălēns, vălĭdŭs, pōllēns. Phr.—Pŏtēstātĕ vălēns. Ēx hŭmĭlī pŏtēns. Rērūm cuī sūmmă pŏtēstās.

Pŏtēntĭă, æ & Pŏtēstās, ātĭs. f. *Power.* Syn.—Īmpĕrĭūm. Phr.—Nūllă pŏtēntĭă lōnga ēst. Ēmĭtūr sōlā vīrtūtĕ pŏtēstās. Cuī tāntă vĭrō cōncēssă pŏtēstās. *Liberty to act.* Syn.—Cōpĭă, făcūltās, vīs, vĕnĭă, vīrtūs.

Pŏtĭŏr, īrĭs, ītŭs sūm, īrī. *To get possession of, to enjoy.* Sī vērō căpĕre Ītălĭām scēptrīsquĕ pŏtīrī Cōntĭgĕrĭt. V. Syn.—Frŭŏr, hăbĕŏ, tĕnĕŏ, ōbtĭnĕŏ, pōssĭdĕŏ, ōccŭpŏ, īnvādŏ, căpĭŏ, răpĭŏ. Phr.—Mĭhĭ vīndĭcŏ.

Pōtŏ, ās, āvī, ātūm, ārĕ. *To drink.* Syn.—Bĭbŏ, pērpōtŏ, haūrĭŏ. Phr.—Vīnō īndūlgĕŏ. Ăquām dūcĕrĕ fōntĕ. Fōntĕ sĭtīm rēstīnguĕrĕ.

Pōtŏr, ōrĭs. m. *One who drinks.* Syn.—Pōtātŏr, bĭbāx, bĭbŭlŭs. Phr.—Dēdĭtŭs Bācchō. Vīnō dēvōtŭs. Gaūdēns mĕrō.

Præbĕŏ, ēs, ŭī, ĭtūm, ērĕ. *To furnish.* Mātĕrĭāmquĕ sŭō præbēt sĕgĕs ārĭdă dāmnō. O. Syn.—Pōrrĭgŏ, ōffĕrŏ, ēxhĭbĕŏ, dō, trĭbŭŏ, mĭnīstrŏ, sūppĕdĭtŏ, sūffĭcĭŏ, præstŏ. Sē præbērĕ. *To show oneself.* Syn.—Ōstēndŏ, præstŏ, gĕrŏ, hăbĕŏ.

Præcēdŏ, ĭs, cēssī, cēssūm, ĕrĕ. *To go before.* Syn.—Āntĕcēdŏ, āntĕŏ, prævērtŏ, præcūrrŏ, praĕĕŏ, prægrĕdĭŏr. Phr.—Prævĭŭs ĕŏ. Ĕgŏ prævĭŭs ībŏ. Præquĕ dĭēm vĕnĭēns.

Præcēps, ĭpĭtĭs. adj. *Headforemost, headlong.* Syn.—Prōnŭs, præcĭpĭtāns, præcĭpĭtātŭs, mīssŭs, dēmīssŭs, dējēctŭs, cădēns, cădūcŭs, dēcĭdŭŭs. Phr.—Hīc sē præcĭpĭtēm tēctō dĕdĭt. *Rapidly, hastily.* Syn.—Cĕlĕr, cĭtŭs, cōncĭtŭs, fēstīnŭs, vēlōx.

Præcēptūm, ī. n. *Teaching, precept.* Syn.—Mŏnĭtūm, dōctrīnă, dŏcŭmēntūm. *Order, command.* Syn.—Māndātūm, jūssūm, īmpĕrĭūm, plăcĭtūm, mŏnĭtūm, præscrīptūm.

Præcĭpĭŏ, ĭs, cēpī, ēptūm, ĕrĕ. *To anticipate, to prevent.* Syn.—Praĕōccŭpŏ, ōccŭpŏ, prævĕnĭŏ, prævērtŏ. Phr.—Præcēpĭt mōrs nōstră fŭgām. *To command.* Syn.—Māndŏ, jŭbĕŏ, īmpĕrŏ, īnjūngŏ, ēdīcŏ, præscrībŏ.

Præcĭpĭtāntĕr. adj. *Hastily.* Syn.—Prŏpĕrē, prŏpĕrāntĕr.

Præcĭpĭtŏ, ās, āvī, ātūm, ārĕ. *To hurl down, to precipitate.* Syn.—Dētūrbŏ, ēxtūrbŏ, dējĭcĭŏ, prōjĭcĭŏ, ēxcŭtĭŏ. Phr.—Præcĭpĭtēm (*or*) īn præcēps ăgĕrĕ, ădĭgĕrĕ. Cōrpŭs ēx āltō dētrūdĕrĕ. (*Intrans.*) *To cast oneself down.* Syn.—Cădŏ, cōncĭdŏ, rŭŏ, cōrrŭŏ, prōlābŏr. Phr.—Præcēps ăgŏr. Vōlvĭtŭr īn căpŭt. Sē dărĕ præcĭpĭtēm.

Præcĭpŭē. adj. *Especially, above all.* Syn.—Præsērtīm, īmprīmīs, māxĭmē.

Præcĭpŭŭs, ă, ūm. *Particular, special.* Syn.—Māxĭmŭs, ēxĭmĭŭs, præstāns, īnsīgnĭs, prīmŭs, pŏtīssĭmŭs.

Præclārŭs, ă, ūm. *Famous, illustrious, remarkable.* Syn.—Clārŭs, īnsīgnĭs, cōnspĭcŭŭs, ēxĭmĭŭs, īllūstrĭs, cĕlĕbĕr. *Brilliant.* Syn.—Clārŭs, nĭtĭdŭs, lūcĭdŭs.

Præclūdŏ, ĭs, ūsī, ūsūm, ĕrĕ. *To shut, to close.* Syn.—Ōcclūdŏ, ōbstrŭŏ. *To prevent, to stop.* Syn.—Īmpĕdĭŏ, cŏērcĕŏ, prŏhĭbĕŏ.

Præcōrdĭă, ōrūm. n. *Membrane situated near the heart, consequently by extension, the heart.* Syn.—Vīscĕră, cŏr, pēctŭs.

Præcūrrŏ ĭs, cūrrī, cūrsūm, ĕrĕ. *To run before.* Syn.—Āntĕvŏlŏ, præcĕlĕrŏ.

Prædă, æ. f. *Plunder.* Vīctōrēs prædā spŏlĭīsquĕ pŏtītī. V. Syn.—Ēxŭvĭæ, spŏlĭă. Phr.—Vīctō ēx hōstĕ rĕlātæ. Hōstīlĭs gāză. Ēt prædæ dūcĕrĕ sōrtēm. *Booty, (in general).* Syn.—Răpīnă, răptūm, fūrtūm.

Prædātŏr, ōrĭs. m. *Plunderer, thief.* Syn.—Prædŏ, rāptŏr, fūr.

Prædĭcŏ, ās, āvī, ātūm, ārĕ. *To announce, to make known.* Syn.—Dīcŏ, dēclārŏ, dēnūntĭŏ, prōfĭtĕŏr.

Prædīcŏ, ĭs, īxī, īctūm, ĕrĕ. *To predict, to forewarn.* Syn.—Cănŏ, præcĭnŏ, nūntĭŏ, prænūntĭŏ, aūgŭrŏr, vātĭcĭnŏr, mōnstrŏ, præmōnstrŏ, mŏnĕŏ, præmŏnĕŏ, ōmĭnŏr, pōrtēndŏ. Phr.—Cāsūs ăpĕrīrĕ fŭtūrōs. Fātăquĕ præmŏnŭĭt.

Prædĭtŭs, ă, ūm. *Endowed with, possessed with.* Syn.—Cōmpŏs, ōrnātŭs, dĕcŏrātŭs, īnstrūctŭs, mūnītŭs, pōllēns, præstāns, īllūstrĭs, īnsīgnĭs, cŭmŭlātŭs.

Prædĭūm, ĭī. n. *Farm, estate, manor.* Syn.—Vīllă, fūndŭs, ăgĕr, jūgĕră.

Prædīvĕs, ĭtĭs. adj. *Very rich.* Syn.—Dīvĕs, ŏpŭlēntŭs, dītīssĭmŭs.

Prædŏ, ōnĭs. m. *Pirate, brigand.* Syn.—Lătrŏ, grāssātŏr, prædātŏr, fūr.

Prædŏr, ārĭs, ātŭs sūm, ārī. *To plunder.* Syn.—Dēprædŏr, fūrŏr, răpĭŏ, ērĭpĭŏ, ābrĭpĭŏ, vāstŏ, pŏpŭlŏ, dēpŏpŭlŏr, spŏlĭŏ. Phr.—

Prǣdās ăgŏ. Prǣdăm făcĕrĕ. Spŏlĭīs gaūdērĕ. Vīvĕrĕ rāptō. Āssuēscĕrĕ prǣdǣ.

Prǣfĕrŏ, fērs, tŭlī, lātūm, fērrĕ. *To bring before or in front of.* Syn.—Āntĕfĕrŏ. *To announce, to show.* Syn.—Ōstēndŏ, prǣbĕŏ. *To prefer.* Syn.—Prǣpōnŏ, āntĕpōnŏ.

Prǣfĭcĭŏ, ĭs, fēcī, fēctūm, ĕrĕ. *To place in command.* Syn.—Prǣpōnŏ. Phr.—Īmpĕrĭūm dō, trādŏ. Sēd mē cūm lūcīs Hĕcātē prǣfēcĭt Ăvērnīs. Rĕgēndūm trādŏ.

Prǣlĭūm (Prœlĭūm), ĭī. n. *Battle, combat.* Syn.—Rīxă, cērtāmĕn, pūgnă. *See Bellum.*

Prǣlūm, ī. n. *A press, wine-press.* Vīnăquĕ fūndūntūr prǣlīs ēlīsă Fălērnīs. Pr. Phr.—Cōlăquĕ prǣlōrūm. Călēnō dŏmĭtă prǣlō ūvă.

Prǣmĭūm, ĭī. n. *Prize, reward.* Syn.—Mērcēs, prĕtĭūm, dōnūm, mūnŭs. Phr.—Prĕtĭī mērcēs. Ēxāctī lăbōrĭs hŏnōs. Prǣmĭă jūstă lăbōrūm. Mĕrĭtǣ prǣmĭă pālmǣ. Sūnt hīc ĕtĭām sŭă prǣmĭă laūdī. *Profit, booty.* Syn.—Frūctŭs, lŭcrūm, quēstŭs, prǣdă, rāptūm.

Prǣmŏnĭtŭs, ūs. m. *Warning.* Syn.—Mŏnĭtŭs, mŏnĭtūm, prǣdīctūm.

Prǣpărŏ, ās, āvī, ātūm, ārĕ. *To prepare, to make ready.* Syn.—Părŏ, āppărŏ, cōmpărŏ, īnstrŭŏ, ōrnŏ, ădōrnŏ, ōrdĭnŏ, cōmpōnŏ. Phr.—Āccīngūnt ōmnēs ŏpĕrī. Īllī sē pūgnae āccīngūnt. Rēbūs jām rītĕ părātīs.

Prǣpĕs, ĕtĭs. adj. *Swift of flight.* Prǣpĕtĭbūs pēnnīs aūsūs sē crēdĕrĕ cœlō. V. Syn.—Cĕlĕr, cĭtŭs, cōncĭtŭs, pērnīx, vēlōx.

Prǣpōnŏ, ĭs, ŏsŭī, ŏsĭtūm, ĕrĕ. *To place before, to prefer.* Syn.—Āntĕpōnŏ, prǣfĕrŏ, āntĕfĕrŏ, mālŏ. Phr.—Plūrĭs făcĭŏ. Mājōrĭs pēndŏ. Mĭhĭ sătĭŭs ēst.

Prǣrĭpĭŏ, ĭs, ĭpŭī, ēptūm, ĕrĕ. *To seize first.* Syn.—Praĕōccŭpŏ. *To ravish, to take away.* Syn.—Răpĭŏ, aūfĕrŏ, ōccŭpŏ.

Prǣsāgĭŏ, īs, īvī & ĭī, ītūm, īrĕ. *To predict.* Syn.—Prǣsēntĭŏ, prǣscīscŏ, prǣvĭdĕŏ, aūgŭrŏr, vātĭcĭnŏr. *To indicate in advance.* Syn.—Prǣmōnstrŏ, prǣdīcŏ, prǣmŏnĕŏ.

Prǣsāgĭūm, ĭī. n. *Augury, omen.* Syn.—Aūgŭrĭūm, ōmĕn.

Prǣscrībŏ, ĭs, psī, ptūm, ĕrĕ. *To prefix in writing.* Syn.—Scrībŏ. *To order.* Syn.—Jŭbĕŏ, īmpĕrŏ, prǣcĭpĭŏ, prǣmōnstrŏ, mŏnĕŏ, prǣmŏnĕŏ. *To determine, to regulate.* Syn.—Stătŭŏ, prǣstĭtŭŏ, dēfīnĭŏ, īndīcŏ.

Prǣsēns, ēntĭs. adj. *Present.* Syn.—Ādstāns. *A spectator.* Syn.—Spēctāns, spēctātŏr, tēstĭs, ārbĭtĕr, ādstāns, ādsīstēns, prŏpĭŏr. *Ready.* Syn.—Prōmptŭs, părātŭs. *Favorable.* Syn.—Mĕlĭŏr, făvēns, sĕcūndŭs.

Præsēntĭŏ, īs, sēnsī, sēnsūm, īrĕ. *To feel beforehand, to divine.* Syn.—Præsāgĭŏ, aūgŭrŏr, præscĭŏ, præscīscŏ, prævĭdĕŏ.

Præsĕs, ĭdĭs. m. f. *One who presides, chief.* Syn.—Prīncēps, dūx, tūtŏr, cūstōs.

Præsĭdĕŏ, ēs, ēdī, ērĕ. *To preside.* Syn.—Præsūm, dŏmĭnŏr, īmpĕrŏ. Phr.—Sūm præsĕs.

Præsĭdĭūm, ĭī. n. *Guard, garrison.* Syn.—Cūstōdĭă. Fig.—*Help, protection.* Syn.—Tūtēlă, aūxĭlĭūm, sūbsĭdĭūm.

Præstŏ, ās, ĭtī, ĭtūm, ārĕ. *To be in advance.* Syn.—Āntĕ stō. *To excel. Syn.*—Ēxcēllŏ, præcēllŏ, ēxsŭpĕrŏ, vīncŏ, praĕĕŏ, ānteĕŏ, prævērtŏ. Præstăt (impers). *It is better.* Phr.—Sătĭŭs, pŏtĭŭs, mĕlĭŭs ēst, vĭdētŭr, vīsūm ēst. Măgĭs expĕdĭt, cōnvĕnĭt. *To represent.* Syn.—Ēxhĭbĕŏ, rĕfĕrŏ.

Præsūm, praĕĕs, præfŭī, praĕēssĕ. *To be in charge.* Syn.—Præsĭdĕŏ, īmpĕrŏ.

Prætēndŏ, ĭs, dī, sūm, ĕrĕ. *To stretch, to stretch before.* Syn.—Ōbtēndŏ, prætēntŏ, ōbjĭcĭŏ, ōppōnŏ. Phr.—Mōrtī prætēndĕrĕ mūrōs.

Prætĕr. prep. *Except, beyond.* Syn.—Nĭsĭ, ēxcēptō, ēxcēptā, ūltrā.

Prætĕrĕā. adv. *Furthermore.* Syn.—Deīndĕ, pōsthāc, deīncēps.

Prætĕrĕŏ, īs, īvī & ĭī, ĭtūm, īrĕ. *To pass by.* Syn.—Prætērgrĕdĭŏr, trānsĕŏ, prætērvĕhŏr, prætērlābŏr, flŭŏ, lābŏr, ēlābŏr, ăbĕŏ, fŭgĭŏ. *To omit.* Syn.—Ōmīttŏ, nēglĕgŏ.

Prætēxŏ, ĭs, ŭī, ēxtūm, ĕrĕ. *To cover.* Syn.—Tĕgŏ, īndūcŏ, ōbdūcŏ. Fig.—*To palliate.* Syn.—Prætēndŏ, cēlŏ, caūsŏr, tĕgŏ.

Prævĕnĭŏ, īs, vēnī, vēntūm, īrĕ. *To come before.* Syn.—Prævērtŏ, prægrĕdĭŏr, ōccŭpŏ, praĕĕŏ, præcūrrŏ.

Prævērtŏ, ĭs, tī, sūm, ĕrĕ. *To advance before.* Cūrsūquĕ pĕdūm prævērtĕrĕ vēntōs. V. Syn.—Præcūrrŏ, praĕĕŏ, ānteĕŏ, prævĕnĭŏ. *To anticipate.* Syn.—Praĕōccŭpŏ, ōccŭpŏ, præcĭpĭŏ.

Prævĭdĕŏ, ēs, vīdī, vīsūm, ērĕ. *To foresee.* Cūnctăquĕ mēns ŏcŭlīs prævĭdĕt īllă sŭīs. O. Syn.—Āntĕvĭdĕŏ, prōspĭcĭŏ, præsēntĭŏ, præsāgĭŏ, prænōscŏ, præscĭŏ, præscīscŏ, aūgŭrŏ, aūgŭrŏr.

Prāndĕŏ, ēs, dī, sūm, ērĕ. *To dine.* Syn.—Cœnŏ, cōnvīvŏr, ĕdŏ.

Prātūm, ī. n. *Meadow.* Rīpārūmquĕ tŏrōs ēt prātă rĕcēntĭă rīvīs. V. Phr.—Prātēnsĕ vĭrētūm. Vĭrĭdāntĭă prātī Jūgĕră. Flōrĭdă rūră. Fūlgēns cŏlōrĕ. Vērĕ nŏvō rīdēns. Fūlgēns vĭrĭdāntĕ cŏlōrĕ. Āprīcī grāmĭnă cāmpī.

Prāvē. adv. *Wrongly, badly.* Syn.—Mălĕ, pērvērsē, pērpĕrām.

Prāvŭs, ă, ūm. *Ill-shapen, twisted.* Syn.—Dīstōrtŭs, pērvērsŭs. *Mean, vicious.* Syn.—Mălŭs, īmprŏbŭs, pērvērsŭs, scĕlĕrātŭs.

Prĕcēs, cūm. f. *Prayers.* Cōncĭpĭt īllă prĕcēs ēt vērbă prĕcāntĭă dīcĭt. O. Syn.—Prĕcātŭs, vōtă. Phr.—Vērbă rŏgāntĭă sūpplĭcĭă. Vērbă prĕcāntĭs. Sūpplēx vōtūm. Prĕcūm vīs. Dĕūm plācāntēs. Aūdĭŏ vōtă. Ōrāntī făvĕŏ. Ōrāntī bĕnīgnŭs. Prĕcĭbŭs mŏvĕŏr. Vōtă rătă făcĭŏ. Aūdītĕ prĕcēs ēt vōtă prĕcāntūm. Prĕcēs spērnŏ, rĕpēllŏ, rēspŭŏ. Vōtă rŏgāntĭs spērnĕrĕ. Nēglĕgĭt aūrĕ prĕcēs.

Prĕcŏr, ārĭs, ātŭs sūm, ārī. *To pray.* Sæpĕ prĕcōr mōrtēm, mōrtēm quŏquĕ dēprĕcŏr īdēm. O. Syn.—Ōrŏ, ōbtēstŏr, ōbsĕcrŏ, rŏgŏ, īmplōrŏ, īnvŏcŏ, pōscŏ, ēxpōscŏ, dēprĕcŏr, flāgĭtŏ, ēfflāgĭtŏ, quærŏ, pōstŭlŏ. Phr.—Sūpplēx pĕtŏ. Vōcĕ prĕcŏr. Prĕcĭbŭs pōscŏ. Prĕcēs fūndŏ. Aūxĭlĭō vŏcŏ. Dŭplĭcēs tēndīt sūpplēx ād sīdĕră pālmās. Sīc vōcĕ prĕcātŭr. Sŏlĭtā prĕcĕ nūmĕn ădōrăt.

Prĕhēndŏ (Prēndŏ), ĭs, dī, sūm, ĕrĕ. *To take, to seize.* Syn.—Căpĭŏ, cōmprĕhēndŏ, āpprĕhēndŏ, ārrĭpĭŏ, cōrrĭpĭŏ, āssĕquŏr.

Prĕmŏ, ĭs, prēssī, prēssūm, ĕrĕ. *To press, to bear down upon.* Syn.—Prēssŏ, ŏnĕrŏ, cōmprĭmŏ, grăvŏ. *To press hard in pursuit, to pursue.* Syn.—Ūrgĕŏ, ăgŏ, ăgĭtŏ, ēxērcĕŏ, pērsĕquŏr, īnsĕquŏr, īnstŏ. *To overwhelm.* Syn.—Ūrgĕŏ, ōbrŭŏ, ōpprĭmŏ, vēxŏ. *To hold back.* Syn.—Tĕnĕŏ, cōntĭnĕŏ, cōmprĭmŏ, rĕprĭmŏ, sīstŏ.

Prĕtĭūm, ĭī. n. *Price, value.* Syn.—Præmĭūm. *Money, riches.* Syn.—Aūrūm, dīvĭtĭæ, pĕcūnĭă. *Chastisement, punishment.* Syn.—Mērcēs, præmĭūm, pœnă.

Prīdēm. adv. *For a long time.* Syn.—Dūdūm, jām. Phr.—Jām prīdēm, jām dūdūm.

Prīmævŭs, ă, ūm. *Young.* Syn.—Jŭvĕnīlĭs, jŭvĕnĭs. Phr.—Prīmævō flōrĕ jŭvēntūs.

Prīmĭtĭæ, ārūm. f. *First fruits.* Phr.—Prīmă dōnă, mūnĕră. *The beginning.* Syn.—Prīmōrdĭă, ēxōrdĭă, ēxōrsă.

Prīmōrdĭūm, ĭī. n. *Beginning.* Syn.—Ēxōrdĭūm, prīncĭpĭūm, ēxōrsă, ŏrīgŏ.

Prīmōrēs, ūm. m. *The chief men of the state.* Syn.—Prīmī, prŏcĕrēs.

Prīmŭs, ă, ūm. *First.* Syn.—Prĭŏr, prīncēps, prīmŏr. *Ancestors.* Syn.—Prīmī, āntīquī, vĕtĕrēs. *Prince, chief.* Syn.—Prīncēps, præcĭpŭŭs, ōptĭmŭs, prŏcĕrēs (pl.).

Prīncēps, ĭpĭs. m. *Chief, head, prince.* Syn.—Prīmŭs, præcĭpŭŭs, dūx, præsĕs, rēx.

Prīncĭpĭūm, ĭī. n. *Beginning.* Āb Jŏvĕ prīncĭpĭūm, Mūsæ: Jŏvīs ōmnĭă plēnă. V. Syn.—Ĭnĭtĭūm, prīmōrdĭūm, ŏrīgŏ, fōns, căpŭt, aūctŏr, caūsă.

Prĭŏr, ŭs, ōrĭs. *First.* Syn.—Prīmŭs, prīstĭnŭs, prīscŭs, vĕtŭs, āntīquŭs, prætĕrĭtŭs. *The more distinguished.* Syn.—Mĕlĭŏr, præstāntĭŏr.

Prīscŭs, ă, ūm. *Old.* Syn.—Āntīquŭs, vĕtŭs, vĕtūstŭs. *First.* Syn.—Prĭŏr, prīstĭnŭs, prīmŭs.

Prĭŭs. adv. *Before, rather.* Syn.—Āntĕ, cĭtĭŭs, pŏtĭŭs, măgĭs. *Formerly.* Syn.—Āntĕ, āntĕā, quōndām, ōlīm.

Prīvātŭs, ă, ūm. *Private.* Syn.—Prīvŭs, prŏprĭŭs.

Prīvŏ, ās, āvī, ātūm, ārĕ. *To despoil.* Syn.—Spŏlĭŏ, ēxspŏlĭŏ, ŏrbŏ, fraūdŏ, nūdŏ, dēnūdŏ, ērĭpĭŏ, aūfĕrŏ, ădĭmŏ, tōllŏ.

Prō. prep. *For the sake of.* Syn.—Caūsā, ērgŏ. *In the place of.* Syn.—Lŏcō, vĭcĕ. *According to.* Syn.—Ēx, ăd, sĕcūndūm. *Before.* Syn.—Āntĕ.

Prŏbē. adv. *Honestly, rightly, well.* Syn.—Bĕnĕ, rēctē, pūlchrē, ēgrĕgĭē. *Completely, wholly.* Syn.—Plānē, ōmnīnō, prōrsŭs.

Prŏbĭtās, ātĭs. f. *Honesty, probity.* Prŏbĭtās laūdātŭr ĕt ālgĕt. J. Syn.—Bŏnĭtās, pĭĕtās, vīrtūs, fĭdēs, cāstĭtās. Phr.—Tĕnĕrō mātūrĭŏr ævō. Ādvērsīs ēxērcĭtă rēbŭs.

Prŏbŏ, ās, āvī, ātūm, ārĕ. *To prove.* Syn.—Dēmōnstrŏ, cōnfīrmŏ, mōnstrŏ, ōstēndŏ, ārgŭŏ. *To approve.* Syn.—Āpprŏbŏ, cōmprŏbŏ, laūdŏ, āssēntĭŏr.

Prŏbrōsŭs, ă, ūm. *Shameful, disgraceful.* Syn.—Pŭdēndŭs, ĭnhŏnēstŭs, īgnōmĭnĭōsŭs, tūrpĭs, īnfāmĭs.

Prŏbrūm, ī. n. *Disgrace, dishonor.* Vĕtĭtō tĕmĕrāt sācrārĭă prōbrō. O. Syn.—Ōpprŏbrĭūm, īnfāmĭă, dēdĕcŭs, īgnōmĭnĭă. *Insult, outrage.* Syn.—Cōnvīcĭă, ōpprŏbrĭă, mălĕdīctă.

Prŏbŭs, ă, ūm. *Honest, upright.* Syn.—Bŏnŭs, pĭŭs, īnnŏcēns, jūstŭs, æquŭs, hŏnēstŭs, sānctŭs, īntĕgĕr, frūgī. Phr.—Prŏbāmquĕ Paūpĕrĭēm sĭnĕ dōtĕ quærŏ.

Prŏcācĭtās, ātĭs. f. *Impudence, insolence.* Syn.—Prŏtērvĭă, pĕtŭlāntĭă, aūdācĭă. *Wantonness, licentiousness.* Syn.—Īmprŏbĭtās, nēquĭtĭă, pĕtŭlāntĭă, lāscīvĭă.

Prŏcācĭtĕr. adv. *Wantonly.* Syn.—Prŏtērvē, pĕtŭlāntĕr, lāscīvē.

Prŏcāx, ācĭs. adj. *Forward, insolent, bold.* Syn.—Prŏtērvŭs, aūdāx, lāscīvŭs. *Immodest, impure.* Syn.—Īmpŭdīcŭs.

Prōcēdŏ, ĭs, cēssī, cēssūm, ĕrĕ. *To advance.* Syn.—Prōgrĕdĭŏr. *To appear.* Syn.—Āppārĕŏ. *To be useful.* Syn.—Jŭvāt, prōsūm.

Prŏcēllă, æ. f. *Storm, tempest.* Ēffŭgĭt hībērnās dēmīssa āntēnnă prŏcēllās. O. Syn.—Tēmpēstās, hĭēms, tūrbŏ, nīmbŭs, īmbĕr. Phr.—Strīdēns Ȧquĭlōnĭbŭs prŏcēllă. Sălĭūnt īn vēlă prŏcēllæ.

Prŏcēllōsŭs, ă, ūm. *Stormy.* Syn.—Nīmbōsŭs, vēntōsŭs, hībērnŭs, tūrbātŭs, ăgĭtātŭs. Phr.—Prŏcēllīs plēnŭs, crēbĕr, frĕquēns. *Raging.* Syn.—Fŭrēns, īnsānŭs, præcēps.

Prŏcĕrēs, ūm. m. *The chief men, nobles.* Syn.—Prīmī, prīmōrēs, prīncĭpēs, dŭcēs, præcĭpŭī, lēctī, dēlēctī. Phr.—Prŏcĕrūm mănŭs, tūrbă. Ūrbĭs dūctōrēs. Māgnănĭmī dŭcēs. Dĕcŭs ūrbĭs. Flōs pŏpŭlī. Dŭcūm gĕnĕrōsă cŏhōrs, īllūstrĭs cōnsēssŭs. Cāstrōrūm prŏcĕrēs. Rērūm prŏcĕrēs.

Prōcērŭs, ă, ūm. *Lofty, high.* Sōlō prōcērās ērĭgĭt ālnōs. V. Syn.—Māgnŭs, āltŭs, ēxcēlsŭs, īngēns, ārdŭŭs, sūblīmĭs. Phr.—Īngēntī cōrpŏrĕ. Ērēctŭs ĭn aūrās. Ēt tōtō vērtĭcĕ sūpra ēst. Lōngā prōcērĭŏr ālnō.

Prōcĭdŏ, ĭs, ī, ĕrĕ. *To fall.* Syn.—Cădŏ, prōcūmbŏ, prōlābŏr.

Prōcĭdŭŭs, ă, ūm. *About to fall, falling.* Syn.—Cădūcŭs, cădēns, lābēns, lāpsŭs, prōlāpsŭs.

Prōclāmŏ, ās, āvī, ātūm, ārĕ. *To proclaim.* Ādjŭvăt ēt māgnā prōclāmăt vōcĕ Dĭōrēs. V. Syn.—Clāmŏ, prædĭcŏ (ās), dēclārŏ, nūntĭŏ.

Prōclīvĭs, ĭs, ĕ. *Bending, leaning.* Syn.—Ācclīvĭs, dēclīvĭs, prōnŭs, præcēps. *Inclined towards, prone to.* Syn.—Īnclīnātŭs, prōpēnsŭs, prōnŭs.

Prōcrāstĭnŏ, ās, āvī, ātūm, ārĕ. *To put off, to delay.* Sēd prŏpĕrā, nēc tē vēntūras dīffĕr ĭn hōrās. O. Syn.—Dīffĕrŏ, cūnctŏr, tārdŏ, mŏrŏr.

Prōcrĕŏ, ās, āvī, ātūm, ārĕ. *To bring forth, to produce.* Syn.—Gĕnĕrŏ, gīgnŏ, prōdūcŏ, părĭŏ.

Prōcŭbŏ, ās, ŭī, ĭtūm, ārĕ. *To lie down.* Prōcŭbŭīt, săcrāmquĕ dĕdīt pēr mēmbră quĭētēm. V. Syn.—Īncūmbŏ, īncŭbŏ, prōcūmbŏ. *To hang over.* Syn.—Īmmĭnĕŏ.

Prōcūdŏ, ĭs, dī, sūm, ĕrĕ. *To forge.* Nōn īră quæ prōcūdĭt ēnsēs. H. Syn.—Cūdŏ, ēxcūdŏ. Phr.—Fērrūm īgnĕ mōllīrĕ, rĕcōquĕrĕ. Tēlă nŏvānt.

Prŏcŭl. adv. *Afar, far off.* Syn.—Lōngē, lōngĭŭs, rĕmōtē. Phr.—Prŏcŭl ēstĕ, prŏfānī. Prŏcŭl dīscōrdĭbŭs ārmīs. Sīnt prŏcŭl ā nōbīs.

Prōcūlcŏ, ās, āvī, ātūm, ārĕ. *To trample underfoot.* Syn.—Cālcŏ, cōncūlcŏ, prōtĕrŏ. Fig.—*To despise.* Syn.—Cōntēmnŏ.

Prōcūmbŏ, ĭs, ŭbŭī, ŭbĭtūm, ĕrĕ. *To fall.* Syn.—Cădŏ, dēcĭdŏ, prōcĭdŏ, prōstērnŏr, lābŏr, rŭŏ, cōrrŭŏ. *To fall in ruins.* Syn.—

Cōrrŭŏ, rŭŏ, prōlābŏr. Phr.—Pōndĕrĕ tūrrĭs Prōcŭbŭ t sŭbĭtō. *To perish, to die.* Syn.—Pĕrĕŏ, cădŏ. *To lie down.* Syn.— Cŭbŏ, jăcĕŏ.

Prŏcūrŏ, ās, āvī, ātūm, ārĕ. *To care for.* Lætī bĕnĕ gēstīs cōrpŏră rēbŭs Prōcūrātĕ, vĭrī. V. *To purify, to expiate.* Syn.—Pĭŏ, ēxpĭŏ.

Prōcūrsŭs, ūs. m. *Course.* Syn.—Cūrsŭs, īmpĕtŭs.

Prōdĕŏ, īs, īvī, ĭtūm, īrĕ. *To advance.* Īllæ tāntūm prōdīrĕ vŏlāndō. V. Syn.—Prōcēdŏ, prōgrĕdĭŏr. *To go out, to appear.* Syn.— Ĕŏ, ēxĕŏ, prōcēdŏ. *To be shown.* Syn.—Āppārĕŏ, ŏrĭŏr, ēdŏr.

Prōdēst. impers. *It helps, it serves.* Syn.—Jŭvăt, ūtĭlĕ ēst.

Prōdĭgĭum, ĭī. n. *Prodigy.* Prōdĭgĭīs āctī cœlēstĭbŭs ōssă pĭābūnt. V. Syn.—Monstrum, pŏrtēntūm, mīrācŭlă. *Monster.* Syn.— Mōnstrūm.

Prōdĭgŭs, ă, ūm. *Lavish, prodigal.* Syn.—Prŏfūsŭs, ēffūsŭs, lūxŭrĭōsŭs, pērdĭtŭs. *Generous.* Syn.—Lārgŭs. Phr.—Prōdĭgŭs ærĭs. Prōdĭgă mēns.

Prōdĭtĭŏ, ōnĭs. f. *Treason.* Syn.—Dŏlŭs, fraūs, pērfĭdĭă.

Prōdŏ, ĭs, dĭdī, dĭtūm, ĕrĕ. *To bring forth to light.* Syn.—Ăpĕrĭŏ, pāndŏ, ōstēndŏ, dētĕgŏ, ēxsĕrŏ, ēdūcŏ, prōfĕrŏ, ārgŭŏ. *To betray.* Syn.—Fāllŏ, dēcĭpĭŏ. *To deliver up.* Syn.—Trādŏ, dēdŏ, prōjĭcĭŏ. Phr.—Ūnĭŭs ŏb īrām Prōdĭmŭr. *To abandon, to desert.* Syn.—Dēsĕrŏ, rēlīnquŏ, dēstĭtŭŏ.

Prōdūcŏ, ĭs, ūxī, ūctūm, ĕrĕ. *To conduct outside.* Syn.—Ēdūcŏ, prōmŏvĕŏ, ēffĕrŏ. *To accompany.* Syn.—Dēdūcŏ, sĕquŏr, cŏmĭtŏr. *To beget.* Syn.— Gīgnŏ, ēdūcŏ. *To prolong.* Syn.—Prōtrăhŏ, trăhŏ.

Prŏfānŏ, ās, āvī, ātūm, ārĕ. *To profane, to pollute.* Syn.—Vĭŏlŏ, pōllŭŏ, tĕmĕrŏ, īncēstŏ.

Prŏfānŭs, ă, ūm. *Profane.* Syn.—Īmpĭŭs, nĕfāndŭs. *Impious.* Syn.—Īmpĭŭs, scĕlĕrātŭs, nĕfāndŭs.

Prŏfēctŭs, ūs. m. *Advantage, success.* Syn.—Ēffēctŭs, ūtĭlĭtās.

Prŏfĕrŏ, fērs, tŭlī, lātūm, fērrĕ. *To carry ahead.* Syn.—Āffĕrŏ, dūcŏ, prōmŏvĕŏ. Phr.—Prōfērrĕ pĕdēm. *To produce, to make appear.* Syn.—Ēffĕrŏ, ēdūcŏ, prōmŏ, ēxsĕrŏ, ēxprōmŏ, ēdŏ. *To generate.* Syn.—Ēffĕrŏ, ēdūcŏ, gīgnŏ, prōcrĕŏ. *To defer.* Syn.—Prōdūcŏ, dĭffĕrŏ, prōrŏgŏ, prōcrāstĭnŏ.

Prŏfĭcĭŏ, ĭs, fēcī, fēctūm, ĕrĕ. *To profit, to serve.* Vērbă mĭsēr frūstrā nōn prōfĭcĭēntĭă pērdŏ. O. Syn.—Prōsum, prōcēdŏ, sŭccēdŏ. *To make progress.* Syn.—Prōgrĕdĭŏr, prōcēdŏ.

Prŏfĭcīscŏr, ĕrĭs, fēctŭs sūm, ī. *To set out.* Syn.—Ĕŏ, ăbĕŏ, prōdĕŏ, dīscēdŏ, vādŏ, tēndŏ, cōntēndŏ. Phr.—Vĭăm, ĭtĕr tēntŏ, cōrrĭpĭŏ, cārpŏ. Grēssūs dīrĭgŏ. Ĭtĕr īncĭpĭŏ. Pōrtīs sēse ēxstŭlĭt. Mēque ēxtrā tēctă fĕrēbām. Ō quŏtĭēs īngrēssŭs ĭtĕr.

Prŏfĭtĕŏr, ērĭs, fēssŭs sūm, ērī. *To avow, to declare.* Syn.—Fătĕŏr, cōnfĭtĕŏr, dēclārŏ. *To reveal, to show.* Syn.—Prōdŏ, ārgŭŏ, dēclārŏ, īndĭcŏ. Phr.—Dūcēm prŏfĭtētūr ĭn ārmīs.

Prōflīgŏ, ās, āvī, ātūm, ārĕ. *To cast down, to overwhelm.* Syn.—Āfflīgŏ, stērnŏ, prōstērnŏ, dējĭcĭŏ, cædŏ, cōncīdŏ, dīssĭpŏ, fūndŏ, vīncŏ, dŏmŏ.

Prōflŭŏ, ĭs, ūxī, ūxūm, ĕrĕ. *To flow.* Īn mĕdĭūm seū stābĭt ĭnērs, seū prōflŭĭt hūmŏr. V. Syn.—Flŭŏ, dēflŭŏ, ēfflŭŏ, lābŏr, dēlābŏr, mānŏ, prōmānŏ, cūrrŏ, dēcūrrŏ, fĕrŏr.

Prŏfŭgŭs, ī. m. *Exile, fugitive.* Syn.—Fŭgĭtīvŭs, fŭgĭēns, ēxsŭl.

Prŏfūndŏ, ĭs, fūdī, fūsūm, ĕrĕ. *To pour out.* Syn.—Fūndŏ, ēffūndŏ. *To dissipate.* Syn.—Dīssĭpŏ, ēffūndŏ, prōdĭgŏ.

Prŏfūndŭs, ă, m. *Deep, profound.* Syn.—Āltŭs, dēprēssŭs, īmŭs.

Prōgĕnĭēs, ēī. f. *Progeny, lineage.* Syn.—Prōlēs, sŏbŏlēs, gĕnŭs, stīrps, prŏpāgŏ.

Prŏgnē, ēs. f. *A swallow.* (*See Appendix under list of Birds.*)

Prŏhĭbĕŏ, ēs, ŭī, ĭtūm, ērĕ. *To prevent.* Syn.—Īmpĕdĭŏ, ōbstŏ, ĭnhĭbĕŏ, āmŏvĕŏ, rĕmŏvĕŏ, sūbmŏvĕŏ, ārcĕŏ, rĕpēllŏ. Phr.—Hōspĭtĭō prŏhĭbēmŭr ărēnæ. Prŏhĭbēntĕ Dĕō.

Prŏīn, Prŏīndĕ, Proīndĕ. adv. *Then.* Syn.—Ĭdĕō, ērgō, prōptĕrĕā.

Prōjĭcĭŏ, ĭs, jēcī, pēctūm, ĕrĕ. *To throw ahead.* Syn.—Jăcĭŏ, jăcŭlŏr. *To reject.* Syn.—Ābjĭcĭŏ, rĕjĭcĭŏ, mīttŏ, ŏmīttŏ. *To lie down.* Syn.—Stērnŏ.

Prōlābŏr, ĕrĭs, psŭs sūm, ī. *To fall.* Syn.—Cădŏ, prōcĭdŏ, rŭŏ, lābŏr.

Prōlātŏ, ās, āvī, ātūm, ārĕ. *To prolong.* Syn.—Prōdūcŏ, prōfĕrŏ, ēxtēndŏ. Phr.—Mūtābĭlĭs hōræ Prōlātārĕ dĭēm.

Prōlēctŏ, ās, āvī, ātūm, ārĕ. *To allure by flattery.* Syn.—Āllĭcĭŏ, pēllĭcĭŏ.

Prōlēs, ĭs. f. *Race, lineage.* Hīc gĕnŭs āntīquūm Teūcrī, pūlchērrĭmă prōlēs. V. Syn.—Prōgĕnĭēs, stīrps, gĕnŭs, prŏpāgŏ, sŏbŏlēs. *Child.* Syn.—Prōgĕnĭēs, sŏbŏlēs, fīlĭŭs, fīlĭă, nātŭs, nātă, nātī, pŭĕr, lībĕrī. Phr.—Pūlchrā făcĭāt. . . .prōlĕ părēntēm. Īgnāră părēntĭs.

Prōlīxŭs, ă, ūm. *Long, extended.* Squālĭdă prōlīxīs quī tĕgĭt ōră cŏmīs. O. Syn.—Lōngŭs, prōmīssŭs, prōlātŭs. *Generous.* Syn.—Lībĕrālĭs, lārgŭs, prōdĭgŭs.

Prōlŭŏ, ĭs, ŭī, ūtūm, ĕrĕ. *To inundate, to water well.* Plēnō sē prōlŭĭt aūrō. V. Syn.—Lăvŏ, āblŭŏ, hūmēctŏ, īrrĭgŏ. *To roll or drag along in its course.* Syn.—Ābrĭpĭŏ, vōlvŏ.

Prōmĭnĕō, ēs, ŭī, ērĕ. *To advance.* Prōmĭnĕt īn pōntūm cŭnĕātŭs ăcūmĭnĕ lōngō Cōllĭs. O. Syn.—Prōcūrrŏ, ēxcūrrŏ, ēxstŏ, prōpēndĕŏ.

Prōmīscŭŭs, ă, ūm. *Mixed, promiscuous.* Syn.—Cōnfūsŭs, mīxtŭs, īndīscrētŭs.

Prōmīssūm, ī. n. *Promise.* Mūnĕră prōmīssīs ūbĕrĭōră fĕrēs. O. Syn.—Pōllĭcĭtūm, prōmīssĭō. Phr.—Rēs prōmīssă. Dătă, prōmīssă fĭdēs. Fœdĕră līnguæ. Pīgnŏră pōllĭcĭtī. Mūltă fĭdēm prōmīssă lĕvānt. Prōmīssīs stō, mănĕō. Fĭdēm, prōmīssūm sērvārĕ. Prōmīssă īmplĕō, dō, pērfĭcĭō. Pāctă sērvŏ. Rēddĕ fĭdēm.

Prōmīttŏ, ĭs, mīsī, mīssūm, ĕrĕ. *To send on ahead.* Syn.—Mīttŏ, māndŏ. *To promise.* Syn.—Pōllĭcĕŏr, pōllĭcĭtŏr, spōndĕŏ, āssĕrŏ, āffīrmŏ, prŏfĭtĕŏr. Phr.—Fĭdēm, prōmīssūm dō, præbĕŏ.

Prōmŏ, ĭs, psī, ptūm, ĕrĕ. *To bring forth.* Flāvăquĕ dē rūbrō prōmĕrĕ mēllă cădō. M. Syn.—Dēprōmŏ, ēxprōmŏ, ēdūcŏ, ēxtrăhŏ, ēffĕrŏ, prōfĕrŏ, prōtrăhŏ, prōdūcŏ, ēdŏ, ēxpĕdĭŏ, ēxsĕrŏ. Phr.—Lætīquĕ căvō sē rōbŏrĕ prōmūnt. Gĕmĭtūs dē pēctŏrĕ prōmĭt. Dīgnă gĕrī prōmēs īn scēnām. *To publish.* Syn.—Ēdŏ, vūlgŏ, prōfĕrŏ. *To explain.* Syn.—Ēxplĭcŏ, ēxpōnŏ.

Prōmōntōrĭūm, ĭī. n. *Promontory.* Īndĕ lĕgĭt Căprĕās prōmōntōrĭūmquĕ Mĭnērvæ. O. Phr.—Prōcūrrēntēs, prōjēctī scŏpŭlī. Prōcūrrēntĭă sāxă. Prōjēctăquĕ sāxă. Rūpēs vāstūm quæ prōcēdĭt ĭn æquŏr. Ēxpōstăquĕ pōntō.

Prōmŏvĕō, ēs, mōvī, mōtūm, ērĕ. *To move forward, to cause to advance.* Syn.—Prōvĕhŏ, mŏvĕŏ, īmpēllŏ, ăgŏ. *To put, to send forth.* Syn.—Ēffĕrŏ, prōfĕrŏ, ēdūcŏ, prōdūcŏ, prōmŏ. *To extend, to develop.* Syn.—Prōvĕhŏ, ēxtēndŏ, prŏpāgŏ, aūgĕŏ.

Prōmptŭs, ă, ūm. *Ready, resolved.* Syn.—Ălăcĕr, părātŭs, ēxpĕdītŭs, strēnŭŭs. Phr.—Prōmptŭs ăd ārmă. Īn fērrūm răbĭēs prōmptīssĭmă. *Quick.* Syn.—Cĕlĕr.

Prōmptŭs, ūs. m. (*Used only in the ablative, in the phrase* Īn prōmptū.) *Ready, on the spot.* Syn.—Præstō, prōmptūm, făcĭlĕ. Phr.—Īn mănū, ăd mănūm.

Prōmūlgŏ, ās, āvī, ātūm, ārĕ. *To make known, to promulgate.* Syn.—Vūlgŏ, prōvūlgŏ, ēdīcŏ. Phr.—Præcōnīs vōcī cōmmīttŏ. Vōcĕ præcōnĭs ēdīcŏ. Pălām făcĕrĕ, rĕfērrĕ.

Prōnūntĭŏ, ās, āvī, ātūm, ārĕ. *To pronounce, to recite.* Syn.—Prōfĕrŏ, ēffĕrŏ, dīcŏ. *To announce publicly.* Syn.—Nūntĭŏ.

Prōnŭs, ă, ūm. *Bent, inclined forward.* Ūt prōnă jŭgō lævum īncūmbēbăt ăd āmnēm. V. Syn.—Pēndēns, præcēps, cērnŭŭs, īnclīnātŭs. Phr.—Aūrīgæ pēndēnt īn vērbĕră prōnī. *Falling.* Syn.—Cădēns, cădūcŭs. *Sloping.* Syn.—Dēclīvĭs, præcēps. *Yielding.* Syn.—Făcĭlĭs, făvēns, bĕnīgnŭs.

Prŏpāgŏ, ās, āvī, ātūm, ārĕ. *To propagate.* Syn.—Mūltĭplĭcŏ, prōcrĕŏ, prōdūcŏ. *To extend, to multiply.* Syn.—Prōdūcŏ, prōfĕrŏ, prōlātŏ, ēxtēndŏ, aūgĕŏ, prōtēndŏ, āmplĭfĭcŏ.

Prŏpāgŏ, ĭnĭs. f. *Race, lineage.* Sīt Rōmānă pŏtēns Ĭtălā vīrtūtĕ prŏpāgŏ. V. Syn.—Gĕnŭs, stīrps, prōlēs, prōgĕnĭēs, sŏbŏlēs. *Of animals.* Syn.—Prōlēs, pūllī, cătŭlī.

Prŏpĕ. prep. *Near, close at hand.* Syn.—Jūxtā, prōptĕr, ăd, sĕcūndūm. adv. Syn.—Fĕrē, pēnĕ, fērmē, prŏpĕmŏdūm.

Prōpēllŏ, ĭs, pŭlī, pūlsūm, ĕrĕ. *To push before.* Hānc ăgĭte, Ō sŏcĭī, prōpēllĭte ĭn æquŏră nāvēm. Pr. Syn.—Pēllŏ, prōpūlsŏ, ārcĕŏ.

Prŏpĕrŏ, ās, āvī, ātūm, ārĕ. *To hasten.* Quōd sī fōrtĕ tĭbī prŏpĕrārēnt fātă quĭētēm. Pr. Syn.—Cĕlĕrŏ, āccĕlĕrŏ, mātūrŏ, āpprŏpĕrŏ, fēstīnŏ.

Prŏphētă, æ. m. *Prophet.* Syn.—Vātēs. Phr.—Dĕī īntērprĕs. Fŭtūrī dōctŭs. Fŭtūră pāndēns. Cuī mēns dīvīnō cōncĭtă mōtū.

Prŏpīnquŏ, ās, āvī, ātūm, ārĕ. *To approach.* Jāmquĕ prŏpīnquābānt cāstrīs, mūrōsquĕ sŭbībānt. V. Syn.—Āccēdŏ, āpprŏpīnquŏ, ādstŏ, īnstŏ, ādvēntŏ. Phr.—Prŏpĭŏr fīŏ, ādsūm. Prŏpĭŭs āccēdŏ. Haūd prŏcŭl ādsūm.

Prŏpīnquŭs, ă, ūm. *Near, close to.* Syn.—Prŏpĭŏr, prōxĭmŭs, vīcīnŭs, fīnĭtĭmŭs. *Related to.* Syn.—Cōnsānguĭnĕŭs, āffīnĭs.

Prŏpĭtĭŭs, ă, ūm. *Propitious, favorable.* Syn.—Āmīcŭs, bĕnīgnŭs, clēmēns, dēxtĕr, făcĭlĭs, făvēns, mītĭs, sĕcūndŭs, ŏpĭfĕr.

Prōpōnŏ, ĭs, pŏsŭī, ĭtūm, ĕrĕ. *To set before one's eyes.* Syn.—Ēxpōnŏ, ōbjĭcĭŏ, prōfĕrŏ, ōstēndŏ. Phr.—Ŏcŭlīs sūbjĭcĭŏ, ōffĕrŏ. *To offer.* Syn.—Ōffĕrŏ, prōmīttŏ. *To propose.* Syn.—Stătŭŏ, cōnstĭtŭŏ, dēcērnŏ.

Prōpŏsĭtūm, ī. n. *Resolution, design.* Syn.—Cōnsĭlĭūm, mēns, sēntēntĭă, vŏlūntās, cœptūm, īncœptūm. Phr.—Prōpŏsĭtīquĕ tĕnāx.

Prŏprĭŭs, ă, ūm. *One's own.* Syn.—Sŭŭs, mĕŭs, tŭŭs, pĕcūlĭārĭs. *Stable, firm.* Syn.—Pērpĕtŭŭs, mānsūrŭs, fīrmŭs, stăbĭlĭs, cērtŭs.

Prōptĕr. prep. *Near.* Syn.—Prŏpĕ, jūxtā. *On account of.* Syn.—Præ, ŏb, caūsā, ērgō.

Prōptĕrĕā. adv. *Therefore.* Syn.—Ĭdĕō, īdcīrcō, īndĕ, quārē, quāprōptĕr.

Prōpūgnācŭlūm, ī. n. *Fortification, defense.* Syn.—Mūnīmĕn, mūnīmēntūm, mūrī, mœnĭă, præsĭdĭūm, ārx, āggĕr, tūrrĭs, vāllūm, fōssæ. Phr.—Claūsī mūnīmĭnă vāllī. Cāstră cīrcūmdătă vāllō. Sērvābānt ăggĕrĕ mūrōs.

Prōpūgnŏ, ās, āvī, ātūm, ārĕ. *To fight for, to defend.* Syn.—Tŭĕŏr, tūtŏr, dēfēndŏ, prōtĕgŏ.

Prōră, æ. f. *Prow of a vessel.* Vēlă lĕgūnt sŏcĭi ĕt prōrās ăd līttŏră tōrquēnt. V. Syn.—Aēs, rōstrūm. Phr.—Stĕtĕrānt ăd līttŏră prōræ. Dūm prōram ăd sāxă sŭbūrgĕt. Ānchŏră dē prōrā jăcĭtŭr. Vērtĕrĕ prōrās.

Prōrŏgŏ, ās, āvī, ātūm, ārĕ. *To prolong.* Syn.—Prōdūcŏ, prōtrăhŏ, prōfĕrŏ, ēxtēndŏ. Phr.—Prōrŏgăt ævūm. *To defer.* Syn.—Dīffĕrŏ, prōcrāstĭnŏ.

Prōrūmpŏ, ĭs, rūpī, rūptūm, ĕrĕ. *To burst forth with violence.* Tōtō prōrūmpĭt cōrpŏrĕ sūdŏr. V. Syn.—Ērūmpŏ, rŭŏ, ēxsĭlĭŏ, prōsĭlĭŏ. *To enter by force.* Syn.—Īrrūmpŏ, īnvādŏ, īrrŭŏ. *To eject violently.* Syn.—Ēmīttŏ, ējēctŏ, prōrŭŏ, ērūctŏ, ēvŏmŏ.

Prōsă, æ. f. *Prose.* Phr.—Prōsă ōrātĭŏ. Prōsă lŏquēlă. Sŏlūtŭs, pĕdēstrĭs sērmŏ. Nŭmĕrī lēgĕ sŏlūtī. Vērbă sŏlūtă mŏdīs.

Prōsĭlĭŏ, īs, ŭī & īvī, īrĕ. *To jump forth, to leap.* Syn.—Ēxsĭlĭŏ, prōrūmpŏ, rŭŏ, ēmĭcŏ.

Prōspĕr, ĕră, ĕrūm. *Propitious, favorable.* Ōmnēm cūrsūm mĭhĭ prōspĕră dīxĭt Rēlĭgĭŏ. V. Syn.—Fēlīx, præsēns, dēxtĕr, făvēns. *Prosperous.* Syn.—Faūstŭs, fōrtūnātŭs, sĕcūndŭs, fēlīx, lætŭs.

Prōspĕrĭtās, ātĭs. f. *Prosperity.* Syn.—Fēlīcĭtās. Phr.—Sōrs prōspĕră, fōrtūnă sĕcūndă, făvēns, rīdēns. Rēs sĕcūndæ, prōspĕræ.

Prōspĭcĭŏ, ĭs, ēxī, ēctūm, ĕrĕ. *To see, to observe from afar.* Ē sūmmō prōspĭcĭēns tŭmŭlō cœlūm spēctābăt. V. Syn.—Prōspēctŏ. Phr.—Prŏcŭl āspĭcĭŏ. Ŏcŭlōs vīsūm prōtēndŏ ĭn. Ŏcŭlīs cāmpōs lūstrārĕ. *To provide for.* Syn.—Cōnsŭlŏ, căvĕŏ, prōvĭdĕŏ, īnvĭgĭlŏ.

Prōstērnŏ, ĭs, strāvī, strātūm, ĕrĕ. *To overwhelm, to lay low.* Syn.—Hŭmī stērnŏ, āffīgŏ, ăbjĭcĭŏ, dējĭcĭŏ, dēprĭmŏ, ēvērtŏ, dīrŭŏ, prōtĕrŏ.

Prōsūm, dĕs, fŭī, dēssĕ. *To serve, to profit, to assist.* Syn.—Jŭvŏ, prōfĭcĭŏ. Phr.—Ūtĭlĭs sūm. Impers. *It is good, useful.* Syn.—Jŭvăt, ēxpĕdĭt, cōndūcĭt, prōfĭcĭt.

Prōtĕgŏ, ĭs, ēxī, ēctūm, ĕrĕ. *To cover, to protect.* Syn.—Tĕgŏ. *To protect, to defend.* Syn.—Tĕgŏ, cōntĕgŏ, tŭĕŏr, dēfēndŏ.

Prōtēndŏ, ĭs, dī, tūm, ĕrĕ. *To stretch forward, to extend.* Syn.—Prōdūcŏ, prōfĕrŏ, prōtrăhŏ, pōrrĭgŏ. *To prolong.* Syn.—Ēxtēndŏ, prōfĕrŏ, prōdūcŏ, pōrrĭgŏ.

Prōtĕnŭs. adv. *Afar.* Syn.—Lōngē, prŏcŭl. *Straightway.* Syn.—Cōntĭnŭō, ēxīndĕ, jām.

Prōtĕrŏ, ĭs, trīvī, trītūm, ĕrĕ. *To tread under foot.* Quācūnque īngrĕdĭtūr flōrēntĭă prōtĕrĭt ārvă. O. Syn.—Cālcŏ, prōcūlcŏ, tĕrŏ. *To follow in the footsteps.* Syn.—Ūrgĕŏ, trūdŏ.

Prŏtērvē. adv. *Boldly, forwardly.* Syn.—Aūdāctĕr, prŏcācĭtĕr, pĕtŭlāntĕr.

Prŏtērvĭă & Prŏtērvĭtās, ātĭs. f. *Boldness, wantonness.* Syn.—Pĕtŭlāntĭă, prŏcācĭtās, aūdācĭă, lāscīvĭă.

Prŏtērvŭs, ă, ūm. *Bold, insolent.* Syn.—Aūdāx, prŏcāx, īmpŭdēns, sŭpērbŭs, īnfrēnĭs. *Lascivious, wanton.* Syn.—Aūdāx, lāscīvŭs, sălāx, pĕtŭlāns, īmprŏbŭs, īmpŭdīcŭs, ōbscœnŭs.

Prōtĭnŭs. adv. *Straightway.* Syn.—Cōnfēstīm, cōntĭnŭō, īllĭcō, sŭbĭtō, stătīm. Phr.—Sĭnĕ mŏrā. Nūllă mŏra ēst. Nēc mŏră quīn. *Afar. See Protenus.*

Prōtrăhŏ, ĭs, trāxī, trāctūm, ĕrĕ. *To drag forward. See Traho. To bring forward to view.* Syn.—Prōfĕrŏ, prōdŏ, prōdūcŏ, ēdūcŏ, ēffĕrŏ, ēxprōmŏ. *To reveal.* Syn.—Dētĕgŏ, prōdŏ, īndīcŏ. *To prolong.* Syn.—Prōdūcŏ, prōfĕrŏ, trăhŏ, prōlātŏ, ēxtēndŏ.

Prōtūrbŏ, ās, āvī, ātūm, ārĕ. *To drive in disorder.* Syn.—Ēxtūrbŏ, ăbĭgŏ, pēllŏ. *To overwhelm.* Syn.—Stērnŏ, prōstērnŏ, dējĭcĭŏ, ēvērtŏ.

Prōvĕhŏ, ĭs, ēxī, ēctūm, ĕrĕ. *To carry.* Syn.—Vĕhŏ, īnvĕhŏ. *To send forward, to advance.* Syn.—Prōmŏvĕŏ, īmpēllŏ, ăgŏ, fĕrŏ.

Prōvĕnĭŏ, īs, vēnī, vēntūm, īrĕ. *To advance, to appear.* Syn.—Prōcēdŏ, ēxĕŏ, prōfĕrŏr. *To be born.* Syn.—Ŏrĭŏr, nāscŏr, crēscŏ, sūccēdŏ. Fig.—*To happen.* Syn.—Ēvĕnĭŏ, cōntīngŏ.

Prōvēntŭs, ūs. m. *Revenue, fruit.* Syn.—Rĕdĭtŭs, cōpĭă, frūctŭs, frūgēs, mēssĭs.

Prōvērbĭūm, ĭī. n. *Proverb.* Syn.—Ădăgĭūm, dīctūm, sēntēntĭă.

Prōvĭdĕŏ, ēs, vīdī, vīsūm, ērĕ. *To foresee.* Syn.—Prævĭdĕŏ. *To be on one's guard against, to prevent.* Syn.—Prōspĭcĭŏ, căvĕŏ, præcăvĕŏ, cūrŏ, cōnsŭlŏ.

Prōvĭdŭs, ă, ūm. *Foreseeing.* Syn.—Præscĭŭs, præsāgŭs. *Prudent.* Syn.—Prōspĭcĭēns, prūdēns, săpĭēns, caūtŭs.

Prōvŏcŏ, ās, āvī, ātūm, ārĕ. *To call forth.* Syn.—Vŏcŏ, ēvŏcŏ, ārcēssŏ. *To provoke.* Syn.—Vŏcŏ, pōscŏ, lăcēssŏ, ădŏrĭŏr. *To irritate.* Syn.—Lăcēssŏ, īrrītŏ, īncĭtŏ.

Prōvŏmŏ, ĭs, ŭī, ĭtūm, ĕrĕ. *To vomit forth.* Syn.—Ējĭcĭŏ, ējēctŏ, ērūctŏ.

Prūdēns, ēntĭs. adj. *Prudent, knowing.* Syn.—Scĭēns, dōctŭs, pĕrītŭs, cāllĭdŭs, cāllēns, gnārŭs. *Far-seeing.* Syn.—Prōvĭdŭs, prōspĭcĭēns, săpĭēns, caūtŭs, cāllĭdŭs, săgāx, sōlērs, cīrcūmspēctŭs. Phr.—Cōnsĭlĭō, sōlērtī mēntĕ prædĭtŭs. Ănĭmī mātūrŭs. Ōmnĭă prōspĭcĭēns. Cōnsĭlĭī plēnŭs. Cuī prōvĭdă mēns. Mēntēm sŭă nōn căpĭt ætās. Ānte ānnōs ănĭmūmquĕ gĕrēns.

Prūdēntĕr. adv. *Prudently.* Syn.—Caūtē, prōvĭdē, săpĭēntĕr. *See Sapienter.*

Prūdēntĭă, æ. f. *Knowledge, science.* Syn.—Scĭēntĭă, pĕrītĭă, sōlērtĭă, ārs. *Prudence.* Syn.—Săgācĭtās, săpĭēntĭă, sōlērtĭă, cōnsĭlĭūm, jūdĭcĭūm, pĕrītĭă, cāllĭdĭtās. Phr.—Rērūm prūdēntĭă, ēxpĕrĭēntĭă. Prōvĭdă mēns. Rērūm prūdēntĭă majŏr.

Prūnă, æ. f. *Burning coal, live coal.* Syn.—Cārbŏ, cārbūncŭlŭs, īgnĭs.

Prūnŭs, ī. f. *A plum tree.* (*See Appendix under list of Trees, etc.*)

Psīttăcŭs, ī. m. *A parrot.* (*See Appendix under list of Birds.*)

Pūbĕŏ, ēs, ŭī, ērĕ & Pūbēscŏ, ĭs, ĕrĕ. *To reach the age of puberty.* Syn.—Jŭvĕnēscŏ, ădŏlēscŏ. *To increase, to grow.* Syn.—Crēscŏ, ădŏlēscŏ.

Pūbĕr & Pūbĕs, ĕrĭs. adj. *Of ripe years.* Syn.—Pūbēns, pūbēscēns, ădūltŭs. Fig.—*Flourishing, vigorous.* Syn.—Flōrēns, crēscēns, vĕgĕtŭs.

Pŭdēntĕr. adv. *Modestly.* Syn.—Mŏdēstē, vĕrēcūndē.

Pŭdĕt, ŭĭt, ērĕ. *To be ashamed.* Syn.—Ērŭbēscŏ. Phr.—Pŭdŏr ēst ūltĕrĭōră lŏquī. Vīdīt pŭdŭītquĕ vĭdērĕ. Hăbĕāt jām Rōmă pŭdōrēm! Nēc tūrpĕ pŭtārēnt prædōnēs fĭĕrī.

Pŭdĭbūndŭs, ă, ūm. *Modest, reserved.* Pŭdĭbūndăquĕ cēlăt ămīctū ōră. O. Syn.—Pŭdēns, pŭdīcŭs, mŏdēstŭs, vĕrēcūndŭs. Phr.—Tăcĭtō vīctă pŭdōrĕ.

Pŭdīcē. adv. *Modestly, chastely.* Syn.—Pŭdēntĕr, vĕrēcūndē, cāstē, hŏnēstē, sānctē.

Pŭdīcĭtĭă, æ. f. *Modesty, chastity.* Nūllā rĕpărābĭlĭs ārtĕ Læsă pŭdīcĭtia ēst; dēpĕrĭt īllă sĕmĕl. O. Syn.—Pŭdŏr, cāstĭtās, vīrgĭnĭtās. Phr.—Pŭdīcĭtĭæ laūs, hŏnŏr, dĕcŭs. Vītă sĭnĕ lābĕ.

Pŭdīcŭs, ă, ūm. *Modest, chaste.* Nēc tĭbĭ cōntīngăt mātrōnă pŭdīcĭŏr īllā. O. Syn.—Pŭdēns, pŭdĭbūndŭs, mŏdēstŭs, cāstŭs, pūrŭs, īntĕgĕr, vĕrēcūndŭs, hŏnēstŭs. Phr.—Nōn ōblītă pŭdōrĭs.

Pŭdŏr, ōrĭs. m. *Shame, confusion.* Ēt tĭmĭdūs lătĕbrās spērăt hăbērĕ pŭdŏr. O. Syn.—Rŭbŏr, vĕrēcūndĭă. Phr.—Rŭbŏr īgnĕŭs īnfĭcĭt ōră. *Modesty.* Syn.—Vĕrēcūndĭă, rŭbŏr, mŏdēstĭă. Phr.—Mājēstās grātă pŭdōrĭs. Ōră cŏlōrāns. Dējĭcĭēns ŏcŭlōs. Īndēx īngĕnŭæ mēntĭs. Īn ōrĕ sĕdēt pŭdŏr. Pŭdŏr ōră dĕcēt. Lūmĭnă plēnă pŭdōrĭs. *Chastity.* Syn.—Pŭdīcĭtĭă, cāstĭtās. Phr.—Fīnēs trānsīrĕ pŭdōrĭs. Flōs īntĕmĕrātĕ pŭdōrĭs.

Pŭēllă, æ. f. *Girl, maiden.* Syn.—Vīrgŏ, pŭēllŭlă. Phr.—Lōngā cōmptă pŭēllă cŏmā.

Pŭĕr, ĕrī. m. *Boy*. Ōră pŭēr prīmā sīgnāns īntōnsă jŭventā. V. Syn.—Ĕphēbŭs, ădŏlēscēns, īnfāns. Phr.—Aēvī rŭdĭs. Prīmīs, tĕnĕrīs ānnīs. Nōn ūtĭlīs ārmīs. Aētās pŭĕrōrum īmprōvĭdă. Īnnŏcŭa ēst ætas. Āgmēn pŭĕrīlĕ. Sŭīs mātūrĭŏr ānnīs. *Slave*. Syn.—Fămŭlŭs, mĭnīstĕr, sērvŭs.

Pŭĕrīlĭs, ĭs, ĕ. *Childlike, boyish*. Syn.—Jŭvĕnīlĭs, tĕnĕr, mōllĭs.

Pŭĕrĭtiă & Pŭērtĭă, æ. f. *Childhood, boyhood*. Phr.—Tĕnĕră, pŭĕrīlĭs ætās. Tĕnĕrī ānnī. Prīmūm ævūm. Prīmă pārs ævī. Tēmpŭs pŭĕrīlĕ jŭvēntæ. Aētās īnfīrmă. Aētās mōllĭs ĕt āptă rĕgī.

Pŭgĭl, ĭlĭs. m. *Athlete*. Syn.—Āthlētă, pălēstrītă, lūctātŏr. Phr.—Frōntēm rĕdĭmīrĕ cŏrōnā.

Pūgĭŏ, ōnĭs. m. *Dagger*. Syn.—Sīcă, glădĭŭs, ēnsĭs.

Pūgnă, æ. f. *Battle, combat*. Sēmpĕr ĕquōs ātque ārmă vĭrūm pūgnāsquĕ cănēbăt. V. Syn.—Cērtāmĕn, prœlĭūm, cōngrēssŭs, cōnflīctŭs, cōncūrsŭs, (*sometimes*) ārmă, bēllūm, ăcĭēs. Phr.—Cērtāmĭnă Mārtĭs. Dīscrīmĭnă pūgnæ. Cōnsērtæ cāmpīs ăcĭēs. Ācrĭŏr ād pūgnām rĕdĭt. Āncēps pūgnæ fōrtūnă. Pūgnæ mēmbră părānt. Dēsīstĕrĕ pūgnā. Ēvādĕrĕ pūgnā. Fĕrūs Māvōrs cĭĕt ūndĭquĕ pūgnām. *Fight (without arms)*. Syn.—Cērtāmĕn, rīxă.

Pūgnātŏr, ōrĭs. m. *Combatant*. Syn.—Pūgnāns, mīlĕs, bēllātŏr, ārmātŭs.

Pūgnāx, ācĭs. adj. *Warlike*. Syn.—Bēllātŏr, bēllĭcōsŭs, fōrtĭs. *Opposed to, contrary to*. Syn.—Pūgnāns, dīscōrs, ādvērsŭs, ōppŏsĭtŭs, cōntrārĭŭs.

Pūgnŏ, ās, āvī, ātūm, ārĕ. *To fight*. Crās, ŭt rūmŏr ăĭt, tōtā pūgnābĭtŭr ūrbĕ. Prop. Syn.—Cērtŏ, cōncērtŏ, cōnflīgŏ, cōngrĕdĭŏr, cōncūrrŏ, prœlĭŏr, dīmĭcŏ. Phr.—Pūgnām, cērtāmēn tēntŏ, cōmmīttŏ, ŏbĕŏ. Pūgnā, fērrō, ārmīs dīmĭcŏ, cōntēndŏ. Mārtēm lăcēssŏ. Ārmīs cōncūrrĕrĕ cāmpō. Sē crēdĕrĕ pūgnæ. Īn pūgnām fĕrŏr. Pūgnās ĭnĕūnt. Pūgnātūr cōmĭnŭs ārmīs. Ītūr pēr tēlă, pĕr hōstēs. Dānt prœlĭă cērvī. Ād prœlĭă vēntum ēst. Mārtēmquĕ fătīgānt. Glădĭīs pūgnātŭr ăcūtīs. Īmmīscēntquĕ mănūs mănĭbŭs. Fērvēbāt Māvōrs. Pūgna āspĕră sūrgĭt. *To resist*. Syn.—Ōblūctŏr, ōbnītŏr, ōbsīstŏ, rĕsīstŏ. *To be opposed to*. Syn.—Ōbstŏ, dīssĭdĕŏ, ādvērsŏr.

Pūgnŭs, ī. m. *Fist*. Jŭvĕnīlī gūttŭră pūgnō Rūpĭt. O. Syn.—Mănŭs, pŭgīllŭs. Phr.—Cōmprēssă, claūsă mănŭs. Īn pūgnūm cōmprēssă mănŭs. Ārctă mănŭs. Cæsŭs pūgnīs. Plēnī sānguĭnĕ pūgnī.

Pūlchĕr, chră, chrūm. *Beautiful*. Grātĭŏr ēt pūlchrō vĕnĭēns īn cōrpŏrĕ vīrtūs. V. Syn.—Fōrmōsŭs, dĕcōrŭs, dĕcēns, spĕcĭōsŭs, vĕnūstŭs. Phr.—Făcĭē, fōrmā, fōrmæ dĕcōrĕ, nĭtōrĕ, mūnĕrĕ præstāns, īnsīgnĭs, cōnspĭcĭēndŭs. Fōrmā præstāntī, ēgrĕgĭā. Quæ fōrmā ōmnēs vīncĭt. Dĕcōrĕ fēlīx. Fōrmā sŭpĕrāntĕ pŭēllæ. Quēm vūltŭs hŏnēstăt. Quā nūllă dĕcēntĭŏr. Quō pūlchrĭŏr āltĕr Nōn fŭĭt. Īnsīgnĭs făcĭē jŭvĕnĭs. Fōrmā pūlchērrĭmŭs. Rădĭānt ūt sīdŭs ŏcēllī. Nīgrō crīnĕ dĕcōră. *Beautiful, fine (in speaking of objects).* Syn.—Nĭtĭdŭs, dĕcōrŭs, splēndĭdŭs, laūtŭs, māgnĭfĭcŭs, cōnspĭcĭēndŭs, dīvĕs. *Fine, excellent (in speaking of the works of the mind).* Syn.—Dĕcōrŭs, hŏnēstŭs, laūdāndŭs, splēndĭdŭs, clārŭs, nōbĭlĭs, præclārŭs.

Pūlchrē. adv. *Well, excellently.* Syn.—Bĕnĕ, rēctē, prŏbē, āptē.

Pūlchrĭtūdŏ, ĭnĭs. f. *Beauty.* Syn.—Dĕcŏr, fōrmă, spĕcĭēs, vĕnūstās.

Pūllŭlŏ, ās, āvī, ātūm, ārĕ. *To send forth roots.* Pūllŭlăt āb rādīce ălĭīs dēnsīssĭmă sīlvă. V. Syn.—Gērmĭnŏ, frŭtĭcŏ, sūccrēscŏ, lūxŭrĭŏ.

Pūllŭs, ī. m. *Chicken, young bird.* Syn.—Fœtŭs, nīdī, nātī, prōlēs, prōgĕnĭēs, prŏpāgŏ. Phr.—Ăvĭūm prōgĕnĭēs, prōlēs.

Pūlmēntārĭūm, ĭī. n. *Stew, broth.* Syn.—Pūls, pūlmēntūm, pūlpāmĕn, pūlpāmēntūm. Phr.—Vĕnĭēt quī pūlmēntārĭă cōndĭt. Tū pūlmēntārĭă quærĕ Sūdāndō.

Pūlmŏ, ōnĭs. m. *The lungs.* Phr.—Pūlmōnĭs fĭbræ. Cōrdĭs flăbră, flăbēllă, ănĭmæ spīrāmĭnă. Spīrācŭlă vītæ. Ănĭmæ lătĕbræ. Căptăt rēddĭtque aūrās. Fīxō fērrum īn pūlmōnĕ tĕpēscĭt.

Pūlpĭtūm, ī. n. *Stage.* Pūlpĭtă sōlēmnēs nōn ŏlŭērĕ crŏcōs. Prop. Syn.—Thĕātrūm, prōscēnĭūm, scēnă.

Pūls, tĭs. f. *Pottage, stew.* Grāndēs fūmābānt pūltĭbŭs ōllæ. J. Syn.—Pŏlēntă, pūlmēntūm, pūlmēntārĭūm.

Pūlsātŏr, ōrĭs. m. *A player of any stringed instrument.* Cĭthăræ pūlsātŏr Ăpōllŏ. V. Syn.—Cĭthărœdŭs, fīdĭcĕn, lўrĭcĕn. Phr.—Quī sēmpĕr ŏbērrăt ĕādēm chōrdā. Cĭthărām pūlsāns. Cĭthăræ pūlsāndæ pĕrītŭs. Nērvōs pūlsārĕ pĕrītŭs. Stŭdĭō cĭthăræ dēdĭtŭs. Fĭdĭbūs plēctrōquĕ pŏtēns. Mŏvēns sāxă fĕrāsquĕ lўrā. Cĭthără quī pērsŏnăt aūrĕā. Plēctră mŏvēns.

Pūlsŏ, ās, āvī, ātūm, ārĕ. *To beat, to strike.* Ēxsūltāntĭăque haūrĭt Cōrdă păvor pūlsāns. Prop. Syn.—Fĕrĭŏ, quătĭŏ, pērcŭtĭŏ, vērbĕrŏ. Phr.—Mūrūs pūlsātŭr ăb hōstĕ. *To agitate, to excite.* Syn.—Ăgŏ, ăgĭtŏ, mŏvĕŏ, cōmmŏvĕŏ, tūrbŏ. *To overturn.* Syn.—Dējĭcĭŏ, ēvērtŏ.

Pūlsŭs, ūs. m. *Stroke, blow.* Pūlsūquĕ pĕdūm trĕmĭt ēxcĭtă tēllūs. V. Syn.—Īmpūlsŭs, īmpĕtŭs, ĭctŭs, vērbĕr.

Pūlvīllŭs & Pūlvīnŭs, ī. m. *Cushion, couch.* Syn.—Pulvīnăr, cērvīcăl, cūlcĭtă, cŭbĭtăl. Phr.—Căpĭtī sūppŏsĭtŭs.

Pūlvīnăr, ārĭs. n. *Couch. See Pulvillus.*

Pūlvĭs, ĕrĭs. m. *Dust, powder.* Pūlvĕrĭs ēxĭgŭī jăctū cōmprēssă quĭēscēnt. V. Syn.—Ărēnă. Phr.—Pūlvĕrĭs, pūlvĕrĕŭs glŏbŭs, tūrbŏ. Pūlvĕrĕă nūbēs. Tūrbĭnĕ cōllēctūs pūlvĭs. Mīscētūr pūlvĕrĕ cæcō cāmpŭs. Fūmāntēs pūlvĕrĕ cāmpī. Pūlvĭs cālīgĭnĕ cæcā. Pūlvĕrĕ spārgŏ. Pūlvĕrĕ tūrpāns.

Pūnctūm, ī. n. *Point.* Syn.—Pūnctŭs. *Opening, small hole.* Syn.—Fŏrāmĕn, fĕnēstră. *Moment of time.* Syn.—Mōmēntūm. *Vote.* Syn.—Sūffrāgĭūm.

Pūngŏ, ĭs, pūnxī & pĕpŭgī, pūnctūm, pūngĕrĕ. *To pierce, to prick.* Syn.—Cōmpūngŏ, fŏdĭŏ, fŏdĭcŏ, lāncĭnŏ, stĭmŭlŏ.

Pūnĭŏ, īs, īvī & ĭī, ītūm, īrĕ. *To punish, to chastise.* Syn.—Cāstīgŏ, mūlctŏ, plēctŏ, ūlcīscŏr, sævĭŏ, ănĭmādvērtŏ ĭn (acc.). Phr.—Pœnās rĕpĕtŏ, āccĭpĭŏ, rĕpōscŏ, pōscŏ, sūmŏ. Pœnās dēcērnŏ, ēxērcĕŏ. Pœnīs āffĭcĭŏ. Crīmĕn ūlcīscŏr, vīndĭcŏ. Sūpplĭcĭīs dēlīctă cŏērcĕt. (*In the passive*) *To be punished.* Syn.—Cāstīgŏr, mūlctŏr, plēctŏr. Phr.—Pœnās sūbĕŏ, pătĭŏr, sōlvŏ, dō. Pœnīs āffĭcĭŏr, tōrquĕŏr. Ĭn pœnām trăhŏr. Pătī sĭnĕ crīmĭnĕ pœnām.

Pūrē. adv. *Cleanly, purely, chastely.* Syn.—Cāstē, pĭē, sānctē, hŏnēstē, pūlchrē.

Pūrgŏ, ās, āvī, ātūm, ārĕ. *To clean, to purify.* Dī pătrĭī, pūrgāmŭs ăgrōs pūrgāmŭs ăgrēstēs. Tib. Syn.—Ēxpūrgŏ, mūndŏ, ēmūndŏ, āblŭŏ, ēlŭŏ, ābstērgŏ, pĭŏ, ēxpĭŏ. *To cure.* Syn.—Cūrŏ, sānŏ. *To justify.* Syn.—Ēxcūsŏ, dīlŭŏ.

Pūrpŭră, æ. f. *A shell-fish from which they procured the purple color, hence purple dye or color.* Syn.—Mūrēx, ōstrūm, cōccŭs, cōnchȳlĭūm. Phr.—Tȳrĭūm stāmĕn, vēllŭs. Tȳrĭŭs cŏlŏr. Tȳrĭōs īncōctă rūbōrēs vēllĕră.

Pūrpŭrĕŭs, ă, ūm. *Of purple.* Syn.—Cōccĭnĕŭs, cōnchȳlĭŭs, ōstrīnŭs, pūnĭcĕŭs, Tȳrĭŭs, Sīdŏnĭŭs. Phr.—Fūlgēntī mūrĭcĕ pīctă Vēstĭs. Ōstrō pērfūsæ vēstēs.

Pūrŭs, ă, ūm. *Clean, neat.* Syn.—Mūndŭs, sīncērŭs, tērsŭs, laūtŭs. Phr.—Sĭnĕ lābĕ. Măcŭlīs cărēns. *Clear, bright.* Syn.—Clārŭs, nĭtĭdŭs, līmpĭdŭs, pērlūcĭdŭs. *Free from, immune.* Syn.—Văcŭŭs, lībĕr, īmmūnĭs. *Chaste.* Syn.—Cāstŭs, īntĕmĕrātŭs, īntāctŭs, īntĕgĕr, īncōrrūptŭs, sīncērŭs, īnnŏcŭŭs, īnnŏcēns.

Pŭsīllŭs, ă, ūm. *Little, small, slender.* Tērră mălōs hŏmĭnēs nūnc ēdŭcăt ātquĕ pŭsīllōs. J. Syn.—Pārvŭs, pŭmĭlŭs, pērpārvŭs, mĭnĭmŭs, ēxĭgŭŭs.

Pūsĭŏ, ōnĭs. m. *Small boy.* Syn.—Pŭĕr, pŭēllŭs, pūsŭs, pūpŭs pūpŭlŭs.

Pūtĭdŭs, ă, ūm. *Ill-smelling, infected.* Syn.—Fœtĭdŭs, grăvĭs.
Pŭtŏ, ās, āvī, ātūm, ārĕ. *To cut, to prune.* Syn.—Āmpŭtŏ, rĕsĕcŏ, rĕcīdŏ, dēcīdŏ, cædŏ, tōndĕŏ, āttōndĕŏ, prĕmŏ. Phr.—Fālcĕ prĕmŏ. *To think, to believe.* Syn.—Ārbĭtrŏr, ŏpīnŏr, cēnsĕŏ, sēntĭŏ, ēxīstĭmŏ, rĕŏr, rĕpŭtŏ, aŭtŭmŏ, jūdĭcŏ, crēdŏ, cōnjĭcĭŏ, sūspĭcŏr. Phr.—Nē vānă pŭtēs. *To meditate upon.* Syn.—Rĕpŭtŏ, vōlvŏ, cōgĭtŏ, ăgĭtŏ, vŏlūtŏ.
Pŭtrēdŏ, ĭnĭs. f. *Corruption.* Syn.—Cărĭēs, pŭtrŏr, tābēs, tābūm.
Pŭtrĕfīŏ, fīs, fāctŭs sūm, fĭĕrī. *To become corrupt.* Syn.—Pŭtrĕŏ, pŭtrēscŏ, tābēscŏ, īntābēscŏ, cōrrūmpŏr, vĭtĭŏr. Phr.—Pŭtrēdĭnĕ vĭtĭŏr, cōrrūmpŏr.
Pūtrĭdŭs, ă, ūm. *Putrid, corrupt.* Syn.—Pŭtrĭs, pŭtrĕfāctŭs, pŭtrēscēns, cōrrūptŭs, cărĭōsŭs, tābĭdŭs, tābēscēns, vĭtĭātŭs.
Pȳră, æ. f. *Funeral-pyre.* Syn.—Būstūm, rŏgŭs.
Pȳrămĭs, ĭdĭs. f. *Pyramid.* Phr.—Pȳrămĭdīs mōlēs. Nōbĭlĕ ŏpŭs. Aūdācĭă sāxă pȳrămĭdūm. Pȳrămĭdūm sūmptūs ād sīdĕră dūctī. Rēgālīquĕ sĭtū pȳrămĭdum āltĭŭs.
Pўrŭs, ī. f. *A pear-tree.* (*See Appendix under list of Trees, etc.*)
Pȳxĭs, ĭdĭs. f. *Box.* Syn.—Cāpsă, ārcă, ārcŭlă.

Q

Quădrāgīntă. indecl. *Forty.* Syn.—Quădrāgēnī. Phr.—Bīs vīcēnī. Quătēr dēnī.
Quădrīgæ, ārūm. f. *Chariot, car.* Quădrĭjŭgēs, cūrrŭs. Phr.—Quădrĭjŭgēs ĭn ĕquōs ādvērsăquĕ pēctŏră tēndĭt. Quādrĭjŭgō vĕhĭtūr cūrrū.
Quădrŭpĕdāns, ntĭs. adj. *Four-footed.* Quādrŭpĕdāntĕ pŭtrēm sŏnĭtū quătĭt ūngŭlă cāmpūm. V. Syn.—Quădrŭpēs.
Quærŏ, ĭs, sīvī & ĭī, ītūm, ĕrĕ. *To seek.* Nātām Sōlĭs ăd ōccāsūs, sōlĭs quærēbăt ăd ōrtūs. O. Syn.—Dīsquīrŏ, ēxquīrŏ, īnquīrŏ, pērquīrŏ, rĕquīrŏ, īndāgŏ, rīmŏr, scrūtŏr, pērscrūtŏr, vēstīgŏ, īnvēstīgŏ, cīrcūmspĭcĭŏ. Phr.—Ŏcŭlīs lūstrāns vēstīgŏ. Vēstīgĭă sĕquŏr, ōbsērvŏ. *To ask.* Syn.—Rŏgŏ, rŏgĭtŏ, īntērrŏgŏ, pērcōntŏr, scīscĭtŏr, pōscŏ, flāgĭtŏ, pĕtŏ (ab).
Quæsītŏr, ōrĭs. m. *Judge.* Quæsītōr Mīnōs ūrnām mŏvĕt. V. Syn.—Jūdēx. Phr.—Quæsītōr scĕlĕrūm, vīndēxquĕ rĕōrūm.
Quæsītūm, ī. n. *Question, demand.* Syn.—Quæstĭŏ. *Asquisition.* Syn.—Pārtūm, quæstŭs.
Quæsŏ, quæsŭmŭs. *Defective verb. I beg of you.* Syn.—Ōrŏ, prĕcŏr, ōbtēstŏr, rŏgŏ.

Quālĭtĕr. adv. *How.* Syn.—Quōmŏdŏ. *As, just as.* Syn.—Vĕlŭt, ŭt, vĕlŭtī, sīcŭt, sīcŭtī.

Quām. conj. *As.* Syn.—Ŭtī, ŭt. (*With an adjective*). *How.*—Syn.—Quāntūm.

Quāmprīmūm. adv. *As soon as possible.* Syn.—Cĭtō, īllĭcō, prōtĭnŭs, sŭbĭtō.

Quāmvīs. conj. *Although.* Syn.—Ētsī, lĭcĕt, quāmquām, quāntūmvīs.

Quāndŏ. adv. *When.* Syn.—Cūm. *Since.* Syn.—Quŏnĭām, quāndŏquĭdēm, cūm, quātĕnŭs.

Quāndŏcūnquĕ & Quāndŏquĕ. conj. *Wherever, whenever.* Syn.—Cūm. *Sometime.* Syn.—Ōlīm, ălĭquāndŏ.

Quāndŏquĭdēm. conj. *Since.* Syn.—Quāndŏ, sīquĭdēm, quŏnĭām, cūm, ŭt.

Quāntō. adv. (*with a comparative*). *The more.* Syn.—Quō, quām. *How much the more.* Syn.—Quō, ŭt.

Quāntūmvīs. adv. *As much as you will, however.* Syn.—Quāntūmlĭbĕt, quāntūmcūnquĕ, quāmlĭbĕt, quāmvīs.

Quāprōptĕr. conj. *Therefore.* Syn.—Ĭdĕō, īdcīrcō, prōptĕrĕā, hīnc, īndĕ.

Quārē. conj. *Why, wherefore.* Syn.—Cūr, cūrnām, ūndĕnām. *Therefore.* Syn.—Ērgō, ĭgĭtŭr, quāprōptĕr.

Quăsĭ. adv. *As.* Syn.—Vĕlŭt, vĕlŭtī, tānquām, ŭt. *As if.* Syn.—Tānquām, sīcŭt, sīcŭtī, vĕlŭt, vĕlŭtī. *About, almost.* Syn.—Fĕrē, pēnĕ.

Quătĭŏ, ĭs, quāssūm, ĕrĕ. *To shake.* Syn.—Quāssŏ, ăgĭtŏ, tōrquĕŏ, vĭbrŏ, cōncŭtĭŏ, ēxcŭtĭŏ, sūccŭtĭŏ, cōmmŏvĕŏ. Phr.—Hōrrōr mēmbră quătĭt. Quătĕ cȳmbălă. Gĕmĭtū quătĭūntūr pēctŏră. *To strike.* Syn.—Fĕrĭŏ, pērcŭtĭŏ, cōncŭtĭŏ. *Fig.*—*To disturb, to trouble.* Syn.—Mŏvĕŏ, cōmmŏvĕo, pērcēllŏ, quāssŏ, tūrbŏ.

Quĕ. encl. conj. *And.* Syn.—Ātque, ĕt, nēcnōn.

Quĕŏ, quīs, quīvī, quĭtūm, quīrĕ. *To be able.* Nāmque ălĭūd quōd sīt quōd jam īmplōrārĕ quĕāmŭs. V. Syn.—Pōssūm, vălĕŏ.

Quērcŭs, ūs. f. *An oak.* (*See Appendix under list of Trees, etc.*)

Quĕrēlă, ǣ. f. *Complaint, lamentation.* Ērgō nē dŭbĭtā blāndās ădhĭbērĕ quĕrēlās. O. Syn.—Gĕmĭtŭs, quēstŭs, quĕrĭmōnĭă, lāmēntūm. Phr.—Trīstĭă vērbă. Quĕrŭlī, flēbĭlēs sŏnī. Quĕrŭlǣ vōcēs. Tūrpēs dēpōnĕ quĕrēlās. *Reproaches, charge.* Syn.—Quĕrĭmōnĭă, cōnvīcĭūm.

Quĕrŏr, ĕrĭs, quēstŭs sūm, quĕrī. *To complain.* Īnvĭdĕt, ātque hŏmĭnūm quĕrĭtūr cūrārĕ trĭūmphōs. V. Syn.—Cōnquĕrŏr, lāmēntŏr, dŏlĕŏ, gĕmŏ, cōngĕmŏ, flĕŏ, dēflĕŏ, lūgĕŏ, sūspīrŏ, plāngŏ. Phr.—Quĕrēlās, quēstūs fūndŏ, ēffūndŏ, dō, ēdŏ, mīttŏ, tōllŏ. Mūltă gĕmŏ. Quēstū pēctŏră rūmpŏ. Īn flētūm ērūmpŏ. Lāmēntīs īndūlgĕŏ. Mœstō dĕdĭt ōrĕ quĕrēlās. Stābăt mūltă quĕrēns. Nēc plūră quĕrēntēm Pāssă Vĕnŭs. *To accuse.* Syn.—Īncūsŏ, īncrĕpŏ, cūlpŏ.

Quĕrŭlŭs, ă, ūm. *Complaining.* Syn.—Quĕrĭbūndŭs, quĕrēns, gĕmēns, gĕmĕbūndŭs. *Querulous, hard to please.* Syn.—Mōrōsŭs, dīffĭcĭlĭs.

Quī, quæ, quŏd. *Who, which.*

Quī? adv. *How?* Syn.—Cūr, ūndĕ, quārē, quōmŏdŏ.

Quĭă. conj. *Because.* Syn.—Quŏnĭăm, quŏd, nām, nāmquĕ, ĕnīm, ĕtĕnīm.

Quĭănām? conj. *Why?* Syn.—Cūr, quārē, quĭd, ūndĕ.

Quīcūnquĕ, quæcūnquĕ, quōdcūnquĕ. *Whosoever.* Syn.—Quīvīs, quīlĭbĕt, quīsquĭs.

Quĭd? conj. *Why?* Syn.—Cūr, quārē, quĭănām, ūndĕ.

Quīdām, quædām, quōddām. *A certain one, someone.* Syn.—Ălĭquĭs, nōnnūllŭs.

Quĭdēm. adv. *Truly, in truth.* Syn.—Ĕquĭdēm, cērtē, sānē, prŏfēctō.

Quĭēs, ētĭs. f. *Repose, quiet.* Ōmnĭbŭs ūnă quĭēs ŏpĕrūm, lăbŏr ōmnĭbŭs ūnŭs. V. Syn.—Ōtĭūm, rĕquĭēs, pāx. Phr.—Ămīcă quĭēs. Plăcĭdūm tēmpŭs. Trānquīllæ grāta ōtĭă mēntĭs. Cōrpŭs rĕcrĕāns. Tēmpēstīvă quĭēs vīrēs ălĭt. *Sleep.* Syn.—Sōmnŭs. *See Somnus.*

Quĭēscŏ, ĭs, ēvī, tūm, ēscĕrĕ. *To rest oneself.* Nōctĭvăgūm quī cārpĭt ĭtĕr, nōn aūrĕ quĭēscīt, Nōn ŏcŭlīs. O. Syn.—Rĕquĭēscŏ, ōtĭŏr. Phr.—Quĭētī īndūlgĕŏ, mē dō, văcŏ. Quĭētēm căpĭŏ. Quĭētĕ frŭŏr. Vīrēs frāctās rĕcrĕŏ. *To sleep. See Dormio. To become calm.* Syn.—Cēssŏ, rĕsīdŏ, dēsĭnŏ, plăcŏr, sēdŏr.

Quĭētē. adv. *Quietly, tranquilly.* Syn.—Plăcĭdē, trānquīllē.

Quĭētŭs, ă, ūm. *Peaceful, tranquil.* Hīc Sŭpĕrīs lăbŏr ēst, ĕă cūră quĭētōs Sōllĭcĭtăt. V. Syn.—Plăcĭdŭs, trānquīllŭs. Phr.—Mōx āĕrĕ lāpsă quĭētō. *Calm in spirit.* Syn.—Plăcĭdŭs, trānquīllŭs, sēcūrŭs.

Quīlĭbĕt, quælĭbĕt, quōdlĭbĕt, quīdlĭbĕt. *Anyone or anything whatsoever.* Syn.—Quīvīs, quīsquĕ.

Quīn. conj. *But that, why not.* Syn.—Quīdnī. *Nay even.* Syn.—Īmmŏ.

Quīppĕ. conj. *For, because.* Syn.—Nām, ĕnīm, ĕtĕnīm. *Forsooth.* Syn.—Nēmpĕ, scīlĭcēt, ūtpŏtĕ.

Quĭrīs, ītĭs. m. *Citizen of Rome* (*generally used in the plural*). Syn.—Rōmānī, Rōmŭlĭdæ. Phr.—Mōbĭlĭūm tūrbă Quĭrītĭūm. Prīscīquĕ Quĭrītēs.

Quĭs, quæ, quŏd & quĭd? *Who, what?* Syn.—Quīsnām.

Quīsquĕ, quæquĕ, quōdquĕ & quīdquĕ. *Each.* Syn.—Quīlĭbĕt, quīvīs, ūnūsquīsquĕ, ōmnĭs, cūnctī.

Quīvīs, quævīs, quōdvīs & quīdvīs. *Whosoever, whatsoever.* Syn.—Quīlĭbĕt, quīcūnquĕ, ōmnĭs, quīvīscūnquĕ.

Quō. adv. *Where.* Syn.—Quōrsūm. *As an interrogative.* Syn.—Quōnām, īn quā pārtĕ. *In order that.* Syn.—Ītă ŭt, ŭt. *The more.* Syn.—Quāntō.

Quōcīrcā. conj. *Therefore.* Syn.—Quāprōptĕr, quārē, īdcīrcō, ĭdĕō, ērgŏ, ĭgĭtŭr.

Quōcūnquĕ. adv. *Wherever.* Syn.—Quōvīs, quōlĭbĕt, quōquō.

Quōmĭnŭs. conj. *That....not.* Syn.—Quīn, nē.

Quōmŏdŏ? adv. *How?* Syn.—Quī, quā, ŭt.

Quōndām. adv. *Formerly.* Syn.—Ōlīm, āntĕ, prĭŭs, āntehāc. *Some day in the future.* Syn.—Ōlīm.

Quŏnĭām. conj. *Because.* Syn.—Quĭă, quŏd.

Quōvīs. adv. *Wherever.* Syn.—Quōlĭbĕt, quōcūnquĕ.

Quūm (*more correctly,* Cūm). conj. *When.* Syn.—Quāndŏ, pōstquām, quāndŏquĕ, ŭt, ŭbĭ, dūm, quŏtĭēs. Phr.—Quō tēmpŏrĕ. Sī fōrtĕ. Sī quāndŏ. *Since.* Syn.—Quāndŏ, ŭt, quŏnĭām, sĭquĭdēm.

R

Răbĭdŭs, ă, ūm. *Enraged, furious.* Fūlmĭnĕō răbĭdōs dūm rŏtăt ōrĕ cănēs. O. Syn.—Fŭrēns, fŭrĭōsŭs, īnsānŭs, fŭrĭbūndŭs, ēffĕrŭs. Phr.—Āccēnsŭs fŭrōrĕ. Nĭmĭōquĕ fŭrōrĕ īnsānŭs. Ănĭmūs răbĭē stĭmŭlātŭs.

Răbĭēs, ēī. f. *Rage.* Sævă cănūm răbĭēs mōrsūs āvērtĭt hĭāntēs. Prop. Syn.—Fŭrŏr, īră, vēsānĭă, vĭŏlēntĭă, cŭpīdŏ. Phr.—Cōllĭgĭt ōs răbĭēm. Bēllī răbĭēs. Hīnc cănĭbūs blāndīs răbĭēs vĕnĭt.

Rādīcĭtŭs. adv. *Right to the root, utterly.* Phr.—Ā rādīcĕ, ā stīrpĕ. Ā rādīcĭbūs īmīs. Ārbŏr īmā dē stīrpĕ rĕcīsă.

Rădĭŏ, ās, āvī, ātūm, ārĕ. *To send forth light, to be radiant.* Ārgēntī bĭfŏrēs rădĭābānt lūmĭnĕ vālvæ. O. Syn.—Īrrădĭŏ, rŭtĭlŏ, cŏrūscŏ, splēndĕŏ, mĭcŏ, fūlgĕŏ, fūlgŭrŏ, scīntīllŏ. Phr.—Rădĭōs, rădĭōrūm spīcŭlă mīttŏ, spārgŏ. Rădĭīs cŏrūscŏ, mĭcŏ. Rădĭāntī lūcī fūlgĕŏ. Rădĭābăt īn ārmīs. Rădĭānt, ūt sīdŭs, ŏcēllī. *See Luceo.*

Rădĭŭs, ĭī. m. *Ray of light.* Rădĭīs gĕlĭdī cālŭĕrĕ Trĭōnēs. O. Syn.—Lūx, lūmĕn, jŭbăr, splēndŏr. Phr.—Rădĭōrūm lūx. Jāmquĕ rŭbēscēbāt rădĭīs mărĕ. Ērūmpūnt rădĭī. Nūbēm rădĭīs ārdēntēm lūcĭs ĕt aūrō.

Rādīx, īcĭs. f. *Root.* Cōncrētām pătĭtūr rādīcem āffīgĕrĕ tērræ. V. Syn.—Stīrps, fībră. Phr.—Rāmōsæ fībræ. Rādīxquĕ mĕdēndī Ūtĭlĭs. Nītī rādīcĭbūs āltīs. Rādīcĭbūs hærĕt.

Rādŏ, ĭs, sī, sūm, ĕrĕ. *To scrape, to smooth, to polish.* Syn.—Ābrādŏ, ērādŏ, dērādŏ, cōmplānŏ, lævĭgŏ, pŏlĭŏ, āllŭŏ, lībŏ, lāmbŏ, mōrdĕŏ.

Rāmŭs, ī. m. *Branch of a tree.* Jām frăgĭlēs pŏtĕram ā tērrā cōntĭngĕrĕ rāmōs. V. Syn.—Rāmŭlŭs, frŭtĕx, pālmĕs, sūrcŭlŭs. Phr.—Ārbŏrĭs brāchĭă, mănŭs. Pōndĕră rāmī. Rāmōrūm ūmbræ. Lēntō vīmĭnĕ rāmŭs. Pēndēns rōbŏrĕ rāmŭs. Māgno āmbĭtū dīffūsă rāmīs Ārbŏr. Rāmōs fīgĕre hŭmō. Dēnūdāt fŏlĭīs rāmōs. Fālx rāmō lūcūm spŏlĭāvĭt ŏpācō. *To send forth branches.* Syn.—Rāmōs, sūrcŭlōs ăgŏ, frŭtĭcŏ, gērmĭnŏ.

Răphănŭs, ī. m. *A radish.* (*See Appendix under list of Trees, etc.*)

Răpĭdŭs, ă, ūm. *Rapid, violent, vehement.* Aēstŭăt ūt claūsīs răpĭdūs fōrnācĭbŭs īgnĭs. V. Syn.—Răpāx, cĕlĕr, cĭtŭs, cĭtātŭs, præcēps, vēlōx, vĕhĕmēns. Phr.—Răpĭdō cōntēndĕrĕ cūrsū. Răpĭdā vēlōcĭŭs aūrā. Răpĭdōquĕ vŏlāns.

Răpīnă, æ. f. *Rapine, pillage.* Trīstī spŏlĭāntūr tēmplă răpīnā. Syn.—Lătrōcĭnĭūm, fūrtūm. *Booty.* Syn.—Prædă, fūrtūm. *See Præda.*

Răpĭŏ, ĭs, răpŭī, rāptūm, ĕrĕ. *To seize.* Ēt vălĭdām dēxtrā răpĭt īndēfēssă bĭpēnnēm. V. Syn.—Cŏrrĭpĭŏ, ārrĭpĭŏ, prĕhēndŏ, căpĭŏ. *To take by force.* Syn.—Ābrĭpĭŏ, prōrĭpĭŏ, aūfĕrŏ, ābdūcŏ, rāptŏ, ērĭpĭŏ, tŏllŏ, ădĭmŏ, ēxtōrquĕŏ, sūbrĭpĭŏ. Phr.—Ōmnĕ săcrūm răpĭēntĕ dēxtrā.

Rāptŏr, ōrĭs. m. *Ravisher, plunderer.* Syn.—Prædātŏr, prædŏ, răpāx, lătrŏ.

Rāptūm, ī. n. *Theft, larceny, plunder.* Syn.—Præda, răpīnă, fūrtūm.

Rārŭs, ă, ūm. *Thin.* Syn.—Lāxŭs. Phr.—Nōn dēnsŭs. Rētĭă rāră. Quā rāra ēst ăcĭēs. *Rare, infrequent.* Syn.—Īnfrĕquēns. *Scanty, slight, sparing.* Syn.—Mŏdĕrātŭs, pārcŭs, īnfrĕquēns. *Rare, precious.* Syn.—Ēxcēllēns, ēxĭmĭŭs, ēgrĕgĭŭs, præstāns.

Rāsĭlĭs, ĭs, ĕ. *Easily polished, polished.* Syn.—Rāsŭs, lævĭs, pŏlītŭs.

Rāstrūm, ī. n. Rāstră, ōrūm. n. & Rāstrī, ōrūm. m. *Rake.* Phr.—Rāstrī ŏnŭs. Rārūm pēctĕn. Glēbās vērsāns. Ēt ĭnīquō pōndĕrĕ rāstrī. Cūrvīs pūrgātūr vīnĕā rāstrīs. Rāstrīs tēllūs īntāctă.

Rătĭō, ōnĭs. f. *Reason, motive.* Syn.—Caūsă, mēns, ănĭmŭs, jūdĭcĭūm, cōnsĭlĭūm, prūdēntĭă. Phr.—Sānă mēns. Mēntĭs sōlērtĭă. *Manner, method.* Syn.—Mŏdŭs, vĭă, ārs, pāctūm.

Rătĭs, ĭs. f. *Raft, vessel.* Ēt pāndās rătĭbūs pŏsŭērĕ cărīnās. V. Syn.—Nāvĭs, nāvĭgĭūm.

Raūcĭsŏnŭs, ă, ūm. *Hoarse-sounding.* Syn.—Raūcŭs. Phr.—Raūcă sŏnāns. Raūcō mūrmŭrĕ strĕpĭtāns.

Raūcŭs, ă, ūm. *Hoarse, hoarse-sounding.* Syn.—Raūcĭsŏnŭs. Phr. —Raūcă strĕpēns vōcĕ. Cōrnŭă raūcă sŏnānt. Raūcīs rĕsŏnānt ārbūstă cĭcādīs. Vāllĭs raūcă sŏnăt. Frāctīsquĕ raūcī flūctĭbŭs Ādrĭæ.

Rĕbēllĭs, ĭs, ĕ. *Rebellious, revolting.* Nĕc ārmă rĕbēllēs Aēnĕădæ rĕfĕrēnt, fērrōve hæc rēgnă lăcēssēnt. V. Syn.—Rĕbēllāns, īndŏmĭtŭs, īndŏcĭlĭs. Phr.—Jŭgă dētrēctāns, rĕcūsāns, ēxcŭtĭēns. Jŭgī īmpătĭēns. Īndŏcĭlĭs rĕgī. Īndŏcĭlīs sērvĭtĭūm pătī.

Rĕbŏō, ās, āvī, ātūm, ārĕ. *To re-echo, resound.* Syn.—Rĕmūgĭō, rĕsŏnō, rĕclāmō, rĕsūltō. Phr.—Cūm gĕmĭtū rĕbŏānt sīlvæ.

Rĕcēdō, ĭs, cēssī, cēssūm, ĕrĕ. *To retire, to go away.* Nēc vēro ā stăbŭlīs, plŭvĭa īmpēndēntĕ, rĕcēdūnt. V. Syn.—Cēdō, dēcēdō, cōncēdō, dīscēdō, ābscēdō, ăbĕō. Phr.—Īn sīlvām pēnnīs āblātă rĕcēssĭt. *To retreat.* Phr.—Grēssūs rĕmŏvĕō, rĕvŏcō. Pĕdēm rĕfĕrō.

Rĕcēns, tĭs. adj. *Recent, new.* Vōs mŏdŏ frātērnī, mānēs ănĭmæquĕ rĕcēntēs. O. Syn.—Nŏvŭs, īnsŏlĭtŭs. Phr.—Sērtīsquĕ rĕcēntībŭs hālānt. Flŭvĭōs præbērĕ rĕcēntēs. Fŏlĭō vēlātă rĕcēntī.

Rĕcēnsĕō, ēs, ŭī, ūm & ĭtūm, ērĕ. *To count.* Fōrtĕ rĕcēnsēbāt nŭmĕrūm cārōsquĕ nĕpōtēs. V. Syn.—Nŭmĕrō, rĕcōgnōscō, pērlūstrōr, lūstrō. *To review in thought.* Syn.—Pērcūrrō, rĕvōlvō, ēvōlvō, pērcēnsĕō, rĕcŏlō. *To recount.* Syn.—Nārrō, rĕcĭtō, rĕfĕrō.

Rĕcēssŭs, ūs. m. *Retreat, solitude.* Syn.—Sēcēssŭs, lătĕbræ, pĕnĕtrālĕ, ădўtūm, sēcrētūm, sēcrētă. Phr.—Īn vāllĕ rĕdūctā. Ēst īn sēcēssū lōngō lŏcŭs.

Rĕcĭdīvŭs, ă, ūm. *That which is reborn.* Syn.—Rĕdĭvīvŭs, rĕnāscēns, rĕnŏvātŭs.

Rĕcīdō, ĭs, dī, sūm, ĕrĕ. (*Cædo*). *To cut.* Ūt fās sīt, lōngās, Phœbĕ, rĕcīdĕ cŏmās. M. Syn.—Rĕsĕcō, sĕcō, cædō, ābscīdō, āmpŭtō. Phr.—Cērāsquĕ rĕcīdĕre ĭnānēs. Bārbām rĕcīdĕrĕ fālcĕ. Fig.—*To take away.* Syn.—Tōllō, ădĭmō.

Rĕcīngō, ĭs, xī, ctūm, ĕrĕ. *To unbind, to detach.* Syn.—Ēxŭō, dīscīngō, pōnō, sōlvō.

Rĕcĭnŏ, ĭs, ŭī, ĕrĕ. *Repeat.* Syn.—Rĕcāntŏ, rĕfĕrŏ, gĕmĭnŏ, īngĕmĭnŏ.

Rĕcĭpĭŏ, ĭs, cēpī, cēptūm, ĕrĕ. *To retake, to recover.* Syn.—Rĕcēptŏ, rĕsūmŏ, rĕcŭpĕrŏ. *To take, receive.* Syn.—Căpĭŏ, āccĭpĭŏ, sūmŏ, āssūmŏ. *To welcome, to receive.* Syn.—Rĕcēptŏ, ēxcĭpĭŏ, āccĭpĭŏ. *To save.* Syn.—Ērĭpĭŏ, aūfĕrŏ, sērvŏ. (*Reflexsive*) *To retreat, to go away.* Syn.—Dēcēdŏ, rĕcēdŏ, ābscēdŏ, ĕŏ, ăbĕŏ, rĕdĕŏ. Syn.—Mē cōnfĕrŏ.

Rĕcĭprŏcŭs, ă, ūm. *Reciprocal.* Syn.—Āltērnŭs, rĕflŭŭs.

Rĕcĭtŏ, ās, āvī, ātūm, ārĕ. *To recite, to read.* Syn.—Lĕgŏ, dīcŏ, rĕfĕrŏ.

Rĕclāmŏ, ās, āvī, ātūm, ārĕ. *To cry out against.* Syn.—Clāmŏ. *To re-echo.* Syn.—Rĕbŏŏ, rĕsŏnŏ, rĕsūltŏ.

Rĕclīnĭs, ĭs, ĕ. *Reclining, bending.* Hūnc ŭbĭ rēclīnēm strātīs ēt pācĕ frŭēntēm Āspĭcĭt. V. Syn.—Ācclīvĭs, jăcēns, rĕcŭbāns, strātŭs, rĕclīnātŭs.

Rĕclīnŏ, ās, āvī, ātūm, ārĕ. *To bend down, to recline.* Dēfīgūnt tēllūre hāstās āc scūtă rĕclīnānt. V. Syn.—Ācclīnŏ, īnclīnŏ, īnflēctŏ, dēflēctŏ, pōnŏ, stērnŏ.

Rĕclūdŏ, ĭs, sī, sūm, ĕrĕ. *To open.* Aērātās hōstī rēclūdĕrĕ pōrtās. O. Syn.—Ăpĕrĭŏ, pătĕfăcĭŏ, rĕsĕrŏ. Phr.—Trīstēsquĕ rĕclūdĕrĕ pōrtās. Sānctōs aūsūs rēclūdĕrĕ fōntēs. *To discover, to unfold.* Syn.—Ăpĕrĭŏ, pătĕfăcĭŏ, ēdūcŏ, ēffĕrŏ, dētĕgŏ.

Rĕcōgnōscŏ, ĭs, ōvī, ĭtūm, ĕrĕ. *To recognize.* Syn.—Āgnōscŏ, rĕcēnsĕŏ, pērcēnsĕŏ, pērlūstrŏ.

Rĕcōllĭgŏ, ĭs, ēgī, ēctūm, ĕrĕ. *To collect.* Syn.—Cōllĭgŏ, cōgŏ, rĕcĭpĭŏ. *To recover.* Syn.—Rĕsūmŏ, rĕcĭpĭŏ, rĕcēptŏ.

Rĕcŏlŏ, ĭs, ŭī, cūltūm, ĕrĕ. *To cultivate anew.* Hŭmī pōst tēmpŏră lōngă rĕcūltæ̆. O. Syn.—Cŏlŏ. *To renew, to restore.* Syn.—Rĕnŏvŏ, rĕpărŏ, īnstaūrŏ. *To recall to mind.* Syn.—Rĕcēnsĕŏ, rĕvōlvŏ, rĕcōrdŏr, mĕmĭnī, vōlvŏ.

Rĕcōncĭlĭŏ, ās, āvī, ātūm, ārĕ. *To reconcile.* Syn.—Cōncĭlĭŏ, cōmpōnŏ.

Rĕcōndŏ, ĭs, dĭdī, dĭtum, ĕrĕ. *To conceal.* Aūt sŭpĕr Īdălĭūm, săcrātā sēdĕ, rĕcōndām. V. Syn.—Cōndŏ, ābscōndŏ, ābdŏ, tĕgŏ, cōntĕgŏ. *To bury.* Syn.—Cōndŏ, mērgō, īnfīgŏ, īnfŏdĭŏ.

Rĕcōrdŏr, ārĭs, ātŭs sūm, ārī. *To remember.* Mēcūm lŏquŏr hæ̆c, tăcĭtūsquĕ rĕcōrdŏr. H. Syn.—Mĕmĭnī, rĕmĭnīscŏr. Phr.—Sūm mĕmŏr. Nōn sūm īmmĕmŏr. Nōn sūm ōblītŭs.

Rĕcrĕŏ, ās, āvī, ātūm, ārĕ. *To restore, to refresh, to refit.* Syn.—Rĕpărŏ, rĕfĭcĭŏ, rĕlĕvŏ, ēxcĭtŏ. Phr.—Lūdō, cāntū mēntēm rĕfĭcĭō. Vīrēs rĕcrĕō. Frāctōs ănĭmōs rĕfĭcĭō. Rĕfĭcītque īn prœlĭă vīrēs. Ārbŏr æstīvā rĕcrĕātŭr aūrā.

Rĕcrūdēscō, ĭs, ŭī, ĕrĕ. *To increase, to grow larger.* Syn.—Crūdēscō, ægrēscō, īngrăvēscō, aūgĕŏr, aūgēscō, īnvălĕō.

Rēctē. adv. *Well.* Syn.—Bĕnĕ, prŏbē, pūlchrē. *Rightly, with good reason.* Syn.—Bĕnĕ, jūrĕ, mĕrĭtō.

Rēctŏr, ōrĭs. m. *Director, ruler.* Nĕque ĕnīm tūnc Aĕŏlŭs īllīs Rēctŏr ĕrăt. V. Syn.—Dūx, dūctŏr, mŏdĕrātŏr, gŭbērnātŏr, rēx, dŏmĭnŭs, præsĕs, ārbĭtĕr. *Bishop, prelate.* Syn.—Āntīstĕs, præsŭl, pōntĭfēx.

Rēctūm, ī. n. *Law, right, equity.* Sĭnĕ lēgĕ fĭdēm rēctūmquĕ cŏlēbānt. O. Syn.—Aēquūm, jūstūm, hŏnēstūm, bŏnūm, jūs. Phr.—Rēctūm sērvārĕ. Præpōnĕrĕ rēctūm. Mŏdŏ rēctă căpēssēns.

Rēctŭs, ă, ūm. *Straight, direct.* Syn.—Stāns, ērēctŭs, fīxŭs, īmmōtŭs, īrrĕtōrtŭs. *Right, just.* Syn.—Jūstŭs, æquŭs, hŏnēstŭs, bŏnŭs.

Rĕcŭbō, ās, ŭī, ĭtūm, ārĕ. *To lie down.* Sūb quā nūnc rĕcŭbās ārbŏrĕ, vīrgă fŭĭt. O. Syn.—Rĕcūmbō, stērnŏr, ēxtēndŏr, jăcĕō, quĭēscō, rĕquĭēscō.

Rĕcūmbō, ĭs, ŭī, ŭbĭtūm, ĕrĕ. *To lie down.* Syn.—Jăcĕō, rĕcŭbō, quĭēscō. *To recline at table.* Syn.—Āccūmbō, dīscūmbō. *To bend down.* Syn.—Īnclīnŏr, rĕsīdō. Phr.—Īnque hŭmĕrōs cērvīx cōllāpsă rĕcūmbĭt. Sēd fēssă lăbāt mĭhĭ pōndĕrĕ cērvīx. *To place upon.* Syn.—Īncūmbō, fūlcĭŏr. *To fall upon.* Syn.—Prōcūmbō, īncĭdō, cōllābŏr.

Rĕcūrrō, ĭs, cūrrī & (*sometimes*) cŭcūrrī, cūrsūm, ĕrĕ. *To run back.* Syn.—Rĕdĕō, rĕvērtŏr. *To have recourse to.* Syn.—Cōnfŭgĭō. *To recommence.* Syn.—Ĭtĕrō, rĕpĕtō, gĕmĭnō, īngĕmĭnō, īntĕgrō, rĕdīntĕgrō, īnstaūrō.

Rĕcūrsō, ās, āvī, ātūm, ārĕ. *To run, to come to.* Syn.—Rĕcūrrō. *To recollect.* Syn.—Ōbvērsŏr, rĕdĕō, sŭbĕō.

Rĕcūrvŭs, ă, ūm. *Bent in the opposite direction.* Syn.—Cūrvŭs, īncūrvŭs, rĕcūrvātŭs, īnflēxŭs, rĕflēxŭs, rĕtōrtŭs.

Rĕcūsō, ās, āvī, ātūm, ārĕ. *To refuse.* Cēdo ĕquĭdēm, nēc, nātĕ, tĭbī cŏmĕs īrĕ rĕcūsō. V. Syn.—Ābnĕgō, dētrēctō, rĕfŭgĭō, rĕnŭō, nōlō, īndīgnŏr. Phr.—Nēc jūssă rĕcūsăt. Ūxōrēm grāndī cūm dōtĕ rĕcūsăt.

Rĕdārgŭō, ĭs, ŭī, ūtūm, ĕrĕ. *To refute, to confound.* Syn.—Ārgŭō, rĕfūtō, rĕfēllō, dētĕgō, ōstēndō.

Rēddō, ĭs, ĭdī, ĭtūm, ĕrĕ. *To restore, to give back.* Quæ tĭbĭ quæ tālī rēddām prō cārmĭnĕ dōnă? V. Syn.—Rēstĭtŭō, rĕfĕrō, rĕsīgnō, sōlvō, ēxsōlvō, pērsōlvō, dō, fĕrō, trĭbŭō, trādō. Phr.—

Dătă rēddĕrĕ nōlūnt. Ērēptūm rēddī sĭbĭ pōscĭt hŏnōrēm. Cūm fœnŏrĕ rēddŏ. *To give up, to send away.* Syn.—Rĕmīttŏ, rĕpēllŏ, rēĭcĭŏ. *To reject.* Syn.—Mīttŏ, ēmīttŏ, ēgĕrŏ, ējēctŏ. *To make.* Syn.—Făcĭŏ, ēffĭcĭŏ, præstŏ.

Rĕdĕŏ, īs, īvī & ĭī, ĭtūm, īrĕ. *To return.* Tītўrĕ, dūm rĕdĕō, brĕvĭs ēst vĭă, pāscĕ căpēllās. V. Syn.—Rĕgrĕdĭŏr, rĕvērtŏ, rĕvērtŏr, rĕmĕŏ, rĕmĭgrŏ. Phr.—Mē rĕcĭpĭŏ. Mē rēddŏ, mē rĕfĕrŏ. Sūm rĕdūx. Ĭtĕr rĕpētŏ. Pĕdēm, grēssūm, grădūm rĕfĕrŏ. Cūrsūs ĭtĕrŏ. Rūrsūs tēndĭt ăd. Pĕnātēs rĕpētŏ. Ītquĕ rĕdītquĕ vĭām tŏtĭēs. Vēstīgĭă sĕquŏr.

Rĕdĭgŏ, ĭs, ēgī, āctūm, ĕrĕ. *To bring back, to recall, to gather again.* Syn.—Rĕdūcŏ, āddūcŏ, cōmpēllŏ, ăbĭgŏ, rĕvŏcŏ. *To reduce.* Syn.—Sŭbĭgŏ, sūbjĭcĭŏ.

Rĕdĭmĭŏ, īs, īvī & ĭī, ītūm, īrĕ. *To crown, to girt.* Syn.—Cĭngŏ, vīncĭŏ, cŏrōnŏ, cīrcūmdŏ.

Rĕdĭmŏ, ĭs, ēmī, ēmptūm, ĕrĕ. *To redeem, to ransom.* Sī mĕă mōrs rĕdĭmēndă tŭă. O. Syn.—Ĕmŏ, rĕpēndŏ. Phr.—Aūrō, prĕtĭō rĕpēndŏ. Aūrō rĕdĭmāt jūs trīstĕ sĕpūlcrī. *To save, to liberate.* Syn.—Ēxĭmŏ, lībĕrŏ, sērvŏ, sālvŏ. *To repair.* Syn.—Rĕpărŏ, sārcĭŏ, rĕsārcĭŏ.

Rĕdīntĕgrŏ, ās, āvī, ātūm, ārĕ. *To renovate, to restore, to renew.* Syn.—Īntĕgrŏ, īnstaūrŏ, rĕnŏvŏ, rĕpărŏ.

Rĕdĭtŭs, ūs. m. *Return.* Hī nōstrī rĕdĭtūs, ēxspēctātīquĕ trĭūmphī! V. Syn.—Rĕgrēssŭs, rĕcūrsŭs. Phr.—Sānguĭnĕ quærēndī rĕdĭtūs. Rĕdĭtūs ābscīndĕrĕ dūlcēs. Vōtūm prō rĕdĭtū sĭmŭlānt. Vēlă cărēnt rĕdĭtū. *Revenue.* Syn.—Prōvēntŭs, cēnsŭs.

Rĕdĭvīvŭs, ă, ūm. *That which is born anew, returned to life.* Syn.—Rĕsūrgēns, rĕnāscēns, rĕnātŭs, rĕpărātŭs. Phr.—Ā mōrtĕ rĕvŏcātŭs. Sŭpĕrīs aūrīs rēddĭtŭs. Īn vītām rĕdūx.

Rĕdŏlĕŏ, ēs, ŭī, ērĕ. *To smell, to have the odor of.* Syn.—Ŏlĕŏ, hālŏ, spīrŏ.

Rĕdūcŏ, ĭs, xī, ctūm, ĕrĕ. *To lead back.* Vēspĕr ŭbi ē pāstū vĭtŭlōs ăd tēctă rĕdūcĭt. V. Syn.—Rĕfĕrŏ, rĕdĭgŏ, rĕvŏcŏ, rĕtrăhŏ. *To render, to give up.* Syn.—Rēddŏ, rĕfĕrŏ, rĕvĕhŏ, rēstĭtŭŏ.

Rĕdūncŭs, ă, ūm. *Curved, bent.* Syn.—Ūncŭs, ădūncŭs, rĕcūrvŭs, rĕflēxŭs.

Rĕdūndŏ, ās, āvī, ātūm, ārĕ. *To flow over.* Gūttŭrĕ fāc plēnō sūmptă rĕdūndĕt ăquă. O. Syn.—Ăbūndŏ, ēfflŭŏ, sŭpērflŭŏ. *To fall back upon.* Syn.—Rĕlābŏr, rĕcĭdŏ.

Rĕdūx, ŭcĭs. adj. *That which is brought back or returned.* Syn.—Rĕdĭēns, rēddĭtŭs, rĕvērsŭs.

Rĕfēllŏ, ĭs, ī, ĕrĕ. *To refute, to contradict.* Ēt sōlūs fērrō crīmēn cōmmūnĕ rĕfēllām. V. Syn.—Rĕfūtŏ, cōnfūtŏ, cŏārgŭŏ, rĕdārgŭŏ, īnfīrmŏ, dīssōlvŏ, frāngŏ.

Rĕfērcĭŏ, īs, sī, tūm, īrĕ. *To fill.* Syn.—Īmplĕŏ, rĕplĕŏ, cŭmŭlŏ.

Rĕfĕrŏ, fērs, rĕtŭlī & rēttŭlī, rĕlātūm, fērrĕ. *To bring back.* Sēdĭbŭs hūnc rĕfĕr āntĕ sŭīs, āc cōndĕ sĕpūlcrō. V. Syn.—Rĕpōrtŏ, rĕvĕhŏ, rĕdūcŏ. —grātĭām. *To show or give thanks.* Syn.—Rēddŏ, rĕpēndŏ. *To vomit* Syn.—Ēgĕrŏ, ējēctŏ. *To relate.* Syn.—Nārrŏ, dīcŏ. Phr.—Tālĭă vōcĕ rĕfērt. Mōnstră Dĕūm rĕfĕrŏ. Rēs ēst hōrrēndă rĕlātū.

Rĕfĭcĭŏ, ĭs, fēcī, fēctŭm, ĕrĕ. *To refit, to repair.* Āh! lăcĕrās ĕtĭām pūppēs fŭrĭōsă rĕfēcī. O. Syn.—Rĕpărŏ, rĕnŏvŏ, īnstaūrŏ. *To acquire new strength.* Syn.—Rĕcrĕŏ, rĕpărŏ, rĕfŏvĕŏ. *To restore one's courage.* Syn.—Ēxcĭtŏ, ēxsūscĭtŏ, ērĭgŏ.

Rĕfīgŏ, ĭs, xī, xūm, ĕrĕ. *To snatch from, to tear from.* Syn.—Vēllŏ. Fig.—*To abolish a law.* Syn.—Ăbŏlĕŏ, āntīquŏ, rēscīndŏ.

Rĕfīngŏ, ĭs, fīnxī, fīctūm, ĕrĕ. *To fashion anew, to refit.* Syn.—Rĕpărŏ, rĕfĭcĭŏ, rĕnŏvŏ.

Rĕflēctŏ, ĭs, xī, xūm, ĕrĕ. *To bend back, to curve back.* Syn.—Rĕtōrquĕŏ, cūrvŏ, īnflēctŏ, flēctŏ, rĕcūrvŏ, rĕclīnŏ, rĕplĭcŏ.

Rĕflŭŏ, ĭs, ūxī, ūxūm, ĕrĕ. *To flow back.* Dīssūltānt rīpæ, rĕflŭītque ēxtērrĭtŭs āmnĭs. V. Syn.—Rĕcūrrŏ, rĕdĕŏ, rĕcēdŏ, rĕlābŏr. Phr.—Rētrō fĕrŏr. Īn fōntēs rĕdĭērĕ sŭōs. Ād fōntēm vērsă rĕcūrrăt ăquă.

Rĕflŭŭs, ă, ūm. *That which flows back.* Syn.—Rĕlābēns, rĕflŭēns, rĕcūrrēns, rĕfŭgŭs.

Rĕfōrmīdŏ, ās, āvī, ātūm, ārĕ. *To fear.* Saūcĭă tāctūm Mēmbră rĕfōrmīdānt. O. Syn.—Fōrmīdŏ, mĕtŭŏ, hōrrĕŏ.

Rĕfōrmŏ, ās, āvī, ātūm, ārĕ. *To reform, to repair.* Dūm, quōd fŭĭt āntĕ, rĕfōrmĕt. O. Syn.—Rĕfĭcĭŏ, rĕfīngŏ, īnstaūrŏ, rēstaūrŏ, rĕpărŏ, rĕnŏvŏ.

Rĕfrēnŏ, ās, āvī, ātūm, ārĕ. *To check.* Īllă rĕfrēnăt ăquās, ōblīquăquĕ flūmĭnă sīstĭt. O. Syn.—Frēnŏ, rĕprĭmŏ, cŏērcĕŏ, cŏhĭbĕŏ, cōntĭnĕŏ.

Rĕfrīgĕrŏ, ās, āvī, ātūm, ārĕ. *To cool, to refresh.* Phr.—Aēstūm, călōrēm tēmpĕrŏ, lēnĭŏ, frāngŏ, sēdŏ, rĕlĕvŏ, mītĭgŏ, mĭnŭŏ. Nĭmĭōs sōlēs frāngŏ, dēfēndŏ, ārcĕŏ.

Rĕfrīgēscŏ, ĭs, frīxī, ĕrĕ. *To become cool, to refresh oneself.* Syn.—Dēfrīgēscŏ, rĕfrīgĕrŏr, dēfērvĕŏ, dēfērvēscŏ. Phr.—Călōrēm pērdŏ, āmīttŏ, pōnŏ. Frīgŏrĕ cōrrĭpĭŏr. Ōrĕ ănhēlō aūrās căptŏ. Ŏpācī quærĕrĕ frīgŏrĭs ūmbrās. Mītĭgăt ūmbră.

Rĕfŭgĭŏ, ĭs, fūgī, ĕrĕ. *To fly from.* Saŭcĭŭs āt quădrŭpēs nōta īntĕr tēctă rĕfūgĭt. V. Syn.—Fŭgĭŏ, aūfŭgĭŏ, ābscēdŏ, rĕcēdŏ. *To avoid.* Syn.—Fŭgĭŏ, ēffŭgĭŏ. *To refuse to.* Syn.—Āvērsŏr, rĕcūsŏ, dētrēctŏ, ābnŭŏ, nōlŏ.

Rĕfŭgŭs, ă, ūm. *One who flies, escapes.* Syn.—Prŏfŭgŭs, fŭgĭtīvŭs, fŭgĭēns, fŭgāx.

Rĕfūlgĕŏ, ēs, sī, ērĕ. *To shine brightly.* Pūrpŭrĕā lūcĕ rĕfūlsĭt hŭmŭs. O. Syn.—Fūlgĕŏ, rĕnīdĕŏ, rĕnĭtĕŏ, mĭcŏ, cŏrūscŏ, rădĭŏ, rŭtĭlŏ. Phr.—Rŏsĕā cērvīcĕ rĕfūlsĭt.

Rĕfūtŏ, ās, āvī, ātūm, ārĕ. *To repulse, to reject.* Syn.—Cōnfūtŏ, rĕdārgŭŏ, rĕfēllŏ.

Rĕgĕrŏ, ĭs, gēssī, gēstūm, ĕrĕ. *To carry back, to send back, to reject.* Syn.—Rējĭcĭŏ, rĕfĕrŏ, rēddŏ, rējēctŏ, rĕfūndŏ.

Rēgĭă, æ. f. *Royal palace.* Fēstăquĕ cōnfūsā rĕsŏnābāt rēgĭă tūrbā. O. Syn.—Aūlă, ātrĭă, pălātĭă. Phr.—Rēgĭă tēctă. Rēgālĭs dŏmŭs. Sŭpērbă rēgūm ātrĭă. Rēgālĭs prīncĭpĭs aūlă. Vĕtĕrūm pĕnĕtrālĭă rēgūm. Rēgālĭs līmĭnă clără dŏmūs.

Rēgĭfĭcē. adv. *Royally.* Syn.—Rēgĭē, rēgālĭtĕr, māgnĭfĭcē, laūtē. Phr.—Rēgālī pōmpā. Rēgĭfĭcō lūxū, părātū, mōrĕ.

Rĕgĭmĕn, ĭnĭs. n. *Government, rule.* Syn.—Mŏdĕrāmĕn, īmpĕrĭūm, dūctŭs.

Rēgīnă, æ. f. *Queen.* Rēgīna ăd tēmplūm fōrmā pūlchērrĭmă Dīdō. V. Syn.—Rēgnātrīx, dŏmĭnātrīx, dŏmĭnă. Phr.—Rēgĭă cōnjūx, ūxŏr, spōnsă.

Rĕgĭŏ, ōnĭs. f. *Line, direction, way.* Syn.—Līnĕă, vĭă. *Region, country.* Syn.—Plăgă, tērră, ōră, lĭttŭs, trāctŭs, fīnēs, rēgnūm.

Rēgĭŭs, ă, ūm. *Royal, regal.* Syn.—Rēgālĭs, rēgĭfĭcŭs, māgnĭfĭcŭs, splēndĭdŭs.

Rēgnātŏr, ōrĭs. m. *One who reigns as king.* Syn.—Dŏmĭnātŏr, mŏdĕrātŏr, rēx. Phr.—Sŭpĕrī rēgnātŏr Ŏlÿmpī. Quō frēnă rĕgūntŭr Īmpĕrĭī.

Rēgnŏ, ās, āvī, ātūm, ārĕ. *To rule, to command.* Nēc tĭbĭ rēgnāndī vĕnĭāt tām dīră cŭpīdŏ. V. Syn.—Īmpĕrŏ, dŏmĭnŏr, præsūm. Phr.—Rēgnă Tÿrī Gērmānŭs hăbēbāt. Hūmānūm cūrārĕ gĕnŭs. Lōngō rēgnābĭtŭr ævō.

Rēgnūm, ī. n. *Kingdom.* Ārmă Jŏvĭs fŭgĭēns ē rēgnīs ēxsŭl ădēmptīs. V. Syn.—Īmpĕrĭūm. Phr—Rēgnī fīnēs. Dūm rēgnă mănēbānt. Fās rēgnă rĕsūrgĕrĕ Trōjæ. Pūlsūm rēgnīs cēssīssĕ pătērnīs. Quæ sūrgĕrĕ rēgnă vĭdēbĭs! *Power, control.* Syn.—Dŏmĭnātŭs, dĭtĭŏ, sŏlĭūm, scēptrūm. Phr.—Rēgnī pŏtēstās, mŏdĕrāmĕn, frēnă, dĕcŭs, hŏnŏr, pōndŭs. Rēgĭă pŏtēstas. Scēptrī dĕcŭs.

Rĕgŏ, ĭs, rēxī, rēctūm, ĕrĕ. *To guide, to conduct.* Cæcă rĕgēns fīlō vēstīgĭă. V. Syn.—Dūcŏ, dīrĭgŏ. *To rule.* Syn.—Mŏdĕrŏr, gŭbērnŏ, dīrĭgŏ, īmpĕrŏ, īmpĕrĭtŏ. Phr.—Rĕgēt pătrĭīs vīrtūtĭbŭs ōrbēm. Īllĕ rĕgīt dīctīs ănĭmōs. Fōrtūnă sŭă tēmpŏră lēgĕ rĕgĭt.

Rēgŭlă, æ. f. *Rule.* Syn.—Lēx, nōrmă, mŏdŭs, ēxēmplūm.

Rējĭcĭŏ, ĭs, jēcī, jēctūm, ĕrĕ. *To throw back, to cast away.* Syn.—Mīttŏ, ābjĭcĭŏ, dēpōnŏ, pōnŏ. *To reject, to repulse.* Syn.—Rĕpēllŏ, āmŏvĕŏ, āvērtŏ, ārcĕŏ. *To send away, to send back.* Syn.—Rĕpēllŏ, rēddŏ, rĕfĕrŏ, rĕpērcŭtĭŏ. *To refuse.* Syn.—Rēspŭŏ, cōntēmnŏ, āvērsŏr, fāstīdĭŏ, āspērnŏr, dēdīgnŏr.

Rĕlābŏr, ĕrĭs, psŭs sūm, ī. *To fall back.* Syn.—Rĕcĭdŏ, cădŏ. *To mount back.* Syn.—Rĕflŭŏ, rĕmānŏ.

Rĕlāxŏ, ās, āvī, ātūm, ārĕ. *To relax, to become loose.* Syn.—Lāxŏ, rĕmīttŏ, sōlvŏ, dīssōlvŏ, ăpĕrĭŏ. Phr.—Vīnclă rĕlāxăt. Dēnsă rĕlāxăt. *To let loose, to lighten.* Syn.—Lāxŏ, lĕvŏ, rĕcrĕŏ, rĕmīttŏ.

Rĕlēgŏ, ās, āvī, ātūm, ārĕ. *To exile, to send away.* Syn.—Āblēgŏ, āmāndŏ, pēllŏ, rĕmŏvĕŏ, rējĭcĭŏ.

Rĕlĕgŏ, ĭs, lēgī, lēctūm, ĕrĕ. *To gather together.* Syn.—Cōllĭgŏ, rĕcōllĭgŏ. *To run over, to revise.* Syn.—Rĕpĕtŏ, rĕvīsŏ, rĕmētĭŏr.

Rĕlĕvŏ, ās, āvī, ātūm, ārĕ. *To raise up.* Ā tērrā cōrpŭs rĕlĕvārĕ vŏlēntēm. O. Syn.—Lĕvŏ, āllĕvŏ, sūblĕvŏ, ērĭgŏ. *To help, to assist.* Syn.—Lĕvŏ, ēxĭmŏ, ādjŭvŏ, rĕcrĕŏ, rĕfĭcĭŏ, mĕdĕŏr, sōlŏr.

Rĕlĭgĭŏ & Rēllĭgĭŏ, ōnĭs. f. *Religion, worship.* Ēt pŏpŭlum āntīquā sūb rēllĭgĭōnĕ tŭērī. V. Syn.—Pĭĕtās, cūltŭs. Phr.—Săcĕr cūltŭs. Dīvūm rēlĭgĭŏ. Rītūs mōrēsquĕ săcrōrūm.

Rĕlĭgĭōsŭs (Rēllĭgĭōsŭs), ă, ūm. *Religious, holy, sacred.* Ēt rēllĭgĭōsă dĕōrūm līmĭnă. V. Syn.—Săcĕr, sānctŭs, dīvīnŭs.

Rĕlĭgŏ, ās, āvī, ātūm, ārĕ. *To bind, to attach.* Rĕlĭgāvĭt ăb āggĕrĕ clāssēm. V. Syn.—Lĭgŏ, āllĭgŏ, rĕvīncĭŏ.

Rĕlīnquŏ, ĭs, līquī, līctūm, ĕrĕ. *To leave, to abandon.* Ārdĕt ăbīrĕ fŭgā, dūlcēsquĕ rĕlīnquĕrĕ tērrās. V. Syn.—Līnquŏ, dēsĕrŏ, fŭgĭŏ, dīscēdŏ, ăbĕŏ, ābscēdŏ, rĕcēdŏ, dēpōnŏ, pōnŏ.

Rĕlĭquĭæ, ārūm. f. *Remains.* Phr.—Pārs rĕlĭquă, cētĕră. *Remains, ashes or body of the dead.* Syn.—Cĭnĭs, cĭnĕrēs, ōssă.

Rĕlĭquŭs, ă, ūm. *Remaining.* Syn.—Rĕsĭdŭŭs, ălĭŭs, cētĕrŭs, sŭpērstĕs.

Rĕlūcĕŏ, ēs, xī, ērĕ. *To shine.* Sīgæa īgnī frĕtă lātă rĕlūcēnt. V. Syn.—Rĕfūlgĕŏ, rĕnīdĕŏ, rēsplēndĕŏ. *See Luceo.*

Rĕlūctŏr, ārĭs, ātŭs sūm, ārī. *To be reluctant, to refuse.* Syn.—Ōblūctŏr, rĕsīstŏ, ōbnītŏr, rĕpūgnŏ. *See Resisto.*

Rĕmĕŏ, ās, āvī, ātūm, ārĕ. *To return, to come back.* Syn.—Rĕdĕŏ, rĕvērtŏr. *See Redeo.*

Rĕmētĭŏr, īrĭs , mēnsŭs sūm, īrī. *To remeasure.* Syn.—Mētĭŏr. *To run over again.* Syn.—Rĕlĕgŏ, rĕcūrrŏ, rĕpĕtŏ. Phr.—Lĕgŏ rĕtrōrsūm. *To pass over in one's mind.* Syn.—Rĕvōlvŏ, rĕcōgnōscŏ, rĕcēnsĕŏ.

Rēmĭgĭūm, ĭī. n. *Rowing.* Syn.—Rēmī, rēmōrūm vērbĕră, īctūs, aūxĭlĭūm.

Rēmĭgŏ, ās, āvī, ātūm, ārĕ. *To row.* Phr.—Rēmōs dūcŏ, īmpēllŏ, mŏvĕŏ, ăgĭtŏ. Rēmīs ūtŏr, ēnītŏr, brāchĭă īntēndŏ. Rēmis ăquās, ūndās, æquŏră, flūctūs, frĕtă fĕrĭŏ, sĕcŏ, fīndŏ, dīvĭdŏ, vērrŏ. Rēmīs, rēmĭgĭō nāvēm mŏvĕŏ. Vălĭdīs īncūmbĭtĕ rēmīs. Īmpēllĕrĕ rēmĭgĕ clāssēm. Lēntōs īncūrvānt gūrgĭtĕ rēmōs.

Rĕmīttŏ, ĭs, mīsī, mīssūm, ĕrĕ. *To send back.* Syn.—Rēddŏ, mīttŏ. *To reecho.* Syn.—Rēddŏ, ĭtĕrŏ, īngĕmĭnŏ, rĕpĕtŏ. *To relax.* Syn.—Lāxŏ, rĕlāxŏ. *To pardon.* Syn.—Cōndōnŏ, pārcŏ, īgnōscŏ, īndūlgĕŏ.

Rĕmŏrŏr, ārĭs, ātŭs sūm, ārī. *To delay, to stop.* Syn.—Mŏrŏr, tārdŏ, rĕtārdŏ, rĕtĭnĕŏ, ōbstŏ.

Rĕmŏvĕŏ, ēs, mōvī, mōtūm, ērĕ. *To separate from.* Ēt mŏnĕt ārcānīs ŏcŭlōs rĕmŏvērĕ prŏfānōs. O. Syn.—Āmŏvĕŏ, dīmŏvĕŏ, sūbmŏvĕŏ, ābdūcŏ, āvērtŏ, ārcĕŏ, āmāndŏ, rējĭcĭŏ, rĕpēllŏ. *To take away.* Syn.—Tōllŏ, aūfĕrŏ, ērĭpĭŏ, sūbdūcŏ, ădĭmŏ.

Rĕmūgĭŏ, īs, īvī & ĭī, īrĕ. *To reecho loudly.* Syn.—Rĕbŏŏ, rĕclāmŏ, rĕsŏnŏ.

Rĕmūnĕrŏ, ās, āvī, ātūm, ārĕ. *To reward.* Syn.—Pēnsŏ, cōmpēnsŏ. Phr.—Grātĭăm, vĭcēm rĕfĕrŏ, rĕpōnŏ, rēddŏ, rĕtrĭbŭŏ. Prĕtĭūm, mērcēdēm rĕpēndŏ, sōlvŏ, pērsōlvŏ.

Rĕmūrmŭrŏ, ās, āvī, ātūm, ārĕ. *To murmur.* Nēc frāctă rĕmūrmŭrăt ūndă. V. Syn.—Ōbmūrmŭrŏ, ōblŏquŏr. *To reecho.* Syn.—Ōbmūrmŭrŏ, rĕsŏnŏ.

Rēmŭs, ī. m. *An oar.* Āgmĭnĕ rēmōrūm cĕlĕrī, vēntisquĕ vŏcātīs. V. Syn.—Rēmĭgĭūm, ārbŏr, pālmĕs, pālmŭlă, tōnsæ. Phr.—Rēmī pālmă. Rēmōrūm āgmĕn. Cōnsūrgūnt tērno ōrdĭnĕ rēmī.

Rĕnāscŏr, ĕrĭs, nātŭs sūm, ī. *To be born again.* Syn.—Rĕvīvīscŏr, rĕvīvŏ, rĕsūscĭtŏr, rĕsūrgŏ, rĕnŏvŏr, rĕvĭrĕŏ. Phr.—Rĕdĕŏ ād līmĭnă vītæ.

Rĕnīdĕŏ, ēs, ērĕ. *To shine brightly.* Syn.—Rĕnīdēscŏ, rĕfūlgĕŏ, rĕlūcĕŏ, rēsplēndĕŏ.

Rĕnŏvŏ, ās, āvī, ātūm, ārĕ. *To renew.* Rĕpĕtītăquĕ fōrmă lŏcōrūm Ēxsĭlĭūm rĕnŏvāt trīstĕ, rĕcēnsquĕ făcĭt. O. Syn.—Īnstaūrŏ, īntĕgrŏ, rĕdīntĕgrŏ, ĭtĕrŏ, rĕpĕtŏ. Phr.—Rĕnŏvārĕ dŏlōrēm. Stāt cāsūs rĕnŏvāre ōmnēs. *To re-animate, to re-invigorate.* Syn.—Rĕpărŏ, rĕcrĕŏ, rĕfĭcĭŏ.

Rĕnūntĭŏ, ās, āvī, ātūm, ārĕ. *To announce.* Syn.—Nūntĭŏ, rĕfĕrŏ, nārrŏ. *To countermand, to give up.* Syn.—Rĕcāntŏ, rĕtrāctŏ.

Rĕnŭŏ, ĭs, ī, ĕrĕ. *To reject with a nod, to refuse.* Syn.—Ābnŭŏ, nĕgŏ, ābnĕgŏ, nōlŏ, vĕtŏ, rĕcūsŏ.

Rĕŏr, rērĭs, rătŭs sūm, rērī. *To think, to believe.* Sīc ĕquĭdēm dūcēbam ănĭmō rēbārquĕ fŭtūrūm. V. Syn.—Cēnsĕŏ, ēxīstĭmŏ, jūdĭcŏ, ŏpīnŏr, pŭtŏ.

Rĕpāgŭlă, ōrūm. n. *Bar, barriers.* Syn.—Ŏbēx, vēctĭs.

Rĕpărŏ, ās, āvī, ātūm, ārĕ. *To acquire anew.* Syn.—Rĕcĭpĭŏ, rĕcŭpĕrŏ. *To restore.* Syn.—Rĕfĭcĭŏ, nŏvŏ, rĕnŏvŏ, rēstaūrŏ, īntĕgrŏ, rĕdīntĕgrŏ, sārcĭŏ, rĕsārcĭŏ. Phr.—Ăd āntīquūm rĕvŏcārĕ dĕcŭs. Vĕtĕrēs sārcīrĕ rŭīnās. *To re-animate.* Syn.—Rĕfĭcĭŏ, rĕcrĕŏ, lĕvŏ, rĕlĕvŏ, ērĭgŏ. Phr.—Vīrēs rĕddŏ, rĕnŏvŏ, āddŏ. *To create anew.* Syn.—Rĕsūscĭtŏ, ēxsūscĭtŏ.

Rĕpēllŏ, ĭs, rĕpŭlī & rēppŭlī, pūlsūm, ĕrĕ. *To repel, to repulse.* Ōcĕănī sprētōs pĕdĕ rēppŭlĭt āmnēs. V. Syn.—Pēllŏ, dēpēllŏ, ēxpēllŏ, prōpēllŏ, prōpūlsŏ, ārcĕŏ, āmōlĭŏr, āmŏvĕŏ, rĕmŏvĕŏ, āvērtŏ, prŏhĭbĕŏ. Phr.—Hŭmĭlī rēppŭlĭt ārtĕ fămēm. *To refuse.* Syn.—Rĕcūsŏ, rējĭcĭŏ, rēspŭŏ, dētrēctŏ, āspērnŏr, dēdīgnŏr.

Rĕpēndŏ, ĭs, dī, sūm, ĕrĕ. *To repay.* Syn.—Sōlvŏ, pērsōlvŏ, rĕtrĭbŭŏ, rĕfĕrŏ. *To make compensation, to compensate for.* Syn.—Rĕpēnsŏ, cōmpēnsŏ, pēnsŏ, rĕdĭmŏ.

Rĕpēntĕ. adv. *Suddenly, unexpectedly.* Syn.—Āctūtūm, cōnfēstīm, ēxtēmplō, cōntĭnŭō, prōtĭnŭs, sŭbĭtō, stătīm.

Rĕpēntīnŭs, ă, ūm. *Sudden, unforeseen.* Syn.—Rĕpēns, sŭbĭtŭs, īmprōvīsŭs, ĭnōpīnŭs.

Rĕpĕrĭŏ, īs, ī & rēppĕrī, rĕpērtūm, īrĕ. *To discover, to find.* Syn.—Īnvĕnĭŏ, nāncīscŏr, cōmpĕrĭŏ. *To imagine.* Syn.—Īnvĕnĭŏ, ēxcōgĭtŏ.

Rĕpĕtŏ, ĭs, īvī & ĭī, ītūm, ĕrĕ. *To return to.* Syn.—Rĕdĕŏ. *To repeat.* Syn.—Ĭtĕrŏ, īngĕmĭnŏ. *To recall.* Syn.—Rĕcōrdŏr, rĕvŏcŏ. *To seek anew.* Syn.—Rĕpōscŏ, rĕquīrŏ.

Rĕplĕŏ, ēs, ēvī, ētūm, ērĕ. *To refill.* Syn.—Īmplĕŏ, ădīmplĕŏ, cŭmŭlŏ. Phr.—Fōssă rĕplētŭr hŭmō. Līttŏră vōcĕ rĕplĕt.

Rēpŏ, ĭs, sī, tūm, ĕrĕ. *To creep, to crawl.* Syn.—Ādrēpŏ, rēptŏ, sērpŏ. Phr.—Sērpĕrĕ hŭmī. Cōrpŭs hŭmī trăhĕrĕ. Vērrĕrĕ pēctŏrĕ tērrăm. *To glide into, to insinuate oneself into.* Syn.—Sērpŏ, īnsĭnŭŏ.

Rĕpōnŏ, ĭs, pŏsŭī, pŏsĭtūm, ĕrĕ. *To replace, to re-establish.* Sīc nōs īn scēptră rĕpōnĭs? V. Syn.—Rĕpărŏ, rĕfĭcĭŏ, īnstaūrŏ, stătŭŏ. *To place in reserve.* Syn.—Rĕcōndŏ, cōndŏ, sērvŏ, sēpōnŏ. *To place or put.* Syn.—Dēpōnŏ, pōnŏ, cōllŏcŏ, lŏcŏ, stătŭŏ.

Rĕpōrtŏ, ās, āvī, ātūm, ārĕ. *To bring back.* Syn.—Rĕfĕrŏ, rĕdūcŏ, rĕvĕhŏ. *To relate.* Syn.—Rĕfĕrŏ, nūntĭŏ. *See Nuntio.*

Rĕpōscŏ, ĭs, pŏpōscī, pōscĭtūm, ĕrĕ. *To demand again.* Syn.—Rĕpĕtŏ, pĕtŏ, pōscŏ.

Rĕprĕhēndŏ (Rĕprēndŏ), ĭs, dī, sūm, ĕrĕ. *To take, to bring back.* Syn.—Rĕtrăhŏ, rĕvŏcŏ. *To find fault with.* Syn.—Ārgŭŏ, īncrĕpĭtŏ, īncūsŏ, ŏbjūrgŏ.

Rĕprĕhēnsŏr, ōrĭs. m. *One who blames, censor.* Syn.—Cēnsŏr, cāstīgātŏr.

Rĕprĭmŏ, ĭs, prēssī, prēssūm, ĕrĕ. *To check, to hold back.* Rētrōquĕ pĕdēm cūm vōcĕ rĕprēssĭt. V. Syn.—Cōmprĭmŏ, tĕnĕŏ, cōntĭnĕŏ, rĕtĭnĕŏ, cŏērcĕŏ, cŏhĭbĕŏ, cōmpēscŏ, frēnŏ, rĕfrēnŏ, sīstŏ. Phr.—Dēxtrāmquĕ rĕprēssĭt. Gĕmĭtūm vīrtūtĕ rĕprēssĭt. Īrāmquĕ pŭdōrĕ rĕprēssĭt.

Rĕpŭdĭŏ, ās, āvī, ātūm, ārĕ. *To reject, to repudiate.* Syn.—Rĕcūsŏ, rējĭcĭŏ, rĕpēllŏ, rēspŭŏ, āspērnŏr, dēdīgnŏr.

Rĕpūgnŏ, ās, āvī, ātūm, ārĕ. *To resist.* Cēdĕ rĕpūgnāntī, cēdēndō vīctŏr ăbĭbĭs. O. Syn.—Ādvērsŏr, rĕsīstŏ, rĕlūctŏr. *To differ from, to be contrary to.* Syn.—Pūgnŏ, dīffĕrŏ, dīscrĕpŏ.

Rĕpūrgŏ, ās, āvī, ātūm, ārĕ. *To cleanse, to purge.* Dūmquĕ rĕpūrgăt hŭmūm, cōllēctăquĕ săxă rĕmīttĭt. O. Syn.—Pūrgŏ, ēxpūrgŏ, mūndŏ. *To purify.* Syn.—Ēlŭŏ, pūrgŏ.

Rĕpŭtŏ, ās, āvī, ātūm, ārĕ. *To think, to consider.* Syn.—Cōgĭtŏ, rĕvōlvŏ, rĕpĕtŏ, mĕdĭtŏr.

Rĕquĭēs, ētĭs. f. *Repose, quiet.* Īs lŏcŭs ūrbĭs ĕrīt, rĕquĭēs ĕă cērtă lăbōrūm. V. Syn.—Quĭēs, pāx. Phr.—Rĕquĭēm pūgnæ rēbūsquĕ sălūtēm. Nēc mŏră, nēc rĕquĭēs. Nūllă mălī rĕquĭēs ĕrăt. Tū rĕquĭēs fēssō grātă lăbōrĭs ĕrăt.

Rĕquĭēscŏ, ĭs, ēvī, ētūm, ĕrĕ. *To rest, to take repose.* Lōngām rĕquĭēscĕrĕ nōctēm. V. Syn.—Quĭēscŏ, ōtĭŏr. *To lie upon.* Syn.—Īncūmbŏ, īnnītŏr.

Rĕquīrŏ, ĭs, sīvī, sītūm, ĕrĕ. *To seek carefully.* Ŏcŭlīs ănĭmōquĕ rĕquīrĭt. O. Syn.—Quærŏ, ēxquīrŏ, īnvēstīgŏ, scrūtŏr. *To long for.* Syn.—Dēsīdĕrŏ.

Rēs, rĕī. f. *Thing.* Fēlīx quī pŏtŭĭt rērūm cōgnōscĕrĕ caūsās. V. *Deed, action.* Syn.—Āctă, fāctūm, făcĭnŭs. *The world.* Syn.—

Ōrbĭs. *Power.* Syn.—Īmpĕrĭum, ŏpēs, rēgnūm. *Fortune.*
Syn.—Fōrtūnă. *Deeds.* Syn.—Gēstă.

Rĕsārcĭŏ, īs, īvī & ĭī, ītūm, īrĕ. *To refit, repair.* Syn.—Sārcĭŏ, rĕfĭcĭŏ, rĕpārŏ, rĕnŏvŏ, rēstaūrŏ.

Rēscĭndŏ, ĭs, scĭdī, scīssūm, ĕrĕ. *To retrench, to cut off.* Syn.—
Scīndŏ, ābscīndŏ, rĕcīdŏ, sĕcŏ, rĕsĕcŏ, rĕvēllŏ. *To reopen a
wound.* Syn.—Rĕnŏvŏ, rĕfrĭcŏ. *To destroy.* Syn.—Dēstrŭŏ,
dīrŭŏ, ēvērtŏ. *To abolish, to abrogate.* Syn.—Ăbŏlĕŏ, ābrŏgŏ,
āntīquŏ, īnfīrmŏ, frāngŏ, rūmpŏ, ēvērtŏ.

Rĕsĕcŏ, ās, ŭī, ctūm, ārĕ. *To cut off.* Syn.—Sĕcŏ. *See Seco.*
Fig.—*To retrench.* Syn.—Ēxcīdŏ, tōllŏ, ădĭmŏ, aūfĕrŏ.

Rĕsĕrŏ, ās, āvī, ātūm, ārĕ. *To open.* Ūrbem ălĭī rĕsĕrārĕ jŭbēnt ēt
pāndĕrĕ pōrtās. V. Syn.—Ăpĕrĭŏ, rĕclūdŏ, rĕsīgnŏ, pāndŏ.
To commence. Syn.—Īncĭpĭŏ, ōrdĭŏr, ăpĕrĭŏ. *To unveil.* Syn.—
Syn.—Dēclārŏ, mănĭfēstŏ, ōstēndŏ, rĕtĕgŏ.

Rĕsērvŏ, ās, āvī, ātūm, ārĕ. *To reserve, to keep for someone.*
Syn.—Sērvŏ, rĕcōndŏ, rĕpōnŏ, dēstĭnŏ.

Rĕsĕs, ĭdĭs. adj. *Lazy, sluggish.* Jām prīdēm rĕsĭdēs ănĭmōs dēsuētăquĕ cōrdă. V. Syn.—Dēsĕs, ōtĭōsŭs, pĭgĕr, sēgnĭs.

Rĕsĭdĕŏ, ēs, sēdī, sēssūm, ērĕ. *To seat oneself.* Syn.—Cōnsĭdĕŏ.
To remain. Syn.—Mănĕŏ, rĕmănĕŏ, rēstŏ. *To settle, to subside.* Syn.—Cōncĭdŏ, cōnsīdŏ, rĕlābŏr. Fig.—*To become appeased.* Syn.—Quĭēscŏ, rĕquĭēscŏ, cădŏ, pōnŏ, plācŏr.

Rĕsīgnŏ, ās, āvī, ātūm, ārĕ. *To open, unseal.* Syn.—Ăpĕrĭŏ, rĕsōlvŏ.
To destroy. Syn.—Sōlvŏ, rūmpŏ, frāngŏ, tōllŏ.

Rĕsĭlĭŏ, īs, ĭī & ŭī, sūltūm, īrĕ. *To rebound.* Syn.—Rĕsūltŏ, rĕflēctŏ,
rĕpērcŭtĭŏr, rĕtōrquĕŏr, rĕpēllŏr. Phr.—Rĕtrō sălĭŏ, ēxsĭlĭŏ,
fĕrŏr.

Rĕsīstŏ, ĭs, stĭtī, ĕrĕ. *To stop, to rest.* Rēstĭtĭt ād nōstrās fēssă lăbōrĕ fŏrēs. O. Syn.—Sīstŏ, cōnsīstŏ, stō, mănĕŏ, hærĕŏ, mŏrŏr.
To resist. Syn.—Ōbsīstŏ, ōbstŏ, ōbsūm, rĕnītŏr, ōbnītŏr, rĕlūctŏr, ōblūctŏr, rēspōnsŏ, ādvērsŏ, rĕpūgnŏ. Phr.—Cōntrā
nītŏr, stō. Hōstēm īnstāntēm, hōstīlēm īncūrsūm sūstĭnĕŏ, rĕtārdŏ. Dēnsīs ōbsīstĕrĕ tūrmīs. Cæcŏ Mārtĕ rĕsīstūnt.

Rĕsōlvŏ, ĭs, ōlvī, ŏlūtūm, ĕrĕ. *To dissolve.* Syn.—Sōlvŏ, dīssōlvŏ.
To weaken, to enervate. Syn.—Sōlvŏ, frāngŏ, ēnērvŏ. *To dissipate.* Syn.—Lāxŏ, rĕlāxō, rĕmīttŏ, fŭgŏ, dīscŭtĭŏ. *To absolve.* Syn.—Ābsōlvŏ.

Rĕsŏnŏ, ās, ŭī, ārĕ. *To resound, to re-echo.* Āvĭă tūm rĕsŏnānt ăvĭbūs vīrgŭltă cănōrīs. V. Syn.—Sŏnŏ, āssŏnŏ, cōnsŏnŏ, īnsŏnŏ,
rĕbŏŏ, rĕmūgĭŏ, rĕclāmŏ, rēspōnsŏ, rĕmūrmŭrŏ, rĕsūltŏ. Phr.—

Sŏnūm rēddŏ, rĕfĕrŏ. Rĕsŏnāt clāmōrībŭs æthēr. *To repeat.* Syn.—Rĕmūrmŭrŏ, ōbmūrmŭrŏ, ĭtĕrŏ, īngĕmĭnŏ, rĕpĕtŏ.

Rĕsŏnŭs, ă, ūm. *Resounding, sonorous.* Dīxĕrăt; hæc rĕsŏnīs ĭtĕrābăt vōcĭbŭs, ēheū! O. Syn.—Rĕsŏnāns, rĕsŏnābĭlĭs, sŏnōrŭs.

Rēspērgŏ, ĭs, sī, sūm, ĕrĕ. *To scatter, to sprinkle.* Syn.—Spārgŏ, āspērgŏ, pērfūndŏ.

Rēspĭcĭŏ, ĭs, ēxī, ēctūm, ĕrĕ. *To look back.* Syn.—Rēspēctŏ. Phr.—Rĕtrō āspĭcĭŏ, vĭdĕŏ, cērnŏ, tŭĕŏr. Ŏcŭlōs vērtŏ, cōnvērtŏ. Flēctŏ ăcĭēm. Ŏcŭlōs ăd tēctă rĕtōrsĭt. *To consider, to examine.* Syn.—Āttēndŏ, rĕpŭtŏ, mĕdĭtŏr, ēxpēndŏ.

Rēspīrŏ, ās, āvī, ātūm, ārĕ. *To breathe.* Nēc rēspīrārĕ pŏtēstās. V. Syn.—Ēxhālŏ, spīrŏ, hālŏ. Phr.—Spīrĭtūm, aūrām trăhŏ, dūcŏ, cāptŏ. Ănĭmām rĕcĭpĭŏ.

Rēspōndĕŏ, ēs, dī, sūm, ērĕ. *To respond.* Ōllī sēdātō rēspōndĭt cōrdĕ Lătīnŭs. V. Syn.—Rēspōnsŏ, rĕfĕrŏ, rĕsĕquŏr, ēxcĭpĭŏ. Phr.—Rēspōnsă dō, rēddŏ, fĕrŏ, rĕfĕrŏ. Vōcēm, dīctă rēddŏ. Cōntrā ōrdĭŏr. Dīctīs dīctă sĕquŏr. Tūrnŭs ăd hæc. Aeŏlŭs hæc cōntrā. Tūm sīc ēxcēpĭt. Rēspōnsūm prīmŭs dĕdĭt īllĕ pĕtēntī. Sīc rēddĭdĭt ōrĕ. *To be reflected (in speaking of objects).* Syn.—Īngĕmĭnŏr, rēddŏr, rĕflēctŏr. *To correspond to.* Syn.—Cōngrŭŏ, cōnvĕnĭŏ.

Rēspōnsūm, ī. n. *Reply.* Nēc rēspōnsă pŏtēst cōnsūltūs rēddĕrĕ vātēs. V. Syn.—Rēspōnsĭŏ. *Oracle.* Syn.—Ōrăcŭlūm. Phr.—Hōc ūnō rēspōnso ănĭmūm dēlūsĭt Ăpōllŏ. Rēspōnsīs hōrrēnt Dīvūm.

Rēspūblĭcă, rĕīpūblĭcæ. f. *State, republic.* Syn.—Īmpĕrĭūm, rēs. *Public affairs.* Syn.—Pūblĭcă nĕgōtĭă.

Rēspŭŏ, ĭs, ī, ĕrĕ. *To spit forth, to eject, to vomit.* Syn.—Ējĭcĭŏ, rējĭcĭŏ, ēvŏmŏ, ēgĕrŏ. *To reject with scorn.* Syn.—Āspērnŏr, fāstīdĭŏ, rĕnŭŏ, rējĭcĭŏ, spērnŏ, dēdīgnŏr.

Rēstāgnŏ, ās, āvī, ātūm, ārĕ. *To overflow.* Syn.—Stāgnŏ, ēxūndŏ, ēffūndŏr, sŭpērfūndŏr, ēxspătĭŏr.

Rēstĭtŭŏ, ĭs, ī, tūtūm, ĕrĕ. *To restore, to put in place.* Syn.—Rĕpōnŏ, rĕfĭcĭŏ, rĕpărŏ. *To render back.* **Syn.—Rēddŏ, rĕfĕrŏ.**

Rēstŏ, ās, stĭtī, ārĕ. *To stop, to halt.* Syn.—Rĕsīstŏ, mănĕŏ, mŏrŏr, cōnsīstŏ. *To remain, to be left.* Syn.—Sŭpērsūm. Phr.—Sūm sŭpērstēs, rĕlĭquŭs. Nēc spēs jām rēstăt Iūlī.

Rĕsūltŏ, ās, āvī, ātūm, ārĕ. *To leap back.* Syn.—Rĕsĭlĭŏ. *To be repulsed.* Syn.—Rĕsĭlĭŏ, rĕpēllŏr.

Rĕsūmŏ, ĭs, ūmpsī, ūmptūm, ĕrĕ. *To retake, to seize again.* Syn.—Rĕcĭpĭŏ, rĕprēndŏ, căpĭŏ. *To recover.* Syn.—Rĕcĭpĭŏ, rĕcōllĭgŏ.

Rĕsŭpīnŭs, ă, ūm. *Bent backward.* Syn.—Sŭpīnŭs, rĕsŭpīnātŭs, rĕclīnĭs. *Overwhelmed, prostrate.* Syn.—Strātŭs, prōstrātŭs, dējēctŭs, ēvērsŭs.

Rĕsūrgŏ, ĭs, sūrrēxī, sūrrēctūm, ĕrĕ. *To rise again.* Vīctă tămēn vīncēs, ēvērsăquĕ, Trōjă, rĕsūrgēs. O. Syn.—Sūrgŏ, āssūrgŏ, rĕnŏvŏr, (et fig.) rĕpărŏr, īnstaūrŏr, rĕnāscŏr, rĕvīvīscŏ.

Rĕsūscĭtŏ, ās, āvī, ātūm, ārĕ. *To arouse anew.* Syn.—Ēxcĭtŏ, sūscĭtŏ, ēxsūscĭtŏ, rĕvŏcŏ, āccēndŏ. *To resuscitate, to bring back to life.* Syn.—Sūscĭtŏ, ēxsūscĭtŏ. Phr.—Ēxstīnctūm, fūnctūm cădāvĕr ād vītām rĕvŏcŏ, rĕdūcŏ. Ăb īnfērnīs ūmbrīs rĕdūcŏ. Vītām ădēmptām, ănĭmām rēddŏ. Ād mūnĕră, lūmĭnă vītæ, dĭēm ērēptūm rĕvŏcŏ. Ārtūs īn vīvūm rĕvŏcārĕ călōrēm.

Rĕsūscĭtŏr, ārĭs, ātŭs sūm, ārī. *To be resuscitated, to be revived.* Syn.—Rĕvīvīscŏ, rĕnāscŏr, rĕsūrgŏ. Phr.—Ād vītām rĕsūrgŏ, rĕdĕŏ. Tŭmŭlō ēxĕŏ. Vītām rĕcĭpĭŏ. Sŭpĕrās ăd aūrās rĕdĕŏ. Ēdūcī rūrsŭs ĭn aūrās. Nūm vānæ rĕdĕāt sānguĭs ĭmāgĭnī.

Rĕtārdŏ, ās, āvī, ātūm, ārĕ. *To delay.* Ĕquōs ōbjēctă rĕtārdānt Flūmĭnă. V. Syn.—Tārdŏ, mŏrŏr, dēmŏrŏr, rĕmŏrŏr, tĕnĕŏ, dētĭnĕŏ, rĕtĭnĕŏ, sīstŏ. Phr.—Mŏrām făcĭŏ, īnfĕrŏ. Sēgnīs rĕtĭnēt mŏră.

Rētĕ, ĭs. n. *Net, snare.* Sī dūm sēctārĭs ăprōs, ĕgŏ rētĭă sērvŏ. V. Cāssēs, lăquĕī, plăgæ, līnă, fīlă, pĕdĭcæ, īndāgŏ. Phr.—Plăgārūm fraūs, dŏlī, īnsĭdĭæ. Hūmēntĭă līnă. Nōdōsī cāssēs. Dūcēntĭă rētĭă pīscēs. Ăgĭtāre īn rētĭă cērvōs. Rētĭă pōnŏ, lāxŏ. Rētĭbŭs claūdŏ, cīngŏ.

Rĕtĕgŏ, ĭs, tēxī, tēctūm, ĕrĕ. *To uncover.* Cæcūmquĕ dŏmŭs scĕlŭs ōmnĕ rĕtēxĭt. V. Syn.—Dētĕgŏ, ăpĕrĭŏ, rĕclūdŏ, rĕsĕrŏ, pāndŏ, ēxplĭcŏ, nūdŏ, dēnūdŏ, rĕvēlŏ. Phr.—Scīssō rĕtĕgīt vēlāmĭnĕ vūltūs.

Rĕtēxŏ, ĭs, xŭī, xtūm, ĕrĕ. *To unravel.* Syn.—Rĕsōlvŏ, dīssŭŏ. Fig.—*To commence.* Syn.—Rĕpĕtŏ, rĕnŏvŏ, ĭtĕrŏ. *To relate.* Syn.—Ēvōlvŏ, rĕfĕrŏ, nārrŏ, ēnārrŏ.

Rĕtĭcĕŏ, ēs, ŭī, ērĕ. *To be silent.* Syn.—Sĭlĕŏ. *See Sileo. To pass over in silence.* Syn.—Sĭlĕŏ, prætērmīttŏ, prætĕrĕŏ, tăcĕŏ.

Rĕtĭnācŭlūm, ī. n. *Check, bridle, rein.* Syn.—Lōrūm, hăbēnă. *Anchor.* Syn.—Ānchŏră.

Rĕtĭnĕŏ, ēs, ŭī, tēntūm, ērĕ. *To hold back.* Tū tămĕn ēt fīrmīs quāmvīs rĕtĭnēbĕrĕ vīnclīs. O. Syn.—Tĕnĕŏ, cōntĭnĕŏ, cŏhĭbĕŏ, cŏērcĕŏ. *To delay.* Syn.—Tārdŏ, rĕtārdŏ, mŏrŏr, rĕmŏrŏr. *To reserve, to hold.* Syn.—Tĕnĕŏ, sērvŏ.

Rĕtōrquĕŏ, ēs, sī, tūm, ērĕ. *To turn back.* Āvērsōs tŏtĭēs cūrrūs Jūtūrnă rĕtōrsĭt. V. Syn.—Flēctŏ, rĕflēctŏ, dēflēctŏ, āvērtŏ.

Phr.—Căpŭt īn sŭă tērgă rĕtōrsĭt. Fĕrōcĭs Cōllă rĕtōrsĭt ĕquī. *To repel.* Syn.—Rĕpēllŏ.

Rĕtrāctŏ, ās, āvī, ātūm, ārĕ. *To draw back.* Syn.—Rĕtrăhŏ. *To revolve in one's mind.* Syn.—Rĕvōlvŏ, vōlvŏ, rĕlĕgŏ, rĕpĕtŏ, rĕvŏcŏ.

Rĕtrăhŏ, ĭs, trāxī, trāctūm, ĕrĕ. *To draw back.* Syn.—Rĕdūcŏ, rĕtrāctŏ, rĕvŏcŏ, ābstrăhŏ, āvērtŏ.

Rĕtrō. adv. *Back, backwards.* Syn.—Rĕtrōrsūm, rĕtrōrsŭs, pōnĕ, ā tērgō.

Rĕtrōgrĕdĭŏr, ĕrĭs, grēssŭs sūm, grĕdī. *To go backwards.* Syn.—Rĕcēdŏ, cēdŏ, ābscēdŏ, dīscēdŏ, rĕfŭgĭŏ, rĕfĕrŏr. Phr.—Pĕdēm, grēssūm rĕfĕrŏ, āvērtŏ, Mē rĕfĕrŏ. Cūrsūm tōrquĕŏ.

Rĕtrōrsŭs, Rĕtrōrsūm. adv. *Backwards.* Syn.—Rĕtrō.

Rĕŭs, rĕă. m. f. *Guilty, accused, defendant.* Phr.—Āctŭs crīmĭnĭs rĕŭs. Crīmĭnĕ ĭnīquō dēlātŭs. Sōrdĭdā mœstūs tŏgā. Sprētārūmque ăgĭtūr lēgūm rĕŭs. Fālsī crīmĭnĭs āctă rĕa ēst. Āspĕră cōnfēssō vērbă rĕmīttĕ rĕō.

Rĕvălĕŏ, ēs, ŭī, ĭtūm, ērĕ. *To recover one's health.* Syn.—Rĕvălēscŏ, cōnvălēscŏ, rĕfĭcĭŏr, rĕcrĕŏr. Phr.—Vīrēs rĕcĭpĭŏ, rĕsūmŏ.

Rĕvĕhŏ, ĭs, vēxī, vēctūm, ĕrĕ. *To carry back, to lead back.* Syn.—Rĕfĕrŏ, rĕdūcŏ, rĕpōrtŏ.

Rĕvēllŏ, ĭs, vēllī & vūlsī, vūlsūm, ĕrĕ. *To tear away, to snatch.* Ārrĭpĭt ĭpsūm Pēndēntem ēt māgnā mūrī cūm pārtĕ rĕvēllĭt. V. Syn.—Āvēllŏ, ābstrăhŏ, ērĭpĭŏ, aūfĕrŏ, tōllŏ. Phr.—Dēntĕ rĕvēllĭt hŭmūm.

Rĕvēlŏ, ās, āvī, ātūm, ārĕ. *To unveil, to uncover.* Mēntītăquĕ sācră rĕvēlāt Aĕŏlŭs. O. Syn.—Ăpĕrĭŏ, dētĕgŏ, rĕclūdŏ, rĕsĕrŏ, pāndŏ, ēxplĭcŏ, mănĭfēstŏ, pătĕfăcĭŏ, prōdŏ.

Rĕvĕrēntĭă, æ. f. *Reverence, respect.* Māgnă fŭīt quōndām căpĭtĭs rĕvĕrēntĭă cānī. O. Syn.—Ōbsērvāntĭă, vĕnĕrātĭŏ, cūltŭs, hŏnŏr, cūră. Phr.—Māxĭmă dēbētūr pŭĕrō rĕvĕrēntĭă. *Modesty.* Syn.—Pŭdŏr, mŏdŭs.

Rĕvĕrĕŏr, ērĭs, ĭtŭs sūm, ērī. *To respect.* Syn.—Cŏlŏ, hŏnōrŏ, ōbsērvŏ. *See Veneror.*

Rĕvērtŏ, ĭs, tī, sūm, ĕrĕ. (*Pass. also used as a deponent*). *To return.* Syn.—Rĕdĕŏ, rĕmĕŏ. *To fall back upon.* Syn.—Rĕcĭdŏ, rĕvōlvŏr, rĕlābŏr.

Rĕvīncĭŏ, īs, vīnxī, vīnctūm, īrĕ. *To bind, to attach.* Syn.—Vīncĭŏ, lĭgŏ, rĕlĭgŏ.

Rĕvĭrĕŏ, ēs, ērĕ, & Rĕvĭrēscŏ, ĭs, ĕrĕ. *To be rejuvenated.* Ārtĕ sŭūm părĭlī rĕvĭrēscĕrĕ sīlvās. O. Syn.—Jŭvĕnēscŏ, rĕnŏvŏr, rĕvīvīscŏ, rĕvĭrēscŏ.

Rĕvīsŏ, ĭs, ī, ūm, ĕrĕ. *To revisit.* Prōgĕnĭēm pārvām dūlcēsquĕ rĕvīsĕrĕ nātōs. V. Syn.—Rĕvīsĭtŏ. Phr.—Ĭtĕrūm, rūrsŭs vīsŏ, īnvīsŏ, ădĕŏ. Ārcēmquĕ rĕvīsŏ. Īndĕ rĕdīt răbĭēs ĕădem ēt fŭrŏr īllĕ rĕvīsĭt.

Rĕvŏcŏ, ās, āvī, ātūm, ārĕ. *To recall, to summon back.* Vērum ŭbĭ rēctōrēs ăcĭē rĕvŏcābĕrĭs āmbō. V. Syn.—Rĕdūcŏ, ābdūcŏ, āvŏcŏ, rĕtrăhŏ, ābstrăhŏ, āmŏvĕŏ, rĕmŏvĕŏ, āvērtŏ. *To turn from.* Syn.—Āvŏcŏ, āvērtŏ, āmŏvĕŏ, dētērrĕŏ. Fig.— *To revive a law, or custom.* Syn.—Rĕdūcŏ, rĕfĕrŏ, rĕnŏvŏ.

Rĕvōlvŏ, ĭs, vōlvī, vŏlūtūm, ĕrĕ. *To roll.* Syn.—Vōlvŏ. *To fall back.* Syn.—Rĕlābŏr, rĕcĭdŏ, rĕvērtŏr, rĕdĕŏ.

Rēx, rēgĭs. m. *King, sovereign.* Ān nēscīs lōngās rēgĭbŭs ēssĕ mănūs. O. Syn.—Rēgnātŏr, rēctŏr, prīncēps, īmpĕrātŏr, dūctŏr, dŏmĭnŭs, tўrānnŭs. Phr.—Pŏpŭlī rēctŏr. Pŏtēns rērūm. Scēptră, rēgnă tĕnēns. Rēgālī jūrĕ pŏtēns. Rēgīs frōntēm dĭădēmă cŏrōnăt. Scēptrūm dēxtră gĕrĭt. Fūlgēntī dāt jūră thrŏnō. Quĭbŭs īn pŏpŭlōs pērmīssă pŏtēstās.

Rhēdă, æ. f. *Chariot, any four-wheeled vehicle.* Sēd dūm tōtă dŏmūs rhēdā cōmpōnĭtŭr ūnā. J. Syn.—Ēssĕdūm, cārpēntūm, cārrūcă, cūrrŭs, cŏvīnŭs.

Rhŏdŏdāphnē, ēs. f. *The oleander, rose-bay.* (*See Appendix under list of Trees, etc.*)

Rhŏdŏdēndrŏn, ī. n. *The oleander.* (*See Appendix under list of Trees, etc.*)

Rhōncŭs, ī. m. *Snort, snore.* Syn.—Prōflātŭs. *Sneer, scoff.* Syn.—Sānnă, căchīnnŭs, rīsŭs.

Rīdĕŏ, ēs, sī, sūm, ērĕ. *To laugh.* Syn.—Căchīnnŏ, căchīnnŏr. Phr.—Īn rīsūm, īn rīsūs, īn căchīnnōs sōlvŏr. Rīsūm ēdŏ. Rīsū cōncŭtĭŏr, rūmpŏ. Mūltō nōn sĭnĕ rīsū. *To smile upon someone.* Syn.—Ārrīdĕŏ. *To joke.* Syn.—Lūdŏ, jŏcŏr. *To smile brightly.* Syn.—Rĕnīdĕŏ, nĭtĕŏ, flōrĕŏ. *To mock at.* Syn.—Dērīdĕŏ, īrrīdĕŏ, īllūdŏ.

Rīdĭcŭlē. adv. *Jokingly, pleasantly.* Syn.—Lĕpĭdē, făcētē, jŏcōsē.

Rīdĭcŭlŭs, ă, ūm. *Witty, jocose.* Syn.—Jŏcŭlārĭs, jŏcōsŭs, făcētŭs. *Ridiculous.* Syn.—Rīdēndŭs, īrrīdēndŭs, dērīdēndŭs.

Rĭgĕŏ, ēs, ŭī, ērĕ. *To grow hard.* Syn.—Dūrēscŏ, īndūrēscŏ, ōbdūrēscŏ, īndūrŏr, rĭgēscŏ. *To become stiff with the cold.* Syn.—Dūrēscŏ, ālgĕŏ, frīgĕŏ. Phr.—Glăcĭē rĭgēt hōrrĭdă bārbă. Prātă rĭgēnt. *To shudder.* Syn.—Hōrrĕŏ, hōrrēscŏ, stō.

Rĭgĭdē. adv. *Rigidly, severely.* Syn.—Dūrē. sĕvērē.

Rĭgĭdŭs, ă, ūm. *Hard.* Syn.—Dūrŭs. *That which stands stiff, rigid.* Syn.—Stāns, rĭgēns, rēctŭs, ērēctŭs. *Frozen.* Syn.—Gĕlĭdŭs. *Severe.* Syn.—Sĕvērŭs. *Hardy.* Syn.—Dūrŭs, pătĭēns.

Rĭgŏ, ās, āvī, ātūm, ārĕ. *To water, to moisten.* Dīsjĭcĭt, ēt spārsō lātē rĭgăt ārvă crŭōrĕ. V. Syn.—Īrrĭgŏ, hūmēctŏ, mădĕfăcĭŏ, īmbŭŏ, tīngŏ, spārgŏ, āspērgŏ, rēspērgŏ, rōrŏ, īrrōrŏ. Phr.—Ăquīs spārgŏ, ăquās mīttŏ ĭn. Rōrēm lātē dīspērgĕrĕ. Spārgĕrĕ sēmĕn ăquā. Flŭvĭōsquĕ mĭnīstrăt.

Rĭgŏr, ōrĭs. m. *Hardness, roughness.* Syn.—Dūrĭtĭēs, āspĕrĭtās, fĕrĭtās. *Coldness.* Syn.—Frīgŭs. *Severity.* Syn.—Aūstērĭtās, grăvĭtās.

Rĭgŭŭs, ă, ūm. *Watered, irrigated.* Īpsĕ pŏtēs rĭgŭīs plāntām dīspōnĕre ĭn hōrtīs. O. Syn.—Īrrĭgŭŭs, hūmĭdŭs, mădĭdŭs, mădēfāctŭs, ūdŭs.

Rīmă, æ. f. *Rift, cleft, opening.* Āccĭpĭūnt ĭnĭmīcum īmbrēm, rīmīsquĕ fătīscūnt. V. Syn.—Hĭātŭs, fīssūră, fĕnēstră, fŏrāmĕn, ōs.

Rīmŏr, ārĭs, ātŭs sūm, ārī. *To open, to pierce.* Aēgrē rāstrīs tērrām rīmāntŭr. V. Syn.—Fīndŏ, īnfīndŏ, fŏdĭŏ, īnfŏdĭŏ. *To search for, to scrutinize.* Syn.—Scrūtŏr, quærŏ.

Rīmōsŭs, ă, ūm. *Full of holes, leaky.* Syn.—Ăpērtŭs, hĭāns, hĭūlcŭs, dĕhīscēns, fătīscēns Phr.—Tĕnŭī rīmā fīssŭs.

Rīpă, æ. f. *Bank, border.* Rīpārūmquĕ tŏrōs ēt prātă rĕcēntĭă rīvīs. V. Syn.—Ōră, mārgŏ, āggĕr. Phr.—Rīpæ mārgŏ, ōră, āggĕr. Crĕpĭtāntĭbŭs ūndīs gārrŭlă. Vĭrĭdīssĭmă grāmĭnĕ rīpă. Mōllĭs dēclīvī trāmĭtĕ rīpă. Ād rīpās lēnĕ sŏnāntĭs ăquæ.

Rīsŭs, ūs. m. *Smile, laughter.* Īncĭpĕ, pārvĕ pŭĕr, rīsū cōgnōscĕrĕ mātrēm. V. Syn.—Căchīnnŭs. Phr.—Blāndō prætēxĕrĕ rīsū. Rīsūm mŏvĕŏ, ēxcŭtĭŏ, ēlĭcĭŏ, præbĕŏ. *Derision.* Syn.—Dērīsŭs, jŏcŭs, căchīnnŭs, sānnă.

Rītĕ. adv. *According to rite, form, custom.* Phr.—Dē mōrĕ, ēx mōrĕ, sŏlĭtō dē mōrĕ, ŭt fĭt. *Well.* Syn.—Bĕnĕ, prŏbē, rēctē.

Rītŭs, ūs. m. *Rite, ceremony.* Hīnc pŏpŭlī rītūs ēdĭdĭcērĕ nŏvōs. O. Syn.—Săcră, cūltŭs, rēllĭgĭŏ. Phr.—Mōrēm rītūsquĕ săcrōrūm. Măgĭcō lūstrābĕrĕ rītū. Rītĭbŭs īnstrŭĭtŭr.

Rītū. adv. *After the manner of, like.* Syn.—Mōrĕ, mŏdō, īnstăr, vĕlŭt, vĕlŭtī, sīcŭt.

Rīvŭs, ī. m. *Stream.* Āspĭcĕ lābēntēs jūcūndō mūrmŭrĕ rīvōs. O. Syn.—Rīvŭlŭs, flŭvĭŭs, flūmĕn, ūndă, lÿmphă, ăquă, fōns. Phr.—Lēnĕ flŭēns ēt gūrgĭtĕ pūrō Cōnspĭcŭŭs. Ārĭdă prātă fŏvēt lÿmphīs. Lābēntīs mūrmŭră rīvī. Rīvūs cūm mūrmŭrĕ lābēns.

Rīxă, æ. f. *Quarrel, dispute.* Tūrpĭs ĭn ārcānā sŏnŭīt cūm rīxă tăbērnā. Prop. Syn.—Jūrgĭūm, dīssĭdĭūm, līs, cērtāmĕn. Phr.—Līnguæ cōntēntĭō, prœlĭă. Āmāræ prœlĭă līnguæ.

Rīxŏr, ārĭs, ātŭs sūm, ārī. *To dispute, to quarrel.* Syn.—Āltērcŏr, jūrgŏr, cōntēndŏ, lītĭgŏ, dīscēptŏ, pūgnŏ, cērtŏ. Phr.—Dīssĭdĭīs cōntēndŏ. Līnguām īn jūrgĭă sōlvŏ. Rīxās ēxcĭtŏ. Līnguæ ămāræ prœlĭă ĭnīrĕ.

Rōbŏrĕŭs, ă, ūm. *Of oak.* Syn.—Quērnŭs, quērnĕŭs, īlīgnŭs.

Rōbŏrŏ, ās, āvī, ātūm, ārĕ. *To strengthen.* Syn.—Cōrrōbŏrŏ, fīrmŏ, cōnfīrmŏ. Phr.—Rōbŭr, vīm, vīrēs dō, āddŏ, sūppĕdĭtŏ, mĭnīstrŏ. Vīrēs aūgĕŏ, sūggĕrŏ.

Rōbŭr, ŏrĭs. n. *Oak. See Appendix.* Fig.—*Strength, force.* Syn.—Vīs, vīrēs, vĭgŏr, nērvī, lăcērtī. *Strength of character.* Syn.—Ănĭmī vīs, vīrtūs, cōnstāntĭă. Phr.—Rōbŭr pēctŏrĭs ænĕī. Sŏlĭdæ jŭvĕnīli īn pēctŏrĕ vīrēs.

Rōbūstŭs, ă, ūm. *Of oak.* Syn.—Rōbŏrĕŭs, quērnŭs. *Strong, robust.* Syn.—Vălēns, vălĭdŭs, fōrtĭs, vĕgĕtŭs, lăcērtōsŭs, nērvōsŭs. Phr.—Rōbŏrĕ, vīrĭbŭs prǣstāns, īnsīgnĭs, fīdēns, sŭpērbŭs. Vīr fīrmō pēctŏrĕ. Cuī cōrpūs rōbūstūm. Cuī īntĕgĕr ævī Sānguĭs ĭnēst.

Rōdŏ, ĭs, sī, sūm, ĕrĕ. *To gnaw, to nibble.* Syn.—Ārrōdŏ, cōrrōdŏ, cīrcūmrōdŏ, cīrcūmcīdŏ. Phr.—Vīvōs ēt rōdĕrēt ūnguēs. *To wear away anything.* Syn.—Ēxĕdŏ, mōrdĕŏ, pĕrĕdŏ. Fig.—*To criticize.* Syn.—Cārpŏ, mōrdĕŏ, ōbtrēctŏ, īmpĕtŏ.

Rŏgŏ, ās, āvī, ātūm, ārĕ. *To question, to ask.* Ōccīdĭs sæpĕ rŏgāndō. H. Syn.—Rŏgĭtŏ, īntērrŏgŏ, quærŏ, scīscĭtŏr. *To beg, beseech.* Syn.—Ōrŏ, ōbsĕcrŏ, ōbtēstŏr, flāgĭtŏ, ēfflāgĭtŏ. Phr.—Sūpplĭcĕ vōcĕ rŏgānt. Sūbmīssā vōcĕ rŏgāvĭt ŏpēm. Nām mē rŏgăt ēt prĕcĕ cōgĭt.

Rŏgŭs, ī. m. *Funeral pyre.* Tēr cīrcum āccēnsōs, cīnctī fūlgēntĭbŭs ārmīs Dēcūrrērĕ rŏgōs. V. Syn.—Pўră, būstūm. Phr.—Līgnōrūm strŭēs, cōngĕrĭēs. Līgnă fūnĕrĭs. Āră sĕpūlcrī. Ērēctă ăd īgnēs fūnĕbrĭs strŭēs. Fig.—*Destruction.* Syn.—Mōrs, Lĭbĭtīnă, fūnŭs, tŭmŭlŭs, sĕpūlcrūm.

Rōrŏ, ās, āvī, ātūm, ārĕ. *To bedew, to sprinkle.* Spārsī rōrābānt sānguĭnĕ vēprēs. V. Syn.—Rōrēscŏ, stīllŏ, mānŏ, flŭŏ. Phr.—Rōrĕ stīllŏ. Rōrēm ēmīttŏ. Lăcrĭmīs spārgūnt rōrāntĭbŭs ōră.

Rōs, rōrĭs. m. *Dew.* Cūm rōs īn tĕnĕrā pĕcŏrī grātīssĭmŭs hērba ēst. V. Phr.—Rōrĭs ăquă. Rōscĭdŭs, mātūtīnŭs hūmŏr. Nōctĭs lēntŭs hūmŏr. Rōrĭs īmbĕr. Mānĕ cădēns. Ārvă rĭgāns. Lǣtās făcĭēns sĕgĕtēs. Spārsă mădēt tēllūs. Cœlēstī rōrĕ mădēscĭt hŭmŭs.

Rŏsă, æ. f. *The rose.* (*See Appendix under list of Trees, etc.*)

Rōscĭdŭs, ă, ūm. *Moistened with dew, dewy.* Syn.—Rōrātŭs. Phr.—Rōrĕ mădēns, spārsŭs, hūmĭdŭs, ūdŭs, hūmēns. *That which sprinkles the dew.* Syn.—Rōrĭfĕr, rōrāns, stīllāns, mānāns, hūmēns.

Rŏsĕŭs, ă, ūm. *Rosy, rose-colored.* Dīxĭt, ĕt āvērtēns rŏsĕā cērvīcĕ rĕfūlsĭt. V. Syn.—Rŭbēns, rŭbĭcūndŭs, pūrpŭrĕŭs. Phr.— Rŏsĕīs Aūrōrā quădrīgīs. Ēt rŏsĕās lănĭātă gĕnās.

Rōstrūm, ī. n. *Beak of a bird.* Rōstrūm lătĕrī dēfīgĭt ăcūtūm. O. Syn.—Ōs. Phr.—Rōstrī ăcūmĕn. Spīcŭlăque ēxăcŭŭnt rōstrīs. *The prow of a ship.* Syn.—Prōră.

Rŏtă, ǣ. f. *Wheel.* Hǣc ĕrĭt ādmīssā mētă tĕrēndā rŏtā. O. Syn.— Ōrbĭs, ōrbĭtă, āxĭs. Phr.—Rŏtǣ ōrbĭs, cūrvāmĕn, cūrvātūră. Fērrātŭs ōrbĭs. Cĭtātō āxĕ vŏlūbĭlĭs. Rŏtārūm lāpsūs. Rŏtārūm strĕpĭtŭs. Vŏlāt vī fērvĭdŭs āxĭs. Fig.—*Turn, revolution, circuit.* Syn.—Ōrbĭs, gȳrŭs, cūrsŭs.

Rŏtō, ās, āvī, ātūm, ārĕ. *To move in a circle.* Āc rŏtăt ēnsēm Fūl-mĭnĕūm. V. Syn.—Tōrquĕō, vērtŏ, vērsŏ, cīrcŭmăgŏ, cīrcūm-vōlvŏ. Phr.—Ĭn ōrbēm, īn gȳrūm dūcŏ, ăgŏ. Mŏrĕ rŏtăt fūndǣ.

Rŏtūndŭs, ă, ūm. *Round, circular.* Syn.—Glŏbōsŭs, tĕrĕs. Phr.— Ĭn ōrbēm āctŭs. Ōrbĭs ĭn fīgūrām vērsŭs.

Rŭbēcŭlă, ǣ. f. *The robin redbreast.* (*See Appendix under list of Birds.*)

Rŭbĕfăcĭŏ, ĭs, fēcī, fāctūm, ĕrĕ. *To redden.* Phr.—Rŭbōrĕ tīngŏ, īmbŭŏ, īnfĭcĭŏ, cŏlōrŏ. Rŭbōrēm āddŏ, īnfūndŏ.

Rŭbĕŏ, ēs, ŭī, ērĕ. *To become red.* Syn.—Rŭbēscŏ. Phr.—Rŭbōrĕ tīngŏr, īnfĭcĭŏr. Rŭbōrēm trăhŏ. Vēntō sēmpēr rŭbĕt aūrĕă Phœbē. Sānguĭnĕ tērră rŭbĕt.

Rŭbĕr, rŭbră, rŭbrūm. *Red.* Flāvăquĕ dē rūbrō prōmĕrĕ mēllă cădō. M. Syn.—Rŭbēns, rŭbĭcūndŭs, rŭbēscēns, rŏsĕŭs, pūnĭ-cĕŭs, pūrpŭrĕŭs, sānguĭnĕŭs, rŭtĭlŭs. Phr.—Cŏlōrĕ rŭbrō, pūr-pŭrĕō tīnctŭs. Tȳrĭōs īncōctă rŭbōrēs Vēllĕră.

Rūbīgŏ, ĭnĭs. f. *Rust.* Nōn scăbĭe ēt sālsā lǣdēt rūbīgĭnĕ fērrūm. V. Syn.—Aērūgŏ, fērrūgŏ, sĭtŭs. Phr.—Scăbrǣ mōrsŭs rūbīgĭnĭs. Fērrūm rūbīgŏ īnfĭcĭt. Nĭgrǣ rūbīgĭnĕ fālcēs. Plēnī rūbī-gĭnĭs ēnsēs. Fig.—*Inertia.* Syn.—Sĭtŭs, vĕtērnūm, tōrpŏr, tōr-pēdŏ.

Rŭbŭs, ī. m. *Bramble, thorn.* Āt rŭbŭs ēt sēntēs tāntūmmŏdŏ lǣ-dĕrĕ nātǣ. O. Syn.—Sēntĭs, vĕprēs, spīnă.

Rŭdēns, tĭs. m. *Cable, cord, rope.* Īnsĕquĭtūr clāmōrquĕ vĭrūm strīdōrquĕ rŭdēntūm. V. Syn.—Fūnĭs, rĕtĭnācŭlă, vīncŭlă, cān-nābĭs. Phr.—Ēxcūssōsquĕ jŭbĕt lāxārĕ rŭdēntēs. Vēlīs īmmīttĕ rŭdēntēs. Dūrōs trāctārĕ rŭdēntēs.

Rŭdīmēntūm, ī. n. *Apprenticeship, beginning.* Syn.—Prīmĭtĭǣ, tīrōcĭnĭūm.

Rŭdĭs, ĭs, ĕ. *Rude, unfashioned.* Syn.—Āspĕr. *Uncultivated.* Syn. —Īncūltŭs. Fig.—*Neglected.* Syn.—Īncōmptŭs, īncōncīnnŭs.

Open, sincere. Syn.—Sīncērŭs, cāndĭdŭs, ăpērtŭs, sīmplēx, īngĕnŭŭs. *Barbarous, uncivilized.* Syn.—Īncūltŭs, fĕrŭs, āspĕr, ăgrēstĭs, bārbărŭs. *Ignorant.* Syn.—Īndōctŭs, īnscītŭs, īmpĕrītŭs. *Inexperienced.* Syn.—Īgnārŭs, ĭnēxpērtŭs, īnscĭŭs, nēscĭŭs, īnsŏlēns, tīrŏ, nŏvīcĭŭs. *Unripe.* Syn.—Īmmātūrŭs, vĭrĭdĭs, ăcērbŭs.

Rūgă, æ. f. *Wrinkle, fold.* Jām vĕnĭēnt rūgæ quæ tĭbĭ cōrpŭs ărēnt. O. Phr.—Rūgōsă frōns, făcĭēs. Gĕnārūm, frōntĭs sūlcī. Āspĕră sūlcăt Rūgă cŭtēm. Tē rūgæ tūrpānt. Dūm tārdă sĕnēctūs. Īndūcăt rūgās. Lāxāntūr cōrpŏră rūgīs.

Rŭīnă, æ. f. *Ruin, downfall.* Hæc lŏcă vī quōndam ēt vāstā cōnvūlsă rŭīnā. V. Syn.—Lāpsŭs, cāsŭs, ēxcĭdĭūm. Phr.—Fātālī quāssă rŭīnā Cūnctă lăbēnt. Hōrrĭfĭcīs jūxtā tŏnăt Aētnă rŭīnīs. Quā jăcĕānt pērcūlsă rŭīnā. Fig.—*Misfortune.* Syn.—Clādēs, pērnĭcĭēs.

Rŭīnōsŭs, ă, ūm. *Ready to fall.* Syn.—Rŭēns, cădūcŭs, lăbāns, rūptŭs. *In ruins.* Syn.—Jăcēns, ēvērsŭs, dīrŭtŭs, strātŭs, lāpsŭs, cōllāpsŭs.

Rūmŏr, ōrĭs. m. *Rumor, report.* Fīnĭtĭmās īn bēllă fĕrām rūmōrĭbŭs ūrbēs. V. Syn.—Fāmă, nūntĭŭs, sērmŏ, fābŭlă. Phr.—Aūră rūmōrĭs. Īt rūmŏr ăd ūrbēs. Tōtă rūmŏr ĭn ūrbĕ sŏnăt. Rūmŏr ĭn āmbĭgŭo ēst. Fāctūm rūmōr dīssĭpăt. *Reputation.* Syn.—Fāmă.

Rūmpŏ, ĭs, rūpī, rūptūm, ĕrĕ. *To break, to shatter.* Rūmpĕrĕ claūstră mănū, sŏcĭōsque īmmīttĕrĕ pōrtīs. V. Syn.—Dīsrūmpŏ, pērrūmpŏ, frāngŏ, ēffrīngŏ, rĕfrīngŏ. *To separate violently.* Syn.—Dīsrūmpŏ, scīndŏ, dīscīndŏ, dīssōlvŏ, ăpĕrĭŏ, dīvēllŏ, rĕvēllŏ, dīvĭdŏ, fīndŏ, dīffīndŏ. *To break, to violate.* Syn.—Frāngŏ, rēscīndŏ, ābrūmpŏ, sōlvŏ, dīssōlvŏ, rĕvēllŏ, vĭŏlŏ. *To interrupt.* Syn.—Ābrūmpŏ, tūrbŏ, pēllŏ, ēxcŭtĭŏ. *To break down under a weight.* Syn.—Fătīscŏ, sūccūmbŏ, prĕmŏr, grăvŏr, ōpprĭmŏr, cōnsīdŏ.

Rŭŏ, ĭs, rŭī, ĕrĕ. *To drive ahead.* Spūmās sălĭs ærĕ rŭēbānt. V. Syn.—Prōrŭŏ, ăgŏ, pēllŏ, prōpēllŏ. *To push violently, to overturn.* Syn.—Stērnŏ, prōstērnŏ, dējĭcĭŏ, ēvērtŏ, āfflīgŏ. *To fall violently.* Syn.—Cōrrŭŏ, prōrŭŏ, cădŏ, cōncĭdŏ, dēcĭdŏ, lābŏr, dēlābŏr, prōlābŏr, præcĭpĭtŏ, prōcūmbŏ. Phr.—Ād tērrām lābŏr. Præcēps ăgŏr. Scōpŭli īngēntēm trāxērĕ rŭīnām. Rŭīnām cūm sŏnĭtū trăhĭt. Rŭĭt ālto ā cūlmĭnĕ Trōjă. *To rush on headlong.* Syn.—Fĕrŏr, īrrŭŏ, īrrūmpŏ, prōsĭlĭŏ, prōcūrrŏ, prōvŏlŏ. *To rush forth from.* Syn.—Ērūmpŏ, ēxsĭlĭŏ, prōrūmpŏ.

Rūpēs, ĭs. f. *Rock, cliff.* Īllĕ vĕlūt pĕlăgī rūpēs īmmōtă rĕsīstĭt. V. Syn.—Caūtēs, sāxūm, scōpŭlŭs, sĭlēx. Phr.—Jŭgūm sāxōsūm, scŏpŭlōsūm. Sāxūm prǣcĕps. Sāxĕă mōlēs. Sāxīs ārdŭă caūtēs. Scŏpŭlīs pēndēntĭbŭs āntrūm.

Rūrĭcŏlă, æ. m. *Farmer, tiller of the soil.* Lānĭgĕrūmquĕ pĕcūs rūrĭcŏlǣquĕ bŏvēs. O. Syn.—Āgrĭcŏlă. *One who lives in the country.* Syn.—Rūstĭcŭs, ăgrēstĭs, āgrĭcŏlă.

Rūrsŭs (Rūrsūm). adv. *Again.* Syn.—Dēnŭō, ĭtĕrūm, ăb īntĕgrō.

Rūs, rūrĭs. n. *Fields, country.* Sī tē dīgnă mănēt dīvīnī glōrĭă rūrĭs. V. Syn.—Cāmpī, ăgrī. Phr.—Rūrĭs ŏpēs, dēlĭcĭæ, ōtĭă, gaūdĭă, sēcēssŭs. Pīctī vĭrĭdārĭă cāmpī. Fēcūndī rūră bĕātă sŏlī. Īnnŏcŭī rūrĭs lăbŏr. Pēr flōrĕă rūră. *Territory, country.* Syn.—Rĕgĭŏ, tērră, tēllūs, cāmpī.

Rūstĭcĭtās, ātĭs. f. *Rudeness, roughness.* Syn.—Āspĕrĭtās, fĕrĭtās. Phr.—Incūltī mōrēs. Rŭdĭs āspĕr cūltŭs.

Rūstĭcŏr, ārĭs, ātŭs sūm, ārī. *To spend the time in the country.* Phr.—Rūrĕ mŏrŏr, hăbĭtō, dēgŏ, vīvŏ. Rūră hăbĭtō. Rūrĭs ōtĭă sĕquŏr.

Rūstĭcŭs, ă, ūm. *Rustic, rural.* Syn.—Rūrālĭs, ăgrēstĭs. Fig.—*Rough, coarse.* Syn.—Īnūrbānŭs, īncūltŭs, rŭdĭs, hōrrĭdŭs, āspĕr, rūstĭcŭlŭs, ăgrēstĭs.

Rūstĭcŭs, ī. m. *Farmer, villager.* Syn.—Rūrĭcŏlă, āgrĭcŏlă, cŏlōnŭs, vīllĭcŭs.

Rūtă, æ. f. *The herb rue.* (*See Appendix under list of Trees, etc.*)

Rŭtĭlŏ, ās, āvī, ātūm, ārĕ. *To sparkle, to shine.* Syn.—Cŏrūscŏ, mĭcŏ, fūlgĕŏ, splēndĕō. *See Fulgeo, Splendeo.*

Rŭtĭlŭs, ă, ūm. *Yellow, golden.* Syn.—Īgnĕŭs, flāvŭs, aūrĕŭs. *Brilliant.* Syn.—Splēndĭdŭs. *See Splendidus.*

S

Sāccŏ, ās, āvī, ātūm, ārĕ. *To strain through a bag.* Syn.—Lĭquŏ, pērcōlŏ, cōlŏ.

Sāccŭs, ī. m. *Sack, pouch.* Syn.—Sāccŭlŭs, pēră, crŭmēnă, lŏcŭlī.

Săcēllūm, ī. n. *Chapel.* Syn.—Aēdĭcŭlă, ēcclēsĭă.

Săcĕr, săcră, săcrūm. *Sacred, holy.* Cōntrāctōs ārtūs săcĕr īgnĭs ĕdēbăt. Syn.—Sānctŭs, rēllĭgĭōsŭs, săcrātŭs, pĭŭs, aūgūstŭs, vĕrēndŭs, vĕnĕrāndŭs. *Consecrated to, under the protection of.* Syn.—Săcrātŭs, cōnsĕcrātŭs, dĭcātŭs, dīctŭs. Phr.—Dĕō dĭcātŭs. Ēst lūcūs lātē săcĕr. Săcĕr īgnĭs.

Săcērdōs, ōtĭs. m. *Priest.* Quām fērrō māctāvĕrăt āntĕ săcērdōs. V. Syn.—Pōntĭfēx, āntīstĕs, mĭnīstĕr, săcrĭfĭcŭs. Phr.—Vĭr săcĕr. Săcrōrūm prǣsĕs. Săcrīs ŏpĕrātŭs. Cuī cūră săcrōrum ēst. Lŏcūm dātĕ săcră fĕrēntī. *Priestess.* Syn.—Āntīstĭtă. (*Eccles.*) *Priest.* Syn.—Prēsbȳtĕr.

Săcrāmēntūm, ī. n. *Oath.* Syn.—Jūs jūrāndūm, jūrāmēntūm, fĭdēs. *Military oath, service.* Phr.—Fērrĕ ārmă, cāstră sĕquŏr. Stīpēndĭă mĕrĕō. (*Eccles.*) *Sacrament.*

Săcrārĭūm, ĭī. n. *Vestry, sacristy, chapel.* Syn.—Săcēllūm, dēlūbrūm, tēmplūm, pĕnĕtrālĕ. Fig.—*Holy place, sanctuary.* Syn.—Ădўtūm, pĕnĕtrālĕ, pĕnĕtrālĭă.

Săcrĭfĭcĭūm, ĭī. n. *Sacrifice.* Săcrĭfĭcī gĕnŭs ēst, sīc īnstĭtŭērĕ prĭōrēs. O. Syn.—Săcrum, lībāmĕn, pĭăcŭlūm, sōlēmnĭă, vīctĭmă, hōstĭă, hŏnōrēs. Phr.—Rēs săcră, dīvīnă. Săcră mūnĕră. Cŏlēndă dĕī mўstērĭă. Tēmplōrūm hŏnōs. Săcrīs āddĭtă flāmmīs.

Săcrĭfĭcŏ, ās, āvī, ātūm, ārĕ. *To offer sacrifice.* Ādmŏnĕt ēt fōrtī săcrĭfĭcārĕ Dĕæ. O. Syn.—Lībŏ, făcĭŏ, ŏpĕrŏr. Phr.—Săcrūm, săcră făcĭŏ. Săcrīs ŏpĕrŏr. Ārīs hŏnōrēs, dōnă, mūnĕră īmpōnŏ. Săcrīs dĕūm, nūmĕn ădōrŏ. Ād tēmplă mūnĕră fĕrŏ. Săcră rītĕ fĕrŏ. Vīctĭmām, vōtīvām pĕcŭdēm jŭgŭlŏ, cædŏ. Mĕrĭtōs ārīs māctāvĭt hŏnōrēs. Aūt ārīs sūpplēx īmpōnĭt hŏnōrēm. Pĭă săcră părābānt.

Săcrĭlĕgŭs, ă, ūm. *Sacrilegious.* Syn.—Īmpĭŭs, nĕfāndŭs.

Săcrŏ, ās, āvī, ātūm, ārĕ. *To consecrate, to dedicate.* Sīlvānō fāma ēst vĕtĕrēs săcrāssĕ Pĕlāsgōs. V. Syn.—Cōnsĕcrŏ, dĭcŏ, dēdĭcŏ, dēstĭnŏ, rĕsērvŏ.

Săcrūm, ī. n. *Sacrifice.* Syn.—Săcrĭfĭcĭūm. Phr.—Săcră făcīt dĕæ. Cāstīs āccēdĕrĕ săcrīs. *Sacred ceremony.* Syn.—Rītŭs, cūltŭs.

Sæpĕ. adv. *Often.* Syn.—Frĕquēntĕr, crēbrō, pērsæpĕ, āssĭdŭē, cōntĭnŭō, plērūmquĕ. Phr.—Haūd, nōn rārō. Nōn sĕmĕl. Ĭtĕrūm ātquĕ ĭtĕrūm. Ĕtĭam ātque ĕtĭām.

Sævĭŏ, īs, ĭī, ītūm, īrĕ. *To rage, to be furious.* Syn.—Īrāscŏr, fŭrŏ, bācchŏr.

Sævĭtĭă, æ. f. *Cruelty.* Dā brĕvĕ sævĭtĭæ spătĭūm pĕlăgīquĕ tŭæquĕ. O. Syn.—Bārbărĭēs, crūdēlĭtās, fĕrĭtās, īmmānĭtās. *Rage, anger.* Syn.—Īră, fŭrŏr, răbĭēs.

Sævŭs, ă, ūm. *Raging.* Syn.—Īrātŭs. *See Iratus. Cruel, inhuman.* Syn.—Bārbărŭs, crūdēlĭs, fĕrŭs, ēffĕrŭs, īmmītĭs. *Formidable.* Syn.—Mĕtŭēndŭs, ătrōx.

Săgă, æ. f. *Sorceress.* Syn.—Măgă, īncāntātrīx, vĕnēfĭcă.

Săgācĭtĕr. adv. *Wisely, prudently.* Syn.—Ăcūtē, ārgūtē, scītē, cāllĭdē.

Săgāx, ācĭs. adj. *That which has a penetrating odor.* Syn.—Ŏdōrŭs. Fig.—*Subtle, penetrating, keen.* Syn.—Pērspĭcāx, ăcĕr, ăcūtŭs, cāllĭdŭs, prōvĭdŭs, prūdēns, sōlērs, pĕrītŭs.

Săgīttă, æ. f. *Arrow.* Nōn sĕcūs āc nērvō pēr nūbem īmpūlsā săgīttā. V. Syn.—Ărūndŏ, călămŭs, jăcŭlūm, tēlūm, spīcŭlūm, cūspĭs, fērrūm, mīssĭlĕ, pēnnă. Phr.—Săgīttæ ăcūmĕn. Pĕnĕtrābĭlĕ tēlūm. Tēlă vĕnēno īmbūtă. Fŭgĭēns strīdōrĕ pĕr aūrās. Hærēt lătĕrī lētālĭs ărūndŏ. Fērrōquĕ mĭcāntĭă tēlă.

Săgīttārĭŭs, ĭī. m. *Archer, bowman.* Syn.—Jăcŭlātŏr. Phr.—Ărcūm tēndĕrĕ, săgīttām vĭbrārĕ dōctŭs, pĕrītŭs. Săgīttīs ārmātŭs. Tēlă sŏnānt hŭmĕrīs. Tēlīs mĕtŭēndŭs ĕt ārcū. Mīssĭlĭbūs mĕlĭōr săgīttīs. *The constellation.* Syn.—Ărcĭtĕnēns, Săgīttĭfĕr, Săgīttĭpŏtēns, Cēntaūrŭs, Chīrōn.

Săgūm, ī. n. *Military cloak.* Syn.—Săgŭlūm. *General's cloak.* Syn.—Pălūdāmēntūm. Phr.—Īnsīgnĕ dĕcŭs săgŭlī, săgī.

Sāl, sălĭs. m. & n. (pl. m.) *Salt.* Aūt pārcō sălĕ cōntīngūnt. V. Phr.—Sălĭbūs vĭtĭāntăr ămārīs. Grānă sălĭs. Pūrī cāndĭdă mīcă sălĭs. Cĭbōrūm cōndīmēntūm. *Sea-water. See Mare.*

Sălēs, ĭūm. m. *Wit, jokes, humor.* Plaūtīnōs ēt nŭmĕrōs ēt Laūdāvērĕ sălēs. H. Syn.—Jŏcī, dīctērĭă, ārgūtĭæ, făcētĭæ. Phr.—Dīctă sălĕ tīnctă. Dīctōrūm lĕpŏr. Sălēs īntrā pōmœrĭă nātī. Nōn sŏlĭtī lūsĕrĕ sălēs. Sălĭbūs tīngĕt.

Sălĭŏ, īs, ŭī & ĭī, sāltūm, īrĕ. *To leap, to jump.* Mōllĭbŭs īn prātīs ūnctōs sălĭērĕ pĕr ūtrēs. V. Syn.—Sāltŏ, ēxsĭlĭŏ, ēxsūltŏ, ēmĭcŏ. Phr.—Sāltū cŏrpŭs tōllŏ. Sāltū fĕrŏr. Ăgĭlī sāltū vŏlŏ. *To jump down.* Syn.—Ēxsĭlĭŏ, dēsĭlĭŏ, præcĭpĭtŏ. Phr.—Sē cŏrpŏre ăd ūndās mīsĭt. Fīnĭbŭs ōmnēs Prōsĭlŭērĕ sŭīs. *To palpitate, to tremble.* Syn.—Sūbsĭlĭŏ, sūbsūltŏ, pālpĭtŏ, mĭcŏ, trĕmŏ, trĕpĭdŏ. *To leap forth.* Syn.—Prōsĭlĭŏ, ēxsĭlĭŏ, sūrgŏ, ēxĕŏ, ēffĕrŏr.

Sălīvă, æ. f. *Saliva.* Syn.—Spūtūm. *Taste, savor.* Syn.—Gūstŭs, săpŏr.

Sălĭx, ĭcĭs. f. *A willow.* (*See Appendix under list of Trees, etc.*)

Sālsē. adv. *Wittily, smartly.* Syn.—Lĕpĭdē, ārgūtē, ăcūtē, făcētē. Phr.—Lĕpĭdōs spārgĭt ăb ōrĕ sălēs.

Sālsŭs, ă, ūm. *Salted.* Syn.—Ămārŭs. Fig.—*Witty, piquant.* Syn.—Ārgūtŭs, făcētŭs, lĕpĭdŭs, ăcērbŭs, ămārŭs.

Sāltēm. adv. *At least.* Syn.—Cērtē, mŏdŏ, tāntūm. Phr.—Āt cērtē. Āt sāltēm.

Sāltŏ, ās, āvī, ātūm, ārĕ. *To dance.* Brāchĭă sāltāntīs, vōcēm mīrārĕ cănēntĭs. O. Syn.—Mŏvĕŏr. Phr.—Chŏrōs, chŏrēās ăgŏ, dūcŏ, cĕlĕbrŏ. Chŏrīs, chŏrēīs īndūlgĕŏ. Dō mōtūs cōmpŏsĭtōs. Ād nŭmĕrūm lūdŏ. Āltērnō pĕdĕ tērrām pūlsŏ, quătĭŏ. Lætō sē tōllĕrĕ sāltū. Mōtūs dŏcērī gaūdĕt Īōnĭcōs.

Sāltŭs, ūs. m. *Leap, bound. Dance.* Syn.—Sāltātŭs, sāltātĭŏ.

Sāltŭs, ūs. m. *Woods, grove.* Sāltĭbŭs īn văcŭīs pāscānt, ēt plēnă sĕcūndūm Flūmĭnă. V. Syn.—Sīlvă, nĕmŭs. *See Silva.*

Sălūbĕr (Sălūbrĭs), sălūbrĭs, sălūbrĕ. *Healthful.* Nēc pŏtŭīt cūrās sānārĕ sălūbrĭbŭs hērbīs. Tib. Syn.—Sălūtārĭs, sălūtĭfĕr, ūtĭlĭs, præsēns, sānŭs.

Sălūs, ūtĭs. f. *Safety.* Ūnă sălūs vīctīs nūllām spērārĕ sălūtēm. V. Syn.—Īncŏlŭmĭtās, (*sometimes*) vītă, pōrtŭs, ēffŭgĭūm, pērfŭgĭūm. Phr.—Ūnă sălūs āmbōbŭs ĕrĭt. Ēă vīsă sălūs mŏrĭēntĭbŭs ūnă. Spōndēt fōrtūnă sălūtēm. Fōrtūnă sălūtĭs Mōnstrăt ĭtĕr. *Health.* Syn.—Sānĭtās, vĭgŏr.

Sălūtŏ, ās, āvī, ātūm, ārĕ. *To salute.* Sæpĕ sălūtātūs, nūmquām prĭŏr īpsĕ sălūtās. M. Syn.—Sălūtēm dō, dīcŏ, nūntĭŏ, āffĕrŏ. Phr.—Sālvērĕ jŭbĕŏ. Ăvē fĕrŏ. Sălūtātūm vĕnĭŏ. Sălūtāndī mūnŭs fĕrŏ. Sālvūs sīs. Vādĕ sălūtātūm prō mē. *To salute by name.* Syn.—Āppēllŏ.

Sālvĭă, æ. f. *The herb sage.* (*See Appendix under list of Trees, etc.*)

Sālvŭs, ă, ūm. *Sound, healthy.* Syn.—Sānŭs, vălēns. *Safe, preserved.* Syn.—Īncŏlŭmĭs, sērvātŭs, īllæsŭs, īntĕgĕr, sōspĕs, tūtŭs. *Protected from.* Syn.—Īncŏlŭmĭs, īntāctŭs, īllæsŭs.

Sāncĭŏ, īs, xī, ctūm, īrĕ. *To ordain, to establish.* Syn.—Dēcērnŏ, dēfīnĭŏ, stătŭŏ, cōnstĭtŭŏ. *To sanction, to confirm.* Syn.—Fīrmŏ, cōnfīrmŏ.

Sānctē. adv. *Holily.* Syn.—Cāstē, pĭē.

Sānctŭs, ă, ūm. *Holy, sacred.* Īngrĕdĭŏr, sānctōs aūsūs rēclūdĕrĕ fōntēs. V. Syn.—Săcĕr, săcrātŭs, vĕrēndŭs, vĕnĕrāndŭs, īnvĭŏlābĭlĭs, īntĕmĕrāndŭs. Phr.—Ēt sānctām vĭŏlārĕ fĭdēm. Sānctārum īnscītĭă lēgūm. *Pure, chaste.* Syn.—Pĭŭs, rĕlĭgĭōsŭs, īnsōns, īntĕgĕr, cāstŭs, īnnŏcēns. Phr.—Āntĕ dĭēm dĕō plēnŭs. Āddēndūs sŭpĕrīs. *The saints.* Syn.—Cœlĭtēs, cœlĭcŏlæ, dīvī, sŭpĕrī, bĕātī. Phr.—Bĕātī prŏcĕrēs. Īmmōrtālēs ănĭmæ. Nūmĭnă dīvūm. Gēns ēlēctă. Fōrtūnātă pĭōrūm Āgmĭnă. Quōs vīrtūs āddĭdĭt āstrīs.

Sānē. adv. *Wisely.* Syn.—Săpĭēntĕr. *Surely, without doubt.* Syn.—Cērtē, næ, prŏfēctō, quĭdēm. Phr.—Sĭnĕ dŭbĭō, prŏcŭl dŭbĭŏ.

Sānguĭnĕŭs, ă, ūm. *Bloody.* Syn.—Crŭēntŭs. *See Cruentus. Red, the color of blood.* Syn.—Pūrpŭrĕŭs, rŭbĕŭs. *Cruel.* Syn.—Crŭēntŭs, crūdēlĭs.

Sānguĭnŏlēntŭs, ă, ūm. *Bloody.* Pēctŏră jāctāntēm sānguĭnŏlēntă vĭrūm. O. Syn.—Sānguĭnĕŭs, crŭēntŭs, crŭēntātŭs. Phr.—Sānguĭnĕ spārsŭs, āspērsŭs, īmbūtŭs, mădēns, īnfēctŭs, tūrpĭs, mānāns, pīnguĭs. Stĕtĭt īmbrĕ crŭēntō Īnfōrmīs făcĭēs. Ēnsēmque crŭōrĕ Spūmāntēm. Mūltō rŭbĕfāctă crŭōrĕ.

Sānguĭs, ĭnĭs. m. *Blood.* Gĕlĭdūs cōncrēvīt frīgŏrĕ sānguĭs. V. Syn.—Crŭŏr. Phr.—Sānguĭnĕŭs ĭmbĕr. Ātrō sānguĭnĕ gūttæ. Sānguĭnĕ tērrām rĭgăt. Tōtō cōrpŏrĕ sānguĭs mānăt. Īnūndānt sānguĭnĕ fōssæ. Nōstrō sĕquĭtūr dē vūlnĕrĕ sānguĭs. Mānăt pĕnĕtrālĭă tābō. *Race, lineage.* Syn.—Gēns, ōrtŭs, ŏrīgŏ, stīrps, prōlēs, prŏpāgŏ, prōgĕnĭēs. *See Genus.*

Sănĭēs, ēī. f. *Pus, matter, decomposed blood.* Syn.—Crŭŏr, tābēs. Phr.—Stīllāntīs tābī sănĭēs. Vūlnĕrĕ mānāns. Tābō flŭēns. Pīnguī cōncrētōs sānguĭnĕ crīnēs. *Poison of animals and serpents.* Syn.—Vīrŭs, tābūm, vĕnēnūm.

Sānŏ, ās, āvī, ātūm, ārĕ. *To cure.* Cōrpŏră vīx quædām fērrō sānāntŭr. O. Syn.—Mĕdĕŏr, mĕdĭcŏr, cūrŏ. Phr.—Sălūtēm dō, rēddŏ. Fīrmās rēstĭtŭŏ vīrēs. Mōrbūm pēllŏ, dēpēllŏ, ēxpēllŏ. Aēgrūm rĕfĭcĭŏ. Sānăt mĕdĕcīnă dŏlōrēs. *Pass. To be cured.* Syn.—Cōnvălĕŏ, rĕcrĕŏr, rĕfĭcĭŏr. Phr.—Ād vītām rĕdĕŏ. Vīrēs rĕcĭpĭŏ. Nŏvæ rĕdĭēre īn prīstĭnă vīrēs.

Sānŭs, ă, ūm. *Sound, healthy.* Sī mē vīvĕrĕ vīs sānūm rēctēquĕ vălēntēm. H. Syn.—Vălēns, vĭgēns, īntĕgĕr, īncŏlŭmĭs, sōspĕs. Phr.—Fīrmō cōrpŏrĕ sānŭs. Sālvŭs āc vălēns. Sōspēs ĕt īntĕgĕr. Sānō, vălĭdō cōrpŏrĕ. Fīrmīs vīrĭbŭs.

Săpĭēns, ēntĭs. adj. *Wise, prudent.* Syn.—Prūdēns, dōctŭs, pĕrītŭs. Phr.—Cuī săpĭēntĭă mēntēm Īmbŭĭt. *A wise man.* Syn.—Sŏphŭs. Phr.—Vĭr jūstŭs. Ūnūs dē grĕgĕ Sōcrătĭcō.

Săpĭēntĕr. adv. *Wisely, prudently.* Syn.—Prūdēntĕr, scītē, cōrdātē, sānĭŭs.

Săpĭēntĭă, æ. f. *Wisdom, science.* Nūnquam ălĭŭd nātūra, ălĭŭd săpĭēntĭă dīcĭt. J. Syn.—Prūdēntĭă, rătĭŏ, cōnsĭlĭūm, sēnsŭs, jūdĭcĭūm. Phr.—Vēră, rēctă, rătĭŏ. Sānă mēns. Prīncēps vīrtūtūm.

Săpŏr, ōrĭs. m. *Taste, savour.* Syn.—Gūstŭs. Phr.—Āspĕr īn ōrĕ săpŏr. Dūrūm dŏmĭtūră săpōrēm. Fœdō pērtōrquēnt ōră săpōrĕ.

Sārcĭnă, æ. f. *Baggage.* Syn.—Ŏnŭs, pōndŭs, sārcĭnŭlæ, fāscĭs. *Embarrassment, burden.* Syn.—Āngŏr, cūră. *See Angor.*

Sārcĭŏ, īs, sārsī, sārtūm, īrĕ. *To repair.* Īncūmbūnt gĕnĕrīs lāpsī sārcīrĕ rŭīnās. V. Syn.—Rĕsārcĭŏ, rĕpārŏ, pēnsŏ, cōmpēnsŏ. *See Reparo.*

Sătă, ōrūm. n. *Fields that are sown.* Ēt plŭvĭa īngēntī sătă lætă bŏūmquĕ lăbōrēs Dīlŭĭt. V. Syn.—Sĕgĕs, cūltă, ăgĕr. Phr.—Ănĭmōs tōllūnt sătă.

Sătēllĕs, ĭtĭs. m. *Guard, companion.* Syn.—Cūstōs, mīlĕs. Phr.—Mīlĭtūm, cūstōdūm cŏhōrs, cūstōdĭă, tūtēlă. Strīctō cūstōdĭă fērrō. *Guardian, protector.* Syn.—Cūstōs, mĭnĭstĕr, dēfēnsŏr, mūnīmĕn, tūtēlă.

Sătĭs. adv. *Enough.* Syn.—Săt, ăbūndē. Phr.—Sătĭs sŭpērquĕ. Jām sătĭs āc nĭmĭūm. Sătĭs ēst, sūffĭcĭt.

Sătīsfăcĭŏ, ĭs, fēcī, fāctūm, ĕrĕ. *To satisfy.* Syn.—Plăcĕō. Phr.—Sătĭs ăgĕrĕ. Dēbĭtūm sōlvŏ, ēxsōlvŏ, pērsōlvŏ.

Sătĭŭs. adv. *Better.* Syn.—Pŏtĭŭs, mĕlĭŭs.

Sătŏr, ōrĭs. m. *Sower.* Syn.—Sēmĭnāns. Fig.—*Creator, author.* Syn.—Cōndĭtŏr crĕātŏr, aūctŏr. Phr.—Hŏmĭnūm sătŏr ātquĕ dĕōrūm. *See Auctor.*

Sătŭr, ŭră, ŭrūm. *Satisfied.* Dūx ărĭēs sătŭrās īpsĕ rĕdūxĭt ŏvēs. Prop. Syn.—Sătŭrātŭs, sătĭātŭs, rĕfēctŭs, rĕplētŭs, plēnŭs Phr.—Cĭbīs rĕplētŭs. Pūlsā, dēpūlsā fămē. Sīt mĭhĭ vērnă sătŭr. Fig.—*Fertile.* Syn.—Fērtĭlĭs. *See Fertilis.* *Saturated, imbued with.* Syn.—Sătŭrātŭs, īmbūtŭs.

Sătŭrŏ, ās, āvī, ātūm, arĕ. *To satisfy, to satiate.* Syn.—Sătĭŏ, ēxsătŭrŏ, ēxplĕŏ, rĕplĕŏ. *Pass. To be satisfied.* Syn.—Sătĭŏr, ēxsătĭŏr, ēxplĕŏr. Phr.—Sătŭr fīŏ. Cĭbīs fămēm pēllŏ, dēpēllŏ, ēxstīnguŏ, cōmprĭmŏ, plācŏ, ēxplĕŏ. Īnglŭvĭēm ēxplĕŏ. Pōstquam ēxēmptă fămēs.

Saūcĭŭs, ă, ūm. *Wounded.* Pēnĕ mănūs tēlō saūcĭă fāctă tŭo ēst. O. Syn.—Læsŭs, vūlnĕrātŭs, ōffēnsŭs, īctŭs, pērcūssŭs, cōnfōssŭs, cōnfīxŭs. Phr.—Grăvī vūlnĕrĕ saūcĭŭs.

Sāxōsŭs, ă, ūm. *Rocky.* Nāscūntūr stĕrĭlēs sāxōsīs mōntĭbŭs ōrnī. V. Syn.—Lăpĭdōsŭs, pĕtrōsŭs, scrūpĕŭs, sălĕbrōsŭs, scŏpŭlōsŭs, scăbĕr. Phr.—Sāxīs, scŏpŭlīs āspĕr, crēbĕr, plēnŭs, rĕfērtŭs, hōrrēns. Sīlvīs hōrrēntĭă sāxă frăgōsīs. Præcĭpĭtēs caūtēs. Āspĕrĭtās ĭnīquă lŏcī.

Sāxūm, ī. n. *Rock, cliff.* Ēccĕ pĕtūnt rūpēs prærūptăquĕ sāxă căpēllæ. O. Syn.—Sĭlēx, caūtēs, rūpēs, scŏpŭlŭs. Phr.—Sāxă frĕmūnt. Clāmōrēm căvă sāxă dĕdērĕ. Rōscĭdă rīvīs Sāxă cŏlānt. Cīrcūmlĭtă mūscō.

Scăbēllūm, ī. n. *Little bench.* Syn.—Scāmnūm, sĕdīlĕ, sēdēs. *See Sedes.*

Scăbĕr, scăbră, scăbrūm. *Rough.* Ēxēsa īnvĕnĭēt scābrā rūbīgĭnĕ pīlă. V. Syn.—Āspĕr, rĭgĭdŭs, rŭdĭs. Phr.—Scābrī rūbīgĭnĕ dēntēs. *Filthy.* Syn.—Sōrdĭdŭs, spūrcŭs, īmmūndŭs, squālĭdŭs, squālēns, scăbĭōsŭs.

Scăbĭēs, ēī. f. *Itch, mange.* Syn.—Scăbrĭtĭēs, prūrīgŏ. Phr.—Scăbĭē īnfēctă. Scăbĭēī āspĕrĭtās. Cŭtēm scăbĭēs rōdĭt. Tūrpĭs ŏvēs tēntāt scăbĭēs. Ēt mălă quēm scăbĭēs ūrgĕt. Fig.—*Contagion.* Syn.—Pēstĭs, lŭēs, cōntăgĭă (pl.).

Scālpŏ, ĭs, psī, ptūm, ĕrĕ. *To scrape, to scratch.* Syn.—Scăbŏ, frĭcŏ, rādŏ. *To engrave.* Syn.—Scūlpŏ. *See Sculpo.*

Scăphă, æ. f. *Skiff, boat.* Tūnc mē, bĭrēmĭs præsĭdĭō scăphæ, Aūră fĕrĕt. H. Syn.—Cȳmbă, lēmbŭs, lĭntĕr, nāvĭs, rătĭs. *See Navis.*

Scătĕō, ēs, ŭī, ērĕ. *To burst forth, to flow forth.* Syn.—Ērūmpŏ, ēxĕō, ēfflŭō, sălĭō, prōsĭlĭō, ēxsĭlĭō.

Scĕlĕrātŭs, ă, ūm. *Wicked, criminal.* Syn.—Scĕlēstŭs, nĕfārĭŭs, nĕfāndŭs, īmprŏbŭs, flāgĭtĭōsŭs, nēquām, pērdĭtŭs, mălŭs, pērvērsŭs, nŏcēns, sōns, īmpĭŭs. Phr.—Scĕlĕrĭs, crīmĭnĭs ārtĭfēx. Scĕlĕrūm sēctātŏr. Prōnŭs ăd ōmnĕ nĕfās. Prāvī cuī cōnscĭă mēns ēst. Aūdāx ĭn aūsūs. Dīssuāsŏr hŏnēstī. Scĕlĕre ānte ălĭōs īmmānĭŏr ōmnes. Mājŭs ădōrsă nĕfās.

Scĕlēstŭs, ă, ūm. *Wicked, criminal. See Sceleratus.*

Scĕlŭs, ĕrĭs. n. *Crime.* Quŏd ĕnīm scĕlŭs ērrŏr hăbēbăt? O. Syn.—Făcĭnŭs, flāgĭtĭūm, nĕfās, crīmĕn, pĭăcŭlŭm, dēlīctūm, cūlpă, pēccātūm. Phr.—Scĕlēstūm, nĕfāndūm făcĭnŭs, fāctūm. Īmpĭă fāctă. Cūlpæ crīmĕn ătrōx. Scĕlĕrūm lābēs. Mēns ăgĭt īn făcĭnŭs. Nĭtĭmŭr īn vĕtĭtūm. Cērtăt ĭn ōmnĕ scĕlŭs.

Scēptrūm, ī. n. *Sceptre.* Aūrĕă cūr dēxtræ scēptră dĕdērĕ mĕæ? O. Phr.—Rēgĭs, rēgĭūm īnsīgnĕ. Vīrgă nōbĭlĭs. Scēptrī dĕcŭs. Scēptrī grăvĭtās. Aūrō gēmmīsquĕ dĕcōrūm.

Schŏlă, æ. f. *School.* Sī schŏlă dāmnātūr, fŏră lītĭbŭs ōmnĭă fērvēnt. M. Syn.—Gȳmnăsĭūm, pălæstră, lūdŭs. Phr.—Mūsārūm sēdēs, lŏcŭs. Quī rhētŏrĭcā dēscēndĭt ăb ūmbrā.

Scĭēntĭă, æ. f. *Knowledge, science.* Jāmjam ēffĭcācī dō mănūs scĭēntĭæ. H. Syn.—Dŏctrīnă, dīscĭplīnă, ārs, stŭdĭūm. Phr.—Cāstæ Pāllădĭs ārtēs.

Scīlĭcĕt. adv. *To be sure, forsooth.* Syn.—Crēdŏ, nēmpĕ, vĭdēlĭcĕt, prŏfēctō, nīmīrūm. *In other words.* Syn.—Vĭdēlĭcĕt, nēmpĕ, quīppĕ.

Scīllă, æ. f. *A sea-onion.* (*See Appendix under list of Trees, etc.*)

Scīndŏ, ĭs, scĭdī, scīssūm, ĕrĕ. *To cleave, to cut, to split.* Nām prīmī cŭnĕīs scīndēbānt fīssĭlĕ līgnūm. V. Syn.—Ābscīndŏ, dīscīndŏ, prōscīndŏ, rēscīndŏ, dīvĭdŏ, dīdūcŏ, sĕcŏ, ēxsĕcŏ, rĕsĕcŏ, dīssĕcŏ, ēxcīdŏ, īncīdŏ, rĕcīdŏ, āmpŭtŏ, trūncŏ, mŭtĭlŏ, lăcĕrŏ, cædŏ. Phr.—Fērrō, fālcĕ, sĕcūrī fĕrĭō, dīscīndŏ. Īn frūstă sĕcŏ. Ābstŭlĭt ēnsĕ fĕrō. Fīndĭt ĭn āmbās.

Scīntīllŏ, ās, āvī, ātūm, ārĕ. *To sparkle.* Scīntīllāre ŏlĕūm tēstā cūm ārdēntĕ vĭdērēnt. V. Phr.—Scīntīllās, mīttŏ, ăgŏ, dō, jăcĭō. *To send forth light.* Syn.—Fūlgŭrŏ, mĭcŏ, ārdĕō.

Scĭŏ, īs, scīvī, scītūm, īrĕ. *To know.* Scīs ĕtĕnīm jūstūm gĕmĭnā sūspēndĕrĕ lāncĕ. Pers. Syn.—Nōscŏ, cōgnōscŏ, cāllĕŏ, īntēllĕgŏ, těněŏ. Phr.—Nōn īgnōrŏ. Nōn nēscĭŏ. Nōn sūm īgnārŭs. Nōn mē lătĕt, fŭgĭt, prætĕrĭt. Mĭhĭ lĭquĕt.

Scīrpŭs & Sīrpŭs, ī. m. *A reed, bulrush.* (*See Appendix under list of Trees, etc.*)

Scīscĭtŏr (Scītŏr), ārĭs, ātŭs sūm, ārī. *To demand, to seek.* Syn.—Pērcōntŏr, quærŏ, īnquīrŏ, pōscŏ, pōstŭlŏ, rŏgŏ, rŏgĭtŏ, īntērrŏgŏ. Phr.—Scītārīs dīgnă rĕlātū. Vĕnĭēndī pōscĕrĕ caūsās. Scītāri ēt quærĕrĕ caūsās.

Scītē. adv. *Learnedly.* Syn.—Dōctē, pĕrītē, cāllĭdē.

Scŏpŭlŭs, ī. m. *Rock, cliff.* Dīdūxīt scŏpŭlōs, ēt mōntēm rūpĭt ăcētō. J. Syn.—Săxūm, caūtēs, sĭlēx, rūpēs. Phr.—Scŏpŭlī, scŏpŭlōrūm, sāxōrūm caūtēs, mĭnæ, fraūdēs. Săxă lătēntĭă. Scŏpŭlūs brĕvĭs ēmĭnĕt āltē. Scŏpŭlīs pēndēntĭbŭs āntrūm. Gĕmĭnīquĕ mĭnāntŭr Īn cœlūm scŏpŭlī. *See Rupes, Saxum.*

Scŏpŭs, ī. m. *End proposed.* Syn.—Mētă, fīnĭs, prōpŏsĭtūm. Phr.—Īn scŏpūm īntēndĕrĕ. Scŏpūm, mētām tāngĕrĕ.

Scōrpĭŭs, ĭī. m. *Scorpion.* Scōrpĭūs ēxībīt, caūdāquĕ mĭnābĭtūr ūncā. O. Phr.—Ăcūtō ūnguĕ, caūdā ūncā. Dīrō vĕnēnō. Mĕtŭēndŭs ăcūmĭnĕ caūdæ. Vĭŏlēntā cūspĭdĕ sævŭs. Quī caūdā dīrĭgĭt īctūm. *The constellation.* Syn.—Nĕpă.

Scrībŏ, ĭs, psī, ptūm, ĕrĕ. *To trace lines.* Syn.—Ărŏ, ēxărŏ, pĕrărŏ, sūlcŏ, īnscrībŏ. *To write.* Syn.—Cōnscrībŏ, īnscrībŏ, pērscrībŏ, ēxărŏ, ărŏ, pĕrărŏ. Phr.—Stȳlō, călămō tăbēllās ēxărŏ. Chārtīs, cērīs vērbă nŏtŏ, cōmmīttŏ. Chārtīs īllĭnŏ. Sīgnārĕ tăbēllās. *To compose.* Syn.—Cōnscrībŏ, cōmpōnŏ, ēdŏ. *To set forth.* Syn.—Dēscrībŏ, pīngŏ.

Scrīnĭūm, ĭī. n. *Casket, desk.* Syn.—Căpsă, ārcă, ārcŭlă. *Tablet.* Syn.—Tăbēllæ.

Scrīptŏr, ōrĭs. m. *Writer, copyist.* Syn.—Lĭbrārĭŭs, scrībă. *Author.* Syn.—Aūctŏr, cōndĭtŏr.

Scrīptūm, ī. n. *Work, writing.* Scrīptă fĕrūnt ānnōs, scrīptīs Ăgămēmnŏnă nōstī. O. Syn.—Ŏpŭs, lĭbĕr, lĭbēllŭs, chārtă, vŏlūmĕn.

Scrūpĕŭs, ă, ūm. *Rocky.* Scrūpĕă tūtă lăcū nīgrō nĕmŏrūmquĕ lătēbrīs (spelunca). V. Syn.—Lăpĭdōsŭs, sălĕbrōsŭs, sāxōsŭs, scăbĕr, āspĕr, hōrrēns.

Scrūpŭlŭs, ī. m. *Small stone.* Syn.—Lăpīllŭs, cālcŭlŭs. Fig.—*Scruple.* Syn.—Dŭbĭūm.

Scrūtŏr, ārĭs, ātŭs sūm, ārī. *To seek, to investigate.* Syn.—Pērscrūtŏr, quærŏ, īnquīrŏ, ēxquīrŏ, īnvēstīgŏ, īndāgŏ, ēxplōrŏ.

Scūlpŏ, ĭs, psī, ptūm, ĕrĕ. *To cut, to chisel, to carve.* Nĭvĕūm mīrā fēlīcĭtĕr ārtĕ Scūlpsĭt ĕbŭr. O. Syn.—Scālpŏ, cælŏ, īncīdŏ, īnscūlpŏ. Phr.—Scālprō, cǣlō mārmŏr, ǣs, ĕbŭr, aūrūm ēffīngŏ, cūdŏ, īncīdŏ. Tĕnĕrōs ē mārmŏrĕ dūcĕrĕ vūltūs.

Scūlptŏr, ōrĭs. m. *Sculptor, engraver.* Syn.—Stătŭārĭŭs, cǣlātŏr. Phr.—Ārtĭs Phīdĭăcǣ dōctŭs, pĕrītŭs. Dōctūs spīrāntēs ănĭmārĕ fĭgūrās. Cǣlāndī pĕrītŭs.

Scūlptūră, ǣ. f. *Sculpture, engraving.* Syn.—Stătŭārĭă, cǣlātūră. Phīdĭăcǣ ārtēs. Pŏlўclētī ārs, lăbŏr, ŏpŭs. Mēntŏrĭs, Mēntŏrĕǣ ārtēs.

Scŭtĭcă, ǣ. f. *Scourge.* Syn.—Lōrūm, hăbēnă, flăgēllūm.

Scūtūm. ī. n. *Shield.* Scūtīs prōtēctī cōrpŏră lōngīs. V. Syn.—Clўpeŭs, umbŏ, pārmă. *See Clypeus.*

Scўphŭs, ī. m. *Cup.* Făgĭnūs ādstābāt cūm scўphŭs āntĕ dăpēs. Tib. Syn.—Crātēr, călīx, pōcŭlūm. Ēt săcĕr īmplēvīt dēxtrām scўphŭs. Nātīs ĭn ūsūm lǣtĭtĭǣ scўphīs.

Sēcēdŏ, ĭs, cēssī, cēssūm, ĕrĕ. *To withdraw from.* Quōs hăbŭīt văcŭōs sēcēdĕre ĭn hōrtōs. O. Syn.—Ābscēdŏ, dēcēdŏ, rĕcēdŏ. Phr.—Sēcēssūm pĕtŏ.

Sēcērnŏ, ĭs, crēvī, crētūm, ĕrĕ. *To separate, to put aside.* Pūblĭcă prīvātīs sēcērnĕrĕ, săcră prŏfānīs. H. Syn.—Sēpōnŏ, sēlĭgŏ, dīscērnŏ, dīvĭdŏ, sēgrĕgŏ, sēpărŏ. *To distinguish.* Syn.—Dīscērnŏ, dīstīnguŏ.

Sēcēssŭs, ūs. m. *Retreat, hidden place.* Cārmĭnă sēcēssūm scrībēntĭs ĕt ōtĭă quǣrūnt. O. Syn.—Rĕcēssŭs, lătĕbrǣ, pĕnĕtrālĕ, sēcrētă, sĭlēntĭă. Phr.—Lŏcŭs sēcrētŭs. Ēst īn sēcēssū lōngō lŏcŭs. Ēt grātūm līttŭs ămœ̄nī Sēcēssŭs.

Sēclūdŏ, ĭs, sī, sūm, ĕrĕ. *To separate from, to shut off.* Syn.—Sēpărŏ, claūdŏ. *To banish.* Syn.—Rĕmŏvĕŏ, pēllŏ, prōpēllŏ, mīttŏ.

Sĕcŏ, ās, ŭī, sēctūm, ārĕ. *To cut.* Āh! tĭbĭ nē tĕnĕrās glăcĭēs sĕcĕt āspĕră plāntās. V. Syn.—Fīndŏ, lăcĕrŏ, dīvĭdŏ, cǣdŏ.

Sēcrētūm, ī. n. *Secret place.* Aēnēǣ sēdem āc sēcrētă pĕtēbānt. V. Syn.—Sēcēssŭs, rĕcēssŭs. *Secret.* Syn.—Rēs ōccūltă, ābdĭtă, tēctă.

Sēctă, ǣ. f. *Sect, party, band.* Syn.—Īnstĭtūtūm, scītă, plăcĭtă, dōctrīnă, tūrbă, āgmĕn, grēx.

Sēctŏr, ārĭs, ātŭs sūm, ārī. *To pursue.* Sī dūm tū sēctārĭs ăprōs, ĕgŏ rētĭă sērvŏ. V. Syn.—Īnsĕquŏr, pērsĕquŏr, ūrgĕŏ, īnstŏ. *To follow after eagerly, to seek after.* Syn.—Āssēctŏr, sĕquŏr, pērsĕquŏr, pĕtŏ, āppĕtŏ, cāptŏ, aŭcŭpŏr, vēnŏr.

Sēcŭlūm (sēclūm), ī. n. *Century.* Syn.—Aētās. *Generation, age.* Syn.—Aētās, ǣvūm. *Posterity.* Syn.—Pōstĕrī.

Sĕcūndŏ, ās, āvī, ātūm, ārĕ. *To favor, to second.* Rītĕ sĕcūndārēnt vīsūs, ōmēnquĕ lĕvārēnt. V. Syn.—Ādjŭvŏ, făvĕŏ, prōspĕrŏ, āspīrŏ, ādsūm. Phr.—Dī nōstra īncœptă sĕcūndēnt. Aūră sĕcūndĕt ītĕr.

Sĕcūndūm. adv. & prep. *Near.* Syn.—Jūxtā, prŏpĕ, prōptĕr, ăd. *After.* Syn.—Pōst. *According to.* Syn.—Prō.

Sĕcūndŭs, ă, ūm. *Second.* Syn.—Āltĕr. *Inferior.* Syn.—Īnfĕrĭŏr, mĭnŏr. *Favorable.* Syn.—Fēlīx, faūstŭs, fōrtūnātŭs, prōspĕr, făvēns, præsēns. Phr.—Fōrtūnă sĕcūndă, Aūt ādvērsă cădăt. Īrĕ sĕcūndīs ōmĭnĭbŭs.

Sĕcūrĭs, ĭs. f. *Axe, hatchet.* Sŏnăt īctă sĕcūrĭbŭs īlēx. V. Syn.—Āscĭă, bĭpēnnĭs, fērrūm. Phr.—Fērrūm bĭpēnnĕ. Sĕcūrĭs īctŭs. Sĕcūrī căpŭt āmpŭtŏ. Dūrīs ēxcīsă sĕcūrĭbŭs īlēx. Crēbrīsquĕ bĭpēnnĭbŭs īnstānt ērŭĕrĕ. Īncērtam ēxcūssīt cērvīcĕ sĕcūrīm. *Plural, the Fasces.* Syn.—Fāscēs.

Sēcūrŭs, ă, ūm. *Free from fear.* Mōllĭă sēcūræ pĕrăgēbānt ōtĭă gēntēs. O. Syn.—Tūtŭs, quĭētŭs, trānquīllŭs, plăcĭdŭs. Phr.—Cūrīs lībĕr, văcāns, văcŭŭs, sŏlūtŭs. Sēcūrōs rūmpĕrĕ sōmnōs.

Sĕcŭs. adv. *Otherwise.* Syn.—Ălĭtĕr, nōn sĕcŭs. Phr.—Haūd sĕcŭs āc jūssī făcĭūnt. Nōn sēcĭŭs. *None the less.* Syn.—Nōn mĭnŭs, nĭhĭlōmĭnŭs. Prep. *Near to.* Syn.—Jūxtā, prŏpĕ, sĕcūndūm.

Sĕd. conj. *But.* Syn.—Āst, ăt, vērūm, sĕdĕnĭm, vērō, aūtēm.

Sēdāmĕn, ĭnĭs. n. *Solace.* Syn.—Sōlāmĕn, sōlātĭūm, lĕvāmĕn.

Sĕdĕŏ, ēs, sēdī, sēssūm, ērĕ. *To sit down.* Sĕdĕt ætērnūmquĕ sĕdēbĭt Īnfēlīx Thēseūs. V. Syn.—Sīdŏ, cōnsĭdĕŏ, āssĭdĕŏ, rĕsĭdĕŏ, cōnsīdŏ. Phr.—Sĕdīlĕ prĕmŏ, īn sēdĕ lŏcŏr. Sŏlĭōque āltē sūbnīxă rĕsēdĭt. Sŏlĭō cōnsēdĭt ăvītō. *To stop, to delay.* Syn.—Stō, mănĕŏ, hærĕŏ, cōnsīstŏ, cēssŏ. *To remain fixed.* Syn.—Stō, hærĕŏ, mănĕŏ. *To be situated.* Syn.—Sūbjăcĕŏ, jăcĕŏ. *To settle into, to penetrate into.* Syn.—Dēscēndŏ, dēmīttŏr, pĕnĕtrŏ, sŭbĕŏ.

Sēdēs, ĭs. f. *Seat.* Quī pōstquām nĭvĕōs flēxērūnt sēdĭbŭs ārtūs. *Cat.* Syn.—Sĕdīlĕ, scāmnūm, sēllă, scăbēllūm, sūbsēllĭă, căthĕdră, sŏlĭūm. *Dwelling, sojourn.* Syn.—Dŏmŭs, lŏcŭs, stătĭŏ, pĕnātēs.

Sĕdīlĕ, ĭs. n. *Seat. See Sedes.*

Sēdĭtĭŏ, ōnĭs. f. *Sedition, rebellion.* Crēscītquĕ făvōrĕ Tūrbĭdă sēdĭtĭŏ. O. Syn.—Dīssĭdĭūm, dīscōrdĭă, tūrbæ, mōtŭs, tŭmūltŭs. Phr.—Prōnŭbă bēllī. Sēdĭtĭōsŭs rūmŏr. Pŏpŭlārĭs mōtŭs. Cīvīlĭă bēllă. Fŭrēns vūlgī mōtŭs. Fērvēntĕ tŭmūltū. Īn mūtŭă vūlnĕră cīvēs ārmāntŭr. Plēbs vēsānă sēdĭtĭōnĕ fŭrĭt.

Sēdĭtĭōsŭs, ă, ūm. *Seditious, rebellious.* Phr.—Sēdĭtĭōnĭs ămāns, aūctŏr, căpŭt, ŏrīgŏ. Sēdĭtĭōnĕ fŭrēns, pŏtēns. Gēns ĭnĭmīcă pācĭs, quĭētĭs.

Sēdŏ, ās, āvī, ātūm, ārĕ. *To appease, to soothe.* Dūmquĕ sĭtīm sēdārĕ cŭpīt, sĭtĭs āltĕră crēvĭt. O. Syn.—Lēnĭŏ, mītĭgŏ, plācŏ. Phr.—Cārnĕ fĕræ sēdānt jējūnĭă. Mĕtūm sēdāt dĭēs. Sēdārĕ lĕōnĭbŭs īrām. Sēdāre īncēndĭă tēntēs. *See Placo.*

Sēdūcŏ, ĭs, dūxī, dūctūm, ĕrĕ. *To lead apart.* Syn.—Sēvŏcŏ, ābdūcŏ. *To separate.* *See Separo.* *To deceive.* Syn.—Dēcĭpĭŏ. *See Decipio.*

Sēdŭlĭtās, ātĭs. f. *Care, diligence.* Ēt nōn sēntītūr sēdŭlĭtātĕ lăbŏr. O. Syn.—Cūră, stŭdĭūm, īndūstrĭă, ŏpĕră, lăbŏr.

Sēdŭlŭs, ă, ūm. *Careful, diligent.* Nōn ăpĭs īndĕ tŭlīt cōllēctās sēdŭlă flōrēs. O. Syn.—Dīlĭgēns, īmpĭgĕr, āssĭdŭŭs, vĭgĭl, ācĕr, āttēntŭs, gnāvŭs, īndūstrĭŭs. *Officious.* Syn.—Ōffĭcĭōsŭs, ōbsĕquĭōsŭs.

Sĕdūm, ī. n. *House-leek.* (*See Appendix under list of Trees, etc.*)

Sĕgĕs, ĕtĭs. f. *Land for sowing.* Syn.—Ăgĕr. *Sown field, harvest.* Syn.—Sătă, frūgēs, ărīstæ, spīcæ, frūmēntūm, trītĭcūm, Cĕrēs. Phr.—Cĕrĕrĭs, tēllūrĭs, tērræ ŏpēs, mūnĕră. Cĕrĕālĭă dōnă. Sĕgĕtūm mūnŭs. Hūmānō cūltă lăbōrĕ sĕgĕs. Īmbrĭbŭs aūctă bĕnīgnīs. Cānīs flāvēns ărīstīs. Vĭrĭdĭs ārvă sĕgĕs tĕgĭt. Pīnguīs flāvēscīt cāmpŭs ărīstīs. Grăvĭdīs prōcūmbĭt ărīstīs. Prīmīs sĕgĕtēs mŏrĭūntŭr ĭn hērbīs. Nōndūm sūrgēntĭbŭs āltām Īn sĕgĕtēm cūlmīs. Sĕgĕtī prætēndĕrĕ sēpēm. Ōbdūcūnt hērbæ sĕgĕtēm.

Sēgnĭs, ĭs, ĕ. *Lazy, slothful.* Nēc Tūrnūs sēgnĭŏr īnstăt. V. Syn.—Tārdŭs, īgnāvŭs, pĭgĕr, lēntŭs, ĭnērs. Phr.—Sēgnēs rūmpĕ mŏrās. Haūd sēgnīs strātō sūrgĭt.

Sēgnĭtĕr. adv. *Slowly, tardily.* Syn.—Sēgnĭŭs, īgnāvē, lēntē, pĭgrē, tārdē, gĕlĭdē.

Sēgnĭtĭēs, ēī (Sēgnĭtĭă, æ). f. *Laziness, sloth.* Syn.—Īgnāvĭă, dēsĭdĭă, sōcōrdĭă, pĭgrĭtĭă.

Sēgrĕgŏ, ās, āvī, ātūm, ārĕ. *To separate.* Syn.—Sēpărŏ, sējūngŏ, sēmŏvĕŏ, sēpōnŏ.

Sēgrēx, ĕgĭs. adj. *Separated, solitary.* Syn.—Rĕmōtŭs, sējūnctŭs, sēclūsŭs.

Sēlĭgŏ, ĭs, lēgī, lēctūm, ĕrĕ. *To choose, to set aside.* Quīdquĭd ĕrīs, mĕă sēmpĕr ĕrīs, tū sēlĭgĕ tāntūm. O. Syn.—Lĕgŏ, dēlĭgŏ, ēlĭgŏ. *See Eligo.*

Sēllă, æ. f. *Seat, chair, throne.* Ēt sēllām rēgnī trăbĕāmque īnsīgnĭă nōstrī. V. Syn.—Sēdēs, sēdīlĕ, sŏlĭūm. *Portable chair.* Syn.—Lēctīcă. *Curule chair.* Syn.—Cŭrūlĭs.

Sēmĕn, ĭnĭs. n. *Seed, grain.* Prīmă Cĕrēs dŏcŭĭt tūrgēscĕrĕ sēmĕn ĭn āgrīs. O. Syn.—Sēmĭnĭs hērbă. Plāntæ īncrēmēntă fŭtūræ. Vīvācī nūtrītă sŏlō. Hŭmō dătă sēmĭnă. *Young plant.* Syn.—Vīrgūltūm, sārcŭlŭs, gērmĕn. *Source, origin.* Syn.—Gĕnŭs, ŏrīgŏ. *Source, cause.* Syn.—Ŏrīgŏ, prīncĭpĭūm, fōns, caūsă. *Principles, elements.* Syn.—Ĕlĕmēntă, prīmōrdĭă, prīncĭpĭă.

Sēmĭfĕr, ă, ūm. *Half-man, half-beast.* Syn.—Sēmĭvĭr, sēmĭhŏmŏ, bĭfōrmĭs. *Centaur.* Syn.—Cēntaūrŭs. *Wild, barbarous.* Syn.—Bārbărŭs, hōrrĭdŭs, ăgrēstĭs.

Sēmĭnŏ, ās, āvī, ātūm, ārĕ. *To sow.* Frōndĕ vĭrērĕ nŏvā, quōd nōn sŭă sēmĭnăt ārbŏr. V. Syn.—Sĕrŏ, cōnsĕrŏ, īnsĕrŏ, īnsēmĭnŏ. Phr.—Sēmĕn spārgŏ, mīttŏ. Tērræ sēmĭnă dō, māndŏ, cōmmīttŏ.

Sēmĭtă, æ. f. *Path.* Syn.—Cāllĭs, ĭtĕr, trāmĕs. Fig.—*Trace.* Syn.—Sūlcŭs, trāmĕs, trāctŭs.

Sēmiūstŭs, ă, ūm. *Half-burned.* Sēmiūstūm fūlmĭnĕ cōrpŭs. V. Syn.—Sēmiāmbūstŭs, sēmĭcrĕmātŭs, sēmĭcrĕmŭs.

Sēmĭvĭr, ĭrī. m. *Eunuch.* Syn.—Eūnūchŭs, spădŏ, sēmĭmās. *Half-man, half-animal.* Syn.—Sēmĭfĕr, bĭfōrmĭs, cēntaūrŭs. *Effeminate.* Syn.—Mōllĭs, īmbēllĭs, gnāvŭs, fēmĭnĕŭs.

Sēmpĕr. adv. *Always.* Syn.—Ūsquĕ, pērpĕtŭō, ætērnūm, cōntĭnŭō, āssĭdŭē. Phr.—Ōmnī tēmpŏrĕ. Nūnquām nōn. Sĭnĕ fīnĕ. Nūllō fīnĕ. Nōctēsquĕ dĭēsquĕ. Ōmnēs pĕr ānnōs. Tēmpŭs ĭn ōmnĕ. Ĭn ōmne ævūm. Fūlgēbānt dūm sīdĕră cœlō. Dūm sōl lūstrābĭt Ōlȳmpūm. Nĕc ūllă rĕquĭēs. Nēc mŏră nēc rĕquĭēs.

Sĕnātŏr, ōrĭs. m. *Senator.* Pāscēbātquĕ sŭās īpsĕ sĕnātŏr ŏvēs. O. Syn.—Pătrēs cōnscrīptī. Phr.—Cōnsĭlĭō pŏtēns. Īngĕnĭō māgnŭs. Jūdĭcĭī dēxtĕrĭtātĕ grăvĭs. Tŏgātī prŏcĕrēs.

Sĕnātŭs, ūs. m. *Senate.* Syn.—Cūrĭă, pătrēs cōnscrīpti, sĕnātōrēs. Phr.—Pătrūm, sĕnātōrūm cœtŭs, ōrdŏ. Vĕrēndī pătrēs. Sānctūm cōncĭlĭūm pătrūm. Lēctī prŏcĕrēs. Sĕnātōrūm aūlă. Āmplīssĭmŭs ōrdŏ. Āmplīssĭmă sēdēs.

Sĕnēctă, æ & Sĕnēctūs, ūtĭs. f. *Old age.* Dīscĭtĕ vēntūrām jām nūnc sēntīrĕ sĕnēctām. Pr. Syn.—Sĕnĭūm, cānĭtĭēs, cānī, rūgæ. Phr.—Sĕnēctæ ætās, tēmpŏră. Grăvĭs ætās. Grāndĕ ævūm. Pārs vītæ dētĕrĭŏr. Lōngævī tēmpŏrĭs ætās. Ūltĭmă tēmpŏră vītæ. Ōbrēpīt nōn īntēllēctă sĕnēctūs. Prōxĭmă lētō. Vīrĭbŭs ægră. Tārdō cūrvă sĕnēctă pĕdĕ. Tārdă sĕnēctūs.

Sĕnēscŏ, ĭs, sĕnŭī, ĕrĕ. *To grow old.* Tēmpŏră lābūntūr, tăcĭtīsquĕ sĕnēscĭmŭs ānnīs. O. Syn.—Cōnsĕnēscŏ. Phr.—Sĕnēx, sĕnĭŏr fīŏ. Vērgēntĭbŭs ānnīs īn sĕnĭūm. Jām vīrēs sĕnēctūs dēbĭlĭtāt.

Cānī nīgrōs læsērĕ căpīllōs. Sērpīt pēr mēmbră sĕnēctūs. *To become feeble.* Syn.—Tābēscŏ. Phr.—Fōrmă sĕnēscĭt. Sĕnēscĭt ămŏr.

Sĕnēx, sĕnĭs. m. *Old man.* Fōrtūnātĕ sĕnēx, ērgō tŭă rūră mănēbūnt. V. Syn.—Sĕnĭŏr, vĕtŭlŭs. *See Senectus.* Phr.—Ānnīs, ævō, ætātĕ grăvĭs, cōnfēctŭs, lānguĭdŭs. Lōngīs cōnsūmptūs ăb ānnīs. Aēvō măcĭēquĕ sĕnēscēns. Mātūrĭŏr ānnīs. Prōvēctĭŏr ānnīs. Cānīs āspērsŭs. Cuī rūgīs cōntrăctă cŭtĭs. Sĕnĭō trānscēndīt Nēstŏrĭs ānnōs.

Sēnsīm. adv. *Little by little.* Syn.—Paūlātīm, pĕdĕtēntīm.

Sēnsŭs, ūs. m. *Sense of feeling, sensation.* Phr.—Vītālēm dēpērdĕrĕ sēnsūm. Āttŏnĭtō cēssērūnt pēctŏrĕ sēnsūs. *Sentiment, affection, feeling.* Syn.—Pēctŭs, ănĭmŭs, cŏr, āffēctŭs, ămŏr. *Reason.* Syn.—Rătĭŏ, mēns, cōnsĭlĭūm, jūdĭcĭūm. *Taste.* Syn.—Săpŏr, gūstŭs.

Sēntēntĭă, æ. f. *Opinion, feeling.* Hōc plăcĕt ēt dŭbĭām vīcīt sēntēntĭă mēntēm. O. Syn.—Mēns, ănĭmŭs, cōnsĭlĭūm, sēnsŭs, ŏpīnĭŏ. Phr.—Ănĭmī sēnsă. Prūdēns ănĭmī sēntēntĭă. Mĕlĭŏr sēntēntĭă mēntī. Nĕquĕ tē sēntēntĭă fāllĭt. Sīc stāt sēntēntĭă. *Meaning.* Syn.—Sēnsŭs. *Sentence, judgment.* Syn.—Jūdĭcĭūm, sūffrāgĭūm.

Sēntēs, sēntĭūm. m. & f. *Bushes, thorns.* Dēnsī cōmplērūnt ūndĭquĕ sēntēs. V. Syn.—Rŭbī, vĕprēs, dūmŭs, spīnæ. Phr.—Sēntēs crūră nŏtānt. Hāmātīs præcōrdĭă sēntĭbŭs īmplĕt.

Sēntĭŏ, īs, sēnsī, sēnsūm, īrĕ. *To feel, perceive.* Quīn pōrrō vărĭōs rērūm sēntīmŭs ŏdōrēs. Lr. Syn.—Pērcĭpĭŏ, ŏdōrŏr, gūstŏ. *To judge.* Syn.—Aūtŭmŏ, ārbĭtrŏr, cēnsĕŏ, ēxīstĭmŏ, jūdĭcŏ, ŏpīnŏr, pŭtŏ, rĕŏr. Phr.—Hæc mĭhī mēns ēst. Hæc ănĭmō sēntēntĭă sĕdĕt. Fīxūm ēst. Mēns ōmnĭbŭs ūna ēst. *To know.* Syn.—Nōscŏ, ēxpĕrĭŏr. *To recognize.* Syn.—Āgnōscŏ, cōmpĕrĭŏ, ădvērtŏ, vĭdĕŏ.

Sēpărŏ, ās, āvī, ātūm, ārĕ. *To separate.* Syn.—Dīvĭdŏ, dīsjūngŏ, sējūngŏ, sēcērnŏ, sēgrĕgŏ, sēpōnŏ, rĕmŏvĕŏ, sēmŏvĕŏ, dīssōlvŏ, dīssŏcĭŏ, ābscīndŏ, dīscīndŏ, dĭrĭmŏ, dīstrăhŏ, dīvēllŏ, dīstīnguŏ, dīspērtĭŏr. Phr.—Ēxĭgŭă prŏhĭbēmŭr ăquā. Ābjūnctīs dīssŏcĭāmŭr ăquīs. Ēt tērrīs ābscĭdĭt ūndās.

Sĕpĕlĭŏ, īs, sĕpĕlīvī & sĕpĕlĭī, sĕpūltūm, īrĕ. *To bury.* Syn.—Hŭmŏ, tŭmŭlŏ, cōndŏ, cōmpōnŏ. Phr.—Tērræ, sōlō īnfĕrŏ, māndŏ. Sĕpūlcrō, tŭmŭlō dō, rēddŏ, cōndŏ, tĕgŏ. Ōssă cōntĕgŏ. Fūnŭs, cădāvĕr īngēstā hŭmō sĕpĕlĭŏ. Dĕcŏrārĕ sĕpūlcrō. Ēxsĕquĭās făcĭŏ, cĕlĕbrŏ. Fūnĕrĕōs hŏnōrēs rĕfĕrŏ. Cōrpūsque ēxsānguĕ sĕpūlcrō Rĕddĭdĭt. Dărĕ cōrpŭs ĭnānĕ rŏgō. *To ruin.* Syn.—Ēvērtŏ, dēlĕō.

Sēpēs, ĭs. f. *Hedge.* Tēxēndæ sēpēs ĕtĭam, ēt pĕcŭs ōmnĕ tĕnēndum ēst. V. Syn.—Sēptūm, vāllūm. Phr.—Spīnīs, sēntĭbŭs hōrrēns. *Enclosure.* Syn.—Claūstră, sēptă (ōrūm).

Sēpĭŏ, īs, psī, ptūm, īrĕ. *To enclose with hedges.* Syn.—Ōbsēpĭŏ, vāllŏ. Phr.—Sēpĭbŭs, spīnīs, dūmētīs āmbĭŏ, cīngŏ, cŏrōnŏ, claūdŏ, mūnĭŏ. Sĕgĕtī prætēndĕrĕ sēpēm. Prætēxīt sēpĭbŭs hōrtōs. Cīrcūmdărĕ sēpĭbŭs āgrōs. (*In general*) *To surround.* Syn.—Claūdŏ, cīrcūmdŏ, cīngŏ. *See Cingo.*

Sēpōnŏ, ĭs, pŏsŭī, pŏsĭtūm, ĕrĕ. *To set aside.* Dē mīllĕ săgīttīs Ūnām sēpŏsŭĭt. O. Syn.—Sēmŏvĕŏ, sēcērnŏ, sēgrĕgŏ, sēpărŏ, rĕsērvŏ. *To banish.* Syn.—Sēclūdŏ, rĕmŏvĕŏ, pēllŏ. *See Pello. To distinguish.* Syn.—Dīstīnguŏ, sēcērnŏ, dīscērnŏ.

Sēptūm, ī. n. *Enclosure.* Syn.—Claūstrūm, cōnsēptūm, sēpēs. *Sheepfold.* Syn.—Ŏvīlĕ.

Sĕpūlcrālĭs, ĭs, ĕ. *Sepulchral, funereal.* Syn.—Fūnĕrĕŭs, fērālĭs, fūnĕbrĭs.

Sĕpūlcrūm, ī. n. *Tomb, sepulchre.* Grāndĭăque ĕffōssīs mīrābĭtŭr ōssă sĕpūlcrīs. V. Syn.—Būstūm, mŏnŭmēntūm, tŭmŭlŭs, āggĕr. Phr.—Sĕpūlcrī, tŭmŭlī sēdēs, ūrnă. Mārmŏrĕī mōlēs ŏpĕrōsă sĕpūlcrī. Tŭmŭlī quĭēs. Mārmŏrĕă ūrnă. Dŏmŭs ūltĭmă. Tērrēno ēx āggĕrĕ būstūm.

Sĕquāx, ācĭs. adj. *That which follows constantly.* Ōrĕ fŏvē, fūmōsquĕ mănū prætēndĕ sĕquācēs. V. Syn.—Sĕquēns. *Flexible.* Syn.—Dūctĭlĭs, flēxĭlĭs, lēntŭs.

Sĕquŏr, ĕrĭs, sĕcūtŭs sūm, sĕquī. *To follow.* Nēc pŏtīs Īŏnĭōs flūctūs æquārĕ sĕquēndō. V. Syn.—Sūbsĕquŏr, sēctŏr, cŏmĭtŏr. Phr.—Pōnĕ sĕquŏr, ĕŏ, sŭbĕŏ. Vēstīgĭă sērvŏ. Tērgă sĕquŏr. Āddŏ mē sŏcĭūm. Pāssĭbŭs īnstŏ. Sĕquūntŭr ā tērgō. *To pursue.* Syn.—Īnsĕquŏr, pērsĕquŏr, prĕmŏ, ūrgĕŏ, īnstŏ. *To seek after.* Syn.—Sēctŏr, āppĕtŏ, āmplēctŏr, quærŏ. *To imitate.* Syn.—Īmĭtŏr. *To follow from, to depend upon.* Syn.—Pēndĕŏ, ĭnhærĕŏ.

Sĕră, æ. f. *Bar, bolt, barrier.* Tēmpŏră nōctĭs ĕūnt, ēxcŭtĕ pōstĕ sĕrām. O. Syn.—Claūstrūm, ŏbēx, vēctĭs, pēssŭlŭs, rĕpāgŭlă, claūstră. Phr.—Sĕræ ŏbēx, mūnīmĕn. Claūsæ mūnīmĭnă pōrtæ. Pōnĕ sĕrām.

Sĕrēnĭtās, ātĭs. f. *Clear sky, clear weather.* Syn.—Sĕrēnūm, sūdūm. Phr.—Sĕrēnŭs, pūrŭs, cāndĭdŭs, clārŭs dĭēs, āēr, pŏlŭs, sōl. Dĭēs īnnūbĭs. Sĕrēnă lūx. Plăcĭdī cœlī īndūlgēntĭă, clēmēntĭă. Lībēr nūbĭbŭs æthēr. Rĭdēns pūrō lūmĭnĕ cœlūm. Făvēt īnnūbīs clēmentĭă cœlī. Clāră dĭēs. Sōl trīstī dēpēllĭt nūbĭlă cœlō. Nĕbūlās rĕcēdĕrĕ jūssĭt.

Sĕrēnŏ, ās, āvī, ātūm, ārĕ. *To make clear, to clear up.* Vūltū quō cœlūm tēmpēstātēsquĕ sĕrēnăt. V. Syn.—Trānquīllŏ, sēdŏ, plācŏ. Phr.—Pūrum āĕră rēddĭt. Dētērsă rĕmōvĭt Nūbĭlă.

Sĕrēnŭs, ă, ūm. *Serene, clear.* Mūltă fŏrēnt cœlō quæ mōx prŏpĕrāndă sĕrēnŏ. V. Syn.—Sĕrēnātŭs, īnnūbĭlŭs, īnnūbĭs, pūrŭs, clārŭs, lūcĭdŭs, cāndĭdŭs, lĭquĭdŭs, pūrgātŭs, dētērsŭs. Phr.—Nōn nūbĭlŭs, nōn tūrbĭdŭs. Sĭnĕ nūbĕ. Sĭnĕ nūbĭbŭs. Nūbĭbŭs cărēns. Nūllā nūbĕ tĕmĕrātŭs. Nūllīs nīmbīs cōndĭtŭs, dēnsŭs, ōbsĭtŭs. Plŭvĭā vēntīsquĕ cărēns. Hĭĕmēs ōrātĕ sĕrēnās. Cœlī dē pārtĕ sĕrēnā. Fig.—*Calm, tranquil.* Syn.—Plăcĭdŭs, quĭētŭs, trānquīllŭs, lætŭs, mītĭs, lēnĭs, bĕnīgnŭs.

Sĕrēscŏ, ĭs, ĕrĕ. *To dry up.* Syn.—Sīccŏr, ārēscŏ.

Sērĭcūm, ī. n. *Silk.* Quīd rĕlĕvānt vărĭīs sērĭcă tēxtĭlĭbŭs? Prop. Syn.—Bōmbȳx, sērĭcă, bōmbȳcĭnă (pl.). Phr.—Sērĭcūm stāmĕn, vēllŭs. Sērĭcă fīlă. Vēllĕră Sērūm.

Sĕrĭēs, ēī. f. *Order, course, proceedings.* Dēbĭlĭtāt sĕrĭēs īmmēnsă lăbōrūm. O. Syn.—Ōrdŏ. Phr.—Sĕrĭēs lōngīssĭmă rērūm. Sĕrĭēmque ēvōlvĕrĕ fātī.

Sērmŏ, ōnĭs. m. *Discourse, talk.* Āmīssōs lōngō sŏcĭōs sērmōnĕ rĕquīrūnt. V. Syn.—Cōllŏquĭūm, vērbă, dīctă. Phr.—Hāc vĭcĕ sērmōnūm. Dētĭnŭīt sērmōnĕ dĭēm. Vărĭō sŭpĕrī sērmōnĕ frĕmēbānt. Hŏmō sērmōnĭs ămārī. Vărĭō nōctēm sērmōnĕ trăhēbăt. *Report, rumor.* Syn.—Rūmŏr, fāmă. *Language.* Syn.—Līnguă.

Sĕrŏ, ĭs, ŭī, rtūm, ĕrĕ. *To weave.* Syn.—Nēctŏ, tēxŏ, cōnsĕrŏ.

Sĕrŏ, ĭs, sēvī, sătūm, ĕrĕ. *To sow.* Ēt dŭbĭtānt hŏmĭnēs sĕrĕre ātque īmpēndĕrĕ cūrām! V. Syn.—Sēmĭnŏ, cōnsĕrŏ. Phr.—Sēmĭnă jūssĭt Spārgĕre hŭmō. Sĕrĭte hōrdĕă cāmpīs. Mōtā spārgĕrĕ sēmĕn hŭmō.

Sērō. adv. *Late.* Syn.—Tārdē, sērĭŭs, tārdĭŭs. Phr.—Sērĭŭs ēgrĕdĭtŭr. Sēro ēst.

Sērpēns, ēntĭs. m. *Serpent.* Cīnctāmquĕ gĕrīt sērpēntĭbŭs hȳdrām. V. Syn.—Ānguĭs, drăcŏ, cŏlŭbĕr, cŏlŭbră, hȳdrŭs, hȳdră, āspĭs, vīpĕră. Phr.—Squāmĕă tūrbă. Vīpĕrĕūm, rēptĭlĕ gĕnŭs. Sērpēntĭs ōrbēs, vŏlūmĭnă, nōdī, trāctūs. Sĭnŭōsă vŏlūmĭnă tōrquēns. Sĭnŭōsō flēxu ēlābĭtŭr ānguĭs. Sĭnŭāt vēstīgĭă sērpēns. Tōrtō cōrpŏrĕ vērrĭt hŭmūm. Sĭnŭāns īmmēnsă vŏlūmĭnĕ tērgă. Sēptēnă trăhēns vŏlūmĭnă. Hōrrēndă sībĭlă dāns. Hōrrēndūm sībĭlăt ōrĕ. Vĕnēnō tŭmēns. Ārmātŭs ēt īrā Tērrĭbĭlĭs. Ōrĕ mĭnāx līnguāquĕ trĭsŭlcā. Līnguīs mĭcāt ōrĕ.

Ārdēns ŏcŭlōs. Āttōllēns īrās. Cærŭlă cōllă tŭmēns. Măcŭlīs īnsīgnĭs ĕt aūrō. Ārrēctīs hōrrēns squāmīs. Aūrātō nĭtĭdūs fūlgōrĕ.

Sērpŏ, ĭs, psī, ĕrĕ. *To crawl along the ground.* Vīpĕră sērpĭt hŭmī. O. Syn.—Rēpŏ, rēptŏ, ādrēptŏ, prōsērpŏ. Phr.—Hŭmī sērpŏ, cōrpŭs trăhŏ. *To glide along slowly.* Syn.—Īnsērpŏ, rēpŏ, ādrēpŏ, ōbrēpŏ, īrrēpŏ, īnsĭnŭŏ, spārgŏr, ĕŏ.

Sērtūm, ī. n. *Bouquet, crown, garland.* Sērtă prŏcŭl tāntūm căpĭtī dēlāpsă jăcēbānt. V. Syn.—Cŏrōnă, cŏrōllă, flōrēs. Phr.—Sērtī dĕcŭs, hŏnŏr, ŏdŏr, grātĭă. Flōrēs īntēxĕrĕ sērtīs. Flōrĭbŭs ē văriīs sērtūm. Cŏrōllām nēctĕrĕ. Văriōs īn sērtă flōrēs jūngŏ, strīngŏ, lĭgŏ, cōllĭgŏ. Sērtīs ōrnŏ. Sērtīs ŏdōrīs rĕcēntĭbŭs hālānt. Mȳrtĕă sērtă gĕrĭt.

Sērŭs, ă, ūm. *Late, tardy.* Syn.—Tārdŭs, lēntŭs, sēgnĭs. *That which comes last.* Syn.—Ūltĭmŭs, nŏvīssĭmŭs, ēxtrēmŭs, sŭprēmŭs. *Nocturnal, by night.* Syn.—Nōctūrnŭs, vēspērtīnŭs. *Of advanced (age).* Syn.—Prōvēctŭs, tārdŭs, tārdĭŏr.

Sērvă, æ. f. *Maid-servant.* Syn.—Āncīllă, fămŭlă, mĭnīstră.

Sērvātŏr, ōrĭs. m. *Saviour, protector.* Syn.—Cūstōs, tūtŏr, dēfēnsŏr, āssērtŏr, tūtēlă. *One who observes faithfully.* Syn.—Sērvāns, ōbsērvāns, cūltŏr, tĕnāx.

Sērvīlĭs, ĭs, ĕ. *Servile, pertaining to a slave.* Syn.—Fămŭlārĭs, fămŭlŭs. *Low, humble.* Syn.—Ābjēctŭs, vīlĭs.

Sērvĭŏ, īs, īvī & ĭī, ītūm, īrĕ. *To serve, to be a slave.* Sērvĭĕrāt quīdām, quāntōlĭbĕt ōrdĭnĕ dīgnŭs. O. Syn.—Fămŭlŏr. Phr.—Sūm mĭnīstĕr, sērvŭs, fămŭlŭs, māncĭpĭūm. Sērvi īmplērĕ vĭcēs. Nĕquĕ sērvĭtĭō me ēxīrĕ lĭcēbăt. *To become a slave.* Syn.—Pārĕŏ, fămŭlŏr, sūbjĭcĭŏr. Phr.—Jŭgūm āccĭpĭŏ, sŭbĕŏ, fĕrŏ, pătĭŏr. Sērvĭtĭō prĕmŏr. Jūgō cōllă dărĕ. Sērvīrĕ rĕcūsăt.

Sērvĭtĭūm, ĭī. n. *Slavery.* Nĕquĕ sērvĭtĭō me ēxīrĕ lĭcēbăt. V. Syn.—Fămŭlātŭs, mĭnīstĕrĭūm. Phr.—Sērvīlĭs lābŏr. Fămŭlāre ŏpŭs. Hĕrīlĕ jŭgūm. Īnīquūm jŭgī pōndŭs. *Subjugation of the conquered.* Syn.—Fămŭlātŭs, jŭgūm, vīncŭlă, vīnclă. Phr.—Sērvĭtĭī jŭgūm, ŏnŭs, pōndŭs.

Sērvŏ, ās, āvī, ātūm, ārĕ. *To serve, to keep, to guard.* Sī, dūm tū sēctārĭs ăprōs, ĕgŏ rētĭă sērvŏ. V. Syn.—Āssērvŏ, cūstōdĭŏ, īnvĭgĭlŏ, cōnsērvŏ, rĕtĭnĕŏ. *To defend, to save.* Syn.—Tŭĕŏr, tūtŏr, prōtĕgŏ. *To observe faithfully.* Syn.—Cūstōdĭŏ, cŏlŏ, ōbsērvŏ, fŏvĕŏ. *To preside over.* Syn.—Tŭĕŏr, cūstōdĭŏ, prōtĕgŏ. *To dwell in a place.* Syn.—Cŏlŏ, īncŏlŏ, sĕdĕŏ.

Sērvŭs, ī. m. *Slave, man-servant.* Syn.—Māncĭpĭūm, fămŭlŭs, mĭnīstĕr, vērnă, pŭĕr. Phr.—Fămŭlārĭs, fămŭlōrūm grēx, ōrdŏ.

Tūrbăquĕ vērnārūm. Ād jūssă dŏmĭnī părātŭs, prōmptŭs, ălăcĕr, făcĭlĭs. Nūtūs hĕrīlēs ōbsērvāns. Pătī jŭgūm īndŏcĭlĭs.

Sērvŭs, ă, ūm. *Pertaining to a slave.* Syn.—Sērvīlĭs, fămŭlārĭs, fămŭlŭs.

Seū. conj. *Whether, or.* Syn.—Sīvĕ, aūt, vĕl, ăn.

Sĕvērĭtās, ātĭs. f. *Severity, harshness.* Syn.—Sŭpērcĭlĭūm, aūstērĭtās, āspĕrĭtās, tētrĭcĭtās, mōrōsĭtās, grăvĭtās, dūrĭtĭēs, dūrĭtĭă, īnclēmēntĭă.

Sĕvērŭs, ă, ūm. *Austere, severe.* Syn.—Aūstērŭs, rĭgĭdŭs, tētrĭcŭs, mōrōsŭs, grăvĭs, dūrŭs, īnclēmēns, āspĕr, trīstĭs. Phr.—Frōntĕ sĕvērā, cōntrāctā. Sĕvēræ frōntĭs. Sŭpērcĭlĭī mātrōnă sĕvērī. *Cruel.* Syn.—Dūrŭs, fĕrŭs, ăgrēstĭs. *Bitter (in speaking of wine).* Syn.—Ācĕr, āspĕr, aūstērŭs. *Sombre, sad.* Syn.—Ātĕr, sævŭs, hōrrēndŭs, mĕtŭēndŭs, īnfēstŭs, trīstĭs.

Sēvŏcŏ, ās, āvī, ātūm, ārĕ. *To call apart.* Sēvŏcăt hūnc gĕnĭtŏr, nēc caūsām fāssūs ămōrĭs. O. Syn.—Āvŏcŏ, ābdūcŏ, sēdūcŏ.

Sēxŭs, ūs. m. *Sex.* Phr.—Sēxŭs vĭrīlĭs, māscŭlŭs; mŭlĭēbrĭs, fēmĭnĕŭs; āmbĭgŭŭs.

Sī. conj. *If.* Syn.—Sī quāndŏ, sī fōrtĕ, sī fōrs, quōd sī, sī ūnquām. *When.* Syn.—Cūm, quāndŏ, ŭbĭ, pōstquām.

Sībĭlŏ, ās, āvī, ātūm, ārĕ. *To hiss.* Dīrĭgŭēre ŏcŭlīs, tŏt Ĕrīnnȳs sībĭlăt hȳdrīs. V. Syn.—Sībĭlă dō, ēdŏ, fūndŏ, tōllŏ, vĭbrŏ.

Sīc. adv. *Thus.* Syn.—Ĭtă. Phr.—Hāc rătĭōnĕ, hōc pāctō, hōccĕ mŏdō, ăd hūnc mōrēm. *So, likewise.* Syn.—Ĭtă, părĭtĕr, æquĕ. Phr.—Haūd sĕcŭs, haūd ălĭtĕr. Haūd mĭnŭs.

Sīcă, æ. f. *Dagger, poniard.* Syn.—Ēnsĭs, glădĭŭs, pūgĭŏ, măchæră.

Sīccĭtās, ātĭs. f. *Dryness.* Syn.—Ārĭdĭtās, sĭtĭs, æstŭs, Cănĭs, Sīrĭŭs, Cănīcŭlă. Phr.—Aēstīvī tēmpŏră sīccă Cănĭs. Ēt dēsērtă sĭtī rĕgĭŏ.

Sīccŏ, ās, āvī, ātūm, ārĕ. *To dry.* Īnjēctōs hŭmĕrīs sīccānt ē sōlĕ căpīllōs. O. Syn.—Ēxsīccŏ. Phr.—Āquās, hūmōrēm călŏr ēxtrăhĭt, sōrbĕt. Dūm rētĭă līttŏrĕ sīccăt. Ārĭēs nūnc vēllĕră sīccăt. Lăcrĭmās sīccāvĕrăt ārdŏr. *To exhaust.* Syn.—Ēxhaūrĭŏ, ābsōrbĕŏ. *To burn up, to become withered.* Syn.—Ēxsīccŏ, cŏquŏ, ūrŏ, ădūrŏ, pĕrūrŏ, ēxūrŏ, ēxhaūrĭŏ.

Sīccŭs, ă, ūm. *Dry, withered.* Pĕdĭbūs sīccīs sŭpĕr æquŏră cūrrĭt. O. Syn.—Ārĭdŭs, ārēns, ārēscēns, sīccātŭs, ēxsīccātŭs, sĭtĭēns, ūstŭs, pĕrūstŭs. Phr.—Hūmōrĭs ĕgēns. Ārdōrĕ dĕhīscēns. *Exhausted.* Syn.—Ēxhaūstŭs, sīccātŭs, văcŭŭs.

Sīcŭt. conj. *As, just as.* Syn.—Sīcŭtī, ŭt, ŭtĭ, vĕlŭt, vĕlŭtĭ.

Sīdĕrĕŭs, ă, ūm. *Starry.* Syn.—Cœlēstĭs. *Heavenly.* Syn.—Cœlēstĭs, æthĕrĕŭs, sŭpĕrŭs. *Divine.* Syn.—Dīvīnŭs, cœlēstĭs.

Sīdŏ, ĭs, sēdī, ĕrĕ. *To sit down.* Syn.—Sĕdĕō, cōnsīdŏ, cōnsīdĕō. *To become feeble, collapse.* Syn.—Sūbsīdŏ, dēsīdŏ, cōnsīdŏ, fătīscŏ.

Sīdŭs, ĕrĭs. n. *Star.* Mĭsĕrōs fāllēntĭă naūtās Sīdĕră. V. Syn.—Āstrūm, stēllă. Phr.—Sīdĕrĭs īgnēs. Ārdŭă tēstŏr Sīdĕră. Dūm sīdĕră pāscĕt. Tăcĭtō vōlvūntūr sīdĕră lāpsū. Tōtĭdēm sĭnĕ sīdĕrĕ nōctēs. *Season.* Syn.—Tēmpēstās, tēmpŭs, hōră. Fig.—*Glory, ornament.* Syn.—Dĕcŭs.

Sīgnĭfĭcŏ, ās, āvī, ātūm, ārĕ. *To indicate.* Sīgnĭfĭcātquĕ mănu, ēt māgnō sĭmŭl īncĭpĭt ōrĕ. V. Syn.—Īndĭcŏ, īnnŭŏ. *To make known.* Syn.—Īndĭcŏ, ăpĕrĭŏ, ēxplĭcŏ. *To show, to testify.* Syn.—Ēxprĭmŏ, ēxhĭbĕŏ, nūdŏ, mōnstrŏr, tēstŏr.

Sīgnŏ, ās, āvī, ātūm, ārĕ. *To mark, to trace.* Quīn ĕtĭām cœlī rĕgĭōnem īn cōrtĭcĕ sīgnānt. V. Syn.—Īmprĭmŏ, scrībŏ, īnscrībŏ, nŏtŏ. *To ingrave.* Syn.—Scrībŏ, īnscrībŏ, scālpŏ, īnscūlpŏ. *To remark, to note.* Syn.—Nŏtŏ, dēprēndŏ, ādvērtŏ. *To adorn, to decorate.* Syn.—Ōrnŏ, dĕcŏrŏ, cōmmēndŏ, īnsīgnĭŏ. *To seal.* Syn.—Ōbsīgnŏ, sĭgīllŏ.

Sīgnūm, ī. n. *Mark, trace.* Quærēntēm nūlla ād spēlūncām sīgnă fĕrēbānt. V. Syn.—Nŏtă, vēstīgĭūm. *Indication, proof.* Syn.—Īnsīgnĕ, spĕcĭmĕn, ārgūmēntūm, vēstīgĭūm. *Sign, symptom.* Syn.—Īndĭcĭūm. *Nod.* Syn.—Gēstŭs, nūtŭs. *Statue.* Syn.—Stătŭă. *Seal.* Syn.—Gēmmă, sĭgīllūm. *Standard.* Syn.—Vēxīllūm, ăquĭlă.

Sĭlēntĭūm, ĭī. n. *Silence.* Sī sērmōnĕ plăcēt, tăcĭtūrnă sĭlēntĭă vītĕt. *Peace, quiet.* Syn.—Ōtĭūm, quĭēs, pāx.

Sĭlĕŏ, ēs, ŭī, ērĕ. *To remain silent, to keep quiet.* Mūtă sĭlēt vīrgō, tērrāmque īmmōtă tŭētŭr. V. Syn.—Sĭlēscŏ, tăcĕŏ, cōntĭcĕŏ, rĕtĭcĕŏ, ōbmūtēscŏ. Phr.—Sĭlēntĭă præstŏ, sērvŏ, tĕnĕŏ. Sĭlēns, mūtŭs sūm, stō, mănĕŏ. Vōcēm tĕnĕŏ. Sĭlēnt ārrēctīsque aūrĭbŭs ādstānt. Vōcēm tĕnŭērĕ sŏrōrēs. Cōntĭcŭēre ōmnēs. Vōx vōcĭbŭs hæsĭt. Līnguă dēfĭcĭt. Āspēctu ōbmūtŭĭt āmēns. Tĕnŭērĕ sĭlēntĭă cūnctī. Vōcēs cōmpēscĕ mŏlēstās. *To be calm. See Quiesco. To pass over in silence.* Syn.—Tăcĕŏ, ŏmīttŏ, cēlŏ, tĕgŏ, prĕmŏ.

Sĭlĕr, ĕrĭs. n. *The brook-willow.* Phr.—Mōllĕ sĭlēr, lēntæquĕ gĕnīstæ.

Sĭlēx, ĭcĭs. m. & f. *Rock, stone.* Syn.—Lăpĭs, sāxūm, caūtēs, rūpēs.

Sĭlīgŏ, ĭnĭs. f. *A fine kind of wheat.* Syn.—Fār, sĭmĭlă, sĭmĭlāgŏ, trītĭcūm.

Sīlvă, æ. f. *Woods, forest.* Sīlvă vĕtūs stābāt nūllā vĭŏlātă sĕcūrī. O. Syn.—Nĕmŭs, sāltŭs, lūcŭs. Phr.—Sīlvārūm, nĕmŏrūm sāltŭs, rĕcēssŭs, ūmbræ. Ūmbrōsī nĕmŏrĭs lātĕbræ. Jŭgă frōndĕă sīlvīs. Fĕrārūm dēsērtă. Frōndĭfĕræ ăvĭūm dŏmūs. Ārbŏrĭbūs lŏcă cōnsĭtă. Dēnsūm trăbĭbūs nĕmŭs. Sīlvă rōbŏrĕ dēnsă. Hōrrĭdă dūmīs. Ŏpācīs ūmbrōsă rāmīs. Sōlī īmpērvĭă. Nĕmūs vēnātĭbŭs āptūm. Cālīgāns nīgrā fōrmīdĭnĕ lūcŭs.

Sīlvēstrĭs, ĭs, ĕ. *Woody.* Syn.—Sīlvātĭcŭs, sīlvōsŭs, nĕmŏrōsŭs. *Wild, savage.* Syn.—Īncūltŭs, fĕrŭs. *Rustic.* Syn.—Rūstĭcŭs, ăgrēstĭs. *Fierce, savage (in speaking of men).* Syn.—Īncūltŭs, fĕrŭs, ăgrēstĭs, āspĕr, sēmĭfĕr.

Sĭmĭlĭs, ĭs, ĕ. *Similar, like.* Syn.—Cōnsĭmĭlĭs, părĭlĭs, æquālĭs, æquŭs, īdēm, prōxĭmŭs, pār. Phr.—Haūd īmpār. Ōrĕ, cŏlōrĕ ălĭquēm sĭmĭlāns. Ōrĕ pătrēm rĕfĕrēns. Ōs dĕō sĭmĭlĭs. Plūrĭmă vūltū Mātĕr ĭnēst.

Sĭmĭlĭtĕr. adv. *Similarly, likewise.* Syn.—Aēquē, æquālĭtĕr, părĭtĕr. Phr.—Sĭmĭlī mŏdō.

Sīmĭŭs, ĭī. m. *Monkey, ape.* Syn.—Sīmĭă, cērcōps, cērcŏpĭthēcŭs. Phr.—Ōrĭs hūmānī sĭmŭlātŏr. Hūmānī sīmĭŭs ōrĭs.

Sīmplēx, ĭcĭs. adj. *Single, one.* Syn.—Ūnŭs, ūnĭcŭs. *Unadorned, simple.* Syn.—Īncōmptŭs, ĭnōrnātŭs, īncūltŭs. *Sincere, open.* Syn.—Cāndĭdŭs, sīncērŭs, ăpērtŭs, īngĕnŭŭs, īnnŏcŭŭs. Phr.—Nōn făllĕrĕ dōctŭs. Vērā sīmplĭcĭtātĕ bŏnŭs. *Simple, credulous.* Syn.—Crēdŭlŭs. Phr.—Quī dīctīs făcĭlēm sē præbĕt.

Sīmplĭcĭtās, ātĭs. f. *Simplicity, lack of parts.* Syn.—Ūnĭcĭtās. *Lack of art, refinement.* Syn.—Rūstĭcĭtās, mŏdēstĭă. *Simplicity, sincerity.* Syn.—Cāndŏr, sīncērĭtās. Phr.—Nēscĭă fraūdĭs. *Credulity.* Syn.—Crēdŭlĭtās.

Sīmplĭcĭtĕr. adv. *Artlessly.* Syn.—Tĕmĕrĕ. Phr.—Sĭnĕ ārtĕ. *Candidly.* Syn.—Īngĕnŭē, ăpērtē, cāndĭdē, vērē, sīncērē.

Sĭmŭl. adv. *At the same time, together.* Syn.—Īnsĭmŭl ūnā, părĭtĕr.

Sĭmŭl, Sĭmŭl āc, Sĭmŭl ātquĕ. conj. *As soon as.* Syn.—Cūm, ŭt, ŭbĭ, pōstquăm.

Sĭmŭlācrūm, ī. n. *Image, likeness, statue.* Syn.—Ēffĭgĭēs, fĭgūră, sīgnūm, ĭmāgŏ, stătŭă. Phr.—Fōrmă dĕī. Sĭmŭlācrăquĕ cērĕă fīngĭt. *Appearance.* Syn.—Ĭmāgŏ, spĕcĭēs, ēffĭgĭēs, sĭmŭlāmĕn. *Spectre.* Syn.—Ĭmāgŏ, spĕcĭēs, lārvă, fĭgūră, ūmbră. Phr.—Nōtă mājŏr ĭmāgŏ. Fōrmă dĕī vūltū. Sĭmŭlācri āppārŭĭt ūmbră.

Sĭmŭlātĭŏ, ōnĭs. f. *Imitation.* Syn.—Fīctĭŏ, ĭmĭtātĭŏ, sĭmŭlāmĕn. *Pretence.* Syn.—Fāllācĭă, mēndācĭūm. Phr.—Fīctă, sĭmŭlāntĭă vērbă.

Sĭmŭlātŏr, ōrĭs. m. *One who imitates.* Syn.—Ĭmĭtātŏr, sĭmŭlāns. *Dissembler.* Syn.—Dīssĭmŭlātŏr, făllāx, mēndāx, fālsŭs. Phr.—Cuī sĭmŭlāns ănĭmŭs. Sĭmŭlātă mēns. Sĭmŭlātō pēctŏrĕ fāllāx. Fāndī fīctŏr.

Sĭmŭlŏ, ās, āvī, ātūm, ārĕ. *To counterfeit, to imitate.* Nōn ĭmĭtābĭlĕ fūlmĕn Aēre ēt cōrnĭpĕdūm pūlsū sĭmŭlārăt ĕquōrūm. V. Syn.—Ĭmĭtŏr. *To represent.* Syn.—Ĭmĭtŏr, āssĭmŭlŏ, fīngŏ, ēffīngŏ, rĕfĕrŏ, pīngŏ, dēpīngŏ, cūdŏ, cælŏ. *To feign.* Syn.—Fīngŏ, mēntĭŏr.

Sĭmūltās, ātĭs. f. *Resentment, anger.* Syn.—Īră, ŏdĭūm, ĭnĭmīcĭtĭă.

Sĭnāpī. n. indecl. & Sĭnāpĭs, ĭs. f. *Mustard seed or tree.* (*See Appendix under list of Trees, etc.*)

Sīncērē. adv. *Sincerely.* Syn.—Vērē, cāndĭdē, īngĕnŭē, sīmplĭcĭtĕr. Phr.—Bŏnā, sīncērā fĭdē. Sīncērō cōrdĕ, pēctŏrĕ.

Sīncērĭtās, ātĭs. f. *Sincerity.* Syn.—Cāndŏr, prŏbĭtās, sīmplĭcĭtās. Phr.—Ănĭmī cāndŏr. Fraūdĭs nēscĭă. Sīncērŭs ănĭmŭs.

Sīncērŭs, ă, ūm. *Pure, unadulterated.* Syn.—Pūrŭs, īntĕgĕr, īncōrrūptŭs. *Intact.* Syn.—Īntĕgĕr, sānŭs, īntāctŭs, īllæsŭs, īncŏlŭmĭs. *Sincere.* Syn.—Cāndĭdŭs, sīmplēx, ăpērtŭs. Phr.—Fāllĕrĕ nēscĭŭs. Nōn fāllĕrĕ dōctŭs. Nōn fālsă lŏquī dōctŭs. Ēxpērs dŏlī. Sĭnĕ fraūdĕ. Cuī pēctŏră nēscĭă fālsī.

Sĭnĕ. prep. *Without.* Syn.—Ābsquĕ, ēxtrā. Phr.—Rē dēmptā, sūblātā, rĕmōtā, pŏsĭtā. Pōscĭt spē prœlĭă nūllā. Nāvĭs ēxcūssā măgīstrō.

Sīngīllātīm. adv. *Singly, one by one.* Syn.—Sĕōrsīm, seōrsīm, seōrsŭs, sējūnctūm, sīgīllātīm.

Sīngŭlārĭs, ĭs, ĕ. *Single, alone.* Syn.—Sōlŭs. *Remarkable, singular.* Syn.—Ēxĭmĭŭs, ēxcēllēns, īnsīgnĭs, sūmmŭs, rārŭs, īnfrĕquēns, īnsŏlĭtŭs.

Sīngŭlī, æ, ă. *One by one.* Syn.—Quīsquĕ, ūnūsquīsquĕ, ōmnēs, cūnctī.

Sīngūltŏ, ās, āvī, ātūm, ārĕ, (Sīngūltĭŏ, īs, īvī & ĭī, īrĕ). *To palpitate.* Syn.—Pālpĭtŏ, ēmĭcŏ. *To sob.* Phr.—Sīngūltūs ēmīttŏ, cĭĕŏ. Sīngūltū, sīngūltĭbŭs pēctŭs, pēctŏră quătĭŏ, cōncŭtĭŏ.

Sĭnīstĕr, tră, trūm. *Left.* Sæpĕ sĭnīstră căvā prædīxĭt ăb īlĭcĕ cōrnīx. V. Syn.—Lævŭs. Fig.—*Contrary, ill-omened.* Syn.—Lævŭs, ĭnĭmīcŭs, īnfaūstŭs, nōxĭŭs, īmpōrtūnŭs.

Sĭnŏ, ĭs, sīvī, sĭtūm, ĕrĕ. *To permit, to allow.* Nēc sĭnĭt aūdīrī vōcēm frăgŏr æquŏrĭs ūllām. O. Syn.—Cōncēdŏ, pērmīttŏ, pătĭŏr. Phr.—Nūllā sĭnĭmūr cōnsīstĕrĕ tērrā. Nēc lōngĭŭs īrĕ sĭnēbăt. *To suffer, to leave.* Syn.—Pătĭŏr, rĕlīnquŏ, līnquŏ, pērmīttŏ.

Sĭnŭŏ, ās, āvī, ātūm, ārĕ. *To bend, to curve.* Īmpŏsĭtĭs călămĭs pătŭlōs sĭnŭāvĕrăt ārcūs. O. Syn.—Cūrvŏ, īncūrvŏ, flēctŏ. Phr.—Sērpēns sĭnŭātŭr ĭn ārcūs.

Sĭnŭōsŭs, ă, ūm. *Curved, crooked, with windings.* Syn.—Cūrvŭs, cūrvātŭs, īnflēxŭs, flēxŭs, rĕvŏlūtŭs. Phr.—Sērpēns sĭnŭōsă vŏlūmĭnă vērsăt. Sĭnŭōsă vēstĭs.

Sĭnŭs, ūs. m. *Recess, cavity.* Syn.—Rĕcēssŭs, ānfrāctŭs, lătĕbræ, īntĭmă, īntĕrĭōră, ābdĭtă. *The breast, the lap.* Syn.—Grēmĭūm, pēctŭs, ūlnæ, cōmplēxŭs. *Gulf.* Syn.—Rĕcēssŭs.

Sĭquĭdēm. conj. *For, since.* Syn.—Quŏnĭām, quĭă, nām, ĕnīm, ĕtĕnīm.

Sīstŏ, ĭs, stĭtī, stătūm, ĕrĕ. *To stop.* Syn.—Dētĭnĕŏ, dīstĭnĕŏ, cōntĭnĕŏ, rĕtĭnĕŏ, sūstĭnĕŏ, cŏhĭbĕŏ, mŏrŏr. Phr.—Sīstĕre ăquām flŭvĭīs. Sīstĕrĕ bēllūm. Īmmēnsōs sīstĕ lăbōrēs. Sīstĕ grădūm. *To sustain.* Syn.—Sūstĭnĕŏ, fŭlcĭŏ. *To hold back.* Syn.—Āstrīngŏ, cŏhĭbĕŏ. *To place, to establish.* Syn.—Stătŭŏ, pōnŏ, dēpōnŏ, cōllŏcŏ.

Sĭsȳmbrĭūm, ĭī. n. *Spearmint, thyme.* (*See Appendix under list of Trees, etc.*)

Sĭtĭŏ, īs, īvī & ĭī, īrĕ. *To be thirsty.* Quō plūs sūnt pōtæ, plūs sĭtĭūntŭr ăquæ. O. Phr.—Sĭtī ārdĕŏ, lăbōrŏ, prĕmŏr, ūrgĕŏr, ūrŏr, īncēndŏr, tōrquĕŏr, pĕrĕŏ. Faūcēs, gūttŭr, ōră sĭtĭs ūrgĕt, prĕmĭt, tōrquĕt. Sīccă hĭānt pēndŭlă lābră sĭtī. Răbĭdō quōs sĭtĭs ūrgĕt ĭn æstū. Sĭtĭs ēxhaūsĕrăt ārtūs. Sīccō tŏrrēt sĭtĭs ōră pălātō. *To desire ardently.* Syn.—Ārdĕŏ, ĭnhĭŏ, āppĕtŏ, cŭpĭŏ, pērcŭpĭŏ.

Sĭtĭs, ĭs. f. *Thirst.* Quī pōtūs dŭbĭum ēst sīstăt ălātvĕ sĭtīm. O. Phr.—Pōtūs cŭpīdŏ, dēsīdĕrĭūm. Bĭbēndī ārdŏr. Sĭtĭs răbĭēs. Āddūxērĕ sĭtīm Tēmpŏră. Sĭtīm ēxstīnguŏ. Fōntĕ sĭtīm lĕvārĕ. Sĭtīm pēllŏ. *Drought.* Syn.—Sīccĭtās, æstŭs, æstās mĕdĭă. *Desire.* Syn.—Cŭpīdŏ, dēsīdĕrĭūm.

Sĭtŭs, ūs. m. *Situation.* Nēc rĕvŏcārĕ sĭtūs, aūt jūngĕrĕ cārmĭnă cūrăt. V. Syn.—Pŏsĭtŭs, lŏcŭs. *Mould, dirt.* Syn.—Squālŏr, sōrdēs, īllŭvĭēs, pædŏr. *Apathy, sloth.* Syn.—Ōtĭūm, dēsĭdĭă, tōrpŏr, sŏpŏr, vĕtērnūm. *Disorder.* Syn.—Squālŏr, sōrdēs.

Smīlăx, ăcĭs. f. *Smilax.* (*See Appendix under list of Trees, etc.*)

Sŏbŏlēs, ĭs. f. *Race, progeny.* Cāră dĕūm sŏbŏlēs. V. Syn.—Prōlēs, prōgĕnĭēs, gĕnŭs, prŏpāgŏ, nātī. *See Proles.*

Sōbrĭĕtās, ātĭs. f. *Sobriety, self-restraint.* Syn.—Tēmpĕrāntĭă, ābstĭnēntĭă.

Sōbrĭŭs, ă, ūm. *One who abstains from wine.* Syn.—Ābstēmĭŭs. *Moderate, temperate.* Syn.—Tēmpĕrāns, frūgī, pārcŭs, mŏdēstŭs.

Sŏcĭĕtās, ātĭs. f. *Society, alliance.* Syn.—Cōmmērcĭūm, fœdŭs, cōncōrdĭă.

Sŏcĭŏ, ās, āvī, ātūm, ārĕ. *To join, to associate with.* Syn.—Āssŏcĭŏ, cōnsŏcĭŏ, jūngŏ, ādjūngŏ, cōnjūngŏ. Phr.—Sŏcĭūm dō, āddŏ, ādjūngŏ, āccĭpĭŏ. Cārmĭnă nērvīs sŏcĭārĕ.

Sŏcĭŭs, ă, ūm. *Joined to, associated with.* Syn.—Sŏcĭātŭs, jūnctŭs, cōnjūnctŭs.

Sŏcĭŭs, ĭī. m. (Sŏcĭă, æ. f.). *Associate, companion.* Mēne ĭgĭtūr sŏcĭūm sūmmīs ādjūngĕrĕ rēbŭs, Nīsĕ, fŭgĭs? V. Syn.—Cŏmĕs, sŏdālĭs, ămīcŭs, cōnsōrs, pārtĭcēps, ādjūtŏr ,aūxĭlĭātŏr. Phr.—Lăbōrūm, ŏpĕrūm cŏmĕs, cōnsōrs. Jūnctī frātērnō mōrĕ sŏdālēs. Sŏcĭă āgmĭnă. Fœdĕrĕ jūnctī.

Sŏdālĭs, ĭs. m. *Companion.* Syn.—Sŏcĭŭs, cŏmĕs, ămīcŭs. *See Socius.*

Sōdēs (*sync. for Si audes*). *Please, I beg of you.* Syn.—Quæsŏ, ōrŏ, vĕlīm.

Sōl, sōlĭs. m. *Sun.* Ōrbēm Pēr dŭŏdēnă rĕgīt mūndī sōl aūrĕŭs āstră. V. Syn.—Ăpōllŏ, Dēlĭŭs, Tītān, Hўpĕrīōn, Phœbŭs, dĭēs, jŭbăr. Phr.—Sōlĭs jŭbăr. Phœbēī rădĭī, īgnēs. Phœbī lūcĭdŭs ōrbĭs. Cœlēstĕ jŭbăr. Rŏtă fērvĭdă sōlĭs. Lūx, lūmĭnĭs aūctŏr. Vīvō cūnctă călōrĕ fŏvēns. Nĭtĭdīssĭmă sōlĭs ĭmāgŏ. Pūrpŭrĕō quī mŏvĕt āxĕ dĭēm. Pūrpŭrĕō tēmōnĕ sĕdēns. Quī lōngūm mētītŭr ānnūm. Quī tēmpĕrăt ōrbēm. Rădĭīs ōmnĭă lūstrăt. Cūrrū nĭtĭdō dĭēm prōmĭt ēt cēlăt. Ŏrĭēntĭă sōlĭs lūmĭnă. Sōl vĭtrĕĭs prōcēdĭt ăb ūndīs. Sōl rĕvŏcābăt ĕquōs. Sŭprēmō sōlĕ. Sōl cădĭt ōrbēm sŭb īmūm. Ēmēnsō dēcēdĭt Ŏlўmpō. Rădĭōs cōndĭt. Dēscēndĭt ĭn ūndās. Tītān jām prōnŭs ĭn ūndās ībăt. Mĕdĭō sōl lūcĕt. Ālmă lūcĕ īllūstrāns. Īgnĭpĕdēs flēctĭt ĕquōs. Sūmmō Phœbūs rēsplēndĕt Ŏlўmpō. Lūcĕ sĕrēnă sōl mĭcăt. Īncērtī cæcā cālīgĭnĕ sōlēs. (*By extension*) *Heat.* Syn.—Călŏr, æstŭs, ārdŏr, fērvŏr. *Climate.* Syn.—Cœlūm, sīdŭs.

Sōlātĭūm, ĭī. n. *Consolation.* Syn.—Sōlāmĕn, lēnīmĕn, lĕvāmĕn. Phr.—Lĕvāmĕn dūlcĕ lăbōrūm, lăbōrĭs. Cūrārūm mĕdĕcīnă. Sĕnēctæ grātūm sōlāmĕn, lēnīmĕn. 'Mœstæ, sōllĭcĭtæ sōlātĭă mēntĭs. Lēnĭă dīctă. Ăvēs, sōlātĭă rūrĭs. Ămīcī, blāndī ādmŏnĭtŭs. Cūræ cāsūsquĕ lĕvāmĕn.

Sōlēmnĭs & Sōlēnnĭs, ĭs, ĕ. *That which is done or happens each year.* Syn.—Fēstŭs, ānnŭŭs, cĕlĕbĕr. Phr.—Sōlēmnĭă rēddĕrĕ vōtă. Sōlēmnēs taūrūm māctābăt ăd ārās. *Solemn.* Syn.—Săcĕr, săcrātŭs. *Customary.* Syn.—Sŏlĭtŭs, āssuētŭs, suētŭs. Phr.—Mōs ēst.

Sŏlĕŏ, ēs, ĭtŭs sūm, ērĕ. *To be accustomed to.* Ūtquĕ sŏlēbāmūs cōnsūmĕrĕ lōngă lŏquēndō Tēmpŏră. O. Syn.—Āssŏlĕŏ, cōnsuēvī, suēvī, āssuēvī. Phr.—Cōnsuētūm hăbĕŏ. Sŏlĭtŭs, cōnsuētŭs sūm. Mōs ēst mĭhĭ. Ēst crēbĕr ūsŭs. Sæpĕ, frĕquēntĕr ăgŏ. Quō mōrĕ sŏlēnt. Mōs plăcĕt mĭhĭ.

Sōlērs, ērtĭs. adj. *Skilful, industrious.* Pĕcŭdūm cūstōdĭă sōlērs. V. Syn.—Īndūstrĭŭs, pĕrītŭs, īngĕnĭōsŭs, prūdēns, săgāx, scītŭs, cătŭs, cāllĭdŭs, ācĕr. Phr.—Mūsă lÿræ sōlērs. Sōlērs cūnctāndī.

Sōlērtĕr. adv. *Skilfully.* Syn.—Pĕrītē, scītē, dōctē, cāllĭdē.

Sōlērtĭă, æ. f. *Skill.* Grāndĕ dŏlōrĭs Īngĕnĭum ēst, mĭsĕrīsquĕ vĕnīt sōlērtiă rēbŭs. O. Syn.—Īndūstrĭă, dēxtĕrĭtās, pĕrītĭă, prūdēntĭă, īngĕnĭūm, ăcūmĕn. Phr.—Vīvāx ănĭmī sōlērtĭă. Mēntĭs ăcūtæ dēxtĕrĭtās. Ărtēs părīt sōlērtĭă.

Sŏlĭdŏ, ās, āvī, ātūm, ārĕ. *To strengthen, to make firm.* Ēt vērtēndă mănu ēt crētā sŏlĭdāndă tĕnācī. V. Syn.—Fīrmŏ, stăbĭlĭŏ. *To harden, to make compact.* Syn.—Fīrmŏ, dūrŏ, āstrīngŏ. *To sustain.* Syn.—Fīrmŏ, fūlcĭŏ, stăbĭlĭŏ.

Sŏlĭdŭs, ă, ūm. *Solid, firm.* Sŏlĭdō sŏnăt ūngŭlă cōrnū. V. Syn.—Dūrŭs, fīrmŭs. Fig.—*Firm, immovable.* Syn.—Fīrmŭs, īmmōtŭs, īncōncūssŭs. *Entire.* Syn.—Tōtŭs, īntĕgĕr.

Sōlĭtārĭŭs, ă, ūm. *Solitary, isolated, one who lives alone.* Syn.—Sōlŭs, sōlĭvăgŭs. Phr.—Lŏcă sōlă cŏlēns. Căvō rĕcēssū vīvēns. Hōrrēndă īntĕr lūstră ābdĭtŭs. Tĭmĭdūs vĭdērī. *Monk, religious.* Syn.—Mŏnăchŭs.

Sōlĭtūdŏ, ĭnĭs. f. *Solitude.* Syn.—Rĕcēssŭs, sēcēssŭs, dēsērtă (pl.). Phr.—Lŏcă sōlă, dēsērtă. Dēsērtæ, īgnōtæ sīlvæ, lātĕbræ. Lŏcŭs ăb ōmnī tēstĕ rĕmōtŭs.

Sŏlĭūm, ĭī. n. *Elevated seat, throne.* Præfātūs dīvōs, sŏlĭō rēx īnfĭt ăb āltō. V. Syn.—Sēdēs, sĕdīlĕ, sēllă, thrŏnŭs. Phr.—Rēgālĭs, rēgūm sēdēs. Rēgālĕ trĭbūnăl. Sŏlĭō fūltūs ĕbūrnō. Sŏlĭō mĕdĭūs cōnsēdĭt ăvītō.

Sōllĭcĭtŏ, ās, āvī, ātūm, ārĕ. *To shake violently.* Syn.—Mŏvĕŏ. *To pursue.* Syn.—Ăgŏ, ăgĭtŏ, prĕmŏ, pērsĕquŏr, ūrgĕŏ, īnstŏ. *To solicit, to beg.* Syn.—Prĕcŏr, ūrgĕŏ, fătīgŏ. *To render restless, to torment.* Syn.—Vēxŏ, tōrquĕŏ, crŭcĭŏ, prĕmŏ. *To attempt to seduce.* Syn.—Tēntŏ, ēxpĕrĭŏr. *To invite.* Syn.—Īnvītŏ, tēntŏ, āllĭcĭŏ.

Sōllĭcĭtūdŏ, ĭnĭs. f. *Solicitude, anxiety.* Syn.—Cūră, ānxĭĕtās. Phr.—Īnquĭētī pēctŏrĭs æstŭs.

Sōllĭcĭtŭs, ă, ūm. *Agitated, disturbed.* Ūt mărĕ sōllĭcĭtūm strīdēt rĕflŭēntĭbŭs ūndīs. V. Syn.—Cōmmōtŭs, ăgĭtātŭs, tūrbĭdŭs, īnquĭētŭs, īrrĕquĭētŭs. *Anxious, restless.* Syn.—Ānxĭŭs, ăncēps, dŭbĭŭs, sūspēnsŭs, tūrbātŭs, tĭmēns, păvēns, păvĭdŭs, trĕpĭdŭs.

Sōlŏr, ārĭs, ātŭs sūm, ārī. *To console.* Ēt tēlā cūrās sōlābŏr ănīlēs. V. Syn.—Cōnsōlŏr. Phr.—Sōlātĭă dō, fĕrŏ, præbĕŏ, mĭnīstrŏ. Cūrās, lūctūm, dŏlōrēm lĕvŏ, lēnĭŏ, mītĭgŏ. Mœstūm ănĭmūm lēnĭŏ, mūlcĕŏ. Āspĕră fātă sōlāndō lĕvŏ. Dūlcĭbŭs vērbīs sōlŏr. Rēddĕrĕ cōnfūsæ mēntī sōlātĭă. Tū pŏtĕs īnsānōs ănĭmī cōmpēscĕrĕ lūctūs. Fig.—*To appease the hunger.* Syn.—Sēdŏ, plācŏ, lēnĭŏ, pēllŏ, dēpēllŏ.

Sŏlūm, ī. n. *Base, foundation.* Syn.—Fūndāmēntūm, fūndāmĕn. *Soil, ground.* Syn.—Hŭmŭs, tērră, tēllūs. *Imprint of the foot.* Syn.—Pēs, plāntă, vēstīgĭūm.

Sōlūm. adv. *Only.* Syn.—Tāntūm, tāntūmmŏdŏ, dūntāxăt, mŏdŏ.

Sōlŭs, ă, ūm. *Alone, only.* Syn.—Ūnŭs, ūnĭcŭs. *Unaccompanied.* Syn.—Īncŏmĭtātŭs, sĭnĕ cŏmĭtĕ. Phr.—Nūllō cŏmĭtāntĕ. *Solitary, deserted.* Syn.—Dēsērtŭs, văcŭŭs, vāstŭs.

Sōlvŏ, ĭs, sōlvī & sŏlŭī, sŏlūtūm, ĕrĕ. *To disunite, to part, to break.* Syn.—Frāngŏ, rūmpŏ, ābrūmpŏ, dīstūrbŏ. *To dissolve.* Syn.—Ēxsōlvŏ, rĕsōlvŏ, mōllĭŏ, rĕlāxŏ, lĭquĕfăcĭŏ. *To free, to deliver.* Syn.—Ēxsōlvŏ, ēxĭmŏ, lībĕrŏ, ēxpĕdĭŏ. *To unbind.* Syn.—Rĕsōlvŏ, rĕlāxŏ, lāxŏ. *To enervate, to enfeeble.* Syn.—Rĕsōlvŏ, vīncŏ, frāngŏ. *To pay.* Syn.—Ēxsōlvŏ, pērsōlvŏ, pēndŏ, rĕpēndŏ. *To free from debt.* Syn.—Ābsōlvŏ, ēxĭmŏ.

Sōmnĭfĕr, ĕră, ĕrūm. *Sleep-bringing, soporific.* Syn.—Sōmnĭfĭcŭs, sŏpōrĭfĕr, sŏpōrŭs.

Sōmnĭŏ, ās, āvī, ātūm, ārĕ. *To dream.* Phr.—Pēr sōmnūm, īn sōmnīs vĭdĕŏ. Mēntēm sōmnĭă lūdūnt. Sōpītōs dēlūdūnt sōmnĭă sēnsūs. Quæ mē sūspēnsam īnsōmnĭă tērrēnt. *To fancy, to vainly imagine.* Syn.—Dēlīrŏ, ĭnēptĭŏ, fīngŏ.

Sōmnĭūm, ĭī. n. *Dream.* Sōmnĭă, quæ vērās æquānt ĭmĭtāmĭnĕ fōrmās. O. Syn.—Īnsōmnĭūm. Phr.—Sōmnī, nōctĭs, ĭmāgĭnēs, ĭmāgŏ, spĕcĭēs. Sōmnī tērrŏr ĭnānĭs. Fālsă sŏpōrĭs Lūdĭbrĭă. Fālsī vīsūs. Sĭmŭlācrăque ĭnānĭă sōmnī. Tĭbĭ trīstĭă sōmnĭă pōrtāns. Sōmnĭă vērōs nārrāntĭă cāsūs. Pōst mĕdĭām nōctēm cūm sōmnĭă vēră. Fig. Syn.—Dēlīrĭūm, vānă, dēlīrĭă (pl.).

Sōmnŭs, ī. m. *Sleep.* Vēnīt tăcĭtūs nīgrīs cīrcūmdătŭs ālīs. Tib. Syn.—Mōrpheūs, sŏpŏr, quĭēs, rĕquĭēs. Phr.—Mēntī dĕŭs ūtĭlĭs ægræ. Cōnsāngŭĭnĕūs lētī sŏpŏr. Gĕlĭdæ mōrtīs frātēr lānguĭdŭs. Sōmnī quĭēs. Dōnă sŏpōrĭfĕræ nōctĭs. Dūlcĭs ĕt āltă quĭēs. Pēctŏră mūlcēns. Mōrtĭs ĭmāgŏ. Vērīs mīscēns fālsă. Ŏcŭlīs īndūlgērĕ sŏpōrēm. Sōmnūm spārgŏ. Sōmnō sōlvŏ. Lūmĭnă sōmnō vīncĭŏ. Sōmnō ēxcŭtĭŏ. Mĭhĭ gĕlĭdŭs hōrrŏr sōmnūm ēxpēllĭt. *Dream.* Syn.—Sōmnĭūm. *Inertia.* Syn.—Sŏpŏr, īgnāvĭă, ĭnērtĭă, tōrpŏr.

Sŏnĭtŭs, ūs. m. *Sound, noise.* Dūm flāmmās Jŏvĭs ēt sŏnĭtūs ĭmĭtātŭr Ŏlȳmpī. V. Syn.—Sŏnŭs, sŏnŏr, strĕpĭtŭs, clāmŏr, mūrmŭr, frăgŏr, strīdŏr, tŭmūltŭs. Phr.—Fĭt frăgŏr. Sŏnĭtŭs ēxŏrĭtŭr. Quătĭt āstră frăgŏr. Sŏnĭtūmquĕ pĕdūm vōcēmquĕ trĕmīscŏ. Dānt sŏnĭtūm gălĕæ. Rēddīt chōrdă sŏnūm. Frăgŏr īntŏnăt īngēns.

Sŏnŏ, ās, ŭī, ĭtūm, ārĕ. *To sound, to resound.* Scūtă sŏnānt, pūlsūquĕ pĕdūm trĕmĭt ēxcĭtă tēllūs. V. Syn.—Rĕsŏnŏ, īnsŏnŏ, strĕpŏ, pērstrĕpŏ, frĕmŏ, īnfrĕmŏ, mūgĭŏ, crĕpŏ, strīdĕŏ, mūrmŭrŏ, clāmŏ. Phr.—Sŏnĭtūm dō, rēddŏ. Mūrmŭră mīscĕŏ. Aūrās mŭrmŭrĕ cōmplĕŏ, īmplĕŏ. Strĕpĭtūs īngĕmĭtŏ. Mūrmŭrĕ cæco īntūs sāxă sŏnānt. *To speak.* Syn.—Lŏquŏr.

Sŏnōrŭs, ă, ūm. *Sonorous, resounding.* Lūctāntēs vēntōs tēmpēstātēsquĕ sŏnōrās. V. Phr.—Sŏnō, sŏnĭtū sævŭs, hōrrēndŭs. Raūcă sŏnāns āmnĭs. Cēntum ōră sŏnāntĭă līnguīs.

Sŏnŭs, ī. m. *Sound. See Sonitus. Voice, word.* Syn.—Vōcēs, vērbă.

Sōpĭŏ, īs, īvī & ĭī, ītūm, īrĕ. *To sleep.* Syn.—Sŏpōrŏ. Phr.—Sōmnūm īndūcŏ. Īn sōmnōs sōlvŏ. Cūstōdēm sōmnō sōpīstĭs.

Sŏpŏr, ōrĭs. m. *Sleep.* Syn.—Sōmnŭs, quĭēs, rĕquĭēs.

Sŏpōrĭfĕr, ĕră, ĕrūm. *Narcotic, that which puts to sleep.* Syn.—Sōmnĭfĕr, sōmnĭfĭcŭs, sŏpōrŭs.

Sŏpōrŭs, ă, ūm. *Causing sleep. See Soporifer.*

Sōrbĕŏ, ēs, ŭī, ptūm, ērĕ. *To absorb.* Syn.—Ābsōrbĕŏ, haūrĭŏ, dēglūtĭŏ, vŏrŏ. *To engulf.* Syn.—Haūrĭŏ, ābsōrbĕŏ, trăhŏ, dūcŏ, vŏrŏ.

Sōrdĕŏ, ēs, ērĕ. *To become sordid, dirty.* Syn.—Sōrdēscŏ, squālĕŏ. Phr.—Sōrdĭbŭs āspērgŏr. Sūm dēfōrmīs, ōbscœnŭs, ōbsĭtŭs. Sĭtū squālĕŏ. Fig.—*To be despised.* Syn.—Cōntēmnŏr, tēmnŏr, dēspĭcĭŏr, nēglĕgŏr, spērnŏr, ābjĭcĭŏr. Phr.—Hăbĕŏr vīlĭs.

Sōrdēs, ĭūm. f. *Dirt, filth.* Syn.—Squālŏr, īmmūndĭtĭæ, cōllŭvĭēs, īllŭvĭēs, spūrcĭtĭēs, pædŏr, lŭtūm. Phr.—Sōrdĭdă cōllŭvĭēs, squālŏr. Sōrdĭdŭs īmmūndō cōrpŏrĕ squālŏr. Squālēns sĭtŭs. Fig.—*Avarice. See Avaritia. Stain, dishonest action.* Syn.—Lābēs, măcŭlă.

Sōrdĭdŭs, ă, ūm. *Dirty, filthy.* Syn.—Sōrdēns, squālēns, fœdātŭs, fœdŭs, īmmūndŭs, tūrpĭs, spūrcŭs, ōbscœnŭs. Phr.—Squālōrĭs plēnŭs. Plēnŭs sōrdĭbŭs.

Sŏrŏr, ōrĭs. f. *Sister.* Āst ĕgŏ quæ dīvum īncēdō rēgīnă, Jŏvīsquĕ Ēt sŏrŏr ēt cōnjūx. V. Syn.—Gērmānă, cōnsōrs, sŏrōrcŭlă. Phr.—Gērmānă Jŏvĭs. Prōlēs frātērnă. Pœnĭtĕăt scĕlĕrĭs Dănăūm sævāsquĕ sŏrōrēs.

Sōrs, sōrtĭs. f. *Chance, lot.* Ārmă, Cāsĭbŭs īncērtīs ēt cæcā sōrtĕ pārārēnt. L. Syn.—Ālĕă, cāsŭs, fōrs. Phr.—Aūdācēm sōrsquĕ Vĕnūsquĕ jŭvānt. Quŏnĭām sōrs ōmnĭă vērsăt. *Destiny, lot.* Syn.—Fātūm. *Result, issue.* Syn.—Ēvēntŭs, ēxĭtŭs, fātūm. *Lots.* Syn.—Tăbēllă, sōrtītŭs. Phr.—Stāt dūctīs sōrtĭbŭs ūrnā. Crīstāsquĕ cŏmāntēs Ēxcĭpĭūnt sōrtī. *Condition, state.* Syn.—Cōndĭtĭō, stătŭs. *Principal, sum.* Syn.—Sūmmă, căpŭt.

Sōrtĭŏr, īrĭs, ītŭs sūm, īrī. *To allot, to cast lots.* Nēc rēgnă vīnī sōrtĭērĕ tālīs. H. Phr.—Sōrtēs dūcŏ, mīttŏ. Sōrtĕ dărī. Lĕgĭō sōrtītă pĕrīclūm. Ēt prædæ dūcērĕ sōrtēm. Lŏcă sōrtĕ lĕgūnt. Sōrtītī rēmōs. *To assign by lot.* Syn.—Dīvĭdō, pārtĭŏr, dīstrĭbŭō. Phr.—Sōrtĕ dīvĭdŏ. *To obtain by chance.* Syn.—Ōbtĭnĕō, āssĕquŏr, cōnsĕquŏr, nāncīscŏr. Phr.—Mĭhĭ cōntīngĭt. Sōrtĕ hăbĕō.

Sōrtītō. adv. *By chance.* Syn.—Sōrtĕ, fātō.

Sōspĕs, ĭtĭs. adj. *Safe, sound, healthy.* Syn.—Sālvŭs, īncŏlŭmĭs, īntĕgĕr, sŭpērstĕs, sērvātŭs, īllæsŭs. Phr.—Nāvīs sōspēs ăb īgnĭbŭs. Pōst prœlĭă sōspĕs.

Spārgŏ, ĭs, sī, sūm, ĕrĕ. *To scatter, to spread here and there.* Jām cōrnū pĕtăt ēt pĕdĭbūs quī spārgĭt ărēnām. V. Syn.—Dīspērgŏ, fūndŏ, dĭffūndŏ, ēffūndŏ, sĕrŏ, mīttŏ, jāctŏ, dīssēmĭnŏ, prŏjĭcĭŏ. Phr.—Sēmĭnă spārgĭt hŭmō. *To divide.* Syn.—Dīspērgŏ, dīsjĭcĭŏ, dīssĭpŏ. Fig.—*To spread a rumor.* Syn.—Vūlgŏ, pērvūlgŏ, sĕrŏ, dīssēmĭnŏ, dĭffūndŏ. *To water.* Syn.—Āspērgŏ, cōnspērgŏ. *To strew, to cover.* Syn.—Stērnŏ, tĕgŏ, vēstĭŏ.

Spătĭōsŭs, ă, ūm. *Spacious, wide.* Mētām spătĭōsō cīrcŭĭt ōrbĕ. O. Syn.—Āmplŭs, vāstŭs, căpāx, īngēns, lātŭs, īmmēnsŭs, ăpērtŭs, pătŭlŭs. Phr.—Lātē pătēns. Pătēntēm īn cīrcūm ēxtēnsŭs. Īngēntīs tūrbæ căpāx lŏcŭs. *Great.* Syn.—Īngēns, prōcērŭs, āltŭs, māgnŭs. *Long.* Syn.—Lōngŭs, dĭūtūrnŭs.

Spătĭūm, ĭī. n. *Space, interval.* Īnvĭdă mē spătĭō nātūră cŏērcŭĭt ārctō. O. Syn.—Īntērvāllūm, dīscrīmĕn. Phr.—Spătĭī dīscrīmĭnă. Pōrrēctūs spătĭī lŏcŭs. Ŏcŭlīs spătĭum ēmēnsŭs. *Great extent, size.* Syn.—Mōlēs, prōcērĭtās. *Space of time.* Syn.—Mŏră, tēmpŭs, īntērvāllūm. *Place for promenading.* Syn.—Āmbŭlācrūm, pōrtĭcŭs.

Spĕcĭēs, ēī. f. *Sight, aspect.* Syn.—Vīsŭs, āspēctŭs, spēctācŭlūm. *Appearance.* Syn.—Fōrmă, fĭgūră, ĭmāgŏ. *Decorum.* Syn.—Dĕcŏr. *Pretence, form, pretext.* Syn.—Cŏlŏr, ūmbră, ĭmāgŏ, nōmĕn. *Beauty.* Syn.—Pūlchrĭtūdŏ, fōrmă. *Spectre, shade.* Syn.—Spēctrūm, lārvă, sĭmŭlācrūm.

Spĕcĭmĕn, ĭnĭs. n. *Mark, proof, model.* Syn.—Ēxēmplūm, īndĭcĭūm, nŏtă, sīgnūm, ārgūmēntūm. *Ornament.* Syn.—Īnsīgnĕ.

Spĕcĭōsē. adv. *Elegantly.* Syn.—Pūlchrē, vĕnūstē, bĕnĕ.

Spĕcĭōsŭs, ă, ūm. *Beautiful.* Syn.—Pūlchĕr, cōnspĭcŭŭs, spēctābĭlĭs, īnsīgnĭs.

Spēctābĭlĭs, ĭs, ĕ. *Worthy of being seen.* Īpsĕ sŭpĕr cūrrūm plăcĭdō spēctābĭlĭs ōrĕ. O. Syn.—Spēctāndŭs, cōnspĭcŭŭs, īnsīgnĭs, cōnspĭcĭēndŭs, spĕcĭōsŭs. Phr.—Mūltō spēctābĭlĭs aūrō. Pŭĕr făcĭē spēctābĭlĭs. Spēctābĭlĭs hērōs.

Spēctăcŭlūm, ī. n. *Sight, spectacle.* Syn.—Vīsŭs, āspēctŭs, spĕcĭēs.

Spēctācŭlă, ōrūm. n. *Public games.* Syn.—Lūdī. Phr.—Scēnæ spēctācŭlă. Sōlēmnēs pōmpæ, lūdī. Nŏvæ mīrācŭlă pōmpæ. *Amphitheatre.* Syn.—Āmphĭthĕātrūm, thĕātrūm.

Spēctātŏr, ōrĭs. m. *Spectator.* Syn.—Spēctāns, tēstĭs, ārbĭtĕr, sēssŏr.

Spēctŏ, ās, āvī, ātūm, ārĕ. *To look at.* Spēctātūm vĕnĭūnt, vĕnĭūnt spēctēntŭr ŭt īpsæ. O. Syn.—Āspēctŏ, āspĭcĭŏ, cōnsīdĕrŏ, cōntēmplŏr, īntŭĕŏr, tŭĕŏr, cōntŭĕŏr, ōbsērvŏ, cērnŏ, vĭdĕŏ. Phr.—Ŏcŭlīs spēctārĕ prŏtērvīs. Quīdquĭd spēctātŭr ĭn cīrcō. *To turn towards.* Syn.—Vērtŏr, cōnvērtŏr, ōbvērtŏr, vērgŏ. *To prove.* Syn.—Prŏbŏ, ēxpĕrĭŏr, æstĭmŏ, īnspĭcĭŏ, jūdĭcŏ, nōscŏ, ēxplōrŏ.

Spēctrūm, ī. n. *Spectre, shadow, phantom.* Syn.—Sĭmŭlăcrūm, lĕmŭrēs, mānēs, ūmbræ, lārvæ. Phr.—Nōctūrnæ, ĭnānēs ūmbræ. Ūmbræ nōctĕ vŏlāntēs. Nīgră sōmnĭă. Căvă sŭb īmāgĭnĕ fōrmæ.

Spĕcŭlă, æ. f. *Place of observation, top of a hill.* Præcēps āĕrĭī spĕcŭlā dē mēntĭs ĭn ūndās Dēfĕrăr. V. Syn.—Cūlmĕn, ārx, căcūmĕn.

Spĕcŭlŏr, ārĭs, ātŭs sūm, ārī. *To observe, to consider.* Ābdĭtă frōndĕ lĕvī dēnsā spĕcŭlātŭr ăb ūlmō. O. Syn.—Spēctŏ, īntŭĕŏr, ōbsērvŏ, ēxplōrŏ, cōnsīdĕrŏ, cōntēmplŏr. Phr.—Tūrrī spĕcŭlātŭr ăb āltā. Ōmnēm āccēssūm lūstrāns. Tăcĭtīs ŏcŭlīs pĕrērrāns. Hæc sŭpĕr ē vāllō prōspēctānt. Fig.—*To spy upon.* Syn.—Īnspēctŏ, ēxplōrŏ, ōbsērvŏ.

Spĕcŭlūm, ī. n. *Mirror.* Ēlīgăt ēt spĕcŭlūm cōnsŭlăt āntĕ sŭūm. O. Phr.—Spĕcŭlī vĭtrūm, æquŏr, splēndŏr, nĭtŏr. Spĕcŭlī nĭtĭdīssĭmŭs ōrbĭs. Crȳstāllĭnă lāmĭnă. Nĭtĭdō splēndōrĕ cŏrūscāns. Fōrmās rēddēns. Īn spĕcŭlō sŏlĕt āppārērĕ fĭgūră.

Spĕcŭs, ūs. m. f. & n. *Deep cavern, trench.* Syn.—Spēlūncă, spēlæūm, āntrūm, căvērnă. Phr.—Spēlūncæ rĕcēssŭs, lātĕbræ, căvūm, āmbĭtŭs.

Spērnāx, ācĭs. adj. *One who despises.* Syn.—Cōntēmptŏr, sprētŏr.

Spērnŏ, ĭs, sprēvī, sprētūm, ĕrĕ. *To despise.* Syn.—Āspērnŏr, cōntēmnŏ, rējĭcĭŏ.

Spērŏ, ās, āvī, ātūm, ārĕ. *To hope.* Grātă sŭpērvĕnĭēt, quæ nōn spērābĭtŭr hōră. H. Syn.—Cōnfīdŏ, ēxspēctŏ. Phr.—Spēm căpĭŏ, cōncĭpĭŏ, hăbĕŏ. Spē dūcŏr. Ănĭmūm spēs ēxcĭtăt. Crēdŭlă mēntēm spēs hăbĕt. Spēs mĭhĭ māgnă ēst. Īn spēm vĕnĭŏ. Fāllācī spēm pōnĭt ĭn aūrō. Spēm frōntĕ sĕrēnăt. Tūm spēs ārrēctæ jŭvĕnūm. *To foresee, to expect.* Syn.—Prævĭdĕŏ, tĭmĕŏ, præmĕtŭŏ.

Spēs, ĕī. f. *Hope.* Cūră făcīt dŭbĭūm, vēl spēs īncērtă fătīgăt. M. Syn.—Ēxspēctātĭŏ, fīdūcĭă, vōtă. Phr.—Fīdūcĭă rērūm. Spēs īncērtă fŭtūrī. Spēs āltrīx ēt cŏmēs jŭvēntæ. Tōllēns tædĭă vītæ. Īncūsăt spēs ægră mŏrās. Spēmquĕ mĕtūmque īntēr dŭbĭī. Āltērnānt spēsquĕ tĭmōrquĕ fĭdēm. Spēs āddĭtă ēxcĭtăt īrās. Spēs mĕă mīxtă mĕtū. Spēm dō, āddŏ, āccēndŏ, ōstēndŏ. Spē īmplĕŏ. Spēm vānăm, ĭnānēm căpĭŏ, fŏvĕŏ. Spē dēcĭpĭŏr. Ănĭmūm spēs ĭnānĭs hăbĕt. Spē mēndācī, ĭnānī dūcŏr. Ĭnānĭă vōtă fŏvēns. Spēs ăbĭt, mē dēsĕrĭt. Spēs mĭhĭ vānă cădĭt, flŭĭt. Spēm ădĭmŏ.

Spīcŭlūm, ī. n. *Point.* Hāstārūm trĕmŭlō quătĭēbăt spīcŭlă mōtū. O. Syn.—Ăcĭēs, cūspĭs, mūcrŏ, ăcūmĕn. *Dart.* Syn.—Ăcŭlĕŭs, cūspĭs, ărūndŏ, jăcŭlūm, săgīttă, tēlūm. Phr.—Tīnctă vĕnēnō. Lævātō lūcĭdă fērrō. Ădhūc sōrdēntĭă tābō. Spīcŭlă cāstrīs Dēnsă cădūnt mĕdĭīs. Spīcŭlă dēxtrā Tōrtă vŏlānt.

Spīnă, æ. f. *Thorn.* Ēt rĭgĕt āmīssā spīnă rĕlīctă rŏsā. O. Syn.—Rŭbŭs, sēntēs, vĕprēs.

Spīnētūm, ī. n. *Place where thorns or briars grow.* Nūnc vĭrĭdēs ĕtĭam ōccūltānt spīnētă lăcērtōs. V. Syn.—Dūmētūm, rŭbētūm. Phr.—Spīnōsŭs, dūmōsŭs, spīnīs cōnsĭtŭs lŏcŭs, ăgĕr, cāmpŭs.

Spīnōsŭs, ă, ūm. *Thorny.* Spīnōsī rōscĭdă tērgă jŭgī. Prop. Syn.—Spīnĭfĕr, spīnĕŭs, dūmōsŭs. Fig.—*Irritating.* Syn.—Āspĕr, dūrŭs, ăcūtŭs, sævŭs.

Spīră, æ. f. *Spiral line.* Syn.—Gȳrŭs, sĭnŭs, ōrbĭs, nōdŭs, flēxŭs, vŏlūmĕn.

Spīrācŭlūm, ī. n. *Breathing-place, vent.* Syn.—Ōs, faūcēs, hĭātŭs, spīrāmēntūm.

Spīrāmĕn, ĭnĭs. n. *Opening.* Syn.—Spīrācŭlūm, ōs, faūcēs, hĭātŭs, fŏrāmĕn.

Spīrĭtŭs, ūs. m. *Breath.* Syn.—Hālĭtŭs, ănhēlĭtŭs, flāmĕn, flātŭs, āfflātŭs, aūră, ănĭmă, spīrāmĕn, rēspīrāmĕn, spīrāmēntūm. Phr. Ōrĭs spīrĭtŭs. Vītālĭs aūră. Pūrī æthĕrĭs haūstŭs. *Spirit of life.* Syn.—Ănĭmă, vītă, ănĭmŭs. Fig.—*Soul.* Syn.—Ănĭmă, mēns, ănĭmŭs. *Pride, haughtiness.* Syn.—Sŭpērbĭă, fāstŭs. *Inspiration.* Syn.—Flātŭs, āfflātŭs.

Spīrŏ, ās, āvī, ātūm, ārĕ. *To breathe.* Syn.—Āspīrŏ, vīvŏ. *To come forth (from the mouth or nose).* Syn.—Ēxĕŏ, ērūmpŏ, ējĭcĭŏ. *To exhale an odor.* Syn.—Rĕdŏlĕŏ, frăgrŏ. *To favor. See Faveo.*

Spīssŏ, ās, āvī, ātūm, ārĕ. *To thicken.* Syn.—Dēnsŏ, cōndēnsŏ, cōgŏ, ăgglŏmĕrŏ.

Spīssŭs, ă, ūm. *Thick, condensed.* Nē spīssæ rīsūm tōllānt īmpūnĕ cŏrōnæ. H. Syn.—Spīssātŭs, dēnsŭs, dēnsātŭs. Phr.—Spīssō vīmĭnĕ quālī. Spīssă rāmīs laūrĕă.

Splēndĕŏ, ēs, ŭī, ērĕ. *To shine brightly, to be resplendent.* Syn.—Rēsplēndĕŏ, lūcĕŏ, cōllūcĕŏ, rĕlūcĕŏ, nĭtĕŏ, fūlgĕŏ, ēffūlgĕŏ, rĕnīdĕŏ, fūlgŭrŏ, scīntīllŏ. Phr.—Lūcēm cŏrūscām, fūlgōrēm dō, ēmīttŏ, rădĭŏ. Splēndōrĕ, rădĭīs rĕnīdĕŏ. Rădĭīs ārdēscō lūcĭs ĕt aūrō. Nŏvă lūx ŏcŭlīs ēffūlsĭt.

Splēndĭdŭs, ă, ūm. *Brilliant, shining.* Āt dŏmŭs īntĕrĭōr rēgālī splēndĭdă lūxū. V. Syn.—Splēndēns, fūlgēns, fūlgĭdŭs, nĭtĭdŭs, lūcĭdŭs, cŏrūscŭs, rŭtĭlŭs, rŭtĭlāns, mĭcāns, ārdēns, nĭtēns, rădĭāns. Phr.—Nĭtĭdā lūcĕ, nĭtĭdō splēndōrĕ cŏrūscāns. Cŏrūscō splēndōrĕ ārdēns. Cŏrūscām lūcēm vĭbrāns. Splēndĭdŭs ōstrō crīnĭs. *Celebrated, famous.* Syn.—Cĕlĕbĕr, clārŭs, prǣclārŭs, īllūstrĭs. *Magnificent.* Syn.—Māgnĭfĭcŭs, sŭpērbŭs.

Splēndŏr, ōrĭs. m. *Splendor, brilliancy.* Syn.—Lūx, nĭtŏr, lūmĕn, fūlgŏr, jŭbăr, flāmmă, īgnĭs, rădĭī. Phr.—Splēndĭdă lūx. Splēndĭdŭs nĭtŏr. Lūcĭdă flāmmă. Cŏrūscŭs splēndŏr ăppārĕt. Hūnc căpĭt ārgēntī splēndŏr.

Spŏlĭŏ, ās, āvī, ātūm, ārĕ. *To despoil, to rob.* Āddĭt ĕquōs ēt tēlă quĭbūs spŏlĭāvĕrăt hōstēm. V. Syn.—Ēxspŏlĭŏ, nūdŏ, dēnūdŏ, ēxŭŏ, dīrĭpĭŏ, răpĭŏ, prǣdŏr. Phr.—Pārs spŏlĭānt ārās. Īllūm vītā spŏlĭāvĭt Āchīllēs. Pŏpŭlīs spŏlĭāvĕrăt ūrbēs. Vīctūm spŏlĭārĕ părābăt. Spŏlĭātūr lūmĭnĕ tērră.

Spŏlĭă, ōrūm. n. *Spoils.* Syn.—Ēxŭvĭæ. Phr.—Vīctō ēx hōstĕ rĕlātæ ēxŭvĭæ. Bēllōrūm ēxŭvĭæ. Spŏlĭă ēx hōstĕ pārtă. Prǣdă spŏlĭīsquĕ pŏtītī. Tūrnŭs ŏvāt spŏlĭō. Spŏlĭīs aūctŭs, ōrnātŭs, īnsīgnĭs.

Spōndĕŏ, ēs, spŏpōndī, spōnsūm, ērĕ. *To promise with assurance.* Spōndĕō dīgnă tŭīs īngēntĭbŭs ōmnĭă cœptīs. V. Syn.—Pōllĭcĕŏr, prōmīttŏ. Phr.—Spōndēt fōrtūnă sălūtēm.

Spōnsă, æ. f. *Spouse, affianced.* Flēbĭlī spōnsæ jŭvĕnēmquĕ rāptūm Plōrăt. H. Syn.—Dēspōnsă. Phr.—Dēspōnsă pŭēllă. Nŏvă nūptă. Pāctă vīrgŏ.

Spōnsŭs, ī. m. *Husband, affianced.* Syn.—Vĭr, mărītŭs, cōnjūx.

Spōntĕ (*abl. of Spons, obsolete*). f. *Of one's own accord.* Spōntĕ sŭā sāndȳx pāscēntēs vēstĭĕt āgnōs. V. Syn.—Ūltrō, lĭbēntĕr, lĭbēns, vŏlēns, īpsĕ. Phr.—Prŏprĭā spōntĕ. Aēquō, lĭbēntī ănĭmō. Nōn īnvītŭs, nōn cŏāctŭs. Vŏlēns făcĭlīsquĕ. Nūllō cōgēntĕ crĕātī. Pēr sē dăbăt ōmnĭă tēllūs.

Sprētŏr, ōrĭs. m. *One who despises.* Syn.—Cōntēmptŏr, spērnāx.

Spūmă, æ. f. *Foam.* Phr.—Spūmĕŭs lĭquŏr, hūmŏr. Spūmāns ăquă, ūndă. Nĭvĕŭs sălĭs lĭquŏr. Spūmæ sălĭs. Mărĭs āspērgŏ, cānĭtĭēs.

Spūmĕŭs, ă, ūm. *Foamy.* Syn.—Spūmāns, spūmĭfĕr, spūmōsŭs. Phr.—Spūmīs plēnŭs, ālbēns, pērfūsŭs, spārsŭs, ōblĭtŭs.

Spūmŏ, ās, āvī, ātūm, ārĕ. *To foam.* Ōbjēctæ sālsā spūmānt āspērgĭnĕ caūtēs. V. Syn.—Spūmēscŏ. Phr.—Spūmās rējĭcĭŏ, fūndŏ, ēffūndŏ, spārgŏ, ēmīttŏ, æstŭŏ. Spūmă flŭĭt. Spūmās ăgĭt ōrĕ crŭēntās. Spūmānt frĕtă vērsă lăcērtīs. Spūmās sălĭs ærĕ rŭēbānt.

Spŭŏ, ĭs, ŭī, ūtūm, ĕrĕ. *To expectorate.* Syn.—Ēxspŭŏ, dēspŭŏ, scrĕŏ, ēxscrĕŏ.

Spūrcŏ, ās, āvī, ātūm, ārĕ. *To defile.* Syn.—Fœdŏ, măcŭlŏ, vĭtĭŏ, cōntămĭnŏ, pōllŭŏ.

Spūrcŭs, ă, ūm. *Defiled, unclean.* Syn.—Īmmūndŭs, īmpūrŭs, ōbscœnŭs, fœdŭs, squālēns, squālĭdŭs, sōrdĭdŭs.

Squālĕŏ, ēs, ŭī, ērĕ. *To be roughened, to have scales.* Syn.—Īntĕgŏr, cōntĕgŏr, ŏpĕrĭŏr. *To be neglected, to be untilled.* Syn.—Sōrdĕŏ, sōrdēscŏ. Phr.—Sūm īncūltŭs, īncōmptŭs.

Squālĭdŭs, ă, ūm. *Neglected, dirty.* Syn.—Squālēns, sōrdĭdŭs. Phr.—Squālōrĕ sōrdĭdŭs, fœdŭs, ātĕr. Sōrdĭdă lūctū mātĕr. Squālĭdă mōrs.

Squālŏr, ōrĭs. m. *Roughness.* Syn.—Āspĕrĭtās. *Neglect, disorder.* Syn.—Pædŏr, sōrdēs, sĭtŭs. Phr.—Tērrĭbĭlī squālōrĕ jăcĕt. *Darkness.* Syn.—Hōrrŏr, ūmbră, cālīgŏ.

Squāmă, æ. *Scale.* Ārrēctīs hōrrēt squāmīs ēt sībĭlăt ōrĕ. V. Phr.—Squāmōsūm tēgmĕn. Squāmōsă pēllĭs. Pēllĭs dūrĭtĭēs. Squāmārūm nēxĭlĭs ōrdŏ, sĕrĭēs.

Squāmĕŭs, ă, ūm. *Covered with scales.* Squāmĕă cōnvōlvēns sūblātō pēctŏrĕ tērgă. V. Syn.—Squāmōsŭs, squāmĭfĕr, squālēns. Phr.—Squāmīs vēlāntĭbŭs ārtūs. *That which has a rough skin.* Syn.—Scăbĕr, scăbĭōsŭs, āspĕr.

Stăbĭlĭŏ, īs, īvī, ītūm, īrĕ. *To establish, to make firm.* Syn.—Fīrmŏ, cōnfīrmŏ, fūlcĭŏ, cōrrōbŏrŏ, stătŭŏ, cōnstĭtŭŏ.

Stăbĭlĭs, ĭs, ĕ. *Firm.* Quæ mănĕăt stăbĭlī, cūm fŭgĭt īllă pĕdĕ. O. Syn.—Cōnstāns, fīrmŭs, fīrmātŭs, sŏlĭdŭs, īmmūtābĭlĭs, īmmōbĭlĭs, īmmōtŭs, cērtŭs.

Stăbŭlūm, ī. n. *Stable.* Cōgĕrĕ jūssĭt ŏvēs stăbŭlīs nŭmĕrūmquĕ rĕfērrī. O. Syn.—Sēptūm, præsēpĕ, (*for horses*) ĕquīlĕ, (*for cattle*) būbīlĕ, (*for goats*) hædīlĕ, (*for sheep*) ŏvīlĕ, caūlă, (*for pigs*) sŭīlĕ, hără, vŏlūtābrūm. Phr.—Stăbŭlī claūstră, sēptă, sēpēs, tēctă, hōspĭtĭūm. Pĕcŏrūm dŏmŭs. Stăbŭlīs quālīs lĕō sævĭt ŏpīmīs. Quīs răpĭăt stăbŭlīs ārmēntă rĕclūsīs. Stăbŭlīs ēxpēllĕrĕ vāccās. Īn stăbŭlă cōgĕrĕ taūrōs. Claūsă tĕnēnt stăbŭlīs ārmēntă. *The herd.* Syn.—Ārmēntūm, pĕcŭs.

Stădĭūm, ĭī. n. *Stadium.* Syn.—Cūrrĭcŭlūm, spătĭă. Phr.—Ālphēūs stădĭō nōtŭs Ŏlўmpĭcō.

Stāgnŏ, ās, āvī, ātūm, ārĕ. *To overflow.* Syn. Ēxūndŏ, ēffūndŏ, sŭpērfūndŏr, ēxspătĭŏr, ēxcūrrŏ. *To be inundated.* Syn.—Ĭnūndŏ, nătŏ, mădĕŏ.

Stāgnūm, ī. n. *Marsh, stagnant water.* Syn.—Lăcŭs, pălūs. Phr.—Stāgnāns ăquă. Stāns ūndă. Stāgnă pălūdĭs. Stāgnă jăcēntĭs ăquæ. Stāgnă pĕtīt pătŭlōsquĕ lăcūs. Īnnābĭlĭs ūndă. Hūmĭdă cīrcūm stāgnă sŏnānt.

Stāmĕn, ĭnĭs. n. *Thread of flax.* Syn.—Fīlūm. *Warp.* Syn.—Fīlūm, līcĭă, sūbtēmĕn.

Stātēră, æ. f. *Roman balance, scales.* Syn.—Lībră, trŭtĭnă, lānx.

Stătĭm. adv. *Immediately.* Syn.—Āctūtūm, brĕvī, cĭtŏ, cōnfēstĭm, cōntĭnŭō, ēxtēmplō, īlĭcĕt, īllĭcō, jāmjām, mōx, ōcĭŭs, prōtĭnŭs, rĕpēntĕ, sŭbĭtō, prŏpĕrē, mātūrē, mōmēntō. Phr.—Nēc mŏră. Nūllă, pārvă mŏra ēst. Nēc lōngūm. Haūd mŏră. Dīctō cĭtĭŭs. Nēc mūltă mŏrātŭs. Vīx ĕă fātŭs ĕrāt. Stătĭm āc. *As soon as.* Syn.—Sĭmŭl āc, sĭmŭl ātquĕ, ŭt, ŭbĭ. Phr.—Ūt prīmūm fārī pŏtŭĭt. Vīx ēdĭdĕrāt cūm prōtĭnŭs.

Stătĭŏ, ōnĭs. f. *Delay.* Syn.—Mŏră. *Military post.* Syn.—Cūstōdĭă, ēxcŭbĭæ. *Harbor.* Syn.—Pōrtŭs.

Stătŭă, æ. f. *Statue.* Īnsānīt vĕtĕrēs stătŭās Dămăsīppŭs ĕmēndō. H. Syn.—Ēffĭgĭēs, sĭmŭlācrūm, sīgnūm, spĕcĭēs, ĭmāgŏ. Phr.—Aūrūm, ārgēntūm, līgnūm scūlptĭlĕ, scūlptūm, spīrāns. Fōrmātum ē mārmŏrĕ sīgnūm. Vīvīs cērtāntĭă vūltĭbŭs ærā. Vīvī dē mārmŏrĕ vūltūs. Ēffĭgĭēs sāxō ēxprēssă. Vītā cărēns. Stāt Jūpĭtĕr aūrĕŭs.

Stătŭŏ, ĭs, ŭī, ūtūm, ĕrĕ. *To establish, to place.* Ūrbēm præclārām stătŭī. V. Syn.—Pōnŏ, lŏcŏ, cōllŏcŏ, cōnstĭtŭŏ, ērĭgŏ, fūndŏ, ædĭfĭcŏ. *To stop.* Syn.—Sīstŏ. *To establish, to prescribe.* Syn.—Pōnŏ, īmpōnŏ, cōnstĭtŭŏ, dō, præscrībŏ. *To arrange.* Syn.—Dīrĭmŏ, dījūdĭcŏ, cōmpōnŏ. *To determine.* Syn.—Dēcērnŏ, cōnstĭtŭŏ.

Stătŭs, ūs. m. *Position, attitude.* Syn.—Pōsĭtūră, pŏsĭtŭs, hăbĭtŭs. *State, condition.* Syn.—Cōndĭtĭō, fōrtūnă, sōrs. Phr.—Quō rēs sūmmă lŏcō?

Stēllă, æ. f. *Star.* Nām nĕquĕ tūnc stēllīs ăcĭēs ōbtūsă vĭdētŭr. V. Syn.—Āstrūm, sīdŭs. Phr.—Fīxă pŏlō flāmmă. Spārsă mĭcānt stēllārūm lūmĭnă cœlō. Cœlūm vōlvīt răpĭdā vērtīgĭnĕ stēllās.

Stēmmă, ătĭs. n. *Garland or wreath placed upon the busts of ancestors, therefore title of nobility.* Syn.—Nōbĭlĭtās. Phr.—Gēntīlĕ sīgnūm. Prīscæ mājōrūm ĭmāgĭnēs. Nōbĭlĕ vīctrīcĭs stēmmă dŏmŭs. Stēmmătĕ mātērnō fēlīx.

Stērcŏrŏ, ās, āvī, ātūm, ārĕ. *To fertilize.* Phr.—Sătă fĭmō, stērcŏrĕ tĕgŏ, ōbdūcŏ, ŏpĕrĭŏ, spārgŏ, rĕplĕŏ. Fēcūndāt stērcŏrĕ tērrām.

Stĕrĭlĭs, ĭs, ĕ. *Sterile, barren.* Īnfēlīx lŏlĭum ēt stĕrĭlēs dŏmĭnāntŭr ăvēnæ. V. Syn.—Īnfēcūndŭs, ārĭdŭs, ărēnōsŭs, dīffĭcĭlĭs, trīstĭs, ĭnērs, sēgnĭs, mălŭs, mălīgnŭs, mēndāx, fāllāx, jējūnŭs. Phr.—Nōn fēcūndŭs. Mălĕ fēcūndŭs. Īnvīsŭs ăgĕr. Trīstĕ sŏlūm, cūltōrĕ cărēns. Stĕrĭlēs ād sēmĭnă tērræ. Aēgră sŏlŏ măcĭēs. Nūllās tērră frūgēs părĭt. Cāmpī cūltōrĕ cărēntēs. Sæpĕ fĕfēllĭt ăgĕr. Tūrpĭs sĭnĕ grāmĭnĕ cāmpŭs. Prīmĭs sĕgĕtēs mŏrĭūntŭr ĭn hērbīs. Fig.—*Sterile, useless, vain.* Syn.—Vānŭs, ĭnānĭs, cāssŭs, īrrĭtŭs.

Stērnŏ, ĭs, strāvī, strātūm, ĕrĕ. *To strew upon the ground.* Mōllĭt hŭmūm fŏlĭīs nātāsquĕ sŭb æquŏrĕ vīrgās Stērnĭt. V. Syn.—Sūbstērnŏ, īnstērnŏ, ēxtēndŏ. *To cover. See Tego. To overwhelm.* Syn.—Prōstērnŏ, āfflīgŏ, dējĭcĭŏ, ēvērtŏ, dētūrbŏ, præcĭpĭtŏ, prōrŭŏ, ēxcŭtĭŏ. Phr.—Hŭmī fūndŏ. Prōnūm stērnŏ. Sŏlō ēffūndŏ. Strāvĭt hŭmī prōnām.

Stīgmă, ătĭs. n. *Mark, brand upon the forehead.* Syn.—Nŏtă, sīgnūm. Phr.—Īnūstūm frōntī. Sīgnāns vūltūm. Frōntēm pĕrūrēns. Rĭgĭdō nŏtātām, sīgnātām stīgmătĕ frōntēm.

Stīllŏ, ās, āvī, ātūm, ārĕ. *To trickle down, to distil.* Flāvăquĕ dē vĭrĭdī stīllābānt īlĭcĕ mēllă. V. Syn.—Flŭŏ, ēfflŭŏ, dīstīllŏ, sūdŏ. Phr.—Gūttātĭm cădŏ, flŭŏ. Stīllās mīttŏ. Sānguĭnēĭs stīllāvĭt rōrĭbŭs ărbŏr. Stīllābāt Tȳrĭō cŏmă rōrĕ. Fig.—*See Insinuo.*

Stĭmŭlŏ, ās, āvī, ātūm, ārĕ. *To urge, to spur on, to excite.* Syn.—Ēxstĭmŭlŏ, īnstĭmŭlŏ, fŏdĭcŏ, lāncĭnŏ, pūngŏ, cōncĭtŏ, ēxcĭtŏ. Phr.—Stĭmŭlūm ădhĭbĕŏ, āddŏ, ādjĭcĭŏ. Ūrgēt stĭmŭlīs aūrīgă crŭēntĭs. Pārcĕ, pŭĕr, stĭmŭlīs, ēt fōrtĭŭs ūtĕrĕ lōrīs. Ācrēs stĭmŭlōs sūb pēctŏrĕ vērtĭt.

Stĭmŭlŭs, ī. m. *Goad, spur.* Phr.—Stĭmŭlī cūspĭs, ăcūmĕn. *Whip. See Flagellum.* Fig.—*Encouragement.* Syn.—Cālcăr. *Suffering, torment.* Syn.—Crŭcĭātŭs, dŏlŏr, āngŏr, vūlnŭs, cūră.

Stīpĕs, ĭtĭs. m. *Trunk, and by extention tree.* Cōnstĕrnūnt tĕrrăm cōncūssō stīpĭtĕ frōndēs. V. Syn.—Trūncŭs, ārbŏr. Phr.—Nōdīs grăvĭdŭs. Prŏpĕrāntī fālcĕ dŏlātŭs. Sēdūctō stīpĭtĕ flāmmă pĕrĭt. *Stick, club.* Syn.—Sŭdēs, fūstĭs. Fig.—*A fool.* Syn.—Stūltŭs, ăsĭnŭs.

Stīpŏ, ās, āvī, ātūm, ārĕ. *To condense.* Aūt cūm līquēntĭă mēllă Stīpānt. V. *See Denseo. To heap together.* Syn.—Cŭmŭlŏ, āccŭmŭlŏ, cōngĕrŏ. *To surround.* Syn.—Āmbĭŏ, cīngŏ, cīrcūmdŏ, cīrcūmstŏ, cŏmĭtŏr, sĕquŏr.

Stĭpŭlă, æ. f. *Straw.* Ātquĕ lĕvēm stĭpŭlām crĕpĭtāntĭbŭs ūrĕrĕ flāmmīs. V. Syn.—Cūlmŭs, călămŭs, pălĕă, strāmĕn. Phr.—Stĭpŭlă crĕpĭtāvĭt ĭnānī Īgnĭs ĭnērs.

Stīrpĭtŭs. adv. *Down to the roots.* Syn.—Rādīcĭtŭs, pĕnĭtŭs. Phr.—Ā stīrpĕ, ā rādīcĕ. Cūm stīrpĭbŭs īmīs.

Stīrps, īrpĭs. m. & f. *Root.* Īmmō dē stīrpĕ rĕcīsūm. V. Syn.—Rādīx. Phr.—Ā stīrpĕ, ā stīrpĭbŭs. *Race.* Syn.—Gĕnŭs.

Stō, stās, stĕtī, stătūm, ārĕ. *To stand.* Ēt cōrnū dūctūs stābāt săcĕr hīrcŭs ăd ārām. V. Syn.—Sīstŏ. *To exist.* Syn.—Mănĕŏ, pērmănĕŏ, dūrŏ, vĭgĕŏ, vīvŏ. *To stop.* Syn.—Sīstŏ, sūbsīstŏ, rĕsīstŏ, cōnsīstŏ, mănĕŏ, mŏrŏr, cōmmŏrŏr. Phr.—Quæ fīnĭs stāndī? Ăcĭēs stĕtĭt ōrdĭnĕ cērtō. Stāt vī tĕrrā sŭā. *To be calm, immovable.* Syn.—Quĭēscŏ, tōrpĕŏ, sĭlĕŏ. *To stand firmly.* Syn.—Ōbsīstŏ, rĕsīstŏ, cōnsīstŏ.

Strāgēs, ĭs. f. *Ruin, disaster.* Dăbĭt īllĕ rŭīnām Ārbŏrĭbūs strāgēmquĕ sătĭs. V. Syn.—Rŭīnă, cāsŭs, ēxcĭdĭūm, ēxĭlĭūm. *Defeat.* Syn.—Clādēs. *Slaughter.* Syn.—Cædēs, ōccīsĭŏ.

Strāgŭlūm, ī. n. *Coverlet, counterpane.* Syn.—Gaūsăpĕ, pĕrīstrōmă, vēstĭs, pāllĭūm, vēlāmĕn.

Strāmĕn, ĭnĭs. n. *Bed of straw, or leaves.* Hīc jŭvĕnem āgrēstī sūblīmem īn strāmĭnĕ pōnūnt. V. Syn.—Stĭpŭlă, pălĕă, fŏlĭă, frōndēs, hērbæ. Phr.—Mīxtă cūm fŏlĭīs præbŭĭt hērbă tŏrūm. Strātīs pōrrēxĭt ĭn hērbīs. Pălĕā pōrrēctŭs ĭn hōrnā.

Strāngŭlŏ, ās, āvī, ātūm, ārĕ. *To choke, to throttle.* Ēt tŭă sīc Stўgĭŭs strangŭlĕt ōră lĭquŏr. O. Syn.—Sūffōcŏ, præfōcŏ, ēlīdŏ. Phr.—Faūcēs, cōllūm, gūttŭr, prĕmŏ, cōnstrīngŏ. Ănĭmām lăquĕō claūdŏ, sūffōcŏ, ōbstrŭŏ. Cōllō lăquĕūm āptŏ. Gūttŭră ēlīsă prĕmŏ. Āptābāt pāllēntī vīncŭlă cōllō. Fig.—*To press.* Syn.—Ārctŏ, cōnstrīngŏ.

Strātūm, ī. n. *Bed.* Syn.—Lēctŭs, cŭbīlĕ, thălămŭs. *Covering.* Syn.—Strāgŭlūm. (*In the plural*) *Street.* Syn.—Vĭă, ĭtĕr. Phr.—Strātūm ĭtĕr. Vĭă strātă, mūnītă, sāxĕă.

Strēnŭŭs, ă, ūm. *Strenuous, active.* Syn.—Gnāvŭs, īmpĭgĕr, ācĕr, ălăcĕr, prōmptŭs, cĭtŭs, dīlĭgēns, īndūstrĭŭs.

Strĕpĭtŏ, ās, āvī, ātūm, ārĕ. *To resound.* Syn.—Ōbstrĕpŏ, mūrmŭrŏ, sŏnŏ, rĕsŏnŏ. Phr.—Mūrmŭră mīscērĕ. Raūcūm dărĕ mūrmŭr. Tēctă frĕmūnt. Raūcō strĕpŭērūnt cōrnŭă cāntū. Tōt părĭbūs strĕpĕrēt clўpĕīs.

Strĕpĭtŭs, ūs. m. *Noise, tumult.* Fīt strĕpĭtūs tēctīs, vōcēmquĕ pĕr āmplă vŏlūtānt Ātrĭă. V. Syn.—Mūrmŭr, sŏnŭs, sŏnĭtŭs, tŭmūltŭs, strīdŏr. Phr.—Hōrrĭsŏnōs Bŏrĕǽ strĕpĭtūs. Nēc vānōs hōrrēt strĕpĭtūs. Māgnō pūlsă dŏmūs strĕpĭtū.

Strīctīm. adv. *Briefly, in passing.* Syn.—Brĕvĭtĕr, ŏbĭtĕr, sūmmātīm.

Strīdĕŏ, ēs, ī, ērĕ. *To make a sharp noise.* Syn.—Strĕpŏ, strĕpĭtŏ, crĕpĭtŏ, frĕmŏ. Phr.—Strīdōrēm dō, cĭĕŏ, tōllŏ, āttōllŏ. Strīdēnt hāstīlĭbŭs aūrǣ. Fūsūm strīdĕt ĭn īgnĕ mĕrūm. Prēssōquĕ diū strīdērĕ mŏlārī. Strīdĕt sūb pēctŏrĕ vūlnŭs.

Strīdŏr, ōrĭs. m. *Piercing, sharp noise.* Ēcce ĭnĭmīcŭs, ătrōx, māgnō strīdōrĕ pĕr aūrās Īnsĕquĭtŭr. V. Syn.—Strĕpĭtŭs, sŏnĭtŭs, mūrmŭr, sībĭlŭs, sībĭlă. Phr.—Frĕmĭt ūndĭquĕ strīdŏr Hōrrĭbĭlĭs. Tūm vălĭdās strīdōrĕ fŏrēs. Māgnīs ăcŭūnt strīdōrĭbŭs īrās.

Strīdŭlŭs, ă, ūm. *That which makes a creaking or sharp sound.* Strīdŭlă Saūrŏmătēs plaūstră bŭbūlcŭs ăgĭt. O. Syn.—Strīdēns, crĕpĭtāns, sŏnōrŭs, ārgūtŭs. Phr.—Trăhūnt strīdēntĭă plaūstră. Fāx lăcrĭmōsō strīdŭlă fūmō.

Strīngŏ, ĭs, strīnxī, strīctūm, ĕrĕ. *To bind, to press together.* Syn.—Cōnstrīngŏ, āstrīngŏ, lĭgŏ, vīncĭŏ, prĕmŏ, cōmprĭmŏ, cŏārctŏ. *To draw forth.* Syn.—Dīstrīngŏ, ēdūcŏ, nūdŏ. *To wound slightly.* Syn.—Pērstrīngŏ, lǣdŏ, tāngŏ. *To gather.* Syn.—Cārpŏ, dēcērpŏ, lĕgŏ, cōllĭgŏ.

Strīx, ĭgĭs. f. *The owl.* (*See Appendix under list of Birds.*)

Strŏphă, ǣ. f. *Part of the chorus.* Syn.—Strŏphē. *Ruse, deceit.* Syn.—Ārtēs, dŏlŭs, fāllācĭă, mēndācĭūm.

Strŭēs, ĭs. f. *Heap, pile.* Syn.—Cōngĕrĭēs, cŭmŭlŭs, āggĕr, ăcērvŭs.

Strŭŏ, ĭs, ūxī, ūctūm, ĕrĕ. *To heap together, to pile up, to accumulate.* Āltăquĕ cōngēstōs strūxīsse ād sīdĕră mōntēs. O. Syn.—Ēxstrŭŏ, cōngĕrŏ, ăcērvŏ, cŭmŭlŏ, āggĕrŏ. *To construct.* Syn.—Cōnstrŭŏ, ēxstrŭŏ, ǣdĭfĭcŏ. *To prepare.* Syn.—Părŏ, āppărŏ, īnstrŭŏ. *To meditate.* Syn.—Īnstrŭŏ, părŏ, mĕdĭtŏr, cōmpărŏ, mōlĭŏr.

Stŭdĕŏ, ēs, ŭī, ērĕ. *To desire, to be inclined towards.* Quī stŭdĕt ōptātām cūrsū cōntīngĕrĕ mētām. H. Syn.—Pĕtŏ, āppĕtŏ, cŭpĭŏ, ārdĕŏ, īncūmbŏ, ēxpōscŏ, ēxōptŏ. *To study.* Syn.—Dīscŏ. Phr.—Stŭdĭīs, ārtĭbŭs văcŏ, īndūlgĕŏ, īncūmbŏ. Mūsīs sērvĭŏ. Stŭdĭă, ārtēs cŏlŏ, dīscŏ. Mēntēm stŭdĭīs cŏlŏ. Pĭĕrĭīs īnvĭgĭlārĕ chŏrīs. Dētĭnĕō stŭdĭīs ănĭmūm. Stŭdĭīs frēnă rĕmīttĕrĕ.

Stŭdĭōsē. adv. *Carefully, zealously.* Syn.—Stŭdĭō, gnāvĭtĕr, dīlĭgēntĕr, strēnŭē, āttēntē, āccūrātē, sōllĭcĭtē, āssĭdŭē, ācrĭtĕr, ēnīxē, sēdŭlō, cŭpĭdē, ămāntĕr.

Stŭdĭōsŭs, ă, ūm. *Desirous.* Syn.—Ămāns, cŭpĭdŭs. *Favorable.* Syn.—Făvēns. *Studious.* Phr.—Stŭdĭīs āddīctŭs, dēdĭtŭs. Stŭdĭōrūm, ārtĭūm, ārtĭs cūltŏr, ămāns. Flōrēns stŭdĭīs.

Stŭdĭūm, ĭī. n. *Desire, inclination.* Syn.—Cŭpīdŏ, vŏlūntās. *Work.* Syn.—Lăbŏr. *Passion.* Syn.—Ămŏr. *Zeal.* Syn.—Sēdŭlĭtās, cūră. *Care.* Syn.—Cūră.

Stūltē. adv. *Foolishly.* Syn.—Īnēptē, stŏlĭdē, fătŭē, īnsĭpĭēntĕr.

Stūltĭtĭă, æ. f. *Folly.* Syn.—Īnsānĭă, āmēntĭă, dēmēntĭă, vēcōrdĭă, vēsānĭă. Phr.—Mēns stūltă, stŏlĭdă. Stūltă pēctŏră. Mălă mēns fŭrōrquĕ vēcōrs.

Stūltŭs, ă, ūm. *Foolish.* Syn.—Stŏlĭdŭs, īnēptŭs, īnsĭpĭēns, īnsūlsŭs, stŭpĭdŭs, fătŭŭs, āmēns, dēmēns, dēlīrŭs, īnsānŭs, mălĕsānŭs, bārdŭs, plūmbĕŭs, hĕbĕs. Phr.—Mēntĭs, rătĭōnĭs, cōnsĭlĭī ĭnŏps, cărēns. Ōbtūsūm īngĕnĭūm. Nōn sānæ mēntĭs. Hĕbĕtī pēctŏrĕ. Dēlīră mēntĕ. Cui ōbtūsă pēctŏră. Quæ mentem īnsānĭă mūtăt?

Stŭpĕfīŏ, īs, fāctŭs sūm, fĭĕrī. *To be astonished.* Syn.—Stŭpĕŏ, stŭpēscŏ, ōbstŭpēscŏ.

Stŭpĕŏ, ēs, ŭī, ērĕ. *To be immovable.* Syn.—Stō, tōrpĕŏ. *To be amazed, to wonder at.* Syn.—Ōbstŭpēscŏ, ōbstŭpĕfīŏ, mīrŏr, ādmīrŏr, hĭŏ. Phr.—Stŭpĕfāctŭs, āttŏnĭtŭs mănĕŏ, hærĕŏ. Stŭpēt īnscĭă tūrbă. Prōdĭgĭūm mīrātă nŏvūm. Hīc stŭpēt āttŏnĭtŭs rōstrīs. Ōbstŭpŭērĕ sĭlēntēs.

Stŭpĭdŭs, ă, ūm. *Astonished, amazed.* Syn.—Stŭpĕfāctŭs, stŭpēns. *Stupid.* Syn.—Bārdŭs, hĕbĕs, stŏlĭdŭs.

Stŭpŏr, ōrĭs. m. *Languor, torpor.* Syn.—Tōrpŏr. *Amazement, fright.* Syn.—Tērrŏr, păvŏr, fōrmīdŏ, mĕtŭs. *Stupidity.* Syn.—Stūltĭtĭă.

Stūrnŭs, ī. m. *A starling.* (*See Appendix under list of Birds.*)

Stȳlŭs, ī. m. *Point.* Syn.—Ăcūmĕn, cūspĭs. *Stylus, instrument for writing.* Syn.—Grăphĭūm, călămŭs, ărūndŏ, pēnnă. Fig.—*Manner of writing, style.* Syn.—Dīcēndī, scrībēndī gĕnŭs, cŏlŏr, fōrmă, mŏdŭs, rătĭŏ.

Suādĕŏ, ēs, sī, sūm, ērĕ. *To counsel, to advise.* Nōx ĕt ămōr vīnūmquĕ nĭhĭl mŏdĕrābĭlĕ suādēnt. O. Syn.—Hōrtŏr, īndūcŏ, īncĭtŏ, īmpēllŏ, īnvītŏ. Phr.—Aūctŏr sūm. Quĭd făcĭām suādĕ? Ān mĕlĭūs quĭd hăbēs suādērĕ. Nĕfās suāsĭt ĕgēstās. Sōmnōs nōx hūmĭdă suādĕt.

Suāsŏr, ōrĭs. m. *One who counsels, an adviser.* Syn.—Aūctŏr, hōrtātŏr, īmpūlsŏr.

Suāvĭs, ĭs, ĕ. *Sweet to the taste.* Syn.—Dūlcĭs. *Sweet-smelling.* Syn.—Dūlcĭs, frăgrāns, ŏdōrŭs. Fig.—*Sweet, agreeable.* Syn.—Dūlcĭs, blāndŭs, ămœnŭs, grātŭs, āccēptŭs, jūcūndŭs, lætŭs, bĕnīgnŭs.

Suāvĭtĕr. adv. *Sweetly.* Syn.—Suāvĕ, dūlcĕ.

Sŭb. prep. *Under.* Syn.—Sūbtĕr. *Within.* Syn.—Sūbtĕr, ĭn, īntrā. *In the neighborhood of.* Syn.—Cīrcā, cīrcĭtĕr.

Sūbdŏ, ĭs, dĭdī, dĭtūm, ĕrĕ. *To place under.* Syn.—Sūbjĭcĭŏ, sūppōnŏ. *To substitute.* Syn.—Sūffĭcĭŏ, sūppōnŏ, sūbstĭtŭŏ.

Sūbdŏlŭs, ă, ūm. *Deceitful.* Syn.—Āstūtŭs, dŏlōsŭs, cāllĭdŭs, fāllāx, văfĕr.

Sūbdūcŏ, ĭs, dūxī, dūctūm, ĕrĕ. *To draw out.* Syn.—Sūbtrăhŏ, aūfĕrŏ, tōllŏ, rĕmŏvĕŏ. *To get rid of.* Syn.—Sūbtrăhŏ, ērĭpĭŏ, dēmŏ, ădĭmŏ, tōllŏ.

Sŭbĕŏ, īs, īvī & ĭī, ĭtūm, īrĕ. *To go underneath.* Syn.—Sūbjĭcĭŏr, sūccēdŏ. *To enter.* Syn.—Īngrĕdĭŏr, īntrŏ, pĕnĕtrŏ, pērmĕŏ, pērvādŏ. *To approach.* Syn.—Ădĕŏ, āccēdŏ, prŏpīnquŏ. *To creep on one unawares, to approach insensibly.* Syn.—Ōbrēpŏ, ādrēpŏ, īnsĭnŭŏ. *To undertake.* Syn.—Āggrĕdĭŏr, ŏbĕŏ, sūscĭpĭŏ. *To suffer.* Syn.—Fĕrŏ, tŏlĕrŏ, pătĭŏr.

Sŭbĭgŏ, ĭs, ēgī, āctūm, ĕrĕ. *To push forward, to direct.* Īpsĕ rătēm cōntō sŭbĭgĭt. V. Syn.—Ăgŏ, īmpēllŏ. *To turn the soil, to labor.* Syn.—Vērtŏ, īnvērtŏ, vērsŏ, ēxērcĕŏ. *To subdue.* Syn.—Vīncŏ, dŏmŏ, sūbjĭcĭŏ. *To force.* Syn.—Cōgŏ.

Sŭbĭtō. adv. *Suddenly.* Syn.—Stătīm, rĕpēntĕ, brĕvī. *See Statim, Brevi.*

Sūbjĭcĭŏ, ĭs, jēcī, jēctūm, ĕrĕ. *To place beneath.* Rāmĕă cōstĭs Sūbjĭcĭūnt frāgmēntă. V. Syn.—Sūbdŏ, sūppōnŏ, sūbstērnŏ, sŭbĭcĭŏ. Fig.—*To subdue.* Syn.—Sūbdŏ, sŭbĭgŏ, dŏmŏ, frēnŏ, sūbmīttŏ, dēbēllŏ. *To present.* Syn.—Ōbjĭcĭŏ, ēxpōnŏ. *To furnish, to suggest.* Syn.—Sūggĕrŏ, āffĕrŏ, præbĕŏ.

Sūblĕvŏ, ās, āvī, ātūm, ārĕ. *To raise up.* Cūnctāntēs sŏcĭōs, ēt tērrā sūblĕvăt īpsūm. V. Syn.—Lĕvŏ, ērĭgŏ. Fig.—*To help.* Syn.—Jŭvŏ, ādjŭvŏ.

Sūblīmĕ. adv. *On high.* Syn.—Āltē, sūrsūm. Phr.—Īn sūblīmĕ, ĭn āltūm.

Sūblīmĭs, ĭs, ĕ. *High, elevated.* Īpsă Păphōn sūblīmĭs ăbĭt. V. Syn.—Āltŭs, ēxcēlsŭs, ērēctŭs. Fig.—*Sublime, lofty, noble.* Syn.—Āltŭs, ēxcēlsŭs, sūmmŭs, grāndĭs, ēlātŭs.

Sūbmērgŏ, ĭs, sī, sūm, ĕrĕ. *To submerge.* Īpsōs pŏtŭīt sūbmērgĕrĕ pōntō. V. Syn.—Mērgŏ, dēmērgŏ, īmmērgŏ. *See Mergo.*

Sūbmīssē. adv. *Submissively, humbly.* Syn.—Sūpplĭcĭtĕr, dēmīssē.

Sūbmīttŏ, ĭs, mīsī, mīssūm, ĕrĕ. *To place beneath.* Syn.—Sūbdŏ, sūbjĭcĭŏ, sūppōnŏ. *To lower.* Syn.—Dēmīttŏ. *To furnish.* Syn.—Mĭnīstrŏ, sūffĭcĭŏ, fūndŏ, prǣbĕŏ. Fig.—*To submit.* Syn.—Sūbjĭcĭŏ, sūbdŏ.

Sūbmŏvĕŏ, ēs, mōvī, mōtūm, ērĕ. *To drive away.* Aūdĭīt, ēt sī quēm tēllūs ēxtrēmă rĕfūsō Sūbmŏvĕt Ōcĕănō. V. Syn.—Rĕmŏvĕŏ, āmŏvĕŏ, dēpēllŏ, ārcĕŏ.

Sūbōrnŏ, ās, āvī, ātūm, ārĕ. *To deceive by flattery.* Syn.—Instrŭŏ, părŏ. *To swear falsely.* Syn.—Cōrrūmpŏ, sōllĭcĭtŏ.

Sūbrēpŏ, ĭs, sī, tūm, ĕrĕ. *To drag oneself along, to creep along stealthily.* Jām sūbrēpĭt ĭnērs ǣtās nĕc ămārĕ dĕcēbĭt. Tib. Syn.—Īrrēpŏ, ōbrēpŏ, sūblābŏr, īllābŏr, īnsĭnŭŏ.

Sūbrīdĕŏ, ēs, sī, sūm, ērĕ. *To smile upon.* Syn.—Ārrīdĕŏ, rīdĕŏ. Phr.—Līmīs sūbrīsĭt ŏcēllīs. Sūbrīsĭt mōllĕ pŭēllă. Sūbrīsī mŏdĭcē lĕvīquĕ nūtū.

Sūbrĭpĭŏ, ĭs, ŭī, ēptūm, ĕrĕ. *To make away with, to bear away.* Syn.—Răpĭŏ, fūrŏr, sūbdūcŏ. *To conceal.* Syn.—Tĕgŏ.

Sūbscrībŏ, ĭs, psī, ptūm, ĕrĕ. *To sign, to subscribe.* Syn.—Sūbsīgnŏ. *To favor.* Syn.—Ānnŭŏ, cōncēdŏ, āssēntĭŏr, prŏbŏ, cōmprŏbŏ, āpprŏbŏ.

Sūbsĭdĭūm. ĭī. n. *Aid, assistance.* Sūbsĭdĭō Trōjǣ tēr dēnīs nāvĭbūs ībăt. V. Syn.—Aūxĭlĭūm, jŭvāmĕn, sūppĕtĭǣ. *Reserve corps.* Syn.—Prǣsĭdĭūm.

Sūbsīdŏ, ĭs, sēdī, sēssūm, ĕrĕ. *To subside.* Syn.—Dēsīdŏ, cōnsīdŏ, sīdŏ. Fig.—*To grow calm.* Syn.—Quĭēscŏ, pōnŏ.

Sūbsīstŏ, ĭs, tĭtī, tĭtūm, ĕrĕ. *To stop, to halt.* Tăcĭtā rĕflŭēns ĭtă sūbstĭtĭt ūndā Tībrĭs. V. Syn.—Sīstŏ, cōnsīstŏ, rĕsīstŏ, stō.

Sūbstērnŏ, ĭs, strāvī, strātūm, ĕrĕ. *To extend, to place beneath.* Syn.—Sūppōnŏ, sūbjĭcĭŏ, stērnŏ.

Sūbstĭtŭŏ, ĭs, ŭī, ūtūm, ĕrĕ. *To place under.* Syn.—Sūbjĭcĭŏ, ōbjĭcĭŏ, sūppōnŏ. *To substitute.* Syn.—Sūbdŏ, sūppōnŏ, sūffĭcĭŏ.

Sūbsūm, ĕs, fŭī, ēssĕ. *To be near, to be present.* Syn.—Ādsūm, sūccūrrŏ, ōbvērsŏr.

Sūbtērfŭgĭŏ, ĭs, fūgī, ĭtūm, ĕrĕ. *To avoid.* Syn.—Vītŏ, ēvītŏ, dēclīnŏ, dētrēctŏ, fŭgĭŏ, ēffŭgĭŏ.

Sūbtērlābŏr, ĕrĭs, psūs sūm, ī. *To flow under.* Syn.—Sūblābŏr, sūbtērflŭŏ, sūbtērmĕŏ.

Sūbtēxŏ, ĭs, ŭī, xtūm, ĕrĕ. *To weave.* Syn.—Īntēxŏ, sūbnēctŏ, īnnēctŏ, jūngŏ. *To cover.* Syn.—Ŏpĕrĭŏ, tĕgŏ, ōbdūcŏ, vēlŏ, cōndŏ, ābscōndŏ. *To place before.* Syn.—Ōbdūcŏ, īndūcŏ.

Sūbtīlĭs, ĭs, ĕ. *Subtile, delicate, minute.* Syn.—Tĕnŭĭs, grăcĭlĭs, mĭnūtŭs. *Fine, ingenious.* Syn.—Ăcĕr, ăcūtŭs, săgāx, cāllĭdŭs, sōlērs.

Sūbtīlĭtĕr. adv. *Skilfully, ingeniously.* Syn.—Ăcutē, sōlērtĕr, cāllĭdē.

Sūbtrăhŏ, ĭs, trāxī, trāctūm, ĕrĕ. *To take away from.* Sūbtrăhĭtūr prēssō mōllĭs ărēnă pĕdĕ. Syn.—Sūbdūcŏ, sūbrĭpĭŏ, răpĭŏ, ērĭpĭŏ, aūfĕrŏ.

Sŭbūrbānŭs, ă, ūm. *Close to a city, suburban.* Phr.—Ūrbī vīcīnŭs, prŏpĭŏr. *Dweller in the suburbs.* Syn.—Sūmmœnĭānŭs. Phr.—Sŭbūrbānī dāns mĭhĭ mūnŭs ĭdēm.

Sūccēdŏ, ĭs, cēssī, cēssūm, ĕrĕ. *To go under, to enter.* Nōstrīs sūccēdĕ pĕnātĭbŭs, hōspĕs. V. Syn.—Sŭbĕŏ, īngrĕdĭŏr. *To approach.* Syn.—Ăccēdŏ, sŭbĕŏ. *To succeed, to take the place of.* Syn.—Ĕxcĭpĭŏ, sŭbĕŏ, sūffĭcĭŏr, sūbstĭtŭŏr.

Sūccēssŭs, ūs. m. *Success.* Syn.—Ĕxĭtŭs, ēvēntŭs, ēvēntă (n. pl.). Phr.—Faūstă, prōspĕră sōrs, fōrtūnă. Sĕcūndŭs, fōrtūnātŭs cāsŭs, ēxĭtŭs. Faūstă rērūm ēvēntă. Sūccēssūque ācrĭŏr īpsō. Sūccēssū cædĭs ŏvāns.

Sūccĭdŭŭs, ă, ūm. *That which falls easily.* Syn.—Lăbāns, tĭtŭbāns, cădēns.

Sūccrēscŏ, ĭs, crēvī, crētūm, ĕrĕ. *To increase.* Syn.—Crēscŏ, aūgĕŏr.

Sūccūmbŏ, ĭs, cŭbŭī, cŭbĭtūm, ĕrĕ. *To fall beneath.* Vīctă pŏtēst flēxō sūccŭbŭīssĕ gĕnū. O. Syn.—Sūccĭdŏ, cădŏ, prōcĭdŏ. *To yield to.* Syn.—Cēdŏ, vīncŏr, frāngŏr. Phr.—Sūccūmbĕrĕ nēscĭă sōmnō Lūmĭnă. Vīrtūtēm tūrbæ sūccūmbĕrĕ vīdĭt. Sūccūmbĕrĕ fātĭs.

Sūccŭtĭŏ, ĭs, cūssī, cūssūm, ĕrĕ. *To shake.* Syn.—Cōncŭtĭŏ, quătĭŏ, quāssŏ.

Sŭdēs, ĭs. f. *Stake, sharpened piece of wood.* Syn.—Trūncŭs, pālŭs, stīpĕs.

Sūdŏ, ās, āvī, ātūm, ārĕ. *To sweat.* Mūltă tŭlīt fēcītquĕ pŭēr, sūdāvĭt ĕt ālsĭt. H. Phr.—Sūdōrēm fūndŏ, mīttŏ. Sūdōrĕ mānŏ, mădĕŏ, flŭŏ. Sūdŏr ĭt, mānăt, flŭĭt. Sūdŏr flŭĭt pēr mēmbră, pĕr ārtūs, cōrpŏrĕ tōtō. Sālsæquĕ flŭūnt dē cōrpŏrĕ gūttæ. Gĕlĭdūs tōtō mānābāt cōrpŏrĕ sūdŏr. Flŭĭt tōtō dē cōrpŏrĕ sūdŏr. Pŭēr sūdāvĭt ĭn ārmīs. Fig.—*To be moist.* Syn.—

Stīllŏ, mānŏ, mădĕŏ. *To distil from.* Syn.—Stīllŏ, fūndŏ. *To bear a heavy burden, labor.* Syn.—Dēsūdŏ, ēxsūdŏ, pērfĕrŏ, tŏlĕrŏ.

Sūdŏr, ōrĭs. m. *Sweat.* Phr.—Sūdōrĭs hūmŏr, gūttæ, rōs, lătēx. Sūdātŭs hūmŏr. Flŭēns dē cōrpŏrĕ tōtō. Vĭdĕt ēxhaūstōs sūdōrĭbŭs ārtūs. Fig.—*Work.* Syn.—Lăbŏr, ŏpŭs.

Sūffĕrŏ, fērs, fērrĕ. *To sustain, to bear.* Cūstōdēs sūffērrĕ vălēnt. V. Syn.—Sūstĭnĕŏ, fĕrŏ, pērfĕrŏ, pătĭŏr.

Sūffĭcĭŏ, ĭs, fēcī, fēctūm, ĕrĕ. *To be able.* Syn.—Vălĕŏ, pōssūm. Phr.—Sătĭs sūm. Săt ēst. Ăbūnde ēst. *To present oneself, to offer oneself.* Syn.—Sūccūrrŏ, ōccūrrŏ, sūppĕtŏ. *To furnish.* Syn.—Præbĕŏ, sūppĕdĭtŏ, mĭnīstrŏ, sūggĕrŏ, āffĕrŏ. *To substitute.* Syn.—Sūbstĭtŭŏ.

Sūffōcŏ, ās, āvī, ātūm, ārĕ. *To suffocate, to stifle.* Sūffōcēnt ănĭmām dīră vĕnēnă sŭām. O. Syn.—Præfōcŏ, ēlīdŏ, strāngŭlŏ, āngŏ. Phr.—Ănĭmām īntērclūdŏ. Prēssīs ēlīdĕrĕ faūcĭbŭs. Sīlvă prĕmīt faūcēs.

Sūffrāgĭūm, ĭī. n. *Vote, suffrage.* Nōn ĕgŏ vēntōsæ plēbīs sūffrāgĭă vēnŏr. H. Phr.—Sūffrāgĭūm fērrĕ, ăgĕrĕ. Īnīre īn cāmpūm.

Sūffūndŏ, ĭs, fūdī, fūsūm, ĕrĕ. *To spread out.* Ēt tĕpĭdō sūffūndīt lūmĭnă rōrĕ. O. Syn.—Īnfūndŏ, pērfūndŏ, īnspērgŏ, spārgŏ, āspērgŏ, īrrōrŏ. *To cover.* Syn.—Tĕgŏ, ŏpĕrĭŏ, ābscōndŏ.

Sūggĕrŏ, ĭs, gēssī, gēstūm, ĕrĕ. *To carry, place beneath.* Syn.—Sūbjĭcĭŏ, sūppōnŏ, sūbdŏ. *To furnish.* Syn.—Præbĕŏ, mĭnīstrŏ, sūppĕdĭtŏ, sūffĭcĭŏ. *To substitute.* Syn.—Sūbjĭcĭŏ, sūbstĭtŭŏ.

Sūggēstūm, ī. n. *Elevation, height, mound.* Syn.—Ăpēx, fāstīgĭūm.

Sūlcŏ, ās, āvī, ātūm, ārĕ. *To plow.* Prēssō vōmĕrĕ sūlcăt hŭmūm. O. Syn.—Prōscīndŏ. Phr.—Sūlcōs īnfīndŏ, īmprĭmŏ, īnfīgŏ, īnscrībŏ. Tēllūrēm tĕnŭī sūspēndĕrĕ sūlcō. Sūlcum īmprēssō pătĕfēcĭt ărātrō. Fig.—Sūlcăt mărĭa āltă cărīnă. Sūlcārĕ cŭtēm rūgīs.

Sūlcŭs, ī. m. *Furrow.* Hērbăquĕ quæ lătŭīt cĕrĕālĭbŭs ōbrŭtă sūlcīs. O. Syn. Phr.—Sūlcī cūlmĭnă, āggĕrēs. Vōmĕrĕ dūctăs. Cūm sūlcōs aēquānt sătă. Plāntās dēpŏsŭīt sūlcīs. Lŏcūm cōnclūdĕrĕ sūlcō. *Scar.* Syn.—Cĭcātrīx.

Sūlphŭr, ŭrĭs. n. *Sulphur.* Phr.—Sūlphŭrĭs īgnĭs, ŏdŏr, aūră. Sūlphŭrĕă vīs. Cærŭlĕī pūrō dē sūlphŭrĕ fūmī. *Match.* Syn.—Sūlphŭrātūm.

Sūm, ĕs, fŭī, ēssĕ. *To be.* Quō pūlchrĭŏr āltĕr Nōn fŭīt Aēnĕădūm. V. Syn.—Ēxsīstŏ, ēxstŏ, vīvŏ. *To dwell.* Syn.—Hăbĭtŏ, dēgŏ, mănĕŏ, mŏrŏr, vērsŏr.

Sūmmātīm. adv. *On the whole, to be brief.* Syn.—Lĕvĭtĕr, ŏbĭtĕr, strīctīm.

Sūmmŭs, ă, ūm. *The highest, the top.* Hī sūmmo īn flūctū pēndēnt. V. Syn.—Āltīssĭmŭs, sūblīmĭs, sŭprēmŭs. Phr.—Īmīs pērmīscēt sūmmă. Sūmmĕ dĕūm rēctŏr. *The last.* Syn.—Ūltĭmŭs, pōstrēmŭs, nŏvīssĭmŭs. *Great, glorious.* Syn.—Nōbĭlĭs, īnclўtŭs, ēgrĕgĭŭs, dĕcōrŭs, pūlchĕr, clārŭs.

Sūmŏ, ĭs, sūmpsī, sūmptūm, ĕrĕ. *To take.* Sūmĕrēt āgrēstēm pŏsĭtō dĭădēmătĕ fālcēm. J. Syn.—Āssūmŏ, căpĭŏ, prĕhēndŏ, āccĭpĭŏ. Phr.—Sūmĕre ăquam ē flŭvĭō. Paūlātīm sūmĕrĕ fōrmām. *To assume, to don.* Syn.—Căpĭŏ, āssūmŏ, īndŭŏ. *To use, to employ.* Syn.—Īnsūmŏ, īmpēndŏ, ădhĭbĕŏ. *To undertake.* Syn.—Sūscĭpĭŏ, īngrĕdĭŏr, ĭnĕŏ.

Sūmptŭōsē. adv. *Magnificently, sumptuously.* Syn.—Laūtē, māgnĭfĭcē, splēndĭdē, sŭpērbē.

Sūmptŭōsŭs, ă, ūm. *Sumptuous, splendid.* Syn.—Prĕtĭōsŭs, dīvĕs, māgnĭfĭcŭs, splēndĭdŭs, sŭpērbŭs.

Sūmptŭs, ūs. m. *Expense.* Syn.—Īmpēnsă, īmpēndĭūm. Phr.—Ēx rē sūmptūs præbētŭr ăvītā. Sūmptūm īnsūmĕrĕ, făcĕrĕ. Sūmptūm ēxērcērĕ.

Sŭpĕr. prep. *Above, upon.* Syn.— Sŭprā, ĭn. *In regard to.* Syn.—Dē. *Because of.* Syn.—Prōptĕr, ŏb. *Beyond (with acc.).* Syn.—Ūltrā.

Sŭpĕrātŏr, ōrĭs. m. *Conqueror.* Syn.—Dŏmĭtŏr, vĭctŏr, dēbēllātŏr.

Sŭpērbē. adv. *Proudly, haughtily.* Syn.—Ēlātē, ārrŏgāntĕr. *Luxuriously.* Syn.—Laūtē, splēndĭdē, māgnĭfĭcē.

Sŭpērbĭă, æ. f. *Pride.* Nōn ĕă vīs ănĭmō, nēc tāntă sŭpērbĭă vĭctīs. V. Syn.—Fāstŭs, ănĭmī (ōrūm), spīrĭtŭs, fīdūcĭă, ārrŏgāntĭă, fāstīdĭă (ōrūm). Phr.—Sŭpērbŭs, vēntōsŭs tŭmŏr. Vēsānĭă fāstūs. Mēntĭs ēlātæ tŭmŏr. Tŭmĭdæ fāstīdĭă mēntĭs. Frēnī, vērī īmpătĭēns. Dŏmĭnæ fāstīdĭă Rōmæ. Spīrĭtūs māgnōs fŭgĕ.

Sŭpērbĭŏ, īs, īvī & ĭī, īrĕ. *To be proud.* Ūt nōstrīs tŭmĕfāctă sŭpērbĭăt Ūmbrĭă lĭbrīs. Prop. Syn.—Ēffĕrŏr, glōrĭŏr, īnsŏlēscŏ, tŭmĕŏ, īntŭmĕŏ, tūrgĕŏ. Phr.—Ănĭmō, ănĭmīs ēffĕrŏr. Fāstū pēctŏră, cōrdă tŭmēnt. Dōtēs ōstēntārĕ sŭās. Ēxĭmĭūm jāctārĕ gĕnŭs. Vērbīs īmmŏdĭcīs, sŭpērbīs sē ēxtōllĕrĕ. Căpūt cœlō ēffērt, ērĭgĭt. Vānă tŭmēntēs.

Sŭpērbŭs, ă, ūm. *Proud, haughty.* Ăchīllēæ fāstūs jŭvĕnēmquĕ sŭpērbūm (tulimus). V. Syn.—Ārrŏgāns, ēlātŭs, fĕrōx, tŭmēns, īnsŏlēns, fāstōsŭs, sūblīmĭs. Phr.—Īnānī fāstū tŭmēns. Vānō tŭmĭdŭs præcōrdĭă fāstū. Ănĭmīs ēlātŭs sŭpērbīs. Quēm sŭpērbĭă dēmēns īnflăt. Tūrgĭdă cōrdă gĕrēns. Ēlātā frōntĕ sŭpērbŭs. Fāstū tūrgĭdŭs āltō. Nĭmĭūm gaūdēns pŏpŭlārĭbŭs aūrĭs. Fōrtūnā dūlcī ēbrĭŭs. *Disdainful.* Syn.—Fāstīdĭōsŭs, cōntēmptŏr, spērnāx. *Cruel, tyrannical.* Syn.—Crūdēlĭs, ĭnīquŭs, tўrānnŭs. *Glorious.* Syn.—Pūlchĕr, glōrĭōsŭs, nōbĭlĭs, dĕcōrŭs, ēgrĕgĭŭs, clārŭs. *Rich, magnificent.* Syn.—Splēndĭdŭs, māgnĭfĭcŭs, laūtŭs, dīvĕs, ŏpŭlēntŭs, rēgālĭs.

Sŭpērcĭlĭūm, ĭī. n. *Eye-brow.* Fig.—*Severity, gravity.* Syn.—Sĕvērĭtās, tētrĭcĭtās, grăvĭtās, āspĕrĭtās, trīstĭtĭă, dūrĭtĭēs. Phr.—Vūltŭs sĕvērŭs, grăvĭs. Rĭgĭdī vūltūs. Dūrīs tōrvă sŭpērcĭlĭīs. Dēmĕ sŭpērcĭlĭō nūbēm. *Will, authority.* Syn.—Nūtŭs, īmpĕrĭūm, vŏlūntās.

Sŭpĕrēmĭnĕō, ēs, ŭī, ērĕ. *To surpass, to be above.* Vīctōrquĕ vĭrōs sŭpĕrēmĭnĕt ōmnēs. V. Syn.—Sŭpĕrō, ēxsŭpĕrō. Phr.—Căpŭt tōllō, āttōllō. Sēd cūnctīs āltĭŏr ībăt. Nĭtēt sŭpĕr āltĭŏr ōmnēs.

Sŭpĕrī, ōrūm. m. *Gods, dwellers of heaven.* Syn.—Dĭī, Dī, dīvī, cœlĭcŏlæ, cœlĭtēs, nūmĭnă. Phr.—Rēx sŭpĕrōrūm. Pār sŭpĕrīs. Sŭpĕrōs prĕcārī. Plēbs sŭpĕrūm.

Sŭpĕrīmpōnō, ĭs, ŏsŭī, ŏsĭtūm, ĕrĕ. *To place above.* Syn.—Sŭpērpōnō, sŭpĕrīnjĭcĭō, sŭpērjăcĭō, sŭpĕrīngĕrō.

Sŭpērnŭs, ă, ūm. *Celestial, divine.* Syn.—Sŭpĕrŭs, dīvīnŭs, cœlēstĭs.

Sŭpĕrō, ās, āvī, ātūm, ārĕ. *To pass over.* Syn.—Trānscēndō, trājĭcĭō, sŭpērgrĕdĭŏr, prætērvĕhŏr. *To surpass.* Syn.—Ēxsŭpĕrō, præstō, vīncō, ēxcēllō, præcēllō, praĕēō, prævērtō, prægrĕdĭŏr, āntĕcēllō. Phr.—Sūm præstāntĭŏr. *To conquer.* Syn.—Vīncō. *To abound in.* Syn.—Ăbūndō, rĕdūndō, lūxŭrĭō. *To survive.* Syn.—Sŭpērsūm, ēxīstō.

Sŭpērsĕdĕō, ēs, sēdī, ērĕ. *To desist, to cease.* Syn.—Cēssō, dēsīstō, ābstĭnĕō, ŏmīttō, prætĕrĕō.

Sŭpērstĕs, ĭtĭs. adj. *Safe, sound, surviving.* Syn.—Sālvŭs, sōspĕs, īncŏlŭmĭs.

Sŭpērstĭtĭō, ōnĭs. f. *Superstition.* Phr.—Vānă, ĭnānĭs, fālsă rĕllĭgĭō. Vānī rītūs. Stūltæ rēllīgĭōnĭs ămŏr. Crēdŭlă cōrdă fătīgāns. Sĭbĭ quæ vărĭīs fīnxĭt sĭmŭlācră fĭgūrīs.

Sŭpērsūm, ĕs, sŭpērfŭī, ēssĕ. *To come forth from.* Syn.—Ēxstō, ēxsīstō, ēmĭnĕō. *To remain.* Syn.—Sŭpĕrō, rēstō, ēxstō, mănĕō. Phr.—Sūm rĕlĭquŭs. Nāmquĕ sŭpēr tĭbi ĕrūnt. *To survive.* Syn.—Sŭpĕrō. *To be in abundance.* Syn.—Ăbūndō, sŭpĕrō, lūxŭrĭō, āffluō.

Sŭpĕrŭs, ă, ūm. *From on high.* Syn.—Sŭpērnŭs. *Heavenly.* Syn.—Aēthĕrĕŭs, cœlēstĭs.

Sŭpērvăcŭŭs, ă, ūm. *Superfluous, redundant.* Syn.—Sŭpērvăcānĕŭs, vānŭs, ĭnānĭs, ĭnūtĭlĭs.

Sŭpīnŭs, ă, ūm. *Turned over, prostrate.* Syn.—Sŭpīnātŭs, rĕsŭpīnŭs, rĕsŭpīnātŭs, strātŭs, prōstrātŭs, rĕcūmbēns. *Bent over.* Syn.—Prōnŭs. *Sloping.* Syn.—Dēclīvĭs, prōclīvĭs, ācclīvĭs, clīvōsŭs. *Indolent.* Syn.—Mōllĭs, sēgnĭs, īgnāvŭs, ĭnērs. *Backwards, going back.* Syn.—Rĕflŭŭs, rĕflŭēns, rĕcūrrēns.

Sūppĕdĭtŏ, ās, āvī, ātūm, ārĕ. *To furnish.* Syn.—Mĭnīstrŏ, præbĕŏ, sūffĭcĭŏ, sūggĕrŏ, dō. *To be sufficient, to be in abundance.* Syn.—Sūffĭcĭŏ, sūppĕtŏ.

Sūppĕtŏ, ĭs, ĕrĕ. *To be present.* Syn.—Ādsūm. *To suffice.* Syn.—Sūffĭcĭŏ, sūppĕdĭtŏ, sŭpērsūm. Phr.—Sătĭs sūm. Sūppĕtĭt mĭhĭ lŭcrūm.

Sūpplĕŏ, ēs, ēvī, ētūm, ērĕ. *To complete.* Syn.—Ădīmplĕŏ, cōmplĕŏ. *To repare.* Syn.—Rĕpărŏ, rĕsārcĭŏ.

Sūpplēx, ĭcĭs. adj. *Suppliant.* Īlle hŭmĭlĭs sūpplēxque ŏcŭlōs dēxtrāmquĕ prĕcāntēm Prōtēndēns. V. Syn.—Sūbmīssŭs, ābjēctŭs, prōstrātŭs, jăcēns, ōrāns, rŏgāns. Phr.—Sĭmĭlĭs prĕcāntī. Tū mūnĕră sūpplēx Tēndĕ, pĕtēns pācēm.

Sūpplĭcĭtĕr. adv. *Suppliantly.* Syn.—Ābjēctē, dēmīssē. Phr.—Sūpplĭcĕ vōcĕ, sūpplĭcĭbŭs vōcĭbŭs. Ārām sūpplĭcĭtēr vĕnĕrāns.

Sūpplĭcĭūm, ĭī. n. *Prayer.* Syn.—Prĕcēs. *Punishment.* Syn.—Crŭcĭātŭs, pœnă, tōrmēntūm. Phr.—Gĕnūs mĭsĕrābĭlĕ pœnă. Scĕlĕrūm vīndēx. Pœnārūm gĕnŭs ōmnĕ. Sævī crŭcĭātūs hōrrŏr. Ād sūpplĭcĭūm dēdĕrĕ. Scĕlĕrĭs sūpplĭcĭum ēxērcēnt cūræ.

Sūpplĭcŏ, ās, āvī, ātūm, ārĕ. *To beg, to beseech.* Ārĭdă nēc plŭvĭō sūpplĭcăt hērbă Jŏvī. Tib. Syn.—Ōbsĕcrŏ, ōrŏ, ōbtēstŏr, prĕcŏr. Phr.—Sūpplēx āccēdŏ. Sūpplĭcĭtĕr rŏgŏ. Supplĭcĕ vōcĕ rŏgăt.

Sūppōnŏ, ĭs, pŏsŭī, ĭtūm, ĕrĕ. *To place above, upon.* Nĕque āntĕ Fālcēm mātūrĭs quīsquām sūppōnăt ărīstīs. V. Syn.—Sūbjĭcĭŏ, sūbmĭttŏ. Phr.—Cōllă jŭgō taūrī sūppōnūnt. Lāssō sūppōnĕrĕ brāchĭă mēntō. Sūppōnūnt ălĭī cūltrōs. *To substitute.* Syn.—Sūbstĭtŭŏ. *To submit.* Syn.—Sūbmīttŏ.

Sūpprĭmŏ, ĭs, prēssī, prēssūm, ĕrĕ. *To repress, to hold back.* Sūpprĭmĭt ēxtēmplō vōcēm. O. Syn.—Cŏhĭbĕŏ, cŏērcĕŏ, rĕtĭnĕŏ, cōntĭnĕŏ.

Sŭprā. prep. *Above.* Syn.—Sŭpĕr. *Beyond.* Syn.—Ūltrā. (*As an adverb*) *Above, beyond.* Syn.—Sŭpĕr, īnsŭpĕr, dēsŭpĕr.

Sŭprēmă, ōrūm. n. *The last rites.* Syn.—Fūnĕră, ēxsĕquĭæ.

Sŭprēmŭs, ă, ūm. *Last.* Syn.—Ēxtrēmŭs, nŏvīssĭmŭs, ūltĭmŭs. Fig.—*Greatest, extreme.* Syn.—Māxĭmŭs, īngēns.

Sūrcŭlŭs, ī. m. *Shoot, scion, sprig.* Nēc sūrcŭlūs īdēm Crūstŭmĭīs Sўrĭīsquĕ pўrīs. V. Syn.—Vīrgūltūm, pālmĕs, frūtēx.

Sūrdŭs, ă, ūm. *Deaf.* Syn.—Nōn sēntĭēns, aūdĭēns. Fig.—*Insensible, inexorable.* Syn.—Īmmītĭs, īnclēmēns, īnsēnsĭbĭlĭs. Phr.—

Sūrdōs īn tŭă vōtă dĕōs. Nēscĭă mānsuēscĕrĕ cōrdă. *Unknown, obscure.* Syn.—Īgnōtŭs, ōbscūrŭs, īnglōrĭŭs.

Sūrgŏ, ĭs, rēxī, rēctūm, ĕrĕ. *To arise, to get up.* Ēxcūssērĕ mĕtūs sōmnūm cōntĕrrĭtă sūrgĭt. V. Syn.—Ēxsūrgŏ. Phr.—Lēctīs, strātīs sūrgŏ, ēxsūrgŏ, ēxsĭlĭŏ. Lēctūm, cŭbīlĕ līnquŏ, rĕlīnquŏ. Cōrrĭpĭŏ ē strātīs cōrpŭs. Mōllī fūrtīm dēcēdĕrĕ lēctō. Crŏcĕūm līnquēns Aūrōră cŭbīlĕ. Tēr sēse āttōllēns cŭbĭtōque īnnīxă lĕvāvĭt. *To stand up.* Syn.—Āssūrgŏ, cōnsūrgŏ, īnsūrgŏ. Phr.—Mē, cōrpŭs tōllŏ, lĕvŏ. Hŭmō mēmbră lĕvārĕ. Sūrgĭt hŭmō pīgrē. *To rise (speaking of the stars).* Syn.—Ŏrĭŏr, nāscŏr. *To be raised, to be elevated.* Syn.—Āssūrgŏ, cōnsūrgŏ, ēxsūrgŏ, tōllŏr, āttōllŏr, ērĭgŏr, crēscŏ.

Sūs, sŭĭs. m. *Hog, boar, pig.* Īmmūndī mĕmĭnērĕ sŭēs jāctārĕ mănīplōs. V. Syn.—Pōrcŭs, pōrcŭlŭs, pōrcēllŭs. Phr.—Fīĕt ĕnīm sŭbĭtō sūs hōrrĭdŭs. Glāndĕ sŭēs lætī rĕdĕūnt.

Sūscĭpĭŏ, ĭs, cēpī, cēptūm, ĕrĕ. *To hold, to gather together.* Sūscĭpĭūnt fămŭlæ cōllāpsăquĕ mēmbră Mārmŏrĕō rĕfĕrūnt thălămō. V. Syn.—Sūstĭnĕŏ, āccĭpĭŏ. *To undertake, to enter upon.* Syn.—Īncĭpĭŏ, ĭnĕŏ, āggrĕdĭŏr, ădŏrĭŏr, ōrdĭŏr. Phr.—Nōbĭlĕ ŏpŭs mōlīrī. Nŏvōs āssūrgĕre ĭn aūsūs. Nŏvō tēntāt mōlīmĭnĕ vīrēs. Mūnĕră Mārtĭs Sūscĭpĕrĕ. *To take, to gather.* Syn.—Ēxcĭpĭŏ, rĕcĭpĭŏ, āccĭpĭŏ, cōllĭgŏ. *To admit, to receive.* Syn.—Cōncĭpĭŏ, pērcĭpĭŏ, cōntrăhŏ.

Sūscĭtŏ, ās, āvī, ātūm, ārĕ. *To raise, to arouse.* Syn.—Ēxcĭtŏ, āttōllŏ, ērĭgŏ. *To awaken.* Syn.—Ēxpērgēfăcĭŏ. *To excite.* Syn.—Ēxcĭtŏ, āccēndŏ.

Sūspēndŏ, ĭs, dī, sūm, ĕrĕ. *To suspend.* Ēnsēm cōllō sūspēndĭt ĕbūrnō. V. Phr.—Fūnĕ ĭn āltūm tōllŏ, ēffĕrŏ, ērĭgŏ. Hŭmĕrīs sūspēndĕrăt ārcūm. Tīgnīs nīdūm sūspēndăt hĭrūndŏ. Vŏlŭcrēm mălō sūspēndĭt ăb āltō. Hāmō sūspēndĕrĕ pīscēm. *To labor.* Phr.—Vōmĕrĕ, ărātrō sūspēnsō lĕvĭtĕr prōscīndĕrĕ.

Sūspĭcĭŏ, ĭs, pēxī, pēctūm, ĕrĕ. *To look up at.* Sūspĭcĭēns haūsĭt cœlūm mēntēmquĕ rĕcēpĭt. V. Syn.—Sūspēctŏ. Phr.—Ŏcŭlīs sūspēctāns sīdĕră. Sūrsūm āspĭcĭŏ. Ŏcŭlōs, lūmĭnă tōllŏ, āttōllŏ. Ād cœlūm, sīdĕră ērĭgŏ lūmĭnă. Fāstīgĭă sūspĭcĭt ūrbĭs. Ŏcŭlōs ād sīdĕră lætŭs Ēxtŭlĭt. Ōrăque īn cœlum ērĭgăt.

Sūspĭcŏr, ārĭs, ātŭs sūm, ārī. *To suspect, to doubt.* Syn.—Aūgŭrŏr, cōnjĭcĭŏ, ārbĭtrŏr, ŏpīnŏr.

Sūspīrĭūm, ĭī. n. *Breathing.* Syn.—Spīrĭtŭs. *Sigh, groan.* Syn.—Gĕmĭtŭs, sīngūltŭs, lūctŭs, lāmēntūm. Phr.—Sūspīrĭă lūctūs Præsāgă. Pēr nūllă trăhām sūspīrĭă sōmnōs.

Sūspīrŏ, ās, āvī, ātūm, ārĕ. *To sigh, to groan.* Sūspīrāns, āltōquĕ trăhēns dē pēctŏrĕ vōcēm. V. Syn.—Gĕmŏ. Phr.—Sūspīrĭă dō, ēdŏ, dūcŏ, ēffūndŏ, gĕmĭnŏ. Lōngīs sīngūltĭbŭs īlĭă pūlsăt. Sūspīrĭă pēctŏre ăb īmō Cūră dŏlōrquĕ trăhĭt. Āssĭdŭō rĕnŏvāns sūspīrĭă plānctū. Tăcĭtō sūspīrĭă pēctŏrĕ. *To long for.* Syn.—Dēsīdĕrŏ. *To complain.* Syn.—Quĕrŏr. *To breathe forth.* Syn.—Spīrŏ, ēxspīrŏ, ēfflŏ, ēxhālŏ.

Sūstēntŏ, ās, āvī, ātūm, ārĕ. *To support, to sustain.* Syn.—Sūstĭnĕŏ. *To stop, to hold back.* Syn.—Cŏhĭbĕŏ. *To support, to nourish.* Syn.—Ălŏ, nūtrĭŏ.

Sūstĭnĕŏ, ēs, ŭī, ēntūm, ērĕ. *To sustain.* Sūstĭnĕās ŭt ŏnūs, nītēndum ēst vērtĭcĕ rēctō. O. Syn.—Fĕrŏ, gĕrŏ, sūstēntŏ, fūlcĭŏ. *To bear, to have, to hold.* Syn.—Hăbĕŏ, tĕnĕŏ, fĕrŏ. *To check, to stop.* Syn.—Cōntĭnĕŏ, prĕmŏ, rĕprĭmŏ, sīstŏ, cŏhĭbĕŏ. Fig.—*To sustain.* Syn.—Fĕrŏ, sŭbĕŏ. *To protect, to defend.* Syn.—Dēfēndŏ, tŭĕŏr, prōpūgnŏ. *To support, to nourish.* Syn.—Ălŏ. *To resist.* Syn.—Fĕrŏ, pătĭŏr, tŏlĕrŏ. *To console, to strengthen.* Syn.—Fīrmŏ, ērĭgŏ, sōlŏr. *To be able.* Syn.—Pōssūm, quĕŏ, vălĕŏ.

Sŭsūrrŏ, ās, āvī, ātūm, ārĕ. *To murmur, to whisper.* Tūm sŏnŭs aūdītūr grăvĭŏr, trāctīmquĕ sŭsūrrānt. V. Syn.—Mūrmŭrŏ, īmmūrmŭrŏ, strĕpŏ, strĕpĭtŏ, strīdĕŏ. Phr.—Sŭsūrrūm dō, ēdŏ, cĭĕŏ. Plăcĭdīs īmmūrmŭrăt ūndă sŭsūrrīs. Sŏpōrĭfĕrōs tĕnŭī strīdōrĕ sŭsūrrōs Ūndă cĭĕt. Strĕpĭtānt ārgūtō mūrmŭrĕ rīvī. Sībĭlăt mōllī sīlvă sŭsūrrō. *To speak secretly.* Syn.—Mūrmŭrŏ, īmmūrmŭrŏ. Phr.—Tăcĭtās aūrĭbŭs cōmmīttĕrĕ vōcēs. Ōccūltō crīmĕn māndārĕ sŭsūrrō. Pārs quīd vĕlĭt ōrĕ sŭsūrrăt. Fūrtīm līnguā tĭtŭbāntĕ lŏcūtŭs.

Sŭsūrrŭs, ī. m. *Murmur, whisper, light sound.* Sæpĕ lĕvī sōmnūm suādēbĭt ĭnīrĕ sŭsūrrō. V. Syn.—Mūrmŭr, strĕpĭtŭs, sŏnŭs, sŏnĭtŭs, bōmbŭs. Phr.—Ārgūtūs rīvī strĕpĭtŭs. Tăcĭtæ vōcēs. Fūrtīvæ mūrmŭră vōcĭs. Dŭbĭōque aūctōrĕ sŭsūrrī.

Sūtĭlĭs, ĭs, ĕ. *Sewed, joined.* Syn.—Sūtŭs, cōnsūtŭs. Phr.—Cȳmbă sūtĭlĭs.

Sŭŭs, ă, ūm. *His, their, one's own.* Syn.—Prŏprĭŭs. *Just, legitimate.* Syn.—Jūstŭs, dēbĭtŭs.

Sȳmphōnĭă, æ. f. *Symphony, harmony.* Ūt grātās īntēr mēnsās sȳmphōnĭă dīscōrs. H. Syn.—Cōncēntŭs, chŏrŭs. *See Musica.*

Sȳrmă, ătĭs. n. *Trailing robe.* Syn.—Cȳclăs. Phr.—Aūrō dĕcōrūm sȳrmă bārbărĭcūm trăhĭt. Lōngō sȳrmătĕ vērrĭt hŭmūm. Pīctæ Sārrānă fĕrēntēm Ēx hŭmĕrīs aūlæă tŏgæ. Fig.—*Tragedy. See Tragoedia.*

T

Tābĕfăcĭŏ, ĭs, fēcī, făctūm, ĕrĕ. *To dry up, to rot away.* Syn.—Ēxtābĕfăcĭŏ. Phr.—Tābĕ cōnfĭcĭŏ, ēxĕdŏ, pĕrĕdŏ, āttĕnŭŏ, dēfōrmŏ.

Tābĕŏ, ēs, ŭī, ērĕ. *To melt.* Syn.—Tābēscŏ. *To dissolve.* Syn.—Cōntābĕŏ, cōntābēscŏ, sōlvŏr, cōrrūmpŏ, pŭtrēscŏ. Fig.—*To be consumed.* Syn.—Cōntābĕŏ, cōntābēscŏ, ēxtābēscŏ, ābsūmŏr, cōnsūmŏr, ēxĕdŏr, pĕrĕdŏr, lānguĕŏ. Phr.—Tābĕ pĕrĕdŏr. Aētērnō tābēscĕrĕ lūctū. Āssĭdŭīs cūrīs ănĭmūs tābēscĭt.

Tăbērnă, æ. f. *Tavern.* Tūrpĭs ĭn ārcānā sŏnŭīt cūm rīxă tăbērnā. Prop. Syn.—Caūpōnă, pŏpīnă.

Tābēs, ĭs. f. *Putrid matter, gore.* Tīnctăquĕ mōrtĭfĕrā tābĕ săgĭttă mădĕt. O. Syn.—Tābūm, sănĭēs. Phr.—Fūnēstā tābĕ vĕnēnī. Nĭgrā dīstīllāns tābĕ. Fig.— *Consumption, wasting away.* Syn.—Lānguŏr, pēstĭs, mōrbŭs, lŭēs, vĕnēnūm. Phr.—Pāllĭdă tābēs. Cæcā lĭquĕfāctæ tābĕ mĕdūllæ. Nēc lĭvĭdă tābēs Īnvĭdĭæ.

Tābĭdŭs, ă, ūm. *Corrupting.* Syn.—Tābĭfĭcŭs, pēstĭfĕr, vĕnēnĭfĕr. *Corrupted.* Syn.—Tābēns, tābēscēns, lĭquĕfāctŭs, lĭquēscēns, rĕsōlūtŭs, cōrrūptŭs. *Dried up, wasted away.* Syn.—Tābēns, tābēscēns, lānguĭdŭs.

Tābĭfĭcŭs, ă, ūm. *That which wastes away, or corrupts.* Syn.—Tābĭdŭs, pēstĭfĕr, vĕnēnĭfĕr, ĕdāx.

Tăbŭlă, æ. f. *Plank.* Syn.—Āssĕr, tăbēllă. *Picture.* Syn.—Tăbēllă, ĭmāgŏ, ēffĭgĭēs.

Tābūm (*used only in the ablative*). n. *Pus, putrid matter.* Ōră vĭrūm trīstī pēndēbānt pāllĭdă tābō. V. Syn.—Tābēs, sănĭēs. Phr.—Stīllāntīs tābī sănĭēs. Vūlnĕrĕ mānāns, flŭēns. Sănĭē tābōquĕ flŭēntēs. Tābō ōblĭtă.

Tăcĕŏ, ēs, cŭī, cĭtūm, ērĕ. *To be silent.* Vērĕ prĭŭs vŏlŭcrēs tăcĕānt æstātĕ cĭcādæ. V. Syn.—Cōntĭcēscŏ, rĕtĭcĕŏ, sĭlĕŏ, ōbmūtēscŏ. Phr.—Vōcēm prĕmĕrĕ. Cōmmīssă cēlārĕ. Nēc tăcŭī dēmēns. *To pass over in silence.* Syn.—Prætĕrĕŏ, ŏmīttŏ, prætērmīttŏ.

Tăcĭtūrnŭs, ă, ūm. *Silent.* Quī sērmōnĕ plăcēt, tăcĭtūrnă sĭlēntĭă vītĕt. O. Syn.—Mūtŭs, tăcēns, sĭlēns, tăcĭtŭs. Phr.—Ūltrō quī sĭlĕăt. Rāro ēt pērpaūcă lŏquēntĭs. Lŏquēndī pārcŭs. *Calm, peaceful.* Syn.—Plăcĭdŭs, trānquīllŭs, quĭētŭs, sĭlēns, mūtŭs.

Tædă, æ. f. *Pine-wood.* Syn.—Ăbĭēs, pīnŭs. *Torch.* Syn.—Fāx, fūnālĕ. Phr.—Īndūtō cērātæ sūlphŭrĕ tædæ. Pĭcĕūm fērt fūmĭdă lūmĕn Tædă. Cāstīs ădŏlēt dum āltārĭă tædīs. Tædās sīlva āltă mĭnīstrăt. (*By extension*) *Marriage.* Syn.—Cōnjŭgĭūm. Phr.—Fēlīcēs tædæ. Tēmpŏră tædīs āptă. Tædās cĕlĕbrārĕ jŭgālēs. Tædās ēxōsă jŭgālēs.

Tædĕt. impers. *It disgusts.* Syn.—Pērtæsūm ēst, pĭgĕt. Phr.—Tædĭō, fāstīdĭō āffĭcĭŏr. Tædĭă, fāstīdĭă ănĭmūm tĕnēnt. Ūt lōngī tædĭă bēllī Lōngă fĕrām. Tædēt nĕmŏrūm.

Tædĭūm, ĭī. n. *Disgust, weariness.* Syn.—Fāstīdĭūm, sătĭĕtās.

Tænĭă, æ. f. *Long ribbon, fillet.* Syn.—Vīttă, tænĭŏlă, fāscĭŏlă. Phr.—Fīt lōngæ tænĭă vīttæ.

Tālĕă, æ. f. *Branch, slip, a stock to set in the ground.* Syn.—Sūrcŭlŭs, rāmŭs, rāmŭlŭs, vīrgūltūm, frŭtēx.

Tālĭs, ĭs, ĕ. *Such.* Tālĭs ĕrāt Dīdō, tālēm sē lætă fĕrēbăt. V. Syn.—Hīc, ĭs, hūjūsmŏdī. Phr.—Tālĭă vōcĕ rĕfērt.

Tămĕn. conj. *Nevertheless, however.* Syn.—Āttămĕn, vērūm, vērūmtămĕn, nĭhĭlōmĭnŭs. Phr.—Nĭhĭlō sēcĭŭs, nōn mĭnŭs.

Tāndēm. adv. *Finally.* Syn.—Dēmūm, dēnĭquĕ, pōstrēmō. Phr.—Ăd ēxtrēmūm.

Tāngŏ, ĭs, tĕtĭgī, tāctūm, ĕrĕ. *To touch.* Tāngĕre ĕnim ēt tāngī nĭsī cōrpŭs, nūllă pŏtēst rēs. Lr. Syn.—Āttīngŏ, cōntīngŏ, trāctŏ, āttrēctŏ. *To attain.* Syn.—Āttīngŏ, āssĕquŏr, pērvĕnĭŏ ăd. Phr.—Tāngĕrĕ pōrtūs. Thrācĭă nōctūrnō tāngĕrĕ cāstră dŏlō. *To strike.* Syn.—Fĕrĭŏ, pērcŭtĭŏ, vērbĕrŏ. *To move.* Syn.—Mŏvĕŏ. Phr.—Mēntēm mōrtālĭă tāngūnt. Tē sī quă părēntĭs Tāngĕrĕ cūră pŏtēst. Nēc tāngĭtŭr īră.

Tānquām. conj. *As.* Syn.—Vĕlŭt, ŭt, vĕlŭtī, sīcŭt, quăsī, ceū, īnstăr, mōrĕ, mŏdō, rītū. Phr.—Īn mōrēm, īn mŏdūm, īn spĕcĭēm. Mōrĕ mŏdōquĕ. *Just as.* Syn.—Ceū, quăsī, vĕlŭt, vĕlŭtī.

Tāntūm. adv. *So.* Syn.—Sīc, ădĕō. *Only.* Syn.—Sōlŭm.

Tăpētūm, ī. n. *Tapestry, carpet.* Phr.—Tăpētēs mūltĭplĭcī cŏlōrĕ dīstīnctī. Mīră ārtĕ, dōctā mănū pīctī, lăbōrātī, cōntēxtī. Ăcū Bārbărĭcā lăbōrātī. Grăvēs aūrō. Vărĭīs spīrāntēs fĭgūrīs. Āttălĭcā spīrāntēs ārtĕ tăpētās.

Tārdē, ĭŭs. adv. *Slowly.* Syn.—Lēntē, sērō, pĭgrē, sēgnĭtĕr, cūnctāntĕr.

Tārdēscŏ, ĭs, ĕrĕ. *To become slow, tardy.* Syn.—Tārdŏr, īmpĕdĭŏr, tōrpēscŏ, mŏrŏr.

Tārdĭtās, ātĭs. f. *Slowness.* Syn.—Sēgnĭtĭă, sēgnĭtĭēs, ĭnērtĭă, mŏră, pĭgrĭtĭă.

Tārdŏ, ās, āvī, ātūm, ārĕ. *To delay, to retard.* Tārdātūr, cārōque ŏnĕrī tĭmĕt ōmnĭă sēcūm. V. Syn.—Rĕtārdŏ, mŏrŏr, rĕmŏrŏr, rĕtĭnĕŏ, īmpĕdĭŏ. Phr.—Mŏrām āffĕrŏ. Nōs tārdăt ĭnērtĭă. Gĕlĭdūs tārdāntĕ sĕnēctæ Sānguĭs hĕbĕt.

Tārdŭs, ă, ūm. *Tardy, slow.* Tārdīs vēl quæ mŏră nōctĭbŭs ōbstĕt. V. Syn.—Lēntŭs, pĭgĕr, īgnāvŭs, sēgnĭs, rĕmīssŭs. Phr.—Tārdōque īncēdĕrĕ pāssū. Vūlnĕrĕ tārdŭs Ŭlyssei. *Stupid.* Syn.—Hĕbĕs, stŭpĭdŭs.

Taūrĕă, æ. f. *Whip made from a bull's hide.* Syn.—Scŭtĭcă, lōrūm.

Taūrŭs, ī. m. *Bull.* Ēheū! quām pīnguī măcĕr ēst mĭhĭ taūrŭs ĭn ărvō. V. Syn.—Jŭvēncŭs, bōs. Phr.—Ārmēntī dūx, dūctŏr. Frōntĕ mĭnāns. Frōns taūrī mĕtŭēndă mĭnācĭs. Īrātō răpĭdūs cōrnū. Cōrnĭbŭs pŏtēns. Mūltā pāllēns fērrūgĭnĕ. Mūgītū hōrrĭfĭcāns cœlūm. Dūrō fūmāt sūb vōmĕrĕ taūrŭs. Pīnguĕ sŏlum īnvērtānt taūrī. Fōrtĭă taūrōrūm cōrpŏră. Præstāntī cōrpŏrĕ taūrŭs. Taūrūs quī spārgĭt ărēnām.

Tāxŭs, ī. f. *The yew-tree.* (*See Appendix under list of Trees, etc.*)

Tēctē. adv. *Secretly.* Syn.—Ārcānō, fūrtīm, clām.

Tēctūm, ī. n. *Roof.* Tēr flāmma ād sūmmūm tēctī sūbjēctă rĕlūxĭt. V. Syn.—Tēgmĕn. Phr.—Tēctī ăpĕx, cūlmĕn, fāstīgĭūm, vērtēx. Āngūstī sūbtēr fāstīgĭă tēctī. Rāră dŏnōrūm tēctă vĭdēnt. Sūmmīquĕ fĕrīt lăquĕārĭă tēctī. (*In general*) *House, dwelling.* Syn.—Dŏmŭs. Phr.—Tēctăquĕ dīgnă dĕō. Nĭgrō dēfōrmĭă fūmō. Laūrūs ĕrāt tēctī mĕdĭō.

Tēgmĕn, ĭnĭs. n. *Covering.* Syn.—Tĕgŭmēntūm. *Skin.* Syn.—Pēllĭs, cōrtēx. *Vestment.* Syn.—Tĕgŭmēntūm, vēlāmĕn, vēlāmēntūm, vēstĭs, ămīctŭs, īnvŏlŭcrūm. *Roof, house.* Syn.—Tēctūm, dŏmŭs.

Tĕgŏ, ĭs, tēxī, tēctūm, ĕrĕ. *To cover, to conceal.* Sīt tĭbĭ tērră lĕvīs, mōllīquĕ tĕgārĭs ărēnā. M. Syn.—Cōntĕgŏ, ōbtĕgŏ, ŏpĕrĭŏ, ădŏpĕrĭŏ, vēlŏ, ōbdūcŏ, cōndŏ, ōccūltŏ, ōbnūdŏ, īnvōlvŏ, sĕpĕlĭŏ. Phr.—Pĭā tĕgĕ tēmpŏră vīttā. Sēmĕn hŭmō tĕgĕrĕ. Rārā tĕgĭt ārbŭtŭs ūmbrā. Cōrpŭs hŭmō pătĭārĕ tĕgī. *To protect.* Syn.—Prōtĕgŏ, dēfēndŏ, tŭĕŏr. *To surround.* Syn.—Cīngŏ, stīpŏ, cīrcūmdŏ. Fig.—*To conceal, to dissemble.* Syn.—Ŏpĕrĭŏ, cōndŏ, ābscōndŏ, prĕmŏ, cēlŏ, dīssĭmŭlŏ, īnvōlvŏ.

Tēgŭlă, æ. f. *Tile.* Syn.—Lătĕr, lătērcŭlŭs, īmbrēx, tēstă.

Tēlă, æ. f. *Web, warp.* Lāssārēt vĭdŭās pēndŭlă tēlă mănūs. O. Syn.—Stāmĕn, tēxtūm, tēxtūră. Phr.—Stāmĭnă tēlæ. Pērcūrrĕrĕ pēctĭnĕ tēlās. Tēlă jŭgō jūncta ēst.

Tēllūs, ūrĭs. f. *Earth.* Syn.—Rĕgĭŏ, tērră. *See both these words.*

Tēlūm, ī. n. *Weapon.* Tēlum īmmānĕ, mănū vălĭdā quōd fōrtĕ gĕrēbăt. V. Syn.—Mīssĭlĕ, spīcŭlūm, hāstă, hāstīlĕ, jăcŭlūm, fērrūm, cūspĭs. Phr.—Tēlī cūspĭs. Tēlūm fērrō mĭcāns. Sŏlĭdūm nōdīs ēt rōbŏrĕ cōctō. Fērrō præfīxūm rōbŭr ăcūtō. Tēlōrūm sĕgĕs fērrĕă. Strīdēntīs sībĭlă tēlī. Tēlă sŏnānt hŭmĕrīs. Quā tēlă vĭdēt dēnsīssĭmă, vādĭt. Pēr mīllĕ sĕquēntĭă tēlă. Hæsūrūm clŷpĕī cūrvāmĭnĕ tēlūm. Tēlūm cōntōrsit ĭn hōstēm. Sūmmā tēlūm lībrābăt ăb aūrĕ. Cōncūrrūnt ūndĭquĕ tēlīs. Tēlō dāt pēctŭs ĭnērmēm. Sūccūmbĕrĕ tēlīs.

Tĕmĕrārĭŭs, ă, ūm. *Who acts by chance, incautious.* Ābstŭlĕrāt tōtām tĕmĕrārĭŭs īnstĭtŏr ūrbēm. M. Syn.—Lĕvĭs, vānŭs, īmprūdēns, īncōnsūltŭs, īncaūtŭs, cæcŭs, præcēps. *Rash.* Syn.—Aūdāx, cæcŭs, præcēps. Phr.—Ănĭmī præcēps, fīdēns.

Tĕmĕrĕ. adv. *By chance.* Syn.—Pāssīm, fōrtŭĭtō. Phr.—Sĭnĕ ōrdĭnĕ, sĭnĕ lēgĕ. *Rashly.* Syn.—Īncaūtē, lĕvĭtĕr, īncōnsūltē, stūltē, īmprūdēntĕr.

Tĕmĕrĭtās ātĭs. f. *Rashness.* Syn.—Aūdācĭă, īmprūdēntĭă. Phr.—Mēns īncōnsūltă. Vīs cōnsĭlĭī ēxpērs. Aūsă, cœptă tĕmĕrārĭă. Ŏpūs mălĕ caūtī pēctŏrĭs.

Tĕmĕrŏ, ās, āvī, ātūm, ārĕ. *To soil holy, sacred things.* Syn.—Vĭŏlŏ, cŏīnquĭnŏ, fœdŏ, īnfĭcĭŏ, cōntāmĭnŏ. *To corrupt.* Syn.—Cōrrūmpŏ, īnfĭcĭŏ.

Tēmnŏ, ĭs, tēmpsī, tēmptūm, ĕrĕ. *To despise.* Dīscĭtĕ jūstĭtĭām mŏnĭti ēt nōn tēmnĕrĕ dīvōs. V. Syn.—Cōntēmnŏ, dēspĭcĭŏ, nēglĕgŏ, āspērnŏr, rēspŭŏ, spērnŏ.

Tēmpĕrāntĭă, æ. f. *Moderation, temperance.* Syn.—Ābstĭnēntĭă, mŏdĕrātĭŏ, mŏdēstĭă, sōbrĭĕtās, tēmpĕrĭēs. Phr.—Sōbrĭă mēns, cūltŭs, hăbĭtŭs, vīctŭs. Mŏdĭcæ dăpēs ēt sōbrĭă pōcŭlă.

Tēmpĕrŏ, ās, āvī, ātūm, ārĕ. *To temper, to flavor.* Syn.—Mīscĕŏ. *To rule, to govern.* Syn.—Rĕgŏ, mŏdĕrŏr, gŭbērnŏ. Phr.—Tēmpĕrăt ārtĕ dŏmūm. *To regulate, to limit.* Syn.—Mŏdĕrŏr, cŏērcĕŏ, cōntĭnĕŏ, frēnŏ. *To appease.* Syn.—Mōllĭŏ, lēnĭŏ, plācŏ, mītĭgŏ. *To abstain. See Abstineo.*

Tēmpēstās, ātĭs. f. *Time, epoch.* Syn.—Tēmpŭs, ætās, ævūm. *See Tempus. Season.* Syn.—Tēmpŏră, hōræ, sīdŭs. *Weather, state of the atmosphere. See Coelum.* Phr.—Ūnde hæc tām clāră rĕpēntĕ Tēmpēstās? Cūm fŭĕrīt lĭquĭdīssĭmă cœlī Tēmpēstās. *Storm, tempest.* Syn.—Hĭēms, nīmbŭs, tūrbŏ, prŏcēllă, īmbĕr. Phr.—Mărĭs, pōntī, frĕtī, æquŏrĭs æstūs. Cœlī răbĭēs, fŭrŏr, īră. Nōn trāctābĭlĕ cœlūm. Vīs prŏcēllæ. Aēquŏră tūrbĭdă. Mărĭă vēntīs cōncĭtă. Nēptūnī quāssă trĭdēntī. Āspĕră cœlī Tēmpēstās. Hībērnæ mĭnæ. Cœlī rūīnă. Ūndă mĭnāx. Tēmpēstās ăgēns hĭĕmēm. Nīmbīs ēt grāndĭnĕ fērvēns. Strīdēntĭbūs hōrrĭdă nīmbīs. Cōncūssū trĕmŭērĕ pŏlī. Vēntī vōlvūnt mărĕ. Tōtō tēmpēstās æquŏrĕ sævĭt. Tēmpēstās sēdātŭr. Jūpĭtĕr ātră sĕrēnăt Nūbĭlă. Mărĕ trānquīllūm. Fig.—*Calamity, disaster.* Syn.—Pērnĭcĭēs, clādēs, rŭīnă. *Rain, hail.* Syn.—Grāndŏ, īmbĕr.

Tēmpēstīvŭs, ă, ūm. *Opportune.* Vĕnĭēt nārrātĭbūs hōră Tēmpēstīvă mĕīs. O. Syn.—Cōmmŏdŭs, ōppōrtūnŭs. *Mature.* Syn.—Mātūrŭs.

Tēmplūm, ī. n. *Temple, consecrated place.* Hīc tēmplūm Jūnōni īngēns Sīdōnĭă Dīdō Cōndēbăt. V. Syn.—Aēdēs, dēlūbrūm, fānūm, ădy̆tūm, să̆crārĭūm, săcēllūm. Phr.—Tēmplă dĕōrūm. Să̆cră dŏmŭ̆s. Tēmplī līmĕ̆n. Līmĭnă dīvūm. Să̆cră tēctă, līmĭnă, lŏcă. Săcræ tēctă vĕrēndă dŏmūs. Tērrēstrĕ Jŏvĭ̆s dŏmĭcĭlĭūm. Sŏlĭdō dē mārmŏrĕ tēmplă īnstĭtŭām. Clārō sūrgēbāt mārmŏrĕ tēmplūm. Tēmplă nŏvō dĕcŏrārĕ sāxō. *Tomb. See Sepulcrum.*

Tēmpŏrĭŭs. adv. *Sooner, earlier.* Syn.—Cĭtĭŭs, mātūrĭŭ̆s, ōcĭŭs.

Tēmpŭ̆s, ŏrĭ̆s. n. *Time, age.* Stāt sŭă cuīquĕ dĭēs; brĕve ĕt īrrĕpărābĭlĕ tēmpŭ̆s ōmnĭbŭs ēst vītæ. V. Syn.—Aētās, ævūm, dĭēs, ānnī. Phr.—Tēmpŏrĭ̆s ætās, spătĭūm. Ānnōrūm mŏră. Lūcīs nōctīsquĕ vĭcēs. Lōngă dĭēs. Āngūstī tērmĭnŭs ævī. Lōngī tēmpŏrūm trāctŭ̆s. Nēc lōngūm īn mĕdĭō tēmpŭ̆s. Ēx īllō tēmpŏrĕ. Tēmpŏrĭs ēxĭgŭūm. Tēmpŏră tārdă flŭūnt. Vēnīt sūmmă dĭēs ĕt īnēlūctābĭlĕ tēmpŭ̆s. Tēmpŭs vĕlŭt ūndă lābēns. Nĭhĭl ēst vēlōcĭŭs ānnīs. Clām tăcĭtūm tēmpŭ̆s ăbīrĕ sŏlĕ̆t. Fŭgĭt īrrĕpărābĭlĕ tēmpŭ̆s. Ānnōrūm vērtūntūr tēmpŏră. Lēntēscūnt tēmpŏră cūræ. Mēssīsquĕ dĭēm, tēmpūsquĕ sĕrēndī. Nūnc tēmpŭ̆s ĕquōs, nūnc pōscĕrĕ cūrrūs.

Tĕnāx, ācĭ̆s. adj. *Tenacious, clinging, that which holds fast.* Dēntĕ tĕnācī Ānchŏră fūndābāt nāvēs. V. Syn.—Hærēns, ădhærēns. Phr.—Flōs āpprīmă tĕnāx. Tĕnācĭă vīnclă. *Firm, immovable.* Syn.—Cōnstāns, fīrmŭ̆s. *Untamable.* Syn.—Īndŏcĭlĭ̆s, rĕlūctāns, rĕnītēns.

Tēndŏ̆, ĭ̆s, tĕtēndī, tēnsūm, & tēntūm, ĕrĕ. *To stretch, to extend.* Pālmās ād sīdĕră tēndūnt. V. Syn.—Cōntēndŏ̆, īntēndŏ̆, prōtēndŏ̆, pōrrĭgŏ̆. Phr.—Īnfēstām cūm tēndĕrēt hāstām. Tēndĕrĕ rētĭă cērvīs. Tēndūnt vēlă Nŏtī. *To present.* Syn.—Pōrrĭgŏ̆, prōtēndŏ̆, ōffĕrŏ̆. *To prolong.* Syn.—Ēxtēndŏ̆, prōdūcŏ̆, dūcŏ̆, prōfĕrŏ̆. *To direct one's steps towards.* Syn.—Ĕŏ̆, ădĕŏ̆, prōgrĕdĭŏ̆r. *To strive.* Syn.—Cōnŏ̆r, nītŏ̆r.

Tĕnĕ̆bræ, ārūm. f. *Darkness, obscurity, night.* Quīd făcĭam? ōbdūctīs cōmmīttām mēnĕ tĕnēbrīs? Prop. Syn.—Cālīgŏ̆, nōx, ūmbră, nĕbŭlă. Phr.—Spīssæ ūmbræ. Cālīgĭnĭs hōrrŏr. Ŏpācæ nūbēs. Sĭnĕ sōlĕ dĭēs. Claūsæ tĕnĕbrīs ēt cārcĕrĕ cæcō. Ōffūsæ tĕnĕbræ cœlūm, dĭēm ērĭpĭūnt. Pōntō nōx īncŭbāt ātră. Tĕnĕbrās īndūcĕrĕ rēbŭ̆s. Tĕnĕbrīs nīgrēscūnt ōmnĭă cīrcūm. Ōbtēntā dēnsāntūr nōctĕ tĕnēbræ. Īnhōrrŭĭt ūndă tĕnēbrīs. Cālīgĭnĕ cœlūm Cōndĭtūr īn tĕnĕbrās. Cœlūmque ōbtēxĭtūr ūmbrā. Dēnsīs ădŏpērtīs nūbĭbŭs æthēr. Tĕnĕbrās dīscŭtĭŏ̆, pēllŏ̆. Fūlgēt tĕnĕbrīs Aūrōră fŭgātīs. Dēpŭlĕrāt gĕlĭdās Aūrōră tĕnēbrās. Tĕnĕbrīsquĕ rĕmōtīs. *Blindness. See Caecitas.*

Tĕnĕ̆brōsŭ̆s, ă, ūm. *Dark, obscure.* Hānc mĕtŭēns clādēm tĕnĕbrōsā sēdĕ ty̆rānnŭ̆s Ēxĭĕrāt. O. Syn.—Ōbscūrŭ̆s, cālīgĭnōsŭ̆s, cæcŭ̆s, ŏpācŭs, nūbĭlŭs, ātĕr, nĭgĕr, nĭgrāns. Phr.—Tĕnēbrīs, cālīgĭnĕ ōbdūctŭs, ŏpērtŭs, īnvŏlūtŭs, dēnsŭs. Aēquŏră sōlĭbŭs ōrbă. Lŏcŭs Phœbī īnscĭŭs. Cæcă tĕnēbrīs vĭă. Sōlĕ cărēns.

Tĕnĕŏ, ēs, ŭī, tēntūm, ērĕ. *To hold, to sustain.* Īllĕ tĕnēns dēxtrā băcŭlūm clāvēmquĕ sĭnīstrā. O. Syn.—Sūstĭnĕŏ, gĕrŏ, fĕrŏ, gēstŏ, pōrtŏ, hăbĕŏ. Phr.—Āvērsī tĕnŭērĕ făcēm. *To retain, to hold back.* Syn.—Cōntĭnĕŏ, cŏērcĕŏ, cŏhĭbĕŏ, cōmprĭmŏ, cōmpēscŏ. *To contain, to shut in.* Syn.—Cōntĭnĕŏ, āmplēctŏr, cōmplēctŏr. *To occupy, to inhabit.* Syn.—Ōccŭpŏ, hăbĭtŏ, cŏlŏ, ōbtĭnĕŏ. *To govern.* Syn.—Rĕgŏ, mŏdĕrŏr. *To guard, to preserve.* Syn.—Sērvŏ, rĕtĭnĕŏ. *To attain.* Syn.—Āttīngŏ, tāngŏ, āssĕquŏr. *To retard.* Syn.—Dētĭnĕŏ, mŏrŏr, tārdŏ, sīstŏ. *To bind.* Syn.—Ōbstrīngŏ, ōblĭgŏ, vīncĭŏ.

Tĕnĕr, ĕră, ĕrūm. *Tender, soft.* Sŭpĕrēst tĕnĕr ōmnĭbŭs hūmŏr. V. Syn.—Tĕnēllŭs, tĕnēllŭlŭs, mōllĭs. Phr.—Tĕnĕrās ārcēbānt vīncŭlă pālmās. Tĕnĕrōs ūrīt lōrīcă lăcērtōs. *Young.* Syn.—Mōllĭs, tĕnēllŭs, rŭdĭs, jŭvĕnĭs. Phr.—Ŏvĭūm tĕnĕrōs dēpēllĕrĕ fœtūs. *Effeminate.* Syn.—Mōllĭs, frāctŭs. *Feeble.* Syn.—Mōllĭs, dēbĭlĭs, īnfīrmŭs.

Tēntāmĕn, ĭnĭs & Tēntāmēntūm, ī. n. *Experience, proof, trial.* Syn.—Pĕrīclūm, pĕrīcŭlūm. Phr.—Vōcīsquĕ dătæ tēntāmĭnă sūmpsĭt.

Tēntŏ, ās, āvī, ātūm, ārĕ. *To attempt, to essay, to try.* Tēntāmūsquĕ vĭam ēt vēlōrūm pāndĭmŭs ālās. V. Syn.—Ēxpĕrĭŏr, ēxplōrŏ, ădĕŏ, āggrĕdĭŏr, quærŏ. Phr.—Nīl īntēntūm, ĭnēxpērtūm, ĭnaūsūm rĕlīnquŏ. Cūnctă prĭŭs tēntāndă. Flŭvĭōs tēntārĕ mĭnācēs. Fŭgām cūrsū tēntāvĭt ĕquōrūm. Sēd quīd tēntārĕ nŏcēbĭt? Pōllĭcĭtī tēntārĕ fĭdēm. *To tempt.* Syn.—Ădĕŏ, āggrĕdĭŏr, sōllĭcĭtŏ. *To attack.* Syn.—Āggrĕdĭŏr, lăcēssŏ, prōvŏcŏ.

Tēntōrĭūm, ĭī. n. *Tent.* Syn.—Tăbērnācŭlūm, tăbērnāclūm. Phr.—Nĭvĕīs tēntōrĭă vēlīs. Tēntōrĭă pōnĕrĕ.

Tĕnŭĭs, ĭs, ĕ & Tēnuĭs, ĭs, ĕ. *Delicate, fine, small, tender.* Vīx hăbĕō tĕnŭēm, quæ tĕgăt ōssă cŭtēm. O. Syn.—Ēxīlĭs, grăcĭlĭs, sūbtīlĭs. Fig.—*Delicate, fine, subtle.* Syn.—Ācĕr, ăcūtŭs, sūbtīlĭs, sōlērs. *Small, narrow.* Syn.—Pārvŭs, ēxĭgŭŭs, āngūstŭs, mĭnūtŭs. Phr.—Tĕnŭĭs mĭhī cāmpŭs ărātŭr. Glōrĭă nōn tĕnŭĭs. *Low, humble. See Humilis. Poor. See Pauper. Moderate.* Syn.—Mŏdĭcŭs, pārcŭs, mŏdĕrātŭs.

Tĕnŭŏ, ās, āvī, ātūm, ārĕ. *To make small, thin or tender.* Syn.—Ēxtĕnŭŏ, mĭnŭŏ, īmmĭnŭŏ, tĕrŏ, āttĕnŭŏ. Fig.—*To diminish. See Minuo.*

Tĕpĕō, ēs, ŭī, ērĕ. *To be warm.* Sēmpērquĕ rĕcēntī Cædĕ tĕpēbăt hŭmŭs. V. Syn.—Tĕpĕfīō, tĕpēscŏ, călĕō. Phr.—Ēst ŭbĭ plūs tĕpĕānt hĭĕmēs? Fig.—*To be filled with passion.* Syn.—Călĕō. *To become tepid, to cool.* Syn.—Dēfērvĕō, rĕfrīgĕrŏr, frīgēscŏ.

Tĕpēscŏ, ĭs, ĕrĕ. *To become warm. See Tepeo.*

Tĕpĭdŭs, ă, ūm. *Warm, moderately hot.* Syn.—Tĕpēns, tĕpĕfāctŭs, tĕpēscēns, ēgĕlĭdŭs, călĭdŭs. *Cool.* Syn.—Gĕlĭdŭs.

Tĕpŏr, ōrĭs. m. *Warmth. See Calor.*

Tĕrĕbrŏ, ās, āvī, ātūm, ārĕ. *To pierce.* Syn.—Fŏrŏ, pērfŏrŏ, fŏdĭŏ, pērfŏdĭō. Phr.—Lūmēn tēlō tĕrĕbrāmŭs ăcūtō.

Tērgĕŏ, ēs, ērĕ & Tērgŏ, ĭs, sī, sūm, ĕrĕ. *To clean, to rub, to polish.* Clўpĕōs ēt lūcĭdă spīcŭlă tērgēnt Ārvīnā pīnguī. Syn.—Ābstērgŏ, dētērgŏ, pŏlĭŏ, mūndŏ, pūrgŏ. Phr.—Plēnōs rūbīgĭnĭs ēnsēs Tērgĕrĕ. *To correct.* Syn.—Emēndŏ, līmŏ.

Tērgūm, ī. n. *Back.* Ōssăquĕ pōst tērgūm māgnæ jāctātă părēntĭs. O. Syn.—Dōrsūm. Phr.—Mănūs pōst tērgă rĕvīnctūm. Vērbĕrĕ tērgă sĕcăt. Hōrrēntĭă tērgă bŏūm. Tērgūm īmmānĕ lĕōnĭs. Tērgă dō, vērtŏ.

Tērmĭnŏ, ās, āvī, ātūm, ārĕ. *To end, to limit.* Syn.—Dīstērmĭnŏ, fīnĭŏ, dēfīnĭŏ, cīrcūmscrībŏ, claūdŏ, īnclūdŏ, sēpărŏ, dīvĭdŏ, sēcērnŏ, dīscrīmĭnŏ. Phr.—Mētās, fīnēs, līmĭtēs pōnŏ, fīgŏ, cōnstĭtŭŏ. Līmĭtĭbŭs dīvĭdŏ. Cērtīs spătĭīs īnclūdŏ. Īmmōtō dīvīsĭt līmĭtĕ mūndūm.

Tērmĭnŭs, ī. m. *End, limit.* Syn.—Fīnĭs, līmĕs, mētă. Phr.—Āngūstī tērmĭnŭs ævī.

Tĕrŏ, ĭs, trīvī, trītūm, ĕrĕ. *To press.* Tōstās æstū tĕrĭt ārĕă frūgēs. V. Syn.—Āttĕrŏ, cōntĕrŏ, mŏlŏ, tūndŏ, cōmmĭnŭŏ. *To rub, to polish.* Syn.—Frĭcŏ, rādŏ, pŏlĭŏ. *To rub away, to consume.* Syn.—Cōntĕrŏ, dētĕrŏ, cōnsūmŏ, ĕdŏ, ēxĕdŏ, mĭnŭŏ, cōmmĭnŭŏ. Fig.—*To waste (time).* Syn.—Īnsūmŏ, cōnsūmŏ, cōntĕrŏ, pērdŏ.

Tērră, æ. f. *Land, earth.* Tērrăquĕ cœlēstēs ārĭdă sōrbēt ăquās. O. Syn.—Tēllūs, hŭmŭs, sŏlūm, cāmpŭs, ăgĕr, ārvūm. Phr.—Tērræ sĭnŭs, grĕmĭūm. Frūgūm ālmă, māgnă părēns, mātĕr. Ōptĭmă mātrūm. Fēcūndæ tēllūrĭs ŏpēs. Dūlcī līgĭnĕ lætă. Ēx īmbrĭbŭs hūmĭdă tēllūs. Nōn ōmnĭs fērt ōmnĭă tēllūs. Nēc tēllūs ĕădēm părĭt ōmnĭă. Tēllūs vĭrĭdāntēs pārtŭrĭt hērbās. Pēr sē dăbăt ōmnĭă tēllūs. Flūmĭnă cīrcūm Fūndĭt hŭmūs flōrēs. *The world.* Syn.—Ōrbĭs, mūndŭs. Phr.—Ōrbĭs tērrārūm. Dēspĭcĭēns mărĕ vēlĭvŏlūm tērrāsquĕ jăcēntēs. *Region, country.* Syn.—Rĕgĭŏ, nātĭŏ. Phr.—Sŏcĭōs īgnōtā līnquĕrĕ tērrā. Quĭbūs tērrārūm mīlĭtĕt ōrīs.

Tērrēnŭs, ă, ūm. *Earthen, made of earth.* Tērrēno ēx āggĕrĕ būstūm. V. Syn.—Tērrĕŭs. Phr.—Ē tērrā cŏāctŭs, fīctŭs, cōnflātŭs.

Tērrĕŏ, ēs, ŭī, ĭtūm, ērĕ. *To frighten.* Aētērnūm lātrāns ēxsānguēs tērrĕāt ūmbrās. V. Syn.—Tērrĭtŏ, tērrĭfĭcŏ, cōntērrĕŏ, ēxtērrĕŏ, tūrbŏ, cōntūrbŏ, trĕmĕfăcĭŏ. Phr.—Tērrōrēm, tĭmōrēm, mĕtūm, hōrrōrēm āffĕrŏ, īncŭtĭŏ, īmmĭttŏ. Fōrmīdĭnĕ, tērrōrĕ mŏvĕŏ, īnfĭcĭŏ, īmplĕŏ. Ănĭmōs tērrōrĕ cōncŭtĭŏ. Quī tērrēt plūs īpsĕ tĭmĕt. Aūdācī tū tĭmŏr ēssĕ pŏtĕs. Tāntūm trăhĭt īllĕ tĭmōrĭs.

Tērrĕŏr, ērĭs, ĭtŭs sūm, ērī. *To be frightened.* Syn.—Ēxtērrĕŏr, cōntērrĕŏr, tūrbŏr, cōntūrbŏr, păvĕŏ, ēxpăvēscŏ, păvĭtŏ, trĕmŏ, trĕpĭdŏ, ēxhōrrēscŏ, hōrrĕŏ, pĕrhōrrĕŏ, fōrmīdŏ. Phr.—Tĭmōrĕ, tērrōrĕ īmplĕŏr, cōncŭtĭŏr, pērcēllŏr, ēxstērnŏr. Hōrrōrĕ quătĭŏr. Tērrŏr mēmbră quătĭt, ōccŭpăt ārtūs. Pāllēt tērrōrĕ pŭēllă. Īmplētūr tērrōrĕ văgō.

Tērrĭbĭlĭs, ĭs, ĕ. *Terrible, frightful.* Fŭrĭīs āccēnsŭs ĕt īrā Tērrĭbĭlĭs. V. Syn.—Tērrĭfĭcŭs, tĭmēndŭs, mĕtŭēndŭs, fōrmīdābĭlĭs, fōrmīdāndŭs, stŭpēndŭs, hōrrĭdŭs, hōrrĭbĭlĭs, hōrrēndŭs, hōrrĭfĭcŭs, trĕmēndŭs, grăvĭs, sævŭs, ătrōx. Phr.—Tērrĭbĭlēs vīsū fōrmæ. Ădĕrăt tērrōrĕ mĭnācī.

Tērrĭgĕnă, æ. m. & f. *Earth-born.* Syn.—Tērrēnŭs, tērrēstrĭs. Phr.—Tērrā, tēllūrĕ gĕnĭtŭs, sătŭs, ōrtŭs. Tērræ fīlĭŭs.

Tēstă, æ. f. *Earthenware vessel.* Syn.—Āmphŏră, cădŭs. *Cup.* Syn.—Pōcŭlūm. *Urn.* Syn.—Ūrnă. *Lamp.* Lŭcērnă. *Tile.* Syn.—Lătĕr, tēgŭlă.

Tēstāmēntūm, ī. n. *Testament, last will.* Syn.—Tăbŭlæ, tăbēllæ. Phr.—Tēstātæ, sŭprēmæ tăbŭlæ. Sŭprēmă vŏlūntās. Ūltĭmæ vōcēs. Sŭprēmæ cēræ. Nŏvīssĭmă scrīptă.

Tēstĭmōnĭūm, ĭī. n. *Testimony, proof.* Ŏvīs dāmnātă fālsō tēstĭmōnĭō. Phaed. Syn.—Īndĭcĭūm, sīgnūm.

Tēstĭs, ĭs. m. & f. *Witness.* Vēndūnt pērjūrĭă tēstēs. O. Syn.—Ārbĭtĕr. Phr.—Tēstĭs ăbēst sōmnō. Quĭs hōc crēdāt, nĭsĭ sīt prō tēstĕ vĕtūstās? *Spectator, eye-witness.* Syn.—Ārbĭtĕr, spēctātŏr. Phr.—Prŏcŭl ēst, ăĭt, ārbĭtĕr ōmnĭs. Fōrs mē sērmōnī tēstēm dĕdĭt. Īllĕ dŏlēt vērē quī sĭnĕ tēstĕ dŏlĕt.

Tēstŏr, ārĭs, ātŭs sūm, ārī. *To show, to testify.* Lōngum Āndrŏmăchēs tēstēntŭr ămōrēm. V. Syn.—Dēclārŏ, ōstēndŏ, ārgŭŏ, sīgnĭfĭcŏ, īndĭcŏ. Phr.—Tēstāntĭă mōrēs Cārmĭnă. Tēstōr gaūdĭă dīctīs. *To call to witness.* Syn.—Jūrŏ, āttēstŏr, vŏcŏ, āppēllŏ.

Tēstūdŏ, ĭnĭs. f. *Tortoise.* Phr.—Mănēns dūræ sūb tēgmĭnĕ tēstæ. Lēntō rēpēns. *Lyre.* Syn.—Cĭthără, lўră. Phr.—Rĕsŏnārĕ sēptēm callĭdă nērvīs. Lēsbĭō prīmūm mŏdŭlātă cīvī. Dĕcūs Phœbī. Grātă dăpĭbūs sŭprēmī Jŏvĭs. Lăbōrūm dūlcĕ lĕvāmĕn. Căvă tēstūdĭnĕ flēvĭt ămōrēm. Tālĕ făcĭs cārmēn dōctă tēstūdĭnĕ. *See Cithara. A military maneuvre.* Syn.—Crātēs. *Vault. See Fornix.*

Tētĕr, tră, trūm. *Sombre, black.* Syn.—Ātĕr, ōbscūrŭs, nĭgĕr, fūscŭs. *Dirty.* Syn.—Fœdŭs, tūrpĭs, sōrdĭdŭs, squālĭdŭs, īmmūndŭs, spūrcŭs, ōbscœnŭs. Fig.—*Horrible, terrible, cruel.* Syn.—Dīrŭs, fĕrŭs, sævŭs, īmpĭŭs, nĕfāndŭs, hōrrĭdŭs, hōrrēndŭs.

Tētrĭcĭtās, ātĭs. f. *Harsh appearance, gravity, ill-humor.* Lætă sēd tētrĭcĭtātĕ dĕcōrūm. O. Syn.—Grăvĭtās, sĕvērĭtās, āspĕrĭtās, sŭpērcĭlĭūm. Phr.—Frōntĭs nūbēs.

Tĕtrĭcŭs, ă, ūm. *Austere, severe.* Āt quām nōn tĕtrĭcūs, quām nūllā nūbĭbūs īrā. M. Syn.—Aūstērŭs, sĕvērŭs, trīstĭs, rĭgĭdŭs. *Sad, funereal.* Syn.—Sævŭs, trīstĭs, dīrŭs, lūctĭfĭcŭs, hōrrēndŭs, fērālĭs.

Tēxŏ, ĭs, ŭī, tūm, ĕrĕ. *To interweave.* Nūnc făcĭlĭs rŭbĕā tēxātūr fīscĭnă vīrgā. V. Syn.—Cōntēxŏ, īntēxŏ, īnsērŏ, īnsērtŏ, nēctŏ, īnnēctŏ, cōnnēctŏ. Phr.—Lēntæ tēxūnt ūmbrācŭlă vītēs. Tēxĕrĕ flōrēs. *To weave a tissue.* Syn.—Īntēxŏ, cōntēxŏ, nĕŏ.

Tēxtĭlĭs, ĭs, ĕ. *Woven.* Syn.—Tēxtŭs, īntēxtŭs. Tēxtĭlĕ, ĭs. (*noun*). n. *Web, fabric.* Syn.—Tēxtūm.

Tēxtūm, ī. n. *Tissue, anything woven.* Pūrpŭră nāmquĕ tĭbī prĕtĭōsăquĕ tēxtă dăbāntŭr. O. Syn.—Tēxtĭlĕ, tēxtūră, tēxtŭs, tēlă. Phr.—Pāllădĭæ ārtĭs ŏpŭs. Pīctīs īntēxtūm vēstĭbūs aūrūm.

Thălămŭs, ī. m. *Sleeping-room.* Syn.—Cŭbīlĕ. *Couch, bed.* Syn.—Tŏrŭs, lēctŭs, cŭbīlĕ. Fig.—*Marriage.* Syn.—Cōnjŭgĭūm. *See Conjugium. Dwelling, retreat.* Syn.—Sēdēs, cŭbīlĕ.

Thĕātrūm, ī. n. *Theatre.* Cīvĭcă nōbĭlĭbūs plēbs ēst īmmīxtă thĕātrīs. J. Syn.—Căvĕă, cīrcŭs, spēctācŭlūm, scēnă, pūlpĭtă (pl.). Phr.—Thĕātrī lūdī. Clāmōsī tūrbă thĕātrī. Thĕātrī cīrcŭs ĕrăt. Cōnsēssum īngēntēm căvĕæ. Māgnīs Cīrcēnsĭbūs āctīs. Scēnīs ăgĭtātŭs Ŏrēstēs.

Thēsaūrŭs, ī. m. *Treasure.* Vĕtĕrēsquĕ rĕclūdĭt Thēsaūrōs, īgnōtum ărgēntī pōndŭs ĕt aūrī. V. Syn.—Gāză, ŏpēs, dīvĭtĭæ, pĕcūnĭă. Phr.—Ŏpūm ăcērvŭs, cōngĕrĭēs, cŭmŭlŭs. Cōllēctī pōndĕrĭs aūrī.

Thōrāx, ācĭs. m. *Breast, chest.* Syn.—Pēctŭs. *Breastplate.* Syn.—Lōrīcă, crātēs. Phr.—Grăvēm sŭbĕūnt thōrācă lăcērtī. Thōrācă sĭmŭl cūm pēctŏrĕ rūpĭt. Nēctĭlĭs ēmīssā pĕnētrātŭr ărūndĭnĕ thōrāx.

Thūs (Tūs), ūrĭs. n. *Incense*. Āspĭcĭt ārā prĕcēs vōtīvăquĕ thūră pĭōrūm. O. Phr.—Thūrĕā mīcā. Thūrĭs ărēnæ, glŏbŭlī, lăcrĭmæ. Thūrĕā dōnā. Tūrĭs ŏdōrēs. Ŏdōrātā sĕgĕs. Ŏdōrātæ ărīstæ. Săbæŭs ŏdŏr. Ărăbūm gāzæ. Mīttūnt mōllēs sŭă thūră Săbæī. Thūs ădŏlĕō, crĕmō. Thūs āltārĭbūs āddō. Tūrĭs hŏnōrēs fĕrō. Thūrĭs hŏnōrĕ dīgnŏr. Fūmōsīs āddĕrĕ thūră fŏcīs. Ŭbī thūrĕ pĭāvĕrĭs ārās. Āltārĭă fūmānt fēstă Jŏvĭs.

Thўmūm, ī. n. *Thyme*. Phr.—Ăpĭbūs grātūm. Suāvī flōrĕ, ŏdōrĕ frăgrāns, hālāns. Dūmquĕ thўmō pāscēntŭr ăpēs.

Tĭārā, æ. f. *Crown, tiara*. Tēmpŏră pūrpŭrĕīs tēntāt vēlārĕ tĭārās. O. Syn.—Tĭārās (æ), mĭtră, cŏrōnă. Phr.—Phrўgĭă vēstītūr būccă tĭārā.

Tībĭă, æ. f. *Flute*. Īncĭpĕ Mænălĭōs mēcūm, mĕă tībĭă vērsūs. V. Syn.—Fīstŭlă, călămŭs, ărūndŏ, būxŭs, ĕbŭr. Phr.—Phrўgĭă lōtōs. Ădūncō tībĭă cōrnū. Tībĭă dūctă sŏnăt. Bĭfŏrīs dēt tībĭă cāntūm. Tībĭă būxō tĭbī mūltĭfŏrā Sōlēmnĕ cănĭt.

Tīgnūm, ī. n. *Beam*. Mŏdĭcīs īnstrāvīt pūlpĭtă tīgnīs. H. Syn.—Trābs, līgnūm. Phr.—Hīc tīgnūm căpĭti īncŭtĭt.

Tĭgrĭs, ĭs (ĭdĭs). f. *Tiger*. Ūtquĕ fĕræ tīgrēs nūnquām pŏsŭērĕ fŭrōrēm. L. Phr.—Fĕră Cāspĭă. Hўrcānă fĕră. Cædĭs ănhēlāns. Sĭtĭēns, ūt tīgrĭs ăcērbă, crŭōrēm. Tīgrĭdĭs ēxŭvĭæ pēr dōrsum ā vērtĭcĕ pnēdēnt.

Tĭlĭă, æ. f. *The linden-tree*. (*See Appendix under list of Trees, etc.*)

Tĭmĕō, ēs, ŭī, ērĕ. *To fear*. Mĭnūs gaūdēnt quī tĭmŭērĕ nĭhĭl. M. Syn.—Ēxtĭmēscŏ, pērtĭmēscŏ, mĕtŭŏ, vĕrĕŏr, fōrmīdŏ, rĕfōrmīdŏ, păvĕŏ, trĕpĭdŏ, hōrrĕŏ, hōrrēscŏ, pĕrhōrrēscŏ, ēxhōrrēscŏ. Phr.—Tĭmōrĕ, mĕtū pērcēllŏr, tūrbŏr. Tĭmŏr ārtūs ŏccŭpăt. Mĕtŭs mēntēm prĕmĭt. Āttŏnĭtīs hæsēre ănĭmīs. Sŭbĭt hōrrĭdă mēntēm fōrmīdŏ. Tōrpŭĕrăt līnguă rĕtēntā mĕtū. Quīd tūtă tĭmēs?

Tĭmĭdē. adv. *Fearfully, timidly*. Syn.—Cūnctāntĕr. Phr.—Tĭmĭdē gĕlĭdēquĕ mĭnīstrăt.

Tĭmĭdŭs, ă, ūm. *Fearful, timid*. Aēquī cūltōr tĭmĭdūsquĕ dĕōrūm. O. Syn.—Vĕrĭtŭs, tĭmēns, mĕtŭēns. Phr.—Tĭmĭdūsquĕ prŏcēllæ. Pĕrīcŭlă, vūlnĕră fōrmīdāns. *Frightened*. Syn.—Tĭmēns. păvĭdŭs, trĕpĭdŭs, īgnāvŭs, īmbēllĭs. Phr.—Mĕtū ēxsānguĭs. Fōrmīdĭnĕ cāptŭs. Mēntĭs ĭnōps. Tērrōrĕ păvēns.

Tĭmŏr, ōrĭs. m. *Fear*. Vōtă mĕtū dŭplĭcānt mātrēs, prŏpĭūsquĕ pĕrīclō Īt tĭmŏr. V. Syn.—Fōrmīdŏ, păvŏr, mĕtŭs, tērrŏr, trĕmŏr, hōrrŏr. Phr.—Gĕlĭdŭs tōrpŏr. Sēmpĕr ānxĭŭs. Ēxpērs quĭētĭs. Pēctŭs cōnstrīngēns. Pārcŭs sŭī. Mălŭs īntērprēs rērūm mĕtŭs. Aūdācēm fēcĕrăt īpsĕ tĭmŏr. Vēntūrī tĭmŏr īpsĕ mălī. Sōllĭcĭtām tĭmŏr ānxĭŭs ūrgĕt. Rēs ēst īmpĕrĭōsă tĭmŏr. Mēns trĕpĭdō pălpĭtăt ægră mĕtū. Trĕpĭdī fōrmīdĭnĕ pōrtās Ēxplōrănt. Sŭbĭtūs trĕmŏr ōccŭpăt ārtūs. Pārcĕ mĕtū. Sōlvĕ mĕtūs. Sōlvĭtĕ cōrdĕ mĕtūm. Tĭmōrēm lēnĭĭt. Păvŏr ōssă rĕlīquĭt. Mĕtŭs hīnc ăbsĭt. Sōlvĕ mĕtūs ănĭmō.

Tīngŏ, ĭs, xī, ctūm, ĕrĕ. *To moisten.* Spārsā tīngĕrĕ cōrpŭs ăquā. O. Syn.—Mădĕfăcĭŏ, hūmēctŏ, mērgŏ, īmmērgŏ, īmbŭŏ, spārgŏ, āspērgŏ, rĭgŏ, īrrĭgŏ, ūngŏ, pērfūndŏ, īrrōrŏ. Phr.—Cĕlĕrēs nēc tīngĕrĕt æquŏrĕ plāntās. Tīngĕre ĭn āmnĕ cŏmās. *To tint.* Syn.—Īmbŭŏ, fūcŏ, cŏlōrŏ, lĭnŏ, īllĭnŏ, mĕdĭcŏ, sătūrŏ. Phr.—Lānām, vēllĕră cŏlōrĕ, fūcō, vĕnēnō tīngĕrĕ. Crŏcĕō mūtābĭt vēllĕră lūtō. Tȳrĭūm quæ pūrpŭră sēnsĭt ăhēnūm.

Tīnnĭŏ, īs, ĭī, ītūm, īrĕ. *To ring, to sound, to tinkle.* Syn.—Tīnnītŏ, tīntīnnŏ, strīdĕŏ, strīdŏ, crĕpŏ, crĕpĭtŏ, strĕpŏ. Phr.—Tīnnītūm ēdŏ. Tīnnītū āĕră pūlsŏ.

Tīnnŭlŭs, ă, ūm. *That which renders a clear sound.* Syn.—Ārgūtŭs, rĕsŏnāns, sŏnōrŭs, strīdēns.

Tīnŭs, ī. f. *A kind of bay-tree.* (*See Appendix under list of Trees, etc.*)

Tīrŏ, ōnĭs. m. *New recruit, soldier just enrolled.* Syn.—Tīrūncŭlŭs. Phr.—Ārtĕ rŭdĭs, īmpĕrītŭs, īgnārŭs. Rŭdĭs ārmōrūm.

Tĭtīllŏ, ās, āvī, ātūm, ārĕ. *To tickle, to allure pleasantly.* Syn.—Mūlcĕŏ, dēmūlcĭŏ, pērmūlcĕŏ, āllĭcĭŏ, dēlīnĭŏ, ōblēctŏ.

Tĭtŭbŏ, ās, āvī, ātūm, ārĕ. *To hesitate, to falter.* Īllĕ mĕrō sōmnōquĕ grăvīs tĭtŭbārĕ vĭdētŭr. O. Syn.—Lăbŏ, lăbāscŏ, nūtŏ, văcīllŏ, hæsĭtŏ. Phr.—Dŭbĭī stāntquĕ lăbāntquĕ pĕdēs.

Tĭtŭlŭs, ī. m. *Title, inscription.* Syn.—Nōmĕn, ĕpĭgrāmmă. Phr.—Tĭtŭlō sīgnētŭr ĭmāgŏ. *Title of honor.* Syn.—Nōmĕn, hŏnŏr, laūs, dĕcŭs, stēmmă. Phr.—Tĭtŭlīs īnsīgnĭs ăvōrūm. *Pretext.* Syn.—Caūsă, nōmĕn, spĕcĭēs.

Tŏgă, æ. f. *Toga, Roman robe.* Ēfflŭĭt ēffūsō cuī tŏgă lāxă sĭnū. Tib. Phr.—Rūstĭcĭūs tōnsō tŏgă dēflŭĭt. *See Vestis.* Fig.—*Roman.* Syn.—Rōmānŭs. *Client.* Syn.—Tŏgātī, clĭēntēs. *Peace.* Syn.—Pāx.

Tŏgātŭs, ă, ūm. *Clothed in the toga.* Rōmānōs rērūm dŏmĭnōs gēntēmquĕ tŏgātām. V. Phr.—Tŏgā īndūtŭs. *Roman.* Syn.—Rōmānŭs. *Clients.* Syn.—Tŏgă, clĭēntēs.

Tŏlĕrŏ, ās, āvī, ātūm, ārĕ. *To bear, to sustain.* Quā nūnc ārtĕ grăvīs tŏlĕrābĭs ĭnūtĭlĭs ānnōs. M. Syn.—Fĕrŏ, pătĭŏr, pērfĕrŏ, pērpĕtĭŏr, sūstĭnĕŏ. Cāsĭbŭs ēxērcĕŏr. Fōrtī, cōnstāntī pēctŏrĕ fērrĕ mălūm. Sævōs tŏlĕrābĭmŭs īmbrēs.

Tōllŏ, ĭs, sūstŭlī, sūblātūm, ĕrĕ. *To raise.* Āc sē tōllĕrĕ hŭmō, rēctōque āssīstĕrĕ trūncō. O. Syn.—Āttōllŏ, ēxtōllŏ, ēffĕrŏ, ērĭgŏ, ēvĕhŏ, lĕvŏ, sūblĕvŏ. Phr.—Flūctūs ād sīdĕră tōllĭt. Clāmōr sē tōllĭt ăd aūrās. *To animate, to give courage.* Syn.—Ērĭgŏ. *To nourish.* Syn.—Ălŏ, ēdūcŏ, nūtrĭŏ. *To take, to receive.* Syn.—Sūmŏ, āssūmŏ. *To take away, to bear away.* Syn.—Ābdūcŏ, aūfĕrŏ, dēmŏ, ădĭmŏ, rĕmŏvĕŏ, mīttŏ. Phr.—Hās ārtēs tōllĕ. Tōllĕ, pŭēr, călĭcēs. Tōllĕ mŏrās. *To put an end to.* Syn.—Mīttŏ, ōmīttŏ. *To kill.* Syn.—Ōccīdŏ, īntĕrĭmŏ, cædŏ, nĕcŏ.

Tōndĕŏ, ēs, tŏtōndī, tōnsūm, ērĕ. *To shave.* Syn.—Āttōndĕŏ, dētōndĕŏ, tōnsĭtŏ, sĕcŏ, rĕsĕcŏ, mĕtŏ, rādŏ, ābrādŏ, ābscīndŏ. Phr.—Bārbām fērrō sĕcŏ. Cōllūm tōnsōrī cōmmīttŏ. *To cut the hair.* Syn.—Dētōndĕŏ, sĕcŏ, rĕsĕcŏ, mĭnŭŏ, sūccīdŏ, cūrtŏ. Phr.—Crīnĕ sŭūm spŏlĭăt. *To reap.* Syn.—Mĕtŏ. *To graze.* Syn.—Pāscŏr, dēpāscŏr, cārpŏ.

Tŏnĭtrŭs, ūs. m. & Tŏnĭtrū. (*indecl. in sing.*) n. *Thunder.* Fūlgōrēm cērnĭmŭs āntĕ Quām tŏnĭtrum āccĭpĭmŭs. O. Syn.—Fūlmĕn. Phr.—Aēthĕrĭŭs frăgŏr, tŭmūltŭs, strĕpĭtŭs. Īctī æthĕrĭs sŏnĭtŭs, sŏnŭs. Aēthĕrĭūm mūrmŭr. Frāctō dīsplōsă tŏnītrŭă cœlō. Frāctæquĕ tŏnītrŭă nūbĭs.

Tŏnŏ, ās, ŭī, ĭtūm, ārĕ. *To thunder.* Pōrtă tŏnāt cœli, ēt scŏpŭlīs īllīsă rĕclāmānt Aēquŏră. V. Syn.—Īntŏnŏ. Phr.—Cœlūm tŏnăt ōmnĕ frăgōrĕ, tŭmūltū. Īngēns frăgŏr æthĕră cōmplĕt. Māgnō mīscētūr mūrmŭrĕ cœlūm. Tōtō rĕsŏnānt tŏnītrŭă cœlō. Rŭĭt īgnĕŭs æthēr Cūm tŏnĭtrū. Cōncūssī trĕmŭĕrĕ pŏlī. Tŏnăt āltī rēgĭă cœlī. Pătĕr ōmnĭpŏtēns tŏnăt. Fūlmĭnă vĭbrăt. Trĕmēndō Jūpĭtĕr īpsĕ rŭĭt tŭmūltū. Cœlīquĕ sĕrēnă Cōncŭtĭēns tŏnĭtrū. Fig.—*To resound.* Syn.—Īntŏnŏ, sŏnŏ, rĕsŏnŏ, strĕpŏ, pērstrĕpŏ, mūgĭŏ, rĕbŏŏ, clāmŏ.

Tōrtmēntūm, ī. n. *Cord, bond, chain.* Syn.—Vīncŭlūm, cătēnă. *Engine of war.* Syn.—Bālīstă, māchĭnă. *Cannon* (*modern*). Phr.—Sūlphŭrātīs fœtă tŏnītrĭbŭs. Aērĕă fūlmĭnă. Māchĭnă fūlmĭnĭs æmŭlă. Fūnĕră spārgēns. Sŏnĭtūm cōncūssi ĭmĭtātŭr Ŏlŷmpī. Īngēntēm lātō vŏmĭt ōrĕ făvīllām. *Torment, torture.* Syn.—Crŭcĭātŭs, pœnă, sūpplĭcĭūm. Fig.—*Anguish, pain.* Syn.—Dŏlŏr, crŭcĭātŭs, āngŏr, ærūmnă, cūră.

Tŏrōsŭs, ă, ūm. *Strong, muscular.* Syn.—Lăcērtōsŭs, nērvōsŭs rōbūstŭs. Phr.—Tŏrīs lūxŭrĭāns.

Tōrpĕŏ, ēs, ŭī, ērĕ. *To become heavy, languid, immovable.* Nēc tōrpērĕ grăvī pāssūs sŭă rēgnă vĕtērnō. V. Syn.—Stŭpĕŏ, stŭpēscŏ, ōbtōrpēscŏ, lānguĕŏ, lānguēscŏ, hærĕŏ, ādstrīngŏr, cōnstrīngŏr. Phr.—Īmmōbĭlĭs, īmmōtŭs, tōrpēns hærĕō. Mēmbră tōrpŏr hăbĕt. Mēmbră nŏvūs sōlvīt fōrmīdĭnĕ tōrpŏr. Ănĭmōque ēt cōrpŏrĕ tōrpĕt. Tōrpēnt ăd prœlĭă vīrēs.

Tōrpŏr, ōrĭs. m. *Languor, stupor.* Syn.—Tōrpēdŏ, stŭpŏr, lānguŏr, ĭnērtĭă, sĭtŭs.

Tōrquĕō, ēs, tōrsī, tōrtūm, ērĕ. *To twist.* Ēt stāmĭnă pōllĭcĕ tōrquēnt. O. Syn.—Īntōrquĕō, flēctŏ, īnflēctŏ, vōlvŏ, vērtŏ, īnvērtŏ, vērsŏ. *To roll.* Syn.—Vōlvŏ, ăgŏ, ābrĭpĭŏ, vērsŏ. *To turn, to direct.* Syn.—Vērtŏ, tēndŏ, flēctŏ, dētōrquĕŏ, āvērtŏ, dēflēctŏ. *To carry.* Syn.—Gĕrŏ, pōrtŏ, fĕrŏ, sūstĭnĕŏ. *To hurl.* Syn.—Īntōrquĕŏ, cōntōrquĕŏ, lībrŏ, jăcŭlŏr, vĭbrŏ. *To torture.* Syn.—Crŭcĭŏ, pūnĭŏ. *To torment.* Syn.—Vēxŏ, āngŏ, crŭcĭŏ.

Tōrrēns, tĭs. m. *Torrent.* Quā sāxă rŏtāntĭă lātē Īntŭlĕrāt tōrrēns ārbūstăquĕ dīrŭtă rīpīs. V. Syn.—Rīvŭs, āmnĭs. Phr.—Ūndæ răpācēs. Tōrtō vōrtĭcĕ tōrrēns. Rŭēns dē mōntĭbŭs āmnĭs. Rīpīs căpācĭbŭs ēffūsŭs. Mūltō tŭmĕfāctŭs ăb īmbrĕ. Hībērnā nĭvĕ nūtrītŭs. Răpāx cădĭt. Tŭmĭdūs cūm vōrtĭcĕ tōrrēns Sāxă rŏtăt. Spătĭōsās ēxplĭcăt ūndās. Mōntĕ dēcūrrēns vĕlŭt āmnĭs.

Tōrrĕō, ēs, ŭī, tōstūm, ērĕ. *To burn, to dry up.* Syn.—Ūrŏ, ēxūrŏ, ădūrŏ, pĕrūrŏ. Phr.—Tōrrēns sĭtĭēns Sīrĭŭs Īndōs. Tōrrēntūr fēbrĭbŭs ārtūs. *To burn.* Syn.—Īncēndŏ, ūrŏ, cōmbūrŏ, crĕmŏ. *To cook.* Syn.—Cŏquŏ, āssŏ.

Tōrrĭdŭs, ă, ūm. *Burnt, dried up.* Sēmpēr sōlĕ rŭbēns ēt tōrrĭdă sēmpĕr ăb īgnĕ. V. Syn.—Ūstŭs, ēxūstŭs, pĕrūstŭs, ārēns, ārĭdŭs, sīccŭs, sĭtĭēns. *Burning.* Syn.—Tōrrēns, flăgrāns, fērvĭdŭs.

Tōrtĭlĭs, ĭs, ĕ. *Twisting, spinning, spiral.* Syn.—Tōrtŭs, īntōrtŭs, flēxŭs, īnflēxŭs.

Tōrtŭs, ūs. m. *Fold.* Syn.—Spīră, nēxŭs, nōdŭs, vŏlūmĕn.

Tŏrŭs, ī. m. *Muscle.* Lūxŭrĭătquĕ tŏrīs ănĭmōsūm pēctŭs. V. Syn.—Mūscŭlŭs. Phr.—Mŏvĕt ārmă lĕō, gaŭdētquĕ cŏmāntēs Ēxcŭtĭēns cērvīcĕ tŏrōs. *Bed.* Syn.—Lēctŭs, cŭbīlĕ. Phr.—Sīgnīs tŏrŭs āspĕr ĕbūrnīs. Strātīquĕ cŭbīlĭă lēctī. *Nuptial couch.* Syn.—Thălămŭs. *Marriage.* Syn.—Cōnjŭgĭūm.

Tōrvă, tōrvē, tōrvūm. adv. *Crosswise, severely.* Syn.—Ōblīquē, mĭnācĭtĕr.

Tōrvŭs, ă, ūm. *Grim, stern.* Syn.—Trūx, ătrōx, mĭnāx, hōrrĭdŭs, hōrrēndŭs, tērrĭbĭlĭs, sævŭs, dūrŭs, āspĕr, sĕvērŭs, tĕtrĭcŭs, fĕrŭs.

Tōtŭs, ă, ūm. *Whole, entire.* Syn.—Ŏmnĭs, ūnĭvērsŭs, plēnŭs, sŏlĭdŭs, īntĕgĕr. Phr.—Tōtō dīvīsōs ōrbĕ Brĭtānnōs. Hăbēs tōtā quōd mēntĕ pĕtīstī.

Trābs, trăbĭs. f. *Beam, heavy piece of timber.* Aūrātāsquĕ trăbēs, vĕtĕrūm dĕcŏra āltă părēntūm. V. Syn.—Tīgnūm, tĭgīllūm, rōbŭr. Phr.—Nēxǣ ǣrĕ trăbēs. Aūrō nĭtĭdǣ.

Trāctābĭlĭṣ, ĭs, ĕ. *Tractable, easily handled.* Syn.—Făcĭlĭs. Fig.— *Sweet, pleasant.* Syn.—Făcĭlĭs, mītĭs, lēnĭs, mānsuētŭs, ăffābĭlĭs. *Flexible.* Syn.—Flēxĭbĭlĭs, cērĕŭs, mōllĭs, tĕnĕr.

Trāctīm. adv. *Uninterruptedly.* Syn.—Jūgĭtĕr, cōntĭnŭō.

Trāctŏ, ās, āvī, ātūm, ārĕ. *To drag.* Syn.—Trăhŏ, răpĭŏ, rāptŏ. *To touch.* Syn.—Āttrēctŏ, cōntrēctŏ, tāngŏ, pērtēntŏ, vērsŏ, vŏlūtŏ. Fig.— *To treat, to conduct.* Syn.—Rĕgŏ, gĕrŏ, cūrŏ, hăbĕŏ. *To discuss.* Syn.—Ăgĭtŏ, dīssĕrŏ. *To pass over in one's mind.* Syn.—Vērsŏ,vōlvŏ, ăgĭtŏ.

Trāctŭs, ūs. m. *Course, march.* Syn.—Cūrsŭs, ĭtĕr. *Trail, path of fire.* Syn.—Sūlcŭs, trāmĕs, sēmĭtă. *Space, extent.* Syn.— Spătĭūm, plăgă. *Country, region.* Syn.—Rĕgĭŏ, ōră, lŏcŭs.

Trādŏ, ĭs, ĭdī, ĭtūm, ĕrĕ. *To deliver up, to entrust.* Trādĭt ēquūm cŏmĭtī părĭbūsque āssīstĭt ĭn ārmīs. V. Syn.—Dō, prǣbĕŏ, cōmmīttŏ, māndŏ, trĭbŭŏ. *To submit.* Syn.—Dēdŏ, sūbmīttŏ, sūbjĭcĭŏ, sūbdŏ. *To betray.* Syn.—Prōdŏ. *To relate.* Syn.—Mĕmŏrŏ, rĕfĕrŏ, nārrŏ.

Trādūcŏ, ĭs, xī, ctūm, ĕrĕ. *To lead across.* Ātquĕ sătās ălĭō vīdī trādūcĕrĕ mēssēs. V. Syn.—Trānsfĕrŏ, trānsvĕhŏ, trānsmīttŏ, trānspōrtŏ, trājĭcĭŏ. *To pass the time.* Syn.—Ăgŏ, dūcŏ, dēgŏ, trānsĭgŏ.

Trăgĭcŭs, ă, ūm. *Tragic, pertaining to tragedy.* Syn.—Cŏthūrnātŭs, Sŏphŏclĕŭs. Phr.—Sūblīmĭbŭs āptă cŏthūrnīs Mătĕrĭă. Nōn hŭmĭlī mĕmŏrāndă cŏthūrnō. Vērsĭbŭs trăgĭcīs.

Trăgĭcŭs, ī. m. *Tragic poet.* Phr.—Grāndĕ sŏnānt trăgĭcī. Cŏthūrnātŭs vātēs. Māgnūm spīrāns.

Trăgœdĭă, ǣ. f. *Tragedy.* Ōmnĕ gĕnūs scrīptī grăvĭtātĕ trăgœdĭă vīncĭt. O. Syn.—Cŏthūrnŭs, cŏthūrnī. Phr.—Trăgĭcūm cārmĕn. Cĕcrŏpĭŭs, Aēschўlĕŭs cŏthūrnŭs. Grāndēs cŏthūrnī. Cōmpōnĕrĕ vērbă cŏthūrnō. Sĕvērǣ Mūsă trăgœdĭǣ. Trăgĭcă mūsă.

Trăgœdŭs, ī. m. *Tragic actor.* Phr.—Quī āltē grădĭtŭr mājōrĕ cŏthūrnō. Mīrōs aūdĭrĕ trăgœdōs. Aūdītūră trăgœdōs.

Trăhŏ, ĭs, trāxī, trāctūm, ĕrĕ. *To drag.* Ēccĕ trăhēbātūr pāssīs Prĭămēĭă vīrgŏ Crīnĭbŭs. V. Syn.—Āttrăhŏ, prōtrăhŏ, răpĭŏ, rāptŏ, dūcŏ, ābdūcŏ, trāctŏ. Trăhĕrētŭr ărūndĭnĕ prǣdă. Trăhūntūr pēr sīlvām. *To draw out from.* Syn.—Ēxtrăhŏ, ēdūcŏ, ērĭpĭŏ, ēvēllŏ. *To contract, to fold.* Syn.—Cōntrăhŏ, āddūcŏ. *To take, to contract.* Syn.—Dūcŏ, sūmŏ, āccĭpĭŏ, cōncĭpĭŏ, īndŭŏ. *To attract, to allure.* Syn.—Āttrăhŏ, āllĭcĭŏ, dūcŏ, răpĭŏ. *To protract.* Syn.—Prōdūcŏ, prōtrăhŏ, dūcŏ, prōfĕrŏ. Phr.—Sīc ănĭmūm tēmpūsquĕ trăhŏ. Dătūm trăhĕrēnt pēr tālĭă tēmpŭs. *To pass, to spend.* Syn.—Dūcŏ, ăgŏ, dēgŏ, trānsĭgŏ, cōnsūmŏ.

Trājĭcĭŏ, ĭs, jēcī, jēctūm, ĕrĕ. *To transport.* Trājĭcĭt āltērnō quī lĕvĕ pōndŭs ĕquō. V. Syn.—Trānsdūcŏ, trānsfĕrŏ, trānsmīttŏ, trānsvĕhŏ, trānspōrtŏ. *To pass.* Syn.—Trānsĕŏ, trānsgrĕdĭŏr, sŭpĕrŏ, prætĕrĕŏ, trānŏ, trānsmĕŏ, prætērvŏlŏ.

Trāmĕs, ĭtĭs. m. *Path, track.* Ēccĕ sŭpērcĭlĭō clīvōsī trāmĭtĭs ūndām Ēlĭcĭt. V. Syn.—Sēmĭtă, cāllĭs, vĭă. Phr.—Făcĭlī tē trāmĭtĕ sīstām. Cĭtō dēcūrrīt trāmĭtĕ vīrgŏ.

Trānŏ, ās, āvī, ātūm, ārĕ. *To swim through.* Sŭpĕrānt mōntēs ēt flūmĭnă trānānt. V. Syn.—Trānsnŏ, trānsnătŏ, trānsjĭcĭŏ, trānsmīttŏ. Phr.—Nāndō, nătātū trājĭcĭŏ. *To traverse the air.* Syn.—Trānsĕŏ, trānsmĕŏ, trājĭcĭŏ, trānsvŏlŏ, trānscūrrŏ. *To escape. See Evado.*

Trānquīllē. adv. *Peacefully, quietly.* Syn.—Plăcĭdē, quĭētē, lēnĭtĕr, lēnĕ. Phr.—Cūm pācĕ. Trānquīllă rŭēns.

Trānquīllŏ, ās, āvī, ātūm, ārĕ. *To calm.* Syn.—Pācŏ, sēdŏ, lēnĭŏ, tēmpĕrŏ.

Trānquīllŭs, ă, ūm. *Peaceful, quiet, calm.* Syn.—Plăcĭdŭs, quĭētŭs, mītĭs, pācātŭs, sēcūrŭs, sĕrēnŭs. *Speaking of persons.* Syn.—Plăcĭdŭs, quĭētŭs, sĕrēnŭs, sēcūrŭs. Phr.—Cūrīs văcāns. Cūrārūm ēxpērs.

Trāns. prep. *Across.* Syn.—Ūltrā. *On the other side.* Syn.—Cōntrā, ūltrā.

Trānsădĭgŏ, ĭs, ădēgī, ădāctūm, ĕrĕ. *To pierce through.* Syn.—Trānsfīgŏ, trānsfŏdĭŏ, trānsvērbĕrŏ.

Trānscēndŏ, ĭs, dī, sūm, ĕrĕ. *To pass beyond, over.* Syn.—Sŭpĕrŏ, trānsgrĕdĭŏr.

Trānscrībŏ, ĭs, psī, ptūm, ĕrĕ. *To transcribe.* Syn.—Scrībŏ, ēxscrībŏ. Fig.—*To transport.* Syn.—Trānsfĕrŏ, trānsmīttŏ.

Trānscūrrŏ, ĭs, rī, cūrsūm, ĕrĕ. *To traverse, to run beyond.* Syn.—Trājĭcĭŏ, trānsgrĕdĭŏr, prætērvĕhŏr, trānsvŏlŏ, prætērvŏlŏ.

Trānsĕŏ, īs, īvī & ĭī, ĭtūm, īrĕ. *To pass over, to cross.* Ēt mărĭs Īŏnĭī trānsĭĕrītĭs ăquās. O. Syn.—Trānsgrĕdĭŏr, prætĕrĕŏ, trānsmĕŏ, trānsmĭgrŏ, trānscēndŏ, trānsĭlĭŏ, trājĭcĭŏ, trānsmīttŏ, pērmĕŏ, pĕnĕtrŏ, prætērvĕhŏr, trānsvĕhŏr, sŭpĕrŏ, trānslābŏr.

To pass, to go by. Syn.—Ăbĕō, flŭō, ēfflŭō. *To pass over in silence.* Syn.—Mīttŏ, ŏmīttŏ, trānsĭlĭō, prætĕrĕō, prætērmīttŏ.

Trānsfĕrŏ, fērs, tŭlī, lātūm, fērrĕ. *To transport, to carry.* Rēgnūmque ā sēdĕ Lăvīnī Trānsfĕrĕt. V. Syn.—Trānspōrtŏ, trānsmīttŏ, trānsvĕhŏ, trādūcŏ, vērtŏ, trājĭcĭŏ.

Trānsfīgŏ, ĭs, fīxī, fīxūm, ĕrĕ. *To pierce through.* Syn.—Trānsădĭgŏ, trānsfŏdĭŏ, cōnfŏdĭŏ, trānsvērbĕrŏ, trājĭcĭŏ, trānsăbĕŏ, trānsfŏrŏ. Phr.—Cōrpŭs, pēctŭs, vīscĕră fērrō fīgŏ, fŏdĭŏ. Fērrūm pēr vīscĕră ăgŏ. Ēnsēm pēctŏrĕ cōndŏ. Lătŭs mŭcrōnĕ rĕsōlvŏ. Trānsfīgēns ūnguĭbŭs ānguēm.

Trānsflŭō, ĭs, flūxī, flūxūm, ĕrĕ. *To flow by.* Syn.—Flŭŏ, ēfflŭŏ, trānsĕŏ, ăbĕŏ.

Trānsfŏdĭō, ĭs, fōdī, fōssūm, ĕrĕ. *To pierce through and through.* Gĕmĭnō trānsfōdīt vūlnĕrĕ pēctŭs. O. Syn.—Cōnfŏdĭŏ, trānsădĭgŏ, trānsfīgŏ, trānsvērbĕrŏ. Phr.—Crūdūm pēr cōstās ēxĭgĭt ēnsēm. Huĭc glădĭō lătŭs haūrĭt ăpērtūm.

Trānsfōrmŏ, ās, āvī, ātūm, ārĕ. *To change.* Ōmnĭă trānsfōrmāt sēse īn mīrācŭlă rērūm. V. Syn.—Mūtŏ, īmmūtŏ, vărĭŏ. Phr.—Vĕtĕrēs mūtārĕ fĭgūrās. Vērsāmquĕ vĕnēnīs Fēcĭt ăvēm. Fĭgūrās Sūmĕrĕ quās vēllĕt.

Trānsgrĕdĭŏr, ĕrĭs, grēssŭs sūm, ī. *To pass beyond.* Syn.—Trānsĕŏ, trānsăbĕŏ, trānscēndŏ, sŭpĕrŏ.

Trānsĭgŏ, ĭs, ēgī, āctūm, ĕrĕ. *To pierce through.* Trānsēgīt pēctŏră mūcrŏ. Syn.—Trājĭcĭŏ. *To pass the time.* Syn.—Ăgŏ, dūcŏ, trādūcŏ, ēxĭgŏ, dēgŏ. *To execute, to finish.* Syn.—Pĕrăgŏ, cōnfĭcĭŏ, ābsōlvŏ.

Trānsĭlĭō, īs, ŭī & ĭī, ūltūm, īrĕ. *To leap over, to jump.* Strīdēns ēt cĕlĕrēs īncōgnĭtă trānsĭlĭt ūmbrās. V. Syn.—Trānsĕŏ, prætĕrĕŏ, trānscēndŏ, trānsgrĕdĭŏr, sŭpĕrŏ, trānsūltŏ. Phr.—Sāltū sŭpĕrŏ. Nōn tāngēndă rătēs trānsĭlĭūnt vădă. *To pass over in silence.* Syn.—Trānsĕŏ, prætĕrĕŏ, ŏmīttŏ.

Trānslūcĕō, ēs, xī, ērĕ. *To shine through, to be transparent.* Syn.—Pērlūcĕŏ. *To reflect light.* Syn.—Rĕflēctŏr, rĕdĕŏ, rĕmīttŏr.

Trānsmīttŏ, ĭs, mīsī, mīssūm, ĕrĕ. *To carry over, to transport.* Syn.—Trānsfĕrŏ, trājĭcĭŏ, trānsvĕhŏ, trānspōrtŏ. *To bury.* Syn.—Trājĭcĭŏ, īmmīttŏ, īnjĭcĭŏ.

Trānspōrtŏ, ās, āvī, ātūm, ārĕ. *To carry. See Transmitto, Transveho.*

Trānsvĕhŏ, ĭs, ēxī, ēctūm, ĕrĕ. *To carry over.* Syn.—Trājĭcĭŏ, trānspōrtŏ, trānsmīttŏ, prætērvĕhŏ, trānsfĕrŏ.

Trānsvŏlŏ, ās, āvī, ātūm, ārĕ. *To fly over, to traverse.* Syn.—Prætērvŏlŏ, prætĕrĕŏ, trānsĕŏ, trānscūrrŏ. *To omit.* Syn.—Prætērmīttŏ, ŏmīttŏ, prætĕrĕŏ, trānsĕŏ, trānsĭlĭŏ, nēglĕgŏ.

Trĕmĕbūndŭs, ă, ūm. *Trembling, palpitating.* Syn.—Trĕpĭdŭs, trĕmŭlŭs. *Frightened.* Syn.—Trĕmĕfāctŭs, trĕmēns, păvĭdŭs, tērrĭtŭs.

Trĕmĕfăcĭŏ, ĭs, fēcī, fāctūm, ĕrĕ. *To make tremble.* Ānnŭĭt ēt tōtūm nūtū trĕmĕfēcĭt Ŏlȳmpūm. V. Syn.—Quătĭŏ, cōncŭtĭŏ, quāssŏ, mŏvĕŏ.

Trĕmŏ, ĭs, ŭī, ĕrĕ. *To tremble with fear.* Tārdă trĕmēntī Gĕnuă lăbānt. V. Syn.—Trĕmīscŏ, cōntrĕmīscŏ, trĕpĭdŏ, hōrrĕŏ. Phr.—Tōtūs trĕmo, hōrrĕōquĕ. Ēt cōrde ēt gĕnĭbūs trĕmĭt. Cŏr āttŏnĭtūm sălĭt. Trĕmŏr ōccŭpăt ārtūs. Gĕlĭdūsquĕ cŭcūrrĭt Īmă pĕr ōssă trémŏr. Pōplĭtĕ sūccĭdŭō gĕnŭa īntrĕmŭĕrĕ. Ōrĕ trĕmente lŏqui. *To tremble, to agitate.* Pūlsūquĕ pĕdūm trĕmĭt ēxcĭtă tēllūs. V. Syn.—Trĕmīscŏ, īntrĕmŏ, cōntrĕmŏ, cōntrĕmīscŏ, trĕpĭdŏ, ăgĭtŏr, mŏvĕŏr, cōmmŏvĕŏr, vĭbrŏr, cōncŭtĭŏr, quătĭŏr, nūtŏ, văcīllŏ.

Trĕmŏr, ōrĭs. m. *Trembling.* Syn.—Mōtŭs. *Fear.* Syn.—Trĕpĭdātĭŏ, hōrrŏr, păvŏr, tĭmŏr.

Trĕmŭlŭs, ă, ūm. *Trembling.* Grădū trĕmŭlō vĕnĭt ǣgră sĕnēctūs. Prop. Syn.—Trĕmĕbūndŭs, trĕmēns, trĕmīscēns, trĕpĭdāns, mōtŭs, ăgĭtātŭs, crīspŭs, mĭcāns, vĭbrāns. Phr.—Hĭēms trĕmŭlō vĕnĭt hōrrĭdă pāssū. Ŏcŭlī trĕmŭlō fūlgōrĕ mĭcāntēs. Splēndĕt trĕmŭlō sŭb lūmĭnĕ pōntŭs. *Fearful, timid.* Syn.—Trĕmēns, trĕmĕbūndŭs, trĕmĕfāctŭs, trĕpĭdāns, păvĭdŭs, tĭmĭdŭs, tērrĭtŭs, pērtērrĭtŭs.

Trĕpĭdŏ, ās, āvī, ātūm, ārĕ. *To be agitated.* Syn.—Cōncūrsŏ, cūrsĭtŏ. *To hasten.* Syn.—Fēstīnŏ, cūrrŏ. *To tremble.* Syn.—Tērrĕŏr, tĭmĕŏ, mĕtŭŏ.

Trĕpĭdŭs, ă, ūm. *Trembling, agitated.* Syn.—Trĕmŭlŭs. *Excited, rushing.* Syn.—Trĕpĭdŭs, fēstīnŭs, fēstīnāns, ănhēlŭs. *Anxious.* Syn.—Sōllĭcĭtŭs, ānxĭŭs, tūrbātŭs.

Trĭbūnăl, ālĭs. n. *Tribunal.* Quōd făcĭăt māgnās tūrpĕ trĭbūnăl ŏpēs. O. Syn.—Sŏlĭūm. Phr.—Jūdĭcĭs, jūrĭdĭcūm sŏlĭūm, sĕdīlĕ. Fŏrēnsĭs sēdēs. Stāt jūdĭcĭs āntĕ trĭbūnăl.

Trĭbūnŭs, ī. m. *Tribune, Roman magistrate.* Sūmĕrĕ dēpŏsĭtūm clāvūm fĭĕrīquĕ trĭbūnūm. H. Phr.—Trĭbūnĭtĭă plēbēiūs sīgnĭfĕr ārcĕ. Cūm cōnsŭlĭbŭs Tūrbāntēs jūră trĭbūnī.

Trĭbŭŏ, ĭs, ŭī, ūtūm, ĕrĕ. *To grant, to give.* Hǣc bŏnă nōn prīmǣ trĭbŭĭt nātūră jŭvēntǣ. O. Syn.—Dō, prǣbĕŏ, trādŏ, lārgĭŏr, īmpērtĭŏr, dēfĕrŏ, cōncēdŏ, prǣstŏ, cōndōnŏ, pērmīttŏ. *To attribute.* Syn.—Āttrĭbŭŏ, āssīgnŏ.

Trĭbūtūm, ī. n. *Tribute.* Syn.—Aĕră, vēctīgăl. Phr.—Ēx ōmnī gēntĕ trĭbūtă pĕtĭt. Tĭbĭ pōrtĭtŏr ǣră rĕcēpĭt.

Trĭdēns, ēntĭs. adj. *That which has three teeth or points.* Cōnvūlsūm rēmĭs rōstrīsquĕ trĭdēntĭbŭs æquŏr. V. Syn.—Trĭcūspĭs, trĭfĭdŭs. Phr.—Trĭsūlcă cūspĭs, hāstă. Fūscĭnă dēntĕ mĭnāx.

Trĭfĭdŭs, ă, ūm. *Three-pointed.* Syn.—Trĭcūspĭs, trĭsūlcŭs, trĭplēx, trĭdēns.

Trĭplēx, ĭcĭs. adj. *Triple.* Syn.—Tērgĕmĭnŭs, tērnŭs, trĭplŭs.

Trĭpŭdĭō, ās, āvī, ātūm, ārĕ. *To dance.* Syn.—Sāltō, ēxsūltō. Phr.—Gaūdēt īnvīsām pĕpŭlīssĕ fōssŏr Tēr pĕdĕ tērrām. *See Chorea.*

Trīstĭs, ĭs, ĕ. *Sad, mournful.* Trīstĭŏr ēt lăcrĭmīs ŏcŭlōs sūffūsă nĭtēntēs. V. Syn.—Mœrēns, mœstŭs, dŏlēns, āfflīctŭs, ānxĭŭs, sōllĭcĭtŭs. Phr.—Mœrōrĕ, trīstĭtĭă prēssŭs, sōllĭcĭtŭs. Cuī frōns nūbĭlă. Mœstă jăcēt tūndītquĕ gĕnās. Ēt trīstēs sĭnĕ sōlĕ dŏmōs. *Severe, grave.* Syn.—Grăvĭs, tētrĭcŭs, sĕvērŭs, hōrrĭdŭs. *Fatal, deplorable.* Syn.—Fūnēstŭs, fātālĭs, dīrŭs, āspĕr, īnfaūstŭs, lūctĭfĭcŭs, crūdēlĭs, mĭsĕr, dēplōrāndŭs. *Horrible, menacing.* Syn.—Hōrrēndŭs, hōrrĭfĭcŭs, dīrŭs, ātĕr, fœdŭs, mĭnāx, tērrĭbĭlĭs.

Trīstĭtĭă, æ. f. *Sadness.* Sīmque ĕgŏ trīstĭtĭæ caūsă mŏdūsquĕ tŭæ. O. Syn.—Mœrŏr, mœstĭtĭă, dŏlŏr, āngŏr, squālŏr, lūctŭs, ærūmnă, ānxĭĕtās. Phr.—Vūltūs, frōntĭs trīstĭtĭă. Trīstĭtĭæ ŏnŭs. Dūrī lăbōrēs ănĭmī. Cūræ trīstēs. Frōns trīstĭs. Trīstĭs sōllĭcĭtūdŏ. Cōntrāctæ nūbĭlă frōntĭs. Mœrēntĭă pēctŏră.

Trīstŏr, ārĭs, ātŭs sūm, ārī. *To be sad.* Syn.—Mœrĕō, cōntrīstŏr, lūgĕō, gĕmŏ. Phr.—Dŏlōrĕ, mœrōrĕ prĕmŏr, ōpprĭmŏr.

Trĭsūlcŭs, ă, ūm. *Three-pointed.* Syn.—Trĭcūspĭs, trĭdēns, trĭfĭdŭs, trĭplēx. Phr.—Līnguīs mĭcăt ōrĕ trĭsūlcīs.

Trītĭcūm, ī. n. *Wheat.* Syn.—Fār, frūmēntūm. *See Frumentum, Seges.*

Trĭūmphŏ, ās, āvī, ātūm, ārĕ. *To triumph.* Vīctŏr ăb hōstĕ rĕdīt, lætāquĕ trĭūmphăt ĭn ūrbĕ. Prop. Syn.—Ŏvŏ. Phr.—Trĭūmphūm ăgŏ, dūcŏ. Trĭūmphō īnvĕhŏr. Cūrrū sūblīmĭs ĕŏ. Ād tēmplă dĕōrūm trĭūmphōs dūcŏ. Trĭūmphī dĕcŭs. Trĭūmphālī dēvīnctūs tēmpŏră laūrōs. Vīctrīcēs gĕrĕrĕ laūrōs. Laūrĭgĕrōs trānscēndĕrĕ cūrrūs. Vīctŏr ăgēt cūrrūm. Præmĭă bēllī.

Trĭūmphŭs, ī. m. *Triumph.* Ērgo ŭbī præclārōs pōscēnt tŭă fātă trĭūmphōs. Tib. Phr.—Trĭūmphī pōmpă, dĕcŭs, hŏnŏr. Trĭūmphālĭs pōmpă, cūrrŭs. Trĭūmphālēs ĕquī. Vīctōr cūrrŭs cŏrōnātīs dūctŭs ĕquīs. Aētērnī trĭūmphī pōmpă sōlēmnĭs. Cūrrŭs vīctŏr, laūrĭgĕr. Fig.—*Victory.* Syn.—Vīctōrĭă, trŏpæūm, pālmă.

Trŏpæūm, ī. n. *Trophy, monument of victory.* Ēt dŭō rāptă mănū dīvērso ēx hōstĕ trŏpæă. V. Syn.—Ēxŭvĭæ, spŏlĭă. Phr.—Vīctī hōstĭs mŏnŭmēntă, sīgnă. Clārī mŏnŭmēntă trŏpæă. Trĭūmphātī hōstĭs ēxŭvĭǣ. Vīctrīcīs pīgnŏră dēxtrǣ. Spŏlĭātī glōrĭă Pārthī. Fig.—*Victory.* Syn.—Trĭūmphŭs, vīctōrĭă, pālmă, laūrŭs.

Trŭcīdŏ, ās, āvī, ātūm, ārĕ. *To kill.* Fīt vĭă vī, rūmpūnt ădĭtūs, prīmōsquĕ trŭcīdānt. V. Syn.—Cǣdŏ, ōccīdŏ, īntērfīcĭŏ, īntĕrĭmŏ, jŭgŭlŏ, nĕcŏ, ōbtrūncŏ. *See Occido.*

Trŭcŭlēntŭs, ă, ūm. *Fierce, threatening.* Spēctāt trŭcŭlēntă lŏquēntēm. O. Syn.—Trūx, tōrvŭs, āspĕr, ătrōx, mĭnāx, tērrĭbĭlĭs, dūrŭs, hōrrĭdŭs, hōrrēndŭs. *Cruel, barbarous.* Syn.—Bārbărŭs, ēffĕrŭs, ĭnhūmānŭs, īmmītĭs, crūdēlĭs, sǣvŭs, īmmānĭs.

Trūdŏ, ĭs, sī, sūm, ĕrĕ. *To push violently.* Syn.—Ădĭgŏ, ăgŏ, prōpēllŏ, īmpēllŏ, pēllŏ, cōmpēllŏ. Phr.—Īn prœlĭă trūdĭt ĭnērmēm. Trūdĭtūr dĭēs dĭē.

Trūncŭs, ă, ūm. *Cut, mutilated.* Trūncă mănūm pīnūs rĕgĭt, ēt vēstīgĭă fīrmăt. V. Syn.—Trūncātŭs, ōbtrūncātŭs, āmpŭtātŭs, mŭtĭlŭs, lăcĕr, scīssŭs, ābscīssŭs, rēscīssŭs, sēctŭs, dēsēctŭs. Phr.—Trūncās ĭnhŏnēstō vūlnĕrĕ nārēs. Trūncă tēmpŏră.

Trūncŭs, ī. m. *Trunk of a tree.* Gēnsquĕ vĭrūm trūncīs ēt dūrō rōbŏrĕ nātă. V. Syn.—Stīpĕs, caūdēx, ārbŏr. Phr.—Trūncī rōbŭr. Cǣlēbs sĭnĕ pālmĭtĕ trūncŭs. *Trunk of a body.* Syn.—Cōrpŭs.

Trŭtĭnă, ǣ. f. *The upper part of a scales, scales in general.* Syn.—Lānx, bĭlānx, lĭbră, stătēră, ēxāmĕn.

Trūx, trŭcĭs. adj. *Frightful, severe. See Truculentus.*

Tŭbă, ǣ. f. *Trumpet.* Ēxŏrĭtūr clāmōrquĕ vĭrūm clāngōrquĕ tŭbārūm. V. Syn.—Clāssĭcūm, cōrnū, būccĭnă, lĭtŭŭs, ǣs. Phr.—Aēs, cōrnū căvūm, sŏnōrūm. Cōrnū tŭbă flēxĭlĭs ūncō. Tŭbǣ sīgnă, sŏnĭtŭs. Mārtĭă clāssĭcă. Dāns bēllō sīgnūm. Quǣ fĕră bēllă cănĭt. Tērrĭfīcō strīdēns clāngōrĕ. Īmmītī mūrmŭrĕ sǣvǣ Īntēr bēllă tŭbǣ. Tŭbǣ frĕmĭtŭs trŭcēs. Nōn ǣră sŏnānt. Quōs ǣrĕ rĕcūrvō Strīdēntēs ăcŭĕrĕ tŭbǣ. Nūllās tŭbă vērbĕrĕt aūrēs. Dāt sīgnūm pūgnǣ. Clāră dĕdīt sŏnĭtūm tŭbă.

Tŭĕŏr, ērĭs, tŭĭtŭs sūm, ērī. *To look at.* Ēxplērī mēntēm nĕquĭt ārdēscĭtquĕ tŭēndō. V. Syn.—Īntŭĕŏr, āspĭcĭŏ, spēctŏ. Phr.—Ŏcŭlīsquĕ tŭēns īmmītĭbŭs. *To guard.* Syn.—Cūstōdĭŏ, sērvŏ. *To defend, to protect.* Syn.—Tūtŏr, dēfēndŏ, tĕgŏ, prōtĕgŏ, sērvŏ, āssērvŏ.

Tūm. adv. *Then.* Syn.—Tūnc. *Next, besides.* Syn.—Īnsŭpĕr, deīndĕ, prǣtĕrĕă.

Tŭmĕŏ, ēs, ŭī, ērĕ. *To swell up.* Ēt tŭă jām flētū lūmĭnă fēssă tŭmēnt. Tib. Syn.—Īntŭmĕŏ, īnflŏr, tūrgĕŏ, tūrgēscŏ. *To rise up.* Syn.—Sūrgŏ, crēscŏ. *To be filled with pride.* Syn.—Sŭpērbĭŏ. *See Superbio.*

Tŭmĭdŭs, ă, ūm. *Swollen.* Tŭmĭdæque īn vītĭbŭs ūvæ. O. Syn.—Tŭmēns, tŭmĕfāctŭs, tūrgēns, tūrgēscēns, dīstēntŭs. Phr.—Sībĭlă cōllă tŭmēns. Quā tŭmĭdūs rĭgăt ārvă Nīlŭs. Fig.—*Proud.* Syn.—Īnflātŭs, tŭmĕfāctŭs, tŭmēns, tūrgĭdŭs, sŭpērbŭs, ēlātŭs. Phr.—Sūccēssū tŭmĭdŭs. Tŭmĭdūs gĕnĭtōrĭs ĭmāgĭnĕ fālsī. Fūlgēntem ārmīs āc vānă tŭmēntēm. *Angry.* Syn.—Īrātŭs.

Tŭmūltŭŏr, ārĭs, ātŭs sūm, ārī. *To cause a tumult.* Syn.—Trĕpĭdŏ, ăgĭtŏr.

Tŭmūltŭōsŭs, ă, ūm. *Noisy, tumultous.* Tŭmūltŭōsūm sōllĭcĭtāt mărĕ. H. Syn.—Tūrbātŭs, tūrbĭdŭs, tūrbŭlēntŭs, sēdĭtĭōsŭs.

Tŭmūltŭs, ūs. m. *Tumult, noise.* Āt dŏmŭs īntĕrĭŏr gĕmĭtū mĭsĕrōquĕ tŭmūltū Mīscētŭr. V. Syn.—Strĕpĭtŭs, frăgŏr, mūrmŭr. Phr.—Cœlūm tŏnăt ōmnĕ tŭmūltū. *Sedition, revolt.* Syn.—Tūrbă, mōtŭs, sēdĭtĭŏ. Phr.—Sēdĭtĭōsŭs rūmŏr. Cīvīlēs tūrbæ. Mīstōque īngēns ēxōrtă tŭmūltū Lætĭtĭă. Tūrbā cŏĕūntĕ. *Quarrel.* Syn.—Rīxă, jūrgĭūm. *Trouble of the mind.* Syn.—Ānxĭĕtās, cūră.

Tūnc. adv. *Then.* Syn.—Tūm. Phr.—Tūnc tēmpŏrĭs. Hōc tēmpŏrĕ.

Tūndŏ, ĭs, tŭtŭdī, tūnsūm, ĕrĕ. *To beat, to strike.* Gēns ēffrēnă vĭrūm Rīphæō tūndĭtūr Eūrō. V. Syn.—Cōntūndŏ, cædŏ, fĕrĭŏ, pūlsŏ, plāngŏ, vērbĕrŏ. *To break, to knock down.* Syn.—Tĕrŏ, cōntĕrŏ, frāngŏ, cōnfrīngŏ, cōmmĭnŭŏ.

Tŭnĭcă, æ. f. *Tunic, worn under the toga.* Ēt tŭnĭcām mōllī mātēr quām nēvĕrăt aūrō. V. Syn.—Vēstĭs. *See Vestis. Covering (in general).* Syn.—Mēmbrānă, tĕgŭmēntūm, tēgmĕn, cōrtēx. *Coat-of-mail.* Syn.—Fōllĭcŭlŭs, lōrīcă.

Tūrbă, æ. f. *Trouble, confusion.* Syn.—Tŭmūltŭs. *Trouble of mind.* Syn.—Cūră, ānxĭĕtās. *Crowd, multitude.* Syn.—Āgmĕn, cătērvă, cŏhōrs, cœtŭs, cōncĭŏ, mănŭs, mūltĭtūdŏ, frĕquēntĭă, glŏbŭs, nŭmĕrŭs, cōpĭă, vīs. Phr.—Tūrbæ glŏbŭs. Vīs hŏmĭnūm. Plūrĭmă tūrbă vĭrūm. Dēnsum hŭmĕrīs vūlgŭs. Rŭĭt ōmnĭs ĭn ūnūm Tūrbă fŭrēns. Māgnā jŭvĕnūm stīpāntĕ cătērvā. Tāntō cōmplērīnt āgmĭnĕ rīpās.

Tūrbĭdŭs, ă, ūm. *Agitated.* Syn.—Ăgĭtātŭs, tŭmēns, tŭmūltŭōsŭs, īrātŭs, mōtŭs, cōmmōtŭs, sōllĭcĭtŭs, fērvĭdŭs, æstŭāns. *Threatening, obscure (in speaking of the sky).* Syn.—Ātĕr, nĭgĕr, ōbscūrŭs, pĭcĕŭs, prŏcēllōsŭs. Fig.—(*Speaking of the mind*). Syn.—Ăgĭtātŭs, cōmmōtŭs, pērtūrbātŭs, ēxstērnātŭs, āmēns.

Tūrbŏ, ās, āvī, ātūm, ārĕ. *To disturb, to trouble.* Ēvērsæ tūrbānt cōnvīvĭă mēnsæ. O. Syn.—Cōntūrbŏ, pērtūrbŏ, mīscĕŏ, pērmīscĕŏ, cōnfūndŏ, vērsŏ, ăgĭtŏ. Phr.—Hūnc sĭnĕ mē tūrbārĕ lŏcūm. Ūsque ădĕō tūrbātŭr ăgrīs. *To put in disorder.* Syn.—Prōtūrbŏ, ăgĭtŏ, ēxăgĭtŏ, ăgŏ, īnsĕquŏr, īnsēctŏr.

Tūrbŏ, ĭnĭs. m. *Wind, whirlwind.* Vēntī, Quā dătă pōrtă, rŭūnt ēt tērrās tūrbĭnĕ pērflānt. V. Syn.—Vēntŭs, tēmpēstās. Phr.—Vīs sævī tūrbĭnĭs. Nĭgĕr īntōrtō ceū tūrbĭnĕ nīmbŭs. Īntōrquēns nīgrāntī tūrbĭnĕ nūbēm. Vŏlāt ātrī tūrbĭnĭs īnstăr. Ăgēns hĭĕmēm rŭĭt. Quōs æquŏrĕ tūrbŏ Dīspŭlĕrāt. *Any rotary movement.* Syn.—Gȳrŭs, vērtīgŏ. *Violence.* Syn.—Vīs, īmpĕtŭs.

Tūrbŭlēntŭs, ă, ūm. *Troubled, disturbed.* Syn.—Tūrbĭdŭs, tūrbātŭs. *One who causes trouble.* Syn.—Sēdĭtĭōsŭs, ĭnĭmīcŭs.

Tūrdŭs, ī. m. *A thrush.* (*See Appendix under list of Birds.*)

Tūrgĭdŭs, ă, ūm. *Swollen.* Syn.—Tŭmēns, tŭmĭdŭs, tŭmĕfāctŭs, īnflātŭs. Fig.—*Filled with pride.* Syn.—Sŭpērbŭs.

Tūrmă, æ. f. *Squadron.* Syn.—Cătērvă, ālă, cŏhōrs. Phr.—Fōrtēs ăd prœlĭă tūrmæ. Ālĭpĕdēs răpĭt ăd cērtāmĭnă tūrmās. *Crowd. See Turba.*

Tūrmātīm. adv. *In troops, in bands.* Syn.—Cōngrĕgātīm, ūnā, sĭmŭl.

Tūrpĭs, ĭs, ĕ. *Ill-shaped, deformed.* Nāmque ălĭæ tūrpēs hōrrēnt. V. Syn.—Dēfōrmĭs, īnfōrmĭs, tētĕr, fœdŭs, hōrrĭdŭs, prāvŭs. *Dirty. See Sordidus. Base, disgraceful.* Syn.—Ābjēctŭs, vīlĭs, īndĕcōrŭs, ĭnhŏnēstŭs, fœdŭs, īnfāmĭs, īndīgnŭs, sōrdĭdŭs, prŏbrōsŭs, pŭdēndŭs. *Immodest, licentious.* Syn.—Flāgĭtĭōsŭs fœdŭs, īmpūrŭs, ōbscœnŭs, spūrcŭs.

Tūrpĭtĕr. adv. *Basely.* Syn.—Fœdē, prŏbrōsē, tūrpĕ, pŭdēndūm. *Indecently.* Syn.—Ōbscœnē, prŏtērvē, lāscīvē.

Tūrpĭtūdŏ, ĭnĭs. f. *Deformity.* Syn.—Dēfōrmĭtās. *Shame, dishonor.* Syn.—Dēdĕcŭs, flāgĭtĭūm, īnfāmĭă, nŏtă, vĭtĭūm.

Tūrpŏ, ās, āvī, ātūm, ārĕ. *To deform, to disfigure.* Syn.—Dētūrpŏ, fœdŏ, dēfōrmŏ, cōrrūmpŏ. *To soil.* Syn.—Pōllŭŏ. *To dishonor.* Syn.—Dēdĕcŏrŏ.

Tūrrĭfĕr, ĕră, ĕrūm. *Crowned with towers.* Syn.—Tūrrītŭs, tūrrĭgĕr. Phr.—Tūrrĭbŭs cīnctŭs, mūnītŭs, īnstrūctŭs.

Tūrrĭs, ĭs. f. *Tower.* Ārmātīquĕ căvīs ēxspēctānt tūrrĭbŭs hōstēm. V. Syn.—Ārx, cāstrūm, cāstēllūm, spĕcŭlă, mūnīmĕn, prōpūgnācŭlūm. Phr.—Tūrrĭs mūnīmĕn. Tūrrītūm prōpūgnācŭlūm. Vālĭdæ bēllō tūrrēs. Stāt fērrĕă tūrrĭs ăd aūrās. Cēlsæ grăvĭōrĕ cāsū Dēcĭdūnt. Stāt tūrrīs mūnītă lŏcō.

Tūrtŭr, ŭrĭs. m. *A turtle-dove.* (*See Appendix under list of Birds.*)

Tūssĭō, īs, īvī, īrĕ. *To cough.* Phr.—Tūssĭs pūlmōnēm, pēctūs quāssāt, cōncŭtĭt. Āspĕră pūlmōnēm tūssīs quătĭt. Raūcā cōnspērgĕrĕt ōmnĭă tūssī. Tūssīm pătī.

Tūssĭs, ĭs. f. *Cough.* Syn.—Tūssēdŏ. Phr.—Mălă pēctŏrĭs hōspĕs.

Tūtămĕn, ĭnĭs. n. *Defense.* Syn.—Mūnīmĕn, tūtēlă.

Tūtēlă, æ. f. *Protection.* Rērūm tūtēlă mĕārūm. H. Syn.—Tūtămĕn, tūtămēntūm, pătrōcĭnĭūm, præsĭdĭūm.

Tūtŏr, ārĭs, ātŭs sūm, ārī. *To defend, to protect.* Tūtātūr făvŏr Eūrўălūm lăcrĭmæquĕ dĕcōræ. V. Syn.—Tŭĕŏr, dēfēndŏ, prōtēgŏ. Phr.—Hānc prīmūm tūtārĕ dŏmūm.

Tūtŏr, ōrĭs. m. *Defender, protector.* Syn.—Cūstōs, dēfēnsŏr, pătrōnŭs, præsĭdĭūm, tūtēlă.

Tūtŭs, ă, ūm. *Safe, free from harm.* Sērpĭt hŭmī tūtūs nĭmĭūm tĭmĭdūsquĕ prŏcēllæ. H. Syn.—Sēcūrŭs. Phr.—Mĕtū văcāns, văcŭŭs. Tūtŭs ăb īnsĭdĭīs. Ōmnĭă tūtă vĭdēs. Vĭă tūtă frĕquēnsquĕ.

Tўrānnĭcŭs, ă, ūm. *Tyrannical, cruel.* Syn.—Crūdēlĭs, īmpŏtēns, sŭpērbŭs.

Tўrānnĭs, ĭdĭs. f. *Tyranny.* Phr.—Ĭnīquūm, crūdēlĕ, grăvĕ īmpĕrĭūm. Īmpĭī tўrānnī sērvīlĕ jŭgūm. Rēgnī sævūs fŭrŏr. Ŏdĭōquĕ tўrānnĭdĭs ēxsŭl.

Tўrānnŭs, ī. m. *Absolute ruler.* Syn.—Rēx, prīncēps. *Tyrant.* Phr.—Rēx, rēctŏr, prīncēps, dŏmĭnātŏr ĭnīquŭs, crūdēlĭs, sŭpērbŭs. Flēctī nēscĭŭs. Pŏpŭlī ōpprēssŏr. Ērēptŏr lībērtātĭs. Īmpătĭēns frēni ēt sĭnĕ lēgĕ tўrānnŭs. Pătrĭām tўrānnĭdĕ prĕmēns. Rēgnă sŭpērbă gĕrēns. Gēntēm rēx deīndĕ sŭpērbō Īmpĕrĭō tĕnŭĭt.

U

Ūbĕr, ĕrĭs. adj. *Abundant, fertile.* Dōnăquĕ prōmīssīs ūbĕrĭōră fĕrānt. O. Syn.—Ăbūndāns, fēcūndŭs, fĕrāx, fērtĭlĭs. Phr.—Ūbĕrĭbūs fēcūndŭs ăquīs. Mōrūs nĭvĕīs ūbērrĭmă pōmīs. Fig.—*See Abundans.*

Ūbērtās, ātĭs. f. *Fertility.* Syn.—Ūbĕr (*as a noun*), fērtĭlĭtās, ăbūndāntĭă, cōpĭă. Fig. Syn.—Fācūndĭă.

Ūbērtīm. adv. *Abundantly.* Syn.—Ăbūndē, āfflŭēntĕr, cōpĭōsē.

Ŭbĭ. conj. *When.* Syn.—Cūm, quāndŏ, ŭt, pōstquām. *Where.* Syn.—Ŭbĭnām, quō. Phr.—Quō lŏcō, quā pārtĕ, quā rĕgĭōnĕ? Quā vōs rĕgĭōnĕ rĕquīrām?

Ŭbĭcūnquĕ. adv. *Wherever.* Syn.—Quōcūnquĕ.

Ŭbīquĕ. adv. *Everywhere.* Syn.—Pāssīm, ŭbĭcūmquĕ, ŭbĭvīs. Phr.—Pēr tōtūm ōrbēm. Ōrbĕ tōtō. Quā tērră pătĕt. Pēr mărĕ, pēr tērrās. Ōmnĭbŭs ūmbră lŏcīs ădĕrŏ. Tōtō sūrgēt gēns aūrĕă mūndō. Tōtūm vūlgātă pĕr ōrbēm. Quā sōl hăbĭtābĭlēs īllūstrăt ōrās.

Ūbĭvīs. adv. *In any place whatsoever.* Syn.—Ūbĭlĭbĕt, ŭbĭcūnquĕ.

Ūdŭs, ă, ūm. *Moist, damp.* Nīgră sŭbēst ūdō tāntūm cuī līnguă pălātō. V. Syn.—Hūmĭdŭs, hūmēns, mădēns mădĭdŭs, mădĕfāctŭs, ūvĭdŭs. Fig.—*Drunk, one who had imbibed too much.* Syn.—Pōtŭs, ēbrĭŭs, mădēns.

Ūlcīscŏr, ĕrĭs, ūltŭs sūm, ī. *To punish.* Ūltŭs ĕs ōffēnsās, ūt dĕcĕt, īpsĕ tŭās. O. Syn.—Pūnĭō, pērsĕquŏr. Phr.—Mē ūlcīscŏr, vīndĭcŏ. Pœnās ēxĭgŏ, sūmŏ, rĕpĕtŏ. Ūlcīscī stătŭĭt. *To take revenge.* Syn.—Vīndĭcŏ. Phr.—Ūlcīscī fūnĕră gēntĭs. Cæsōs ūlcīscĕrĕ frātrēs.

Ūlmŭs, ī. f. *The elm-tree.* (*See Appendix under list of Trees, etc.*)

Ūlnă, æ. f. *Forearm.* Syn.—Brāchĭūm, lăcērtŭs. Phr.—Cŭpĭdīs āmplēctĭtŭr ūlnīs.

Ūltĭmŭs, ă, ūm. *Farthest.* Syn.—Ēxtrēmŭs, lōngīnquŭs, rĕmōtŭs. *Last.* Syn.—Pōstrēmŭs ēxtrēmŭs, nŏvīssĭmŭs, sŭprēmŭs, sūmmŭs. Phr.—Mōrs ūltĭmă līnĕă rērum ēst. Pārs ūltĭmă vītæ. Ēxtrēmō sūb fīnĕ lăbōrūm. Vēnīt sūmmă dĭēs. *Least.* Syn.—Mĭnĭmŭs.

Ūltŏr, ōrĭs. m. & Ūltrīx, īcĭs. f. *Avenger.* Prōmīsi ūltōrem ēt vērbīs ŏdĭa āspĕră mōvī. V. Syn.—Vīndēx, pūnītŏr. Phr.—Pœnārūm ēxāctŏr. Ūltrīcēm prōnŭs ăd īrām. Īmmēnsīs āccēssīt clādĭbŭs ūltŏr.

Ūltrā. adv. *Beyond.* Syn.—Lōngĭŭs. *More, later, further (in point of time).* Syn.—Āmplĭŭs, ūltĕrĭŭs, lōngĭŭs, măgĭs. Prep. Syn.—Sŭpĕr.

Ūltrō. adv. *Of one's own accord.* Syn.—Spōntĕ, lĭbēntĕr, lĭbēns, vŏlēns, īpsĕ. Phr.—Nūllō cōgēntĕ. Nūllīs cōgēntĭbŭs. Īpsĕ vŏlēns. Sŭā spōntĕ.

Ŭlŭlă, æ. f. *A screech-owl.* (*See Appendix under list of Birds.*)

Ŭlŭlātŭs, ūs. m. *Howl, shout, cry.* Īmplēvīt săcrūm quĕrŭlīs ŭlŭlātĭbŭs Īdām. O. Syn.—Clāmŏr, quēstŭs, gĕmĭtŭs, lāmēntūm, plāngŏr. Phr.—Mœstæ lūgŭbrēs. Ŭlŭlātūs flēbĭlīs aūrēs Īmpŭlĭt.

Ŭlŭlŏ, ās, āvī, ātūm, ārĕ. *To shout, to cry out, to complain.* Pēr nōctēm rĕsŏnārĕ, lŭpīs ŭlŭlāntĭbŭs, ūrbēs. V. Syn.—Ēxŭlŭlŏ, vōcĭfĕrŏr, clāmŏ. Phr.—Ŭlŭlātū, quĕrēlīs, quēstĭbŭs, clāmōrĕ cœlūm, aūrās, æthĕră cōmplĕŏ, īmplĕŏ, mīscĕŏ. Ŭlŭlātūm mīttŏ. Ŭlŭlātūm spārgŏ īn aūrās. Crēbrīs fĕrĭūnt ŭlŭlātĭbŭs aūrēs.

To groan, to howl mournfully. Syn.—Mūgĭō, rĕbŏō, rĕsŏnō, gĕmō.

Ūmbŏ, ōnĭs. m. *Boss of a shield, and by extension the shield.* Syn.—Clўpĕŭs, scūtūm. *An eminence.* Syn.—Āggĕr, tŭmŭlŭs, tŭmŏr.

Ūmbră, æ. f. *Shade, shadow.* Ēt sōl dēcēdēns crēscēntēs dūplĭcăt ūmbrās. V. Syn.—Tĕnĕbræ, nōx, cālīgŏ. Phr.—Āgnōvītquĕ pĕr ūmbrām Ōbscūrām. Cæcīs sē cōndĭdĭt ūmbrīs. Nōctūrnās vŏlĭtārĕ pĕr ūmbrās. Nōx ūmbrās tērrīs īndūcĭt. Nōx ātră sĭlēntĭbŭs ūmbrīs. Rāmōrūm ūmbræ. Lŏcŭs ūmbrōsŭs. Nĕmŏră sōlī īnvĭă. Ŏpācī frīgŏrĭs ūmbræ. Tēgmĕn ārbŏrĭs. Pĕcŏrī jām grātĭŏr ūmbra ēst. Nŏcēnt ēt frūgĭbŭs ūmbræ. Vĕtĕrīs sūb nŏctĕ cŭprēssī. Frīgŏră dānt rāmī. Ūmbrōsam ēxquīrĕrĕ vāllēm. Sūb tēgmĭnĕ fāgī. *Shade, ghost.* Syn.—Mānēs, sĭmŭlācrūm. Phr.—Cœtūsquĕ sĭlēntūm. Dēscēndĭt ăd ūmbrās. Ūmbræ nŏctĕ vŏlāntēs. Dēfūnctăquĕ cōrpŏră vītæ. *Appearance, pretext.* Syn.—Spĕcĭēs, ĭmāgŏ, nōmĕn.

Ūmbrācŭlūm, ī. n. *Shady place.* Ēt lēntæ tēxūnt ūmbrācŭlă vītēs. V. Syn.—Ūmbră. Phr.—Lŏcŭs nĕmŏrōsŭs, sīlvēstrĭs, ŏpācŭs. Sācrīs tēndēns ūmbrācŭlă sērtīs.

Ūmbrŏ, ās, āvī, ātūm, ārĕ. *To give shade.* Syn.—Īnūmbrŏ, ŏbūmbrŏ, ŏpācŏ, tĕgŏ. Phr.—Ūmbrā tĕgŏ. Ūmbrās īndūcŏ. Rāmīs tĕgŏ. Grāndĭs ŏpācăt Ārbŏr ăquās. Vĭrĭdī fōntēs īndūcĕrĕt ūmbrā. Ōbtēntū frōndĭs ĭnūmbrānt. Mōntēs ūmbrāntŭr ŏpācī.

Ūmbrōsŭs, ă, ūm. *Shady.* Tāntum īntēr dēnsās ūmbrōsă căcūmĭnă fāgōs Āssĭdŭē vĕnĭēbăt. V. Syn.—Ūmbrĭfĕr, ūmbrātĭlĭs, ŏpācŭs, dēnsŭs. Phr.—Lætīssĭmŭs ūmbrā. Īnscĭŭs Phœbī. Pērvĭă nūllīs sīlvă sōlĭbŭs. Crīnēs ūmbrōsă tĕgēbăt ărūndŏ.

Ūnā. adv. *Together.* Syn.—Sĭmŭl, părĭtĕr.

Ūncŭs, ă, ūm. *Curved, bent.* Ūncō nōn āllĭgăt ānchŏră mōrsū. V. Syn.—Ădūncŭs, ŏbūncŭs, rĕdūncŭs, cūrvŭs, īncūrvŭs, rĕcūrvŭs, rĕflēxŭs. Phr.—Tēllūs cūm dēntĕ rĕclūdĭtŭr ūncō.

Ūndă, æ. f. *Wave.* Cūrvāta īn mōntīs făcĭēm cīrcūmstĕtĭt ūndă. V. Syn.—Flūctŭs. Phr.—Fērvēntēs æstĭbŭs ūndæ. Ūndāque īmpēllĭtŭr ūndă. Īncūrsu ūndārūm sŏnăt ūndă. *Sea. See Mare. Water.* Syn.—Ăquă, lўmphă, lătēx, fōns, rīvŭs, āmnĭs, flūmĕn, flŭvĭŭs. Phr.—Fūlmĭnĕī lătĭcēs. Ūndārūm cūrsŭs. Căpūt fōntānā spārgĭtŭr ūndā.

Ūndĭquĕ. adv. *From everywhere.* Syn.—Ūbīquĕ. Phr.—Ēx ōmnī pārtĕ.

Ūndŏ, ās, āvī, ātūm, ārĕ. *To boil, to rise up in waves.* Syn.—Ēxūndŏ, æstŭŏ, ēxæstŭŏ, ĭnūndŏ, flūctŭŏ. *To undulate.* Syn.—Flūctŭŏ.

Ūndōsŭs, ă, ūm. *Agitated, stormy, seething.* Syn.—Ūndāns, flūctŭāns, æstŭōsŭs, ăgĭtātŭs, prŏcēllōsŭs. Phr.—Ūndīs tūrgĭdŭs,
tŭmēns, sŏnōrŭs.

Ūngŏ, ĭs, xī, ctūm, ĕrĕ. *To anoint, to smear.* Ūngĕrĕ tēlă mănū.
fērrūmque ārmārĕ vĕnēnō. V. Syn.—Ĭnūngŏ, pĕrūngŏ, lĭnŏ, īllĭnŏ, ōblĭnŏ, pērlĭnŏ, cīrcūmlĭnŏ, īmbŭŏ, tīngŏ, pērdūcŏ, mădĕfăcĭŏ *To perfume.* Syn.—Tīngŏ, pērfūndŏ, ŏdōrŏ, lĭnŏ, īllĭnŏ,
ōbdūcŏ. Phr.—Ūngŏr ŏlīvō. Nārēs mўrrhĕŭs ūngăt ŏnўx.

Ūnguēntūm, ī. n. *Ointment, essence, perfume.* Īllĭŭs ē nĭtĭdō spīrānt ūnguēntă căpīllō. Tib. Syn.—Bālsămūm, ŏpŏbālsămūm,
ămōmūm, ŏdōrēs, mўrrhă, nārdŭs. Phr.—Rōs Tўrĭŭs. Mўr-
rhĕă gūttă. Āssўrĭūm ŏlĕūm. Āssўrĭæ lăcrĭmæ. Lĭquĭdī ŏdōrēs.
Sўrĭō munērĕ plēnŭs ŏnўx. Pērfūsŭs ŏdōrĕ spīrāntĭs ămōmī.

Ūnguĭs, ĭs, m. *Finger-nail, claw.* Flōs mŏdŏ dēcērptŭs tĕnūī pŭĕrī-
lĭtĕr ūnguĕ. Prop. Syn.—Ūnguĭcŭlŭs. Phr.—Ūnguēs cūltēllō
pūrgārĕ. Prāvē sēctŭs ūnguĭs. Ēt sīnt sĭnĕ sōrdĭbŭs ūnguēs.
Hand. Syn.—Dĭgĭtŭs, pōllēx, mănŭs. Fig.—Ăd ūnguēm. *Perfectly, to the minutest detail.* Syn.—Ădămūssīm. Phr.—Hŏmŏ
făctŭs ăd ūnguēm.

Ūngŭlă, æ. f. *Hoof.* Quădrŭpĕdāntĕ pŭtrēm sŏnĭtū quătĭt ūngŭlă
cāmpūm. V. Syn.—Ūnguĭs. Phr.—Pĕdūm cōrnū. Pĕdēs ūncī.
Sŏlĭdō grăvĭtēr sŏnăt ūngŭlă cōrnū. Īn quīnōs ūnguēs dīlāpsă.

Ūnĭcŭs, ă, ūm. *Only, sole.* Syn.—Sōlŭs, ūnŭs. *Unique, remarkable.* Syn.—Rārŭs, ēxĭmĭŭs, præstāns, pūlchērrĭmŭs.

Ūnĭŏ, ōnĭs. m. *Pearl.* Syn.—Mārgărītă, băccă, gēmmă. Phr.—
Lăpĭs Gāngētĭcŭs. Băccæ cōnchă. Īndī mărĭs dōnă. Lăpĭs Ēōă
lēctŭs ĭn ūndă.

Ūnŭs, ă, ūm. *One, alone.* Ūnŭs ĕrăt tōtō nātūræ vūltŭs ĭn ōrbĕ. O.
Syn.—Ūnĭcŭs, sōlŭs. Phr.—Ūnŭs mūltōrūm. Ūna ē mūltīs.
Ūnŭs ĕt āltĕr.

Ūrbānŭs, ă, ūm. *Belonging to the city.* Syn.—Ūrbĭcŭs. *Polite, re-
fined.* Syn.—Mītĭs, cōmĭs, bĕnīgnŭs, āffābĭlĭs, lĕpĭdŭs, făcētŭs.
Phr.—Mōrēs nōn sătĭs ūrbĭs hăbēs.

Ūrbs, ūrbĭs. f. *City.* Ūrbs āntīquă fŭīt mūltōs dŏmĭnātă pĕr ānnōs.
V. Syn.—Ārx, ārcēs, ōppĭdūm, mœnĭă, cīvĭtās. Phr.—Sĭtū
āmplă, clără. Ēxcēlsō stāns ĭn vērtĭcĕ mōntĭs. Pŏsĭtū dēfēnsă.
Tūrrĭbŭs ārdŭă. Cĕlĕbrī hōspĭtă pōrtū. Pŏpŭlōsă vĭrīs. Dīvĭtĭīs
fœtă. Dīvĕs ŏpūm. Ūrbs aūgūstă, pŏtēns. Stŭdĭīs āspērrĭmă
bēllī. Pācĕ flōrēns. Ūrbĭūm dĕcŭs. Vĭdŭāntūr cīvĭbŭs ūrbēs.

Ūrgĕŏ, ēs, sī, ērĕ. *To press hard, to push, to pursue.* Ūrgĕt ĕnīm
dŏmĭnūs mēntēm nōn lēnĭs. H. Syn.—Prĕmŏ, īmpēllŏ, īnstŏ,
īnsēctŏr, īnsĕquŏr. Phr.—Īn brĕvĭa ēt sўrtēs ūrgĕt. Ūrgēt dĭēm
nōx. *To hurry.* Syn.—Fēstīnŏ, prŏpĕrŏ, cĕlĕrŏ, āccĕlĕrŏ, īnstŏ.

To impel, to excite. Syn.—Īmpēllŏ, ēxcĭtŏ. *To overwhelm.* Syn.—Prĕmŏ, ōpprĭmŏ, ŏnĕrŏ, ōbrŭŏ. *To torment.* Syn.—Prĕmŏ, ăgĭtŏ, crŭcĭŏ, vēxŏ, īnsēctŏr.

Ūrnă, æ. f. *Urn, case, vessel.* Syn.—Ūrnŭlă, ūrcĕŭs, hȳdrĭă, ăquālĭs, āmphŏră. *Vessel in which they placed the lots or the votes.* Syn.—Sĭtŭlă, sĭtēllă, sērĭă. Phr.—Stāt dūctīs sōrtĭbŭs ūrnă. Quæsītōr Mīnōs ūrnām mŏvĕt. Ōmnĕ căpāx mŏvĕt ūrnă nōmēn.

Ūrŏ, ĭs, ūssī, ūstūm, ĕrĕ. *To burn.* Ātquĕ lĕvēm stĭpŭlām crĕpĭtāntĭbŭs ūrĕrĕ flāmmīs. V. Syn.—Ădūrŏ, cōmbūrŏ, ēxūrŏ, pĕrūrŏ, crĕmŏ, cōncrĕmŏ, tōrrĕŏ, īncēndŏ, sūccēndŏ, īnflāmmŏ, cōnsūmŏ. Phr.—Flāmmīs, īgnĕ dēlĕŏ, ăbŏlĕŏ, cōnsūmŏ, ēxūrŏ. Īgnēm, flāmmās sūbjĭcĭŏ, ādmŏvĕŏ. Īn cĭnĕrēm, făvīllās vērtŏ. Vūlcānō māndŏ. Sūbjēctīs ūrĕrĕ flāmmīs. Dāt sūccēnsæ mēmbră crĕmāndă pȳræ. Ūrĕ fŏcō cāncrōs. Rāmōs ūrēntĕ cămīnō. Īgnīs sūppōnĭtŭr hērbīs. *To light, to set on fire.* Syn.—Īncēndŏ, īnflāmmŏ, crĕmŏ, cōmbūrŏ. Phr.—Făcĭbŭs īncēndŏ. Flāmmās jăcĭŏ. Tōtīs Vūlcānūm spārgĕrĕ tēctīs. *To make suffer.* Syn.—Lædŏ, crŭcĭŏ, āngŏ, ūrgĕŏ. *To irritate.* Syn.—Āccēndŏ, pūngŏ, crŭcĭŏ, āngŏ, tōrquĕŏ, vēxŏ, cŏquŏ.

Ūsūrpŏ, ās, āvī, ātūm, ārĕ. *To use, to employ. See Utor. To seize, to appropriate.* Syn.—Căpĭŏ, āccĭpĭŏ, pērcĭpĭŏ.

Ūsŭs, ūs. m. *Use.* Syn.—Ūsūră, făcūltās. *Practice, experience.* Syn.—Ēxpĕrĭēntĭă, pĕrĭtĭă, scĭēntĭă. *Custom.* Syn.—Mōs, cōnsuētūdŏ. *Utility.* Syn.—Ūtĭlĭtās.

Ŭt. conj. *In order that.* Syn.—Ūtī, quō. *Although.* Syn.—Quāmvīs, ētsī, lĭcĕt, cūm, quāmquām. *As.* Syn.—Cūm, quāndŏ, ŭbĭ.

Ŭtĕrŭs, ī. m. *Womb.* Syn.—Vēntĕr, ālvŭs, vīscĕră, īlĭă.

Ūtĭlĭs, ĭs, ĕ. *Useful.* Ōmnĕ tŭlīt pūnctūm, quī mīscŭĭt ūtĭlĕ dūlcī. H. Syn.—Cōmmŏdŭs, āccōmmŏdŭs, ōppōrtūnŭs, āptŭs, ĭdōnĕŭs, bŏnŭs, prōfĭcĭēns, sălūtārĭs. Phr.—Bīs pōmīs ūtĭlĭs ārbōs. Cĭbŭs ūtĭlĭs ægrō.

Ūtĭlĭtās, ātĭs. f. *Usefulness, profit.* Syn.—Cōmmŏdĭtās, cōmmŏdūm, ōppōrtūnĭtās, ūsŭs, frūctŭs, lŭcrūm, quæstŭs, ēmŏlŭmēntūm. Phr.—Ūtĭlĭtātĭs ŏpēs. Vūlgŭs ămīcĭtĭās ūtĭlĭtātĕ prŏbăt.

Ŭtĭnām. interj. *Would that!* Syn.—Ūtī, ŭt, sī. Phr.—Ō ŭtĭnām! Ō sī! Quām vēllēm! Dī făcĭānt! Dī, prĕcŏr, hōc jŭbĕānt! Fātă sĭnānt! Dī tĭbĭ dēnt! Fāxīt Dĕŭs!

Ūtŏr, ĕrĭs, ūsŭs sūm, ī. *To use.* Sērvĭĕt ætērnūm, quī pārvō nēscĭĕt ūtī. H. Syn.—Ūsūrpŏ, ădhĭbĕŏ, frŭŏr. Phr.—Ūtĕrĕ sōrtĕ tŭă. Ān nūnquam ūtārĕ părātĭs? Vērbīs mōllĭbŭs ūtī. Vīrĭbŭs ūtēndum ēst.

Ūvă, æ. f. *Grape*. Dūcĕrĕt āprīcīs īn cōllĭbŭs ūvă cŏlōrēm. V. Syn.—Răcēmŭs, (*for the vine*) vītĭs, vīnĕă, vīndēmĭă, vīnūm. Phr.—Vītĭs frūctŭs, mūnĕră. Bācchēă dōnă. Cērtāns ūvă pūrpŭræ. Aūrō sĭmĭlĭs.

Ūvēns, tĭs & Ūvĭdŭs, ă, ūm. adj. *Moist, wet*. Syn.—Ūdŭs, mădēns, mădĭdŭs. Phr.—Ūvĭdŭlam ā flētū. *Intoxicated*. Syn.—Pōtŭs, ēbrĭŭs, mădēns.

Ūxŏr, ōrĭs. f. *Wife*. Syn.—Spōnsă, cōnjūx, nūptă, mărītă, ūxōrcŭlă. Phr.—Jūnctă cōnnūbĭō. Vīnclō sŏcĭātă jŭgālī. Pŭdōrĭs ămāns. Sŏcĭō fīdă vĭrō, mărītō. Nūptă sŏrōrquĕ Jŏvĭs. Făcĕ nūptĭālī dīgnă.

V

Vāccă, æ. f. *Cow*. Ūbĕră vāccæ Lāctĕă dēmīttūnt. V. Syn.—Vāccŭlă, bōs, būcŭlă, jŭvēncă, jŭvēncŭlă, vĭtŭlă. Phr.—Bīs cūrvāns jām cōrnŭă frōntĕ. Ūbĕrĭbŭs lāc gĕrēns. Lāctĭs ălĭmēntă mĭnīstrāns. Nĭvĕūm fūndĭt ēx ūbĕrĕ nēctăr. Rēddĭdĭt ūnă bŏūm vōcēm. Raūcōs ēdēns mūgītūs. Ōptĭmă tōrvæ Fōrmă bŏvĭs.

Vāccīnĭūm, ĭī. n. *The blueberry*. (*See Appendix under list of Trees, etc.*)

Văcīllŏ, ās, āvī, ātūm, ārĕ. *To totter, to tremble*. Syn.—Lābŏ, lābāscŏ, nūtŏ, tĭtŭbŏ, trĕmŏ, trĕmīscŏ. Fig.—*To hesitate*. Syn.—Hæsĭtŏ, tĭtŭbŏ.

Văcŏ, ās, āvī, ātūm, ārĕ. *To be free, to be empty*. Phr.—Sūm văcŭŭs. Lōngē sāltūs lātēquĕ văcāntēs. *To lack*. Syn.—Cărĕŏ. Phr.—Crīmĭnĕ fāmă văcăt. Lītĕ văcēnt aūrēs. Văcăt īnsŭlă cūltū. *To be free from care or anxiety*. Syn.—Ōtĭŏr, cēssŏ, quĭēscŏ. *To give oneself up to*. Syn.—Īncūmbŏ, īnsūdŏ, īnvĭgĭlŏ, stŭdĕŏ. Phr.—Ănĭmūm īntēndŏ, ŏpĕrām dŏ.

Văcŭŏ, ās, āvī, ātūm, ārĕ. *To empty*. Syn.—Ēvăcŭŏ, ēxhaūrĭŏ, ĭnānĭŏ.

Văcŭŭs, ă, ūm. *Empty*. Pērquĕ dŏmōs Dītīs văcŭās ĕt ĭnānĭă rēgnă. V. Syn.—Văcāns, văcŭātŭs, ĭnānĭs, lībĕr, ăpērtŭs, āmplŭs, vāstŭs, pătēns. Phr.—Āĕră pēr văcŭūm fērrī. *Free from, exempt*. Syn.—Īmmūnĭs, ēxpērs, cărēns, văcāns, lībĕr, sŏlūtŭs. Vītă lăbōrĭbŭs văcŭă. Crīmĭnĕ nōx văcŭă. Văcŭās cædĭs hăbētĕ mănūs.

Vādŏ, ĭs, ĕrĕ. *To go forward*. Vādĭmŭs īmmīxtī Dănăīs, haūd nūmĭnĕ nōstrō. V. Syn.—Ĕŏ, pērgŏ, grădĭŏ, fēstīnŏ. Phr.—Vādĭmŭs haūd dŭbĭam īn mōrtēm. Vādĕ sălūtātūm prō mē.

Vădūm, ī. n. *Shoals.* Syn.—Brĕvĭă. Phr.—Īn vădă cæcă tŭlĭt. Īllīdītquĕ vădīs. Flūmĭnĕīs vīx tūtă vădīs.

Væ. interj. *Woe to!* Phr.—Væ tĭbĭ! Āt tē Dī pērdānt! Dī mălă mūltă dēnt clĭēntī!

Văfĕr, văfră, văfrūm. *Shrewd, cunning.* Quā văfĕr ēlūdī pōssēt rătĭōnĕ mărītŭs. O. Syn.—Āstūtŭs, cāllĭdŭs, caūtŭs, dŏlōsŭs, pēllāx, vērsūtŭs.

Vāgīnă, æ. f. *Sheath, scabbard.* Vāgīnāquĕ căvā fūlgēntēm dērĭpĭt ēnsēm. V. Phr.—Ēnsĭs tēgmĕn. Văcŭūm, căvūm ĕbŭr. Lătĕrī āffīxă, Hăbĭlēm vāgīna āptārăt ĕbūrnā. Vāgīnāque ērĭpĕ fērrūm. Vāgīnā dūcĕrĕ fērrūm. Vāgīnā lībĕrăt ēnsēm. Ēnsīs vāgīnā tēctŭs. Claūsūsque ēt cōndĭtŭs ēnsĭs.

Vāgĭŏ, īs, īvī & ĭī, ītūm, īrĕ. *To cry as a child or an infant.* Vāgĭĕrānt āmbō, părĭtēr sēntīrĕ pŭtārēs. O. Syn.—Flĕŏ, plōrŏ. Phr.—Vāgītūs, plānctūm ēdŏ, dō, ēmīttŏ. Vāgītū, vāgītĭbŭs aūrās īmplĕŏ. Īnfāntūmque ănĭmæ flēntēs.

Vāgītŭs, ūs. m. *Weeping, cries of children.* Syn.—Plōrātŭs, flētŭs. Phr.—Pŭĕrīlĭs flētŭs, plōrātŭs. Aūdītæ vōcēs, vāgītūs ēt īngēns.

Văgŏr, ārĭs, ātŭs sūm, ārī. *To wander.* Stēllæ spōntĕ sŭā jūssænĕ văgēntŭr ēt ērrēnt. H. Syn.—Ērrŏ, ŏbērrŏ, deērrŏ, dīscūrrŏ, pālŏr. Phr.—Vĭæ īnscĭŭs. Īncērtŭs ērrŏ. Hūc īllūc fĕrŏr. Īncērtō cūrsū fĕrŏr. Văgāntem īncērtum ērrŏr ăgĭt. Tōtāquĕ văgātŭr Ūrbĕ fŭrēns.

Văgŭs, ă, ūm. *Wandering.* Jām văgă prōsĭlĭēt frēnīs nātūră rĕmōtīs. H. Syn.—Văgāns, văgābūndŭs, ērrāns, ērrātĭcŭs, ērrābūndŭs. Phr.—Ērrōrĕ āctŭs. Ēxcūssŭs vĭā. Pēr dēvĭă lūstră văgāntēs. *Overflowing, inundating.* Syn.—Īnūndāns, ēffūsŭs, ēxūndāns, ēxspătĭātŭs. *Inconstant, light, fickle.* Syn.—Īncōnstāns, lĕvĭs.

Vāldē. adv. *Very, much.* Syn.—Mūltūm, plūrĭmūm.

Vălē, Vălētĕ. *Farewell, good-bye.* Syn.—Vălĕās, vīvĕ. Phr.—Vīvĕ vălēquĕ.

Vălĕdīcŏ, ĭs, xī, ctūm, ĕrĕ. *To say farewell.* Īdquĕ quŏd īgnōtī făcĭūnt, vălĕdīcĕrĕ sāltēm. O. Phr.—Ēxtrēmūm āffārī. Sŭprēmūm vălĕdīcĕrĕ. Vīvĭtĕ sīlvæ. Dīctōquĕ vălē, văle, īnquĭt ēt Ēchō. Aētērnūmquĕ vălē. Nūnquām dīxīssĕ vălē.

Vălĕŏ, ēs, ŭī, ĭtūm, ērĕ. *To be strong, robust.* Sī tămĕn īpsă vălēs, ălĭquā nōs pārtĕ vălēmŭs. O. Syn.—Vĭgĕŏ. Phr.—Sūm sānŭs, īncŏlūmĭs. Vălērĕ stŏmăchō. Mēns sāna īn cōrpŏrĕ sānō. Fig.—*To be able.* Syn.—Pōssūm, pŏllĕŏ.

Vălētūdŏ, ĭnĭs. f. *Health.* Syn.—Sānĭtās. *Good-health.* Syn.—Sānĭtās, sălūs, vĭgŏr. *Bad-health.* Syn.—Aēgrĭtūdŏ. *See Aeger, Morbus.*

Vălĭdŭs, ă, ūm. *Strong, robust.* Sēd quĭă mēntĕ mĭnūs vălĭdūs quām cōrpŏrĕ tōtō. H. Syn.—Vălēns, fīrmŭs, fōrtĭs, rōbūstŭs. Phr.—Vălĭdās rēscīndĕrĕ lēgēs. *Violent.* Syn.—Vĭŏlēntŭs, ācĕr, īngēns, māgnŭs. *Powerful.* Syn.—Vălēns, præsēns, pŏtēns, ūtĭlĭs.

Vāllēs (ĭs), ĭs. f. *Valley.* Rūră mĭhi ēt rĭgŭĭs plăcĕānt īn vāllĭbŭs āmnēs. V. Syn.—Cōnvāllēs, Tēmpē. Phr.—Vāllĭs īrrĭguæ lŏcă. Vāllĭs lătĕbræ. Ūndĭquĕ sēptă jŭgīs. Īn vāllĕ rĕdūctā. Claūdĕrĕ vāllēs īnsĭdĭīs. Vāllīs sŏnăt āmnĕ prŏpīnquō. Vāllīs dēnsīs lătĕt ābdĭtă sīlvīs. Vāllĭs ĭn āmplēxū nĕmŏrūm.

Vāllŏ, ās, āvī, ātūm, ārĕ. *To fortify.* Cōnsīdūnt cāstrīs ēt mœnĭă vāllānt. V. Syn.—Ōbvāllŏ, mūnĭŏ. Phr.—Vāllūm dūcŏ. Vāllō cīngŏ, cīrcūmdŏ. Dūctō vāllō fīrmō. Nūllī vāllārānt ōppĭdă mūrī. Pārvūmquĕ lĕvī strŭĭt āggĕrĕ vāllūm. (*In general*) *To surround.* Syn.—Cīngŏ, cŏrōnŏ.

Vāllūm, ī. n. *Palisade, wall, fortification.* Syn.—Āggĕr, mūnīmĕn, prōpūgnācŭlūm. Phr.—Mĕdĭī fīdūcĭă bēllī. Nōn ēxsŭpĕrābĭlĕ vāllūm. Claūsō fīdĕrĕ bēllō.

Vānēscŏ, ĭs, ŭī, ĕrĕ. *To vanish.* Cārmĭnĕ læsă Cĕrēs stĕrĭlēs vānēscĭt ĭn hērbās. O. Syn.—Ēvānēscŏ. Phr.—Ăbĕo ĭn aūrās. Tĕnŭēs vānēscĭt ĭn aūrās. Vānēscītque ābsēns.

Vānĭtās, ātĭs. f. *Vanity, uselessness.* Syn.—Īnānĭtās, lĕvĭtās, fāllācĭă, mēndācĭūm. *Vain glory.* Syn.—Āmbĭtĭŏ, jāctāntĭă, sŭpērbĭă. Phr.—Cădūcārūm sĭmŭlācră rērūm. Rērum ūmbræ mēndācēs.

Vānŭs, ă, ūm. *Vain, unreal.* Sĕd īllōs Ēxspēctātă sĕgēs vānīs ēlūsĭt ăvēnīs. V. Syn.—Văcŭŭs, ĭnānĭs, cāssŭs, īrrĭtŭs. *Useless, frivolous, without effect.* Syn.—Īrrĭtŭs, ĭnūtĭlĭs, fāllāx, ĭnānĭs, frīvŏlŭs, fūtĭlĭs, lĕvĭs, cădūcŭs, fŭgāx. *Proud. See Superbus.*

Văpŏr, ōrĭs. m. *Vapor.* Nēc jām sē căpĭt ūndă, vŏlāt văpŏr ātĕr ăd aūrās. V. Phr.—Quī tĕnŭēs vānēscĭt ĭn aūrās. *Smoke. See Fumus. Heat, steam.* Syn.—Călŏr.

Văpōrŏ, ās, āvī, ātūm, ārĕ. *To give forth vapor, or odors.* Phr.—Văpōrēs ēxhālŏ, spīrŏ, ēmīttŏ. *To fill with vapor, steam or smoke.* Phr.—Văpōrĕ, văpōrĭbŭs, fūmō īmplĕŏ, rĕplĕŏ, spārgŏ, mīscĕŏ. *To warm.* Syn.—Călĕfăcĭŏ.

Vāpŭlŏ, ās, āvī, ātūm, ārĕ. *To be beaten.* Sī rīxa ēst, ŭbĭ tū pūlsās, ĕgŏ vāpŭlŏ tāntūm. J. Syn.—Vērbĕrŏr, pērcŭtĭŏr, cædŏr, fĕrĭŏr. Phr.—Tērgō flēctŏr. Tērgă, lătŭs vērbĕrĭbŭs, flăgēllīs dō, præbĕŏ, sūbjĭcĭŏ. Hīc frāngĭt fĕrŭlās, rŭbĕt īllĕ flăgēllīs.

Vărĭŏ, ās, āvī, ātūm, ārĕ. *To stain.* Īlle ŭbĭ nāscēntēm măcŭlīs vărĭāvĕrĭt ōrtūm. V. Syn.—Dīstīnguŏ, pīngŏ, măcŭlŏ. *To vary.*

Syn.—Mūtŏ. *To vary, to be changeable.* Syn.—Vărĭŏr, mūtŏr, īmmūtŏr. Phr.—Sūm mōbĭlĭs, vărĭŭs, dīvērsŭs.

Vărĭŭs, ă, ūm. *Stained, spotted.* Syn.—Vărĭātŭs, dīstīnctŭs, pīctŭs. *Diversified, varied.* Syn.—Dīvērsŭs, dīssĭmĭlĭs, dīspār, mūltŭs, mūltĭplēx. Phr.—Ārbŏrĭbūs vărĭa ēst nātūră crĕāndīs. Dīvĕs ŏpūm vărĭārūm. Vărĭō dīstīnctă lĕpōrĕ Ōmnĭă. Nōctēm vărĭō sērmōnĕ trăhēbānt. *Changeable, inconstant.* Syn.—Lĕvĭs, īncōnstāns, īnstăbĭlĭs, mūtābĭlĭs.

Vās, vāsĭs. n. *Vase, vessel.* Sīncērum ēst nĭsĭ vās, quōdcūnque īnfūndĭs, ăcēscĭt. H. Syn.—Vāscŭlūm, ūrcĕŭs, hȳdrĭă, ăquālĭs, ūrnă, sērĭă, sĭtŭlă, sĭtēllă, ōllă, tēstă, cānthărŭs, cўăthŭs, pōcŭlūm, āmphŏră, călīx, crātēr, scўphŭs. Phr.—Aūrō rĭgēns. Sīgnīs āspĕrūm. Mīră, dōctă ārtĕ lăbōrātūm, scūlptūm. Pērfēctūm ārgēntō.

Vāsă, ōrūm. n. *Baggage, utensils.* Syn.—Sŭpēllēx, īnstrūmēntă, ārmă.

Vāstātŏr, ōrĭs. m. *One who devastates.* Syn.—Pŏpŭlātŏr, ēvērsŏr. Phr.—Trōjæ vāstātŏr Ăchīllēs. Fĕrārūm Vāstātōrem Ămўcūm.

Vāstĭtās, ātĭs. f. *Immensity.* Syn.—Dēsērtūm, sōlĭtūdŏ. *Ravage, ruin.* Syn.—Vāstātĭŏ, pŏpŭlātĭŏ, rŭīnă, cædēs, strāgēs.

Vāstŏ, ās, āvī, ātūm, ārĕ. *To ravage.* Dūm bēllo Ārgŏlĭcī vāstābānt Pērgămă rēgēs. V. Syn.—Pŏpŭlŏr, pŏpŭlŏ, dēpŏpŭlŏr, dīrŭŏ, ēvērtŏ, ēxpīlŏ. Phr.—Īncūltūm, vāstūm dēsērtūm făcĭŏ. Fūndĭtŭs ēvērtĕrĕ. Ōmnĭă nām lātē vāstānt. Vāstānt cūltōrĭbŭs āgrōs. Vāstāvīt dūctōrĭs ĭtĕr.

Vāstŭs, ă, ūm. *Devastated, deserted.* Syn.—Vāstātŭs, dēvāstātŭs, dēsērtŭs, dēsōlātŭs, sōlātŭs, sōlŭs. *Vast, spacious.* Syn.—Īmmēnsŭs, īngēns, lātŭs, āmplŭs, spătĭōsŭs, ēffūsŭs, pătēns. Phr.—Vāstūm mărĭs æquŏr ărāndūm. Vāstōque īmmānĭs hĭātū spēlūncă. *Great, colossal.* Syn.—Māgnŭs, īngēns, īmmānĭs, grăvĭs.

Vātēs, ĭs. m. & f. *Soothsayer.* Dēlĭŭs īnspīrāt vātēs, ăpĕrītquĕ fŭtūră. V. Syn.—Vātĭcĭnātŏr, săcērdōs, dīvīnŭs, aūgŭr, sĭbўllă. Phr.—Fŭtūrī, ævī vēntūrī prænūntĭŭs, prōvĭdŭs, haūd īnscĭŭs, haūd īgnārŭs. Īntērprĕs dĕōrūm. Fātă cănēns. Ēvēntūră vĭdēns. Plēnŭs Phœbō. *Poet. See Poeta.*

Vātĭcĭnŏr, ārĭs, ātŭs sūm, ārī. *To predict, to prophesy.* Dīctă tĭbī vātĭcĭnāntĕ nōtā. O. Syn.—Prædīcŏ. Phr.—Vēntūrăquĕ bēllă Ēxpĕdĭĕt. Cūrsūm mĭhĭ prōspĕră dīxĭt Rēllĭgĭŏ. Īrātōs fībră lŏcūtă dĕōs. Crūdēlĕ cănēbānt Ārtĭfĭcīs scĕlŭs. Cĕcĭnērūnt ōmĭnă vātēs. Hōs mĭhĭ prædīxīt lūctūs.

-Vĕ. conj. *Or.* Syn.—Vĕl, aūt, sīvĕ, seū.

Vēcōrdĭă, æ. f. *Madness, delirium.* Syn.—Āmēntĭă, fŭrŏr, īnsānĭă. *Cowardice.* Syn.—Īgnāvĭă.

Vēcōrs, cōrdĭs. adj. *Mad, insane.* Syn.—Āmēns, fŭrēns, fŭrĭōsŭs, īnsānŭs, vēsānŭs.

Vēctīgăl, ālĭs. n. *Tribute.* Syn.—Trĭbūtūm, pōrtōrĭūm. *Rent, revenue.* Syn.—Rĕdĭtŭs.

Vĕgĕtŭs, ă, ūm. *Full of strength, vigor.* Syn.—Vălēns, vălĭdŭs, vīvĭdŭs, ăcĕr, strēnŭŭs, fōrtĭs, fīrmŭs, rōbūstŭs. *Entire, intact.* Syn.—Īncŏlŭmĭs, īntĕgĕr.

Vĕhĕmēns, ēntĭs. adj. *Violent, vehement.* Syn.—Vĭŏlēns, vĭŏlēntŭs, ăcĕr, vălĭdŭs, grăvĭs, īmmŏdĕrātŭs, ēffrēnĭs, īmmŏdĭcŭs, præcēps. Fig. Syn.—Ăcĕr, vīvĭdŭs. *Biting, keen.* Syn.—Ăcĕr, mōrdāx, ăcērbŭs, āspĕr. *Irritated, furious, terrible.* Syn.—Ăcĕr, īrātŭs, răbĭdŭs, fŭrēns, fŭrĭōsŭs, tērrĭbĭlĭs.

Vĕhĕmēntĕr (Vēmēntĕr). adv. *Violently, vehemently.* Syn.—Ăcrĭtĕr, grăvĭtĕr, vĭŏlēntĕr, fōrtĭtĕr. *Very, much.* Syn.—Vāldē, mūltūm.

Vĕhŏ, ĭs, vēxī, vēctūm, ĕrĕ. *To carry, to bear, to transport.* Nāvēm quæ Lȳcĭōs fīdūmquĕ vĕhēbăt Ŏrōntēm. V. Syn.—Vēctŏ, dēvĕhŏ, īnvĕhŏ, sūbvĕhŏ, trānsvĕhŏ, fĕrŏ, gĕrŏ, gēstŏ, pōrtŏ, trānspōrtŏ, dūcŏ, trăhŏ. Phr.—Dēfērrĕ cūrrū, ĕquō, nāvī. *To roll.* Syn.—Vōlvŏ, trăhŏ, fĕrŏ. *To carry away.* Syn.—Aūfĕrŏ, ābdūcŏ, răpĭŏ, ābrĭpĭŏ.

Vĕl. conj. *Or.* Syn.—Aūt, sīvĕ, seū, -vĕ. *Even.* Syn.—Ĕtĭām, quŏquĕ, īpsĕ. *At least.* Syn.—Sāltēm.

Vēlāmĕn, ĭnĭs. n. *Veil, covering, vesture.* Ēt cīrcūmtēxtūm crŏcĕō vēlāmĕn ăcānthō. V. Syn.—Tēgmĕn, ămīctŭs, tĕgŭmēntūm, vēlāmēntūm. *Fillet.* Syn.—Vīttæ.

Vēlĭfĭcŏ, ās, āvī, ātūm, ārĕ. *To make sail, to sail.* Syn.—Vēlă dō, făcĭŏ. Phr.—Pĕnĭtūsquĕ prŏfūndō Vēlă dăbĭt. Vēntīs īntēndĕrĕ vēlă sĕcūndīs. Dărĕ fātīs vēlă jŭbēbăt. Vēlōrūm pāndĭmŭs ālās. Aūrās vēlă vŏcānt. Sōlvĭtĕ vēlă.

Vēllŏ, ĭs, vēllī, & vūlsī, vūlsūm, ĕrĕ. *To snatch.* Nām quæ prīmă sŏlō rūptīs rādīcĭbŭs ārbŏs Vēllĭtŭr. V. Syn.—Āvēllŏ, rĕvēllŏ, cōnvēllŏ, ābstrăhŏ, ērŭŏ, ēxstīrpŏ, aūfĕrŏ. Phr.—Ālbŏs ā stīrpĕ căpīllŏs Vēllĕrĕ. Dēntĭbŭs hērbās Vēllēns. Ā cārdĭnĕ pōstēs Vēllĕrĕ. *To separate.* Syn.—Āvēllŏ, dīvēllŏ, ābstrăhŏ. *To torment.* Syn.—Crŭcĭŏ, pūngŏ, lăcĕrŏ, tōrquĕŏ, vēxŏ.

Vēllŭs, ĕrĭs. n. *Wool.* Syn.—Lānă. Phr.—Vēllĕră lānæ. Mūtēntūr vēllĕră. Vēllŭs aūrĕūm. Ŏvĭs, ărĭēs vēllĕrĕ dīvĕs. Pēllĭs ŏvĭs. *(In general) Sheep-skin.* Syn.—Pēllĭs, spŏlĭūm, ēxŭvĭæ, tēgmĕn.

Vēlŏ, ās, āvī, ātūm, ārĕ. *To veil, to cover.* Pūrpŭrĕō vēlārĕ cŏmās ădŏpērtŭs ămīctū. V. Syn.—Ōbvēlŏ, ămīcĭŏ, ōbdūcŏ, ōccūltŏ, ŏpĕrĭŏ, tĕgŏ. Phr.—Vēlārūnt flāmmĕă vūltūs. Vēlāvĭt ărānĕă fānūm. *To vest.* Syn.—Tĕgŏ, vēstĭŏ. *To adorn.* Syn.—Ōrnŏ. *To crown.* Syn.—Cīngŏ, cīrcūmdŏ, rĕdĭmĭŏ.

Vēlōcĭtās, ātĭs. f. *Quickness, speed.* Syn.—Cĕlĕrĭtās, lĕvĭtās, īmpĕtŭs.

Vēlōcĭtĕr. adv. *Quickly.* Syn.—Cĭtŏ, ōcĭŭs, sŭbĭtō, rĕpēntĕ.

Vēlōx, ōcĭs. adj. *Quick, prompt.* Vēlōcēs Spārtæ cătŭlōs ācrēmquĕ Mŏlōssūm. V. Syn.—Cĭtŭs, cōncĭtŭs, cĕlĕr, lĕvĭs, pērnīx, præcēps, præpĕs, prōmptŭs, prŏpĕrŭs, răpĭdŭs, vŏlāns, vŏlŭcrĭs, ālĭgĕr, ālĭpĕs. Phr.—Pĕdĭbūs cĕlĕr ēt pērnīcĭbŭs ālīs. Fūlmĭnĕ pērnĭcĭŏr. Nĭhĭl ēst vēlōcĭŭs ānnīs. Vēlōcĭă crūră. Ŏcŭlō vēlōcī præcūrrĕrĕ. Pĭlă vēlōx. Vēlōx ād făcĭnŭs.

Vēlūm, ī. n. *Covering, tapestry.* Syn.—Aūlæă, vēlāmĕn, tēgmĕn, ămīctŭs, vēlārĭūm. *Veil for the head.* Syn.—Flāmmĕă, rētĭcŭlūm, vēlāmĕn. *Sail.* Syn.—Cārbăsă, līntĕă, līnă, sĭnŭs. Phr.—Vēlōrūm sĭnūs. Āntēnnīs pēndēntĭă vēlă. Ānnēxă mālō. Præcĭpĭtī cārbăsă tēnsă Nŏtō. Sĕcūndīs īnflātă Nŏtīs vēlă. Pāndĕrĕ vēlă. Mĕdĭō stānt vēlă tŭmēntĭă pōntō. Vēntūs cōncăvă vēlă tĕnĕt. Vēlōrūm pāndĭmŭs ālās. Vēlīs flēctĕ vĭām. Clāssēm prōcēdĕrĕ vēlīs. Jŭbĕt ūtī nāvĭtă vēlīs.

Vĕlŭt, vĕlŭtī. conj. *As, just as.* Syn.—Ŭtī, ŭt, sīcŭt, sīcŭtī, tānquām. Phr.—Nōn sĕcŭs āc. Haūd ălĭtĕr.

Vēnă, æ. f. *Vein.* Aūt quīd tēntārēt sălĭēntīs tēmpŏră vēnæ. O. Phr.—Trĕpĭdæquĕ sĭne ūllā Pēllĕ mĭcānt vēnæ. Sălĭūnt tēntātæ pōllĭcĕ vēnæ. Pāllēnt āmīssō sānguĭnĕ vēnæ. Plēnīs tŭmŭĕrūnt gūttŭră vēnīs. Īgnĕă vēnīs Ōmnĭbŭs āctă sĭtĭs. *Vein of metal.* Syn.—Fŏdīnă. *Source of a river.* Syn.—Fōns, rīvŭs. *Poetic vein, poetic genius.* Syn.—Īngĕnĭūm, Mĭnērvă. Phr.—Vēna īngĕnĭī bĕnīgnă.

Vēnālĭă, ĭūm. n. *Merchandise, goods for sale.* Phr.—Părābĭlĭs aūrō. Vēnālēs ănĭmæ. Vēnālĭs līnguæ. Vēnālīsquĕ fĭdēs. Ōmnĭă Rōmæ Cūm prĕtĭō. Plūrĭmŭs aūrō Vēnĭt hŏnōs.

Vēnālĭs, ĭs, ĕ. *Exposed for sale.* Syn.—Vēnālĭtĭŭs, ēxpŏsĭtŭs.

Vēnātŏr, ōrĭs. m. *Hunter.* Vēnātōr tĕnĕræ cōnjŭgĭs īmmĕmŏr. H. Syn.—Vēnāns. Phr.—Fĕrārūm sēctātŏr. Vēnātŭī, Dīānæ stŭdĭīs, nĕmŏrūm cūltŏr, stŭdĭōsŭs. Ăgĭtāns īn sāltĭbŭs āprōs. Mānēns sūb Jŏvĕ frīgĭdō. Fĕrās sŏlĭtūs tērrērĕ fŭgācēs.

Vēndŏ, ĭs, dĭdī, dĭtūm, ĕrĕ. *To sell.* Ēxănĭmūmque aūrō cōrpūs vēndēbăt Ăchīllēs. V. Syn.—Vēnūmdŏ, vēnūmtrādŏ, vēndĭtŏ. Phr.—Sī vēndās ōmnĭă plūrĭs. Mīlēsĭă māgnō Vēllĕră mūtēntŭr.

Vĕnēfĭcă, æ. f. *Magician, sorceress.* Syn.—Măgă, sāgă, īncāntātrīx. Phr.—Thēssălīs pŏtēns vĕnēnīs. Vĕnēnī ārtĭfēx.

Vĕnēfĭcĭūm, ĭī. n. *Sorcery, witchcraft.* Dēmĕ vĕnēfĭcĭīs cārmĭnĭbūsquĕ fĭdēm. O. Syn.—Cārmĕn, cāntŭs. Phr.—Vĕnēfĭcĭī ārs īmpĭă. Thēssălă, măgĭcă vĕnēnă. Nōxĭă, vĕnēfĭcă vērbă.

Vĕnēfĭcŭs, ī. m. *Magician, poisoner.* Syn.—Măgŭs, īncāntātŏr.

Vĕnēnō, ās, ārĕ. *To saturate, to tinge.* Syn.—Mĕdĭcŏ, tīngŏ, īmbŭŏ. *To poison.* Syn.—Īnfĭcĭŏ, cōrrūmpŏ, vĭtĭŏ.

Vĕnēnūm, ī. n. *Poison.* Pērfūsūs sănĭē vīttās ātrōquĕ vĕnēnō. V. Syn.—Vīrŭs, tōxĭcūm, tābūm, ăcōnītă. Phr.—Vĕnēnī tābēs. Vīpĕrĕŭs crŭŏr, sānguĭs. Vĕnēnĭfĕræ, mōrtĭfĕræ, lētālēs hērbæ. Hērbă nŏcēns. Fūnēstă, mălă grāmĭnă. Sērpēntūm sănĭēs. Nēssī crŭŏr. Trītīs ăcōnītă cĭcūtīs. Nĭgră pōcŭlă. Pōcŭlă Cīrcēs. Tābēs fūnēstă vĕnēnī. Tābĭfĭcam ēxspīrāt sănĭēm. Tēlă, săgīttās vĕnēnō tīngŏ, ūnguŏ. Călămōs ārmārĕ vĕnēnō. Īllĭtă tēlă dŏlīs. Vĕnēnūm dō. Vĕnēnō tōllĕrĕ. Vēlōcĭūsvĕ mīscŭīssĕ tōxĭcūm. Lētālēs cōmpōnĕrĕ sūccōs. Cōrpūs tŭmēt ōmnĕ vĕnēnō. Īnfūndās ăcōnītă pălām. Vĕnēnūm bĭbŏ. Ātrūm cōrpŏrĕ cōmbĭbĕrĕ vĕnēnūm. Fig.—*Poison of calumny.* Syn.—Fĕl, vīrŭs, tābēs, tābūm. Phr.—Ātră vĕnēnō Īnvĭdĭæ. Lingua ēst sūffūsă vĕnēnō. *Drug.* Syn.—Mĕdĭcāmĕn.

Vēnĕō, īs, īvī & ĭī, ĭtūm, īrĕ. *To be sold.* Syn.—Vēndōr, vēnūmdŏr, vēnŭmĕŏ.

Vĕnĕrābĭlĭs, ĭs, ĕ. *Venerable, worthy of respect.* Īllŭd ămīcĭtĭæ sānctum āc vĕnĕrābĭlĕ nōmĕn. O. Syn.—Vĕnĕrāndŭs, vĕrēndŭs, rĕvĕrēndŭs, cŏlēndŭs, ădōrāndŭs, aūgūstŭs, sānctŭs, săcĕr. Phr.—Mājēstātĕ vĕrēndŭs. Dĕcūs vĕnĕrābĭlĕ mōrūm Ēxēmplūm. Vĕnĕrābĭlĭōr Lărĕ Dīvĕs.

Vĕnĕrātĭŏ, ōnĭs. f. *Veneration, respect.* Syn.—Cūltŭs, hŏnŏr, hŏnōs, ōbsērvāntĭă, rĕvĕrēntĭă.

Vĕnĕrŏr, ārĭs, ātŭs sūm, ārī. *To venerate, to respect.* Plācātum Eūrўdĭcēn vĭtŭlā vĕnĕrābĕrĕ cæsā. V. Syn.—Vĕrĕŏr, rĕvĕrĕŏr, cŏlŏ, ădōrŏ, hŏnōrŏ, ōbsērvŏ, plācŏ. Phr.—Vōtīsquĕ dĕōs vĕnĕrābĕrĕ sērīs. Sūpplēx plēnā vĕnĕrātŭr ăcērrā.

Vĕnĭă, æ. f. *Grace, pardon.* Mātĕrĭām vĕnĭæ sōrs tĭbĭ nōstră dĕdĭt. O. Syn.—Pāx, īndūlgēntĭă. Phr.—Vĕnĭā cărēt ēt cĭthărœdŭs. Tū mŏdŏ pōscĕ Dēlōs vĕnĭām. Vĕnĭām dō. Nōxām rĕmīttŏ. Haūd āspērnātă prĕcāntēs Prōsĕquĭtŭr vĕnĭā. *Permission, favor.* Syn.—Cōpĭă, lĭcēntĭă, făcūltās, lībērtās. Phr.—Pācĕ tŭā.

Vĕnĭŏ, īs, vēnī, vēntūm, īrĕ. *To come, to arrive.* Fāc vĕnĭās ŏcŭlīs ūmbră bĕnīgnă mĕīs. Prop. Syn.—Ādvĕnĭŏ, ādvēntŏ, dēvĕnĭŏ, pērvĕnĭŏ, āccēdŏ, sūccēdŏ, prŏpīnquŏ, fĕrŏr, āffĕrŏr, dēfĕrŏr, ādsūm, ādvŏlō, ădĕō, pĕtō, tāngŏ, āttīngŏ, cōntīngŏ. Phr.—Hūc flēctĕ grădūm. Hūc ădēs. Sēdēm vĕnĭēmŭs ĭn ūnām. Ēn sūpplēx vĕnĭō. Mīssŭs ĭn hānc ūrbēm vĕnĭō. Vēntum ĕrăt ād rīpās. Vĕnĭēns ād līttŏră clāssĭs. Vĕnĭēndī pōscĕrĕ caūsās. Vēnĭt ăd aūrēs. Vĕnĭt īn mēntēm. Vĕnĭēntĕ dĭē. Ārbŏrĭbūs mĭsĕrāndă lŭēs vēnĭt. Vēntum ēst īn fīnēm.

Vēnŏr, ārĭs, ātŭs sūm, ārī. *To hunt.* Ēt cănĭbūs lĕpŏrēm, cănĭbūs vēnābĕrĕ dāmās. V. Phr.—Vēnātūm ĕō. Fĕrās sēctŏr, ēxăgĭtō. Fĕrīs īnstō, īnsĭdĭās mōlĭŏr. Fĕrās īn rētĭă ăgō. Sīlvās, nĕmŏră cănĭbŭs, plăgīs claūdō. Fĕrārūm lătĕbrās tūrbō. Vēnāndō pēr jŭgă. Trĕpĭdōs ăgĭtāre īn rētĭă cērvōs. Aūt ācrēs vēnābŏr āprōs. Spēlūncās cănĭbūs rīmātŭr. Nēc rētĭă cērvīs Ūllă dŏlūm mĕdĭtāntŭr. Lătēbrās īntrārĕ fĕrārūm. Fig.—*To pursue, to search for.* Syn.—Cāptō, aūcŭpŏr.

Vēntĕr, trĭs. m. *Belly, womb.* Quīdquīd quæsĭĕrāt vēntrī dōnābăt ăvārō. H. Syn.—Ālvŭs, ŭtĕrŭs, īlĭă, vīscĕră, stŏmăchŭs. Phr.—Pĕnĕtrālĭă vēntrĭs. Aēgrūm sōllĭcĭtāt stŏmăchūm mălă cōpĭă. Fig.—*Appetite.* Syn.—Fămēs, īnglŭvĭēs. Phr.—Plācāt jējūnĭă vēntrĭs. Vēntrīs văcŭī fŭrŏr. Vēntrī bēllūm īndīcĕrĕ. Lūxŭrĭæ vēntrīquĕ văcārĕ.

Vēntĭlō, ās, āvī, ātūm, ārĕ. *To breathe, to blow.* Syn.—Flō, āfflō, āspīrō. Phr.—Īgnēm quătĭō, cōncŭtĭō. Fōllēs ēxănĭmō. Īncēndĭă flātŭs Vēntĭlăt. *To agitate, to whirl around.* Syn.—Rŏtō, cŏrūscō, vĭbrō, tōrquĕō. *To handle often.* Syn.—Vērsō, trāctō, mŏvĕō, ăgĭtō.

Vēntŭs, ī. m. *Wind.* Quæ cūncta āĕrĭī dīscērpūnt īrrĭtă vēntī. Cat. Syn.—Aūră, spīrĭtŭs, flāmĕn, flātŭs, flābrūm; (*also*) Āfrĭcŭs, Aūstĕr, Nŏtŭs, Ăquĭlō, Bŏrĕās, Eūrŭs, Zĕphȳrŭs, Făvōnĭŭs. Phr.—Vēntōrūm flāmmă. Vēntī vīs, vīrēs, mĭnæ, răbĭēs, īră. Aēŏlĭī frātrēs. Aēŏlĭī cārcĕrĭs āgmĭnă. Vĕnĭēntīs sībĭlŭs Aūstrī. Vēntōsī mūrmŭrĭs aūræ. Făcĭēntēs frīgŏră vēntī. Vēntōs pērpēssŭs ĕt īmbrēs. Dūm nūbĭlă vēntŭs ăgēbăt. Ănĭmæ vērīs cŏmĭtēs. Lēnī crĕpĭtābāt brāctĕă vēntō. Lēnī rĕcrĕārĕ vēntō. Āspīrānt aūrae īn nōctēm. Vēntī tūrbŏ. Vēntī vīrēs vălĭdæ. Prŏcēllæ strīdŏr. Cæcō tūrbĭnĕ vēntī. Vēntī, quæquĕ rŭūnt, stērnūnt. Mărĭa ōmnĭă cœlō mīscŭĭt. Sævītquĕ mĭnācī mūrmŭrĕ pōntŭs. Īnsŏnŭīt vēntō nĕmŭs. Vēntŭs ŭt āmīttīt vīrēs. Cūm fĕră pōnĭt hĭēms.

Vĕnūstās, ātĭs. f. *Beauty, grace.* Syn.—Vĕnŭs, fōrmă, dĕcŏr, hŏnŏr, grātĭă, lĕpŏr.

Vĕprēs, ĭs. m. *Thorn.* Syn.—Rŭbŭs, spīnă, dūmŭs, sēntēs. Phr.—Hīrsūtī sĕcŭērūnt cōrpŏră vēprēs. Spārsī rōrābānt sānguĭnĕ vēprēs. Ăcūtīs āspĕrī vĕprēs rŭbīs.

Vēr, vērĭs. n. *Spring.* Hīc vēr āssĭdŭum ātque ălĭēnīs mēnsĭbŭs æstās. V. Phr.—Vērnūm tēmpŭs. Vērnī dĭēs. Vērnă tēmpēstās. Tēmpŏră vērĭs. Nŏvă tēmpŏrĭs ætās. Vērĭs hŏnōs. Pārs ānnī mĕlĭŏr. Vērĭs ămœnă dĭēs. Blāndīsquĕ sălūbrĕ Vēr Zĕphȳrīs. Rīdēntĭă flōrĭbŭs ānnī Tēmpŏră. Vērnō tēmpŏrĕ. Vērĕ nŏvō. Vēr flōrĭbŭs ārvă nŏvīs dĕcŏrăt. Vēr æthĕră mūlcĕt. Vērnī rīdēnt dĭēs. Cūm lætīs dĕcŏrāntūr flōrĭbŭs ārvă. Fig.—*Youth. See Juventus.*

Vērātrūm, ī. *Hellebore.* (*See Appendix under list of Trees, etc.*)

Vērāx, ācĭs. adj. *True, sincere.* Ĕrāt vērāx vātĭcĭnātă sŏrŏr. O. Syn.—Vērŭs, sīncērŭs, vērĭdĭcŭs. Phr.—Vīr līngua ēt pēctŏrĕ vērŭs.

Vērbēnă, æ. f. *The herb vervain.* (*See Appendix under list of Trees, etc.*)

Vērbĕr, ĕrĭs. n. *Wand, whip, scourge.* Cōncūssērĕ jŭgīs, prōnīque īn vērbĕră pēndēnt. V. Syn.—Flăgēllūm, flăgrūm, scŭtĭcă, vīrgă, hăbēnă, lōrūm. Phr.—Vērbĕră īnsŏnŭĭt. Īlli īnstānt vērbĕrĕ tōrtō. Vērbĕrĭs īctū Īncrĕpŭĭt. Vērbĕrĭbūs præbērĕ mănūs. Vērbĕră sævă sŏnānt. *Blow. See Ictus. Flapping of wings.* Syn.—Plaūsŭs.

Vērbĕrŏ, ās, āvī, ātūm, ārĕ. *To beat, to lash.* Syn.—Dīvērbĕrŏ, cædŏ, tūndŏ, fĕrĭŏ, pērcŭtĭŏ, pūlsŏ, cāstīgŏ, mūlctŏ. Phr.—Vērbĕră, īctūs dō, īnflīgŏ. Mănū pērcŭtĭŏ. Tērgă, lătŭs scīndĕrĕ. Īntōrtō vērbĕrĕ tērgă sĕcăt. Vĕhĕmēntī pērcŭlĭt īctū. Fig.—*To beat the air.* Syn.—Fĕrĭŏ, quătĭŏ, pērcŭtĭŏ, pūlsŏ, plāngŏ. Sĭmŭl æthĕră vērbĕrăt ālīs. Ēt cālcĭbŭs aūrās Vērbĕrăt. Cēntēnāque ārbŏrĕ flūctūm Vērbĕrăt.

Vērbūm, ī. n. *Word.* Syn.—Dīctĭŏ, dīctūm, vōx, vōcābŭlūm. *Discourse, language.* Syn.—Dīctă, vōcēs, sērmŏ, lŏquēlă.

Vĕrēcūndē. adv. *Modestly.* Syn.—Pŭdīcē, cāstē, pŭdēntĕr, īngĕnŭē.

Vĕrēcūndŏr, ārĭs, ātŭs sūm, ārī. *To have shame, to be modest.* Syn. —Pŭdĕt mē, ērŭbēscŏ.

Vĕrēcūndŭs, ă, ūm. *Modest.* Īllĕ vĕrēcūndō vīx tōllēns lūmĭnă vūltū. O. Syn.—Pŭdēns, pŭdīcŭs, pŭdĭbūndŭs, mŏdēstŭs. *Honest, virtuous.* Syn.—Cāstŭs, prŏbŭs.

Vĕrēndŭs, ă, ūm. *Venerated.* Syn.—Vĕnĕrābĭlĭs. *To be feared.* Syn.—Mĕtŭēndŭs, fōrmīdāndŭs, tērrĭbĭlĭs.

Vĕrĕŏr, ērĭs, ĭtŭs sūm, ērī. *To reverence, to respect.* Syn.—Cŏlŏ, rĕvĕrĕŏr, vĕnĕrŏr. *To fear.* Syn.—Tĭmĕŏ, rĕvĕrĕŏr, mĕtŭŏ. *To hesitate about, to scruple.* Syn.—Tĭmĕŏ, dŭbĭtŏ. Phr.—Nōn aūdĕŏ.

Vērgŏ, ĭs, ĕrĕ. *To be turned towards, to be bent towards.* Syn.—Vērgŏr, flēctŏr, vērtŏr, spēctŏ, tēndŏ, īnclīnŏ, pēndĕŏ, prōpēndĕŏ, īncūmbŏ, īmmĭnĕŏ. Phr.—Quō vērgāt pōndĕrĕ lētūm. Vērgēntĕ dĭē. Vērgēntĭbŭs ānnīs Īn sĕnĭūm.

Vērĭdĭcŭs, ă, ūm. *True, truly spoken.* Syn.—Vērŭs, vērāx, sīncērŭs.

Vērĭtās, ātĭs. f. *Truth.* Syn.—Vērūm. Phr.—Nēscĭă fraūdūm. Nēscĭă fāllĕrĕ vīrtūs. Vērī fĭdēs. Vērāx dīctūm. Nōn fŭgĭēns lūcēm. Īnscĭă fūcī. Rīdēntēm dīcĕrĕ vērūm Quīd vĕtăt? Vērō dīstīnguĕrĕ fālsūm. Ābsīt rĕvĕrēntĭă vērō. Vērī prōvĭdŭs aūgŭr. Me īgnōrāntĭă vērī Dēcĭpĭt.

Vērmĭs, ĭs. m. *Worm.* Syn.—Vērmĭcŭlŭs, lūmbrĭcŭs. Phr.—Fœdō se īn pūlvĕrĕ vōlvēns.

Vērnă, æ. m. & f. *Slave born in the house, bondsman.* Syn.—Vērnācŭlŭs, fămŭlŭs, sērvŭs, māncĭpĭūm.

Vērnācŭlŭs, ă, ūm. *Belonging to a country, proper to a country.* Syn.—Dŏmēstĭcŭs, prŏprĭŭs. Phr.—Vērnācŭlă līnguă, vōx.

Vērō. adv. *Truly.* Syn.—Sānē, rēvērā, quĭdēm, īmmō vērō. *But.* Syn.—Vērūm, ăt, sĕd.

Vērrŏ, ĭs, rī, sūm, ĕrĕ. *To drag along the ground.* Syn.—Trăhŏ. *To sweep.* Syn.—Ādvērrŏ, cōnvērrŏ. Phr.—Caūdā vērrūntŭr ărēnæ. Quīdquīd dē Lĭbўcīs vērrĭtŭr ārĕīs. *To push before.* Syn.—Ăgŏ, īmpēllŏ, răpĭŏ, ābrĭpĭŏ.

Vērsĭcŏlŏr, ōrĭs. adj. *Of varied hue, color.* Āstŭr ĕquō fīdēns ēt vērsĭcŏlōrĭbŭs ārmīs. V. Syn.—Dīscŏlŏr, mūltĭcŏlŏr, vărĭŭs. Phr.—Vărĭō cŏlōrĕ dīstīnctŭs. Vărĭīs cŏlōrĭbŭs nĭtēns, fūlgēns, īnsīgnĭs. Cūltū vērsĭcŏlōrĕ dĕcēns.

Vērsĭpēllĭs, ĭs, ĕ. *That which can be changed in form, variable.* Syn.—Vărĭŭs, mūtābĭlĭs. Fig.—*Deceiver.* Syn.—Āstūtŭs, cāllĭdŭs, dŏlōsŭs, sĭmŭlātŏr, văfĕr.

Vērsŏ, ās, āvī, ātūm, ārĕ. *To turn often.* Hūc īllūc vīnclōrum īmmēnsă vŏlūmĭnă vērsăt. V. Syn.—Vōlvŏ, vērtŏ, vŏlūtŏ, tōrquĕŏ, cīrcŭmăgŏ. Phr.—Vērsāntquĕ tĕnācī fōrcĭpĕ fērrūm. Bŏūmquĕ lăbōrēs Vērsāndō terram ēxpērtī. Vērsāvĭt ĭn ōmnĭă vūltūs. Sōrs ōmnĭă vērsăt. Fig.—*To ponder over.* Syn.—Vŏlūtŏ, vōlvŏ, ăgĭtŏ, mĕdĭtŏr. *To put to use.* Syn.—Ēxērcĕŏ, ăgĭtŏ. *To agitate.* Syn.—Ăgĭtŏ, jāctŏ, vōlvŏ, ēxērcĕŏ. *To put in confusion, to overwhelm.* Syn.—Mīscĕŏ, tūrbŏ. (*In the passive*) *To remain, to dwell in.* Syn.—Mănĕŏ, mŏrŏr, hăbĭtŏ, sūm, hærĕŏ.

Vērsŭs, ūs. m. *Rank, order.* Syn.—Ōrdŏ, sĕrĭēs. *Verse.* Syn.—Cārmĕn, mŏdī, vērsĭcŭlŭs. Phr.—Ēffūtīrĕ lĕvēs vērsūs. Lūctōr dēdūcĕrĕ vērsūm. Vērbă fĭdĭbŭs mŏdŭlāndă.

Vērsūtē. adv. *Cunningly.* Syn.—Dŏlōsē, āstūtē, fāllācĭtĕr.

Vērsūtŭs, ă, ūm. *Cunning, skilful.* Ālĭpĕdīs dē stīrpĕ dĕī vērsūtă prŏpāgŏ. V. Syn.—Āstūtŭs, cāllĭdŭs, dŏlōsŭs, văfĕr, fāllāx.

Vērtēx, ĭcĭs. m. *Vortex.* Syn.—Vōrtēx. *Axis, pole.* Syn.—Pŏlŭs. *The top of the head.* Syn.—Cŏrōnă, căpŭt, ăpēx. *Top, summit.* Syn.—Ăpēx, căcūmĕn, cūlmĕn, fāstīgĭūm. Phr.—Cēlsō vērtĭcĕ quērcŭs. Vērtĭcĕ cēlsō Cānŭs ăpēx. Cēlsā nīmbōsī vērtĭcĭs ārcĕ.

Vērtŏ, ĭs, tī, sūm, ĕrĕ. *To turn.* Gōrgŏnă dēsēctō vērtēntēm lūmĭnă cōllō. O. Syn.—Vŏlūtŏ, vōlvŏ, vērsŏ, tōrquĕŏ, flēctŏ. Phr.—Vērtĭtur īntĕrĕā cœlūm. *To turn towards.* Syn.—Cōnvērtŏ, ādvērtŏ, tōrquĕŏ, dīrĭgŏ. *To turn over.* Syn.—Ēvērtŏ. *To change.* Syn.—Mūtŏ. (*As an intransitive verb*) *To be changed.* Syn.—Mūtŏr, cōnvērtŏr.

Vērūm. conj. *But.* Syn.—Sĕd, āst, ăt, vērō, vērūmtămĕn.

Vērŭs, ă, ūm. *True.* Syn.—Sīncērŭs, īngĕnŭŭs, vērāx, vērĭdĭcŭs, cāndĭdŭs. Phr.—Vērīs īmmīscēns fālsă. Ōbscūrīs īnvōlvēns vēră. Vērō vērĭŭs.

Vēsānĭă, æ. f. *Folly.* Syn.—Āmēntĭă, dēmēntĭă, fŭrŏr, īnsānĭă.

Vēsānŭs, ă, ūm. *Foolish, stupid.* Syn.—Īnsānŭs, stūltŭs, āmēns. *Mad.* Syn.—Īnsānŭs, fŭrĭōsŭs, fŭrēns.

Vēscŏr, ĕrĭs, ī. *To eat, to nourish oneself.* Syn.—Dēvēscŏr, pāscŏr, ălŏr, nūtrĭŏr, sūstēntŏr, vīvŏ, ĕdŏ. Phr.—Vīctū pāscūntūr sīmplĭcĭs hērbæ. Quīcūmquĕ tērræ mūnĕrĕ vēscĭmŭr.

Vēscŭs, ă, ūm. *Eatable.* Vērbēnāsquĕ prĕmēns vēscūmquĕ păpāvĕr. V. Phr.—Ēt vēscās sălĭcūm frōndēs. *Dry, feeble.* Syn.—Pārvŭs, grăcĭlĭs, ēxĭgŭŭs, tĕnŭĭs.

Vēspă, æ. f. *Wasp.* Syn.—Fūcŭs, crābrŏ. Phr.—Īnvīsă cĭcādīs.

Vēspĕr, ĕrĭs & Vēspĕrŭs, ī. m. *Vesper, the evening star.* Īllīc sēră rŭbēns āccēndīt lūmĭnă vēspĕr. Syn.—Nōctĭfĕr, Hēspĕrŭs. Phr.—Sērūm Vĕnĕrĭs sīdŭs. Sēræ nūntĭūs hōræ. Prīmās rĕfĕrēns tĕnĕbrās. *Evening.* Syn.—Vēspĕră, crĕpūscŭlūm.

Vēspĕrī & Vēspĕrĕ. adv. *In the evening.* Syn.—Sērō. Phr.—Dīē vērgēntĕ, ōccĭdŭō, lābēntĕ, prōnō. Sōlĕ fŭgĭēntĕ. Sōlĕ sŭb ōccĭdŭō. Sūb nōctēm. Prīmă nōctĕ. Īn nōctēm vērgēntĕ dĭē. Vēspērtīnīs sŭb hōrīs. Nōctēm dūcēntĭbŭs āstrīs. Cūm sōl rădĭōs æquŏrĕ cōndĭt. Cūm sōl Ōcĕănō sŭbēst. Nōx ĕrăt īncĭpĭēns. Jāmquĕ dĭēs ēxāctŭs ĕrăt. Āscēndīt vēspĕr Ōlȳmpūm. Jām nōx jūngĭt ĕquōs. Dēcēdēntĕ dĭē.

Vēspērtīnŭs, ă, ūm. *Evening, nocturnal.* Syn.—Sērŭs, sērōtĭnŭs.

Vēstālĭs, ĭs. f. *Vestal virgin.* Quæ sērvāt cāstæ pĕnĕtrālĭă Vēstæ. Prop. Phr.—Vēstālĭs vīrgŏ, pŭēllă, săcērdōs. Vēstæ săcrātă. Vēstæ mĭnīstrāns. Vīrgĭnĕō lēctă mĭnīstră fŏcō.

Vēstĭbŭlūm, ī. n. *Vestibule, porch.* Syn.—Ātrĭūm, ātrĭă (pl.), līmĕn, pōrtĭcŭs, ădĭtŭs.

Vēstīgĭūm, ĭī. n. *Trace, track.* Vēstīgĭă rētrō Ōbsērvātă sĕquōr pēr nōctem ēt lūmĭnĕ lūstrŏ. V. Syn.—Sīgnă, īndĭcĭă, nŏtæ. Phr.—Pĕdūm īmprēssūm īndĭcĭūm. Sīgnātæ pĕdūm nŏtæ. Vĭæ sīgnă. Sūmmō vēstīgĭă pūlvĕrĕ sīgnēnt. *Step.* Syn.—Grēssŭs, grădŭs, pāssŭs. *March.* Syn.—Ĭtĕr, vĭă. Fig.—*Debris, remains.* Syn.—Rĕlĭquĭæ, frāgmĕn, frāgmēntă.

Vēstīgŏ, ās, āvī, ātūm, ārĕ. *To search diligently.* Ērgo āltē vēstīga ŏcŭlīs. V. Syn.—Īnvēstīgŏ, īnquīrŏ, scrūtŏr.

Vēstĭŏ, īs, īvī & ĭī, ītūm, īrĕ. *To clothe.* Ātque ūnām vēstīrĕ trĭbūm tŭă vēllĕră pōssūnt. M. Syn.—Īndŭŏ, vēlŏ, tĕgŏ, cōntĕgŏ, ŏpĕrĭŏ, īndūcŏ, ōbdūcŏr, ămīcĭŏ, cīrcūmdŏ, cīngŏ. Phr.—Vēstĕ tĕgŏ, ămīcĭŏ. Ămīctū, tēgmĭnĕ vēstĭŏ. Cōrpūs spŏlĭīs vēstīrĕ fĕrārūm. Căpūt glaūcō cōntēxĭt ămīctū. Īn lōngīs vēstĭbŭs īrĕ. (*In general*) *To cover.* Syn.—Īndŭŏ, tĕgŏ, cōntĕgŏ, ŏpĕrĭŏ, ōbdūcŏ.

Vēstĭs, ĭs. f. *Vestment, garment, habit.* Aūrĕă pūrpŭrĕām sūbnēctīt fībŭlă vēstēm. V. Syn.—Vēstīmēntūm, vēstītŭs, tēgmĕn, tŏgă, tŭnĭcă, pāllĭūm, vēlāmĕn, vēlāmēntūm, cārbăsŭs, līnūm, stŏlă, sĭnŭs. Phr.—Ārtĕ tēxtă. Ōstrō, mūrĭcĕ tīnctă. Aūrō rĭgēns, āspĕră. Gēmmīs ŏnūstă. Ārtĭs ŏpūs rāræ. Lōngæ tēgmĭnĕ pāllæ. Pĕdēs vēstīs dēflūxĭt ăd īmōs. Vēstēm prætēxŭĭt ōstrō. Squālēntēs pūlvĕrĕ vēstēs. Cīnctāsquĕ sōlvĭtĕ vēstēs. *Covering in general.* Syn.—Strāgŭlūm. *Cloth.* Syn.—Tēxtă.

Vĕtērnŭs, ī. m. *Languor, weakness.* Syn.—Tōrpŏr, lānguŏr, sĭtŭs, ĭnērtĭă, īgnāvĭă.

Vĕtĭtūm, ī. n. *That which is forbidden.* Syn.—Nĕfās, īllĭcĭtūm, scĕlŭs. Phr.—Quōd nōn lĭcēt. Hæc īn vĕtĭtīs nŭmĕrānt.

Vĕtŏ, ās, ŭī, ĭtūm, ārĕ. *To forbid.* Sūppŏsŭīt tŭmŭlō, rēgĕ vĕtāntĕ, sŏrŏr. O. Syn.—Prŏhĭbĕŏ, ābstērrĕŏ. Phr.—Nōn sĭnŏ, nōn pērmīttŏ, jŭbĕŏ nē. Tālī vĕtŭīt mē vōcĕ Quĭrīnŭs. *To prevent, to oppose.* Syn.—Prŏhĭbĕŏ, ōbstŏ, ōbsūm. Phr.—Prīmāquĕ vĕtānt cōnsīstĕrĕ tērrā. *To turn away, to turn off.* Syn.—Ārcĕŏ, prŏhĭbĕŏ, ābstērrĕŏ, āvērtŏr.

Vĕtŭlŭs, ă, ūm. *Quite old.* Syn.—Ānnōsŭs, vĕtŭs, vĕtūstŭs.

Vĕtŭs, ĕrĭs. adj. *Old, ancient.* Nōn mĭhĭ rēspōndēnt vĕtĕrēs īn cārmĭnĕ vīrēs. O. Syn.—Āntīquŭs, prīscŭs, vĕtūstŭs, vĕtŭlŭs, prīstĭnŭs, prætĕrĭtŭs, ānnōsŭs, lōngævŭs, sĕnēx. (*In the plural*)

The elders. Syn.—Mājōrēs, ăvī, prŏăvī, prīscī, āntīquī, prīmī, prĭōrēs.

Vĕtūstās, ātĭs. f. *Antiquity.* Syn.—Āntīquĭtās, tēmpŏră prīscă. Phr.—Prīscī tēmpŏrĭs ætās. Vĕtūstum ætātĭs spătĭūm. Mĕmŏrāndă cănēns. Laūdātōr tēmpŏrĭs āctī, sē pŭĕrō. *Time.* Syn.—Aētās, ævūm, tēmpŭs, ānnī, dĭēs. Phr.—Tēmpŏrĭs ætās. Lōngī fŭgă mōbĭlĭs ævī. Fĕrūnt scrīptă vĕtūstātēm. *Old age.* Syn.—Sĕnēctūs, sĕnēctă, sĕnĭūm.

Vēxātĭŏ, ōnĭs. f. *Persecution, torment.* Syn.—Mŏlēstĭă, crŭcĭātŭs, ærūmnă, āngŏr.

Vēxīllūm, ī. n. *Standard, ensign.* Syn.—Sīgnūm, dĕcŭs, ăquĭlă. Phr.—Ādvērsīs cōncūrrĕrĕ sīgnīs. Cāstrīs āvūlsă mŏvērī sīgnă jŭbĕt. Sīgnă sēquāntŭr.

Vēxŏ, ās, āvī, ātūm, ārĕ. *To shake, to agitate.* Syn.—Jāctŏ, ăgĭtŏ, ēxăgĭtŏ, quătĭŏ, cōncŭtĭŏ, quāssŏ. *To vex, to torment.* Syn.—Āngŏ, āfflīgŏ, āfflīctŏ, crŭcĭŏ, dīscrŭcĭŏ, tōrquĕŏ, lăcĕrŏ, lædŏ, prĕmŏ, ōpprĭmŏ. Phr.—Pœnīs, crŭcĭātĭbŭs āffĭcĭŏ. Vēxāt cōrpŏră fēssă călŏr. Me īnsōmnĭă vēxānt. *To trouble.* Syn.—Ăgĭtŏ, ēxăgĭtŏ, tūrbŏ.

Vĭă, æ. f. *Route, street, way.* Jāmquĕ prŏpīnquābām pōrtīs, ōmnēmquĕ vĭdēbăr Ēvāsīssĕ vĭām. V. Syn.—Ĭtĕr, cāllĭs, trāmĕs, sēmĭtă, ădĭtŭs, mĕātŭs. Phr.—Trītūm spătĭūm. Sēmĭtă cāllĭs. Strātă vĭārūm. Pārtēs ŭbī sē vĭă fīndĭt ĭn āmbās. Mīllĕ fŭgīt rĕfŭgītquĕ vĭās. Vĭārūm āmbāgēs. Ădĭtūmquĕ pĕr āvĭă quærĭt. Pĕr ŏpācă vĭārūm. Lōngās īrĕ vĭās. Mētă vĭārūm. Vĭām cārpĕrĕ. Vĭæ sē cōmmīttĕrĕ. Hæc īngrēssă vĭām. Pēr tūtās āmbŭlăt īllĕ vĭās. Nĕgātă tēntăt ĭtēr vĭă. Quō lātī dūcūnt ădĭtūs. Īgnārōsquĕ vĭæ. Mātrĕ dĕā mōnstrāntĕ vĭām. Sī quă vĭa ēst. Vĭă fāllĭt ĕūntēs. Fīt vĭă vī, rūmpūnt ădĭtūs. Vĭă fāctă pĕr hōstēs. *March, journey.* Syn.—Ĭtĕr, cūrsŭs, grădŭs, grēssŭs. *Conduit, canal.* Syn.—Ădĭtŭs, ĭtĕr, mĕātŭs, ēxĭtŭs, fŏrāmĕn. Fig.—*Method.* Syn.—Mŏdŭs, rătĭŏ.

Vĭātŏr, ōrĭs. m. *Voyager.* Cūm vĕnĭt ēt tērrām sīccō spŭĭt ōrĕ vĭātŏr Ārĭdŭs. V. Syn.—Pĕrĕgrīnŭs, ādvĕnă. Phr.—Quī cārpĭt ĭtĕr. Fĕrēns tædĭă lōngă vĭæ. Ēxpŏsĭtŭs mīllĕ pĕrīclīs. Caūtūs præcīngĭtŭr ēnsĕ vĭātŏr.

Vĭbrŏ, ās, āvī, ātūm, ārĕ. *To shake, to agitate.* Ādvērsās vībrābānt flāmĭnă vēstēs. O. Syn.—Quătĭŏ, ăgĭtŏ, jāctŏ, mŏvĕŏ, tōrquĕŏ, rŏtŏ, cŏrūscŏ. *To hurl, to send forward.* Syn.—Jăcĭŏ, cōnjĭcĭŏ, jăcŭlŏr, mīttŏ, tōrquĕŏ, cōntōrquĕŏ. (*Intransitively*) *To be agitated, vibrated.* Syn.—Vĭbrŏr, cŏrūscŏ, mĭcŏ, trĕmŏ.

Vĭcĭă, æ. f. *Vetch, tare.* (*See Appendix under list of Trees, etc.*)

Vīcīnĭă, æ. f. *Vicinity, proximity*. Syn.—Vīcīnĭtās, prōxĭmĭtās. Phr.—Vīcīnĭă Pērsĭdĭs. Sĭcŭlæ vīcīnĭă tērræ. Vīcīnĭă dāmno ēst.

Vīcīnŭs, ă, ūm. *Nearby, close, neighboring*. Heū! Quām vīcīna ēst ūltĭmă tērră mĭhĭ. O. Syn.—Prŏpīnquŭs, prŏpĭŏr, prōxĭmŭs, cōntērmĭnŭs, cōnfīnĭs, cōntĭgŭŭs, fīnĭtĭmŭs. Phr.—Cōntĭgŭās hăbŭērĕ dŏmōs. Prŏpĭūsquĕ mălum ēst. *Impending, imminent*. Syn.—Prŏpĭŏr, prōxĭmŭs, prŏpīnquŭs, īnstāns, īmmĭnēns.

Vĭcĭs. f. *Change, turn*. (*Used only in the forms*, vĭcēm, vĭcĕ, vĭcēs, vĭcĭbŭs.) Sōlvĭtŭr ācrĭs hĭēms grātā vĭcĕ vērĭs ēt Făvōnī. H. Phr.—Sūccēdūnt sērvāntquĕ vĭcēs. Dīscūrrūnt, vărĭāntquĕ vĭcēs. Ŏpĕrūmquĕ vĭcēs dīspōnĕrĕ. Vĭcēm nōn pĕrăgĭt. Āltērnārĕ vĭcēs. Ārmōrūm vĭcĭbŭs. *Compensation, return*. Syn.—Mūnŭs, mērcēs, pœnă. Phr.—Pār rĕfĕrŏ. Rēddĕ vĭcēm mĕrĭtīs. *Chance, peril*. Syn.—Pĕrīcŭlă, dīscrīmĕn, cāsŭs. Phr.—Pēr grăvēs bēllī vĭcēs.

Vĭcīssīm. adv. *By turns*. Phr.—Pēr vĭcēs. Īn vĭcēm, āltērnā vĭcĕ, āltērnīs vĭcĭbŭs.

Vīctĭmă, æ. f. *Victim for the sacrifice*. Ēt cădĕt ānte ārās īnfēlīx vīctĭmă taūrŭs. O. Syn.—Hōstĭă, pĭăcŭlŭm; (*sometimes*) taūrŭs, jŭvēncŭs, bōs, ŏvĭs, etc. Phr.—Taūrōrūm sānguĭs. Vōtīvŭs sānguĭs. Vōtīvæ cædĭs hŏnŏr. Āltārĭs hŏnōrēs. Rēddĕrĕ vīctĭmās. Māxĭmă taūrīs Vīctĭmă. Ānte ārās sīstŏ. Taūrūm cædŏ. Vīctĭmă cædĭtŭr. Plăcārĕ dĕōs vĭtŭlī sānguĭnĕ dēbĭtō. Taūrūm stērnĕrĕ. Mĕrĭtōs ārīs māctābăt hŏnōrēs. Ālbăquĕ prōfūsā vīctĭmă frōntĕ cădăt.

Vīctŏr, ōrĭs. m. *Victor, conqueror*. Cȳprūm vīctōr dĭtĭōnĕ tĕnēbăt. V. Syn.—Trĭūmphātŏr, dŏmĭtŏr, sŭpĕrātŏr, dēbēllātŏr, dŏmātŏr. Phr.—Dŏmĭtŏr hōstĭūm. Spŏlĭīs hōstīlĭbŭs īnsīgnĭs. Spŏlĭīs dĕcōrŭs, ōrnātŭs. Pālmām vīctō hōstĕ rĕfĕrēns. Vīctō hōstĕ sŭpērbŭs. Mūltō sūblīmĭs hŏnōrĕ. Vīctōrquĕ vĭrōs sŭpĕrēmĭnĕt ōmnēs. Vīctŏr ăgēt cūrrūm. Vīctōrēsque ōstēntăt ĕquōs.

Vīctŏr, ōrĭs, m. & Vīctrīx, īcĭs, f. adj. *Victorious*. Syn.—Trĭūmphāns, ŏvāns, trĭūmphālĭs.

Vīctōrĭă, æ. f. *Victory*. Ārdŭă sōllĭcĭtīs vīctōrĭă quærĭtŭr ārmīs. O. Syn.—Trĭūmphŭs, pālmă, trŏpæūm. Phr.—Vīctōrĭs hŏnōs. Pālmæ dĕcŭs. Vīctrīcēs laūrī. Mūltō sānguĭnĕ pārtă. Mūltō sūdōrĕ pārātă. Āmāt vīctōrĭă cūrām. Dŭbĭās æquāt vīctōrĭă sōrtēs.

Vīctŭs, ūs. m. *Living, food, nourishment*. Syn.—Ălĭmēntūm, cĭbŭs, ēscă, ĕpŭlæ, nūtrīmēntūm, pābŭlūm, dăpēs. Phr.—Vīctu ălĭtŭr cōrpŭs. Vīctūm sĕgĕs ǣgră nĕgābăt. Quērnā pēllĕrĕ glāndĕ fămēm.

Vĭdēlĭcĕt. adv. *Namely*. Syn.—Scīlĭcĕt, nēmpĕ, nīmīrūm.

Vĭdĕō, ēs, vīdī, vīsūm, ērĕ. *To see, to perceive*. Aūt vĭdĕt aūt vīdīssĕ pŭtāt pēr nūbĭlă lūnām. V. Syn.—Āspĭcĭŏ, cōnspĭcĭŏ, cērnŏ, tŭĕŏr, īntŭĕŏr. Phr.—Ŏcŭlīs, lūmĭnĭbŭs āspĭcĭŏ. Vīsū, lūmĭnĕ pērcĭpĭŏ. Spēctăt ĭnēxplētō lūmĭnĕ. Nĕquĕūnt ēxplērī cōrdă tŭēndō. Cērnīt vānēscĕrĕ mōntēs. Quōd vĭdĕānt ŏcŭlī. *To comprehend*. Syn.—Īntēllĕgŏ, căpĭŏ, sēntĭŏ, āgnōscŏ, nōvī. *To guard, to watch*. Syn.—Căvĕŏ, cōnsŭlŏ, āttēndŏ. (*In the passive*) *To be seen, to seem, to appear*. Syn.—Hăbĕŏr, dūcŏr. Phr.—Spĕcĭēm gerō. Mĕrŭīt fōrmōsă vĭdērī. Īpsĕ vĭdērētūr sĭbĭ nēquĭŏr. Mĭhĭ vĭdētŭr.

Vĭdŭă, ǣ. f. *Widow*. Vĭdŭās vēnātŭr ăvārās. H. Phr.—Ōrbă, ōrbātă, vĭdŭātă, spŏlĭātă vĭrō, cōnjŭgĕ, mărītō. Pārtĕ sŭī mĕlĭōrĕ cărēns. Vīvēns sĭnĕ cōnjŭgĕ cǣlēbs. Vĭdŭō fūndīt sūspīrĭă lēctō.

Vĭdŭĭtās, ātĭs. f. *Widowhood*. Syn.—Vĭdŭŭs lēctŭs, vītă cǣlēbs, cǣlĭbēs ānnī. Phr.—Vĭdŭō vīvĕrĕ lēctō. Vĭdŭās ēxĭgĕrĕ nōctēs.

Vĭdŭŏ, ās, āvī, ātūm, ārĕ. *To render a widow*. Phr.—Spŏlĭārĕ vĭrō. *To despoil*. Syn.—Ōrbŏ, spŏlĭŏ, nūdŏ, ēxŭŏ. Phr.—Ēt fŏlĭīs vĭdŭāntŭr ōrnī. Quīn ēnsĕ vĭdŭās dēxtĕrām.

Vĭdŭŭs, ă, ūm. *Widowed*. Īn vĭdŭō jăcĕō sōlŭs ĕt īpsĕ tŏrō. O. Phr.—Cōnjŭgĕ, ūxōrĕ ōrbŭs, ōrbātŭs, vĭdŭātŭs. Quō sē rāptā bĭs cōnjŭgĕ fērrĕt? (*In general*) *Despoiled, deprived*. Syn.—Vĭdŭātŭs, ōrbātŭs, ōrbŭs, spŏlĭātŭs, cărēns, ēxpērs, ēxsōrs. Phr.—Vĭdŭūs phărĕtrā.

Vĭētŭs, ă, ūm. *Languishing, lifeless*. Syn.—Flāccĭdŭs, mārcēns, mārcĭdŭs, vĕtŭs, vĕtūstŭs, ōbsŏlētŭs.

Vĭgĕŏ, ēs, ŭī, ērĕ. *To have strength, vigor*. Syn.—Vălĕŏ. Fig.—*To be flourishing*. Syn.—Vĭgēscŏ, vălĕŏ, pōllĕŏ, vĭrĕŏ, flōrĕŏ, flōrēscŏ. Phr.—Vīrĭbŭs pōllĕō. Vĕgĕtō sūm cōrpŏrĕ. Vĭgōrĕ plēnŭs sūm. Āssĭdŭō vĭgĕăt cērtāmĭnĕ mīlĕs. Fāmă Mōbĭlĭtātĕ vĭgĕt. Sūmmōque ĭn hŏnōrĕ vĭgērĕ.

Vĭgĭl, ĭlĭs. adj. *One who guards, on guard*. Dūmquĕ vĭgīl Phrўgĭōs sērvāt cūstōdĭă mūrōs. O. Syn.—Pērvĭgĭl, vĭgĭlāns, īnsōmnĭs, īnsōpītŭs, pērnōx. Phr.—Īnōps sōmnī. Ēt vĭgĭlāns stērtĭs. *Sleepless*. Syn.—Vĭgĭlātŭs, īnsōmnĭs. *Vigilant*. Syn.—Vĭgĭlāns, ācĕr, īmpĭgĕr, āttēntŭs, dīlĭgēns, ārrēctŭs.

Vĭgĭlāntĭă, ǣ. f. *Vigilance*. Āt sī quōs haūd ūllă vĭrōs vĭgĭlāntĭă fŭgĭt. V. Syn.—Stŭdĭūm, cūră, sēdŭlĭtās. Phr.—Cūră vĭgĭl. Vĭgĭlēs ănĭmī. Vĭgĭlāntĭă cōrdă.

Vĭgĭlēs, ūm. m. *Guards, sentinels.* Syn.—Cūstōdēs, cūstōdĭă, ēx-cŭbĭæ. Phr.—Vĭgĭlūm ēxcŭbĭæ. Pōrtārūm vĭgĭlēs.

Vĭgĭlŏ, ās, āvī, ātūm, ārĕ. *To watch.* Sēd vĭgĭlŏ, vĭgĭlāntquĕ mĕī sĭnĕ fĭnĕ dŏlōrēs. O. Syn.—Pērvĭgĭlŏ, ēvĭgĭlŏ, ēxcŭbŏ. Phr.— Īnsōmnēm, vĭgĭlēm nōctēm dūcŏ. Nōctēm vĭgĭlŏ. Nūllī sōmnō sŭccūmbŏ. Nōctēs vĭgĭlārĕ sĕrēnās. Nēc dūlcī dēclīnānt lūmĭnă sōmnō. Nōctēs vĭgĭlābăt ăd īpsūm Mānĕ. Ēxănĭmēm vĭgĭlārĕ mĕtū. *To go on watch.* Syn.—Ēxcŭbŏ. Phr.—Ēxcŭbĭās ăgŏ. Nōctēmquĕ vĭgĭl dūcēbăt ĭn ārmīs. Vĭgĭl sērvāt cūstōdĭă mūrōs. *To awake.* Syn.—Ēvĭgĭlŏ, ēxpērgīscŏr. Phr.—Ēxcŭtī sōmnō. *To be on one's guard.* Syn.—Căvĕŏ, prōspĭcĭŏ.

Vĭgŏr, ōrĭs. m. *Strength, vigor, force.* Dēbĭlĭtāt vīrēs ănĭmī mūtātquĕ vĭgōrēm. V. Syn.—Vīs, vīrēs, rōbŭr. Phr.—Ātque hăbĭlīs mēmbrīs vēnīt vĭgŏr. Grātŭs ĭn ōrĕ vĭgŏr. Mēmbrīs cōnstāt vĭgŏr. Īgnĕŭs ēst ōllīs vĭgŏr.

Vīlĭs, ĭs, ĕ. *Cheap.* Vīlĭbŭs aūt ŏnĕrāt pōmīs. V. Syn.—Vūlgārĭs, nĭhĭlī. Phr.—Quădrāntĕ lăvārī. Tū pōscīs vīlĭă rērūm. Fig.— *Cheap, contemptible.* Syn.—Ābjēctŭs, cōntēmptŭs, cōntēmnēndŭs, spērnēndŭs, āspērnāndŭs, dēdīgnāndŭs, dēspēctŭs, nēglēctŭs, hŭmĭlĭs, sōrdĭdŭs. Phr.—Prētĭūm nōn vĭlĕ lăbōrĭs. Prōjēctā vīlĭŏr ālgā. Vīlĭsquĕ sŭpēllēx. Vēstīs vīlĭsquĕ vĕtūsquĕ. Āquā rērūm vīlĭssĭmā.

Vīllă, æ. f. *Villa, country-house.* Syn.—Prædĭūm, fūndŭs, rūs. Phr.—Dŏmŭs rūstĭcă. Sēcēssū vīllā bĕātō. Lōngē strĕpĭtū. Pŏpŭlārĭbŭs ūndīs āmōtā.

Vīllĭcŭs, ī. m. *Farmer, rustic, countryman.* Syn.—Cŏlōnŭs, ăgrĭcŏlă, rūstĭcŭs, cŏlōnă, rūstĭcă.

Vīllōsŭs, ă, ūm. *Hairy, shaggy.* Prēcĭpŭūmquĕ tŏro ēt vīllōsī pēllĕ lĕōnĭs. H. Syn.—Pĭlōsŭs, sētōsŭs, hīrsūtŭs. Phr.—Vīllīs cŏmāns. Vīllōsūm sētīs pēctŭs. Cŏmāntēs Ēxcŭtĭēns cērvīcĕ tŏrōs. Cōrpūs vīllōsā vēstĕ tĕgēbăt. Vīllōsă cŏlūbrīs Pēctŏră.

Vīmĕn, ĭnĭs. n. *Osier, twig.* Mōllĕ fĕrētrūm Ārbŭtĕīs tēxū vīrgīs ēt vīmĭnĕ quērnō. V. Syn.—Vīrgă, vīrgūltūm, frŭtēx. Phr.— Vīmĭnĕă vīrgă. Vīmĭnĕī frŭtĭcēs. Āspĕră rūscī Vīmĭnă. Mōllī dētēxĕrĕ jūncō. *Basket.* Syn.—Fīscĭnă, fīscēllā.

Vīncĭŏ, īs, xī, ctūm, īrĕ. *To bind, to attach.* Pūrpŭrēās āltē sūrās vīncīrĕ cŏthūrnō. V. Syn.—Dēvīncĭŏ, ēvīncĭŏ, rĕvīncĭŏ, līgŏ, āllĭgŏ, cōllĭgŏ, rĕlĭgŏ, strīngŏ, ādstrīngŏ, cōnstrīngŏ, ōbstrīngŏ, nēctŏ, īnnēctŏ, cōnnēctŏ, nōdŏ, cŏērcĕŏ, cŏhĭbĕŏ, īmpēdĭŏ, ārctŏ, cŏārctŏ, cīngŏ, īncīngŏ, rĕtĭnĕŏ, īllăquĕŏ, īrrētĭŏ, prēmŏ, rĕdĭmĭŏ. Phr.—Nōdō, nēxū cŏērcĕŏ. Aūrō vīncīrĕ lăcērtōs. Vīncīrĕ cŏmās vīttā. Vīnclīs cŏērcĕŏ, cŏhĭbĕŏ. Vīncŭlă, vīnclă, cătēnās dō, īmpōnŏ. Ārctō nēxū vīnclōquĕ tĕnācī Ādstrīngŏ. Vīncŭlă nēctĕ. Cōntēndĕ tĕnācĭă vīnclă. Īnjĭcĕ vīnclă mĭhī. Hūnc tū cōmpēscĕ cătēnā. Cōllō sŏnŭērĕ cătēnæ. Mēntēm vīncīrĕ Lȳæō. Ūncō nōn āllĭgăt ānchŏră mōrsū.

Vīncŏ, ĭs, vīcī, vīctūm, ĕrĕ. *To conquer.* Āspĭcĭt ēt dŭbĭtāt sŭpĕrāri ān vīncĕrĕ mālĭt. O. Syn.—Dēvīncŏ, dēbēllŏ, dŏmŏ, sŭbĭgŏ, sūbjĭcĭŏ, sŭpĕrŏ, ēxpūgnŏ, fūndŏ, stērnŏ, frāngŏ, cōntūndŏ. Phr.—Bēllō, cērtāmĭnĕ, pūgnā vīncŏ. Ārmīs dēbēllŏ. Frāngō vīctrīcĭbŭs ārmīs. Pālmām, vīctōrĭs prǣmĭă, dĕcŭs fĕrŏ. Ē cērtāmĭnĕ vīctŏr mūltā cūm laūdĕ rĕdĕŏ. Rĕdĭt sŭpĕrātō vīctĕ ăb hōstĕ. Mœnĭă vīctōr cōrrĭpŭĭt. Caūsā quī vīncĭt, vīncăt ĕt ārmīs. *To persuade. See Persuadeo. To prove, to show.* Syn.—Convīncŏ, prŏbŏ, ōstēndŏ.

Vīncŭlūm & Vīnclūm, ī. n. *Bond, attachment.* Tēxtăquĕ cōmpŏsĭtīs jūncĕă vīnclă rŏsā. O. Syn.—Nēxŭs, nōdŭs, līgāmĕn, rĕtĭnācŭlūm, rēstĭs, fūnĭs, fāscĭă, lōrūm. *Chains, bonds, prison.* Syn.—Cătēnă, nōdī, mănĭcæ, cōmpāgēs, cōmpĕdēs. Phr.—Vīnclōrūm ǣrātī nōdī, nēxūs, cōmpāgēs. Trītō vīncŭlă cōllō. Sī vīncŭlă sævă rĕmīttĭs. Vīncla ōmnĭă rūpī. Vīnclīs ēt cārcĕrĕ frēnăt. Nōdōs ēt līnĕă vīncŭlă rūpĭt. Pūppēs ābrūmpūnt vīncŭlă rīpīs. Fig.—*Attachment, connection.* Syn.—Cătēnă, nēxŭs. Phr.—Vīncŭla ămīcĭtĭæ. Cōnnūbĭālĭă vīnclă.

Vīndēmĭă, æ. f. *Vintage.* Phr.—Ūvās cārpŏ, cālcŏ, prĕmŏ.

Vīndēx ĭcĭs. m. & f. *One who protects.* Syn.—Dēfēnsŏr, āssērtŏr. *Guardian.* Syn.—Cūstōs. *Avenger.* Syn.—Ūltŏr, ūltrīx.

Vīndĭcŏ, ās, āvī, ātūm, ārĕ. *To assert for oneself, to take for oneself.* Syn.—Ādscrībŏ, ārrŏgŏ, āssĕrŏ, āssūmŏ, āttrĭbŭŏ. *To set free.* Syn.—Līběrŏ, āssĕrŏ. *To protect.* Syn.—Prŏhĭbĕŏ, tŭĕŏr, dēfēndŏ, prōtĕgŏ. *To avenge.* Syn.—Ūlcīscŏr, pūnĭŏ.

Vīndīctă, æ. f. *Rod placed on the head of a slave when he was set free, therefore liberty, freedom.* Syn.—Lībērtās. *Protection, defense.* Syn.—Cūstōdĭă, tūtēlă, pătrōcĭnĭūm. *Vengeance.* Syn.—Ūltĭŏ.

Vīnĕă, æ. f. *Vine, vineyard.* Nōn rāstrōs pătĭētŭr hŭmūs, nōn vīnĕă fālcēm. V. Syn.—Vīnētūm, vītĭs, pālmĕs. Phr.—Pāmpĭnĕūm, vītĭfĕrūm nĕmŭs. Āmīctī pālmĭtĕ cōllēs. Vītĭfĕrī cōllīs ămœnă prǣdĭă. Lārgō pūbēscēns vīnĕă fœtū. Pāmpĭnĕīs pīcta ārvă jŭgīs. Vītĭbŭs cōnsĭtī cōllēs. Ārvă fēlīcĭă Bācchī. Ūvīs, răcēmīs pīctă, dīstīnctă vīnĕă. *Sheds, or coverings used in war.* Phr.—Vīnĕăque īndūctūm lōngŏ tĕgēbăt ŏpŭs. Mĕdĭīs sūbrēpsĭt vīnĕă mūrīs. Vīnĕæ sūb tēgmĭnĕ tūtō.

Vīnētŭm, ī. n. *Vineyard.* Nēvĕ tĭbi ăd sōlĕm vērgānt vīnētă cădēntēm. V. Syn.—Vīnĕă, vītĭs, pālmĕs. Phr.—Lŏcă cōnsĭtă vītĭbŭs. Pāmpĭnĕī, ūnĭfĕrī cōllēs. Jŭgă fēlīcĭă Bācchī. Cāmpŭs fērtĭlĭs ūvæ̆. Nĭtĭdās frūgēs vīnētăquĕ lætă. Ōptĭmă vīnētīs stătĭŏ. Ăpērtōs Bācchŭs ămăt cōllēs. Quō vĭrĕt ūvă jŭgō.

Vīnōsŭs, ă, ŭm. *Given to wine.* Syn.—Bĭbāx, pōtŏr, pōtātŏr, ēbrĭōsŭs. Phr.—Vīnō dēdĭtŭs. Clĭēns Bācchī. Vīnō dēvōtŭs.

Vīnŭm, ī. n. *Wine.* Ēt pāssīm rīvīs cūrrēntĭă vīnă rĕprēssĭt. V. Syn.—Mĕrŭm, mūstŭm, ūvă, vītĭs nēctăr; Bācchŭs, Lyæ̆ŭs, Fălērnŭm, Māssĭcŭm, Cæcŭbŭm, pōcŭlă, scȳphī. Phr.—Bācchī, Lyæ̆ī hūmŏr, lătēx, lĭquŏr. Mūnĕră Bācchī. Mūnĕră vītĭs. Vītĕă pōcŭlă. Ūvæ sūccī. Māssĭcŭs hūmŏr. Ēxhĭlărāns ănĭmōs. Cūrās pēllēns. Ŏpērtă rĕclūdēns. Lætĭtĭæ dătŏr. Pătĕră fūmāntĭă vīnă căpācī. Cūrām dūlcī Lyæ̆ō sōlvĕrĕ. Mūnĕră vītĭs ămăt. Vīlĕ pōtābīs mŏdĭcīs Săbīnŭm Cānthărīs. Vīnŭm pōnŏ, dō, præbĕŏ. Ēt vīnă rĕpōnĭtĕ mēnsīs. Trĕmŭlā dānt vīnă rŭbēntĭă dēxtrā. Īmplēvīt mĕrō pătĕrăm. Chīō sōlvĭtĕ vīnclă cădō. Nēctărĕ mīscĕt ăquās. Nēc bĭbĕrīs dīlūtă. Pōcŭlă haūrĭŏ. Vīnō īndūlgĕō. Ăd vīnă rĕdīt lætŭs. Ūnă vīnă jŏcōsă cŏlūnt. Mădĕānt gĕnĕrōsō pōcŭlă Bācchō. Vīnōquĕ lĕvānt cūrāsquĕ sĭtīmquĕ. Vīnŭm dīssĭpăt cūrās. Trīstĭtĭăm vītæquĕ lăbōrēs mōllī fīnīrĕ mĕrō. Dūlcī mălă vīnō lăvĕrĕ. Vīnō cōrrūmpĭtŭr ætās. Ēt dătă nōn āptō tēmpŏrĕ vīnă nŏcēnt.

Vĭŏlă, æ. f. *The violet.* (*See Appendix under list of Trees, etc.*)

Vĭŏlēns, ēntĭs. adj. *Violent.* Vĭŏlēntăquĕ pēctŏră Tūrnī. V. Syn.—Īrācūndŭs, fĕrōx, āspĕr, ācĕr, vĕhĕmēns, ătrōx, ēffrēnŭs, īmpŏtēns, aūdāx, præcēps, tĕmĕrārĭŭs. *Terrible.* Syn.—Tērrĭbĭlĭs.

Vĭŏlēntĕr. adv. *With violence.* Syn.—Vī, īmpĕtĕ, vĕhĕmēntĕr, vălĭdē. Phr.—Vī māgnā. Răpĭdō īmpĕtĕ. Īmpĕtĕ māgnō.

Vĭŏlēntĭă, æ. f. *Violence.* Syn.—Vīs, īmpĕtŭs. Phr.—Vī īrrŭŏ, īrrūmpŏ. Vīm făcĭŏ. Fīt vĭă vī, rūmpūnt ădĭtūs. Nēc tē ūllīŭs vĭŏlēntĭă vīncăt.

Vĭŏlŏ, ās, āvī, ātŭm, ārĕ. *To use violence towards.* Quīcūnquĕ săcrŭm vĭŏlārĭt vūlnĕrĕ cōrpŭs. V. Syn.—Ōffēndŏ, lædŏ, āggrĕdĭŏr, īnvādŏ, īncēssŏ, vūlnĕrŏ, saūcĭŏ. *To profane, to violate.* Syn.—Tĕmĕrŏ, pōllŭŏ, cōnscĕlĕrŏ, prŏfānŏ. *To dirty, to contaminate.* Syn.—Cōntāmĭnŏ, fœdŏ, măcŭlŏ, spūrcŏ, tĕmĕrŏ, īnfĭcĭŏ, cōrrūmpŏ. *To violate or infringe upon a law.* Syn.—Rūmpŏ, ābrūmpŏ, rēscīndŏ, rĕvēllŏ.

Vīpĕră, æ. f. *Snake, serpent.* Syn.—Sērpēns, cŏlŭbĕr.

Vĭr, vĭrī. m. *Man.* Syn.—Măs. *Husband. See Conjux. Male (among animals).* Syn.—Mās, mărītŭs. *Hero.* Syn.—Hērōs. *Man (in general).* Syn.—Hŏmŏ, hŏmĭnēs, mōrtālēs, cīvēs.

Vĭrĕŏ, ēs, ŭī, ērĕ. *To be green.* Phīllȳdĭs ādvēntū nōstræ nĕmŭs ōmnĕ vĭrēbĭt. V. Syn.—Vērnŏ, vĭrēscŏ, frōndēscŏ. Phr.—Frōndĕ vĭrērĕ nŏvā. Pēctŏră fēllĕ vĭrēnt. Fig.—*To be vigorous, strong.* Syn.—Vălĕŏ, flōrĕŏ, pōllĕŏ. Phr.—Lūxŭrĭānt ănĭmī, cōrpŏrăque īpsă vĭrēnt.

Vīrēs, ĭūm. f. pl. *Force, vigor.* Pār vĭgŏr ēst mēmbrīs, prōmptæque ād fōrtĭă vīrēs. V. Syn.—Vīs, vĭgŏr, rōbŭr, nērvī. Phr.—Īntēr sē cōntēndūnt vīrĭbŭs. Vīrēs tēmpĕrăt īllĕ sŭas. Armōrūm vīrĭbŭs ūsŭs. Tūm vīctū rĕvŏcānt vīrēs. Vīrēs ăcquīrĭt ĕūndō. Nŏvæ rĕdĭēre īn prīstĭnă vīrēs. Vīrĭbŭs aūdāx. Prædūrūs vīrĭbŭs. Nūnc īllās prōmĭtĕ vīrēs. Tōtās ēffūndĭtĕ vīrēs. Frīgēnt ēffœtae īn cōrpŏrĕ vīrēs. Tōrpēnt īnfrāctae ād prœlĭă vīrēs. *(By extension) Power, resources.* Syn.—Vīs, pŏtēntĭă, ŏpēs, īmpĕrĭūm.

Vĭrēscŏ, ĭs, ĕrĕ. *To become green.* Īnjūssă vĭrēscūnt grāmĭnă. V. Syn.—Vĭrĭdŏr, vĭrĕŏ, rĕvĭrēscŏ, frōndēscŏ. Fig.—*To become strong.* Syn.—Īnvălĕŏ, vĭgēscŏ.

Vĭrētūm, ī. n. *Meadow, prairie.* Syn.—Vĭrĭdārĭă, prātūm.

Vīrgă, æ. f. *Branch.* Tūm læves călămōs ēt rāsae hāstīlĭă vīrgæ. V. Syn.—Vīmĕn, vīrgūltūm, rāmŭlŭs. *Wand of mercury.* Syn.—Cādūcĕŭs. *Whip.* Syn.—Flăgēllūm, vērbĕr.

Vīrgĭnĭtās, ātĭs. f. *Virginity.* Syn.—Cāstĭtās, pŭdŏr, pŭdīcĭtĭă, īntĕgrĭtās. Phr.—Vīrgĭnĕī flōs pŭdōrĭs. Pŭdōrĭs hŏnōs. Īntāctūm cōrpŭs. Vīrgĭnĕī flōs īntĕmĕrātŭs hŏnōrĭs.

Vīrgŏ, ĭnĭs. f. *Virgin.* Syn.—Pŭēllă, cælēbs. Phr.—Īnnŭbă vīrgŏ. Īnnūptă pŭēllă. Pērpĕtŭā vīrgĭnĭtātĕ frŭēns. Vīrgĭnĭtātĭs ămāns, stŭdĭōsă. Laūdēm quæ cāstæ vīrgĭnĭtātĭs hăbēt. Vīrgĭnĭs ōs hăbĭtūmquĕ gĕrēns. Pŭdĭbūndăquĕ cēlāt ămīctū Ōră. *Vestal virgin.* Syn.—Vēstālĭs. *The constellation.* Syn.—Āstræă, Ērĭgŏnē.

Vīrgūltūm, ī. n. *Shrub, bush, twigs.* Āvĭă tūm rĕsŏnānt ăvĭbūs vīrgūltă cănōrīs. V. Syn.—Ārbūstūm, frŭtēx. Phr.—Māgnōquĕ cădūnt vīrgūltă frăgōrĕ. Vīrgūltă sŏnāntĭă sīlvīs. *Branch, shoot, twig.* Syn.—Frŭtēx, rāmŭs, rāmŭlŭs, rāmūscŭlŭs, sūrcŭlŭs, vīmĕn, vīrgă, pālmĕs. *Young plant, quick-set.* Syn.—Sūrcŭlŭs, pālmĕs, plāntă, vīrgă, gērmĕn, māllĕŏlŭs.

Vĭrĭdĭs, ĭs, ĕ. *Green, verdant.* Pērpĕtŭōs vĭrĭdīs sēmpēr gĕrĕ frōndĭs hŏnōrēs. O. Syn.—Vĭrĭdāns, vĭrēns, vĭrēscēns, frōndēns, vērnāns. Phr.—Ēt stāgnă vĭrēntĭă mūscō. Cūltōrquĕ vĭrēntĭs ăgēllī. Vĭrĭdī tēgĭt ārbŭtŭs ūmbrā. Vĭrĭdī prōjēctŭs ĭn āntrō. Vĭrĭdāntĕ tŏrō. Fig.—*Strong, vigorous.* Syn.—Vĭrēns, vĭgēns, fīrmŭs, rōbūstŭs, vălĭdŭs. Phr.—Aēvī flōrĕ vĭrēns.

Vĭrīlĭs, ĭs, ĕ. *Pertaining to man, manly.* Syn.—Māscŭlŭs, mās. Fig.—*Strong.* Syn.—Rōbūstŭs, vălĭdŭs.

Vĭrīlĭtĕr. adv. *Courageously, manly.* Syn.—Ănĭmōsē, aūdāctĕr, fōrtĭtĕr, gĕnĕrōsē.

Vīrtūs, ūtĭs. f. *Valor, courage.* Præstāntēs vīrtūtĕ lĕgĭt. V. Syn.—Ănĭmŭs, fōrtĭtūdō. Phr.—Sŭpĕrāt vīrtūtĕ dŏlōrēm. Vīrtūs bēllī. Nŏcēt tĕmĕrārĭă vīrtūs. *Force, power.* Syn.—Vīs, rōbŭr, pŏtēntĭă. *Virtue.* Syn.—Pĭĕtās, prŏbĭtās, æquĭtās, īntĕgrĭtās, sānctĭtās, cāstĭtās, fĭdēs, jūstĭtĭă, æquūm, bŏnūm, rēctūm. Phr.—Bŏnæ ārtēs. Vīrtūtĭs hŏnōs, dĕcŭs. Māgnæ rōbŭr mēntĭs. Dĕō grātīssĭmă. Hōc vīrtūtĭs ŏpŭs. Vīrtūs ēst vĭtĭūm fŭgĕrĕ. Vīrtūs ōmnĭă vīncĭt.

Vīrŭs, ī. n. (No pl.). *Secretion, pus.* Syn.—Sūccŭs, vĕnēnūm. *Poison.* Syn.—Vĕnēnūm. *See Venenum.* Fig.—*Bitterness, rancor.* Syn.—Vīs, æstŭs, vĭŏlēntĭă.

Vīs, ĭs. f. *Force, vigor.* Māgnā vī flēxă dŏmātŭr Ūlmŭs. V. Syn.—Rōbŭr, vĭgŏr, vīrtūs. Phr.—Vīs jŭvĕnīlĭs ĕrăt. Vīs ănĭmæ. *Violence.* Syn.—Vĭŏlēntĭă. *See Violentia.* Phr.—Ăpĕrīt sī nūllă vĭăm vīs. Vīs hōrrĭdă lētī. Aūrō vī pŏtĭtūr. Ād vīmquĕ părātŭs. *Nature, essence.* Syn.—Nātūră, vīrtūs. *Power, strength.* Syn.—Pŏtēntĭă, pŏtēstās, nūmĕn. *Virtue, efficacity.* Syn.—Vīrtūs, vīrēs, pŏtēntĭă, pŏtēstās, ēffēctŭs. *Worth, force of a word.* Syn.—Sēnsŭs, sēntēntĭă.

Vīscōsŭs, ă, ūm. *Sticky.* Syn.—Glūtĭnĕŭs, vīscātŭs, pĭcĕātŭs. Phr.—Vīscō īllĭtŭs, mĕdĭcātŭs, cīrcūmlĭtŭs.

Vīscŭs, ĕrĭs & Vīscĕră, ĕrūm. n. *Vitals, entrails.* Vīscĕrĭbūs mĭsĕrōrum ēt sānguĭnĕ vēscĭtŭr ātrō. V. Syn.—Ēxtă, īlĭă, īntēstīnă, fībræ, præcōrdĭă. Phr.—Jŭgŭlānt pĕcŭdēs, ēt vīscĕră vīvīs Ērĭpĭūnt. Lōngīs sīngūltĭbūs īlĭă pūlsānt. Trājēcĭt vīscĕră fērrō. Vīscĕră nūdānt.

Vīsŏ, ĭs, ī, ūm, ĕrĕ. *To visit.* Ārvă rĕlēgātūm jūssīstī vīsĕrĕ Pōntī. O. Syn.—Īnvīsŏ, vīsĭtŏ, ădĕŏ, cōnvĕnĭŏ. Phr.—Pĕrĕgrīnum ūt vīsĕrēt ōrbēm. Vīsēntēm rēgnă sŏrōrĭs. Vīsēndī stūdĭō.

Vīsūm, ī. n. *Sight, spectacle.* Syn.—Spēctācŭlūm. *Vision, apparition.* Syn.—Vīsŭs, sĭmŭlācrūm, făcĭēs, spĕcĭēs. Phr.—Tālĭbŭs āttŏnĭtūs vīsīs. Tērrēbānt sĭmŭlācră mălī.

Vīsŭs, ūs. m. *Sight, vision.* Mōrtālēs vīsūs mĕdĭō sērmōnĕ rĕlīquĭt. V. Syn.—Āspēctŭs, īntŭĭtŭs, lūmĭnă, ŏcŭlī. Phr.—Mōrtālēs hĕbĕtāt vīsūs tĭbĭ. *Sight, spectacle.* Syn.—Vīsūm, āspēctŭs, spēctācŭlūm. *Vision, apparition.* Syn.—Vīsūm, sĭmŭlācrūm, pōrtēntūm, mōnstrūm. Phr.—Īmmūndō sōmnĭă vīsū. Hōrrĭbĭlī vīsū pōrtēntă sĕquūntŭr.

Vītă, æ. f. *Life.* Ō mĭhĭ tām lōngæ mănĕăt pārs ūltĭmă vītæ. V. Syn.—Lūx, spīrĭtŭs, ănĭmă, ævūm, ānnī, dĭēs, ætās. Phr.—Vītæ tēmpŭs, tēmpŏră, spătĭūm. Mūnĕră lūcĭs. Vītālēs aūræ. Lūcĭs ūsūră. Lūcĭs dūlcĕ mūnŭs. Vītālĕ lūmĕn. Vītæ mōrtālĭs hŏnōs. Brĕvĭs cūrsŭs ævī. Sōlātĭă vītæ dūlcĭă. Vărĭĭs jāctātă prŏcēllĭs. Trīstĭbŭs ānxĭă cūrīs. Sī līmĭnă vītæ Āttĭgĕrīnt. Īpsōque īn līmĭnĕ vītæ. Īn vēntōs vītă rĕcēssĭt. Ād mānēs cōncēssĭt vītă pĕr aūrās. Vītāmque āmīsĭt ĭn ūndīs. Ēxācto cōntēntūs tēmpŏrĕ vītæ. Vītām dīspērgĭt ĭn aūrās. Vītām mūltō cūm sāngŭĭnĕ fūdĭt. Ārtūs vītă rĕlīnquĭt. Āngūstī tērmĭnŭs ævī. Pūlvĭs ĕt ūmbră lĕvĭs. Ēxĭgŭī brĕvĕ dōnūm tēmpŏrĭs. Rŏtă præcĭpĭtĭs vērtĭtŭr ānnī. *Conduct, manner of living.* Syn.—Mōrēs, āctă, fāctă.

Vĭtĭō, ās, āvī, ātūm, ārĕ. *To corrupt, to soil.* Īstă dĕcēns făcĭēs lōngīs vĭtĭābĭtŭr ānnīs. O. Syn.—Cōrrūmpŏ, vĭŏlŏ, dēprāvŏ, pōllŭŏ. Phr.—Vĭtĭāntŭr ŏdōrĭbŭs aūræ.

Vĭtĭōsŭs, ă, ūm. *Corrupted, spoiled.* Cōrtĭcĭbūsquĕ căvīs, vĭtĭōsæque īlĭcĭs ālvō. V. Syn.—Pŭtrĭs, pŭtrĭdŭs, vĭtĭātŭs, īnfēctŭs, cōrrūptŭs. Fig.—*Vicious, corrupt.* Syn.—Cōrrūptŭs, flāgĭtĭōsŭs, mălŭs, īmprŏbŭs, pērdĭtŭs, nēquām. Phr.—Vĭtĭīs āddīctŭs. Āffīnīs vĭtĭō. Vĭtĭīs sūpprēssă lĕvābŏ Pēctŏră.

Vītĭs, ĭs. f. *Vine.* Vītĭs ŭt ārbŏrĭbūs dĕcŏri ēst, ŭt vītĭbŭs ūvæ. V. Syn.—Vīnĕă, ūvă, pālmĕs, pāmpĭnŭs, Bācchŭs. Phr.—Ădūltă vītĭūm prōpāgŏ. Cōmplēxă tĕnācĭtĕr ūlmūm. Fērtĭlĭs ūvīs. Răcēmīs grăvĭdă, tŭmēns. Grăvĭdōs frūctūs præbēns. Lætĭs īntēxĕrĕ vītĭbŭs ūlmōs. Pārvās ūlmīs āttōllĕrĕ vītēs. Pāmpĭnĕā dūlcīs lātĕt ūvă sŭb ūmbrā.

Vĭtĭūm, ĭī. n. *Corruption.* Ārĕt ăgĕr, vĭtĭō mŏrĭēns sĭtĭt āĕrĭs hērbă. V. Syn.—Lābēs, lŭēs, pēstĭs, mōrbŭs, mălūm. *Defect.* Syn.—Mălă, īncōmmŏdă. *Vice, vicious habit.* Syn.—Mălă (pl.), crīmĕn, cūlpă, scĕlŭs, flāgĭtĭūm. Phr.—Vĭtĭī lābēs, măcŭlă. Vĭtĭōrūm sōrdēs. Cōrrūptī mōrēs. Mēntĭs, ănĭmī vĭtĭūm tūrpĭs. Prāvă lĭbīdŏ. Pūrūm vĭtĭō cŏr. Vĭtĭō rĕmōtŭs ăb ōmnī. Vĭtĭīs tĕnērī. Cērĕŭs īn vĭtĭūm flēctī. Sērvūm vĭtĭīs pēctŭs hăbērĕ. *Fault in a work.* Syn.—Mēndūm, cūlpă, ērrŏr.

Vītŏ, ās, āvī, ātūm, ārĕ. *To avoid.* Vītāvī dēnĭquĕ cūlpām, Nōn laūdēm mĕrŭī. H. Syn.—Dēvītŏ, ēvītŏ, fŭgĭŏ, ēffŭgĭŏ, dēclīnŏ, căvĕŏ, dīscēdŏ, rĕcēdŏ. Phr.—Mē sūbdūcŏ. Mē āvērtŏ. Quæ prīmă pĕrīcŭlă vītĕt. Vītāt sūb frōndĭbŭs æstūm. Īnsĭdĭās vītārĕ dŏlūmquĕ. Tēlīs ēlāpsŭs Ăchīvūm. Cāsūs ēvāsĕrāt ōmnēs. Săpĭēns vītātū. Vītāvīssĕ vĭcēs Dănăūm. Cănĕ pējŭs ĕt ānguĕ Vītābĭt.

Vĭtrĕŭs, ă, ūm. *Of glass, crystal.* Syn.—Crȳstāllĭnŭs. Phr.—Ēx vĭtrō. (*By extension*) *Clear, transparent.* Syn.—Clārŭs, nĭtĭdŭs, līmpĭdŭs, lūcĭdŭs, pēllūcĭdŭs. Phr.—Vĭtrōquĕ măgīs pēllūcĭdŭs āmnĭs. Fōns splēndĭdĭōr vĭtrō. *Fragile.* Syn.—Cădūcŭs.

Vīttă, æ. f. *Fillet, band, garland.* Lānĕă dūm nĭvĕā cīrcūmdătŭr īnfŭlă vīttā. V. Syn.—Tænĭă, fāscĭă, īnfŭlă. Phr.—Crīnālĭs fāscĭă. Căpĭtĭs tænĭă. Tēmpŏră cīngēns. Crīnēs, căpīllōs āstrīngēns, cŏērcēns. Fīt lōngæ tænĭă vīttæ. Fērālēs sūmĕrĕ vīttās. Mōllī cīnge hæc āltārĭă vīttā. Strīngīt vīttă cŏmās. Crīnālēs sōlvĕrĕ vīttās.

Vĭtŭlă, æ. f. *Calf, heifer.* Syn.—Jŭvēncă, văccă, vĭtŭlŭs.

Vĭtŭlŭs, ī. m. *Calf.* Tūm vĭtŭlūs bīmā cūrvāns jām cōrnŭă frōntĕ. V. Syn.—Jŭvēncŭs. Phr.—Māgnī pārvŭs ārmēntī cŏmĕs. Nēcdūm fīrmātīs cōrnĭbŭs aūdāx. Quī lūdīt prātō līběr ăpērtō. Tēmplīs mātūrŭs. Īntăctā vĭtŭlūs cērvīcĕ.

Vĭtŭpĕrŏ, ās, āvī, ātūm, ārĕ. *To blame.* Syn.—Ārgŭŏ, cūlpŏ, dāmnŏ, īmprŏbŏ. Phr.—Dīctīs ămārīs, vērbīs sĕvērīs cāstīgārĕ, īncrĕpārĕ. Ăcērbīs vērbīs ārgŭĕrĕ.

Vīvāx, ācĭs. adj. *Long-lived.* Syn.—Lōngævŭs, ānnōsŭs, pĕrēnnĭs. *Lively.* Syn.—Ăcĕr, ănĭmōsŭs, vălĭdŭs. *See Vividus.*

Vīvĭdŭs, ă, ūm. *Living.* Syn.—Spīrāns. Fig.—*Lively, vigorous.* Syn.—Ăcĕr, ănĭmōsŭs, vĭgēns, vīvāx, fōrtĭs, vălĭdŭs, vĕgĕtŭs, rōbūstŭs.

Vīvŏ, ĭs, xī, vīctūm, ĕrĕ. *To live.* Nūnc vīvō nĕc ădhūc hŏmĭnēs lūcēmquĕ rĕlīnquŏ. V. Syn.—Spīrŏ, rēspīrŏ. Phr.—Vītā, lūcĕ frŭŏr. Vītālēs aūrās cārpŏ. Aēthĕrĕā lūcĕ frŭŏr. Lūmēn vītālĕ vĭdĕŏ. Dĭēm, lūmĕn āspĭcĭŏ. Vēscī vītālĭbŭs aūrīs. Dūm vītă mănēbĭt. Īnvīsūs cælēstĭbŭs aūrās Cārpĭs. Īnūtĭlĭs ānnōs Dēmŏrŏr. Vīvĕ mĕmōr nōstrī. Sī vēscĭtŭr aūrā. Vītām prōfĕrŏ. Lōngă mănēt seū vītă. Prōdūcĕrĕ vītām. Vītām, ānnōs ăgŏ, trăhŏ. Nūllō Vīvĕrĕ cōnsĭlĭō. Ōmnēs tēcum ēxĭgăt ānnōs. Aēvūm trānsēgĭt ĭn ārvīs. *To nourish oneself.* Syn.—Vēscŏr, ălŏr, nūtrĭŏ, vīctĭtŏ. *To endure, to last.* Syn.—Ălŏr, fŏvĕŏr, mănĕŏ.

Vīvŭs, ă, ūm. *Alive, living.* Ēn quō vīvī pērvēnĭmŭs. V. Syn.—Vīvēns, spīrāns, sŭpērstĕs, īncŏlŭmĭs. Phr.—Vīvūsquĕ pĕr ōră fĕrētŭr. Vīvēntī pēctŏrĕ fībrās Ērĭpĭūnt. Āltĭŭs ād vīvūm pērsēdĭt. Vīvă sŭā plāntārĭă tērrā. *Animated.* Syn.—Vīvēns, spīrāns. *Lively, animated, vigorous.* Syn.—Vīvĭdŭs, vīvāx, ācĕr.

Vīx. adv. *Hardly, scarcely.* Syn.—Vīxdūm. Phr.—Vīx bĕnĕ dēsĭĕrăt. Vīx ădĕo āgnōvī. Vīx mē cōntĭnĕō. *With difficulty.* Syn.—Aēgrē.

Vŏcābŭlūm, ī. n. *Word.* Spĕcĭōsă vŏcābŭlă rērūm. H. Syn.—Vōx, dīctūm, vērbūm. *Name.* Syn.—Nōmĕn.

Vōcālĭs, ĭs, ĕ. *Re-echoing, clear.* Syn.—Sŏnāns, sŏnōrŭs, ārgūtŭs. Phr.—Vōcālī cārmĭnĕ clārŭs. Tūrrĭs vōcālĭbŭs āddĭtă mūrīs.

Vōcĭfĕrōr, ārĭs, ātūs sūm, ārī. *To cry out, to shout out.* Tālĭă vōcĭfĕrāns gĕmĭtū tēctum ōmnĕ rĕplēbăt. V. Syn.—Clāmŏ, exclāmŏ, cōnclamŏ. Phr.—Vōcĕ, vōcĭbŭs aūrās īmplĕō. Ārmātūs sōlīs clāmōrĭbŭs hostĭs.

Vŏcŏ, ās, āvī, ātūm, ārĕ. *To call.* Dīcāmūs lēgēs, sŏcĭōsque īn rēgnă vŏcēmŭs. V. Syn.—Ādvŏcŏ, āppēllŏ, cōmpēllŏ (ās), ārcēssŏ, cĭĕŏ, clāmŏ, īnclāmŏ, nōmĭnŏ. Phr.—Nōmĭnĕ vŏcŏ, clāmŏ. Ōrĕ, clāmōrĕ, vōcĕ māgnā nōmĭnŏ. Nōmĕn vŏcŏ. Nōmĭnĕ quēmquĕ vŏcăt. Īngĕmĭnāns ĭtĕrūmque ĭtĕrūmquĕ vŏcāvī. *To summon.* Syn.—Cōnvŏcŏ, ādvŏcŏ. *To implore.* Syn.—Ōrŏ, īmplōrŏ, rŏgŏ, pĕtŏ, pōscŏ, rĕpōscŏ. *To claim.* Syn.—Pōscŏ, rĕpōscŏ, rĕquīrŏ. *To invite to dine.* Syn.—Īnvītŏ. *To name.* Syn.—Nōmĭnŏ, dīcŏ, nūncŭpŏ. *To invoke.* Syn.—Īnvŏcŏ, prĕcŏr.

Vŏlātĭlĭs, ĭs, ĕ. *Winged.* Tēlīsquĕ vŏlātĭlĕ fērrūm Spārgĭtŭr. V. Syn.—Vŏlāns, vŏlŭcrĭs, ālĕs, ālātŭs, ālĭgĕr.

Vŏlātŭs, ūs. m. *Flight of birds.* Sīc cĕlĕrī mīssō præcēps pĕr ĭnānĕ vŏlātū. O. Syn.—Lāpsŭs, cūrsŭs, fŭgă, mĕātŭs, īmpĕtŭs, ālă, pēnnă, ālæ, pēnnæ. Phr.—Āĕrĭŭs, vŏlŭcrĭs cūrsŭs. Cĕlĕr pĕr āĕră lāpsŭs. Cūrsŭs ăvĭs. Rēmĭgĭūm ālārūm. Fig.—*Rapid course, flight.* Syn.—Cūrsŭs, īmpĕtŭs, fŭgă.

Vŏlŏ, ās, āvī, ātūm, ārĕ. *To fly.* Īpsă vŏlāns tĕnŭēs sē sūstŭlĭt ālēs ĭn aūrās. V. Syn.—Vŏlĭtŏ. Phr.—Āĕră, aūrās, æthĕră, nūbĭlă ālīs, pēnnīs, rēmĭgĭō ālārūm sĕcŏ, scīndŏ, pĕtŏ, vērbĕrŏ, trānŏ. Pēnnās, ālās pĕr āĕră quătĭŏ, mŏvĕŏ, īmpēllŏ. Vŏlātū, pēnnīs pĕr ĭnānĕ fĕrŏr, lābŏr. Ād cœlūm pēnnīs āssūrgŏ. Vŏlāns ĭn āltūm fĕrŏr. Ĭtĕr lĭquĭdūm tēntŏ. Vŏlātūs ēxērcĕō. Ālīs nītŏr. Ēt tūrbĭdă trānăt Nūbĭlă. Trĕpĭdō pĕtĭt ārvă vŏlātū. Āĕrĭōs aūdēt tēntārĕ vŏlātūs. Mŏvērĕ pĕr aūrās pēnnās. Ārdŭă pēnnīs Āstră sĕquī. Āltām sūprā vŏlăt ārdĕă nūbēm. Cĕlĕrīquĕ fŭgā sūb sīdĕră lāpsæ. Nōctĕ vŏlăt cœlī mĕdĭō. Ārdŭŭs īn nūbēs ăbĭĭt. Spērnĭt hŭmūm fŭgĭēntĕ pēnnā. Nūbēs sūb pĕdĭbūs vĭdĕt. Ātquĕ vŏlāns dēspēctăt hŭmūm. *To run, to go quickly.* Syn.—Vŏlĭtŏ, fĕrŏr, prŏpĕrŏ, fēstīnŏ, cūrrŏ. Phr.—

Vŏlāt vī fērvĭdŭs āxĭs. Ĕquōs ĭnhĭbērĕ vŏlāntēs. Pāssū vŏlăt ālĭtĕ vīrgŏ. Īgnēs ād tēctă vŏlārĕ. Fāmă vŏlăt.

Vŏlŏ, vīs, vŏlŭī, vēllĕ. *To wish.* Mē sī cœlĭcŏlæ vŏlŭīssēnt dūcĕrĕ vītăm. V. Syn.—Cŭpĭŏ, ōptŏ, ăvĕŏ, plăcĕt, jŭvĕt, jŭbĕŏ, īm-pĕrŏ. Phr.—Fērt ănĭmŭs. Mēns, ănĭmŭs ēst. Sīc fērt cōrdĕ vŏlūntās. Mēns ōmnĭbŭs ūnă sĕquēndī. Vŏlūntās ēst mĭhĭ. *To permit.* Syn.—Sĭnŏ, pērmīttŏ, pătĭŏr. *To pretend.* Syn.—Cōn-tēndŏ, āssĕrŏ.

Vŏlūbĭlĭs, ĭs, ĕ. *Revolving.* Syn.—Vōlvēns. Fig.—*Fickle, incon-stant.* Syn.—Lĕvĭs, mūtăbĭlĭs, īncōnstāns, īnstăbĭlĭs, vērsātĭlĭs, mōbĭlĭs, lūbrĭcŭs.

Vŏlŭcrĭs (Vŏlŭcĕr), crĭs, crĕ. *Winged, flying.* Syn.—Ālĕs, ālātŭs, ālĭgĕr, pēnnātŭs, vŏlāns, vŏlātĭlĭs. *Quick, light, nimble.* Syn.— Vŏlāns, ălăcĕr, cĭtŭs, cōncĭtŭs, cĕlĕr, pērnīx, vēlōx.

Vŏlŭcrĭs, ĭs. f. *Bird. See Avis.*

Vŏlūmĕn, ĭnĭs. n. *Fold, coil.* Syn.—Gŷrŭs, spīră, ōrbĭs, sĭnŭs, glŏ-mĕrāmĕn, rŏtātŭs. Phr.—Sĭnŭātque ĭmmēnsă vŏlūmĭnĕ tērgă. Tāntōsquĕ trăhīt sĭnŭs ūltĭmŭs ōrbēs. Sĭnŭātque āltērnă vŏlūm-ĭnă crūrūm. *Volume, book.* Syn.—Lĭbĕr, lĭbēllŭs, cōdēx, chārtă.

Vŏlūntās, ātĭs. f. *Will, desire.* Tŭă sī mĭhĭ cērtă vŏlūntās. V. Syn.—Ānĭmŭs, mēns, ārbĭtrĭūm, plăcĭtūm, prōpŏsĭtūm, cōn-sĭlĭūm, vōtūm, ōptātūm, stŭdĭūm, cŭpīdŏ. Phr.—Sŭă cuīquĕ vŏlūntās. Mēns ĭmmōtă mănĕt. Nūnc quŏquĕ mēns ĕădēm pērstăt. Dīvērsă vŏlūntās Ēst mĭhĭ. *Affection, good will.* Syn.— Stŭdĭūm, făvŏr. Phr.—Ĕrĭt ōffĭcĭōsă vŏlūntās. Cœlĭcŏlūm nō-bīs prōpēnsă vŏlūntās. Sŭpĕrīs āvērsă vŏlūntās. Āvērsă dĕæ mēns.

Vŏlūptās, ātĭs. f. *Pleasure.* Ēst ĭn ăquā dūlcī nōn īnvĭdĭōsă vŏlūp-tās. O. Syn.—Lætĭtĭă, gaūdĭūm, gaūdĭă, dēlĭcĭæ. Phr.—Cūrā-rūm īgnāră. Cārĕ pŭĕr, mĕă sōlă vŏlŭptās. Trăhīt sŭă quēm-quĕ vŏlūptās. Ūrbī mălĕ nōtă vŏlūptās. Nūlla ēst sīncērā vŏlūptās. *Sensual pleasure.* Syn.—Lāscĭvĭă, lĭbīdŏ, lūxŭs, lūx-ŭrĭă, lūxŭrĭēs, dēlĭcĭæ. Phr.—Tūrpēs dēlĭcĭæ. Mălă mēntīs gaūdĭă. Ēnērvāns vīrēs. Ēscă mălōrūm. Vīrtūti ĭnĭmīcă vŏlūptās.

Vōlvŏ, ĭs, vōlvī, vŏlūtūm, ĕrĕ. *To roll, to cause to roll.* Vōlvĭtŭr Īxīōn, ēt sē sĕquĭtūrquĕ fŭgītquĕ. O. Syn.—Vŏlūtŏ, vērtŏ, vērsŏ, ăgĭtŏ, cōnvōlvŏ, tōrquĕŏ, cōntōrquĕŏ, cīrcŭmăgŏ, rŏtŏ. Phr.—Īn gŷrūm, ĭn ōrbēm tōrquĕŏ, vērsŏ. Vōlvēndō dūcĕrĕ. Mănĭbŭs sūbvōlvĕrĕ sāxă. Vāstōs vōlvŭnt ād lĭttŏră flūctŭs. Vōlvēns ŏcŭlōs. Aēstūs īncēndĭă vōlvŭnt. Vōlvĭtŭr īn præcēps. Præcēps pĕr dēvĭă vōlvĭtŭr āmnĭs. Vōlvĭtŭr īn căpŭt. Tŏt vōlvĕrĕ cāsūs. *To run through a book.* Syn.—Dēvōlvŏ, vērsŏ, lĕgŏ. *To think over in one's mind. See Meditor.* (*In the passive*) *To fall.* Syn.—Cădŏ, dēcĭdŏ, lābŏr. *To fall prostrate.* Syn.—Ădvōlvŏr, prōvōlvŏr, cădŏ, prōcūmbŏ.

Vōmĕr, ĕrĭs. m. *Plow-share.* Syn.—Vōmĭs. Phr.—Ărātrī, vōmĕrĭs dēns, fērrūm. Dēns ūncŭs. Tērrām scīndēns. Nūllō sūlcāntūr vōmĕrĕ cāmpī. Saūcĭă vōmĕrĭbŭs. Pătĭēns vōmĕrĭs ūncī. Rĭgĭdī vērsātūr vōmĕrĭs ĭctū. Dūrō fūmāns sūb vōmĕrĕ taūrŭs. Rŭtŭlōs ēxērcēnt vōmĕrĕ cāmpōs.

Vŏmŏ, ĭs, ŭī, ĭtūm, ĕrĕ. *To eject, to vomit.* Syn.—Ēvŏmŏ, rĕvŏmŏ, ērūctŏ, ējĭcĭŏ, ējēctŏ, ēmīttŏ, rēddŏ, ēxspŭŏ. Phr.—Pūrpŭrĕām vŏmit īlle ănĭmām. Vŏmēns călĭdūm dē pēctŏrĕ flūmĕn.

Vŏrāgŏ, ĭnĭs. f. *Whirlpool.* Tūrbĭdŭs hīc cœnō vāstāquĕ vŏrāgĭnĕ gūrgĕs Aēstŭăt. V. Syn.—Gūrgĕs, vōrtēx. Phr.—Īntōrtō vōrtĭcĕ gūrgĕs. *Opening in the ground, chasm.* Syn.—Hĭātŭs, bărăthrūm. Phr.—Spēcŭs īngēns. Cæcæ vŏrāgĭnĕ faūcēs.

Vŏrāx, ācĭs. adj. *Voracious.* Syn.—Gŭlōsŭs. *Eager, greedy.* Syn.—Ăvārŭs, ăvĭdŭs. *Consuming.* Syn.—Ĕdāx, ēxĭtĭōsŭs.

Vŏrŏ, ās, āvī, ātūm, ārĕ. *To devour.* Syn.—Dēvŏrŏ, sōrbĕŏ, ābsōrbĕŏ, glūtĭŏ, ĕdŏ, cŏmĕdŏ, pāscŏr, dēpāscŏr, hēllŭŏr, ābsūmŏ, cōnsūmŏ, lănĭŏ. Phr.—Ăvĭdō, vŏrācī dēntĕ dīrĭpĭŏ. Mĭsĕrōs mōrsū dēpāscĭtŭr ārtūs. Vīscĕrĕ pāscēt ăvēs. *To engulf.* Syn.—Haūrĭŏ, sōrbĕŏ, mērgŏ, dēmērgŏ, ōbrŭŏ. *To consume.* Syn.—Ĕdŏ, ēxĕdŏ, pĕrĕdŏ, ābsūmŏ, cōnfĭcĭŏ, dēvŏrŏ.

Vōrtēx, ĭcĭs. m. *Whirlpool.* Vōrtĭcĭbūsquĕ frĕquēns ĕrăt ātque īmpērvĭŭs āmnĭs. O. Syn.—Gūrgĕs, vŏrāgŏ, æstŭs. Phr.—Īma ēxæstŭăt ūndă. Vōrtĭcĭbŭs răpĭdīs. Fŭrĭt ūndă sŏnōrĭs Vōrtĭcĭbŭs. Mĭnōrēs vōlvĕrĕ vōrtĭcēs. *Whirlwind. See Turbo.*

Vōtīvŭs, ă, ūm. *Votive, that which is vowed.* Syn.—Vōtŭs, săcĕr, dēbĭtŭs. Phr.—Ārās vōtīvō sānguĭnĕ tīngĭt.

Vōtūm, ī. n. *Vow, votive offering.* Dīs Ĭtălīs vōtum īmmōrtālĕ săcrābăt. V. Syn.—Prōmīssūm, dōnārĭă (pl.). Phr.—Dēbĭtă vōtă. Vōtīvūm mūnŭs. Vōtī mūnŭs. Vōtīvæ prĕcēs. Dōnă vōtīvă. Pēnsĭlĕ vōtūm. Vōtūm prō rĕdĭtū sĭmŭlānt. Vōtūm sōlvŏ. Pĭă vōtă rĕpēndēnt. Vōtă trānscēndī mĕă.

Vŏvĕŏ, ēs, vōvī, vōtūm, ērĕ. *To vow, to promise.* Hānc Mārtī prō dŭcĕ vōvĭt ăvēm. M. Syn.—Prōmĭttŏ, dēvŏvĕŏ, cōnsĕcrŏ, dīcŏ (ās). Phr.—Vōtūm cōncĭpĭŏ, făcĭŏ, nūncŭpŏ, dīcŏ, vŏvĕŏ. Vōtō mē ōbstrīngŏ. Vōtī sūm rĕŭs. Vōtīs căpŭt ōblĭgŏ. Vōtă mētū dŭplĭcānt mātrēs. Tăcĭtō sūspēndĭt vōtă lăbēllō. Quĭd prōdēst cœlūm vōtīs īmplēssĕ? *To ask for, to desire.* Syn.—Ōptŏ, ēxōptŏ, rŏgŏ, pōscŏ, cŭpĭŏ, vŏlŏ.

Vōx, vōcĭs. f. *Voice, the sound of the voice.* Hæc quĭă dūlcĕ cănīt, flēctītquĕ făcīllĭmă vōcĕm. O. Syn.—Sŏnŭs, lŏquēlă, līnguă, vērbă (pl.). Phr.—Vōcĭs sŏnŭs, sŏnĭtŭs, mūrmŭr, mūrmŭră. Vōcĭs, līnguæ ūsŭs. Vōcālĭs sŏnŭs. Vōx ēdĭtă ĭn aūrās. Spārsă pĕr aūrās. Cōnsŏnă mēntī. Cănōră vōcĕ lŏquī. Vōx fērtŭr ăd aūrēs. Quæ vōx pĕnĕtrāvĭt ăd aūrēs. Vōx ĕrăt īn cūrsū. Vōx fēssă lŏquēndō. Vīscĕră vōcĕ rĕplĕt. Īmōquĕ trăhēns ā pēctŏrĕ vōcĕm. Vōcĕ vŏcăt. Nēc vōx hŏmĭnĕm sŏnăt. Tālĭă vōcĕ rĕfērt. Vōx faūcĭbŭs haūsĭt. Pārvæ mūrmŭră vōcĭs. Sūmmīssā vōcĕ rŏgāvĭt ŏpĕm. Māgnā prōclāmăt vōcĕ. Ănhēlam ēxprōmĕrĕ vōcĕm. *Word.* Syn.—Vērbūm, vŏcăbŭlūm. Phr.—Nēscīt vōx mīssă rĕvērtī. Prōfūdīt pēctŏrĕ vōcēs. Tālī fŭgĭēntem ēst vōcĕ sĕcūtŭs. Spārgĕrĕ vōcēs. Tālēs ēffūndĭt ăd æthĕră vōcēs. Blāndīsquĕ mŏrātŭr Vōcĭbŭs. *Language.* Syn.—Līnguă, sērmŏ.

Vūlgārĭs, ĭs, ĕ. *Cheap, common.* Jējūnūs rārō stŏmăchūs vūlgārĭă tēmnĭt. H. Syn.—Plēbēiŭs, cōmmūnĭs, trītŭs, vīlĭs. Phr.—Cœtūsquĕ vūlgārēs.

Vūlgŏ, ās, āvī, ātūm, ārĕ. *To divulge, to make known.* Hīnc tōtam īnfēlīx vūlgātūr fāmă pĕr ŏrbĕm. V. Syn.—Dīvūlgŏ, ēvūlgŏ, pērvūlgŏ, spārgŏ, dīffūndŏ, dīssēmĭnŏ. Phr.—Pĕr (*or*) ĭn vūlgŭs, pĕr pŏpŭlōs ēdŏ, spārgŏ.

Vūlgō. adv. *On all sides.* Syn.—Pāssīm, ŭbīquĕ. *Commonly, ordinarily, often.* Syn.—Sæpĕ, sæpĭŭs, crēbrō, plērūmquĕ, frĕquēntĕr, ăpērtē.

Vūlgŭs, ī. n. *People, the crowd.* Mōbĭlĕ mūtātūr sēmpēr cūm prīncĭpĕ vūlgŭs. Syn.—Tūrbă, plēbs, pŏpŭlŭs, plēbēcŭlă, pŏpēllŭs. Phr.—Nōn trāctābĭlĕ vūlgŭs. Ănĭmæ vīlēs. Vūlgārĭs cœtŭs. Mūltām sĭnĕ nōmĭnĕ plēbēm. Mĭsĕrī pārs māxĭmă vūlgī. Sprētūm sĭnĕ nōmĭnĕ vūlgŭs. Vărĭum ēt mūtābĭlĕ vūlgŭs. Nūnc hūc, nūnc flēctĭtŭr īllūc. Clāmōsī mūrmŭră vūlgī. Ārdēscīt vūlgŭs ĭn īrās. Vūlgŭs ĭnērs. Āncĭpĭtīs pūgnăt sēntēntĭă vūlgī. Scīndĭtŭr īn cōntrārĭă vūlgŭs. Sævītque ănĭmīs īgnōbĭlĕ vūlgŭs. Ēxpērs ēt rŭdĕ vūlgŭs ĕrăt.

Vūlnĕrŏ, ās, āvī, ātūm, ārĕ. *To wound.* Nūnc lătĕrūm cōstās fālcātō vūlnĕrăt ēnsĕ. O. Syn.—Lædŏ, saūcĭŏ, vĭŏlŏ. Phr.—Ēnsĕ, fērrō, tēlō, glădĭō cædŏ. Vūlnŭs dō, īncŭtĭŏ, īnflīgŏ. Ēnsĕ, fērrō pēctŭs, lătŭs ăpĕrĭŏ, rĕclūdŏ. Ēnsēm īn pēctŭs cōndŏ. Dārĕ cūspĭdĕ vūlnŭs. Glădĭō pērstrīngĕrĕ pēctŭs. Fērrūm sūb pēctŏrĕ cōndĭt. Lătŭs haūsĭt ăpērtūm. Fēcīt mănŭs īmpĭă vūlnŭs. Īn vūlnĕre ēnsem ābscōndĭt. Tūm lătĕbrās ănĭmæ pēctūs mūcrōnĕ rĕclūdĭt.

Vūlnŭs, ĕrĭs. n. *Wound.* Āffīxæ vēnīs, ănĭmāsque īn vūlnĕrĕ pōnūnt. V. Syn.—Plāgă, īctŭs. Phr.—Vūlnĕrĭs īctŭs, dŏlŏr, āspĕrĭtās. Lētālĕ mălūm. Vūlnĕrĭs ōs, hĭātŭs, cĭcātrīx. Vĭā fāctă fērrō. Mūltā vī prœlĭă mīscēnt Vūlnĕrĭbŭs. Stĕtĭt īmmō vūlnĕrĕ sānguĭs. Hŭmĕrōs ād vūlnĕră dūrăt. Nūdāns īn pēctŏrĕ vūlnŭs. Nŏtām sĭnĕ vūlnĕrĕ fēcĭt. Nīl lētālĕ dătūm. Vūlnūs lētālĕ. Ēxhālāns crūdēlī vūlnĕrĕ vītām. Pătēns īn pēctŏrĕ vūlnŭs Cūspĭdĭs. Ēxstīnctūs mĭsĕrāndō vūlnĕrĕ. Nōtīsquĕ dĕcōrūm Vūlnĕrĭbŭs. Călĭdō dē vūlnĕrĕ tēlūm Ēxtrăhĭt. Fōmēntă lĕvāntĭă vūlnŭs. Ēt vūlnĕră crūdă rĕtrāctānt. Fig. Syn.—Īctŭs, mălūm, dŏlŏr. Phr.—Tăcĭtūm vīvīt sūb pēctŏrĕ vūlnŭs. Pārvō cōr vūlnĕrĕ læsum. Aētērnūm sērvāns sūb pēctŏrĕ vūlnŭs. Vūlnĕră mēntĭs.

Vūltŭr, ŭrĭs & Vūltŭrĭŭs, ĭī. m. *A vulture.* (*See Appendix under list of Birds.*)

Vūltŭs, ūs. m. *Face, countenance.* Huīc sē fōrmă dĕī vūltū rĕdĕūntĭs ĕōdēm Ōbtŭlĭt. V. Syn.—Făcĭēs, ōs, ōră (pl.), frōns, āspēctŭs. Phr.—Vūltūs, frōntĭs, ōrĭs dĕcŏr, vĕnūstās, dĕcŭs, mŏdēstĭă. Plēnūs grăvĭtātĕ. Īn vūltu ēst rĕvĕrēntĭă tāntă vĕnūstō. Cōnsĭlĭūm vūltū tĕgĭt. Spēm vūltū sĭmŭlăt. Vĕnĭēntūm dīscĕrĕ vūltūs. Ācēr vūltŭs ĭn hōstēm. Vūltū lōngævă dĕcōrō. Ēgrĕgĭō dĕcūs ēnĭtĕt ōrĕ. Dīvīnī sīgnă dĕcōrĭs. Spēctābĭlĭs ōrĕ. Vūltūm sērvăt fōrtūnă bĕnīgnūm. Tūrbātō prōdĭtă vūltū Īră. Cōntrāctæ sĕrĭă frōntĭs. Mœstō dēfīxūs lūmĭnă vūltū. Ēt vūltūs mĕlĭōrĭs ĕrĭs. Dējēctōs ĭn hŭmūm vūltūs. Vūltū mūtābĭlĭs. Nĭvĕōs īnfēcĭt pūrpŭră vūltūs. *Sight, aspect.* Syn.—Āspēctŭs, făcĭēs, vīsŭs.

X

Xĕnĭūm, ĭī. n. *Guest-present.* Syn.—Mūnŭs, mūnūscŭlūm, dōnūm.

Xȳstūm (Xȳstŭs. m.), ī. n. *Porch, portico under which athletes exercised in the winter-time.* Syn.—Pōrtĭcŭs, ūmbrācŭlūm, āmbŭlācrūm.

Z

Zēlŭs, ī. m. *Jealousy.* Syn.—Īnvĭdĭă. *Rivalry.* Syn.—Īnvĭdĭă, stŭdĭūm. *Zeal.* Syn.—Stŭdĭūm, īndūstrĭă.

Zĕphȳrŭs, ī. m. *West wind.* Zĕphȳrīs cūm lætă vŏcāntĭbŭs æstās. V. Syn.—Făvōnĭŭs. Phr.—Făvōnī aūră, flātŭs. Zĕphȳrī plăcĭdæ aūræ, flātŭs. Vērĭs pătĕr. Tĕpēntĭbŭs aūrīs mūlcēns ārvă. Aūră vērnō cŏmĕs. Mōllĭŏr aūră Spīrăt. Zĕphȳrōs aūdīs spīrārĕ sĕcūndōs. Vērīs prænūntĭŭs. Zĕphȳrīs ăgĭtātă Tēmpē.

Zīzănĭă, ōrūm. n. *Cockle.* (*See Appendix under list of Trees, etc.*)
Zōnă, æ. f. *Cincture, girdle.* Dāt tĕrĕtēm zōnām quā mŏdŏ cīnctă fŭĭt. O. Syn.—Cīngŭlūm, cīnctŭs, bāltĕŭs, līmbŭs, zōnŭlă.
Zōnæ cœlēstēs. (pl.). f. *The zones.* Syn.—Cœlī fāscĭă. Phr.—Quīnquĕ pŏlī, cœlī plăgæ. Quōt cœlūm strīngūnt cīngŭlă. *The torrid zone.* Phr.—Vīttă ārdēns. Ēxūstă mūndī. Quā pārtĕ dēbācchēntŭr īgnēs. Trītă zōnă flāmmĕā Phœbī rŏtā. *The frigid zone.* Syn.—Ārctŏs, ūrsă. Phr.—Āxĭs nĭvālĭs, glăcĭālĭs. Quā nĕbŭlæ plŭvĭīquĕ rōrēs. Nĭvĭūmquĕ rĭgēt sūb pōndĕrĕ tēllūs.
Zȳthūm, ī. n. *Beer, ale.* Syn.—Cērvīsĭă, cĕrĕvīsĭă. Phr.—Cĕrĕālĕ pōcŭlūm. Cĕrĕālĭs pōtŭs. Cĕrĕālīs pōcŭlă zȳthī. Bācchum ĭmĭtātă Cĕrēs. Cōctă Cĕrēs sĭmŭlāt spūmāntīs pōcŭlă Bācchī.

APPENDIX.

LIST OF PROPER NAMES, ANCIENT AND MODERN, COMMON TO POETRY.

Āărōn, ōnĭs. m. *Aaron, the brother of Moses.* Syn.—Āmrămĭdēs. Phr.—Mōsĭs frātĕr. Āmrămō sătŭs. Săcrōrūm āntīstĕs, præsŭl. Vīrgā clārŭs. Săcrīs āccīnctŭs. Ēlŏquĭō præstāns.

Ăbĕl, ĕlĭs & Ăbēlŭs, ī. m. *Abel, son of Adam, killed by his brother Cain.* Phr.—Căīnī frātĕr. Ădāmī sŏbŏlēs. Scĕlĕrātī vīctĭmă frātrĭs. Frātērnō tēlō cæsŭs, māctātŭs.

Ăbrăhām, Ăbrām. indec. Ăbrăhămŭs, Ăbrămŭs, ī. & Ăbrās, æ. m. *Abraham, the father of the Jewish nation.* Syn.—Thārīdēs, Thārĭădēs. Phr.—Thārā gĕnĭtŭs. Sāræ cōnjūx. Īsăăcī pătĕr, gĕnĭtŏr. Dĕō fīdīssĭmŭs Ăbrām. Hēbrææ stīrpĭs ŏrīgŏ.

Ābsālŏn, ōnĭs. m. *Absalom, the son of David.* Syn.—Ābsālŏ, Ābsālŏmŭs, Ābēssālŏn, Māăchĭdēs. Phr.—Jŭvĕnĭs Dāvĭdĭcŭs. Pēnsĭlī nōtŭs cŏmā. Īncēstā cædĕ crŭēntŭs. Măcŭlātŭs sānguĭnĕ frātrĭs. Pērsōlvĭt ĭn ārbŏrĕ pœnās.

Ăcădēmĭă, æ. f. *The Academe, a grove near Athens, where Plato taught philosophy.* Īnque Ăcădēmīa ūmbrĭfĕrā nĭtĭdōquĕ Lўcæō. Cic. Syn.—Gўmnăsĭūm, Lўcæūm. Phr.—Ăcădēmĭæ spătĭă. Dōctōrūm ălūmnă vĭrōrūm. Schŏlă Ăcădēmī nōmĭnĕ dīctă. Ăcădēmĭæ dōctūm nĕmŭs, dōctæ sīlvæ. Dōctæ nūtrīx Ăcădēmĭă tūrbæ.

Ăchĕrōn, ōntĭs. m. *The Acheron, one of the rivers of the lower world.* Hīnc vĭă Tārtărĕī quæ fērt Ăchĕrōntĭs ăd ūndās. V. Phr.—Ăchĕrōntĭcŭs āmnĭs. Ăchĕrōntĭs ūndă, flūmĕn, lăcŭs, pălūs, vōrtēx. Īnfērnă pălūs. Tārtărĕæ stāgnă pălūdĭs. Tĕnĕbrōsă pălūs Ăchĕrōntĕ rĕfūsō.

Ăchīllēs, ĭs, ĕī & eī. m. *Achilles, son of Peleus, hero of the Trojan war.* Ēxĭtĭūm Trōjæ nōstrīque ōrbātŏr Ăchīllēs. O. Syn.—Aēăcĭdēs, Pēlīdēs. Phr.—Thēssălŭs hērōs. Dūx Pēllæŭs. Thĕtĭdĭs prōlēs, fīlĭŭs, nātŭs. Gĕnŭs Aēăcī. Dănăūm fōrtīssĭmŭs. Prĭămī rēgnōrum ēvērsŏr. Fātālĭs Prĭămō. Ēxpērs tērrōrĭs. Bēllō crŭēntĭŏr īpsō. Cēdĕrĕ nēscĭŭs. Grăvĭs Pēlīdæ stŏmăchŭs. Pŏpŭlātŏr Ăchīllēs. Tāntōrūm vīctŏr Ăchīllēs. Īnsŭpĕrābĭlĕ bēllō.

Ăchīvī, ōrūm. m. *Greeks in general.* Syn.—Ăchæī, Ārgīvī, Dănăī, Grāiī, Græcī, Pĕlāsgī.

Ădām. indecl. *or with gen.* Ădæ̅ & Ădămŭs, ī. m. *Adam, the father of all mankind.* Phr.—Prīmŭs hŏmŏ. Prīmævŭs pătĕr. Prīmŭs ōrbĭs īncŏlă. Hūmānæ̅ gēntĭs ŏrīgŏ. Prīmŭs ĭn ōrbĕ părēns hŏmĭnūm. Hūmānī gĕnĕrĭs prīncēps. Aŭctōr cūnctōrūm.

Ădōnĭs, ĭs & ĭdĭs. m. *Adonis, son of the king of Cyprus, supposed to have been changed at his death into the flower anemone.* Ēt fōrmōsŭs ŏvēs ād flūmĭnă pāvĭt Ădōnĭs. V. Phr.—Cўnĭrēĭŭs hērōs, jŭvĕnĭs. Mўrrhæ̅ fīlĭŭs, nātŭs. Fūlmĭnĕō pērcūssŭs ăb āprō.

Ădrĭă, æ̅. f. *The Adriatic sea.* Nōn ĕgŏ nūnc Ădrĭæ̅ vĕrĕōr mărĕ nōscĕrĕ tēcūm. Prop. Phr.—Ădrĭăs ūndă. Mărĕ Ădrĭătĭcūm, Īllўrĭcūm. Ădrĭæ̅ sĭnŭs. Vēntōsī tŭmŏr Ădrĭæ̅. Frĕtĭs ācrĭŏr Ădrĭæ̅.

Aēăcŭs, ī. m. *Aeacus, one of the judges of the lower world.* Aēăcŭs īn pœ̄nās īngĕnĭōsŭs ĕrĭt. O. Syn.—Āsōpĭădēs. Phr.—Jūdēx, ārbĭtĕr Ōrcī. Rēddĭt quī jūră sĭlēntĭbŭs ūmbrīs. Ūrnām Tārtărĕĭs mŏvĕt Aēăcŭs ūmbrīs. Jūdēx sĕdĕt Aēăcŭs.

Aēgīsthŭs, ī. m. *Aegisthus, son of Thyestes.* Syn.—Thўēstæ̅ŭs, Thўēstĭădēs, Thўēstæ̅ nātŭs, prōlēs.

Aēgўptŭs, ī. f. *Egypt.* Ēt vĭrĭdem Aēgўptūm nīgrā fēcūndăt ărēnā. V. Syn.—Cănōpŭs, Mēmphĭs. Phr.—Tēllūs Aēgўptĭă. Āgrī trāctūs Phărĭī. Ārvă Mărĕōtĭcă. Nīlō fēcūndă rĕgĭŏ. Mātĕr ārtĭūm. Dĕōrūm prōdĭgĭōsă părēns.

Aēnēās, æ̅. m. *Aeneas, son of Anchises.* Sūm pĭŭs Aēnēās fāmā sŭpĕr æ̅thĕră nōtŭs. V. Syn.—Ānchīsĭădēs, Dārdănĭdēs. Phr.—Dūx Īlĭăcŭs. Nātūs Dĕā. Ānchīsā gĕnĕrātŭs. Teūcrōrūm, Trōjānōrūm dūx, pătĕr. Trōjāno ā sānguĭnĕ dūctŭs. Pĭĕtāte īnsīgnĭs ĕt ārmīs. Dīvūm cērtīssĭmă prōlēs. Trōjānæ̅ dūx īnclўtĕ gēntĭs. Nēc pĭĕtātĕ nĕc ārmīs Mājŏr. Quō jūstĭŏr āltēr nēc pĭĕtātĕ fŭĭt.

Aēŏlŭs, ī. m. *Aeolus, the god of the winds.* Hīc vāstō rēx Aēŏlŭs āntrō lūctāntēs vēntōs...prĕmĭt. V. Syn.—Hīppŏtădēs. Phr.—Aēŏlĭŭs tўrānnŭs. Rēx tēmpēstātūm. Vēntōrūm rēx. Cuī vēntī pārēnt. Vēntōs cārcĕrĕ tĕnēns, frēnāns. Quī vēntīs vīm īncŭtĭt. Ēt mūlcērĕ dĕdīt flūctūs ēt tōllĕrĕ vēntōs. Mōllītque ănĭmōs ēt tēmpĕrăt īrās.

Aēscŭlāpĭŭs, ĭī. m. *Aesculapius, a famous physician deified at his death.* Plăcēt săcrātŭs ānguĭs Aēscŭlāpĭō. Prop. Syn.—Āsclēpĭŭs, Phœbĭgĕnă, Ĕpĭdaŭrĭŭs. Phr.—Mĕdĭcīnæ̅ rĕpērtŏr. Clārŭs ārtĕ mĕdēndī.

Aētnă, æ. f. *Aetna, a volcano in Italy.* Fŭrĭt īgnĭbŭs īmpĕtŭs Aētnæ. L. Phr.—Mōns Trīnăcrĭŭs, Sĭcŭlŭs. Sĭcŭlŭs ăpēx. Rūpēs Trīnăcrĭă. Flāmmīs ūndāntĭbŭs Aētnă. Dēpāstī flāmmīs scŏpŭlī. Īmmūgĭĭt Aētnă căvērnīs. Lōngē făvīllām dīffērt. Crāssā vōlvēns cālīgĭnĕ fūmūm. Sūlphŭrĕīs ārdēt fōrnācĭbŭs Aētnă.

Ăgămēmnōn, ŏnĭs. m. *Agamemnon, king of Mycenæ, one of the leaders in the Trojan war.* Syn.—Ăgămēmnŏ, Tāntălĭdēs, Ătrīdēs. Phr.—Tŷndărĕī gĕnĭtŏr. Dūx Mўcēnæŭs. Dūctōr Dănăūm. Tēllūrīs dĕcŭs Ārgŏlĭcæ. Dūctŏr Ăchīvūm.

Ājāx, ācĭs. m. 1. *Ajax, the son of Telamon, one of the heroes of the Trojan war.* Nēc quīsquam Ājācēm pōssīt sŭpĕrārĕ nĭsi Ājāx. O. Syn.—Tĕlĕmōnĭădēs. Phr.—Tĕlĕmōnĭŭs hērōs. Tĕlĕmōnĭă prōlēs. Aēmŭlŭs Ŭlўssĭs. Mārtĕ fĕrōx ēt vīrĭbŭs Ājāx. Clўpĕō īntērrĭtŭs. Hērōs ăb Ăchīllĕ sĕcūndŭs.

Ājāx, ācĭs. m. 2. *Ajax, son of Oileus, noted for his bravery in the Trojan war.* Ūnĭŭs ōb nōxam ēt fŭrĭās Ājācĭs Ŏīleī. V. Syn.—Ŏīlīdēs. Phr.—Cōntēmptōr sŭpĕrūm. Fūlmĭnĕ pērcūssŭs, ēxūstŭs. Nōn aūdēt Ŏīlĕōs Ājāx.

Ālbă, æ. f. *Alba, a city in Latium.* Āscănĭūs clārī cōndēt cōgnōmĭnĭs Ālbām. V. Phr.—Ālbă Lōngă. Ālbānă mœnĭă. Ālbă pŏtēns. Ālbæ sŭīs ōmĭnĕ nātă. Lōngām mūltā vī mūnĭēt Ālbām.

Ālcæŭs, ī. m. *Alceus, a Greek lyric poet.* Ālcæūs sŏnāns aūrĕō plēctrō. H. Phr.—Lēsbĭŭs pŏētă, vātēs, cīvĭs. Ēxāctōsquĕ cănīs, pūgnāx Ālcæĕ, tўrānnōs. Ālcæī mĭnācēs Cămœnæ.

Ălēxāndĕr, drī. m. *Alexander, son of Philip, king of Macedon.* Grātŭs Ălēxāndrō rēgī māgnō fŭĭt īllĕ. H. Phr.—Prōlēs īnvīctă Phĭlīppī. Pēllæŭs jŭvĕnĭs, dūx, hērōs. Dūx Măcĕdŏ. Ăsĭæ dŏmĭtŏr. Īnsŭpĕrābĭlĭs ārmīs. Cuī fōrtīs dēxtĕră. Tōtĭŭs mūndī trĕmŏr. Căpŭt īnsŭpĕrābĭlĕ bēllō. Fūlmĕn bēllī. Bēllātōr mūndī.

Ālpēs, ĭūm. f. *The Alps.* Ārcēs Ālpĭbŭs īmpŏsĭtæ. H. Phr.—Ālpīnī mōntēs. Rūpēs, ārcēs Ālpīnæ. Ālpīnī āggĕrēs. Aūstrō ēxpŏsĭtæ. Ārdŭă mōntĭs Ālpīnī făcĭēs. Ālpīs nūbĭfĕræ cōllēs. Quŏt ĭn Ālpĕ fĕræ.

Ālphēŭs, ī. m. *Alpheus, a famous hunter, according to mythology, changed into a stream.* Phr.—Mīrācŭlă fōntĭs ēt āmnĭs. Ēlĭdĭs āmnĭs. Ālphēă flūmĭnă Pīsæ. Trānsfŭgă Pīsæ.

Ămāzŏnĕs, ūm. f. *The Amazons, race of female warriors.* Phr.—Tūrmă, cŏhōrs, cătērvă Thērmōdōntĭăcă. Scўthĭcæ pŭēllæ. Hŏmĭnĭbŭs pārēs, sĭmĭlēs.

Āmphīōn, ŏnĭs. m. *Amphion, founder of Thebes.* Phr.—Nātŭs Jŏvĕ. Quī lăpĭdēs mōvīssĕ, flēxīssĕ cănēndō Dīcĭtŭr. Cănōrō mŏdŭlātū sāxă trăhēns. Dūcēns dūrās tēstūdĭnĕ caūtēs. Ănĭmās tēstūdĭnĕ sāxă. Thēbānæ cōndĭtŏr ūrbĭs.

Ānchīsēs, æ. m. *Anchises, father of Aeneas.* Āt pătĕr Ānchīsēs ŏcŭlōs ād sīdĕră lætŭs Ēxtŭlĭt. V. Phr.—Aēnēæ pătĕr, părēns, gĕnĭtŏr. Phrȳx sĕnēx, sārcĭnă nātī. Vĕtĕrem Ānchīsēn āgnōscĭt ămīcūm.

Āndrŏmăchē, ēs. f. *Andromache, wife of Hector.* Lībābāt cĭnĕri Āndrŏmăchē, mānēsquĕ vŏcābăt. V. Phr.—Hēctŏrĭs cōnjūx, ūxŏr.

Āndrŏmĕdă, æ. f. *Andromeda, wife of Perseus, placed among the stars after death.* Phr.—Āndrŏmĕdam īnvŏcāt naūtă. Pērsēĭă cōnjūx. Pērsēī nōbĭlĭs ūxŏr. Pātrĭæ fūscă cŏlōrĕ sŭæ. Clārĭssĭmă stēllă.

Ānglĭă, æ. f. (*modern*) *England.* Syn.—Ālbĭōn, Brĭtānnĭă. Phr.—Clāră ŏpĭbŭs, dīvĭtĭs ūbĕrĕ cāmpī. Dīvĕs ăgrī, ŏvĭūm, pĕcŏrūm. Cīrcūmflŭă pōntō.

Āntæŭs, ī. m. *Antæus, a giant who wrestled with Hercules.* Hērcŭlĭs Āntæūm prŏcŭl ā tēllūrĕ tĕnēntĭs. J. Phr.—Cāstīgātūm Lĭbȳcæ cērōmă pălæstræ. Hērcŭlēĭs prēssūm sīc fāmă lăcērtĭs Tērrĭgĕnām sūdāssĕ Lĭbȳn.

Āntēnŏr, ŏrĭs. m. *Antenor, Trojan prince, founder of Padua.* Syn.—Māvōrtĭŭs, Phrȳgĭŭs prŏfŭgŭs. Fūndātŏr Pădŭæ.

Āntĭcȳră, æ. f. *Anticyra, an island in the Aegean.* Trĭbŭs Āntĭcȳrĭs căpŭt īnsānābĭlĕ. H. Phr—Pūrgāntēs pēctŏră sūccī. Nāvĭgĕt Āntĭcȳrām.

Ăphrŏdītă, æ. f. *See Venus.*

Ăpōllŏ, ĭnĭs. m. *Apollo, the god of poetry, music, divination and prophecy.* Sānctī cūstōs Sōrāctĭs Ăpōllŏ. V. Syn.—Phœbŭs, Sōl, Tītān, Smīnthēus, Cȳnthĭŭs, Dēlĭŭs, Pȳthĭŭs, Lātōnĭŭs. Phr.—Phœbŭs Ăpōllŏ. Lātōnĭă prōlēs. Mūsārūm præsĕs. Vātūm pătĕr. Cārmĭnĭs aūctŏr. Crīnĭbŭs īnsīgnĭs. Mĕdĭcīnæ īnvēntŏr. Trōjæ mūnītŏr. Cĭthăræ pūlsātŏr. Nūbĕ cāndēntēs hŭmĕrōs ămīctŭs. Ārcū fūlgēntĕ dĕcōrŭs. Āccēptūsquĕ nŏvēm Cămœnīs. Dōctŏr ārgūtæ fĭdĭcēn Thălīæ. Quī nērvīs tēmpĕrăt ārcūm. Flāvŭs Ăpōllŏ.

Ăpōstŏlī, ōrūm. m. *The Twelve Apostles of our Lord.* Syn.—Dīscĭpŭlī. Phr.—Bīs sēnī cŏmĭtēs Chrīstī. Bīs sēnă vĭrūm vīs. Dŭŏdēnă tūrbă. Chrīstī cŏmĭtēsquĕ vĭæ. Tēstēsquĕ lăbōrūm Chrīstī. Nŭmĕro ēx ōmnī dēlēgĭt ămīcōs Bīs sēnōs. Quī fūnĕrĕ sprētō tērrās Chrīstum īnsŏnŭērĕ pĕr ōmnēs.

Āppĭă, æ. f. *The Appian Way.* Ēt Āppĭām mānnīs tĕrĭt. H. Phr.—Āppĭă trītă rŏtīs. Aūsŏnĭæ māxĭmă fāmă vĭæ.

Ăpūlĭă, æ. f. *Apulia, a province of Italy.* Āltrīcĭs ēxtrā līmĕn Ăpūlĭæ. H. Syn.—Daūnĭă. Phr.—Jūgĕră Daūnĭæ.

Ăquārĭŭs, ĭī. m. *Aquarius, one of the signs of the Zodiac.* Īnvērsūm cōntrīstăt Ăquārĭŭs āmnēm. H. Syn.—Hȳdrŏchŏŭs. Phr.—Sīdŭs Ăquārī. Ūndĕcĭm sīgnūm. Fūsŏr ăquæ. Jŭvĕnĭs gēstātŏr ăquæ. Sīgnă tĕnēntĭs ăquās. Gĕlĭdōs pōrtēndĭt Ăquārĭŭs īmbrēs.

Ărăbēs, ūm. m. *Arabians.* Syn.—Năbăthæī, Săbæī. Phr.—Mĭtrā vēlātī. Pālmĭfĕrōsque Ărăbēs, Pānchæăquĕ rūră rĕlīnquĭt.

Ărăbĭă, æ. f. *Arabia.* Ēt dŏmŭs īntāctæ tē trĕmĭt Ărăbĭæ. Prop. Syn.—Pānchāĭă. Phr.—Pānchāĭă, Pānchāĭcă tēllūs. Ărăbūm rĕgĭŏ. Săbæī dīvĕs ŏdōrĭs. Ārvă Săbæă. Ŏdōrūm tērră fĕrāx. Rĕgĭō tūrĭs ăbūndāns. Ēōæ dŏmŭs Ărăbūm.

Ărāchnē, ēs. f. *Arachne, a most skilful spinner, turned into a spider by Pallas.* Mæŏnĭæque ănĭmūm fātĭs īntēndĭt Ărāchnēs. O. Phr.—Vīrgŏ Mæŏnĭă. Pāllădĭs æmŭlă. Rădĭō pērcūssă Mĭnērvæ.

Ārchĭlŏchŭs, ī. m. *Archilochus, inventor of the iambic metre.* Ārchĭlŏchūm prŏprĭō răbĭēs ārmāvĭt ĭāmbō. H. Phr.—Fāmōsī cārmĭnĭs aūctŏr. Rĕpērtŏr pūgnācĭs ĭāmbī. Mūsĭs ămīcŭs.

Ārchĭmēdēs, ĭs. m. *Archimedes, a famous geometrician.* Phr.—Ămāns pătrĭæ. Quī Sȳrăcŭsĭī trāxīt cērtāmĭnă bēllī.

Ārctŏs, ī & Ārctī, ōrūm. f. *The constellations of the Great Bear and Little Bear.* Āltăquĕ cærŭlĕūm dūm Nērĕă nēscĭĕt Ārctŏs. V. Syn.—Ūrsă, Pārrhăsĭs, Hĕlĭcē, Plaūstrūm, Ārctūrŭs. Phr.—Pārrhăsĭdēs stēllæ. Gĕlĭdō prōxĭmă sīgnă pŏlō. Plaūstrī præbēntĭă fōrmām Sīdĕră. Plaūstrūm glăcĭālĕ sŭb ūrsā.

Ārctūrŭs, ī. m. *Arcturus, a star in the constellation of the Bear.* Syn.—Ārctŏphȳlāx. Phr.—Sævŭs Ārctūrī cădēntĭs Īmpĕtŭs. Sŭb īpsūm Ārctūrūm.

Ārēŏpăgŭs, ī. m. *The Areopagus, a famous hill in Athens.* Phr.—Mārtīsquĕ fŏrēnsĕ trĭbūnăl. Cēcrŏpĭă Māvōrtĭs ĭn ārcĕ. Cūrĭă Mārtĭs.

Ărĕthūsă, æ. f. *Arethusa, a nymph changed into a fountain.* Ōre, Ărĕthūsă, tŭō Sĭcŭlĭs cōnfūndĭtŭr ūndīs. V. Phr.—Ārcădĭă vīrgŏ. Fōns Ărĕthūsĭŭs. Ărĕthūsĭdĕs ūndæ, Ărĕthūsæī lătĭcēs.

Ārgō. f. indecl. *Argo, the boat of the Argonauts.* Phr.—Ārgō săxă păvēns pōstquăm Scȳllæĭă lēgĭt. Pūppĭs, rătĭs, nāvĭs, cărīnă Thēssălĭă, Ārgōă, Ĭāsŏnĭă. Ārgō suētă lŏquī. Pēlĭăs ārbŏr. Dīvīnā Pāllădĭs ārtĕ Strūctă rătĭs.

Ārgŏnaūtæ, ārūm. m. *The Argonauts, who went in search of the Golden Fleece.* Phr.—Hērōĕs jŭvĕnēs. Naūtæ, hērōĕs Ārgīvī. Ārgōæ lĕgĭō rătĭs. Ārgīvæ rōbŏră pūppĭs. Aūrĭcŏmam Hērōēs cōnāti āvēllĕrĕ pēllēm.

Ārgŏs. n. (*Used only in the nom., acc., voc. sing.*) & Ārgī, ōrūm, m. (*for the plural*). *Argos, a part of the Peloponnesus.* Syn.—Ūrbs, pătrĭă, Īnăchĭă. Phr.—Īnăchĭdēs ōræ. Ārgōs nōbĭlĭbūs nōbĭlĕ cīvĭbūs. Ōmĭnă nī rĕpĕtānt Ārgīs.

Ārgŭs, ī. m. *Argus, a monster with a hundred eyes.* Syn.—Ārēstŏrĭdēs. Phr.—Pāstŏr Aēmŏnĭūs. Cūstōs Jūnōnĭūs. Cūstōs Vīrgĭnĭs Ārgūs. Cēntēnō lūmĭnĕ cīnctūs.

Ărĭādnē, ēs. f. *Ariadne, daughter of Minos, king of Crete.* Syn.—Syn.—Mīnōĭs, Gnōssĭs. Phr.—Vīrgŏ, pŭēllă Crēssă. Gnōssĭă, Mīnōĭă vīrgŏ. Dīgnă vĭrō mĕlĭōrĕ. Īgnōtō sōlă rĕlīctă mărī.

Ărĭēs, Ărĭĕtĭs & Ărĭētĭs. m. *The Ram, one of the signs of the Zodiac.* Syn.—Lānĭgĕr, Āgnūs. Phr.—Sīgnōrūm prīncēps. Phrȳxæūm sīgnūm. Pōrtĭtŏr Hēllēs. Nōbĭlĕ Lānĭgĕrī sīdūs. Dōctōrque ēt jānĭtŏr ānnī. Aūrātō, aūrĕō vīllō īnsīgnĭs. Tōrtūs īn cōrnŭă.

Ărīōn, ŏnĭs. m. *Arion, a famous lyric poet and musician of Lesbos.* Quōd mărĕ nōn nōvīt, quæ nēscĭt Ărīŏnă tēllūs? O. Phr.—Lēsbĭūs, Mēthȳmnæūs vātēs. Cāntū īnsīgnĭs Ărīōn. Aēquŏrĕō pōrtāvĭt Ărīŏnă dōrsō.

Ărīstæūs, ī. *Son of Apollo, the first to make oil and honey.* Pāstŏr Ărīstæūs fŭgĭēns Pēnēĭă Tēmpē. V. Phr.—Ārcădĭūs măgīstĕr. Rĕnŏvātŏr ăpūm.

Ărīstārchūs, ī. m. *Aristarchus, a famous Greek critic.* Māgnūs Ărīstārchō mājŏr Hŏmērūs ĕrăt. O. Phr.—Fīĕt Ărīstārchūs. Ācrī jūdĭcĭō līmātūs. Vĭr nārĭs ēmūnctæ.

Ărīstīdēs, ĭs. m. *Aristides, a Greek noted for his justice.* Pūlsūs Ărīstīdēs pătrĭā Lăcĕdæmŏnă fūgĭt. O. Phr.—Jūstī spēctātŏr ēt æquī. Jūstīssĭmūs hŏmŏ.

Ărīstŏphănēs, ĭs. m. *Aristophanes, a Greek comic poet.* Eūpŏlĭs ātquĕ Crătīnūs Ărīstŏphănēsquĕ pŏētæ. H. Phr.—Ărīstŏphănĭs īngēns mĭcāt sōlērtĭă.

Ărīstŏtĕlēs, ĭs. m. *Aristotle, a famous Greek philosopher.* Sī quĭs Ărīstŏtĕlēm sĭmĭlēm vēl Pīttăcōn ēmĭt. J. Syn.—Stăgȳrītēs, Stăgȳræūs. Phr.—Ărīstŏtĕlēs dīvīnūs, sōlērs, sūbtīlĭs, dōctūs, pĕrītūs, cĕlĕbĕr. Mōnstrātŏr vērī. Nātūrae āc vērī nōn sōrdĭdūs aūctŏr. Suāsŏr hŏnēstī.

Ărīūs, ĭī. m. *Arius, a famous heretic.* Phr.—Nŏvĭtātĭs ămāns. Hōstĭs fĭdĕī. Nŏvĭs rēbūs stūdēns. Lēgēs ăbŏlērĕ părēntūm āntīquās cŭpĭt. Hærĕsĕōs lētālī āfflātūs cūlpā.

Ārmĕnĭūs, ĭī. m. *An Armenian.* Phr.—Hīnc crīnĕ dĕcōrō Ārmĕnĭūs. Ārmĕnĭās cūrrū sūbjūngĕrĕ tīgrēs.

Āscănĭūs, ĭī. m. *Ascanius, son of Aeneas.* Āt pŭĕr Āscănĭūs cuī nūnc cōgnōmĕn Īūlō. V. Syn.—Īlūs, Īūlūs, Aēnĕădēs. Phr.—

Dārdănĭŭs pŭĕr. Cōndĭtŏr Ālbæ. Māgnæ spēs āltĕră Rōmæ. Ōmnĭs ĭn Āscănĭō cārī stāt cūră părēntĭs.

Ăsĭă, æ. f. *Asia.* Tē dŭcĕ māgnĭfĭcās Ăsĭæ pērrēxĭmŭs ūrbēs. O. Phr.—Ăsĭæ tēllūs. Ăsĭātĭcă tēllūs. Hūmānæ cūnābŭlă gēntĭs. Quā nūllă bĕātĭŏr ōră. Rēs Ăsĭæ. Quōndām clārīssĭmă tēllūs. Ăsĭæ vīctŏr.

Āstўănāx, āctĭs. m. *Astyanax, the son of Hector.* Ō mĭhĭ sōlă mĕī sŭpĕr Āstўănāctĭs ĭmāgŏ. V. Syn.—Hēctŏrĭdēs. Phr.—Spēs Trōjæ mĭsĕræquĕ părēntĭs. Hēctŏrĕŭs pŭĕr. Ĕt ăvō pŭĕrum Āstўănāctă trăhēbăt.

Ăthēnæ, ārūm. f. *Athens, city of Attica.* Quīd Pāndīŏnĭæ rēstānt nĭsĭ nōmĕn Ăthēnæ? O. Phr.—Ūrbs Cĕcrŏpĭă, Pāllădĭs. Mūsārūm ūrbs, nūtrīx Mūsārūm, dōctrīnārūm īnvēntrīx, dŏmŭs. Āltĕră Rōmă. Ūrbs stŭdĭīs clārīssĭmă. Cĕcrŏpĭs tērră. Ūrbs āddīctă Mĭnērvæ. Dīctæ ā Pāllădĕ tērræ.

Ăthēnĭēnsēs, ĭūm. m. *Athenians.* Syn.—Cĕcrŏpĭdæ, Cĕcrŏpĭī, Ĕrēchthīdæ, Āttĭcī.

Ăthŏ (Ăthōn), ōnĭs & thōs. m. *Athos, a mountain dividing Macedonia and Thrace.* Āut Ātho aūt Rhŏdŏpēn aūt āltă Cĕraūnĭă tēlō Dējĭcĭt. V. Phr.—Quōt lĕpŏrēs ĭn Ăthō. Vēlĭfĭcātŭs Ăthōs. Glăcĭālĭs Ăthō. Mōns sūblīmĭs.

Ătlās, āntĭs. m. *Atlas, who was said to have supported the heavens on his shoulders.* Ŭbĭ stēllĭfĕr Ātlās Āxem hŭmĕrō tōrquēt stēllĭs ārdēntĭbŭs āptūm. V. Syn.—Īăpĕtīŏnĭdēs. Phr.—Tāngēns vērtĭcĕ cœlūm. Căpŭt īntēr nūbĭlă cōndēns. Hŭmĕrĭs quī cœlūm sūstĭnĕt. Āstrōrūm pōndĕrĕ prēssŭs. Aēthĕrĕōs hŭmĕrō quī sūstĭnĕt ōrbēs. Quī fērt cērvīcĭbŭs āxēm. Hŭmĕrĭs ārdēntēm sūstĭnĕt āxēm.

Ătreŭs, ĕŏs, ĕī & eī. m. *Atreus, father of Agamemnon and Menelaus.* Aūt hūmānă pălām cŏquăt ēxtă nĕfārĭŭs Ātreūs. H. Syn.—Tāntălĭdēs. Phr.—Pĕlŏpēĭă prōlēs. Ātreūs ătrōx, īmmānĭs.

Ātrŏpŏs, ī. f. *Atropos, one of the fates.* Ātrŏpŏs ēt Lăchĕsĭs jūngēbānt stāmĭnă dīctĭs. Phr.—Nēscĭă flēctī, nōn ēxōrābĭlĭs, īgnāră mŏvērī. Rūmpīt vītæ fātālĭă stāmĭnă. Ēt sēmpēr dē trĭbŭs ūnă sĕcăt.

Āttĭcă, æ. f. *Attica.* Syn.—Ātthĭs. Phr.—Āttĭcă tēllūs, tērră. Āctă Cĕcrŏpĭă. Cĕcrŏpĭī fīnēs.

Āttĭlă & Ătĭlă, æ. m. *Attila, king of the Huns.* Phr.—Tērrĭfĭcĭs dīffūdĕrāt Āttĭlă tūrmĭs. Rēx dīrŭs, fĕrōx. Fāx ōrbĭs. Flăgēllūm Dŏmĭnī.

Aūgūstīnŭs, ī. m. *Saint Augustine, doctor of the Church.* Phr.—Hīppōnĭs præsŭl, āntīstĕs. Pēlāgiī tērrŏr. Pătrĭtĭō sătŭs, gĕnĕrātŭs. Dĕcŭs īmmōrtālĕ Tăgāstæ. Dōctōrūm ăpĕx.

Aūgūstŭs, ī. m. *Octavian Augustus, the first Roman emperor.* Cœpĕrăt Aūgūstūs dēcēptae īgnōscĕrĕ cūlpæ. O. Syn.—Cæsăr, Ōctāvĭŭs. Phr.—Aūgūstŭs Cæsăr, dīvūm gĕnŭs. Ōrtŭs ăb Aēnēā. Hīc ămēs dīcī pătĕr ātquĕ prīncēps. Pătĕr Aūgūstīssĭmŭs ōrbĭs. Pācēm dĕdĭt ōrbī.

Aūgūstŭs, ī. m. *August, the eighth month of the year.* Phr.—Aūgūstūm mēnsēm Lĕō fērvĭdŭs īgnĕ pĕrūrĭt. Mēnsĭs sēxtīlĭs. Quō răpĭdĭs sōl tērgă Lĕōnĭs Ūrĭt ĕquīs. Mēnsĭs nōmĭnĕ Cæsărĕō gaūdēns. Ăb Aūgūstō dūcēns sŭă nōmĭnă mēnsĭs. Aūgūstī mūnĕrĕ frūgēs.

Aūlĭs, ĭdĭs. f. *Aulis, a port in Boeotia whence the Greeks sailed against Troy.* Bœōtĭcă tēllūs Aūlĭdĕ pīscōsā pūppēs tĕnŭīssĕt ĭtūrās. O. Phr.—Aūlĭdĭs pōrtŭs. Prīmă rătēs Dănăās Hĕcătēĭă cōngrĕgăt Aūlĭs.

Aūrōră, æ. f. *Aurora, goddess of the dawn.* Ōcĕănum īntĕrĕā sūrgēns Aūrōră rĕlīnquĭt. V. Syn.—Ēōs, Pāllāntĭs, Tīthŏnĭs, Tīthōnĭă, Thaūmāntĭs. Phr.—Tīthōnī fūlgĭdă cōnjŭx. Lūcĭs nūntĭă. Clārī prænūntĭă sōlĭs. Āstră fŭgāns. Crŏcĕō vēlāmĭnĕ fūlgēns. Aūrōræ lūmĭnă. Dĭēmque Aūrōră rĕdūcĭt. Spārgēbānt lūmĭnĕ tērrās. Aūrōră rūbēbăt. Rŏsĕīs Aūrōră quădrīgīs. Rŏsĕīs Aūrōră căpīllīs. Tīthōnī rōscĭdă cōnjŭx. Aūrōra īngrĕdĭēns. Ēxŏrĭēns Aūrōră.

Aūsŏnĕs, ūm. m. *Italians.* Syn.—Aūsŏnĭī, Lătīnī. *See Romani.*

Aūsŏnĭă, æ. f. *Italy.* Syn.—Ītălĭă, Lătĭūm. Phr.—Aūsŏnĭī fīnēs. Ītălă tēllūs. Sātūrnĭă rēgnă. *See Italia.*

Ăvērnŭs, ī. m. & Ăvērnă, ōrūm. n. *Avernus, a lake in Campania, supposed to be the entrance to the Lower World.* Dīvīnōsquĕ lăcūs ēt Ăvērnă sŏnāntĭă sīlvīs. V. Syn.—Īnfērnŭs, Īnfĕrī, Ōrcŭs, Tārtărŭs, Ĕrĕbŭs, Stȳx, Ăchĕrōn. Phr.—Tārtărĕæ sēdēs. Rēgnă Plūtōnĭă. Ăvērnă pălūs. Ăvērnæ vāllēs. Ōrcī ădĭtŭs. Dītĭs jānŭă. Faūcēs grăveōlēntĭs Ăvērnī. Cœtūsquĕ sĭlēntĭs Ăvērnī. Făcĭlĭs dēscēnsŭs Ăvērnī.

B

Băbȳlōn, ōnĭs. f. *Babylon, city of Chaldea and Assyria.* Cūmquĕ sŭpērbă fŏrĕt Băbȳlōn spŏlĭāndă trŏpæīs. L. Phr.—Băbȳlōnĭă mœnĭă. Ūrbs Băbȳlōnĭs. Sĕmīrămĭdĭs ārcēs. Cīrcūmdātă mūrīs. Dīvĕs ŏpūm. Ŏpĭbŭs sŭpērbă. Căpŭt Āssȳrĭæ gēntĭs. Āssȳrĭī pālātĭă cēlsă tȳrānnī.

Bācchă, æ. f. *A Bacchante, a devotee of Bacchus.* Quālĭs ăb Ōgȳgĭō cōncĭtă Bācchă dĕō. O. Syn.—Bācchē, Bācchĭs, Thȳăs, Mænăs, Bāssărĭs. Phr.—Mātrēs Cādmēæ, Thēbānæ. Bācchī cŏmĭtēs. Bācchō āfflātæ. Cĕlĕbrāntēs ōrgĭă Bācchī. Fēmĭnĕī chŏrī. Fŭrĭīs āccēnsæ pēctŏră mātrēs.

Bācchānăl, ĭs (Bācchānālĭă, ĭūm). n. *The Bacchanalia, feast of Bacchus.* Phr.—Bācchō fēstă. Bācchī săcră. Săcră Bācchō tēmpŏră. Ōrgĭă Bācchī.

Bācchŭs, ī. m. *Bacchus, god of wine.* Syn.—Ĭācchŭs, Lȳæŭs, Lībĕr, Lēnæŭs, Ēvān, Bāssărēŭs, Ēvĭŭs. Phr.—Sĕmĕlēĭă prōlēs. Thēbānæ Sĕmĕlēs pŭĕr. Bīs gĕnĭtŭs. Dĕŭs vītĭsătŏr. Vīnī rĕpērtŏr. Jūcūndæ cōndĭtŏr ūvæ. Lætĭtĭæ dătŏr. Aūrĕō cōrnū dĕcōrŭs.

Bāiæ, ārūm. f. *Baiæ, city in Campania, a famous watering-place.* Nūllŭs ĭn ōrbĕ sĭnūs Bāiīs prælūcĕt ămœnīs. H. Phr.—Eūbŏĭcūm Bāiārūm līttŭs. Līttŏră Bāiārūm. Hūmĭdă Bāiārūm stāgnă.

Bēllĕrŏphōn, ōntĭs. m. *Bellerophon, who overcame the Chimæra.* Phr.—Chĭmæræ dŏmĭtŏr. Glaūcī cāstīssĭmă prōlēs. Cuī prædă Chĭmæră.

Bēllōnă, æ. f. *Bellona, the goddess of war.* Quām cūm sānguĭnĕō sĕquĭtūr Bēllōnă flăgēllō. V. Syn.—Ēnȳō. Phr.—Bēllōrūm dĕă. Māvōrtĭă Dīvă. Dīgnă Mārtĭs sŏrŏr. Bēllōnæ īmplācābĭlĕ nūmĕn. Sānguĭnĕ sōrdĭdă vēstēm. Bēllōnă fŭrēns.

Bĕthlĕhēm & Bĕthlēm. indecl., Bĕthlĕhĕmă & Bĕthlēmă, æ. f. *Bethlehem, where our Lord was born.* Phr.—Īndĕ pĕtīt Bēthlēm. Dūx Bĕthlēm. Ūrbs Bĕthlĕmĭcă. Sācră mœnĭă Bĕthlēm. Chrīstī īncūnābŭlă.

Bœōtĭă, æ. f. *Boeotia, province of Greece.* Phr.—Bœōtăquĕ tēllūs. Hȳānthĭă, Āŏnĭs, Cādmēĭă tērră.

Bŏōtēs, æ. m. *Bootes, the constellation.* Haūd ōbscūră cădēns mīttīt tĭbĭ sīgnă Bŏōtēs. V. Syn.—Ārctūrŭs, Ārctŏphȳlāx. Phr.—Cūstōs Ĕrȳmānthĭdŏs ūrsæ. Sīdŭs Hȳpērbŏrĕūm. Plaūstrīquĕ prŏpīnquŭs Pārrhăsĭī. Sævīs frīgŏrĭbŭs rĭgēns. Ā tērgō nĭtĕt Ārctŏphȳlāx.

Bōsphŏrŭs, Bōspŏrŭs, ī. m. & Bōsphŏră, ōrūm. n. *The straits of Bosporus.* Phr.—Scȳthĭcās āstrīngēns Bōspŏrŭs ūndās. Eūxīnī ōstĭă Pōntī. Quā Bōspŏrŭs æstŭăt ūndās.

Brĭăreūs, ĕŏs, ĕī & eī. m. *Briareus, a giant who had a hundred hands.* Ēt cēntūmgĕmĭnūs Brĭăreūs ēt bēllŭă Lērnæ. V. Syn.—Aĕgēōn. Phr.—Gĭgās cēntĭmănŭs, cēntūmgĕmĭnŭs. Sūb Aētnā gĕmēns. Īmpŏsĭtă quēm Aētnă prĕmĭt.

Brĭtānnī, ōrūm. m. *The people of Britain.* Syn.—Brĭtŏnēs. Phr.—Hōspĭtĭbŭs fĕrī. Mĭnĭmā nōctĕ cōntēntī.

Brĭtānnĭă, æ. f. *Britain.* Syn.—Brĭtānnĭs, Ānglĭă. Phr.—Nōstrō dīdūctă Brĭtānnĭă mūndō. Pīctōquĕ Brĭtānnĭă cūrrū.

Brūtŭs, ī. m. (1) *Marcus Brutus, one of the conspirators against Cæsar.* Phr.—Dĕcŭs īmpĕrĭī. Spēs ūltĭmă Rōmæ. Ēxtrēmūm clārī gĕnĕrīs nōmĕn. (2) *Lucius Brutus, the first Roman consul.* Phr.—Ănĭmă sŭpērbă Ūltōrĭs Brūtī. Ănĭmō sŭă nōmĭnă fāllĭt.

Bȳzāntĭūm, ĭī. n. *Byzantium, the modern Constantinople.* Syn.—Cōnstāntīnŏpŏlĭs. Phr.—Bȳzāntī ārcēs. Bȳzāntĭă mœnĭă, līttŏră. Āltĕră Rōmă. Nŏvă Rōmă. Ūrbs Cōnstāntīnī dē nōmĭnĕ dīctă.

C

Cādmŭs, ī. m. *Cadmus, the founder of Thebes.* Cādmŭs ĭn Āŏnĭā cōnstĭtĭt ēxsŭl hŭmō. O. Syn.—Āgēnŏrĭdēs. Phr.—Āgēnŏrĕ nātŭs. Sīdŏnĭŭs hōspĕs. Tȳrĭā dē gēntĕ prŏfēctŭs. Jŭvĕnĭs Hȳāntĭŭs. Prīmūs Thēbānæ cōndĭtŏr ūrbĭs. Tȳrĭīs quī pūlsŭs ăb ōrīs. Bœōtĭă mœnĭă cōndĭt.

Cādūcĕŭs, ī. m. & Cādūcĕūm, ī. n. *The Caduceus, the wand of Mercury.* Syn.—Vīrgă. Phr.—Lēthæūm vīmĕn. Quā sōmnōs dūcĭt ĕt ārcĕt. Aūrĕă quī tōrtō vīrgă drăcōnĕ nĭtĕt.

Cæsăr, ărĭs. m. *Julius Cæsar.* Nāscētūr pūlchrā Trōjānŭs ŏrīgĭnĕ Cæsăr. V. Phr.—Dūx Lătĭŭs, Aūsŏnĭŭs. Īllūstrī stīrpĕ crĕātŭs. Dē sānguĭnĕ nātŭs Īūlī. Mārtĕ tŏgāquĕ Præcīpŭŭs. Hēspĕrĭī fōrtūnă dŭcĭs.

Căīn, indecl. & Căīnŭs, ī. m. *Cain, the brother of Abel.* Phr.—Cœlō īnvīsŭs. Ĕdācī ānxĭŭs īnvĭdĭā. Vēsānă tŭmēns præcōrdĭă. Frātērnō cædĕ crŭēntŭs. Frātērnō tērrām quī sānguĭnĕ tīnxĭt. Cōgnātō măcŭlāvīt sānguĭnĕ dēxtrām.

Călĭgŭlă, æ. m. *Caligula, Roman emperor.* Syn.—Căĭŭs, Cāiŭs. Phr.—Dūx īmpĭŭs, scĕlēstŭs, nĕfāndŭs.

Cāllĭŏpē, ēs & Cāllĭŏpēă, æ. f. *Calliope, the muse of epic poetry.* Cāllĭŏpē quĕrŭlās prætēntāt pōllĭcĕ chōrdās. V. Phr.—Mūsă cāllĭdă. Rĕquĭēs hŏmĭnūm dīvūmquĕ vŏlūptās. Prīmă sŭī chŏrī. Īmmīstōs hĕdĕrā cōllēctă căpīllōs. *See Musæ.*

Călȳpsō, ūs. f. *Calypso, the nymph who befriended Ulysses.* Ān grăvĕ sēx ānnīs pūlchrām fōvīssĕ Călȳpsō? O. Phr.—Aēæă pŭēllă. Ātlāntĭs fīlĭă. Īncōmptīs mœstă căpīllīs.

Cămœnæ, ārūm. f. *The Muses. See Musæ.*

Cāncĕr, crī & ĕrĭs. m. *Cancer, one of the signs of the Zodiac.* Cāncrī cūm sīgnă rŭbēscūnt. O. Phr.—Cāncrī tōrrĭdŭs īgnĭs. Cāncēr sōlĕ pĕrūstŭs. Brāchĭă cūrvāns. Clārō cōllūcēns lūmĭnĕ. Ōctĭpĕdīs sērpēntĭă brāchĭă Cāncrī.

Cănīcŭlă, æ. f. *The Dog-star.* Sīccās Cănīcŭlă mēnsēs. Pers. Syn.—Cănĭs, Sīrĭŭs. Phr.—Aēstīvī Cănĭs stēllă. Īcărĭūm sīdŭs. Sīrĭŭs ārdŏr. Aēstĭfĕr Cănĭs. Mălĕsānă Cănīcŭlă. Ătrōx hōră Cănīcŭlæ. Cănīcŭlă tārdĕt.

Cānnæ, ārūm. f. *Cannæ, a town in Apulia, noted for the defeat of the Romans by Hannibal.* Phr.—Īnsīgnēs Rōmānō sānguĭnĕ Cānnæ. Ēt Trĕbĭām sævō gĕmĭnāssēnt fūnĕrĕ Cānnæ. Lĭbўcā sūccēnsæ lāmpădĕ. Cānnās cĕlĕbrēs Vārrōnĕ fŭgātō.

Căpĭtōlĭūm, ĭī. n. *The Capitol of Rome.* Stābāt prō tēmplo ēt Căpĭtōlĭă cēlsă tĕnēbăt. V. Phr.—Ārx, sēdēs Tārpēĭă. Jūlĭă, tārpēĭă tēmplă. Aēdēs sācră Jŏvī. Tārpēĭī tēmplă Tŏnāntĭs. Căpĭtōli īmmōbĭlĕ sāxūm.

Căprĭcōrnŭs, ī. m. *Capricorn, one of the signs of the Zodiac.* Hæc ŭbī trānsĭĕrīnt, Căprĭcōrnō, Phœbĕ, rĕlīctō. O. Syn.—Aēgŏcĕrōs, Căpĕr. Phr.—Căprĭcōrnī sīdŭs. Aēthĕrĭs hīrcŭs. Cōrnĭfĕr hīrcŭs. Cōrnŭă Căprī. Pōrtĭtŏr Hēllēs. Cōrnĭbŭs ārmātŭs. Caūdā cōrnūquĕ mĭnāx. Tўrānnŭs Hēspĕrĭæ Căprĭcōrnŭs ūndæ. Gĕlĭdūm dē pēctŏrĕ frīgŭs ănhēlāns. Cōrpŏrĕ sēmĭfĕrō Căprĭcōrnŭs.

Căpŭă, æ. f. *Capua, a city of Campania.* Tālēm dīvĕs ărāt Căpŭa ēt vīcīnă Vĕsēvō Ōră jŭgō. V. Phr.—Āltĕră Rōmă. Mœnĭă Dārdănĭī Cāmpānă cŏlōnī.

Cārthāgĭnĭēnsēs, ĭūm. m. *The Carthaginians.* Hōstēm quī fĕrĭēt, mĭhi ĕrīt Cārthāgĭnĭēnsēs. Enn. Syn.—Pœnī, Pūnĭcī, Sīdŏnĭī, Tўrĭī, Ăgēnŏrĕī Ăgēnŏrĭdæ. Phr.—Cārthāgĭnĕ nātī. Tўrĭī cŏlōnī. Gēns Pūnĭcă.

Cārthāgŏ, ĭnĭs. f. *Carthage, city in Africa.* Sūrgēntēmquĕ nŏvæ Cārthāgĭnĭs ārcēm. V. Syn.—Bўrsă. Phr.—Ūrbs Ăgēnŏrĭs, Pūnĭcă, Tўrĭă. Tўrĭæ ārcēs. Tўrĭīs hăbĭtātă cŏlōnīs. Aēmŭlă Rōmæ. Tūrrītă cēlsă fĭgūrā. Dīvĕs ŏpūm.

Cāssāndră, æ. f. *Cassandra, daughter of Priam.* Sōlă mĭhī tālēs cāsūs Cāssāndră cănēbăt. V. Syn.—Phœbās. Phr.—Prĭămēĭă vīrgŏ, vātēs. Āntīstĭtă Phœbī. Fātīs ăpĕrīt Cāssāndră fŭtūrīs. Nōn ūnquām crēdĭtă.

Cāstălĭă, æ. f. *Castalia, a famous fountain.* Pōcŭlă Cāstălĭă plēnă mĭnīstrăt ăquā. O. Phr.—Cāstălĭs ăquă. Ăquæ Cāstălĭæ. Fōntĭs dōctī lўmphă. Cāstălĭī fōns Āŏnĭŭs.

Cāstŏr, ŏrĭs. m. *Castor, the brother of Pollux.* Cāstōr gaūdēt ĕquīs, ōvō prōgnātūs ĕōdēm. H. Syn.—Tȳndărĭdēs. Phr.—Lēdæ gĕnŭs. Lēdā sătŭs. Pōllūx āltĕr.

Cătŏ, ōnĭs. m. *Cato, a celebrated Roman.* Măctĕ Vīrtūte ēsto, īnquīt, sēntēntĭă dīă Cătōnĭs. H. Phr.—Mājōr Cārthāgĭnĭs hōstĭs. Vērbă sĕvēră Cătōnĭs.

Caūcăsŭs, ī. m. *The Caucasus mountains.* Dūrīs gĕnŭīt tē caūtĭbūs hōrrēns Caūcăsŭs. H. Phr.—Caūcăsĕī mōntēs, fāstīgĭă mōntĭs. Caūcăsĭæ rūpēs. Caūcăsĭŭs vērtēx. Jŭgă Caūcăsĭă.

Cēntaūrī, ōrūm. m. *The Centaurs.* Cēntaūri īn fŏrĭbūs stăbŭlānt, Scȳllæquĕ bĭfōrmēs. V. Syn.—Īxīŏnĭdæ, nūbĭgĕnæ, bĭmēmbrēs. Phr.—Īxīŏnĕ nātī.

Cērbĕrŭs & Cērbĕrŏs, ī. m. *Cerberus, the dog who guarded the gate of the Lower World.* Tĕnŭītque ĭnhĭāns trĭă Cērbĕrŭs ōră. V. Phr.—Cănĭs Mĕdūsæŭs, Stȳgĭŭs, Tārtărĕŭs, tērgĕmĭnŭs. Bēllŭă cēntĭcēps. Cūstōs Tārtărĕŭs. Īmmānīs jānĭtŏr aūlæ. Rēgnūm cănĭs īnquĭētī. Jānĭtŏr Ōrcī.

Cĕrēs, ĕrĭs. f. *Ceres, the goddess of agriculture.* Flāvă Cĕrēs āltō nēquīcquām spēctăt Ŏlȳmpō. V. Phr.—Mātĕr Ĕleūsīnă, Ĕleūsĭs. Dĕă frūgĭfĕră. Frūgūm gĕnĭtrīx. Frūgūm mītīssĭmă mātĕr. Ālmă părēns. Dīvă pōtēns frūgūm. Flāvă cŏmās. Nūtrīt rūră Cĕrēs.

Chărĭtĕs, ūm. f. *The Graces.* Prōtĭnŭs ārrĭpĭūnt Chărĭtēs, nēctūntquĕ cŏrōnās. O. Syn.—Grātĭæ. Phr.—Sŏrōrēs Īdălĭæ. Chărĭtūm chŏrŭs. Trĭplĭcī nēxū jŭgātæ. Vĕnĕrĭs cŏmĭtēs.

Chărōn, ōnĭs. m. *Charon, the ferryman of the Lower World.* Pōrtĭtŏr īllĕ Chărōn; hī quōs vĕhĭt ūndă sĕpūltī. V. Syn.—Pōrthmeūs. Phr.—Pōrtĭtŏr Ōrcī, ūmbrārūm. Stȳgĭŭs sĕnēx. Īnfērnæ nāvĭtă tūrpĭs ăquæ. Stȳgĭæ rēmĭgātŏr ūndæ.

Chărȳbdĭs, ĭs. f. *Charybdis, a famous whirlpool off Sicily.* Īncĭdĭt īn Scȳllām cŭpĭēns vītārĕ Chărȳbdĭn. O. Phr.—Scȳllæ ādvērsă. Rătĭbŭs ĭnĭmīcă. Vŏrāgŏ Chărȳbdĭs.

Chĭmæră, æ. f. *The Chimæra, a fabulous monster.* Prīmă lĕō, pōstrēmă drăcō, mĕdĭa īpsă Chĭmæră. Lr. Phr.—Mōnstrūm flāmmĭvŏmūm. Flāmmīs ārmăt. Flāmmās ōrĕ vŏmēns. Flāmmām spīrāntēs ōrĕ Chĭmæræ. Caūdām sērpēntĭs hăbēbăt.

Chĭŏs, ĭī. f. *Chios, an island in the Aegean.* Rōmæ laūdātūr Sămŏs ēt Chĭŏs ēt Rhŏdŏs ābsēns. H. Phr.—Ēt quās Chĭŏs āspĕrăt ūndās. Dōctæ psāllĕrĕ Chīæ. Chīō sōlvĭtĕ vīnclă cădō.

Chīrōn, ōnĭs. m. *Chiron, one of the Centaurs.* Syn.—Phīllȳrĭdēs. Phr.—Sĕnēx bĭfōrmĭs. Ārtĭs mĕdĭcæ pĕrītŭs. Ārmātŭs ārcū. Ăchīllĭs dōctŏr.

Chrīstĭānī, ōrūm. m. *Christians.* Syn.—Chrīstĭădæ, Chrīstĭcŏlæ. Phr.—Chrīstī cūltōrēs. Gĕnŭs ēlēctūm. Gēns Chrīstō săcră. Dīlēctă Dĕō. Dēdĭtă Chrīstō. Dĭcātă Chrīstō pēctŏră. Chrīstī præcēptă sĕcūtī. Gēns ā Chrīstō quæ dŭcĕ nōmĕn hăbĕt. Chrīstī dē nōmĭnĕ dĭctī. Āgmĭnă pĭōrūm.

Chrīstŭs, ī. m. *Jesus Christ, the Son of God.* Syn.—Vērbūm, Rĕdēmptŏr, Jēsŭs, Sālvātŏr, Dŏmĭnŭs, Dĕŭs. Phr.—Chrīstĕ pŏtēns rērūm rĕdĕūntĭs cōndĭtŏr ævī. Vērbūm ĭnēnārrābĭlĕ. Aētērnī Săpĭēntĭă Pātrĭs. Vōx sūmmī Dĕī. Vēră Dĕī sŏbŏlēs. Vīrgĭnĭs īntāctæ prōlēs. Spēs cērtīssĭmă tērræ.

Cĭcĕrŏ, ōnĭs. m. *Cicero, the great Roman orator.* Rōmă pătrēm pătrĭæ, Cĭcĕrōnēm lībĕră dīxĭt. J. Syn.—Tūllĭŭs. Phr.—Rōmānæ glōrĭă līnguæ. Rōmānī fŏrī glōrĭă, lūx, lūmĕn, splēndŏr. Rōmānī fāmă dĕcūsquĕ fŏrī. Ēlŏquĭō pōllēns. Ēlŏquĭī fūlmĕn. Lătĭæ fācūndĭă līnguæ. Dīsērtīssĭmŭs Rōmŭlī nĕpōtūm. Tē Cătĭlīnă mĭnāntēm Fūgĭt hĭāns.

Cīrcē, ēs. f. *Circe, a famous sorceress.* Cārmĭnĭbūs Cīrcē sŏcĭōs mūtāvĭt Ŭlȳssĭs. V. Syn.—Cīrcă, Tītānĭs. Phr.—Fīlĭă Pērsēs. Aēēă pŭēllă. Āptă hērbīs.

Clĕōpātră, æ. f. *Cleopatra, a famous queen of Egypt.* Ēxpūgnārĕ sĕnēm pŏtŭĭt Clĕōpātră vĕnēnīs. L. Phr.—Aēgȳptĭă cōnjūx. Phărĭă cōnjūx. Blāndă rēgīnă.

Clȳtēmnēstră, æ. f. *Clytemnestra, the wife of Agamemnon.* Clȳtēmnēstrām nūllūs nōn vīcŭs hăbēbĭt. J. Syn.—Tȳndărĭs. Phr.—Sævă Ăgămēmnŏnĭs ūxŏr. Lēdā sătă.

Cōnstāntīnŏpŏlĭs, ĭs. f. *Constantinople.* Syn.—Bȳzāntĭūm. Phr.—Ūrbs Cōnstāntīnī dē nōmĭnĕ dĭctă. Āltĕră Rōmă. Bȳzāntĭă lĭttŏră. Bȳzāntī ārcēs.

Cŏrīnthŭs & ŏs, ī. f. *Corinth, city of Greece.* Nōn cuīvīs hŏmĭnī cōntīngĭt ădīrĕ Cŏrīnthūm. H. Syn.—Ĕphȳrē. Phr.—Ārcēs Ĕphȳrēæ, Cŏrīnthĭăcæ. Ĕphȳrēă mœnĭă. Nōbĭlĭs ærĕ Cŏrīnthŭs. Īsthmŭs Cŏrīnthĭŭs.

Crāssŭs, ī. m. *Crassus, triumvir with Cæsar and Pompey.* Phr.—Trādĭt ŏpēs Crāssī dīvĭtĭs ārcă pŏtēns. Dīvĭtĭīs pŏtēns. Cæsărĭs æmŭlŭs. Ūmbrāque ērrārēt Crāssŭs ĭnūltă.

Crētă, æ. f. *Crete, an island in the Mediterranean.* Crētă Jŏvīs māgnī mĕdĭō jăcēt īnsŭlă pōntō. V. Phr.—Mīnōĭă tēllūs. Ārvă Mīnōĭă, Gnōssĭă. Cēntūm nōbĭlĭs ūrbĭbŭs. Ūbērrĭmă rēgnă. Trōjæ cūnābŭlă gēntĭs. Crētă pŏtēns ŏpĭbŭs.

Crœsŭs, ī. m. *Croesus, celebrated for his riches.* Phr.—Dīvĭtĭs ŏpŭlēntĭă Crœsī. Māgnī pătrĭmōnĭă Crœsī. Quīd Crœsī rēgĭă Sārdĭs.

Cȳbĕlē, ēs. f. *Cybele, mother of the gods.* Vērtĭcĕ tūrrĭgĕrō jūxtā dĕā Māgnă Cȳbēlē. Prop. Syn.—Ōps, Rhĕā, Vēstă, Dīndȳmĕnē, Mātĕr. Phr.—Mātĕr Bĕrĕcȳnthĭă. Dĕūm gĕnĭtrīx. Māgnă mātĕr. Tūrrĭgĕrā căpŭt ēxōrnātă cŏrōnā.

Cȳclădĕs, ūm. f. *Cyclades, islands in the Aegean.* Hīnc ădĭt Aēgēūm quō Cȳclădăs āspĭcĭt ōmnēs. O. Phr.—Spārsāsquĕ pĕr æquŏr Cȳclădăs. Frāngūnt ŭbĭ sāxă prŏcēllæ. Īntērfūsă nĭtēntēs Vītēs æquŏră Cȳclădăs.

Cȳclōpĕs, ūm. m. *Cyclops.* Īmmĕmŏrēs sŏcĭī vāstō Cȳclōpĭs ĭn āntrō Dēsĕrŭērĕ. V. Phr.—Aētnæī frātrēs. Vūlcānī cŏmĭtēs. Cœlō căpĭta āltă fĕrēntēs. Vāstō Cȳclōpēs ĭn āntrō.

Cȳprŭs & Cȳprŏs, ī. f. *Cyprus, an island in the Aegean.* Ō quæ bĕātām Dīvă tĕnēs Cȳprūm. H. Phr.—Aēquŏrĕīs ūndīs cīrcūmflŭă Cȳprŭs. Săcră Vĕnĕrī. Vĕnĕrĭs tēllūs pūlchērrĭmă.

Cȳrŭs, ī. m. *Cyrus, king of the Persians.* Phr.—Āsĭæ dŏmĭtŏr. Pērsārūm dĕcŭs, rōbŭr.

D

Dædălŭs, ī. m. *Dædalus, a famous artisan.* Dædălŭs īpsĕ dŏlōs tēcti āmbāgēsquĕ rĕsōlvĭt. V. Phr.—Gōrtȳnĭŭs ālĭgĕr. Lăbȳrīnthī cōndĭtŏr. Aēdĭs cōndĭtŏr. Ēxpērtūs văcŭūm Dædălŭs āĕră Pēnnīs nōn hŏmĭnī dătīs. Vēlōrūm pāndĭdĭt ālīs. Făbrūmquĕ vŏlāntēm.

Dæmōn, ŏnĭs. m. *Devil, the Evil Spirit.* Syn.—Dæmŏnĭūm, căcŏdæmōn, Sătān, Sătănās, dĭăbŏlŭs. Phr.—Tȳrānnŭs īnfērnŭs. Tārtărĕŭs hōstĭs. Īnvēntōr scĕlĕrūm. Hōrtātōr scĕlĕrūm. Hūmānī nōmĭnĭs hōstĭs. Mĭsĕræ dēcēptōr sūbdŏlŭs Ēvæ. Hōstĭs nōctĭpŏtēns.

Dănăē, ēs. f. *Danae, mother of Perseus.* Dīcĭtŭr ūrbēm Ācrĭsĭōnēĭs Dănăē fūndāssĕ cŏlōnīs. V. Syn.—Ācrĭsĭŏnē. Phr.—Pērseī gĕnĭtrīx, mātĕr, părēns. Făcĭē cōnspĭcŭă. Aūrō dēlūsă. Fūlvī dēcēptă cŭpīdĭnĕ nīmbī.

Dănăĭdĕs, ūm. f. *The Danaœ, daughters of Danaus.* Syn.—Bēlĭdĕs, Bēlĭădĕs. Phr.—Dănăī prōlēs. Scĕlēstæ sŏrōrēs. Crŭēntă tūrbă sŏrōrūm.

Dănĭēl, ēlĭs. m. *Daniel, the great Hebrew prophet.* Phr.—Fātĭdĭcŭs jŭvĕnĭs. Hĕbræūmquĕ dĕcŭs. Fātī cōnscĭŭs ārcānī. Ōbjēcto īmpāstī pārsērĕ lĕōnēs.

Dānŭbĭŭs, ĭī. m. *River Danube.* Syn.—Īstĕr. Phr.—Ŏpācŭs vītĭbŭs. Tăcĭtās prætērmĕăt īngēns, Dānŭbĭās rīpās. Māgnās āllŭĭt ūrbēs.

Dāphnē, ēs. f. *Daphne.* Syn.—Fīlĭă Pēnē (*or*) Pēnēŏs. Phr.—Pēnēĭă nȳmphă. Phœbēĭă vīrgŏ.

Dāphnĭs, ĭdĭs. m. *Daphnis, inventor of bucolic poetry.* Dāphnĭ, quĭd āntīquōs sīgnōrūm rēspĭcĭs ōrtūs? V. Phr.—Mĕă cārmĭnă dūcĭtĕ Dāphnīm. Quēm nȳmphæ pēllĭcĭs īră Cōntŭlĭt īn sāxūm.

Dāvīd, ĭdĭs. m. *David, king of Judea.* Syn.—Jēssīdēs, Jēssĭădēs. Phr.—Rēx ātquĕ prŏphētă. Jēssēĭă prōlēs. Īsăcĭŭs vātēs. Rēx vātēsquĕ sĭmŭl. Cĭthărāquĕ dĕcōrŭs.

Dēĭphŏbē, ēs. f. *Deiphobe, priestess of Apollo.* Dēĭphŏbē Glaūcī, fātūr quæ tālĭă rēgī. V. Phr.—Vātēs Cūmæă. Phœbī lōngævă săcērdōs. Fīlĭă Glaūcī. Cūmæă Sĭbȳllă. Aēnēæ dōctă cŏmēs.

Dēlŏs, ī. (Dēlŭs) f. *Delos, an island in the Aegean.* Syn.—Ōrtȳgĭă. Phr.—Ēt gēntĭbŭs hōspĭtă Dēlŏs. Clărĭō Dēlŏs ămātă dĕō. Quām vīx ērrātĭcă Dēlŏs.

Dēlphī, ōrūm. m. *Delphi, celebrated for the oracle of Apollo.* Vēl Bācchō Thēbās vĕl Ăpōllĭnĕ Dēlphōs Īnsīgnēs. H. Phr.—Ūrbs Ăpōllĭnĕă. Dēlphĭcă tēllūs, sēdēs. Ōrācŭlă Phœbī. Dēlphĭcă Phœbī pĕnĕtrālĭă.

Dēmōsthĕnēs, ĭs. m. *Demosthenes, the Athenian orator.* Pērsĕquăr aūt stŭdĭūm līnguæ, Dēmōsthĕnĭs ārmă. Prop. Phr.—Dēmōsthĕnĭs ōră dĭsērtī. Ēlŏquĭō pŏtēns. Grāndī vōcĕ tŏnāns. Grāiæ fācūndĭă līnguæ. Tērrōr clādēsquĕ Phĭlīppī.

Deūcălĭōn, ōnĭs. m. *Deucalion, son of Prometheus.* Ēt pōst āntīquās Deūcălĭōnĭs ăquās. Prop. Syn.—Prŏmēthīdēs. Phr.—Īăpĕtī nĕpōs. Hūmānī gĕnĕrĭs rĕpărātŏr. Ămāntĭŏr æquī.

Dĭānă, æ. f. *Diana, the goddess of the chase.* Quæquĕ cŏlūnt Scȳthĭcæ stāgnūm nĕmŏrālĕ Dĭānæ. O. Syn.—Lātōĭs, Lātōnĭgĕnă, Lātōnĭă, Lūnă, Lūcīnă, Dēlĭă, Cȳnthĭă. Phr.—Phœbī sŏrŏr. Lātōnĭă vīrgŏ, pŭēllă. Vīrgŏ pŏtēns nĕmŏrūm. Nĕmŏrūm cūltrīx. Nȳmphārūm cŏmĭtātă chŏrō. Vēnātrīx dĕă. Vīrgŏ phărĕtrātă. Āstrōrūm dĕcŭs. Cāstă Dĭānă.

Dīdō, ōnĭs & ūs. f. *Dido, queen of Carthage.* Īpsă sŭā Dīdō cōncĭdĭt ūsă mănū. O. Syn.—Ĕlīsă, Phœnīssă. Phr.—Sīchæĭă cōnjūx. Sīdŏnĭă rēgīnă. Tȳrĭām quæ cōndĭdĭt ūrbēm. Phrȳgĭō mălĕ nūptă vĭrō. Īnfēlīx Dīdō.

Dĭŏgĕnēs, ĭs. m. *Diogenes.* Syn.—Cȳnĭcŭs. Phr.—Ănĭmō fīxūs sēd mōbĭlĭs ædĕ.

Dĭŏmēdēs, ī. m. *Diomede.* Vĕnŭs ōdĕrĭt ōmnēs Sūb Dĭŏmēdĕ vĭrōs. O. Syn.—Oēnīdēs, Tȳdīdēs. Phr.—Cālȳdōnĭŭs dūx, rēx, hērōs. Cŏmēs fāllācĭs Ŭlȳsseī. Tȳdīdēn Sŭpĕrīs părēm.

Dōdōnă, æ. (Dōdōnē, ēs). f. *Dodona, city in Epirus, famous for its oracles.* Phr.—Vīctūm Dōdōnă nĕgārĕt. Sīlvăquĕ Dōdōnēs.

Drȳădēs, ūm. f. *Dryads, nymphs of the woods.* Īntĕrĕā Drȳădūm sīlvās sāltūsquĕ sĕquāmŭr. V. Syn.—Hămădrȳădēs, Năpææ. Phr.—Drȳădēs pŭēllæ. Nĕmŏrūm dĕæ. Nȳmphæ sīlvĭcŏlæ.

E

Ēchō, ūs. f. *Echo, a nymph.* Nēc prĭŏr īpsă lŏquī dĭdĭcīt rĕsŏnābĭlĭs Ēchō. O. Phr.—Vōcālĭs nȳmphă. Quæ Dīvă căvōs cŏlīt rĕcēssūs.

Ēlīās, æ. m. *Elias, the prophet.* Phr.—Nūmĭnĕ plēnŭs Ēlīās. Quī vīvĭt ădhūc. Quēm cōrvī quōndām pāvērĕ mĭnīstrī. Flāmmĭfĕro īnvēctūs cūrrū. Trānsvēctŭs ăd æthĕră. Tūrbĭnĕ rāptŭs.

Ēlȳsĭūm, ĭī. n. & Ēlȳsĭī, ōrūm. m. *The Elysian fields.* Tū cŏlĭs Ēlȳsĭōs nĕmŏrīsque hăbĭtātŏr ămœnī. M. Phr.—Ēlȳsĭī cāmpī, lūcī. Dŏmūs plăcĭdæ. Ēlȳsĭă sēdēs, vāllĭs. Ēlȳsĭŭs ăgĕr. Dīscrētæ pĭōrūm sēdēs. Lætă nĕmŏrĭs Ēlȳsĭī lŏcă. Sēdēsquĕ bĕātæ. Cāmpōquĕ pĭōrūm.

Ēndȳmĭōn, ōnĭs. m. *Endymion, shepherd in Thessaly.* Phr.—Lātmĭŭs hērōs. Lātmĭŭs vēnātŏr.

Ēnnĭŭs, ĭī. m. *Ennius, first Roman epic poet.* Ūtquĕ sŭō Mārtēm cĕcĭnīt grăvĭs Ēnnĭŭs ōrĕ. O. Phr.—Quēm Rŭdĭæ gĕnŭērĕ. Ārtĕ cărēns. Īngĕnĭō māxĭmŭs, ārtĕ rŭdĭs. Ēnnĭŭs īpsĕ pătĕr.

Ĕnōch & Ĕnōs, indecl. & Ĕnōchŭs, ī. m. *Enoch, one of the Patriarchs of Israel.* Syn.—Jārīdēs. Phr.—Jārēdĭcă prōlēs. Ăd æthĕrĕās rāptūs sēdēs. Pōllēns vīrtūtĭbŭs Ĕnōch.

Ĕpĭcūrŭs, ī. m. *Epicurus, the philosopher.* Quēm rīdērĕ vōlēs Ĕpĭcūrī dē grĕgĕ pōrcūm. H. Phr.—Gārgētĭcŭs sĕnĭŏr. Cĕcrŏpĭŭs sĕnēx. Ĕpĭcūrī sōmnĭă, mūndōs.

Ĕrĕbŭs, ī. m. *Erebus, the Infernal regions.* Syn.—Ăvērnŭs, Ōrcŭs, Stȳx, Tārtărŭs. Phr.—Īmās Ĕrĕbī dēscēndĭt ăd ūmbrās.

Ērĭdănŭs, ī. m. *The river Eridanus, now the Po.* Plūrĭmŭs Ērĭdănī pēr sīlvām vōlvĭtŭr āmnĭs. V. Syn.—Pădŭs. Phr.—Flŭvĭōrūm rēx, prīncēps. Pătĕr īpsĕ sŭpērbŭs ăquārūm Aūsŏnĭdūm. Īnsānō cōntōrquēns vōrtĭcĕ sīlvās.

Ĕrīnȳs, ȳŏs. f. *Erinnys, one of the Furies.* Hōrrĭfĭcāmque ŏcŭlīs ănĭmōque ōbjēcĭt Ĕrīnȳm. O. Phr.—Sătă, ēdĭtă nōctĕ. Tĕnĕbrārūm īncŏlă. Fĕră rēgnăt Ĕrīnȳs.

Ĕrĭphȳlă, æ. f. *Eriphyle, who betrayed her husband.* Mœstāmque Ĕrĭphȳlēn Crūdēlīs nātī mōnstrāntēm vūlnĕră cērnĭt. V. Phr.—Pērfĭdă cōnjūx. Quīd dōnīs Ĕrĭphȳla īnvēnĭt ămārīs.

Ētrūrĭă, æ. f. *Etruria, a province of Italy.* Ērgo ōmnīs fŭrĭīs sūrrēxĭt Ĕtrūrĭă jūstīs. V. Syn.—Tūscĭă. Phr.—Īnfēnsa Ētrūrĭă Tūrnō. Mæŏnĭdūm tēllūs.

Eūbœă, æ. f. *Euboea, an island near Greece.* Syn.—Ăbāntĭs. Phr.—Tēllūs Eūbŏĭs.

Eūmĕnĭdēs, ŭm. f. *The Furies.* Fērreīque Eūmĕnĭdūm thălămī. V. Syn.—Dīræ, Fŭrĭæ. Phr.—Īmpĭă dōnĕc Eūmĕnĭs ēx ŏcŭlīs fŭgĭt. *See Furiæ.*

Eūphrātēs, ĭs. m. *The river Euphrates.* Hīnc mŏvĕt Eūphrātēs, īllīnc Gērmānĭă bēllūm. V. Phr.—Sĕcāns lēni āgmĭnĕ rūră. Āgrōs ūbĕrĭbūs fēcūndăt ăquis. Căpūt răpĭdō tōllĭt cūrsū.

Eūrōpă, æ. f. *Europa, daughter of Agenor.* Syn.—Ăgēnŏrĭs, Sīdōnĭs. Phr.—Ăgēnŏrĕ nātă. Cādmī sŏrŏr. Āssўrĭă pŭēllă.

Eūrōpă, æ. f. *Europe.* Eūrōpae ātque Ăsĭæ fātīs cōncūrrĕrĭt ōrbĭs. V. Phr.—Rēgnă Eūrōpæă. Eūrōpææ ōræ. Māgnōrūm gĕnĭtrīx Eūrōpă vĭrōrūm. Frūgum āltrīx, vīnīquĕ fĕrāx, fēcūndă vĭrōrūm.

Eūrŭs, ī. m. *Eurus, the East wind (deified).* Eūrŭs ăd Aūrōrām Năbăthæăquĕ rēgnă rĕcēssĭt. O. Phr.—Lætŭs Ĕōīs Eūrŭs ĕquīs. Īnsībĭlăt Eūrŭs. Mĭnātūr flūctĭbŭs Eūrŭs. Nūbĭfĕr Eūrŭs. Naūfrăgĭūm spārgēns. Vŏlŭcrīquĕ cĭtātĭŏr Eūrō. Vērīs cŏmĭtēs. Quæ mărĕ tēmpĕrānt.

Eūrўdĭcē, ēs. f. *Eurydice, wife of Orpheus.* Eūrўdĭcēn tōtō rĕfĕrēbānt flūmĭnĕ rīpæ. V. Phr.—Ōrpheī cōnjūx. Quām Ōrpheūs rĕvŏcāvĭt ăb Ōrcō.

Ēvă, æ. f. *Eve, the first woman.* Phr.—Crēdŭlă cōnjūx. Quām sērpēns prōdĭdĭt. Mātĕr dēcēptă. Cāptă vĕnēnīs. Mŭlĭēr mălĕ crēdŭlă.

Ēvāndĕr, drī. m. *Evander, king of Palanteum.* Ēxsŭl ăb Ārcădĭā Lătĭōs Ēvāndĕr ĭn āgrōs Vĕnĕrăt. Phr.—Dūx Ārcădĭŭs. Pāllāntĭŭs hērōs. Rōmānæ cōndĭtŏr ārcĭs.

F

Făbĭŭs, ĭī. m. *Quintus Fabius Maximus, a great Roman general.* Phr.—Sōlērs cūnctāndī. Cūnctātōrquĕ sĕnēx. Īnvīctūsquĕ mŏrā. Făbĭæ laūs, Māxĭmĕ, gēntĭs. Ūnūs quī nōbīs cūnctāndō rēstĭtŭĭs rēm.

Fābrĭcĭŭs, ĭī. m. *Fabricius, the conqueror of Pyrrhus.* Phr.—Pēctŏră Fābrĭcĭī dōnīs īnvīctă. Pārvōquĕ pŏtēntēm Fābrĭcĭūm. Paūpĕrĭs ūmbră Fābrĭcĭī.

Faūnī, ōrūm. m. *The Fauns.* Syn.—Pānēs, Sătўrī, Sīlvānī. Phr.—Sīlvēstrĭă nūmĭnă. Plēbs sŭpĕrūm. Rūrĭcŏlæ, sīlvārūm nūmĭnă, Faūnī.

Fĕbrŭārĭŭs, ĭī. m. *The month of February.* Syn.—Fĕbrŭŭs. Phr.—Mēnsīs Nūmæ. Fērālī mēnsĕ. Mēnsīs făcĭūnt ān fēbrŭă nōmĕn.

Flōră, æ. f. *Flora, the goddess of flowers.* Syn.—Chlōrĭs, Zĕphȳrītĭs. Phr.—Zĕphȳrī pūlchĕrrĭmă cōnjūx. Īmpĕrĭūm quæ Dĕă flōrĭs hăbĕt. Cuī Zĕphȳrī dōtālēs trādĭdĭt hōrtōs. Flōrĭbŭs ārvă cŏrōnāns. Lūdīs cĕlĕbrātă jŏcōsīs. Vĭrĭdī rĕsĭdēns īn grāmĭnĕ. Cīnctă flōrĭbŭs. Vūltū vērsĭcŏlōrĕ dĕcēns.

Fōrtūnă, æ. f. *The goddess Fortune.* Nōs tē, Nōs făcĭmūs, Fōrtūnă, dĕām. J. Syn.—Sōrs, fātūm. Phr.—Dĕă Rhāmnūsĭă, Prænēstīnă. Dĕă cæcă, īmmītĭs, mōbĭlĭs. Fōrtūnæ nūmĕn, ārbĭtrĭūm. Cērtō stārĕ lŏcō nēscĭă. Fōrtūnă sævō lætă nĕgōtĭō. Trānsmūtăt īncērtōs hŏnōrēs. Fōrtūnă nūnc mĭhĭ nūnc ălĭī bĕnīgnă. Ūt cāsūs Fōrtūnă rŏtăt. Cāsĭbŭs ōmnĭă pōnūnt. Ō Fōrtūnă pŏtēns, quām vărĭābĭlĭs! Pāssĭbŭs āmbĭgŭīs ērrăt.

Fŭrĭæ, ārūm. f. *The Furies.* Nēscĭă sē Fŭrĭīs āccŭbŭīssĕ nŏvīs. Prop. Syn.—Dīræ, Eūmĕnĭdēs, Ĕrīnȳēs. Phr.—Nōctĕ sātæ. Nōctĭs ălūmnæ. Sŏrōrēs īnfērnæ. Dīræ ūltrīcēs. Ūltrīcēs scĕlĕrūm Dĕæ. Dītīsquĕ Mĭnīstræ. Tūrbă sĕvēră Eūmĕnĭdūm. Āgmĕn Īnfērnūm, ānguĭbŭs hōrrēndūm. Dīră Fŭrĭārūm cŏhōrs. Āgmĭnă sævă sŏrōrūm. Queīs dătūm scĕlĕră ūlcīscī. Fāctă vĭrūm mūlctānt vīndĭcĕ pœnā. Sōntēs fūnēstō sūpplĭcĭō crŭcĭānt. Trīstēs sūmūnt dē crīmĭnĕ pœnās. Flāmmĕă tōrquēns lūmĭnă. Cōgnōmĭnĕ Dīræ.

G

Găbrĭēl, ēlĭs. m. *The Archangel Gabriel.* Phr.—Dēscēndīt nūntĭŭs āltō Gābrīēl Pătrĭs ēx sŏlĭō. Āngĕlŭs ālĭgĕr. Āngĕlŭs hūmānæ sălūtĭs nūntĭŭs. Nūntĭŭs vīrgĭnĕī pārtūs. Fīdŭs sŭprēmī cōnsĭlĭī mĭnīstĕr. *See Angelus.*

Gādēs, ĭūm. f. *Cadiz, town in Spain.* Phr.—Gādītānă īnsŭlă. Gādītānæ ōræ. Tērrārūm fīnēs.

Gălătēă, æ. f. *Galatea, a nymph.* Cāndĭdĭōr fŏlĭō nĭvĕī, Gălătēă, lĭgūstrī. O. Syn.—Nērĕĭs, Nērīnē. Phr.—Cuī pătĕr ēst Nēreūs. Cāndĭdĭōr cȳcnīs. Hĕdĕrā fōrmōsĭōr ālbā. Păvōnĕ sŭpērbĭōr.

Gălīlæă, æ. f. *Galilee.* Phr.—Gălīlæă tēllūs, rĕgĭō, ōră. Gălīlæī fīnēs, āgrī. Gălīlæām īn rĕgĭōnēm. Gălīlæă pĕr ārvă. Pēr tērrās Gălīlææ.

Gāllī, ōrūm. m. *Gauls.* Cīnctă prĕmēbāntūr trŭcĭbūs Căpĭtōlĭă Gāllīs. O. Syn.—Cēltæ, Frāncī, Frāncĭgĕnæ. Phr.—Fĕrōcēs Gāllōrūm pŏpŭlī. Gāllōrūm īnvīctă gēns. Īn gȳrūm flēxīs gēns ōptĭmă frēnīs.

Gāllĭă, æ. f. *Gaul, France.* Phr.—Gāllĭcă tēllūs, rĕgĭō. Fēcūndă vĭvōrūm. Frūgum āltrīx vīnīquĕ fĕrāx. Dīvĕs ŏpūm stŭdĭīsque āspērrĭmă bēllī. Īnclȳtă fāmā.

Gāngēs, ĭs & ētĭs. m. *The river Ganges.* Gāngētīsquĕ rĕplēt pŏpŭlōs ātque Īndĭcă rēgnă. V. Phr.—Gāngētĭdēs ūndæ. Gāngētĭs flūmĭnă. Līttŏră Gāngĭs. Quēm bĭbĭt Īndĭă. Lātō spătĭāns flūmĭnĕ. Cīngĭtŭr Īndĭă Gāngē. Tĕpĭdūs Gāngēs.

Gănȳmēdēs, ĭs. m. *Ganymede, who became cup-bearer to Jupiter.* Ēt rāptī Gănȳmēdĭs hŏnōrēs. V. Syn.—Īlĭădēs. Phr.—Pŭĕr, jŭvĕnĭs Trōs, Phrȳgĭŭs. Pŭĕr rēgĭŭs Īdæ. Quī pōcŭlă tēmpĕrāt tŏnāntī. Rāptūsquĕ Jŏvī Gănȳmēdēs. Ūndĕ pŭēr rāptūs cœlō. Stāt Jŏvĭs ād cȳăthūm. Īnvītāquĕ Jŏvī nēctār Jūnōnĕ mĭnĭstrāt.

Gārgānŭs, ī. m. *Garganus, a mountain in Apulia.* Phr.—Mōns Āpŭlŭs. Gārgānī cūlmĭnă, jŭgă. Āpŭlă jŭgă. Āquĭlōnĭbŭs Quērcētă Gārgānī lăbōrānt.

Gĕmĭnī, ōrūm. m. *Gemini, one of the signs of the Zodiac.* Īn gĕmĭnōs ēx quō tēmpŏrĕ Phœbūs ădĭt. O. Phr.—Cūm Cāstŏrĕ Pōllūx. Lēdæ Sŏbŏlēs. Tȳndărĭdæ jŭvĕnēs. Clāră, Gĕmĭnī, sīgnă. Naūtīs sīdŭs ămīcūm. Frātrēs Hĕlĕnæ, lūcĭdă sīdĕră.

Gērmānī, ōrūm. m. *Germans.* Syn.—Ălĕmānnī, Teūtŏnī, Teūtŏnĕs, Sĭcāmbrī.

Gērmānĭă, æ. f. *Germany.* Phr.—Gērmānĭcă tēllūs. Gērmānæ ōræ. Gērmānĭă quōndām Īllă fĕrōx pŏpŭlīs.

Gērȳōn, ŏnĭs. m. *Geryon, a Spanish king.* Tērgĕmĭnī nĕcĕ Gērȳŏnĭs spŏlĭīsquĕ sŭpērbŭs. V. Phr.—Tēr āmplŭs. Fōrmă trĭcōrpŏrĭs ūmbræ. Pāstōrĭs Ĭbērī fōrmă trĭplēx. Pāstŏr trĭfōrmĭs līttŏrĭs Tārtēssī.

Gĭgāntĕs, ūm. m. *The Giants or Titans.* Syn.—Ānguĭpĕdēs, Tērrĭgĕnæ, Tītānĕs. Phr.—Tītānĭă prōlēs. Gĭgāntūm cŏhōrs. Tērrĭgĕnæ frātrēs. Tēllūrĭs jŭvĕnēs. Īmpĭă tūrbă Gĭgāntūm. Cœlō căpĭta āltă fĕrēntēs. Cœlō īrātă jŭvēntūs. Fīdēns jŭvēntūs hōrrĭdă brāchĭīs. Īngēntēs hŭmĕrōs. Āggrēssī rēscīndĕrĕ cœlūm, sŭpĕrīsquĕ Jŏvēm dētrūdĕrĕ rēgnīs.

Gŏlĭās, æ. m. *Goliath, the giant whom David overthrew.* Cf. Gigantes.

Gōrgōn, ŏnĭs. f. *Medusa, one of the Gorgons.* Syn.—Mĕdūsă, Phōrcĭs, Phōrcȳnĭs. *In the plural, the Gorgons.* Phr.—Phōrcī tērnă prŏpāgŏ. Sāxĭfĭcæ sŏrōrēs. Ānguĭfĕræ Phōrcī nātæ. Sērpēntĭgĕrī crūdēlĭă lūmĭnă mōnstrī.

Græcī, ōrūm. m. *The Greeks.* Quā rŭdĭs ēt Græcīs īntāctī cārmĭnĭs aūctŏr. H. Syn.—Grāiī, Grājŭgĕnæ, Āchæī, Ārgīvī, Dănăī, Pĕlāsgī. Phr.—Grāiūm, Grāiōrūm pŏpŭlī. Gēns Dănăūm, Āttĭcă, Ārgīvă, Pĕlāsgă. Gēns īnstrūctă dŏlīs. Fācūndūm gĕnŭs. Gēns ōptĭmă mōrūm, clāra īngĕnĭīs.

Græcĭă, æ. f. *Greece.* Ēt quīdquīd Græcĭă mēndāx Aūdĕt ĭn hīstŏrĭā. J. Syn.—Hēllăs, Ăchāĭă, Ăchāĭs. Phr.—Grāiă, Ăchīvă, Ăchāĭcă, Dōrĭcă, Pĕlāsgă tēllūs. Grāiōrūm rĕgĭō. Ārgīvæ jūgĕră tērræ. Ārgŏlĭcī cāmpī. Līttŭs Īnăchĭūm.

H

Hălȳs, ȳs. m. *Halys, a river in Asia Minor.* Phr.—Crœsō fātālĭs Hălȳs. Crœsŭs Hălȳn pĕnĕtrāns māgnām pērvērtĭt ŏpūm vīm. Crēbrō vōrtĭcĕ tōrtŭs. Tūrbĭdŭs Aēgēā nĭvĕ.

Hārpyīæ, ārūm. f. *The Harpies, a fabled class of monsters.* Āt sŭbĭtae hōrrĭfĭcō lāpsū dē mōntĭbŭs ādsūnt Hārpyīæ. V. Phr.—Fœdă ăvĭūm mōnstră. Tūrbă sŏnāns. Pōllŭīt ōrĕ dăpēs. Cōntāctūque ōmnĭă fœdānt. Pāllĭdă sēmpĕr Ōră fămē.

Hēbē, ēs. f. *Hebe, the goddess of youth and cup-bearer to Jove.* Hōc īllī dĕdĕrāt Jūnōnĭă mūnĕrĭs Hēbē. O. Syn.—Jŭvēntās, Jŭvēntă. Phr.—Jūnōnĭă vīrgŏ. Dīvă jŭvēntæ. Jŭvēntūtĭs præsĕs. Hērcŭlĭs ūxŏr.

Hēbrŭs, ī. m. *Hebrus, a river in Thrace.* Phr.—Aūrātīs tūrbĭdŭs ūndīs. Vŏlŭcrēmquĕ fŭgā prævērtĭtŭr Hēbrūm.

Hĕcătē, ēs. f. *Hecate, the goddess of night, dreams and the Lower World.* Tērgĕmĭnāmque Hĕcătēn, trĭă vīrgĭnĭs ōră Dĭānæ. V. Syn.—Lūnă, Dĭānă, Prōsērpĭnă, Trĭvĭă. Phr.—Dĕă, Dīvă trĭfōrmĭs. Dĭānă trĭplēx. Dĕă fērālĭs. Tērnīs vărĭātă fĭgūrīs. Măgĭcīs cōnscĭă cœptīs.

Hēctŏr, ŏrĭs. m. *Hector, son of Priam.* Tēr cīrcum Īlĭăcōs rāptāvĕrăt Hēctŏră mūrōs. V. Phr.—Trōĭŭs hērōs. Trōjæ dēfēnsŏr. Dănăūm tērrŏr. Lūx Dārdănĭæ. Spēs fīdīssĭmă Trōjæ. Rāptŭs Aēmŏnĭīs flēbĭlĭs Hēctŏr ĕquīs.

Hĕcŭbă, æ. f. *Hecuba, the wife of Priam, king of Troy.* Vīdi Hĕcŭbām, cēntūmquĕ nŭrūs, Prĭămūmquĕ. V. Syn.—Cīssæĭs, Dȳmāntĭs. Phr.—Prĭămēĭă cōnjūx, ūxŏr. Mātĕr Hēctŏrĭs. Tŏt īllă rĕgūm mātĕr.

Hĕlĕnă, æ & Hĕlĕnē, ēs. f. *Helen, wife of Menelaus.* Lēdēāmque Hĕlĕnām Trōjānūs vēxĭt ăd ārcēs. V. Syn.—Lăcænă, Lēdæă, Tȳndărĭs. Phr.—Bīs rāptă pēllēx. Părĭdĭs ădūltĕră cōnjūx. Trōjānī caūsă ēxcĭdĭī. Trōjae ēt pătrĭæ cōmmūnĭs Ĕrīnȳs. Lăcænă ădūltĕră. Māgnō Eūrōpae ātquĕ Ăsĭæ rĕpĕtēndă tŭmūltū.

Hĕlĕnŭs, ī. m. *Helenus, son of Priam.* Prīămĭdēn Hĕlĕnūm Grāiās rēgnārĕ pĕr ūrbēs. V. Phr.—Īntērprēs dīvūm. Quī nūmĭnă Phœbī sēnsĭt. Cōnjŭgĭī Pȳrrhī scēptrīsquĕ pŏtītŭs.

Hēlĭădĕs, ūm. f. *Heliades, the daughters of the sun.* Hēlĭădēs lūgēnt ēt mānĭă mōrtī Mūnĕră dānt lăcrĭmās. O. Syn.—Clўmĕnēĭdĕs. Phăĕthōntĭdĕs, Phăĕthōntĭădĕs. Phr.—Clўmĕnēĭă prōlēs. Frōndōsæ sŏrōrēs.

Hĕlĭcōn, ōnĭs. m. *Mount Helicon.* Phr.—Hĕlĭcōnĭŭs cōllĭs, mōns. Hĕlĭcōnĭă rūpēs. Ūmbrōsæ Hĕlĭcōnĭs ōræ. Hĕlĭcōnĭs sīlvă. Mōns sŏrōrūm. Hĕlĭcōnă vĭrēntēm.

Hēllēspōntŭs, ī. m. *The Hellespont.* Quæ pāssīm răpĭdō dīffūndĭtŭr Hēllēspōntō. *Cat.* Phr.—Hēllēspōntĭăcūm mărĕ. Hēllespōntĭăcă ōră. Pontŭs Hēllēs. Ăbȳdēnă ăquă. Pĕr āngūstās mălĕ vēctæ vīrgĭnĭs ūndās.

Hēlvĕtĭī, ōrūm. m. *The Helvetians, Swiss.* Phr.—Fĕră gēns ārmīs Hēlvĕtĭă. Āssuētī vīvĕrĕ pārvō.

Hērcŭlēs, ĭs. m. *Hercules.* Vīctōrēsque ōstēntăt ĕquōs sătŭs Hērcŭlĕ pūlchrō. V. Syn.—Ālcīdēs, Āmphĭtrȳōnĭădēs, Tīrȳnthĭŭs. Phr. —Ālcmēnæ sătŭs, sŏbŏlēs. Mōnstrōrūm dŏmĭtŏr. Stȳgĭī dŏmĭtŏr cănĭs. Jŏvĕ nātŭs. Phărĕtra ārmātūs spŏlĭīsquĕ lĕōnĭs. Hēspĕrĭdūm aŭrĕă pōmă sūrrĭpŭĭt. Fāctă Hērcŭlĕă. Nōn pŏtŭĭt Jūnō vīncĕrĕ, vīncĭt ămŏr.

Hērŏ, ūs. f. *Hero, beloved by Leander.* Sæpĕ pĕtēns Hērō jŭvĕnīs trānsnāvĕrăt ūndās. O. Syn.—Sēstĭăs. Phr.—Sēstă pŭēllă. Sĕdēt ānxĭă tūrrĕ sŭprēmā Sēstĭăs, īn spĕcŭlīs.

Hērōdēs, ĭs. m. *Herod, son of Antipater, king of Judæa.* Phr.— Īdūmæŭs rēx. Hĕbrææ fĕrŭs ārbĭtĕr aūlæ. Sævūs rēgnātŏr. Īnsōntēs pŭĕrōs fērro īmpĭŭs haūsĭt. Chrīstūm, quī mĕtŭēns pŭĕrūm tōt mīllĭă lētō Cōrpŏră dīmīsĭt. Vērmĭbŭs ēscă fŭĭt.

Hēsĭŏdŭs, ī. m. *Hesiod, Greek poet.* Phr.—Āscræŭs sĕnēx, pŏētă, vātēs. Vātēs Hĕlĭcōnĭŭs. Āgrĭcŏlæ mūsă sĕnĭs. Āscræī vĕtĕrĭs præcēptă pŏētæ.

Hēspĕrŭs, ī. m. *Hesperus, son of Aurora and Atlas, placed among the stars.* Ītĕ dŏmūm sătŭræ, vĕnĭt Hēspĕrŭs. V. Phr.—Nōctīs nūntĭŭs. Prīmās rĕfĕrēns tĕnĕbrās. Mŏdŏ lōtŭs ūndīs. Lūcĭfĕr īdēm. Ălĭōs prĕmĭt Hēspĕrŭs ignes.

Hĭbērnĭă, æ. f. *Ireland.* Syn.—H[illegible]ē, Jŭvērnă, Īĕrnē.

Hĭĕrōsŏlȳmă, ōrūm. n. *Jerusalem, city in Palestine.* Syn.—Hĭĕrūsălēm, Jērūsălēm, Sŏlȳmă (æ), Sĭōn. Phr.—Ūrbs Sŏlȳmōrūm. Ūrbs Dāvĭdĭcă. Ārx Sĭōnĭs. Jŭdææ dĕcŭs. Pīnguĭs Sŏlȳmæ pālmĕtă. Grātīssĭmă tēllūs.

Hīppŏlȳtŭs, ī. m. *Hippolytus, son of Theseus.* Hīc lătĕt Hīppŏlȳtūs lōrīs dīscērptŭs ĕquōrūm. O. Syn.—Thēsīdēs. Vīrbĭŭs. Phr.—Thēsēĭŭs hērōs. Vĭr Ămāzŏnĭŭs. Dīscērptŭs ĕquīs. Nĕpōs Aēthræ. Phædræ prīvīgnŭs.

Hīppŏmĕnēs, ĭs. m. *Hippomenes, who vanquished Atalanta.* Phr.—Prōlēs Nēptūnĭă. Mĕgărēĭŭs hērōs. Āŏnĭŭs jŭvĕnĭs.

Hīspānī, ōrūm. m. *Spaniards.* Syn.—Hēspĕrĭī, Ībērī, Bētĭcŏlæ, Bētĭgĕnæ, Cāntăbrī. Phr.—Hīspānă gēns, nātĭŏ. Gēns āspĕră bēllō. Pătĭēns lăbōrūm. Tŭmĭdō sŭpērbă fāstū. Gĕnŭs īntrāctābĭlĕ bēllō.

Hīspānĭă, æ. f. *Spain.* Hōrrĭdă vītānda ēst Hīspānĭă, Gāllĭcŭs āxĭs. J. Syn.—Hēspĕrĭă, Ībērĭă. Phr.—Hīspānă, Tārtēssĭă, Ībērĭcă tēllūs, ōră. Dīvĕs ăgrīs. Lātīs aūdāx Hīspānĭă tērrīs. Dīvĕs ĕquīs, frūgūm făcĭlīs, prĕtĭōsă mĕtāllīs.

Hŏmērŭs, ī. m. *Homer, the epic poet.* Quāndōquĕ bŏnūs dōrmītāt Hŏmērŭs. H. Syn.—Mæŏnĭdēs. Phr.—Mæŏnĭŭs, Smȳrnæŭs vātēs, sĕnēx. Cæcŭs vātēs. Cŏlŏphōnĭs ălūmnŭs. Cōndĭtŏr Īlĭădĭs. Quō nīl Græcĭă mājŭs hăbēt.

Hŏrātĭŭs, ĭī. m. *Horace, the lyric poet.* Sătŭr ēst, cūm dīcĭt Hŏrātĭŭs Ēvœ. J. Syn.—Flāccŭs. Phr.—Vātēs Vĕnŭsīnŭs. Aŭsŏnĭæ lȳræ dĕcŭs. Rōmānæ fĭdĭcēn lȳræ. Cūjŭs Āttĭcō lĕpōrĕ tīnctī sălēs. Dŭplĭcī rĕdĭmītŭs tēmpŏră laūrō.

Hȳăcīnthŭs, ī. m. *Hyacinth, the youth beloved by Apollo.* Nēc gĕnŭīssĕ pŭdēt Spārtēn Hȳăcīnthŏn, hŏnōrquĕ. O. Syn.—Āmȳclīdēs, Oēbălĭdēs. Phr.—Oēbălĭŭs pŭĕr, jŭvĕnĭs. Quēm dīscī pērcŭlĭt ērrŏr.

Hȳădĕs, ūm. f. *The Hyades, daughters of Atlas, changed into a constellation at their death.* Ārctūrūm, plŭvĭāsque Hȳădās, gĕmĭnōsquĕ Trĭōnēs. V. Syn.—Ātlāntĭdĕs, Plēĭădĕs, Plīădĕs. Phr.—Prōgĕnĭēs Ātlāntĭs. Nīmbōsăquĕ Taūrūm Dūcăt Hȳăs.

Hȳblă, æ. f. *Hybla, mountain in Sicily famous for honey.* Ēt cărĕāt dūlcī Trīnăcrĭs Hȳblă thȳmō. O. Phr.—Thȳmī fĕrāx. Vărĭīs pīctă cŏlōrĭbŭs. Thȳmō mĭhĭ dūlcĭŏr Hȳblæ. Quŏt ăpēs pāscūntŭr ĭn Hȳblā.

Hȳmēn, ĕnĭs. m. *Hymen, the god of marriage.* Vūlgŭs Hȳmēn, Hȳmĕnæĕ vŏcānt, fŭgĭt īllĕ vŏcāntēs. Prop. Syn.—Hȳmĕnæŭs. Phr.—Cōnjŭgĭī præsĕs. Cuī sūnt cōnnūbĭă cūræ. Quī făcĭbŭs lēgĭtĭmīs ădēst. Nĭvĕō [illegible] Lūtĕūm pĕdĕ sōccūm. Crŏcĕō vēlātŭs ămīctū. Hŏnēstŭ[illegible] Hȳmēn.

Hȳmēttŭs, ī. m. *Hymettus, a mountain in Attica, famous for its honey.* Vērtĭcĕ dē sūmmō sēmpēr flōrēntĭs Hȳmēttī. O. Phr.—Thȳmī fĕrāx. Mārmŏrĕ dīvĕs.

Hȳpsĭphĭlē & Hȳpsĭpy̆lē, ēs. f. *Hypsipile, queen of Lemnos, a friend of Jason.* Syn.—Lēmnĭăs, Thŏāntĭăs. Phr.—Clārō gĕnĕrātă Thŏāntĕ. Cōnjŭgĭō fraūdātă. Ā dŭcĕ Aēsŏnĭō rĕlīctă.

I

Ĭāsōn, ŏnĭs. m. *Jason, who went in search of the Golden Fleece.* Quēm nĭsĭ crūdēlēm nōn tāngĭt Ĭāsŏnĭs ǣtās? O. Syn.—Aēsŏnĭdēs, Crēthīdēs. Phr.—Aēsŏnĕ nātŭs. Dūx Aēsŏnĭŭs. Prīmǣquĕ rătīs, mōlītŏr Ĭāsōn. Aūrātǣ vēllĕrĕ dīvĕs ŏvīs. Prŏfŭgām quī Cōlchĭdă lūsĭt. Quī tŭlĭt aūrātǣ nōbĭlĕ vēllŭs ŏvĭs.

Īcărŭs, ī. m. *Icarus, son of Dædalus.* Dūm pĕtĭt īnfīrmīs nĭmĭūm sūblīmĭă pēnnīs Īcărŭs, Īcărĭīs nōmĭnă fēcĭt ăquīs. O. Phr.—Dǣdălĭŭs pŭĕr. Quī sē mălĕ crēdĭdĭt ālīs. Ēxūtūsvĕ pŭēr pēnnīs lābēntĭbŭs. Cērātīs ŏpĕ Dǣdălēā Nītĭtūr pēnnīs, vĭtrĕō dătūrŭs Nōmĭnă pōntō. Aēthĕrĭs āltă pĕtēns, ǣquŏrĭs īmă sŭbĭt. Īcărŭs aūdācī fōrtĭŭs ārtĕ vŏlăt. Pŭēr tĕmĕrārĭŭs.

Īdă, ǣ. f. *Ida, a mountain in Phrygia.* Clāssēm sūb Phrȳgĭǣ mōlīmūr mōntĭbŭs Īdǣ. V. Phr.—Mōns Īdǣŭs, Īlĭăcŭs. Phrȳgĭŭs. Āltrīx Īdă fĕrārūm. Īdǣūm nĕmŭs. Cĕlĕbērrĭmă fōntĭbŭs Īdă. Nĕmŭs Cy̆bĕlēs.

Īndī, ōrūm. m. *The people of India.* Ārmă Dĕūs Cǣsār dītēs mĕdĭtātŭr ăd Īndōs. O. Phr.—Īndōrūm pŏpŭlŭs. Īndī pŏpŭlī. Īndĭcă gēns. Ĕōǣ gēntēs. Ēxtrēmī cūltōrēs ōrbĭs Ĕōī. Pōsĭtīquĕ sŭb īgnĭbŭs Īndī Sīdĕrĕīs. Quōs Aūrōră sŭīs rūbră cŏlōrăt ăquīs.

Īndĭă, ǣ. f. *India.* Dĕcŏlŏr ēxtrēmō quā cīngĭtŭr Īndĭă Gāngĕ. O. Phr.—Īndă, Īndĭcă, Hy̆dāspǣă, Mēmnŏnĭă tērră, tēllūs, ōră. Ĕōīs trāctūs. Ōrbĭs Ĕōŭs. Ūltĭmă tērră. Tērrā ūltĭmō sūbmōtă mūndō. Dītī quǣ Gāngĕ rĭgātŭr Īndĭă. Quǣ lŏcă fābŭlōsŭs Lāmbĭt Hy̆dāspēs. Īndĭă mīttĭt ĕbŭr.

Īnfĕrī, ōrūm. m. *The Lower World, Hell, Hades.* Syn.—Īnfērnŭs, Īnfērnī, Īnfērnă, Ōrcŭs, Ăvērnŭs, Ăvērnă, Tārtărŭs, Tārtără, Cōcy̆tŭs, Sty̆x, Ĕrĕbŭs, Ăchĕrōn. Phr.—Īnfērnǣ sēdēs, dŏmŭs, pălūdēs, ūmbrǣ, tĕnĕbrǣ. Plūtōnĭă rēgnă. Ty̆rānnī rēgĭă cǣcă Dĕī. Rēgnă īnfērnī Jŏvĭs. Eūmĕnĭdūm sēdēs. Dīră Fŭrĭārūm lŏcă. Īmmānēs Ĕrĕbī hĭātŭs. Īmǣ sēdēs Ĕrĕbī. Cǣcă ōstĭă Dītĭs. Trīstēs sĭnĕ sōlĕ dŏmūs. Ūmbrārūm dŏmŭs. Sīlēntēs nōctĕ pērpĕtŭā dŏmūs. Lūcĕ cărēntĭă rēgnă. Aētērnǣ cālīgĭnĭs ūmbrǣ. Īmī rēgĭă mūndī. Ūmbrārūm cārcĕr. Īmpĭă rĕgĭŏ. Faūcēs grăveŏlēntĭs Ăvērnī. Vĭdŭātăquĕ lūmĭnĕ rēgnă.

Īnō, ūs. f. *Ino, daughter of Cadmus and Hermione.* Sīt Mēdēă fĕrōx īnvīctăquĕ, flēbĭlĭs Īnō. H. Syn.—Cādmēĭs, Leūcŏthĕă, Mātūtă. Phr.—Nūtrīx Bācchī. Ăthămāntĭă cōnjūx. Sĕmĕlēs sŏrŏr.

Īŏ, Īūs. f. *Io, daughter of Inachus.* Quæ tĭbĭ caūsă fŭgæ? quĭd, Īō, frĕtă lōngă pĕrērrās? Prop. Syn.—Īsĭs, Īnăchĭs, Phŏrōnĭs. Phr.—Īnăchĭă jŭvēncă. Ēx bŏvĕ fāctă dĕă.

Īphĭgĕnīă, æ. f. *Iphigenia, daughter of Agamemnon.* Prō quā māctāta ēst Īphĭgĕnīă mŏrā. Prop. Syn.—Īphĭănāssă, Mўcēnĭs. Phr.—Pĕlŏpēĭă vīrgŏ. Ānte ārām stĕtĭt Īphĭgĕnīă.

Īrĭs, ĭdĭs. f. *Iris, messenger of Juno.* Īrīm dē cœlō mīsĭt Sātūrnĭă Jūnŏ. V. Syn.—Thaūmāntĭs, Thaūmantĭăs. Phr.—Jūnōnĭă Vīrgŏ. Vărĭō dĕcŏrātă cŏlōrĕ. Vărĭīs dīstīnctă cŏlōrĭbŭs. Nūntĭă Jūnōnĭs. Īrĭ, dĕcūs cœlī. Sūccīnctām nūbĭbŭs Īrīm. Rŏsĕō Thaūmāntĭăs ōrĕ lŏcūta ēst. Aūt āctām nūbĭbŭs Īrīm. Īllă vĭām cĕlĕrāns pēr mīllĕ cŏlōrĭbŭs ārcūm.

Īsĭs, ĭdŏs. f. *Isis, an Egyptian deity.* Syn.—Īŏ, Īnăchĭs. Phr.—Nīlĭăcă, Phărĭă jŭvēncă. Mēmphītĭs vāccă. Līnĭgĕră jŭvēncă. Mărĕōtĭcăque ārvă Quæ cŏlĭs.

Ĭtălī, ōrūm. m. *The Italians.* Īngrŭĭt Aēnēās Ĭtălīs ēt prœlĭă mīscĕt. V. Syn.—Oēnŏtrĭī, Hēspĕrĭī, Lătĭī, Lătīnī. Phr.—Gēns Ĭtălūm. Ĭtălūm gĕnŭs. Ĭtălă gēns, nātĭŏ. Sātūrnĭă gēns. Pŏtēns Ītălā vīrtūtĕ prŏpāgŏ.

Ītălĭă, æ. f. *Italy.* Ītălĭām, fātō prŏfŭgūs, Lāvīnĭăquĕ vēnĭt Līttŏră. Syn.—Aūsŏnĭă, Oēnŏtrĭă, Hēspĕrĭă, Lătĭūm. Phr.—Tēllūs Ĭtălă, Aūsŏnĭă, Hēspĕrĭă, Sātūrnĭă. Aūsŏnĭī fīnēs. Sātūrnĭă rēgnă. Aūsŏnĭæ tēllūs. Rēgnūm Ītălĭæ, Rōmānăquĕ tēllūs. Fīnēs Ĭtălūm. Pŏtēns ārmīs ātque ūbĕrĕ glēbæ. Ītălĭām dīxīssĕ dŭcīs dē nōmĭnĕ gēntēm.

Īxīōn, ŏnĭs. m. *Ixion, father of the Centaurs.* Vōlvĭtŭr Īxīōn ēt sē sĕquĭtūrquĕ fŭgītquĕ. O. Phr.—Tōrtōsque Īxīŏnĭs ānguēs. Răpĭtūr vŏlŭcrī tōrtŭs Īxīōn rŏtā. Tăcĕānt Īxīŏnĭs ōrbēs. Răpĭdæ vīnctŭs ăb ōrbĕ rŏtæ.

J

Jānŭs, ī. m. *Janus, whose temple was open in time of war and closed in time of peace.* Tūm săcĕr āncĭpĭtī mīrāndŭs ĭmāgĭnĕ Jānŭs. O. Syn.—Clūsĭŭs, Pătūlcĭŭs, mātūtīnŭs. Phr.—Jānŭs pătĕr. Bĭcēps dĕŭs, nūmĕn. Dīvūm vĕtērrĭmŭs. Īmmēnsī rĕpărātŏr māxĭmŭs ævī. Jānīquĕ bĭfrōntĭs ĭmāgŏ. Cœlī Jānĭtŏr. Mātūtīnĕ pătĕr.

Jāsōn. *See Iason.*

Jĕrĕmĭăs & Jĕrēmĭās, ǣ. m. *Jeremias, one of the prophets of Israel.* Phr.—Cārmĭnĕ lūctĭfĭcō quām dēflēns Jĕrēmĭās. Vātēs pĭŭs, săcĕr. Prŏphētă īllăcrĭmāns, gĕmēns.

Jĕrūsălēm. *See Hierosolyma.*

Jēsŭs (Iēsŭs), ū. m. *Jesus Christ.* Syn.—Chrīstŭs, Dŏmĭnŭs, Rĕdēmptŏr. Phr.—Ālmŭs hŏmĭnūm sătŏr ātquĕ Rĕdēmptŏr. Hūmānī gĕnĕrĭs rĕpărātŏr. Cērtă sălūs. Auctŏr dūxquĕ sălūtĭs. Spēs mĭsĕrĭs. Sălūtĭs ŏrīgŏ. Mūndī mĕlĭōrĭs ŏrīgŏ. Nōstĕr ămŏr. Spērātūm pēr sæcŭlă. Nōmĕn ădōrāndūm. Quī crīmĭnă nōstră pĭāvĭt, ēlŭĭt āffīxŭs crŭcī. Rĕdĕūntĭs cōndĭtŏr ǣvī. Quēm tōtă cănūnt ōrācŭlă vātūm. Vēntūrŭs sūb cārnĕ Dĕŭs. Quēm sānctī cĕcĭnērĕ prŏphētæ.

Jŏānnēs, ĭs. m. *John the Baptist.* Syn.—Bāptīstă, Zāchărĭdēs. Phr. —Zāchărĭæ sŏbŏlēs. Sŏbŏlēs sānctōrūm sēră părēntūm. Præmĭă sāltātrīx pōscĭt fūnēbrĭă vīrgŏ Jŏānnīs căpŭt. Cūjŭs ĭn ādvēntu ēxsĭlŭĭt dē vēntrĕ Jŏānnēs.

Jōsēph. indecl. m. (1) *Joseph, son of Jacob.* Phr.—Īsăcĭdæ nātŭs. Frātrĭbŭs īnvīsŭs. Cāstă Jăcōbī sŏbŏlēs. (2) *Joseph, spouse of the Blessed Virgin.* Phr.—Spōnsŭs Mărĭæ. Cūstōs sŏcĭæ Vīrgĭnĭs ĭntĕgĕr. Rēgĭă prōgĕnĭēs. Vĕnĭēns Dāvīdĭs ŏrīgĭnĕ Jōsēph. Cānō crīnĕ vĕrēndūm Jōsēph. Mŏnĭtĭs cœlēstĭbŭs āctŭs.

Jōsŭă, ǣ. m. *Josua, one of the judges of Israel.* Syn.—Nūnnĭădēs. Phr.—Prŏpĭōrĕ nūmĭnĕ fīdēns. Cūjŭs ād vōcēm sōl ĭmmōtŭs dēclīvī trāmĭtĕ sīstĭt Cūrrŭs. Jōsŭă dīvīnōs ăgĭtāns sūb pēctŏrĕ sēnsūs. Stătŭās prōstrāvĭt Jōsŭă dīvūm.

Jūdǣă, ǣ. f. *Judæa.* Ēt dēdĭtă săcrĭs Īncērtī Jūdǣă dĕī. L. Syn.— Chănāān, Chănănǣă, Īdūmǣă, Pălēstīnă. Phr.—Īsăcĭdūm tēllūs. Rūră Pălēstīnæ. Jūdǣī trāctŭs rēgnī. Jōrdānĭs ăquĭs īrrĭgŭă.

Jūdǣī, ōrūm. m. *The Jews.* Pērsuādērĕ cŭpĭt; crēdāt Jūdǣŭs Ăpēllă, Nōn ĕgŏ. H. Syn.—Ābrămĭdæ, Hĕbrǣī, Īsăcĭdæ, Īsrăēlītæ, Īdūmǣī. Phr.—Jūdǣă, Jūdăĭcă, Hĕbrǣă gēns, prŏpāgŏ. Īsăcĭdūm gĕnŭs. Gĕnŭs ōrtum ā sānguĭnĕ Jūdæ. Gēns quōndām dīlēctă Dĕō. Plēbs īngrātă. Sōrtītī mĕtŭēntēm sābbăthă pātrēm.

Jūdās (Iūdās), ǣ. m. *Judas Iscariot.* Syn.—Īscărĭōtēs. Phr.—Prŏdĭtŏr Īscărĭōtēs. Fālsī sĭmŭlātŏr ămōrĭs. Hŏrtātŏr scĕlĕrīsque īnvēntŏr Iūdās.

Jūnŏ, ōnĭs. f. *Juno, daughter of Saturn and wife of Jupiter.* Cōnscĭă sīt Jūnō săcrĭs præfēctă mărītĭs. O. Syn.—Sātūrnĭă, Lūcīnă. Phr.—Jŏvĭs ūxŏr. Jŏvĭs ēt sŏrŏr ēt cōnjūx. Sŭī gērmānă mărītī. Nūptă sŏrōrquĕ Jŏvĭs. Dĕārūm prīncēps. Dĕūm rēgīnă. Māgnă dĕūm gĕnĭtrīx.

Jūpĭtĕr, Jŏvĭs. m. *Jupiter, the god of heaven and earth.* Jūpĭtĕr, hōspĭtĭbūs nām tē dărĕ jūră lŏquūntŭr. V. Syn.—Sātūrnĭŭs, Tŏnāns, Dĭēspĭtĕr, Pătĕr, Gĕnĭtŏr, dĕŭs. Phr.—Pătĕr ōmnĭpŏtēns. Dĕūm, dĕōrūm, dīvūm pătĕr, rēx, sătŏr, mŏdĕrātŏr. Ŏlȳmpī rēgnātŏr. Dīvūm pătĕr ātque hŏmĭnūm. Tōrquēt quī sīdĕră mūndī. Aēthĕrĭūs vīndēx. Răpĭdūs quī tŏnăt āltŭs ĕquīs. Cūnctă sŭpērcĭlĭō mŏvēns. Īllĕ pătēr, rēctōrquĕ dĕūm.

Jūstĭtĭă, æ. f. *The goddess Justice.* Ēxtrēmă pĕr īllōs Jūstĭtĭa ēxcēdēns tērrīs vēstīgĭă fēcĭt. V. Syn.—Āstrææă, Thĕmĭs. Phr.—Fāctă æquātō ēxāmĭnĕ pēndĭt, lībrăt. Jām rĕdĭt ēt vīrgŏ. Jūstĭtĭa, īnvĭŏlātă mălīs, plăcĭdīssĭmă vīrgŏ.

L

Lăcĕdæmōn, ŏnĭs. f. *Lacedæmon, famous city in Laconia.* Syn.—Spārtă, Spārtē. Phr.—Tūtĭūs ōbjēcĭt nūdām Lăcĕdæmŏnă bēllīs. Ūrbs āntīquă, Hērcŭlĕă. Īnclȳtă bēllō. Ūrbs īnclȳtă.

Lăcōnĕs, ūm. m. *Lacedæmonians.* Syn.—Lăcænī, Spārtānī, Lăcĕdæmŏnĭī.

Lāŏmĕdōn, ōntĭs. m. *Laomedon, father of Priam.* Īndĕ nŏvæ prīmūm mōlīrī mœnĭă Trōjæ Lāŏmĕdōntă vĭdĕt. O. Phr.—Trōjæ cōndĭtŏr. Prĭămī pătĕr.

Lărēs, ĭūm & ūm. m. *The two protecting deities of Rome.* Ēt vĭgĭlānt nōstrā sēmpĕr ĭn ūrbĕ lărēs. O. Syn.—Pĕnātēs. Phr.—Paūpĕrĭs āgrī cūstōdēs.

Lātōnă, æ. f. *Latona, the mother of Diana and Apollo.* Lātōnæ tăcĭtūm pērtēntānt gaūdĭă pēctŭs. V. Syn.—Tītānĭs, Tītānĭă. Phr.—Fīlĭă Cœī. Cœō gĕnĭtă. Dŭōrūm fāctă părēns dīvūm. Mātĕr Ăpōllĭnĭs. Dĭānæ gĕnĭtrīx.

Lĕāndĕr & Lĕāndrŭs, ī. m. *Leander, lover of Hero.* Phr.—Aūdāx jŭvĕnĭs. Ăbȳdēnŭs jŭvĕnĭs. Phrȳxēī cōntēmptŏr ĕphēbŭs Aēquŏrĭs. Nōctĕ nătāt cæcā sērūs frĕtă. Tŭmĭdīs jām prĕmĕrētŭr ăquīs.

Lībĕr, ĕrī. m. *See Bacchus.*

Lĭbȳă, æ. & Lĭbȳē, ēs. f. *Libya, the northern part of Africa, generally a name for the whole of Africa.* Īpse īgnōtŭs, ĕgēns, Lĭbȳæ dēsērtă pĕrăgrŏ. V. Syn.—Āfrĭcă. Phr.—Pēr călĭdās Lĭbȳæ sĭtĭēntĭs ărēnās. Nĭmĭō mūnītă călōrĕ. Īnfēstăquĕ tērră cŏlŭbrīs. Vīcīnă pĕrūstī Aēthĕrĭs. Lĭbȳæ, quæ tōrrĭdă sēmpĕr.

Lūcrētĭă, æ. f. *Lucretia, wife of Tarquinius Collatinus.* Phr.—Gĕnĕrōsă vĭrāgŏ. Ănĭmī mātrōnă vĭrīlĭs. Nōn hŭmĭlĭs mŭlĭĕr. Pŭdōrĭs īpsă sŭī vīndēx. Ūltă pŭdīcĭtĭām. Cēlātō fīgĭt sŭă pēctŏră fērrō. Pēctŏrĕ sūbnĭvĕō glădĭūm mŏrĭbūndă rĕcōndĭt.

Lūnă, æ. f. *The moon, deified.* Lūnăquĕ nōctūrnōs āltă rĕgēbăt ĕquōs. O. Syn.—Dēlĭă, Cȳnthĭă, Dĭānă, Lātōnĭă, Phœbē. Phr.—Phœbī sŏrŏr. Sŏrŏr īgnĕă Phœbī. Dĕă nōctĭvăgă. Āstrōrūm rēgīnă. Sīdĕrūm rēgīnă bĭcōrnĭs. Tăcĭtæ mŏdĕrātrīx Cȳnthĭă nōctĭs. Phœbē nōctĭbŭs īmpĕrāns. Nĭvĕīs īnvēctă bīgīs. Quæ sĭlēntĭūm rĕgĭt. Cĕlĕrēm prōnōs vōlvĕrĕ mēnsēs. Lūcĭdūm cœlī dĕcŭs. Mētĭēns ĭtĕr ānnŭūm. Phœbē mĕdĭūm pūlsābăt Ŏlȳmpūm. Īrātōs āttōllăt Cȳnthĭă vūltūs. Āstrōrūm dĕcŭs ēt nĕmŏrūm Lātōnĭă cūstōs.

M

Măcĕdŏnĭă, æ. f. *Macedonia.* Syn.—Aēmăthĭă, Aēmŏnĭă. Phr.—Rēgnātăquĕ tērră Phĭlīppō.

Măcĕdŏnĭŭs, ă, ūm. *Macedonian.* Syn.—Măcĕdŏ, Pēllæŭs, Aēmăthĭŭs, Aēmŏnĭŭs.

Mæcēnās, ātĭs. m. *Mæcenas, Prime Minister of Augustus.* Mæcēnās ĕquĕs Ētrūscō dē sānguĭnĕ nātŭs. Prop. Phr.—Dōctōrūm faūtŏr. Lārgŭs ŏpūm. Fāmā īnclȳtŭs. Ătăvīs ēdĭtĕ rēgĭbŭs. Mūsārūm præsĭdĭum ēt dūlcĕ dĕcūs mĕūm. Grāndĕ dĕcūs cŏlŭmēnquĕ vātūm.

Mænălă, ōrūm. n. *Mount Mænalos, a mountain in Arcadia consecrated to Pan.* Īntĕrĕā mīstīs lūstrābō Mænălă nȳmphīs. V. Phr.—Mōns Ārcădĭŭs. Pānī săcĕr. Mænălă Pānī săcră. Lătĕbrīs hōrrēndă fĕrārūm.

Māgdălēnă, æ. f. *Mary Magdalen.* Syn.—Māgdălĭs, Māgdălă. Phr.—Pēctŭs ĭnēxplētīs Māgdălĭs īmplĕt ăquīs.

Măgī, ōrūm. m. *The Magi.* Phr.—Hūjūs prīmōrēs nōmēn tĕnŭērĕ Măgōrūm. Dĕōque hŏmĭnīquĕ Dōnă fĕrūnt. Sīdūsquĕ, stēllāmquĕ sĕcūtī. Ădōrāntēs sācra ād cūnābŭlă gēntēs. Aūrĕă nāscēntī fūdērūnt mūnĕră Rēgī.

Māntŭă, æ. f. *Mantua, birthplace of Vergil.* Māntŭă Vērgĭlĭō gaūdĕt Vērōnă Cătūllō. O. Phr.—Vērgĭlĭī nātālĕ sŏlūm. Dīvĕs ăvīsī Māntŭă væ mĭsĕræ nĭmĭūm vīcīnă Crĕmōnæ. Fēlīx Mărōnĕ Māntŭă. Māntŭă mūsārūm dŏmŭs. Smȳrnæīs æmŭlă plēctrĭs.

Mărĭă, æ. f. *The Blessed Virgin Mary.* Phr.—Jēssæă vīrgŏ. Jēssææ glōrĭă stīrpĭs. Vīrgŏ părēns. Cāstă pŭērpără. Ēxcēlsī rēgīnă pŏlī. Cœlī dŏmĭnă. Vīrgŏ, dĕcŭs cœlī. Tērrārūm glōrĭă. Stēllă mărĭs. Vīrgĭnĭtātĭs hŏnŏr. Īntāctæ vīrgĭnĭtātĕ părēns. Pāx hŏmĭnūm rērūmquĕ sălūs. Rēbūs sōlāmĕn ĭn ārctīs. Cuī mīllĕ jŭvāndi ārtēs. Īnnūptă mātĕr ĕt vīrgŏ. Rēgĭă Vīrgŏ. Ūltă tŭī gĕnĕrĭs. Mātrūm māxĭmă mātĕr. Fīlĭă fīlī.

Maūrī, ōrūm. m. *The Moors.* Ēt Maūrī cĕlĕrēs ēt Maūro ōbscūrĭŏr Īndŭs. J. Phr.—Maūră, Maūrĭcă gēns. Maūrŭs cōncŏlŏr Īndō. Pīctī tŭnĭcā Nīlōtĭdĕ Maūrī. Nĭgrīs prōrūmpīt Maūrŭs ĭn ārmīs.

Mēdēă, æ. f. *Medea, the famous sorceress who helped Jason.* Sīt Mēdēă fĕrōx īnvīctăquĕ. H. Syn.—Aēētĭs, Aēētĭās, Cōlchĭs, Phāsĭās. Phr.—Aēæīs ārmātă vĕnēnīs. Jāsŏnĭs ūxŏr. Frātērnā cædĕ crŭēntă. Cōlchĭs nŏvērcă. Bārbără mātĕr. Rēspērsă nātōrūm sānguĭnĕ. Fŭgĭēns Mēdēă mărītūm. Nē pŭĕrōs cōrām pŏpŭlō Mēdēă trŭcīdĕt.

Mĕdūsă, æ. f. *Medusa, one of the Gorgons.* Syn.—Phōrcȳs, Gōrgōn, Gōrgō. Phr.—Mĕdūsæūm mōnstrūm. Sāxĭfĭcæ ōră Mĕdūsæ. Sāxĭfĭcī Mĕdūsæ vūltūs. Gōrgŏnĕūm căpŭt. Crīnītă cŏlūbrīs. Ānguĭnĕīs cīnctă cŏmīs. Gĕrēns āltērnīs īmmīstōs crīnĭbŭs ānguēs. Ānguĕ cŏmās nēxă. Sævīssĭmă vīsū.

Mĕlĕāgĕr & Mĕlĕāgrŭs, ī. m. *Meleager, king of Aetolia.* Īnscĭŭs ātque ābsēns flāmmā Mĕlĕāgrŭs ăb īllā Ūrĭtŭr. O. Syn.—Oēnīdēs, Thēstĭădēs.

Mĕnĕlāŭs & Mĕnĕlāŏs, ī. m. *Menelaus, husband of Helen and brother of Agamemnon.* Tū fŏrĕ tām lēntūm crēdīs Mĕnĕlāŏn ĭn īrā? O. Syn.—Ătrīdēs, Tāntălĭdēs. Phr.—Ătrīdēs mĭnŏr. Frātēr mājōrĭs Ătrīdæ. Hĕlĕnæ mărītŭs, cōnjūx.

Mērcŭrĭŭs, ĭī. m. *Mercury, the messenger of the gods.* Ōmnĭă Mērcŭrĭō sĭmĭlīs, vōcēmquĕ cŏlōrēmquĕ. V. Syn.—Mājŭgĕnă, Ătlāntĭădēs, cādūcĭfĕr, Hērmēs, Cȳllēnĭŭs. Phr.—Cȳllēnĭŭs ālĕs. Īntērprēs dīvūm. Māiā gĕnĭtŭs, nātŭs, sātŭs. Ătlāntĭs nĕpōs. Cȳllēnĭă prōlēs. Cĭthăræ rĕpērtŏr, īnvēntŏr. Cūrvæ lўræ părēns. Fraūdīs fūrūmquĕ măgīstĕr. Fūrĭbŭs āptŭs.

Mĭdās (Mĭdă), æ. m. *Midas, the king of Phrygia.* Quī māvūlt hērēs dīvĭtĭs ēssĕ Mĭdæ. M. Phr.—Aūrĭcŭlās ăsĭnī Mĭdă rēx hăbĕt. Bĕrĕcȳnthĭŭs hērōs. Rēx Mæŏnĭŭs. Dīvēs Phrўgĭæ rēx. Rēx aūrītŭs.

Mĭlŏ, ōnĭs. m. *Milo, a famous athlete.* Flētquĕ Mĭlōn sĕnĭŏr cūm spēctĕt ĭnānēs....Pēndērĕ lăcērtōs. O. Phr.—Clārŭs pŭgĭl. Quī pĕrĭĭt cōnfīsŭs vīrĭbŭs, ādmīrāndīsquĕ lăcērtīs.

Mĭnērvă, æ. f. *Minerva, goddess of wisdom and the arts.* Āccĭpĕ bēllĭgĕræ crūdūm thōrācă Mĭnērvæ. M. Syn.—Pāllās, Trītōnĭă, Trītōnĭs. Phr.—Dīvă Jŏvĭs sŏbŏlēs. Sōlō Jŏvĕ nātă. Sĭnĕ mātrĕ crĕātă. Fīlĭă nātă Jŏvĕ. Māgnī nātă tŏnāntĭs. Trītōnĭă vīrgŏ. Dĕă, vīrgŏ bēllĭcă. Dīvă bēllātrīx. Bēllō mĕtŭēndă vĭrāgŏ. Trīstĭbŭs āspĕră bēllīs. Dīvă fĕrōx. Pūlchērquĕ sĕvērō Ārmātūr tērrōrĕ pŭdŏr.

Mīnōs, ōĭs. m. *Minos, king of Crete.* Māgnănĭmum ād Mīnōă vĕnīt, sēdēsquĕ sŭpērbās. *Cat.* Phr.—Ăgēnŏrĕŭs, Gnōssĭŭs, Crētēnsĭs rēx, dūx, hērōs, jūdēx. Ārbĭtĕr Ōrcī. Mīnōs ūrnām mŏvĕt.

Mīnōtaūrŭs, ī. m. *Minotaur, the monster of the Cretan Labyrinth.* Phr.—Mīnōĭŭs, Mīnōŭs taūrŭs. Vīr sēmĭbōs, bōs sēmĭvĭr. Taūrūs bĭfōrmĭs. Gĕmĭnā taūrī jŭvĕnīsquĕ fĭgūrā.

Mōrpheūs, ĕōs, ĕī & eī. m. *Morpheus, the father of dreams.* Cūnctīsque ē frātrĭbŭs ēlĭgĭt ūnūm Mōrphĕă. O. Phr.—Sōmnī mĭnĭstĕr. Pīctŭs ĭmāgĭnĭbūs fōrmīsquĕ.

Mŏȳsēs & Mōsēs, ĭs & ĕōs. m. *Moses, the brother of Aaron.* Syn.—Āmrămĭdēs. Phr.—Hĕbræōrūm, gēntĭs Hĕbrææ lēgĭfĕr, dūx, rĕcēptŏr. Pāstŏr, dūx Īsăcĭdēs. Cōrnĭgĕr hērōs. Dĕī săcĕr īnterprĕs. Aūxĭlĭīs frētūs cœlēstĭbŭs hērōs.

Mūsæ, ārūm. f. *The nine muses.* Mūsă mĭhī mĕmŏrā. V. Syn.—Cămœnæ, Pīĕrĭdēs, Āŏnĭdĕs, Cāstălĭdĕs, Hĕlĭcōnĭădĕs, Mæŏnĭdĕs. Phr.—Cāstălĭæ sŏrōrēs. Nŏvēm sŏrōrēs. Pīĕrĭī mōntĭs ălūmnæ, dŏmĭnæ. Phœbī, Ăpōllĭnĭs chŏrŭs. Nŏvī Phœbī cŏmĭtēs. Vīrgĭnĕŭs Mūsārūm chŏrŭs. Mūsă pŏtēns lȳræ. Rĕquĭēs hŏmĭnūm dīvūmquĕ vŏlūptās.

N

Năĭădĕs & Năĭdĕs, ūm. f. *The Naiads, water-nymphs.* Năĭdĕs æquŏrĕæ dūrīsque īn mōntĭbŭs ōrtæ. O. Phr.—Năĭădūm chŏrŭs, cŏhōrs, tūrbă. Flŭvĭōrūm, fōntĭūm, ăquārūm Dĕæ, nȳmphæ, dŏmĭnæ. Flŭvĭālĭă nūmĭnă. Nȳmphă dĕcūs flŭvĭōrūm.

Nārcīssŭs, ī. m. *Narcissus.* Ērgo ŭbĭ Nārcīssūm pēr dēvĭă lūstră văgāntēm. O. Syn.—Cēphīsĭŭs. Phr.—Cēphīsĭă prōlēs. Ămāns sŭī. Quōndām pŭĕr. Nĭmĭūm quī crēdĭdĭt ūndīs.

Nāzărĕth. indecl. & Nāzără, æ. f. *Nazareth, village of Galilee.* Phr.—Nāzără, fēlīx pătrĭă. Dĕī pătrĭă. Chrīstī tēllūs ălūmnă. Nātālĕ sŏlūm Chrīstī. Āltrīx tērră Dĕī.

Nĕmĕsĭs, ĭs. f. *Nemesis, the avenger.* Syn.—Pœnă, Ădrāstēă. Phr.—Dĕă scĕlĕrūm ūltrīx. Nūmĕn crīmĭnūm vīndēx. Nĕmĕsīsquĕ fătīgăt ĕūntēm.

Nēptūnŭs, ī. m. *Neptune, the god of the ocean.* Prōxĭmă cuī cœlō cēssīt, Nēptūnĕ, pŏtēstās. O. Syn.—Pōrtūnŭs. Phr.—Mărĭs, æquŏrĭs, frĕtī, pōntī dĕŭs, dŏmĭnŭs, dŏmĭnātŏr, rēx, rēctŏr. Trĭdēntĭfĕr dĕŭs. Nūmĕn ăquārūm. Ōcĕănī pătĕr. Cærŭlĕŭs Jŏvĭs pătĕr. Dĕŭs mărĭs pŏtēns. Sævō trĭdēntĕ pŏtēns. Tŭmĭda æquŏră tēmpĕrăt. Tŭmĭdīs quī rēgnăt ĭn ūndīs. Prōspĭcĭēns summā flāvūm căpŭt ēxtŭlĭt ūndā.

Nērēĭdēs, ūm. f. *Nereids, nymphs of the sea.* Ēt tĭbi ōb īnvĭdĭām Nērēĭdēs īncrēpĭtārēnt. Prop. Syn.—Nērīnē. Phr.—Nēreī, Dōrĭdĭs nātæ. Ōcĕănī, Thĕtĭdĭs pŭēllæ, nўmphæ. Ūndārūm dĕæ. Nērēĭă tūrbă, prōlēs, prŏpāgŏ. Nērĕĭdūm chŏrŭs. Fōrmōsā Dōrĭdĕ nātæ.

Nĕrŏ, ōnĭs. m. *Nero, emperor of Rome.* Heū! Nĕrō crūdēlĭs, nūllāque īnvīsĭŏr ūmbrā. M. Phr.—Īmpĭŭs Aēnĕădēs. Tērræ pōndŭs. Mōnstrūm ēxsĕcrābĭlĕ. Quīd Nĕrōnĕ pējŭs. Sūstŭlĭt hīc mātrēm.

Nēstŏr, ŏrĭs. m. *Nestor, king of Pylos.* Pēlĕōs ēt Prĭămī trānsīt vēl Nēstŏrĭs ætās. M. Phr.—Nēlēĭă prōlēs. Nēlēĭŭs, Pўlĭŭs dūx, hērōs, sĕnēx. Īllĕ sĕnēx, tĕr ævō fūnctŭs. Trĭă quī sæcŭlă vīxĭt. Pўlĭŭs dūx, īllĕ dĭsērtŭs. Lārgă cuī cōpĭă fāndī. Cuī dūlcīs flŭĭt ăb ōrĕ sŏnŭs. Cōnsĭlĭō clārŭs ĕt ēlŏquĭō. Fācūndĕ sĕnēx.

Nīlŭs, ī. m. *The river Nile.* Ăccŏlĭt ēffūsō stāgnāntēm flūmĭnĕ Nīlūm. V. Phr.—Sēptēmplēx āmnĭs. Sēptēm, sēptēnă ōstĭă Nīlī. Flŭvĭŭs Phărĭŭs. Nīlī ālvĕŭs. Īn vădă Pēlūsĭă flŭēns. Stāgnāns ēffūsō flūmĭnĕ. Sēptēno īmpēllīt tŭmĕfāctūm gūrgĭtĕ pōntūm. Lēnĕ flŭĭt Nīlŭs. Aēgўptūm nīgrā fēcūndăt ărēnā. Fērtĭlĭs æstīvā Nīlŭs ăbūndăt ăquā.

Nĭŏbē, ēs. f. *Niobe, wife of Amphion.* Ēccĕ vĕnīt cŏmĭtūm Nĭŏbēs cĕlĕbērrĭmă tūrbă. O. Syn.—Tāntălĭs. Phr.—Tāntălī fīlĭă, nātă. Pĕlŏpĭs sŏrŏr. Āmphīŏnĭs ūxŏr. Mūltā Lātōnām prōlĕ lăcēssēns. Flēt mœstă sĭlēx Nĭŏbē. Māgnĭlŏquōs lŭĭt īmpĭă flātūs Tāntălĭs.

Nŏē. indecl. & Nŏēmŭs, ī. m. *Noah.* Syn.—Nŏă, Nŏăcŭs, Lāmĕchĭdēs. Phr.—Vītĭsātŏr pătĕr. Vīnī īnvēntŏr. Hŏmĭnūm rĕpărātŏr. Ārcæ mōlītŏr, făbrĭcātŏr ăcērnæ. Tūtā sērvātŭs ĭn ārcā.

Nŏvēmbĕr, brĭs. m. *November.* Phr.—Mēnsīs quō brūmă rĭgĕt. Quō cānēnt Bŏrĕālĭbŭs ārvă prŭīnīs.

Nŭmă, æ. m. *Numa Pompilius, second king of Rome.* Hæc fŭĭt āntīquī rēgĭă pārvă Nŭmæ. O. Syn.—Pōmpĭlĭŭs. Phr.—Cūltŏr dĕōrūm. Lēgūm sērvātŏr ĕt æquī.

Nўmphæ, ārūm. f. *The Nymphs.* Jūnctæquĕ Nўmphīs Grātĭæ dĕcēntēs. H. Syn.—Ōcĕănītĭdēs, Nērĕĭdēs, Năĭdēs. Phr.—Nўmphārūm chŏrŭs, cŏhōrs, tūrbă, āgmĕn, grēx. Nўmphæ sŏrōrēs. Ēt cūm sōlēmnĭă vōtă Rēddēmūs Nўmphīs.

O

Oēdĭpŭs, ī. & Oēdĭpūs, ŏdĭs. m. *Oedipus, son of Jocasta.* Syn.—Lāĭădēs, Oēdĭpŏdēs. Phr.—Quīquĕ nēc mōs ēst fĕrīs, Frātrēs sĭbi īpsĕ gĕnŭĭt. Īpsĕ părēns frātrūm, cōnjūxquĕ părēntĭs. Ēxpēndīt prŏprĭīs fātōrūm crīmĭnă pœnīs.

Ŏlўmpŭs, ī. m. *Olympus, a mountain in Thessaly.* Ōssăquĕ cūm Pīndō mājōrque āmbōbŭs Ŏlўmpŭs. O. Phr.—Āstrīs, cœlō vīcīnŭs. Ŏlўmpī ăpēx, jŭgă, cūlmĕn. Nūbēs ēxcēdĭt Ŏlўmpŭs. Āltŭs Ŏlўmpī vērtēx. Cēlsĭŏr ēxsūrgīt plŭvĭīs.

Ōps, Ŏpĭs. f. *Ops, the wife of Saturn.* Īdææ cūrrūs īllĕ sĕquātŭr Ŏpĭs. Tib. Syn.—Cўbĕlē, Rhĕă, Mātĕr, Tēllūs.

Ŏrēădĕs, ūm. f. *The mountain nymphs.* Hīnc ātque hīnc glŏmĕrāntŭr Ŏrēădĕs. V. Phr.—Mōntĭūm dĕæ. Mōntānæ, mōntĭcŏlæ Nўmphæ. Mōntānă nūmĭnă. Quæ văgāntŭr ĭn āltīs Mōntĭbŭs.

Ŏrēstēs, æ. m. *Orestes, son of Agamemnon and Clytemnestra.* Ēt vīndēx īn mōrtĕ pātrīs, mălŭs ūltŏr Ŏrēstēs. O. Syn.—Ăgămēmnŏnĭdēs, Tāntălĭdēs. Phr.—Ăgămēmnŏnĭs īnclўtă prōlēs. Ăgămēmnŏnĕ nātŭs. Pĕlŏpēŭs Ŏrēstēs. Mātrĭs īntērfēctŏr. Fīdŭs Pўlădīs cŏmĕs, sŏcĭŭs. Scĕlĕrūm fŭrĭīs ăgĭtātŭs. Dŭbĭūm pĭŭs ān scĕlĕrātŭs. Sēd mīxtūm pĭĕtātĕ nĕfās sĭbĭ.

Ŏrīōn, ŏnĭs. m. *Orion, a famous hunter, after death placed among the constellations.* Phr.—Tēstĕ tŭlīt cœlō vīctī dĕcŭs Ōrīōnĭs Scōrpĭŭs. Vălĭdō prōlēs Hўrææ lăcērtō. Vīrgĭnĕā dŏmĭtŭs săgīttā. Māgnŭs Ŏrīōn. *The Constellation.* Phr.—Ŏrīōnĭs āstrūm, sīdŭs, stēllă. Naūtīs īnfēstŭs Ŏrīōn. Fērrō, ēnsĕ mĭnāx. Āssūrgēns flūctū nīmbōsŭs Ŏrīōn. Īnsānūs dūm nūbĭlă dēnsăt Ŏrīōn.

Ōrpheūs, ĕŏs, ĕī & eī. m. *Orpheus, a famous poet and musician.* Sāxă fĕrāsquĕ lўrā tĕnŭĭt Rhŏdŏpēĭŭs Ōrpheūs. O. Phr.—Thrācĭŭs, Thrāx, Rhŏdŏpēĭŭs vātēs, săcērdōs, cĭthărœdŭs. Nērvīs cĭthărāquĕ pŏtēns. Blāndŭs tēstūdĭnĕ. Căllĭŏpæ gĕnŭs. Sāxă cāntū mūlcĕt. Sīlvīs cŏmĭtātŭs ĕt āmnĭbŭs Ōrpheūs. Thrēĭcĭā frētūs cĭthărā fĭdĭbūsquĕ cănōrīs. Īntērprēsquĕ dĕōrūm. Lēnīrĕ tĭgrēs răbĭdōsquĕ lĕōnēs. Cūjŭs ād chōrdās mŏdŭlāntĕ plēctrō Rēstĭtĭt tōrrēns.

Ŏvĭdĭŭs, ĭī. m. *Ovid, a famous Roman poet.* Syn.—Nāsŏ. Phr.—Pēlīgnūs vātēs. Pēlīgnæ glōrĭă gēntĭs. Pārnāssī dĕcŭs īmmōrtālĕ Lătīnī. Lătīnōrūm vātēs ŏpĕrōsĕ dĭērūm. Quēm sŭă Mūsă fŭgāvĭt.

P

Pāllădĭūm, ĭī. n. *The Palladium, the famous statue of Pallas in Troy.* Syn.—Pāllăs. Phr.—Pāllădĭs, Mĭnērvæ, Pāllădĭă ēffĭgĭēs, sĭmŭlācrūm. Sīgnūm fātālĕ Mĭnērvæ. Phrўgĭæ sīgnūm pĕnĕtrālĕ Mĭnērvæ.

Pāllăs, ădĭs. f. *Pallas. See Minerva.*

Pān, ānŏs. m. *Pan, the god of shepherds.* Pān ŏvĭūm cūstōs. V. Phr.—Dĕŭs Ārcădĭæ, sīlvārūm, pĕcŏrūm. Sīlvēstrĭs dĕŭs. Cūltōr nĕmŏrūm. Nĕmŏrūm bēllīquĕ pŏtēns. Cūrăt ŏvēs ŏvĭūmquĕ măgīstrōs. Prīmūs călămōs nōn pāssŭs ĭnērtēs. Pān prīmūs călămōs cērā cōnjūngĕrĕ plūrēs Īnstĭtŭĭt. Cērātā mŏdŭlātŭr ărūndĭnĕ cārmĕn.

Pāpă, æ. m. *The Pope, successor of St. Peter and Bishop of Rome.* Phr.—Sūmmŭs Pōntĭfēx. Chrīstī vĭcārĭŭs. Dĕī, Chrīstī săcĕr īntērprĕs. Trĭplĭcī căpŭt dĭădēmătĕ cīnctŭs. Trĭplĭcēm gĕrĭt, gēstăt quī frōntĕ cŏrōnām. Cuī sūmmă pŏtēstās Tērrārūm cœlīquĕ dăta ēst. Scēptră vĭcēsquĕ Dĕī gĕrēns. Tērgĕmĭnūmquĕ cīngīt cuī dĭădēmă căpŭt.

Părădīsŭs, ī. m. *Paradise, where God placed Adam and Eve.* Syn.—Ēdēn. Phr.—Bĕātæ sēdēs. Ēlўsĭī cāmpī. Lætă ārvă. Rēgnă īnvĭă vīvīs. Sēmpēr sĭnĕ nūbĭbŭs āēr Līmpĭdŭs.

Pārcæ, ārūm. f. *The Fates, Clotho, Lachesis and Atropos.* Syn.—Fātă, fātūm, Lĭbĭtīnă. Phr.—Stўgĭæ, fātĭdĭcæ sŏrōrēs. Nēscĭă flēctī nūmĭnă. Fīlă sŏrōrūm. Quās nūllă mŏvēnt fātă prĕcēsquĕ. Dūm sŏrōrūm Fīlă trĭūm pătĭūntŭr ātră. Tēmpŏră Pārcæ Dēbĭtă.

Părĭs, ĭdĭs. m. *Paris, son of Priam and Hecuba.* Jūdĭcĭūm Părĭdĭs, sprētæque īnjūrĭă fōrmæ. V. Syn.—Ălēxāndĕr, Prĭămĭdēs. Phr.—Phrўgĭŭs pāstŏr, Īdæŭs pāstŏr. Lăcænæ fămōsŭs hōspĕs. Īntērfēctŏr Ăchīllĭs. Pāstōr pērfĭdŭs.

Pārnāssŭs, ī. m. *Parnassus, a famous mountain in Phocis.* Sēd mē Pārnāssī dēsērtă pĕr ārdŭă dūlcĭs Rāptăt ămŏr. V. Syn.—Cāstălĭs, Ăgănīppē. Phr.—Pārnāssĭă, Pārnāssĭs rūpēs. Pārnāssĭă jŭgă. Āŏnĭŭs vērtēx. Mōns Pĭĕrĭŭs. Mōns Phœbō Mūsīsquĕ săcĕr. Gĕmĭnă Pārnāssī ārx. Lŏcă Mūsīs cūltă. Ŭbĭ fōns mānăt Bēllĕrŏphōntĭs ĕquī. Sŭpĕrātquĕ căcūmĭnĕ nūbēs.

Pārthī, ōrūm. m. *Parthians.* Fīdēntēmquĕ fŭgā Pārthūm vērsīsquĕ săgīttīs. V. Syn.—Mēdī, Pērsæ. Phr.—Tērgă făllăcīs mĕtŭēndă Pārthī. Vērsīs ănĭmōsŭs ĕquīs Pārthŭs. Nōn fīctā trĕpĭdārĕ fŭgā. Pōssīt Rōmă fĕrōx dărĕ jūră Mēdīs. Mārtĭă gēns Pārthī. Tēlīs ārcūquĕ pŏtēntēs.

Paūlŭs, ī. m. *Saint Paul, the Apostle.* Syn.—Saūlŭs, Tārsīdēs. Phr.—Dĕī īntērprĕs lēctīssĭmŭs.

Pēgăsŭs, ī. m. *Pegasus, the winged horse.* Ānte ălĭōs quāntūm Pēgăsŭs ībăt ĕquōs. O. Phr.—Ālātŭs ĕquŭs. Cœlō volāns. Ālātă prŏpāgŏ Mĕdūsæ. Sŏnĭpēs Pārnāssĭŭs. Ēt Pēgăsŭs hūjŭs ŏrīgo ēst. Pēnnīsquĕ fŭgācēm Pēgăsŏn.

Pĕlōps, ŏpĭs. m. *Pelops, son of Tantalus.* Syn.—Tāntălĭdēs. Phr.—Tŷndărĕī gĕnŭs. Trūncātūsquĕ Pĕlōps. Phrўgĭŭs Hīppŏdămīæ mărītŭs.

Pĕnātēs, ūm. m. *Penates, the household gods.* Hōs tĭbĭ sācră sŭōs cōmmēndāt Trōjă Pĕnātēs. V. Syn.—Lărēs. Phr.—Dĭī, Dī, dīvī pĕnātēs. Dī pătrĭī, īndĭgĕtēs.

Pēnĕlŏpē, ēs. f. *Penelope, wife of Ulysses.* Hānc tŭă Pēnĕlŏpē lēntō tĭbĭ mīttĭt, Ŭlŷssĕ. O. Syn.—Īcărĭs, Īcărĭōtĭs. Phr.—Cāstă sēmpĕr Ŭlŷssĭs Cōnjūx. Ābsēntī fīdă mărītō. Mūltīs ūnă pĕtītă prŏcīs. Īllūsōs dōctă fŭgārĕ prŏcōs. Dīffĭcĭlīs prŏcīs. Pēnĕlŏpēn sōlērs ābsēns tōrquēbăt Ŭlŷssēs.

Pĕrīllŭs, ī. m. *Perillus, a famous artist.* Ēt gĕmĕre īn taūrō, sævĕ Pĕrīllĕ, tŭō. Prop. Phr.—Taūrī făbrĭcātŏr ăhēnī. Quī pĕrĭt ārtĕ sŭā. Claūsūs bŏvĕ mūgĭt ăhēnō Īnfēlīx făbĕr.

Pērseūs, ĕŏs, ĕī & eī. m. *Perseus, conqueror of Medusa.* Cāndĭdă sī nōn sūm, plăcŭīt Cēphēĭă Pērseō. O. Syn.—Ăbāntĭădēs, Īnăchĭdēs, Ăcrĭsĭōnĭădēs. Phr.—Jŏvĕ nātŭs. Mĕdūsæ vīctŏr. Dănăēă prŏpāgŏ. Dănăēĭă prōlēs. Ālĭgĕr hērōs. Fīlĭŭs aūrĭgĕnă. Quī Gōrgŏnă vīcĭt. Tēla hōrrēntĭă quāssāns. Gōrgŏnĭs ānguĭcŏmæ Pērseūs sŭpĕrātŏr.

Pĕtrŭs, ī. m. *Saint Peter.* Syn.—Cēphăs. Phr.—Ăpōstŏlĭcī cœtūs prīncēps, căpŭt. Bēthsāĭdŏs ācĕr ălūmnŭs. Bēthsāĭdĕ nātŭs. Cœlūm quī clāvĕ rĕclūdĭt. Gĕmĭnæquĕ mĭcānt īn pēctŏrĕ clāvēs.

Phăĕtōn, ōntĭs. m. *Phaeton, son of Apollo.* Pœnām, Phăĕtōn, prō mūnĕrĕ pōscĭs. O. Phr.—Clŷmĕnēĭŭs, Clŷmĕnēs pŭĕr. Clŷmĕnēĭă prōlēs. Sōlĕ nātŭs. Fūlmĭnĕ pērcūlsŭs, cōmbŭstŭs. Pătrĭīs ēxcĭdĭt āctŭs ĕquīs. Flāmmĭgĕrōs ōptāvīt tāngĕrĕ cūrrūs. Phăĕtōn tĕmĕrārĭŭs.

Phărăō & Phărăōn, ōnĭs. m. *Pharaoh.* Phr.—Phărĭŭs, Aēgŷptĭŭs rēx, tŷrānnŭs. Ăquīs, ūndīs sūbmērsŭs, ōbrŭtŭs. Sĕpūltŭs ĭn æquŏrĕ.

Phărŏs & Phărŭs, ī. f. *Pharos, an island off Alexandria, Egypt.* Phr.—Ptŏlĕmæē līttŏră Phărī. Flūctĭbŭs āmbītă. Pēllæīs prōxĭmă mūrīs. Claūstrūm pĕlăgī.

Phĭlŏctētēs, æ. m. *Philoctetes, companion of Hercules.* Tārdă Phĭlŏctētæ sānāvīt crūră Măchāōn. Prop. Syn.—Pœāntĭădēs,

Pœāntĭŭs. Phr.—Pœāntĭŭs hērōs, Pœāntĭă prōlēs. Pœāntĕ nātŭs, sătŭs. Gĕnŭs Pœāntĭūm. Ālcīdæ cŏmēs. Hērcŭlĭs hērēs.

Phlĕgĕthōn, ōntĭs. m. *Phlegethon, one of the rivers of the Lower World.* Ēt Chăŏs, ēt Phlĕgĕthōn, lŏcă nōctĕ sĭlēntĭă lātē. V. Phr.—Tārtărĕŭs lăcŭs. Īgnĕŭs āmnĭs. Fŭrēns ārdēntĭbŭs ūndīs. Ātră vădīs īncēndĭă vōlvēns. Nĭgrīs vōlvēns īncēndĭă rīpīs. Nŏcēntēs īgnĕō cīngēns vădō.

Phœbŭs, ī. m. *Phoebus Apollo:* Quæ Phœbō pătĕr ōmnĭpŏtēns, mĭhĭ Phœbŭs Ăpōllŏ Prædīxĭt. V. Syn.—Ăpōllŏ, Cȳnthĭŭs, Dēlĭŭs. *See Apollo.*

Phœnīcĕs, ūm. m. *Phenicians.* Syn.—Ăgēnŏrĭdæ, Sīdŏnĭī, Tȳrĭī. Phr.—Phœnīssă, Sīdŏnĭă, Sīdŏnĭs gēns, prŏpāgŏ.

Phrȳxŭs, ī. m. *Phryxus, son of Athamas.* Phr.—Dēlāpsæ pōrtĭtŏr Hēllēs. Aēŏlĭŭs jŭvĕnĭs. Aŭrātō vēllĕrĕ dīvĕs.

Pīndărŭs, ī. m. *Pindar, the famous Theban poet.* Pīndărūm quīsquīs stŭdĕt æmŭlārī. H. Phr.—Dīrcæŭs cȳcnŭs. Pīndărĭcæ fĭdĭcēn lȳræ. Thēbānă ăquĭlă. Rŭĭt prŏfūndō Pīndărŭs ōrē.

Pīrĭthŏŭs, ī. m. *Pirithous, son of Ixion.* Nōn Lēthæă vălēt Thēseūs ābrūmpĕrĕ cārō Vīncŭlă Pīrĭthŏō. H. Phr.—Aūdāci Īxīŏnĕ nātŭs. Īxīŏnĭs prōlēs.

Plătŏ & Plătōn, ōnĭs. m. *Plato, the Greek philosopher.* Quōrsūm pērtĭnŭīt stīpārĕ Plătōnă Mĕnāndrō? H. Phr.—Hŏmŏ săgāx, īnsīgnĭs. Īngĕnĭō clārŭs.

Plēĭădĕs, Plēĭădĕs & Plĭădĕs, ūm. f. *The Pleiades.* Nōn hæc Plēĭădēs făcĭūnt, nĕc ăquōsŭs Ŏrīōn. Prop. Syn.—Vērgĭlĭæ, Ătlāntĭdĕs. Phr.—Ătlāntĭs nātæ. Ătlāntēæ sŏrōrēs. Plēĭădūm grēx, chŏrŭs, sīdĕră, sīgnă. Stēllæ rătĭbūs tĭmēndæ. Sēptēm rădĭāntĭă stēllīs Sīdĕră.

Plūtŏ & Plūtōn, ōnĭs. m. *Pluto, the god of the Lower World.* Syn. – Dīs, Ōrcŭs. Phr.—Tārtărĕŭs, Stȳgĭŭs, nĭgĕr Jūpĭtĕr, tȳrānnŭs. Rēx Ōrcī. Sĭlēns dŏmĭnŭs. Dŏmĭnātŏr Ăvērnī. Nōctĭs ārbĭtĕr, ūmbrārūmquĕ pŏtēns. Īnămœnă tĕnēns rēgnă. Nĭgrī rēgĭă cæcă Dĕī. Dŏmĭnūmquĕ rēgnī trīstĭs. Ūmbrārūm dŏmĭnŭs. Ō sævīssĭmĕ frātrūm.

Pōllūx, ūcĭs. m. *Pollux, the brother of Castor.* Tālĭs Ămȳclæī dŏmĭtūs Pōllūcĭs hăbēnĭs. V. Syn.—Lēdæŭs, Tȳndărĭdēs, Oēbălĭdēs. Phr.—Cæstĭbŭs præstāns, āptĭŏr. Ōvō prōgnātŭs ĕōdēm. Qui frātrem āltērnā mōrtĕ rĕdēmĭt.

Pŏlȳphēmŭs, ī. m. *Polyphemus, one of the Cyclops.* Nām quālīs quāntūsquĕ căvō Pŏlȳphēmŭs ĭn āntrō. V. Phr.—Aētnæŭs Cȳclōps. Pāstŏr Aētnæŭs. Lūmĭnĕ fraūdātŭs Cȳclōps. Īpsīs hōrrēndūs sīlvīs. Vīsŭs ăb hōspĭtĕ nūllō Īmpūnĕ. Māgnī cūm dīs cōntēmptŏr Ŏlȳmpī. Mōnstrum hōrrēndum, īnfōrme, īngēns cuī lūmĕn ădēmptūm.

Pŏlȳxĕnă, æ. f. *Polyxena, daughter of Priam and Hecuba.* Plăcĕt Ăchīllĕōs māctātă Pŏlȳxĕnă mānēs. O. Phr.—Prĭămēĭă vīrgŏ. Părĭdĭs sŏrŏr. Jūssă mŏrī. Plūsquām fœmĭnă vīrgŏ. Scīssāquĕ Pŏlȳxĕnă pāllā.

Prĭămŭs, ī. m. *Priam, king of Troy.* Fōrsĭtăn ēt Prĭămī fŭĕrīnt quæ fātă rĕquīrās. V. Syn.—Lāŏmĕdōntĭădēs. Phr.—Dārdănŭs, Lāŏmĕdōntĭŭs rēx, rēctŏr, hērōs, sĕnēx. Hæc fīnīs Prĭămī fātōrūm. Sŭpērbūm rēgnātōrem Ăsĭæ.

Prĭāpŭs, ī. m. *Priapus, the god of gardens.* Cūm fālcē sālīgnā Hēllēspōntĭăcī sērvēt tūtēlă Prĭāpī. V. Syn.—Lāmpsăcĭdēs. Phr.—Dĕŭs Lāmpsăcĭŭs, Hēllēspōntĭăcŭs. Hōrtōrūm dĕŭs, cūstōs. Rūrĭs cūstōs. Bācchī rūstĭcă prōlēs. Cūstōs vītĭs ēt hōrtī.

Prōgnē, ēs. f. *Procne, daughter of King Pandion.* Dīssĭmŭlārĕ nĕquīt crūdēlĭă gaūdĭă Prōgnē. O. Syn.—Daūlĭăs, Daūlĭs, Pāndīōnĭs, Ātthȳs. Phr.—Rhŏdŏpēĭă cōnjūx. Pāndīŏnĕ nātă. Tērĕōs ūxŏr, mărītă. Ūltă mănū thălămōs. Plōrăt Ĭtȳn vŏlŭcrīs pĭă, mātĕr ăcērbă.

Prŏmētheŭs, ĕŏs, ĕī & eī. m. *Prometheus, son of Iapetus.* Caūcăsĕāsquĕ rĕfērt vŏlŭcrēs fūrtūmquĕ Prŏmētheī. V. Syn.—Īăpĕtĭŏnĭdēs, Jāpĕtĭdēs. Phr.—Sătŭs Īăpĕtō. Gĕnŭs aūdāx. Quī fūrtō gēntĭbŭs Īntŭlĭt īgnēm. Caūcăsĭă sūb rūpĕ lĭgātŭs. Cuī Ăquĭlă rōdĭt ūnguĕ jĕcŭr. Dīrīquĕ Prŏmēthĕōs ārtēs. Mōrtālĭbŭs īntŭlĭt īgnēm.

Prŏsērpĭnă, æ. f. *Proserpina, daughter of Ceres.* Fūrvæ rēgnă Prŏsērpĭnæ. H. Syn.—Pērsĕphŏnē, Hĕcătē, Brīmō. Phr.—Nātă Cĕrĕrĭs. Dītĭs cōnjūx. Ēlȳsĭī spōnsă tȳrānnī. Nĭgrī Jŏvĭs ūxŏr. Jūnă īnfērnă. Rēgīnă Ĕrĕbī. Ōrcī Dīvă trĭfōrmĭs. Hĕcătē cœlōque Ĕrĕbōquĕ pŏtēns.

Prōteŭs, ĕŏs, ĕī & eī. m. *Proteus, the guardian of the seals of Neptune.* Quālĭs ĭn ūmbrōsō Prōteŭs mīrābĭlĭs āntrō. M. Phr.—Aēquŏrĕŭs, āmbĭgŭŭs vātēs. Cārpăthĭŭs sĕnēx. Nēptūnī pāstŏr. Cārpăthĭīs quī rēgnăt ăquīs. Vărĭōs mūtāns vūltūs. Dūm sōllĭcĭtīs nōn vūlt ăpĕrīrĕ fŭtūră Spūmăt ăpēr, flŭĭt ūndă, frĕmĭt lĕŏ, sībĭlăt ānguĭs.

Pȳgmæŭs, ī. & Pȳgmæī, ōrūm. m. *The Pygmies.* Pȳgmæŭs pārvīs cūrrīt bēllātŏr ĭn ārmīs. J. Phr.—Pŭsīllă gēns, prŏpāgŏ. Īnērs plēbēcŭlă. Gēns cŭbĭtō, pĕdĕ nōn āltĭŏr ūnō. Gēns grŭĭbŭs ĭnĭmīcă. Pȳgmæă prŏpāgŏ.

Pȳrrhŭs, ī. m. *Pyrrhus, son of Achilles.* Pȳrrhŭs Ăchīllīdēs, ănĭmōsŭs ĭmāgĭnĕ pātrĭs. O. Syn.—Nĕŏptŏlĕmŭs, Ăchīllīdēs, Pēlīdēs, Aēăcĭdēs. Phr.—Hērōs Aēăcĭdēs. Scȳrĭŭs jŭvĕnĭs, hērōs.

Pȳthăgŏrās, æ. m. *Pythagoras, the famous philosopher of Samos.* Nēc tē Pȳthăgŏræ fāllānt ārcānă rĕnātī. H. Phr.—Sămĭŭs vĭr, sĕnēx, sŏphŭs. Sămĭæ tēllūrĭs ălūmnŭs. Quī cūnctīs ănĭmālĭbŭs ābstĭnŭĭt. Vērī nōn sōrdĭdŭs aŭctŏr.

Q

Quĭrites, ūm. m. *Romans.* Mĭnĭmūm dē plēbĕ Quĭrītem. O. Syn.—Rōmānī, Rōmŭlĭdæ. Phr.—Mōbĭlĭūm tūrbă Quĭrītĭūm. Prīscīquĕ Quĭrītēs.

R

Rēgŭlŭs, ī. m. *Regulus, Roman consul, killed by the Carthaginians.* Pătrĭae īnflāmmātŭs ămōrĕ Rēgŭlŭs, īn mĕdĭīs sērvāvīt săcră fĭdēmquĕ. V. Phr.—Ămāns pătrĭæ. Vītæ, lūcĭs cōntēmptŏr, prōdĭgŭs.

Rhădămānthŭs, ī. m. *Rhadamanthus, king of Lycia and one of the judges of the Lower World.* Syn.—Ăgēnŏrĭdēs. Phr.—Nēc mūnĕrĭbŭs, prĕcĭbŭs nēc flēctĭtŭr ūllīs. Cāstīgātque aŭdītquĕ dŏlōs. Jūdēx sævīssĭmŭs Ŏrcī.

Rhēnŭs, ī. m. *The river Rhine.* Phr.—Īmmēnsī vădă cærŭlă Rhēnī. Cūrsū vĭŏlēntŭs ĕt ūndā. Flēxō sĭnŭōsŭs gūrgĭtĕ. Rhēnūmquĕ mĭnācēm.

Rhŏdănŭs, ī. m. *The river Rhone.* Phr.—Rhŏdănī ūndă, flŭēntă. Quā Rhŏdănŭs răptūm vēlōcĭbŭs ūndīs Īn mărĕ fērt Ărărīm. Rhŏdănŭs lātō flŭĭt āgmĭnĕ præcēps.

Rhŏdŭs & Rhŏdŏs, ī. f. *The island of Rhodes.* Phr.—Īnsŭlă sōlĭs. Līttŏrĕ clāră sŭō. Fērtĭlĭs aŭrō. Pĕlăgī pŏtēns.

Rōmă, æ. f. *Rome.* Rōmă, tŭūm nōmēn tērrīs fātālĕ rĕgēndīs. Tib. Phr.—Ūrbs Rōmānă, Rōmŭlă. Āltæ mœnĭă Rōmæ. Ūrbs āltă Quĭrīnī. Tērrārūm căpŭt, dŏmĭnă, rēgīnă, vīctrīx. Ōrbīs trĭūmphātī căpŭt. Īnclȳtă bēllīs. Rērūm pūlchērrĭmă. Rōmă pŏtēns ŏpĭbŭs. Prīmă ūrbēs īntĕr, aŭrĕă Rōmă.

Rōmānī, ōrūm. m. *Romans.* Īllīc rēs Ĭtălās Rōmānōrūmquĕ trĭūmphōs Fēcĕrăt. V. Syn.—Rōmŭlĭdæ, Quĭrītēs, Aēnĕădæ, Aŭsŏnĭdæ. Phr.—Rōmānă, Rōmŭlă gēns, prŏpāgŏ, stīrps. Pŏpŭlŭs Rōmānŭs. Mārtĭă tūrbă. Gēns tŏgātă. Pŏpŭlŭs lātē rēx bēllōquĕ sŭpērbŭs. Trōjānă prŏpāgŏ. Rōmānōs rērūm dŏmĭnōs gēntēmquĕ tŏgātām.

Rōmŭlŭs, ī. m. *Romulus, founder of Rome.* Rōmŭlŭs Āssărăcī quēm sānguĭnĭs Īlĭă mātĕr Ēdūxĭt. V. Syn.—Quĭrīnŭs, Īlĭădēs. Phr.—Mārtĕ sătŭs. Mārtĭă prōlēs. Rĕmī frātĕr. Rōmānæ ūrbĭs pătĕr. Rōmānŭs prīncēps. Rōmæ cōndĭtŏr. Māvōrtĭă cōndēt Mœnĭă.

S

Săbæī, ōrūm. m. *The people of Arabia Felix, Sabæans.* Īndĭă mīttĭt ĕbūr, mōllēs sŭă tūră Săbæī. V. Phr.—Tūrĭfĕrī fēlīcĭă rūră Săbæī. Pīnguĭă rūră Săbæōrūm. Sōlīs ēst tūrĕă vīrgă Săbæīs.

Săgīttārĭŭs, ĭī. m. *The constellation, Sagittarius.* Syn.—Ārcĭtĕnēns, Săgīttĭfĕr, Săgīttĭpŏtēns, Cēntaūrŭs, Chīrōn. Phr.—Săgīttĭfĕrī sīdŭs, āstrūm. Jăcŭlīs ārmătŭs ĕt ārcū. Sēmĭvĭr ārcĭpŏtēns. Aēmŏnĭī ārcŭs.

Sălŏmōn (Sŏlŏmōn), ōnĭs. m. *Solomon, son of David.* Phr.—Dāvīdĭcă sŏbŏlēs. Dāvīdĭs īnclȳtă prōlēs. Rēx săpĭēns. Aūrātō spēctābĭlĭs ōstrō. Pācĭfĭcŭs rēctŏr Īdūmēs. Mēntĭs ŏpūmquĕ pŏtēns.

Sāpphō, ūs. f. *Sappho, the poetess of Lesbos.* Grātă lȳrām pŏsŭĭt tĭbĭ, Phœbē, pŏētrĭă Sāpphō. O. Phr.—Lēsbĭă vātēs. Lēsbĭ, Aēŏlĭă pŭēllă. Pĭērĭĭs sŏrŏr āddĭtă Mūsīs. Mūsīs Lēsbĭs ămīcă săcrīs. Aēŏlĭæ Lēsbĭs ămīcă lȳræ. Sāpphĭcă Mūsă.

Sātūrnŭs, ī. m. *Saturn, father of the gods.* Sātūrnīs rēgnīs āb Jŏvĕ pūlsŭs ĕrăt. O. Phr.—Fālcĭfĕr, fālcĭtĕnēns, fālcĕ pŏtēns Dĕŭs. Sātūrnŭs pătĕr. Aūreī rēx ārbĭtĕr ævī. Prōgĕnĭtōr dīvūm cūrvātā fālcĕ mĭnāns. Ārmă Jŏvīs fŭgĭēns.

Sătȳrī, ōrūm. m. *The satyrs.* Syn.—Faūnī, Sīlvānī, Pānĕs, cōrnĭpĕdēs. Phr.—Dĕī āgrēstēs, sīlvēstrēs. Sīlvārūm, rūrĭs dĕī. Rūstĭcă nūmĭnă. Sătȳrōrūm tūrbă, cŏhōrs. Aūrēs cāprĭpĕdūm Sătȳrōrum ăcūtās.

Scȳllă, æ. f. *Scylla, a sea-monster dwelling near Charybdis.* Scȳllăquĕ vīrgĭnĕām cănĭbūs sūccīnctă fĭgūrām. Tib. Phr.—Scȳllēŭs scŏpŭlŭs. Scȳllēĭă sāxă. Tērrĭbĭlēs quæ pāndĭt hĭātūs. Naūtīs īnfēstă. Vīrgĭnĭs ōră gĕrēns. Āttrāctāns lăcĕrāns nāvēs.

Scȳthæ, ārūm. m. *The Scythians.* Syn.—Scȳthēs (sing.), Sārmătă, Saūrŏmătæ, Māssăgĕtæ, Gĕtæ, Gĕlōnī. Phr.—Scȳthĭæ bēllācĭs ălūmnī. Ērrāntēs Scȳthĭæ pŏpŭlī. Scȳthĭcă gēns. Gēns Hȳpērbŏrĕă. Gēns Rīphæă. Rīphæī pŏpŭlī.

Sēptēmbĕr, brĭs. m. *The month of September.* Phr.—Mēnsĭs pōmĭfĕr, răcēmĭfĕr. Mēnsīs quō fœtō dē pălmĭtĕ pōmă nĭtēnt. Quō prēssō spūmăt vīndēmĭă Bācchō. Quō plēnīs spūmăt vīndēmĭă lābrīs. Quō Lībră dĭēs cūm nōctĭbŭs æquăt.

Sĭbyllă, æ. f. *One of the Sibyls, a famous set of prophetesses, of which there were ten, the most famous being the Cumæan Sibyl.* Hōrrēndǣquĕ prŏcūl sēcrētă Sĭbyllǣ, Āntrum īmmānĕ pĕtīt. V. Syn.—Vātēs, săcērdōs. Phr.—Ănūs, vīrgŏ, vātēs fēmĭnă. Phœbī lōngǣvă māgnă săcērdōs. Vēntūrī īntērprēs. Dĕī āfflātă nūmĭnĕ. Hōspĭtĕ plēnă dĕō. Phœbī pătĭēns.

Sĭcĭlĭă, æ. f. *Sicily.* Syn.—Sĭcănĭă, Trīnăcrĭs, Trīnăcrĭă. Phr.—Sĭcănĭŭs, Sĭcănŭs, Trīnăcrĭs tērră, ōră, īnsŭlă, tēllūs. Ĕrўcĭs fīnēs. Gĭgāntūm, Cўclōpūm tēllūs, ōrǣ. Sĭcŭlūm līttŭs. Ārvăquĕ frūgĭfĕrǣ pīnguĭă sĭcănĭǣ.

Sīnă, æ & Sīnăī. indecl. f. *Mount Sinai.* Syn.—Hōrēb. Phr.—Sīnǣŭs mōns. Sīnǣī mōntĭs ăpēx. Sīnǣī cūlmĭnă mōntĭs. Īn quō mārmŏrĕīs dătă lēx īnscrīptă tăbēllīs.

Sīōn. indecl. f. *Mount Sion in Jerusalem.* Phr.—Ēxsūltă fīlĭă Sīōn. Tēmplō vĕnĕrāndă Sīōn. Sŏlўmǣ quī mōns sŭpĕrēmĭnĕt ūrbī.

Sīrēnēs, ūm. f. *The Sirens.* Jāmque ădĕō scŏpŭlōs Sīrēnum ădvēctă sŭbībăt. V. Syn.—Ăchĕlōĭdēs, Ăchĕlōĭădēs. Phr.—Ăchĕlōĭǣ, Sĭcŭlǣ, Tўrrhēnǣ vīrgĭnēs, pŭēllǣ, pēstēs. Sĭcŭlī mōnstră mărĭs. Blāndă pĕrīclă mărĭs. Fraŭdēs cāntū părăt īmprŏbă Sīrēn. Trēs vŏlŭcrēs, trēs sēmĭdĕǣ, trēs sēmĭpŭēllǣ. Hĭlărēm nāvĭgāntĭūm pœnām. Quās nēmō quōndām dēsĕrēbăt aŭdītās.

Sīsўphŭs, ī. m. *Sisyphus, son of Aeolus.* Aŭt pĕtĭs aŭt ūrgēs rŭĭtūrūm, Sīsўphĕ, sāxūm. O. Syn.—Aĕōlĭdēs. Phr.—Aĕōlī nātŭs īnfēlīx. Sāxūm vōlvēnsquĕ pĕtēnsquĕ. Sĕnĭs pĕrēnnĭs Aĕōlĭī lăbŏr. Īmmēnsūsquĕ lăpīs dēfēssūm Sīsўphŏn ūrgĕt.

Sōcrătēs, ĭs. m. *Socrates, the Athenian philosopher.* Sī Rōmănă fŏrēnt hǣc Sōcrătĭs ōră. M. Phr.—Cĕcrŏpĭŭs sĕnēx. Sōrbĭtĭō tōllīt quēm dīră cĭcūtǣ. Ănўtī rĕŭs. Īllĕ sĕnēx dīctūs săpĭēns ăb Ăpōllĭnĕ. Dūlcīquĕ sĕnēx vīcīnŭs Hўmēttō.

Sphīnx, ngĭs & gŏs. f. *The Sphinx.* Phr.—Thēbārūm dīră lŭēs. Sēmĭfĕrō nēctēns ōrĕ dŏlōs. Īnvōlvēns cǣcīs ăbdĭtă vērbă mŏdīs. Īnfēctă crŭōrĕ. Sphīnx, vŏlŭcrīs pēnnīs, pĕdĭbūs fĕră, frōntĕ pŭēllă.

Stўx, Stўgĭs. f. *The river Styx of the Lower World.* Prōmīssī Stўx mĭhĭ tēstĭs ĕrĭt. O. Phr.—Stўgĭŭs āmnĭs, lăcŭs, vōrtēx. Stўgĭă pălūs. Stўgĭs āltă pălūs. Dīs jūrāndă pălūs. Stўgĭǣ stāgnă pălūdĭs. Stўgĭs īrrĕmĕābĭlĭs ūndă. Stўgĭǣ nūmĕn ăquǣ. Īgnāvă lūrĭdă ăquă.

Sўrăcūsǣ, ārūm. f. *Syracuse, a city in Sicily.* Ūtquĕ Sўrăcūsās Ărĕthūsĭdās ăbstŭlĭt ārmīs Claŭdĭŭs. O. Phr.—Ūrbs Sўrăcūsĭă. Ărcēs Sўrăcūsĭǣ. Mœnĭă Ĕphўrēă.

T

Tāntălŭs, ī. m. *Tantalus, condemned in the Lower World to stand in water which retreated at his touch.* Tĭbĭ, Tāntălĕ, nūllæ Dēprēndūntŭr ăquæ; quæque īmmĭnĕt, ēffŭgĭt ārbŏr. O. Phr.—Pĕlŏpĭs părēns, pătĕr. Phrȳgĭŭs sĕnēx. Phrȳgĭŭs nātī lănĭātŏr ătrōx. Sŭpĕrūm crūdēlĭs, bārbărŭs hōspĕs. Rāmōs frūstrā quī căptăt ĕt ūndās. Īn mĕdĭā gārrŭlŭs ārĕt ăquā. Īn mĕdĭō Tāntălŭs āmnĕ sĭtĭt.

Tărēntūm, ī. n. *Tarentum, city in Italy.* Syn.—Tărēntŭs, Tărās, Oēbălĭă. Phr.—Māllĕt tŭă mītĭs Ōră Tărās. Nēptūnōquĕ săcrī cūstōdĕ Tărēntī.

Tārtărŭs, ī. m. & Tārtără, ōrūm. n. *The Lower World, Hell.* Syn.—Īnfērnī. Phr.—Lūcĭs ĕgēnŭs. Nōn hūc ŭt ŏpācă vĭdērem, Tārtără dēscēndī. Sŭb ĭnānĭă cōrpŭs Tārtără dētrūsūm.

Tēmpē. indecl. n. (pl.). *Tempe, vale in Thessaly.* Pāstŏr Ărīstæūs, fŭgĭēns Pēnēĭă Tēmpē. V. Phr.—Thēssălă Tēmpē. Tēmpē nĕmŏrōsă. Nĕmŭs Aēmŏnĭæ. Frīgĭdă Tēmpē. Tēmpē Zĕphȳrīs ăgĭtātă.

Tērmĭnŭs, ī. m. *Terminus, the god of boundaries.* Tū quŏquĕ săcrōrūm, Tērmĭnĕ, fīnĭs ĕrās. O. Phr.—Tūtŏr fīnĭūm. Ārbĭtĕr fūndī, lăpĭs. Sēpărăt īndĭcĭō quī dĕŭs ārvă sŭō.

Thēseūs, ĕŏs, ĕī & eī. m. *Theseus, king of Athens.* Jāmque ădĕrāt Thēseūs prōlēs īgnāră părēntĭs. O. Syn.—Aēgīdēs. Phr.—Trœzēnĭŭs hērōs. Vīctŏr Mĭnōtaūrī. Āssērtā Mărăthōnĕ sŭpērbŭs. Pīrĭthŏī cŏmĕs.

Thĕtĭs, ĭdĭs. f. *Thetis, mother of Achilles.* Jūpĭtĕr æquŏrĕæ Thĕtĭdīs cōnnūbĭă fŭgĭt. O. Syn.—Nērīnē. Phr.—Fīlĭă Nēreī. Mātĕr Ăchīllĭs. Aēăcĭdæ mātĕr, gĕnĭtrīx. Prō nātō cærŭlă mātĕr Āmbĭtĭōsă fŭĭt.

Thrācĕs, ūm. m. *The Thracians.* Syn.—Sīthŏnĭī, Thrēĭcĭī, Ēdōnī, Bīstŏnĕs, Bīstŏnĭī, Īsmărĭī, Ōdrȳsĭī.

Thrācă, Thrācĭă, æ & Thrācē, ēs. f. *Thrace.* Rhŏdōnquĕ nōbĭlem, hōrrĭdāmquĕ Thrācĭām. Tib. Syn.—Sīthŏnĭă, Bīstŏnĭă, Bīstŏnĕs. Phr.—Tēllūs, tērră Bīstŏnĭă, Bīstŏnĭs, Sīthŏnĭă. Nĭvĕ cāndĭdă. Fŭrĭōsă bēllō.

Tĭbĕrĭs, ĭs & Tĭbrĭs, ĭs & ĭdĭs. m. *The river Tiber.* Vīcīnăquĕ Tībrĭdĭs ārvă. V. Syn.—Ālbŭlă. Phr.—Tūscŭs, Tĭbĕrīnŭs āmnĭs. Tĭbrĭdĭs ūndă. Hēspĕrĭdūm flŭvĭūs rēgnātŏr ăquārūm. Tĭbĕrīnă flŭēntă. Ētrūscīs mānăt quæ fōntĭbŭs ūndă. Āspērque īmmānī cōrpŏrĕ Tĭbrĭs. Lēnī flŭĭt āgmĭnĕ Tĭbrĭs.

Tībŭr, ŭrĭs. n. *Tibur or Tivoli, a village near Rome.* Rōmæ̅ Tībŭr ămēm vēntōsūs, Tībŭrĕ Rōmăm. H. Phr.—Ārgēō pŏsĭtūm cŏlōnō. Ārgēī rēgnūm cŏlōnī.

Tĭgrĭs, ĭs & ĭdĭs. m. *The river Tigris.* Phr.—Tĭgrĭdĭs ūndă, āmnĭs, flŭēntă.

Tīsĭphŏnē, ēs. f. *Tisiphone, one of the Furies.* Tīsĭphŏnēs ātrō sī fŭrĭt āngue căpŭt. Prop. Phr.—Nōctĭs ălūmnă. Cæ̅dīs vīndēx, ūltrīx. Hy̆drīs crīnītă. Īmpēxă fĕrōs prō crīnĭbŭs ānguēs. Ăccīnctă flăgēllō.

Tĭty̆ŭs & ŏs, y̆ī. m. *Tityus the giant, son of Jupiter.* Vīscĕră præ̅bēbāt Tĭty̆ūs lănĭāndă, nŏvēmquĕ Jūgĕrĭbūs dīstrāctŭs ĕrăt. O. Phr.—Aētērnās vŏlŭcrī præ̅bēns dăpēs. Īncōntĭnēntīs Tĭty̆ī. Tērrae ōmnĭpărēntĭs ălūmnŭs. Sēmpĕr rĕnāscēns.

Trōăs, ădĭs. f. *The Troad.* Syn.—Dārdănĭă, Teūcrĭă. *Used as an adjective, Trojan.* Syn.—Īlĭăs, Dārdănĭs, Trōjānă.

Trōjă, æ̅. f. *Troy.* Trōjăquĕ nūnc stārēs, Prĭămīque ārx āltă, mănērēs. V. Syn.—Īlĭūm, Īlĭŏn, Īlĭŏs, Pērgămūm, Pērgămă. Phr.—Āltæ̅ mœ̅nĭă Trōjæ̅. Trōjānă ūrbs, tēllūs. Pērgămĕæ̅ ārcēs. Phœ̅bī, Nēptūnī mœ̅nĭă. Nēptūnī făbrĭcātă mănū. Ăpōllĭnĭs ārcēs. Prĭămī dūm rēgnă mănēbūnt. Dūm rēs stĕtĭt Īlĭă rēgnō. Dănăīs īnvīsă pŭēllĭs Trōjă jăcĕt. Ēt cāmpōs ŭbĭ Trōjă fŭĭt. Quīs Trōjæ̅ nēscĭăt ūrbēm?

Trōjānī, ōrūm. m. *The Trojans.* Sīn ēt Trōjānīs cūm mūltō glōrĭă vēnĭt Sānguĭnĕ. V. Syn.—Trōjŭgĕnæ̅, Trōĕs, Dārdănĭdæ̅, Teūcrī, Lāŏmĕdōntĭădæ̅, Hēctŏrĭdæ̅, Aēnēădæ̅, Phry̆gĭī, Phry̆gĕs. Phr.—Dārdănī, Dārdănĭī vĭrī, cŏlōnī, sŏcĭī. Trōjānă gēns, stīrps. Trōjānŭs pŏpŭlŭs. Āssărăcī gēns. Gĕnŭs ālto ā sānguĭnĕ dīvūm.

Tūrnŭs, ī. m. *Turnus, king of the Rutulians, vanquished by Aeneas.* Præ̅stāntī cōrpŏrĕ Tūrnŭs Vērtĭtŭr ārmă tĕnēns. V. Phr.—Daūnĭŭs hērōs. Rŭtŭlŭs hērōs, dūx, dūctŏr. Pāctā fŭrēns prō cōnjŭgĕ.

Ty̆phōeūs, ōĕŏs, ōĕī & ōeī. m. *Typhoeus, one of the giants destroyed by Jupiter.* Nōn tērrŭĭt īpsĕ Ty̆phōeūs Ārdŭŭs, ārmă tĕnēns. V. Syn.—Ty̆phōn. Phr.—Sæ̅vŭs ĕt īngēns. Tērrĭbĭlēm quōndām fŭgĭēns Ty̆phōnă Dĭōnē. Jŏvēm tūrbāntĕ Ty̆phōeō.

Ty̆rŏs & Ty̆rŭs, ī. f. *Tyre, city in Phenicia.* Prīmă rătēm vēntīs crēdĕrĕ dŏctă Ty̆rōs. Tib. Syn.—Sīdōn. Phr.—Rēgnă Ty̆rī. Ty̆rĭæ̅ ārcēs. Ty̆rĭī pŏsŭērĕ cŏlōnī.

U

Ŭlÿssēs & Ŭlÿxēs, ĭs, ĕī, eī & ī. m. *Ulysses, king of Ithaca.* Cārmĭnĭbūs Cīrcē sŏcĭōs mūtāvĭt Ŭlÿssēs. Syn.—Ĭthăcŭs, Lāērtĭădēs, Aēŏlĭdēs, Sīsÿphĭdēs. Phr.—Dūlĭchĭŭs, Lāērtĭŭs hērōs, dūx, rēctŏr, Lāērtĭă prōlēs. Lāērtĕ sătŭs. Aēmŭlŭs Ājăcĭs. Fūrtīs āptŭs. Cāsūs tārdē rĕmĕāntĭs Ŭlÿssĭs. Mōrēs hŏmĭnūm īnspēxĭt.

V

Vĕnĕtĭæ, ārūm. f. *Venice.* Phr.—Ūrbs Vĕnĕtă. Ūrbs Vĕnĕtōrūm. Vĕnĕtī, Eūgănĕī lăcŭs. Ādrĭăcī rēgīnă mărĭs. Mĕdĭo īn pĕlăgō mōlīmĭnĕ mūltō Ēxstrūctă. Aēmŭlă Rōmæ.

Vĕnŭs, ĕrĭs. f. *Venus, the goddess of beauty.* Sīc Vĕnŭs; āt Vĕnĕrĭs cōntrā sīc fīlĭŭs ōrsŭs. V. Syn.—Cÿthĕrēă, Cÿthĕrēĭă, Cÿthĕrēĭs, Cÿprĭs, Āphrōdītē, Ĕrÿcīnă, Dĭōnē. Phr.—Dĕă Păphĭă, Īdălĭă. Dīvă Păphī. Păphĭă mātĕr. Nātă frĕtō. Ōrtă mărī. Cÿprĭă vīrgŏ. Dīvă pŏtēns Cÿprī. Cōnchō vēctă.

Vērgĭlĭŭs, ĭī. m. *Vergil, the Roman epic poet.* Vērgĭlĭūm laūdāt, pĕrĭtūrae īgnōscĭt Ĕlīssæ. J. Syn.—Mărŏ. Phr.—Rōmŭlĕŭs pŏētă, vātēs. Lătĭālĭs Hŏmērŭs. Āltĕr Hŏmērŭs. Aēnĕĭdŏs sūmmŭs vātēs, cōndĭtŏr, aūctŏr. Sŏbŏlēs cērtīssĭmă Phœbī. Stŭdĭīs flōrēns īgnōbĭlĭs ōtī. Quī Phœbum æquāvĭt hŏnōrĕ. Dĕcŭs Ītălĭæ, lūx Ō **clārīssĭmă vātūm.**

Vĕsēvŭs, ī. m. *Mount Vesuvius near Naples.* Syn.—Vĕsŭvĭŭs, Vēsvĭŭs, Vēsbĭŭs. Phr.—Vĕsēvī jŭgūm. Vēsvīnŭs ăpēx, mōns. Vēsvīnŭs sæpĕ ērūctāns ĭn āstră făvīllās. Lŏcŭs Hērcŭlĕō nōmĭnĕ clārŭs. Vēsvĭŭs Aūsŏnĭīs fŭrĭt ōrĭs, Aētnă Sĭcānĭs. Prōrūmpĭt ăd æthĕră fūmūm. Vŏmēns pĭcĕă cālīgĭnĕ nīmbōs.

Vēstă, æ. f. *Vesta, goddess of the hearth.* Phr.—Quæque īgnēs Trōĭcă sērvăt. Cæsărĕōs īntēr săcrātă pĕnātēs. Vēstæ vĭgĭlēs ēxstīnguĕrĕ flāmmās. Fŏcī vēstālēs.

Vēstālĭs, ĭs. f. *A Vestal, virgin.* Cūr mŏdŏ Vēstālĭs tædās īnvītŏr ăd ūllās? O. Phr.—Vēstālĭs vīrgŏ, pŭēllă, săcērdōs. Vēstæ mĭnīstră. Vēstæ săcră. Vēstæ vĕnĕrāndă săcērdōs. Quæ cāstæ sērvāt pĕnētrālĭă Vēstæ. Īlĭăcæ tūtēlă făvīllæ. Aētērnūm sērvāns ădўtĭs pĕnētrālĭbŭs īgnēm.

Vūlcānŭs, ī. m. *Vulcan, the god of fire.* Vūlcānŭs ārdēns ūrĭt ōffĭcīnās. H. Syn.—Īgnĭpŏtēns, Mūlcĭbĕr. Phr.—Lēmnĭŭs dĕŭs. Īgnĭs dĕŭs. Dĕŭs īgnĭpŏtēns. Ŏpĭfēx trĭsūlcī fūlmĭnĭs dĕŭs. Fŭrĭt īmmīssīs Vūlcānŭs hăbēnīs.

X

Xērxēs, ĭs. m. *Xerxes, son of Darius and king of Persia.* Xērxĭs ēt īmpĕrĭō bīnă cŏīssĕ vădă. Prop. Phr.—Dūx, dūctŏr Pērsĭcŭs, Mēdŭs. Dărĭō gĕnĭtŭs.

Z

Zĕphy̆rŭs, ī. m. *Zephyrus, the west wind (deified).* Cōnflīgūnt Zĕphy̆rūsquĕ, Nŏtūsque ēt lætŭs Ĕōīs Eūrŭs ĕquīs. V. Syn.—Făvōnĭŭs. Phr.—Făvōnī, Zĕphy̆rī aūră, ănĭmă, flātŭs. Zĕphy̆rī plăcĭdæ, tĕpēntēs, lēnēs aūræ, mōllĭs āfflātŭs, lĕvĕ flāmĕn. Vērnī clēmēntĭŏr aūră Făvōnī. Vēntōrūm plăcĭdīssĭmŭs. Flātū, aūrā rĕfrīgĕrāns. Zĕphy̆rī nŏvă flāmĭnă. Vērnæ spīrānt aūræ. Ā Zĕphy̆rīs mītĭŏr aūră vĕnĭt. Mōllĭŏr aūră vĕnĭt. Zĕphy̆rō nīx vīctă tĕpēntī. Zĕphy̆rīs ăgĭtātă Tēmpē. Quĕrŭlō pēr rūră sŭsūrrō Mūrmŭrăt. Nīvĕ quæ Zĕphy̆rō vīctă tĕpēntĕ flŭĭt.

Zōdĭăcŭs, ī. m. *The Zodiac.* Syn.—Sīgnĭfĕr, Bāltĕŭs. Phr.—Āstrĭfĕr, sīgnĭfĕr, stēllātŭs cœlī līmĕs, ārcŭs, cīrcŭlŭs. Sōlĭs ĭtĕr. Cīrcŭlŭs āstră, sīgnă bīssēnă gĕrēns. Sīgnă pōlī dŭŏdēnă gĕrēns.

LIST OF TREES, PLANTS, FLOWERS AND SHRUBS MENTIONED IN POETRY.

Ăbĭēs, ăbĭĕtĭs & ābiĕtĭs. f. *Spruce, fir or hemlock.* Pōpŭlŭs īn flŭvĭīs, ăbĭēs īn mōntĭbŭs āltīs. V. Phr.—Sŭpĕr æthĕră sūrgēns. Āptă frĕtīs. Ūtĭlĭs ārbŏr ăquīs. Cāsūs vīsūră mărīnōs. Hīnc aūdāx ăbĭēs. Ād cœlūm rāmōs ăbĭēs ēxtēndĭt.

Ābsīnthĭūm, ĭī. n. *Wormwood.* Cānă prĭūs gĕlĭdō dēsīnt ābsīnthĭă Pōntō. O. Phr. Pōntō crēscēns, nātūm. Pērpotēt amarūm Ābsīnthī lătĭcēm. Părĭūnt ābsīnthĭă cāmpī.

Ăcācĭă, æ. f. *Acacia.* Phr.—Spīnīs ārmātă, hōrrēns, mĕtŭēndă. Sævīs mīstă rŭbīs. Cuī mĕtŭēndă lătēnt spīnæ pēr brāchĭă.

Ăcānthŭs, ī. m. *The acanthus or bears-foot.* Mīstăquĕ rīdēntī cŏlŏcāsĭă fūndĕt ăcānthō. V. Phr.—Flōs ăcānthĭnŭs. Īnflēxī vīmĕn ăcānthī. Flēxī vīmĕn ăcānthī. Bāccās sēmpēr frōndēntĭs ăcānthī.

Ăcĕr, ĕrĭs. n. *A maple tree.* Āt nūpēr vīlĕ fŭīstĭs ăcĕr. O. Phr.—Ēst ăcĕr īn sīlvīs. Ārbŏr ăcērnă. Ăcērnæ frōndĭs hŏnōs. Ăcērquĕ cŏlōrĭbŭs īmpār. Līgnō bĭcŏlōrĕ nŏtātūm. Tĭlĭæ fōrmā fŏlĭīquĕ cŏlōrĕ Nōn mūltum ābsĭmĭlĭs. Rĭgĭdī sēd cōrtĭcĭs ārbŏr. Hōrrĭdă rūgīs.

Ăcŏnītūm & Ăcŏnītŏn, ī. n. *Aconite, wolfsbane, monksbane.* Lūrĭdă tērrĭbĭlēs mīscēnt ăcŏnītă nŏvērcæ. O. Phr.—Lētālĕ vĕnēnūm. Dīctæīs nāscēntĭă sāxīs. Scȳthĭcīs ăcŏnītŏn ăb ōrīs.

Ădĭāntūm, ī. n. *The herb maidenhair.* Syn.—Căpīllī Vĕnĕrĭs. Phr. —Rōrĭs ēxpērs. Tēstātūm Vĕnĕrīs nīgrāntī crīnĕ dŏlōrēm.

Ădōnĭūm, ĭī. n. *The anemone. See Anemone.*

Ālĭūm, ĭī. n. *Garlic, leeks, onion.* Ālĭă sērpȳllūmque, hērbās cōntūndĭt ŏlēntēs. V. Syn.—Būlbŭs, cæpĕ. Phr.—Grăvĭtēr rĕdŏlēns. Grăvēm spīrāns ŏdōrēm. Tēr mānĕ căpūt gūstāvĕrĭs ālī. Pīstīllō frāgrāntĭă mōllĭt Ālĭă.

Ālnŭs, ī. f. *An alder tree.* Flōrĭdĭōr prātō; lōngā prōcērĭōr ālnō. O. Phr.—Ālnūs ămīcă frĕtīs. Āptă mărī, ūndīs. Flūctĭbŭs āptĭōr ālnŭs. Ātquĕ sōlō prōcērās ērĭgĭt ālnōs.

Ălŏē, ēs. f. *The herb aloe.* Plūs ălŏēs quām mēllĭs hăbĕt. J.

Ămārăcŭs, ī. m. & Ămārăcūm, ī. n. *Sweet-marjoram.* Sīc ŭbi ŏdōrātās prætēxĭt ămārăcŭs ūmbrās. Syn.—Sāmpsūchūm, sāmpsūchŭs. Phr.—Mōllĭs ămārăcŭs. Gĕnĭālĭs ămārăcŭs.

Ămărānthŭs, ī. m. *Everlasting, a flower that never fades.* Ūt cūm cōntēxūnt ămărānthīs ālbă pŭēllă Sērtă. Tib. Phr.—Mārcēscĕrĕ nēscĭŭs. Nūmquām mārcēscēns. Nēscĭēns mōrtĭs. Cuī flōs pērpĕtŭŭs. Nūmquam āmīttīt flōrĭs hŏnōrēm. Sūstĭnĕt ūrēntēs æstūs nēc frīgŏrĕ læsŭs Brūmālī mŏrĭtŭr.

Ămȳgdălă, æ. f. *An almond tree.* Phr.—Phȳllĭdĭs ārbŏr frōndōsă, pătŭlă. Phȳllĭdă quīn ĕtĭām grāndī mītēscĕrĕ frūctū Īnstĭtŭēns, dūræ dāt sŭă mēmbră cŭtī. Ămȳgdălĭnūm ŏlĕūm.

Ănĕmōnē, ēs & Ănĕmōnă, æ. f. *The anemone.* Syn.—Ădōnĭūm. Phr.—Nāmque ĕt ămāt Zĕphȳrōs ănĕmōnē. Flōs brĕvĭs ūsū. Vērĭs hŏnōrēs. Nĭmĭā lĕvĭtātĕ cădūcŭs. Hĭĕmĭs vūltūm hōrrēntēm sŭō sōlābĭtŭr ōstrō. Crīspō rĕcrĕăt mūrĭcĕ cāmpōs. Hōrtōrūm dĕcŭs. Fōrmōsī glōrĭă rūrĭs. Tēmpŏrĕ dīgna ălĭō. Nōn ūllūs flōrūm nŭmĕrō tĭbĭ cērtĕt ăb ōmnī.

Ănēthūm, ī. n. *The herb anise.* Ēt flōrēm jūngīt bĕne ŏlēntĭs ănēthī. V. Phr.—Ănēthī flōs, grāmĕn.

Ārbŭtŭs, ī. f. *Wild strawberry or cherry-tree.* Dūlcĕ sătīs hūmōr dēpūlsīs ārbŭtŭs hædīs. V. Phr.—Pōmōque ŏnĕrātă rŭbēnt. Tĕgĭt ārbŭtŭs ūmbrā.

Ărūndŏ, ĭnĭs. f. *Reed or cane.* Hīc vĭrĭdēs tĕnĕrā prætēxĭt ărūndĭnĕ rīpās. V. Syn.—Ăvēnă, călămŭs, cānnă. Phr.—Pārvæ lōngā sŭb ărūndĭnĕ cānnæ. Grăcĭlĭs vībrātŭr ărūndŏ. Flŭvĭālĭs ărūndŏ.

Aūrāntĭă, ōrūm. n. *Oranges.* Phr.—Ēst ĕtĭām pōmūm cuī prīmum Aūrāntĭă nōmĕn Ūrbs āntīquă dĕdĭt. Aūrĕă mālă, pōmă. Mālă Hēspĕrĭdūm. Măgĭs ūbĕrĕ rōrĭdă sūccō.

Ăvēnă, æ. f. *Oats, oaten straw.* Īllōs ēxspēctātă sĕgēs vānīs ēlūsĭt ăvēnīs. V. Syn.—Cūlmŭs. Phr.—Ēt lĕvĭs ōbsēssō stābăt ăvēnă sŏlō. Stĕrĭlēs dŏmĭnāntŭr ăvēnæ.

Bāccăr, ărĭs. n. *Lady's glove, or perhaps digitalis.* Ērrāntēs hĕdĕrās pāssīm cūm bāccărĕ tēllūs. V. Syn.—Bāccărĭs (f.). Phr.—Bāccărĕ frōntēm cīngĭte.

Bālsămūm, ī. n. *The balsam tree.* Quīs tĭbi ŏdōrātō rĕfĕrām sūdāntĭă līgnō Bālsămă? V. Syn.—Ŏpŏbālsămūm. Phr.—Bālsămĕŭs ŏdŏr. Sȳrĭūm mūnŭs. Ēōŭs lĭquŏr. Lætōs spīrăt ŏdōrēs. Bālsămă mē căpĭūnt; hæc sūnt ūnguēntă vĭrōrūm. Tārdăquĕ sūdāntī prōrēpūnt bālsămă sūccō. Bālsămūm mŏdĭcă ārbŏr.

Bēllĭs, ĭdĭs. f. *The marguerite.* Syn.—Bēllŭs (m.). Phr.—Tŭō flōrēbūnt bēllĭdēs hōrtō. Glōrĭă cāmpī. Flōs fōrmōsă.

Būlbŭs, ī. m. *Onion.* Daūnĭŭs ān Lĭbȳcīs būlbūs tĭbĭ mīssŭs ăb ōrīs. O. Syn.—Ālĭūm, cæpĕ. Phr.—Gĕnĭtālĭă sēmĭnă būlbī.

Būxŭs, ī. f. & Būxūm, ī. n. *The box-tree.* Ēt dēnsūm fŏlĭīs būxūm, frăgĭlēsquĕ mўrīcæ. O. Phr.—Flūctŭăt hīc dēnsō crīspātă căcūmĭnĕ būxŭs. Tōrnō rāsĭlĕ būxūm. Pērpĕtŭōquĕ vĭrēns būxŭs. Nē lūbrĭcă būxŭs Āntĭcĭpēt sēdēm. Flāvăquĕ pērpĕtŭō būxŭs hŏnōrĕ vĭrĕt. Dāt thălămōs ĕădēm mōllīquĕ sĕdīlĭă frōndĕ. Tĕnĕrōs lōngō flēctēns cūrvāmĭnĕ rāmōs. Ēxhĭbĕt æstīvīs īmpērvĭă sōlĭbŭs āntră.

Călămŭs, ī. m. *Reed or cane.* Cōrpŏrĕ prō Nўmphæ călămōs tĕnŭīssĕ pălūstrēs. O. Syn.—Ărūndŏ, cānnă. Phr.—Călămŭs ărōmătĭcŭs. Tū călămōs īnflārĕ lĕvēs. Călămōs nōn pāssŭs ĭnērtēs.

Cālthă, æ. f. *The marigold.* Mōllĭă lūtĕōlā pīngīt vāccīnĭă cālthā. V. Phr.—Pāllēntī flāvēntēs lūmĭnĕ cālthæ.

Cānnă, æ. f. *Reed, or cane.* Āră vĕtūs stābāt trĕmŭlūs cīrcūmdătă cānnīs. O. Syn. Ărūndŏ, călămŭs, jūncŭs. Phr.—Prætēxēns vĭrĭdēs rīpās. Pĭgrām vēlēbāt cānnă pălūdēm. Lōngæ pārvā sŭb ărūndĭnĕ cānnæ. Dŏmūs jūncō cānnāque īntēxtă pălūstrī.

Cārpĭnŭs, ī. f. *A kind of plane-tree, maple or yoke-tree.* Phr.—Ămīcā cārpĭnŭs ūmbrā. Īrĕ pĕr ōmnēs Ōbsĕquĭōsă mŏdōs. Mōllēs tēndēns rāmōs. Præbēbīt vĭrĭdēm dīvērso ē mārgĭnĕ scēnām.

Cāstănĕă, æ. f. *Chestnut-tree.* Phr.—Stānt ēt jūnĭpĕrī ēt cāstănĕæ hīrsūtæ. Ăvĭbūs frōndōsă præbēns hōspĭtă. Frūctĭbŭs ūtĭlĭs. Ēxtēndēns lātē sŭă brāchĭă. Rāmīs dīffūsă. Tōllēns sē vērtĭcĕ ăd aūrās.

Cĕdrŭs, ī. f. *The Cedar tree.* Ūrĭt ŏdōrātām nōctūrna īn lūmĭnĕ cēdrūm. V. Phr.—Aētērnūm vĭrēns. Lōngæ sĕnēctæ. Nōn mĕtŭēns cărĭēm. Cărĭe īmpĕnĕtrābĭlĭs ārbōs. Ārdŭă cēdrŭs hăbĕt. Cĕdrŭs ŏdōrātă.

Cĕrăsŭs, ī. f. *The cherry-tree.* Hīc dūlcēs cĕrăsōs, hīc aūtūmnālĭă pōmă. Prop. Phr.—Frūctĭfĕră ārbŏr. Dūlcĭs ārbŏr.

Chærĕphўlūm, ī. n. *The herb chervil.* Jām brĕvĕ chærĕphўlum ēt tōrpēntī grātă pălātō Īntŭbă. Syn.—Chærĕphўllōn, chærŏphўllūm, cærĕfŏlĭūm.

Chrўsānthĕmūm, ī. n. *Chrysanthemum or crowfoot.* Syn.—Chrўsānthĕmŏn. Phr.—Āgnātō flōrēns chrўsānthĕmŏn aūrō.

Cĭcĕr, ĕrĭs. n. *Chick peas.* Nĕque īllĕ Sēpōsĭtī cĭcĕrīs, nēc lōngae īnvīdĭt ăvēnæ. H. Phr.—Tēllūrĭs ĕdāx. Cĭcĕr ārĭĕtīnūm. Cĭcĕrīs mŏdĭī trēs.

Cĭchŏrēūm, ī. n. *Chicory or succory.* Mē pāscūnt ŏlīvæ, Mē cĭchŏrēă lĕvēsquĕ mālvæ. H. Syn.—Īntŭbŭs, īntўbūm. Phr.—Lāctūcæquĕ grăvēs sōmnīs cĭchŏrēăquĕ rēnūm Pūrgātrīx.

Cĭcūtă, æ. f. *Hemlock.* Sēd mălă tōllēt ănūm vĭtĭātō mēllĕ cĭcūtă. H. *See Venenum.* Phr.—Mīsta ăcōnītă cĭcūtīs. Pīnguēscĕrĕ sæpĕ cĭcūtā bārbĭgĕrās pĕcŭdēs.

Cīnnămōn, ī. n. *The Cinnamon tree.* Syn.—Cīnnămūm, cīnnămōmūm. Phr.—Ădŏlēbūnt cīnnămă flāmmæ. O. Mūltūmquĕ mădēntī Īnfūdĕrĕ cŏmæ cīnnămōn. Pānchæăquĕ sūrgūnt Cīnnămă. Rāră sŭō mīscēntūr cīnnămă nārdō. *See Odor.*

Cĭtrŭs, ī. f. *A citron-tree.* Sēd cītrī cōntēntă cŏmīs vīvēbăt ĕt ūmbrā. L. Phr.—Sēctōs Ātlāntĭdĕ sīlvā Īmpŏsŭēre ōrbēs. Maūræque Ātlāntĭcă sīlvæ Prōgĕnĭēs. Rāmīsque ēxsūltăt Ădōnĭăs ārbōs. Cĭtrĕă rōbŏră. Ātlāntĭcă mūnĕră. Cĭtrōs nĕcăt hūmĭdă tēllūs. Īntĕr ŏdōrātās, fēlīcĭă gērmĭnă, cītrōs. Īllæsūm rĕtĭnēt cĭtrŭs aūrĕă frōndĭs hŏnōrēm. Lĭbÿssă cĭtrŭs.

Cōrnŭs, ī. f. *The cornel-tree.* Phr.—Tĕrĕs ārbŏr. Bŏnă bēllō. Ītălă cōrnŭs. Ārmātă fērrō cōrnŭs.

Cŏrÿlŭs, ī. f. *The hazel-tree.* Phÿllĭs ămāt cŏrÿlōs; īllās dūm Phÿllĭs ămābăt. V. Phr.—Nēc mÿrtūs vīncēt cŏrÿlōs, nēc laūrĕă Phœbī. Plāntīs ēdūræ cŏrÿlī nāscūntŭr.

Crŏcŭs, ī. m. *The saffron.* Īllĕ crŏcūm sĭmŭlăt, crŏcĕō vēlātŭs ămīctū. O. Phr.—Crŏcĕī flōrēs. Spīcă Cĭlīssă, Cĭlĭcūm mēssĭs, flōrēs. Vōbīs pīctă crŏcō. Spīrāntēsquĕ crŏcōs, ĕt ĭn ūrnā pērpĕtŭūm vēr. Cōrÿcĭæquĕ cŏmæ.

Cŭprēssŭs, ī & ūs. f. *A cypress-tree.* Āræ Cærŭlĕīs mœstīs vīttīs ātrāquĕ cŭprēssō. V. Syn.—Cÿpărīssŭs. Phr.—Lūctūs tēstātă. Brūmă īllæsă. Tŭmŭlōs tēctūră. Tōndērī dŏcĭlĭs. Pēr sē pătĭēns īn quāslĭbĕt īrĕ fĭgūrās. Īn cœlūm cōnō pōrrēctă. Dēnsă cŭprēssū. Fērālī cīnctă cŭprēssū. Īnvĭŏlātă cŭprēssŭs. Cōmmŏda rūrī. Tēndĭt ĭnæquālēs rāmōs crīstāmquĕ cŏmāntēm. Vēntīs ăgĭtātă cŭprēssŭs.

Dāphnē, ēs. f. *A laurel-tree.* Hīc nĕmŏrōsă vĭrēnt Dāphnē lŏcă. *See Laurus.*

Ērvūm, ī. n. *A kind of pulse like the vetch.* Phr.—Mē sīlvă căvūsquĕ Tūtŭs ăb īnsĭdĭīs, tĕnŭī sōlābĭtŭr ērvō. Nĕc ērvi ŏpĕrōsă cūra ēst.

Fāgŭs, ī. f. *A beech-tree.* Sūb tēgmĭnĕ fāgī. V. Phr.—Tāntum īntēr dēnsās, ūmbrōsă căcūmĭnă, fāgōs. V. Rūgōsō cōrtĭcĕ fāgŭs. Āspĕră rāmōs āltē spārgēns. Lātē rāmōs ānnōsăquĕ brāchĭă pāndēns. Rŭdĭbūs fāgīs tēxūntŭr ĕt ōrnīs.

Frāgă, ōrūm. n. *Strawberries.* Sīlvēstrī nātă sŭb ūmbrā Mōllĭă frāgă lĕgēs. O. Phr.—Ēt hŭmī nāscēntĭă frāgă. Pārvīs vūlsă dūmētīs. Făcĭlēs cĭbī. Pūnĭcă frāgōrūm pūrpŭra sērpĭt hŭmī.

Frāxĭnŭs, ī. f. *An ash-tree.* Frāxĭnŭs īn sīlvīs pūlchērrĭmă. V. Syn.—Ōrnŭs. Phr.—Frāxĭnŭs ūtĭlĭs hāstīs. Frāxĭnŭs ămīcĭŏr ūndīs. Frāxĭnŭs bēllō. Frāngī pătĭēns sēd nēscĭă flēctī. Sŏnăt āltă bĭpēnnī Frāxĭnŭs.

Fūngŭs, ī. m. *Mushroom.* Vīlĭbŭs āncĭpĭtēs fūngī pōnēntŭr ămīcīs. J. Syn.—Bōlētŭs. Phr.—Prātēnsĭbŭs ōptĭma fūngīs Nātūra ēst. Cōrpŏră plŭvĭālĭbŭs ēdĭtă fūngīs. Īrrītāmēntă gŭlæ. Fūngōrūm ŏrīgŏ ēx pītuītā ārbŏrūm.

Gĕnīstă, æ. f. *Broom-plant.* Mōllĕ sĭlēr, lēntæquĕ gĕnīstæ. V. Syn.—Spārtūm. Phr.—Gĕnīstă hŭmĭlĭs. Gĕnīstă spīnōsă, sīlvēstrĭs.

Hĕdĕră, æ. f. *Ivy.* Ūtquĕ sŏlēnt hĕdĕræ lōngōs īntēxĕrĕ trūncōs. O. Phr.—Frōndēntēs bāccīs hĕdĕræ. Cŏrȳmbīs vĭrēscēns. Frōndĕ sĕquācī rōbŏră lĭgāns, āmplēctēns. Grātīssĭmă Bācchō. Īnsīgnĭă Bācchī. Bācchĭă sērtă. Dōctārūm præmĭă frōntĭūm. Nōbĭlĭs cŏrōnă vātūm. Lāscīvīs hĕdĕrīs āmbĭtĭōsĭŏr. Hĕdĕrā fōrmōsĭŏr ālbā. Hĕdĕrā crīnēs rĕlĭgātă fūlgēs. Hĕdĕrā tēmpŏră vīnctă fĕrās. Hĕdĕrā prōcēra āstrīngĭtŭr īlēx. Prōcēdĭt Īācchŭs Crīnālī flōrēns hĕdĕrā. Vūltūs hĕdĕrārūm frōndĭbŭs ābdĭt.

Hўăcīnthŭs & Hўăcīnthŏs, ī. m. *The hyacinth.* Suāvĕ rŭbēns hўăcīnthŭs. V. Phr.—Tē quŏquĕ flēbĭlĭbŭs mœrēns Hўăcīnthĕ fĭgūrīs. Flōs Ămȳclæŭs, Oēbălĭŭs, Spārtānŭs, Tænărĭŭs, Thĕrāpnæŭs. Nātŭs Ămȳclīs. Mūltā fērrūgĭnĕ lūcēns. Nōmĭnă rēgūm Īnscrīptūs fŏlĭīs. Ĕt āi, āi Flōs hăbēt īnscrīptūm.

Hȳssōpŭs, ī. m. *The herb hyssop.* Phr.—Īn vīnō prĭŭs hȳssōpūm, vălĭdām quŏquĕ rūtām. Mĕdĭcōs hȳssōpŭs ĭn ūsūs.

Īlēx, ĭcĭs. f. *A kind of oak-tree.* Cōrtĭcĭbūsquĕ căvīs vĭtĭōsæque īlĭcĭs ālvō. V. Syn.—Quērcŭs. Phr.—Īlīgnūm, īlĭcēūm rōbŏr. Īlēx plēnă făvīs. Cūrvātăquĕ glāndĭbŭs īlēx. Dūrīs ŭt īlēx tōnsă bĭpēnnĭbŭs. Sŭb ārgūtā cōnsēdĕrāt īlĭcĕ Dāphnē.

Īrĭs, ĭdĭs. f. *The iris.* Īllȳrĭcā quæ vĕnĭt Īrĭs hŭmō. O. Phr.—Quæ dīcĭtŭr Īrĭs ăb ārcū. Flōrēs vărĭātă cŏlōrĭbŭs ārcūs.

Jūncŭs, ī. m. *A bulrush.* Līmōsōquĕ pălūs ōbdūcāt pāscŭă jūncō. V. Syn.—Ărūndŏ, scīrpŭs. Phr.—Jūncī vīmĕn. Nēc ăcūtā cūspĭdĕ jūncī.

Jūnĭpĕrŭs, ī. f. *The juniper-tree.* Jūnĭpĕrī grăvĭs ūmbră, nŏcēnt ēt frūgĭbŭs ūmbræ. V.

Lāctūcă, æ. f. *Lettuce.* Claūdĕrĕ quæ cœnās lāctūcă sŏlēbăt ăvŏrūm. M. Syn.—Lāctūcŭlă. Phr.—Grātă nōbĭlĭūm rĕquĭēs cĭbōrūm. Lāctūcă cŏchlĕās ĭmĭtātă. Lāctūcă plēxīs frōndĭbŭs. Lāctūcă dēntātās crīspātă cŏmās. Sălūtārī lāctūcā săpōrĕ.

Laūrŭs, ī & ūs. f. *The laurel or bay-tree.* Ītĕ trĭūmphālēs cīrcūm mĕă tēmpŏră laūrī. O. Syn.—Laūrĕă. Phr.—Laūrī frōndēs.

Ārbŏr Phœbī, Phœbēă, Pārnāssĭă, Pārnāssĭs. Phœbī dĕcŭs. Laūrī pērpĕtŭūm dĕcŭs. Phœbō săcră, dĭcātă. Săcră cŏmāns. Ămāns cārmĭnă. Laūrō dēvīnctŭs ăgrēstī. Cāstā rĕdĭmītūs tēmpŏră laūrō. Dēpōnĕ sūb laūrū mĕā. Vĭrēt sēmpēr laūrūs nēc frōndĕ cădūcā Cārpĭtŭr. Ōrnārī laūrō sĕcūndā.

Lēns, lēntĭs. f. *Lentils.* Nēc Pēlūsĭăcæ cūram āspērnābĕrĕ lēntĭs. V. Syn.—Lēntĭcŭlă. Phr.—Pēlūsĭă, Pēlūsĭăcă mūnĕră. Lēns ămāt sŏlūm tĕnŭĕ.

Leūcŏĭŏn & Leūcŏĭūm, ī. n. *The white violet.* Phr.—Cāndĭdă leūcŏĭa, ēt flāvēntĭă lūmĭnă cālthæ. Fŏlĭō văriātă rūbēntī Leūcŏĭă.

Lĭgūstrūm, ī. n. *Privet.* Ālbă lĭgūstră cădūnt, vāccīnĭă nīgră lĕgūntŭr. V. Phr.—Cāndĭdĭōr fŏlĭō nĭvĕī, Gălātēă, lĭgūstrī. Cāndĭdĭōr pŭēllă nĭvĕ, līlĭō, lĭgūstrī.

Līlĭūm, ĭī. n. *The lily.* Sæpĕ tŭlīt blāndīs ārgēntēă līlĭă nўmphīs. Prop. Phr.—Līlĭă lūtĕōlīs īntērlūcēntĭă sērtīs. Mĭcānt pūrīs līlĭă mīxtă rŏsīs. Rōscĭdă līlĭă cāmpīs. Vĭrĭdī sē līlĭă caūdĭcĕ tōllūnt. Brĕvĕ līlĭūm. Cāndĭdă līlĭă. Līlĭă hĭāntĭă. Līlĭūm rŏsæ nōbĭlĭtātĕ prōxĭmūm ēst.

Līnūm, ī. n. *Flax.* Ūrĭt ĕnīm cāmpūm līnī sĕgĕs, ūrĭt ăvēnă. V. Phr.—Quī līnă mădēntĭă dūcūnt.

Lŏlĭūm, ĭī. n. *Cockle.* Īnfēlīx lŏlĭum, ēt stĕrĭlēs dŏmĭnāntŭr ăvēnæ. V. Syn.—Zīzānĭă. Phr.—Ārvīs, sĕgĕtī ĭnĭmīcūm. Cĕrĕrĭs lŭēs, pēstĭs. Cărĕānt āgrī lŏlĭīs. Āgrĭcŏlīs ĭnĭmīcūm.

Lŭpīnŭs, ī. m. *A kind of pulse, called lupins.* Aūt tĕnŭīs fœtūs vĭcĭæ, trīstīsquĕ lŭpīnī. V. Syn.—Lŭpīnūm. Phr.—Trīstĭs lŭpīnī frăgĭlēs călămī.

Mālŭs, ī. f. *An apple-tree* Ēt stĕrĭlēs plătănī mālōs gēssērĕ vălēntēs. V. Phr.—Nĭtĕt ĭn ārvō. Pōmă mĭcānt. Frūctĭbŭs ūtĭlĭs. Mālŭs bĭfĕră. Cūjūs rĕdŏlēntĭă mālă. Frūctūque ēt flōrĕ sŭpērbă. Īmplēbīt tĕrētēs ārbōr spē dīvĭtĕ rāmōs.

Mālvă, æ. f. *The herb mallows.* Ūtĕrĕ lāctūcīs ēt mōllĭbŭs ūtĕrĕ mālvīs. M. Phr.—Sălūbrĭs grăvī cōrpŏrī.

Mărīscă, æ. f. *A large inferior kind of fig.* Phr.—Vīlēsquĕ mărīscæ. Fătŭæ mărīscæ. Fīcī mărīscæ. Pīnguēs mărīscæ.

Mārrŭbĭūm, ĭī. n. *Hore-hound.* Phr.—Mārrŭbĭūm nĭgrūm. Prōfŭĭt ēt plāntīs lătĭcēs īnfūndĕre ămārōs Mārrŭbĭī.

Mĕlīsphўllūm, ī. n. *The balm-gentle, apiastrum.* Trītă mĕlīsphўlla ēt cērīnthae īgnōbĭlĕ grāmĕn. V. Syn.—Mĕlīssă, mĕlīssōphўllŏn. Phr.—Hŭmĭlī dē cæspĭtĕ, rūfō Flōrĕ mĭcāns. Tĕnŭēmquĕ mĕlīssām.

Mēntă (Mēnthă), æ. f. *Mint.* Hæc tĭbĭ quæ tōrtā vēnērūnt cōndĭtă mēntă. M. Phr.—Suāvēm quæ spīrāt ŏdōrēm. Mēntă rūctātrīx, sērpēns. Rūta ēt mēntă, rēcte ŭtrūmquĕ.

Mĭlĭūm, ĭī. n. *Millet.* Mĭlĭō vĕnĭt ānnŭă cūră. V. Phr.—Lībā dē mĭlĭō.

Mōrŭs, ī. f. *A mulberry-tree.* Ārdŭă mōrŭs ĕrāt gĕlĭdō cōntērmĭnă fōntī. O. Phr.—Ārbōs Sērĭcă, Thīsbææ. Ārbŏrūm săpĭēntīssĭmă mōrŭs. Nĭvĕīs ūbērrĭmă pōmīs.

Mȳrīcă, æ. f. *The tamarisk.* Nōn ōmnēs ārbūstă jŭvānt, hŭmĭlēsquĕ mȳrīcæ. V. Phr.—Ēt rārā frōndĕ mȳrīcæ.

Mȳrrhă (Mūrră), æ. f. *Myrrh-tree.* Nōndūm pērtŭlĕrāt lăcrĭmātūs cōrtĭcĕ mȳrrhās. O. Phr.—Stīllātăquĕ cōrtĭcĕ Mȳrrhă Nōmĕn hĕrīlĕ tĕnĕt. Mȳrrhæ lăcrĭmæ, gūttæ, ārbŏr, cōrtēx. Mȳrrhĕă gūttă. Ŏdōrātō stīllātă, stīllāns cōrtĭcĕ mȳrrhă. Pīnguī dē cōrtĭcĕ mānāns, cădēns. Dōnă fĕrūnt Pŭĕrō mȳrrhæque ēt tūrĭs ēt aūrī.

Nārcīssŭs, ī. m. *The daffodil.* Prō mōllī vĭōlā, prō pūrpŭrĕō nārcīssō. V. Phr.—Suāvĕ rŭbēns. Sēră cŏmāns. Dē cōrpŏrĕ flōrēm. Sūblīmi āttōllīt jūncō, fŏlĭōquĕ cŏmāntī.

Nārdŭs, ī. f. & Nārdūm, ī. n. *Nard.* Nārdī lēnĭs ărīstās, Quāssăquĕ cūm fūlvā sūbstrāvīt cīnnămă mȳrrhā. O. Phr.—Sērtās nārdō flōrēntĕ cŏrōnās. Nārdī gērmĕn. Nārdŭs Gāllĭcŭs.

Nāstūrtĭūm, ĭī. n. *A kind of cress.* Phr.—Cæcīs nāstūrtĭă dīră cŏlŭbrīs.

Ŏlĕă, æ. f. *Olive-tree.* Sēd trūncīs ŏlĕæ mĕlĭūs prōpāgĭnĕ vītēs Rēspōndēnt. V. Syn.—Ŏlīvă. Phr.—Pāllădĭs ārbŏr, rāmī. Ārbŏr Pāllădĭă. Ŏlĕæ, ŏlīvæ rāmī. Rādīx ŏlĕāgĭnă. Pācĭs ārbŏr. Frōns Mĭnērvæ. Tārdē crēscēns. Aētērnūm vĭrēns. Aētērnōs gĕrēns frōndĭs hŏnōrēs. Rāmūmquĕ tĕnēns pŏpŭlārĭs ŏlīvæ. Frōntī præpōnĕre ŏlīvām.

Ŏlĕāstĕr, trī. m. *The wild olive.* Īndĭcĭo ēst trāctū sūrgēns ŏlĕāstĕr ĕōdēm. V. Phr.—Sŭpĕrāt fŏlĭīs ŏlĕāstĕr ămārīs. Sīlvēstrĭs ŏlīvī Sūrcŭlŭs.

Ōrnŭs, ī. f. *Wild ash.* Nāscūntūr stĕrĭlēs sāxōsīs mōntĭbŭs ōrnī. V. Syn.—Frāxĭnŭs. Phr.—Īngēntēs ādvōlvūnt mōntĭbŭs ōrnōs. Ōrnūsquę īncānŭĭt ālbō Flōrĕ pȳrī. Āntīqua īn mōntĭbŭs ōrnŭs.

Păpāvĕr, ĕrĭs. n. *Poppy.* Crēbră sŏpōrĭfĕrūm grānă păpāvĕr hăbĕt. O. Phr.—Căpŭt grăvāns. Sōmnūm īndūcēns. Grātūm Cĕrĕrī plēnūmquĕ sŏpōrĕ. Lēthæō rōrĕ mĕdĭcātūm. Lāssōvĕ păpāvĕră cōllō Dēmīsērĕ căpŭt. Lēthæō pērfūsă păpāvĕră sōmnō. Caūsæquĕ păpāvĕră sōmnī. Crīspātōs ĭmĭtātă păpāvĕră cīrrōs. Lĭlĭă pūrpŭrĕīs mīxtă păpāvĕrĭbŭs. Cĕrĕālĕ păpāvĕr. Mĕdĭcōs ădhĭbēntŭr ĭn ūsūs.

Păpȳrŭs, ī. f. & Păpȳrūm, ī. n. *Papyrus.* Pērdĭtĕ Nīlĭăcās, Mūsæ, mĕă dāmnă, păpȳrōs. M. Syn.—Bĭblŭs. Phr.—Crēscĭt mūltă păpȳrō Pāgĭnă.

Pērsĭcŭs, ī. f. *Peach-tree.* Phr.—Pērsĭcūm mālūm, pōmūm. Mīssūm ā Pērsĭdĕ mālūm. Quōd Pērsīs gĕnŭĭt. Quōd pūrpŭră tīnxĭt. Pūrpŭrĕō sūffūsūm cŏlōrĕ. Ūnă sŭpēr frūctūs lōngē laūdātĭŏr ōmnēs.

Pĭcĕă, æ. f. *The pitch-pine.* Syn.—Pīnŭs, pĭcĕāstĕr. Phr.—Vāllĭs ĕrāt pĭcĕīs ĕt ăcūtā dēnsă cŭprēssū. Lūcūs nīgrāntī pĭcĕa ōbscūrŭs. Pīnŭs sīlvēstrĭs.

Pīnŭs, ī & ūs. f. *A pine-tree.* Ēt sūccīnctă cŏmās hīrsūtăquĕ vērtĭcĕ pīnŭs. O. Syn.—Pĭcĕă, pĭcĕāstĕr. Phr.—Ēvērtūnt āctās ād sīdĕră pīnūs. Pōntĭcă pīnŭs. Sūdāntī cōrtĭcĕ. Ŏdōrō vūlnĕrĕ pīnŭs. Ārcădĭō pīnūs ămātă dĕō. Grātă dĕūm mātrī. Sīlvæ fīlĭă nōbĭlĭs. Cŏmāns sīlvārūm glōrĭă. Līttŭs ămāns. Līttŏrĭbŭs gaūdēns. Pērpĕtŭōquĕ vĭrēns ēt sēmpēr flōrĭdă pīnŭs. Sē lātē pārtēs prōfūndĭt ĭn ōmnēs. Tĕrēs trūncō pāssīsque āmplīssĭmă rāmīs. Frōndĭs hŏnōrēm sērvăt. Sīlvām dŏmĭnātŭr. Vēntōs ămăt ēt mōntēs.

Pĭrŭs, ī. f. *A pear-tree.* Īnsĕrĕ nūnc, Mĕlĭbœĕ, pĭrōs. V. Phr.—Quēm pĭrŭs īnvītō stīpĭtĕ mālă tŭlĭt. Īnsĭtīvă dēcērpēns pĭră. Sȳrĭīsquĕ pĭrīs plēnă.

Plătănŭs, ī. f. *A plane-tree.* Jāmquĕ mĭnīstrāntēm plătănūm pōtāntĭbŭs ūmbrām. V. Phr.—Hīc vērnō plătănūs fŏlĭō vĭrĕt. Nōbĭlĭŏr pōmīs, plătănō cōnspēctĭŏr āltā. Stĕrĭlēs plătănī. Ēxplĭcăt hīc frōndēs plătănūs gĕnĭālĭs ŏpācās. Plătănūs pătŭlīs dīffūsă rāmīs. Sūb plătănō ūmbrĭfĕrā. Plătănŭs cælēbs.

Pōpŭlŭs, ī. f. *A poplar-tree.* Pōpŭlūs īn flŭvĭīs, ăbĭēs īn mōntĭbŭs āltīs. V. Phr.—Ārbŏr Hērcŭlĕă. Ālcīdæ grātīssĭmă. Flŭvĭīs ămīcă. Flūmĭnĭbŭs gaūdēns. Ūndā nūtrītă. Hērcŭlĕæ ārbōs ūmbrōsă cŏrōnæ. Ālbă cŏmās. Prætēxēns vĭrĭdēs ūndās. Phăĕtōntĭs sŏrŏr. Clȳmĕnēūm gērmĕn. Hīc cāndĭdă pōpŭlūs āntrō Īmmĭnĕt. Pōpŭlŭs flŭvĭālī cōnsĭtă rīpā.

Prūnŭs, ī. f. *A plum-tree.* Ēt prūnīs lăpĭdōsă rŭbēscĕrĕ cōrnă. V. Phr.—Frūctĭbŭs ūtĭlĭs. Prūnŭs sīlvēstrĭs. Dūlcēsquĕ fĕrēntēs frūctūs.

Pȳrŭs, ī. f. *A pear-tree.* Nēc sūrcŭlŭs īdēm Crūstŭmĭīs, Sȳrĭīsquĕ pȳrīs, grăvĭbūsquĕ vŏlēmīs. V. *See Pirus.*

Quērcŭs, ūs. f. *An oak-tree.* Cōncūssăquĕ fămem īn sīlvīs sōlābĕrĕ quērcū. V. Syn.—Aēscŭlŭs, īlēx, rōbŭr. Phr.—Ārbōs Dōdōnĭs.

Jŏvī ămīcă. Dūrīs ŏnūstă glāndĭbŭs īlēx. Sŭĭbŭs grātīssĭmă. Lātē brāchĭă tēndēns. Sūblīmī vērtĭcĕ nūtāns. Īnfīxīs āltē rādīcĭbŭs hǣrēns. Āttōllēns īntōnsă căcūmĭnă cœ̄lō. Frōndĭbŭs ǣscŭlŭs āltīs. Āntīquō rōbŏrĕ quērcŭs. Lōngā căriōsă sĕnēctā. Īnnātăquĕ rūpĭbŭs āltīs Rōbŏră. Sŏnăt īctă sĕcūrĭbŭs īlēx. Īn quērcū mēllă rĕpērtă căvā. Nūdăquĕ rāmōsǣ tēndēbānt brāchĭă quērcūs. Tēndēbăt ăd ǣthĕră rāmōs. Īngēntēm nām lāte āmplēctĭtŭr ūmbrām. Nĕmūs făcĭt ūnă. Cōnsūrgūnt gĕmĭnǣ quērcūs. Quērcŭs glāndĭfĕră. Māgnă Jŏvīs quērcŭs. Quērcūs ĕt īlēx Mūltā frūgĕ pĕcūs jŭvăt. Dūrĭŏr ānnōsā quērcū.

Răphănŭs, ī. m. *A radish.* Pērcūrrēnt răphănīquĕ mūgĭlēsquĕ. *Cat.* Syn.—Rapa, rapum, radix.

Rhŏdŏdāphnē, ēs. f. *The oleander, rose-bay.* Syn.—Rhŏdŏdēndrŏn, rhŏdŏdēndrŏs, nērĭūm, nērĭŏn. Phr.—Laūrūs ĭtēm Phœ̄bī sūrgēns dĕcŭs, hīc rhŏdŏdāphnē. V.

Rhŏdŏdēndrōn, ī. n. *The Oleander. See Rhododaphne.*

Rŏsă, ǣ. f. *The rose.* Quālĕ rŏsǣ fūlgēnt īntēr sŭă līlĭă mīxtǣ. O. Phr.—Flōs Īdălĭŭs, Vĕnĕrĭs, Vĕnĕrī săcĕr, grātīssĭmŭs. Vērĭs hŏnŏr. Flōrūm rēgīnă. Hāmātīs vāllātă spīnīs. Sānguĭnĕō fūlgōrĕ mĭcāns. Glōrĭă rūrĭs. Nātīvīs fūlgĕt ămīctă cŏmīs. Nĭmĭūm brĕvēs flōrēs ămœ̄nǣ fērrĕ jŭbē rŏsǣ. Spīnārūm tūtǣ sūb stătĭōnĕ cŏmǣ. Hōrtōrūm rēgīnă.

Rŭbŭs, ī. m. *A bramble, blackberry bush.* Āt rūbŭs ēt sēntēs tāntūmmŏdŏ lǣdĕrĕ nātǣ. O. Syn.—Sēntĭs, vĕprēs, spīnă. Phr.—Hŏrrēntēsquĕ rŭbōs ĕt ămāntēs ārdŭă dūmōs. Hīrsūtīs brāchĭă sēctă rŭbīs. Seū vĭrĭdēs rŭbūm dīmōvērĕ lăcērtǣ. Hōrrēntēs rŭbī.

Rūtă, ǣ. f. *The herb rue.* Īndĕ cŏmās ăpĭī grăcĭlēs rūtāmquĕ vĭrēntēm. V. Phr.—Ăcŭēntēs lūmĭnă rūtǣ. Aūt sī quĭd ŏlēntĭūs īllīs. Quǣquĕ mănūs ĭnŏdōrăt rūtă lĕgēntēs. Mēmbrīs ăgĭt ātrūm rūtă vĕnēnūm.

Sălīx, ĭcĭs. f. *A willow-tree.* Mēcum īntēr sălĭcēs lēntā sūb vītĕ jăcērĕt. V. Syn.—Sălīctūm. Phr.—Sălĭcĭs, sălīctī flōrēs, frōndēs. Sălīgnǣ frōndēs, ūmbrǣ. Īrrĭgŭī fōntĭs ămīcă sălīx. Flūmĭnă, līttŏră ămāns. Gaūdēnt flūmĭnĭbūs sălĭcēs. Vīmĭnĭbūs sălĭcēs fēcūndǣ, frōndĭbŭs ūlmī.

Sālvĭă, ǣ. f. *The herb sage.* Phr.—Crāssīs sālvĭă rāmīs. Cuī sālvĭă crēscĭt ĭn hōrtō?

Scīllă, ǣ. f. *A sea-onion.* Scīllāmque hēllĕbŏrōsquĕ grăvēs nīgrūmquĕ bĭtūmĕn. V. Phr.—Scīllă mărĭtĭmă. Scīllăquĕ lēntīscō sĭmĭlĭs. Trĭă tēmpŏră mōnstrăt ărāndī.

Scīrpŭs (Sīrpŭs), ī. m. *A reed, bulrush.* Syn.—Jūncŭs. Phr.—Nōdūm īn scīrpō quǣrĕrĕ. Aūt scīrpōs ālgāsquĕ lĕvēs dēdūcĕrĕ mōs ēst.

Sĕdūm, ī. n. *House-leek.* Syn.—Dĭgĭtēllūm. Phr.—Mūltōquĕ sĕdī cōntīngĕrĕ sūccō.

Sĭnāpī. n. indecl. & Sĭnāpĭs, ĭs. f. *Mustard-seed.* Phr.—Sēquĕ lăcēssēntī flētūm fāctūră sĭnāpĭs. Sēmĕn ŏlēns. Mĭnĭmō sēmĭnĕ nātŭs.

Sĭsȳmbrĭūm, ĭī. n. *Spearmint.* Cūmquĕ sŭā dŏmĭnǣ dătă grātă sĭsȳmbrĭă mȳrtō. O. Phr.—Pĕr īrrĭgŭās quǣrēndă sĭsȳmbrĭă vāllēs Crēscūnt. Cūm mȳrtō nātă.

Smīlāx, ăcĭs. f. *Smilax.* Phr.—Āspĕră smīlāx. (*Also*) *The yew-tree. See Taxus.*

Tāxŭs, ī. f. *The yew-tree.* Ēst vĭă dēclīvīs, fūnēstā nūbĭlă tāxō. O. Phr.—Sī fŭgĭānt ēxāmĭnă tāxōs. Sūccō mĕtŭēndă. Āmāntēs frīgŏră tāxī. Tāxŭs ĭn īrrĭgŭīs crēscēt fōrmōsĭŏr hōrtīs. Aēthĕrĭōs ĭmĭtātūr flēxĭlĭs ārcūs Vēl sōlĭs rădĭōs. Āltǣ pȳrămĭdīs rītū.

Thȳmūm, ī. n. *Thyme.* Rĕdŏlēntquĕ thȳmō frāgrāntĭă mēllă. V. Phr.—Āpĭbŭs grātūm. Suāvī flōrĕ. Ŏdōrĕ frăgrāns, hālāns. Dūmquĕ thȳmō pāscēntŭr ăpēs.

Tĭlĭă, ǣ. f. *The linden-tree.* Nēc tĭlĭǣ laēvēs, ēt tōrnō rāsĭlĕ būxūm. V. Phr.—Tĭlĭă lēvĭs cǣdĭtŭr. Stŏmăchūm tĭlĭǣ sōlāntŭr ŏnūstūm, Mārcēntēmquĕ cĭbīs.

Tīnŭs, ī. f. *A kind of bay-tree.* Ēt bĭcŏlōr mȳrtūs, ēt bāccīs cǣrŭlă tīnŭs. O. *See Laurus.*

Ūlmŭs, ī. f. *The elm-tree.* Pāmpĭnĕǣ vītēs ĕt āmīctǣ vītĭbŭs ūlmī. O. Phr.—Vītĭbŭs ārbŏr ămīcă. Nĕc ĭnhōspĭtă vītĭbŭs ūlmŭs. Rāmōs ānnōsăquĕ brāchĭă pāndēns. Spĕcĭōsă nĭtēntĭbŭs ūvīs. Fēcūndǣ frōndĭbŭs ūlmī. Vītēs ūlmīs ādjūngĕrĕ. Cōnjūncta ūlmō mărītō. Ūlmī vĭdŭǣ.

Vāccīnĭūm, ĭī. n. *The blueberry.* Ālbă lĭgūstră cădūnt, vāccīnĭă nīgră lĕgūntŭr. V.

Vērātrūm, ī. n. *Hellebore.* Prǣtĕrĕā nōbīs vērātrum ēst ācrĕ vĕnēnūm. L. Syn.—Hēllĕbŏrŭs. Phr.—Īlĭăs Āccī Ēbrĭă vērātrō.

Vērbēnă, ǣ. f. *The herb vervain.* Vērbēnās ădŏlē pīnguēs ēt māscŭlă tūră. V. Syn.—Vērbēnācă. Phr.—Vērbēnā tēmpŏră vīnctī. Ēx ārā sūme hīnc vērbēnās tĭbĭ.

Vĭcĭă, ǣ. f. *Vetch, tare.* Phr.—Ēt tĕnŭēs vĭcĭǣ fœtūs. Flōrĕ sĕmēl lǣsō, pĕrĕūnt vĭcĭǣquĕ făbǣquĕ.

Vĭŏlă, ǣ. f. *The violet.* Pāllēntēs vĭŏlās ēt sūmmă păpāvĕră cārpēns. V. Phr.—Flōrēns vērĕ nŏvō. Quǣ pāllĕt hŭmī. Quǣ frōndēns pūrpŭrăt aūrō. Ōbscūra īnfĭcĭēns fērrūgĭnĕ vūltūm. Prīmŭlă prātōrūm sŏbŏlēs ēt prǣvĭă vērĭs. Nōn lōngūm cēlābĭt ŏdōrēs. Hŭmĭlī dē cǣspĭtĕ sūrgĭt. Tĕrrǣ prĕtĭōsūm mūnŭs ăgrēstĭs. Pūrpŭrĕūm pīngūnt vĭŏlārĭă cāmpūm.

Vītĭs, ĭs. f. *Vine, grape-vine.* Vītĭs ŭt ārbŏrĭbŭs dĕcŏri ēst, ūt vītĭbŭs ūvǣ. V. Syn.—Vīnĕă, ūvă, pālmĕs, pāmpĭnŭs, Bācchŭs. Phr.— Ădūltă vītĭūm prōpāgŏ. Cōmplēxă tĕnācĭtĕr ūlmūm. Fērtĭlĭs ūvīs. Răcēmīs grăvĭdă, tŭmēns, pīctă, dīstīnctă. Tĕnĕrō dāns pālmĭtĕ frūctūm. Grăvĭdōs frūctūs, fœtūs, lǣtă mūnĕră prǣbēns. Grātīssĭmă vītĭs Ĭācchō. Āmīctǣ vītĭbŭs ūlmī. Pāmpĭnĕĭǝ ŏnĕratūm vītĭbŭs ūlmūm. Tĕnĕrīs jūngūntūr vītĭbŭs ūlmī. Pāmpĭnĕīs ŏnĕrātūm vītĭbŭs ūlmūm. Tĕnĕrīs jūngūntūr vītĭbŭs ūlmī. Āppŏsĭtīs vīncĭtūr vītĭbŭs ūlmŭs. Lǣtīs īntēxĕrĕ vītĭbŭs ūlmōs. Ūlmīs, pālīs ādjūngĕrĕ vītēs. Pārvās ūlmīs āttŏllĕrĕ vītēs. Pālmēs vĭdŭās dēsīdĕrăt ūlmōs. Plēnăquĕ pūrpŭrĕō sŭbrŭbĕt ūvă mĕrō. Ūlmŭs ămāt vītĭm, vītīs nōn dēsĕrĭt ūlmūm.

Zīzănĭă, ōrūm. n. *Cockle.* Syn.—Lŏlĭūm, ǣgĭlŏps, ǣră. Phr.—Spīnīs fūltă sŭbīt sĕgĕs hōrrĭdă zīzănĭōrūm.

LIST OF BIRDS MENTIONED IN CLASSICAL POETRY.

Ăcānthĭs & Ăcălānthĭs, ĭdĭs. f. *Goldfinch or linnet.* Lītŏrăque Ālcyŏnēm rĕsŏnānt, ăcălānthĭdă dūmī. V. Syn.—Cārdŭēlĭs. Phr.—Vīncĭt ăcānthīs cāntū. Ārgūtăt rĕlĭquās īntĕr ăcānthĭs ăvēs. Frīngīllă cārdŭēlĭs.

Āccĭpĭtĕr, trĭs. m. *Hawk.* Ēt nūnc āccĭpĭtēr, nūllī sătĭs æquŭs, ĭn ōmnēs Sævĭt ăvēs. O. Syn.—Āstŭr. Phr.—Āccĭpĭtrūm mōrēs. Prædātrīx, prædātŏr ālēs. Ācēr pēnnīs ēt cūrvīs ūnguĭbŭs ālēs. Īnfēstūs cŏlūmbīs. Chāŏnĭæ tūrbæ ĭnĭmīcă vŏlŭcrĭs. Rōstro īnmānĭs ŏbūncō. Ācēr sĕquĭtūr pĕr ĭnānĕ cŏlūmbām. Vŏlŭcrīs rāptō quæ vīvĭt ĕt ōmnēs Tērrĕt ăvēs. Dēsŭpĕr āccĭpĭtrēs ēxsūltāvērĕ răpīnīs. Dēlāpsūs cœlō cēlsā dē sēdĕ cŏlūmbām Sūstŭlĭt. Ūt sŏlĕt āccĭpĭtēr trĕpĭdās ūrgērĕ cŏlūmbās.

Ălaūdă, æ. f. *A lark.* Syn.—Cāssītă, gălērītă. Phr.—Gălĕātă căpŭt. Āltă pĕtēns. Līnquēns tērrās ēt sīdĕră vōcĕ sĕquēns. Dūlcēs ĭtĕrāns quĕrēlās. Trĕmŭlō fūndēns dē gūttŭrĕ cāntūs. Vărĭōs quæ dūcĭt ĭn āĕrĕ gȳrōs. Nūntĭă vērĭs Lætă lăbōrĭfĕrī. Gaūdēns ŏpĕrīs rūrĭs ădēssĕ cŏmĕs. Gălĕāque īnsīgnĭs ălaūdă. Cāntăt ĕt āscēndĭt. Sē lĕvăt īn nūbēs. Sīdĕră cārmĭnĕ mūlcĕt.

Ālcēdŏ (Hālcēdŏ), ĭnĭs. f. *The kingfisher, halcyon.* Syn.—Ālcyŏn, ālcyŏnē. Phr.—Dīlēctæ Thĕtĭdī ālcyŏnēs. Phr.—Cēycĭs ăvĭs. Ālēs mĭsĕrābĭlĭs. Fœtūs nīdō tĭtŭbāntĕ fŏvēns. Ēxclūdēns ĭn æquŏrĕ pūllōs. Pēnnās īn līttŏrĕ pāndūnt. Īncŭbăt Ālcyŏnē pēndēntĭbŭs æquŏrĕ nīdīs. Cēycĭs ăvēs rĕpĕtūnt īn līttŏrĕ quēstūs. Cēycĭs cōnjūx.

Āltĭlĭs, ĭs. m. & f. *Capon.* Syn.—Pūllŭs. Āltĭlĭs ăvĭs, gāllīnă.

Ănās, ătĭs. f. *Duck.* Syn.—Gēns ănătīnă. Phr.—Ănās flŭvĭātĭlĭs. Grĕgēs ănătūm. Cærŭlă pēnnīs. Crūrĕ rŭbră pūnĭcō. Dēpīctæ cērvīcĭs ănās. Stāgnūm sŭpēr pĕdĕ rēmĭgăt ūdō. Nūnc ēxstăt ăquīs, nūnc mērgĭtŭr. Lātĭpĕdēmque ănătēm.

Ānsĕr, ĕrĭs. m. *Goose.* Ūnĭcŭs ānsĕr ĕrăt, mĭnĭmæ cūstōdĭă vīllæ. O. Syn.—Ānsērcŭlŭs. Phr.—Ānsĕr ăquīs gaūdēns. Cănĭbŭs săgācĭŏr ānsĕr. Strĕpĭt īmprŏbŭs ānsĕr. Gārrŭlŭs ānsēr nūntĭăt. Rōmŭlĭdārum ārcīs sērvātŏr. Tārpēiæ fēlīx cūstōdĭă rūpĭs. Dīgnă sĕd ārgūtōs īntēr strĕpĕre ānsĕr ŏlōrēs.

Ăquĭlă, æ. f. *An eagle.* Sīc ăquĭlām fŭgĭūnt pēnnā trĕpĭdāntĕ cŏlūmbæ. O. Phr.—Jŏvĭs ārmĭgĕr ālĕs. Rēgĭă ālĕs. Flāmmĭgĕr ālĕs. Cūstōs fūlmĭnĭs. Fămŭlă Jŏvĭs. Ālĕs săcră Jŏvī. Fīdă mĭnīstră Jŏvĭs. Mĭnīstēr fūlmĭnĭs ālĕs. Vēctōr fūlmĭnĭs ārdēns. Ālĭtŭūm rēgīnă. Rēgnātōr vŏlŭcrūm. Ārdŭŭs āspēctū. Īpsa īngēns ālĕs. Sŭpra hŏmĭnūm tēcta āc mōntēs sūprāquĕ vŏlŭcrēs Fērtŭr. Cūrsū pĕtĭt ōbvĭă nūbēs. Văgās spătĭātă pĕr aūrās. Lūmĭnă sōlĭs Sūspĭcĭt.

Ārdĕă, æ. f. *Heron.* Īpsă sŭīs dēplāngĭtŭr ārdĕă pēnnīs. O. Syn.—Ārdĕŏlă, ăvēs Dĭŏmēdēæ. Phr.—Plūmă tēgīt grăcĭlēs ārtūs. Nūllŭs ĭn ēxtēntō rōstrō mŏdŭs. Nōtāsquĕ pălūdēs dēsĕrĭt. Ārdĕă pălūstrĭs.

Āstŭr, ŭrĭs. m. *Hawk. See Accipiter.*

Āttăgēn, ēnĭs. m. *Grouse, heath-cock or hazel-hen.* Nōn āfra ăvĭs .....Nōn āttăgēn Īōnĭcūs jūcūndĭŏr. H. Syn.—Āttăgēnă, lăgōĭs. Phr.—Īōnĭcārūm gūstŭs āttăgēnārūm.

Būbŏ, ōnĭs. m. (*rarely feminine*). *An owl.* Īgnāvūs būbō, dīrūm mōrtālĭbŭs ōmĕn. O. Syn.—Nōctŭă, ŭlŭlă, strīx. Phr.—Nōctĭs ăvĭs. Pāllădĭs ăvĭs. Trīstĕ cănēns. Lūctūs prænūntĭŭs ālĕs. Vŏlŭcrĭs prænūntĭă fātī. Dāmnă cănēns fērālĭă. Trīstĭă fātă cănēns. Lōngās īn flētūm dūcĕrĕ vōcēs. Nōctĕ sĕdēns tētrūm cănĭt. Fūnĕrĕōquĕ sŏnōs ēdĭdĭt ōrĕ grăvēs. Tēr ōmĕn Fūnĕrĕūs būbō lētālī cārmĭnĕ fēcĭt.

Cārdŭēlĭs, ĭs. f. *A goldfinch, thistlefinch.* Syn.—Ăcānthĭs, ăcălānthĭs. Phr.—Frīngīllă cārdŭēlĭs. *See Acanthis.*

Cĭcōnĭă, æ. f. *Stork.* Tūtŭs ĕrāt rhōmbūs, tūtōquĕ cĭcōnĭă nīdō. H. Phr.—Cāndĭdă pēnnīs cĭcōnĭă. Nūntĭă vērĭs. Īnsīgnĭs pĭĕtātĕ. Īnvīsă cŏlūbrīs. Crēpĭtāntĕ cĭcōnĭă rōstrō.

Cŏlūmbă, æ. f. *Dove, pigeon.* Ūt fŭgĭūnt ăquĭlās, tĭmĭdīssĭmă tūrbă, cŏlūmbæ. O. Syn.—Pălūmbēs. Phr.—Ālĕs, ăvĭs, vŏlŭcrĭs Chāŏnĭă, Chāŏnĭs, Cўprĭă. Vĕnĕrĭs cūră. Āccĭpĭtrēm mĕtŭēns. Trĕpĭdāntĭbŭs ālīs. Sĭnĕ lābĕ cŏlūmbæ. Āspĭcĭs ūt vĕnĭānt ād cāndĭdă tēctă cŏlūmbæ. Āmīcām blāndă rŏgāntēs Ōscŭlă cīrcŭmĕūnt.

Cōrnīcŭlă, æ. f. *Jackdaw, or little crow.* Syn.—Mŏnēdŭlă, cōrnīx. Phr.—Mŏvĕāt cōrnīcŭlă rīsūm. *See Cornix.*

Cōrnīx, īcĭs. f. *A crow.* Tūm cōrnīx plēnā plŭvĭām vŏcāt īmprŏbă vōcĕ. V. Phr.—Īnvīsă Mĭnērvæ. Sēcŭlă pāssă nŏvēm. Sēclīs vīx mŏrĭtūră nŏvēm. Plŭvĭæ vātēs. Plŭvĭōsæ nūntĭă lūcĭs. Īmbrĭūm dīvīna ăvĭs īmmĭnēntĭūm. Aūgŭr ăquæ. Præsāgō clāngōrĕ lŏquāx. Gārrŭlă cōrnīx. Sæpĕ sĭnīstră căvā prædīxĭt ăb īlĭcĕ cōrnīx. Raūcă sŏnāns.

Cōrvŭs, ī. m. *A raven.* Īntĕr ăvēs ālbās vĕtŭīt cōnsīstĕrĕ cōrvūm. O. Phr.—Phœbēĭŭs ālĕs. Ăpōllĭnĭs ālĕs. Phœbī săcĕr nūntĭŭs īmbrĭs. Trīstĕ mĭnāns. Ŏvāntēs gūttŭrĕ cōrvī. Hĭāntēm cōrvūm dēlūdĕrĕ. Cōrvĕ lŏquāx. Cōrvūs rīdētūr Lēdæōs īntĕr ŏlōrēs. Cōrvōrum īncrĕpŭīt dēnsīs ēxērcĭtŭs ālīs.

Cŏtūrnīx, īcĭs. f. *A quail.* Sēdŭlă pēr stĭpŭlās tĕnĕrā cūm prōlĕ cŏtūrnīx Pāscĭtŭr. O. Phr.—Quĕrĭtūr pĕrĕgrīnă cŏtūrnīx. Rēgūm grātīssĭmă mēnsīs. Mātērtĕră Phœbī. Māgnō quōndām dīlēctă Tŏnāntī.

Cŭcūlŭs (Cŭcūllŭs), ī. m. *A cuckoo.* Syn.—Cōccȳx.

Cȳcnŭs (Cȳgnŭs), ī. m. *Swan.* Dānt sŏnĭtūm raūcī pēr stāgnă lŏquācĭă cȳcnī. V. Syn.—Ŏlŏr. Phr.—Căȳstrĭŭs ālĕs. Mæāndrī īncŏlă. Flūmĭnă cȳcnŭs ămāns. Ālbūm mūtŏr ĭn ālĭtēm. Cāntātōr cȳcnūs fūnĕrĭs īpsĕ sŭī. Cārmĭnă jām mŏrĭēns cănĭt. Dēflērĕ....Dīcĭtŭr ōrĕ sŭām dēfĭcĭēntĕ nĕcēm. Cȳcnŭs ĭn aūgŭrĭīs naūtīs grātīssĭmŭs ālĕs. Pāscēntēs nīvĕōs hērbōsō flūmĭnĕ cȳcnōs. Quīd cōntēndăt hĭrūndō cȳcnīs? Cērtānt cȳcnīs ŭlŭlæ.

Daūlĭăs (ālĕs), ădĭs. f. *A nightingale.* Cōncĭnĭt Īsmărĭūm Daūlĭăs ālĕs Ĭtȳn. O. Syn.—Phĭlŏmēlă, lūscĭnĭă. *See Philomela.*

Fālcŏ, ōnĭs. m. *A falcon, or sparrow-hawk.* Syn.—Āccĭpĭtĕr. Phr.—Fālcātĭs ŭnguĭbŭs ālĕs. Pēnnīs ēt cūrvīs ŭnguĭbŭs ăcĕr. Lĭquĭdūm sĕcăt āĕră fālcŏ. Tīnnŭlă pēr văcŭūm quătĭēns crĕpĭtācŭlă fālcŏ. Ăvĭdūsquĕ vŏrāx.

Fīcēdŭlă, æ. f. *A fig-pecker, becafico.* Phr.—Cērĕă quæ pătŭlō lūcēt fīcēdŭlă lūmbō. Ĕōdēm jūrĕ nătāntēs Mērgĕrĕ fīcēdŭlās dĭdĭcĭt.

Frīngīllă (Frīgīllă & Frīnguīllă), æ. f. *Chaffinch.* Nūnc stūrnōs ĭnŏpēs, frīngīllārūmquĕ quĕrēlās Aūdĭt. M. Phr.—Hĭlărī rĕcrĕāns ăvĭārĭă cāntū. Aūrōram īncrĕpĭtāns cāntū frīngīllă mŏrāntēm.

Fŭlĭcă, æ. f. *A coot.* Nūnc cĕlĕbrēs mērgīs fŭlĭcīsquĕ pălūstrĭbŭs ūndæ. O. Syn.—Fŭlīx, phălăcrŏcŏrāx. Phr.—Cōrvŭs ăquātĭcŭs. Īmbrĭs, plŭvĭæ prænūntĭă. Cūmquĕ mărīnæ Īn sīccō lūdūnt fŭlĭcæ. Fŭgĭēns ā gūrgĭtĕ pōntī, Nūntĭăt hōrrĭbĭlēs clāmāns īnstārĕ prŏcēllās.

Gālgŭlŭs, ī. m. & Gālbŭlă, æ. f. *Witwall or thrush.* Gālbŭlă dēcĭpĭtūr călămīs ēt rētĭbŭs ālĕs, Tūrgĕt ădhūc vĭrĭdī cūm rŭdĭs ūvă mĕrō. M. *For thrush, see Turdus.*

Gāllīnă, æ. f. *A hen.* Nēc gāllīnă mălō rēspōndēt dūră pălātō. H. Phr.—Pūllōrūm fīdīssĭmă cūstōs. Crīstātī fēmĭnă gāllī. Cōnjūx crīstātī fœtă mărītī. Quæ fœtūs stŭdĭōsă fŏvĕt. Tĕgēns ālārūm tēgmĭnĕ pūllōs. Pūllīs tŭmĭdās ālās ēxpāndēns.

Gāllŭs, ī. m. *Cock, rooster.* Nōndūm crīstātī rūpērĕ sĭlēntĭă gāllī. M. Phr.—Crīstātŭs ālĕs. Lūmĭnĭs aūctŏr ăvĭs. Phœbēĭŭs ālĕs. Tītānĭŭs ālĕs. Pērsĭcŭs ālĕs. Ālĕs sīdĕrūm cōnscĭŭs. Nūntĭŭs lūcĭs ālĕs. Aūrōræ præcŏ vĭgĭl. Ăvĭs crīstātă. Ādmŏnĭtŏr ŏpĕrūm. Crīstă spēctābĭlĭs āltā. Aūrōrām vŏcăt ōrĕ mŏrāntēm. Sūb gāllī cāntūm. Jām dĕdĕrăt cāntūm lūcĭs prænūntĭŭs ālĕs. Vĭgĭlī prōvŏcăt ōrĕ dĭēm. Sīgnă cănēns dāt gāllŭs Ĕōī. Crīstātæquĕ sŏnānt ūndĭquĕ lūcĭs ăvēs. Vōcĕ sĭlēntĭă rūmpĭt. Mānĕ cănōrā Vōcĕ dĭēm cĭtăt, ēt sōmnōs ābrūmpĭt ĭnērtēs.

Grūs & Grŭĭs, ĭs. f. *A crane.* Tūm grŭĭbūs pĕdĭcās ēt rētĭă tēndĕrĕ cērvīs. V. Phr.—Pălămēdĭs ăvēs. Thrēĭcĭă vŏlŭcrĭs. Raūcă āgmĭnă grŭūm. Quæ Pȳgmæō sānguĭnĕ gaūdĕt ăvĭs. Grūs ōrdĭnĕ lōngō Cūm clāmōrĕ vŏlăt. Rĕdĕūntquĕ grŭēs, ēt sēmĭnă sūlcīs Jāctă lĕgūnt. Cīnxērĕ grŭēs lōngo ōrdĭnĕ cœlūm. Aūdītūr grăvĭs ĭntēr nūbĭlă clāngŏr. Æthĕră trānānt Cūm sŏnĭtū. Fŭgĭūntquĕ Nŏtōs clāmōrĕ sĕcūndō. Dēcēdūnt āgmĭnă Nīlō Cūm fĕră pōnĭt hĭēms. Īngēntī clāngōrĕ grŭēs æstīvă rĕlīnquūnt Thrācĭă.

Hĭrūndŏ, ĭnĭs. f. *Swallow.* Aūt ārgūtă lăcūs cīrcūmvŏlĭtāvĭt hĭrūndŏ. V. Syn.—Prōgnē, ăvĭs Pāndĭŏnĭă. Phr.—Pāndĭŏnĭs, Cĕcrŏpĭă, Daūlĭs ālĕs, ăvĭs, vŏlŭcrĭs. Ăvĭs Āttĭcă. Vērĭs nūntĭă, prænūntĭă. Āmīssūm quæ gĕmĭt ālēs Ĭtȳn. Īmpĭă dīrī fūrtă mărĭtī dēflēns. Tīgnīs nīdūm sūspēndĭt hĭrūndŏ. Sūb lūcēm mŏdŭlōs ĭtĕrăt, mĕdĭtātŭr, fūndĭt. Nīdōsquĕ rĕvērsă lŭtābĭt hĭrūndŏ. Nīdūm pōnĭt. Īnfēlīx ăvĭs. Gārrŭlă līmōsās sēdēs mōlītūr hĭrūndŏ. Pābŭlă pārvă lĕgēns. Cīrcūm stāgnă sŏnānt.

Ībĭs, ĭdĭs. f. *The ibis.* Pīscĕ Vĕnūs lătŭĭt, Cȳllēnĭŭs Ībĭdĭs ālĭs. O. Phr.—Aēgȳptĭăcă ăvĭs, vŏlŭcrĭs. Aēgȳptĭīs săcră.

Lūscĭnĭă, æ. f. *Nightingale.* Lūscĭnĭæ tŭmŭlūm sī Thĕlĕsīnă dĕdĭt. M. Syn.—Phĭlŏmēlă, lūscĭnĭŭs, lūscĭnĭŏlă. Phr.—Sīrēn nĕmŏrūm. Pēnnātæ glōrĭă gēntĭs. Lūscĭnĭās sŏlĭti īmpēnsō prāndērĕ cŏēmptās. Vōx lūscĭnĭī. *See Philomela.*

Mĕlĕāgrĭs, ĭdĭs. f. *Turkey, or guinea-hen.* Syn.—Āfră ăvĭs, mēlĭcă.

Mērgŭs, ī. m. *A comorant, sea-gull, or sea-coot.* Cūm mĕdĭō cĕlĕrēs rĕvŏlānt ēx æquŏrĕ mērgī. V. Syn.—Mērgŭlŭs, ālcȳŏn. Phr.—Īncŏlă mērgŭs ăquæ. Hŭmĭlĭs vŏlăt æquŏră jūxtā. Nāntī sĭmĭlĭs sĭmĭlīsquĕ vŏlāntī. Aēquŏr ămāns. Nōmēnquĕ mănēt quĭă mērgĭtŭr īllō.

Mĕrōps, ŏpĭs. m. *The bee-eater.* Pīnguĭbŭs ā stăbŭlīs, ălĭæquĕ vŏlŭcrēs. V. Syn.—Ăpĭāstră.

Mĕrŭlă, æ. f. *Blackbird.* Sī vĕlŭtī mĕrŭlīs īntēntūs dēcīdĭt aūceps Īn pŭtēūm. H.

Mīlŭŭs (Mīlvŭs), ī. m. *A kite.* Phr.—Hīnc prŏpĕ sūmmă răpāx mīlvŭs ĭn āstră vŏlăt. Vŏlŭcrĭs răpĭdīssĭmă. *See Accipiter.*

Mŏnēdŭlă, æ. f. *Jackdaw.* Nīgră pĕdēs, nīgrīs vēlātă mŏnēdŭlă pēnnīs. O. Syn.—Cōrnīcŭlă.

Nōctŭă, æ. f. *Owl.* Sērōs ēxērcēt nōctŭă cāntūs. V. Syn.—Ŭlŭlă, būbŏ, strīx. Phr.—Pāllădĭs, Cĕcrŏpĭă vŏlŭcrĭs. Nōctĭs, nōctĭvăgă ăvĭs, ālĕs, vŏlŭcrĭs. Fūnēstă gĕmēns tēctīs. Prænūntĭă fātī. Cārmēn trīstĕ cănēns. Nōctūrnā vŏlŭcrīs fūnēstă quĕrēlā.

Ŏlŏr, ōrĭs. m. *Swan.* Ārgūtōs īntēr strĕpĕre ānsĕr ŏlōrēs. V. Syn.—Cȳcnŭs. Phr.—Cārmĭnă mœstă cănēns. Rĕsŏnāns mŏrĭbūndō gūttŭrĕ dūlcĕ mĕlŏs. *See Cycnus.*

Pălūmbēs, ĭs. f. & Pălūmbŭs, ī. m. *A wood-pigeon, ring-dove.* Nŏtāvī Ĭpsĕ lŏcum āĕrĭæ quō cōngrēssērĕ pălūmbēs. V. Syn.—Cŏlūmbă. Phr.—Gĕmĭt hīnc pălūmbēs, īndĕ cērĕūs tūrtŭr. Raūcæ, tŭă cūră, pălūmbēs. Frōndĕ nŏvā pŭĕrūm pălūmbēs tēxĕrĕ.

Pāssĕr, ĕrĭs. m. *A sparrow.* Ārgūtō pāssĕrĕ vērnăt ăgĕr. M. Syn.—Pāssērcŭlŭs. Phr.—Vērnōs cāntābăt ămōrēs.

Pāvŏ, ōnĭs. m. *A peacock.* Īngrĕdĭtūr lĭquĭdūm pāvōnĭbŭs āĕră pīctīs. O. Syn.—Pāvă. Phr.—Jūnōnĭŭs ālĕs. Vŏlŭcrĭs Jūnōnĭă. Stēllāntēm pāndēns caūdām. Quī caūdā sīdĕră pōrtăt. Gēmmīs caūdām stēllāntĭbŭs īmplĕt. Stēllātæ pāndīt spēctācŭlă caūdæ. Caūdæ spĕcĭōsă, gēmmātă vŏlūmĭnă vērsăt. Cōnscĭă fōrmæ Cōllă tŭmēnt. Stēllāntĭbŭs ālīs sē rŏtăt īn gȳrōs. Pēnnārūm fūlgēnt ŏcŭlī. Sī tăcĭtūs spēctēs, īllĕ rĕcōndĭt ŏpēs. Gēmmāntēs ēxplĭcăt ālās. Pūrpŭrĕō fūlgēt rădĭātă cŏlōrĕ. Sē mīrātŭr ĕūntēm. Crīstāquĕ sŭpērbŭs. Vărĭōsquĕ trăhēns ā sōlĕ cŏlōrēs.

Pērdīx, īcĭs. m. & f. *A partridge.* Ēt pīctă pērdīx, nŭmĭdĭcæquĕ gūttātæ. M. Phr.—Quīquĕ rĕfērt jūngēns ĭtĕrātă vŏcābŭlă pērdīx. Jŏvī săcră. Lātōnæquĕ vŏlŭcrĭs. Lōngūm tĭbĭ, Dædălĕ, crīmĕn. Īmplūmēs pērdīx vĭdĕt ānxĭă pūllōs. Āvŏlăt īrrīdēns hōstēs, nīdōsquĕ rĕvīsĭt.

Phāsĭānŭs, ī. m. *A pheasant.* Phr.—Phāsĭdĭs ālĕs. Scȳthĭcă, Cōlchă vŏlŭcrĭs. Phāsĭăcă gāllīnă. Ā Scȳthĭcō mīssæ Phāsĭde ăvēs. Jām Phāsĭdĭs ūndă Ōrbāta ēst ăvĭbŭs. Nēc Lĭbȳē mīttīt, nēc tĭbĭ Phāsĭs ăvēs.

Phĭlŏmēlă, æ. f. *A nightingale.* Dūlcēs vărĭăt Phĭlŏmēlă quĕrēlās. Syn.—Lūscĭnĭă, Āēdōn, Āttĭs, Daūlĭăs ăvĭs. Phr.—Āvĭs Pāndĭōnĭă. Cĕcrŏpĭs ăvĭs. Pēndēt sūmmō strīdŭlă rāmō. Nātūmquĕ sŏnăt flēbĭlĭs Āttĭs. Aēmŭlă dīvīnī suāvīssĭmă cārmĭnĭs ālĕs.

Quæ vĭrĭdēs ūmbrās ēt lŏcă sācră tĕnĕt. Mīllĕ pŏtēs văriōs īpsă rĕfērrĕ sŏnōs. Suāvĕ cănīt rĕsŏnō mŏdŭlāmĭnĕ cārmĕn. Dēnsīs rāmōrūm cōncĭnĭt ūmbrīs. Pōpŭlĕā mœrēns phĭlŏmēlă sŭb ūmbrā Āmīssōs quĕrĭtūr fœtūs. Rāmōquĕ sĕdēns mĭsĕrābĭlĕ cārmĕn Īntĕgrăt. Lŏcă quēstĭbŭs īmplĕt.

Phœnīcōptĕrŭs, ī. m. *A flamingo.* Ēt Scȳthĭcæ vŏlŭcrēs, ēt Phœnīcōptĕrŭs īngēns. J.

Phœnīx, īcĭs. m. *The phoenix, a mythical bird of Arabia.* Ēt vīvāx Phœnīx, ūnĭcă sēmpĕr ăvĭs. O. Phr.—Sōlĭs ăvĭs. Vŏlŭcrĭs Gāngētĭcă. Ălūmnŭs Phœbī. Sōlă sŭī gĕnĕrīs, sĭbī sōlă sŭpērstĕs. Ēōīs rĕnŏvātă būstīs. Āssȳrĭōs rĕnŏvānt īncēndĭă nīdōs. Ūnă dĕcēm quŏtĭēs sēcŭlă vīxĭt ăvĭs. Quī spōntĕ crĕmātŭr Ūt rĕdĕăt, gaūdētquĕ mŏrī fēstīnŭs ĭn ōrtūm. Sēxū sōlă cărĕt. Īpsă sĭbī prōlēs, sŭŭs ēst pătĕr, ēt sŭŭs hērēs. Nūtrīx īpsă sŭī. Ūt pŏssīt nāscī, āppĕtĭt āntĕ mŏrī.

Pīcŭs, ī. m. *A woodpecker.* Mārtĭă pīcŭs ăvĭs. O. Phr.—Tēquĕ nēc lævŭs vĕtĕt īrĕ pīcŭs. Pīcŭs ĭn aūspĭcĭīs ăvĭs ōbsērvātă Lătīnīs. Pīcŭs rōstrō prædūră lăcēssēns Rōbŏră, sēcūrōs mĕdĭā căvăt ārbŏrĕ nīdōs.

Prŏgnē, ēs. f. *A swallow.* Syn.—Hĭrūndŏ, ăvĭs Pāndīŏnĭă. *See Hirundo.*

Psīttăcŭs, ī. m. *A parrot.* Psīttăcŭs, Ēōīs ālēs mĭhĭ mīssŭs ăb ūndīs. O. Syn.—Sīttăcŭs. Phr.—Īndă, Īndĭcă ăvĭs, ālĕs, vŏlŭcrĭs. Hūmānæ vōcĭs, līnguæ ĭmĭtātŏr, sĭmŭlātŏr, æmŭlŭs ālĕs. Lŏquāx hūmānæ vōcĭs ĭmāgŏ. Ăvĭs dōctă lŏquī. Ēxtrēmō mūnŭs ăb ōrbĕ dătūm. Hūmānās dēprōmēns vōcĕ quĕrēlās. Hūmānæ rĕfĕrēns ĭmĭtāmĭnă līnguæ. Hūmānæ sōlērs ĭmĭtātŏr, psīttăcĕ, līnguæ. Plūmă vĭrĕt.

Rŭbēcŭlă, æ. f. *The robin redbreast.* Phr.—Quæ căpĭt ā rūbrō pēctŏrĕ nōmĕn ăvĭs. Rŭbĭcūndī pēctŏrĭs ālĕs. Tīnctă crŭōrĕ Crŭcĭs.

Strīx, ĭgĭs. f. *The owl.* Quōd trĕpĭdūs būbō, quōd strīx nōctūrnă quĕrūntŭr. L. Syn.—Būbŏ, nōctŭă, ŭlŭlă. Phr.—Grāndĕ căpŭt, stāntēs ŏcŭlī, rōstra āptă răpīnæ. Nōctĕ vŏlăt. Nōmĭnĭs hūjŭs Caūsă, quŏd hōrrēndā strīdĕrĕ nōctĕ sŏlēnt. *See Bubo.*

Stūrnŭs, ī. m. *A starling.* Nūnc stūrnōs ĭnŏpēs, frīngīllārūmquĕ quĕrēlās. M. Syn.—Stūrnēllă. Phr.—Stūrnŭs vūlgārĭs.

Tūrdŭs, ī. m. *A thrush.* Ŏbēsō Nīl mĕlĭūs tūrdō. H. Phr.—Dē tūrdīs fāctă cŏrōnă plăcĕt. Nēc tĕnŭēs sōlērs tūrdārūm nōssĕ sălīvās. Īntĕr ăvēs tūrdūs prīmōs tĭbĭ jăctăt hŏnōrēs.

Tūrtŭr, ŭrĭs. m. *A turtle-dove.* Nēc gĕmĕre āĕrĭă cēssābīt tūrtŭr ăb ūlmō. V. Syn.—Cŏlūmbă, pălūmbēs. Phr.—Āmīssā cōmpărĕ mœstūs Cuī cāntūs gĕmĕre ēst. Raūcă gĕmīt, dūlcēsquĕ mĭsēr sūspīrăt ămōrēs. *See Columba.*

Ŭlŭlă, æ. f. *A screech-owl.* Cērtēnt ēt cȳcnīs ŭlŭlæ. V. Syn.—Būbŏ, strīx, nōctŭă. Phr.—Trīstĕ gĕmēns. Prænūntĭă fātī, clādĭs, mōrtĭs. *See Bubo.*

Vūltŭr, ŭrĭs, & Vūltŭrĭŭs, ĭī. m. *A vulture.* Aūt ŭt ĕdāx vūltūr cōrpūs cīrcūmspĭcĭt. O. Phr.—Ăvĭs Caūcăsĕă. Rōstrōque īmmānīs vūltŭr ădūncō. Ūnguĭbŭs ŏbūncīs mĭnāx. Sævīt prædătŏr ădūncīs Ūnguĭbŭs, ēt dūrō dīscērpīt vīscĕră rōstrō. Ēt quī vūltŭrĭbūs sērvābāt vīscĕră Dācīs.

FINIS